The Longman Anthology of British Literature

✦╍═◆═╍✦

VOLUME 1C

THE RESTORATION AND THE 18TH CENTURY

David Damrosch
COLUMBIA UNIVERSITY

Christopher Baswell
UNIVERSITY OF CALIFORNIA, LOS ANGELES

Clare Carroll
QUEENS COLLEGE, CITY UNIVERSITY OF NEW YORK

Kevin J. H. Dettmar
SOUTHERN ILLINOIS UNIVERSITY

Heather Henderson

Constance Jordan
CLAREMONT GRADUATE UNIVERSITY

Peter J. Manning
STATE UNIVERSITY OF NEW YORK, STONY BROOK

Anne Howland Schotter
WAGNER COLLEGE

William Chapman Sharpe
BARNARD COLLEGE

Stuart Sherman
FORDHAM UNIVERSITY

Jennifer Wicke
UNIVERSITY OF VIRGINIA

Susan J. Wolfson
PRINCETON UNIVERSITY

The Longman Anthology
of British Literature
Second Edition

David Damrosch

General Editor

VOLUME 1C

THE RESTORATION AND THE 18TH CENTURY
Stuart Sherman

New York   San Francisco   Boston
London   Toronto   Sydney   Tokyo   Singapore   Madrid
Mexico City   Munich   Paris   Cape Town   Hong Kong   Montreal

Vice President and Editor-in-Chief: *Joseph Terry*
Development Editor: *Mark Getlein*
Assistant Development Editor: *Lai Moy*
Development Manager: *Janet Lanphier*
Senior Marketing Manager: *Melanie Craig*
Supplements Editor: *Donna Campion*
Media Supplements Editor: *Nancy Garcia*
Senior Production Manager: *Valerie Zaborski*
Project Coordination, Text Design, and Page Makeup: *TechBooks*
Cover Design Manager: *Nancy Danahy*
Cover Designer: *Kay Petronio*
On the Cover: *Joshua Reynolds*, Mrs. Abington as "Miss Prue." *1771. Yale Center for British Art,
    Paul Mellon Collection.*
Photo Researcher: *Julie Tesser*
Manufacturing Buyer: *Lucy Hebard*
Printer and Binder: *Quebecor-World/Taunton*
Cover Printer: *The Lehigh Press, Inc.*

For permission to use copyrighted material, grateful acknowledgment is made to the copyright
holders on page 2991, which are hereby made part of this copyright page.

Library of Congress Cataloging-in-Publication Data

The Longman anthology of British literature / David Damrosch, general
    editor. — 2nd ed.
        p.   cm.
    Includes bibliographical references and index.
    Contents: v. 1. The Middle Ages / Christopher Baswell and Anne Howland
Schotter. The early modern period / Constance Jordan and Clare
Carroll. The Restoration and the 18th century / Stuart Sherman —
v. 2. The romantics and their contemporaries / Susan Wolfson and Peter
Manning. The Victorian age / Heather Henderson and William Sharpe.
The twentieth century / Kevin Dettmar and Jennifer Wicke.
    ISBN 0-321-09388-7 (v. 1). — ISBN 0-321-09389-5 (v. 2)
    1. English literature.   2. Great Britain—Literary collections.
I. Damrosch, David.
PR1109.L67   2002
820.8—dc21   2002066148

Please visit our website at http://www.ablongman.com/damrosch.

ISBN Single Volume Edition, Volume I: 0-321-09388-7
ISBN Volume 1A, The Middle Ages: 0-321-10667-9
ISBN Volume 1B, The Early Modern Period: 0-321-10578-8
ISBN Volume 1C, The Restoration and the 18th Century: 0-321-10668-7

567890—QWT—05 04

CONTENTS

LIST OF ILLUSTRATIONS

PREFACE

Literature has a double life. Born in one time and place and read in another, literary works are at once products of their age and independent creations, able to live on long after their original world has disappeared. The goal of this anthology is to present a wealth of poetry, prose, and drama from the full sweep of the literary history of the British Isles, and to do so in ways that will bring out both the works' original cultural contexts and their lasting aesthetic power. These aspects are, in fact, closely related: Form and content, verbal music and social meanings, go hand in hand. This double life makes literature, as Aristotle said, "the most philosophical" of all the arts, intimately connected to ideas and to realities that the writer transforms into moving patterns of words. The challenge is to show these works in the contexts in which, and for which, they were written, while at the same time not trapping them within those contexts. The warm response this anthology received from the hundreds of teachers who adopted it in its first edition reflects the growing consensus that we do not have to accept an "either/or" choice between the literature's aesthetic and cultural dimensions. Our users' responses have now guided us in seeing how we can improve our anthology further, so as to be most pleasurable and stimulating to students, most useful to teachers, and most responsive to ongoing developments in literary studies. This preface can serve as a road map to the new phase in this book's life.

LITERATURE IN ITS TIME—AND IN OURS

When we engage with a rich literary history that extends back over a thousand years, we often encounter writers who assume their readers know all sorts of things that are little known today: historical facts, social issues, literary and cultural references. Beyond specific information, these works will have come out of a very different literary culture than our own. Even the contemporary British Isles present a cultural situation—or a mix of cultures—very different from what North American readers encounter at home, and these differences only increase as we go farther back in time. A major emphasis of this anthology is to bring the works' original cultural moment to life: not because the works simply or naively reflect that moment of origin, but because they do refract it in fascinating ways. British literature is both a major heritage for modern North America and, in many ways, a very distinct culture; reading British literature will regularly give an experience both of connection and of difference. Great writers create imaginative worlds that have their own compelling internal logic, and a prime purpose of this anthology is to help readers to understand the formal means—whether of genre, rhetoric, or style—with which these writers have created works of haunting beauty. At the same time, as Virginia Woolf says in A Room of One's Own, the gossamer threads of the artist's web are joined to reality "with bands of steel." This anthology pursues a range of strategies to bring out both the beauty of these webs of words and their points of contact with reality.

The Longman Anthology brings related authors and works together in several ways:

☞ PERSPECTIVES: Broad groupings that illuminate underlying issues in a variety of the major works of a period.

☞ AND ITS TIME: A focused cluster that illuminates a specific cultural moment or a debate to which an author is responding.

☞ COMPANION READINGS: Pairings of works in dialogue with each other.

These groupings provide a range of means of access to the literary culture of each period. The Perspectives sections do much more than record what major writers thought about an issue: they give a variety of views in a range of voices, to illustrate the wider culture within which the literature was being written. An attack on tobacco by King James the First; theological reflections by the pioneering scientist Isaac Newton; haunting testimony by Victorian child workers concerning their lives; these and many other vivid readings give rhetorical as well as social contexts for the poems, plays, and stories around them. Perspectives sections typically relate to several major authors of the period, as with a section on Government and Self-Government that relates broadly to Sir Thomas More's *Utopia*, to Spenser's *Faerie Queene*, and to Milton's *Paradise Lost*. Most of the writers included in Perspectives sections are important figures of the period who could be neglected if they were listed on their own with just a few pages each; grouping them together has proven to be useful pedagogically as well as intellectually. Perspectives sections may also include work by a major author whose primary listing appears elsewhere in the period; thus, a Perspective section on the abolition of slavery—a hotly debated issue in England from the 1790s through the 1830s—includes poems and essays on slavery by Wordsworth, Coleridge, and Barbauld, so as to give a rounded presentation of the issue in ways that can inform the reading of those authors in their individual sections.

When we present a major work "And Its Time," we give a cluster of related materials to suggest the context within which the work was written. Thus Sir Philip Sidney's great *Apology for Poetry* is accompanied by readings showing the controversy that was raging at the time concerning the nature and value of poetry. Some of the writers in these groupings and in our Perspectives sections have not traditionally been seen as literary figures, but all have produced lively and intriguing works, from medieval clerics writing about saints and sea monsters, to a polemical seventeenth-century tract giving *The Arraignment of Lewd, Idle, Froward, and Unconstant Women*, to rousing speeches by Winston Churchill as the British faced the Nazis during World War II.

Also, we include "Companion Readings" to present specific prior texts to which a work is responding: when Sir Thomas Wyatt creates a beautiful poem, *Whoso list to hunt*, by making a free translation of a Petrarch sonnet, we include Petrarch's original (with a literal translation) as a companion reading. For Conrad's *Heart of Darkness*, companion texts include Conrad's diary of the Congo journey on which he based his novella, and a bizarre lecture by Sir Henry Morton Stanley, the explorer-adventurer whose travel writings Conrad parodies.

CULTURAL EDITIONS

This edition also sees the establishment of an important new series of companion volumes, the Longman Cultural Editions, which carry further the anthology's emphases by presenting major texts along with a generous selection of contextual material. Five initial volumes are devoted to *King Lear*; a pairing of *Othello* and Elizabeth Cary's *Tragedie of Mariam*; *Pride and Prejudice*; *Frankenstein*; and *Hard Times*. More are currently being developed. The *Othello/Mariam* and *Frankenstein* volumes build on material derived from the first edition of the anthology; presenting these works separately—available free, for course use, with the anthology itself—has helped to free up space for our many additions to this edition, from the medieval play *Mankind*, to a substantial increase in seventeenth-century lyric poetry, to the addition of Sheridan's hilarious eighteenth-century play *The School for Scandal*, to *Doctor Jekyll and Mr. Hyde* in the Victorian period and *Mrs. Dalloway* in the twentieth century. Taken together, our new edition and the Longman Cultural Editions offer an unparalleled set of materials for the enjoyment and study of British literary culture from its first beginnings to the present.

ILLUSTRATING VISUAL CULTURE

Another important context for literary production has been a different kind of culture: the visual. We have newly added in this edition a suite of color plates in each volume, and we also have one hundred black-and-white illustrations throughout the anthology, chosen to show artistic and cultural images that figured importantly for literary creation. Sometimes, a poem refers to a specific painting, or more generally emulates qualities of a school of visual art. At other times, more popular materials like advertisements may underlie scenes in Victorian or Modernist writing. In some cases, visual and literary creation have merged, as in Hogarth's series *A Rake's Progress*, included in Volume 1, or Blake's illustrated engravings of his *Songs of Innocence and of Experience*, several of whose plates are reproduced in color in Volume 2.

AIDS TO UNDERSTANDING

We have attempted to contextualize our selections in suggestive rather than exhaustive ways, trying to enhance rather than overwhelm the experience of reading the texts themselves. Thus, when difficult or archaic words need defining in poems, we use glosses in the margins, so as to disrupt the reader's eye as little as possible; footnotes are intended to be concise and informative, rather than massive or interpretive. Important literary and social terms are defined when they are used; for convenience of reference, there is also an extensive glossary of literary and cultural terms at the end of each volume, together with useful summaries of British political and religious organization, and of money, weights, and measures. For further reading, carefully selected, up-to-date bibliographies for each period and for each author can be found at the end of each volume.

LOOKING—AND LISTENING—FURTHER

Beyond the boundaries of the anthology itself, along with this edition we are introducing a pair of CDs, one for each semester, giving a wide range of readings of texts in the anthology and of selections of music from each period. It is only in the past century or two that people usually began to read literature silently; most literature has been written in the expectation that it would be read aloud, or even sung in the case of lyric poetry ("lyric" itself means a work meant to be sung to the accompaniment of a lyre or other instruments). The aural power and beauty of these works is a crucial dimension of their experience. For further explorations, we have also expanded our Web site, available to all users at www.awlonline.com/damrosch; this site gives a wealth of information, annotated links to related sites, and an archive of texts for further reading. For instructors, we have revised and expanded our popular companion volume, *Teaching British Literature*, written directly by the anthology editors, 600 pages in length, available free to everyone who adopts the anthology.

WHAT IS BRITISH LITERATURE?

Turning now to the book itself, let us begin by defining our basic terms: What is "British" literature? What is literature itself? And just what should an anthology of this material look like at the present time? The term "British" can mean many things, some of them contradictory, some of them even offensive to people on whom the name has been imposed. If the term "British" has no ultimate essence, it does have a history. The first British were Celtic people who inhabited the British Isles and the northern coast of France (still called Brittany) before various Germanic tribes of Angles and Saxons moved onto the islands in the fifth and sixth centuries. Gradually the Angles and Saxons amalgamated into the Anglo-Saxon culture that became dominant in the southern and eastern regions of Britain and then spread outward; the old British people were pushed west, toward what became known as Cornwall, Wales, and Ireland, which remained independent kingdoms for centuries, as did Celtic Scotland to the north. By an ironic twist of linguistic fate, the Anglo-Saxons began to appropriate the term British from the Britons they had displaced, and they took as a national hero the early, semi-mythic Welsh King Arthur. By the seventeenth century, English monarchs had extended their sway over Wales, Ireland, and Scotland, and they began to refer to their holdings as "Great Britain." Today, Great Britain includes England, Wales, Scotland, and Northern Ireland, but does not include the Republic of Ireland, which has been independent from England since 1922.

This anthology uses "British" in a broad sense, as a geographical term encompassing the whole of the British Isles. For all its fraught history, it seems a more satisfactory term than to speak simply of "English" literature, for two reasons. First: most speakers of English live in countries that are not the focus of this anthology; second, while the English language and its literature have long been dominant in the British Isles, other cultures in the region have always used other languages and have produced great literature in these languages. Important works by Irish, Welsh, and Scots writers appear regularly in the body of this anthology, some of them written directly in their languages and presented here in translation, and others written in an English inflected by the rhythms, habits of thought, and modes of expression characteristic of these other languages and the people who use them.

We use the term "literature" in a similarly capacious sense, to refer to a range of artistically shaped works written in a charged language, appealing to the imagination at least as much as to discursive reasoning. It is only relatively recently that creative writers have been able to make a living composing poems, plays, and novels, and only in the past hundred years or so has creating "belles lettres" or high literary art been thought of as a sharply separate sphere of activity from other sorts of writing that the same authors would regularly produce. Sometimes, Romantic poets wrote sonnets to explore the deepest mysteries of individual perception and memory; at other times, they wrote sonnets the way a person might now write an Op-Ed piece, and such a sonnet would be published and read along with parliamentary debates and letters to the editor on the most pressing contemporary issues.

WOMEN'S WRITING, AND MEN'S

Literary culture has always involved an interplay between central and marginal regions, groupings, and individuals. A major emphasis in literary study in recent years has been the recovery of writing by women writers, some of them little read until recently, others major figures in their time. The first edition of this anthology included more women, and more writing by the women we included, than any other anthology had ever done or does even today. This edition increases the presence of women writers still more, with new inclusions of such important voices as Christine de Pizan, Stevie Smith, and Eavan Boland, while also highlighting Virginia Woolf with the inclusion of the complete text of her great novel *Mrs. Dalloway*. Attending to these voices gives us a new variety of compelling works, and helps us rethink the entire periods in which they wrote. The first third of the nineteenth century, for example, can be defined more broadly than as a "Romantic Age" dominated by six male poets; looking closely at women's writing as well as at men's, we can deepen our understanding of the period as a whole, including the specific achievements of Blake, William Wordsworth, Coleridge, Keats, Percy Shelley, and Byron, all of whom continue to have a major presence in these pages as most of them did during the nineteenth century.

VARIETIES OF LITERARY EXPERIENCE

Above all, we have striven to give as full a presentation as possible to the varieties of great literature produced over the centuries in the British Isles, by women as well as by men, in outlying regions as well as in the metropolitan center of London, and in prose, drama, and verse alike. We have taken particular care to do justice to prose fiction: we include entire novels or novellas by Charles Dickens, Robert Louis Stevenson, Joseph Conrad, and Virginia Woolf, as well as a wealth of short fiction from the eighteenth century to the present. For the earlier periods, we include More's entire *Utopia*, and we give major space to narrative poetry by Chaucer, Spenser, and Milton, among others. Drama appears throughout the anthology, from the medieval *Second Play of the Shepherds* and *Mankind* to a range of twentieth-century plays: George Bernard Shaw's *Pygmalion*, a radio play by Dylan Thomas, Samuel Beckett's *Krapp's Last Tape*, and Caryl Churchill's gender-bending comedy *Cloud 9*. Finally, lyric poetry appears in profusion throughout the anthology, from early lyrics by anonymous Middle English poets and the trenchantly witty Dafydd ap Gwilym to the powerful contemporary voices of Philip Larkin, Seamus Heaney, Eavan Boland, Thom Gunn, and Derek Walcott—himself a product of colonial British education, heir of Shakespeare and James Joyce—who closes the anthology with poems about Englishness abroad and foreignness in Britain.

As topical as these contemporary writers are, we hope that this anthology will show that the great works of earlier centuries can also speak to us compellingly today, their value only increased by the resistance they offer to our views of ourselves and our world. To read and reread the full sweep of this literature is to be struck anew by the degree to which the most radically new works are rooted in centuries of prior innovation. Even this preface can close in no better way than by quoting the words written eighteen hundred years ago by Apuleius of Madaura—both a consummate artist and a kind of anthologist of extraordinary tales—when he concluded the prologue to his masterpiece *The Golden Ass*: Attend, reader, and pleasure is yours.

David Damrosch

ACKNOWLEDGMENTS

In planning and preparing the second edition of our anthology, the editors have been fortunate to have the support, advice, and assistance of many people. Our editor, Joe Terry, has been unwavering in his enthusiasm for the book and his commitment to it; he and his associates Roth Wilkofsky, Janet Lanphier, and Melanie Craig have supported us in every possible way throughout the process, ably assisted by Michele Cronin, Lai Moy, and Alison Main. Our developmental editor Mark Getlein guided us and our manuscript from start to finish with unfailing acuity and Wildean wit. Our copyeditor, Stephanie Magean, marvelously integrated the work of a dozen editors. Daniel Kline and Peter Meyers have devoted enormous energy and creativity to revising our Web site and developing our new audio CD. Joyce Riemer cleared our many permissions, and Julie Tesser tracked down and cleared our many new illustrations. Finally, Valerie Zaborski oversaw the production with sunny good humor and kept the book successfully on track on a very challenging schedule, working closely with Kevin Bradley, and then Kelly Ricci at TechBooks.

Our plans for the new edition have been shaped by comments and suggestions from many faculty who have used the book over the past four years. We are specifically grateful for the thoughtful advice of our reviewers for this edition, Robert Barrett (University of Pennsylvania), Mary Been (Clovis Community College), Stephen Behrendt (University of Nebraska), James Campbell (University of Central Florida), Linda McFerrin Cook (McLellan Community College), Kevin Gardner (Baylor University), Peter Greenfield (University of Puget Sound), Natalie Grinnell (Wofford College), Wayne Hall (University of Cincinnati), Donna Hamilton (University of Maryland), Carrie Hintz (Queens College), Eric Johnson (Dakota State College), Roxanne Kent-Drury (Northern Kentucky University), Adam Komisaruk (West Virginia University), John Laflin (Dakota State University), Paulino Lim (California State University, Long Beach), Ed Malone (Missouri Western State College), William W. Matter (Richland College), Evan Matthews (Navarro College), Lawrence McCauley (College of New Jersey), Peter E. Medine (University of Arizona), Charlotte Morse (Virginia Commonwealth University), Mary Morse (Rider University), Richard Nordquist (Armstrong Atlantic State University), John Ottenhoff (Alma College), Joyce Cornette Palmer (Texas Women's University), Leslie Palmer (University of North Texas), Rebecca Phillips (West Virginia University), William Rankin (Abilene Christian University), Sherry Rankin (Abilene Christian University), Luke Reinsma (Seattle Pacific University), David Rollison (College of Marin), Kathryn Rummel (California Polytechnic), R. G. Siemens (Malaspina University-College), Brad Sullivan (Florida Gulf Coast University), Brett Wallen (Cleveland Community College), Daniel Watkins (Duquesne University), and Julia Wright (University of Waterloo).

We remain grateful as well for the guidance of the many reviewers who advised us on the creation of the first edition, the base on which this new edition has been built. In addition to several of the people named above, we would like to thank Lucien Agosta (California State University, Sacramento), Anne W. Astell (Purdue University), Derek Attridge (Rutgers University), Linda Austin (Oklahoma State University), Joseph Bartolomeo (University of Massachusetts, Amherst), Todd Bender (University of Wisconsin, Madison), Bruce Boehrer (Florida State University),

Joel J. Brattin (Worcester Polytechnic Institute), J. Douglas Canfield (University of Arizona), Paul A. Cantor (University of Virginia), George Allan Cate (University of Maryland, College Park), Eugene R. Cunnar (New Mexico State University), Earl Dachslager (University of Houston), Elizabeth Davis (University of California, Davis), Andrew Elfenbein (University of Minnesota), Margaret Ferguson (University of California, Davis), Sandra K. Fisher (State University of New York, Albany), Allen J. Frantzen (Loyola University, Chicago), Kate Garder Frost (University of Texas), Leon Gottfried (Purdue University), Mark L. Greenberg (Drexel University), James Hala (Drew University), Wendell Harris (Pennsylvania State University), Richard H. Haswell (Washington State University), Susan Sage Heinzelman (University of Texas, Austin), Standish Henning (University of Wisconsin, Madison), Jack W. Herring (Baylor University), Maurice Hunt (Baylor University), Colleen Juarretche (University of California, Los Angeles), R. B. Kershner (University of Florida), Lisa Klein (Ohio State University), Rita S. Kranidis (Radford University), Elizabeth B. Loizeaux (University of Maryland), John J. Manning (University of Connecticut), Michael B. McDonald (Iowa State University), Celia Millward (Boston University), Thomas C. Moser, Jr. (University of Maryland), Jude V. Nixon (Baylor University), Violet O'Valle (Tarrant County Junior College, Texas), Richard Pearce (Wheaton College), Renée Pigeon (California State University, San Bernardino), Tadeusz Pioro (Southern Methodist University), Deborah Preston (Dekalb College), Elizabeth Robertson (University of Colorado), Deborah Rogers (University of Maine), Brian Rosenberg (Allegheny College), Charles Ross (Purdue University), Harry Rusche (Emory University), Kenneth D. Shields (Southern Methodist University), Clare A. Simmons (Ohio State University), Sally Slocum (University of Akron), Phillip Snyder (Brigham Young University), Isabel Bonnyman Stanley (East Tennessee University), Margaret Sullivan (University of California, Los Angeles), Herbert Sussmann (Northeastern University), Ronald R. Thomas (Trinity College), Theresa Tinkle (University of Michigan), William A. Ulmer (University of Alabama), Jennifer A. Wagner (University of Memphis), Anne D. Wallace (University of Southern Mississippi), Jackie Walsh (McNeese State University, Louisiana), John Watkins (University of Minnesota), Martin Wechselblatt (University of Cincinnati), Arthur Weitzman (Northeastern University), Bonnie Wheeler (Southern Methodist University), Dennis L. Williams (Central Texas College), and Paula Woods (Baylor University).

Other colleagues brought our developing book into the classroom, teaching from portions of the work-in-progress. Our thanks go to Lisa Abney (Northwestern State University), Charles Lynn Batten (University of California, Los Angeles), Brenda Riffe Brown (College of the Mainland, Texas), John Brugaletta (California State University, Fullerton), Dan Butcher (Southeastern Louisiana University), Lynn Byrd (Southern University at New Orleans), David Cowles (Brigham Young University), Sheila Drain (John Carroll University), Lawrence Frank (University of Oklahoma), Leigh Garrison (Virginia Polytechnic Institute), David Griffin (New York University), Rita Harkness (Virginia Commonwealth University), Linda Kissler (Westmoreland County Community College, Pennsylvania), Brenda Lewis (Motlow State Community College, Tennessee), Paul Lizotte (River College), Wayne Luckman (Green River Community College, Washington), Arnold Markely (Pennsylvania State University, Delaware County), James McKusick (University of Maryland, Baltimore), Eva McManus (Ohio Northern University), Manuel Moyrao (Old Dominion University), Kate Palguta (Shawnee State University, Ohio), Paul Puccio (University of Central Florida), Sarah Polito (Cape Cod Community College), Meredith Poole (Virginia Western Community College), Tracy Seeley (University of San Francisco), Clare Simmons (Ohio State University), and Paul Yoder (University of Arkansas, Little Rock).

As if all this help weren't enough, the editors also drew directly on friends and colleagues in many ways, for advice, for information, sometimes for outright contributions to headnotes and footnotes, even (in a pinch) for aid in proofreading. In particular, we wish to thank David Ackiss, Marshall Brown, James Cain, Cathy Corder, Jeffrey Cox, Michael Coyle, Pat Denison, Tom Farrell, Andrew Fleck, Jane Freilich, Laurie Glover, Lisa Gordis, Joy Hayton, Ryan Hibbet, V. Lauryl Hicks, Nelson Hilton, Jean Howard, David Kastan, Stanislas Kemper, Andrew Krull, Ron Levao, Carol Levin, David Lipscomb, Denise MacNeil, Jackie Maslowski, Richard Matlak, Anne Mellor, James McKusick, Melanie Micir, Michael North, David Paroissien, Stephen M. Parrish, Peter Platt, Cary Plotkin, Desma Polydorou, Gina Renee, Alan Richardson, Esther Schor, Catherine Siemann, Glenn Simshaw, David Tresilian, Shasta Turner, Nicholas Watson, Michael Winckleman, Gillen Wood, and Sarah Zimmerman for all their guidance and assistance.

The pages on the Restoration and the eighteenth century are the work of many collaborators, diligent and generous. Michael F. Suarez, S. J. (Campion Hall, Oxford) edited the Swift and Pope sections; Mary Bly (Fordham University) edited Sheridan's *School for Scandal*; Michael Caldwell (University of Chicago) edited the portions of "Reading Papers" on *The Craftsman* and the South Sea Bubble. Steven N. Zwicker (Washington University) co-wrote the period introduction, and the headnotes for the Dryden section. Bruce Redford (Boston University) crafted the footnotes for Dryden, Gay, Johnson, and Boswell. Susan Brown, Christine Coch, Tara Czechowski, Paige Reynolds, and Andrew Tumminia helped with texts, footnotes, and other matters throughout; William Pritchard gathered texts, wrote notes, and prepared the bibliography. To all, abiding thanks.

It has been a pleasure to work with all of these colleagues in the ongoing collaborative process that has produced this book and brought it to this new stage of its life and use. This book exists for its readers, whose reactions and suggestions we warmly welcome, as these will in turn reshape this book for later users in the years to come.

Thomas Bowles, *The Bubblers' Medley, or a Sketch of the Times,* 1720.

The Restoration and
the Eighteenth Century

On 25 May 1660, Charles II set foot on the shore of Dover and brought his eleven-year exile to an end. The arrival was recorded by the great diarist Samuel Pepys, and his words preserve for us a form of the event:

> I went, and Mr. Mansell, and one of the King's footmen, with a dog that the King loved (which beshat the boat, which made us laugh, and methink that a king and all that belong to him are but just as others are), in a boat by ourselves, and so got on shore when the King did, who was received . . . with all imaginable love and respect at his entrance upon the land of Dover. Infinite the crowd of people and the horsemen, citizens, and noblemen of all sorts. The Mayor of the town came and gave him his white staff, the badge of his place, which the King did give him again. The Mayor also presented him from the town a very rich Bible, which he took and said it was the thing that he loved above all things in the world. . . . The shouting and joy expressed by all is past imagination.

Pepys captures and creates a brilliant mix of materials and experiences: his words compound jubilation and skepticism, images of authority and obeisance, tropes of spirituality and irony, and they remind us of the elements and passions by which all men live. Every gesture and exchange in this scene forecast the world to come, but what most signals the future is the paradox of remembering and forgetting that the diarist performs even as he records this scene. And all who witnessed the King's descent at Dover committed similar acts of memory and oblivion. Many of those (Pepys included) who were drunk with pleasure at the return of Charles Stuart had endorsed the destruction of his father eleven years before. The entire Restoration and the events that would follow over the ensuing years would prove a complex unfolding of memory and forgetfulness.

The jubilant crowds at Dover thought to make flux stop here: forever to banish the turbulence of civil war and political innovation, to restore all the old familiar forms, utterly to erase what had come between the death of the father and the restoration of the son. Charles II would soon institute an Act of Oblivion to those ends, forgiving proponents of rebellion by officially forgetting their misdeeds. But civil war and revolution would not be erased, nor could monarchy, the Anglican Church, aristocratic privilege, political patronage, and the old social hierarchies be revived as though nothing had intervened. Much of the old was brought back with the return of the Stuart monarchy, but the consequence of layering the present over a willfully suppressed past was an instability of feelings and forms that ensured the ever-changing triumph of different memories and different oblivions during the ensuing decades. No one celebrating the return of ancient ways in 1660 could have foreseen the ruptures and innovations that lay ahead in the next half of the century, when crises of conspiracy and the birth of party politics would produce further shifts in monarchy through a sequence of three ruling houses from three different countries. But even in 1660 the innocent acclaim on the shores of Dover was accompanied by hidden guilts and ironies, by vindictive desires, even for some by millenarian hopes. And while such stresses and tensions were unacknowledged in May 1660, they soon enough surfaced, and they unsettled not only the pleasures of this king's rule but the politics of an entire age.

MONARCHS, MINISTERS, EMPIRE

The coronation of Charles II in May 1661 marked the beginning of both the first and the eleventh year of his rule. The King's laws were named as if he had taken possession of the crown at the moment of his father's execution in 1649. And fictions, legal and not so legal, were to prove a hallmark of Stuart rule. The King openly proclaimed his love of parliaments, his devotion to the immemorial constitution of balance and moderation, his Protestant fervor, and his pious hopes for a national church. Yet he often postponed his parliaments; he claimed a tender conscience for Protestant dissenters, but he maneuvered for the toleration of Roman Catholics; he conducted an aggressive, nationalist program against European powers, but he signed a secret and deeply compromising treaty with Louis XIV; he took communion in the Anglican Church, but on his deathbed he sealed his own conversion to Catholicism; he was tenderly affectionate to his barren queen, yet he publicly flaunted his whoring tastes; he repeatedly exiled his unpopular brother James, Duke of York, while promoting and indulging his own bastard sons, yet he staunchly resisted any effort to displace his brother from the line of succession. The dominance of masquerade surely derived from Charles's temper, but fiction and falsehood were also the structural principles and aesthetic features of an entire world.

In December 1678, a series of events started to unfold that proved the very emblem of the masking, the fears, and the psychology of Charles II's rule. It began with legal depositions: one Titus Oates, a baker's son and self-anointed savior of a Protestant people, claimed to have knowledge of a secret plot to kill the King, crown his Catholic brother, and begin the wholesale conversion of English souls—and, just as frightening, English properties—to Rome. Oates offered to a public hungry for scandal and change a Popish plot and a familiar mix of images and idioms: priests and idols, the Roman Antichrist, conspiracy, murder, and mayhem. His depositions and fabrications played brilliantly on memories of the past and on fears of a future under a Catholic king. Nor did it help that the Duke of York's private secretary, Edward Coleman, was caught with treasonous correspondence in his chamber. The plot seemed compounded of sufficient truths to challenge the stability of the Crown. From the midst of the plot, and under the hand of the Earl of Shaftesbury, a political party emerged that took advantage of Popish facts and fears by proposing the Bill of Exclusion in Parliament, which would have barred the Duke of York and any future Catholic monarchs from the English throne. In the event, the bill failed, Charles died of natural causes, and the Duke succeeded his brother in February 1685.

During James's brief reign, no plots, conspiracies, or political parties proved so costly to his rule as did the new king himself. He succeeded his brother in a mood of surprising public affirmation. At his accession, James returned the embrace of Anglican England by promising to honor the national church and that most beloved of Protestant properties, a tender conscience. There would be no forcing of religious uniformity in this reign. But soon enough James began to move against Anglican interests: he staffed his army with Catholic officers, he imposed Catholic officials on

Oxford University, and he insisted that his Declarations of Toleration be read aloud from the pulpits of Anglican churches. Such a program challenged interest, property, and propriety, and it spelled the quick demise of Catholic rule.

As Duke of York, James had been famed for martial valor. But now, when confronted in November 1688 by the army of his Dutch son-in-law, William of Orange, he fled under cover of night to France. What had in part provoked James's flight were memories of the past—of civil war and of the execution of his father, Charles I. What had provoked the invasion by William of Orange was not merely the specter of Louis XIV hovering behind James's rule or the open presence of Jesuits at James's court. It was the birth of James Francis Edward Stuart, son of James II and Mary of Modena. Protestants would suffer not only the inconvenience of one Catholic monarch but the possibility of an endless Catholic succession. The prospect was too much to bear. Secret negotiations were begun between powerful English artistocrats—Whigs and Tories alike—and William, the governor (stadholder) of Holland, resulting in what many called the Glorious Revolution. But the deceits and pretenses—the gaps and silences—of this palace coup did not strike all contemporaries as glorious. The stadholder who chased a Catholic king from England was not only an invading hero (though some did call him William the Conqueror), he was also the son-in-law of James II. Those who clung to the binding ties of loyalty and gratitude accused William and Mary of deep impiety, indeed, of parricide.

But the astonishing invitation to William of Orange produced no bloodshed. What it did produce was a Protestant monarchy under the rule of King William III and Queen Mary. Members of Parliament, meeting to invent the laws that would sanctify this revolutionary change, decided that it would be best to say they had discovered the throne of England mysteriously vacant and that this William was no conqueror but a rightful claimant on a vacant throne. Of course, not everyone was pleased by such a revolution—sacred oaths had been broken, binding ties were cast aside, vows were juggled as mere words. Those who would not accept a convenient revolution were called Jacobites, that is, supporters of King James (*Jacobus* in Latin); they remained a force that would trouble British political life by threatening a Stuart restoration in the fervent but failed Jacobite rebellions of 1715 and 1745.

Most of William's subjects, though, were content with the evasions of this Glorious Revolution. Many were not content, though, with the program of European war in which the English were now plunged by their new king, intent on thwarting the ambitions of Louis XIV, his lifelong nemesis. The ruinous expense of war demanded taxes and fiscal innovation; it produced a stream of grumbling satire, complaint against Dutch favorites, and more than one conspiracy and attempted assassination. No such disaffection or turbulence disturbed the reign (1702–1714) of William's successor, Queen Anne. Her years were the twilight of Stuart monarchy, a time of political nostalgia and commercial confidence whose mood the young Alexander Pope captured in the lines of *Windsor-Forest* (1713), where softened memories and strategic elisions of the years of Stuart rule are mingled with images of triumph—of imperial expansion and a swelling commerce of domestic and foreign trade.

But luxury was not England's only import. At the death of Queen Anne, an entire court and new ruling house were shipped to England from the German state of Hanover. George I was the grandson of James I; beyond lineage, George's communion in a Protestant church was the virtue that most recommended his succession.

He spoke no English, knew nothing of his new subjects, and could not be bothered to learn. Nor was he much implicated in the management of a state whose rule would successively become less the prerogative of kings than the business of ministers and the function of parties, interest, and corruption. This displacement of monarch by minister was cemented during the period caustically nicknamed "Robin's Reign": two decades (1721–1742), transversing the reigns of George I and George II, when politics were dominated by Robert Walpole, who bought loyalties, managed kings, and ran the state with such ruthless efficency as to earn him the new label "prime minister" (the phrase was meant as an insult, aimed at the perceived excess of his power in a government where ministers were only supposed to advise their colleagues and their king). The South Sea Bubble, a state-endorsed investment scheme that ruined many, was the making of Robert Walpole. As the only cabinet minister untainted by the scandal (he had initially argued against the scheme, then lost money in it), he was put in charge of the subsequent governmental housecleaning. Once empowered, he cheerfully shed his scruples, devising a political machine fueled by patronage that made his cronies rich, his opposition apoplectic. By the firmness of his rule and the prudence of his policies, Walpole consolidated a long period of Whig supremacy that supplanted the party contest of the preceding decades, when Whigs and Tories had see-sawed more swiftly in and out of power.

The parties had begun to crystallize during the Exclusion crisis of the early 1680s, when Whigs fought to bar the king's Catholic brother from the throne and Tories upheld the established continuity of the Stuart line. Like "prime minister," the two party names began as insult, "Tory" denoting an Irish-Catholic bandit, "Whigs" identifying a group of Scottish rebels during the civil wars. Late in the eighteenth century, Samuel Johnson summed up their polarities: "The prejudice of the Tory is for establishment; the prejudice of the Whig is for innovation." "Establishment" meant preserving monarchic prerogatives, upholding the Anglican church, lamenting the advent of the Hanoverians, and—for some Tories, not all—actively yearning for the restoration of the Stuart line and abetting the attempts to achieve this in the Jacobite rebellions of 1715 and 1745. Whig "innovation" entailed enthusiastic support for both the Glorious Revolution and the House of Hanover, for policies of religious tolerance, and for all measures that advanced the interests of the newly prosperous and powerful merchant class. In the late seventeenth century, party politics had begun for the first time to supplant long-running religious conflicts as the main articulation of interest and power. For all its noise and rage, the new structure produced a paradoxical calm, not by the suppression of difference but by its recognition. The division into parties amounted to a sanctioned fragmentation of the whole. Even during the reign of Anne, when party conflict was at its most feverish, what the machinery of party seemed to ensure was the containment of partisan interest within the dynamic, even organic, coherence of the state.

During Walpole's "reign," portions of the two parties coalesced in an uneasy alliance. The arrogance, obstinacy, and efficacy of Walpole's methods galvanized an opposition consisting of both Tories and alienated Whigs; their endeavors acquired luster from the contributions of a remarkable array of writers (the Tories Jonathan Swift, Alexander Pope, John Gay, and Henry Fielding, and the Whig James Thomson) who opposed the prime minister on grounds of personality, principle, and of course self-interest. Walpole, recognizing that the best writers worked for the opposition, strove to suppress them by all the strategies of censorship he could devise. But by his greatness as a character and his force as an opponent, Walpole loomed for a long while as both literature's nemesis and its muse.

In fact, Walpole enforced the policies endorsed by only a fraction of his party—those moderate Whigs deeply interested in cultivating the country's wealth by commerce, deeply resistant to waging war. "My *politics*," he once wrote emphatically, "*are to keep free from all engagements, as long as we possibly can*"; by "engagements," he meant military commitments abroad. By the late 1730s, he discovered that he could keep free from them no longer. Britons feared that powers on the Continent—Spain, Austria, and above all France—were encroaching on their rights, and the popular clamor to wage European war prevailed. "When trade is at stake," the oppositionist William Pitt warned the British, "it is your last retrenchment; you must defend it or perish." Under the pressure of such sentiments Walpole eventually resigned, having led the state through two decades of comparative peace, growing national prosperity, and a new stability in government, but leaving behind him an army and a navy debilitated by disuse. Nonetheless, with trade at stake and the navy rebuilt, Britain embarked on a series of wars that ran almost unbroken for the rest of the century. Pitt presided brilliantly over many of them, wars waged directly or indirectly against France for trading privileges and territories abroad. By 1763, Britain had secured possession of Bengal in India, many islands and coastal territories in the Caribbean, and virtually all of North America (including Canada) east of the Mississippi, as well as half of all the international trade transpiring on the planet. So great was the impetus toward empire that even Britain's humiliating defeat in the American War of Independence (1775–1783) could not really halt the momentum; territories in India were still expanding, and settlement of Australia lay in the offing.

By now, the throne was occupied by the first Hanoverian monarch born in Britain—George III. His long reign (1760–1820) teemed with troubles: the popular scorn for his chosen ministers, the loss of the American war, the aftershocks of the French Revolution, the defiance of his heirs, the torments of his own slow-encroaching madness. But almost from beginning to end he ruled over the richest nation and the widest empire in the world. In 1740, a new song could be heard with a catchy refrain: "Rule, Britannia, rule the waves / Britons never will be slaves." The words were the work of the Scots-born poet James Thomson, now a proud adherent of "Britannia" by virtue of the Act of Union (1707), which had fused Scotland with England and Wales into a new nation, newly named: Great Britain. Over the ensuing years the song took hold because of the seductively prophetic ways in which it forecast Britain's greatness and partly because of the proud but peculiar resonances of the refrain's last line. There, Thomson contrasts British liberties with the slave-like constraints supposedly suffered by subjects of absolute monarchy elsewhere. Less directly, "slaves" also points to those peoples upon whose subjugation British privilege and British prosperity were increasingly to depend. Throughout the century, Britons profited spectacularly from the capture, transport, sale, and labor of African slaves in current and former colonies; "no nation," William Pitt the Younger proclaimed in 1792, had "plunged so deeply into this guilt as Great Britain."

There were also whole populations whose condition often evoked the analogy of slavery in the minds of the few who paid reformist attention to their plight: the oppressed indigenous peoples of the colonies, and women and the poor at home.

Conversation about such issues became louder and more purposeful near the end of the eighteenth century, as particular champions began to turn social questions into moral causes: John Wilkes on the widening of liberties and voting rights; Mary Wollstonecraft on the rights of women; William Blake (and later, William Cobbett) on the economic inequities of the whole social structure. The problems themselves did not even begin to find redress until the following century, but the emergence of such advocacies, quickened by the audacities of the French Revolution, marked a turning point toward the Romanticism that seized poetic and political imaginations in the 1790s. For most Britons of the eighteenth century, however, the new prosperity produced no special promptings of conscience. As their Restoration forebears had actively encouraged oblivion in an effort to anesthetize themselves to their past, men and women now sustained a moral and social oblivion that eased their use of others and their pleasure in new wealth. Out of such adroitly managed oscillations, Britons fabricated a new sense of themselves as a nation and an empire.

This new construct was in large measure the work of a prominent breed of economic architects: the capital-wielding middle classes. For centuries, wealth had derived primarily from land: tenant farmers performed the labor; the landed gentry collected the often enormous profits. The new wealth was amassed, even created, by people situated between these two extremes, constituting what was often referred to as "the middling rank," "the middling station," or "the middling orders." What set the middling orders apart was the comparatively new way in which they made their money: not by landed inheritance, not by tenancy or wage work, but by the adroit deployment of money itself. Having acquired a sum by inheritance, wage, or loan, they used it as capital, investing it, along with their own efforts, in potentially lucrative enterprises: in shops, in factories, and in the enormous new financial structures (banks, stocks) that underwrote the nation's economic expansiveness. They hired helpers, reinvested profits, and when their schemes succeeded, they made their money grow. With wealth, of course, grew clout. The interests of the "City"—that is, of the eastern half of London where bustling merchants made their deals—increasingly shaped the affairs of state, the appetites for empire. Empire also shaped the progress of the arts: members of the middle class became the chief consumers and energetic producers of the period's most conspicuous new forms of literature: newspapers and novels. But nowhere were the new powers of the burgeoning bourgeoisie more striking than in the theater, that cultural site they often visited and ultimately revised.

MONEY, MANNERS, AND THEATRICS

No event more exactly and more economically signals the return of an aristocratic court to the center of English culture than the reopening of the London theaters in 1662. The intimacy, indeed the complicity, of court with theater throughout the early modern period was such that when in the 1640s Parliament took aim at monarchy, aristocracy, and privilege, it not only struck off the heads of the Earl of Strafford and Archbishop Laud, it also banished play acting and shut tight the doors of the London stage. But Puritans could not banish the theater from the English imagination, and no sooner were the playhouses closed than publishers issued new editions of old plays and the theater made a secret return in domestic spaces and before private audiences. Print and memory would be the preservative of an entire culture. In 1660, monarchy and theater were restored in tandem. But this artistic restoration, like the political one that made it possible, irresistibly mingled the old with the new. Pepys captured all the excitement and splendor of this restoration; as usual he proves adroit at reckoning innovation:

> [T]he stage is now . . . a thousand times better and more glorious than heretofore. Now, wax-candles, and many of them; then, not above three pounds of tallow. Now, all things civil, no rudeness anywhere; then, as in a bear garden. Then, two or three fiddlers; now, nine or ten of the best. Then, nothing but rushes upon the ground and everything mean; and now all otherwise. Then the Queen seldom and the King never would come; now not the King only for state but all civil people do think they may come as well as any.

One reason that "all civil people" thought so was a matter of simple geography. Whereas the theaters of Shakespeare's day had been located in seedy districts on the outskirts of the city, this new and sumptuous theatrical world was ensconced in new neighborhoods strategically located for maximum social confluence, on the border between Westminster—home of the court—and the City of London, dwelling place of a "mighty band of citizens and prentices" whose sudden convergence with royalty seemed a dramatic innovation. They had all gathered to witness the most astonishing new spectacle of all: women on stage in a public theater.

Before the Restoration, aristocratic women had tantalized the court in private and privileged masquing; now the pleasures of display and consumption were democratized in several ways. For women, theatricality was no longer a pastime reserved for the very few but a plausible—though precarious—profession. For audiences at the new theaters, actresses represented the possibility of erotic spectacle for the price of a ticket—a chance to gaze on women who everyone knew were managing the pleasures, and often the policies, of kings and courtiers. Inevitably new strategies of theatricality suffused this audience, where women might model seductive conduct on the teasing combinations of concealment and display enacted before them. Pepys eavesdropped on the libertine Sir Charles Sedley in urgent banter with two women: "And one of the women would and did sit with her mask on, all the play. He would fain know who she was, but she would not tell; yet did give him many pleasant hints of her knowledge of him, by that means setting his brains at work to find out who she was, and did give him leave to use all means but pulling off her mask." Display and disguise not only animated the stage, they quickened social exchange in the intimate spaces of stalls and boxes. The traffic between revelation and concealment defined this theater. It drove the plots of plays and galvanized audiences, modeling and scripting their fashions, their language, their lives.

In such a world the theater provided a national mask, a fantasy of empire and heroism, and yet at the same time sustained a critique of masquerade, a brutal exposure of deceptions rampant in the culture. On the one hand, the heroic drama displayed, indeed reveled in, outsized acts of conquest in exotic lands, valor, and virtue: on stage, princes slaughtered infidels by the thousands; virgins sustained honor through impossible ordeals of abduction and assault. Yet in 1667, at the same moment such dramas were thriving in the king's and the duke's playhouses, the royal fleet was being burned and sunk by a Dutch navy that breached all defenses, invading the very precincts and privacy of London's docks and shipyards. And while the fleet burned, the king busied himself with other depradations, sustaining a series of intrigues, some with the very actresses who wore such incomparable honor and virtue on the stage. (The mix of myth and mischief was popular in pictures too—for example, in the portrait of Barbara Villiers, Countess of Castlemaine, perhaps the most notorious of all the king's mistresses, gotten up in the guise of Minerva, Roman goddess of wisdom; see Color Plate 21.) The heroic drama celebrated military conquest and colonial glory, and displayed them at a moment in national history that produced nothing so much as shame and humiliation: defeat at the hands of Dutch ships and Dutch commerce.

At the same time, but in a far different dramatic mode, the stage sustained a brilliant critique of a whole culture of incongruity, masquerade, and self-delusion. Restoration comedy took as its subject appetite and opportunism, social hypocrisy and sexual power play. The London audience watched scenes of seduction and connivance set in the very vicinities they had traversed to reach the playhouse: St. James's Park, Covent Garden. Such aristocratic libertines as Sir Charles Sedley and Lord Rochester, intent on their own intrigues, might admire themselves in a theatrical mirror, where the rake-hero conducted endless parry-and-thrust with his equals, brutalized his inferiors, and laid hands and claim on any moveable object of desire: fruits and foodstuffs, silks and sonnets, housemaids and women of high estate. But the rakes in the playhouse might see themselves mocked as well. The best comic writers—Wycherley, Etherege, Behn, Congreve—showed the libertines equaled and often bested in cunning by the women they pursued, baffled where they would be most powerful, enslaved where they would be most free. In brilliant volleys of dialogue, these lovers mixed passion and poison in volatile measures, chasing one another through a maze of plots, counterplots, and subplots so convoluted as to suggest a world of calculation run mad. Over the thirty years of its triumphs, Restoration comedy, in an astounding fugue of excesses and depravities, laid bare the turbulence and toxins of this culture.

That the heroic drama, with all its exaggerations and flatteries, found a market is hardly surprising; what is more puzzling is the commercial triumph of Restoration comedy, a theatrical mode that entertained by punishing and humiliating its audience—though it is hardly surprising that this theater should itself have fallen victim in the 1690s to prudery and what would come to be called "taste." In the wake of the Protestant revolution of 1688, which typed Stuart rule as the very emblem of self-indulgence, agents of moral improvement and social propriety made their assault on Restoration comedy the stalking horse for a broad program of Christian reform. Restoration comedy, which had erupted as a repudiation of Puritan prohibitions, now seemed to prompt a new wave of moral rectitude.

Under such pressures, the playhouse redirected its mirror away from the aristocracy toward the upper strata of the "middling sort": London merchants, colonial profiteers. During the Restoration, the newly prosperous mercantile classes who converged with courtiers at the theater had watched themselves either derided or ignored on stage, their social pretensions and ineptitudes put down in the comedies, their commercial concerns absent from the heroic drama. In the early eighteenth century, they saw themselves glorified instead, in "domestic tragedy," which displayed the tribulations of commercial households, and in sentimental comedy, which sought by a mix of tears and modest laughter to inculcate family values and to portray the merchant class as the nation's moral core. Richard Steele's *The Conscious Lovers* (1722) sounded the fanfare for a newly theatric social self-conception. "We merchants," a businessman informs an aristocrat, "are a species of gentry that have grown into the world this last century, and are as honorable and almost as useful as you landed folk, that have always thought yourself so much above us."

Nor was the stage the only venue to promulgate this new cultural self-awareness. By its very title *The Spectator* (1711–1713), one of the most widely read periodicals of the century, assured its largely middle-class audience that they moved under the constant, thoughtful scrutiny of a virtual playgoer, the paper's fictive author, "Mr. Spectator," who made all London a kind of theater, in which he (and his eagerly imitative readers) might perpetually enjoy the privileges of making observations and forming judgments. The very energies that had been drained away from the stage now found a new home in the theatricalized world of commerce, fashion, manners, taste.

The cast members in this new theater were numerous, varied, and eager for direction, mostly because, as a "new species of gentry," they aspired to roles for which they had formerly been deemed unfit. Terms like "esquire" and "gentleman" had operated in previous centuries as proof of literal "entitlement." They were secured by registration with the College of Heralds, and they calibrated not merely monetary wealth but lineage, landholdings, education, and social standing. In the eighteenth century, men and women with sufficient money and nerve assumed these titles for themselves, confident enough that they might learn to play the part. "In our days," noted a 1730 dictionary, "all are accounted gentlemen that have money." But since "the money" was now so variously attainable—by shopkeeping, by manufacture, by international trade—the "middle station" was itself subdivided into many strata, and since the very point of capital was accumulation and improvement, ascent by emulation became a master plot in the new social theater. "Everyone," observed one commentator, "is flying from his inferiors in pursuit of his superiors, who fly from him with equal alacrity."

Amid the flux, fashion and commodity—what one wore, what one owned—mattered enormously. Wigs, fans, scarves, silks, petticoats, and jewels; china, silver, family portraits—these were the costumes, these the props of the new commercial theater, by which members of the middle orders pleased themselves and imitated the gentry. The commercial classes who had begun by catering to the aristocracy gradually became, in their waxing prosperity, their own best customers, selling garb and goods to one another. Shrewd marketers saw that novelty itself possessed an intrinsic and urgent appeal for people constantly in social flight, tirelessly engaged in remaking themselves. Advertising came into its own, filling the pages and underwriting the costs of the daily, weekly, and monthly periodicals. The listing of consumables became a prevalent mode of print, in everything from auction catalogues (the still-dominant houses of Christie's and Sotheby's got their start near the middle of the century) to poems and novels, where long lists of products and possessions became a means of recording the culture's appetites, and at times of satirizing them. In the hands of Swift and Pope, the catalogue itself became a form of art. The taste in literary miscellany reflected a more general taste for omnivorous consumption: variety indexed abundance and proved power. Tea from China, coffee from the Caribbean, tobacco from Virginia—all were relatively new, comparatively inexpensive, and enormously popular. In daily rituals of drink and smoke, the middling orders imbibed and inhaled a pleasing sense of their global reach, their comfortable centrality on a planet newly commercialized.

Commodities formed part of a larger discourse, involving speech and gesture as well as prop and costume. A cluster of precepts, gathered under the umbrella-term "politeness," supplied the stage directions, even at times the script, for the new social theater in which everyone was actor and everyone was audience. Eager to shine in their recently acquired roles, the merchant classes pursued the polish implicit in the word "polite." They hired "dancing masters" to teach them graceful motions and proper manners, "bear leaders" (tutors) to guide their sons on the Grand Tour of France and Italy in the footsteps of the nobility, elocution coaches to help them purge inappropriate accents, teachers of painting and music to supply their daughters with marriageable competence. For the newly prosperous, politeness was the epitome of distinction: it went beyond gesture and accomplishment to suggest a state of mind, a refinement of perception, a mix of knowledge, responsiveness, and judgment often summarized as "taste." "The man of polite imagination," said the *Spectator*, "is let into a great many pleasures that the vulgar are not capable of receiving." Eager to gain access, middle-class readers avidly sought instruction.

Politeness (which Samuel Johnson once defined as "fictitious benevolence") required considerable self-control; the passions (rage, greed, lust) were to be contained and channeled into the appearance of abundant and abiding goodwill. The middle classes embraced such constraints partly to allay widespread suspicion of their commercial aggressions, their social ambitions. Their preoccupation with politeness has helped to foster a recurrent misimpression of the period: that, setting aside the occasional rake or wench, it was all manners and morals, dignity and decorum, fuss and formality, reason and enlightenment. Not so. Even among the merchant classes, politeness afforded only provisional concealment for roiling energies; amid the impoverished and the gentry, it held less purchase still. In no succeeding epoch until our own was language so openly and energetically obscene, drunkenness so rampant, sexual conduct so various and unapologetic. Even among the "officially" polite, the very failure of containment could produce a special thrill. In one of the century's most often-used phrases, a speaker announces that "I cannot forbear"—that is, cannot restrain myself—from saying or doing what the verb itself suggests were better left unsaid or undone. The formula declares helpless and pleasurable surrender to an unmastered impulse, and the condition was apparently endemic. James Boswell records the memorable self-summary of an elderly lawyer: "I have tried . . . in my time to be a philosopher, but—I don't know how—cheerfulness was always breaking in." Such "breakings-in" (and breakings-out) of feeling were common, even cherished. The scholar Donald Greene has argued well that the eighteenth century was less an "age of reason" (as has often been said) than an age of exuberance. Certainly much of what the middle classes read and wrote is a literature of outburst: of hilarity, of lament, of rage, of exaltation. The copious diaries that the century brought forth deal in all such exclamations; they are the prose of people who have chosen to write rather than repress the thoughts and actions that strict politeness might proscribe. Even the *Spectator*, that manual of polished taste, presents itself as the daily outpouring of a writer who, after maintaining an eccentric lifelong silence, has found that he can no longer keep his "discoveries"—moral, social, experiential—to himself.

Such self-publicizing was more complex for women than for men. When women represented their own lives—in manuscript (letters, journals) and increasingly in print—they sometimes chafed at the paradoxical mix of tantalizing possibilities and

Color Plate 21 Sir Peter Lely, *Barbara Villiers, Countess of Castlemaine*, c. 1665. Theatricality disseminated: Charles II's favorite painter portrays Charles II's favorite mistress, in costume as Minerva, Roman goddess of wisdom, against a stormy background. Castlemaine's countenance was reproduced in less costly ways as well, in engravings from Lely's portraits that made the visage of the King's mistress possessible by ordinary mortals. The diarist Samuel Pepys records a visit to Lely's sumptuous studio, where he "saw the so-much-by-me-desired picture of my Lady Castlemaine, which is a most blessed picture and that I must have a copy of." (Sir Peter Lely [1618–80], Barbara Villiers, Duchess of Cleveland, c. 1641–1709. Photograph: SC/SKY. The Royal Collection © 2002, Her Majesty Queen Elizabeth II.)

Color Plate 22 Johann Zoffany, *Queen Charlotte with Her Two Eldest Sons*, 1764. Theatricality domesticated: a century after Lely painted the king's mistress in the garb of the goddess of wisdom (Color Plate 21), such mythological trappings are reduced to dress-up for George III's two young sons at play. Amid sumptuous furnishings, Zoffany's conversation piece emphasizes not the grandeur of the royal family but its intimacy and affection; a new era of majesty as "good example" has commenced. (Johann Zoffany [1733/4–1810], Queen Charlotte with her Two Eldest Sons. Photograph: A.C. Cooper Ltd. The Royal Collection © 2002, Her Majesty Queen Elizabeth II.)

Color Plate 23 Joshua Reynolds, *Mrs. Abington as "Miss Prue,"* 1771. Restoration theatricality transposed and transformed: the comic actress Frances Abington (1737–1815) here traverses time and rank, reincarnating Miss Prue, an "awkward country girl" in William Congreve's late-17th-century comedy *Love for Love* (1695), in garb that epitomizes late-18th-century high fashion. Abington later scored her greatest triumph in a similar role, modeled on Restoration antecedents and crafted especially for her: Lady Teazle, the country wife ardent for London life in Richard Brinsley Sheridan's *School for Scandal* (page 2083). (The Bridgeman Art Library International Ltd.)

Color Plate 24 Marcellus Laroon, *Charles II as President of the Royal Society*, 1684. Science enthroned: in this portrait of the King painted a year before his death, the traditional trappings of royalty—crown, throne, and orb—literally take a back seat (in the background at left) to the advancements of the new science. Charles gestures toward the instruments of seeing, modeling, mapping, and calibrating that the Royal Society he sponsored had done much to devise and develop. By their placement, the painter suggests that these tools make possible the naval commerce and conquest depicted in the distance—as though the telescope were the world's new scepter, and the globe the monarch's proper sphere. (Picture Desk, Inc./Kobal Collection.)

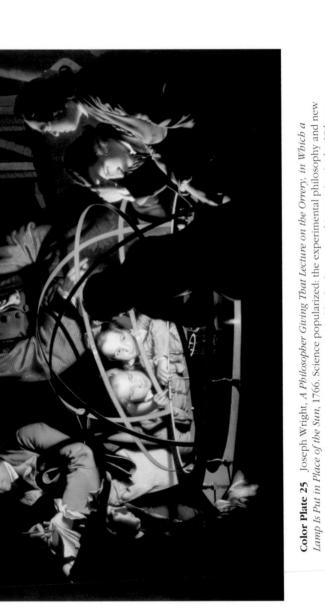

Color Plate 25 Joseph Wright, *A Philosopher Giving That Lecture on the Orrery, in Which a Lamp Is Put in Place of the Sun*, 1766. Science popularized: the experimental philosophy and new science pioneered during the 17th century provided both pleasure and instruction in the 18th, as teachers and textbooks strove to distill and redistribute recondite discoveries as common knowledge. The orrery, a working model of the solar system, figured prominently in this new educational endeavor; it could supply, wrote Richard Steele, "the pleasures of science to any one." The spheres within the circle, coordinated by clockwork, enacted the orbits of the planets and their moons. The sun's stand-in was often a brass ball, but more rarely (as here) a lit oil lamp at the center of the machine. In Wright's painting, the flame sheds light on the lecturer and his listeners, each of them different, all of them enthralled. (Derby Museums and Art Gallery.)

Color Plate 26 Joseph Wright, *An Experiment on a Bird in the Air Pump*, 1768. Science interrogated: the experiment's purpose is to demonstrate the effects of a vacuum on a breathing creature; its outcome, unless the experimenter restores air to the glass chamber, will be the death of the bird. Such experiments, though widely performed, were deemed by one lecturer "too shocking to every spectator who has the least degree of humanity." This time, Wright depicts a mixture of reactions. The lecturer, gesturing like a conjurer, stares out at the viewer as though in a kind of trance, oblivious both to the bird and to his audience, whose faces and forms variously evince absorption, meditation, distraction, and distress. (© National Gallery, London.)

Color Plate 27 William Hogarth, *The Beggar's Opera, Act 3, Scene 11,* 1792. Theatricality encompasses all: audience and actors encounter each other on stage. Hogarth here replicates icons of art history much as *The Beggar's Opera*, a theatrical sensation of 1728, echoed popular ballads (see page 2588). Macheath, the criminal-hero of the play, is shown poised in the center between Lucy (left) and Polly (right)—a grouping that evokes the hero Hercules at his mythic moment of choosing between Virtue and Vice. Meanwhile, Polly and her father, Mr. Peachum (in black at right), strike poses bizarrely reminiscent of Christ and Mary Magdalen. Another kind of pairing is in play too. Lavinia Fenton, the actress playing Polly, gestures not so much toward her stage father as to the audience member standing starstruck just beyond him: the Duke of Bolton, so taken with her in the role that he became her lover and eventually her husband. In this, the fifth version he painted of the same scene, Hogarth has expanded the scope of the stage set so that the prison walls appear to enclose the spectators too within the *Opera's* bright, bleak world, where everything and everyone have become commodities—objects of desire and items of exchange engulfed in intricate, energetic, precarious transactions. (The Bridgeman Art Library International Ltd.)

Color Plate 28   William Hogarth, *Hogarth's Servants*, mid-1750s. In this late painting, Hogarth's lifelong brilliancies of satire cede place to an approach both documentary and tender, as he traces, with painstaking attention and evident affection, the faces of six people deeply familiar to him. (Copyright Tate Gallery, London/Art Resource, NY.)

Color Plate 29   Thomas Gainsborough, *Cottage Door with Children Playing*, c. 1788. As the critic John Barrell has pointed out, Gainsborough's painting mingles two different perceptions of the rural poor. The gracious women and boisterous children basking in the day's last light conjure up the sort of sentimental idealization of pastoral joys that also found expression in such poems as Oliver Goldsmith's *The Deserted Village* (page 2874). George Crabbe's contrapuntal insistence on the misery of the laborer's lot in such works as *The Village* and *The Parish Register* (pages 2884 and 2886) is figured here in the form of the returning husband at bottom left, bent with his burden of firewood and nearly buried by the shadows. (Thomas Gainsborough, The Cottage Door. Cincinnati Art Museum. Given in honor of Mr. and Mrs. Charles F. Williams by their children.)

painful limitations that their privilege produced. Post-Restoration prosperity and politeness supplied women with many new venues for self-display and sociability, in playhouses and pleasure gardens, ballrooms, spas, and shops. Society exalted and paraded women as superior consumers: wearing the furs, fragrances, and fabrics of distant climes, they furnished evidence of empire, proud proof of their fathers' and husbands' economic attainments. They consumed print, too; near the start of the eighteenth century, male editors invented the women's periodical and found the new genre immensely profitable. Increasingly, women not only purchased print but produced it, deploying their words and wit as a kind of cultural capital, which when properly expended might reap both cash and fame. During the eighteenth century, for the first time, books by women—of poems, of precepts, and above all of fiction— became not exotic but comparatively commonplace.

Still, books by women remained controversial, as did all manifestations of female autonomy and innovation. The very excitement aroused by women's new conspicuousness in the culture provoked counter-efforts at containment. Preachers and moralists argued endlessly that female virtue resided in domesticity. Marriage itself offered an age-old instrument of social control, newly retooled to meet the needs of ambitious merchants, for whom daughters were the very currency of social mobility. If parents could arrange the right marriage, the whole family's status promptly rose. The dowry that the bride brought with her was an investment in future possibilities: in the rank and connections that the union secured, in the inheritance that would descend to its heirs, in the annual income ("jointure") that the wife herself would receive following the death of the husband. Financially, a widow (or for that matter, a well-born woman who never married) was often far more independent than a wife, whose wedding led to a kind of sanctioned erasure. She possessed little or no control over marital property (including the wealth she had brought to the union); "in marriage," wrote the codifier of English law William Blackstone, "husband and wife are one person, and that person is the husband." The sums that the husband undertook to hand over to his wife were dubbed "pin money" (a suggestive trivialization): funds for managing the household, that sphere wherein, as the moral literature insisted, a woman might best deploy her innate talents and find her sanctioned satisfactions. These consisted first and foremost in producing children and in shaping their manners and morals. In a time of improvisatory birth control, precarious obstetrics, and high infant mortality, the bearing of children was a relentless, dangerous, and emotionally exhausting process. The upbringing of children provided more pleasure and possessed a new cachet: the conduct literature endorsed busy, attentive child-rearing as the highest calling possible for women whose prosperity freed them from the need to work for wages. (Guidebooks for parents and pleasure books for children both had their origins in the eighteenth century.) Apart from the duties of motherhood and household management—the supervision of servants, meals, shopping, and social occasions—the woman of means was encouraged to pursue those pleasures for which her often deliberately constricted education had prepared her: music, embroidery, letter writing, and talk at the tea table—the domestic counterpart of the clubs and coffeehouses, where women were not permitted to appear.

In the late seventeenth century, the possibilities for women had seemed at moments more various and more audacious. In the plays of Aphra Behn, female characters pursued their pleasures with an almost piratical energy and ingenuity; in A

Serious Proposal to the Ladies (1694), the feminist Mary Astell imagined academies where women could withdraw to pursue the pleasures of learning and escape the drudgeries of marriage. In the eighteenth century, though, despite women's increasing authorial presence, these early audacities tended to go underground. Protests by women against their secondary status are most overt in manuscript—in the acerbic poems and letters that Mary Wortley Montagu circulated among her friends, in the journal entries wherein the brewer's wife Hester Thrale vented her frustrations. In print, women's desire for autonomy became a tension in the text, rather than its explicit point or out-come. Novelists explored women's psyches with subtlety; their plots, however, nearly always culminated in marriage, and more rarely in catastrophe, as though those were the only alternatives. Even the Bluestocking Circle, an eminent late-century group of intellectual women, preached tenets of essential sexual difference and subordination; they argued (for example) in favor of improving girls' educations, but as a way of preparing them for better and happier work within the home rather than for adventures abroad. During the eighteenth century, the middle classes did much to spell out the gendered divison of labor—father as the family's champion in the marketplace, mother as cheerfully efficient angel in the house—that remained a cultural commonplace, among families who could afford it, for the next two hundred years.

Among the poor, such divisions were not tenable; most manual labor paid so lit-tle that everyone in the family had to work if all were to survive. Wives not only managed their frugal households, they also worked for wages, in fields, in shops, or in cottage manufacture of fabrics, gloves, basketry. Children often began wage work at age four or five, treading laundry, scaring crows, sweeping chimneys; boys began the more promising role of apprenticeships around the age of ten. For many of the poor, domestic service offered employment comparatively secure and endlessly demanding. Darker prospects included prostitution, and crime: shoplifting was punishable by death. In the case of the helplessly indigent, local government was responsible for providing relief, but the Poor Law provided large loop-holes by which the parish could drive out any unwanted supplicant—an unwed mother, for example—who could not meet the intricate and restrictive criteria for legal residence. The poor had no vote, no voice in government; as the century progressed, their predicament attracted increasing attention and advocacy. Philanthropists instituted charity schools designed, in the words of their proponent Hannah More, "to train up the lower classes in habits of industry and piety." Two convictions informed even the most ambitious philanthropy: that poverty was part of a divine plan and that it was the fault of the indolent poor themselves; they thus found themselves caught between the rock of providence and the hard place of reproach. Yet charity schools did increase literacy, and with it perhaps the sense of possibilities. Other late-century developments, too, were mixed. Improvements in sanitation, medicine, and hygiene contributed to a surge in population, which in turn produced among the rural poor a labor surplus: too many people, too little work. At the same time, wealthy landhold-ers increased the practice of "enclosure," acquiring and sequestering acreage formerly used by the poor for common pasturage and family farming. As a result, many rural families left the land on which they had worked for centuries and traveled to alien terrain: the textile mills that capitalists had newly built and the industrial cities developing rapidly around them.

As the poor became poorer, the very rich—landowning lords and gentry—became very much richer, both by the means they now shared with the middle class (capital investment in banks and stocks) and through their own long-held resources. Land increased in value, partly because there were now so many merchant families passionately eager to buy into the landscape and the life of their aristocratic betters, among whom the spectacle of emulation provoked amusement and revulsion. The landed gentry preserved their distance by many means: social practices (they often flaunted their adulteries, for example, as contrast to middle-class proprieties), artistic allegiance (with the advent of the bourgeois drama, aristocratic audiences defected from the theater to the opera house, where elaborate productions and myth-based plots sustained the aristocratic values of the heroic drama), and the sheer ostentation of their leisure and magnitude of their consumption. But the pivotal difference remained political: by the award of offices, by the control of elections, landowners maintained their strangle-hold on local and national power, despite all the waxing wealth of trade.

At the same time, their very absorption in pleasure and power demanded a continual traffic with their inferiors. Merchants and shopkeepers catered to them; professionals managed their transactions; household servants contrived their comforts; aspiring artists sought to cultivate their taste and profit by their patronage. Transactions among the aristocracy and the middle classes took other forms as well. A lord low on money often found it lucrative to marry the daughter of a thriving merchant. And middle-class modes of life could exert a subtler magnetism, too—particularly for George III, who prized mercantile decorum over aristocratic swagger. In the portrait of his queen and her two eldest sons in Color Plate 22, the artist Johann Zoffany (himself an expensive German import) celebrates not their royal state but their domestic felicity: the heroic trappings (helmet, spear, turban) so conspicuous in Lely's portrait of the scandalous Lady Castlemaine (see Color Plate 21) are here reduced to the props of child's play in the domestic theater of family relations.

King George had commissioned Johann Zoffany in pursuit of precisely this effect. By his eager emulation of the middling orders, George III broke with monarchic traditions, but he inaugurated a new one that would be sustained and expanded in various ways by Queen Victoria in the nineteenth century and her successors in the twentieth. During George's reign, too, the middle classes began to pursue more practical convergence with the aristocracy: a wider distribution of voting rights, a firmer political power base. For the first time, the phrase "middle classes" itself came into use, as a way of registering this cohort's recognition of its own coherence and interests, its unique, often combative relations with the classes above and below; the plural ("classes") registered the abiding diversity—of income, of lifestyle—within the cohesion. In the years since the Restoration, the middle classes had moved themselves energetically in the theater of social and economic relations from a place in the audience toward center stage, exerting enormous power over the working lives of the poor, posing challenges to the elite. Increasingly, their money, manners, appetites, and tastes came to be perceived as the essence of national life, as the part that might stand for the whole. "Trade," Henry Fielding remarked in 1751, "has indeed given a new face to the nation."

It gave the nation new momentum, too, literal as well as figurative. The engineering marvels of the eighteenth century—the harnessing of steam power, the innovations in factory design, the acceleration of production—were instruments of capital. So were improvements in the rate of transport. Over the course of the century, the government collaborated with private investors to construct a proliferating network of smooth turnpikes and inland waterways: canal boats delivered coal and other cargo with new celerity; stagecoaches sped between cities on precise schedules with crowded timetables. Timekeeping itself became a source of national wealth and pride. During the 1660s, British clockmakers established themselves as the best in Europe. A century later, the clockmaker John Harrison invented the "marine chronometer," a large watch so sturdy and so precise that it could keep time to the minute throughout a voyage around the world, amid all vicissitudes of wind and weather. Harrison's invention made it possible to calculate a ship's longitude accurately, thus solving a problem that had bedeviled navigation for centuries (and sometimes sunk whole fleets). The innovation further paved the way for trade and empire-building, and did much to establish Greenwich, a town just east of London, as the reference point for world time-keeping. Trade was giving a new face—a new distribution of power and priority—not only to the nation but also to the globe, placing Britain (so Britons liked to think) at its center.

FAITH AND KNOWLEDGE, THOUGHT AND FEELING

Clockwork functioned another way too: as a new, theologically unsettling metaphor for the relations between God and his creation. In his *Principia Mathematica* (1687), Isaac Newton set forth the mathematical principles—the laws of motion, the workings of gravity—by which, it turned out, the universe could be seen to operate more consistently and efficiently than even the finest clockwork. What need had this flawless mechanism for any further adjustments by its divine clockmaker? Some of Newton's admirers—though never the pious scientist himself—found in his discoveries the cue for a nearly omnivorous skepticism. The boldest deists and "freethinkers" dismissed Christianity as irrational fiction, to be supplanted by the stripped-down doctrine of "natural religion." In the intricate design of nature they found the proof of a creator whose existence and infinite wisdom, they argued, are all we know on earth and all we need to know. The fashion for such thought—at least in its purest form—proved fleeting. To most minds, the "argument from design" simply furnished further proof of God's benevolence. Amid such comfortable conviction, the blasphemies of a virtuoso skeptic like David Hume appeared an aberration, even an entertainment, rather than a trend. "There is a great cry about infidelity," Samuel Johnson remarked in 1775, "but there are, in reality, very few infidels." From deep belief and ingrained habit, Christianity retained its hold over the entire culture; though a few pietists voiced alarm, science tended to enhance faith, not destroy it.

Still, the relation of religion to public life had changed. In the mid-seventeenth century, politics was inevitably suffused with spirituality. Charles I had gone to the scaffold as an Anglican martyr; he had ruled according to the dictum "No bishop, no king." For many English men and women, the war of Parliament against the king was a holy war: Puritans had typed Charles I as that "man of blood"; Cromwell's army had gone to battle singing David's psalms. By the eighteenth century, ardors had cooled: no one went to war for creed alone. But that is not to say that these were lives bereft of the spiritual; deep religious feeling remained, even as violence of expression abated. The Restoration had reinstated Anglicanism as the national faith; its adherents were admitted to the full privileges of education and office. Over the ensuing century, the Church of England pursued a strategic but controversial mix of old exclusions and new accommodations. For dissenters (offspring of the Puritans), new laws proffered certain permissions (to teach, to congregate for public worship) in exchange for certain oaths. Catholics, by contrast, were kept beyond the pale; they received no such concessions until late in the eighteenth century, when even a limited act provoked angry Protestant riots. Early in the century, the Anglican faithful were divided between the "high flyers," who perennially claimed that the church was in danger of dilution, and the Latitudinarians, who argued that all kinds of dissent might finally be accommodated within the structure of the church. Latitudinarians prevailed, but as the Church of England broadened, it began to lose the force of its exclusiveness; attendance at services shrank markedly as the century advanced, but alternative forms of communal worship flourished. In the eighteenth century, evangelical religions came to occupy the crucial space of fervent spirituality that the church of Donne and Herbert had once claimed as its own. By midcentury, in the new movement called Methodism, John Wesley expressed a vehement response against the skeptical rationalism of the freethinkers and the monied complacency of the established church. Wesley preached the truth of scriptural revelation. He urged his followers to purge their sins methodically—by a constant self-monitoring, partly modeled on earlier Puritan practices—and enthusiastically, by attending revival meetings, hearing electrifying sermons. Wesley delivered some 40,000 sermons over the course of a phenomenally energetic life, and his no less relentless brother Charles composed some 6,000 hymns to quicken evangelical spirits. Methodism found its most ardent following among the poor, who discovered in the doctrine a sympathy for their condition and a recognition of their worth, epitomized in one of Charles Wesley's verses: "Our Savior by the rich unknown / Is worshipped by the poor alone." Their worship was loud and fervent; intensity of feeling attested authenticity of faith.

The middle class and gentry located their own fervor in the more polished idioms of sentiment and sensibility. The terms named a code of conduct and of feeling current in the mid-eighteenth century, when men and women increasingly came to pride themselves on an emotional responsiveness highly cultivated and conspicuously displayed: tears of pity at the spectacle of suffering, admiration for the achievements of art or the magnificence of nature. For many in the middle class, the cult of sentiment held out the appealing prospect of a democratization of manners; the elaborate protocols of the aristocracy might remain elusive, but pure *feeling* was surely more accessible, to anyone with the leisure and the training. For many women, the cult afforded the added attraction of honoring that very susceptibility to feeling and that renunciation of reason that had long and pejoratively been gendered female. The sufferings of the poor, of children, of animals, became a testing ground for empathy; majestic mountains became favorite proving grounds for heightened response. The fashion for benevolence helped focus attention on the plight of the poor and the oppressed, prompting new charities and social movements. For many of the conventionally religious, sentimentality became an adjunct article of faith. They found their scriptures in treatises that posited proper feeling as a chief measure of human worth—Adam Smith's *Theory of Moral Sentiments* (1759); in sentimental dramas that modeled the cultivation (and the performance) of elaborate emotion; in novels that paid minute attention to the protagonist's every emotional nuance— Samuel Richardson's *Pamela* (1740–1741) and *Clarissa* (1747–1749), Laurence Sterne's *Life and Opinions of Tristram Shandy* (1759–1767) and *A Sentimental Journey* (1768), Henry Mackenzies's *The Man of Feeling* (1771); in travel books that transported readers geographically and emotionally by charged descriptions of mighty vistas. For both deists and pietists earlier in the century, nature had testified the existence of a God; for connoisseurs of the sublime near century's end, nature itself was beginning to serve as surrogate for the divine.

In the articulation of eighteenth-century faith and science, thought and feeling, the most conspicuous and continuous voice was that of the first person. The "I" was omnipresent, observing world and self alike: in the experiment-reports of the scientists and the thought-experiments of the philosophers; in the Methodists' self-monitoring, the sentimentalist's self-approbation, the sublimity-seekers' recorded raptures; in the copious autobiographical writings—diaries, letters, memoirs—of characters in novels and people in the real world. Always and everywhere, it seems, someone was setting down the nuances of his or her experience. The self-reckoning promulgated in the past by dissenters was now a broad cultural preoccupation. Its dominion may help to explain why the literature of this era famed for the dominance and delight of its conversation returns us, again and again, to a sense of fundamental solitude.

WRITERS, READERS, CONVERSATIONS

The century and a half from the English Civil Wars to the brink of the French Revolution brought startling change to the structures of politics, social relations, scientific knowledge, and the economy, and no change was more intimate to all these revolutions than the transformations in the relations between writers and readers. From our present perspective, perhaps no scene seems more familiar, even eternal, than that of reader with book in hand. We imagine Virgil's readers and Dante's, Austen's and Wilde's, Pound's and Pynchon's similarly situated, alone with a book, communing silently with an oracular author. But these configurations have changed radically from age to age—sometimes driven by shifts in technology, at other times by social changes. In the eighteenth century, the sea change in relations between writers and readers derived from new social transactions and a new marketplace of letters. And this change did much to shape the modern reckoning of the mix of the solitary and the social, the commerical and the therapeutic within the act of reading. In its refiguring of the social contract between writers and readers, the eighteenth century was nearly as eruptive as our own time with its marketplace of e-mail and Internet, where everyone can potentially operate as both consumer and purveyor—and no one knows for sure the shape of literary things to come.

In 1661, the Earl of Argyle wrote to his son with advice on books, their acquisition, and their proper use:

Think no cost too much in purchasing rare books; next to that of acquiring good friends I look upon this purchase; but buy them not to lay by or to grace your library, with the name of such a manuscript, or by such a singular piece, but read, revolve him, and lay him up in your memory where he will be far the better ornament. Read seriously whatever is before you, and reduce and digest it to practice and observation, otherwise it will be Sisyphus's labor to be always revolving sheets and books at every new occurence which will require the oracle of your reading. Trust not to your memory, but put all remarkable, notable things you shall meet with in your books *sub salva custodia* [under the sound care] of pen and ink, but so alter the property by your own scholia and annotations on it, that your memory may speedily recur to the place it was committed to.

The earl's account displays all the elements of the traditional reading program of Renaissance humanism: book or manuscript as surrogate friend, as "ornament" of the gentleman's mind and library, as "oracle" of enduring truths, as "property" to be possessed, marked, transcribed, and committed to memory. In the decades that followed, all these constructions remained in play, yet every one of the earl's crucial terms broadened in application to include print genres and transactions that Argyle would not have imagined: the periodical review, the monthly miscellany; epistolary fiction; the three-volume novel; as well as the coffeehouses and penny lending libraries that broadly circulated these new forms of print. With these new genres and modes of distribution, the text's status as friend, ornament, oracle, and property changed markedly.

Nothing had demonstrated (some even thought created) the material force and oracular authority of print so much as the English Civil Wars. Sermons and prophecies bearing the names of "oracles" and "revelations" forecast the demise of the Beast, the triumph of Parliament, indeed the imminence of the thousand-year rule of Christ on earth. Nor had the restoration of the Stuart monarchy wholly denatured print as prophecy—royalists and radicals continued to publish apocalyptic claims. And yet, over the ensuing decades the repeated threat of contest and rebellion began to exhaust both the authority of print as prophecy and the appetite of readers for a textual diet of frenzy and apocalypse—not that party warfare in print forms declined, but rather that partisanship yoked political contest to forms of confrontation that cooled apocalyptic tempers and supplanted military combat with paper controversy. The uneven course of government censorship, the issuing and lapsing of the licensing laws that governed press freedom, meant that paper wars with their full armory of ephemera—pamphlets, broadsides, pasquinades—raged at moments of crisis and parliamentary inattention when printers might cash in on the market for opposition and confrontation.

But not all the action of print contest was situated in the gutter of journalism. Satire, that most venerable mode of attack and advocacy, flourished in England as it had in Augustan Rome. Horace and Juvenal were indeed the models for Dryden, Pope, and Swift, who not only translated the forms of Roman satire into native idioms but were themselves possessed by all the Roman delight in outrage and invective, in civic engagement and political contest. But the genius of satire is never solely political. Satirists always score their most important points by wit, by cool savagery, by the thrust and parry of language, by the most brilliant and damaging metaphors and rhymes. Their peers, their rivals, even their enemies ruefully conceded that Dryden, Pope, and Swift had brought the verse couplet and the prose sentence to an unprecedented suppleness and precision. Satire in the years of civil war and Stuart agitations had begun in politics; pamphlet wars, swelled by periodicals, continued to rage through the Georgian age. But the classic verse satire had moved to a more exalted ground where the aesthetic often overwhelmed the political, and satire itself became an object of admiration, even of theorizing, and of the most vivid and polite conversation.

"Conversation" had once meant the entire conduct of life itself; now, "conversation" had narrowed to signify social exchange; yet social exchange in its turn had expanded to govern the conduct of life itself. Many of the most striking literary developments in the period—its poetic modes and tastes, the popularity and prominence of letter and journal writing, the advent of the newspaper and the novel—can perhaps best be understood as new ways devised by writers for performing conversation on the page—conversation with readers, with other writers, and within the texts themselves. The cultural critic Mikhail Bakhtin has pinpointed as one key feature of the novel its "heteroglossia": its capacity to speak, almost concurrently, many different languages, in the various voices and viewpoints of its characters and narrators; the range of its concerns (across social ranks and geographical spaces); even the variabilities of its style (each with its own cultural connotations) from page to page, paragraph to paragraph. But in this respect as in so many, the novel, usually reckoned the greatest literary invention of the period, is the product of a time when virtually all modes of writing were involved with diversity and dialogue.

One of the most popular ways of buying and reading poetry, for example, was in the form of "miscellanies"—anthologies of work by many hands ancient and modern in many modes, brought together in intriguing juxtapositions. Such juxtapositions could also take place within a single poem. For poets, a crucial procedure was the "imitation"—a poem in English that closely echoes the tone, structure, and sequence of a classical model while applying the predecessor's form and thought to contemporary topics. Where the Roman poet Juvenal, for example, begins his tenth Satire by declaring that wise men are hard to find even if you search every country from Spain to India (roughly the extent of the known Roman world), Samuel Johnson begins his imitation of Juvenal's poem (*The Vanity of Human Wishes*) this way:

> Let Observation, with extensive view,
> Survey mankind, from China to Peru . . .

The known world, Johnson tacitly reminds his knowing reader, is much larger than it was when Juvenal wrote (and hence the rarity of discerning mortals will be all the more striking). The opening couplet prepares us for the poem's close, where it will turn out that moral possibilities are larger too: there, Johnson will supplant Juvenal's characteristically Roman resignation to "Fortune" with an expressly Christian reliance on the cardinal virtues (faith, hope, charity) as a means of protection from the delusions of desire. The writer of a poetic imitation always conducts at least a double dialogue: between poet and predecessor, and between the present writer and the ideal reader who knows enough of the "original" to savor the poetic exchange, the cultural cross-talk, in all its echoes, divergences, and diversions.

Johnson here practices a more general kind of imitation as well, by casting his poem in heroic couplets: iambic pentameter lines paired in a sequence of successive rhymes. The rhymed pairs are often "closed," so that the moment of the rhyme coincides with and clinches the completion of a sentence and a thought. The verse form was called "heroic" because of its frequent use in the heroic drama and other high-aspiring poetry of the Restoration; the rhymed, closed pentameter was also thought to imitate, as closely as English allowed, the grandeur and the sonority of the lines in which ancient poets composed their epics. Throughout the century following the Restoration, the heroic couplet prevailed as the most commonly used poetic structure, adaptable to all genres and occasions, deployed by every sort of poet from hacks to John Dryden and Alexander Pope, the supreme masters of the mode. It was in this form that Dryden translated Virgil's *Aeneid* (1697) and Pope translated Homer's *Iliad* (1715–1720) and *Odyssey* (1725–1726), it was in this form that they wrote original poems of high seriousness and savage satire, and it was in this form that they aspired (like many of their contemporaries) to write new epics of their own. Neither ever did; both complained intermittently that they lived in an unheroic age. But the mesh of mighty ancient models with trivial modern subjects produced a new mode of satire, the mock-heroic, and disclosed astonishing suppleness in the heroic couplet itself.

In the hands of Dryden, Pope, and many others, the mock mode—high style, low subject matter—performed brilliant accommodations and solved large problems. It allowed poets to turn what they perceived as the crassness of modern culture to satiric advantage. If the triviality of modern life prevented them from recapturing epic grandeur whole, they could at least strive to match the epic's inclusiveness, its capacity to encompass all the things and actions of the world: the accessories of a young woman's dressing table (Pope's *Rape of the Lock*), the clutter in a gutter after rain (Swift's *Description of a City Shower*), the glut of print itself and the folly of those who produce so much bad writing (Pope's *Dunciad*). After Pope's death, though, this vein of mockery seemed exhausted. The heroic couplet persisted in poetry to the end of the century, but other verse forms became prominent too, partly in the service of an even wider inclusiveness, of paying new kinds of attention to modes of life and literature that lay outside the heroic and the mock: the predicament of the poor, the pleasures of domesticity, the discoveries of science, the tones and textures of medieval English balladry, the modalities of melancholy, the improvisatory motions of human thought and feeling. Blank verse—iambic pentameter without rhyme—offered one manifestation of the impulse to open-endedness. James Thomson's *The Seasons* (1730) and William Cowper's *The Task* (1785), huge works in blank verse, are epic in their own kind: they mingle genres and move from topic to topic with the improvisatory energy of a barely stoppable train of thought. They perform the world's miscellany, the mind's conversation with itself and others, in a new poetic language—one that Wordsworth had absorbed by century's end, when he cast his *Prelude* in a capacious blank verse and praised in the preface to *Lyrical Ballads* that kind of poetry which deploys "the real language" of "a man speaking to men."

In the new prose forms of the eighteenth century—both nonfiction and fiction—the dominion of miscellany, the centrality of conversation, is if anything more palpable than in poetry. The first daily newspaper and the first magazines both appeared early in the century, providing a regularly recurrent compendium of disparate items intended to appeal to a variety of tastes and interests. These periodicals formed part of a larger and highly visible print mix: coffeehouses attracted a burgeoning clientele of urbanites by laying out copies of the current gazettes, mercuries, newsletters, playbooks, and satiric verses. Customers took pleasure in the literary montage, the ever-shifting anthology on the tabletops (of which the pictorial medley on page 2060 conveys a vivid visual idea). Coffeehouse customers gathered to consume new drink and new print in a commerce of pleasure, intellect, and gossip. Some read silently, others aloud to listeners who eagerly seized on texts and topics. Habits of social reading that would have been familiar to Chaucer and his audience (even to Virgil performing his epic at the court of Augustus Caesar) contributed to sociable debate on the persons and personalities of public life, foreign potentates, military campaigns, theatrical rivalries, monsters, and prodigies. In the eighteenth century, the papers and the consequent conversations broadened to encompass questions of personal conduct, relations between the sexes, manner and fashion. Writers of papers still claimed oracular authority: "Isaac Bickerstaff" of the *Tatler* dubbed himself the Censor of Great Britain, Mr. Spectator claimed to watch everyone who read his paper, and the *Athenian Gazette* dispensed advice as though with the authority of a supremely learned society. But writers made such claims at least partly with tongue in cheek; they knew that their oracular "truths" would trickle down into the commerce of conversation.

The press not only stimulated but also simulated conversation. Newspapers had always depended on "correspondents"—not (as now) professional reporters, but local letter writers who sent in the news of their parish and county in exchange for free copies of the paper. To read a newspaper was to read in part the work of fellow readers. Other periodicals—the scientific monthly as well as the journal of advice and the review of arts—adopted the practice of printing letters as a reliable source of copy and as an act and model of sociability. Printed correspondence ran longer, more ambitiously, and more lucratively. For the first time, the collected letters of the eminent became an attractive commercial genre (Pope was a pioneer), and travel books in the form of copious letters home sold by the thousands.

The printed letter would prove crucial too to the development of the newest form of all, the "novel." Aphra Behn had pioneered epistolary fiction in the Restoration, and Samuel Richardson recast the mode on an epic scale in *Pamela* and *Clarissa*, among the most important and talked-about fictions of the eighteenth century. In discussing the fate of his characters, Richardson's readers joined a conversation already in progress; Richardson's characters, in their lively exchange of letters, performed and modeled what their creator called "the converse of the pen."

Yet letters were only one among the many kinds of conversation that novelists contrived to carry on. "The rise of the novel"—the emergence over the course of the eighteenth century of so curious, capacious, and durable a genre—has long excited interest and controversy among scholars, who explain the phenomenon in various ways: by the emergence of a large middle-class readership with the money to obtain, the leisure to read, and the eagerness to absorb long narratives that mirrored their circumstances, their aspirations, and their appetites; by a tension between the aristocratic virtues central to older forms of fiction and the constructs of human merit prized by a proud commercial culture; by the passion for journalistic and experiential fact (in newspapers, criminal autobiographies, scientific experiments, etc.), shading over imperceptibly into new practices of fiction.

All of these explanations are true, and each is revelatory when applied to particular clusters of novels. Still, definition and explanation remain elusive, as they clearly were for the genre's early readers and practitioners. The very word "novel"—identifying the genre by no other marks than newness itself—performs a kind of surrender in the face of a form whose central claim to novelty was its barely definable breadth. Mimicry, motion, and metamorphosis are the genre's stock in trade. Novels absorbed all the modes of literature around them: letters, diaries, memoirs, news items, government documents, drawings, verses, even sheet music all crop up within the pages of the early novels, one representational mode supplanting another with often striking speed. Novelists moved with equal alacrity through space: through England (Henry Fielding's *Tom Jones*), Britain more broadly (Tobias Smollett's *Humphry Clinker*), Europe (Smollett's *Roderick Random*), the entire globe as it is ordinarily mapped (Behn's *Oroonoko*, Defoe's *Robinson Crusoe*) or as it could be extraordinarily imagined (Swift's *Gulliver's Travels*). Traversing geographies, the genre crossed cultures too, mostly by means of mimicry, and parroted a range of accents, for purposes either of mockery—the malapropisms of a semiliterate housemaid, the fulminations of a Scots soldier, the outrage of an Irish cuckold—or of pathos: the lamentations of the African slave Oroonoko, the delirium of the violated Clarissa. Many novels, too, made a point of spanning the social spectrum, often compassing destitution and prosperity, labor and luxury within the career of a single ambitious character. Social mobility was perhaps the one plot element that novel readers savored most.

But the novel's supplest means of self-conveyance, its subtlest modes of conversation, were grounded in its attention to the workings of the mind. In his *Essay Concerning Human Understanding* (1690), the philosopher John Locke had explained the mind as a capacious, absorptive instrument engaged in constant motion, linking mixed memories, impressions, and ideas in a ceaseless chain of "associations." In the eighteenth century, novelists took Locke's cue: their works both mimicked the mind's capacity, heterogeneity, and associativeness, and explored them too, tracking over many pages the subtlest modulations in the characters' thoughts and feelings. Richardson famously boasted that his epistolary mode, featuring "familiar letters written as it were to the moment" by characters in their times of crisis, enabled him to track the course of their "hopes and fears" with unprecedented precision—and he trusted that the value of such a process would surely excuse the "bulk" of the huge novels themselves. In the nine volumes of Laurence Sterne's *Life and Opinions of Tristram Shandy*, the title narrator is so committed to following his digressive trains of thought wherever they may lead that the pronouncement of his opinions leaves him preposterously little time to narrate his life. Moving widely over space, freely through society, minutely through time, and deeply into mind, the novelists devised new strategies for achieving that epic inclusiveness that writers sought, in various ways, throughout the century.

The new tactics of miscellany, the new conversations conducted by means of pen and printing press, poetry and prose, refigured the practices of reading that the Earl of Argyle had wished to transmit to his son. In the aristocratic world of Renaissance letters, the book as friend had intimated a sphere of male pedagogy and sociability. The grammar school classroom, the college lecture hall, the estate library, the world of the tutor and his high-born protégé, all these figured reading principally as the privilege and the pleasure of a limited few, mostly males in positions of some leisure, comfort, and power. The links between reading and power were sustained through patterns of production and consumption in which authors received benefits from aristocratic patrons, and manuscripts passed from hand to hand. Donne refused to imagine his verse circulating in any other fashion. After the Restoration, Dryden, Behn, and Pope all pursued the compensations of print, but they nonetheless remained eager to participate in patronage and coterie circulation. Even when printed, their satires purveyed the pleasurable sense of shared knowledge that had constituted the *frisson* of coterie reading. Printers and poets understood that concealing a public name behind initials and dashes provided safety from censors and litigants, at the same time garnering a market share among readers who pleased themselves by decoding "dangerous matter."

By the middle of the eighteenth century, the patronage model of literary production and the coterie mode of distribution had been complicated (some thought ruined) by the commerce of print, for print had become the principal mode of literary distribution. Samuel Johnson, a bookseller's son, thought of literature as print and rarely circulated a manuscript as a gesture of literary sociability. ("None but a blockhead," he famously intoned, "ever wrote except for money.") As a consequence of the dominance of print and its broad distribution, the audiences for texts proliferated into new mixtures. Readers from many strata could afford a penny paper; apprentices and merchants' daughters might read the same novel. Assumptions of commonality that had underwritten the intimate sociability of Renaissance reading had been exploded by civil conflict in the mid-seventeenth century, by the profusion of print and the proliferation of genres that drove and were driven by the appetite of contest and conversation. During the eighteenth century, the print marketplace generated audiences on a scale vaster than ever before, circulating widely across the boundaries of class and gender. Print may have canceled some of the intimacies of the coterie, but it generated new convergences, even new consciousness—a public sphere in which aesthetics, politics, conduct, and taste were all objects of perpetual, often pleasurable debate. To an unprecedented extent, print furnished its readers with the substance for sustained conversation and continual contact.

It also kept them apart. Nothing was more evident to eighteenth-century men and women than the burgeoning of their domestic economy, the vastness of their colonial empire, and the growth in wealth and population which both entailed. The proliferation of consumables was evident in the village market, the Royal Exchange, and the bookstalls of country towns and capitol. The sheer bulk and variety of these consumables were strikingly evident in the length and scope of that capacious new genre, the novel. But even in the midst of abundance and sociability, eighteenth-century consumers were instructed in their paradoxical solitude. Defoe inscribes the condition of the novel as isolation—Robinson Crusoe, a man alone on an island, opines that human life "is, or ought to be, one universal act of solitude." And in novel after novel the very transactions of commerce produce isolation, as ambition and acquisition drive each character into the solitary, often melancholy corner of his or her own self-interest. The novel itself as a reading experience produced comparable sensations. Readers might now empathize with an entire world of fictional characters, but in order to savor such imaginative pleasures, they spent long hours in the privacy of their own quarters, in silent acts of reading.

A sense of solitude underwrote all this century's celebrated gregariousness. This held true even for sociable transactions that might take place between a reader and a text. In the Renaissance, it had long been a practice to annotate texts with comments echoing and endorsing the author's oracular wisdom. Under the pressure of civil war, the dialogue between author and reader often became more heated as the manuscript marginalia expressed anger and outrage at the partisan zeal of the printed text. But one form of textual reverence persisted. Throughout the seventeenth century readers took pleasure in writing marginalia that epitomized the text, making its wisdom portable. They filled blank books with pithy sentences, "commonplaces" drawn from their favorite works and organized in ways that would allow them to recirculate these sayings in their own writing and conversation.

By the eighteenth century, print had managed to appropriate all these modes of study and sociability. Through print, the manuscript collation of wit and wisdom turned into popular commodities—the printed commonplace book, the miscellany, the anthology. Even annotation itself migrated from manuscript markings into print, as Swift and Pope (among others) found ways of exploding scholarly pretension and of rendering the breath of gossip and scandal in the elaborate apparatus of the printed page. By century's end, all of manuscript's august authority and its most cherished genres—letters and memoirs—had been commandeered by print. In the mid-1730s, Pope alarmed and outraged his contemporaries by publishing his letters as if they deserved to partake of eternity with Cicero's. By the early nineteenth century, even that most secretive mode of self-communion, the private journal, had made its way into the marketplace. In 1825, Pepys's *Diary* appeared in two large printed folios, laying bare the elaborate machinery of public life, the secrets and scandals of the Restoration court, and the diarist's own experiences, transgressions, and sequestered musings, which he had written in shorthand code and shown to no one. The communal and commodified medium of print had found yet another way to market signal acts of solitude.

CODA

Mrs. Abington as "Miss Prue" (1771), by the pre-eminent portraitist Sir Joshua Reynolds (see Color Plate 23), shows a solitary figure engaged in intricate conversation with the viewer. Some of the intricacy inheres in the life history of the sitter, whose career many of the painting's first viewers would have known well. The daughter of a cobbler, Frances Abington had worked in childhood as a flower seller and in her teens as an actress, quickly establishing herself as "by far the most eminent performer in comedy of her day" (these words, and others to follow, are the testimony of contemporaries); she would eventually score one of her greatest hits in the role of that latter-day country wife Lady Teazle, in Richard Brinsley Sheridan's *The School for Scandal* (1777). When an unknown, Abington had married her music teacher; as fame increased, she carried on several well-publicized affairs with members of parliament and the aristocracy. By her sexual frankness, she scandalized—and of course fascinated—the multitudes. By her grace and taste, she became "a favorite of the public" and "the high priestess of fashion"; her cos-

Joshua Reynolds, *Mrs. Abington as "Miss Prue,"* 1771.
Restoration theatricality transposed and transformed.

tumes on stage instantly set new trends among her audience. Reynolds, who greatly admired her, here captures the complexity of her character and reputation. Her
dress is supremely stylish, her pose deliberately provocative. For a woman to lean
casually over the back of a chair this way violated all propriety; in earlier portraits,
only men had struck such a pose. The thumb at her lips suggests vulgarity verging
on the lascivious. The portrait's title purports to explain such seeming aberra-
tions: the actress here appears in her celebrated role as Miss Prue, the "silly, awkward country girl" in William Congreve's Restoration comedy *Love for Love*
(1695), who comes to London with the intention, frankly lustful and loudly
declared, of getting herself a husband. In Reynolds's painting, of course, Mrs.
Abington plays a role more layered: a hybrid of Miss Prue, of the matchlessly fashionable figure into which the actress had transformed herself, and of the whole
range of experiences, the prodigious lifelong motion from poverty to polish, which
formed part of her self-creation and her fame. Impersonating Miss Prue some seventy-five years after the comedy's first production, Mrs. Abington here infuses
Restoration wantonness with Georgian elegance, transgression with high taste,
theatricality with self-assertive authenticity. Like the century she inhabits, she is
miscellany incarnate.

Stuart Sherman and
Steven N. Zwicker

━╍═╍═ ╍

Samuel Pepys
1633–1703

Twice in his life, Samuel Pepys embarked on long projects that allowed him to fuse the methods of the bureaucrat with an inventiveness that amounted to genius. The longer project, which occupied him from his mid-twenties through his mid-fifties, was a fundamental restructuring of the Royal Navy. The shorter project began just a few months earlier. Starting on January 1, 1660, and continuing for the next nine years, Pepys devised the diary form as we know it today: a detailed, private, day-by-day account of daily doings.

Halfway through the diary, Pepys delights to describe himself as "a very rising man," and he wrote the diary in part to track his ascent. The rise began slowly. Born in London to a tailor and a butcher's sister, Pepys studied at Puritan schools; he then attended Magdalene College, Cambridge, as a scholarship student. His B.A. left him well educated but short on cash. A year later he married the fifteen-year-old Elizabeth St. Michel, a French Protestant whose poverty surpassed his own. By his mid-twenties (when the diary commences), neither his accomplishments nor his prospects were particularly striking: he was working as factotum for two powerful men, one of them his high-born cousin Edward Mountagu, First Earl of Sandwich, an important naval officer once devoted to Cromwell but recently turned Royalist.

The diary begins at a calendrical turning point (the first day of a new week, a new year, and a new decade) and on a kind of double bet: that the coming time would bring changes worth writing up, both in the life of the diarist and in the history of the state. The two surmises quickly proved true. As a schoolboy taught by Puritans, Pepys had attended and applauded the execution of Charles I, but the Restoration of Charles II was the making of him, and he recalibrated his loyalties readily enough. His cousin secured for him the Clerkship of the Acts in the Navy Office, a secretarial post that Pepys transformed into something more. By mastering the numberless details of shipbuilding and supplying—from the quality of timber to the composition of tar and hemp—he contrived to control costs and produce results to an extent unmatched by any predecessor.

He managed all these matters so carefully that he soon became the ruler of the Royal Navy, in effect if not in name. When the Test Act of 1673 forced Charles's Catholic brother James to resign as Lord High Admiral, Pepys took his place (in the newly created post of Admiralty Secretary) and ran the operation. He immediately launched a systematic reform of the institution, which he had come to see as dangerously slipshod. By devising (in the words of one biographer) "a rule for all things, great or small" and by enforcing the new disciplines through a method of tireless surveillance and correspondence with ports extending from the Thames to Tangier, Pepys made the navy immeasurably more efficient than ever before. His efforts were interrupted by the political tribulations of his patron James: Pepys spent two brief terms in prison on trumped-up charges of Catholic sympathies, and in 1688 the Glorious Revolution drove him from office into a prosperous retirement. At the height of his power, though, as his biographer Richard Ollard observes, Pepys was the "master builder" of the permanent, professional navy that made possible the expansion of trade and the conquest of colonies over the ensuing century. Energetic in his king's service and in his own (the taking of bribes was one of the perquisites of office that Pepys mastered most adroitly), the tailor's son functioned formidably as an early architect of empire.

Pepys's schooling and profession had immersed him in the two practices most central to earlier English diaries, Puritanism and financial bookkeeping. But where account books and religious diaries emphasize certain kinds of moment—exchanges of money and goods, instances of moral redemption and relapse—Pepys tries for something more comprehensive. He implicitly commits himself to tracking the whole day's experience: the motions of the body as it makes its way through the city in boats, in coaches, and on foot, and the motions of the mind as it shuttles between business and pleasure. He sustained his narrative over a virtually unbroken series of daily entries before stopping out of fear that his work on the diary had helped to damage his eyesight to the brink of blindness. "None of Pepys's contemporaries," writes his editor Robert Latham, "attempted a diary in the all-inclusive Pepysian sense and on the Pepysian scale." To the efficiency of the bookkeeper and the discipline of the Puritan, Pepys added the ardor of the virtuoso, eager (as he observes at one point) "to see any strange thing" and capable of finding wonder in ordinary things: music, plays, books, food, clothes, conversation. The phrase "with great pleasure" recurs in the diary as a kind of leitmotiv, and superlatives play leapfrog through the pages: many, many experiences qualify in turn as the "best" thing that the diarist ever ate, read, thought, saw, heard. To achieve the diary's seeming immediacy, Pepys put his entries through as many as five stages of revision, sometimes days or even months after the events recorded. Even at the final stage, in the bound, elegantly format- ted volumes of the diary manuscript, he often crammed new detail or comment into margins and between the lines. Comparable pressures operated in connection with the diary's complex privacy. Pepys took pains to secure secrecy for his text. He hid it from view in drawers or in cabinets. He wrote most of it in a secretarial shorthand, and where he most wanted secrecy, as in the accounts of his many flirtations and infidelities, he obscured things further by an impro- vised language made up of Spanish, French, Latin, and other tongues. (Elizabeth Pepys figures throughout the diary as a kind of muse and countermuse, the narrative's most recurrent and obsessive subject, and the person most urgently to be prevented from reading it.) At the same time, the manuscript makes notable gestures toward self-display. Pepys frequently shifts to a readily readable longhand, especially for names, places, titles of books, plays, and persons; at times even his secret sexual language opens out into longhand.

This ambivalent secrecy persisted past the diarist's death. Pepys bequeathed the manu- script to Magdalene College without calling any special attention to it. It was included among his many collections: of naval books and papers, of broadsheet ballads, and of instruction man- uals on shorthand methods—including the one Pepys used to write the diary. The manuscript kept its secrets long. In the early nineteenth century, the diary was discovered and painstak- ingly decoded (by a transcriber who, missing the connection between the manuscript and the shorthand manuals on adjacent shelves, treated the text as a million-word cryptogram); it was finally published, in a severely shortened and expurgated version, in 1825. Readers and reviewers soon called for more, recognizing that Pepys possessed (in the words of one re- viewer) "the most indiscriminating, insatiable, and miscellaneous curiosity, that ever . . . sup- plied the pen, of a daily chronicler." Expanded (but still bowdlerized) editions appeared throughout the century, and only in the 1970s did the semisecret manuscript make its way wholly into print.

from **The Diary**

[FIRST ENTRIES][1]

$16\frac{59}{60}$.

Blessed be God, at the end of the last year I was in very good health, without any sense of my old pain[2] but upon taking of cold.

---

1. England still adhered to the Old Style calendar, in which the new year officially began on March 25. Pepys wrote this "prelude" in early January 1659 according to the English reckoning, but 1660 (New Style) in the rest of Europe.

2. Pepys had suffered from stones in the bladder from babyhood until 1658, when he underwent a risky but suc- cessful operation.

I lived in Axe Yard,[3] having my wife and servant Jane, and no more in family than us three.

My wife, after the absence of her terms[4] for seven weeks, gave me hopes of her being with child, but on the last day of the year she hath them again. The condition of the state was thus. *Viz.* the Rump, after being disturbed by my Lord Lambert, was lately returned to sit again.[5] The officers of the army all forced to yield. Lawson lies still in the river and Monck is with his army in Scotland.[6] Only my Lord Lambert is not yet come in to the Parliament; nor is it expected that he will, without being forced to it.

The new Common Council of the City doth speak very high; and hath sent to Monck their sword-bearer, to acquaint him with their desires for a free and full Parliament, which is at present the desires and the hopes and expectation of all—22 of the old secluded members having been at the House door the last week to demand entrance; but it was denied them, and it is believed that they nor the people will not be satisfied till the House be filled.[7]

My own private condition very handsome; and esteemed rich, but indeed very poor, besides my goods of my house and my office, which at present is somewhat uncertain. Mr Downing master of my office.[8]

1 January 1659/60. Lord's Day. This morning (we lying lately in the garret) I rose, put on my suit with great skirts,[9] having not lately worn any other clothes but them.

Went to Mr. Gunning's church at Exeter House, where he made a very good sermon upon these words: that in the fullness of time God sent his Son, made of a woman, etc., showing that by "made under the law" is meant his circumcision, which is solemnized this day.[1]

Dined at home in the garret, where my wife dressed the remains of a turkey, and in the doing of it she burned her hand.

I stayed at home all the afternoon, looking over my accounts.

Then went with my wife to my father's; and in going, observed the great posts which the City hath set up[2] at the Conduit in Fleet Street.

Supped at my father's, where in came Mrs. Theophila Turner and Madam Morris[3] and supped with us. After that, my wife and I went home with them, and so to our own home.

---

3. In Westminster.
4. Menstrual periods.
5. John Lambert, a skilled general under Oliver Cromwell, now opposed the convening of the Rump Parliament, which had governed England since the fall of Cromwell's son Richard in 1659.
6. At this point, the political intentions and allegiance of General George Monck were the object of much speculation; he led his army back from Scotland into England on January 1 and became one of the principal engineers of the Restoration. Vice-Admiral John Lawson supported the Rump.
7. A Parliament that would include the "old secluded members"—the representatives expelled in 1648—was understood to be a first step toward restoration of the

monarchy.
8. Pepys was at this point a clerk in the office of the Exchequer.
9. I.e., with a long coat.
1. Peter Gunning had held illegal Anglican services during the Commonwealth. His sermon text is Galatians 4.4: "But, when the fullness of the time was come, God sent forth his Son, made of a woman, made under the law."
2. As defensive barriers during its opposition to the Rump Parliament.
3. A relative and a friend, respectively. "Mistress" ("Mrs.") was applied to unmarried as well as to married women; Theophila was eight years old.

[THE CORONATION OF CHARLES II][4]

[23 April 1661] I lay with Mr. Shiply,[5] and about 4 in the morning I rose.

Coronation Day.

And got to the Abbey,[6] where I followed Sir J. Denham the surveyor with some company that he was leading in. And with much ado, by the favor of Mr. Cooper his man, did get up into a great scaffold across the north end of the Abbey—where with a great deal of patience I sat from past 4 till 11 before the King came in. And a pleasure it was to see the Abbey raised in the middle, all covered with red and a throne (that is a chair) and footstool on the top of it. And all the officers of all kinds, so much as the very fiddlers, in red vests.

At last comes in the Dean and prebends of Westminster with the Bishops (many of them in cloth-of-gold copes); and after them the nobility all in their Parliament robes, which was a most magnificent sight. Then the Duke[7] and the King with a scepter (carried by my Lord of Sandwich) and sword and mond before him, and the crown too.

The King in his robes, bare-headed, which was very fine. And after all had placed themselves, there was a sermon and the service. And then in the choir at the high altar he passed all the ceremonies of the coronation—which, to my very great grief, I and most in the Abbey could not see. The crown being put upon his head, a great shout begun. And he came forth to the throne and there passed more ceremonies: as, taking the oath and having things read to him by the Bishop, and his lords (who put on their caps as soon as the King put on his crown) and bishops came and kneeled before him.

And three times the King-at-Arms went to the three open places on the scaffold and proclaimed that if any one could show any reason why Charles Stuart should not be King of England, that now he should come and speak.

And a general pardon also was read by the Lord Chancellor;[8] and medals flung up and down by my Lord Cornwallis—of silver; but I could not come by any.

But so great a noise, that I could make but little of the music; and indeed, it was lost to everybody. But I had so great a list[9] to piss, that I went out a little while before the King had done all his ceremonies and went round the Abbey to Westminster Hall, all the way within rails, and 10,000 people, with the ground covered with blue cloth—and scaffolds all the way. Into the hall I got—where it was very fine with hangings and scaffolds, one upon another, full of brave[1] ladies. And my wife in one little one on the right hand.

Here I stayed walking up and down; and at last, upon one of the side-stalls, I stood and saw the King come in with all the persons (but the soldiers) that were yesterday in the cavalcade;[2] and a most pleasant sight it was to see them in their several robes. And the King came in with his crown on and his scepter in his hand—under a canopy borne up by six silver staves, carried by Barons of the Cinqueports—and little bells at every end.

---

4. Charles II had returned to England in May 1660; he scheduled his coronation for St. George's Day, honoring England's patron saint.
5. Edward Shipley was steward to Pepys's cousin Edward Mountagu.
6. Westminster Abbey, site of English coronations.
7. Charles's brother James, Duke of York, later James II.

8. Charles II's Act of Oblivion forgave the crimes of all those on the parliamentary side, with the principal exception of those who had participated in the trial, sentencing, and execution of his father.
9. Desire.
1. Splendid.
2. The previous day's procession.

And after a long time he got up to the farther end, and all set themselves down at their several tables—and that was also a rare sight. And the King's first course carried up by the Knights of the Bath. And many fine ceremonies there was of the heralds leading up people before him and bowing; and my Lord of Albemarle's[3] going to the kitchen and eat[4] a bit of the first dish that was to go to the King's table.

But above all was these three Lords, Northumberland and Suffolk and the Duke of Ormond, coming before the courses on horseback and staying so all dinner-time; and at last, to bring up Dymock the King's champion, all in armor on horseback, with his spear and target carried before him. And a herald proclaim that if any dare deny Charles Stuart to be lawful King of England, here was a champion that would fight with him; and with those words the champion flings down his gauntlet; and all this he doth three times in his going up toward the King's table. At last, when he is come, the King drinks to him and then sends him the cup, which is of gold; and he drinks it off and then rides back again with the cup in his hand.

I went from table to table to see the bishops and all others at their dinner, and was infinite pleased with it. And at the lords' table I met with Will Howe and he spoke to my Lord for me and he did give him four rabbits and a pullet; and so I got it, and Mr. Creed and I got Mr. Mitchell to give us some bread and so we at a stall eat it, as everybody else did what they could get.[5]

I took a great deal of pleasure to go up and down and look upon the ladies—and to hear the music of all sorts; but above all, the 24 violins.

About 6 at night they had dined; and I went up to my wife and there met with a pretty lady (Mrs. Franklin, a doctor's wife, a friend of Mr. Bowyer's) and kissed them both—and by and by took them down to Mr. Bowyer's. And strange it is, to think that these two days have held up fair till now that all is done and the King gone out of the Hall; and then it fell a-raining and thundering and lightening as I have not seen it do some years—which people did take great notice of God's blessing of the work of these two days—which is a foolery, to take too much notice of such things.

I observed little disorder in all this; but only the King's footmen had got hold of the canopy and would keep it from the Barons of the Cinqueports; which they endeavored to force from them again but could not do it till my Lord Duke of Albemarle caused it to be put into Sir R. Pye's hand till tomorrow to be decided.

At Mr. Bowyer's, a great deal of company; some I knew, others I did not. Here we stayed upon the leads[6] and below till it was late, expecting to see the fireworks; but they were not performed tonight. Only, the City had a light like a glory round about it, with bonfires.

At last I went to King Street; and there sent Crockford to my father's and my house to tell them I could not come home tonight, because of the dirt and a coach could not be had.

And so after drinking a pot of ale alone at Mrs. Harper's, I returned to Mr. Bowyer's; and after a little stay more, I took my wife and Mrs. Franklin (who I proferred the civility of lying with my wife at Mrs. Hunt's tonight) to Axe Yard. In which, at the further end, there was three great bonfires and a great many great gallants, men and women; and they laid hold of us and would have us drink the King's

---

3. In 1660 Charles II had made George Monck Duke of Albemarle as a reward for his role in the Restoration.
4. Ate (pronounced "ett"), to test for poison.
5. Will Howe and John Creed served as clerks to Sand-

wich, whom the diarist invariably refers to as "my Lord." Miles Mitchell was a local bookseller.
6. Rooftop.

health upon our knee, kneeling upon a fagot; which we all did, they drinking to us one after another—which we thought a strange frolic. But these gallants continued thus a great while, and I wondered to see how the ladies did tipple.

At last I sent my wife and her bedfellow to bed, and Mr. Hunt and I went in with Mr. Thornbury (who did give the company all their wines, he being yeoman of the wine-cellar to the King) to his house; and there, with his wife and two of his sisters and some gallant sparks that were there, we drank the King's health and nothing else, till one of the gentlemen fell down stark drunk and there lay spewing. And I went to my Lord's pretty well. But no sooner a-bed with Mr. Shiply but my head begun to turn and I to vomit, and if ever I was foxed[7] it was now—which I cannot say yet, because I fell asleep and sleep till morning—only, when I waked I found myself wet with my spewing. Thus did the day end, with joy everywhere; and blessed be God, I have not heard of any mischance to anybody through it all, but only to Sergeant Glynne, whose horse fell upon him yesterday and is like to kill him; which people do please themselves with, to see how just God is to punish that rogue at such a time as this—he being now one of the King's sergeants and rode in the cavalcade with Maynard, to whom people wished the same fortune.[8]

There was also this night, in King Street, a woman had her eye put out by a boy's flinging of a firebrand into the coach.

Now after all this, I can say that besides the pleasure of the sight of these glorious things, I may now shut my eyes against any other objects, or for the future trouble myself to see things of state and show, as being sure never to see the like again in this world.

[24 April 1661] Waked in the morning with my head in a sad taking through the last night's drink, which I am very sorry for. So rise and went out with Mr. Creed to drink our morning draught, which he did give me in chocolate to settle my stomach. And after that to my wife, who lay with Mrs. Franklin at the next door to Mrs. Hunt's.

And they were ready, and so I took them up in a coach and carried the lady to Paul's[9] and there set her down; and so my wife and I home—and I to the office.

That being done, my wife and I went to dinner to Sir W. Batten;[1] and all our talk about the happy conclusion of these last solemnities.

After dinner home and advised with my wife about ordering things in my house; and then she went away to my father's to lie, and I stayed with my workmen, who do please me very well with their work.

At night set myself to write down these three days' diary; and while I am about it, I hear the noise of the chambers and other things of the fireworks, which are now playing upon the Thames before the King. And I wish myself with them, being sorry not to see them.

So to bed.

[THE PLAGUE YEAR]

[7 June 1665] This morning my wife and mother rose about 2 a-clock, and with Mercer, Mary, the boy, and W. Hewer,[2] as they had designed, took boat and down to refresh themselves on the water to Gravesend. I lay till 7 a-clock; then up, and to the

---

7. Drunk.
8. Sir John Glynne and Sir John Maynard were lawyers who had served under Cromwell.
9. St. Paul's Cathedral.

1. Surveyor of the Navy.
2. Mary Mercer was Elizabeth Pepys's paid companion; Will Hewer was Pepys's office clerk and lifelong friend; Mary and "the boy" are household servants.

office upon Sir G. Carteret's accounts again—where very busy.[3] Thence abroad and to the Change, no news of certainty being yet come from the fleet.[4] Thence to the Dolphin Tavern, where Sir J. Mennes, Lord Brouncker, Sir Thomas Harvey and myself dined upon Sir G. Carteret's charge—and very merry we were, Sir Thomas Harvey being a very droll.[5] Thence to the office; and meeting Creed, away with him to my Lord Treasurer's, there thinking to have met the goldsmiths, or at Whitehall; but did not, and so appointed another time for my lord to speak to them to advance us some money. Thence, it being the hottest day that ever I felt in my life, and it is confessed so by all other people the hottest they ever knew in England in the beginning of June—we to the New Exchange and there drunk whey; with much entreaty, getting it for our money, and would not be entreated to let us have one glass more. So took water, and to Foxhall[6] to the Spring Garden and there walked an hour or two with great pleasure, saving our minds ill at ease concerning the fleet and my Lord Sandwich, that we have no news of them, and ill reports run up and down of his being killed, but without ground. Here stayed, pleasantly walking and spending but 6d, till 9 at night; and then by water to Whitehall, and there I stopped to hear news of the fleet, but none come, which is strange; and so by water home—where, weary with walking and with the mighty heat of the weather, and for my wife's not coming home—I staying walking in the garden till 12 at night, when it begun to lighten exceedingly through the greatness of the heat. Then, despairing of her coming home, I to bed.

This day, much against my will, I did in Drury Lane see two or three houses marked with a red cross upon the doors, and "Lord have mercy upon us" writ there[7]—which was a sad sight to me, being the first of that kind that to my remembrance I ever saw. It put me into an ill conception of myself and my smell, so that I was forced to buy some roll-tobacco to smell to and chaw—which took away the apprehension.[8]

[30 July 1665] Lord's Day. Up, and in my nightgown, cap, and neck-cloth, undressed all day long; lost not a minute, but in my chamber setting my Tangier accounts to rights, which I did by night, to my very heart's content; not only that it is done, but I find everything right and even beyond what, after so long neglecting them, I did hope for. The Lord of Heaven be praised for it.

Will was with me today and is very well again. It was a sad noise to hear our bell to toll and ring so often today, either for deaths or burials; I think five or six times.

At night, weary with the day's work but full of joy at my having done it—I to bed, being to rise betimes tomorrow to go to the wedding at Dagnams.

So to bed—fearing I have got some cold sitting in my loose garment all this day.

[31 July 1665[9]] Up, and very betimes, by 6 a-clock, at Deptford; and there find Sir G. Carteret and my lady ready to go—I being in my new colored-silk suit and coat, trimmed with gold buttons and gold broad lace round my hands, very rich and fine. By water to the ferry, where, when we came, no coach there—and tide of ebb so far

3. George Carteret was Navy Treasurer.
4. The Royal Exchange was the City's central location for luxury shopping, business dealings, and news gathering. Pepys wanted news of the ongoing Second Dutch War; his patron Sandwich was in command of the fleet.
5. All these men were colleagues on the Navy Board. *Droll*: jester.
6. Vauxhall, a cluster of riverside gardens, immensely

popular for its avenues, covered walks, and wine stalls.
7. The red cross marked houses infected by plague.
8. Tobacco was thought to prevent infection.
9. The wedding day of Lady Jemimah Mountagu, Sandwich's eldest daughter, and Philip Carteret, eldest son of Pepys's colleague Sir George. Pepys had helped to arrange the match.

spent as the horse-boat could not get off on the other side the river to bring away the coach. So we were fain to stay there in the unlucky Isle of Dogs—in a chill place, the morning cool and wind fresh, above two if not three hours, to our great discontent. Yet being upon a pleasant errand, and seeing that could not be helped, we did bear it very patiently; and it was worth my observing, I thought as ever anything, to see how upon these two scores, Sir G. Carteret, the most passionate man in the world and that was in greatest haste to be gone, did bear with it, and very pleasant all the while, at least not troubled much so as to fret and storm at it.

Anon the coach comes—in the meantime there coming a citizen thither with his horse to go over, that told us he did come from Islington this morning, and that Proctor the vintner of the Mitre in Wood Street, and his son, is dead this morning there—of the plague. He having laid out abundance of money there—and was the greatest vintner for some time in London for great entertainments.

We, fearing the canonical hour would be past before we got thither,[1] did with a great deal of unwillingness send away the license and wedding ring. So that when we came, though we drove hard with six horses, yet we found them gone from home; and going toward the church, met them coming from church—which troubled us. But however, that trouble was soon over—hearing it was well done—they being both in their old clothes. My Lord Crew giving her—there being three coach-fulls of them. The young lady mighty sad, which troubled me; but yet I think it was only her gravity, in a little greater degree than usual. All saluted her,[2] but I did not till my Lady Sandwich did ask me whether I had not saluted her or no. So to dinner, and very merry we were; but yet in such a sober way as never almost any wedding was in so great families—but it was much better. After dinner, company divided, some to cards—others to talk. My Lady Sandwich and I up to settle accounts and pay her some money—and mighty kind she is to me, and would fain have had me gone down for company with her to Hinchingbrooke—but for my life I cannot.

At night to supper, and so to talk and, which methought was the most extraordinary thing, all of us to prayers as usual, and the young bride and bridegroom too. And so after prayers, soberly to bed; only, I got into the bridegroom's chamber while he undressed himself, and there was very merry—till he was called to the bride's chamber and into bed they went. I kissed the bride in bed, and so the curtains drawn with the greatest gravity that could be, and so good-night.

But the modesty and gravity of this business was so decent, that it was to me, indeed, ten times more delightful than if it had been twenty times more merry and jovial.

Whereas I feared I must have sat up all night, we did here all get good beds—and I lay in the same I did before, with Mr. Brisband, who is a good scholar and sober man; and we lay in bed, getting him to give me an account of Rome, which is the most delightful talk a man can have of any traveler. And so to sleep—my eyes much troubled already with the change of my drink.

Thus I ended this month with the greatest joy that ever I did any in my life, because I have spent the greatest part of it with abundance of joy and honor, and pleasant journeys and brave entertainments, and without cost of money. And at last live to see that business ended[3] with great content on all sides.

---

1. Church law stipulated that weddings could be performed only during certain hours of the day.

2. Greeted her with a kiss.

3. The marriage concluded.

This evening with Mr. Brisband speaking of enchantments and spells, I telling him some of my charms,[4] he told me this of his own knowledge at Bourdeaux in France. The words these—

Voicy un corps mort
Royde comme un baston
Froid comme marbre
Leger comme un esprit,
Levons te au nom de Jesus Christ.[5]

He saw four little girls, very young ones, all kneeling, each of them upon one knee; and one begin the first line, whispering in the ear of the next, and the second to the third, and the third to the fourth, and she to the first. Then the first begun the second line, and so round quite through. And putting each one finger only to a boy that lay flat upon his back on the ground, as if he was dead. At the end of the words they did with their four fingers raise this boy as high as they could reach. And he being there and wondering at it (as also being afeared to see it—for they would have had him to have bore a part in saying the words in the room of one of the little girls, that was so young that they could hardly make her learn to repeat the words), did, for fear there might be some sleight used in it by the boy, or that the boy might be light, called the cook of the house, a very lusty fellow, as Sir G. Carteret's cook, who is very big, and they did raise him just in the same manner.

This is one of the strangest things I ever heard, but he tells it me of his own knowledge and I do heartily believe it to be true. I inquired of him whether they were Protestant or Catholic girls, and he told me they were Protestant—which made it the more strange to me.

Thus we end this month, as I said, after the greatest glut of content that ever I had; only, under some difficulty because of the plague, which grows mightily upon us, the last week being about 1,700 or 1,800 [dead] of the plague.

My Lord Sandwich, at sea with a fleet of about 100 sail to the Norward, expect De Ruyter or the Dutch East-India fleet.

My Lord Hinchingbrooke[6] coming over from France, and will meet his sister at Scott's Hall.

Myself having obliged both these families in this business very much, as both my lady and Sir G. Carteret and his lady do confess exceedingly; and the latter two also now call me cousin, which I am glad of.

So God preserve us all friends long, and continue health among us.

[15 August 1665] Up by 4 a-clock and walked to Greenwich, where called at Captain Cocke's[7] and to his chamber, he being in bed—where something put my last night's dream into my head, which I think is the best that ever was dreamed—which was, that I had my Lady Castlemaine[8] in my arms and was admitted to use all the dalliance I desired with her, and then dreamed that this could not be awake but that it

4. At the end of the previous year, Pepys had written into his diary a set of incantations ("charms") for healing cuts, burns, etc.
5. Here is a dead body / Stiff as a rod / Cold as marble / Light as a spirit, / We raise thee in the name of Jesus Christ.

6. Sandwich's son.
7. George Cocke, supplier to the navy and Pepys's colleague on the board.
8. Barbara Palmer, Countess of Castlemaine, was a celebrated beauty and at this point the foremost among the King's mistresses.

was only a dream. But that since it was a dream and that I took so much real pleasure in it, what a happy thing it would be, if when we are in our graves (as Shakespeare resembles it),[9] we could dream, and dream but such dreams as this—that then we should not need to be so fearful of death as we are this plague-time. * * *

It was dark before I could get home; and so land at church-yard-stairs, where to my great trouble I met a dead corpse, of the plague, in the narrow ally, just bringing down[1] a little pair of stairs—but I thank God I was not much disturbed at it. However, I shall beware of being late abroad again.

[10 September 1665] *Lord's day*. Walked home, being forced thereto by one of my watermen falling sick yesterday; and it was God's great mercy I did not go by water with them yesterday, for he fell sick on Saturday night and it is to be feared of the plague. So I sent him away to London with his fellow.

But another boat came to me this morning, whom I sent to Blackwell for Mr. Andrews; I walked to Woolwich,[2] and there find Mr. Hill, and he and I all the morning at music and a song he hath set, of three parts; methinks very good. Anon comes Mr. Andrews, though it be a very ill day. And so after dinner we to music and sang till about 4 or 5 a-clock, it blowing very hard, and now and then raining—and, wind and tide being against us, Andrews and I took leave and walked to Greenwich—my wife before I came out telling me the ill news that she hears, that her father is very ill; and then I told her I feared of the plague, for that the house is shut up.[3] And so, she much troubled, she did desire me to send them something, and I said I would, and will do so.

But before I came out, there happened news to come to me by an express from Mr. Coventry, telling me the most happy news of my Lord Sandwich's meeting with part of the Dutch; his taking two of their East India ships and six or seven others, and very good prize—and that he is in search of the rest of the fleet, which he hopes to find upon the Well Bank—with the loss only of the *Hector*, poor Captain Cuttle. This news doth so overjoy me, that I know not what to say enough to express it; but the better to do it, I did walk to Greenwich;[4] and there sending away Mr. Andrews, I to Captain Cocke's, where I find my Lord Brouncker and his mistress and Sir J. Mennes—where we supped (there was also Sir W. Doyly and Mr. Evelyn);[5] but the receipt of this news did put us all into such an ecstasy of joy, that it inspired into Sir J. Mennes and Mr. Evelyn such a spirit of mirth, that in all my life I never met with so merry a two hours as our company this night was. Among other humors, Mr. Evelyn's repeating of some verses made up of nothing but the various acceptations of May and Can, and doing it so aptly, upon occasion of something of that nature, and so fast, did make us all die almost with laughing, and did so stop the mouth of Sir J. Mennes in the middle of all his mirth (and in a thing agreeing with his own manner of genius) that I never saw any man so outdone in all my life; and Sir J. Mennes's mirth too, to see himself outdone, was the crown of all our mirth.

---

9. Shakespeare compares ("resembles") death to sleep in Hamlet's famous soliloquy, though Hamlet fears what he might dream when dead: "To die, to sleep; / To sleep, perchance to dream. Ay, there's the rub, / For in that sleep of death what dreams may come, / When we have shuffled off this mortal coil, / Must give us pause." (*Hamlet* 3.1.65–69).
1. Being carried down.
2. A navy yard on the Thames, east of London, where Pepys, his wife, and their servants had taken lodgings in

an effort to avoid the plague.
3. Quarantined.
4. A town on the Thames, east of London, where the Navy Office had temporarily relocated during plague time.
5. John Evelyn (1620–1706), author, virtuoso, and fellow diarist. During the Second Dutch War, both Evelyn and William Doyly served the Navy as Commissioners for the Sick and Wounded.

In this humor we sat till about 10 at night; and so my Lord and his mistress home, and we to bed—it being one of the times of my life wherein I was the fullest of true sense of joy.

[14 September 1665] Up, and walked to Greenwich and there fitted myself in several businesses to go to London, where I have not been now a pretty while. But before I went from the office, news is brought by word of mouth that letters are now just now brought from the Fleet of our taking a great many more of the Dutch fleet—in which I did never more plainly see my command of my temper, in my not admitting myself to receive any kind of joy from it till I had heard the certainty of it. And therefore went by water directly to the Duke of Albemarle, where I find a letter of the 12th from Solebay, from my Lord Sandwich, of the fleet's meeting with about 18 more of the Dutch fleet and his taking of most of them; and the messenger says they had taken three after the letter was wrote and sealed; which being 21, and the 14 took the other day, is 45 sail—some of which are good, and others rich ships—which is so great a cause of joy in us all, that my Lord and every body is highly joyed thereat. And having taken a copy of my Lord's letter, I away back again to the Bear at the bridge-foot, being full of wind and out of order, and there called for a biscuit and a piece of cheese and gill of sack[6]—being forced to walk over the bridge toward the Change, and the plague being all thereabouts. Here my news was highly welcome, and I did wonder to see the Change so full, I believe 200 people; but not a man or merchant of any fashion, but plain men all. And Lord, to see how I did endeavor all I could to talk with as few as I could, there being now no observation of shutting up of houses infected, that to be sure we do converse and meet with people that have the plague upon them. I to Sir Robert Viners, where my main business was about settling the business of Debusty's 5000*l* tallies—which I did for the present to enable me to have some money. And so home, buying some things for my wife in the way. So home and put up several things to carry to Woolwich—and upon serious thoughts, I am advised by W. Griffin to let my money and plate[7] rest there, as being as safe as any place, nobody imagining that people would leave money in their houses now, when all their families are gone. So for the present, that being my opinion, I did leave them there still. But Lord, to see the trouble that it puts a man to to keep safe what with pain a man hath been getting together; and there is good reason for it. Down to the office, and there wrote letters to and again about this good news of our victory, and so by water home late—

Where when I came home, I spent some thoughts upon the occurrences of this day, giving matter for as much content on one hand and melancholy on another as any day in all my life—for the first, the finding of my money and plate and all safe at London and speeding in my business of money this day—the hearing of this good news, to such excess after so great a despair of my Lord's doing anything this year—adding to that, the decrease of 500 and more, which is the first decrease we have yet had in the sickness since it begun—and great hopes that the next week it will be greater. Then on the other side—my finding that though the Bill[8] in general is abated, yet the City within the walls[9] is increased and likely to continue so and is close to our house there—my meeting dead corpses of the plague, carried to be buried close to me

6. Quarter pint of white wine.
7. Silver.
8. The Bill of Mortality, a weekly, parish-by-parish account of the deaths in London.
9. London had spread beyond its original walls, but the area within those walls was still known as "the City."

at noonday through the City in Fanchurch Street—to see a person sick of the sores carried close by me by Grace Church in a hackney-coach—my finding the Angel Tavern at the lower end of Tower Hill shut up; and more than that, the ale-house at the Tower stairs; and more than that, that the person was then dying of the plague when I was last there, a little while ago at night, to write a short letter there, and I overheard the mistress of the house sadly saying to her husband somebody was very ill, but did not think it was of the plague—to hear that poor Payne my waterman hath buried a child and is dying himself—to hear that a laborer I sent but the other day to Dagnams to know how they did there is dead of the plague; and that one of my own watermen, that carried me daily, fell sick as soon as he had landed me on Friday morning last, when I had been all night upon the water (and I believed he did get his infection that day at Brainford) is now dead of the plague—to hear that Captain Lambert and Cuttle are killed in the taking these ships and that Mr. Sidney Mountagu is sick of a desperate fever at my Lady Carteret's at Scott's Hall—to hear that Mr. Lewes hath another daughter sick—and lastly, that both my servants, W. Hewer and Tom Edwards, have lost their fathers, both in St. Sepulcher's parish, of the plague this week—doth put me into great apprehensions of melancholy, and with good reason. But I put off the thoughts of sadness as much as I can; and the rather to keep my wife in good heart, and family also. After supper (having eat nothing all this day) upon a fine tench[1] of Mr. Sheldon's taking, we to bed.

[THE FIRE OF LONDON]

[2 September 1666] Lord's Day. Some of our maids sitting up late last night to get things ready against our feast today, Jane called us up, about 3 in the morning, to tell us of a great fire they saw in the City. So I rose, and slipped on my nightgown and went to her window, and thought it to be on the back side of Mark Lane at the furthest; but being unused to such fires as followed, I thought it far enough off, and so went to bed again and to sleep. About 7 rose again to dress myself, and there looked out at the window and saw the fire not so much as it was, and further off. So to my closet[2] to set things to rights after yesterday's cleaning. By and by Jane comes and tells me that she hears that above 300 houses have been burned down tonight by the fire we saw, and that it was now burning down all Fish Street by London Bridge. So I made myself ready presently, and walked to the Tower and there got up upon one of the high places, Sir J. Robinson's little son going up with me; and there I did see the houses at that end of the bridge all on fire, and an infinite great fire on this and the other side the end of the bridge—which, among other people, did trouble me for poor little Mitchell and our Sarah on the bridge.[3] So down, with my heart full of trouble, to the Lieutenant of the Tower, who tells me that it begun this morning in the King's baker's house in Pudding Lane, and that it hath burned down St. Magnus's Church and most part of Fish Street already. So I down to the water-side and there got a boat and through bridge,[4] and there saw a lamentable fire. Poor Mitchell's house, as far as the Old Swan, already burned that way and the fire running further, that in a very little time it got as far as the Steelyard while I was there. Everybody endeavoring to remove their goods, and flinging into the river or bringing them into lighters[5] that lay off. Poor people staying in their

---

1. A kind of fish.
2. Private room, study.
3. London Bridge was lined with shops and houses, including the liquor shop of Pepys's friend Michael Mitchell and the residence of his former servant Sarah.
4. Under the bridge.
5. Barges.

houses as long as till the very fire touched them, and then running into boats or clambering from one pair of stair by the water-side to another. And among other things, the poor pigeons I perceive were loath to leave their houses, but hovered about the windows and balconies till they were some of them burned, their wings, and fell down.

Having stayed, and in an hour's time seen the fire rage every way, and nobody to my sight endeavoring to quench it, but to remove their goods and leave all to the fire; and having seen it get as far as the Steelyard, and the wind mighty high and driving it into the City, and everything, after so long a drought, proving combustible, even the very stones of churches, and among other things, the poor steeple by which pretty Mrs. Horsley lives, and whereof my old school-fellow Elborough is parson, taken fire in the very top and there burned till it fall down—I to Whitehall with a gentleman with me who desired to go off from the Tower to see the fire in my boat—to Whitehall, and there up to the King's closet in the chapel, where people came about me and I did give them an account dismayed them all; and word was carried in to the King, so I was called for and did tell the King and Duke of York what I saw, and that unless his Majesty did command houses to be pulled down, nothing could stop the fire. They seemed much troubled, and the King commanded me to go to my Lord Mayor from him and command him to spare no houses but to pull down before the fire every way. The Duke of York bid me tell him that if he would have any more soldiers, he shall; and so did my Lord Arlington afterward, as a great secret. Here meeting with Captain Cocke, I in his coach, which he lent me, and Creed with me, to Paul's; and there walked along Watling Street as well as I could, every creature coming away loaden with goods to save—and here and there sick people carried away in beds. Extraordinary good goods carried in carts and on backs. At last met my Lord Mayor in Canning Street, like a man spent, with a hankercher about his neck. To the King's message, he cried like a fainting woman, "Lord, what can I do? I am spent! People will not obey me. I have been pulling down houses. But the fire overtakes us faster than we can do it." That he needed no more soldiers; and that for himself, he must go and refresh himself, having been up all night. So he left me, and I him, and walked home—seeing people all almost distracted and no manner of means used to quench the fire. The houses too, so very thick thereabouts, and full of matter for burning, as pitch and tar, in Thames Street—and warehouses of oil and wines and brandy and other things. Here I saw Mr. Isaac Houblon, that handsome man—prettily dressed and dirty at his door at Dowgate, receiving some of his brothers' things whose houses were on fire; and as he says, have been removed twice already, and he doubts (as it soon proved) that they must be in a little time removed from his house also—which was a sad consideration. And to see the churches all filling with goods, by people who themselves should have been quietly there at this time.

By this time it was about 12 a-clock, and so home and there find my guests, which was Mr. Wood and his wife, Barbary Shelden, and also Mr. Moone—she mighty fine, and her husband, for aught I see, a likely man. But Mr. Moone's design and mine, which was to look over my closet and please him with the sight thereof, which he hath long desired, was wholly disappointed, for we were in great trouble and disturbance at this fire, not knowing what to think of it. However, we had an extraordinary good dinner, and as merry as at this time we could be.

While at dinner, Mrs. Batelier came to inquire after Mr. Woolfe and Stanes (who it seems are related to them), whose houses in Fish Street are all burned, and they in a sad condition. She would not stay in the fright.

As soon as dined, I and Moone away and walked through the City, the streets full of nothing but people and horses and carts loaden with goods, ready to run over one another, and removing goods from one burned house to another—they now removing out of Canning Street (which received goods in the morning) into Lombard Street and further; and among others, I now saw my little goldsmith Stokes receiving some friend's goods, whose house itself was burned the day after. We parted at Paul's, he home and I to Paul's Wharf, where I had appointed a boat to attend me; and took in Mr. Carkesse and his brother, whom I met in the street, and carried them below and above bridge, to and again, to see the fire, which was now got further, both below and above, and no likelihood of stopping it. Met with the King and Duke of York in their barge, and with them to Queenhithe and there called Sir Richard Browne to them. Their order was only to pull down houses apace, and so below bridge at the water-side; but little was or could be done, the fire coming upon them so fast. Good hopes there was of stopping it at the Three Cranes above, and at Buttolph's Wharf below bridge, if care be used; but the wind carries it into the City, so as we know not by the water-side what it doth there. River full of lighters and boats taking in goods, and good goods swimming in the water; and only, I observed that hardly one lighter or boat in three that had the goods of a house in, but there was a pair of virginals[6] in it. Having seen as much as I could now, I away to Whitehall by appointment, and there walked to St. James's Park, and there met my wife and Creed and Wood and his wife and walked to my boat, and there upon the water again, and to the fire up and down, it still increasing and the wind great. So near the fire as we could for smoke; and all over the Thames, with one's face in the wind you were almost burned with a shower of fire-drops—this is very true—so as houses were burned by these drops and flakes of fire, three or four, nay five or six houses, one from another. When we could endure no more upon the water, we to a little alehouse on the Bankside over against the Three Cranes, and there stayed till it was dark almost and saw the fire grow; and as it grow darker, appeared more and more, and in corners and upon steeples and between churches and houses, as far as we could see up the hill of the City, in a most horrid malicious bloody flame, not like the fine flame of an ordinary fire. Barbary and her husband away before us. We stayed till, it being darkish, we saw the fire as only one entire arch of fire from this to the other side the bridge, and in a bow up the hill, for an arch of above a mile long. It made me weep to see it. The churches, houses, and all on fire and flaming at once, and a horrid noise the flames made, and the cracking of houses at their ruin. So home with a sad heart, and there find everybody discoursing and lamenting the fire; and poor Tom Hayter[7] came with some few of his goods saved out of his house, which is burned upon Fish Street Hill. I invited him to lie at my house, and did receive his goods: but was deceived in his lying there, the noise coming every moment of the growth of the fire, so as we were forced to begin to pack up our own goods and prepare for their removal. And did by moonshine (it being brave,[8] dry, and moonshine and warm weather) carry much of my goods into the garden, and Mr. Hayter and I did remove my money and iron-chests into my cellar—as thinking that the safest place. And got my bags of gold into my office ready to carry away, and my chief papers of accounts also there, and my tallies into a box by themselves. So great was our fear, as Sir W. Bat-

---

6. A small harpsichord.
7. One of Pepys's clerks in the Navy Office.

8. Pleasant.

ten had carts come out of the country to fetch away his goods this night. We did put Mr. Hayter, poor man, to bed a little; but he got but very little rest, so much noise being in my house, taking down of goods.

[3 September 1666] About 4 a-clock in the morning, my Lady Batten sent me a cart to carry away all my money and plate and best things to Sir W. Rider's at Bethnell Green; which I did, riding myself in my nightgown in the cart; and Lord, to see how the streets and the highways are crowded with people, running and riding and getting of carts at any rate to fetch away things. I find Sir W. Rider tired with being called up[9] all night and receiving things from several friends. His house full of goods—and much of Sir W. Batten and Sir W. Penn's.[1] I am eased at my heart to have my treasure so well secured. Then home with much ado to find a way. Nor any sleep all this night to me nor my poor wife. But then, and all this day, she and I and all my people laboring to get away the rest of our things, and did get Mr. Tooker to get me a lighter to take them in, and we did carry them (myself some) over Tower Hill, which was by this time full of people's goods, bringing their goods thither. And down to the lighter, which lay at the next quay above the Tower Dock. And here was my neighbor's wife, Mrs. Buckworth, with her pretty child and some few of her things, which I did willingly give way to be saved with mine. But there was no passing with anything through the postern,[2] the crowd was so great.

The Duke of York came this day by the office and spoke to us, and did ride with his guard up and down the City to keep all quiet (he being now general, and having the care of all).

This day, Mercer being not at home, but against her mistress's order gone to her mother's, and my wife going thither to speak with W. Hewer, met her there and was angry; and her mother saying that she was not a prentice girl, to ask leave every time she goes abroad, my wife with good reason was angry, and when she came home, bid her be gone again. And so she went away, which troubled me; but yet less than it would, because of the condition we are in fear of coming into in a little time, of being less able to keep one in her quality. At night, lay down a little upon a quilt of W. Hewer in the office (all my own things being packed up or gone); and after me, my poor wife did the like—we having fed upon the remains of yesterday's dinner, having no fire nor dishes, nor any opportunity of dressing anything.

[4 September 1666] Up by break of day to get away the remainder of my things, which I did by a lighter at the Iron Gate; and my hands so few, that it was the afternoon before we could get them all away.

Sir W. Penn and I to Tower Street, and there met the fire burning three or four doors beyond Mr. Howell's; whose goods, poor man (his trays and dishes, shovels, etc., were flung all along Tower Street in the kennels, and people working therewith from one end to the other), the fire coming on in that narrow street, on both sides, with infinite fury. Sir W. Batten, not knowing how to remove his wine, did dig a pit in the garden and laid it in there; and I took the opportunity of laying all the papers of my office that I could not otherwise dispose of. And in the evening Sir W. Penn and I did dig another and put our wine in it, and I my parmesan cheese as well as my wine and some other things.

9. Called on, woken.
1. William Penn, Pepys's colleague on the Navy Board

(and father of the founder of Pennsylvania).
2. Back or side gate.

The Duke of York was at the office this day at Sir W. Penn's, but I happened not to be within. This afternoon, sitting melancholy with Sir W. Penn in our garden and thinking of the certain burning of this office without extraordinary means, I did propose for the sending up of all our workmen from Woolwich and Deptford yards (none whereof yet appeared), and to write to Sir W. Coventry to have the Duke of York's permission to pull down houses rather then lose this office, which would much hinder the King's business. So Sir W. Penn he went down this night, in order to the sending them up tomorrow morning; and I wrote to Sir W. Coventry about the business, but received no answer.

This night Mrs. Turner (who, poor woman, was removing her goods all this day—good goods, into the garden, and knew not how to dispose of them)—and her husband supped with my wife and I at night in the office, upon a shoulder of mutton from the cook's, without any napkin or anything, in a sad manner but were merry. Only, now and then walking into the garden and saw how horridly the sky looks, all on a fire in the night, was enough to put us out of our wits; and indeed it was extremely dreadful—for it looks just as if it was at us, and the whole heaven on fire. I after supper walked in the dark down to Tower Street, and there saw it all on fire at the Trinity House on that side and the Dolphin Tavern on this side, which was very near us—and the fire with extraordinary vehemence. Now begins the practice of blowing up of houses in Tower Street, those next the Tower, which at first did frighten people more than anything; but it stopped the fire where it was done—it bringing down the houses to the ground in the same places they stood, and then it was easy to quench what little fire was in it, though it kindled nothing almost. W. Hewer this day went to see how his mother did, and comes late home, but telling us how he hath been forced to remove her to Islington, her house in Pye Corner being burned. So that it is got so far that way and all the Old Bailey, and was running down to Fleet Street. And Paul's is burned, and all Cheapside. I wrote to my father this night; but the post-house being burned, the letter could not go.

COMPANION READING

John Evelyn: from *Kalendarium*[1]

[2 September 1666] This fatal night about ten, began that deplorable fire, near Fish Street in London. 2: I had public prayers at home: after dinner the fire continuing, with my wife and son took coach and went to the Bankside in Southwark,[2] where we beheld that dismal spectacle, the whole City in dreadful flames near the water-side, and had now consumed all the houses from the bridge all Thames Street and upwards

---

1. John Evelyn (1620–1706), versatile author (on air pollution, architecture, gardening, forestry, and other subjects), wrote up his life on a plan very different from that of his friend Pepys. His *Kalendarium*, commenced when he was 40 years old, narrates selected dates (and omits many), starting with his birth and ending shortly before his death; the thousand-page manuscript encompasses (in legible longhand) his extensive travels in Europe during the Civil Wars and his busy social, court, and civic life after the Restoration. Evelyn's vantage on the Fire of London (as on much else) contrasts with Pepys's. A landowning gentleman, Evelyn dwelt at a remove from the City on a country estate across the river. A devout Angli-

can, he saw the catastrophe as an apocalypse steeped in biblical precedent and prophecy. A tireless projector of plans and improvements, he reckoned the City's losses and began to imagine its renewal. Nine days after the fire's outbreak, Evelyn presented the king and queen "with a survey of the ruins and a plot for a new city. . . . [They seemed] extremely pleased with what I had so early thought on"—though in the event, no unified plan for rebuilding was followed. For another account of the fire, see the selection from the *London Gazette* in Perspectives: Reading Papers, pages 2389–90.
2. The southern bank of the Thames, across the river from the fire.

towards Cheapside, down to the Three Cranes, and so returned exceedingly astonished, what would become of the rest. 3: The fire having continued all this night (if I
may call that night, which was as light as day for 10 miles round about after a dreadful manner) when conspiring with a fierce eastern wind, in a very dry season, I went
on foot to the same place, when I saw the whole south part of the City burning from
Cheapside to the Thames, and all along Cornhill (for it likewise kindled back against
the wind, as well as forward) Tower Street, Fenchurch Street, Gracious Street and so
along to Baynard Castle, and was now taking hold of St. Paul's Church, to which the
scaffolds contributed exceedingly. The conflagration was so universal, and the people
so astonished, that from the beginning (I know not by what desponding or fate), they
hardly stirred to quench it, so as there was nothing heard or seen but crying out and
lamentation, and running about like distracted creatures, without at all attempting to
save even their goods; such a strange consternation there was upon them, so as it
burned both in breadth and length, the churches, public halls, Exchange, hospitals,
monuments, and ornaments, leaping after a prodigious manner from house to house
and street to street, at great distance one from the other, for the heat (with a long set
of fair and warm weather) had even ignited the air, and prepared the materials to
conceive the fire, which devoured after an incredible manner, houses, furniture, and
everything. Here we saw the Thames covered with goods floating, all the barges and
boats laden with what some had time and courage to save, as on the other, the carts
etc. carrying out to the fields, which for many miles were strewed with moveables of
all sorts, and tents erecting to shelter both people and what goods they could get
away: O the miserable and calamitous spectacle, such as haply the whole world had
not seen the like since the foundation of it, nor to be outdone, till the universal conflagration of it. All the sky were of a fiery aspect, like the top of a burning oven, and
the light seen above 40 miles round about for many nights. God grant mine eyes may
never behold the like, who now saw above ten thousand houses all in one flame, the
noise and crackling and thunder of the impetuous flames, the shrieking of women
and children, the hurry of people, the fall of towers, houses and churches was like an
hideous storm, and the air all about so hot and inflamed that at the last one was not
able to approach it, so as they were forced to stand still, and let the flames consume
on which they did for near two whole miles in length and one in breadth. The clouds
also of smoke were dismal, and reached upon computation near 50 miles in length.
Thus I left it this afternoon burning, a resemblance of Sodom, or the last day.[3] It
called to mind that of 4 *Heb: non enim hic habemus stabilem Civitatem:*[4] the ruins
resembling the picture of *Troy: London* was,[5] but is no more. Thus I returned.

[4 September 1666] The burning still rages; I went now on horseback, and it was now
gotten as far as the Inner Temple; all Fleet Street, Old Bailey, Ludgate Hill, Warwick
Lane, Newgate, Paul's Chain, Watling Street now flaming and most of it reduced to
ashes, the stones of Paul's flew like granados,[6] the lead melting down the streets in a
stream, and the very pavements of them glowing with fiery redness, so as nor horse
nor man was able to tread on them, and the demolitions had stopped all the passages,

3. In Genesis, the Lord destroys the sinful city of Sodom
by raining "fire and brimstone...out of heaven"
(19.24). "The last day" is the Day of Judgment, when the
city of Babylon (emblem of the corrupt world) "shall be
utterly burned with fire" (Revelation 18.8).
4. For here we have no lasting city (Hebrews 13.14; the

sentence continues: "but we seek one to come").
5. Echoing the account of the fall of Troy in the *Aeneid*
(2.325): on the night the Greeks burn the city, a Trojan
priest declares *fuit Ilium* ("Troy was").
6. Grenades.

so as no help could be applied; the eastern wind still more impetuously driving the flames forwards. Nothing but the almighty power of God was able to stop them, for vain was the help of man. On the fourth it crossed towards Whitehall, but O the confusion was then at that court. It pleased his Majesty to command me among the rest to look after the quenching of Fetter Lane end, to preserve (if possible) that part of Holborn, whilst the rest of the gentlemen took their several posts, some at one part, some at another, for now they began to bestir themselves, and not till now, who till now had stood as men interdict, with their hands a cross,[7] and began to consider that nothing was like to put a stop, but the blowing up of so many houses, as might make a wider gap, than any had yet been made by the ordinary method of pulling them down with engines.[8] This some stout seamen proposed early enough to have saved the whole City; but some tenacious and avaricious men, aldermen etc., would not permit, because their houses must have been of the first. It was therefore now commanded to be practiced, and my concern being particularly for the Hospital of St. Bartholomew's near Smithfield, where I had many wounded and sick men, made me the more diligent to promote it;[9] nor was my care for the Savoy less. So as it pleased Almighty God by abating of the wind, and the industry of people, now when all was lost, infusing a new spirit into them (and such as had if exerted in time undoubtedly preserved the whole) that the fury of it began sensibly to abate, about noon, so as it came no farther than the Temple westward, nor than the entrance of Smithfield north; but continued all this day and night so impetuous toward Cripplegate, and the Tower, as made us even all despair. It also brake out again in the Temple: but the courage of the multitude persisting, and innumerable houses blown up with gunpowder, such gaps and desolations were soon made, as also by the former three days' consumption, as the back fire did not so vehemently urge upon the rest, as formerly. There was yet no standing near the burning and glowing ruins near a furlong's space. The coal and wood wharves and magazines of oil, rosin, chandler, etc.[1] did infinite mischief; so as the invective I but a little before dedicated to his Majesty and published, giving warning what might probably be the issue of suffering those shops to be in the City, was looked on as prophetic.[2] But there I left this smoking and sultry heap, which mounted up in dismal clouds night and day, the poor inhabitants dispersed all about St. George's, Moorfields, as far as Highgate, and several miles in circle, some under tents, others under miserable huts and hovels, without a rag, or any necessary utensils, bed or board, who from delicateness, riches and easy accommodations in stately and well-furnished houses, were now reduced to extremest misery and poverty. In this calamitous condition I returned with a sad heart to my house, blessing and adoring the distinguishing mercy of God, to me and mine, who in the midst of all this ruin, was like Lot, in my little Zoar, safe and sound.[3]

◦◦◦◦◦

7. Immobilized, with their arms crossed (a conventional posture of passivity).
8. Machines.
9. Evelyn served on the Navy Board as a commissioner, charged with the care of sick and wounded seamen.
1. Different sorts of fuel, stored and sold in shops along the Thames.
2. In 1661 Evelyn had warned of these dangers in a pamphlet entitled *Fumifugium: or the Inconveniency of the Air and Smoke of London Dissipated. Together with Some Remedies Humbly Proposed by J. E., Esq; to His Sacred Majesty, and to the Parliament Now Assembled.*
3. Lot, a prosperous inhabitant of Sodom, is warned by angels of the city's impending destruction. He escapes to Zoar, a small city nearby (Genesis 19.20–22).

[THE ROYAL SOCIETY]¹

[14 November 1666] Up, and by water to Whitehall; and thence to Westminister, where I bought several things—as, a hone—ribband—gloves—books. And then took coach and to Knepp's² lodging, whom I find not ready to go home with me, so I away to do a little business; among others, to call upon Mr. Osborne for my Tangier warrant for the last quarter, and so to the New Exchange for some things for my wife, and then to Knepp again and there stayed, reading of Waller's³ verses while she finished her dressing—her husband being by, I had no other pastime. Her lodging very mean, and the condition she lives in; yet makes a show without doors, God bless us. I carried him along with us into the City, and set him down in Bishopsgate Street and then home with her. She tells me how Smith of the Duke's house hath killed a man upon a quarrel in play—which makes everybody sorry, he being a good actor, and they say a good man, however this happens. The ladies of the court do much bemoan him, she says. Here she and we alone at dinner, to some good victuals that we could not put off,⁴ that was intended for the great dinner of my Lord Hinchingbrooke, if he had come. After dinner, I to teach her my new recitative of *It is decreed*⁵—of which she learnt a good part; and I do well like it, and believe shall be well pleased when she hath it all, and that it will be found an agreeable thing. Then carried her home, and my wife and I intended to have seen my Lady Jemima at Whitehall; but the Exchange street was so full of coaches, everybody as they say going thither to make themselves fine against tomorrow night,⁶ that after half an hour's stay we could not do any; but only, my wife to see her brother, and I to go speak one word with Sir G. Carteret about office business. And talk of the general complexion of matters; which he looks upon, as I do, with horror, and gives us all for an undone people—that there is no such thing as a peace in hand, nor a possibility of any without our begging it, they⁷ being as high, or higher, in their terms than ever. And tells me that just now my Lord Hollis had been with him, and wept to think in what a condition we are fallen. He showed me my Lord Sandwich's letter to him, complaining of the lack of money; which Sir G. Carteret is at a loss how in the world to get the King to supply him⁸ with—and wishes him for that reason here, for that he fears he will be brought to disgrace there, for want of supplies. He says the House is yet in a bad humor; and desiring to know whence it is that the King stirs not, he says he minds it not, nor will be brought to it—and that his servants of the House do, instead of making the Parliament better, rather play the rogue one with another, and will put all in fire.⁹ So that upon the whole, we are in a wretched condition, and I went from him in full apprehensions of it. So took up my wife, her brother being yet very bad, and doubtful whether he will recover or no; and so to St. Ellen's and there sent my wife home, and myself to the Pope's Head, where all the Houblons were, and Dr. Croone;¹ and by

---

1. This next selection from Pepys was written two months after the fire, when life had begun to return to normal.

2. Elizabeth Knepp, actress, singer, and friend of Pepys.

3. Sir Edmund Waller (1606—1687), widely read poet and pioneer of the heroic couplet; he wrote much love poetry in praise of "Sacharissa," a woman he wooed without success.

4. Delay (because the food would spoil).

5. Pepys enjoyed composing music (here setting words from Ben Jonson's play *Catiline*).

6. When a court ball was to be held for the queen's birthday.

7. The Dutch.

8. Sandwich, now ambassador to Spain.

9. Into ruin.

1. The Houblons were a merchant family—a father and five sons—whom Pepys and others admired for their affection and generosity. Dr. William Croone, a specialist in anatomy, was an original Fellow and First Secretary of the Royal Society for the Improving of Natural Knowledge.

and by to an exceeding pretty supper—excellent discourse of all sorts; and indeed, are a set of the finest gentlemen that ever I met withal in my life. Here Dr. Croone told me that at the meeting[2] at Gresham College tonight (which it seems they now have every Wednesday again) there was a pretty experiment, of the blood of one dog let out (till he died) into the body of another on one side, while all his own run out on the other side. The first died upon the place, and the other very well, and likely to do well. This did give occasion to many pretty wishes, as of the blood of a Quaker to be let into an archbishop, and such like. But, as Dr. Croone says, may if it takes be of mighty use to man's health, for the amending of bad blood by borrowing from a better body.

After supper James Houblon and another brother took me aside, and to talk of some businesses of their own, where I am to serve them, and will. And then to talk of public matters; and I do find that they, and all merchants else, do give over trade and the nation for lost—nothing being done with care or foresight—no convoys[3] granted, nor anything done to satisfaction. But do think that the Dutch and French will master us the next year, do what we can; and so do I, unless God Almighty makes the King to mind his business; which might yet save all.

Here we sat talking till past one in the morning, and then home—where my people sat up for me, my wife and all; and so to bed.

[30 May 1667] Up, and to the office, where all the morning. At noon dined at home; being, without any words, friends with my wife, though last night I was very angry, and do think I did give her as much cause to be angry with me. After dinner I walked to Arundel House, the way very dusty (the day of meeting of the Society being changed from Wednesday to Thursday; which I knew not before because the Wednesday is a Council day and several of the Council are of the Society, and would come but for their attending the King at Council); where I find much company, indeed very much company, in expectation of the Duchess of Newcastle,[4] who had desired to be invited to the Society, and was, after much debate pro and con, it seems many being against it, and we do believe the town will be full of ballets[5] of it. Anon comes the Duchess, with her women attending her; among others, that Ferrabosco[6] of whom so much talk is, that her lady would bid her show her face and kill the gallants. She is indeed black[7] and hath good black little eyes, but otherwise but a very ordinary woman I do think; but they say sings well. The Duchess hath been a good comely woman; but her dress so antic and her deportment so unordinary, that I do not like her at all, nor did I hear her say anything that was worth hearing, but that she was full of admiration, all admiration.[8] Several fine experiments were shown her of colors, lodestones, microscope, and of liquors: among others, of one that did while she was there turn a piece of roasted mutton into pure blood—which was very rare. Here was Mr. Moore of Cambridge, whom I had not seen before, and I was glad to see him—as also a very pretty black boy that run up and down the room, somebody's child in Arundel House. After they had

2. Of the Royal Society.
3. Protective escort for merchant ships.
4. Margaret Cavendish, Duchess of Newcastle, had published poems, plays, and treatises on natural philosophy highly critical of the Society's methods (see pages 2142–57).
5. Ballads (Evelyn wrote one on Cavendish's visit).
6. An Italian family of this name was eminent in England for its musical talents.
7. I.e., of dark complexion and hair.
8. Wonder, amazement.

shown her many experiments, and she cried still she was "full of admiration," she departed, being led out and in by several lords that were there; among others, Lord George Berkeley and the Earl of Carlisle and a very pretty young man, the Duke of Somerset.

She gone, I by coach home and there busy at my letters till night; and then with my wife in the evening, singing with her in the garden with great pleasure. And so home to supper and to bed.

[21 November 1667] Up, and to the office, where all the morning; and at noon home, where my wife not very well, but is to go to Mr. Mill's child's christening, where she is godmother, Sir. J. Mennes and Sir R. Brookes her companions. I left her after dinner (my clerks dining with me) to go with Sir J. Mennes, and I to the office, where did much business till after candlelight; and then, my eyes beginning to fail me, I out and took coach and to Arundel House, where the meeting of Gresham College was broke up; but there meeting Creed, I with him to the tavern in St. Clement's churchyard, where was Dean Wilkins, Dr. Whistler[9] * * * and others. * * * Among the rest, they discourse of a man that is a little frantic (that hath been a kind of minister, Dr. Wilkins saying that he hath read for him in his church) that is a poor and debauched man, that the college have hired for 20s[1] to have some of the blood of a sheep let into his body; and it is to be done on Saturday next. They purpose to let in about twelve ounces, which they compute is what will be let in in a minute's time by a watch. They differ in the opinion they have of the effects of it; some think that it may have a good effect upon him as a frantic man, by cooling his blood; others, that it will not have any effect at all. But the man is a very healthy man, and by this means will be able to give an account what alteration, if any, he doth find in himself, and so may be useful. On this occasion Dr. Whistler told a pretty story related by Muffett, a good author, of Dr. Caius that built Key's College: that being very old and lived only at that time upon woman's milk, while he fed upon the milk of an angry fretful woman, was so himself; and then being advised to take of a good-natured patient woman, he did become so, beyond the common temper of his age. Thus much nutriment, they observed, might do. Their discourse was very fine; and if I should be put out of my office,[2] I do take great content in the liberty I shall be at of frequenting these gentlemen's companies. Broke up thence and home, and there to my wife in her chamber, who is not well (of those[3]); and there she tells me great stories of the gossiping women of the parish, what this and what that woman was; and among the rest, how Mrs. Hollworthy is the veriest confident bragging gossip of them all, which I should not have believed—but that Sir R. Brookes, her partner,[4] was mighty civil to her and taken with her and what not. My eyes being bad, I spent the evening with her in her chamber, talking and inventing a cipher to put on a piece of plate[5] which I must give, better than ordinary, to the parson's child; and so to bed, and through my wife's illness had a bad night of it, and she a worse, poor wretch.

9. The mathematician John Wilkins was one of the founders of the Royal Society; the physician Daniel Whistler was a Fellow.
1. s: Shillings.
2. Pepys's position was in jeopardy because of a parliamentary investigation into Navy Office mismanagement during the Second Dutch War.
3. Her menstrual period.
4. As godfather at the christening.
5. I.e., a coded message to be engraved on a silver dish (so that the gift includes a kind of game).

[30 November 1667] Then to Cary House, a house now of entertainment, * * * next my Lord Ashly's; and there, where I have heretofore heard Common Prayer in the time of Dr. Mossum,[6] we after two hours' stay, sitting at the table with our napkins open, had our dinners brought; but badly done. But here was good company, I choosing to sit next Dr. Wilkins, Sir George Ent, and others whom I value. And there talked of several things; among others, Dr. Wilkins, talking of the universal speech, of which he hath a book coming out,[7] did first inform me how man was certainly made for society, he being of all creatures the least armed for defense; and of all creatures in the world, the young ones are not able to do anything to help themselves, nor can find the dug without being put to it, but would die if the mother did not help it. And he says were it not for speech, man would be a very mean creature. Much of this good discourse we had. But here above all, I was pleased to see the person who had his blood taken out. He speaks well, and did this day give the Society a relation thereof in Latin, saying that he finds himself much better since, and as a new man. But he is cracked a little in his head, though he speaks very reasonably and very well. He had but 20s for his suffering it, and is to have the same again tried upon him—the first sound man that ever had it tried on him in England, and but one that we hear of in France, which was a porter hired by the virtuosi.

[THEATER AND MUSIC]

[5 October 1667] Up, and to the office and there all the morning, none but my Lord Anglesey and myself. But much surprised with the news of the death of Sir W. Batten, who died this morning, having been but two days sick. Sir W. Penn and I did dispatch a letter this morning to Sir W. Coventry[8] to recommend Colonel Middleton, who we think a most honest and understanding man, and fit for that place. Sir G. Carteret did also come this morning, and walked with me in the garden and concluded not to concern or have any advice made to Sir W. Coventry in behalf of my Lord Sandwich's business; so I do rest satisfied, though I do think they are all mad,[9] that they will judge Sir W. Coventry an enemy, when he is indeed no such man to anybody, but is severe and just, as he ought to be, where he sees things ill done. At noon home, and by coach to Temple Bar to a India shop[1] and there bought a gown and sash, which cost me 26s. And so she and Willett[2] away to the Change, and I to my Lord Crew and there met my Lord Hinchingbrooke and Lady Jemima, and there dined with them and my Lord— where pretty merry. And after dinner, my Lord Crew and Hinchingbrooke and myself went aside to discourse about my Lord Sandwich's business, which is in a very ill state for want of money; and so parted, and I to my tailor's and there took up my wife and Willet, who stayed there for me, and to the Duke of York's playhouse;[3] but the House so full, it being a new play The Coffee-House, that we could not get in, and so to the King's House; and there going in, met with Knepp and she took us up into the tiring-rooms

---

6. Robert Mossum had conducted illegal Anglican services (using the forbidden Book of Common Prayer) during the Interregnum.

7. In his *Essay toward a Real Character, and a Philosophical Language* (1668), Wilkins argued for (and attempted) the creation of a newly precise and logical language based not on an arbitrary alphabet but on written symbols representing ideas and things.

8. A commissioner on the Navy Board.

9. "They" are the Parliament investigators looking into the Board's (and Sandwich's) conduct during the Second Dutch War.

1. Dealing in goods imported from India.

2. Deborah Willett, recently hired as Elizabeth Pepys's companion.

3. There were only two licensed theater companies in Restoration London, one officially sponsored by the duke, the other by the king.

and to the women's shift,[4] where Nell[5] was dressing herself and was all unready; and is very pretty, prettier than I thought; and so walked all up and down the house above, and then below into the scene-room, and there sat down and she gave us fruit; and here I read the Qu's[6] to Knepp while she answered me, through all her part of *Flora's Figarys*, which was acted today. But Lord, to see how they were both painted would make a man mad—and did make me loathe them—and what base company of men comes among them, and how lewdly they talk—and how poor the men are in clothes, and yet what a show they make on the stage by candlelight, is very observable. But to see how Nell cursed for having so few people in the pit was pretty, the other house carrying away all the people at the new play, and is said nowadays to have generally most company, as being better players. By and by into the pit and there saw the play; which is pretty good, but my belly was full of what I had seen in the house; and so after the play done, away home and there to the writing my letters; and so home to supper and to bed.

[27 February 1668] All the morning at the office, and at noon home to dinner; and thence with my wife and Deb[7] to the King's House to see *Virgin Martyr*,[8] the first time it hath been acted a great while, and it is mighty pleasant; not that the play is worth much, but it is finely acted by Becke Marshall; but that which did please me beyond anything in the whole world was the wind-music when the angel comes down, which is so sweet that it ravished me; and indeed, in a word, did wrap up my soul so that it made me really sick, just as I have formerly been when in love with my wife; that neither then, nor all the evening going home and at home, I was able to think of anything, but remained all night transported, so as I could not believe that ever any music hath that real command over the soul of a man as this did upon me; and makes me resolve to practice wind-music and to make my wife do the like.

[20 January 1669], Up, and my wife and I and W. Hewer to White-hall, where she set us down. * * * Thence to my wife at Unthankes and with her and W. Hewer to Hercules-Pillars, calling to do two or three things by the way, and there dined; and thence to the Duke of York's House[9] and saw *Twelfth Night*, as it is now revived, but I think one of the weakest plays that ever I saw on the stage.[1] [This afternoon, before the play, I called with my wife at Dancre's[2] the great lanskip-painter, by Mr. Povy's advice, and have bespoke him to come to take measure of my dining-room panels; and there I met with the pretty daughter of the Coate-seller's that lived in Cheapside, and now in Covent-garden, who hath her picture drawn here, but very poorly; but she is a pretty woman, and now I perceive married, a very pretty black[3] woman.][4] So the play done, we home, my wife letting fall some words of her observing my eyes too mightily employed in the playhouse; meaning, upon women, which did vex me; but however, when we came home we were good friends; and so to read and to supper, and so to bed.

---

4. Attiring rooms; women's dressing room.
5. Nell Gwyn, a popular comic actress; she would later become the king's mistress.
6. Cues.
7. Deborah Willett.
8. A tragedy by Thomas Dekker and Philip Massinger, first performed c. 1620.
9. I.e., playhouse.
1. Pepys had already seen the play twice, and set down similar opinions both times: "the play [was] a burthen to me, and I took no pleasure at all in it" (11 September 1661); "saw *Twelfth Night* acted well, though it be but a silly play and not relating at all to the name or day"—i.e., to the Twelfth Night festivities celebrated on this date (6 January 1663).
2. Hendrick Danckerts, Dutch-born painter of portraits and landscapes.
3. Dark-haired.
4. Pepys squeezed these bracketed sentences into the margin of the entry's pages, as an afterthought.

[Elizabeth Pepys and Deborah Willett]

[25 October 1668] *Lord's Day*. Up, and discoursing with my wife about our house and many new things we are doing of; and so to church I, and there find Jack Fen come, and his wife, a pretty black woman; I never saw her before, nor took notice of her now. So home and to dinner; and after dinner, all the afternoon got my wife and boy to read to me. And at night W. Batelier comes and sups with us; and after supper, to have my head combed by Deb, which occasioned the greatest sorrow to me that ever I knew in this world; for my wife, coming up suddenly, did find me embracing the girl con my hand sub su coats; and indeed, I was with my main in her cunny.[5] I was at a wonderful loss upon it, and the girl also; and I endeavored to put it off, but my wife was struck mute and grew angry, and as her voice came to her, grew quite out of order; and I do say little, but to bed; and my wife said little also, but could not sleep all night; but about 2 in the morning waked me and cried, and fell to tell me as a great secret that she was a Roman Catholic and had received the Holy Sacrament; which troubled me but I took no notice of it, but she went on from one thing to another, till at last it appeared plainly her trouble was at what she saw; but yet I did not know how much she saw and therefore said nothing to her. But after her much crying and reproaching me with inconstancy and preferring a sorry girl before her, I did give her no provocations but did promise all fair usage to her, and love, and foreswore any hurt that I did with her—till at last she seemed to be at ease again; and so toward morning, a little sleep; [26][6] and so I, with some little repose and rest, rose, and up and by water to Whitehall, but with my mind mightily troubled for the poor girl, whom I fear I have undone by this, my wife telling me that she would turn her out of door. However, I was obliged to attend the Duke of York, thinking to have had a meeting of Tangier today, but had not; but he did take me and Mr. Wren into his closet, and there did press me to prepare what I had to say upon the answers of my fellow-officers to his great letter; which I promised to do against his coming to town again the next week; and so to other discourse, finding plainly that he is in trouble and apprehensions of the reformers, and would be found to do what he can towards reforming himself.[7] And so thence to my Lord Sandwich; where after long stay, he being in talk with others privately, I to him; and there he taking physic and keeping his chamber, I had an hour's talk with him about the ill posture of things at this time, while the King gives countenance to Sir Charles Sedley and Lord Buckhurst,[8] telling him their late story of running up and down the streets a little while since all night, and their being beaten and clapped up all night by the constable, who is since chid and imprisoned for his pains.

He tells me that he thinks his matters do stand well with the King—and hopes to have dispatch to his mind; but I doubt it, and do see that he doth fear it too. He told me my Lady Carteret's trouble about my writing of that letter[9] of the Duke of York's lately to the office; which I did not own, but declared to be of no injury to

---

5. I.e., with his hand under her petticoats and his hand in her vagina. Here as often, Pepys reports his illicit sexual activities in a "secret" language compounded of Latin, French, Spanish, and English.

6. Pepys wedges the new date into the margin, beside the run-on narrative.

7. The duke was Lord High Admiral of the navy; on his behalf Pepys had composed a letter to the Navy Board proposing reforms in response to parliamentary investigations of the disastrous Second Dutch War.

8. Notorious libertines (Buckhurst was Nell Gwyn's current lover).

9. The "great letter" on naval reform.

G. Carteret, and that I would write a letter to him to satisfy him therein. But this I am in pain how to do without doing myself wrong, and the end I had, of preparing a justification to myself hereafter, when the faults of the Navy come to be found out. However, I will do it in the best manner I can.

Thence by coach home and to dinner, finding my wife mightily discontented and the girl sad, and no words from my wife to her. So after dinner, they out with me about two or three things; and so home again, I all the evening busy and my wife full of trouble in her looks; and anon to bed—where about midnight, she wakes me and there falls foul on me again, affirming that she saw me hug and kiss the girl; the latter I denied, and truly; the other I confessed and no more. And upon her pressing me, did offer to give her under my hand that I would never see Mrs. Pearse[1] more, nor Knepp, but did promise her particular demonstrations of my true love to her, owning some indiscretion in what I did, but that there was no harm in it. She at last on these promises was quiet, and very kind we were, and so to sleep; [27] and in the morning up, but with my mind troubled for the poor girl, with whom I could not get opportunity to speak; but to the office, my mind mighty full of sorrow for her, where all the morning, and to dinner with my people and to the office all the afternoon; and so at night home and there busy to get some things ready against tomorrow's meeting of Tangier; and that being done and my clerks gone, my wife did toward bedtime begin to be in a mighty rage from some new matter that she had got in her head, and did most part of the night in bed rant at me in most high terms, of threats of publishing my shame; and when I offered to rise, would have rose too, and caused a candle to be lit, to burn by her all night in the chimney while she ranted; while I, that knew myself to have given some grounds for it, did make it my business to appease her all I could possibly, and by good words and fair promises did make her very quiet; and so rested all night and rose with perfect good peace, being heartily afflicted for this folly of mine that did occasion it; but was forced to be silent about the girl, which I have no mind to part with, but much less that the poor girl should be undone by my folly. [28] So up, with mighty kindness from my wife and a thorough peace; and being up, did by a note advise the girl what I had done and owned, which note I was in pain for till she told me that she had burned it. This evening, Mr. Spong came and sat late with me, and first told me of the instrument called parrallogram, which I must have one of, showing me his practice thereon by a map of England.[2]

So by coach with Mr. Gibson[3] to Chancery Lane, and there made oath before a master of chancery to my Tangier account of fees; and so to Whitehall, where by and by a committee met; my Lord Sandwich there, but his report was not received, it being late; but only a little business done, about the supplying the place with victuals; but I did get, to my great content, my account allowed of fees, with great applause by my Lord Ashley and Sir W. Penn. Thence home, calling at one or two places, and there about our workmen, who are at work upon my wife's closet and other parts of my house, that we are all in dirt. So after dinner, with Mr. Gibson all the afternoon in my closet; and at night to supper and to bed, my wife and I at good peace, but yet with some little grudgings of trouble in her, and more in me, about the poor girl.

[14 November 1668] Up, and had a mighty mind to have seen or given a note to Deb or to have given her a little money; to which purpose I wrapped up 40s in a paper, thinking to give her; but my wife rose presently, and would not let me be out of her

---

1. Elizabeth Pearse, wife of a naval surgeon.
2. The parallelogram was a device for making copies of

diagrams and maps on the same or on a different scale.
3. A favorite assistant of Pepys's.

sight; and went down before me into the kitchen, and came up and told me that she was in the kitchen, and therefore would have me go round the other way; which she repeating, and I vexed at it, answered her a little angrily; upon which she instantly flew out into a rage, calling me dog and rogue, and that I had a rotten heart; all which, knowing that I deserved it, I bore with; and word being brought presently up that she was gone away by coach with her things, my wife was friends; and so all quiet, and I to the office with my heart sad, and find that I cannot forget the girl, and vexed I know not where to look for her—and more troubled to see how my wife is by this means likely for ever to have her hand over me, that I shall for ever be a slave to her; that is to say, only in matters of pleasure, but in other things she will make her business, I know, to please me and to keep me right to her—which I will labor to be indeed, for she deserves it of me, though it will be I fear a little time before I shall be able to wear Deb out of my mind. At the office all the morning, and merry at noon at dinner; and after dinner to the office, where all the afternoon and doing much business late; my mind being free of all troubles, I thank God, but only for my thoughts of this girl, which hang after her. And so at night home to supper, and there did sleep with great content with my wife. I must here remember that I have lain with my moher[4] as a husband more times since this falling-out then in I believe twelve months before—and with more pleasure to her than I think in all the time of our marriage before.

[20 November 1668] This morning up, with mighty kind words between my poor wife and I; and so to Whitehall by water, W. Hewer with me, who is to go with me everywhere until my wife be in condition to go out along with me herself; for she doth plainly declare that she dares not trust me out alone, and therefore made it a piece of our league that I should alway take somebody with me, or her herself; which I am mighty willing to, being, by the grace of God resolved never to do her wrong more.[5]

We landed at the Temple, and there I did bid him call at my cousin Roger Pepys's lodgings, and I stayed in the street for him; and so took water again at the Strand stairs and so to Whitehall, in my way I telling him plainly and truly my resolutions, if I can get over this evil, never to give new occasion for it. He is, I think, so honest and true a servant to us both, and one that loves us, that I was not much troubled at his being privy to all this, but rejoiced in my heart that I had him to assist in the making us friends; which he did do truly and heartily, and with good success—for I did get him to go to Deb to tell her that I had told my wife all of my being with her the other night, that so, if my wife should send, she might not make the business worse by denying it. While I was at Whitehall with the Duke of York doing our ordinary business with him, here being also the first time the new treasurers, W. Hewer did go to her and come back again; and so I took him into St. James's Park, and there he did tell me he had been with her and found what I said about my manner of being with her true, and had given her advice as I desired. I did there enter into more talk about my wife and myself, and he did give me great assurance of several particular cases to which my wife had from time to time made him privy of her loyalty and truth to me after many and great temptations, and I believe them truly. I did also discourse the unfitness of my leaving of my employment now in many respects, to go into the

---

4. Spanish *mujer:* wife. For the first time, Pepys applies his secret language to Elizabeth.
5. Two nights earlier, Pepys had traced Deborah Willett to her new lodgings, and caressed her in his coach. The

next day, Elizabeth told him that she knew about the assignation, and he signed a pledge "never to see or speak with Deb while I live."

country as my wife desires—but that I would labor to fit myself for it; which he thoroughly understands, and doth agree with me in it; and so, hoping to get over this trouble, we about our business to Westminster Hall to meet Roger Pepys; which I did, and did there discourse of the business of lending him 500*l* to answer some occasions of his, which I believe to be safe enough; and so took leave of him and away by coach home, calling on my coach-maker by the way, where I like my little coach mightily. But when I came home, hoping for a further degree of peace and quiet, I find my wife upon her bed in a horrible rage afresh, calling me all the bitter names; and rising, did fall to revile me in the bitterest manner in the world, and could not refrain to strike me and pull my hair; which I resolved to bear with, and had good reason to bear it. So I by silence and weeping did prevail with her a little to be quiet, and she would not eat her dinner without me; but yet by and by into a raging fit she fell again worse than before, that she would slit the girl's nose; and at last W. Hewer came in and came up, who did allay her fury, I flinging myself in a sad desperate condition upon the bed in the blue room, and there lay while they spoke together; and at last it came to this, that if I would call Deb "whore" under my hand,[6] and write to her that I hated her and would never see her more, she would believe me and trust in me—which I did agree to; only, as to the name of "whore" I would have excused, and therefore wrote to her sparing that word; which my wife thereupon tore it, and would not be satisfied till, W. Hewer winking upon me, I did write so, with the name of a whore, as that I did fear she might too probably have been prevailed upon to have been[7] a whore by her carriage to me, and therefore, as such, I did resolve never to see her more. This pleased my wife, and she gives it W. Hewer to carry to her, with a sharp message from her. So from that minute my wife begun to be kind to me, and we to kiss and be friends, and so continued all the evening and fell to talk of other matters with great comfort, and after supper to bed.

This evening comes Mr. Billup to me to read over Mr. Wren's alterations of my draft of a letter for the Duke of York to sign, to the board; which I like mighty well, they being not considerable, only in mollifying some hard terms which I had thought fit to put in. From this to other discourse; I do find that the Duke of York and his servant Mr. Wren do look upon this service of mine as a very seasonable service to the Duke of York, as that which he will have to show to his enemies in his own justification of his care of the King's business. And I am sure I am heartily glad of it—both for the King's sake and the Duke of York's, and my own also—for if I continue, my work, by this means, will be the less, and my share in the blame[8] also.

He being gone, I to my wife again and so spent the evening with very great joy, and the night also, with good sleep and rest, my wife only troubled in her rest, but less than usual—for which the God of Heaven be praised. I did this night promise to my wife never to go to bed without calling upon God upon my knees by prayer; and I begun this night, and hope I shall never forget to do the like all my life—for I do find that it is much the best for my soul and body to live pleasing to God and my poor wife—and will ease me of much care, as well as much expense.

[31 May 1669] Up very betimes, and so continued all the morning, with W. Hewer, upon examining and stating my accounts, in order to the fitting myself to go abroad beyond sea,[9] which the ill condition of my eyes, and my neglect for a year or two,

---

6. In writing.
7. Become.
8. For Navy Board misconduct.

9. Pepys and his wife planned a tour of Holland, Flanders, and France. Near journey's end, Elizabeth Pepys caught a fever; she died in London on 10 November 1669.

hath kept me behindhand in, and so as to render it very difficult now, and trouble-some to my mind to do it; but I this day made a satisfactory entrance therein.[1] Dined at home, and in the afternoon by water to Whitehall, calling by the way at Mitchell's,[2] where I have not been many a day till just the other day; and now I met her mother there and knew her husband to be out of town. And here yo did besar ella, but have not opportunity para hazer mas[3] with her as I would have offered if yo had had it. And thence had another meeting with the Duke of York at Whitehall with the Duke of York on yesterday's work, and made a good advance; and so being called by my wife, we to the park, Mary Batelier, a Dutch gentleman, a friend of hers, being with us. Thence to the World's End, a drinking-house by the park, and there merry; and so home late.

And thus ends all that I doubt I shall ever be able to do with my own eyes in the keep-ing of my journal, I being not able to do it any longer, having done now so long as to undo my eyes almost every time that I take a pen in my hand; and therefore, whatever comes of it, I must forbear; and therefore resolve from this time forward to have it kept by my people in longhand, and must therefore be contented to set down no more than is fit for them and all the world to know; or if there be anything (which cannot be much, now my amours to Deb are past, and my eyes hindering me in almost all other pleasures), I must endeavor to keep a margin in my book open, to add here and there a note in shorthand with my own hand.[4] And so I betake myself to that course which is almost as much as to see myself go into my grave—for which, and all the dis-comforts that will accompany my being blind, the good God prepare me.

May. 31. 1669.   S.P.

———— ✦✦✦ ————

Mary Carleton
1642?–1673

Even during her highly publicized life, little was known for certain about the woman called Mary Carleton, and that uncertainty generated fascination. She claimed that she was Maria de Wolway, a German-born, convent-educated noblewoman who had traveled to England, where she had been wooed and wedded by an eighteen-year-old lawyer named John Carleton. He, his family, and others claimed instead that she was a con-woman named Mary Moders, a musi-cian's daughter from Canterbury who had tricked Carleton into false nuptials when she was already married to a shoemaker from her hometown.

The dispute came to a head in 1663, with her arrest and trial on charges of bigamy. While in prison awaiting trial, Carleton became a popular attraction, with Londoners paying fees for the privilege of seeing her, assessing her conduct, and surmising her actual identity. At her trial many in the crowd applauded her lively self-defense and quick acquittal (her accusers almost certainly had the truer case but couldn't muster the necessary evidence). In his diary, Samuel

---

1. Pepys suffered from a painful combination of farsight-edness and astigmatism which doctors did not know how to diagnose or to treat; he feared (mistakenly) that he was going blind.
2. Michael Mitchell sold liquor in a shop on London

Bridge; his wife Betty is the "her" of the ensuing clauses.
3. I did kiss her but had no chance to do more.
4. Pepys never produced the continuation of his journal that he envisions here.

Pepys hinted at some components of Carleton's complex popularity: "My Lady Batten inveighed mightily against the German princess, and I [was] as high in the defense of her wit and spirit, and glad that she is cleared at the sessions." The Lady rages and the tailor's son rejoices at the freedom of a woman who had shown how readily high rank might be counterfeited.

Nine months later, strapped for cash, Carleton appeared in a play *The German Princess*, a comedy based on her story. She played, of course, herself—ineptly by all accounts. ("Never," Pepys observed, "was anything so well done in earnest worst performed in jest upon the stage.") Deception proved precarious in life as well. Following several more arrests, Carleton was hanged for theft in 1673.

Both at her initial trial and her eventual execution, the Carleton enigma fed the presses. Pamphlets appeared in abundance, purportedly written by her accusers, by supporters, by disinterested observers who mocked or moralized, and by the woman herself. *The Case of Madam Mary Carleton*, which appeared shortly after the trial, presents the fullest first-person account; like all the other texts in the controversy, it raises basic questions of authenticity and authorship. Is it truthful autobiography or an outright fiction? Probably a mix: the account of her German childhood is almost certainly false; that of her London escapades is partly corroborated by other sources, though wittily elaborated here. Is the text hers or a ghostwriter's? Again, perhaps a hybrid—and a sturdy one. In an audacious, even defiant, voice, the writer recounts dubious activities and improvisatory impersonations in a purported autobiography whose credibility remains stubbornly open to question. This is one of the early templates for the novel. Daniel Defoe, who sixty years later wrote several long fictions on just such a model, knew of Carleton's case and drew on it ("I might as well have been the German Princess," remarks Roxana, one of his most accomplished self-inventors). The Carleton papers bespeak a culture suffused with the suspicion that identity might be a mere construct, an impersonation.

from The Case of Madam Mary Carleton

To the Noble Ladies and Gentlewomen of England

Madames,

Be pleased to lay aside that severity of your judgment, by which you examine and castigate the licitness and convenience of every of your actions or passages of moment, and therefore seldom run into the misgovernment of Fortune, and cast a favorable eye upon these novels[1] of my life, not much unlike those of Boccace[2] but that they are more serious and tragical.

The breach that is made in my credit and reputation, I do feel and understand to be very wide, and past my repairing, whatever materials of defense, excuse, and purgation I can bring to the scrutiny of men; who are not sensible to what sudden changes our natures are subjected, and that from airy thoughts and motions, things of great influence, sometimes good, sometimes bad, have been exhibited to the world, equal to the most sober and firm resolutions of the valiant and the wise.

It hath been my mishap for one among many others to miscarry in an affair to which there are more intrigues and perplexities of kin and alliance, and necessary dependence, than to any other thing in the world, i.e. marriage (Hymen[3] is as blind as Fortune and gives her favors by guess): the mistaken advantages whereof have

---

1. The word (meaning "new things") refers here to both fictions and factual "news."
2. The Renaissance writer Giovanni Boccaccio (1313?–

1375), whose *Decameron* collects 100 short tales.
3. God of marriage.

turned to my real damage: so that when I might have been happy in myself, I must needs transplant my content into a sterile ungrateful soul, and be miserable by another. Yet have I done nothing dishonorable to your better beloved sex, there is nothing of lewdness, baseness, or meanness in the whole carriage of this noised story, nor which I will not, cannot justify, as the actions of a gentlewoman; with the account of which, from the beginning of my life, I here present you.

My fortune not being competent to my mind, though proportionable to my gentele degree,[4] hath forwardly shrunk into nothing, but I doubt not to buoy both my honor and estate up together, when these envious clouds are dispelled that obscure my brightness; the shadows are at the longest, and my fame shall speedily rise in its due luster. Till then, and ever, I am,

Ladies, your devoted hand-maid,

MARY CARLETON

The Case of Madam Mary Carleton
The Wife of Mr. John Carleton, formerly styled a German Princess

* * *

The time of my deliberated departure being come,[5] and other intervening accidents having confirmed me to the pursuance of that journey (some piecemeal rumors whereof have been scattered up and down, not far distant from the truth, namely constraint and awe of an unliked and unsuitable match, which the freedom of my soul most highly abominated and resented), I privately by night withdrew from my governess, and by the way of Utrecht, where I stayed a while incognito, thence passed to Amsterdam, and so to Rotterdam, I came to the Brill,[6] and there took shipping for England, the Elysium[7] of my wishes and expectations being in hope to find it a land of angels,[8] but I perceive it now to be, as to me, a place of torments.

I am not single,[9] or the first woman, that hath put herself upon such hazards or pilgrimages; the stories of all times abound with such examples, enough to make up a volume. I might as well have given luster to a romance[1] as any of those supposed heroines: and since it is the method of those pieces, and the art of that way of writing, to perplex and intricate[2] the commencement and progress of such adventures with unexpected and various difficulties and troubles, and at last bring them to the long desired fruition of their dear-bought content, I am not altogether out of heart, but that Providence may have some tender and more courteous consideration of me; for I protest I know not what crime, offense, or demerit of mine hath rendered her so averse and intractable as she hath proved to my designs.

Nor do the modern and very late times want examples of the like adventures. I could mention a princess and great personage out of the north,[3] who not long since

---

4. I.e., my high birth.
5. By this point in the text, Carleton has recounted her youth in the German city of Cologne, as the orphaned daughter of wealthy parents. Educated in a nunnery, she rejected the religious life, returned to her family seat, "addicted [her]self to the reading of history," and mastered several languages. Wooed pressingly by two unappetizing bachelors, she resolved to leave Germany for England.
6. Brielle, a Dutch port.
7. A place or condition of ideal happiness; paradise.
8. By an old pun, "England" was deemed to mean "Angelland," because the light-haired inhabitants resembled angels.
9. The only.
1. "A tale of wild adventure in war and love" (Johnson's Dictionary); a genre immensely popular in the 17th century.
2. Complicate.
3. Christina (1626–1689), queen of Sweden (1632–1654), who abdicated in 1654, and thereafter wandered through Europe, often dressed as a man. In A Relation of the Life of Christina Queen of Sweden (1656), she is described as a lady errant (the female counterpart to a knight errant).

came into my country, and hath passed two or three times between Italy and France, and keeps her design yet undiscovered, and is the only lady errant in the world. I could mention another of a far worse consequence in this country, a she-general,[4] who followed the camp to the other world in America, etc., and was the occasion of the loss of the design. Mine compared with those are mere puny stories and inconsiderable. I neither concerned my travail in negotiating peace or carrying war, but was merely my own free agent.

Nor can I be blamed for this course, for besides the necessity and enforcements of forsaking my country, without running into a more insupportable condition of marriage than this I am now in (for my patience and suffering and continence I have, I trust in my own power, and shall endeavor to keep them undisturbed and uncorrupted, whatever temptations or occasions, by reason of this unjust separation, now are, or shall be put upon me hereafter; but my life is not in my disposal or preservation, which I had certainly endangered at home, if I had been bedded to him whom my heart abhorred); and besides other reasons, which I cannot in prudence yet render to the world, the very civility and purity of my design, without any lustful or vicious appertenant,[5] would fairly excuse me.

What harm have I done in pretending to great titles? Ambition and affection of greatness to good and just purposes was always esteemed and accounted laudable and praiseworthy, and the sign and character of a virtuous mind, nor do I think it an unjust purpose in me to contrive my own advancement by such illustrious pretenses as they say I made use of, to grant the question that I am not so honorably descended as I insinuated to the catchdolt[6] my father-in-law (which yet by their favor they shall first better and more evidently disprove than as yet they have done, before I relinquish my just claim to my honor), I think I do rather deserve commendation than reproach; if the best *things are to be imitated*; I had a good precept and warrant for my assumption of such a personage as they were willing to believe me to be. If indeed by any misbecoming act unhandsome and unbefitting such a person, I had profaned that quality and bewrayed and discovered any inconsistent meanness therewith (as it was very difficult to personate greatness for so long a time without slips or mistakes), I had deserved to be severely punished and abominated by all gentlemen; whereas after all these loads of imputations which my enemies have heaped upon me, I do (with my acknowledgments to them for it) enjoy, and am happy in many of their loves and good estimation.

And I will yet continue the same respects, and make the world to know that there is no possibility of such perfections, without a more intent care and elegancy of learning, to which I have by great labor and industry attained.

I need not therefore engage further in this preliminary part of my defense, only as an irrefragable[7] confutation of the poorness of my birth, and in this kingdom I would have my adversaries know, as some of them do, though they don't well understand, that the several languages I have ready and at my command, as the Greek, Latin, French, Italian, Spanish, English, and something of the Oriental tongues, all which I pronounce with a Dutch dialect and idiom, are not common and ordinary endowments of an English spinster, no not of the best rank of the city. And since I must praise myself, in short, I came not here to learn anything for use or ornament of a woman, but only the ways to a better fortune.

---

4. This "she-general" has not been identified.
5. Element.

6. Swindler.
7. Unquestionable.

I come now to the matter of fact. The first place I touched at was Gravesend, where I arrived towards the end of March, and without any stay took a tideboat,[8] came to London in company with a parson or minister, who officiously, but I suppose out of design, gave me the trouble of his service and attendance to the Exchange Tavern right against the stock,[9] betwixt the Poultry and Cornhill, the house of one Mr. King, not having any knowledge of the master or his acquaintance, and free, God knows, from any design, for I would have entered any other house if I had found the doors open or could have raised the folks nearer to my landing, for I was distempered with the night's passage; but it was so early in the morning, five a-clock, that there was nobody stirring elsewhere, only here by mishap Mr. King himself was up and standing at the bar, telling of brass farthings, whom the parson desired to fill a pint of wine, which he readily performed, and brought to a room behind the bar. While the wine was a-drinking (which was Rhenish wine, the compliment being put upon me by the parson as the fruit of my own happy country), Sir John very rudely began to accost me and to offer some incivilities to me, which I found no other way to avoid than by pretending want of rest to the master of the house, and acquainting him with my charge of jewels, and that I was as I do justify myself to be a person of quality. Hereupon a room was provided for me to repose myself in, and the clergyman took his leave with a troublesome promise of waiting upon me another day to give me a visit, which I was forced to admit and to tell him I would leave word wherever I went; but he considering as I suppose of the unfeasibleness of his desires and the publicness of the place, neglected his promise and troubled me no more.

He being gone, Mr. King began to question me, what country-woman I was, and of what religion. I frankly told him, and acquainted him with all what charge I had about me, which to secure from the danger of the town, that was full of cozenage and villainy, he advised me to stay with him till I could better provide for myself.

I rested myself here till eleven a-clock at noon; when I arose, and was very civilly treated by Mr. King, who well knowing I was a stranger and well furnished with money, omitted no manner of respect to me, nor did I spend parsimoniously and at an ordinary rate, but answerable to the quality and account, at their fetching and itching questions, I gave of myself.

This invited him earnestly with all submissive address to request my staying with them till I had dispatched and had provided all things for my public appearance, for the better furnishing and equipping whereof, I acquainted him I would send by post to my steward, for the return of some moneys to defray the expenses thereof, which letters he viewed, and conceived such imaginations in his head thereupon that it never left working till it had wrought the effect of his finely begun and hopefully continued enterprise.

These letters he himself delivered at my desire to have them carefully put into the mail, to the posthouse;[1] and thereafter observed me with most manifest respects.[2] In the interim of [3] the return of these moneys, I was slightly, and as it were by the by, upon discourse of my country (wherein they took occasion to be liberally copious[4]), engaged into some discovery of myself, my estate and quality, and the nature of both, the causes of my coming hither, etc., but I did it so unconcernedly and negligently, as

---

8. A vessel that traveled up the Thames with the tide.
9. Next to the public pillory; the tavern is at the center of the City's commercial district.
1. The post office (King hand-delivers them to prevent tampering).
2. Obvious attention.
3. While awaiting.
4. I.e., King and others at the house often brought up the subject.

a matter of no moment or disturbance to me, though I had hinted at the discontent of my match,[5] that this did assure them that all was real, and therefore it was time to secure my estate to them by a speedy and secret marriage.

Let the world now judge whether being prompted by such plain and public signs of a design upon me, to counterplot them I have done any more than what the rule, and a received principle of justice directs: *to deceive the deceiver is no deceit.*

I knew not nevertheless which way their artifices tended, till Master King brought into my acquaintance old Mr. Carleton his father-in-law, and soon after Mr. John Carleton his son: it seems it had been consulted to have preferred George, the elder brother: he, troubled with a simple modesty, and a mind no way competent to so much greatness, was laid aside, and the younger flushed and encouraged to set upon me. By this time they had obtained my name from me, viz. Maria de Wolway, which passage also hath suffered by another lewder imposture, and allusory sound of De Vulva:[6] in the language of which I am better versed than to pick out no civiller and eleganter impress.[7]

To the addresses of Mr. John Carleton, I carried myself with so much indifference, not superciliously refusing his visits or readily admitting his suit, not disheartening him with a severe retiredness or challenges of his imparity,[8] nor encouraging him with a freedom or openness of heart or arrogance of my own condition, that he and his friends were upon the spur to consummate the match, which yet I delayed and dissembled with convenient pretenses, but herein I will be more particular in the ensuing pages.

In the meanwhile, to prevent all notice of me, and the disturbance of their proceedings that might be occasioned thereby, they kept me close in the nature of a prisoner, which though I perceived, yet I made no semblance thereof[9] at all, but colluded with them in their own arts, and pretended some averseness to all company but only my innamorato,[1] Mr. Carleton: nor was anybody else suffered to come near me or to speak with me; insomuch, as I have been informed, that they promised to one Sackvil (whom for his advice they had too forwardly, as they thought, imparted the business) the sum of £200 to be silent, lest that it should be heard at Court, and so the estate and honor which they had already swallowed[2] would be lost from their son and seized by some courtier, who should next come to hear of this great lady.

After many visits passed betwixt Mr. Carleton and myself, old Mr. Carleton and Mr. King came to me and very earnestly pressed the dispatch of the marriage, and that I would be pleased to give my assent, setting forth with all the qualities and great sufficiencies of that noble person, as they pleased to style him. I knew what made them so urgent, for they had now seen the answers I had received by the post, by which I was certified of the receipt of mine, and that accordingly some thousands of crowns should be remitted instantly to London, and coach and horses sent by the next shipping, with other things I had sent for, and to reinforce this their *commendamus*[3] the more effectually, they acquainted me that if I did not presently grant the suit and their request, Mr. Carleton was so far in love with me, that he would make away with himself, or presently travail beyond sea and see England no more.

---

5. Projected marriage (in Cologne).
6. This sexual pun had been popularized by writers of several pamphlets deriding Carleton's claims.
7. Carleton may mean that she knows all three languages (German, Latin, English) better than to have chosen a name so susceptible to punning. (Her point is that it is her given name; she never chose it.)

8. Inequality to me in rank.
9. Didn't reveal that I saw what they were up to.
1. Beloved.
2. Captured.
3. Their self-recommendation (their argument in favor of the marriage).

I cannot deny but that I could hardly forbear smiling, to see how serious these elders and brokers were in this love-killing story, but keeping to my business, after some demurs and demands, I seemed not to consent, and then they began passionately, urging me with other stories.

* * *

And now my lord spoke nothing but rodomantades[4] of the greatness of his family, of the delights and stateliness of his lands and houses, the game of his parks, the largeness of his stables, and convenience of fish and foul, for furnishing his liberal and open housekeeping, that I should see *England afforded more pleasure than any place in the world,* but they were (without the host) reckoned and charged beforehand to my account,[5] and to be purchased with my estate, which was his, by a figure of anticipation, when we two should be all one, and therefore he lied not but only equivocated a little.

But he did not in the least mention any such thing to me, nor made any offer of inquiry what I was, no not the least semblance or shadow of it; he seemed to take no notice of my fortunes, it was my person he only courted, which having so happily and accidentally seen, he could not live if I cherished not his affections. Nor did I think it then convenient or civil to question the credit of his words and the report given me of him. His demeanor I confess was light, but I imputed that to his youth, and the vanity of a gallant, as necessary a quality and as much admired as wit in a woman.

The last day of my virgin state, Easter eve, the tailor brought me my gown to my lodging. I being dressed and adorned with my jewels, he again renewed his suit to me, with all importunity imaginable. His courteous mother was also now most forward, pressing me to consent by telling me that *she should lose her son* and *he his wits,* he being already impatient with denials and delays, adding withal, that he was a person hopeful, and might deserve my condescension. I withstood all their solicitation, although they continued it until twelve of the clock that night. The young lord, at his taking his leave of me, told me he would attend me betimes the next morning and carry me to St. Paul's Church,[6] to hear the organs, saying, that there would be very excellent anthems performed by rare voices, the morrow being Sunday the 19th of April last. In the morning betimes,[7] the young lord cometh to my chamber door, desiring admittance, which I refused, in regard I was not ready; yet so soon as my head was dressed, I let him have access. He hastened me, and told me his coach was ready at the door, in which he carried me to his mother's in the Greyfriars, London,[8] where I was assaulted by the young lord's tears, and others to give my consent to marry him, telling me that they had a parson and a license ready, which was a mere falsehood and temporary fallacy to secure the match.

So on Easter morning, with three coaches, in which with the bride and bridegroom were all the kindred that were privy to the business, and pretended a license,[9] they carried me to Cloth Fair by Smithfield, and in the church of great St. Bartholomew's, married me by one Mr. Smith, who was well paid for his pains. And now they thought themselves possessed of their hopes, but because they would pre-

---

4. Boasts.
5. To "reckon without the host" is to calculate one's debt without consulting the person to whom one owes it (in this case, the author).
6. The City of London's cathedral, and central place of worship.
7. Early.
8. Once the site of a monastery, this was now an area of prosperous residences.
9. Either they pretended to have a license or they had a fake license and pretended it was real.

vent the noise and fame of their good fortune from public discourse, that no sinister accident might intervene before Mr. Carleton had bedded me, offense being likely to be taken at Court (as they whispered to themselves) that a private subject had married a foreign princess, they had before determined to go to Barnet,[1] and thither immediately after the celebration of the marriage we were driven in the coaches, where we had a handsome treatment, and there we stayed Sunday and Monday, both which nights Mr. Carleton lay with me, and on Tuesday morning we were married again, a license being then obtained to make the match more fast and sure, at their instance with me to consent to it.

This being done, and their fears over, they resolved to put me in a garb befitting the estate and dignity they fancied I had; and they were so far possessed with a belief of it, that they gave out I was worth no less than £80,000 per annum, and my husband, as I must now style him, published[2] so much in a coffeehouse; adding withal, to the extolling of his good hap, that there was a further estate but that it was my modesty or design to conceal it, and that he could not attribute his great fortune to anything but the Fates, for he had not anything to balance with the least of my estate and merits. So do conceited[3] heights of sudden prosperity and greatness dazzle the eyes and judgment of the most, nor could this young man be much blamed for his vainglorious mistake.

My clothes being made at the charge of my father-in-law, and other fineries of the mode and fashion sent me by some of his kindred and friends (who prided themselves in this happy affinity, and who had an eye upon some advantages also, and therefore gave me this early bribe, as testimonies of their early respect), and as for jewels I had of mine own of all sorts, for necklaces, pendants and bracelets, of admirable splendor and brightness. I was in a prince-like attire, and a splendid equipage and retinue, accoutered for public view among all the great ladies of the Court and the town on May Day[4] ensuing. At which time in my Lady Bludworth's[5] coach, which the same friends procured for my greater accommodation, and accompanied with the same lady with footmen and pages, I rode to Hyde Park[6] in open view of that celebrious[7] cavalcade and assembly, much gazed upon by them all, the eximiousness[8] of my fortune drawing their eyes upon me; particularly that that noble lady gave me precedence and the right hand, and a neat treatment after our divertisement of turning up and down the park.

I was altogether ignorant of what estate my husband was, and therefore made no nicety to take those places his friends gave me, and if I be taxed for incivility herein, it was his fault that he instructed me no better in my quality, for I conceited still that he was some landed, honorable, and wealthy man.

Things yet went fairly on, the same observances and distances continued, and lodgings befitting a person of quality taken for me in Durham Yard,[9] at one Mr. Green's, where my husband and I enjoyed one another with mutual complacency, till the return of the moneys out of Germany failing the day and their rich hopes, old Mr. Carleton began to suspect he was deceived in his expectation, and that all was not gold that glistered. But to remove such a prejudice from himself, as if he were the

---

1. A village north of London.
2. Announced.
3. Imagined.
4. May 1, exuberantly celebrated as a spring festival.
5. "Blood-worth": a name concocted by Carleton that indicates high rank and birth.

6. A fashionable gathering place.
7. Fine and crowded.
8. Excellence; Carleton is pointedly showing off her vocabulary and her learning.
9. A fashionable London neighborhood.

author of those scandals that were now prepared against my innocence, a letter is produced and sent from some then unknown hand, which reflected much upon my honor and reputation;[1] and thereupon on the fifth or sixth of May ensuing, I was by a warrant dragged forth of my new lodgings, with all the disgrace and contumely that could be cast upon the vilest offender in the world, at the instigation of old Mr. Carleton, who was the prosecutor, and by him and his agents divested and stripped of all my clothes, and plundered of all my jewels and my money, my very bodice and a pair of silk stockings being also pulled from me, and in a strange array carried before a justice.

* * *

See the fickleness and vanity of human things, today embellished, and adorned with all the female arts of bravery and gallantry, and courted and attended on by the best rank of my sex, who are jealous observers what honor and respect they give among themselves, to a very punctilio;[2] and now disrobed and disfigured in misshapen garments and almost left naked, and haled[3] and pulled by beadles,[4] and such like rude and boisterous fellows, before a tribunal, like a lewd criminal.

The justice's name was Mr. Godfrey,[5] by whose *mittimus*,[6] upon an accusation managed by old Mr. Carleton, that I had married two husbands, both of them in being, I was committed to the Gatehouse. Being interrogated by the justice, whether or no I had not two husbands as was alleged, I answered, if I had, he was one of them, which I believe incensed him something the more against me, but I did not know the authority and dignity of his place, so much am I a stranger to this kingdom.

There were other things and crimes of a high nature objected against me besides: That I cheated a vintner[7] of sixty pounds, and was for that committed to Newgate; but that lie quickly vanished, for it was made appear that I was never a prisoner there, nor was my name ever recorded in their books; and that I picked a Kentish lord's pocket, and cheated a French merchant of rings, jewels, and other commodities, that I made an escape, when sold and shipped for the Barbados,[8] but these were urged only as surmises; and old Carleton bound over to prosecute only for bigamy, for my having two husbands.

Thus the world may see how industrious mischief is to ruin a poor helpless and destitute woman, who had neither money, friends, nor acquaintance left me; yet I cannot deny that my husband lovingly came to me at the Gatehouse the same day I was committed, and did very passionately complain of his father's usage of me, merely upon the disappointment, as he said, of their expectations, and that he could be contented to love me as well as ever, to live with me and own me as a wife, and used several other expressions of tenderness to me.

Nor have I less affection and kind sentiments for him, whom I own and will own till death dissolve the union, and did acquaint him with so much there and protested my innocence to him, nor do I doubt, could he have prevailed with his father, but that these things had never happened. If now after my vindication he prove faithless and renege[9] me, his fault will be doubly greater in that he neither assisted my innocence when endangered, or cherished it when vindicated by the law.

1. The letter (which Carleton quotes in a section omitted here) came from Canterbury, and described her as an "absolute cheat" who had already "married several men in our county."
2. A small detail.
3. Harried; molested.
4. Minor parish officers.
5. Sir Edmund Berry Godfrey (1622–1678), justice of the peace. He became one of the century's most famous corpses; his murder, and the accusations surrounding it, initiated the anti-Catholic furor called the Popish Plot.
6. We send (Latin); a warrant stipulating that the accused be imprisoned.
7. Wine dealer.
8. I.e., as punishment for a previous crime.
9. Denounce.

In this prison of the Gatehouse I continued six weeks, in a far better condition than I promised myself, but the greater civilities I owe to the keeper: as I am infinitely beholding to several persons of quality, who came at first I suppose out of curiosity to see me, and did thereafter nobly compassionate my calamitous, and injurious restraint. * * * I may in some measure thank my stars that out of this misfortune extracted so much bliss as the honor of their acquaintance, which otherwise at large I had been in no capacity to attain.[1]

* * *

And now let all the world judge of the cheat I have put upon this worshipful family of the Carletons. I have of theirs not a thread nor piece of anything, to be a token or remembrance of my beloved lord, which I might preserve and lay up as a sacred relic of a person dear to me (I think indeed the dearest that ever woman had).

I am advised howsoever to prosecute my adversaries[2] in the same manner, and at the same bar where they arraigned me for a suspicion, of a real suit of felony, for that riot against the public peace committed upon my person: which I am resolved to do, in case I receive not better satisfaction from them before the Sessions:[3] nor shall my husband's dilating entreaties and persuasions befool me any longer.[4]

> Either love me, or leave me,
> And do not deceive me.

The fashions and customs here are much different from those of our country, where the wife shares an equal portion with her husband in all things of weal and woe, and can *liber intentare*,[5] begin and commence, and finish a suit in her own name; they buy and sell, and keep accounts, manage the affairs of household and the trade, and do all things relating to their several stations and degrees. I have heard and did believe the proverb *that England was a Heaven for women*. But I never saw that Heaven described in its proper terms. For as to as much as I see of it, 'tis a very long prospect, and almost disappears to view; it is to be enjoyed but at second hand, and all by the husband's title; quite contrary to the custom of the Russians, where it is a piece of their divinity that because it's said that the bishop must be the husband of one wife, they put out of orders[6] and from all ecclesiastical function such clergy-men who by the canon being bound to be married, are by death deprived of their wives; so that their tenure to their livings and preferments clearly depends upon the welfare and long life of their yoke-fellows, in whose choice, as of such moment to their well-being, they are very curious, as they are afterwards in their care and preservation of them.

I could instance in many other customs of nearer nations, in respect to female right and propriety in their own dowers, as well as in their husbands' estates: but, *cum fueris Romae, Romano vivite more*.[7] I will not quarrel with the English laws, which I question not are calculated and well accommodated to the genius and temper of the people.

While I mention these customs, I cannot forbear to complain of a very great rudeness and incivility to which the mass and generality of the English vulgar are most pronely inclined, that is, to hoot and hallow and pursue strangers with their

---

1. Carleton proceeds to recount her trial and her acquittal.
2. I.e., the Carleton family.
3. The period appointed for new trials.
4. Since her arrest, her husband had made intermittent

overtures of reconciliation.
5. Be free to bring an action.
6. Dismiss from office.
7. "When in Rome do as the Romans do." St. Ambrose's advice to St. Augustine had become proverbial.

multitudes through the streets, pressing upon them even to the danger of their lives; and when once a cry or some scandalous humor is bruited[8] among them, they become brutes indeed. A barbarity I thought could not possibly be in this nation, whom I heard famed for so much civility and urbanity. This I experimented the other day in Fenchurch Street, as I was passing through it upon some occasion, which being noised and scattered among the 'prentices, I was forced to bethink of some shift and stratagem to avoid them, which was by putting my maid into a coach that by a good hap was at hand, and stepping into an adjoining tavern; which the herd mistaking my maid for me, and following the coach as supposing there for the convenience thereof, gave me the opportunity of escaping from them. A regulation of this kind of uproar by some severe penalties would much conduce not only to the honor of the government of the city, but the whole nation in general; having heard the French very much complain of the like injuries and affronts: but those to me I may justly place to my husband's account, who hath exposed me to the undeserved wonder, and to be a May-game[9] to the town. ✳ ✳ ✳

1663   1663

---

8. Rumored.   9. A source of entertainment, like the games on May
                                               Day.

≈⊹ PERSPECTIVES ⊹≈
The Royal Society and the New Science

In the late 1600s, the antiquarian John Aubrey looked back to the middle of his century as a turning point in intellectual history: "Till about the year 1649, when experimental philosophy was first cultivated by a club at Oxford, 'twas held a strange presumption for a man to attempt an innovation in learnings; and not to be good manners, to be more knowing than his neighbors and forefathers." The "club" consisted of a group of inquirers for whom the university at Oxford offered a place of retreat in time of civil war. As Aubrey implies, their "innovation" consisted in a kind of bad manners. They refused to take the word of their intellectual "forefathers" (notably Aristotle) for how the natural world worked, and instead pursued knowledge of it through direct experiment, preferring new data to old theory, the testimony of the senses over the constructs of the intellect; the works of Francis Bacon, who had articulated such a method a half-century earlier, served for these investigators as something akin to scripture. The members continued to meet during the Interregnum. In 1662, Charles II granted the group (which had relocated to London) a charter, a seal, and with his patronage, a new prominence. The informal club had become the "Royal Society for the Improving of Natural Knowledge."

That "Improving" was to take place on many fronts. The Society's charter stipulated that its experiments should be aimed at "promoting the knowledge of natural things and useful arts": science and technology. In its first decades, its members made enormous advances in both realms, producing (among innumerable innovations) new explanations of heat, cold, and light; an air pump capable of creating a vacuum; a newly efficient pocket watch; and a newly coherent and durable account of the universe. A Fellow of the Society might work simultaneously at many endeavors that have since become specialties, investigating biology, physics, and astronomy, inventing scientific instruments and domestic appliances, advancing inquiries into theology, astrology, even demonology.

The group liked to portray itself as inclusive demographically too. Its Fellows represented many religious views, political persuasions, and social strata, from dukes to merchants to "mechanicks." Still, the early records evince an initial emphasis on high rank: aristocrats, courtiers, politicians, and "gentlemen" made up more than half the original membership (women were excluded altogether). Many of these men were mere names on the rolls, enlisted to bolster the respectability of the new enterprise; others were occasional spectators, intermittently attending the meetings to observe (amused, amazed, often baffled) the experiments performed there. But the Society also fostered a new category of inquirer: the "Christian virtuoso," a man of birth, means, merit, brains, and leisure, whose dissociation from any one profession was taken to guarantee the objectivity of his investigations, and whose rank and goodness underwrote the integrity of his findings. The Honorable Robert Boyle, who coined the phrase, was also its epitome. Well-born, devout, and dazzlingly gifted at science, he was the Society's prime mover and first star. But the type also found a less rarified, more popular incarnation in a new kind of amateur: the prosperous person who read, contemplated, talked the new philosophy, and kept a "cabinet of curiosities"—a closet or small room in which were arranged, and proudly displayed, antiquarian objects, scientific specimens, anything whose strangeness might arouse interest. The Society was amassing comparable collections on a much larger scale; the history of museums begins within the cabinets of the virtuosi.

The Society's emphasis on gentlemanly virtuosity was partly a form of self-defense against attacks from many quarters, where the "experimental philosophy" was regarded as ludicrous or dangerous or both. The influential wits of the day scoffed at the earnestness of the investigators and the seeming preposterousness of their findings (even Charles II laughed out loud when he learned that the members were busy weighing air); some clergymen and politicians saw in the new enterprise a threat to religion and to social hierarchy, a challenge against past, present, and divine authority, mounted by persons so presumptuous as to suppose that the truths of the world could be determined by human investigation rather than by Christian revelation.

The Society answered (again in the language of its charter) that it was intent upon serving "the glory of God and the good of mankind." The "good of mankind" was to be enhanced by technological improvements, which would make work more productive, life easier, and commerce more abundant, in contrast to the dark old days when (as Aubrey reminisces) "even to attempt an improvement in husbandry [agriculture], though it succeeded with profit, was looked upon with an ill eye." The "glory of God" would be served by a new form of attention to the world God made. A long tradition ascribed to the Deity two sacred texts: the Book of Scripture, and the Book of Nature. The faithful had long pondered the first; the Society now undertook to read the second anew and aright. "Each page in the great volume of nature," observed Boyle, "is full of real hieroglyphs, where (by an inverted way of expression) things stand for words"—objects and actions incarnate truths. To disclose the divine intricacy in the Book of Nature (so the Society's advocates argued) could only enlarge wonder and increase worship.

The new reading of that old text reshaped other texts as well. In the 1660s and after, manuscripts, periodicals, and printed books all explored new forms, as writers attempted to render in language what Michel Foucault has called "the prose of the world," to grapple with new relations between words and things, and to make the written or the printed page (like the closet and the cabinet) a copious repository of newfound curiosities.

━━ ⚒ ━━

Thomas Sprat
1635–1713

Given the date of its first appearance, the *History of the Royal Society* seems puzzlingly titled. The Oxford-educated clergyman Thomas Sprat wrote much of it in 1663, just a year after the Society received its charter, and published it (after delays caused by fire, plague, and other distractions) in 1667. Both title and timing reflect the pressures that produced the book in the first place. As he acknowledges at the outset, Sprat has produced not so much a "plain history" of the Society as an "apology," in the Greek-based sense of the word current in the seventeenth century: an energetic defense of the new institution's policies and methods.

From its inception, the Society's directors felt the need for such a defense, and they brought Sprat in specifically to provide it, appointing him a Founding Fellow and anxiously inquiring after his progress on the book. They had chosen him not for his knowledge of science (negligible) but for his status as a divine and for his skill as a rhetorician. In response to its detractors, Sprat insists that the Society will enhance piety (by detailing the wonders of Creation); will uphold hierarchy (as evidenced by the predominance of gentlemen and aristocrats among the Fellowship); and will cultivate community (in order to appease fears that the Fellows will revive "disputation" when the new Restoration needs it least, Sprat downplays the importance of argument in the new science and stresses instead the accumulation of raw data). Above all, Sprat focuses on the Society's capacity to improve ordinary life by producing "new inventions and shorter ways of labor" that will make possible an easier and more prosperous existence for the English, whose national "Genius" is uniquely suited to such advances.

As Michael Hunter notes, Sprat's "generalized attempt to appeal to everybody and antagonize nobody" fell short. It appealed mainly to adherents, and provided critics with a new target for their attacks. In the selection printed here, Sprat navigates a particularly delicate portion of his argument. He sets forth the Fellows' attempts to simplify the prose style in which they wrote up their inquiries and discoveries. The degree to which the Society actually sought and managed to implement a new "mathematical plainness" has long remained a matter of dispute.

In contemporary writing, clarity and "ornament" were often seen as mutually supportive; even when Sprat is arguing for a "naked" prose, he intermittently resorts to the very "amplifications, digressions, and swellings of style" that he is ruling out. As its sponsors intended, Sprat's *History* applies a polished rhetoric to a pointed claim: that the Royal Society was creating a "common-stock" of knowledge on which all might draw, and from which all might profit.

from The History of the Royal Society of London, for the Improving of Natural Knowledge

Thus they have directed, judged, conjectured upon, and improved experiments. But lastly, in these and all other businesses that have come under their care, there is one thing more about which the Society has been most solicitous, and that is the manner of their discourse, which unless they have been watchful to keep in due temper, the whole spirit and vigor of their design had been soon eaten out by the luxury and redundance of speech. The ill effects of this superfluity of talking have already overwhelmed most other arts and professions, insomuch that when I consider the means of happy living and the causes of their corruption, I can hardly forbear recanting what I said before, and concluding that eloquence ought to be banished out of all civil societies as a thing fatal to peace and good manners. To this opinion I should wholly incline, if I did not find that it is a weapon which may be as easily procured by bad men as good, and that, if these should only cast it away and those retain it, the naked innocence of virtue would be upon all occasions exposed to the armed malice of the wicked. This is the chief reason that should now keep up the ornaments of speaking in any request, since they are so much degenerated from their original usefulness. They were at first, no doubt, an admirable instrument in the hands of wise men, when they were only employed to describe goodness, honesty, obedience, in larger, fairer, and more moving images; to represent truth, clothed with bodies; and to bring knowledge back again to our very senses, from whence it was at first derived to our understandings. But now they are generally changed to worse uses. They make the fancy disgust[1] the best things, if they come sound and unadorned. They are in open defiance against reason, professing not to hold much correspondence with that, but with its slaves, the passions. They give the mind a motion too changeable and bewitching to consist with right practice. Who can behold, without indignation, how many mists and uncertainties these specious tropes and figures[2] have brought on our knowledge? How many rewards, which are due to more profitable and difficult arts, have been still snatched away by the easy vanity of fine speaking? For now I am warmed with this just anger, I cannot withhold myself from betraying the shallowness of all these seeming mysteries upon which we writers and speakers look so big. And, in few words, I dare say that of all the studies of men, nothing may be sooner obtained than this vicious abundance of phrase, this trick of metaphors, this volubility of tongue, which makes so great a noise in the world. But I spend words in vain; for the evil is now so inveterate that it is hard to know whom to blame or where to begin to reform. We all value one another so much upon this beautiful deceit and labor so long after it in the years of our education that we cannot but ever after think kinder of it than it deserves. And indeed, in most other parts of learning, I look on it to be a thing almost utterly desperate in its cure. And I think it may be

---

1. They make the imagination reject.   2. Figures of speech.

placed amongst those general mischiefs such as the dissension of Christian princes,[3] the want[4] of practice in religion and the like, which have been so long spoken against, that men are become insensible about them, every one shifting off the fault from himself to others, and so they are only made bare commonplaces of complaint. It will suffice my present purpose to point out what has been done by the Royal Society towards the correcting of its[5] excesses in natural philosophy, to which it is, of all others, a most professed enemy.

They have therefore been most rigorous in putting in execution the only remedy that can be found for this extravagance. And that has been a constant resolution to reject all the amplifications, digressions, and swellings of style; to return back to the primitive purity and shortness, when men delivered so many *things*, almost in an equal number of *words*. They have exacted from all their members a close, naked, natural way of speaking; positive expressions; clear senses; a native easiness; bringing all things as near the mathematical plainness as they can and preferring the language of artisans, countrymen, and merchants before that of wits or scholars.[6]

And here there is one thing not to be passed by, which will render this established custom of the Society well nigh everlasting; and that is, the general constitution of the minds of the English. I have already often insisted on some of the prerogatives of England, whereby it may justly lay claim to be the head of a philosophical league, above all other countries in Europe. I have urged its situation,[7] its present genius, and the disposition of its merchants, and many more such arguments to encourage us still remain to be used. But of all others, this, which I am now alleging, is of the most weighty and important consideration. If there can be a true character given of the universal temper of any nation under heaven, then certainly this must be ascribed to our countrymen: that they have commonly an unaffected sincerity; that they love to deliver their minds with a sound simplicity; that they have the middle qualities between the reserved, subtle southern and the rough, unhewn northern people; that they are not extremely prone to speak; that they are more concerned what others will think of the strength, than of the fineness of what they say; and that an universal modesty possesses them. These qualities are so conspicuous and proper to our soil that we often hear them objected to us by some of our neighbor satirists in more disgraceful expressions. For they are wont to revile the English with a want of familiarity; with a melancholy dumpishness,[8] with slowness, silence, and with the unrefined sullenness of their behavior. But these are only the reproaches of partiality or ignorance. For they ought rather to be commended for an honorable integrity; for a neglect of circumstances and flourishes; for regarding things of greater moment,[9] more than less; for a scorn to deceive as well as to be deceived, which are all the best endowments that can enter into a philosophical mind. So that even the position of our climate, the air, the influence of the heaven, the composition of the English blood, as well as the embraces of the ocean, seem to join with the labors of the Royal Society to render our country a land of experimental knowledge. And it is a good sign that nature will reveal more of its secrets to the English than to others because it

---

3. Disputes between Christian monarchs.
4. Lack.
5. I.e., eloquence's.
6. For a parody of this position, see Swift's depiction of the Academy in *Gulliver's Travels*, Part 3, ch. 5.
7. I.e., its location. Sprat has earlier emphasized that Eng-

land's status as an island, and as "mistress of the Ocean," gives it a privileged position from which to supervise international scientific experiments and correspondence.
8. Tendency to depression.
9. Importance.

has already furnished them with a genius so well proportioned for the receiving and retaining its mysteries.

And now to come to a close of the second part of the narration. The Society has reduced its principal observations into one common-stock[1] and laid them up in public registers to be nakedly transmitted to the next generation of men, and so from them to their successors. And as their purpose was to heap up a mixed mass of experiments, without digesting them into any perfect model, so to this end, they confined themselves to no order of subjects; and whatever they have recorded, they have done it, not as complete schemes of opinions, but as bare, unfinished histories.

✦ ✦ ✦ ✦

Philosophical Transactions

Philosophical Transactions first appeared in 1665 and continues to the present day; it is the longest running periodical in English and the oldest scientific journal in the world. It was created by Henry Oldenburg (1618–1677), a German-born diplomat who came to England in 1653 as an emissary to Oliver Cromwell and found himself powerfully drawn to the ideas and the company of the practitioners of the new science at Oxford. His gift for copious, accurate reporting on scientific matters prompted the Royal Society to enlist him as Fellow and Secretary, charged with attending the meetings, keeping the minutes, and managing the new institution's huge correspondence with scientific inquirers in England and abroad. Oldenburg produced the monthly *Transactions* as a private venture, but he drew its material from the documents in which his Society work immersed him, particularly from the correspondence that provided so plentiful an account (in the words of the journal's subtitle) "of the present undertakings, studies, and labors of the ingenious in many considerable parts of the world." The *Transactions'* content ranged wide conceptually as well as geographically, readily shifting from systematic searches for natural laws, to reports on technological innovations, to eager surmises about random oddities: monstrous births, human and otherwise, were a recurrent favorite. The new journal combined in text the attractions of the scientific treatise and the cabinet of curiosities; the insatiable curiosity of the journal's most assiduous contributor, Oldenburg's patron Robert Boyle, helped to ensure this variety and texture.

More than any other instrument, the *Transactions* established the Royal Society as central to the new philosophy and fostered the conviction that the advancement of learning was a communal pursuit of truth to which (as Francis Bacon had predicted) everyone from a mariner to a virtuoso could contribute indispensable information. The *Transactions* influenced nonscientific journalism as well: with its topical headlines, variegated matter, and detailed tables of contents, it resembled no periodical of its time, but many that came after.

from **Philosophical Transactions**

[THE INTRODUCTION][1]

Whereas there is nothing more necessary for promoting the improvement of philosophical matters than the communicating, to such as apply their studies and endeavors that way, such things as are discovered or put in practice by others, it is therefore thought fit to employ the press as the most proper way to gratify those whose engage-

---

1. Property and resource for the use of all.

1. This and the following two selections appeared in Vol. 1, No. 1, 6 March 1665.

ment in such studies and delight in the advancement of learning and profitable discoveries doth entitle them to the knowledge of what this kingdom or other parts of
the world do from time to time afford, as well of the progress of the studies, labors,
and attempts of the curious and learned in things of this kind, as of their complete
discoveries and performances. To the end that such productions being clearly and
truly communicated, desires after solid and useful knowledge may be further entertained, ingenious endeavors and undertakings cherished, and those addicted to and
conversant in such matters may be invited and encouraged to search, try, and find
out new things, impart their knowledge to one another, and contribute what they
can to the grand design of improving natural knowledge and perfecting all philosophical arts and sciences. All for the glory of God, the honor and advantage of these
kingdoms, and the universal good of mankind.

* * *

An Account of a Very Odd Monstrous Calf

By the same noble person[2] was lately communicated to the Royal Society an account
of a very odd, monstrous birth produced at Limmington in Hampshire, where a
butcher, having caused a cow (which calved her first calf the year before) to be covered that she might the sooner be fatted, killed her when fat, and opening the womb,
which he found heavy to admiration, saw in it a calf, which had begun to have hair,
whose hinderlegs had no joints and whose tongue was, Cerebus-like,[3] triple—to each
side of his mouth one, and one in the midst. Between the forelegs and the hinderlegs
was a great stone, on which the calf rid.[4] The *sternum*, or that part of the breast
where the ribs lie, was also perfect stone. And the stone on which it rid weighed
twenty pounds and a half. The outside of the stone was of greenish color, but some
small parts being broken off, it appeared a perfect free-stone. The stone, according
to the letter of Mr. David Thomas, who sent this account to Mr. Boyle, is with
Dr. Haughten of Salisbury, to whom he also refers for further information.

* * *

An observation imparted to the noble Mr. Boyle by Mr. David Thomas touching some particulars further considerable in the monster mentioned in the first papers of these Philosophical Transactions.[5]

Upon the strictest inquiry, I find by one that saw the monstrous calf and stone,
within four hours after it was cut out of the cow's belly, that the breast of the calf was
not stony (as I wrote) but that the skin of the breast and between the legs and of the
neck (which parts lay on the smaller end of the stone) was very much thicker than
on any other part, and that the feet of the calf were so parted as to be like the claws of
a dog. The stone I have since seen. It is bigger at one end than the other, of no plain
superficies,[6] but full of little cavities. The stone, when broken, is full of small pebble
stones of an oval figure. Its color is gray—like free-stone, but intermixed with veins
of yellow and black. A part of it I have begged of Dr. Haughten for you, which I have
sent to Oxford, whither a more exact account will be conveyed by the same person.

* * *

2. Robert Boyle.
3. Resembling the mythical three-headed dog that guarded the entrance to Hades, the underworld of the dead.

4. Rode (i.e., straddled).
5. A "follow-up" from Vol. 1, No. 2.
6. Smooth surface.

A letter of the honorable Robert Boyle of Sept. 13, 1673, to the publisher concerning Amber Greece and its being a vegetable production[7]

Sir,

Some occasions calling me this afternoon up to London, I was met there with a very intelligent gentleman, who was ready to go out of it. But before he did so, he willingly spared me some time to discourse with him about some of the affairs of our East Indian Company,[8] of which he was very lately Deputy Governor, and, his year being expired, is still one of the chief of the Court of Committees, which a foreigner would call Directors that manage all the affairs of that considerable society. And among other things, talking with him about some contents of a journal lately taken in a Dutch East Indian prize,[9] I learned from him that he, who understands that language very well, is now perusing that manuscript; and among many things recorded there that concern the economical and political affairs of the said Dutch company, he met with one physical observation which he thought so rare that, remembering the curiosity I had expressed for such things, he put it into English and transcribed it for me; and immediately drawing it out of his pocket, he presented me the short paper, whereof I now show you the copy. Upon perusal of which, you will very easily believe, that not only his civility obliged me, but the information it brought me surprised me too. For the several trials and observations of my own about amber greece have long kept me from acquiescing either in the vulgar opinions[1] or those of some learned men concerning it. Yet I confess, my experiments did much less discover what it is than this paper has done, in case we may safely and entirely give credit to its information, and that it reach to all kinds of amber greece. And probably you will be invited to look on this account, though not as complete, yet as very sincere, and on that score credible if you consider that this was not written by a philosopher to broach[2] a paradox or serve a hypothesis, but by a merchant or factor[3] for his superiors to give them an account of a matter of fact. And that this passage is extant in an authentic journal, wherein the affairs of the company were by public order from time to time registered at their chief colony Batavia.[4] And it appears by the paper itself that the relation was not looked upon as a doubtful thing, but as a thing from which a practical way may be deduced to make this discovery easily lucriferous[5] to the Dutch Company. And I could heartily wish that in those countries that are addicted to long navigations, more notice than is usual were taken and given of the natural rarities that occur to merchants and seamen. On which occasion I remember when I had in compliance with my curiosity put myself into our East Indian Company and had by their civility to me been chosen of their Committee as long as my health allowed me to continue so, I had the opportunity in some register books of merchants English and Dutch to observe some things which would easily justify this wish of mine, if my haste and their interest would permit me to acquaint others with them.

7. Ambergris (Latin, "gray amber") is a gray waxy substance formed in the intestines of sperm whales; it was valued as a component in perfumes and medicines. Because ambergris, once emitted by the whale, often floats along the sea coast, traders and scientists were uncertain about its origins. (Boyle's letter appeared in Vol. 8, No. 97.)

8. A company chartered by Elizabeth I in 1600 to develop trade with India and the Far East.

9. I.e., the ship's log of a Dutch trading vessel recently captured by the English.

1. Received ideas of ordinary people.

2. Penetrate, untangle.

3. Company agent. Boyle reaffirms the Royal Society's interest in raw data over cooked theory, in the testimony of experienced "mechanics" over that of abstract "philosophers."

4. A seaport on the island of Java.

5. Profitable.

But to return to our account of amber greece I think you will easily believe that if I had received it not by a paper but immediately from the writer,[6] I should by proposing diverse questions, have been enabled to give you a much more satisfactory account than this short one contains. But the obliging person that gave it me, being just going out of town, I could not civilly stay him to receive my queries about it, which though (God permitting) I may propose ere long, if I can light on him again, yet I fear he has given me in these few lines all that he found about this matter. However, this relation, as short as it is, being about the nature of a drug so precious and so little known will not, I hope, be unwelcome to the curious. To whom none is so like to convey it so soon and so well as Mr. O.,[7] whose forwardness to oblige others by his various communications challenges returns of the like nature from others and particularly from his affectionate humble servant.

Follows the extract itself out of a Dutch journal belonging to the Dutch East Indian Company:

> Amber greece is not the scum or excrement of the whale, etc., but issues out of the root of a tree, which tree how far soever it stands on the land, always shoots forth its roots towards the sea, seeking the warmth of it, thereby to deliver the fattest gum that comes out of it, which tree otherwise by its copious fatness might be burnt and destroyed. Wherever that fat gum is shot into the sea, it is so tough that it is not easily broken from the root, unless its own weight and the working of the warm sea doth it,[8] and so it floats on the sea.
>
> There was found by a soldier 7/8 of a pound and by the chief two pieces weighing five pounds. If you plant the trees where the stream sets to the shore, then the stream will cast it up to great advantage. March 1, 1672, in Batavia.

--- ⚜ ---

Robert Hooke
1635–1703

In a long life, Robert Hooke got little sleep. From the age of twenty-eight until his death, he lived in rooms at Gresham College, the Royal Society headquarters, in order to make himself maximally available to meet the ceaseless demands of his many concurrent employments, as the Society's first Curator of Experiments, as the College's lecturer in geometry, as surveyor and rebuilder of London after the Great Fire, and as restless, relentless inventor and improver of scientific instruments. Hooke's friend John Aubrey described him as "the greatest mechanick this day in the world"; the jostle between the high superlative and the equivocal noun captures Hooke's uncertain status in the Society to which he devoted his prodigiously productive working life. The mechanical arts were in many ways the lifeblood of the Society's enterprise, but "mechanicks" were not gentry. In an institution founded and headed by aristocrats and gentlemen, this gifted son of a provincial clergyman was often treated (in Stephen Shapin's words) "as a tradesman, as a servant." Hooke's contract as Curator required that he prepare and perform "three or four substantial experiments" at each of the Society's weekly meetings, as well as any other experiments the Fellows might (in the recurrent wording of the meeting minutes) "order" or "direct" him to undertake. The empirical life of the Society during its first

---

6. I.e., in conversation.
7. Henry Oldenburg, editor of the *Transactions*.

8. I.e., breaks it off.

four decades would have been unimaginable without Hooke, but the Fellows registered his indispensability by irritation at the outside interests through which he pursued autonomy and income. "I could wish," wrote Sir Robert Moray, "he had finished the task laid upon him rather than to learn a dozen trades." Hooke's variegated pursuits, though, produced dozens of inventions and discoveries: newly efficient lenses, lamps, telescopes, watches; new theories of optics, chemistry, and gravity that in some cases anticipated Issac Newton's. Constitutionally irascible, Hooke spent much energy asserting, angrily but often accurately, the priority and/or superiority of his many innovations.

Hooke produced *Micrographia* at the Society's behest. The book doubled as a work of science and a piece of institutional propaganda, designed to promote the Society's methods. It fulfilled both purposes. In Hooke's sixty word-and-picture "Observations" of magnified objects, readers could see for the first time how far the useful artifice of the microscope had extended the "knowledge of natural things" into realms unreachable by the eye and mind alone. At the same time, the book touched a cultural pulse point. At its Greek root, Hooke's title suggests "the writing down of small things," and this is what many of his fellow Fellows—Pepys, Oldenburg, Evelyn, Aubrey—were in their different ways newly up to. (Pepys thought *Micrographia* "the most ingenious book that I ever read in my life.") Small things, it had been discovered, could produce large amazements when written up.

from **Micrographia**
Or Some Physiological Description of Minute Bodies Made by Magnifying Glasses with Observations and Inquiries thereupon

TO THE KING

Sir,

I do here most humbly lay this small present at your Majesty's royal feet. And though it comes accompanied with two disadvantages, the meanness of the author and of the subject; yet in both I am encouraged by the greatness of your mercy and your knowledge. By the one I am taught, that you can forgive the most presumptuous offenders. And by the other, that you will not esteem the least work of nature or art unworthy of your observation. Amidst the many felicities that have accompanied your Majesty's happy restoration and government, it is none of the least considerable that philosophy and experimental learning have prospered under your royal patronage.[1] And as the calm prosperity of your reign has given us the leisure to follow these studies of quiet and retirement, so it is just that the fruits of them should, by way of acknowledgment, be returned to your Majesty. There are, Sir, several other of your subjects, of your Royal Society, now busy about nobler matters: the improvement of manufactures and agriculture, the increase of commerce, the advantage of navigation—in all which they are assisted by your Majesty's encouragement and example. Amidst all those greater designs, I here presume to bring in that which is more proportional to the smallness of my abilities and to offer some of the least of all visible things to that mighty king that has established an empire over the best of all invisible things of this world, the minds of men. Your Majesty's most humble and most obedient subject and servant,

Robert Hooke

1. Charles II had granted the Society a royal charter in 1662.

TO THE ROYAL SOCIETY

After my address to our great founder and patron, I could not but think myself obliged, in consideration of those many engagements you have laid upon me, to offer these my poor labors to this most illustrious assembly. You have been pleased former-ly to accept of these rude drafts.[2] I have since added to them some descriptions and some conjectures of my own. And therefore, together with your acceptance, I must also beg your pardon. The rules you have prescribed yourselves in your philosophical progress do seem the best that have ever yet been practiced. And particularly that of avoiding dogmatizing and the espousal of any hypothesis not sufficiently grounded and confirmed by experiments. This way seems the most excellent and may preserve both philosophy and natural history from its former corruptions. In saying which, I may seem to condemn my own course in this treatise, in which there may perhaps be some expressions, which may seem more positive than your prescriptions will permit. And though I desire to have them understood only as conjectures and queries (which your method does not altogether disallow) yet if even in those I have exceeded, 'tis fit that I should declare that it was not done by your directions. For it is most unrea-sonable that you should undergo the imputation of the faults of my conjectures, see-ing you can receive so small advantage of reputation by the slight observations of Your most humble and most faithful servant,

Robert Hooke

from *The Preface*

[A]ll the uncertainty and mistakes of human actions proceed either from the narrowness and wandering of our senses, from the slipperiness or delusion of our memory, from the confinement or rashness of our understanding, so that 'tis no won-der that our power over natural causes and effects is so slowly improved, seeing we are not only to contend with the obscurity and difficulty of the things whereon we work and think, but even the forces of our own minds conspire to betray us.

These being the dangers in the process of human reason, the remedies of them all can only proceed from the real, the mechanical, the experimental philosophy, which has this advantage over the philosophy of discourse and disputation, that whereas that chiefly aims at the subtlety of its deductions and conclusions, without much regard to the first groundwork, which ought to be well laid on the sense and memory, so this intends the right ordering of them all and the making them service-able to each other.

The first thing to be undertaken in this weighty work is a watchfulness over the failings and an enlargement of the dominion of the senses.

To which end it is requisite, first, that there should be a scrupulous choice and a strict examination of the reality, constancy, and certainty of the particulars that we admit.[3] This is the first rise[4] whereon truth is to begin, and here the most severe and most impartial diligence must be employed. The storing up of all, without any regard to evidence or use, will only tend to darkness and confusion. We must not therefore esteem the riches of our philosophical treasure by the number only, but chiefly by the weight. The most vulgar instances[5] are not to be neglected, but above all, the

---

2. Hooke had originally drawn many of the book's illus-trations for use in the public presentation of experiments, which, as the Society's Curator of Experiments, he was obliged to perform regularly.

3. I.e., as experimental data.
4. Elevation (with "truth" imagined as a progressive ascent).
5. Familiar particulars.

most instructive are to be entertained.[6] The footsteps of Nature are to be traced, not only in her ordinary course, but when she seems to be put to her shifts,[7] to make many doublings and turnings, and to use some kind of art in endeavoring to avoid our discovery.

The next care to be taken, in respect of the senses, is a supplying of their infirmities with instruments, and as it were, the adding of artificial organs to the natural; this in one of them has been of late years accomplished with prodigious benefit to all sorts of useful knowledge by the invention of optical glasses. By the means of telescopes, there is nothing so far distant but may be represented to our view; and by the help of microscopes, there is nothing so small as to escape our inquiry; hence there is a new visible world discovered to the understanding. By this means the heavens are opened, and a vast number of new stars and new motions and new productions appear in them to which all the ancient astronomers were utterly strangers. By this the earth itself, which lies so near us under our feet, shows quite a new thing to us; and in every little particle of its matter, we now behold almost as great a variety of creatures as we were able before to reckon up in the whole universe itself. * * *

I here present to the world my imperfect endeavors, which though they shall prove no other way considerable, yet I hope they may be in some measure useful to the main design of a reformation in philosophy, if it be only by showing that there is not so much required towards it any strength of imagination or exactness of method or depth of contemplation (though the addition of these, where they can be had, must needs produce a much more perfect composure) as[8] a sincere hand and a faithful eye to examine and to record the things themselves as they appear.

And I beg my reader to let me take the boldness to assure him that in this present condition of knowledge, a man so qualified as I have endeavored to be, only with resolution and integrity and plain intentions of employing his senses aright, may venture to compare the reality and the usefulness of his services towards the true philosophy with those of other men that are of much stronger and more acute speculations that shall not make uses of the same method by the senses. * * *

from *Observation 1. Of the Point of a Sharp Small Needle*

As in geometry, the most natural way of beginning is from a mathematical point, so is the same method in observations and natural history the most genuine, simple, and instructive. We must first endeavor to make letters, and draw single strokes true, before we venture to write whole sentences, or to draw large pictures. And in physical inquiries, we must endeavor to follow Nature in the more plain and easy ways she treads in the most simple and uncompounded bodies, to trace her steps, and be acquainted with her manner of walking there, before we venture ourselves into the multitude of meanders she has in bodies of a more complicated nature; lest, being unable to distinguish and judge of our way, we quickly lose both Nature our guide, and ourselves too, and are left to wander in the labyrinth of groundless opinions; wanting both judgment, that light, and experience, that clue, which should direct our proceedings.

We will begin these our inquiries therefore with the observations of bodies of the most simple nature first, and so gradually proceed to those of a more compounded one. In prosecution of which method, we shall begin with a physical point; of which

6. Considered.
7. Up to her tricks.
8. But only.

kind the point of a needle is commonly reckoned for one, and is indeed, for the most part, made so sharp, that the naked eye cannot distinguish any parts of it. It very easily pierces and makes its way through all kinds of bodies softer than itself. But if viewed with a very good microscope, we may find that the top of a needle (though as to the sense very sharp) appears a broad, blunt, and very irregular end; not resembling a cone, as is imagined, but only a piece of a tapering body, with a great part of the top removed, or deficient. The points of pins are yet more blunt, and the points of the most curious mathematical instruments so very seldom arrive at so great a sharpness. How much therefore can be built upon demonstrations made only by the productions of the ruler and compasses, he will be better able to consider that shall but view those points and lines with a microscope.

* * *

The image we have here exhibited in the first figure, was the top of a small and very sharp needle, whose point *aa* nevertheless appeared through the microscope above a quarter of an inch broad, not round nor flat, but irregular and uneven; so that it seemed to have been big enough to have afforded a hundred armed mites room enough to be ranged by each other without endangering the breaking one another's necks, by being thrust off on either side. The surface of which, though appearing to the naked eye very smooth, could not nevertheless hide a multitude of holes and scratches and ruggednesses from being discovered by the microscope to invest it, several of which inequalities (as A, B, C, seemed holes made by some small specks of rust; and D some adventitious[9] body, that stuck very close to it) were casual.[1] All the rest that roughen the surface, were only so many marks of the rudeness and bungling of art.[2] So unaccurate is it, in all its productions, even in those which seem most neat, that if examined with an organ more acute than that by which they were made, the more we see of their shape, the less appearance will there be of their beauty; whereas in the works in nature, the deepest discoveries show us the greatest excellencies. An evident argument, that He that was the author of all these things, was no other than omnipotent; being able to include as great a variety of parts and contrivances in the yet smallest discernible point, as in those vaster bodies (which comparatively are called also points) such as the earth, sun, or planets. Nor need it seem strange that the earth itself may be by an analogy called a physical point: for as its body, though now so near us as to fill our eyes and fancies with a sense of the vastness of it, may by a little distance, and some convenient diminishing glasses, be made vanish into a scarce visible speck, or point (as I have often tried on the moon, and—when not too bright—on the sun itself), so, could a mechanical contrivance successfully answer our theory, we might see the least spot as big as the earth itself; and discover, as Descartes also conjectures,[3] as great a variety of bodies in the moon, or planets, as in the earth.

But leaving these discoveries to future industries, we shall proceed to add one observation more of a point commonly so called, that is, the mark of a full stop, or period. And for this purpose I observed many both printed ones and written; and among multitudes I found few of them more round or regular than this which I have delineated in the * * * second scheme, but very many abundantly more disfigured; and for the most part if they seemed equally round to the eye, I found those points that had

---

9. Chance-encountered.
1. Accidental.
2. Artifice; human (as opposed to natural) creation.

3. René Descartes (1596–1650); French mathematician and philosopher.

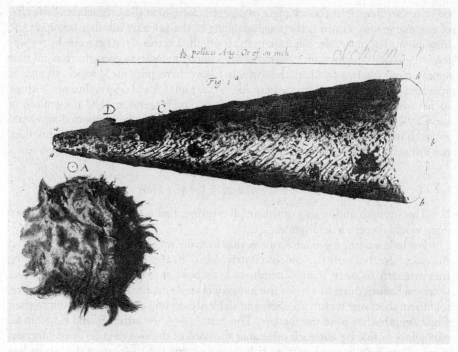

Robert Hooke, *Schema ii: Needle Point and Period,* from *Micrographia*, 1665.

been made by a copper plate, and roll-press, to be as misshapen as those which had
been made with types, the most curious and smoothly engraven strokes and points
looking but as so many furrows and holes, and their printed impressions but like smutty
daubings on a mat or uneven floor with a blunt extinguished brand[4] or stick's end. And
as for points made with a pen they were much more rugged and deformed. Nay, having
viewed certain pieces of exceeding curious writing of the kind (one of which in the
breadth of a two-pence comprised the Lord's Prayer, the Apostles' Creed, the Ten
Commandments, and about half a dozen verses besides of the Bible[5]), whose lines were
so small and near together, that I was unable to number them with my naked eye, a
very ordinary microscope, I had then about me, enabled me to see that what the writer
of it had asserted was true, but withal discovered of what pitiful bungling scribbles and
scrawls it was composed, Arabian and China characters being almost as well shaped;
yet thus much I must say for the man, that it was for the most part legible enough,
though in some places there wanted a good fantasy well prepossessed[6] to help one
through. If this manner of small writing were made easy and practicable (and I think I
know such a one,[7] but have never yet made trial of it, whereby one might be enabled to
write a great deal with much ease, and accurately enough in a very little room) it might
be of very good use to convey secret intelligence without any danger of discovery or
mistrusting. But to come again to the point. The irregularies of it are caused by three or
four coadjutors,[8] one of which is the uneven surface of the paper, which at best appears

4. Torch.
5. In the mid-17th century, this minuscule writing was
practiced as a craft; specimens (often of the scriptural
texts Hooke lists here) were prized by collectors.

6. Imagination kindly disposed.
7. I.e., an instrument.
8. Factors.

no smoother than a very coarse piece of shagged cloth; next the irregularity of the type of engraving; and a third is the rough daubing of the printing ink that lies upon the instrument that makes the impression; to all which, add the variation made by the different lights and shadows, and you may have sufficient reason to guess that a point may appear much more ugly than this, which I have here presented, which though it appeared through the microscope gray, like a great splatch of London dirt, about three inches over; yet to the naked eye it was black, and no bigger than that in the midst of the Circle A. And could I have found room in this plate to have inserted an O you should have seen that the letters were not more distinct than the points of distinction, nor a drawn circle more exactly so, than we have now shown a point to be a point.

from *Observation 53. Of a Flea*

The strength and beauty of this small creature, had it no other relation at all to man, would deserve a description.

For its strength, the microscope is able to make no greater discoveries of it than the naked eye, but only the curious contrivance of its legs and joints, for the exerting that strength, is very plainly manifested, such as no other creature I have yet observed has anything like it; for the joints of it are so adapted, that he can, as 'twere, fold them short one within another, and suddenly stretch, or spring them out to their whole length, that is, of the forelegs. The part A ∗ ∗ ∗ lies within B, and B within C, parallel to, or side by side each other; but the parts of the two next lie quite contrary, that is, D without E, and E without F, but parallel also; but the parts of the hinder legs G, H, and I, bend one within another, like the parts of a double jointed ruler, or like the foot, leg, and thigh of a man; these six legs he clitches[9] up altogether, and when he leaps, springs them all out, and thereby exerts his whole strength at once.

But, as for the beauty of it, the microscope manifests it to be all over adorned with a curiously polished suit of sable armor, neatly jointed, and beset with multitudes of sharp pins, shaped almost like porcupine's quills, or bright conical steel bodkins[1]; the head is either side beautified with a quick and round black eye K, behind each of which also appears a small cavity, L, in which he seems to move to and fro a certain thin film beset with many small transparent hairs, which probably may be his ears. In the forepart of his head, between the two forelegs, he has two small long jointed feelers, or rather smellers, M M, which have four joints, and are hairy, like those of several other creatures. Between these, it has a small proboscis, or probe, N N O, that seems to consist of a tube N N, and a tongue or sucker O, which I have perceived him to flip in and out. Besides these, it has also two chaps or biters P P, which are somewhat like those of an ant, but I could not perceive them toothed; and were opened and shut just after the same manner. With these instruments does this little busy creature bite and pierce the skin, and suck out the blood of an animal, leaving the skin inflamed with a small round red spot. These parts are very difficult to be discovered, because for the most part, they lie covered between the forelegs. There are many other particulars, which, being more obvious, and affording no great matter of information, I shall pass by, and refer the reader to the figure.

1663–1665   1665

---

9. Clutches.

1. "An instrument with a small blade and sharp point, used to bore holes" (Johnson's *Dictionary*).

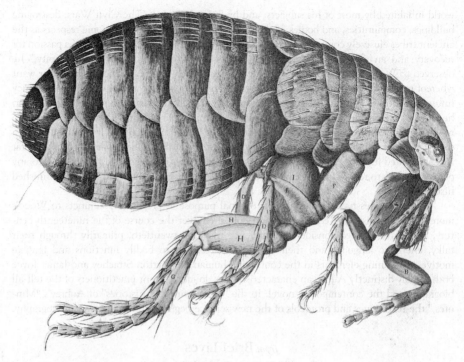

Robert Hooke, *Schema xxxiv: A Flea,* from *Micrographia,* 1665.

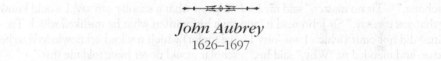

John Aubrey
1626–1697

One of the original Fellows of the Royal Society, John Aubrey possessed in abundance two of its defining characteristics: an omnivorous curiosity and a reluctance to impose arbitrary order on collections of raw data. Prosperous by birth, sickly throughout his life, and prevented by the Civil Wars from completing the Oxford education he craved, Aubrey devoted himself to the study of natural history, folklore, and archaeology. His discovery of the prehistoric stone circle at Avebury remains one of the most important finds in Britain, but he is now best known as an innovator in biography. In the 1670s he agreed to help his friend Anthony à Wood with research for a "history of all the writers and bishops" educated at Oxford since 1500. He began compiling a cluster of manuscripts he called "Minutes of Lives": notes on eminent men and women of the century, dealing in data gathered from documents, conversation, and correspondence with the subjects and their survivors, and from Aubrey's own prodigious (if at times unreliable) memory.

The life stories thus produced display an obsessive particularity, an abiding preference for the telling detail over the big picture (which in the conventional biographies of Aubrey's time took the form of hagiography: pious summations of pious lives). Aubrey's *Lives,* notes his editor Oliver Lawson Dick, "were the first biographies that did not point a moral."

Throughout his "Minutes," Aubrey performs a kind of textual archaeology. He dwells on the physical objects, natural and manufactured, which marked the early seventeenth-century world inhabited by most of his subjects, and by his younger self. The Civil Wars, destroying buildings, communities, and bodies, had rendered that world as remote in some respects as the ancient tribes elusively commemorated at Avebury. Aubrey writes the *Lives* out of a passion for recovery and an awareness of the precariousness of his whole enterprise. "'Tis pity," he observed to Wood, "that such minutes had not been taken 100 years since or more: for want whereof many worthy men's names and notions are swallowed up in oblivion." This urgency infuses the *Lives'* odd form. Aubrey cares more to get the facts down than to set them in order: he repeatedly describes himself as writing his notes "tumultuarily," that is, "as they occurred to my thoughts or as occasionally I had information" or (more succinctly) as if "tumbled out of a sack." Such an unmethodical method sorted well with the Royal Society's program as Sprat had elaborated it: "to heap up a mixed mass of experiments, without digesting them into any perfect model"; to record findings not "as complete schemes of opinions, but as bare unfinished histories."

Aubrey's notes have outlasted their original purpose as preparatory adjuncts to Wood's more "finished" history. Rediscovered and published over the course of the nineteenth century, they have exerted considerable influence over the twentieth, primarily through their talky, energetic language and their unabashed attention to bodily functions and ignoble motives as defining elements in the course of a human life. Lytton Strachey and James Joyce both display distinctly Aubreyan characteristics, as do more recent practitioners of the tell-all biography and the contemporary novel. In the "bare unfinished histories" of Aubrey's "Minutes," the techniques and protocols of the new science begin to infuse the craft of biography.

from **Brief Lives**

[FRANCIS BACON][1]

* * * He came often to Sir John Danvers[2] at Chelsea. Sir John told me that when his lordship had wrote the *History of Henry 7*, he sent the manuscript copy to him to desire his opinion of it before 'twas printed. Qd.[3] Sir John, "Your lordship knows that I am no scholar." "'Tis no matter," said my lord, "I know what a scholar can say; I would know what *you* can say." Sir John read it, and gave his opinion what he misliked which Tacitus[4] did not omit (which I am sorry I have forgot) which my lord acknowledged to be true, and mended it: "Why," said he, "a scholar would never have told me this."

Mr. Thomas Hobbes (Malmesburiensis[5]) was beloved by his lordship, who was wont to have him walk with him in his delicate groves where he did meditate: and when a notion darted into his mind, Mr. Hobbes was presently to write it down, and his lordship was wont to say that he did it better than anyone else about him; for that many times, when he read their[6] notes he scarce understood what they writ, because they understood it not clearly themselves.

In short, all that were *great* and *good* loved and honored him. * * *

His lordship would many times have music in the next room where he meditated.

The aviary at York House[7] was built by his lordship; it did cost £300.

---

1. Statesman, scholar, philosopher, and writer (1561–1626); in his *Advancement of Learning* (1605) and *Novum Organum* (1620) he articulated the experimental methods that would later be championed by the Royal Society.
2. Danvers was a relative of Aubrey's and "a great acquaintance and favorite" of Bacon's.
3. *Quod:* said (Latin).

4. Publius Tacitus (c. A.D. 56–c. 117), Roman historian; the sense here seems to be that Bacon has left out some element in history that Tacitus would have included.
5. Of Malmesbury (Hobbes's birthplace). Hobbes was a close friend of Aubrey's, and his is the longest and the fullest of the *Brief Lives*.
6. Anyone else's.
7. In London; Bacon's birthplace and residence.

At every meal, according to the season of the year, he had his table strewn with sweet herbs and flowers, which he said did refresh his spirits and memory.

When his lordship was at his country house at Gorhambery,[8] St. Albans seemed as if the Court were there, so nobly did he live. His servants had liveries with his crest (a boar . . .[9]); his watermen[1] were more employed by gentlemen than any other, even the King's.

King James sent a buck to him, and he gave the keeper fifty pounds.

He was wont to say to his servant Hunt (who was a notable thrifty man, and loved this world, and the only servant he had that he could never get to become bound for[2] him), "The world was made for man, Hunt; and not man for the world." Hunt left an estate of £1000 per annum in Somerset.

None of his servants durst appear before him without Spanish leather boots:[3] for he would smell the neat's leather which offended him. * * *

He was a παιδεραστής.[4] His Ganimeds[5] and favorites took bribes; but his lordship always gave judgment *secundum aequum et bonum*.[6] His decrees in Chancery[7] stand firm, i.e., there are fewer of his decrees reversed than any other Chancellor.

His dowager[8] married her gentleman-usher,[9] Sir (Thomas, I think) Underhill, whom she made deaf and blind with too much of Venus.[1] She was living since the beheading of the late King.—Quaere[2] where and when she died.

He had a delicate, lively hazel eye; Dr. Harvey told me it was like the eye of a viper. I have now forgot what Mr. Bushnell said, whether his lordship enjoyed his Muse[3] best at night, or in the morning.

Apothegmata[4]

His lordship being in York House garden looking on fishers as they were throwing their net, asked them what they would take for their draught;[5] they answered *so much*: his lordship would offer them no more but *so much*. They drew up their net, and in it were only 2 or 3 little fishes: his lordship then told them it had been better for them to have taken his offer. They replied, they hoped to have had a better draught. "But," said his lordship, "hope is a good breakfast, but an ill supper." * * *

The Bishop of London did cut down a noble cloud of trees at Fulham. The Lord Chancellor told him that he was *a good expounder of dark places*.[6]

Upon his being in disfavor his servants suddenly went away; he compared them to the flying of the vermin when the house was falling.

One told his lordship it was now time to look about him. He replied, "I do not look *about* me, I look *above* me." * * *

---

8. Gornhambry, Bacon's estate on the river Ver, near the city of St. Albans.
9. Aubrey inserts this ellipsis, presumably for filling in later.
1. Ferrymen, busy bringing guests to and from the house.
2. I.e., legally committed to serve.
3. Cordovan leather from Spain was more highly processed than ordinary English "neat's (cattle) leather."
4. Greek: pederast, a homosexual lover of boys.
5. Beloved boys (so called after the Trojan youth Ganymede, Zeus's cupbearer).
6. "Fairly and well." Bacon had served as attorney-general and Lord Chancellor until he was impeached for taking bribes.

7. The law court presided over by the Lord Chancellor.
8. Widow.
9. A gentleman acting as attendant to a person of superior rank.
1. Sex.
2. "Find out" (Aubrey's most frequent instruction to himself in his notes).
3. I.e., wrote and thought.
4. Witty sayings.
5. Catch.
6. Bacon puns on the Bishop's duty to shed light on obscure passages in scripture.

His lordship would often drink a good draught of strong beer (March beer) to-bedwards, to lay his working fancy[7] asleep: which otherwise would keep him from sleeping great part of the night. ✳ ✳ ✳

Mr. Hobbes told me that the cause of his lordship's death was trying an experiment: viz., as he was taking the air in a coach with Dr. Witherborne (a Scotchman, physician to the king) towards Highgate, snow lay on the ground, and it came into my lord's thought, why flesh might not be preserved in snow, as in salt. They were resolved they would try the experiment presently. They alighted out of the coach, and went into a poor woman's house at the bottom of Highgate Hill, and bought a hen, and made the woman exenterate[8] it, and then stuffed the body with snow, and my lord did help to do it himself. The snow so chilled him, that he immediately fell so extremely ill, that he could not return to his lodgings (I suppose then at Gray's Inn), but went to the Earl of Arundel's house at Highgate, where they put him into a good bed warmed with a pan, but it was a damp bed that had not been lain in in about a year before, which gave him such a cold that in 2 or 3 days, as I remember he told me, he died of suffocation.

[WILLIAM HARVEY][1]

He was always very contemplative, and the first that I hear of that was curious in anatomy in England. He had made dissections of frogs, toads, and a number of other animals, and had curious observations on them, which papers, together with his goods, in his lodgings at Whitehall, were plundered at the beginning of the Rebellion, he being for the King, and with him at Oxon;[2] but he often said, that of all the losses he sustained, no grief was so crucifying to him as the loss of these papers, which for love or money he could never retrieve or obtain. When Charles I by reason of the tumults left London, he attended him, and was at the fight of Edgehill with him; and during the fight, the Prince and Duke of York were committed to his care. He told me that he withdrew with them under a hedge, and took out of his pocket a book and read; but he had not read very long before a bullet of a great gun grazed on the ground near him, which made him remove his station. He told me that Sir Adrian Scrope was dangerously wounded there, and left for dead amongst the dead men, stripped; which happened to be the saving of his life. It was cold, clear weather, and a frost that night; which staunched his bleeding, and about midnight, or some hours after his hurt, he awaked, and was fain to draw a dead body upon him for warmth-sake ✳ ✳ ✳

He did delight to be in the dark, and told me he could then best contemplate. He had a house heretofore at Combe, in Surrey, a good air and prospect, where he had caves made in the earth, in which in summer time he delighted to meditate.— He was pretty well versed in the mathematics, and had made himself master of Mr. Oughtred's *Clavis Math.*[3] in his old age; and I have seen him perusing it, and working problems, not long before he died, and that book was always in his meditating apartment. ✳ ✳ ✳

---

7. Busy mind.
8. Clean it; remove its innards.
1. Physician and anatomist (1578–1657); he discovered the circulation of the blood, and set forth his findings in *De Motu Cordis* ("on the heart's motion"), 1628.
2. Oxford, to which Charles I removed himself and his

Court in 1643.
3. William Oughtred (1575–1660), mathematician; his *Clavis Mathematicae* ("the key of mathematics") was a widely used textbook on algebra and arithmetic (it introduced the symbol "×" for multiplication).

At Oxford, he grew acquainted with Dr. Charles Scarborough,[4] then a young physician (since by King Charles II knighted), in whose conversation he much delighted; and whereas before he marched up and down with the army, he took him to him and made him lie in his chamber, and said to him, "Prithee leave off thy gunning, and stay here; I will bring thee into practice."[5]

I remember he kept a pretty young wench to wait on him, which I guess he made use of for warmth-sake as King David did,[6] and took care of her in his will, as also of his man servant. * * *

He was, as all the rest of the brothers, very choleric;[7] and in his young days wore a dagger (as the fashion then was, nay I remember my old schoolmaster, old Mr. Latimer, at 70, wore a dudgeon, with a knife, and bodkin, as also my old grandfather Lyte, and alderman Whitson of Bristowe, which I suppose was the common fashion in their young days), but this Dr. would be too apt to draw out his dagger upon every slight occasion.

He was not tall; but of the lowest stature, round faced, olivaster[8] complexion; little eye, round, very black, full of spirit; his hair was black as a raven, but quite white 20 years before he died. * * *

He was much and often troubled with the gout,[9] and his way of cure was thus: he would then sit with his legs bare, if it were frost, on the leads[1] of Cockaine house, put them into a pail of water, till he was almost dead with cold, and betake himself to the stove, and so 'twas gone.

He was hot-headed, and his thoughts working would many times keep him from sleeping; he told me that then his way was to rise out of his bed and walk about his chamber in his shirt till he was pretty cool, i.e., till he began to have a horror,[2] and then return to bed, and sleep very comfortably.

I remember he was wont to drink coffee; which he and his brother Eliab did, before coffeehouses were in fashion in London.[3] * * *

It is now fit, and but just, that I should endeavor to undeceive the world in a scandal that I find strongly runs of him, which I have met amongst some learned young men: viz. that he made himself away[4] to put himself out of his pain, by opium; not but that, had he labored under great pains, he had been ready enough to have done it; I do not deny that it was not according to his principles upon certain occasions to . . . . [5] But the manner of his dying was really, and bona fide, thus, viz.: The morning of his death about 10 a clock, he went to speak, and found he had the dead palsy[6] in his tongue; then he saw what was to become of him, he knew there was then no hopes of his recovery, so presently sends for his young nephews to come up to him, to whom he gives one his watch ('twas a minute watch with which he made his experiments);[7] to another, another remembrance, etc.; made sign to . . . [8] Sambroke, his apothecary (in Blackfriars), to let him blood in[9] the tongue, which did little or no

4. Charles Scarburgh (1616–1694) assisted Harvey with his work on the generation of animals.
5. I.e., medical practice.
6. In his old age David was warmed in bed at night by a young woman (1 Kings 1.1–4).
7. Prone to anger.
8. Olive-colored.
9. Inflammation of the joints in the hands and feet.
1. Rooftop (lined with lead).
2. Shiver.
3. The drink was rare in England before midcentury,

hugely popular thereafter; London's first coffeehouse opened in 1652.
4. Killed himself.
5. Aubrey leaves the blank, perhaps intending a phrase like "commit suicide."
6. Paralysis caused by stroke.
7. At this time, most clocks and watches told only the hour, not the minutes.
8. Aubrey's blank.
9. Draw blood from.

good; and so he ended his days. His practice was not very great towards his later end; he declined it, unless to a special friend—e.g. my Lady Howland, who had a cancer in her breast, which he did cut off and seared, but at last she died of it.

* * *

I was at his funeral, and helped to carry him into the vault.

1680s   1813

≈⧓ END OF PERSPECTIVES: THE ROYAL SOCIETY AND THE NEW SCIENCE ⧓≈

Margaret Cavendish, Duchess of Newcastle
1623–1674

The youngest child in a wealthy family whose social arrogance and Royalist sympathies brought it near ruin during the Civil Wars, Margaret Lucas combined a near immobilizing shyness with a passion for fame. She spent the years of war and Interregnum on the continent, first as maid of honor to Charles's exiled queen, then as wife to the Royalist general William Cavendish, Marquis of Newcastle; he was made Duke by Charles II after the couple returned to England at the Restoration. Neglected by the Court, they lived far from London on their northern estates, where they cultivated their passions: his, riding and fencing; hers, reading and writing. Words poured from her pen into a variety of genres: verse (*Poems and Fancies*, 1653), fiction (*Nature's Pictures*, 1656), plays (*Love's Adventure, The Matrimonial Trouble, The Female Academy*, and some fifteen others: all printed, none performed); essays (*The World's Olio*, 1655); scientific speculations (*Philosophical and Physical Opinions*, 1663; *Observations upon Experimental Philosophy*, 1665); biography (of her husband); and autobiography (*A True Relation*, 1656; *Sociable Letters*, 1664). Cavendish and her husband published much of her work (and some of his) in sumptuous editions at their own expense.

It was rare for a woman to write and publish, rarer still for an aristocrat to write so revealingly and emphatically about her own fears, desires, opinions, and aspirations. The combination of her gender, rank, and work brought the Duchess an equivocal celebrity, a mix of amazement and derision which her occasional trips to London did much to animate. After one such visit, Mary Evelyn (wife of the diarist John) tried to capture Cavendish's impact in a letter to a friend: "I was surprised to find so much extravagancy and vanity in any person not confined within four walls" (of a madhouse). Her clothing, Evelyn reported, was "fantastical"; her behavior outstripped "the imagination of poets, or the descriptions of a romance heroine's greatness; her gracious bows, seasonable nods, courteous stretching out of hands, twinkling of her eyes, and various gestures of approbation, show what may be expected from her discourse, which is as airy, empty, whimsical, and rambling as her books, aiming at science, difficulties, high notions . . ." Evelyn voices a satiric hostility shared by many London onlookers, but she also pinpoints some of Cavendish's range and intensity: her idiosyncratic engagement with the new science of her day, and her variable, highly conscious self-presentation.

At letter's end, Evelyn despairs of description. The Duchess "is not of mortal race, and therefore cannot be defined." Cavendish, though, knew herself mortal. She repeatedly made clear that the threat of oblivion impelled her pen, and she worked constantly and inventively to define herself, sometimes in familiar genres, sometimes in modes of her own making—most notably that mix of fantasy, science fiction, argument, and autobiography she called *The Blazing World* (1665). The Duchess's extraordinary energies and kaleidoscopic output have transmuted seventeenth-century ridicule into late twentieth-century fascination with a woman's voice in relentless pursuit of (a favorite Cavendish term) "singularity."

from POEMS AND FANCIES[1]

The Poetress's Hasty Resolution

Reading my verses, I liked them so well,
Self-love did make my judgment to rebel;
And thinking them so good, thought more to make,
Considering not how others would them take.
5   I writ so fast, thought, lived I many a year,
A pyramid of fame thereon to rear.[2]
Reason, observing which way I was bent,
Did stay my hand, and asked me what I meant.
"Will you," said he, "thus waste your time in vain,
10   On that which in the world small praise shall gain?
For shame leave off, and do the printer spare:
He'll lose by your ill poetry, I fear.
Besides, the world already hath great store
Of useless books, wherefore do write no more,
15   But pity take, do the world a good turn,
And all you write cast in the fire and burn."
Angry I was, and Reason struck away,
When I did hear what he to me did say.
Then all in haste I to the press it sent,
20   Fearing persuasion might my book prevent.
But now 'tis done, repent with grief do I,
Hang down my head with shame, blush, sigh, and cry.
Take pity, and my drooping spirits raise,
Wipe off my tears with handkerchiefs of praise.

The Poetress's Petition

Like to a fever's pulse my heart doth beat,
For fear my book some great repulse should meet.
If it be naught, let it in silence lie;
Disturb it not; let it in quiet die;
5   Let not the bells of your dispraise ring loud,
But wrap it up in silence as a shroud;
Cause black oblivion on its hearse to lie,
Instead of tapers, let dark night stand by;
Instead of flowers, on its grave to strew,
10   Before its hearse, sleepy, dull poppy throw;
Instead of scutcheons,[3] let my tears be hung,
Which grief and sorrow from my eyes out wrung.
Let those that bear its corpse no jesters be,
But sober, sad, and grave mortality.
15   No satyr° poets by its grave appear,   *satirical*
No altars raised, to write inscriptions there.
Let dust of all forgetfulness be cast

---

1. This was Cavendish's first publication; the first three pieces presented here functioned as a verse preface to the collection. The texts are taken from the second edition (1664), "much altered and corrected."

2. I.e., I thought that if I were to live a long time I would be able to create a poetic monument to myself.
3. Escutcheons: funeral ornaments, shield-shaped, exhibiting the deceased's coat of arms.

Upon its corpse, there let it lie and waste.
Nor let it rise again, unless some know,
20   At Judgments some good merits it can show;
Then shall it live in Heavens of high praise,
And for its glory, garlands have of bays.[4]

An Apology for Writing So Much upon This Book

Condemn me not, I make so much ado
About this book; it is my child, you know;
Just like a bird, when her young are in nest,
Goes in, and out, and hops, and takes no rest;
5   But when their young are fledged,[5] their heads out peep,
Lord! what a chirping does the old one keep.
So I, for fear my strengthless child should fall
Against a door, or stool, aloud I call,
Bid have a care of such a dangerous place.
10   Thus write I much, to hinder all disgrace.

The Hunting of the Hare

Betwixt two ridges of plowed land sat Wat,[6]
Whose body, pressed to the earth, lay close and squat;
His nose upon his two forefeet did lie,
With his gray eyes he glared obliquely;
5   His head he always set against the wind,
His tail when turned, his hair blew up behind,
And made him to get cold; but he being wise,
Doth keep his coat still down, so warm he lies.
Thus rests he all the day, til th' sun doth set,
10   Then up he riseth his relief to get,
And walks about, until the sun doth rise,
Then coming back in's° former posture lies.   *in his*
At last poor Wat was found, as he there lay,
By huntsmen, which came with their dogs that way,
15   Whom seeing, he got up, and fast did run,
Hoping some ways the cruel dogs to shun;
But they by nature had so quick a scent,
That by their nose they traced what way he went,
And with their deep wide mouths set forth a cry,
20   Which answered was by echo in the sky;
Then Wat was struck with terror and with fear,
Seeing each shadow thought the dogs were there,
And running out some distance from their cry,
To hide himself, his thoughts he did employ;
25   Under a clod of earth in sand pit wide
Poor Wat sat close, hoping himself to hide,
There long he had not been, but straight in's ears
The winding° horns and crying dogs he hears;   *blowing*

---

4. Wreaths of laurel leaves, awarded for military victory
or literary excellence.

5. Feathered; ready to fly.
6. Conventional nickname for a hare.

Then starting up with fear, he leaped, and such
30 Swift speed he made, the ground he scarce did touch;
Into a great thick wood straight ways he got,
And underneath a broken bough he sat,
Where every leaf that with the wind did shake
Brought him such terror, that his heart did ache;
35 That place he left, to champaign° plains he went,   *open*
Winding about, for to deceive their scent,
And while they snuffling were to find his track,
Poor Wat being weary, his swift pace did slack;
On his two hinder legs for ease he sat;
40 His forefeet rubbed his face from dust and sweat;
Licking his feet, he wiped his ears so clean
That none could tell that Wat had hunted been;
But casting round about his fair gray eyes,
The hounds in full career he near him 'spies;
45 To Wat it was so terrible a sight,
Fear gave him wings and made his body light;
Though he was tired before by running long,
Yet now his breath he never felt more strong—
Like those that dying are, think health returns,
50 When 'tis but a faint blast which life out-burns;
For spirits seek to guard the heart about,
Striving with death, but death doth quench them out.
The hounds so fast came on, and with such cry,
That he no hopes had left, nor help could 'spy;
55 With that the winds did pity poor Wat's case,
And with their breath the scent blew from that place;
Then every nose was busily employed,
And every nostril was set open wide,
And every head did seek a several way,
60 To find the grass or track where the scent lay;
For witty industry° is never slack,   *cunning diligence*
'Tis like to witchcraft, and brings lost things back;
But though the wind had tied the scent up close,
A busy dog thrust in his snuffling nose
65 And drew it out, with that did foremost run,
Then horns blew loud, the rest to follow on;
The great slow hounds their throats did set a base,
The fleet, swift hounds, as tenors next in place,
The little beagles did a treble sing,
70 And through the air their voices round did ring,
Which made such consort as they ran along,
That, had they spoken words, 't had been a song;
The horns kept time, the men did shout for joy,
And seemed most valiant, poor Wat to destroy;
75 Spurring their horses to a full career,
Swum rivers deep, leaped ditches without fear,
Endangered life and limbs, so fast they'd ride,
Only to see how patiently Wat died;
At last the dogs so near his heels did get,

80 That their sharp teeth they in his breech did set;
Then tumbling down he fell, with weeping eyes
Gave up his ghost; and thus poor Wat he dies.
Men whooping loud, such acclamations made,
As if the Devil they imprisoned had,
85 When they but did a shiftless creature kill;
To hunt, there needs no valiant soldier's skill;
But men do think that exercise and toil,
To keep their health, is best, which makes most spoil,
Thinking that food and nourishment so good,
90 Which doth proceed from others' flesh and blood.
When they do lions, wolves, bears, tigers see
Kill silly sheep, they say, they cruel be,
But for themselves all creatures think too few,
For luxury, wish God would make more new;
95 As if God did make creatures for man's meat,
And gave them life and sense for man to eat,
Or else for sport or recreation's sake
For to destroy those lives that God did make,
Making their stomachs graves, which full they fill
100 With murdered bodies, which in sport they kill;
Yet man doth think himself so gentle and mild,
When of all creatures he's most cruel, wild,
Nay, so proud, that he only[7] thinks to live,
That God a God-like nature him did give,
105 And that all creatures for his sake alone
Were made, for him to tyrannize upon.

                                        1653, 1664

from A True Relation of My Birth, Breeding, and Life[1]

My father was a gentleman,[2] which title is grounded and given by merit, not by princes; and 'tis the act of time, not favor. And though my father was not a peer of the realm, yet there were few peers who had much greater estates, or lived more noble therewith. * * *

As for my breeding, it was according to my birth and the nature of my sex, for my birth was not lost in my breeding; for as my sisters was or had been bred, so was I in plenty, or rather with superfluity. Likewise we were bred virtuously, modestly, civilly, honorably, and on honest principles. As for plenty, we had not only for necessity, conveniency, and decency, but for delight and pleasure to a superfluity. 'Tis true, we did not riot, but we lived orderly; for riot, even in kings' courts and princes' palaces, brings ruin without content or pleasure, when order in less fortune shall live more

7. Alone, with no other creature.
1. Cavendish published her autobiography as the closing piece in a collection of her fiction called *Nature's Pictures* (1656), which she wrote while living in exile at Antwerp during the years of Cromwell's commonwealth. This work (like many of her others) was privately printed, at the author's expense, in a lavish folio, whose title page suggests the autobiography's particular place in the scheme: "In this volume there are several feigned stories

. . . comical, tragical, and tragicomical, poetical, romantical, philosophical, and historical. . . . And a true story at the latter end, wherein there is no feignings." In a later edition (1671), published after she and her husband had returned to England, Cavendish omitted the autobiography.
2. Thomas Lucas (c. 1573–1625), whose forebears had risen to the gentry in the 16th century. He died when Margaret was two years old.

plentifully and deliciously than princes that lives in a hurly-burly, as I may term it, in which they are seldom well served, for disorder obstructs. Besides, it doth disgust life,[3] distract the appetites, and yield no true relish to the senses; for pleasure, delight, peace, and felicity live in method and temperance.

As for our garments, my mother[4] did not only delight to see us neat and cleanly, fine and gay, but rich and costly, maintaining us to the height of her estate, but not beyond it. For we were so far from being in debt, before the wars,[5] as we were rather beforehand with the world, buying all with ready money, not on the score.[6] For although after my father's death the estate was divided between my mother and her sons, paying such a sum of money for portions to her daughters either at the day of their marriage or when they should come to age, yet by reason she and her children agreed with a mutual consent, all their affairs were managed so well as she lived not in a much lower condition than when my father lived. 'Tis true my mother might have increased her daughters' portions by a thrifty sparing, yet she chose to bestow it on our breeding, honest pleasures, and harmless delights, out of an opinion that if she bred us with needy necessity it might chance to create in us sharking[7] qualities, mean[8] thoughts, and base actions, which she knew my father as well as herself did abhor. Likewise we were bred tenderly, for my mother naturally did strive to please and delight her children, not to cross or torment them, terrifying them with threats or lashing them with slavish whips. But instead of threats, reason was used to persuade us, and instead of lashes, the deformities of vices was discovered, and the graces and virtues were presented unto us. Also we were bred with respectful attendance, every one being severally waited upon. And all her servants in general used the same respect to her children (even those that were very young) as they did to herself, for she suffered not her servants either to be rude before us or to domineer over us, which all vulgar servants are apt and ofttimes have leave to do. Likewise she never suffered the vulgar servingmen to be in the nursery amongst the nursemaids, lest their rude lovemaking[9] might do unseemly actions, or speak unhandsome words in the presence of her children, knowing that youth is apt to take infection by ill examples, having not the reason of distinguishing good from bad. Neither were we suffered to have any familiarity with the vulgar servants, or conversation; yet caused us to demean ourselves[1] with an humble civility towards them, as they with a dutiful respect to us. Not because they were servants were we so reserved, for many noble persons are forced to serve through necessity, but by reason the vulgar sort of servants are as ill bred as meanly born, giving children ill examples, and worse counsel. * * *

But some time after this war began, I knew not how they[2] lived. For though most of them were in Oxford, where the King was, yet after the Queen went from Oxford, and so out of England, I was parted from them.[3] For when the Queen was in Oxford, I had a great desire to be one of her Maids of Honor, hearing the Queen had not the same number she was used to have. Whereupon I wooed and won my mother to let me go, for my mother being fond of all her children was desirous to please them, which made her consent to my request. But my brothers and sisters seemed not very well pleased, by reason I had never been from home, nor seldom out of their sight; for

3. I.e., makes life unpleasant.
4. Elizabeth Lucas, née Leighton (?–1647).
5. The English Civil Wars, begun in 1642.
6. On credit.
7. Greedy.
8. Ignoble.
9. Flirtation.

1. To behave.
2. Her mother and siblings.
3. In 1643, Charles I had moved his family, court, and military base to Oxford as the Civil Wars rendered London unsafe. In 1644 his queen, Henrietta Maria, escaped to her native Paris in hopes of raising money and support for the Royalist cause.

though they knew I would not behave myself to their or my own dishonor, yet they thought I might to my disadvantage, being inexperienced in the world. Which indeed I did, for I was so bashful when I was out of my mother's, brothers', and sisters' sight, whose presence used to give me confidence, thinking I could not do amiss while any one of them were by, for I knew they would gently reform me if I did. Besides, I was ambitious they should approve of my actions and behavior, that when I was gone from them I was like one that had no foundation to stand, or guide to direct me, which made me afraid lest I should wander with ignorance out of the ways of honor so that I knew not how to behave myself. Besides, I had heard the world was apt to lay aspersions even on the innocent, for which I dared neither look up with my eyes, nor speak, nor be any way sociable, insomuch as I was thought a natural fool.[4] Indeed I had not much wit, yet I was not an idiot; my wit was according to my years. And though I might have learned more wit, and advanced my understanding by living in a court, yet being dull, fearful, and bashful, I neither heeded what was said or practiced, but just what belonged to my loyal duty and my own honest reputation. And indeed I was so afraid to dishonor my friends and family by my indiscreet actions that I rather chose to be accounted a fool than to be thought rude or wanton. In truth my bashfulness and fears made me repent my going from home to see the world abroad, and much I did desire to return to my mother again, or to my sister Pye,[5] with whom I often lived when she was in London, and loved with a supernatural affection. But my mother advised me there to stay, although I put her to more charges than if she had kept me at home, and the more, by reason she and my brothers were sequestered from their estates and plundered of all their goods.[6] Yet she maintained me so, that I was in a condition rather to lend than to borrow, which courtiers usually are not, being always necessitated by reason of great expenses courts put them to. But my mother said it would be a disgrace for me to return out of the court so soon after I was placed.

So I continued almost two years, until such time as I was married from thence. For my Lord the Marquis of Newcastle[7] did approve of those bashful fears which many condemned, and would choose such a wife as he might bring to his own humors,[8] and not such an one as was wedded to self-conceit, or one that had been tempered to the humors of another, for which he wooed me for his wife. And though I did dread marriage, and shunned men's companies as much as I could, yet I could not nor had not the power to refuse him, by reason my affections were fixed on him, and he was the only person I ever was in love with. Neither was I ashamed to own it, but gloried therein, for it was not amorous love. I never was infected therewith—it is a disease, or a passion, or both, I know by relation, not by experience. Neither could title, wealth, power, or person entice me to love. But my love was honest and honorable, being placed upon merit; which affection joyed at the fame of his worth, pleased with delight in his wit, proud of the respects he used to me, and triumphing in the affections he professed for me; which affections he hath confirmed to me by a deed[9] of time, sealed by constancy, and assigned by an unalterable decree of his promise, which makes me happy in despite of Fortune's frowns. For though misfortunes may and do oft dissolve base, wild, loose, and ungrounded affections, yet she

4. I.e., born mentally defective.
5. Catherine, wife of Edmond Pye.
6. The Lucas family took the king's side in the Civil Wars; its property was raided during anti-Royalist riots in 1642.
7. William Cavendish (1593–1676), a general in the king's army. In 1644, after suffering defeat in a pivotal battle, he departed for the Continent. He married Margaret (his second wife) at Paris in 1645.
8. Inclinations, ways of thinking.
9. A legal document (here used metaphorically).

hath no power of those that are united either by merit, justice, gratitude, duty, fidelity, or the like. And though my Lord hath lost his estate, and banished out of his country for his loyalty to his King and country, yet neither despised poverty nor pinching necessity could make him break the bonds of friendship, or weaken his loyal duty to his King or country.

But not only the family I am linked to is ruined, but the family from which I sprung, by these unhappy wars—which ruin my mother lived to see, and then died, having lived a widow many years, for she never forgot my father so as to marry again. Indeed he remained so lively in her memory, and her grief was so lasting, as she never mentioned his name, though she spoke often of him, but love and grief caused tears to flow, and tender sighs to rise, mourning in sad complaints. She made her house her cloister, enclosing herself as it were therein, for she seldom went abroad, unless to church, but these unhappy wars forced her out by reason she and her children were loyal to the King, for which they plundered her and my brothers of all their goods, plate, jewels, money, corn, cattle, and the like, cut down their woods, pulled down their houses, and sequestered them from their lands and livings. But in such misfortunes my mother was of an heroic spirit, in suffering patiently where there is no remedy, or to be industrious where she thought she could help. She was of a grave behavior, and had such a majestic grandeur, as it were continually hung about her, that it would strike a kind of an awe to the beholders, and command respect from the rudest. I mean the rudest of civilized people; I mean not such barbarous people as plundered her and used her cruelly, for they would have pulled God out of Heaven, had they had power, as they did royalty out of his throne. Also her beauty was beyond the ruin of time, for she had a well-favored loveliness in her face, a pleasing sweetness in her countenance, and a well-tempered complexion, as neither too red nor too pale, even to her dying hour, although in years. And by her dying, one might think death was enamored with her, for he embraced her in a sleep, and so gently, as if he were afraid to hurt her. Also she was an affectionate mother, breeding her children with a most industrious care and tender love. * * * Likewise my mother was a good mistress to her servants, taking care of her servants in their sickness, not sparing any cost she was able to bestow for their recovery. Neither did she exact more from them in their health than what they with ease or rather like pastime could do. She would freely pardon a fault, and forget an injury. Yet sometimes she would be angry, but never with her children; the sight of them would pacify her. Neither would she be angry with others but when she had cause, as with negligent or knavish servants that would lavishly or unnecessarily waste, or subtly and thievishly steal. And though she would often complain that her family was too great for her weak management, and often pressed my brother to take it upon him, yet I observe she took a pleasure and some little pride in the governing thereof. * * *

But howsoever our fortunes are, we are both content, spending our time harmlessly, for my Lord pleaseth himself with the management of some few horses, and exercises himself with the use of the sword. Which two arts he hath brought by his studious thoughts to an absolute perfection. And though he hath taken as much pains in those arts, both by study and practice, as chemists[1] for the philosopher's stone, yet he hath this advantage of them, that he hath found the right and the truth thereof and therein, which chemists never found in their art and I believe never will. Also he recreates himself with his pen, writing what his wit dictates to him. But I

---

1. Alchemists, who devoted themselves to the search for the "philosopher's stone"—the substance that would turn base metals into gold.

pass my time rather with scribbling than writing, with words than wit. Not that I speak much, because I am addicted to contemplation, unless I am with my Lord; yet then I rather attentively listen to what he says, than impertinently speak. Yet when I am writing any sad feigned stories or serious humors or melancholy passions, I am forced many times to express them with the tongue before I can write them with the pen, by reason those thoughts that are sad, serious, and melancholy are apt to contract and to draw too much back, which oppression doth as it were overpower or smother the conception in the brain. But when some of those thoughts are sent out in words, they give the rest more liberty to place themselves in a more methodical order, marching more regularly with my pen on the ground of white paper. But my letters seem rather as a ragged rout, than a well-armed body, for the brain being quicker in creating than the hand in writing, or the memory in retaining, many fancies are lost by reason they ofttimes outrun the pen. Where I, to keep speed in the race, write so fast as I stay not so long as to write my letters plain, insomuch as some have taken my handwriting for some strange character.[2] And being accustomed so to do, I cannot now write very plain. When I strive to write my best, indeed my ordinary handwriting is so bad as few can read it so as to write it fair for the press. But however that[3] little wit I have, it delights me to scribble it out and disperse it about. For I being addicted from my childhood to contemplation rather than conversation, to solitariness rather than society, to melancholy rather than mirth, to write with the pen than to work with a needle, passing my time with harmless fancies, their company being pleasing, their conversation innocent, in which I take such pleasure as I neglect my health. For it is as great a grief to leave their society, as a joy to be in their company. My only trouble is lest my brain should grow barren, or that the root of my fancies should become insipid, withering into a dull stupidity, for want of maturing subjects to write on. * * *

But since I have writ in general thus far of my life, I think it fit I should speak something of my humor, particular practice, and disposition. As for my humor, I was from my childhood given to contemplation, being more taken or delighted with thoughts than in conversation with a society. * * * Also I did dislike any should follow my fashions, for I always took delight in a singularity, even in accoutrements of habits. But whatsoever I was addicted to, either in fashions of clothes, contemplation of thoughts, actions of life, they were lawful, honest, honorable, and modest, of which I can avouch to the world with a great confidence, because it is a pure truth. * * * Likewise I am neither spiteful, envious, nor malicious. I repine not at[4] the gifts that Nature or Fortune bestows upon others, yet I am a great emulator. For though I wish none worse than they are, nor fear any should be better than they are, yet it is lawful for me to wish myself the best, and to do my honest endeavor thereunto. For I think it no crime to wish myself the exactest[5] of Nature's works, my thread of life the longest, my chain of destiny the strongest, my mind the peaceablest, my life the pleasantest, my death the easiest, and the greatest saint in Heaven. * * * As I am not covetous, so I am not prodigal.[6] But of the two I am inclining to be prodigal, yet I cannot say to a vain prodigality, because I imagine it is to a profitable end; for perceiving the world is given or apt to honor the outside more than the inside, worshipping show more than substance; and I am so vain, if it be a vanity, as to endeavor to be worshipped rather than

2. Code, cryptography.
3. Whatever.
4. Do not fret about.

5. Most perfected.
6. Spendthrift, lavish.

not to be regarded. Yet I shall never be so prodigal as to impoverish my friends,[7] or go beyond the limits or facility of our estate. And though I desire to appear at the best advantage whilst I live in the view of the public world, yet I could most willingly exclude myself, so as never to see the face of any creature but my Lord as long as I live, enclosed myself like an anchorite,[8] wearing a frieze gown[9] tied with a cord about my waist. But I hope my readers will not think me vain for writing my life, since there have been many that have done the like, as Caesar, Ovid,[1] and many more, both men and women, and I know no reason I may not do it as well as they. But I verily believe some censuring readers will scornfully say, "Why hath this lady writ her own life, since none cares to know whose daughter she was or whose wife she is, or how she was bred, or what fortunes she had, or how she lived, or what humor or disposition she was of?" I answer that it is true, that 'tis to no purpose, to the readers, but it is to the authoress, because I write it for my own sake, not theirs. Neither did I intend this piece for to delight, but to divulge, not to please the fancy, but to tell the truth, lest after-ages should mistake, in not knowing I was daughter to one Master Lucas of St. Johns near Colchester in Essex, second wife to the Lord Marquis of Newcastle; for my Lord having had two wives, I might easily have been mistaken, especially if I should die, and my Lord marry again.

1656

from Observations upon Experimental Philosophy. To which is added, The Description of a New Blazing World[1]
Of Micrography, and of Magnifying and Multiplying Glasses[2]

Although I am not able to give a solid judgment of the art of micrography and the several dioptrical[3] instruments belonging thereto, by reason I have neither studied nor practiced that art, yet of this I am confident: that this same art, with all its instruments, is not able to discover the interior natural motions of any part or creature of nature. Nay, the question is whether it can represent yet the exterior shapes and motions so exactly as naturally they are, for art[4] doth more easily alter than inform. As, for example, art makes cylinders, concave and convex glasses, and the like, which represent the figure of an object in no part exactly and truly, but very deformed and misshaped. Also a glass that is flawed, cracked, or broke, or cut into the figure of lozenges, triangles, squares, or the like, will present numerous pictures of one object. Besides, there are so many alterations made by several lights, their shadows, refractions, reflections, as also several lines, points, mediums, interposing and intermixing parts, forms, and positions, as the truth of an object will hardly be known.[5]

---

7. Family members.
8. Religious recluse.
9. Coarse woolen robe.
1. Julius Caesar (c. 100–44 B.C.), Roman general and statesman, wrote memoirs of his military campaigns; the Roman poet Ovid (43 B.C.–A.D. 17) wrote many autobiographical poems.
1. The *Observations* is a critique of science, the *Blazing World* a work of fantasy; Cavendish published them together in a single volume as complementary texts. The "experimental philosophy" was that method and outlook pursued and exalted by the Royal Society; the group itself makes a sustained parodic appearance in the *Blazing World*. The Society held that copious experiment was the

necessary basis for reliable study of the natural world. Cavendish challenges any such investigation grounded in human perceptions and the machines (microscopes, telescopes) contrived to enhance them; in the excerpt here she specifically takes on the work of Robert Hooke (see page 2130), whose *Micrographia* (1665) may well have prompted her to write the *Observations*, which includes the first selection given here.
2. Lenses.
3. Vision-enhancing (by means of refraction).
4. Artifice, like that of the lens-makers.
5. Early microscopes in England used simple lenses that blurred the image.

For the perception of sight, and so of the rest of the senses, goes no further than the exterior parts of the object presented, and though the perception may be true when the object is truly presented, yet when the presentation is false, the information must be false also. And it is to be observed that art for the most part makes hermaphroditical,[6] that is, mixed figures, as partly artificial and partly natural. For art may make some metal as pewter, which is between tin and lead, as also brass, and numerous other things of mixed natures; in the like manner may artificial glasses present objects partly natural and partly artificial. Nay, put the case they can present the natural figure of an object; yet that natural figure may be presented in as monstrous a shape as it may appear misshapen rather than natural. For example, a louse by the help of a magnifying glass appears like a lobster,[7] where the microscope enlarging and magnifying each part of it makes them bigger and rounder than naturally they are. The truth is, the more the figure by art is magnified, the more it appears misshapen from the natural, inasmuch as each joint will appear as a diseased, swelled and tumid body, ready and ripe for incision. But mistake me not; I do not say that no glass presents the true picture of an object, but only that magnifying, multiplying, and the like optic glasses may and do oftentimes present falsely the picture of an exterior object. I say the picture because it is not the real body of the object which the glass presents, but the glass only figures or patterns out the picture presented in and by the glass, and there may easily mistakes be committed in taking copies from copies. Nay, artists[8] do confess themselves that flies and the like will appear of several figures or shapes, according to the several reflections, refractions, mediums, and positions of several lights. Which if so, how can they tell or judge which is the truest light, position, or medium, that doth present the object naturally as it is? And if not, then an edge may very well seem flat, and a point of a needle a globe;[9] but if the edge of a knife, or point of a needle were naturally and really so as the microscope presents them, they would never be so useful as they are, for a flat or broad plain-edged knife would not cut, nor a blunt globe pierce so suddenly another body. Neither would or could they pierce without tearing and rending, if their bodies were so uneven. And if the picture of a young beautiful lady should be drawn according to the representation of the microscope, or according to the various refraction and reflection of light through such like glasses, it would be so far from being like her, as it would not be like a human face, but rather a monster than a picture of nature.

Wherefore those that invented microscopes and suchlike dioptrical glasses at first did, in my opinion, the world more injury than benefit. For this art has intoxicated so many men's brains, and wholly employed their thoughts and bodily actions about phenomena, or the exterior figures of objects, as[1] all better arts and studies are laid aside. Nay, those that are not as earnest and active in such employments as they, are by many of them accounted unprofitable subjects to the commonwealth of learning. But though there be numerous books written of the wonders of these glasses, yet I cannot perceive any such; at best, they are but superficial wonders, as I may call them.

But could experimental philosophers find out more beneficial arts than our forefathers have done, either for the better increase of vegetables and brute animals to nourish our bodies, or better and commodious contrivances in the art of architecture

---

6. Composed of two opposite qualities.
7. As in Hooke's *Micrographia* illustration.
8. Technicians.
9. Cavendish evidently refers to Hooke's micrographic depiction of a needle's point, a printed period (her "globe"), and (in the original illustration) a razor's edge; see page 2135.
1. That.

to build us houses, or for the advancing of trade and traffic to provide necessaries for us to live, or for the decrease of nice[2] distinctions and sophistical[3] disputes in churches, schools, and courts of judicature, to make men live in unity, peace, and neighborly friendship, it would not only be worth their labor, but of as much praise as could be given to them. But as boys that play with watery bubbles, or sling dust into each other's eyes, or make a hobbyhorse of snow, are worthy of reproof rather than praise, for wasting their time with useless sports, so those that addict themselves to unprofitable arts spend more time than they reap benefit thereby. Nay, could they benefit men either in husbandry, architecture, or the like necessary and profitable employments, yet before the vulgar sort[4] would learn to understand them, the world would want bread to eat, and houses to dwell in, as also clothes to keep them from the inconveniences of the inconstant weather. But truly, although spinsters[5] were most experienced in this art, yet they will never be able to spin silk, thread, or wool, etc., from loose atoms; neither will weavers weave a web of light from the sun's rays, nor an architect build a house of the bubbles of water and air, unless they be poetical spinsters, weavers, and architects. And if a painter should draw a louse as big as a crab, and of that shape as the microscope presents, can anybody imagine that a beggar would believe it to be true?[6] But if he did, what advantage would it be to the beggar? For it doth neither instruct him how to avoid breeding them, or how to catch them, or to hinder them from biting. Again, if a painter should paint birds according to those colors the microscope presents, what advantage would it be for fowlers to take them? Truly, no fowler will be able to distinguish several birds through a microscope, neither by their shapes nor colors; they will be better discerned by those that eat their flesh than by micrographers that look upon their colors and exterior figures through a magnifying glass.

In short, magnifying glasses are like a high heel to a short leg, which if it be made too high, it is apt to make the wearer fall, and at the best can do no more than represent exterior figures in a bigger, and so in a more deformed shape and posture than naturally they are. But as for the interior form and motions of a creature, as I said before, they can no more represent them, than telescopes can the interior essence and nature of the sun, and what matter it consists of. For if one that never had seen milk before should look upon it through a microscope, he would never be able to discover the interior parts of milk by that instrument, were it the best that is in the world—neither the whey, nor the butter, nor the curds. Wherefore the best optic[7] is a perfect natural eye, and a regular sensitive perception, and the best judge is reason, and the best study is rational contemplation joined with the observations of regular sense, but not deluding arts. For art is not only gross[8] in comparison to nature, but for the most part deformed and defective, and at best produces mixed or hermaphroditical figures—that is, a third figure between nature and art. Which proves that natural reason is above artificial sense, as I may call it. Wherefore those arts are the best and surest informers that alter nature least, and they the greatest deluders that alter nature most—I mean, the particular nature of each particular creature. (For art is so far from altering infinite Nature that it is no more in comparison to it than a little fly

---

2. Minute, subtle, trivial.
3. Complicatedly and falsely argued.
4. Common people.
5. People who spin yarn or thread (possibly, here, with the additional sense of "unmarried woman").

6. Beggars were assumed to be most familiar (because most often afflicted) with lice.
7. Lens.
8. Rough, approximate.

to an elephant;[9] no, not so much, for there is no comparison between finite and infinite.) But wise Nature taking delight in variety, her parts, which are her creatures, must of necessity do so too.

from The Description of a New Blazing World

from To the Reader

If you wonder that I join a work of fancy[1] to my serious philosophical contemplations, think not that it is out of a disparagement to philosophy, or out of an opinion as if this noble study were but a fiction of the mind * * * The end of reason is truth, the end of fancy is fiction. But mistake me not when I distinguish fancy from reason; I mean not as if fancy were not made by the rational parts of matter, but by "reason" I understand a rational search and inquiry into the causes of natural effects, and by "fancy" a voluntary creation or production of the mind, both being effects, or rather actions, of the rational part of matter, of which, as that[2] is a more profitable and useful study than this, so it is also more laborious and difficult, and requires sometimes the help of fancy to recreate the mind and withdraw it from its more serious contemplations.

And this is the reason, why I added this piece of fancy to my philosophical observations, and joined them as two worlds at the ends of their poles; both for my own sake, to divert my studious thoughts, which I employed in the contemplation thereof, and to delight the reader with variety, which is always pleasing. But lest my fancy should stray too much, I chose such a fiction as would be agreeable to the subject treated of in the former parts; it is a description of a new world, not such as Lucian's, or the Frenchman's world in the moon;[3] but a world of my own creating, which I call the Blazing World: the first part whereof is romancical, the second philosophical, and the third is merely fancy, or (as I may call it) fantastical, which if it add any satisfaction to you, I shall account myself a happy creatoress.[4] If not, I must be content to live a melancholy life in my own world; I cannot call it a poor world, if poverty be only want of gold, silver, and jewels; for there is more gold in it than all the chemists ever did, and (as I verily believe) will ever be able to make.[5] As for the rocks of diamonds, I wish with all my soul they might be shared amongst my noble female friends, and upon that condition, I would willingly quit my part;[6] and of the gold I should only desire so much as might suffice to repair my noble Lord and husband's losses:[7] for I am not covetous, but as ambitious as ever any of my sex was, is, or can be; which makes, that though I cannot be Henry the Fifth, or Charles the Second,[8] yet I endeavor to be Margaret the First; and although I have neither power, time, nor

9. Cavendish probably refers to Hooke's illustration of a flea (see page 2137).
1. Imagination.
2. Philosophy.
3. The *True History*, by the Greek satirist Lucian (2nd century A.D.), initiated a long literary tradition of imaginary voyages, to which the French writer Savinien Cyrano de Bergerac's account of a trip to the moon (*Histoire comique contenant les états et empires de la lune* [1657]) was a recent, celebrated contribution.
4. In the first part of *The Blazing World*, a "virtuous lady" survives her abduction at sea and is transported into a "Blazing World" that touches Earth at the North Pole; quickly wooed and wedded by the Emperor of this utopia, she becomes its Empress. In the second, "philosophical,"

section, she hears the testimony of various scholars, scientists, theologians, and philosophers; in the third, "fantastical," section, the Empress summons the soul of Margaret Cavendish to travel from England to the Blazing World, in order to serve as her companion and secretary. The excerpts that follow are from the third part of the narrative.
5. Alchemists sought to turn base metals into gold.
6. Give up my share.
7. During the civil wars, William Cavendish had lost much wealth and property, of which he had recovered only part since the Restoration.
8. Henry V of England (1387–1422) was celebrated for his conquest of France; Charles II for his restoration of the monarchy after the Interregnum.

occasion to conquer the world as Alexander and Caesar did; yet rather than not to be mistress of one, since Fortune and the Fates would give me none, I have made a world of my own: for which nobody, I hope, will blame me, since it is in everyone's power to do the like.

[CREATING WORLDS]

At last, when the Duchess⁹ saw that no patterns would do her any good in the framing of her world, she resolved to make a world of her own invention, * * * which world after it was made, appeared so curious and full of variety, so well ordered and wisely governed, that it cannot possibly be expressed by words, nor the delight and pleasure which the Duchess took in making this world of her own.

In the meantime the Empress was also making and dissolving several worlds in her own mind, and was so puzzled, that she could not settle in any of them; wherefore she sent for the Duchess, who being ready to wait on the Empress, carried her beloved world along with her, and invited the Empress's soul to observe the frame, order, and government of it. Her Majesty was so ravished with the perception of it, that her soul desired to live in the Duchess's world; but the Duchess advised her to make such another world in her own mind; for, said she, your Majesty's mind is full of rational corporeal motions, and the rational motions of my mind shall assist you by the help of sensitive expressions, with the best instructions they are able to give you.

The Empress being thus persuaded by the Duchess to make an imaginary world of her own, followed her advice; and after she had quite finished it, and framed all kinds of creatures proper and useful for it, strengthened it with good laws, and beautified it with arts and sciences; having nothing else to do, unless she did dissolve her imaginary world, or made some alterations in the Blazing World she lived in, which yet she could hardly do, by reason it was so well ordered that it could not be mended.¹

[EMPRESS, DUCHESS, DUKE]

At last, they entered into the Duke's house,² an habitation not so magnificent, as useful; and when the Empress saw it, "Has the Duke," said she, "no other house but this?" "Yes," answered the Duchess, "some five miles from this place, he has a very fine castle, called Bolsover."³ "That place then," said the Empress, "I desire to see." "Alas!" replied the Duchess, "it is but a naked house, and unclothed of all furniture." "However," said the Empress, "I may see the manner of its structure and building." "That you may," replied the Duchess. And as they were thus discoursing, the Duke came out of the house into the court, to see his horses of manage;⁴ whom when the Duchess's soul perceived, she was so overjoyed, that her aerial vehicle⁵ became so splendorous, as if it had been enlightened by the sun; by which we may perceive, that the passions of souls or spirits can alter their bodily vehicles. Then these two ladies' spirits went close to him, but he could not perceive them; and after the Empress had observed the art of manage, she was much pleased with it, and commended it as a

9. Cavendish herself, whose soul has been transported to the Blazing World at the Empress's request. At this point in the story she and the Empress have been experimenting with creating worlds in accordance with the theories established by various experts, ancient and modern (Pythagoras, Plato, Aristotle, Descartes, Hobbes).
1. Instead, the Empress resolves "to see the world the Duchess came from," and so "those two female souls" travel together "as lightly as two thoughts," into England.

2. Welbeck Abbey, north-country birthplace and family seat of Cavendish's husband the Duke of Newcastle.
3. The Duke's favorite residence.
4. Well-disciplined in the actions and paces of *ménage*, or systematic horse training. The Duke, an expert equestrian, had published two books on the subject; when Charles II was a boy, Newcastle had taught him how to ride.
5. Form made out of air.

noble pastime, and an exercise fit and proper for noble and heroic persons; but when the Duke was gone into the house again, those two souls followed him; where the Empress observing, that he went to the exercise of the sword, and was such an excellent and unparalleled master thereof, she was as much pleased with that exercise, as she was with the former. But the Duchess's soul being troubled, that her dear lord and husband used such a violent exercise before meat, for fear of overheating himself, without any consideration of the Empress's soul, left her aerial vehicle, and entered into her lord. The Empress's soul perceiving this, did the like: and then the Duke had three souls in one body; and had there been but some such souls more, the Duke would have been like the Grand Signior in his seraglio,[6] only it would have been a Platonic seraglio.[7] But the Duke's soul being wise, honest, witty, complaisant, and noble, afforded such delight and pleasure to the Empress's soul by her conversation, that these two souls became enamored of each other; which the Duchess's soul perceiving, grew jealous at first, but then considering that no adultery could be committed amongst Platonic lovers, and that Platonism was divine, as being derived from divine Plato, cast forth of her mind that idea of jealousy. Then the conversation of these three souls was so pleasant, that it cannot be expressed; for the Duke's soul entertained the Empress's soul with scenes, songs, music, witty discourses, pleasant recreations, and all kinds of harmless sports; so that the time passed away faster than they expected. At last, a spirit came and told the Empress, that although neither the Emperor, nor any of his subjects knew that her soul was absent; yet the Empress's soul was so sad and melancholy, for want of his own beloved soul, that all the imperial court took notice of it. Wherefore he advised the Empress's soul to return into the Blazing World, into her own body she left there; which both the Duke's and Duchess's soul was very sorry for, and wished, that if it had been possible, the Empress's soul might have stayed a longer time with them; but seeing it could not be otherwise, they pacified themselves. * * *

Epilogue

TO THE READER

By this poetical description, you may perceive, that my ambition is not only to be Empress, but Authoress of a whole world; and that the worlds I have made, both the Blazing and the other Philosophical World, mentioned in the first part of this description, are framed and composed of the most pure, that is, the rational parts of matter, which are the parts of my mind; which creation was more easily and suddenly effected than the conquests of the two famous monarchs of the world, Alexander and Caesar. Neither have I made such disturbances, and caused so many dissolutions of particulars,[8] otherwise named deaths, as they did; for I have destroyed but some few men in a little boat,[9] which died through the extremity of cold, and that by the hand of Justice, which was necessitated to punish their crime of stealing away a young and beauteous lady. And in the formation of those worlds, I take more delight and glory, than ever Alexander or Caesar did in conquering this terrestrial world; and though I have made my Blazing World a peaceable world, allowing it but one religion, one

---

6. Harem.
7. One where the pleasures of the flesh would be repudiated in favor of the contemplation of pure, disembodied Ideas.

8. Individuals.
9. The sailor-abductors of the "virtuous lady," who die during the boat's passage through the North Pole to the Blazing World.

language, and one government; yet could I make another world, as full of factions, divisions, and wars, as this is of peace and tranquility; and the rational figures of my mind might express as much courage to fight, as Hector and Achilles had; and be as wise as Nestor, as eloquent as Ulysses, and as beautiful as Helen.[1] But I esteeming peace before war, wit before policy, honesty before beauty; instead of the figures of Alexander, Caesar, Hector, Achilles, Nestor, Ulysses, Helen, etc. chose rather the figure of honest Margaret Newcastle, which now I would not change for all this terrestrial world; and if any should like the world I have made, and be willing to be my subjects, they may imagine themselves such, and they are such, I mean, in their minds, fancies, or imaginations; but if they cannot endure to be subjects, they may create worlds of their own, and govern themselves as they please: but yet let them have a care, not to prove unjust usurpers, and to rob me of mine; for concerning the Philosophical World, I am Empress of it myself; and as for the Blazing World, it having an Empress already, who rules it with great wisdom and conduct, which Empress is my dear Platonic friend; I shall never prove so unjust, treacherous, and unworthy to her, as to disturb her government, much less to depose her from her imperial throne, for the sake of any other; but rather choose to create another world for another friend.

1666

— ✠ —

John Dryden
1631–1700

In his last years, John Dryden often felt the need to defend his morals, his religion, his politics, even his writing. For nearly a quarter of a century, he had held high literary office and mingled with the great; he had curried royal favor and aristocratic patronage, bolstering officialdom, aiming to injure the Crown's enemies and to caress its friends. He wrote about politics and religion, about trade and empire; he wrote for the theater and for public occasions; he composed songs, fables, odes, and panegyrics, brilliant satire and savage polemic; he translated from many languages and formulated an idiomatic, familiar, and fluent prose style. Dryden virtually invented the idea of a commercial literary career; and through all the turns of a difficult public life, he fashioned from his own unlikely personality—from his privacy, self-doubts, and hesitations—a public figure of literary distinction. But he attained this celebrity at the cost of gossip and scandal, and in the last decade of his life (after the Glorious Revolution and his deposition from the Poet Laureateship) he faced suspicion and scorn.

The poet's beginnings give no hint of literary greatness or the likelihood of fame. He was born in 1631 in a country town and to comfortable circumstance; he was educated at Westminster School and graduated from Trinity College, Cambridge. He held minor public office in the 1650s but had written almost nothing before he was twenty-seven. Dryden then began his long career as public poet. He mourned the Lord Protector in 1659 (*Heroic Stanzas*) and then, in what looks like a convenient turn of allegiance, he celebrated the return of monarchy in 1660, writing poems to Charles II, to the Lord Chancellor, and to the Duchess of York; he praised the Royal Society (*To Doctor Charleton*) and defended the Royal Navy and its aristocratic high command (*Annus Mirabilis*, 1667).

---

1. Characters in the *Iliad*, Homer's epic poem about the Trojan War.

The first years seem a series of calculated moves; and the combination of talent, application, and opportunity was crowned when Dryden was named Poet Laureate in 1667. But in addition to fashioning a career in the 1660s, Dryden also forged a new drama—an epic theater whose themes and language echoed the idioms of heroic verse—and a body of literary criticism that itself would have made his lasting reputation. Indeed, the great text of the first decade was the *Essay of Dramatic Poesy* (1668), Dryden's formulation of a pointedly English poetics and theater. Along with Sir Philip Sidney's *Apology for Poetry*, and Samuel Johnson's *Lives of the Poets*, Dryden's *Essay* is central to the long-standing canon of English literary criticism. Some of Dryden's early plays have been forgotten, but he worked steadily at a craft that would enable him to turn Milton's *Paradise Lost* into theater (*The State of Innocence*, 1677), create a superb adaptation of Shakespeare's *Antony and Cleopatra* in *All for Love* (1678), the finest of Restoration tragedies in *Don Sebastian* (1690), and the texts of one of England's first operas, *King Arthur* (1691), and last masques, *The Pilgrim* (1700).

By the late 1670s Dryden was famed as publicist for the Crown, and his theatrical work had come to dominate the stage; but he had hardly begun the career as satirist by which he is now best known. Its opening move was *Mac Flecknoe* (1676), and in the next few years Dryden fashioned masterpieces of literary mockery and political invective, poems that virtually created literary genres and dominated satire for decades to come. *Mac Flecknoe* allowed Dryden to ridicule and crush his rivals, all the while conjuring the suave tones and elegant manners of literary supremacy. In the abuse of rivals, only Pope surpasses Dryden as a master of scorn. But *Mac Flecknoe* was only the first act in a theater of invective. In the fall of 1681 Dryden wrote *Absalom and Achitophel*, a biblical allegory occasioned by the crisis of succession. The king had failed to beget a legitimate heir, and the king's Catholic brother waited ominously in the wings. It was Dryden's job to defend the Crown, to extenuate royal indulgence, and, especially, to defuse anxieties. With *Absalom and Achitophel*, Dryden wove together the Bible and contemporary politics with such deftness that mere diversionary tactics were spun into an incomparable allegory of envy, ambition, and misdeed. The satire was read, marked, circulated, and treasured as a masterpiece and a menace.

The masterpiece secured Dryden's fame; the menace exacted a cost. The poet had attacked powerful men: aristocrats, politicians, and their partisan hacks who intrigued against the Crown. They failed in the early 1680s to foment rebellion, but by 1688 they were able to effect a revolution that deposed Catholic monarchy and the Poet Laureate himself. Dryden was reputed a brilliant and damaging advocate of Stuart rule; he had collaborated with court publicity and polemic; he had even converted to Roman Catholicism after James ascended the throne. Indeed, Dryden wrote his longest and most elaborate original poem—*The Hind and the Panther* (1687)—in defense of that king's rule and religion, and of his own conversion to Roman Catholicism. Once James II had been chased into exile, the poet felt he had nowhere to turn. In 1688 Dryden was fifty-seven, an old man by contemporary standards. He was forced from office, his pension was canceled, and he was driven back to the venues of commercial writing: the theater, translation, publication by subscription, even editing and anthologizing. He often expressed a keen sense of loss and abandonment in the 1690s, yet the decade would prove to be a remarkable phase of his career. Between his loss of the laureateship in 1689 and his death in 1700, Dryden wrote a series of superb translations that included selections from the satires of Juvenal and Persius, Ovid's *Metamorphoses* and *Amores*, Boccaccio's and Chaucer's tales. In these same years he wrote odes and epitaphs, and collaborated with his publisher Jacob Tonson in the new fashion for literary anthologies. Most remarkably, he produced *The Works of Virgil*, which set the standard for the translation of Latin poetry. He had come to his project late, and more than once he wrote of his inadequacy for this daunting task: "What Virgil wrote in the vigor of his age, in plenty and at ease, I have undertaken to translate in my declining years, struggling with wants, oppressed with sickness, curbed in my genius, liable to be misconstrued in all I write; and my judges . . . already prejudiced against me, by the lying character which has been given them of my morals." But Dryden's *Virgil* was a resounding, rehabilitating commercial and artistic success.

Nor were the twelve thousand lines of translated Virgil the close of this career. What followed was *Fables Ancient and Modern*, an anthology of original verse and new translations that included Ovid, Boccaccio, and Chaucer as well as a trial for what Dryden hoped would be his English Homer. He saw commercial opportunity in this new collection; but he must also have understood it as a crowning achievement in this life of theatricality and ventriloquism. He had begun by seeking a voice in the idioms and gestures of other poets; he now belonged wholly to himself as he casually turned their verse into his own. It is something of a paradox that a life of literary self-assertion, of aggressive, even calculating, careerism, should have closed with Dryden rummaging among other poets' verse, pausing over favorite lines, translating Ovid's Latin and Boccaccio's Italian into what was unmistakably his own voice. And the paradox of self-assertion ending in translation helps us to identify what is so particularly and so brilliantly Dryden's art. In the early modern world, writing meant belonging to others—to the authority of antiquity, to the opinions and fickle pleasure of patrons, to favor, to obligation, to taste, even to the emerging appetites of a reading public. Many of Dryden's contemporaries— Donne, Milton, Rochester—appeal to us by their seeming defiance of such self-denying ordinances. We read Dryden today not just for the skill with which he picked his way through political dangers or negotiated social minefields, not even for the savage cartooning of enemies or baroque praise of friends, but for the achievement of belonging to others as he became more exactly and more generously himself.

ABSALOM AND ACHITOPHEL   Dryden wrote *Absalom and Achitophel* as a piece of propaganda; he was, after all, Poet Laureate. He may even have written it at the personal request of Charles II, and he surely intended to please the king, to entertain his friends, to embarrass their enemies. He performed these offices amidst tangled circumstances and under extraordinary partisan and civic pressures.

Charles had sired many children by many mistresses, but no heir by his wife. These habits and accidents of royal procreation had created a succession crisis: in the absence of a legitimate heir, the crown would pass to Charles's brother James, an openly professed Roman Catholic. This prospect excited every fear of absolute rule—of Popery, slavery, subjugation to France and to Rome. The crisis, in turn, helped crystallize an opposition of Protestants, rebels, republicans, and opportunists who mustered support for an audacious proposal: exclude the duke from succession and appoint as substitute the dim but charming, Protestant but (alas) bastard offspring of the king, James, Duke of Monmouth.

To bolster its program, the opposition made ingenious use of a conspiracy theory, widely entertained though largely false. In 1678 the mysterious murder of an eminent judge, a cloud of perjured witnesses, and a blizzard of broadsides, rumors, and innuendos persuaded many that the Queen, the Duke of York, and a band of Jesuits had conspired in a "Popish Plot" to kill the king and inaugurate Catholic rule. At the height of the mania, thirty-five Catholics were executed for their supposed complicity in this "plot." After the bloodletting, and in the face of much evidence to suggest that the plot itself was fiction, the rage subsided. The Whig opposition, now emerging from thuggery and faction into England's first organized political party, tested its powers by parliamentary maneuver. In 1680 its leader, the Earl of Shaftesbury, tried twice to pass a bill excluding Charles's brother James from the succession. In 1681 Shaftesbury publicly urged Charles to legitimate Monmouth. The king had had enough: he dismissed Parliament in March, and on July 2 had Shaftesbury imprisoned on charges of high treason. Four months later, a packed jury produced the verdict *ignoramus* ("we don't know").

Dryden's poem, appearing the week before the trial, told these busy stories in terms both daring and familiar. He cast the crisis as biblical drama: Charles became King David, Monmouth was David's wayward son Absalom, Shaftesbury the wily counselor Achitophel. Of course, factions of all sorts had long deployed parallels between England and Israel for instruction, for prophecy and exhortation, for mockery and even scandal. But no one had set all the possibilities of irony and celebration simultaneously in motion. Against the king's enemies Dryden turned their own rhetoric of scriptural sanctimony; in support of the king's friends he wrote hymns of praise; but on behalf of that complex client the king himself, Dryden discovered a way of portraying monarchy in a spirit at once appreciative, ironic, and delicately abrasive. In the poem's mischievous opening lines we hear these possibilities fully orchestrated. Charles's sexual energies, mapped as Davidic fecundity, are simultaneously grand and titillating, munificent and comic. Such mixtures of tone suffuse all the actions and arguments of Dryden's poem—its images of authority, its satiric portraits, its theories of governance, its monologues and declamations—all its traffic with the dangerous world of politics, plots, and promiscuity.

Absalom and Achitophel: A Poem.

—Si propiùs stes
Te capiet magis—[1]

TO THE READER

'Tis not my intention to make an apology for my poem: some will think it needs no excuse, and others will receive none. The design, I am sure, is honest, but he who draws his pen for one party must expect to make enemies of the other. For wit and fool are consequents of Whig and Tory, and every man is a knave or an ass to the contrary side. There's a treasury of merits in the fanatic church, as well as in the Papist, and a pennyworth to be had of saintship, honesty, and poetry, for the lewd, the factious, and the blockheads.[2] But the longest chapter in Deuteronomy has not curses enough for an anti-Bromingham.[3] My comfort is, their manifest prejudice to my cause will render their judgment of less authority against me. Yet if a poem have a genius, it will force its own reception in the world. For there's a sweetness in good verse, which tickles even while it hurts, and no man can be heartily angry with him who pleases him against his will. The commendation of adversaries is the greatest triumph of a writer, because it never comes unless extorted. But I can be satisfied on more easy terms: if I happen to please the more moderate sort, I shall be sure of an honest party and, in all probability, of the best judges, for the least concerned are commonly the least corrupt. And, I confess, I have laid in for those, by rebating[4] the satire (where justice would allow it) from carrying too sharp an edge. They who can criticize so weakly as to imagine I have done my worst may be convinced, at their own cost, that I can write severely with more ease than I can gently. I have but laughed at some men's follies, when I could have declaimed against their vices; and other men's virtues I have commended as freely as I have taxed[5] their crimes. And now, if you are a malicious reader, I expect you should return upon me that I affect to be thought more impartial than I am. But if men are not to be judged by their professions,[6] God forgive you commonwealthsmen[7] for professing so plausibly for the government. You cannot be so unconscionable as to charge me for not subscribing of my

---

1. "If you stand closer, it will capture you more readily" (Horace, *Ars Poetica* 361–62); Horace is here developing his argument that a poem works like a picture (*ut pictura poesis*).
2. Roman Catholic doctrine posited the existence in heaven of a fund of surplus "merits," accumulated through the goodness of Christ and the saints, on which ordinary mortals might draw for absolution. Dryden suggests that the dissenting Protestant sects ("the fanatic church"), like the Catholic ("Papist") church, confer for-

giveness (even "saintship") too freely, and too cheaply.
3. Tory (Royalist). Deuteronomy 28 includes a long list of curses against those who "shall not enter into the congregation of the Lord" because they have disobeyed his law.
4. Abating, softening.
5. Denounced.
6. What they say (profess).
7. Here and throughout the poem, Dryden conflates the supporters of Monmouth with the supporters of Cromwell, as enemies of the monarchy.

name, for that would reflect too grossly upon your own party, who never dare, though they have the advantage of a jury to secure them.[8] If you like not my poem, the fault may, possibly, be in my writing (though 'tis hard for an author to judge against himself); but, more probably, 'tis in your morals, which cannot bear the truth of it. The violent on both sides will condemn the character of Absalom as either too favorably or too hardly drawn. But they are not the violent whom I desire to please. The fault, on the right hand, is to extenuate, palliate, and indulge; and, to confess freely, I have endeavored to commit it. Besides the respect which I owe his birth, I have a greater for his heroic virtues; and David himself could not be more tender of the young man's life than I would be of his reputation. But since the most excellent natures are always the most easy,[9] and, as being such, are the soonest perverted by ill counsels, especially when baited with fame and glory, 'tis no more a wonder that he withstood not the temptations of Achitophel than it was for Adam not to have resisted the two devils, the serpent and the woman. The conclusion of the story I purposely forbore to prosecute, because I could not obtain from myself to show Absalom unfortunate.[1] The frame of it was cut out but for a picture to the waist; and if the draught be so far true, 'tis as much as I designed.

Were I the inventor, who am only the historian, I should certainly conclude the piece with the reconcilement of Absalom to David. And who knows but this may come to pass? Things were not brought to an extremity where I left the story. There seems yet to be room left for a composure;[2] hereafter, there may only be for pity. I have not so much as an uncharitable wish against Achitophel, but am content to be accused of a good-natured error and to hope with Origen[3] that the Devil himself may, at last, be saved. For which reason, in this poem he is neither brought to set his house in order nor to dispose of his person afterwards as he in wisdom shall think fit.[4] God is infinitely merciful, and his vicegerent[5] is only not so because he is not infinite.

The true end of satire is the amendment of vices by correction. And he who writes honestly is no more an enemy to the offender than the physician to the patient, when he prescribes harsh remedies to an inveterate disease; for those are only in order to prevent the surgeon's work of an *ense rescindendum*,[6] which I wish not to my very enemies. To conclude all, if the body politic have any analogy to the natural, in my weak judgment, an Act of Oblivion were as necessary in a hot, distempered state as an opiate would be in a raging fever.

Absalom and Achitophel: A Poem

In pious times, ere priestcraft did begin,
Before polygamy was made a sin;[7]
When man on many multiplied his kind,
Ere one to one was cursedly confined;

---

8. Dryden published his politically volatile poem anonymously. He accuses Whig writers of similar caution, and hence of greater cowardice, because the London juries that adjudicated cases of seditious libel were handpicked by Whig sheriffs for their bias in the party's favor.
9. Easily persuaded.
1. I.e., Dryden decided to leave off the end of the biblical story (in which Absalom is killed), because he could not bring himself to show Absalom's misfortune.
2. Reconciliation.
3. An early Christian theologian.
4. Dryden insinuatingly echoes the biblical account of

Achitophel's disappointment and suicide (2 Samuel 23).
5. The king.
6. "Something to be cut out" in order to prevent infection of the whole organism. Dryden next suggests that an "Act of Oblivion" forgiving the rebels, like the one Charles II enacted at his Restoration, might constitute a gentler remedy.
7. "Priestcraft" is "religious fraud" (Johnson's *Dictionary*); Dryden mimics the anti-Catholicism of the Whigs, while insinuating that monogamy is an unnatural restriction imposed by power-hungry priests.

5   When Nature prompted, and no law denied
       Promiscuous use of concubine and bride;
       Then Israel's monarch, after Heaven's own heart,
       His vigorous warmth did variously impart
       To wives and slaves; and, wide as his command,
10   Scattered his Maker's image through the land.
       Michal,[8] of royal blood, the crown did wear,
       A soil ungrateful to the tiller's care:
       Not so the rest, for several mothers bore
       To godlike David several sons before.
15   But since like slaves his bed they did ascend,
       No true succession could their seed attend.[9]
       Of all this numerous progeny was none
       So beautiful, so brave as Absolon:
       Whether, inspired by some diviner lust,
20   His father got° him with a greater gust,°   *begot / pleasure*
       Or that his conscious destiny made way
       By manly beauty to imperial sway.
       Early in foreign fields he won renown,
       With kings and states allied to Israel's crown:
25   In peace the thoughts of war he could remove,
       And seemed as he were only born for love.
       Whate'er he did was done with so much ease,
       In him alone 'twas natural to please.
       His motions all accompanied with grace;
30   And paradise was opened in his face.
       With secret joy indulgent David viewed
       His youthful image in his son renewed:
       To all his wishes nothing he denied,
       And made the charming Annabel[1] his bride.
35   What faults he had (for who from faults is free?)
       His father could not, or he would not see.
       Some warm excesses, which the law forbore,
       Were construed youth that purged by boiling o'er:
       And Amnon's murder,[2] by a specious name,
40   Was called a just revenge for injured fame.
       Thus praised and loved the noble youth remained,
       While David, undisturbed, in Sion[3] reigned.
       But life can never be sincerely blest:
       Heaven punishes the bad, and proves° the best.   *tests*
45   The Jews,[4] a headstrong, moody, murmuring race,
       As ever tried th' extent and stretch of grace;
       God's pampered people whom, debauched with ease,
       No king could govern, nor no God could please
       (Gods they had tried of every shape and size

---

8. Daughter of David's predecessor King Saul; here she represents Charles's childless wife, Catherine of Braganza.
9. Their offspring could not succeed to the throne because of their illegitimacy.
1. Anne, Countess of Buccleuch.

2. In 2 Samuel 8, Amnon rapes Absalom's half sister, and Absalom orders his murder; the correspondence with events in Monmouth's life is uncertain.
3. Jerusalem (hence, London).
4. The English.

50   That god-smiths could produce, or priests devise);
       These Adam-wits, too fortunately free,
       Began to dream they wanted° liberty;   *lacked, desired*
       And when no rule, no precedent was found
       Of men by laws less circumscribed and bound,
55   They led their wild desires to woods and caves,
       And thought that all but savages were slaves.
       They who when Saul was dead, without a blow,
       Made foolish Ishbosheth[5] the crown forgo;
       Who banished David did from Hebron bring,[6]
60   And with a general shout proclaimed him King:
       Those very Jews, who, at their very best,
       Their humor more than loyalty expressed,
       Now wondered why so long they had obeyed
       An idol monarch which their hands had made;
65   Thought they might ruin him they could create,
       Or melt him to that golden calf, a state.
       But these were random bolts; no formed design,
       Nor interest made the factious crowd to join:
       The sober part of Israel, free from stain,
70   Well knew the value of a peaceful reign:
       And, looking backward with a wise afright,
       Saw seams of wounds, dishonest to the sight;
       In contemplation of whose ugly scars
       They cursed the memory of Civil Wars.
75   The moderate sort of men, thus qualified,
       Inclined the balance to the better side:
       And David's mildness managed it so well,
       The bad found no occasion to rebel.
       But when to sin our biased nature leans,
80   The careful Devil is still° at hand with means;   *always*
       And providently pimps for ill desires:
       The Good Old Cause[7] revived, a Plot requires.
       Plots, true or false, are necessary things,
       To raise up commonwealths and ruin kings.
85   Th' inhabitants of old Jerusalem
       Were Jebusites:[8] the town so called from them;
       And theirs the native right—
       But when the chosen people grew more strong,
       The rightful cause at length became the wrong:
90   And every loss the men of Jebus bore,
       They still were thought God's enemies the more.
       Thus, worn and weakened, well or ill content,
       Submit they must to David's government:
       Impoverished, and deprived of all command,
95   Their taxes doubled as they lost their land,

---

5. Ishbosheth briefly succeeded his father Saul; corre-
spondingly, Richard Cromwell was Protector for a few
months after the death of his father, Oliver.
6. David ruled in Hebron seven years before becoming king
of Israel. Charles had been crowned in Scotland in 1651.

7. Popular name for the Cromwellian opposition to the
monarchy.
8. Jebusites inhabited Jerusalem before the Israelites;
here, they represent the Catholics.

And, what was harder yet to flesh and blood,
Their gods disgraced, and burnt like common wood.[9]
This set the heathen priesthood in a flame;
For priests of all religions are the same:
100   Of whatsoe'er descent their godhead be,
Stock, stone, or other homely pedigree,
In his defense his servants are as bold
As if he had been born of beaten gold.
The Jewish rabbins,[1] though their enemies,
105   In this conclude them honest men and wise:
For 'twas their duty, all the learned think,
T' espouse his cause by whom they eat and drink.
From hence began that Plot,[2] the nation's curse,
Bad in itself, but represented worse:
110   Raised in extremes, and in extremes decried;
With oaths affirmed, with dying vows denied:
Not weighed or winnowed by the multitude,
But swallowed in the mass, unchewed and crude.
Some truth there was, but dashed and brewed with lies,
115   To please the fools, and puzzle all the wise.
Succeeding times did equal folly call
Believing nothing, or believing all.
Th' Egyptian rites the Jebusites embraced,
Where gods were recommended by their taste.[3]
120   Such savory deities must needs be good,
As served at once for worship and for food.
By force they could not introduce these gods,
For ten to one[4] in former days was odds.
So fraud was used (the sacrificer's trade):
125   Fools are more hard to conquer than persuade.
Their busy teachers mingled with the Jews,
And raked, for converts, even the court and stews:°   *brothels*
Which Hebrew priests the more unkindly took,
Because the fleece[5] accompanies the flock.
130   Some thought they God's anointed[6] meant to slay
By guns, invented since full many a day:[7]
Our author swears it not; but who can know
How far the Devil and Jebusites may go?
This Plot, which failed for want of common sense,
135   Had yet a deep and dangerous consequence:
For, as when raging fevers boil the blood,
The standing lake soon floats into a flood,
And every hostile humor,[8] which before
Slept quiet in its channels, bubbles o'er;
140   So several factions from this first ferment

---

9. Dryden alludes to a variety of anti-Catholic penal laws.
1. Anglican clergy.
2. The Popish Plot.
3. Here, and in the lines following, Dryden mocks the Catholic belief in transubstantiation.
4. Protestants to Catholics.

5. Tithe, paid by the "flock" (the parishioners).
6. The king.
7. Long since; Dryden playfully acknowledges this anachronism.
8. Bodily fluid, thought to determine temperament.

Work up to foam, and threat the government.
Some by their friends, more by themselves thought wise,
Opposed the power to which they could not rise.
Some had in courts been great, and thrown from thence,
145   Like fiends were hardened in impenitence.
Some, by their monarch's fatal mercy, grown,
From pardoned rebels, kinsmen to the throne,
Were raised in power and public office high:
Strong bands, if bands ungrateful men could tie.
150   Of these the false Achitophel⁹ was first:
A name to all succeeding ages cursed:
For close° designs and crooked counsels fit;   *secret*
Sagacious, bold, and turbulent of wit:
Restless, unfixed in principles and place;
155   In power unpleased, impatient of disgrace:
A fiery soul, which working out its way, ⎫
Fretted the pygmy body to decay: ⎬
And o'er-informed the tenement of clay.¹ ⎭
A daring pilot in extremity;
160   Pleased with the danger, when the waves went high
He sought the storms; but for a calm unfit,
Would steer too nigh the sands, to boast his wit.
Great wits are sure to madness near allied;
And thin partitions do their bounds divide:
165   Else why should he, with wealth and honor blessed,
Refuse his age² the needful hours of rest?
Punish a body which he could not please;
Bankrupt of life, yet prodigal of ease?
And all to leave what with his toil he won,
170   To that unfeathered, two-legged thing, a son:
Got while his soul did huddled notions try;
And born a shapeless lump, like anarchy.
In friendship false, implacable in hate:
Resolved to ruin or to rule the state.
175   To compass this the triple bond³ he broke, ⎫
The pillars of the public safety shook, ⎬
And fitted Israel for a foreign yoke. ⎭
Then, seized with fear, yet still affecting° fame,   *desiring*
Usurped a patriot's all-atoning name.⁴
180   So easy still it proves in factious times,
With public zeal to cancel private crimes:
How safe is treason, and how sacred ill,
Where none can sin against the people's will:
Where crowds can wink,⁵ and no offense be known,
185   Since in another's guilt they find their own.

---

9. David's counselor, who encourages Absalom to rebel against his father; here representing Anthony Ashley Cooper, first Earl of Shaftesbury, counselor to both Cromwell and Charles II.
1. The body; Dryden contrasts Shaftesbury's large ambition with his small and sickly body.

2. Shaftesbury was 60 in 1681.
3. England's 1668 alliance with Sweden and Holland (against France).
4. Name that excuses anything.
5. Turn a blind eye.

Yet fame deserved no enemy can grudge;
The statesman we abhor, but praise the judge.
In Israel's courts ne'er sat an Abbethdin[6]
With more discerning eyes, or hands more clean:
190 Unbribed, unsought, the wretched to redress,
Swift of dispatch, and easy of access.
Oh, had he been content to serve the crown,
With virtues only proper to the gown;
Or had the rankness of the soil been freed
195 From cockle,° that oppressed the noble seed: *weeds*
David for him his tuneful harp had strung,
And heaven had wanted one immortal song.[7]
But wild ambition loves to slide, not stand,
And fortune's ice prefers to virtue's land:
200 Achitophel, grown weary to possess°   *of possessing*
A lawful fame and lazy happiness,
Disdained the golden fruit to gather free,
And lent the crowd his arm to shake the tree.
Now, manifest° of crimes contrived long since,   *clearly guilty*
205 He stood at bold defiance with his prince:
Held up the buckler° of the people's cause   *shield*
Against the crown; and skulked behind the laws.
The wished occasion of the Plot he takes,
Some circumstances finds, but more he makes;
210 By buzzing emissaries fills the ears
Of list'ning crowds with jealousies and fears
Of arbitrary counsels brought to light,
And proves the King himself a Jebusite:
Weak arguments! which yet he knew full well
215 Were strong with people easy to rebel.
For, governed by the moon, the giddy Jews
Tread the same track when she the prime renews;[8]
And once in twenty years, their scribes record,
By natural instinct they change their lord.
220 Achitophel still wants a chief, and none
Was found so fit as warlike Absolon:
Not that he wished his greatness to create
(For politicians neither love nor hate),
But for he knew his title not allowed,
225 Would keep him still depending on the crowd,
That kingly power, thus ebbing out, might be
Drawn to the dregs of a democracy.[9]
Him he attempts with studied arts to please,
And sheds his venom in such words as these.
230   "Auspicious Prince! at whose nativity
Some royal planet ruled the southern sky;
Thy longing country's darling and desire;

6. Chief justice of the Jewish supreme court.
7. David would have composed one psalm fewer because
he would be employed in writing praise of Achitophel.
8. A lunar cycle lasts about 20 years; Dryden alludes to
the constitutional crises of 1640, 1660, and 1680.
9. Like "commonwealth" and "state," a pejorative term
used to suggest a government of mob rule.

Their cloudy pillar, and their guardian fire:
Their second Moses, whose extended wand
235 Divides the seas and shows the promised land:[1]
Whose dawning day, in every distant age,
Has exercised the sacred prophet's rage:
The people's prayer, the glad diviners' theme,
The young men's vision, and the old men's dream!
240 Thee, savior, thee, the nation's vows confess,
And, never satisfied with seeing, bless:
Swift, unbespoken pomps° thy steps proclaim,   *unsought honors*
And stammering babes are taught to lisp thy name.
How long wilt thou the general joy detain,
245 Starve and defraud the people of thy reign?
Content ingloriously to pass thy days
Like one of virtue's fools that feeds on praise;
Till thy fresh glories, which now shine so bright,
Grow stale and tarnish with our daily sight.
250 Believe me, royal youth, thy fruit must be
Or° gathered ripe, or rot upon the tree.   *either*
Heav'n has to all allotted, soon or late,
Some lucky revolution of their fate:
Whose motions, if we watch and guide with skill
255 (For human good depends on human will),
Our Fortune rolls as from a smooth descent,
And from the first impression takes the bent:
But, if unseized, she glides away like wind,
And leaves repenting folly far behind.[2]
260 Now, now she meets you with a glorious prize,
And spreads her locks before her as she flies.
Had thus old David, from whose loins you spring,
Not dared, when Fortune called him, to be King,
At Gath[3] an exile he might still remain,
265 And heaven's anointing oil had been in vain.
Let his successful youth your hopes engage,
But shun the example of declining age:
Behold him setting in his western skies,
The shadows length'ning as the vapors rise.
270 He is not now as when on Jordan's sand
The joyful people thronged to see him land,
Cov'ring the beach, and black'ning all the strand:[4] ⎫
But, like the Prince of Angels[5] from his height,   ⎬
Comes tumbling downward with diminished light; ⎭
275 Betrayed by one poor plot to public scorn
(Our only blessing since his curst return),
Those heaps of people which one sheaf did bind,
Blown off and scattered by a puff of wind.

1. On the way to Canaan, God's "promised land," Moses
led the Israelites across the Red Sea and through the
desert; they followed a pillar of cloud by day and a pillar
of fire by night.
2. Fortune, represented as a woman with streaming hair,
needs to be grasped at the first opportunity.

3. Brussels, where Charles spent the last phase of his
exile.
4. Dryden refers to Charles's triumphant landing at
Dover in May of 1660.
5. Lucifer (light-bearer) rebelled against God and was
cast out from heaven.

What strength can he to your designs oppose,
280 Naked of friends, and round beset with foes?
If Pharaoh's doubtful succor he should use,[6]
A foreign aid would more incense the Jews:
Proud Egypt would dissembled friendship bring,
Foment the war, but not support the King:
285 Nor would the royal party e'er unite
With Pharaoh's arms t' assist the Jebusite;
Or if they should, their interest soon would break,
And with such odious aid make David weak.
All sorts of men by my successful arts,
290 Abhorring kings, estrange their altered hearts
From David's rule; and 'tis the general cry,
'Religion, Commonwealth, and Liberty.'[7]
If you, as champion of the public good,
Add to their arms a chief of royal blood,
295 What may not Israel hope, and what applause
Might such a general gain by such a cause?
Not barren praise alone, that gaudy flower,
Fair only to the sight, but solid power:
And nobler is a limited command,
300 Giv'n by the love of all your native land,
Than a successive° title, long and dark,   *inherited*
Drawn from the moldy rolls of Noah's ark."
     What cannot praise effect in mighty minds,
When flattery soothes, and when ambition blinds!
305 Desire of power, on earth a vicious weed,
Yet, sprung from high, is of celestial seed:
In God 'tis glory, and when men aspire,
'Tis but a spark too much of heavenly fire.
Th' ambitious youth, too covetous of fame,
310 Too full of angel's metal[8] in his frame,
Unwarily was led from virtue's ways,
Made drunk with honor, and debauched with praise.
Half loath, and half consenting to the ill
(For royal blood within him struggled still),
315 He thus replied: "And what pretense have I
To take up arms for public liberty?
My father governs with unquestioned right;
The faith's defender, and mankind's delight:
Good, gracious, just, observant of the laws;
320 And heav'n by wonders has espoused his cause.
Whom has he wronged in all his peaceful reign?
Who sues for justice to his throne in vain?
What millions has he pardoned[9] of his foes,
Whom just revenge did to his wrath expose!

---

6. I.e., if Charles should turn for assistance to Louis XIV, Catholic king of France.
7. A slogan of the Good Old Cause.
8. Dryden puns on "angel" (a coin as well as a supernatu-
ral being) and on "metal / mettle" ("spriteliness, courage"—Johnson's *Dictionary*).
9. By the Act of Oblivion of 1660.

325   Mild, easy, humble, studious of our good,
      Inclined to mercy, and averse from blood.
      If mildness ill with stubborn Israel suit,
      His crime is God's beloved attribute.
      What could he gain, his people to betray,
330   Or change his right for arbitrary sway?
      Let haughty Pharaoh curse, with such a reign,
      His fruitful Nile, and yoke a servile train.
      If David's rule Jerusalem displease,
      The dog star[1] heats their brains to this disease.
335   Why then should I, encouraging the bad,
      Turn rebel and run popularly mad?
      Were he a tyrant who, by lawless might,
      Oppressed the Jews and raised the Jebusite,
      Well might I mourn; but nature's holy bands
340   Would curb my spirits and restrain my hands:
      The people might assert their liberty,
      But what was right in them were crime in me.
      His favor leaves me nothing to require,
      Prevents my wishes, and outruns desire.
345   What more can I expect while David lives?
      All but his kingly diadem he gives;
      And that—" But there he paused; then sighing said,
      "Is justly destined for a worthier head.
      For when my father from his toils shall rest,
350   And late augment the number of the blest,
      His lawful issue shall the throne ascend,
      Or the collateral line[2] where that shall end.
      His brother, though oppressed with vulgar spite,[3]
      Yet dauntless and secure of native right,
355   Of every royal virtue stands possessed;
      Still dear to all the bravest and the best.
      His courage foes, his friends his truth proclaim;
      His loyalty the King, the world his fame.
      His mercy ev'n th' offending crowd will find,
360   For sure he comes of a forgiving kind.°   *family*
      Why should I then repine at Heaven's decree,
      Which gives me no pretense to royalty?
      Yet O that Fate, propitiously inclined,
      Had raised my birth, or had debased my mind;
365   To my large soul not all her treasure lent,
      And then betrayed it to a mean descent.
      I find, I find my mounting spirits bold,
      And David's part disdains my mother's mold.
      Why am I scanted by a niggard[4] birth?
370   My soul disclaims the kindred of her earth:
      And, made for empire, whispers me within,

---

1. Sirius, which presides over the madness-inducing "dog   3. The hostility of the common people.
days" of summer.   4. Stingy; i.e., Monmouth's illegitimacy prevents him
2. That which passed through Charles's brother, James.   from acquiring all he desires.

'Desire of greatness is a godlike sin.' "
   Him staggering so when Hell's dire agent found,[5]
While fainting Virtue scarce maintained her ground,
375 He pours fresh forces in, and thus replies:
   "Th' eternal God, supremely good and wise,
Imparts not these prodigious gifts in vain;
What wonders are reserved to bless your reign?
Against your will, your arguments have shown
380 Such virtue's only given to guide a throne.
Not that your father's mildness I condemn;
But manly force becomes the diadem.
'Tis true, he grants the people all they crave,
And more perhaps than subjects ought to have:
385 For lavish grants suppose° a monarch tame,   *suggest*
And more his goodness than his wit proclaim.
But when should people strive their bonds to break,
If not when kings are negligent or weak?
Let him give on till he can give no more,
390 The thrifty Sanhedrin[6] shall keep him poor:
And every shekel° which he can receive,   *coin*
Shall cost a limb of his prerogative.[7]
To ply him with new plots shall be my care,
Or plunge him deep in some expensive war;
395 Which when his treasure can no more supply,
He must with the remains of kingship buy.
His faithful friends our jealousies and fears
Call Jebusites, and Pharaoh's pensioners:
Whom, when our fury from his aid has torn,
400 He shall be naked left to public scorn.
The next successor,[8] whom I fear and hate,
My arts have made obnoxious to the state;
Turned all his virtues to his overthrow,
And gained our elders[9] to pronounce a foe.
405 His right, for sums of necessary gold,
Shall first be pawned, and afterwards be sold:
Till time shall ever-wanting David draw,
To pass your doubtful title into law:
If not, the people have a right supreme
410 To make their kings, for kings are made for them.
All empire is no more than power in trust,
Which, when resumed, can be no longer just.
Succession, for the general good designed,
In its own wrong a nation cannot bind:
415 If altering that the people can relieve,
Better one suffer than a nation grieve.
The Jews well know their power: ere Saul they chose,

5. The Miltonic inversion of syntax helps to link Achitophel's speech to the temptation of Eve by Satan in Book 9 of *Paradise Lost*.
6. The Jewish council; here the English Parliament.
7. Royal privileges (which Parliament sought to limit).
8. James, Duke of York.
9. Shaftesbury's supporters, who included members of both the gentry and the aristocracy.

God was their King, and God they durst depose.[1]
Urge now your piety, your filial name,
420   A father's right, and fear of future fame;
The public good, that universal call
To which even Heav'n submitted, answers all.
Nor let his love enchant your generous mind;
'Tis Nature's trick to propagate her kind.
425   Our fond begetters, who would never die,
Love but themselves in their posterity.
Or let his kindness by th' effects be tried,
Or let him lay his vain pretense aside.
God said he loved your father; could he bring
430   A better proof than to anoint him King?
It surely showed he loved the shepherd well,
Who gave so fair a flock as Israel.
Would David have you thought his darling son?
What means he then to alienate° the crown?   *give away*
435   The name of godly he may blush to bear:
'Tis after God's own heart to cheat his heir.
He to his brother gives supreme command;
To you a legacy of barren land,[2]
Perhaps th' old harp on which he thrums his lays,[3]
440   Or some dull Hebrew ballad in your praise.
Then the next heir, a prince severe and wise,
Already looks on you with jealous eyes;
Sees through the thin disguises of your arts,
And marks your progress in the people's hearts.
445   Though now his mighty soul its grief contains,
He meditates revenge who least complains;
And like a lion, slumbering in the way,
Or sleep dissembling, while he waits his prey,
His fearless foes within his distance draws,
450   Constrains his roaring, and contracts his paws;
Till at the last, his time for fury found,
He shoots with sudden vengeance from the ground:
The prostrate vulgar passes o'er and spares,
But with a lordly rage his hunters tears.
455   Your case no tame expedients will afford;
Resolve on death, or conquest by the sword,
Which for no less a stake than life you draw;
And self-defense is nature's eldest law.
Leave the warm people no considering time,
460   For then rebellion may be thought a crime.
Prevail° yourself of what occasion gives,   *avail*
But try your title while your father lives:
And that your arms may have a fair pretense,
Proclaim you take them in the King's defense,

1. The prophet Samuel warned the Israelites that in choosing a king they would displace their true king, God (1 Samuel 8).

2. In 1678 Charles had promoted James and in the following year banished Monmouth.
3. David was said to have composed the Psalms.

465 Whose sacred life each minute would expose
To plots from seeming friends and secret foes.
And who can sound the depth of David's soul?
Perhaps his fear his kindness may control.
He fears his brother, though he loves his son,
470 For plighted vows too late to be undone.
If so, by force he wishes to be gained,
Like women's lechery, to seem constrained:
Doubt not, but when he most affects the frown,
Commit a pleasing rape upon the crown.
475 Secure his person to secure your cause;
They who possess the prince, possess the laws."
        He said, and this advice above the rest,
With Absalom's mild nature suited best;
Unblamed of° life (ambition set aside),   *blameless in*
480 Not stained with cruelty, nor puffed with pride;
How happy had he been, if destiny
Had higher placed his birth, or not so high!
His kingly virtues might have claimed a throne,
And blessed all other countries but his own:
485 But charming greatness, since so few refuse,
'Tis juster to lament him than accuse.
Strong were his hopes a rival to remove,
With blandishments to gain the public love;
To head the faction while their zeal was hot,
490 And popularly prosecute the Plot.
To farther this, Achitophel unites
The malcontents of all the Israelites;
Whose differing parties he could wisely join,
For several ends, to serve the same design:
495 The best, and of the princes some were such,
Who thought the power of monarchy too much:
Mistaken men, and patriots in their hearts;
Not wicked, but seduced by impious arts.
By these the springs of property were bent,
500 And wound so high they cracked the government.
The next for interest sought t' embroil the state,
To sell their duty at a dearer rate;
And make their Jewish markets of the throne,
Pretending public good, to serve their own.
505 Others thought kings an useless heavy load,
Who cost too much, and did too little good.
These were for laying honest David by,
On principles of pure good husbandry.°   *economy*
With them joined all th' haranguers of the throng,
510 That thought to get preferment by the tongue.
Who follow next a double danger bring,
Not only hating David, but the King;
The Solymaean rout,⁴ well versed of old

---

4. Solymas was another name for Jerusalem, hence, "the London mob."

In godly faction, and in treason bold;
515   Cowering and quaking at a conqueror's sword,
But lofty° to a lawful prince restored;   *arrogant*
Saw with disdain an ethnic[5] plot begun,
And scorned by Jebusites to be outdone.
Hot Levites[6] headed these; who, pulled before
520   From th' ark, which in the judges' days they bore,[7]
Resumed their cant, and with a zealous cry
Pursued their old beloved theocracy:[8]
Where Sanhedrin and priest enslaved the nation,
And justified their spoils by inspiration;[9]
525   For who so fit for reign as Aaron's race,[1]
If once dominion they could found in grace?
These led the pack; though not of surest scent,
Yet deepest-mouthed against the government.
A numerous host of dreaming saints succeed;
530   Of the true old enthusiastic[2] breed:
'Gainst form and order they their power employ,
Nothing to build and all things to destroy.
But far more numerous was the herd of such
Who think too little, and who talk too much.
535   These out of mere instinct, they knew not why,
Adored their fathers' God and property:
And, by the same blind benefit of fate,
The Devil and the Jebusite did hate:
Born to be saved, even in their own despite,°   *despite themselves*
540   Because they could not help believing right.
Such were the tools, but a whole Hydra[3] more
Remains, of sprouting heads too long to score.
Some of their chiefs were princes of the land:
In the first rank of these did Zimri[4] stand:
545   A man so various, that he seemed to be
Not one, but all mankind's epitome.
Stiff in opinions, always in the wrong;
Was everything by starts, and nothing long:
But, in the course of one revolving moon,
550   Was chemist, fiddler, statesman, and buffoon:
Then all for women, painting, rhyming, drinking;
Besides ten thousand freaks° that died in thinking.   *whims*
Blest madman, who could every hour employ,
With something new to wish, or to enjoy!
555   Railing° and praising were his usual themes;   *criticizing*

5. Here, Catholic.
6. Dissenting clergymen.
7. The 1662 Act of Uniformity deprived Presbyterian clergy of their livings which they had acquired during the commonwealth (the judges' days, when they bore the ark).
8. I.e., sought to restore the commonwealth.
9. Members of dissenting sects sometimes claimed to be inspired directly by God.
1. Priests (who, in Jewish law, had to be descendants of Moses's brother Aaron).
2. A pejorative term, applied to those who claimed special inspiration.
3. Many-headed monster, who would sprout new heads every time one was cut off.
4. An Old Testament conspirator and regicide (1 Kings 16.9–20); here, George Villiers, Second Duke of Buckingham, a prominent Whig. He had satirized the playwright Dryden in *The Rehearsal* (1671).

And both (to show his judgment) in extremes:
So over-violent, or over-civil,
That every man, with him, was god or devil.
In squand'ring wealth was his peculiar art:
560   Nothing went unrewarded but desert.°   *true worth*
Beggared by fools, whom still he found° too late: *found out*
He had his jest, and they had his estate.
He laughed himself from court, then sought relief
By forming parties, but could ne'er be chief:
565   For, spite of him, the weight of business fell
On Absalom and wise Achitophel:
Thus, wicked but in will, of means bereft,
He left not faction, but of that was left.
     Titles and names 'twere tedious to rehearse
570   Of lords below the dignity of verse.
Wits, warriors, commonwealthsmen, were the best:
Kind husbands and mere nobles all the rest.
And therefore, in the name of dullness, be
The well-hung Balaam[5] and cold Caleb free.
575   And canting Nadab[6] let oblivion damn,
Who made new porridge for the paschal lamb.[7]
Let friendship's holy band some names assure:
Some their own worth, and some let scorn secure.
Nor shall the rascal rabble here have place,
580   Whom kings no titles gave, and God no grace:
Not bull-faced Jonas,[8] who could statutes draw
To mean rebellion, and make treason law.
But he, though bad, is followed by a worse,
The wretch who heaven's anointed dared to curse:
585   Shimei,[9] whose youth did early promise bring
Of zeal to God, and hatred to his King;
Did wisely from expensive sins refrain,
And never broke the Sabbath, but for gain:
Nor ever was he known an oath to vent,
590   Or curse, unless against the government.
Thus heaping wealth by the most ready way
Among the Jews, which was to cheat and pray;
The city, to reward his pious hate
Against his master, chose him magistrate:
595   His hand a vare° of justice did uphold;   *staff*
His neck was loaded with a chain of gold.

5. Balaam was a prophet who first resisted and then accepted God's will (Numbers 22–24); here, he probably represents Theophilus Hastings, Earl of Huntingdon, who initially supported Shaftesbury but was subsequently forgiven by Charles. *Well-hung:* Eloquent, or sexually impressive ("Lord Huntingdon," wrote one of the poem's early readers in a marginal inscription, "is said to have a swinging p——"). Caleb (a spy in Numbers 13) has been identified as either Lord Grey, whose wife was reputedly Monmouth's mistress, or Arthur Capel, an efficient administrator and ally of Shaftesbury.
6. The priest Nadab tries to institute improper rites of worship, and is slain by God (Leviticus 10); probably William, Lord Howard of Escrick, a dissenting preacher.
7. Howard was said to have celebrated communion (the commemoration of Christ's sacrifice as "paschal lamb") not with bread and wine but with ale and roasted apples—a concoction known as "lamb's wool." Dissenters such as Howard referred disparagingly to the Anglican Book of Common Prayer as "porridge."
8. Sir William Jones, attorney general and fierce prosecutor of alleged Popish plotters.
9. Shimei cursed David as he fled Absalom's rebellion. Here, he is Slingsby Bethel, one of London's sheriffs.

During his office, treason was no crime;
The sons of Belial[1] had a glorious time:
For Shimei, though not prodigal of pelf,[2]
600   Yet loved his wicked neighbor as himself:
When two or three were gathered to declaim[3] ⎱
Against the monarch of Jerusalem,   }
Shimei was always in the midst of them: ⎰
And, if they cursed the King when he was by,
605   Would rather curse than break good company.
If any durst his factious friends accuse,
He packed a jury of dissenting Jews,
Whose fellow-feeling in the godly cause
Would free the suff'ring saint from human laws.
610   For laws are only made to punish those
Who serve the King, and to protect his foes.
If any leisure time he had from power
(Because 'tis sin to misemploy an hour),
His business was, by writing, to persuade
615   That kings were useless, and a clog to trade:
And that his noble style he might refine,
No Rechabite[4] more shunned the fumes of wine.
Chaste were his cellars, and his shrieval board[5]
The grossness of a city feast abhorred:
620   His cooks, with long disuse, their trade forgot;
Cool was his kitchen, though his brains were hot.
Such frugal virtue malice may accuse,
But sure 'twas necessary to the Jews:
For towns once burnt[6] such magistrates require
625   As dare not tempt God's providence by fire.
With spiritual food he fed his servants well,
But free from flesh that made the Jews rebel:
And Moses's laws he held in more account,
For forty days of fasting in the mount.[7]
630   To speak the rest, who better are forgot,
Would tire a well-breathed witness of the Plot:
Yet, Corah,[8] thou shalt from oblivion pass;
Erect thyself, thou monumental brass,°   *shamelessness*
High as the serpent of thy metal made,[9]
635   While nations stand secure beneath thy shade.
What though his birth were base, yet comets rise
From earthy vapors ere they shine in skies.
Prodigious actions may as well be done
By weaver's issue,[1] as by prince's son.

---

1. Rebellious, debauched men.
2. Free with money.
3. The description of Shimei echoes two of Christ's pronouncements: "Thou shalt love thy neighbor as thyself" (Matthew 22.39); "When two or three are gathered together in my name, there am I in the midst of them" (Matthew 18.20).
4. Rechabites drank no wine.
5. Sheriff's hospitality.
6. A reference to the Fire of London (1666).

7. Shimei attempts to justify his frugality by citing the precedent of Moses, who fasted on Mount Sinai before receiving the Ten Commandments.
8. A rebellious Levite; here, Titus Oates, the ambitious informer who did more than anyone to arouse suspicions of a "Popish Plot."
9. Moses set up a brass serpent that saved the Jews from dying of snakebite (Numbers 21).
1. Oates's father was a weaver.

640   This arch-attestor for the public good
    By that one deed ennobles all his blood.
    Who ever asked the witnesses' high race,
    Whose oath with martyrdom did Stephen[2] grace?
    Ours was a Levite, and as times went then,
645   His tribe were God Almighty's gentlemen.
    Sunk were his eyes, his voice was harsh and loud,
    Sure signs he neither choleric° was, nor proud: *hot-tempered*
    His long chin proved his wit; his saintlike grace
    A church vermilion, and a Moses's face;[3]
650   His memory, miraculously great,
    Could plots, exceeding man's belief, repeat;
    Which therefore cannot be accounted lies,
    For human wit could never such devise.
    Some future truths are mingled in his book;
655   But where the witness failed, the prophet spoke:
    Some things like visionary flights appear;
    The spirit caught him up, the Lord knows where,
    And gave him his rabbinical degree
    Unknown to foreign university.[4]
660   His judgment yet his memory did excel;
    Which pieced his wondrous evidence so well,
    And suited to the temper of the times,
    Then groaning under Jebusitic crimes.
    Let Israel's foes suspect his heav'nly call,
665   And rashly judge his writ apocryphal;[5]
    Our laws for such affronts have forfeits made:
    He takes his life, who takes away his trade.
    Were I myself in witness Corah's place,
    The wretch who did me such a dire disgrace
670   Should whet my memory, though once forgot,
    To make him an appendix of my plot.
    His zeal to heav'n made him his prince despise,
    And load his person with indignities:
    But zeal peculiar privilege affords,
675   Indulging latitude to deeds and words;
    And Corah might for Agag's murder[6] call,
    In terms as coarse as Samuel used to Saul.
    What others in his evidence did join
    (The best that could be had for love or coin)
680   In Corah's own predicament will fall:
    For *witness* is a common name to all.
        Surrounded thus with friends of every sort,
    Deluded Absalom forsakes the court:
    Impatient of high hopes, urged with renown,

2. The first Christian martyr, sworn against and stoned by false witness (Acts 6–7).
3. After Moses received the tables of the law on Mount Sinai, his face shone with divine illumination; Oates's face, by contrast, is flushed with debauchery.
4. Oates pretended to hold a doctorate of divinity from the University of Salamanca.
5. Not part of the canon of biblical texts.
6. Oates denounced Lord Stafford, who was then executed, as Samuel denounced Agag, who was murdered by Saul (1 Samuel 15).

685 And fired with near possession of a crown:
Th' admiring crowd are dazzled with surprise,
And on his goodly person feed their eyes:
His joy concealed, he sets himself to show,
On each side bowing popularly low:
690 His looks, his gestures, and his words he frames,
And with familiar ease repeats their names.
Thus, formed by nature, furnished out with arts,
He glides unfelt into their secret hearts:
Then with a kind compassionating look,
695 And sighs bespeaking pity ere he spoke,
Few words he said, but easy those and fit:
More slow than Hybla° drops, and far more sweet.   honey
     "I mourn, my countrymen, your lost estate,
Though far unable to prevent your fate:
700 Behold a banished man, for your dear cause
Exposed a prey to arbitrary laws!
Yet O! that I alone could be undone,
Cut off from empire, and no more a son!
Now all your liberties a spoil are made, ⎫
705 Egypt and Tyrus° intercept your trade, ⎬   France and Holland
And Jebusites your sacred rites invade. ⎭
My father, whom with reverence yet I name,
Charmed into ease, is careless of his fame:
And bribed with petty sums of foreign gold,
710 Is grown in Bathsheba's[7] embraces old:
Exalts his enemies, his friends destroys,
And all his pow'r against himself employs.
He gives, and let him give, my right away:
But why should he his own, and yours betray?
715 He only, he can make the nation bleed,
And he alone from my revenge is freed.
Take then my tears" (with that he wiped his eyes)
" 'Tis all the aid my present power supplies:
No court informer can these arms accuse,
720 These arms may sons against their fathers use,
And 'tis my wish, the next successor's reign
May make no other Israelite complain."
     Youth, beauty, graceful action seldom fail:
But common interest always will prevail:
725 And pity never ceases to be shown
To him, who makes the people's wrongs his own.
The crowd (that still believe their kings oppress)
With lifted hands their young Messiah bless:
Who now begins his progress to ordain,[8]
730 With chariots, horsemen, and a numerous train:
From east to west his glories he displays:
And, like the sun, the promised land surveys.

7. Louise de Kéroualle, Duchess of Portsmouth, Charles's French, Catholic mistress.

8. Monmouth traveled through the west of England in 1680, rallying popular support.

Fame runs before him, as the morning star,
And shouts of joy salute him from afar:
735 Each house receives him as a guardian god,
And consecrates the place of his abode:
But hospitable treats did most commend
Wise Issachar,[9] his wealthy western friend.
This moving court, that caught the people's eyes,
740 And seemed but pomp, did other ends disguise:
Achitophel had formed it, with intent
To sound the depths, and fathom, where it went,
The people's hearts; distinguish friends from foes,
And try their strength before they came to blows:
745 Yet all was colored with a smooth pretense
Of specious love, and duty to their prince.
Religion, and redress of grievances,
Two names that always cheat and always please,
Are often urged, and good King David's life
750 Endangered by a brother and a wife.[1]
Thus, in a pageant show, a plot is made,
And peace itself is war in masquerade.
O foolish Israel! never warned by ill,
Still the same bait, and circumvented still!
755 Did ever men forsake their present ease,
In midst of health imagine a disease;
Take pains contingent mischiefs to foresee,
Make heirs for monarchs, and for God decree?
What shall we think! can people give away,
760 Both for themselves and sons, their native sway?
Then they are left defenseless to the sword
Of each unbounded, arbitrary lord:
And laws are vain, by which we right enjoy,
If kings unquestioned can those laws destroy.
765 Yet, if the crowd be judge of fit and just,
And kings are only officers in trust,
Then this resuming cov'nant was declared
When kings were made, or is forever barred:
If those who gave the scepter could not tie
770 By their own deed their own posterity,
How then could Adam bind his future race?
How could his forfeit on mankind take place?
Or how could heavenly justice damn us all,
Who ne'er consented to our father's fall?
775 Then kings are slaves to those whom they command,
And tenants to their people's pleasure stand.
Add, that the pow'r for property[2] allowed
Is mischievously seated in the crowd:
For who can be secure of private right,
780 If sovereign sway may be dissolved by might?
Nor is the people's judgment always true:

---

9. Thomas Thynne, a wealthy Whig.
1. Both James and Catherine were Catholic and were

thought by some to be implicated in Popish plotting.
2. Political influence derived from ownership of land.

The most may err as grossly as the few,
And faultless kings run down by common cry
For vice, oppression, and for tyranny.
785   What standard is there in a fickle rout,
Which, flowing to the mark,° runs faster out?   *high-water mark*
Nor only crowds, but Sanhedrins may be
Infected with this public lunacy,
And share the madness of rebellious times,
790   To murder monarchs for imagined crimes.
If they may give and take whene'er they please,
Not kings alone (the Godhead's images),
But government itself at length must fall
To nature's state, where all have right to all.
795   Yet, grant our lords the people kings can make,
What prudent men a settled throne would shake?
For whatsoe'er their sufferings were before,
That change they covet makes them suffer more.
All other errors but disturb a state,
800   But innovation is the blow of fate.
If ancient fabrics nod, and threat to fall,
To patch the flaws, and buttress up the wall,
Thus far 'tis duty; but here fix the mark:
For all beyond it is to touch our ark.³
805   To change foundations, cast the frame anew,
Is work for rebels who base ends pursue,
At once divine and human laws control,
And mend the parts by ruin of the whole.
The tampering world is subject to this curse,
810   To physic their disease into a worse.
      Now what relief can righteous David bring?
How fatal 'tis to be too good a king!
Friends he has few, so high the madness grows;
Who dare be such, must be the people's foes:
815   Yet some there were, ev'n in the worst of days;
Some let me name, and naming is to praise.
      In this short file Barzillai⁴ first appears;
Barzillai crowned with honor and with years:
Long since, the rising rebels he withstood
820   In regions waste, beyond the Jordan's flood:⁵
Unfortunately brave to buoy the state,
But sinking underneath his master's fate:
In exile with his godlike prince he mourned;
For him he suffered, and with him returned.
825   The court he practiced, not the courtier's art:
Large was his wealth, but larger was his heart:
Which well the noblest objects knew to choose,
The fighting warrior, and recording Muse.⁶
His bed could once a fruitful issue boast:

---

3. To touch the ark was to commit sacrilege.
4. James Butler, Duke of Ormonde, loyal to Charles I and II.

5. I.e., in Ireland.
6. I.e., he gave money to support the Stuart cause and was also a patron to authors.

830   Now more than half a father's name is lost:
     His eldest hope,[7] with every grace adorned,
     By me (so Heaven will have it) always mourned,
     And always honored, snatched in manhood's prime
     By unequal Fates, and Providence's crime:
835   Yet not before the goal of honor won, ⎫
     All parts fulfilled of subject and of son; ⎬
     Swift was the race, but short the time to run. ⎭
     Oh narrow circle, but of pow'r divine,
     Scanted in space, but perfect in thy line!
840   By sea, by land, thy matchless worth was known;
     Arms thy delight, and war was all thy own:
     Thy force, infused, the fainting Tyrians[8] propped:
     And haughty Pharaoh found his fortune stopped.
     O ancient honor, O unconquered hand,
845   Whom foes unpunished never could withstand!
     But Israel was unworthy of thy name;
     Short is the date of all immoderate fame.
     It looks as Heaven our ruin had designed,
     And durst not trust thy fortune and thy mind.
850   Now, free from earth, thy disencumbered soul
     Mounts up, and leaves behind the clouds and starry pole:
     From thence thy kindred legions mayst thou bring,
     To aid the guardian angel of thy King.
     Here stop, my Muse, here cease thy painful flight;
855   No pinions° can pursue immortal height: *wings*
     Tell good Barzillai thou canst sing no more,
     And tell thy soul she should have fled before;
     Or fled she with his life, and left this verse
     To hang on her departed patron's hearse?
860   Now take thy steepy flight from heaven, and see
     If thou canst find on earth another *he*;
     Another *he* would be too hard to find,
     See then whom thou canst see not far behind:
     Zadock[9] the priest, whom, shunning power and place,
865   His lowly mind advanced to David's grace:
     With him the Sagan[1] of Jerusalem,
     Of hospitable soul and noble stem;
     Him of the western dome,[2] whose weighty sense
     Flows in fit words and heavenly eloquence.
870   The prophets' sons[3] by such example led,
     To learning and to loyalty were bred:
     For colleges on bounteous kings depend,
     And never rebel was to arts a friend.
     To these succeed the pillars of the laws,
875   Who best could plead and best can judge a cause.
     Next them a train of loyal peers ascend:

---

7. Ormonde's eldest son, who died in 1680.
8. The Dutch, whom Ormonde's son had aided against the French.
9. William Sancroft, Archbishop of Canterbury.

1. Henry Compton, Bishop of London.
2. John Dolben, Dean of Westminster ("the western dome").
3. Students of the Westminster School.

Sharp-judging Adriel,[4] the Muses' friend,
Himself a Muse—in Sanhedrin's debate
True to his prince, but not a slave of state:
880 Whom David's love with honors did adorn,
That from his disobedient son were torn.[5]
Jotham[6] of piercing wit and pregnant thought,
Indued° by nature, and by learning taught   *endowed*
To move assemblies, who but only tried
885 The worse awhile, then chose the better side;
Nor chose alone, but turned the balance too;
So much the weight of one brave man can do.
Hushai,[7] the friend of David in distress,
In public storms of manly steadfastness;
890 By foreign treaties he informed his youth,
And joined experience to his native truth.
His frugal care supplied the wanting throne,
Frugal for that, but bounteous of his own:
'Tis easy conduct when exchequers[8] flow,
895 But hard the task to manage well the low:
For sovereign power is too depressed or high,
When kings are forced to sell, or crowds to buy.
Indulge one labor more, my weary Muse,
For Amiel,[9] who can Amiel's praise refuse?
900 Of ancient race by birth, but nobler yet
In his own worth, and without title great:
The Sanhedrin long time as chief he ruled,
Their reason guided and their passion cooled;
So dexterous was he in the crown's defense,
905 So formed to speak a loyal nation's sense,
That, as their band was Israel's tribes in small,
So fit was he to represent them all.
Now rasher charioteers the seat ascend,
Whose loose careers his steady skill commend:
910 They like th' unequal ruler of the day,[1]
Misguide the seasons and mistake the way;
While he, withdrawn, at their mad labor smiles,
And safe enjoys the sabbath of his toils.
      These were the chief, a small but faithful band ⎫
915 Of worthies, in the breach who dared to stand,   ⎬
And tempt th' united fury of the land.   ⎭
With grief they viewed such powerful engines bent,
To batter down the lawful government:
A numerous faction with pretended frights,
920 In Sanhedrins to plume° the regal rights: *pluck away*

4. John Sheffield, Earl of Mulgrave, poet and a patron of Dryden.
5. In 1679 Mulgrave received two offices that had previously belonged to Monmouth.
6. George Savile, Marquis of Halifax, formerly a critic but now a supporter of Charles's policies, was instrumental in defeating the exclusion bill.
7. Laurence Hyde, Earl of Rochester, negotiated several European treaties and became the first Lord of the Treasury.
8. Treasurers/treasuries.
9. Edward Seymour, Speaker of the Commons (1673–1678) and Treasurer of the Navy (1673–1681); opponent of exclusion.
1. Phaëthon, who drove (with disastrous results) the chariot of the sun that belonged to his father, Apollo.

The true successor from the court removed:[2]
The Plot by hireling witnesses improved.
These ills they saw, and as their duty bound,
They showed the King the danger of the wound:
925 That no concessions from the throne would please,
But lenitives fomented[3] the disease:
That Absalom, ambitious of the crown,
Was made the lure to draw the people down:
That false Achitophel's pernicious hate
930 Had turned the Plot to ruin Church and State:
The council violent, the rabble worse:
That Shimei taught Jerusalem to curse.
  With all these loads of injuries oppressed,
And long revolving, in his careful breast,
935 Th' event of things, at last, his patience tired,
Thus from his royal throne by Heav'n inspired,
The godlike David spoke: with awful fear
His train their Maker in their master hear.
  "Thus long have I, by native mercy swayed,
940 My wrongs dissembled, my revenge delayed:
So willing to forgive th' offending age,
So much the father did the king assuage.
But now so far my clemency they slight,
Th' offenders question my forgiving right.
945 That one was made for many, they contend:
But 'tis to rule, for that's a monarch's end.
They call my tenderness of blood my fear:
Though manly tempers can the longest bear.
Yet, since they will divert my native course,
950 'Tis time to show I am not good by force.
Those heaped affronts that haughty subjects bring,
Are burdens for a camel, not a king:
Kings are the public pillars of the state,
Born to sustain and prop the nation's weight:
955 If my young Samson[4] will pretend a call
To shake the column, let him share the fall:
But O that yet he would repent and live!
How easy 'tis for parents to forgive!
With how few tears a pardon might be won
960 From Nature, pleading for a darling son!
Poor pitied youth, by my paternal care
Raised up to all the height his frame could bear:
Had God ordained his fate for empire born,
He would have given his soul another turn:
965 Gulled with a patriot's name, whose modern sense
Is one that would by law supplant his prince:
The people's brave,° the politicians' tool;   *bully*

---

2. In 1679, at the height of the furor over the Popish Plot, Charles II had ordered his brother to withdraw to the Continent, where James remained for six months.
3. I.e., soothing measures/medicines only encouraged the disease.
4. Monmouth, who threatens, Samson-like, to bring down the nation.

Never was patriot yet, but was a fool.
Whence comes it that religion and the laws
970 Should more be Absalom's than David's cause?
His old instructor,[5] ere he lost his place,
Was never thought indued with so much grace.
Good heavens, how faction can a patriot paint!
My rebel ever proves my people's saint:
975 Would they impose an heir upon the throne?
Let Sanhedrins be taught to give their own.
A king's at least a part of government,
And mine as requisite as their consent:
Without my leave a future king to choose,
980 Infers a right the present to depose:
True, they petition me t' approve their choice,
But Esau's hands suit ill with Jacob's voice.[6]
My pious subjects for my safety pray,
Which to secure they take my power away.
985 From plots and treasons Heaven preserve my years,
But save me most from my petitioners.
Unsatiate as the barren womb or grave;
God cannot grant so much as they can crave.
What then is left but with a jealous eye
990 To guard the small remains of royalty?
The law shall still direct my peaceful sway,
And the same law teach rebels to obey:
Votes shall no more established pow'r control,
Such votes as make a part exceed the whole:
995 No groundless clamors shall my friends remove,
Nor crowds have power to punish ere they prove:
For gods, and godlike kings, their care express,
Still to defend their servants in distress.
O that my power to saving were confined: ⎫
1000 Why am I forced, like Heaven, against my mind, ⎬
To make examples of another kind? ⎭
Must I at length the sword of justice draw?
O cursed effects of necessary law!
How ill my fear they by my mercy scan;[7]
1005 Beware the fury of a patient man.
Law they require, let law then show her face;
They could not be content to look on Grace,
Her hinder parts, but with a daring eye
To tempt the terror of her front, and die.
1010 By their own arts, 'tis righteously decreed,
Those dire artificers of death shall bleed.
Against themselves their witnesses will swear,
Till viper-like their mother Plot they tear:

---

5. Achitophel/Shaftesbury.
6. In Genesis 27, Esau is a hunter and a "hairy man"; his younger brother Jacob steals his birthright by impersonating him before their blind father Isaac, covering his own smooth hands with rough goatskin. David/Charles here

accuses his opposition of Esau-like violence and Jacob-like deception.
7. How wrong ("ill") they are to see ("scan") fear in my mercy.

And suck for nutriment that bloody gore
1015   Which was their principle of life before.
Their Belial with their Belzebub[8] will fight;
Thus on my foes, my foes shall do me right:
Nor doubt th' event: for factious crowds engage,
In their first onset, all their brutal rage;
1020   Then let 'em take an unresisted course,
Retire and traverse, and delude their force:
But when they stand all breathless, urge the fight,
And rise upon 'em with redoubled might:
For lawful pow'r is still superior found,
1025   When long driven back, at length it stands the ground."
He said. Th' Almighty, nodding, gave consent;
And peals of thunder shook the firmament.
Henceforth a series of new time began,
The mighty years in long procession ran:
1030   Once more the godlike David was restored,
And willing nations knew their lawful lord.

1681   1681

COMPANION READING

Charles II: His Majesty's Declaration to all His Loving Subjects, Touching the Causes and Reasons that Moved Him to Dissolve the Two Last Parliaments[1]

It was with exceeding great trouble that We were brought to the dissolving of the two last Parliaments, without more benefit to Our people by the calling of them. But having done Our part in giving so many opportunities of providing for their good, it cannot be justly imputed to Us that the success hath not answered Our expectation.

We cannot at this time but take notice of the particular causes of Our dissatisfaction, which at the beginning of the last Parliament we did recommend to their care to avoid, and expected We should have no new cause to remember them.

We opened the last Parliament, which was held at Westminster, with as gracious expressions of Our readiness to satisfy the desires of Our good subjects and to secure them against all their just fears, as the weighty consideration, either of preserving the established religion, and the liberty and property of Our subjects at home, or of supporting Our neighbors and allies abroad, could fill Our heart with, or possibly require from Us.

---

8. Both devils.

1. In the wake of the Popish Plot, the Whigs tried repeatedly to pass an exclusion bill barring the Catholic Duke of York from succeeding to the throne. In response, the increasingly exasperated Charles dissolved the Parliament twice in quick succession: On 18 January 1681, he dismissed the Commons at Westminster and called for a new Parliament at Oxford; on 28 March he abruptly dissolved this second Parliament after only seven days of bitterly contentious sessions. By his peremptory actions, the King had laid himself open to charges of arbitrary and despotic rule. In His Majesty's Declaration, Charles tried to lay these charges to rest. Recent votes in the House of Commons, he argued, had so encroached upon the King's prerogatives and the country's laws as to endanger the stability of the Restoration and revive the possibility of civil war; throughout the pamphlet, Charles plays adroitly on his audience's memories of midcentury strife. Read aloud from pulpits throughout the land, this unusually direct statement by the monarch to his subjects made a considerable impression—though not so conclusive an impact as Dryden was willing to imagine in the closing lines of Absalom and Achitophel, where the king of Israel's arguments occasionally echo Charles's Declaration.

And We do solemnly declare that We did intend, as far as would have consisted with the very being of the government, to have complied with anything that could have been proposed to Us to accomplish those ends.

We asked of them the supporting the alliances We had made for the preservation of the general peace in Christendom;[2] We recommended to them the further examination of the Plot;[3] We desired their advice and assistance concerning the preservation of Tangier;[4] We offered to concur in any remedies that could be proposed for the security of the Protestant religion, that might consist with preserving the succession of the Crown in its due and legal course of descent; to all which We met with most unsuitable returns from the House of Commons: addresses, in the nature of remonstrances, rather than of answers; arbitrary orders for taking Our subjects into custody, for matters that had no relation to privileges of Parliament; strange illegal votes, declaring diverse eminent persons to be enemies to the King and Kingdom, without any order or process of law, any hearing of their defense, or any proof so much as offered against them.[5] * * *

[The Parliamentary] Votes, instead of giving Us assistance to support our allies, or enable Us to preserve Tangier, tended rather to disable Us from contributing towards either, by Our own revenue or credit; not only exposing Us to all dangers that might happen either at home, or abroad, but endeavoring to deprive Us of the possibility of supporting the government itself, and to reduce Us to a more helpless condition than the meanest of Our subjects. * * *

These were some of the unwarrantable proceedings of the House of Commons, which were the occasion of Our parting with that Parliament.

Which We had no sooner dissolved, but We caused another to be forthwith assembled at Oxford; at the opening of which, We thought it necessary to give them warning of the errors of the former, in hopes to have prevented the like miscarriages; and We required of them to make the laws of the land their rule, as We did, and do, resolve they shall be Ours. We further added, that what We had formerly and so often declared concerning the succession, We could not depart from. But, to remove all reasonable fears that might arise from the possibility of a Popish successor's coming to the Crown, if means could be found that in such a case the administration of the government might remain in Protestant hands, We were ready to hearken to any expedient by which the religion established might be preserved, and the Monarchy not destroyed.

But contrary to Our offers and expectation, We saw that no expedient would be entertained but that of a total Exclusion, which, We had so often declared, was a point that, in Our own royal judgment, so nearly concerned Us both in honor, justice, and conscience, that We could never consent to it. In short, We cannot, after the sad experience We have had of the late Civil Wars, that murdered Our father of blessed memory and ruined the Monarchy, consent to a law that shall establish another most unnatural war, or at least make it necessary to maintain a standing force for the preserving the government and the peace of the Kingdom.

And We have reason to believe, by what passed in the last Parliament at Westminster, that if We could have been brought to give Our consent to a Bill of Exclusion, the intent was not to rest there, but to pass further, and to attempt some other great and important changes even in present. * * *

---

2. Charles had begun to cultivate—and to boast about—a defensive alliance with Spain against France.
3. At the first of the two Parliaments, Charles had consented to the execution of the one of the accused Popish "conspirators."

4. This seaport on the Straits of Gibraltar, claimed by the English, was now under attack by the Moors.
5. At the first of the two Parliaments, the Whigs had demanded the expulsion of several "eminent persons" who had worked successfully to defeat an exclusion bill.

But, notwithstanding all this, let not the restless malice of ill men who are laboring to poison Our people, some out of fondness of their old beloved Commonwealth principles, and some out of anger at their being disappointed in the particular designs they had for the accomplishment of their own ambition and greatness, persuade any of Our good subjects that We intend to lay aside the use of Parliaments. For We do still declare that no irregularities in Parliaments shall ever make Us out of love with Parliaments, which We look upon as the best method for healing the distempers of the Kingdom, and the only means to preserve the Monarchy in that due credit and respect which it ought to have both at home and abroad.

And for this cause We are resolved, by the blessing of God, to have frequent Parliaments, and, both in and out of Parliament, to use Our utmost endeavors to extirpate Popery, and to redress all the grievances of Our good subjects, and in all things to govern according to the laws of the Kingdom.

And We hope that a little time will so far open the eyes of all Our good subjects, that Our next meeting in Parliament shall perfect all that settlement and peace which shall be found wanting either in Church or State.

To which, as We shall contribute Our utmost endeavors, so We assure Ourself that We shall be assisted therein by the loyalty and good affections of all those who consider the rise and progress of the late troubles and confusions, and desire to preserve their country from a relapse.

And who cannot but remember that Religion, Liberty, and Property were all lost and gone when the Monarchy was shaken off, and could never be revived till that was restored.

Given at Our Court at Whitehall, the eighth day of April 1681.

MAC FLECKNOE   In *Mac Flecknoe*, Dryden put on display a literary culture dangerously debased. The poem's title ("Son of Flecknoe") announces a royal succession in the kingdom of bad writing. A literary "father," the priest and minor poet Richard Flecknoe (c. 1605–c. 1677), anoints as his true heir Thomas Shadwell (1640–1692), a playwright whom Dryden loathed as a tiresome controversialist and an ardent (worse, successful) rival for public favor and aristocratic patronage. Dryden wages his attack in an idiom at once elevated and scandalous, in language whose allegiance alternates (even within a single line) between epic poetry and the privy. Like much libelous and bawdy verse, Dryden's demolitionary masterpiece circulated in manuscript for several years; it was eventually printed in a pirated edition (1682) by a publisher seeking to capitalize on the recent success of *Absalom and Achitophel*. Like that poem, *Mac Flecknoe* plays upon the question of monarchic succession, but stages it in such a way as to implicate bad politics in bad taste. Dryden maps a City of London where foul writing chokes the streets, and dim-witted citizens get—and applaud—the poet-monarchs they deserve.

Mac Flecknoe

All human things are subject to decay,
And, when Fate summons, monarchs must obey.
This Flecknoe found, who, like Augustus, young
Was called to empire,[1] and had governed long:
In prose and verse was owned, without dispute,
Through all the realms of Nonsense, absolute.

1. Augustus became the first Roman emperor at the age of 32.

This aged prince, now flourishing in peace,
And blest with issue of a large increase,
Worn out with business, did at length debate
10   To settle the succession of the state:
And, pondering which of all his sons was fit
To reign, and wage immortal war with wit,
Cried, " 'Tis resolved; for Nature pleads that he
Should only rule, who most resembles me:
15   Sh—— alone my perfect image bears,
Mature in dullness from his tender years.
Sh—— alone, of all my sons, is he
Who stands confirmed in full stupidity.
The rest to some faint meaning make pretense,
20   But Sh—— never deviates into sense.
Some beams of wit on other souls may fall,
Strike through and make a lucid interval,
But Sh——'s genuine night admits no ray,
His rising fogs prevail upon the day.
25   Besides, his goodly fabric° fills the eye,   *large body*
And seems designed for thoughtless majesty:
Thoughtless as monarch oaks that shade the plain,
And, spread in solemn state, supinely reign.
Heywood and Shirley were but types of thee,[2]
30   Thou last great prophet of tautology:
Even I, a dunce of more renown than they,
Was sent before but to prepare thy way;
And coarsely clad in Norwich drugget[3] came
To teach the nations in thy greater name.[4]
35   My warbling lute, the lute I whilom° strung   *once*
When to King John of Portugal I sung,[5]
Was but the prelude to that glorious day
When thou on silver Thames didst cut thy way,
With well-timed oars before the royal barge,
40   Swelled with the pride of thy celestial charge;
And big with hymn, commander of an host,
The like was ne'er in Epsom blankets tossed.[6]
Methinks I see the new Arion[7] sail,
The lute still trembling underneath thy nail.
45   At thy well-sharpened thumb from shore to shore
The treble squeaks for fear, the basses roar:
Echoes from Pissing Alley[8] "Sh————" call,
And "Sh————" they resound from A———— Hall.[9]

2. Thomas Heywood and James Shirley, popular and prolific playwrights from the first half of the 17th century.
As "types," they foreshadow or prepare for Shadwell, just
as Old Testament figures such as Moses or Isaac were
interpreted in Christian theology as forerunners of Jesus.
3. Woolen cloth; Shadwell came from Norwich.
4. Here, Flecknoe is John the Baptist ("coarsely clad" in
camel's hair) to Shadwell's Jesus.
5. Flecknoe claimed that, during his travels in Europe,
he had been summoned to perform before the king of
Portugal.
6. A glance at two of Shadwell's plays: *Epsom Wells* and
The Virtuoso, in which Sir Samuel Hearty is tossed in a
blanket; tossing in blankets was also a means of inducing
childbirth.
7. Greek musician-poet rescued from drowning by music-
loving dolphins.
8. West of Temple Bar, it led from the Strand down to
the Thames.
9. Unidentified.

About thy boat the little fishes throng,
50 As at the morning toast° that floats along.   *sewage*
Sometimes as prince of thy harmonious band
Thou wield'st thy papers in thy threshing hand.
St. André's feet[1] ne'er kept more equal time,
Not ev'n the feet of thy own *Psyche*'s rhyme,
55 Though they in number as in sense excel;
So just, so like tautology they fell,
That, pale with envy, Singleton foreswore ⎫
The lute and sword which he in triumph bore, ⎬
And vowed he ne'er would act Villerius[2] more. ⎭
60 Here stopped the good old sire, and wept for joy
In silent raptures of the hopeful boy.
All arguments, but most his plays, persuade,
That for anointed dullness he was made.
        Close to the walls which fair Augusta bind[3]
65 (The fair Augusta much to fears inclined[4]),
An ancient fabric,[5] raised t' inform the sight,
There stood of yore, and Barbican it hight:[6]
A watchtower once, but now, so Fate ordains,
Of all the pile an empty name remains.
70 From its old ruins brothel-houses rise,
Scenes of lewd loves and of polluted joys;
Where their vast courts the mother-strumpets keep
And, undisturbed by watch,° in silence sleep.[7]   *police*
Near these a nursery[8] erects its head,
75 Where queens[9] are formed and future heroes bred;
Where unfledged actors learn to laugh and cry,
Where infant punks° their tender voices try,   *prostitutes*
And little Maximins[1] the gods defy.
Great Fletcher never treads in buskins here,
80 Nor greater Jonson dares in socks appear.[2]
But gentle Simkin[3] just reception finds
Amid this monument of vanished minds:
Pure clinches° the suburbian Muse[4] affords,   *puns*
And Panton[5] waging harmless war with words.
85 Here Flecknoe, as a place to fame well known,
Ambitiously designed his Sh———'s throne.

1. St. André, a French dancer who choreographed the opera *Psyche* (1675), for which Shadwell wrote the libretto.
2. John Singleton, one of the king's musicians; Villerius, a character in William Davenant's opera, *The Siege of Rhodes*.
3. The old wall of the City of London (Augusta).
4. Fears aroused by the Popish Plot.
5. Structure.
6. Was named; the Barbican, a medieval gatehouse, gave its name to a disreputable district of gaming and prostitution; adjoining it was Grub Street, the center of hack journalism.
7. Parodying Abraham Cowley, *Davideis* (1656), "Where their vast court the mother-waters keep, / And undisturbed by moons in silence sleep."

8. A training theater for the two main playhouses.
9. Dryden puns on queen (stage-monarch)/quean (prostitute). During the Restoration, actresses were often thought to moonlight as sexual companions.
1. Maximin is the fulminating protagonist of Dryden's *Tyrannic Love*.
2. John Fletcher and Ben Jonson, major playwrights of the previous generations. The buskin is the symbol of tragedy (Fletcher's forte) and the sock of comedy (Jonson's). Shadwell promoted himself as Jonson's successor in the tradition of "humors" comedy.
3. A clownish character in a series of popular farces.
4. I.e., the muse presiding over the disreputable area outside the City walls.
5. Another farce character.

For ancient Dekker[6] prophesied long since, ⎫
That in this pile should reign a mighty prince, ⎬
Born for a scourge of wit, and flail of sense: ⎭
90   To whom true dullness should some *Psyches* owe,
But Worlds of *Misers* from his pen should flow;
Humorists and *Hypocrites*[7] it should produce,
Whole Raymond families, and tribes of Bruce.
     Now Empress Fame had published the renown
95   Of Sh———'s coronation through the town.
Roused by report of Fame, the nations meet,
From near Bunhill, and distant Watling Street.[8]
No Persian carpets spread th' imperial way,
But scattered limbs of mangled poets lay:
100 From dusty shops neglected authors come,
Martyrs of pies, and relics of the bum.[9]
Much Heywood, Shirley, Ogilby[1] there lay,
But loads of Sh——— almost choked the way.
Bilked stationers for yeomen stood prepared,
105 And H———[2] was captain of the guard.
The hoary prince in majesty appeared,
High on a throne of his own labors reared.
At his right hand our young Ascanius[3] sate,
Rome's other hope, and pillar of the state.
110 His brows thick fogs, instead of glories, grace,
And lambent° dullness played around his face.   *glowing*
As Hannibal did to the altars come,
Sworn by his sire a mortal foe to Rome,[4]
So Sh——— swore, nor should his vow be vain,
115 That he till death true dullness would maintain;
And in his father's right, and realm's defense,
Ne'er to have peace with wit, nor truce with sense.
The king himself the sacred unction[5] made,
As king by office, and as priest by trade:
120 In his sinister° hand, instead of ball,   *left*
He placed a mighty mug of potent ale;
Love's Kingdom[6] to his right he did convey,
At once his scepter and his rule of sway,[7]
Whose righteous lore the prince had practiced young,
125 And from whose loins[8] recorded Psyche sprung.

6. Thomas Dekker (1570?–1632), prolific dramatist whose plays focused on London life.
7. Shadwell was the author of *The Miser* (1672), *The Humorists* (1671), and *The Hypocrite* (1669). Raymond and Bruce appear in *The Humorists* and *The Virtuoso*, respectively.
8. Fame draws her crowd both from cemeteries (like Bunhill Fields) and from mercantile districts (like Watling Street); thus, these devotees of Shadwell include both the dead and the living.
9. Unsold books might be recycled as pie wrappers or as toilet paper; the bones of martyrs were often venerated as relics.
1. John Ogilby, printer, cartographer, and translator (like Dryden) of Virgil.
2. Henry Herringman, a prominent bookseller-publisher; he had published both Shadwell and Dryden.
3. The son of Aeneas, marked for greatness by a heaven-sent flame about his head.
4. According to Livy, Hannibal's father made the young boy swear himself Rome's enemy.
5. The oil with which the king was anointed during the coronation ceremony.
6. A play by Flecknoe.
7. Dryden parodies the rituals and props of the coronation ceremony.
8. Pronounced "lines" (a fact that permits Dryden a significant pun).

His temples last with poppies[9] were o'erspread,
That nodding seemed to consecrate his head:
Just at that point of time, if Fame not lie,
On his left hand twelve reverend owls[1] did fly.
130   So Romulus,[2] 'tis sung, by Tiber's brook,
Presage of sway from twice six vultures took.
Th' admiring throng loud acclamations make,
And omens of his future empire take.
The sire then shook the honors[3] of his head,
135   And from his brows damps of oblivion shed
Full on the filial dullness: long he stood, ⎫
Repelling from his breast the raging God; ⎬
At length burst out in this prophetic mood: ⎭
        "Heavens bless my son, from Ireland let him reign
140   To far Barbados on the western main;[4]
Of his dominion may no end be known,
And greater than his father's be his throne.
Beyond *Love's Kingdom* let him stretch his pen!"
He paused, and all the people cried, "Amen."
145   "Then thus," continued he, "my son, advance
Still in new impudence, new ignorance.
Success let others teach, learn thou from me
Pangs without birth, and fruitless industry.
Let *Virtuosos* in five years be writ,
150   Yet not one thought accuse thy toil of wit.
Let gentle George[5] in triumph tread the stage,
Make Dorimant betray, and Loveit rage;
Let Cully, Cockwood, Fopling charm the pit,
And in their folly show the writer's wit.
155   Yet still thy fools shall stand in thy defense,
And justify° their author's want of sense.   prove
Let 'em be all by thy own model made
Of dullness, and desire no foreign aid:
That they to future ages may be known,
160   Not copies drawn, but issue[6] of thy own.
Nay let thy men of wit too be the same,
All full of thee, and differing but in name;
But let no alien S—dl—y[7] interpose
To lard with wit thy hungry *Epsom* prose.
165   And when false flowers of rhetoric thou would'st cull,
Trust nature, do not labor to be dull;
But write thy best, and top; and in each line,
Sir Formal's[8] oratory will be thine.
Sir Formal, though unsought, attends thy quill,

9. Symbolizing sleep.
1. Symbols of ignorance and darkness (because nocturnal).
2. Cofounder of Rome (through which the Tiber runs).
3. Ornaments, and by extension, hair—a Virgilian expression.
4. His kingdom will be the Atlantic Ocean.
5. Sir George Etherege, comic playwright; characters

from his plays follow.
6. A pun: both progeny and printing.
7. Sir Charles Sedley, courtier, poet, and intimate of Dryden's circle; he wrote a prologue for *Epsom Wells*.
8. Sir Formal Trifle, a character in Shadwell's *The Virtuoso*, described by Shadwell as "the Orator, a florid coxcomb."

170 And does thy northern dedications⁹ fill.
     Nor let false friends seduce thy mind to fame,
     By arrogating Jonson's hostile name.
     Let father Flecknoe fire thy mind with praise,
     And uncle Ogilby thy envy raise.
175 Thou art my blood, where Jonson has no part;
     What share have we in nature or in art?
     Where did his wit on learning fix a brand,
     And rail at arts he did not understand?
     Where made he love in Prince Nicander's¹ vein,
180 Or swept the dust in *Psyche*'s humble strain?
     Where sold he bargains,² "whip-stitch, kiss my arse,"
     Promised a play and dwindled to a farce?
     When did his Muse from Fletcher scenes purloin,
     As thou whole Eth'rege dost transfuse to thine?
185 But so transfused as oil on waters flow,
     His always floats above, thine sinks below.
     This is thy province, this thy wondrous way,
     New humors to invent for each new play:³
     This is that boasted bias of thy mind,
190 By which one way, to dullness, 'tis inclined;
     Which makes thy writings lean on one side still,
     And in all changes that way bends thy will.
     Nor let thy mountain belly make pretense
     Of likeness; thine's a tympany⁴ of sense.
195 A tun of man in thy large bulk is writ,
     But sure thou'rt but a kilderkin⁵ of wit.
     Like mine thy gentle numbers feebly creep;
     Thy tragic Muse gives smiles, thy comic sleep.
     With whate'er gall thou sett'st thyself to write,
200 Thy inoffensive satires never bite.
     In thy felonious heart, though venom lies,
     It does but touch thy Irish⁶ pen, and dies.
     Thy genius calls thee not to purchase fame
     In keen iambics,⁷ but mild anagram:
205 Leave writing plays, and choose for thy command
     Some peaceful province in acrostic land.
     There thou may'st wings display and altars⁸ raise,
     And torture one poor word ten thousand ways.
     Or if thou would'st thy diff'rent talents suit,
210 Set thy own songs, and sing them to thy lute."

9. Both Flecknoe and Shadwell dedicated several of their works to the Duke and Duchess of Newcastle (a town in the north of England).
1. A character in *Psyche*.
2. "To sell bargains" is to respond to an innocent question with a coarse phrase, as in this line. Dryden sharpens the insult by quoting the slangy nonsense phrase "whip-stitch" from Shadwell's own play, *The Virtuoso*.
3. I.e., by these contemptible means, you purport to outdo Ben Jonson.
4. A swelling of the abdomen, caused by air or gas.

5. A tun was a large cask of wine; a kilderkin a quarter of a tun.
6. Neither Flecknoe nor Shadwell was actually Irish; Ireland was regarded in England as an abode of savages.
7. Sharp satire (written in iambic meter by classical satirists).
8. Dryden here mocks the practice of writing emblematic verse, poems in the shape of their subjects (e.g., George Herbert's *Easter Wings* and *The Altar*). He lumps this practice together with other forms of empty ingenuity.

He said, but his last words were scarcely heard,⎫
For Bruce and Longvil had a trap prepared,[9]⎬
And down they sent the yet declaiming bard.⎭
Sinking he left his drugget robe behind,
215   Borne upward by a subterranean wind.
The mantle fell to the young prophet's part,[1]
With double portion of his father's art.

c. 1676   1682

To the Memory of Mr. Oldham[1]

Farewell, too little and too lately known,
Whom I began to think and call my own;
For sure our souls were near allied; and thine
Cast in the same poetic mold with mine.[2]
5   One common note on either lyre did strike,
And knaves and fools[3] we both abhorred alike:
To the same goal did both our studies drive,
The last set out the soonest did arrive.
Thus Nisus[4] fell upon the slippery place,
10   While his young friend performed and won the race.
O early ripe! to thy abundant store
What could advancing age have added more?
It might (what Nature never gives the young)
Have taught the numbers[5] of thy native tongue.
15   But satire needs not those, and wit will shine
Through the harsh cadence of a rugged line:
A noble error, and but seldom made,
When poets are by too much force betrayed.
Thy generous fruits, though gathered ere their prime,⎫
20   Still showed a quickness;[6] and maturing time⎬
But mellows what we write to the dull sweets of rhyme.⎭
Once more, hail and farewell;[7] farewell thou young,
But ah too short, Marcellus of our tongue;
Thy brows with ivy, and with laurels bound;
25   But fate and gloomy night encompass thee around.[8]

1684

9. In Shadwell's *The Virtuoso*, Bruce and Longvil open a trap door beneath the long-winded Sir Formal Trifle.
1. A burlesque of 2 Kings 2.8–14, in which the prophet Elijah is borne up to heaven, while his mantle falls to his successor, Elisha.
1. John Oldham (1653–1683) achieved fame at age 28 with his *Satires upon the Jesuits* (1681). Three years later, an aging Dryden mourned him in a tribute that prefaced the *Remains of Mr. John Oldham in Verse and Prose*. Within his poem's brief compass, Dryden echoes many poets— Virgil, Catullus, Milton, and Oldham himself—and invokes several modes: satire, celebration, elegy.
2. An echo of Oldham's poem *David's Lamentation:* "Oh, dearer than my soul! if I can call it mine, / For sure we had the same, 'twas very thine."
3. Satire's traditional targets.

4. In Book 5 of Virgil's *Aeneid*, Nisus slips near the finish line during a footrace, falling in a manner that permits "his young friend" Euryalus to win.
5. Metrical patterns and harmonies.
6. Liveliness; also, sharpness of taste.
7. Dryden echoes a phrase in Catullus's elegy for his brother: "Ave atque vale" (101.10).
8. In Book 6 of Virgil's *Aeneid*, the hero visits the underworld, where his dead father shows him a vision of Rome's future. This vision concludes with a sight of Augustus Caesar's adopted son and heir Marcellus, who after a glorious military career died at the age of 20. The last line of Dryden's elegy reworks Virgil's conclusion: "But hov'ring mists around his brows are spread, / And night, with sable shades, involves his head." (*Aeneid* 6.866; Dryden's translation).

ODE TO MRS. ANNE KILLIGREW   By her birth and through her accomplishments, Anne Killigrew (1660–1685) moved in an elevated sphere where politics, theater, poetry, and painting were intimately linked. Her uncles, the playwrights Thomas and Sir William Killigrew, were Dryden's associates; her father was chaplain to the Duke of York, and she was Maid of Honor to the Duke's wife. In this aristocratic circle, she wrote and painted. When she died of smallpox at age 25, Dryden made her early death the occasion for an elegy mapping her several worlds. By her varied talents she conquers adjacent provinces in the "spacious empire" of the Muses; by virtue of her family connections she participates in the more material empire of English commerce and conquest; by her saintly chastity she mediates between earth and heaven. To represent such scope, Dryden chose the capacious structure of the Pindaric ode; its formal complexities and varied meters had long provoked admiration and imitation among English poets. A century later, Samuel Johnson deemed Dryden's performance a triumph, "undoubtedly the noblest ode that our language has produced."

To the Pious Memory of the Accomplished Young Lady Mrs. Anne Killigrew[1]
Excellent in the two Sister Arts of Poesy and Painting.
An Ode

1

Thou youngest virgin-daughter of the skies,
Made in the last promotion of the blest;
Whose palms,[2] new plucked from paradise,
In spreading branches more sublimely rise,
5   Rich with immortal green above the rest:
Whether, adopted to some neighboring star,
Thou roll'st above us in thy wandering race,
    Or in procession fixed and regular,
    Moved with the heavens' majestic pace,[3]
10   Or called to more superior bliss,
Thou tread'st with seraphims the vast abyss:
Whatever happy region is thy place,
Cease thy celestial song a little space
(Thou wilt have time enough for hymns divine,
15   Since heav'n's eternal year is thine).
Hear then a mortal Muse thy praise rehearse,
        In no ignoble verse;
But such as thy own voice did practice here,
When thy first fruits of poesy were given,
20   To make thyself a welcome inmate there,
        While yet a young probationer,
        And candidate of heaven.

2

If by traduction[4] came thy mind,
Our wonder is the less to find

---

1. The term Mistress (Mrs.) applied to married and single women alike (Anne Killigrew died unmarried).
2. Symbols of victory (and also of martyrdom).
3. Dryden makes imaginative use of the geocentric cosmos of Ptolemy, which surrounds the earth with nine transparent spheres. Beyond the seven spheres of the luminous bodies that roll "above us" is the sphere of the stars "fix'd and regular"; beyond this is the Prime Mover.
4. By descent, derivation from ancestry.

25   A soul so charming from a stock so good;
        Thy father was transfused into thy blood:
        So wert thou born into the tuneful strain
        (An early, rich, and inexhausted vein).
            But if thy pre-existing soul
30   Was formed at first with myriads more,[5]
        It did through all the mighty poets roll
            Who Greek or Latin laurels wore,
        And was that Sappho[6] last which one it was before.
            If so, then cease thy flight, O heaven-born mind!
35   Thou hast no dross to purge from thy rich ore:
            Nor can thy soul a fairer mansion find,
            Than was the beauteous frame she left behind: ⎤
        Return, to fill or mend the choir of thy celestial kind. ⎦

                              3
        May we presume to say, that at thy birth
40   New joy was sprung in heav'n, as well as here on earth.
            For sure the milder planets did combine ⎤
            On thy auspicious horoscope to shine, ⎬
            And ev'n the most malicious were in trine.[7] ⎦
                Thy brother-angels at thy birth
45   Strung each his lyre and tuned it high,
                That all the people of the sky
        Might know a poetess was born on earth.
                And then, if ever, mortal ears
                Had heard the music of the spheres![8]
50   And if no clustering swarm of bees
        On thy sweet mouth distilled their golden dew,[9]
                'Twas that such vulgar miracles
                Heav'n had not leisure to renew:
            For all the blest fraternity of love
55   Solemnized there thy birth, and kept thy holiday above.

                              4
            O gracious God! How far have we
        Profaned thy heavenly gift of poesy?
        Made prostitute and profligate the Muse,
        Debased to each obscene and impious use,
60   Whose harmony was first ordained above
        For tongues of angels and for hymns of love?
        O wretched we! Why were we hurried down
                This lubric[1] and adult'rate age
                (Nay added fat pollutions of our own)
65   T' increase the steaming ordures of the stage?
        What can we say t' excuse our second fall?

---

5. Dryden offers an alternative explanation for Killigrew's poetic gifts by mentioning the doctrine of metempyschosis, or transmigration of souls.
6. Ancient Greek female poet.
7. Favorably aligned.
8. The celestial music generated by the motion of the planets, inaudible to humans.
9. This "vulgar miracle" was said to have accompanied the birth of the ancient Greek poet Pindar, celebrated for his odes.
1. Lewd.

Let this thy vestal,[2] Heaven, atone for all!
Her Arethusian[3] stream remains unsoiled,
Unmixed with foreign filth, and undefiled;
70   Her wit was more than man, her innocence a child!

5

Art she had none, yet wanted[4] none:
For nature did that want supply,
So rich in treasures of her own,
She might our boasted stores defy:
75   Such noble vigor did her verse adorn,
That it seemed borrowed, where 'twas only born.
Her morals too were in her bosom bred
        By great examples daily fed,
What in the best of books, her father's life, she read.
80   And to be read herself she need not fear;
Each test and every light her Muse will bear,
Though Epictetus[5] with his lamp were there.
Even love (for love sometimes her Muse expressed)
Was but a lambent[6] flame which played about her breast:
85   Light as the vapors of a morning dream,
So cold herself, whilst she such warmth expressed,
'Twas Cupid bathing in Diana's stream.

6

Born to the spacious empire of the Nine,[7]
One would have thought she should have been content
90   To manage well that mighty government:
But what can young ambitious souls confine?
        To the next realm she stretched her sway, ⎤
        For painture near adjoining lay,   ⎟
    A plenteous province, and alluring prey.   ⎦
95   A chamber of dependences[8] was framed
(As conquerors will never want pretense,
        When armed, to justify the offense),
And the whole fief in right of Poetry she claimed.
The country open lay without defense:
100   For poets frequent inroads there had made,
            And perfectly could represent
        The shape, the face, with every lineament;
And all the large domains which the dumb Sister[9] swayed,
            All bowed beneath her government,
105   Received in triumph wheresoe'er she went.
Her pencil drew whate'er her soul designed,
And oft the happy draught surpassed the image in her mind:
        The sylvan scenes of herds and flocks,

2. Virgin tender of a shrine.
3. Arethusa was changed into a spring to save her from the lustful river god Alpheus.
4. Lacked.
5. Stoic philosopher noted for his rigorous system of ethics.
6. Glowing.
7. The nine Muses.
8. This refers to a legislative device used by Louis XIV to annex lands adjoining France.
9. The silent Muse (painting).

And fruitful plains and barren rocks;
110   Of shallow brooks that flowed so clear,
The bottom did the top appear;
Of deeper too and ampler floods,
Which, as in mirrors, showed the woods;
Of lofty trees with sacred shades,
115   And perspectives of pleasant glades,
Where nymphs of brightest form appear, ⎫
And shaggy satyrs standing near,   ⎬
Which them at once admire and fear;   ⎭
The ruins too of some majestic piece,
120   Boasting the pow'r of ancient Rome or Greece,
Whose statues, friezes, columns broken lie,
And though defaced, the wonder of the eye;
What nature, art, bold fiction e'er durst frame,
Her forming hand gave feature to the name.
125   So strange a concourse ne'er was seen before,
But when the peopled ark the whole creation bore.

7

The scene then changed; with bold erected look
Our martial King[1] the sight with reverence strook:
For not content t' express his outward part,
130   Her hand called out the image of his heart;
His warlike mind, his soul devoid of fear, ⎫
His high-designing thoughts, were figured there, ⎬
As when, by magic, ghosts are made appear.   ⎭
Our phoenix Queen[2] was portrayed too, so bright,
135   Beauty alone could beauty take so right:
Her dress, her shape, her matchless grace,
Were all observed, as well as heav'nly face.
With such a peerless majesty she stands,
As in that day she took the crown from sacred hands:[3]
140   Before a train of heroines was seen,
In beauty foremost, as in rank, the queen!
Thus nothing to her[4] genius was denied,
But like a ball of fire, the further thrown, ⎫
Still with a greater blaze she shone,   ⎬
145   And her bright soul broke out on ev'ry side.
What next she had designed, Heaven only knows; ⎫
To such immod'rate growth her conquest rose,   ⎬
That fate alone its progress could oppose.   ⎭

8

Now all those charms, that blooming grace,
150   The well-proportioned shape, and beauteous face,
Shall never more be seen by mortal eyes;
In earth the much-lamented virgin lies!

1. James II, who fought in the Dutch wars, and whose portrait Killigrew had painted.
2. Queen of matchless beauty (James's wife Mary, whom Killigrew also painted).
3. The Archbishop of Canterbury officiated at James's coronation.
4. Killigrew's.

Not wit, nor piety, could fate prevent;
Nor was the cruel destiny content
155　　To finish all the murder at a blow,
To sweep at once her life and beauty too;
But, like a hardened felon, took a pride
　　To work more mischievously slow,
　　And plundered first, and then destroyed.
160　O double sacrilege on things divine,
To rob the relic, and deface the shrine!
　　But thus Orinda[5] died:
Heaven, by the same disease, did both translate,
As equal were their souls, so equal was their fate.

9

165　Meantime her warlike brother[6] on the seas
His waving streamers to the winds displays,
And vows for his return with vain devotion pays.
　　Ah, generous youth, that wish forbear;
　　The winds too soon will waft thee here!
　　Slack all thy sails, and fear to come;
170　Alas, thou know'st not, thou art wrecked at home!
No more shalt thou behold thy sister's face;
Thou hast already had her last embrace.
But look aloft, and if thou ken'st° from far,　　　　　　　　*you see*
175　Among the Pleiads[7] a new-kindled star,
If any sparkles than the rest more bright,
'Tis she that shines in that propitious light.

10

When in mid-air the golden trump shall sound,
　　To raise the nations under ground;
180　　When in the valley of Jehosaphat,
The judging God shall close the book of fate,[8]
　　And there the last assizes[9] keep,
　　For those who wake, and those who sleep;
　　When rattling bones together fly,
185　From the four corners of the sky;
When sinews o'er the skeletons are spread,
Those clothed with flesh, and life inspires the dead;
The sacred poets first shall hear the sound,
　　And foremost from the tomb shall bound: ⎫
190　For they are covered with the lightest ground, ⎬
And straight, with inborn vigor, on the wing, ⎭
Like mounting larks, to the new morning sing.
There thou, sweet saint, before the choir shalt go, ⎫
As harbinger of heaven, the way to show, ⎬
195　The way which thou so well hast learned below. ⎭

1685　　　　　　　　　　　　　　　　　　　　　　　　1685

---

5. The pen name of the poet Katherine Philips, who had died, also of smallpox, in 1664.
6. Henry Killigrew, a naval officer.
7. A cluster of seven stars in the constellation Taurus, associated with a group of 16th-century French poets (who called themselves *la Pléiade*).
8. "Let the heathen be wakened, and come up to the valley of Jehoshaphat: for there will I sit to judge all the heathen round about" (Joel 3.12).
9. Trial session.

Alexander's Feast

or, The Power of Music
An Ode in Honor of St. Cecilia's Day[1]

1

'Twas at the royal feast, for Persia won
       By Philip's warlike son:[2]
   Aloft in awful state
   The godlike hero sate
5   On his imperial throne:
His valiant peers were placed around;
Their brows with roses and with myrtles bound
   (So should desert in arms be crowned).
The lovely Thais[3] by his side
10 Sat like a blooming Eastern bride
In flow'r of youth and beauty's pride.
     Happy, happy, happy pair!
     None but the brave
     None but the brave
15   None but the brave deserves the fair.

Chorus

Happy, happy, happy pair!
None but the brave
None but the brave
None but the brave deserves the fair.

2

20 Timotheus,[4] placed on high
    Amid the tuneful choir,
    With flying fingers touched the lyre:
The trembling notes ascend the sky,
        And heav'nly joys inspire.
25 The song began from Jove,
Who left his blissful seats above
(Such is the power of mighty love).
A dragon's fiery form belied[5] the god:
Sublime on radiant spires° he rode,   *coils*
30   When he to fair Olympia pressed:
    And while he sought her snowy breast:
Then, round her slender waist he curled,
And stamped an image of himself, a sov'reign of the world.

---

1. The early martyr Cecilia is the patron saint of music and musicians. Her feast day (22 November) was annually celebrated in London by a concert featuring a new piece with words by an eminent poet and music by a distinguished composer. The musical society in charge of the occasion commissioned two odes from Dryden, ten years apart: *A Song for St. Cecilia's Day* (1687) and *Alexander's Feast.* Dryden undertook the commission with some reluctance, but after the piece's successful premiere, he noted with pleasure that *Alexander's Feast* "is esteemed the best of all my poetry, by all the town. I thought so myself when I writ it, but being old, I mistrusted my own judgment."

2. Alexander the Great, son of Philip of Macedon; Dryden depicts the feast that Alexander held after defeating the Persians and their emperor Darius in 331 B.C..

3. Alexander's Greek concubine.

4. Celebrated poet and musician.

5. Timotheus tells the alternative story of Alexander's parentage, that he was begotten by Jove—disguised ("belied") as a serpent—upon Philip's wife Olympias.

The listening crowd admire the lofty sound:
35   "A present deity," they shout around:
"A present deity," the vaulted roofs rebound.
    With ravished ears
    The monarch hears,
    Assumes the god,[6]
40   Affects to nod,
And seems to shake the spheres.

Chorus

*   With ravished ears*
*   The monarch hears,*
*   Assumes the god,*
45   *   Affects to nod,*
And seems to shake the spheres.

3

The praise of Bacchus then the sweet musician sung,
    Of Bacchus ever fair and ever young:
        The jolly god in triumph comes;
50   Sound the trumpets; beat the drums:
            Flushed with a purple grace
            He shows his honest face,
Now give the hautboys° breath; he comes, he comes.   *oboes*
        Bacchus, ever fair and young,
55   Drinking joys did first ordain:
Bacchus' blessings are a treasure;
Drinking is the soldier's pleasure;
            Rich the treasure,
            Sweet the pleasure;
60   Sweet is pleasure after pain.

Chorus

*   Bacchus' blessings are a treasure;*
*   Drinking is the soldier's pleasure;*
*   Rich the treasure,*
*   Sweet the pleasure;*
65   *   Sweet is pleasure after pain.*

4

Soothed with the sound, the king grew vain;
    Fought all his battles o'er again;
And thrice he routed all his foes, and thrice he slew the slain.
    The master saw the madness rise,
70   His glowing cheeks, his ardent eyes;
    And, while he heav'n and earth defied,
    Changed his hand, and checked his pride.[7]
        He chose a mournful Muse
        Soft pity to infuse:

---

6. Behaves like Jove, whose nod is said by Virgil to cause earthquakes.

7. Timotheus ("the master") changes the music in order to restrain Alexander's swelling pride.

75   He sung Darius great and good,
                    By too severe a fate
            Fallen, fallen, fallen, fallen,
               Fallen from his high estate
                     And welt'ring in his blood:
80 Deserted at his utmost need,
By those his former bounty fed:
On the bare earth exposed he lies,
With not a friend to close his eyes.

With downcast looks the joyless victor sat,
85   Revolving° in his altered soul   *pondering*
        The various turns of chance below;
And, now and then, a sigh he stole,
        And tears began to flow.

Chorus

        Revolving in his altered soul
90   *The various turns of chance below;*
        And, now and then, a sigh he stole;
          And tears began to flow.

5

The mighty master smiled to see
That love was in the next degree:
95 'Twas but a kindred sound to move;[8]
For pity melts the mind to love.
        Softly sweet, in Lydian measures,[9]
        Soon he soothed his soul to pleasures.
        "War," he sung, "is toil and trouble,
100   Honor but an empty bubble.
              Never ending, still° beginning,   *always*
        Fighting still, and still destroying,
              If the world be worth thy winning,
        Think, O think, it worth enjoying.
105   Lovely Thais sits beside thee,
              Take the good the gods provide thee."

The many[1] rend the skies with loud applause;
So love was crowned, but music won the cause.
        The prince, unable to conceal his pain,
110   Gazed on the fair
                Who caused his care,
             And sighed and looked, sighed and looked,
         Sighed and looked, and sighed again:
At length, with love and wine at once oppressed,
115   The vanquished victor sunk upon her breast.

Chorus

        The prince, unable to conceal his pain,
           Gazed on the fair

---

8. All it took to "move" Alexander to the "next degree" of feeling was to shift ("move") musical registers.
9. In ancient Greek music, the mode associated with pathos.
1. The retinue or company.

Who caused his care,
And sighed and looked, sighed and looked,
120   *Sighed and looked, and sighed again:*
At length, with love and wine at once oppressed,
The vanquished victor sunk upon her breast.

6

Now strike the golden lyre again:
A louder yet, and yet a louder strain.
125   Break his bands of sleep asunder,
And rouse him, like a rattling peal of thunder.
Hark, hark, the horrid sound
Has raised up his head,
As awaked from the dead,
130   And, amazed, he stares around.
"Revenge, revenge," Timotheus cries,
"See the Furies[2] arise!
See the snakes that they rear,
How they hiss in their hair,
135   And the sparkles that flash from their eyes!
Behold a ghastly band,
Each a torch in his hand!
Those are Grecian ghosts, that in battle were slain,
And unburied remain
140   Inglorious on the plain.
Give the vengeance due
To the valiant crew.
Behold how they toss their torches on high,
How they point to the Persian abodes,
145   And glitt'ring temples of their hostile gods!"
The princes applaud, with a furious joy;
And the king seized a flambeau,[3] with zeal to destroy;
Thais led the way,
To light him to his prey,
150   And, like another Helen, fired another Troy.[4]

Chorus

And the king seized a flambeau, with zeal to destroy;
Thais led the way,
To light him to his prey,
And, like another Helen, fired another Troy.

7

155   Thus, long ago,
Ere heaving bellows learned to blow,
While organs yet were mute,
Timotheus, to his breathing flute,
And sounding lyre,
160   Could swell the soul to rage, or kindle soft desire.

2. Spirits of punishment.
3. Torch.
4. Stolen away to Troy by Paris, Helen was blamed for

setting in motion the chain of events that led to the
burning of the city by the Greeks.

At last divine Cecilia came,
Inventress of the vocal frame;[5]
The sweet enthusiast,[6] from her sacred store,
Enlarged the former narrow bounds,
165   And added length to solemn sounds,
With nature's mother wit, and arts unknown before.
Let old Timotheus yield the prize,
Or both divide the crown;
He raised a mortal to the skies;
170   She drew an angel down.[7]

Grand Chorus

At last divine Cecilia came,
Inventress of the vocal frame;
The sweet enthusiast, from her sacred store,
Enlarged the former narrow bounds,
175   *And added length to solemn sounds,*
With nature's mother wit, and arts unknown before.
Let old Timotheus yield the prize,
Or both divide the crown;
He raised a mortal to the skies;
She drew an angel down.

1697   1697

from Fables Ancient and Modern[1]

from *Preface*

'Tis with a poet as with a man who designs to build, and is very exact, as he supposes, in casting up the cost beforehand. But generally speaking, he is mistaken in his account, and reckons short of the expense he first intended. He alters his mind as the work proceeds, and will have this or that convenience more, of which he had not thought when he began. So has it happened to me; I have built a house where I intended but a lodge, yet with better success than a certain nobleman,[2] who beginning with a dog kennel, never lived to finish the palace he had contrived.

From translating the first of Homer's *Iliads* (which I intended as an essay to[3] the whole work) I proceeded to the translation of the twelfth book of Ovid's *Metamorphoses*,[4] because it contains, among other things, the causes, the beginning, and

---

5. Cecilia was believed to have invented the organ.
6. One possessed by spirits or by a god.
7. Dryden alludes to his earlier ode to music, *A Song for St. Cecilia's Day* (1687): as Cecilia plays the organ, "An angel heard and straight appear'd, / Mistaking earth for heaven."
1. Following the triumph of his *Virgil* (1697), Dryden turned again to translation. He had frequently collaborated with others in the assembly of anthologies; now he undertook to make one of his own, containing poets both "Ancient"—Ovid and Homer—and "Modern"—Boccaccio, Chaucer, and Dryden himself. In the *Fables*, Dryden's pleasure and assurance in his own technical mastery are everywhere on display: in the expansiveness of his translations; in the bravado with which he plunders his own works as a treasury of echo and allusion; in the

arrangement of his materials, so that fable talks to fable in an almost calculated sequence; and in his preface, where he lays out the history of his book's development with a conspicuous delight in the improvisatory logic of his creative process, and then proudly argues for the greatness of Chaucer, whose career and craft he celebrates in such a way as to suggest parallels with his own.
2. Probably the Duke of Buckingham (whom Dryden had ridiculed as Zimri in *Absalom and Achitophel* line 544), and Buckingham's house at Cliveden.
3. First attempt at, and "taste of" (Johnson's *Dictionary*).
4. Ovid (43 B.C.–A.D. 17), Roman poet who spent the last decade of his life in exile. His *Metamorphoses* is a collection of ancient legends; in many, the characters undergo bodily transformations, from one form of life into another.

ending, of the Trojan War. Here I ought in reason to have stopped; but the speeches of Ajax and Ulysses lying next in my way, I could not balk 'em. When I had compassed them, I was so taken with the former part of the fifteenth book[5] (which is the masterpiece of the whole *Metamorphoses*) that I enjoined myself the pleasing task of rendering it into English. And now I found, by the number of my verses, that they began to swell into a little volume; which gave me an occasion of looking backward on some beauties of my author, in his former books: there occurred to me the hunting of the boar, Cinyras and Myrrha, the good-natured story of Baucis and Philemon, with the rest, which I hope I have translated closely enough, and given them the same turn of verse, which they had in the original; and this, I may say without vanity, is not the talent of every poet. He who has arrived the nearest to it, is the ingenious and learned Sandys,[6] the best versifier of the former age, if I may properly call it by that name, which was the former part of this concluding century. For Spenser and Fairfax[7] both flourished in the reign of Queen Elizabeth: great masters in our language, and who saw much farther into the beauties of our numbers than those who immediately followed them. Milton was the poetical son of Spenser, and Mr. Waller[8] of Fairfax; for we have our lineal descents and clans, as well as other families. Spenser more than once insinuates that the soul of Chaucer was transfused into his body, and that he was begotten by him two hundred years after his decease. Milton has acknowledged to me that Spenser was his original, and many besides myself have heard our famous Waller own that he derived the harmony of his numbers from the *Godfrey of Bulloign*, which was turned into English by Mr. Fairfax.

But to return: having done with Ovid for this time, it came into my mind that our old English poet Chaucer in many things resembled him, and that with no disadvantage on the side of the modern author, as I shall endeavor to prove when I compare them. And as I am and always have been studious to promote the honor of my native country, so I soon resolved to put their merits to the trial, by turning some of the *Canterbury Tales* into our language, as it is now refined, for by this means, both the poets being set in the same light, and dressed in the same English habit, story to be compared with story, a certain judgment may be made betwixt them by the reader, without obtruding my opinion on him: or if I seem partial to my countryman, and predecessor in the laurel, the friends of antiquity are not few. And besides many of the learned, Ovid has almost all the beaux,[9] and the whole fair sex, his declared patrons. Perhaps I have assumed somewhat more to myself than they allow me, because I have adventured to sum up the evidence. But the readers are the jury; and their privilege remains entire to decide according to the merits of the cause or, if they please, to bring it to another hearing before some other court. In the meantime, to follow the thread of my discourse (as thoughts, according to Mr. Hobbes,[1] have always some connection) so from Chaucer I was led to think on Boccace,[2] who was

---

5. In which Ovid puts into verse the philosophy of the Greek mystic Pythagoras, who propounded a doctrine of reincarnation, arguing that "all things are but altered, nothing dies."
6. George Sandys (1578–1644), poet and translator, whose *Ovid's Metamorphosis Englished* was issued in 1626 and often republished.
7. Edward Fairfax (c. 1580–1635), poet and translator.
8. Edmund Waller (1606–1687), poet, early practitioner of the heroic couplet; Dryden praised him as "the father" of English versification.
9. Fashionable gentlemen.
1. In his *Leviathan* (1651), Thomas Hobbes includes a chapter on "The Consequence or Train of Imaginations" (1.3).
2. Giovanni Boccaccio (1313–1375), Italian writer, authored *The Decameron* (a collection of 100 tales) and was one of Chaucer's chief influences.

not only his contemporary, but also pursued the same studies; wrote novels in prose, and many works in verse; particularly is said to have invented the octave rhyme, or stanza of eight lines, which ever since has been maintained by the practice of all Italian writers who are, or at least assume the title of, heroic poets. He and Chaucer, among other things, had this in common, that they refined their mother tongues; but with this difference, that Dante had begun to file their language,[3] at least in verse, before the time of Boccace, who likewise received no little help from his master Petrarch.[4] But the reformation of their prose was wholly owing to Boccace himself, who is yet the standard of purity in the Italian tongue, though many of his phrases are become obsolete, as in process of time it must needs happen. Chaucer (as you have formerly been told by our learned Mr. Rymer) first adorned and amplified our barren tongue from the Provençal, which was then the most polished of all the modern languages.[5] But this subject has been copiously treated by that great critic, who deserves no little commendation from us his countrymen. For these reasons of time, and resemblance of genius, in Chaucer and Boccace, I resolved to join them in my present work, to which I have added some original papers of my own, which whether they are equal or inferior to my other poems, an author is the most improper judge; and therefore I leave them wholly to the mercy of the reader. I will hope the best, that they will not be condemned; but if they should, I have the excuse of an old gentleman, who mounting on horseback before some ladies, when I was present, got up somewhat heavily, but desired of the fair spectators that they would count fourscore and eight before they judged him. By the mercy of God, I am already come within twenty years of his number, a cripple in my limbs, but what decays are in my mind, the reader must determine. I think myself as vigorous as ever in the faculties of my soul, excepting only my memory, which is not impaired to any great degree; and if I lose not more of it, I have no great reason to complain. What judgment I had increases rather than diminishes; and thoughts, such as they are, come crowding in so fast upon me that my only difficulty is to choose or to reject; to run them into verse, or to give them the other harmony of prose. I have so long studied and practiced both that they are grown into a habit, and become familiar to me. In short, though I may lawfully plead some part of the old gentleman's excuse, yet I will reserve it till I think I have greater need, and ask no grains of allowance for the faults of this my present work but those which are given of course to human frailty. I will not trouble my reader with the shortness of time in which I writ it, or the several intervals of sickness. They who think too well of their own performances are apt to boast in their prefaces how little time their works have cost them, and what other business of more importance interfered. But the reader will be as apt to ask the question, why they allowed not a longer time to make their works more perfect? and why they had so despicable an opinion of their judges, as to thrust their indigested stuff upon them, as if they deserved no better?

With this account of my present undertaking, I conclude the first part of this discourse. In the second part, as at a second sitting, though I alter not the draught, I must touch the same features over again, and change the dead-coloring[6] of the whole.

* * *

3. Dante Alighieri (1265–1321), author of *The Divine Comedy*, was the first great vernacular poet in Italy; *to file*: to smooth (into graceful verse).
4. Italian poet (1304–1374), whose cycle of love sonnets exerted enormous influence over English writers.

5. In his *Short View of Tragedy* (1693), Thomas Rymer writes that Chaucer seized "all Provençal [Old French], French, or Latin that came in his way, gives them a new garb . . . and mingles them amongst our English."
6. The prepatory layer of paint applied to a canvas.

It remains that I say somewhat of Chaucer in particular.

In the first place, as he is the father of English poetry, so I hold him in the same degree of veneration as the Grecians held Homer, or the Romans Virgil. He is a perpetual fountain of good sense; learned in all sciences; and therefore speaks properly on all subjects. As he knew what to say, so he knows also when to leave off, a continence which is practiced by few writers, and scarcely by any of the Ancients, excepting Virgil and Horace. One of our late great poets[7] is sunk in his reputation, because he could never forgive any conceit which came in his way, but swept like a dragnet, great and small. There was plenty enough, but the dishes were ill sorted; whole pyramids of sweet-meats for boys and women, but little of solid meat for men. All this proceeded not from any want of knowledge, but of judgment; neither did he want that in discerning the beauties and faults of other poets, but only indulged himself in the luxury of writing; and perhaps knew it was a fault, but hoped the reader would not find it. For this reason, though he must always be thought a great poet, he is no longer esteemed a good writer; and for ten impressions,[8] which his works have had in so many successive years, yet at present a hundred books are scarcely purchased once a twelvemonth. For, as my last Lord Rochester said, though somewhat profanely, "Not being of God, he could not stand."

Chaucer followed Nature everywhere, but was never so bold to go beyond her. And there is a great difference of being *poeta* and *nimis poeta*,[9] if we may believe Catullus, as much as betwixt a modest behavior and affectation. The verse of Chaucer, I confess, is not harmonious to us; but 'tis like the eloquence of one whom Tacitus commends: it was *auribus istius temporis accommodata*.[1] They who lived with him, and some time after him, thought it musical, and it continues so even in our judgment, if compared with the numbers of Lydgate and Gower, his contemporaries. There is the rude sweetness of a Scotch tune in it, which is natural and pleasing, though not perfect. 'Tis true, I cannot go so far as he who published the last edition of him,[2] for he would make us believe the fault is in our ears, and that there were really ten syllables in a verse where we find but nine. But this opinion is not worth confuting; 'tis so gross and obvious an error that common sense (which is a rule in everything but matters of faith and revelation) must convince the reader that equality of numbers, in every verse which we call heroic,[3] was either not known or not always practiced in Chaucer's age. It were an easy matter to produce some thousands of his verses which are lame for want of half a foot, and sometimes a whole one, and which no pronunciation can make otherwise. We can only say that he lived in the infancy of our poetry, and that nothing is brought to perfection at the first. We must be children before we grow men. There was an Ennius, and in process of time a Lucilius and a Lucretius, before Virgil and Horace; even after Chaucer there was a Spenser, a Harrington, a Fairfax, before Waller and Denham were in being.[4] And our numbers were in their nonage[5] till these last

---

7. Abraham Cowley (1618–1667), whom Dryden admired and imitated.
8. Printings.
9. "A poet" and "too much a poet"; the Latin poet Martial, and not his predecessor Catullus, made this observation.
1. "Suited to the ears of those times": Cornelius Tacitus, Roman historian.

2. Thomas Speght, who argued (correctly) that Chaucer's versification was skillful and smooth but misrepresented by transcribers and misunderstood by readers.
3. I.e., consistent iambic pentameter.
4. Dryden traces a "descent and lineage" of influence first in Latin and then in English poetry.
5. Early youth.

appeared. I need say little of his parentage, life, and fortunes. They are to be found at large in all the editions of his works. He was employed abroad, and favored by Edward the Third, Richard the Second, and Henry the Fourth, and was poet, as I suppose, to all three of them. In Richard's time, I doubt, he was a little dipped in the rebellion of the Commons, and being brother-in-law to John of Gaunt, it was no wonder if he followed the fortunes of that family, and was well with Henry the Fourth when he had deposed his predecessor.[6] Neither is it to be admired[7] that Henry, who was a wise as well as a valiant prince, who claimed by succession, and was sensible that his title was not sound, but was rightfully in Mortimer, who had married the heir of York—it was not to be admired, I say, if that great politician should be pleased to have the greatest wit of those times in his interests, and to be the trumpet of his praises. Augustus had given him the example, by the advice of Maecenas,[8] who recommended Virgil and Horace to him; whose praises helped to make him popular while he was alive, and after his death have made him precious to posterity. As for the religion of our poet, he seems to have some little bias toward the opinions of Wyclif,[9] after John of Gaunt his patron; somewhat of which appears in the *Tale of Piers Plowman*.[1] Yet I cannot blame him for inveighing so sharply against the vices of the clergy in his age. Their pride, their ambition, their pomp, their avarice, their worldly interest deserved the lashes which he gave them, both in that, and in most of his *Canterbury Tales*. Neither has his contemporary Boccace spared them. Yet both those poets lived in much esteem, with good and holy men in orders, for the scandal which is given by particular priests reflects not on the sacred function. Chaucer's Monk, his Canon, and his Friar took not[2] from the character of his Good Parson. A satirical poet is the check of the laymen on bad priests. We are only to take care that we involve not the innocent with the guilty in the same condemnation. The good cannot be too much honored, nor the bad too coarsely used, for the corruption of the best becomes the worst. When a clergyman is whipped, his gown is first taken off, by which the dignity of his order is secured. If he be wrongfully accused, he has his action of slander, and 'tis at the poet's peril if he transgress the law. But they will tell us that all kind of satire, though never so well deserved by particular priests, yet brings the whole order into contempt. Is then the peerage of England any thing dishonored, when a peer suffers for his treason? If he be libeled, or any way defamed, he has his *scandalum magnatum* [legal recourse] to punish the offender. They who use this kind of argument seem to be conscious to themselves of somewhat which has deserved the poet's lash, and are less concerned for their public capacity than for their private. At least, there is pride at the bottom of their reasoning. If the faults of men in orders are only to be judged among themselves, they are all in some sort parties. For, since they say the honor of their order is concerned in every member of it, how can we be sure that they will be impartial judges? How far I may be allowed to speak my opinion in this case I know not, but I am sure a dispute of this nature caused mischief in abundance betwixt a King of England and an Archbishop of Canterbury; one standing up for

---

6. Henry Bolingbroke (son to John of Gaunt) deposed his cousin Richard II in 1399; Chaucer survived political upheaval and received patronage from both kings.
7. Wondered at.
8. Roman patron of the poets Virgil, Horace, and Propertius.

9. John Wyclif (c. 1330–1384), theologian and religious reformer.
1. This tale had been mistakenly attributed to Chaucer; there is no evidence that he was a follower of Wyclif.
2. I.e., did not detract.

the laws of his land, and the other for the honor (as he called it) of God's Church; which ended in the murder of the prelate, and in the whipping of his Majesty from post to pillar for his penance.[3] The learned and ingenious Dr. Drake[4] has saved me the labor of inquiring into the esteem and reverence which the priests have had of old; and I would rather extend than diminish any part of it. Yet I must needs say that when a priest provokes me without any occasion given him, I have no reason, unless it be the charity of a Christian, to forgive him. *Prior laesit*[5] is justification sufficient in the civil law. If I answer him in his own language, self-defense, I am sure, must be allowed me, and if I carry it farther, even to a sharp recrimination, somewhat may be indulged to human frailty. Yet my resentment has not wrought so far, but that I have followed Chaucer in his character of a holy man, and have enlarged on that subject with some pleasure, reserving to myself the right, if I shall think fit hereafter, to describe another sort of priests, such as are more easily to be found than the Good Parson; such as have given the last blow to Christianity in this age, by a practice so contrary to their doctrine. But this will keep cold till another time.

In the meanwhile, I take up Chaucer where I left him. He must have been a man of a most wonderful comprehensive nature, because, as it has been truly observed of him, he has taken into the compass of his *Canterbury Tales* the various manners and humors (as we now call them) of the whole English nation in his age. Not a single character has escaped him. All his pilgrims are severally distinguished from each other; and not only in their inclinations, but in their very physiognomies and persons. Baptista Porta[6] could not have described their natures better than by the marks which the poet gives them. The matter and manner of their tales, and of their telling, are so suited to their different educations, humors, and callings, that each of them would be improper in any other mouth. Even the grave and serious characters are distinguished by their several sorts of gravity: their discourses are such as belong to their age, their calling, and their breeding; such as are becoming of them, and of them only. Some of his persons are vicious, and some virtuous; some are unlearned, or (as Chaucer calls them) *lewd*, and some are learned. Even the ribaldry of the low characters is different: the Reeve, the Miller, and the Cook, are several men, and distinguished from each other, as much as the mincing Lady Prioress and the broad-speaking gap-toothed Wife of Bath. But enough of this: there is such a variety of game springing up before me that I am distracted in my choice, and know not which to follow. 'Tis sufficient to say according to the proverb, that here is God's plenty. We have our forefathers and great grand-dames all before us, as they were in Chaucer's days; their general characters are still remaining in mankind, and even in England, though they are called by other names than those of monks, and friars, and canons, and lady abbesses, and nuns. For mankind is ever the same, and nothing lost out of nature, though everything is altered. May I have leave to do myself the justice (since my enemies will do me none, and are so far from granting me to be a good poet that they will not allow me so much as to be a Christian, or a moral man) may I have leave, I say, to

---

3. Thomas à Becket, Archbishop of Canterbury, was murdered in 1170 on the orders of his king, Henry II, after a long dispute over the powers and rights of the church. (The pilgrims in *The Canterbury Tales* are traveling to Becket's shrine.)
4. James Drake (1667–1707), physician, dramatist, and ally of Dryden in literary controversies.
5. He injured first (i.e., "he started it").
6. Giambattista della Porta (c. 1538–1615), a physician whose book *De humana physiognomia* catalogued the effects of the emotional life on the look of the face.

inform my reader, that I have confined my choice to such tales of Chaucer as savor nothing of immodesty.[7] If I had desired more to please than to instruct, the Reeve, the Miller, the Shipman, the Merchant, the Summoner, and above all, the Wife of Bath, in the Prologue to her Tale, would have procured me as many friends and readers as there are beaux and ladies of pleasure in the town. But I will no more offend against good manners. I am sensible as I ought to be of the scandal I have given by my loose writings;[8] and make what reparation I am able, by this public acknowledgment. If anything of this nature, or of profaneness, be crept into these poems, I am so far from defending it, that I disown it. *Totum hoc indictum volo*.[9] Chaucer makes another manner of apology for his broad speaking, and Boccace makes the like; but I will follow neither of them. Our countryman, in the end of his characters, before the *Canterbury Tales*, thus excuses the ribaldry, which is very gross, in many of his novels.

> But first, I pray you, of your courtesy,
> That ye ne arrete it nought my villany,
> Though that I plainly speak in this mattere
> To tellen you her words, and eke her chere:
> 5 Ne though I speak her words properly,
> For this ye knowen as well as I,
> Who shall tellen a tale after a man
> He mote rehearse as nye as ever he can:
> Everich word of it been in his charge,
> 10 *All speke he never so rudely, ne large*.
> Or else he mote tellen his tale untrue,
> Or feine things, or find words new:
> He may not spare, altho he were his brother,
> He mote as well say o word as another.
> 15 Christ spake himself full broad in holy writ,
> And well I wote no villany is it.
> Eke Plato saith, who so can him rede,
> The words mote been cousin to the dede.[1]

Yet if a man should have inquired of Boccace or of Chaucer, what need they had of introducing such characters, where obscene words were proper in their mouths, but very undecent to be heard, I know not what answer they could have made. For that reason, such tales shall be left untold by me. You have here a specimen of Chaucer's language, which is so obsolete that his sense is scarce to be understood; and you have likewise more than one example of his unequal numbers, which were mentioned before. Yet many of his verses consist of ten syllables, and the words not much behind our present English, as for example, these two lines, in the description of the carpenter's young wife:

> Wincing she was, as is a jolly colt,
> Long as a mast, and upright as a bolt.[2]

---

7. The *Fables* includes Dryden's translations of *The Knight's Tale*, *The Nun's Priest's Tale* (*The Cock and the Fox*), *The Wife of Bath's Tale*, and the portrait of the Parson from the *General Prologue* (*The Character of a Good Parson; Imitated from Chaucer and Inlarg'd*).

8. Throughout his career, Dryden had found it necessary to defend his plays against charges of immorality.
9. I wish all this unsaid.
1. *The General Prologue*, lines 727–744 (see page 318).
2. *The Miller's Tale*, lines 155–156 (see page 324).

I have almost done with Chaucer, when I have answered some objections relating to my present work. I find some people are offended that I have turned these tales into modern English, because they think them unworthy of my pains, and look on Chaucer as a dry, old-fashioned wit, not worth receiving. I have often heard the late Earl of Leicester[3] say that Mr. Cowley himself was of that opinion, who having read him over at my Lord's request, declared he had no taste of him. I dare not advance my opinion against the judgment of so great an author. But I think it fair, however, to leave the decision to the public. Mr. Cowley was too modest to set up for a dictator, and being shocked perhaps with his old style, never examined into the depth of his good sense. Chaucer, I confess, is a rough diamond, and must first be polished ere he shines. I deny not likewise, that living in our early days of poetry, he writes not always of a piece; but sometimes mingles trivial things with those of greater moment. Sometimes also, though not often, he runs riot, like Ovid, and knows not when he has said enough. But there are more great wits, beside Chaucer, whose fault is their excess of conceits, and those ill sorted. An author is not to write all he can, but only all he ought. Having observed this redundancy in Chaucer (as it is an easy matter for a man of ordinary parts to find a fault in one of greater) I have not tied myself to a literal translation, but have often omitted what I judged unnecessary, or not of dignity enough to appear in the company of better thoughts. I have presumed farther in some places, and added somewhat of my own where I thought my author was deficient, and had not given his thoughts their true luster, for want of words in the beginning of our language. And to this I was the more emboldened, because (if I may be permitted to say it of myself) I found I had a soul congenial to his, and that I had been conversant in the same studies. Another poet, in another age, may take the same liberty with my writings, if at least they live long enough to deserve correction. It was also necessary sometimes to restore the sense of Chaucer, which was lost or mangled in the errors of the press. Let this example suffice at present; in the story of Palamon and Arcite,[4] where the Temple of Diana is described, you find these verses in all the editions of our author:

> There saw I Danè turned unto a tree,
> I mean not the goddess Diane,
> But Venus daughter, which that hight Danè.

Which after a little consideration I knew was to be reformed into this sense, that Daphne the daughter of Peneus was turned into a tree. I durst not make thus bold with Ovid, lest some future Milbourn[5] should arise, and say I varied from my author because I understood him not.

But there are other judges who think I ought not to have translated Chaucer into English, out of a quite contrary notion. They suppose there is a certain veneration due to his old language, and that it is little less than profanation and sacrilege to alter it. They are farther of opinion that somewhat of his good sense will suffer in this transfusion, and much of the beauty of his thoughts will infallibly be lost, which appear with more grace in their old habit. Of this opinion was that excellent person whom I mentioned, the late Earl of Leicester, who valued Chaucer as much as Mr. Cowley despised him. My Lord dissuaded me from this attempt (for I was thinking of

---

3. Philip Sidney (1619–1698), patron of Dryden, to whom the poet had dedicated his tragedy *Don Sebastian* (1690).

4. *The Knight's Tale.*
5. Luke Milbourne (1649–1720), a clergyman and translator who had attacked Dryden's *Virgil*.

it some years before his death) and his authority prevailed so far with me as to defer my undertaking while he lived, in deference to him. Yet my reason was not convinced with what he urged against it. If the first end of a writer be to be understood, then as his language grows obsolete, his thoughts must grow obscure: *multa renascentur quae nunc cecidere; cadentque quae nunc sunt in honore vocabula, si volet usus, quem penes arbitrium est & jus & norma loquendi.*[6] When an ancient word for its sound and significancy deserves to be revived, I have that reasonable veneration for antiquity to restore it. All beyond this is superstition. Words are not like landmarks, so sacred as never to be removed. Customs are changed, and even statutes are silently repealed when the reason ceases for which they were enacted. As for the other part of the argument, that his thoughts will lose of their original beauty by the innovation of words: in the first place, not only their beauty, but their being is lost, where they are no longer understood, which is the present case. I grant that something must be lost in all transfusion, that is, in all translations; but the sense will remain, which would otherwise be lost, or at least be maimed, when it is scarce intelligible, and that but to a few. How few are there who can read Chaucer so as to understand him perfectly? And if imperfectly, then with less profit, and no pleasure. 'Tis not for the use of some old Saxon friends[7] that I have taken these pains with him. Let them neglect my version, because they have no need of it. I made it for their sakes who understand sense and poetry as well as they, when that poetry and sense is put into words which they understand. I will go farther, and dare to add, that what beauties I lose in some places, I give to others which had them not originally. But in this I may be partial to myself; let the reader judge, and I submit to his decision. Yet I think I have just occasion to complain of them who, because they understand Chaucer, would deprive the greater part of their countrymen of the same advantage, and hoard him up, as misers do their grandam gold,[8] only to look on it themselves, and hinder others from making use of it. In sum, I seriously protest that no man ever had, or can have, a greater veneration for Chaucer than myself. I have translated some part of his works, only that I might perpetuate his memory, or at least refresh it, amongst my countrymen. If I have altered him anywhere for the better, I must at the same time acknowledge that I could have done nothing without him. *Facile est inventis addere*[9] is no great commendation, and I am not so vain to think I have deserved a greater. I will conclude what I have to say of him singly, with this one remark: a lady of my acquaintance, who keeps a kind of correspondence with some authors of the fair sex in France, has been informed by them, that Mademoiselle de Scudery,[1] who is as old as Sibyl,[2] and inspired like her by the same god of poetry, is at this time translating Chaucer into modern French. From which I gather, that he has been formerly translated into the old Provençal (for how she should come to understand old English, I know not). But the matter of fact being true, it makes me think that there is something in it like fatality; that after certain periods of time, the fame and memory of great wits should be renewed, as Chaucer is both in France and England. If this be wholly chance, 'tis extraordinary; and I dare not call it more, for fear of being taxed with superstition. * * *

---

6. Many terms that have fallen out of use shall be born again, and those shall fall which that are now in use, if usage so will it, in whose hands lies the judgment, the right, and the rule of speech (Horace, *Ars Poetica* 70–72).
7. Friends who were scholars of Anglo-Saxon literature.
8. Long-stored-up wealth.

9. It is easy to add to what has already been discovered.
1. Madeleine de Scudéry (1607–1701), author of chivalric romances.
2. The Sybil of Cumae was a prophetess who served Apollo, god of poetry; he granted her wish to live a thousand years.

The Secular Masque[1]

[Enter Janus.[2]]

JANUS: Chronos,[3] Chronos, mend thy pace,
A hundred times the rolling sun.
Around the radiant belt[4] has run
In his revolving race.

5 Behold, behold, the goal in sight,
Spread thy fans,[5] and wing thy flight.
*[Enter Chronos, with a scythe in his hand, and a great
globe on his back, which he sets down at his entrance.]*

CHRONOS: Weary, weary of my weight,
Let me, let me drop my freight,
And leave the world behind.

10 I could not bear
Another year
The load of humankind.
[Enter Momus[6] laughing.]

MOMUS: Ha! ha! ha! ha! ha! ha! well hast thou done,
To lay down thy pack,

15 And lighten thy back,
The world was a fool, e'er since it begun,
And since neither Janus, nor Chronos, nor I,
Can hinder the crimes,
Or mend the bad times,

20 'Tis better to laugh than to cry.
[Chorus of all three.]
'Tis better to laugh than to cry.

JANUS: Since Momus comes to laugh below,
Old Time, begin the show,
That he may see, in every scene,

25 What changes in this age have been.

CHRONOS: Then, goddess of the silver bow, begin.
[Horns, or hunting music, within. Enter Diana.[7]]

DIANA: With horns and with hounds, I waken the day,
And hie to the woodland walks away;
I tuck up my robe, and am buskined soon,

30 And tie to my forehead a waxing moon,
I course the fleet stag, unkennel the fox,

---

1. "Within this month," Dryden wrote a friend in April 1700, "there will be played for my profit, an old play . . . called *The Pilgrim*, . . . to which I have added a new masque." Dryden called this new portion *The Secular Masque*, because it marked the turn of the century (Latin *saeculum*: age, period, century). Through its nostalgic form, he looked back to the start of the 17th century, and to the courts of Elizabeth, James, and Charles I, where just such masques, dominated by pagan gods mirroring and musing on present events, exerted a hypnotic appeal. In the *Masque*'s short span, Dryden sought both to compass the century—its pursuits and pleasures, its wars and loves—and to dispatch it, in a tone compounded of affection and scorn. The *Masque* proved valedictory in one

other way as well, for on May 1, a few days after the piece's first performance, Dryden died.
2. The Roman god of openings (gates, doors) and beginnings, possessing two faces pointed in opposite directions (past, future). January is named for him.
3. Time, traditionally depicted as described in the ensuing stage direction.
4. The zodiac.
5. Wings.
6. Greek god (the name means "blame") of ridicule, mockery, satire.
7. Roman goddess of chastity and of hunting, here reminiscent of Elizabeth I, the Virgin Queen, and of James I, enthusiastic hunter.

And chase the wild goats o'er summits of rocks,
With shouting and hooting we pierce through the sky,
And Echo turns hunter, and doubles the cry.
                    [*Chorus of all.*]
35   With shouting and hooting we pierce through the sky,
      And Echo turns hunter, and doubles the cry.
JANUS: Then our age was in its prime:
CHRONOS: Free from rage,
DIANA: And free from crime.
MOMUS: A very merry, dancing, drinking,
40   Laughing, quaffing, and unthinking time.
                    [*Chorus of all.*]
          Then our age was in its prime,
          Free from rage, and free from crime;
          A very merry, dancing, drinking,
          Laughing, quaffing, and unthinking time.
             [*Dance of Diana's attendants. Enter Mars.*[8]]
MARS: Inspire the vocal brass,[9] inspire;
          The world is past its infant age:
              Arms and honor,
              Arms and honor,
          Set the martial mind on fire,
50   And kindle manly rage.
          Mars has looked the sky[1] to red;
          And peace, the lazy good, is fled.
          Plenty, peace, and pleasure fly;
              The sprightly green,
55   In woodland walks, no more is seen;
          The sprightly green has drunk the Tyrian dye.[2]
                    [*Chorus of all.*]
          Plenty, peace, etc.
MARS: Sound the trumpet, beat the drum;
          Through all the world around,
60   Sound a reveille, sound, sound,
          The warrior god is come.
                    [*Chorus of all.*]
              Sound the trumpet, etc.
MOMUS: Thy sword within the scabbard keep,
              And let mankind agree;
65   Better the world were fast asleep,
              Than kept awake by thee.
          The fools are only thinner,
              With all our cost and care;
          But neither side a winner,
70   For things are as they were.
                    [*Chorus of all.*]
              The fools are only, etc.

8. Roman god of war, here incarnating the midcentury
civil wars.
9. Sound the speaking trumpet, the call to arms.
1. I.e., has by his stare changed the color of the sky.

2. An ancient purple hue: the color of the soldiers' garments (here displacing the green of the hunters') and of
the blood they shed.

[*Enter Venus*[3]]

VENUS: Calms appear, when storms are past;
          Love will have his hour at last:
          Nature is my kindly care;
75   Mars destroys, and I repair;
          Take me, take me, while you may,
          Venus comes not every day.
              [*Chorus of all.*]
            Take her, take her, etc.

CHRONOS: The world was then so light,
80   I scarcely felt the weight;
          Joy ruled the day, and love the night.
          But since the queen of pleasure left the ground,
            I faint, I lag,
            And feebly drag
85   The ponderous orb around.

MOMUS: All, all of a piece throughout;
          Thy chase had a beast in view;
              [*Pointing to Diana.*]
          Thy wars brought nothing about;
              [*To Mars.*]
          Thy lovers were all untrue.
              [*To Venus.*]

JANUS: 'Tis well an old age is out,
CHRONOS: And time to begin a new.
              [*Chorus of all.*]
          All, all of a piece throughout;
          Thy chase had a beast in view;
          Thy wars brought nothing about;
95   Thy lovers were all untrue.
          'Tis well an old age is out,
          And time to begin a new.
       [*Dance of huntsmen, nymphs, warriors and lovers.*]

                      1700

Aphra Behn

1640?–1689

Aphra Behn's career was unprecedented, her output prodigious, her fame extensive, and her voice distinctive. Her origins, though, remain elusive. We know nothing certain about her birth, family, education, or marriage. She may have been born at the start or at the end of the 1640s, to parents of low or "gentle" station, named Johnson, Amies, or Cooper. Her Catholicism and her firm command of French suggest the possibility of a prosperous upbringing in a convent at home or abroad; the running argument against marriage for money that she sustains through much of her work suggests that her own marriage, to the otherwise unidentifiable "Mr. Behn," may have been obligatory and unhappy. In any case it was brief—and just possibly fictitious, since a widow could pursue a profession more freely than a spinster.

3. Roman goddess of love, here presiding over the amorous court of Charles II.

Behn's first appearances in the historical record suggest a propensity for self-invention. In 1663–1664, during a short stay with her family in the South American sugar colony of Surinam, a government agent there reported that she was conducting a flirtation with William Scott, an antimonarchist on the run from the Restoration. The agent referred to Scott as "Celadon" and Aphra as "Astraea," names the lovers may well have chosen for themselves from a popular French romance; Behn kept hers, as a *nom de plume*, for the whole of her writing life. Within two years, her loyalties had shifted and her self-invention had grown more intricate. In 1666 Behn herself became the king's spy, sent from London to Antwerp to persuade her old flame Scott to turn informer against his fellow Republicans and to apprise King Charles of rebellious plots. She did useful but costly work, garnering good information that her handlers ignored and spending much money that they were slow to reimburse. Returning to England later that year, and threatened with imprisonment for debt, she wrote her supervisor, "I have cried myself dead and could find in my heart to break through all and get to the King and never rise till he were pleased to pay this, but I am sick and weak and unfit for it or a prison . . . Sir, if I have not the money tonight you must send me something to keep [sustain] me in prison, for I will not starve." The king paid up, and Behn forestalled any further threat of starvation by writing plays for money—the first woman in England to earn a living by her pen. She had been "forced to write for bread," she later declared, and she was "not ashamed to own it."

Throughout her career Behn transmuted such "shamelessness" into a positive point of pride and a source of literary substance. Many of her plays, poems, and fictions focus on the difficulty with which intelligent, enterprising women pursue their desires against the current of social convention. In the prologues, prefaces, postscripts, and letters by which she provided a running commentary on her work, Behn sometimes aligned herself with the large fraternity of male authors who "like good tradesmen" sell whatever is "in fashion," but she often stood apart to muse acerbically on her unique position as a *female* purveyor of literary product. Once, surveying the panoply of contemporary male playwrights, she declared that "except for our most unimitable Laureate [Dryden], I dare say I know of none that write at such a formidable rate, but that a woman may well hope to reach their greatest heights." "Formidable rate" suggests both speed and skill; Behn made good on both boasts, producing twenty plays in twenty years, along with much poetry (including fervent pro-Stuart propaganda), copious translations, one of the earliest epistolary novels in English, and a cluster of innovative shorter fiction. In her range and her dexterity, she approached the stature of the "unimitable Laureate" himself, who knew her and praised her repeatedly. With her greatest successes—the comedy *The Rover* (1677), the novella *Oroonoko* (1688)—she secured both an audience and a reputation that continued without pause well into the following century.

Other pieces worked less well. Changes in literary fashion often obliged Behn to try new modes; she switched to fiction, for example, in the 1680s, when plays became less lucrative. Out of her vicissitudes—professional and personal, amorous, financial, literary—she fashioned a formidable celebrity, becoming the object of endless speculation in talk and in ink. "I value fame," she once wrote, and she cultivated it by what seemed an unprecedented frankness. ("All women together," wrote Virginia Woolf, "ought to let flowers fall upon the grave of Aphra Behn . . . for it was she who earned them the right to speak their minds.") In an age of libertines, when men like Rochester paraded their varied couplings in verse couplets, Behn undertook to proclaim and to analyze women's sexual desire, as manifested in her characters and in herself. Her disclosures, though, were intricately orchestrated. Living and writing at the center of a glamorous literary circle, Behn may have fostered, as the critic Janet Todd suggests, the "fantasy of a golden age of sexual and social openness," but she performed it for her readers rather than falling for it herself. Throughout her work Behn adroitly conceals the "self" that she purports to show and sell. She sometimes likens herself to those other female denizens of the theater, the mask-wearing prostitutes who roamed the audience in search of customers. The critic Catherine Gallagher has argued that Behn's literary persona—defiant, vulnerable, hypnotic—functions like the prostitute's vizard, promising the woman's "availability" as commodity while at the same time implying "the impenetrability of the controlling mind" behind the mask.

In Gallagher's reckoning, as in Woolf's, Behn's total career is more important than any particular work it produced. This is fitting tribute to a writer who, in an era of spectacular self-performers (Charles II, Dryden, Rochester), brought off, by virtue of her gender and her art, one of the most intricate performances of all. That performance now looks set for a long second run. After a hiatus in the nineteenth century, when both the writer and the work were dismissed as indecent, Behn's fame has undergone extraordinary revival. She dominates cultural-studies discourse as both a topic and a set of texts. The texts in particular are worth attending to: many are as astonishing as the career that engendered them.

The Disappointment[1]

One day the amorous Lysander,
By an impatient passion swayed,
Surprised fair Cloris, that loved maid,
Who could defend herself no longer.
5   All things did with his love conspire;
The gilded planet of the day,
In his gay chariot drawn by fire,
Was now descending to the sea,
And left no light to guide the world,
10   But what from Cloris' brighter eyes was hurled.

In a lone thicket made for love,
Silent as yielding maid's consent,
She with a charming languishment
Permits his force, yet gently strove;
15   Her hands his bosom softly meet,
But not to put him back designed,
Rather to draw 'em[2] on inclined;
Whilst he lay trembling at her feet,
Resistance 'tis in vain to show;
20   She wants° the power to say, "Ah! What d'ye do?"   *lacks*

Her bright eyes sweet, and yet severe,
Where love and shame confusedly strive,
Fresh vigor to Lysander give;
And breathing faintly in his ear,
25   She cried, "Cease, cease your vain desire,
Or I'll call out—what would you do?
My dearer honor even to you
I cannot, must not give—retire,
Or take this life, whose chiefest part
30   I gave you with the conquest of my heart."

---

1. Behn based this poem partly on a French source, *Sur une impuissance* (1661), itself derived in part from Ovid's poem on impotence in *Amores*, which also provided the model for Rochester's *Imperfect Enjoyment* (see page 2280). Behn's poem and Rochester's first appeared in the same volume, *Poems on Several Occasions* (1680); she later included hers, with alterations, in her own collection, *Poems on Several Occasions* (1684).
2. Behn's earlier version reads "him."

But he as much unused to fear,
As he was capable of love,
The blessed minutes to improve,
Kisses her mouth, her neck, her hair;
35   Each touch her new desire alarms,
His burning trembling hand he pressed
Upon her swelling snowy breast,
While she lay panting in his arms.
All her unguarded beauties lie
40   The spoils and trophies of the enemy.

And now without respect or fear,
He seeks the object of his vows,
(His love no modesty allows)
By swift degrees advancing—where
45   His daring hand that altar seized,
Where gods of love do sacrifice:
That awful° throne, that paradise   awe-inspiring
Where rage is calmed, and anger pleased;
That fountain where delight still flows,
50   And gives the universal world repose.

Her balmy lips encountering his,
Their bodies, as their souls, are joined;
Where both in transports unconfined
Extend themselves upon the moss.
55   Cloris half dead and breathless lay;
Her soft eyes cast a humid light,
Such as divides the day and night;
Or falling stars, whose fires decay:
And now no signs of life she shows,
60   But what in short-breathed sighs returns and goes.

He saw how at her length she lay;
He saw her rising bosom bare;
Her loose thin robes, through which appear
A shape designed for love and play;
65   Abandoned by her pride and shame,
She does her softest joys dispense,
Offering her virgin innocence
A victim to love's sacred flame;
While the o'er-ravished shepherd lies
70   Unable to perform the sacrifice.

Ready to taste a thousand joys,
The too transported hapless swain[3]
Found the vast pleasure turned to pain;
Pleasure which too much love destroys.
75   The willing garments by he laid,
And Heaven all opened to his view,
Mad to possess, himself he threw

---

3. In English pastoral poetry, this is the conventional term for the shepherd/lover.

On the defenseless lovely maid.
But oh what envying god conspires
80 To snatch his power, yet leave him the desire!

Nature's support[4] (without whose aid
She can no human being give)
Itself now wants the art to live.
Faintness its slackened nerves invade.
85 In vain the enraged youth essayed
To call its fleeting vigor back,
No motion 'twill from motion take.
Excess of love his love betrayed.
In vain he toils, in vain commands;
90 The insensible[5] fell weeping in his hand.

In this so amorous cruel strife,
Where love and fate were too severe,
The poor Lysander in despair
Renounced his reason with his life.
95 Now all the brisk and active fire
That should the nobler part inflame,
Served to increase his rage and shame,
And left no spark for new desire.
Not all her naked charms could move
100 Or calm that rage that had debauched° his love.   *corrupted*

Cloris returning from the trance
Which love and soft desire had bred,
Her timorous hand she gently laid
(Or° guided by design or chance)   *either*
105 Upon that fabulous Priapus,[6]
That potent god, as poets feign;
But never did young shepherdess,
Gathering of fern upon the plain,
More nimbly draw her fingers back,
110 Finding beneath the verdant leaves a snake,

Than Cloris her fair hand withdrew,
Finding that god of her desires
Disarmed of all his awful fires,
And cold as flowers bathed in the morning dew.
115 Who can the nymph's confusion guess?
The blood forsook the hinder place,
And strewed with blushes all her face,
Which both disdain and shame expressed.
And from Lysander's arms she fled,
120 Leaving him fainting on the gloomy bed.

Like lightning through the grove she hies,
Or Daphne from the Delphic god,[7]

---

4. I.e., the erect penis.
5. The unfeeling object.
6. Greek god of male fertility, often depicted as possessing

a permanent erection.
7. Apollo, who pursued the nymph Daphne until she was
turned into a laurel tree in order to escape his advances.

No print upon the grassy road
She leaves, to instruct pursuing eyes.
125 The wind that wantoned in her hair,
And with her ruffled garments played,
Discovered in the flying maid
All that the gods e'er made, if fair.
So Venus, when her love was slain,
130 With fear and haste flew o'er the fatal plain.[8]

The nymph's resentments none but I
Can well imagine or condole.
But none can guess Lysander's soul,
But those who swayed his destiny.
135 His silent griefs swell up to storms,
And not one god his fury spares;
He cursed his birth, his fate, his stars;
But more the shepherdess's charms,
Whose soft bewitching influence
140 Had damned him to the hell of impotence.

                                                        1680

To Lysander,[1] on Some Verses He Writ, and Asking More for His Heart than 'Twas Worth

Take back that heart you with such caution give,
    Take the fond[2] valued trifle back;
I hate love-merchants that a trade would drive;
    And meanly cunning bargains make.

5 I care not how the busy market goes,
    And scorn to chaffer° for a price: bargain
Love does one staple° rate on all impose,   fixed
    Nor leaves it to the trader's choice.

A heart requires a heart unfeigned and true,
10   Though subtly you advance the price,
And ask a rate that simple love ne'er knew:
    And the free trade monopolize.

An humble slave the buyer must become,
    She must not bate[3] a look or glance,
15 You will have all, or you'll have none;
    See how love's market° you enhance.°   price / increase

Is't not enough, I gave you heart for heart,
    But I must add my lips and eyes?
I must no friendly smile or kiss impart;
20   But you must dun[4] me with advice?

---

8. When her beloved Adonis was wounded by a boar, the goddess of love rushed to help him, but in vain.
1. "Lysander," the addressee of several of Behn's poems (and, in name at least, the male lover in *The Disappointment*), has not been identified; the poem suggests that he
was a married man.
2. The word meant both "foolish" and "affectionate."
3. Withhold (by way of reducing love's "price").
4. Badger, demand payment from.

And every hour still more unjust you grow.
   Those freedoms you my life deny,
You to Adraste[5] are obliged to show,
   And give her all my rifled° joy.   *stolen*

25 Without control she gazes on that face,
   And all the happy envied night,
In the pleased circle of your fond embrace:
   She takes away the lover's right.

From me she ravishes those silent hours,
30   That are by sacred love my due;
Whilst I in vain accuse the angry powers,
   That make me hopeless love pursue.

Adraste's ears with that dear voice are blest,
   That charms my soul at every sound,
35 And with those love-enchanting touches pressed:
   Which I ne'er felt without a wound.

She has thee all: whilst I with silent grief,
   The fragments of thy softness feel,
Yet dare not blame the happy licensed[6] thief:
40   That does my dear-bought pleasures steal.

Whilst like a glimmering taper still I burn,
   And waste myself in my own flame,
Adraste takes the welcome rich return:
   And leaves me all the hopeless pain.

45 Be just, my lovely swain, and do not take
   Freedoms you'll not to me allow;
Or give Amynta[7] so much freedom back:
   That she may rove as well as you.

Let us then love upon the honest square,[8]
50   Since interest neither have designed.[9]
For the sly gamester,[1] who ne'er plays me fair,
   Must trick for trick expect to find.

                                            1684

To Lysander at the Music-Meeting

It was too much, ye gods, to see and hear,
Receiving wounds both from the eye and ear.
One charm might have secured a victory;
Both, raised the pleasure even to ecstasy.
5 So ravished lovers in each other's arms,
Faint with excess of joy, excess of charms.
Had I but gazed and fed my greedy eyes,

5. Apparently his wife.
6. Permitted (by the marriage license).
7. I.e., the poem's speaker.
8. I.e., by rules that apply to both sides equally.

9. Neither of us has intended to make a profit (on our investment in each other).
1. Trickster or gambler.

Perhaps you'd pleased no farther than surprise.
That heav'nly form might admiration move,
10   But, not without the music, charmed° with love: *have charmed*
At least so quick the conquest had not been;
You stormed without, and harmony within.
Nor could I listen to the sound alone,
But I alas must look—and was undone:
15   I saw the softness that composed your face,
While your attention heightened every grace:
Your mouth all full of sweetness and content,
And your fine killing eyes of languishment:
Your bosom now and then a sigh would move,
20   (For music has the same effects with love).
Your body easy and all tempting lay,
Inspiring wishes which the eyes betray,
In all that have the fate to glance that way.
A careless and a lovely negligence,
25   Did a new charm to every limb dispense.
So look young angels, listening to the sound,
When the tuned spheres glad[1] all the heav'ns around:
So raptured lie amidst the wondering crowd,
So charmingly extended on a cloud.
30   When from so many ways love's arrows storm,
Who can the heedless heart defend from harm?
Beauty and music must the soul disarm;
Since harmony, like fire to wax, does fit
The softened heart impressions to admit:
35   As the brisk sounds of war the courage move,
Music prepares and warms the soul to love.
But when the kindling sparks such fuel meet,
No wonder if the flame inspired be great.

1684

A Letter to Mr. Creech at Oxford[1]
Written in the Last Great Frost[2]

Daphnis, because I am your debtor, ⎫
(And other causes which are better) ⎬
I send you here by debt of letter. ⎭
You should have had a scrap of nonsense,
5   You may remember left at Tonson's.[3]
(Though by the way that's scurvy rhyme Sir,

1. Gladden. In the Ptolemaic view of the universe that
Behn invokes here, the heavens were composed of concentric crystalline spheres, whose motion produced a sublime music. Angels could hear it, humans could not.
1. Thomas Creech (1659–1700), classicist and translator.
Behn had praised his work in a previous poem, in which
(as here) she addresses him by the pastoral name "Daphnis." Here she produces a less solemn piece, explaining
why a love letter from her has failed to reach him, and

conveying (in the postscript) a compliment from an
unnamed well-wisher.
2. The winter of 1683–1684 was so severe that the surface
of the river Thames froze solid.
3. The eminent bookseller Jacob Tonson (1656–1737)
had published several of Behn's plays and her *Poems on
Several Occasions* (1684). The route through London that
Behn traces in this poem would have taken her past Tonson's shop.

But yet 'twill serve to tag° a line Sir.)   *round off*
A *billet-doux°* I had designed then,   *sweet note*
But you may think I was in wine then;
10   Because it being cold, you know
We warmed it with a glass—or so.
I grant you that shy° wine's the devil,   *cheap*
To make one's memory uncivil;
But when, 'twixt every sparkling cup,
15   I so much brisker wit took up;
Wit, able to inspire a thinking;
And make one solemn even in drinking;
Wit that would charm and stock a poet,
Even instruct ———[4] who has no wit;
20   Wit that was hearty, true, and loyal,
Of wit, like Bays'[5] Sir, that's my trial;
I say 'twas most impossible,
That after that one should be dull.
Therefore because you may not blame me,
25   Take the whole truth as —— shall sa'me.[6]
From Whitehall[7] Sir, as I was coming,
His sacred Majesty from dunning—
Who oft in debt is, truth to tell,
For Tory farce, or doggerel—[8]
30   When every street as dangerous was,
As ever the Alpian hills° to pass,   *the Alps*
When melted snow and ice confound one,
Whether to break one's neck or drown one,
And *billet-doux* in pocket lay,
35   To drop as° coach should jolt that way,   *whenever*
Near to that place of fame called Temple,[9] ⎫
(Which I shall note by sad example)   ⎬
Where college dunce is cured of simple,[1]   ⎭
Against that sign of whore called scarlet,[2]
40   My coachman fairly laid pilgarlic.[3]
Though scribbling fist was out of joint,
And every limb made great complaint;
Yet missing the dear assignation,[4]
Gave me most cause of tribulation.
45   To honest H—le[5] I should have shown ye,

---

4. An in-joke, probably referring to some mutually despised Whig poet.
5. John Dryden, Poet Laureate (so nicknamed because in ancient Rome the laureate wore a wreath of bay leaves); Behn here implies that Dryden sets the standard ("trial") for true wit.
6. As Christ shall save me.
7. The royal palace in London; Behn has apparently been trying to collect payment from the king for a poem she wrote in his support.
8. I.e., Charles II frequently owes money to the partisan poets who write for him.
9. A cluster of buildings on Fleet Street containing resi-

dences, offices, and lecture halls for lawyers and students.
1. Simplicity, foolishness.
2. The Pope's Head tavern, so nicknamed because anti-Catholic literature identified the Roman church with the "whore . . . in scarlet" of Revelation 17.
3. The word originally denoted baldness (with "a head like peeled garlic"), but had become slang for any unfortunate person.
4. I.e., with Creech.
5. John Hoyle, a rakish lawyer with whom Aphra Behn had carried on a much-talked-about amorous relationship and to whom she had addressed many poems.

A wit that would be proud t'have known ye;
A wit uncommon, a facetious,
A great admirer of Lucretius.[6]
But transitory hopes do vary,
50   And high designments oft miscarry.
Ambition never climbed so lofty,
But may descend too fair and softly.
But would you'd seen how sneakingly
I looked with this catastrophe.
55   So saucy Whig, when plot broke out,
Dejected hung his sniveling snout;[7]
So Oxford member looked, when Rowley
Kicked out the rebel crew so foully;[8]
So Perkin, once that god of Wapping,
60   Whom slippery turn of state took napping,
From hopes of James the Second fell
Into the native scoundrel.[9]
So lover looked of joy defeated,
When too much fire his vigor cheated.[1]
65   Even so looked I, when bliss-depriving
Was caused by over-hasty driving.
Who saw me could not choose but think,
I looked like brawn in sousing drink,[2]
Or Lazarello[3] who was showed
70   For a strange fish, to the gaping crowd.
      Thus you by fate (to me, sinister)
At shop of book my *billet* missed Sir.
And home I went as discontent,
As a new routed° Parliament,   dismissed
75   Not seeing Daphnis ere he went.
And sure his grief beyond expressing,
Of joy proposed to want the blessing.[4]
Therefore to pardon pray incline,
Since disappointment all was mine.
80   Of Hell we have no other notion,
Than all the joys of Heaven's privation;
So Sir with recommendations fervent,
I rest your very humble servant.

---

6. Roman author of *De rerum natura* (*On the Nature of Things*), which Creech had translated (1683). Lucretius's insistence on worldly pleasure had established him as the patron philosopher of Restoration libertines.
7. Behn imagines a partisan disappointed by the exposure (and hence the failure) of the Rye House plot, an alleged Whig scheme to assassinate the king and his brother in 1683.
8. In March 1681, Charles II (often dubbed "Rowley" in casual talk and satiric ballads) dismissed the Parliament at Oxford to frustrate the ambitions of the Whig faction.
9. "Perkin" is Charles II's illegitimate son James, Duke of Monmouth, who (like the medieval pretender Perkin Warbeck) claimed that he was the legitimate heir to the

crown; his cause was at one point popular in the rough neighborhood of Wapping. Had he made good on his claim, he (rather than his like-named uncle the Duke of York) would have become James II. Disappointed of that prospect, Behn suggests, he has now "fallen back" into what he truly is: a born rascal.
1. I.e., because of premature ejaculation.
2. Like pickled pig's flesh, bruised and discolored.
3. Hero of Juan de Luna's picaresque narrative *Lazarillo de Tormes*, who is rescued in fishermen's nets after a shipwreck and displayed as a sea monster.
4. Certainly he, having missed out on a promised pleasure, suffers inexpressible grief.

Postscript

On Twelfth Night Sir, by that good token,
85   When lamentable cake was broken,[5]
You had a friend, a man of wit,
A man whom I shall ne'er forget,
For every word he did impart,
'Twas worth the keeping in a heart.
90   True Tory all! and when he spoke,
A god of wit, though man in look.
"To this your friend Daphnis, address
The humblest of my services.
Tell him how much—yet do not, too.
95   My vast esteem no words can show.
Tell him—that he is worthy—you."

1685

To the Fair Clarinda, Who Made Love to Me, Imagined More than Woman

Fair lovely maid, or if that title be
Too weak, too feminine for nobler thee,
Permit a name that more approaches truth,
And let me call thee, lovely charming youth.
5   This last will justify my soft complaint,
While that may serve to lessen my constraint;
And without blushes I the youth pursue,
When so much beauteous woman is in view.
Against thy charms we struggle but in vain,
10   With thy deluding form thou giv'st us pain,
While the bright nymph betrays us to the swain.[1]
In pity to our sex sure thou wert sent,
That we might love, and yet be innocent:
For sure no crime with thee we can commit;
15   Or if we should—thy form excuses it.
For who that gathers fairest flowers believes
A snake lies hid beneath the fragrant leaves.
    Thou beauteous wonder of a different kind,
Soft Cloris with the dear Alexis[2] joined;
20   Whene'er the manly part of thee would plead
Thou tempts us with the image of the maid,
While we the noblest passions do extend
The love to Hermes, Aphrodite the friend.[3]

1688

---

5. On the Twelfth Night of Christmas (6 January, "lamentable," perhaps, because it marked the holiday's conclusion), the traditional festivities included the cutting of a cake in which a pea and bean had been concealed. The recipients of the "prize" pieces presided over the celebration as king and queen (cf. the poem's final line, where Behn and Creech are linked in praise).
1. The conventional pastoral term for a male lover or a country lad.
2. "Cloris" is female, "Alexis" male.
3. Named after the offspring of these two gods, a hermaphrodite combines the characteristics of both sexes.

❧ APHRA BEHN AND HER TIME ❧
Coterie Writing

To Lysander, To the Fair Clarinda, A Letter to Mr. Creech: Some of Behn's poetry, like much other verse in the seventeenth century, proffered its readers the voyeuristic sense that they were being let in on the poet's correspondence. Sometimes this was so. In literary families and in friendships, verse often served as a medium of communication. A poem might make its way first from the writer to a designated recipient, then to a larger circle of acquaintants, and finally (with or without the author's consent) to the printing press. The practice of circulating manuscripts has come to be called "coterie writing," and its antecedents were ancient. Theocritus, the Greek poet credited with inventing pastoral verse, cast many of his poems as expressions of love and friendship (sung rather than written) among shepherds and nymphs living in a Golden Age. The Greek names of these ardent Arcadians—all those swooning "Lysanders" and "Clarindas"—came down to the English poets through the *Eclogues* of Virgil, Theocritus's immeasurably influential Roman imitator. Another Roman, Horace, had pioneered the durable paradigm of the verse epistle, a wittily self-conscious poetic performance addressed to a real-life, explicitly identified contemporary. In the seventeenth century, the resurgence of coterie writing began with the work of Katherine Philips, who celebrated her friendships with women in poems published to great acclaim shortly after her early death. (Behn admired Philips enormously, but reworked the tradition by addressing many of her poems to men—lovers and literary colleagues—in a boldly specific, often sexual language that contrasted sharply with Philips's celebrated chastity.) Both men and women produced poems of friendship in great numbers, but for women writers the practice appears to have held a particular attraction. In addressing other women, they could enact a solidarity, cultivate a self-discovery, define and develop a resistance otherwise muted in a male-dominated world; they often depict themselves as building from female friendship what the critic Janet Todd calls "the last buttress against the irrationality always implied in the female condition." The equivocal "privacy" of the coterie poem made it a particularly supple medium, capable of combining fact and fiction, disguise and revelation, intimacy and declamation. The three practitioners sampled here worked many variations in this pliable, powerful mode of writing.

Mary, Lady Chudleigh[1]
To the Ladies

<blockquote>

Wife and servant are the same,
But only differ in the name:
For when that fatal knot is tied,
Which nothing, nothing can divide:
5   When she the word *obey* has said,
And man by law supreme has made,
Then all that's kind is laid aside,
And nothing left but state° and pride: dignity
Fierce as an Eastern Prince he grows,

</blockquote>

---

1. Born Mary Lee, and wed at age 17 into a family as aristocratic as her own, Lady Chudleigh (1656–1710) lived and wrote in the west coast county of Devon. After years of dispatching manuscript verses among a widening circle of writing friends (including the laureate John Dryden and the pioneering feminist Mary Astell), Chudleigh made her first foray into print with *The Ladies Defense* (1701), a satiric retort to a parson who had exhorted all women (in her mocking paraphrase) to "give up their reason, and their wills resign" to the dictates of their husbands. In her *Defense*, and in the two collections of shorter poems that followed (1703, 1710), Chudleigh sought to expand her coterie into a larger collective readership consisting of "all ingenious ladies": women willing, in defiance of male presumption and social convention, "to read and think, and think and read again," and thereby to "make it our whole business to be wise."

10   And all his innate rigor shows:
     Then but to look, to laugh, or speak,
     Will the nuptial contract break.
     Like mutes she signs alone must make,
     And never any freedom take:
15   But still be governed by a nod,
     And fear her husband as her God:
     Him still must serve, him still obey,
     And nothing act, and nothing say,
     But what her haughty lord thinks fit,
20   Who with the power, has all the wit.°   intelligence
     Then shun, oh! shun that wretched state,
     And all the fawning flatterers hate:
     Value your selves, and men despise,
     You must be proud, if you'll be wise.

                                                                1703

To Almystrea[1]

1

     Permit Marissa[2] in an artless lay
     To speak her wonder, and her thanks repay:
     Her creeping Muse can ne'er like yours ascend;
     She has not strength for such a towering flight.
5   Your wit, her humble fancy does transcend;
     She can but gaze at your exalted height:
     Yet she believed it better to expose
         Her failures, than ungrateful prove;
         And rather chose
10   To show a want of sense, than want of love:
     But taught by you, she may at length improve,
     And imitate those virtues she admires.
     Your bright example leaves a tract divine,
     She sees a beamy brightness in each line,
15   And with ambitious warmth aspires,
     Attracted by the glory of your name,
     To follow you in all the lofty roads of fame.

2

     Merit like yours can no resistance find,
     But like a deluge overwhelms the mind;
20   Gives full possession of each part,
     Subdues the soul, and captivates the heart.
     Let those whom wealth, or interest[3] unite,
         Whom avarice, or kindred sway,[4]
         Who in the dregs of life delight,
25   And every dictate of their sense° obey,   appetites
     Learn here to love at a sublimer rate,

---

1. The name is an anagram for Mary Astell, feminist author of *Some Reflections upon Marriage* (see page 2357).
2. Chudleigh's pen name.

3. Self-interest, desire for power and material prosperity.
4. I.e., who are motivated by greed or desire for family status.

To wish for nothing but exchange of thoughts,
   For intellectual joys,
   And pleasures more refined
30 Than earth can give, or fancy can create.
Let our vain sex be fond of glittering toys,
Of pompous titles, and affected noise,
Let envious men by barb'rous custom led
   Descant° on faults,   expound
35   And in detraction° find   criticisms
Delights unknown to a brave generous mind,
While we resolve a nobler path to tread,
   And from tyrannic custom free,
View the dark mansions of the mighty dead,
40   And all their close recesses see;
   Then from those awful shades retire,
     And take a tour above,
And there, the shining scenes admire,
   The opera of eternal love;
45 View the machines,[5] on the bright actors gaze,
Then in a holy transport, blest amaze,
To the great Author our devotion raise,
And let our wonder terminate in praise.

1703

Anne Finch, Countess of Winchilsea[1]
The Introduction

Did I my lines intend for public view,
How many censures would their faults pursue!
Some would, because such words they do affect,
Cry they're insipid, empty, uncorrect.
5 And many have attained, dull and untaught,
The name of wit, only by finding fault.
True judges might condemn their want of wit,
And all might say they're by a woman writ.
Alas! A woman that attempts the pen,
10 Such an intruder on the rights of men,
Such a presumptuous creature is esteemed,
The fault can by no virtue be redeemed.
They tell us we mistake our sex and way;
Good breeding, fashion, dancing, dressing, play
15 Are the accomplishments we should desire;

5. The stage mechanisms used to move scenery and produce striking effects (including the appearances of gods
and angels).
1. In the early 1680s, while serving as Maid of Honor to
Mary of Modena (wife of the future James II), Anne
Kingsmill (1661–1720) met and married Colonel
Heneage Finch, and savored the splendors of the Stuart
court. When that world vanished in the Revolution of
1688, she and her husband withdrew to his country
estate, where she suffered recurrent depression, cultivated
friendships, wrote poetry, and saw her work published in
several miscellanies. In 1713, despite her wariness of the
censures heaped on women writers, she published anonymously a collection of her own, Miscellany Poems on Several Occasions. (The Introduction, in which she most
memorably confronts the censurers, remained like much
of her verse unpublished until the 20th century.) The
book brought her some fame in her own time and much
more a century later, when William Wordsworth proclaimed his admiration for her work. Her poetry moves
adroitly among polarities: city and country, satire and
affection, solitude and friendship.

To write, or read, or think, or to inquire
Would cloud our beauty, and exhaust our time,
And interrupt the conquests of our prime;
Whilst the dull manage of a servile house
20   Is held by some our utmost art, and use.
          Sure 'twas not ever thus, nor are we told
Fables,° of women that excelled of old;   *false stories*
To whom, by the diffusive° hand of heaven   *scattering*
Some share of wit and poetry was given.
25   On that glad day, on which the Ark returned,[2]
The holy pledge for which the land had mourned,
The joyful tribes attend it on the way,
The Levites do the sacred charge convey,
Whilst various instruments before it play;
30   Here, holy virgins in the concert join,
The louder notes to soften, and refine,
And with alternate verse,[3] complete the hymn divine.
Lo! The young poet,[4] after God's own heart,
By Him inspired, and taught the Muse's art,
35   Returned from conquest, a bright chorus meets,
That sing his slain ten thousand in the streets.
In such loud numbers° they his acts declare,   *verses*
Proclaim the wonders of his early war,
That Saul upon the vast applause does frown,
40   And feels its mighty thunder shake the crown.[5]
What can the threatened judgment now prolong?[6]
Half of the kingdom is already gone:
The fairest half, whose influence guides the rest,
Have David's empire o'er their hearts confessed.
45   A woman[7] here leads fainting Israel on,
She fights, she wins, she triumphs with a song,
Devout, majestic, for the subject fit,
And far above her arms, exalts her wit,
Then to the peaceful, shady palm withdraws,
50   And rules the rescued nation with her laws.
How are we fal'n, fal'n by mistaken rules?
And education's, more than nature's fools,
Debarred from all improvements of the mind,
And to be dull, expected and designed°;   *intended*
55   And if someone would soar above the rest,
With warmer fancy[8] and ambition pressed,
So strong the opposing faction still appears,
The hopes to thrive can ne'er outweigh the fears.

2. The Ark of the Covenant was a chest containing the stone tablets of the Ten Commandments. Recovered by King David, it was carried into Jerusalem by members of the Levite tribe (1 Chronicles 15).
3. Responsive singing: the male and the female choruses sing by turns, answering line with line.
4. David, who in his youth was skilled both as a fighter, conquering the Philistines, and as a harper, credited with composing the Psalms.

5. Saul, first king of Israel, had made David his general but tried to kill him after hearing the women of Israel singing, "Saul has slain his thousands, and David his ten thousands" (1 Samuel 18.7).
6. Postpone; the prophet Samuel had foretold an untimely end to Saul's reign.
7. Deborah, judge and prophet who led the Israelites to victory over the Canaanites (Judges 4–5).
8. Livelier imagination.

60 Be cautioned then my Muse, and still retired;
Nor be despised, aiming to be admired;
Conscious of wants, still with contracted wing,
To some few friends and to thy sorrows sing;
For groves of laurel[9] thou wert never meant;
Be dark enough thy shades, and be thou there content.

1903

Friendship Between Ephelia and Ardelia[1]

Eph.   What friendship is, Ardelia, show.
Ard.   'Tis to love, as I love you.
Eph.   This account, so short (though kind)
    Suits not my inquiring mind.
5   Therefore farther now repeat:
    What is friendship when complete?
Ard.   'Tis to share all joy and grief;
    'Tis to lend all due relief
    From the tongue, the heart, the hand;
10   'Tis to mortgage house and land;
    For a friend be sold a slave;
    'Tis to die upon a grave,
    If a friend therein do lie.
Eph.   This indeed, though carried high,
15   This, though more than e'er was done
    Underneath the rolling sun,
    This has all been said before.
    Can Ardelia say no more?
Ard.   Words indeed no more can show:
20   But 'tis to love, as I love you.

1713

A Ballad to Mrs. Catherine Fleming in London
from Malshanger Farm in Hampshire

From me, who whilom° sung the town,   *formerly*
    This second ballad comes;
To let you know we are got down
    From hurry, smoke, and drums:
5 And every visitor that rolls
In restless coach from Mall to Paul's,[1]
    With a fa-la-la-la-la-la.

And now were I to paint the seat[2]
    (As well-bred poets use°)   *do*
10 I should embellish our retreat,
    By favor of the Muse:
Though to no villa we pretend,

---

9. Tree whose leaves were used to crown celebrated poets.
1. "Ardelia" is Finch's pastoral pen name.
1. From Pall Mall, a fashionable promenade in London,
to St. Paul's Cathedral.
2. The "country seat": the farm.

But a plain farm at the best end,
    With a fa-la etc.

15 Where innocence and quiet reigns,
        And no distrust is known;
    His nightly safety none maintains,
        By ways they do in town,
    Who rising loosen bolt and bar;
20 We draw the latch and out we are,
        With a fa-la etc.

    For jarring sounds in London streets,
        Which still are passing by;
    Where "Cowcumbers"[3] with "Sand ho" meets,
25   And for loud mastery vie:
    The driver whistling to his team
    Here wakes us from some rural dream,
        With a fa-la etc.

    From rising hills through distant views,
30   We see the sun decline;
    Whilst everywhere the eye pursues
        The grazing flocks and kine:
    Which home at night the farmer brings,
    And not the post's but sheep's bell rings,
35   With a fa-la etc.

    We silver trouts and crayfish eat,
        Just taken from the stream;
    And never think our meal complete,
        Without fresh curds and cream:
40 And as we pass by the barn floor,
    We choose our supper from the door,
        With a fa-la etc.

    Beneath our feet the partridge springs,
        As to the woods we go;
45 Where birds scarce stretch their painted wings,
        So little fear they show:
    But when our outspread hoops° they spy,   *hoop skirts*
    They look when we like them should fly,
        With a fa-la etc.

50 Through verdant circles as we stray,
        To which no end we know;
    As we o'erhanging boughs survey,
        And tufted grass below:
    Delight into the fancy falls,
55 And happy days and verse recalls,
        With a fa-la etc.

    Oh! Why did I these shades forsake,
        And shelter of the grove;

3. Cucumbers; these are the cries of street peddlers.

The flowering shrub, the rustling brake,°   *thicket*
60   The solitude I love:
Where emperors have fixed their lot,
And greatly chose to be forgot,
     With a fa-la etc.

Then how can I from hence depart,
65   Unless my pleasing friend
Should now her sweet harmonious art
     Unto these shades extend:
And, like old Orpheus' powerful song,[4]
Draw me and all my woods along,
70   With a fa-la etc.

So charmed like Birnam's they would rise,
And march in goodly row,[5]
But since it might the town surprise
     To see me travel so,
75   I must from soothing joys like these,
Too soon return in open chaise°   *carriage*
     With a fa-la etc.

Meanwhile accept what I have writ,
     To show this rural scene;
80   Nor look for sharp satiric wit
     From off the balmy plain:
The country breeds no thorny bays,
     But mirth and love and honest praise,
     With a fa-la etc.

c. 1719   1929

Mary Leapor[1]
The Headache. To Aurelia

Aurelia, when your zeal makes known
Each woman's failing but your own,
How charming Silvia's teeth decay,
And Celia's hair is turning grey;
5   Yet Celia gay has sparkling eyes,
But (to your comfort) is not wise:
Methinks you take a world of pains
To tell us Celia has no brains.

---

4. The mythological poet's music charmed trees and stones into motion.
5. In Shakespeare's *Macbeth*, the forest of Birnam "comes" to Dunsinane (fulfilling the witches' prophecy) when soldiers carry boughs as camouflage.
1. The daughter of a gardener, Mary Leapor (1722–1746) worked as a kitchen maid, read voraciously, wrote plentifully, and sustained the tradition of the social poem (complete with pastoral pseudonyms) into a new era and a new register. Her manuscripts, circulating among neighbors, brought her the attention, friendship, and support of Bridget Freemantle, who undertook to arrange their publication. Leapor died of measles at age 24 before

she could see her work in print. Her *Poems upon Several Occasions* appeared in 1748; its success prompted an additional volume three years later. Though the books were marketed as (in the words of one contemporary) the work of "a most extraordinary, uncultivated genius," the poems themselves prove otherwise. They display influences absorbed from Greek and Roman classics, Restoration drama, and Augustan literature—particularly Swift and Pope. Leapor transports these elements across boundary lines of class and gender to produce a new, arresting voice speaking from an old position: that of the woman who must labor in order to live.

Now you wise folk, who make such a pother°   *fuss*
10   About the wit of one another,
With pleasure would your brains resign,
Did all your noddles° ache like mine.   *heads*

Not cuckolds half my anguish know,
When budding horns[2] begin to grow;
15   Nor battered skull of wrestling Dick,
Who late was drubbed at singlestick;[3]
Nor wretches that in fevers fry,
Not Sappho[4] when her cap's awry,
E'er felt such torturing pangs as I;
20   Not forehead of Sir Jeffrey Strife,
When smiling Cynthio kissed his wife.

Not lovesick Marcia's languid eyes,
Who for her simpering Corin dies,
So sleepy look or dimly shine,
25   As these dejected eyes of mine:
Not Claudia's brow such wrinkles made
At sight of Cynthia's new brocade.

Just so, Aurelia, you complain
Of vapors, rheums, and gouty pain;
30   Yet I am patient, so should you,
For cramps and headaches are our due:
We suffer justly for our crimes,
For scandal you, and I for rhymes;
Yet we (as hardened wretches do)
35   Still the enchanting vice pursue;
Our reformation ne'er begin
But fondly hug the darling sin.

Yet there's a might difference too
Between the fate of me and you;
40   Though you with tottering age shall bow,
And wrinkles scar your lovely brow,
Your busy tongue may still proclaim
The faults of every sinful dame:
You still may prattle nor give o'er,
45   When wretched I must sin no more.
The sprightly Nine° must leave me then,   *Muses*
This trembling hand resign its pen:
No matron ever sweetly sung,
Apollo° only courts the young.   *god of poetry*
50   Then who would not (Aurelia, pray)
Enjoy his favors while they may?
Nor cramps nor headaches shall prevail:
I'll still write on, and you shall rail.

1748

2. Folklore held that the husband of an unfaithful wife
would sprout horns from his forehead.
3. Beaten in a fencing match using short, heavy sticks.

4. Apparently a mutual friend; the ensuing names, too,
refer to either real or imaginary people, otherwise
unidentified.

Advice to Sophronia

When youth and charms have ta'en their wanton flight,
And transient beauty bids the fair good-night;
When once her sparkling eyes shall dimly roll,
Then let the matron dress her lofty soul;
5   Quit affectation, partner of her youth,
For goodness, prudence, purity, and truth.
These virtues will her lasting peace prepare,
And give a sanction to her silver hair.
These precepts let the fond Sophronia prove,
10   Nor vainly dress her blinking eyes with love.
Can roses flourish on a leafless thorn,
Or dewy woodbines grace a wintry morn?
The weeping Cupids languish in your eye;
On your brown cheek the sickly beauties die.
15   Time's rugged hand has stroked your visage o'er;
The gay vermilion stains your lip no more.
None can with justice now your shape admire;
The drooping lilies on your breast expire.
Then, dear Sophronia, leave thy foolish whims:
20   Discard your lover with your favorite sins.
Consult your glass; then prune your wanton mind,
Nor furnish laughter for succeeding time.
'Tis not your own; 'tis gold's all-conquering charms
Invite Myrtillo to your shrivelled arms:
25   And shall Sophronia, whose once-lovely eyes
Beheld those triumphs which her heart despised,
Who looked on merit with a haughty frown,
At five-and-fifty take a beardless clown?
Ye pitying Fates, this withered damsel save,
30   And bear her safely to her virgin grave.

1751

An Essay on Woman

Woman, a pleasing but a short-lived flower,
Too soft for business and too weak for power:
A wife in bondage, or neglected maid;
Despised, if ugly; if she's fair, betrayed.
5   'Tis wealth alone inspires every grace,
And calls the raptures to her plenteous face.
What numbers for those charming features pine,
If blooming acres round her temples twine!!¹
Her lip the strawberry, and her eyes more bright
10   Than sparkling Venus in a frosty night;
Pale lilies fade and, when the fair appears,
Snow turns a negro² and dissolves in tears,
And, where the charmer treads her magic toe,
On English ground Arabian odors grow;

---

1. I.e., if her dowry includes valuable land.   2. I.e., seems black by comparison.

15   Till mighty Hymen° lifts his sceptred rod,   *god of marriage*
      And sinks her glories with a fatal nod,
      Dissolves her triumphs, sweeps her charms away,
      And turns the goddess to her native clay.

          But, Artemisia,³ let your servant sing
20   What small advantage wealth and beauties bring.
      Who would be wise, that knew Pamphilia's⁴ fate?
      Or who be fair, and joined to Sylvia's mate?
      Sylvia, whose cheeks are fresh as early day,
      As evening mild, and sweet as spicy May:
25   And yet that face her partial husband tires,
      And those bright eyes, that all the world admires.
      Pamphilia's wit who does not strive to shun,
      Like death's infection or a dog-day's sun?
      The damsels view her with malignant eyes,
30   The men are vexed to find a nymph so wise:
      And wisdom only serves to make her know
      The keen sensation of superior woe.
      The secret whisper and the listening ear,
      The scornful eyebrow and the hated sneer,
35   The giddy censures of her babbling kind,
      With thousand ills that grate a gentle mind,
      By her are tasted in the first degree,
      Though overlooked by Simplicus and me.
      Does thirst of gold a virgin's heart inspire,
40   Instilled by Nature or a careful sire?
      Then let her quit extravagance and play,
      The brisk companion and expensive tea,
      To feast with Cordia in her filthy sty
      On stewed potatoes or on mouldy pie;
45   Whose eager eyes stare ghastly at the poor,
      And fright the beggars from her hated door;
      In greasy clouts° she wraps her smokey chin,   *rags*
      And holds that pride's a never-pardoned sin.
          If this be wealth, no matter where it falls;
50   But save, ye Muses, save your Mira's⁵ walls:
      Still give me pleasing indolence and ease,
      A fire to warm me and a friend to please.

          Since, whether sunk in avarice or pride,
      A wanton virgin or a starving bride,
55   Or° wondering crowds attend her charming tongue,   *whether*
      Or, deemed an idiot, ever speaks the wrong;
      Though Nature armed us for the growing ill
      With fraudful cunning and a headstrong will;
      Yet, with ten thousand follies to her charge,
60   Unhappy woman's but a slave at large.

                                                            1751

---

3. The name of an ancient ruler celebrated as a patron of literature; Leapor applies it to her friend and sponsor Bridget Freemantle.
4. The lines about "Pamphilia" suggest that she may serve here as Leapor's alter ego; the other pastoral names (Sylvia, Simplicus, etc.) conjure up acquaintances real or imaginary.
5. Leapor's pen name (derived from "Mary").

The Epistle of Deborah Dough

Dearly beloved Cousin, these
Are sent to thank you for your cheese;
The price of oats is greatly fell:
I hope your children all are well
5   (Likewise the calf you take delight in),
As I am at this present writing.
But I've no news to send you now;
Only I've lost my brindled° cow,   *spotted*
And that has greatly sunk my dairy.
10   But I forgot our neighbor Mary;
Our neighbor Mary—who, they say,
Sits scribble-scribble all the day,
And making—what—I can't remember;
But sure 'tis something like December;
15   A frosty morning—let me see—
O! Now I have it to a T:
She throws away her precious time
In scrawling nothing else but rhyme;[1]
Of which, they say, she's mighty proud,
20   And lifts her nose above the crowd;
Though my young daughter Cicely
Is taller by a foot than she,
And better learned (as people say);
Can knit a stocking in a day;
25   Can make a pudding, plump and rare;
And boil her bacon to an hair;
Will coddle° apples nice and green,   *cook*
And fry her pancakes—like a queen.

    But there's a man, that keeps a dairy,
30   Will clip the wings of neighbor Mary:
Things wonderful they talk of him,
But I've a notion 'tis a whim.
Howe'er, 'tis certain he can make
Your rhymes as thick as plums in cake;
35   Nay more, they say that from the pot
He'll take his porridge, scalding hot,
And drink 'em down;—and yet they tell ye
Those porridge shall not burn his belly;
A cheesecake o'er his head he'll throw,
40   And when 'tis on the stones below,
It shan't be found so much as quaking,
Provided 'tis of his wife's making.
From this some people would infer
That this good man's a conjuror:
45   But I believe it is a lie;
I never thought him so, not I,
Though Win'fred Hobble who, you know,
Is plagued with corns on every toe,

1. A pun on "rime" (frost), which is why her work is "like December."

Sticks on his verse with fastening spittle,
50   And says it helps her feet a little.
Old Frances too his paper tears,
And tucks it close behind his ears;
And (as she told me t'other day)
It charmed her toothache quite away.

55   Now as thou'rt better learned than me,
Dear Cos', I leave it all to thee
To judge about this puzzling man,
And ponder wisely—for you can.

         Now Cousin, I must let you know
60   That, while my name is Deborah Dough,
I shall be always glad to see ye,
And what I have, I'll freely gi' ye.

         'Tis one o'clock, as I'm a sinner;
The boys are all come home to dinner,
65   And I must bid you now farewell.
I pray remember me to Nell;
And for your friend I'd have you know
Your loving Cousin,
                    DEBORAH DOUGH

                                                    1751

END OF APHRA BEHN AND COTERIE WRITING

OROONOKO   "I am very ill and have been dying this twelve month," Behn wrote an acquaintance late in 1687; she suffered from degenerative arthritis and had some eighteen months' dying still to do. Now, near the end of her writing career, she set down a narrative of events that had predated its beginnings, a story that she claimed to recall from the months she spent in 1663–1664 as a young woman in Surinam, an English colony on the northeastern coast of South America. A friend records that during the intervening decades Behn had often told the story of an African prince enslaved on the plantation where she dwelt; prompted by his love for a slave from his own country, he mounted a rebellion against his English masters. In *Oroonoko*, Behn displayed Surinam as a world where the appetites of trade and empire had brought several cultures—indigenous "Indians," colonizing Europeans, abducted Africans—into violent and precarious fusion.

     Writing the narrative, Behn undertook volatile fusions of her own. On the title page, the single name "Oroonoko" sits above two subtitles in which both hero and text are implicitly split in two. The hero is both "royal" and a "slave"; the text's "true history" is so suffused with fictional conventions that for a long while historians suspected that Behn had never been to Surinam and had made the whole thing up (the truth of many of the story's details has been neither established nor refuted). Oroonoko and his beloved Imoinda play out the love-and-loss plot of a heroic romance—a genre favored by Restoration aristocracy—within the far more realistic context of a world driven by bourgeois imperatives and political aspirations. Behn's boldest fusion involves not only cultures, identities, and modes but also times. Oroonoko, "the chief actor in this history," comes to embody the history of Stuart sovereignty, playing the roles of all three kings to whom Behn had devoted her own obsessive loyalties: Charles I, whose 1649 execution haunts the narrative, particularly in its last few pages; Charles II, whose 1660 Restoration Behn pointedly invokes at the celebratory moment of the African prince's arrival at Surinam; and James II, the beleaguered Catholic king whose three-year reign was hurtling toward its close at the very moment of *Oroonoko*'s publication, and whose predicament as the embattled champion of an oppressed minority finds many echoes in the royal slave's rebellion and his fate.

Mapping all these convergences—of culture with culture, of monarch with slave, of man with woman—Behn places herself as narrator problematically near their center. The story is driven by her empathy for the slave couple, for whom she acts as mentor, friend, and advocate. Yet her empathy is complicated, perhaps even compromised. She shows less pity for less "royal" slaves, she acknowledges the possibility of her own complicity (however inadvertent) in her hero's pain, and she is oddly absent at the height of his suffering. She also participates in the profitable systems that enmesh him. Even before she tells his story, she presents herself as a kind of trader, who has brought back from Surinam butterflies for the Royal Society and exotic feathers for the dress of the "Indian Queen" in the popular heroic tragedy of that name. As the scholar Laura Brown points out, Behn's "treatment of slavery . . . is neither coherent nor fully critical." The narrative is by turns empathetic with the oppressed and complicit with the powerful; the crossing vectors of Behn's allegiance produce no conclusive sum.

In *Oroonoko*, cultural compounds prove unstable. Again and again in the story, human bodies are torn apart, and these sunderings foretell other dissolutions. Behn repeatedly reminds her readers that shortly after the events she narrates, the entire colony at Surinam disappeared: the English traded it away to the Dutch (they got New York in return). As colonist she laments this loss; as Tory, she anticipates another: the loss of James II in the parliamentary overthrow that would soon supplant the English Catholic with the Dutch Protestant William of Orange. Stuart rule, which had "ended" once with regicide, would end again (like the world of her youth in Surinam) with revolution.

Behn died shortly after publishing her narrative; she was buried in Westminster Abbey, where William would be crowned just five days later. After Behn's death, *Oroonoko* did more than any of her other works to sustain her fame. As a prose narrative and in an oft-revived dramatic adaptation, it became one of the touchstone texts for the antislavery movement that grew in England and America over the next century and a half. Only with the appearance of *Uncle Tom's Cabin* in the 1850s did the advocates of abolition find a more contemporary narrative that could take its place. Behn's intricately fictionalized "true history" had survived its initial moment, and helped shape history thereafter.

Oroonoko
or
The Royal Slave
A True History

I do not pretend, in giving you the history of this royal slave, to entertain my reader with the adventures of a feigned hero, whose life and fortunes Fancy may manage at the poet's pleasure; nor in relating the truth, design to adorn it with any accidents, but such as arrived in earnest to him. And it shall come simply into the world, recommended by its own proper merits, and natural intrigues; there being enough of reality to support it, and to render it diverting, without the addition of invention.

I was myself an eyewitness to a great part of what you will find here set down; and what I could not be witness of, I received from the mouth of the chief actor in this history, the hero himself, who gave us the whole transactions of his youth; and though I shall omit, for brevity's sake, a thousand little accidents of his life, which, however pleasant to us, where history was scarce, and adventures very rare, yet might prove tedious and heavy to my reader, in a world where he finds diversions for every minute, new and strange. But we who were perfectly charmed with the character of this great man were curious to gather every circumstance of his life.

The scene of the last part of his adventures lies in a colony in America called Surinam, in the West Indies.

But before I give you the story of this gallant slave, 'tis fit I tell you the manner of bringing them to these new colonies; for those they make use of there, are not natives of the place; for those we live with in perfect amity, without daring to command them; but on the contrary, caress them with all the brotherly and friendly affection in the world, trading with them for their fish, venison, buffaloes, skins, and little rarities; as marmosets, a sort of monkey as big as a rat or weasel, but of a marvelous and delicate shape, and has face and hands like an human creature; and cousheries,[1] a little beast in the form and fashion of a lion, as big as a kitten; but so exactly made in all parts like that noble beast, that it is it in miniature. Then for little parakeets, great parrots, macaws, and a thousand other birds and beasts of wonderful and surprising forms, shapes, and colors. For skins of prodigious snakes, of which there are some threescore yards in length; as is the skin of one that may be seen at His Majesty's Antiquaries,[2] where are also some rare flies,[3] of amazing forms and colors, presented to them by myself, some as big as my fist, some less; and all of various excellencies, such as art cannot imitate. Then we trade for feathers, which they order into all shapes, make themselves little short habits of them, and glorious wreaths for their heads, necks, arms, and legs, whose tinctures are inconceivable. I had a set of these presented to me, and I gave them to the King's Theater, and it was the dress of the *Indian Queen*,[4] infinitely admired by persons of quality, and were inimitable. Besides these, a thousand little knacks and rarities in nature, and some of art; as their baskets, weapons, aprons, etc. We dealt with them with beads of all colors, knives, axes, pins, and needles, which they used only as tools to drill holes with in their ears, noses, and lips, where they hang a great many little things; as long beads, bits of tin, brass, or silver, beat thin, and any shining trinket. The beads they weave into aprons about a quarter of an ell[5] long, and of the same breadth, working them very prettily in flowers of several colors of beads; which apron they wear just before them, as Adam and Eve did the fig leaves; the men wearing a long strip of linen, which they deal with us for. They thread these beads also on long cotton threads, and make girdles to tie their aprons to, which come twenty times or more about the waist and then cross, like a shoulder-belt, both ways, and round their necks, arms, and legs. This adornment, with their long black hair, and the face painted in little specks or flowers here and there, makes them a wonderful figure to behold. Some of the beauties which indeed are finely shaped, as almost all are, and who have pretty features, are very charming and novel; for they have all that is called beauty except the color, which is a reddish yellow; or after a new oiling, which they often use to themselves, they are of the color of a new brick, but smooth, soft, and sleek. They are extreme modest and bashful, very shy, and nice[6] of being touched. And though they are all thus naked, if one lives forever among them, there is not to be seen an indecent action or glance; and being continually used to see one another so unadorned, so like our first parents before the Fall, it seems as if they had no wishes; there being nothing to heighten curiosity, but all you can see, you see at once, and every moment see; and where there is no novelty, there can be no curiosity. Not but I have seen a handsome young Indian, dying for love of a very beautiful young Indian maid; but all his courtship was, to fold his arms,

1. Other writers mention this animal, but its identity remains uncertain.
2. Probably the "Repository" (museum) of the Royal Society.
3. Butterflies.

4. A heroic drama (1664) by Robert Howard and John Dryden, celebrated for its sumptuous costumes and design.
5. Forty-five inches.
6. Shy.

pursue her with his eyes, and sighs were all his language; while she, as if no such lover were present, or rather, as if she desired none such, carefully guarded her eyes from beholding him; and never approached him, but she looked down with all the blushing modesty I have seen in the most severe and cautious of our world. And these people represented to me an absolute idea of the first state of innocence, before man knew how to sin; and 'tis most evident and plain, that simple Nature is the most harmless, inoffensive, and virtuous mistress. 'Tis she alone, if she were permitted, that better instructs the world than all the inventions of man; religion would here but destroy that tranquillity they possess by ignorance, and laws would but teach them to know offense, of which now they have no notion. They once made mourning and fasting for the death of the English governor, who had given his hand to come on such a day to them, and neither came, nor sent; believing, when once a man's word was past, nothing but death could or should prevent his keeping it. And when they saw he was not dead, they asked him, what name they had for a man who promised a thing he did not do? The governor told them, such a man was a liar, which was a word of infamy to a gentleman. Then one of them replied, "Governor, you are a liar, and guilty of that infamy." They have a native justice which knows no fraud, and they understand no vice, or cunning, but when they are taught by the white men. They have plurality of wives which, when they grow old, they serve those that succeed them, who are young; but with a servitude easy and respected; and unless they take slaves in war, they have no other attendants.

Those on that continent where I was had no king; but the oldest war captain was obeyed with great resignation.

A war captain is a man who has led them on to battle with conduct[7] and success, of whom I shall have occasion to speak more hereafter, and of some other of their customs and manners, as they fall in my way.

With these people, as I said, we live in perfect tranquillity and good understanding, as it behooves us to do; they knowing all the places where to seek the best food of the country, and the means of getting it; and for very small and invaluable trifles, supply us with what 'tis impossible for us to get; for they do not only in the wood, and over the savannahs, in hunting, supply the parts of hounds, by swiftly scouring through those almost impassable places, and by the mere activity of their feet, run down the nimblest deer, and other eatable beasts; but in the water, one would think they were gods of the rivers, or fellow citizens of the deep, so rare an art they have in swimming, diving, and almost living in water, by which they command the less swift inhabitants of the floods. And then for shooting, what they cannot take, or reach with their hands, they do with arrows, and have so admirable an aim, that they will split almost a hair; and at any distance that an arrow can reach, they will shoot down oranges and other fruit, and only touch the stalk with the darts' points, that they may not hurt the fruit. So that they being, on all occasions, very useful to us, we find it absolutely necessary to caress them as friends, and not to treat them as slaves; nor dare we do other, their numbers so far surpassing ours in that continent.

Those then whom we make use of to work in our plantations of sugar are Negroes, black slaves altogether, which are transported thither in this manner.

Those who want slaves make a bargain with a master, or captain of a ship, and contract to pay him so much apiece, a matter of twenty pound a head for as many as he agrees for, and to pay for them when they shall be delivered on such a plantation.

7. Skillful management.

So that when there arrives a ship laden with slaves, they who have so contracted go aboard, and receive their number by lot; and perhaps in one lot that may be for ten, there may happen to be three or four men; the rest, women and children; or be there more or less of either sex, you are obliged to be contented with your lot.

Coramantien,[8] a country of blacks so called, was one of those places in which they found the most advantageous trading for these slaves, and thither most of our great traders in that merchandise trafficked; for that nation is very warlike and brave, and having a continual campaign, being always in hostility with one neighboring prince or other, they had the fortune to take a great many captives; for all they took in battle were sold as slaves, at least, those common men who could not ransom themselves. Of these slaves so taken, the general only has all the profit; and of these generals, our captains and masters of ships buy all their freights.

The King of Coramantien was himself a man of a hundred and odd years old, and had no son, though he had many beautiful black wives; for most certainly, there are beauties that can charm of that color. In his younger years he had had many gallant men to his sons, thirteen of which died in battle, conquering when they fell; and he had only left him for his successor one grandchild, son to one of these dead victors; who, as soon as he could bear a bow in his hand, and a quiver at his back, was sent into the field, to be trained up by one of the oldest generals to war; where, from his natural inclination to arms, and the occasions given him, with the good conduct of the old general, he became, at the age of seventeen, one of the most expert captains, and bravest soldiers, that ever saw the field of Mars; so that he was adored as the wonder of all that world, and the darling of the soldiers. Besides, he was adorned with a native beauty so transcending all those of his gloomy race, that he struck an awe and reverence, even in those that knew not his quality; as he did in me, who beheld him with surprise and wonder, when afterwards he arrived in our world.

He had scarce arrived at his seventeenth year when, fighting by his side, the general was killed with an arrow in his eye, which the Prince Oroonoko (for so was this gallant Moor[9] called) very narrowly avoided; nor had he, if the general, who saw the arrow shot, and perceiving it aimed at the Prince, had not bowed his head between, on purpose to receive it in his own body rather than it should touch that of the Prince, and so saved him.

'Twas then, afflicted as Oroonoko was, that he was proclaimed general in the old man's place; and then it was, at the finishing of that war, which had continued for two years, that the Prince came to court, where he had hardly been a month together, from the time of his fifth year to that of seventeen; and 'twas amazing to imagine where it was he learned so much humanity or, to give his accomplishments a juster name, where 'twas he got that real greatness of soul, those refined notions of true honor, that absolute generosity, and that softness that was capable of the highest passions of love and gallantry, whose objects were almost continually fighting men, or those mangled or dead; who heard no sounds but those of war and groans. Some part of it we may attribute to the care of a Frenchman of wit and learning, who finding it turn to very good account to be a sort of royal tutor to this young black, and perceiving him very ready, apt, and quick of apprehension, took a great pleasure to teach him morals, language, and science, and was for it extremely beloved and valued by

8. Koromantyn, a fort and trading post on the western coast of Africa (in modern Ghana).
9. The word originally meant "Moroccan," but was often used more generally for any person of African descent. Oroonoko's name may echo the river Orinoco in Venezuela, or the African god Oro.

him. Another reason was, he loved, when he came from war, to see all the English gentlemen that traded thither, and did not only learn their language but that of the Spaniards also, with whom he traded afterwards for slaves.

I have often seen and conversed with this great man, and been a witness to many of his mighty actions, and do assure my reader, the most illustrious courts could not have produced a braver man, both for greatness of courage and mind, a judgment more solid, a wit more quick, and a conversation more sweet and diverting. He knew almost as much as if he had read much: he had heard of, and admired the Romans; he had heard of the late Civil Wars in England, and the deplorable death of our great monarch,[1] and would discourse of it with all the sense, and abhorrence of the injustice imaginable. He had an extreme good and graceful mien, and all the civility of a well-bred great man. He had nothing of barbarity in his nature, but in all points addressed himself as if his education had been in some European court.

This great and just character of Oroonoko gave me an extreme curiosity to see him, especially when I knew he spoke French and English, and that I could talk with him. But though I had heard so much of him, I was as greatly surprised when I saw him as if I had heard nothing of him, so beyond all report I found him. He came into the room, and addressed himself to me, and some other women, with the best grace in the world. He was pretty tall, but of a shape the most exact that can be fancied; the most famous statuary[2] could not form the figure of a man more admirably turned from head to foot. His face was not of that brown, rusty black which most of that nation are, but a perfect ebony, or polished jet. His eyes were the most awful that could be seen, and very piercing, the white of them being like snow, as were his teeth. His nose was rising and Roman, instead of African and flat; his mouth, the finest shaped that could be seen, far from those great turned lips which are so natural to the rest of the Negroes. The whole proportion and air of his face was so noble and exactly formed that, bating[3] his color, there could be nothing in nature more beautiful, agreeable, and handsome. There was no one grace wanting that bears the standard of true beauty. His hair came down to his shoulders by the aids of art, which was, by pulling it out with a quill and keeping it combed, of which he took particular care. Nor did the perfections of his mind come short of those of his person, for his discourse was admirable upon almost any subject; and whoever had heard him speak, would have been convinced of their errors, that all fine wit is confined to the white men, especially to those of Christendom; and would have confessed that Oroonoko was as capable even of reigning well, and of governing as wisely, had as great a soul, as politic maxims,[4] and was as sensible of power as any prince civilized in the most refined schools of humanity and learning, or the most illustrious courts.

This Prince, such as I have described him, whose soul and body were so admirably adorned, was (while yet he was in the court of his grandfather) as I said, as capable of love as 'twas possible for a brave and gallant man to be; and in saying that, I have named the highest degree of love; for sure, great souls are most capable of that passion.

I have already said the old general was killed by the shot of an arrow, by the side of this Prince, in battle; and that Oroonoko was made general. This old dead hero had one only daughter left of his race; a beauty that, to describe her truly, one need say only, she was female to the noble male; the beautiful black Venus to our young

1. Charles I, whose beheading in 1649 by sentence of the House of Commons marked the culmination of the wars between Royalists and Parliament.
2. Sculptor.
3. Excepting.
4. Shrewd principles or sayings.

Mars; as charming in her person as he, and of delicate virtues. I have seen an hundred white men sighing after her, and making a thousand vows at her feet, all vain and unsuccessful; and she was, indeed, too great for any but a prince of her own nation to adore.

Oroonoko coming from the wars (which were now ended) after he had made his court to his grandfather, he thought in honor he ought to make a visit to Imoinda, the daughter of his foster-father, the dead general; and to make some excuses to her, because his preservation was the occasion of her father's death; and to present her with those slaves that had been taken in this last battle, as the trophies of her father's victories. When he came, attended by all the young soldiers of any merit, he was infinitely surprised at the beauty of this fair Queen of Night, whose face and person was so exceeding all he had ever beheld; that lovely modesty with which she received him, that softness in her look and sighs, upon the melancholy occasion of this honor that was done by so great a man as Oroonoko, and a prince of whom she had heard such admirable things; the awfulness[5] wherewith she received him, and the sweetness of her words and behavior while he stayed, gained a perfect conquest over his fierce heart, and made him feel the victor could be subdued. So that having made his first compliments, and presented her a hundred and fifty slaves in fetters, he told her with his eyes that he was not insensible of her charms; while Imoinda, who wished for nothing more than so glorious a conquest, was pleased to believe she understood that silent language of new-born love; and from that moment, put on all her additions to beauty.

The Prince returned to court with quite another humor[6] than before; and though he did not speak much of the fair Imoinda, he had the pleasure to hear all his followers speak of nothing but the charms of that maid; insomuch that, even in the presence of the old king, they were extolling her, and heightening, if possible, the beauties they had found in her; so that nothing else was talked of, no other sound was heard in every corner where there were whisperers, but "Imoinda! Imoinda!"

'Twill be imagined Oroonoko stayed not long before he made his second visit; nor, considering his quality, not much longer before he told her he adored her. I have often heard him say that he admired by what strange inspiration he came to talk things so soft and so passionate, who never knew love, nor was used to the conversation of women; but (to use his own words) he said, most happily, some new, and till then unknown power instructed his heart and tongue in the language of love, and at the same time, in favor of him, inspired Imoinda with a sense of his passion. She was touched with what he said, and returned it all in such answers as went to his very heart, with a pleasure unknown before. Nor did he use those obligations ill that love had done him; but turned all his happy moments to the best advantage; and as he knew no vice, his flame aimed at nothing but honor, if such a distinction may be made in love; and especially in that country, where men take to themselves as many as they can maintain, and where the only crime and sin with woman is to turn her off, to abandon her to want, shame, and misery. Such ill morals are only practiced in Christian countries, where they prefer the bare name of religion; and, without virtue or morality, think that's sufficient. But Oroonoko was none of those professors; but as he had right notions of honor, so he made her such propositions as were not only and barely such; but, contrary to the custom of his country, he made

5. Respect.   6. Frame of mind.

her vows she should be the only woman he would possess while he lived; that no age or wrinkles should incline him to change, for her soul would be always fine, and always young; and he should have an eternal idea in his mind of the charms she now bore, and should look into his heart for that idea, when he could find it no longer in her face.

After a thousand assurances of his lasting flame, and her eternal empire over him, she condescended to receive him for her husband; or rather, received him, as the greatest honor the gods could do her.

There is a certain ceremony in these cases to be observed, which I forgot to ask him how performed; but 'twas concluded on both sides that, in obedience to him, the grandfather was to be first made acquainted with the design; for they pay a most absolute resignation to the monarch, especially when he is a parent also.

On the other side, the old king, who had many wives, and many concubines, wanted not court flatterers to insinuate in his heart a thousand tender thoughts for this young beauty; and who represented her to his fancy as the most charming he had ever possessed in all the long race of his numerous years. At this character his old heart, like an extinguished brand, most apt to take fire, felt new sparks of love and began to kindle; and now grown to his second childhood, longed with impatience to behold this gay thing, with whom, alas, he could but innocently play. But how he should be confirmed she was this wonder, before he used his power to call her to court (where maidens never came, unless for the King's private use) he was next to consider; and while he was so doing, he had intelligence brought him, that Imoinda was most certainly mistress to the Prince Oroonoko. This gave him some chagrin; however, it gave him also an opportunity, one day, when the Prince was a-hunting, to wait on a man of quality, as his slave and attendant, who should go and make a present to Imoinda, as from the Prince; he should then, unknown, see this fair maid, and have an opportunity to hear what message she would return the Prince for his present; and from thence gather the state of her heart, and degree of her inclination. This was put in execution, and the old monarch saw, and burned; he found her all he had heard, and would not delay his happiness, but found he should have some obstacle to overcome her heart; for she expressed her sense of the present the Prince had sent her, in terms so sweet, so soft and pretty, with an air of love and joy that could not be dissembled, insomuch that 'twas past doubt whether she loved Oroonoko entirely. This gave the old king some affliction, but he salved it with this, that the obedience the people pay their king was not at all inferior to what they paid their gods, and what love would not oblige Imoinda to do, duty would compel her to.

He was therefore no sooner got to his apartment, but he sent the royal veil to Imoinda, that is, the ceremony of invitation; he sends the lady, he has a mind to honor with his bed, a veil, with which she is covered and secured for the King's use; and 'tis death to disobey; besides, held a most impious disobedience.

'Tis not to be imagined the surprise and grief that seized this lovely maid at this news and sight. However, as delays in these cases are dangerous, and pleading worse than treason, trembling and almost fainting, she was obliged to suffer herself to be covered and led away.

They brought her thus to court; and the King, who had caused a very rich bath to be prepared, was led into it, where he sat under a canopy in state, to receive this longed for virgin; whom he having commanded should be brought to him, they (after disrobing her) led her to the bath and, making fast the doors, left her to descend. The

King, without more courtship, bade her throw off her mantle and come to his arms. But Imoinda, all in tears, threw herself on the marble on the brink of the bath, and besought him to hear her. She told him, as she was a maid, how proud of the divine glory she should have been of having it in her power to oblige her king; but as by the laws he could not, and from his royal goodness would not take from any man his wedded wife, so she believed she should be the occasion of making him commit a great sin, if she did not reveal her state and condition, and tell him she was another's, and could not be so happy to be his.

The King, enraged at this delay, hastily demanded the name of the bold man that had married a woman of her degree without his consent. Imoinda, seeing his eyes fierce and his hands tremble, whether with age or anger I know not, but she fancied the last, almost repented she had said so much, for now she feared the storm would fall on the Prince; she therefore said a thousand things to appease the raging of his flame, and to prepare him to hear who it was with calmness; but before she spoke, he imagined who she meant, but would not seem to do so, but commanded her to lay aside her mantle and suffer herself to receive his caresses; or by his gods, he swore, that happy man whom she was going to name should die, though it were even Oroonoko himself. "Therefore," said he, "deny this marriage, and swear thyself a maid." "That," replied Imoinda, "by all our powers I do, for I am not yet known to my husband." "'Tis enough," said the King, "'tis enough to satisfy both my conscience and my heart." And rising from his seat, he went and led her into the bath, it being in vain for her to resist.

In this time the Prince, who was returned from hunting, went to visit his Imoinda, but found her gone; and not only so, but heard she had received the royal veil. This raised him to a storm, and in his madness they had much ado to save him from laying violent hands on himself. Force first prevailed, and then reason. They urged all to him that might oppose his rage; but nothing weighed so greatly with him as the King's old age, incapable of injuring him with Imoinda. He would give way to that hope, because it pleased him most, and flattered best his heart. Yet this served not altogether to make him cease his different passions, which sometimes raged within him, and sometimes softened into showers. 'Twas not enough to appease him, to tell him his grandfather was old, and could not that way injure him, while he retained that awful[7] duty which the young men are used there to pay to their grave relations. He could not be convinced he had no cause to sigh and mourn for the loss of a mistress he could not with all his strength and courage retrieve. And he would often cry, "O my friends! Were she in walled cities, or confined from me in fortifications of the greatest strength; did enchantments or monsters detain her from me, I would venture through any hazard to free her. But here, in the arms of a feeble old man, my youth, my violent love, my trade in arms, and all my vast desire of glory avail me nothing. Imoinda is as irrecoverably lost to me as if she were snatched by the cold arms of death. Oh! she is never to be retrieved. If I would wait tedious years, till fate should bow the old King to his grave, even that would not leave me Imoinda free; but still that custom that makes it so vile a crime for a son to marry his father's wives or mistress would hinder my happiness; unless I would either ignobly set an ill precedent to my successors, or abandon my country and fly with her to some unknown world, who never heard our story."

7. Reverential.

But it was objected to him that his case was not the same; for Imoinda being his lawful wife, by solemn contract, 'twas he was the injured man, and might, if he so pleased, take Imoinda back, the breach of the law being on his grandfather's side; and that if he could circumvent him, and redeem her from the otan, which is the palace of the King's women, a sort of seraglio, it was both just and lawful for him so to do.

This reasoning had some force upon him, and he should have been entirely comforted, but for the thought that she was possessed by his grandfather. However, he loved so well that he was resolved to believe what most favored his hope, and to endeavor to learn from Imoinda's own mouth what only she could satisfy him in: whether she was robbed of that blessing, which was only due to his faith and love. But as it was very hard to get a sight of the women, for no men ever entered into the otan but when the King went to entertain himself with some one of his wives or mistresses, and 'twas death at any other time for any other to go in, so he knew not how to contrive to get a sight of her.

While Oroonoko felt all the agonies of love, and suffered under a torment the most painful in the world, the old king was not exempted from his share of affliction. He was troubled for having been forced by an irresistible passion to rob his son of a treasure he knew could not but be extremely dear to him, since she was the most beautiful that ever had been seen; and had besides all the sweetness and innocence of youth and modesty, with a charm of wit surpassing all. He found that however she was forced to expose her lovely person to his withered arms, she could only sigh and weep there, and think of Oroonoko; and oftentimes could not forbear speaking of him, though her life were, by custom, forfeited by owning her passion. But she spoke not of a lover only, but of a prince dear to him to whom she spoke; and of the praises of a man, who, till now, filled the old man's soul with joy at every recital of his bravery, or even his name. And 'twas this dotage on our young hero that gave Imoinda a thousand privileges to speak of him without offending, and this condescension in the old king that made her take the satisfaction of speaking of him so very often.

Besides, he many times inquired how the Prince bore himself; and those of whom he asked, being entirely slaves to the merits and virtues of the Prince, still answered what they thought conduced best to his service; which was, to make the old king fancy that the Prince had no more interest in Imoinda, and had resigned her willingly to the pleasure of the king; that he diverted himself with his mathematicians, his fortifications, his officers, and his hunting.

This pleased the old lover, who failed not to report these things again to Imoinda, that she might, by the example of her young lover, withdraw her heart and rest better contented in his arms. But however she was forced to receive this unwelcome news, in all appearance, with unconcern and content, her heart was bursting within, and she was only happy when she could get alone, to vent her griefs and moans with sighs and tears.

What reports of the Prince's conduct were made to the King, he thought good to justify as far as possibly he could by his actions; and when he appeared in the presence of the King, he showed a face not at all betraying his heart; so that in a little time the old man, being entirely convinced that he was no longer a lover of Imoinda, he carried him with him, in his train to the otan, often to banquet with his mistress. But as soon as he entered one day into the apartment of Imoinda with the King, at the first glance from her eyes, notwithstanding all his determined resolution, he was ready to sink in the place where he stood; and had certainly done so, but for the support of Aboan, a young man who was next to him; which, with his change of countenance, had betrayed him, had the King chanced to look that way. And I have observed, 'tis a very great error in those who laugh when one says a Negro can change color; for I have seen them as frequently blush, and look pale, and that as visibly as ever I saw in the most beautiful white. And 'tis certain that both these changes were evident, this day, in both these lovers. And Imoinda, who saw with some joy the change in the Prince's face, and found it in her own, strove to divert the King from beholding either, by a forced caress, with which she met him, which was a new wound in the heart of the poor dying Prince. But as soon as the King was busied in looking on some fine thing of Imoinda's making, she had time to tell the Prince with her angry but love-darting eyes, that she resented his coldness, and bemoaned her own miserable captivity. Nor were his eyes silent, but answered hers again, as much as eyes could do, instructed by the most tender and most passionate heart that ever loved. And they spoke so well, and so effectually, as Imoinda no longer doubted but she was the only delight, and the darling of that soul she found pleading in them its right of love, which none was more willing to resign than she. And 'twas this power- ful language alone that in an instant conveyed all the thoughts of their souls to each other, that they both found there wanted but opportunity to make them both entirely happy. But when he saw another door opened by Onahal, a former old wife of the King's who now had charge of Imoinda, and saw the prospect of a bed of state made ready with sweets and flowers for the dalliance of the King, who immediately led the trembling victim from his sight into that prepared repose, what rage, what wild fren- zies seized his heart! Which forcing to keep within bounds, and to suffer without noise, it became the more insupportable and rent his soul with ten thousand pains. He was forced to retire to vent his groans, where he fell down on a carpet, and lay struggling a long time, and only breathing now and then, "O Imoinda!" When Ona- hal had finished her necessary affair within, shutting the door, she came forth to wait till the King called; and hearing some one sighing in the other room, she passed on, and found the Prince in that deplorable condition which she thought needed her aid. She gave him cordials but all in vain, till finding the nature of his disease by his sighs, and naming Imoinda, she told him he had not so much cause as he imagined to afflict himself; for if he knew the King so well as she did, he would not lose a moment in jealousy, and that she was confident that Imoinda bore, at this minute, part in his affliction. Aboan was of the same opinion; and both together persuaded him to reas- sume his courage; and all sitting down on the carpet, the Prince said so many obliging things to Onahal, that he half persuaded her to be of his party. And she promised him she would thus far comply with his just desires, that she would let Imoinda know how faithful he was, what he suffered, and what he said.

This discourse lasted till the King called, which gave Oroonoko a certain satis- faction; and with the hope Onahal had made him conceive, he assumed a look as gay as 'twas possible a man in his circumstances could do; and presently after, he was called in with the rest who waited without. The King commanded music to be brought, and several of his young wives and mistresses came all together by his com- mand, to dance before him, where Imoinda performed her part with an air and grace so passing all the rest as her beauty was above them, and received the present ordained as a prize. The Prince was every moment more charmed with the new beau- ties and graces he beheld in this fair one; and while he gazed and she danced, Onahal was retired to a window with Aboan.

This Onahal, as I said, was one of the past mistresses of the old king; and 'twas these (now past their beauty) that were made guardians, or governants, to the new and the young ones; and whose business it was, to teach them all those wanton arts of love with which they prevailed and charmed heretofore in their turn; and who now treated the triumphing happy ones with all the severity, as to liberty and freedom, that was possible, in revenge of those honors they rob them of; envying them those satisfactions, those gallantries and presents, that were once made to themselves, while youth and beauty lasted, and which they now saw pass regardless by, and paid only to the bloomings. And certainly, nothing is more afflicting to a decayed beauty than to behold in itself declining charms that were once adored, and to find those caresses paid to new beauties to which once she laid a claim; to hear them whisper as she passes by, "That once was a delicate woman." These abandoned ladies therefore endeavor to revenge all the despites and decays of time on these flourishing happy ones. And 'twas this severity that gave Oroonoko a thousand fears he should never prevail with Onahal to see Imoinda. But, as I said, she was now retired to a window with Aboan.

This young man was not only one of the best quality, but a man extremely well made and beautiful; and coming often to attend the King to the otan, he had subdued the heart of the antiquated Onahal, which had not forgot how pleasant it was to be in love. And though she had some decays in her face, she had none in her sense and wit; she was there agreeable still, even to Aboan's youth, so that he took pleasure in entertaining her with discourses of love. He knew also, that to make his court to these she-favorites was the way to be great; these being the persons that do all affairs and business at court. He had also observed that she had given him glances more tender and inviting than she had done to others of his quality. And now, when he saw that her favor could so absolutely oblige the Prince, he failed not to sigh in her ear, and to look with eyes all soft upon her, and give her hope that she had made some impressions on his heart. He found her pleased at this, and making a thousand advances to him; but the ceremony ending, and the King departing, broke up the company for that day, and his conversation.

Aboan failed not that night to tell the Prince of his success, and how advantageous the service of Onahal might be to his amour with Imoinda. The Prince was overjoyed with this good news, and besought him, if it were possible, to caress her, so as to engage her entirely; which he could not fail to do, if he complied with her desires. "For then," said the Prince, "her life lying at your mercy, she must grant you the request you make in my behalf." Aboan understood him, and assured him he would make love so effectually, that he would defy the most expert mistress of the art to find out whether he dissembled it or had it really. And 'twas with impatience they waited the next opportunity of going to the otan.

The wars came on, the time of taking the field approached, and 'twas impossible for the Prince to delay his going at the head of his army to encounter the enemy; so that every day seemed a tedious year, till he saw his Imoinda, for he believed he could not live if he were forced away without being so happy. 'Twas with impatience therefore that he expected the next visit the King would make; and, according to his wish, it was not long.

The parley of the eyes of these two lovers had not passed so secretly, but an old jealous lover could spy it; or rather, he wanted not flatterers who told him they observed it. So that the Prince was hastened to the camp, and this was the last visit he found he should make to the otan; he therefore urged Aboan to make the best of this last effort, and to explain himself so to Onahal, that she, deferring her enjoyment of her young lover no longer, might make way for the Prince to speak to Imoinda.

The whole affair being agreed on between the Prince and Aboan, they attended the King, as the custom was, to the otan; where, while the whole company was taken up in beholding the dancing and antic[8] postures the women royal made to divert the King, Onahal singled out Aboan, whom she found most pliable to her wish. When

8. Fantastic or grotesque.

she had him where she believed she could not be heard, she sighed to him, and softly cried, "Ah, Aboan! When will you be sensible of my passion? I confess it with my mouth, because I would not give my eyes the lie; and you have but too much already perceived they have confessed my flame. Nor would I have you believe that because I am the abandoned mistress of a king I esteem myself altogether divested of charms. No, Aboan; I have still a rest of beauty enough engaging, and have learned to please too well, not to be desirable. I can have lovers still, but will have none but Aboan." "Madam," replied the half-feigning youth, "you have already, by my eyes, found you can still conquer; and I believe 'tis in pity of me, you condescend to this kind confession. But, Madam, words are used to be so small a part of our country courtship, that 'tis rare one can get so happy an opportunity as to tell one's heart; and those few minutes we have are forced to be snatched for more certain proofs of love than speaking and sighing; and such I languish for."

He spoke this with such a tone that she hoped it true, and could not forbear believing it; and being wholly transported with joy, for having subdued the finest of all the King's subjects to her desires, she took from her ears two large pearls and commanded him to wear them in his. He would have refused them, crying, "Madam, these are not the proofs of your love that I expect; 'tis opportunity, 'tis a lone hour only, that can make me happy." But forcing the pearls into his hand, she whispered softly to him, "Oh! Do not fear a woman's invention when love sets her a-thinking." And pressing his hand she cried, "This night you shall be happy. Come to the gate of the orange groves, behind the otan, and I will be ready, about midnight, to receive you." 'Twas thus agreed, and she left him, that no notice might be taken of their speaking together.

The ladies were still dancing, and the King, laid on a carpet, with a great deal of pleasure was beholding them, especially Imoinda, who that day appeared more lovely than ever, being enlivened with the good tidings Onahal had brought her of the constant passion the Prince had for her. The Prince was laid on another carpet at the other end of the room, with his eyes fixed on the object of his soul; and as she turned or moved so did they; and she alone gave his eyes and soul their motions. Nor did Imoinda employ her eyes to any other use than in beholding with infinite pleasure the joy she produced in those of the Prince. But while she was more regarding him than the steps she took, she chanced to fall, and so near him as that leaping with extreme force from the carpet, he caught her in his arms as she fell; and 'twas visible to the whole presence, the joy wherewith he received her. He clasped her close to his bosom, and quite forgot that reverence that was due to the mistress of a king, and that punishment that is the reward of a boldness of this nature; and had not the presence of mind of Imoinda (fonder of his safety than her own) befriended him in making her spring from his arms and fall into her dance again, he had at that instant met his death; for the old king, jealous to the last degree, rose up in rage, broke all the diversion, and led Imoinda to her apartment, and sent out word to the Prince to go immediately to the camp; and that if he were found another night in court, he should suffer the death ordained for disobedient offenders.

You may imagine how welcome this news was to Oroonoko, whose unseasonable transport and caress of Imoinda was blamed by all men that loved him; and now he perceived his fault, yet cried that for such another moment, he would be content to die.

All the otan was in disorder about this accident; and Onahal was particularly concerned, because on the Prince's stay depended her happiness, for she could no longer expect that of Aboan. So that e'er they departed, they contrived it so that the Prince and he should come both that night to the grove of the otan, which was all of oranges and citrons, and that there they should wait her orders.

They parted thus, with grief enough, till night, leaving the King in possession of the lovely maid. But nothing could appease the jealousy of the old lover. He would not be imposed on, but would have it that Imoinda made a false step on purpose to fall into Oroonoko's bosom, and that all things looked like a design on both sides, and 'twas in vain she protested her innocence. He was old and obstinate, and left her more than half assured that his fear was true.

The King going to his apartment, sent to know where the Prince was, and if he intended to obey his command. The messenger returned and told him he found the Prince pensive, and altogether unpreparing for the campaign; that he lay negligently on the ground, and answered very little. This confirmed the jealousy of the King, and he commanded that they should very narrowly and privately watch his motions; and that he should not stir from his apartment, but one spy or other should be employed to watch him. So that the hour approaching, wherein he was to go to the citron grove, and taking only Aboan along with him, he leaves his apartment, and was watched to the very gate of the otan, where he was seen to enter, and where they left him, to carry back the tidings to the King.

Oroonoko and Aboan were no sooner entered but Onahal led the Prince to the apartment of Imoinda, who, not knowing anything of her happiness, was laid in bed. But Onahal only left him in her chamber to make the best of his opportunity, and took her dear Aboan to her own, where he showed the height of complaisance[9] for his prince, when, to give him an opportunity, he suffered himself to be caressed in bed by Onahal.

The Prince softly wakened Imoinda, who was not a little surprised with joy to find him there, and yet she trembled with a thousand fears. I believe he omitted saying nothing to this young maid that might persuade her to suffer him to seize his own and take the rights of love; and I believe she was not long resisting those arms where she so longed to be; and having opportunity, night and silence, youth, love and desire, he soon prevailed, and ravished in a moment what his old grandfather had been endeavoring for so many months.

'Tis not to be imagined the satisfaction of these two young lovers; nor the vows she made him, that she remained a spotless maid till that night; and that what she did with his grandfather had robbed him of no part of her virgin honor, the gods in mercy and justice having reserved that for her plighted lord, to whom of right it belonged. And 'tis impossible to express the transports he suffered while he listened to a discourse so charming from her loved lips, and clasped that body in his arms for whom he had so long languished; and nothing now afflicted him but his sudden departure from her; for he told her the necessity and his commands; but should depart satisfied in this, that since the old king had hitherto not been able to deprive him of those enjoyments which only belonged to him, he believed for the future he would be less able to injure him. So that abating the scandal of the veil, which was no otherwise so than that she was wife to another, he believed her safe even in the arms of the King, and innocent; yet would he have ventured at the conquest of the world, and have given it all, to have had her avoided that honor of receiving the royal veil. 'Twas thus, between a thousand caresses, that both bemoaned the hard fate of youth and beauty, so liable to that cruel promotion; 'twas a glory that could well have been spared here, though desired and aimed at by all the young females of that kingdom.

But while they were thus fondly employed, forgetting how time ran on and that the dawn must conduct him far away from his only happiness, they heard a great noise in the otan, and unusual voices of men; at which the Prince, starting from the

9. Desire to please.

arms of the frighted Imoinda, ran to a little battle-ax he used to wear by his side; and having not so much leisure as to put on his habit, he opposed himself against some who were already opening the door; which they did with so much violence that Oroonoko was not able to defend it, but was forced to cry out with a commanding voice, "Whoever ye are that have the boldness to attempt to approach this apartment thus rudely, know that I, the Prince Oroonoko, will revenge it with the certain death of him that first enters. Therefore stand back, and know this place is sacred to love and me this night; tomorrow 'tis the King's."

This he spoke with a voice so resolved and assured that they soon retired from the door, but cried, "'Tis by the King's command we are come; and being satisfied by thy voice, O Prince, as much as if we had entered, we can report to the King the truth of all his fears, and leave thee to provide for thy own safety, as thou art advised by thy friends."

At these words they departed, and left the Prince to take a short and sad leave of his Imoinda; who trusting in the strength of her charms, believed she should appease the fury of a jealous king by saying she was surprised, and that it was by force of arms he got into her apartment. All her concern now was for his life, and therefore she hastened him to the camp, and with much ado prevailed on him to go. Nor was it she alone that prevailed; Aboan and Onahal both pleaded, and both assured him of a lie that should be well enough contrived to secure Imoinda. So that at last, with a heart sad as death, dying eyes, and sighing soul, Oroonoko departed, and took his way to the camp.

It was not long after the King in person came to the otan, where beholding Imoinda with rage in his eyes, he upbraided her wickedness and perfidy, and threatening her royal lover, she fell on her face at his feet, bedewing the floor with her tears and imploring his pardon for a fault which she had not with her will committed, as Onahal, who was also prostrate with her, could testify that, unknown to her, he had broke into her apartment, and ravished her. She spoke this much against her conscience; but to save her own life, 'twas absolutely necessary she should feign this falsity. She knew it could not injure the Prince, he being fled to an army that would stand by him against any injuries that should assault him. However, this last thought of Imoinda's being ravished changed the measures of his revenge, and whereas before he designed to be himself her executioner, he now resolved she should not die. But as it is the greatest crime in nature amongst them to touch a woman after having been possessed by a son, a father, or a brother, so now he looked on Imoinda as a polluted thing, wholly unfit for his embrace; nor would he resign her to his grandson, because she had received the royal veil. He therefore removes her from the otan, with Onahal, whom he put into safe hands, with order they should be both sold off as slaves to another country, either Christian or heathen; 'twas no matter where.

This cruel sentence, worse than death, they implored might be reversed; but their prayers were vain, and it was put in execution accordingly, and that with so much secrecy that none, either without or within the otan, knew anything of their absence or their destiny.

The old king, nevertheless, executed this with a great deal of reluctance; but he believed he had made a very great conquest over himself when he had once resolved, and had performed what he resolved. He believed now that his love had been unjust, and that he could not expect the gods, or Captain of the Clouds (as they call the unknown power) should suffer a better consequence from so ill a cause. He now begins to hold Oroonoko excused and to say he had reason for what he did; and now everybody could assure the King, how passionately Imoinda was beloved by the

Prince; even those confessed it now who said the contrary before his flame was abated. So that the King being old and not able to defend himself in war, and having no sons of all his race remaining alive but only this to maintain him on the throne; and looking on this as a man disobliged, first by the rape of his mistress, or rather, wife, and now by depriving him wholly of her, he feared, might make him desperate, and do some cruel thing, either to himself, or his old grandfather the offender; he began to repent him extremely of the contempt he had, in his rage, put on Imoinda. Besides, he considered he ought in honor to have killed her for this offense, if it had been one. He ought to have had so much value and consideration for a maid of her quality, as to have nobly put her to death, and not to have sold her like a common slave, the greatest revenge, and the most disgraceful of any, and to which they a thousand times prefer death, and implore it as Imoinda did, but could not obtain that honor. Seeing therefore it was certain that Oroonoko would highly resent this affront, he thought good to make some excuse for his rashness to him, and to that end he sent a messenger to the camp with orders to treat with him about the matter, to gain his pardon, and to endeavor to mitigate his grief; but that by no means he should tell him she was sold, but secretly put to death; for he knew he should never obtain his pardon for the other.

When the messenger came, he found the Prince upon the point of engaging with the enemy, but as soon as he heard of the arrival of the messenger he commanded him to his tent, where he embraced him and received him with joy; which was soon abated, by the downcast looks of the messenger, who was instantly demanded the cause by Oroonoko, who, impatient of delay, asked a thousand questions in a breath, and all concerning Imoinda. But there needed little return, for he could almost answer himself of all he demanded from his sighs and eyes. At last, the messenger casting himself at the Prince's feet and kissing them with all the submission of a man that had something to implore which he dreaded to utter, he besought him to hear with calmness what he had to deliver to him, and to call up all his noble and heroic courage to encounter with his words, and defend himself against the ungrateful things he must relate. Oroonoko replied, with a deep sigh and a languishing voice, "I am armed against their worst efforts—for I know they will tell me, Imoinda is no more—and after that, you may spare the rest." Then, commanding him to rise, he laid himself on a carpet under a rich pavilion, and remained a good while silent, and was hardly heard to sigh. When he was come a little to himself, the messenger asked him leave to deliver that part of his embassy which the Prince had not yet divined, and the Prince cried, "I permit thee." Then he told him the affliction the old king was in for the rashness he had committed in his cruelty to Imoinda, and how he deigned to ask pardon for his offense, and to implore the Prince would not suffer that loss to touch his heart too sensibly which now all the gods could not restore him, but might recompense him in glory which he begged he would pursue; and that death, that common revenger of all injuries, would soon even the account between him and a feeble old man.

Oroonoko bade him return his duty to his lord and master, and to assure him there was no account of revenge to be adjusted between them; if there were, 'twas he was the aggressor, and that death would be just, and, maugre[1] his age, would see him righted; and he was contented to leave his share of glory to youths more fortunate, and worthy of that favor from the gods. That henceforth he would never lift a

---

1. In spite of; i.e., despite Oroonoko's youth, death will avenge the king by taking Oroonoko first.

weapon, or draw a bow, but abandon the small remains of his life to sighs and tears, and the continual thoughts of what his lord and grandfather had thought good to send out of the world, with all that youth, that innocence, and beauty.

After having spoken this, whatever his greatest officers and men of the best rank could do, they could not raise him from the carpet, or persuade him to action and resolutions of life, but commanding all to retire, he shut himself into his pavilion all that day, while the enemy was ready to engage; and wondering at the delay, the whole body of the chief of the army then addressed themselves to him, and to whom they had much ado to get admittance. They fell on their faces at the foot of his carpet, where they lay, and besought him with earnest prayers and tears to lead them forth to battle, and not let the enemy take advantages of them; and implored him to have regard to his glory, and to the world that depended on his courage and conduct. But he made no other reply to all their supplications but this, that he had now no more business for glory; and for the world, it was a trifle not worth his care. "Go," continued he, sighing, "and divide it amongst you; and reap with joy what you so vainly prize, and leave me to my more welcome destiny."

They then demanded what they should do, and whom he would constitute in his room, that the confusion of ambitious youth and power might not ruin their order, and make them a prey to the enemy. He replied, he would not give himself the trouble; but wished them to choose the bravest man amongst them, let his quality or birth be what it would. "For, O my friends!" said he, "it is not titles make men brave, or good; or birth that bestows courage and generosity, or makes the owner happy. Believe this, when you behold Oroonoko, the most wretched, and abandoned by fortune of all the creation of the gods." So turning himself about, he would make no more reply to all they could urge or implore.

The army beholding their officers return unsuccessful, with sad faces and ominous looks that presaged no good luck, suffered a thousand fears to take possession of their hearts, and the enemy to come even upon them, before they would provide for their safety by any defense; and though they were assured by some, who had a mind to animate them, that they should be immediately headed by the Prince, and that in the meantime Aboan had orders to command as general, yet they were so dismayed for want of that great example of bravery that they could make but a very feeble resistance, and at last downright fled before the enemy, who pursued them to the very tents, killing them. Nor could all Aboan's courage, which that day gained him immortal glory, shame them into a manly defense of themselves. The guards that were left behind about the Prince's tent, seeing the soldiers flee before the enemy and scatter themselves all over the plain in great disorder, made such outcries as roused the Prince from his amorous slumber, in which he had remained buried for two days without permitting any sustenance to approach him. But in spite of all his resolutions, he had not the constancy of grief to that degree as to make him insensible of the danger of his army; and in that instant he leapt from his couch and cried, "Come, if we must die, let us meet death the noblest way; and 'twill be more like Oroonoko to encounter him at an army's head, opposing the torrent of a conquering foe, than lazily, on a couch, to wait his lingering pleasure, and die every moment by a thousand wrecking thoughts; or be tamely taken by an enemy and led a whining, love-sick slave, to adorn the triumphs of Jamoan, that young victor, who already is entered beyond the limits I had prescribed him."

While he was speaking, he suffered his people to dress him for the field; and sallying out of his pavilion, with more life and vigor in his countenance than ever he showed, he appeared like some divine power descended to save his country from destruction; and his people had purposely put him on all things that might make him shine with most splendor, to strike a reverend awe into the beholders. He flew into the thickest of those that were pursuing his men, and being animated with despair, he fought as if he came on purpose to die, and did such things as will not be believed that human strength could perform, and such as soon inspired all the rest with new courage and new order. And now it was that they began to fight indeed, and so, as if they would not be outdone even by their adored hero, who turning the tide of the victory, changing absolutely the fate of the day, gained an entire conquest; and Oroonoko having the good fortune to single out Jamoan, he took him prisoner with his own hand, having wounded him almost to death.

This Jamoan afterwards became very dear to him, being a man very gallant and of excellent graces and fine parts, so that he never put him amongst the rank of captives, as they used to do, without distinction, for the common sale or market, but kept him in his own court, where he retained nothing of the prisoner but the name, and returned no more into his own country, so great an affection he took for Oroonoko; and by a thousand tales and adventures of love and gallantry, flattered his disease of melancholy and languishment, which I have often heard him say had certainly killed him, but for the conversation of this prince and Aboan, [and] the French governor he had from his childhood, of whom I have spoken before, and who was a man of admirable wit, great ingenuity and learning, all which he had infused into his young pupil. This Frenchman was banished out of his own country for some heretical notions he held; and though he was a man of very little religion, he had admirable morals, and a brave soul.

After the total defeat of Jamoan's army, which all fled, or were left dead upon the place, they spent some time in the camp, Oroonoko choosing rather to remain a while there in his tents, than enter into a palace, or live in a court where he had so lately suffered so great a loss. The officers therefore, who saw and knew his cause of discontent, invented all sorts of diversions and sports to entertain their prince: so that what with those amusements abroad and others at home, that is, within their tents, with the persuasions, arguments, and care of his friends and servants that he more peculiarly prized, he wore off in time a great part of that chagrin and torture of despair which the first effects of Imoinda's death had given him; insomuch as having received a thousand kind embassies from the King, and invitations to return to court, he obeyed, though with no little reluctance; and when he did so, there was a visible change in him, and for a long time he was much more melancholy than before. But time lessens all extremes, and reduces them to mediums and unconcern; but no motives or beauties, though all endeavored it, could engage him in any sort of amour, though he had all the invitations to it, both from his own youth and others' ambitions and designs.

Oroonoko was no sooner returned from this last conquest, and received at court with all the joy and magnificence that could be expressed to a young victor, who was not only returned triumphant but beloved like a deity, when there arrived in the port an English ship.

This person had often before been in these countries, and was very well known to Oroonoko, with whom he had trafficked for slaves, and had used to do the same with his predecessors.

This commander was a man of a finer sort of address and conversation, better bred and more engaging than most of that sort of men are; so that he seemed rather never to have been bred out of a court than almost all his life at sea. This captain therefore was always better received at court than most of the traders to those countries were; and especially by Oroonoko, who was more civilized, according to the

European mode, than any other had been, and took more delight in the white nations, and, above all, men of parts and wit. To this captain he sold abundance of his slaves, and for the favor and esteem he had for him made him many presents, and obliged him to stay at court as long as possibly he could. Which the captain seemed to take as a very great honor done him, entertaining the Prince every day with globes and maps, and mathematical discourses and instruments; eating, drinking, hunting, and living with him with so much familiarity that it was not to be doubted but he had gained very greatly upon the heart of this gallant young man. And the captain, in return of all these mighty favors, besought the Prince to honor his vessel with his presence, some day or other, to dinner, before he should set sail; which he condescended to accept, and appointed his day. The captain, on his part, failed not to have all things in a readiness, in the most magnificent order he could possibly. And the day being come, the captain, in his boat richly adorned with carpets and velvet cushions, rowed to the shore to receive the Prince; with another longboat, where was placed all his music and trumpets, with which Oroonoko was extremely delighted, who met him on the shore, attended by his French governor, Jamoan, Aboan, and about an hundred of the noblest of the youths of the court. And after they had first carried the Prince on board, the boats fetched the rest off; where they found a very splendid treat, with all sorts of fine wines, and were as well entertained as 'twas possible in such a place to be.

The Prince having drunk hard of punch, and several sorts of wine, as did all the rest (for great care was taken they should want nothing of that part of the entertainment) was very merry, and in great admiration of the ship, for he had never been in one before; so that he was curious of beholding every place where he decently might descend. The rest, no less curious, who were not quite overcome with drinking, rambled at their pleasure fore and aft, as their fancies guided them: so that the captain, who had well laid his design before, gave the word and seized on all his guests; they clapping great irons suddenly on the Prince when he was leaped down in the hold to view that part of the vessel, and locking him fast down, secured him. The same treachery was used to all the rest; and all in one instant, in several places of the ship, were lashed fast in irons and betrayed to slavery. That great design over, they set all hands to work to hoist sail; and with as treacherous and fair a wind they made from the shore with this innocent and glorious prize, who thought of nothing less than such an entertainment.

Some have commended this act, as brave in the captain; but I will spare my sense of it, and leave it to my reader to judge as he pleases.

It may be easily guessed in what manner the Prince resented this indignity, who may be best resembled to a lion taken in a toil; so he raged, so he struggled for liberty, but all in vain; and they had so wisely managed his fetters that he could not use a hand in his defense, to quit himself of a life that would by no means endure slavery; nor could he move from the place where he was tied to any solid part of the ship against which he might have beat his head, and have finished his disgrace that way; so that being deprived of all other means, he resolved to perish for want of food. And pleased at last with that thought, and toiled and tired by rage and indignation, he laid himself down, and sullenly resolved upon dying, and refused all things that were brought him.

This did not a little vex the captain, and the more so because he found almost all of them of the same humor; so that the loss of so many brave slaves, so tall and goodly to behold, would have been very considerable. He therefore ordered one to go from him (for he would not be seen himself) to Oroonoko, and to assure him he was afflicted for having rashly done so inhospitable a deed, and which could not be now remedied, since they were far from shore; but since he resented it in so high a nature, he assured him he would revoke his resolution, and set both him and his friends ashore on the next land they should touch at; and of this the messenger gave him his oath, provided he would resolve to live. And Oroonoko, whose honor was such as he never had violated a word in his life himself, much less a solemn asseveration, believed in an instant what this man said, but replied he expected for a confirmation of this to have his shameful fetters dismissed. This demand was carried to the captain, who returned him answer that the offense had been so great which he had put upon the Prince, that he durst not trust him with liberty while he remained in the ship, for fear lest by a valor natural to him, and a revenge that would animate that valor, he might commit some outrage fatal to himself and the King his master, to whom his vessel did belong. To this Oroonoko replied, he would engage his honor to behave himself in all friendly order and manner, and obey the command of the captain, as he was lord of the King's vessel, and general of those men under his command.

This was delivered to the still doubting captain, who could not resolve to trust a heathen he said, upon his parole,[2] a man that had no sense or notion of the God that he worshipped. Oroonoko then replied he was very sorry to hear that the captain pretended to the knowledge and worship of any gods who had taught him no better principles, than not to credit as he would be credited; but they told him the difference of their faith occasioned that distrust: for the captain had protested to him upon the word of a Christian, and sworn in the name of a great God, which if he should violate, he would expect eternal torment in the world to come. "Is that all the obligation he has to be just to his oath?" replied Oroonoko. "Let him know I swear by my honor, which to violate, would not only render me contemptible and despised by all brave and honest men, and so give myself perpetual pain, but it would be eternally offending and diseasing all mankind, harming, betraying, circumventing, and outraging all men; but punishments hereafter are suffered by oneself; and the world takes no cognizances whether this god have revenged them, or not, 'tis done so secretly, and deferred so long; while the man of no honor suffers every moment the scorn and contempt of the honester world, and dies every day ignominiously in his fame, which is more valuable than life. I speak not this to move belief, but to show you how you mistake, when you imagine that he who will violate his honor will keep his word with his gods." So turning from him with a disdainful smile, he refused to answer him when he urged him to know what answer he should carry back to his captain; so that he departed without saying any more.

The captain pondering and consulting what to do, it was concluded that nothing but Oroonoko's liberty would encourage any of the rest to eat, except the Frenchman, whom the captain could not pretend to keep prisoner, but only told him he was secured because he might act something in favor of the Prince, but that he should be freed as soon as they came to land. So that they concluded it wholly necessary to free the Prince from his irons that he might show himself to the rest, that they might have an eye upon him, and that they could not fear a single man.

This being resolved, to make the obligation the greater, the captain himself went to Oroonoko; where, after many compliments, and assurances of what he had already promised, he receiving from the Prince his parole, and his hand, for his good behavior, dismissed his irons, and brought him to his own cabin; where, after having treated and

2. Word of honor.

reposed him a while, for he had neither eaten nor slept in four days before, he besought him to visit those obstinate people in chains, who refused all manner of sustenance; and entreated him to oblige them to eat, and assure them of their liberty the first opportunity.

Oroonoko, who was too generous not to give credit to his words, showed himself to his people, who were transported with excess of joy at the sight of their darling prince, falling at his feet, and kissing and embracing them, believing, as some divine oracle, all he assured them. But he besought them to bear their chains with that bravery that became those whom he had seen act so nobly in arms; and that they could not give him greater proofs of their love and friendship, since 'twas all the security the captain (his friend) could have against the revenge, he said, they might possibly justly take, for the injuries sustained by him. And they all, with one accord, assured him they could not suffer enough when it was for his repose and safety.

After this they no longer refused to eat, but took what was brought them and were pleased with their captivity, since by it they hoped to redeem the Prince, who, all the rest of the voyage, was treated with all the respect due to his birth, though nothing could divert his melancholy; and he would often sigh for Imoinda, and think this a punishment due to his misfortune, in having left that noble maid behind him that fatal night in the otan, when he fled to the camp.

Possessed with a thousand thoughts of past joys with this fair young person, and a thousand griefs for her eternal loss, he endured a tedious voyage, and at last arrived at the mouth of the river of Surinam, a colony belonging to the King of England, and where they were to deliver some part of their slaves. There the merchants and gentlemen of the country going on board to demand those lots of slaves they had already agreed on, and amongst those the overseers of those plantations where I then chanced to be, the captain, who had given the word, ordered his men to bring up those noble slaves in fetters, whom I have spoken of; and having put them, some in one, and some in other lots, with women and children (which they call pickaninnies), they sold them off as slaves to several merchants and gentlemen; not putting any two in one lot, because they would separate them far from each other; not daring to trust them together, lest rage and courage should put them upon contriving some great action, to the ruin of the colony.

Oroonoko was first seized on and sold to our overseer, who had the first lot, with seventeen more of all sorts and sizes, but not one of quality with him. When he saw this, he found what they meant; for, as I said, he understood English pretty well; and being wholly unarmed and defenseless, so as it was in vain to make any resistance, he only beheld the captain with a look all fierce and disdainful; upbraiding him with eyes that forced blushes on his guilty cheeks, he only cried in passing over the side of the ship, "Farewell, Sir! 'Tis worth my suffering to gain so true a knowledge both of you and of your gods by whom you swear." And desiring those that held him to forbear their pains, and telling them he would make no resistance, he cried, "Come, my fellow slaves, let us descend, and see if we can meet with more honor and honesty in the next world we shall touch upon." So he nimbly leapt into the boat, and showing no more concern, suffered himself to be rowed up the river with his seventeen companions.

The gentleman that bought him was a young Cornish gentleman, whose name was Trefry, a man of great wit and fine learning, and was carried into those parts by the Lord——, Governor, to manage all his affairs.[3] He reflecting on the last words of

3. John Treffry (?–1674) supervised the plantation at Parham for Francis, Lord Willoughby (1613?–1686), a nobleman long involved with colonization, who received from Charles II both the governorship and a grant of land in Surinam; his appointment of Behn's father to the post of lieutenant-governor appears to account for her sojourn in the colony (though her father died en route).

Oroonoko to the captain, and beholding the richness of his vest,[4] no sooner came into the boat, but he fixed his eyes on him; and finding something so extraordinary in his face, his shape and mien, a greatness of look, and haughtiness in his air, and finding he spoke English, had a great mind to be inquiring into his quality and fortune; which, though Oroonoko endeavored to hide by only confessing he was above the rank of common slaves, Trefry soon found he was yet something greater than he confessed; and from that moment began to conceive so vast an esteem for him, that he ever after loved him as his dearest brother, and showed him all the civilities due to so great a man.

Trefry was a very good mathematician and a linguist, could speak French and Spanish, and in the three days they remained in the boat (for so long were they going from the ship to the plantation) he entertained Oroonoko so agreeably with his art and discourse, that he was no less pleased with Trefry, than he was with the Prince; and he thought himself, at least, fortunate in this, that since he was a slave, as long as he would suffer himself to remain so, he had a man of so excellent wit and parts for a master. So that before they had finished their voyage up the river, he made no scruple of declaring to Trefry all his fortunes and most part of what I have here related, and put himself wholly into the hands of his new friend, whom he found resenting all the injuries were done him, and was charmed with all the greatnesses of his actions, which were recited with that modesty and delicate sense, as wholly vanquished him, and subdued him to his interest. And he promised him on his word and honor, he would find the means to reconduct him to his own country again; assuring him, he had a perfect abhorrence of so dishonorable an action; and that he would sooner have died, than have been the author of such a perfidy. He found the Prince was very much concerned to know what became of his friends, and how they took their slavery; and Trefry promised to take care about the inquiring after their condition, and that he should have an account of them.

Though, as Oroonoko afterwards said, he had little reason to credit the words of a backearary,[5] yet he knew not why, but he saw a kind of sincerity and awful truth in the face of Trefry; he saw an honesty in his eyes, and he found him wise and witty enough to understand honor; for it was one of his maxims, "A man of wit could not be a knave or villain."

In their passage up the river they put in at several houses for refreshment, and ever when they landed numbers of people would flock to behold this man; not but their eyes were daily entertained with the sight of slaves, but the fame of Oroonoko was gone before him, and all people were in admiration of his beauty. Besides, he had a rich habit on, in which he was taken, so different from the rest, and which the captain could not strip him of because he was forced to surprise his person in the minute he sold him. When he found his habit made him liable, as he thought, to be gazed at the more, he begged Trefry to give him something more befitting a slave; which he did, and took off his robes. Nevertheless, he shone through all and his osenbrigs (a sort of brown holland suit he had on)[6] could not conceal the graces of his looks and mien; and he had no less admirers than when he had his dazzling habit on. The royal youth appeared in spite of the slave, and people could not help treating him after a different manner without designing it; as soon as they approached him they vener-

4. Robe.
5. An African-derived term for "white master."

6. Osnaburg and holland were thick cotton or linen fabrics.

ated and esteemed him; his eyes insensibly commanded respect, and his behavior insinuated it into every soul. So that there was nothing talked of but this young and gallant slave, even by those who yet knew not that he was a prince.

I ought to tell you, that the Christians never buy any slaves but they give them some name of their own, their native ones being likely very barbarous, and hard to pronounce; so that Mr. Trefry gave Oroonoko that of Caesar, which name will live in that country as long as that (scarce more) glorious one of the great Roman, for 'tis most evident, he wanted no part of the personal courage of that Caesar, and acted things as memorable, had they been done in some part of the world replenished with people and historians that might have given him his due. But his misfortune was to fall in an obscure world, that afforded only a female pen to celebrate his fame, though I doubt not but it had lived from others' endeavors, if the Dutch, who immediately after his time took that country,[7] had not killed, banished, and dispersed all those that were capable of giving the world this great man's life, much better than I have done. And Mr. Trefry, who designed it, died before he began it, and bemoaned himself for not having undertook it in time.

For the future therefore, I must call Oroonoko Caesar, since by that name only he was known in our western world, and by that name he was received on shore at Parham House, where he was destined a slave. But if the King himself (God bless him) had come ashore, there could not have been greater expectations by all the whole plantation, and those neighboring ones, than was on ours at that time; and he was received more like a governor than a slave. Notwithstanding, as the custom was, they assigned him his portion of land, his house, and his business, up in the plantation. But as it was more for form than any design to put him to his task, he endured no more of the slave but the name, and remained some days in the house, receiving all visits that were made him, without stirring towards that part of the plantation where the Negroes were.

At last, he would needs go view his land, his house, and the business assigned him. But he no sooner came to the houses of the slaves, which are like a little town by itself, the Negroes all having left work, but they all came forth to behold him, and found he was that prince who had, at several times, sold most of them to these parts; and, from a veneration they pay to great men, especially if they know them, and from the surprise and awe they had at the sight of him, they all cast themselves at his feet, crying out, in their language, "Live, O King! Long live, O King!" And kissing his feet, paid him even divine homage.

Several English gentlemen were with him; and what Mr. Trefry had told them was here confirmed, of which he himself before had no other witness than Caesar himself. But he was infinitely glad to find his grandeur confirmed by the adoration of all the slaves.

Caesar, troubled with their over-joy, and over-ceremony, besought them to rise, and to receive him as their fellow slave, assuring them, he was no better. At which they set up with one accord a most terrible and hideous mourning and condoling, which he and the English had much ado to appease. But at last they prevailed with them, and they prepared all their barbarous music, and everyone killed and dressed something of his own stock (for every family has their land apart, on which, at their

---

7. In 1667 Surinam twice changed hands. The Dutch briefly captured the colony and the English won it back, but immediately ceded it to the Dutch (in exchange for New York) at the Treaty of Breda.

leisure times, they breed all eatable things) and clubbing it together, made a most magnificent supper, inviting their grandee captain, their prince, to honor it with his presence, which he did, and several English with him, where they all waited on him, some playing, others dancing before him all the time, according to the manners of their several nations, and with unwearied industry endeavoring to please and delight him.

While they sat at meat Mr. Trefry told Caesar that most of these young slaves were undone in love, with a fine she-slave, whom they had had about six months on their land. The Prince, who never heard the name of love without a sigh, nor any mention of it without the curiosity of examining further into that tale which of all discourses was most agreeable to him, asked, how they came to be so unhappy, as to be all undone for one fair slave? Trefry, who was naturally amorous, and loved to talk of love as well as anybody, proceeded to tell him, they had the most charming black that ever was beheld on their plantation, about fifteen or sixteen years old, as he guessed; that, for his part, he had done nothing but sigh for her ever since she came; and that all the white beauties he had seen never charmed him so absolutely as this fine creature had done; and that no man of any nation ever beheld her, that did not fall in love with her; and that she had all the slaves perpetually at her feet; and the whole country resounded with the fame of Clemene, "for so," said he, "we have christened her. But she denies us all with such a noble disdain, that 'tis a miracle to see that she, who can give such eternal desires, should herself be all ice, and all unconcern. She is adorned with the most graceful modesty that ever beautified youth; the softest sigher—that, if she were capable of love, one would swear she languished for some absent happy man; and so retired, as if she feared a rape even from the God of Day,[8] or that the breezes would steal kisses from her delicate mouth. Her task of work some sighing lover every day makes it his petition to perform for her, which she accepts blushing, and with reluctance, for fear he will ask her a look for a recompense, which he dares not presume to hope, so great an awe she strikes into the hearts of her admirers." "I do not wonder," replied the Prince, "that Clemene should refuse slaves, being as you say so beautiful, but wonder how she escapes those who can entertain her as you can do. Or why, being your slave, you do not oblige her to yield." "I confess," said Trefry, "when I have, against her will, entertained her with love so long as to be transported with my passion even above decency, I have been ready to make use of those advantages of strength and force nature has given me. But oh! she disarms me, with that modesty and weeping so tender and so moving, that I retire, and thank my stars she overcame me." The company laughed at his civility to a slave, and Caesar only applauded the nobleness of his passion and nature, since that slave might be noble, or, what was better, have true notions of honor and virtue in her. Thus passed they this night, after having received from the slaves all imaginable respect and obedience.

The next day Trefry asked Caesar to walk, when the heat was allayed, and designedly carried him by the cottage of the fair slave, and told him, she whom he spoke of last night lived there retired. "But, " says he, "I would not wish you to approach, for I am sure you will be in love as soon as you behold her." Caesar assured him he was proof against all the charms of that sex, and that if he imagined his heart could be so perfidious to love again after Imoinda, he believed he should tear it from his bosom. They had no sooner spoke, but a little shock dog,[9] that Clemene had pre-

---

8. The sun.   9. A thick-haired dog.

sented her, which she took great delight in, ran out, and she, not knowing anybody was there, ran to get it in again, and bolted out on those who were just speaking of her. When seeing them she would have run in again, but Trefry caught her by the hand and cried, "Clemene, however you fly a lover, you ought to pay some respect to this stranger" (pointing to Caesar). But she, as if she had resolved never to raise her eyes to the face of a man again, bent them the more to the earth when he spoke, and gave the Prince the leisure to look the more at her. There needed no long gazing or consideration to examine who this fair creature was. He soon saw Imoinda all over her; in a minute he saw her face, her shape, her air, her modesty, and all that called forth his soul with joy at his eyes, and left his body destitute of almost life. It stood without motion, and, for a minute, knew not that it had a being. And I believe he had never come to himself, so oppressed he was with overjoy, if he had not met with this allay,[1] that he perceived Imoinda fall dead in the hands of Trefry. This awakened him, and he ran to her aid, and caught her in his arms, where, by degrees, she came to herself; and 'tis needless to tell with what transports, what ecstasies of joy, they both a while beheld each other, without speaking, then snatched each other to their arms, then gaze again, as if they still doubted whether they possessed the blessing they grasped. But when they recovered their speech, 'tis not to be imagined what tender things they expressed to each other, wondering what strange fate had brought them again together. They soon informed each other of their fortunes, and equally bewailed their fate; but at the same time, they mutually protested that even fetters and slavery were soft and easy, and would be supported with joy and pleasure, while they could be so happy to possess each other, and to be able to make good their vows. Caesar swore he disdained the empire of the world while he could behold his Imoinda, and she despised grandeur and pomp, those vanities of her sex, when she could gaze on Oroonoko. He adored the very cottage where she resided, and said, that little inch of the world would give him more happiness than all the universe could do, and she vowed, it was a palace, while adorned with the presence of Oroonoko.

Trefry was infinitely pleased with this novel,[2] and found this Clemene was the fair mistress of whom Caesar had before spoke; and was not a little satisfied, that Heaven was so kind to the Prince as to sweeten his misfortunes by so lucky an accident, and leaving the lovers to themselves, was impatient to come down to Parham House (which was on the same plantation) to give me an account of what had happened. I was as impatient to make these lovers a visit, having already made a friendship with Caesar, and from his own mouth learned what I have related, which was confirmed by his Frenchman, who was set on shore to seek his fortunes, and of whom they could not make a slave because a Christian, and he came daily to Parham Hill to see and pay his respects to his pupil prince. So that concerning and interesting myself in all that related to Caesar, whom I had assured of liberty as soon as the governor arrived, I hasted presently to the place where the lovers were, and was infinitely glad to find this beautiful young slave (who had already gained all our esteems, for her modesty and her extraordinary prettiness) to be the same I had heard Caesar speak so much of. One may imagine then, we paid her a treble respect; and though from her being carved in fine flowers and birds all over her body, we took her to be of quality before, yet, when we knew Clemene was Imoinda, we could not enough admire her.

---

1. Reduction; release.   2. New development.

I had forgot to tell you, that those who are nobly born of that country are so delicately cut and raced[3] all over the fore part of the trunk of their bodies, that it looks as if it were japanned;[4] the works being raised like high point[5] round the edges of the flowers. Some are only carved with a little flower or bird at the sides of the temples, as was Caesar; and those who are so carved over the body resemble our ancient Picts,[6] that are figured in the chronicles, but these carvings are more delicate.

From that happy day Caesar took Clemene for his wife, to the general joy of all people, and there was as much magnificence as the country would afford at the celebration of this wedding. And in a very short time after she conceived with child; which made Caesar even adore her, knowing he was the last of his great race. This new accident made him more impatient of liberty, and he was every day treating with Trefry for his and Clemene's liberty; and offered either gold, or a vast quantity of slaves, which should be paid before they let him go, provided he could have any security that he should go when his ransom was paid. They fed him from day to day with promises, and delayed him, till the Lord Governor should come, so that he began to suspect them of falsehood, and that they would delay him till the time of his wife's delivery, and make a slave of that too, for all the breed is theirs to whom the parents belong. This thought made him very uneasy, and his sullenness gave them some jealousies[7] of him, so that I was obliged, by some persons who feared a mutiny (which is very fatal sometimes in those colonies that abound so with slaves that they exceed the whites in vast numbers), to discourse with Caesar, and to give him all the satisfaction I possibly could. They knew he and Clemene were scarce an hour in a day from my lodgings, that they ate with me, and that I obliged them in all things I was capable of: I entertained him with the lives of the Romans, and great men, which charmed him to my company, and her, with teaching her all the pretty works that I was mistress of, and telling her stories of nuns, and endeavoring to bring her to the knowledge of the true God. But of all discourses Caesar liked that the worst, and would never be reconciled to our notions of the Trinity, of which he ever made a jest; it was a riddle, he said, would turn his brain to conceive, and one could not make him understand what faith was. However, these conversations failed not altogether so well to divert him, that he liked the company of us women much above the men, for he could not drink, and he is but an ill companion in that country that cannot. So that obliging him to love us very well, we had all the liberty of speech with him, especially myself, whom he called his Great Mistress; and indeed my word would go a great way with him. For these reasons, I had opportunity to take notice to him, that he was not well pleased of late, as he used to be, was more retired and thoughtful, and told him, I took it ill he should suspect we would break our words with him, and not permit both him and Clemene to return to his own kingdom, which was not so long away, but when he was once on his voyage he would quickly arrive there. He made me some answers that showed a doubt in him, which made me ask him, what advantage it would be to doubt? It would but give us a fear of him, and possibly compel us to treat him so as I should be very loath to behold: that is, it might occasion his confinement. Perhaps this was not so luckily spoke of me, for I perceived he resented that word, which I strove to soften again in vain. However, he assured me, that what-

---

3. Carved.
4. Varnished with a glossy black lacquer.
5. Intricate lace.
6. Ancient inhabitants of northern Britain, possibly so

named by the Romans because of the "pictures" (tattoos and other ornaments) they bore on their skin.
7. Suspicions.

soever resolutions he should take, he would act nothing upon the white people. And as for myself, and those upon that plantation where he was, he would sooner forfeit his eternal liberty, and life itself, than lift his hand against his greatest enemy on that place. He besought me to suffer no fears upon his account, for he could do nothing that honor should not dictate, but he accused himself for having suffered slavery so long; yet he charged that weakness on love alone, who was capable of making him neglect even glory itself, and for which now he reproaches himself every moment of the day. Much more to this effect he spoke, with an air impatient enough to make me know he would not be long in bondage, and though he suffered only the name of a slave, and had nothing of the toil and labor of one, yet that was sufficient to render him uneasy, and he had been too long idle, who used to be always in action, and in arms. He had a spirit all rough and fierce, and that could not be tamed to lazy rest, and though all endeavors were used to exercise himself in such actions and sports as this world afforded, as running, wrestling, pitching the bar,[8] hunting and fishing, chasing and killing tigers of a monstrous size, which this continent affords in abundance; and wonderful snakes, such as Alexander[9] is reported to have encountered at the river of Amazons, and which Caesar took great delight to overcome; yet these were not actions great enough for his large soul, which was still panting after more renowned action.

Before I parted that day with him, I got, with much ado, a promise from him to rest yet a little longer with patience, and wait the coming of the Lord Governor, who was every day expected on our shore. He assured me he would, and this promise he desired me to know was given perfectly in complaisance to me, in whom he had an entire confidence.

After this, I neither thought it convenient to trust him much out of our view, nor did the country who feared him; but with one accord it was advised to treat him fairly, and oblige him to remain within such a compass, and that he should be permitted as seldom as could be to go up to the plantations of the Negroes; or if he did, to be accompanied by some that should be rather in appearance attendants than spies. This care was for some time taken, and Caesar looked upon it as a mark of extraordinary respect, and was glad his discontent had obliged them to be more observant to him. He received new assurance from the overseer, which was confirmed to him by the opinion of all the gentlemen of the country, who made their court to him. During this time that we had his company more frequently than hitherto we had had, it may not be unpleasant to relate to you the diversions we entertained him with, or rather he us.

My stay was to be short in that country, because my father died at sea, and never arrived to possess the honor was designed him (which was lieutenant-general of six and thirty islands, besides the continent[1] of Surinam), nor the advantages he hoped to reap by them, so that though we were obliged to continue on our voyage, we did not intend to stay upon the place. Though, in a word, I must say thus much of it, that certainly had his late Majesty,[2] of sacred memory, but seen and known what a vast and charming world he had been master of in that continent, he would never have parted so easily with it to the Dutch. 'Tis a continent whose vast extent was never yet known, and may contain more noble earth than all the universe besides; for they

---

8. Hurling a heavy rod for purposes of exercise or sport.
9. Legends surrounding Alexander the Great included his encounter with the mythical woman warriors called Amazons, and with the formidable snakes inhabiting their territories.
1. Mainland.
2. Charles II.

say it reaches from east to west, one way as far as China, and another to Peru. It affords all things both for beauty and use; 'tis there eternal spring, always the very months of April, May, and June. The shades are perpetual, the trees, bearing at once all degrees of leaves and fruit from blooming buds to ripe autumn, groves of oranges, lemons, citrons, figs, nutmegs, and noble aromatics, continually bearing their fragrancies. The trees appearing all like nosegays adorned with flowers of different kind; some are all white, some purple, some scarlet, some blue, some yellow; bearing, at the same time, ripe fruit and blooming young, or producing every day new. The very wood of all these trees have an intrinsic value above common timber, for they are, when cut, of different colors, glorious to behold, and bear a price considerable, to inlay withal. Besides this, they yield rich balm and gums, so that we make our candles of such an aromatic substance as does not only give a sufficient light but, as they burn, they cast their perfumes all about. Cedar is the common firing, and all the houses are built with it. The very meat we eat, when set on the table, if it be native, I mean of the country, perfumes the whole room, especially a little beast called an armadillo, a thing which I can liken to nothing so well as a rhinoceros. 'Tis all in white armor so jointed that it moves as well in it as if it had nothing on. This beast is about the bigness of a pig of six weeks old. But it were endless to give an account of all the diverse wonderful and strange things that country affords, and which we took a very great delight to go in search of, though those adventures are oftentimes fatal and at least dangerous. But while we had Caesar in our company on these designs we feared no harm, nor suffered any.

As soon as I came into the country, the best house in it was presented me, called St. John's Hill. It stood on a vast rock of white marble, at the foot of which the river ran a vast depth down, and not to be descended on that side. The little waves still dashing and washing the foot of this rock made the softest murmurs and purlings in the world, and the opposite bank was adorned with such vast quantities of different flowers eternally blowing,[3] and every day and hour new, fenced behind them with lofty trees of a thousand rare forms and colors, that the prospect was the most ravishing that sands can create. On the edge of this white rock, toward the river, was a walk or grove of orange and lemon trees, about half the length of the Mall[4] here, whose flowery and fruity branches meet at the top, and hindered the sun, whose rays are very fierce there, from entering a beam into the grove, and the cool air that came from the river made it not only fit to entertain people in at all the hottest hours of the day, but refreshed the sweet blossoms, and made it always sweet and charming, and sure the whole globe of the world cannot show so delightful a place as this grove was. Not all the gardens of boasted Italy can produce a shade to out-vie this, which Nature had joined with Art to render so exceeding fine. And 'tis a marvel to see how such vast trees, as big as English oaks, could take footing on so solid a rock, and in so little earth, as covered that rock, but all things by nature there are rare, delightful, and wonderful. But to our sports.

Sometimes we would go surprising,[5] and in search of young tigers in their dens, watching when the old ones went forth to forage for prey, and oftentimes we have been in great danger, and have fled apace for our lives, when surprised by the dams. But once, above all other times, we went on this design, and Caesar was with us, who had no sooner stolen a young tiger from her nest, but going off, we encountered the

3. Blossoming.
4. A walk extending alongside London's St. James's Park.
5. I.e., surprise-attacking.

dam, bearing a buttock of a cow, which he[6] had torn off with his mighty paw, and going with it towards his den. We had only four women, Caesar, and an English gentleman, brother to Harry Martin, the great Oliverian.[7] We found there was no escaping this enraged and ravenous beast. However, we women fled as fast as we could from it, but our heels had not saved our lives if Caesar had not laid down his cub, when he found the tiger quit her prey to make the more speed towards him, and taking Mr. Martin's sword desired him to stand aside, or follow the ladies. He obeyed him, and Caesar met this monstrous beast of might, size, and vast limbs, who came with open jaws upon him, and fixing his awful stern eyes full upon those of the beast, and putting himself into a very steady and good aiming posture of defense, ran his sword quite through his breast down to his very heart, home to the hilt of the sword. The dying beast stretched forth her paw, and going to grasp his thigh, surprised with death in that very moment, did him no other harm than fixing her long nails in his flesh very deep, feebly wounded him, but could not grasp the flesh to tear off any. When he had done this, he hollowed to us to return, which, after some assurance of his victory, we did, and found him lugging out the sword from the bosom of the tiger, who was laid in her blood on the ground. He took up the cub, and with an unconcern, that had nothing of the joy or gladness of a victory, he came and laid the whelp at my feet. We all extremely wondered at his daring, and at the bigness of the beast, which was about the height of an heifer, but of mighty, great, and strong limbs.

Another time, being in the woods, he killed a tiger, which had long infested that part, and borne away abundance of sheep and oxen and other things, that were for the support of those to whom they belonged. Abundance of people assailed this beast, some affirming they had shot her with several bullets quite through the body, at several times, and some swearing they shot her through the very heart, and they believed she was a devil rather than a mortal thing. Caesar had often said he had a mind to encounter this monster, and spoke with several gentlemen who had attempted her, one crying, I shot her with so many poisoned arrows, another with his gun in this part of her, and another in that. So that he remarking all these places where she was shot, fancied still he should overcome her, by giving her another sort of a wound than any had yet done, and one day said (at the table), "What trophies and garlands, ladies, will you make me, if I bring you home the heart of this ravenous beast that eats up all your lambs and pigs?" We all promised he should be rewarded at all our hands. So taking a bow, which he chose out of a great many, he went up in the wood, with two gentlemen, where he imagined this devourer to be. They had not passed very far in it, but they heard her voice, growling and grumbling, as if she were pleased with something she was doing. When they came in view, they found her muzzling in the belly of a new ravished sheep which she had torn open, and seeing herself approached, she took fast hold of her prey with her forepaws, and set a very fierce raging look on Caesar, without offering to approach him, for fear, at the same time, of losing what she had in possession. So that Caesar remained a good while, only taking aim, and getting an opportunity to shoot her where he designed. 'Twas some time before he could accomplish it, and to wound her and not kill her would but have enraged her more, and endangered him. He had a quiver of arrows at his side, so that if one failed he could be supplied. At last, retiring a little, he gave her opportunity to

---

6. The "dam" is the cub's mother, but Behn has surprisingly shifted the gender of the pronoun from "she" to "he"; she will do so again in reference to another tiger in the next paragraph.

7. Supporter of Oliver Cromwell.

eat, for he found she was ravenous, and fell to as soon as she saw him retire, being more eager of her prey than of doing new mischiefs. When he going softly to one side of her, and hiding his person behind certain herbage that grew high and thick, he took so good aim that, as he intended, he shot her just into the eye, and the arrow was sent with so good a will, and so sure a hand, that it stuck in her brain, and made her caper and become mad for a moment or two, but being seconded by another arrow, he fell dead upon the prey. Caesar cut him open with a knife, to see where those wounds were that had been reported to him, and why he did not die of them. But I shall now relate a thing that possibly will find no credit among men, because 'tis a notion commonly received with us that nothing can receive a wound in the heart and live; but when the heart of this courageous animal was taken out, there were seven bullets of lead in it, and the wounds seamed up with great scars, and she lived with the bullets a great while, for it was long since they were shot. This heart the conqueror brought up to us, and 'twas a very great curiosity, which all the country came to see; and which gave Caesar occasion of many fine discourses, of accidents in war and strange escapes.

At other times he would go a-fishing, and discoursing on that diversion, he found we had in that country a very strange fish, called a numb eel[8] (an eel of which I have eaten), that while it is alive, it has a quality so cold that those who are angling, though with a line of never so great a length, with a rod at the end of it, it shall, in the same minute the bait is touched by this eel, seize him or her that holds the rod with benumbedness, that shall deprive them of sense for a while. And some have fallen into the water, and others dropped as dead on the banks of the rivers where they stood, as soon as this fish touches the bait. Caesar used to laugh at this, and believed it impossible a man could lose his force at the touch of a fish; and could not understand that philosophy, that a cold quality should be of that nature. However, he had a great curiosity to try whether it would have the same effect on him it had on others, and often tried, but in vain. At last, the sought-for fish came to the bait as he stood angling on the bank; and instead of throwing away the rod, or giving it a sudden twitch out of the water, whereby he might have caught both the eel and have dismissed the rod before it could have too much power over him for experiment sake, he grasped it but the harder, and fainting fell into the river. And being still possessed of the rod, the tide carried him senseless as he was a great way, till an Indian boat took him up, and perceived, when they touched him, a numbness seize them, and by that knew the rod was in his hand, which with a paddle (that is, a short oar) they struck away, and snatched it into the boat, eel and all. If Caesar were almost dead with the effect of this fish, he was more so with that of the water, where he had remained the space of going a league, and they found they had much ado to bring him back to life. But at last they did, and brought him home, where he was in a few hours well recovered and refreshed, and not a little ashamed to find he should be overcome by an eel, and that all the people who heard his defiance would laugh at him. But we cheered him up and he, being convinced, we had the eel at supper, which was a quarter of an ell about, and most delicate meat, and was of the more value, since it cost so dear as almost the life of so gallant a man.

About this time we were in many mortal fears about some disputes the English had with the Indians, so that we could scarce trust ourselves, without great numbers, to go to any Indian towns or place where they abode, for fear they should fall upon

8. An electric eel.

us, as they did immediately after my coming away, and that it was in the possession of the Dutch, who used them not so civilly as the English, so that they cut in pieces all they could take, getting into houses, and hanging up the mother, and all her children about her, and cut a footman I left behind me all in joints, and nailed him to trees.

  This feud began while I was there, so that I lost half the satisfaction I proposed, in not seeing and visiting the Indian towns. But one day, bemoaning of our misfortunes upon this account, Caesar told us we need not fear, for if we had a mind to go he would undertake to be our guard. Some would, but most would not venture. About eighteen of us resolved, and took barge, and after eight days arrived near an Indian town. But approaching it, the hearts of some of our company failed, and they would not venture on shore, so we polled who would, and who would not. For my part, I said, if Caesar would, I would go. He resolved, so did my brother and my woman, a maid of good courage. Now none of us speaking the language of the people, and imagining we should have a half diversion in gazing only and not knowing what they said, we took a fisherman that lived at the mouth of the river, who had been a long inhabitant there, and obliged him to go with us. But because he was known to the Indians, as trading among them, and being, by long living there, become a perfect Indian in color, we, who resolved to surprise them, by making them see something they never had seen (that is, white people) resolved only myself, my brother, and woman should go. So Caesar, the fisherman, and the rest, hiding behind some thick reeds and flowers, that grew on the banks, let us pass on towards the town, which was on the bank of the river all along. A little distant from the houses, or huts, we saw some dancing, others busied in fetching and carrying of water from the river. They had no sooner spied us but they set up a loud cry, that frighted us at first. We thought it had been for those that should kill us, but it seems it was of wonder and amazement. They were all naked, and we were dressed, so as is most commode for the hot countries, very glittering and rich, so that we appeared extremely fine. My own hair was cut short, and I had a taffeta cap, with black feathers, on my head. My brother was in a stuff[9] suit, with silver loops and buttons, and abundance of green ribbon. This was all infinitely surprising to them, and because we saw them stand still, till we approached them, we took heart and advanced, came up to them, and offered them our hands, which they took, and looked on us round about, calling still for more company; who came swarming out, all wondering, and crying out *tepeeme*, taking their hair up in their hands, and spreading it wide to those they called out to, as if they would say (as indeed it signified) "numberless wonders," or not to be recounted, no more than to number the hair of their heads. By degrees they grew more bold, and from gazing upon us round, they touched us, laying their hands upon all the features of our faces, feeling our breasts and arms, taking up one petticoat, then wondering to see another, admiring our shoes and stockings, but more our garters, which we gave them, and they tied about their legs, being laced with silver lace at the ends, for they much esteem any shining things. In fine, we suffered them to survey us as they pleased, and we thought they would never have done admiring us. When Caesar and the rest saw we were received with such wonder, they came up to us, and finding the Indian trader whom they knew (for 'tis by these fishermen, called Indian traders, we hold a commerce with them; for they love not to go far from home, and we never go to them), when they saw him therefore they set up a new joy, and cried, in their language, "Oh! here's our *tiguamy*, and we shall now know whether those things can

9. Woolen.

speak." So advancing to him, some of them gave him their hands, and cried, "*Amora tiguamy*," which is as much as, "How do you," or "Welcome friend," and all, with one din, began to gabble to him, and asked, If we had sense, and wit? If we could talk of affairs of life, and war, as they could do? If we could hunt, swim, and do a thousand things they use? He answered them, we could. Then they invited us into their houses, and dressed venison and buffalo for us; and, going out, gathered a leaf of a tree, called a sarumbo leaf, of six yards long, and spread it on the ground for a tablecloth, and cutting another in pieces instead of plates, setting us on little bow Indian stools, which they cut out of one entire piece of wood, and paint in a sort of japan work. They serve everyone their mess on these pieces of leaves, and it was very good, but too high seasoned with pepper. When we had eaten, my brother and I took out our flutes and played to them, which gave them new wonder, and I soon perceived, by an admiration that is natural to these people, and by the extreme ignorance and simplicity of them, it were not difficult to establish any unknown or extravagant religion among them, and to impose any notions or fictions upon them. For seeing a kinsman of mine set some paper afire with a burning-glass, a trick they had never before seen, they were like to have adored him for a god, and begged he would give them the characters or figures of his name, that they might oppose it against winds and storms, which he did, and they held it up in those seasons, and fancied it had a charm to conquer them, and kept it like a holy relic. They are very superstitious, and called him the great *peeie*, that is, prophet. They showed us their Indian *peeie*, a youth of about sixteen years old, as handsome as Nature could make a man. They consecrate a beautiful youth from his infancy, and all arts are used to complete him in the finest manner, both in beauty and shape. He is bred to all the little arts and cunning they are capable of, to all the legerdemain tricks and sleight of hand whereby he imposes upon the rabble, and is both a doctor in physic and divinity. And by these tricks makes the sick believe he sometimes eases their pains, by drawing from the afflicted part little serpents, or odd flies, or worms, or any strange thing; and though they have besides undoubted good remedies for almost all their diseases, they cure the patient more by fancy than by medicines, and make themselves feared, loved, and reverenced. This young *peeie* had a very young wife, who seeing my brother kiss her, came running and kissed me; after this, they kissed one another, and made it a very great jest, it being so novel, and new admiration and laughing went round the multitude, that they never will forget that ceremony, never before used or known. Caesar had a mind to see and talk with their war captains, and we were conducted to one of their houses, where we beheld several of the great captains, who had been at council. But so frightful a vision it was to see them no fancy can create; no such dreams can represent so dreadful a spectacle. For my part I took them for hobgoblins, or fiends, rather than men. But however their shapes appeared, their souls were very humane and noble, but some wanted their noses, some their lips, some both noses and lips, some their ears, and others cut through each cheek, with long slashes, through which their teeth appeared; they had several other formidable wounds and scars, or rather dismemberings. They had *comitias*, or little aprons before them, and girdles of cotton, with their knives naked, stuck in it, a bow at their backs, and a quiver of arrows on their thighs, and most had feathers on their heads of diverse colors. They cried "*Amora tiguamy*" to us at our entrance, and were pleased we said as much to them. They feted us, and gave us drink of the best sort, and wondered, as much as the others had done before, to see us. Caesar was marveling as much at their faces, wondering how they should all be so wounded in war; he was impatient to know how they all came by those frightful marks of rage or malice, rather than wounds got in noble battle. They told us, by our interpreter, that when any war was waging, two men chosen out by some old captain, whose fighting was past, and who could only teach the theory of war, these two men were to stand in competition for the generalship, or Great War Captain, and being brought before the old judges, now past labor, they are asked, what they dare do to show they are worthy to lead an army? When he who is first asked, making no reply, cuts off his nose, and throws it contemptibly[1] on the ground, and the other does something to himself that he thinks surpasses him, and perhaps deprives himself of lips and an eye. So they slash on till one gives out, and many have died in this debate. And 'tis by a passive valor they show and prove their activity, a sort of courage too brutal to be applauded by our black hero; nevertheless he expressed his esteem of them.

In this voyage Caesar begot so good an understanding between the Indians and the English, that there were no more fears or heartburnings during our stay, but we had a perfect, open, and free trade with them. Many things remarkable, and worthy reciting, we met with in this short voyage, because Caesar made it his business to search out and provide for our entertainment, especially to please his dearly adored Imoinda, who was a sharer in all our adventures; we being resolved to make her chains as easy as we could, and to compliment the Prince in that manner that most obliged him.

As we were coming up again, we met with some Indians of strange aspects, that is, of a larger size, and other sort of features, than those of our country. Our Indian slaves, that rowed us, asked them some questions, but they could not understand us, but showed us a long cotton string with several knots on it, and told us, they had been coming from the mountains so many moons as there were knots. They were habited in skins of a strange beast, and brought along with them bags of gold dust, which, as well as they could give us to understand, came streaming in little small channels down the high mountains, when the rains fell, and offered to be the convoy to anybody, or persons, that would go to the mountains. We carried these men up to Parham, where they were kept till the Lord Governor came. And because all the country was mad to be going on this golden adventure, the governor, by his letters, commanded (for they sent some of the gold to him) that a guard should be set at the mouth of the river of Amazons (a river so called, almost as broad as the river of Thames), and prohibited all people from going up that river, it conducting to those mountains of gold. But we going off for England before the project was further prosecuted, and the Governor being drowned in a hurricane, either the design died, or the Dutch have the advantage of it. And 'tis to be bemoaned what His Majesty lost by losing that part of America.

Though this digression is a little from my story, however since it contains some proofs of the curiosity and daring of this great man, I was content to omit nothing of his character.

It was thus, for some time we diverted him. But now Imoinda began to show she was with child, and did nothing but sigh and weep for the captivity of her lord, herself, and the infant yet unborn, and believed, if it were so hard to gain the liberty of two, 'twould be more difficult to get that for three. Her griefs were so many darts in the great heart of Caesar, and taking his opportunity one Sunday, when all the whites were overtaken in drink, as there were abundance of several trades, and slaves

1. Contemptuously.

for four years,[2] that inhabited among the Negro houses, and Sunday was their day of debauch (otherwise they were a sort of spies upon Caesar), he went pretending out of goodness to them, to feast amongst them, and sent all his music, and ordered a great treat for the whole gang, about three hundred Negroes. And about a hundred and fifty were able to bear arms, such as they had, which were sufficient to do execution with spirits accordingly. For the English had none but rusty swords, that no strength could draw from a scabbard, except the people of particular quality, who took care to oil them and keep them in good order. The guns also, unless here and there one, or those newly carried from England, would do no good or harm, for 'tis the nature of that country to rust and eat up iron, or any metals but gold and silver. And they are very inexpert at the bow, which the Negroes and Indians are perfect masters of.

Caesar, having singled out these men from the women and children, made a harangue to them of the miseries and ignominies of slavery; counting up all their toils and sufferings, under such loads, burdens, and drudgeries as were fitter for beasts than men, senseless brutes than human souls. He told them it was not for days, months, or years, but for eternity; there was no end to be of their misfortunes. They suffered not like men who might find a glory and fortitude in oppression, but like dogs that loved the whip and bell,[3] and fawned the more they were beaten. That they had lost the divine quality of men, and were become insensible asses, fit only to bear. Nay worse, an ass, or dog, or horse, having done his duty, could lie down in retreat, and rise to work again, and while he did his duty endured no stripes; but men, villainous, sense-less men such as they, toiled on all the tedious week till black Friday, and then, whether they worked or not, whether they were faulty or meriting, they promiscuous-ly, the innocent with the guilty, suffered the infamous whip, the sordid stripes, from their fellow slaves till their blood trickled from all parts of their body, blood whose every drop ought to be revenged with a life of some of those tyrants that impose it. "And why," said he, "my dear friends and fellow sufferers, should we be slaves to an unknown people? Have they vanquished us nobly in fight? Have they won us in hon-orable battle? And are we, by the chance of war, become their slaves? This would not anger a noble heart, this would not animate a soldier's soul. No, but we are bought and sold like apes, or monkeys, to be the sport of women, fools, and cowards, and the support of rogues, runagades, that have abandoned their own countries, for raping, murders, thefts, and villainies. Do you not hear every day how they upbraid each other with infamy of life below the wildest savages, and shall we render obedience to such a degenerate race, who have no one human virtue left to distinguish them from the vilest creatures? Will you, I say, suffer the lash from such hands?" They all replied, with one accord, "No, no, no; Caesar has spoke like a great captain, like a great king."

After this he would have proceeded, but was interrupted by a tall Negro of some more quality than the rest. His name was Tuscan, who bowing at the feet of Caesar, cried, "My lord, we have listened with joy and attention to what you have said, and, were we only men, would follow so great a leader through the world. But oh! consider, we are husbands and parents too, and have things more dear to us than life: our wives and children unfit for travel, in these impassable woods, mountains, and bogs. We have not only difficult lands to overcome, but rivers to wade, and monsters to encounter, ravenous beasts of prey—" To this, Caesar replied, that honor was the

---

2. I.e., whites who, as punishment for crime or debt, had been forced into service for fixed periods of time.

3. Because rigorous training has taught them to cherish their punishment.

first principle in nature that was to be obeyed; but as no man would pretend to that, without all the acts of virtue, compassion, charity, love, justice, and reason, he found it not inconsistent with that, to take an equal care of their wives and children, as they would of themselves, and that he did not design, when he led them to freedom and glorious liberty, that they should leave that better part of themselves to perish by the hand of the tyrant's whip. But if there were a woman among them so degenerate from love and virtue to choose slavery before the pursuit of her husband, and with the hazard of her life to share with him in his fortunes, that such an one ought to be abandoned, and left as a prey to the common enemy.

To which they all agreed—and bowed. After this, he spoke of the impassable woods and rivers, and convinced them, the more danger, the more glory. He told them that he had heard of one Hannibal, a great captain, had cut his way through mountains of solid rocks,[4] and should a few shrubs oppose them, which they could fire before them? No, 'twas a trifling excuse to men resolved to die, or overcome. As for bogs, they are with a little labor filled and hardened, and the rivers could be no obstacle, since they swam by nature, at least by custom, from their first hour of their birth. That when the children were weary they must carry them by turns, and the woods and their own industry would afford them food. To this they all assented with joy.

Tuscan then demanded, what he would do? He said, they would travel towards the sea; plant a new colony, and defend it by their valor; and when they could find a ship, either driven by stress of weather, or guided by Providence that way, they would seize it, and make it a prize, till it had transported them to their own countries. At least, they should be made free in his kingdom, and be esteemed as his fellow sufferers, and men that had the courage and the bravery to attempt, at least, for liberty. And if they died in the attempt it would be more brave than to live in perpetual slavery.

They bowed and kissed his feet at this resolution, and with one accord vowed to follow him to death. And that night was appointed to begin their march; they made it known to their wives, and directed them to tie their hamaca[5] about their shoulder, and under their arm like a scarf; and to lead their children that could go, and carry those that could not. The wives, who pay an entire obedience to their husbands, obeyed, and stayed for them where they were appointed. The men stayed but to furnish themselves with what defensive arms they could get, and all met at the rendezvous, where Caesar made a new encouraging speech to them, and led them out.

But, as they could not march far that night, on Monday early, when the overseers went to call them all together to go to work, they were extremely surprised to find not one upon the place, but all fled with what baggage they had. You may imagine this news was not only suddenly spread all over the plantation, but soon reached the neighboring ones, and we had by noon about six hundred men, they call the militia of the county, that came to assist us in the pursuit of the fugitives. But never did one see so comical an army march forth to war. The men of any fashion would not concern themselves, though it were almost the common cause, for such revoltings are very ill examples, and have very fatal consequences oftentimes in many colonies. But they had a respect for Caesar, and all hands were against the Parhamites, as they called those of Parham Plantation, because they did not, in the first place, love the Lord Governor, and secondly, they would have it that Caesar was ill used, and baffled with.[6] And 'tis not impossible but some of the best in the country was of his counsel in this flight, and

---

4. The Carthaginian general (247–182 B.C.) had accomplished this while crossing the Alps to invade Rome.

5. Hammock.
6. Cheated.

depriving us of all the slaves, so that they of the better sort would not meddle in the matter. The deputy governor,[7] of whom I have had no great occasion to speak, and who was the most fawning fair-tongued fellow in the world, and one that pretended the most friendship to Caesar, was now the only violent man against him, and though he had nothing, and so need fear nothing, yet talked and looked bigger than any man. He was a fellow whose character is not fit to be mentioned with the worst of the slaves. This fellow would lead his army forth to meet Caesar, or rather to pursue him. Most of their arms were of those sort of cruel whips they call cat-with-nine-tails; some had rusty useless guns for show; others old basket-hilts, whose blades had never seen the light in this age, and others had long staffs, and clubs. Mr. Trefry went along rather to be a mediator than a conqueror in such a battle, for he foresaw and knew, if by fighting they put the Negroes into despair, they were a sort of sullen fellows that would drown or kill themselves before they would yield, and he advised that fair means was best. But Byam was one that abounded in his own wit, and would take his own measures.

It was not hard to find these fugitives, for as they fled they were forced to fire and cut the woods before them, so that night or day they pursued them by the light they made, and by the path they had cleared. But as soon as Caesar found he was pursued, he put himself in a posture of defense, placing all the women and children in the rear, and himself, with Tuscan by his side, or next to him, all promising to die or conquer. Encouraged thus, they never stood to parley, but fell on pell-mell upon the English, and killed some, and wounded a good many, they having recourse to their whips, as the best of their weapons. And as they observed no order, they perplexed the enemy so sorely, with lashing them in the eyes. And the women and children, seeing their husbands so treated, being of fearful cowardly dispositions, and hearing the English cry out, "Yield and live, yield and be pardoned," they all ran in amongst their husbands and fathers, and hung about them, crying out, "Yield, yield, and leave Caesar to their revenge," that by degrees the slaves abandoned Caesar, and left him only Tuscan and his heroic Imoinda, who, grown big as she was, did nevertheless press near her lord, having a bow, and a quiver full of poisoned arrows, which she managed with such dexterity that she wounded several, and shot the governor into the shoulder, of which wound he had like to have died but that an Indian woman, his mistress, sucked the wound, and cleansed it from the venom. But however, he stirred not from the place till he had parleyed with Caesar, who he found was resolved to die fighting, and would not be taken; no more would Tuscan, or Imoinda. But he, more thirsting after revenge of another sort, than that of depriving him of life, now made use of all his art of talking and dissembling, and besought Caesar to yield himself upon terms which he himself should propose, and should be sacredly assented to and kept by him. He told him, it was not that he any longer feared him, or could believe the force of two men, and a young heroine, could overcome all them, with all the slaves now on their side also, but it was the vast esteem he had for his person, the desire he had to serve so gallant a man, and to hinder himself from the reproach hereafter of having been the occasion of the death of a prince, whose valor and magnanimity deserved the empire of the world. He protested to him, he looked upon this action as gallant and brave, however tending to the prejudice of his lord and master, who would by it have lost so considerable a number of slaves, that this flight of his should

---

7. William Byam, who during a decade as administrator in Surinam had acquired a reputation for arrogance and severity.

be looked on as a heat of youth, and rashness of a too forward courage, and an unconsidered impatience of liberty, and no more; and that he labored in vain to accomplish that which they would effectually perform, as soon as any ship arrived that would touch on his coast. "So that if you will be pleased," continued he, "to surrender yourself, all imaginable respect shall be paid you; and yourself, your wife, and child, if it be here born, shall depart free out of our land." But Caesar would hear of no composition, though Byam urged, if he pursued and went on in his design, he would inevitably perish, either by great snakes, wild beasts, or hunger, and he ought to have regard to his wife, whose condition required ease, and not the fatigues of tedious travel, where she could not be secured from being devoured. But Caesar told him, there was no faith in the white men, or the gods they adored, who instructed them in principles so false that honest men could not live amongst them; though no people professed so much, none performed so little; that he knew what he had to do, when he dealt with men of honor, but with them a man ought to be eternally on his guard, and never to eat and drink with Christians without his weapon of defense in his hand, and, for his own security, never to credit one word they spoke. As for the rashness and inconsiderateness of his action he would confess the governor is in the right, and that he was ashamed of what he had done, in endeavoring to make those free, who were by nature slaves, poor wretched rogues, fit to be used as Christians' tools; dogs, treacherous and cowardly, fit for such masters, and they wanted only but to be whipped into the knowledge of the Christian gods to be the vilest of all creeping things, to learn to worship such deities as had not power to make them just, brave, or honest. In fine, after a thousand things of this nature, not fit here to be recited, he told Byam, he had rather die than live upon the same earth with such dogs. But Trefry and Byam pleaded and protested together so much, that Trefry believing the governor to mean what he said, and speaking very cordially himself, generously put himself into Caesar's hands, and took him aside, and persuaded him, even with tears, to live, by surrendering himself, and to name his conditions. Caesar was overcome by his wit and reasons, and in consideration of Imoinda, and demanding what he desired, and that it should be ratified by their hands in writing, because he had perceived that was the common way of contract between man and man amongst the whites. All this was performed, and Tuscan's pardon was put in, and they surrender to the governor, who walked peaceably down into the plantation with them, after giving order to bury their dead. Caesar was very much toiled with the bustle of the day, for he had fought like a Fury, and what mischief was done he and Tuscan performed alone, and gave their enemies a fatal proof that they durst do anything, and feared no mortal force.

But they were no sooner arrived at the place where all the slaves receive their punishments of whipping, but they laid hands on Caesar and Tuscan, faint with heat and toil; and surprising them, bound them to two several stakes, and whipped them in a most deplorable and inhumane manner, rending the very flesh from their bones; especially Caesar, who was not perceived to make any moan, or to alter his face, only to roll his eyes on the faithless governor, and those he believed guilty, with fierceness and indignation. And, to complete his rage, he saw every one of those slaves, who, but a few days before, adored him as something more than mortal, now had a whip to give him some lashes, while he strove not to break his fetters, though if he had, it were impossible. But he pronounced a woe and revenge from his eyes, that darted fire, that 'twas at once both awful and terrible to behold.

When they thought they were sufficiently revenged on him, they untied him, almost fainting with loss of blood from a thousand wounds all over his body, from which they had rent his clothes, and led him bleeding and naked as he was, and loaded him all over with irons, and then rubbed his wounds, to complete their cruelty, with Indian pepper, which had like to have made him raving mad, and in this condition made him so fast to the ground that he could not stir, if his pains and wounds would have given him leave. They spared Imoinda, and did not let her see this barbarity committed towards her lord, but carried her down to Parham, and shut her up, which was not in kindness to her, but for fear she should die with the sight, or miscarry, and then they should lose a young slave, and perhaps the mother.

You must know, that when the news was brought on Monday morning, that Caesar had betaken himself to the woods, and carried with him all the Negroes, we were possessed with extreme fear, which no persuasions could dissipate, that he would secure himself till night, and then, that he would come down and cut all our throats. This apprehension made all the females of us fly down the river, to be secured, and while we were away, they acted this cruelty. For I suppose I had authority and interest enough there, had I suspected any such thing, to have prevented it, but we had not gone many leagues, but the news overtook us that Caesar was taken, and whipped like a common slave. We met on the river with Colonel Martin, a man of great gallantry, wit, and goodness, and, whom I have celebrated in a character of my new comedy,[8] by his own name, in memory of so brave a man. He was wise and eloquent, and, from the fineness of his parts, bore a great sway over the hearts of all the colony. He was a friend to Caesar, and resented this false dealing with him very much. We carried him back to Parham, thinking to have made an accommodation; when we came, the first news we heard was that the governor was dead of a wound Imoinda had given him, but it was not so well. But it seems he would have the pleasure of beholding the revenge he took on Caesar, and before the cruel ceremony was finished, he dropped down, and then they perceived the wound he had on his shoulder was by a venomed arrow, which, as I said, his Indian mistress healed, by sucking the wound.

We were no sooner arrived, but we went up to the plantation to see Caesar, whom we found in a very miserable and inexpressible condition, and I have a thousand times admired how he lived, in so much tormenting pain. We said all things to him that trouble, pity, and good nature could suggest, protesting our innocence of the fact, and our abhorrence of such cruelties; making a thousand professions of services to him, and begging as many pardons for the offenders, till we said so much, that he believed we had no hand in his ill treatment, but told us, he could never pardon Byam. As for Trefry, he confessed he saw his grief and sorrow for his suffering, which he could not hinder, but was like to have been beaten down by the very slaves, for speaking in his defense. But for Byam, who was their leader, their head—and should, by his justice, and honor, have been an example to them—for him, he wished to live, to take a dire revenge of him, and said, "It had been well for him if he had sacrificed me, instead of giving me the contemptible whip." He refused to talk much, but begging us to give him our hands, he took them, and protested never to lift up his, to do us any harm. He had a great respect for Colonel Martin, and always took his counsel, like that of a parent, and assured him, he would obey him in anything

8. *The Younger Brother: or the Amorous Jilt*, produced posthumously in 1696.

but his revenge on Byam. "Therefore," said he, "for his own safety, let him speedily dispatch me, for if I could dispatch myself, I would not, till that justice were done to my injured person, and the contempt of a soldier. No, I would not kill myself, even after a whipping, but will be content to live with that infamy, and be pointed at by every grinning slave, till I have completed my revenge; and then you shall see that Oroonoko scorns to live with the indignity that was put on Caesar." All we could do could get no more words from him, and we took care to have him put immediately into a healing bath, to rid him of his pepper, and ordered a chirurgeon[9] to anoint him with healing balm, which he suffered, and in some time he began to be able to walk and eat. We failed not to visit him every day, and, to that end, had him brought to an apartment at Parham.

The governor was no sooner recovered, and had heard of the menaces of Caesar, but he called his council, who (not to disgrace them, or burlesque the government there) consisted of such notorious villains as Newgate[1] never transported, and possibly originally were such, who understood neither the laws of God or man, and had no sort of principles to make them worthy the name of men, but at the very council table would contradict and fight with one another, and swear so bloodily that 'twas terrible to hear and see them. (Some of them were afterwards hanged, when the Dutch took possession of the place; others sent off in chains.) But calling these special rulers of the nation together, and requiring their counsel in this weighty affair, they all concluded that (damn them) it might be their own cases, and that Caesar ought to be made an example to all the Negroes, to fright them from daring to threaten their betters, their lords and masters, and, at this rate, no man was safe from his own slaves, and concluded, *nemine contradicente*,[2] that Caesar should be hanged.

Trefry then thought it time to use his authority, and told Byam his command did not extend to his lord's plantation, and that Parham was as much exempt from the law as Whitehall; and that they ought no more to touch the servants of the Lord — (who there represented the King's person) than they could those about the King himself; and that Parham was a sanctuary, and though his lord were absent in person, his power was still in being there, which he had entrusted with him, as far as the dominions of his particular plantations reached, and all that belonged to it; the rest of the country, as Byam was lieutenant to his lord, he might exercise his tyranny upon. Trefry had others as powerful, or more, that interested themselves in Caesar's life, and absolutely said he should be defended. So turning the governor, and his wise council, out of doors (for they sat at Parham House) we set a guard upon our landing place, and would admit none but those we called friends to us and Caesar.

The governor having remained wounded at Parham till his recovery was completed, Caesar did not know but he was still there, and indeed, for the most part, his time was spent there, for he was one that loved to live at other people's expense, and if he were a day absent, he was ten present there, and used to play, and walk, and hunt, and fish, with Caesar. So that Caesar did not at all doubt, if he once recovered strength, but he should find an opportunity of being revenged on him. Though, after such a revenge, he could not hope to live, for if he escaped the fury of the English mobile,[3] who perhaps would have been glad of the occasion to have killed him, he was resolved not to survive his whipping, yet he had, some tender hours, a repenting

9. Surgeon.
1. London prison from which convicts were sent to work in the colonies.

2. No one disagreeing.
3. Mob.

softness, which he called his fits of coward, wherein he struggled with love for the victory of his heart, which took part with his charming Imoinda there; but, for the most part, his time was passed in melancholy thought, and black designs. He considered, if he should do this deed, and die either in the attempt, or after it, he left his lovely Imoinda a prey, or at best a slave, to the enraged multitude; his great heart could not endure that thought. "Perhaps," said he, "she may be first ravished by every brute, exposed first to their nasty lusts, and then a shameful death." No, he could not live a moment under that apprehension, too insupportable to be borne. These were his thoughts, and his silent arguments with his heart, as he told us afterwards, so that now resolving not only to kill Byam, but all those he thought had enraged him, pleasing his great heart with the fancied slaughter he should make over the whole face of the plantation, he first resolved on a deed that (however horrid it at first appeared to us all), when we had heard his reasons, we thought it brave and just. Being able to walk and, as he believed, fit for the execution of his great design, he begged Trefry to trust him into the air, believing a walk would do him good, which was granted him, and taking Imoinda with him, as he used to do in his more happy and calmer days, he led her up into a wood where, after (with a thousand sighs, and long gazing silently on her face, while tears gushed, in spite of him, from his eyes), he told her his design first of killing her, and then his enemies, and next himself, and the impossibility of escaping, and therefore he told her the necessity of dying. He found the heroic wife faster pleading for death than he was to propose it, when she found his fixed resolution, and on her knees besought him not to leave her a prey to his enemies. He (grieved to death) yet pleased at her noble resolution, took her up, and embracing her with all the passion and languishment of a dying lover, drew his knife to kill this treasure of his soul, this pleasure of his eyes. While tears trickled down his cheeks, hers were smiling with joy she should die by so noble a hand, and be sent in her own country (for that's their notion of the next world) by him she so tenderly loved, and so truly adored in this, for wives have a respect for their husbands equal to what any other people pay a deity, and when a man finds any occasion to quit his wife, if he love her, she dies by his hand; if not, he sells her, or suffers some other to kill her. It being thus, you may believe the deed was soon resolved on, and 'tis not to be doubted, but the parting, the eternal leave-taking of two such lovers, so greatly born, so sensible,[4] so beautiful, so young, and so fond, must be very moving, as the relation of it was to me afterwards.

All that love could say in such cases being ended, and all the intermitting irresolutions being adjusted, the lovely, young, and adored victim lays herself down before the sacrificer, while he, with a hand resolved, and a heart breaking within, gave the fatal stroke, first cutting her throat, and then severing her yet smiling face from that delicate body, pregnant as it was with fruits of tenderest love. As soon as he had done, he laid the body decently on leaves and flowers, of which he made a bed, and concealed it under the same coverlid of nature, only her face he left yet bare to look on. But when he found she was dead, and past all retrieve, never more to bless him with her eyes and soft language, his grief swelled up to rage; he tore, he raved, he roared, like some monster of the wood, calling on the loved name of Imoinda. A thousand times he turned the fatal knife that did the deed toward his own heart, with a resolution to go immediately after her, but dire revenge, which now was a thousand times more fierce in his soul than before,

4. Sensitive.

prevents him, and he would cry out, "No, since I have sacrificed Imoinda to my revenge, shall I lose that glory which I have purchased so dear, as at the price of the fairest, dearest, softest creature that ever Nature made? No, no!" Then, at her name, grief would get the ascendant of rage, and he would lie down by her side, and water her face with showers of tears, which never were wont to fall from those eyes. And however bent he was on his intended slaughter, he had not power to stir from the sight of this dear object, now more beloved and more adored than ever.

He remained in this deploring condition for two days, and never rose from the ground where he had made his sad sacrifice. At last, rousing from her side, and accusing himself with living too long now Imoinda was dead, and that the deaths of those barbarous enemies were deferred too long, he resolved now to finish the great work; but offering to rise, he found his strength so decayed, that he reeled to and fro, like boughs assailed by contrary winds, so that he was forced to lie down again, and try to summon all his courage to his aid. He found his brains turn round, and his eyes were dizzy, and objects appeared not the same to him as they were wont to do; his breath was short, and all his limbs surprised with a faintness he had never felt before. He had not eaten in two days, which was one occasion of this feebleness, but excess of grief was the greatest; yet still he hoped he should recover vigor to act his design, and lay expecting it yet six days longer, still mourning over the dead idol of his heart, and striving every day to rise, but could not.

In all this time you may believe we were in no little affliction for Caesar and his wife. Some were of opinion he was escaped never to return; others thought some accident had happened to him. But however, we failed not to send out a hundred people several ways to search for him. A party of about forty went that way he took, among whom was Tuscan, who was perfectly reconciled to Byam. They had not gone very far into the wood, but they smelt an unusual smell, as of a dead body, for stinks must be very noisome that can be distinguished among such a quantity of natural sweets, as every inch of that land produces. So that they concluded they should find him dead, or somebody that was so. They passed on towards it, as loathsome as it was, and made such a rustling among the leaves that lie thick on the ground, by continual falling, that Caesar heard he was approached, and though he had, during the space of these eight days, endeavored to rise, but found he wanted strength, yet looking up, and seeing his pursuers, he rose, and reeled to a neighboring tree, against which he fixed his back. And being within a dozen yards of those that advanced and saw him, he called out to them, and bid them approach no nearer, if they would be safe; so that they stood still, and hardly believing their eyes, that would persuade them that it was Caesar that spoke to them, so much was he altered, they asked him what he had done with his wife, for they smelt a stink that almost struck them dead. He, pointing to the dead body, sighing, cried, "Behold her there." They put off the flowers that covered her with their sticks, and found she was killed, and cried out, "Oh monster! that hast murdered thy wife." Then asking him, why he did so cruel a deed, he replied, he had no leisure to answer impertinent questions. "You may go back," continued he, "and tell the faithless governor he may thank Fortune that I am breathing my last, and that my arm is too feeble to obey my heart in what it had designed him." But his tongue faltering, and trembling, he could scarce end what he was saying. The English taking advantage by his weakness, cried, "Let us take him alive by all means." He heard them; and, as if he had revived from a fainting, or a dream, he cried out, "No, gentlemen, you are deceived, you will find no more Caesars to be whipped, no more find a faith in me. Feeble as you think me, I have strength yet left to secure me from a second indignity." They swore all anew, and he only shook his head, and beheld them with scorn. Then they cried out, "Who will venture on this single man? Will nobody?" They stood all silent while Caesar replied, "Fatal will be the attempt to the first adventurer, let him assure himself," and, at that word, held up his knife in a menacing posture. "Look ye, ye faithless crew," said he, "'tis not life I seek, nor am I afraid of dying," and, at that word, cut a piece of flesh from his own throat, and threw it at them, "yet still I would live if I could, till I had perfected my revenge. But oh! it cannot be. I feel life gliding from my eyes and heart, and, if I make not haste, I shall yet fall a victim to the shameful whip." At that, he ripped up his own belly, and took his bowels and pulled them out, with what strength he could, while some, on their knees imploring, besought him to hold his hand. But when they saw him tottering, they cried out, "Will none venture on him?" A bold English cried, "Yes, if he were the Devil" (taking courage when he saw him almost dead) and swearing a horrid oath for his farewell to the world he rushed on. Caesar with his armed hand met him so fairly, as stuck him to the heart, and he fell dead at his feet. Tuscan seeing that, cried out, "I love thee, oh Caesar, and therefore will not let thee die, if possible." And, running to him, took him in his arms, but at the same time, warding a blow that Caesar made at his bosom, he received it quite through his arm, and Caesar having not the strength to pluck the knife forth, though he attempted it, Tuscan neither pulled it out himself, nor suffered it to be pulled out, but came down with it sticking in his arm, and the reason he gave for it was because the air should not get into the wound. They put their hands across, and carried Caesar between six of them, fainted as he was, and they thought dead, or just dying, and they brought him to Parham, and laid him on a couch, and had the chirurgeon immediately to him, who dressed his wounds, and sewed up his belly, and used means to bring him to life, which they effected. We ran all to see him; and, if before we thought him so beautiful a sight, he was now so altered that his face was like a death's head blacked over, nothing but teeth and eye-holes. For some days we suffered nobody to speak to him, but caused cordials to be poured down his throat, which sustained his life, and in six or seven days he recovered his senses. For you must know, that wounds are almost to a miracle cured in the Indies, unless wounds in the legs, which rarely ever cure.

When he was well enough to speak, we talked to him, and asked him some questions about his wife, and the reasons why he killed her. And he then told us what I have related of that resolution, and of his parting, and he besought us we would let him die, and was extremely afflicted to think it was possible he might live. He assured us, if we did not dispatch him, he would prove very fatal to a great many. We said all we could to make him live, and gave him new assurances, but he begged we would not think so poorly of him, or of his love to Imoinda, to imagine we could flatter him to life again; but the chirurgeon assured him he could not live, and therefore he need not fear. We were all (but Caesar) afflicted at this news; and the sight was gashly.[5] His discourse was sad; and the earthly smell about him so strong, that I was persuaded to leave the place for some time (being myself but sickly, and very apt to fall into fits of dangerous illness upon any extraordinary melancholy). The servants, and Trefry, and the chirurgeons, promised all to take what possible care they could of the life of Caesar, and I, taking boat, went with other company to Colonel Martin's, about three days' journey down the river; but I was no sooner gone, but the governor taking Trefry about some

5. Ghastly.

pretended earnest business a day's journey up the river, having communicated his design to one Banister, a wild Irishman, and one of the council, a fellow of absolute barbarity, and fit to execute any villainy, but was rich, he came up to Parham, and forcibly took Caesar, and had him carried to the same post where he was whipped, and causing him to be tied to it, and a great fire made before him, he told him he should die like a dog, as he was. Caesar replied, this was the first piece of bravery that ever Banister did, and he never spoke sense till he pronounced that word, and, if he would keep it, he would declare, in the other world, that he was the only man, of all the whites, that ever he heard speak truth. And turning to the men that bound him, he said, "My friends, am I to die, or to be whipped?" And they cried, "Whipped! no; you shall not escape so well." And then he replied, smiling, "A blessing on thee," and assured them, they need not tie him, for he would stand fixed, like a rock, and endure death so as should encourage them to die. "But if you whip me," said he, "be sure you tie me fast."

He had learned to take tobacco, and when he was assured he should die, he desired they would give him a pipe in his mouth, ready lighted, which they did, and the executioner came, and first cut off his members,[6] and threw them into the fire. After that, with an ill-favored knife, they cut his ears and his nose, and burned them; he still smoked on, as if nothing had touched him. Then they hacked off one of his arms, and still he bore up, and held his pipe. But at the cutting off the other arm, his head sunk, and his pipe dropped, and he gave up the ghost, without a groan, or a reproach. My mother and sister were by him all the while, but not suffered to save him, so rude and wild were the rabble, and so inhuman were the justices, who stood by to see the execution, who after paid dearly enough for their insolence. They cut Caesar in quarters, and sent them to several of the chief plantations. One quarter was sent to Colonel Martin, who refused it, and swore he had rather see the quarters of Banister and the governor himself than those of Caesar on his plantations, and that he could govern his Negroes without terrifying and grieving them with frightful spectacles of a mangled king.

Thus died this great man, worthy of a better fate, and a more sublime wit than mine to write his praise. Yet, I hope, the reputation of my pen is considerable enough to make his glorious name to survive to all ages, with that of the brave, the beautiful, and the constant Imoinda.

1688

—•—⟩◆⟨—•—

John Wilmot, Earl of Rochester
1647–1680

In one of his many notorious escapades, John Wilmot, Earl of Rochester, drunkenly smashed to pieces one of the king's costliest timekeepers. He always lived at odds with ordinary time, mostly ahead of it: he became Earl at age ten, when his father died; received his M.A. from Oxford at fourteen; conducted a Grand Tour of Europe during the next three years; tried to abduct his future wife Elizabeth Malet (a much-sought woman of wealth, wit, and beauty) when he was eighteen, and was briefly imprisoned for the attempt; married her at twenty; and died, after long libertinage and precipitate piety, at thirty-three. Rochester's wit and beauty, the stupendous energies of his mind (erudite, inventive), of his language (adroit, obscene), of

6. Genitals.

his body (alcoholic, bisexual), and of his convictions (hedonistic, atheistic) made him the fascination of the Restoration court, whose proclivities for theatrics, for combat, and for amorous
entanglement he pushed to matchless extremes. Theatrics: Rochester wrote plays of his own and
produced plays by others; he tutored the stage novice Elizabeth Barry, soon to become the greatest actress of the age (they carried on a volatile affair, and had a daughter); at times he could don
a disguise himself and play a role so successfully (in order to go underground, to escape punishment, to bring off a seduction) that close friends could not recognize him. Combat: Rochester
distinguished himself for courage by plunging into the thick of the fighting during several sea battles; he once disgraced himself for cowardice in running away during a nocturnal street brawl,
"frighted" (he later wrote) "at my own mischiefs" and leaving one of his own defenders dead. In
the lesser combats of the court, those endless verbal cutting contests of improvised insult and
impromptu verse, Rochester was virtually unbeatable (though the king, when cut, could cut
back: the earl's status shifted often and quickly between favorite and outcast). Amorous entanglement: Rochester's letters to his wife bespeak a marriage of extraordinary tenderness; his poems
boast a career of fornication scarcely credible in its range and ferocity. In 1680, ill and exhausted,
Rochester left London for his ancestral country estate where, frighted by his own mischiefs on a
grander scale, he pursued a highly publicized course of penitence under the tutelage of the clergyman Gilbert Burnet, who later published a detailed account of their conversations. The authenticity of this deathbed conversion was questioned then, and has been questioned since, but its
results were real enough: Rochester asked his mother to burn his papers, and she did. Fewer than
a hundred poems survive. Rochester had never troubled to publish any of them himself; a pirated
collection appeared a few months after his death. Yet these pieces, and the conflicting accounts
of the life that produced them, have been enough to make him last. Soon after his death, the
poet Aphra Behn claimed in verse to have received a visit from his "lovely phantom." "The
great, the god-like Rochester" comes before her in order both to praise and to correct her poetry.
Since then he has haunted many—pietists, poets, and others—as object of veneration, or
reproach, or both together: as admonitory example, verbal virtuoso, extraordinary mortal.

Against Constancy

Tell me no more of constancy,
    The frivolous pretense
Of cold age, narrow jealousy,
    Disease, and want of sense.

5 Let duller fools, on whom kind chance
    Some easy heart has thrown,
Despairing higher to advance,
    Be kind to one alone.

Old men and weak, whose idle flame
10   Their own defects discovers,
Since changing can but spread their shame,
    Ought to be constant lovers.

But we, whose hearts do justly swell
    With no vainglorious pride,
15 Who know how we in love excel,
    Long to be often tried.

Then bring my bath, and strew my bed,
    As each kind night returns;
I'll change a mistress till I'm dead—
20   And fate change me to worms.

                                                                        1676

The Disabled Debauchee

As some brave admiral, in former war
    Deprived of force, but pressed with courage still,
Two rival fleets appearing from afar,
    Crawls to the top of an adjacent hill;

5   From whence, with thoughts full of concern, he views
    The wise and daring conduct of the fight,
Whilst each bold action to his mind renews
    His present glory and his past delight;

From his fierce eyes flashes of fire he throws,
10   As from black clouds when lightning breaks away;
Transported, thinks himself amidst the foes,
    And absent, yet enjoys the bloody day;

So, when my days of impotence approach,
    And I'm by pox and wine's unlucky chance
15   Forced from the pleasing billows of debauch
    On the dull shore of lazy temperance,

My pains at least some respite shall afford
    While I behold the battles you maintain
When fleets of glasses sail about the board,[1]
20   From whose broadsides volleys of wit shall rain.

Nor let the sight of honorable scars,
    Which my too forward valor did procure,
Frighten new-listed soldiers from the wars:
    Past joys have more than paid what I endure.

25   Should any youth (worth being drunk) prove nice,
    And from his fair inviter meanly shrink,
'Twill please the ghost of my departed Vice[2]
    If, at my counsel, he repent and drink.

Or should some cold-complexioned sot forbid,
30   With his dull morals, our bold night-alarms,
I'll fire his blood by telling what I did
    When I was strong and able to bear arms.

I'll tell of whores attacked, their lords at home;
    Bawds' quarters beaten up, and fortress won;
35   Windows demolished, watches overcome;
    And handsome ills by my contrivance done.

Nor shall our love-fits, Chloris,[3] be forgot,
    When each the well-looked linkboy[4] strove t' enjoy,
And the best kiss was the deciding lot
40   Whether the boy fucked you, or I the boy.

---

1. I.e., wine glasses passed around the table.
2. A character bearing this name had been a staple figure in medieval morality plays, as the comic, scoffing incarnation of depravity.
3. A woman's name, common in pastoral verse (and in Rochester's).
4. A boy employed to accompany walkers on the city streets at night, lighting their way by means of a torch ("link").

With tales like these I will such thoughts inspire
    As to important mischief shall incline:
I'll make him long some ancient church to fire,
    And fear no lewdness he's called to by wine.

45   Thus, statesmanlike, I'll saucily impose,
    And safe from action, valiantly advise;
Sheltered in impotence, urge you to blows,
    And being good for nothing else, be wise.

1675?   1680

Song

Love a woman? You're an ass!
    'Tis a most insipid passion
To choose out for your happiness
    The silliest part of God's creation.

5   Let the porter and the groom,
    Things designed for dirty slaves,
Drudge in fair Aurelia's womb
    To get supplies for age and graves.

Farewell, woman! I intend
10   Henceforth every night to sit
With my lewd, well-natured friend,
    Drinking to engender wit.

Then give me health, wealth, mirth, and wine,
    And, if busy love entrenches,
15   There's a sweet, soft page of mine
    Does the trick worth forty wenches.

                                                     1680

The Imperfect Enjoyment

Naked she lay, clasped in my longing arms,
I filled with love, and she all over charms;
Both equally inspired with eager fire,
Melting through kindness, flaming in desire.
5   With arms, legs, lips close clinging to embrace,
She clips me to her breast, and sucks me to her face.
Her nimble tongue, Love's lesser lightning, played
Within my mouth, and to my thoughts conveyed
Swift orders that I should prepare to throw
10   The all-dissolving thunderbolt below.
My fluttering soul, sprung with the pointed kiss,
Hangs hovering o'er her balmy brinks of bliss.
But whilst her busy hand would guide that part
Which should convey my soul up to her heart,
15   In liquid raptures I dissolve all o'er,
Melt into sperm, and spend at every pore.
A touch from any part of her had done 't:
Her hand, her foot, her very look's a cunt.

Smiling, she chides in a kind murmuring noise,
20   And from her body wipes the clammy joys,
When, with a thousand kisses wandering o'er
My panting bosom, "Is there then no more?"
She cries. "All this to love and rapture's due;
Must we not pay a debt to pleasure too?"
25   But I, the most forlorn, lost man alive,
To show my wished obedience vainly strive:
I sigh, alas! and kiss, but cannot swive.°   *screw*
Eager desires confound my first intent,
Succeeding shame does more success prevent,
30   And rage at last confirms me impotent.
Ev'n her fair hand, which might bid heat return
To frozen age, and make cold hermits burn,
Applied to my dead cinder, warms no more
Than fire to ashes could past flames restore.
35   Trembling, confused, despairing, limber, dry,
A wishing, weak, unmoving lump I lie.
This dart of love, whose piercing point, oft tried,
With virgin blood ten thousand maids have dyed,
Which nature still directed with such art
40   That it through every cunt reached every heart—
Stiffly resolved, 'twould carelessly invade
Woman or man, nor ought° its fury stayed:°   *anything / stopped*
Where'er it pierced, a cunt it found or made—
Now languid lies in this unhappy hour,
45   Shrunk up and sapless like a withered flower.
Thou treacherous, base deserter of my flame,
False to my passion, fatal to my fame,
Through what mistaken magic dost thou prove
So true to lewdness, so untrue to love?
50   What oyster-cinder-beggar-common whore
Didst thou e'er fail in all thy life before?
When vice, disease, and scandal lead the way,
With what officious haste doest thou obey!
Like a rude, roaring hector° in the streets   *bully*
55   Who scuffles, cuffs, and justles all he meets,
But if his king or country claim his aid,
The rakehell villain shrinks and hides his head;
Ev'n so thy brutal valor is displayed,
Breaks every stew,° does each small whore invade,   *brothel*
60   But when great Love the onset does command,
Base recreant to thy prince, thou dar'st not stand.
Worst part of me, and henceforth hated most,
Through all the town a common fucking post,
On whom each whore relieves her tingling cunt
65   As hogs on gates do rub themselves and grunt,
Mayst thou to ravenous chancres° be a prey,   *syphilis sores*
Or in consuming weepings waste away;
May strangury and stone[1] thy days attend;

---

1. Painful diseases of the bladder and urinary tract that block the flow of urine.

70   May'st thou never piss, who didst refuse to spend
    When all my joys did on false thee depend.
       And may ten thousand abler pricks agree
       To do the wronged Corinna right for thee.

                                                        1680

Upon Nothing

Nothing! thou elder brother even to Shade:
Thou hadst a being ere the world was made,
And well fixed, art alone of ending not afraid.

Ere Time and Place were, Time and Place were not,
5   When primitive Nothing Something straight begot;
Then all proceeded from the great united What.

Something, the general attribute of all,
Severed from thee, its sole original,
Into thy boundless self must undistinguished fall;

10   Yet Something did thy mighty power command,
And from thy fruitful Emptiness's hand
Snatched men, beasts, birds, fire, water, air, and land.

Matter, the wicked'st offspring of thy race,
By Form assisted, flew from thy embrace,
15   And rebel Light obscured thy reverend dusky face.

With Form and Matter, Time and Place did join;
Body, thy foe, with these did leagues combine
To spoil thy peaceful realm, and ruin all thy line;

But turncoat Time assists the foe in vain,
20   And bribed by thee, destroys their short-lived reign,
And to thy hungry womb drives back thy slaves again.

Though mysteries are barred from laic° eyes,   *uninitiated*
And the divine alone with warrant pries
Into thy bosom, where the truth in private lies,

25   Yet this of thee the wise may truly say:
Thou from the virtuous nothing dost delay,
And to be part of thee the wicked wisely pray.

Great Negative, how vainly would the wise
Inquire, define, distinguish, teach, devise,
30   Didst thou not stand to point their blind philosophies!

Is or Is Not, the two great ends of Fate,
And True or False, the subject of debate,
That perfect or destroy the vast designs of state—

When they have racked the politician's breast,
35   Within thy bosom most securely rest,
And when reduced to thee, are least unsafe and best.

But Nothing, why does Something still permit
That sacred monarchs should in council sit
With persons highly thought at best for nothing fit,

40 While weighty Something modestly abstains
From princes' coffers, and from statesmen's brains,
And Nothing there like stately Nothing reigns?

Nothing! who dwellst with fools in grave disguise,
For whom they reverend shapes and forms devise,
45 Lawn[1] sleeves and furs and gowns, when they like thee look wise:

French truth, Dutch prowess, British policy,
Hibernian learning, Scotch civility,
Spaniards' dispatch, Danes' wit are mainly seen in thee;

The great man's gratitude to his best friend,
50 Kings' promises, whores' vows—towards thee they bend,
Flow swiftly into thee, and in thee ever end.

1678   1679

A Satyr[1] Against Reason and Mankind

Were I (who to my cost already am
One of those strange, prodigious creatures, man)
A spirit free to choose, for my own share,
What case of flesh and blood I pleased to wear,
5 I'd be a dog, a monkey, or a bear,
Or anything but that vain animal
Who is so proud of being rational.
  The senses are too gross, and he'll contrive
A sixth, to contradict the other five,
10 And before certain instinct, will prefer
Reason, which fifty times for one does err;
Reason, an *ignis fatuus*[2] in the mind,
Which, leaving light of nature, sense, behind,
Pathless and dangerous wandering ways it takes
15 Through error's fenny bogs and thorny brakes;
Whilst the misguided follower climbs with pain
Mountains of whimseys, heaped in his own brain;
Stumbling from thought to thought, falls headlong down
Into doubt's boundless sea, where, like to drown,
20 Books bear him up awhile, and make him try
To swim with bladders of philosophy;
In hopes still to o'ertake th' escaping light,
The vapor dances in his dazzling sight
Till, spent, it leaves him to eternal night.
25 Then old age and experience, hand in hand,
Lead him to death, and make him understand,

---

1. Linen; worn (like the furs and gowns) as a mark of rank
by eminent professionals: lawyers, scholars, statesmen, etc.
1. Possibly a pun, identifying both the genre (satire) and
the speaker (a satyr: half-man, half-animal).

2. Literally "foolish fire": a marshland phosphorescence
that, appearing now here and now there, was thought to
be created by sprites to mislead night travelers.

After a search so painful and so long,
That all his life he has been in the wrong.
Huddled in dirt the reasoning engine lies,
30   Who was so proud, so witty, and so wise.
    Pride drew him in, as cheats their bubbles° catch,   *victims*
And made him venture to be made a wretch.
His wisdom did his happiness destroy,
Aiming to know that world he should enjoy.
35   And wit was his vain, frivolous pretense
Of pleasing others at his own expense,
For wits are treated just like common whores:
First they're enjoyed, and then kicked out of doors.
The pleasure past, a threatening doubt remains
40   That frights th' enjoyer with succeeding pains.
Women and men of wit are dangerous tools,
And ever fatal to admiring fools:
Pleasure allures, and when the fops escape,
'Tis not that they're belov'd, but fortunate,
45   And therefore what they fear at heart, they hate.
    But now, methinks, some formal band and beard³
Takes me to task. Come on, sir; I'm prepared.
    "Then, by your favor, anything that's writ
Against this gibing, jingling knack called wit
50   Likes° me abundantly; but you take care   *pleases*
Upon this point, not to be too severe.
Perhaps my muse were fitter for this part,
For I profess I can be very smart
On wit, which I abhor with all my heart.
55   I long to lash it in some sharp essay,
But your grand indiscretion bids me stay
And turns my tide of ink another way.
    "What rage ferments in your degenerate mind
To make you rail at reason and mankind?
60   Blest, glorious man! to whom alone kind heaven
An everlasting soul has freely given,
Whom his great Maker took such care to make
That from himself he did the image take
And this fair frame in shining reason dressed
65   To dignify his nature above beast;
Reason, by whose aspiring influence
We take a flight beyond material sense,
Dive into mysteries, then soaring pierce
The flaming limits of the universe,
70   Search heaven and hell, find out what's acted there,
And give the world true grounds of hope and fear."
    Hold, mighty man, I cry, all this we know
From the pathetic pen of Ingelo,

---

3. I.e., clergyman, wearing these marks of office. In 1675 one clergyman in particular, the king's chaplain Edward Stillingfleet, had denounced in a sermon an earlier version of Rochester's *Satyr*, prompting the poet to alter and add some portions of the dialogue that follows.

From Patrick's *Pilgrim*, Stillingfleet's replies,[4]
75   And 'tis this very reason I despise:
This supernatural gift, that makes a mite
Think he's the image of the infinite,
Comparing his short life, void of all rest,
To the eternal and the ever blest;
80   This busy, puzzling stirrer-up of doubt
That frames deep mysteries, then finds 'em out,
Filling with frantic crowds of thinking fools
Those reverend bedlams,° colleges and schools;   *madhouses*
Borne on whose wings, each heavy sot can pierce
85   The limits of the boundless universe;
So charming ointments make an old witch fly
And bear a crippled carcass through the sky.
'Tis this exalted power, whose business lies
In nonsense and impossibilities,
90   This made a whimsical philosopher
Before the spacious world, his tub prefer,[5]
And we have modern cloistered coxcombs who
Retire to think, 'cause they have nought to do.
    But thoughts are given for action's government;
95   Where action ceases, thought's impertinent.
Our sphere of action is life's happiness,
And he who thinks beyond, thinks like an ass.
Thus, whilst against false reasoning I inveigh,
I own[6] right reason, which I would obey:
100   That reason which distinguishes by sense
And gives us rules of good and ill from thence,
That bounds desires with a reforming will
To keep 'em more in vigor, not to kill.
Your reason hinders, mine helps to enjoy,
105   Renewing appetites yours would destroy.
My reason is my friend, yours is a cheat;
Hunger calls out, my reason bids me eat;
Perversely, yours your appetite does mock:
This asks for food, that answers, "What's o'clock?"
110   This plain distinction, sir, your doubt secures:
'Tis not true reason I despise, but yours.
    Thus I think reason righted, but for man,
I'll ne'er recant; defend him if you can.
For all his pride and his philosophy,
115   'Tis evident beasts are, in their degree,
As wise at least, and better far than he.
Those creatures are the wisest who attain,
By surest means, the ends at which they aim.

4. Rochester names three pious inspirational writers: Nathaniel Ingelo (?1621–1683); Simon Patrick, whose *Parable of the Pilgrim* appeared in 1664; and Stillingfleet, Rochester's clerical critic.
5. Diogenes (c. 400–325 B.C.), Greek philosopher who supposedly lived in an earthenware tub, as an emblem of his scorn for the shallowness of more opulent modes of life.
6. Acknowledge. "Right reason" refers to natural instinct or common sense, as opposed to the more elaborate modes of thought Rochester is attacking.

If therefore Jowler[7] finds and kills his hares
120   Better than Meres[8] supplies committee chairs,
Though one's a statesman, th' other but a hound,
Jowler, in justice, would be wiser found.
        You see how far man's wisdom here extends;
Look next if human nature makes amends:
125   Whose principles most generous are, and just,
And to whose morals you would sooner trust.
Be judge yourself, I'll bring it to the test:
Which is the basest creature, man or beast?
Birds feed on birds, beasts on each other prey,
130   But savage man alone does man betray.
Pressed by necessity, they kill for food;
Man undoes man to do himself no good.
With teeth and claws by nature armed, they hunt
Nature's allowance, to supply their want.
135   But man, with smiles, embraces, friendship, praise,
Inhumanly his fellow's life betrays;
With voluntary pains works his distress,
Not through necessity, but wantonness.
        For hunger or for love they fight and tear,
140   Whilst wretched man is still in arms for fear.
For fear he arms, and is of arms afraid,
By fear to fear successively betrayed;
Base fear, the source whence his best passions came:
His boasted honor, and his dear-bought fame;
145   That lust of power, to which he's such a slave,
And for the which alone he dares be brave;
To which his various projects are designed;
Which makes him generous, affable, and kind;
For which he takes such pains to be thought wise,
150   And screws his actions in a forced disguise,
Leading a tedious life in misery
Under laborious, mean hypocrisy.
Look to the bottom of his vast design,
Wherein man's wisdom, power, and glory join:
155   The good he acts, the ill he does endure,
'Tis all from fear, to make himself secure.
Merely for safety, after fame we thirst,
For all men would be cowards if they durst.
        And honesty's against all common sense:
160   Men must be knaves, 'tis in their own defense.
Mankind's dishonest; if you think it fair
Amongst known cheats to play upon the square,
You'll be undone.
Nor can weak truth your reputation save:
165   The knaves will all agree to call you knave.

---

7. A dog's name, emphasizing the animal's appetites.
8. Sir Thomas Meres (1634–1715), politician noted for his energy, efficacy, and self-serving flexibility in questions of party allegiance.

Wronged shall he live, insulted o'er, oppressed,
Who dares be less a villain than the rest.
    Thus, sir, you see what human nature craves:
Most men are cowards, all men should be knaves.
170 The difference lies, as far as I can see,
Not in the thing itself, but the degree,
And all the subject matter of debate
Is only: Who's a knave of the first rate?
    All this with indignation have I hurled
175 At the pretending part of the proud world,
Who, swollen with selfish vanity, devise
False freedoms, holy cheats, and formal lies
Over their fellow slaves to tyrannize.
    But if in court so just a man there be
180 (In court a just man, yet unknown to me)
Who does his needful flattery direct,
Not to oppress and ruin, but protect
(Since flattery, which way soever laid,
Is still a tax on that unhappy trade);
185 If so upright a statesman you can find,
Whose passions bend to his unbiased mind,
Who does his arts and policies apply
To raise his country, not his family,
Nor, whilst his pride owned avarice withstands,
190 Receives close bribes through friends' corrupted hands—
    Is there a churchman who on God relies;
Whose life, his faith and doctrine justifies?
Not one blown up with vain prelatic pride,
Who, for reproof of sins, does man deride;
195 Whose envious heart makes preaching a pretense,
With his obstreperous, saucy eloquence,
To chide at kings, and rail at men of sense;
None of that sensual tribe whose talents lie
In avarice, pride, sloth, and gluttony;
200 Who hunt good livings, but abhor good lives,
Whose lust exalted to that height arrives
They act adultery with their own wives,
And ere a score of years completed be,
Can from the lofty pulpit proudly see
205 Half a large parish their own progeny;
Nor doting bishop who would be adored
For domineering at the council board,
A greater fop in business at fourscore,
Fonder of serious toys, affected more,
210 Than the gay, glittering fool at twenty proves
With all his noise, his tawdry clothes, and loves;
    But a meek, humble man of honest sense,
Who, preaching peace, does practice continence;
Whose pious life's a proof he does believe
215 Mysterious truths, which no man can conceive.

If upon earth there dwell such God-like men,
I'll here recant my paradox to them,
Adore those shrines of virtue, homage pay,
And, with the rabble world, their laws obey.
220   If such there be, yet grant me this at least:
Man differs more from man, than man from beast.

1674–1676   1679

———— ✦⊰✦⊱✦ ————

William Wycherley
1641–1715

The plot of *The Country Wife* turns on a trick. The rakish Harry Horner devises a tactic calculated to secure both a cover-story and a kinky enhancement for his future seductions of
other men's wives. He starts a rumor going round to the effect that he has become a eunuch;
husbands will henceforth not suspect him, and wives, he trusts, will be intrigued. Early in the
play, it becomes clear that Horner has tested his new disguise by making a visit to the theater.
"Come," one of his friends remarks, "your appearance at the play yesterday has, I hope, hardened you for the future" as to the social consequences of his sexless new reputation. "Did I not
bear it bravely?" asks Horner, pleased. "With a most theatrical impudence," answers his
friend.

In London playhouses of the 1660s and the 1670s, theatrical impudence was in high supply. People came to watch not only the performers, but also each other. Pepys records a telling
anecdote (so telling that it is cited also, more compactly, within a fuller discussion of Restoration theater in the introduction to this section, page 2067). Attending a play one evening, he
found himself distracted throughout the performance by the libertine Sir Charles Sedley, seated nearby in conversation with two women.

> And one of the ladies would and did sit with her mask on, all the play and, being exceed-
> ingly witty as ever I heard woman, did talk most pleasantly with him; but was, I believe, a
> virtuous woman and of quality. He would fain know who she was, but she would not tell;
> yet did give him many pleasant hints of her knowledge of him, by that means setting his
> brains at work to find out who she was, and did give him leave to use all means to find out
> who she was but pulling off her mask. He was mighty witty and she also, making sport of
> him very inoffensively, that a more pleasant rencontre I never heard. By that means lost
> the pleasure of the play wholly . . .

But that loss hardly seems to matter, in comparison with the pleasure of the playlet Pepys has
witnessed within the audience. Masks of the kind this woman wears were a widespread item of
Restoration fashion. Characters in the *Country Wife* mention them obsessively, in part because
they were worn both by "virtuous" women and by prostitutes, with the tantalizing effect of rendering those two human categories not quite distinguishable from one another. In Pepys's
anecdote, man and woman engage in a contest for power grounded in wit, concealment, and
artifice; the new plays on stage during the Restoration teemed with just such sexually charged
encounters and combats. For purposes of theatrical impudence and strategic experiment,
Horner could not have picked for himself a better venue.

Neither could William Wycherley. He wrote four comedies while in his early thirties.
The last two—*The Country Wife* (1675) and *The Plain Dealer* (1676)—brought him to the early high point of a career that sloped rather steeply on either side. Before these successes he had

been a law-student, soldier, courtier, traveler in France, and convert to Catholicism. In their wake he was widely celebrated as the deftest wielder alive of those gifts that Dryden enumerated in a single memorable line: "The satire, wit, and strength of manly Wycherley." "Manly" was the name of the forthright protagonist in *The Plain Dealer*; the adjective alternated with "brawny" as the most popular epithets for this vigorous and accomplished playwright in his prime. But by the time Dryden wrote the line, in 1694, it applied more readily to the work than to the man. Before Wycherley turned forty, a serious illness had left his memory permanently damaged and an imprudent marriage with a widowed countess had cost him much in money, serenity, and the patronage of Charles II and his court. He spent years mired in debt, received temporary relief in the form of a pension from that temporary king James II, and found more reliable respite in the estate he inherited from his father in 1697. In old age he published a failed book of ungainly poems, held literary court at Will's Coffee House (where Dryden had previously presided), and basked in the attention of the young, ambitious Alexander Pope. Eleven days before his death he married a second time. His estate passed to his young widow and hence to his cousin, her secret lover; they had spent his last days scheming to secure it.

In the *Country Wife*, alliances prove comparably shifty. The wits (Horner and his friends), though ostensibly relentless in their pursuit of women, nonetheless seem often more interested in their transactions with each other. They array themselves against the "cits"—the prudent, prosperous businessmen of London—and chase after their desirable, precariously domesticated spouses and sisters. Horner the London rake works his charms on Margery the country wife, who proves cheerfully, even ingeniously susceptible. A group of erotically agitated women—headed by the aptly named Lady Fidget—collude with Horner in his deceit, disappear behind closed doors to savor his emphatically non-eunuchoid sexuality while pretending to sample his china, and finally team up, as a suddenly "virtuous gang," to reproach him for his perfidies. Throughout the play, Wycherley works a running comparison between sex and gambling (and, in the famous china scene, a second parallel between sex and shopping). Most of the amorous gamesters play their hands with witty fervor, but the playwright deliberately leaves unclear what exactly is at stake. Deep feelings, real risks, sturdy allegiances seem hard to come by. Most bets are placed instead on power, on cunning, on conquest, perhaps on momentary pleasure; in the end it can be hard to tell who's won, who's lost, and why. *Comedy* takes its name from *komos*, the dance of communal harmony with which so many such plays close. *The Country Wife*, by contrast, ends with a "dance of cuckolds": music for a world where fidelities are faint, and even betrayals, transpiring for muddled motives behind closed doors, are not fully comprehensible.

The Country Wife

PROLOGUE, *SPOKEN BY MR. HART*[1]

Poets, like cudgeled bullies, never do
At first or second blow submit to you;
But will provoke you still, and ne'er have done,
Till you are weary first with laying on.
5   The late so baffled scribbler[2] of this day,
Though he stands trembling, bids me boldly say,
What we before most plays are used to do,
For poets out of fear first draw on you;

---

1. Charles Hart, who starred as Horner in the first production, was famous both as actor and as lover. As actor, he achieved some of his greatest successes playing the preternaturally virile and virtuous protagonists in Dryden's heroic tragedies. As lover, he had been linked with eminent beauties, including Nell Gwyn and Lady Castle-maine (for Pepys's comments on both, see pages 2093 and 2107).

2. Refers to the cold reception of *The Gentleman Dancing Master*, which Wycherley himself recognized as a trivial work.

In a fierce prologue the still pit defy
10   And ere you speak, like Castril,[3] give the lie.
But though our Bayes's battles[4] oft I've fought,
And with bruised knuckles their dear conquests bought;
Nay, never yet feared odds upon the stage,
In prologue dare not hector with the age,
15   But would take quarter from your saving hands,
Though Bayes within[5] all yielding countermands,
Says you confederate wits[6] no quarter give,
Therefore his play shan't ask your leave to live.
Well, let the vain rash fop, by huffing[7] so,
20   Think to obtain the better terms of you;
But we the actors humbly will submit,
Now, and at any time, to a full pit;
Nay, often we anticipate your rage,
And murder poets for you on our stage.
25   We set no guards upon our tiring-room,[8]
But when with flying colors there you come,
We patiently, you see, give up to you
Our poets, virgins, nay, our matrons too.

The Persons

MR. HORNER	MRS. DAINTY FIDGET
MR. HARCOURT	MRS. SQUEAMISH
MR. DORILANT	OLD LADY SQUEAMISH
MR. PINCHWIFE	WAITERS, SERVANTS, AND ATTENDANTS
MR. SPARKISH	A BOY
SIR JASPAR FIDGET	A QUACK
MRS. MARGERY PINCHWIFE	LUCY, ALITHEA'S MAID
MRS. ALITHEA	[CLASP]
MY LADY FIDGET	[A PARSON]

The Scene: *London*

ACT 1

Scene 1

[*Enter Horner, and Quack following him at a distance.*]

HORNER [*aside*]: A quack is as fit for a pimp as a midwife for a bawd;[1] they are still[2] but in their way both helpers of nature.—Well, my dear doctor, hast thou done what I desired?

QUACK: I have undone you forever with the women, and reported you throughout the whole town as bad as an eunuch, with as much trouble as if I had made you one in earnest.

3. An angry character in Ben Jonson's *The Alchemist* (1610), who impulsively challenges ("gives the lie" to) others.
4. The battles that Hart had "fought" onstage in his roles as soldier-hero in Dryden's tragedies, and also the struggles of writers in general (and Wycherley in particular) to secure approval of their work. Bayes was the central character in the Duke of Buckingham's comedy *The Rehearsal* (1671): a foolish, preening playwright, he incarnated in

every particular a merciless, hilarious parody of Dryden. His name soon became a mocking designation for any ambitious poet.
5. I.e., Wycherley, backstage.
6. Critics conjoined to condemn the play.
7. Blustering.
8. Dressing-room.
1. Brothel-keeper.
2. Always.

HORNER: But have you told all the midwives you know, the orange-wenches[3] at the playhouses, the city husbands,[4] and old fumbling keepers[5] of this end of the town? For they'll be the readiest to report it.

QUACK: I have told all the chambermaids, waiting-women, tire-women[6] and old women of my acquaintance; nay, and whispered it as a secret to 'em, and to the whisperers of Whitehall;[7] so that you need not doubt, 'twill spread, and you will be as odious to the handsome young women as—

HORNER: As the smallpox. Well—

QUACK: And to the married women of this end of the town as—

HORNER: As the great ones;[8] nay, as their own husbands.

QUACK: And to the city dames as aniseed Robin[9] of filthy and contemptible memory; and they will frighten their children with your name, especially their females.

HORNER: And cry, "Horner's coming to carry you away." I am only afraid 'twill not be believed. You told 'em 'twas by an English–French disaster and an English–French chirurgeon,[1] who has given me at once, not only a cure, but an antidote[2] for the future against that damned malady, and that worse distemper, love, and all other women's evils.

QUACK: Your late journey into France has made it the more credible and your being here a fortnight before you appeared in public looks as if you apprehended the shame, which I wonder you do not. Well, I have been hired by young gallants to belie 'em t' other way, but you are the first would be thought a man unfit for women.

HORNER: Dear Mr. Doctor, let vain rogues be contented only to be thought abler men than they are, generally 'tis all the pleasure they have; but mine lies another way.

QUACK: You take, methinks, a very preposterous way to it and as ridiculous as if we operators in physic should put forth bills to disparage our medicaments, with hopes to gain customers.

HORNER: Doctor, there are quacks in love as well as physic, who get but the fewer and worse patients for their boasting; a good name is seldom got by giving it one-self, and women no more than honor are compassed[3] by bragging. Come, come, doctor, the wisest lawyer never discovers[4] the merits of his cause till the trial; the wealthiest man conceals his riches, and the cunning gamester his play. Shy husbands and keepers, like old rooks,[5] are not to be cheated but by a new unpracticed trick; false friendship will pass now no more than false dice upon 'em; no, not in the city. [Enter Boy.]

BOY: There are two ladies and a gentleman coming up.   [Exit.]

HORNER: A pox! Some unbelieving sisters of my former acquaintance, who, I am afraid, expect their sense should be satisfied of the falsity of the report. No—this formal[6] fool and women!

[Enter Sir Jaspar Fidget, Lady Fidget, and Mrs. Dainty Fidget.]

---

3. Orange-sellers.
4. Respectable men of business who (according to stereotype) would loathe the likes of Horner.
5. Men who keep mistresses.
6. Ladies' maids, also dressmakers.
7. The royal residence, a center for news and gossip.
8. Syphilis.
9. A famous hermaphrodite; hence (from the vantage of respectable "city dames") a repellent monster.
1. In muddled phrasing, Horner appears to blame both

English and French personnel (women, doctors) for both his supposed illness (syphilis, often called "the French pox") and its drastic cure. The muddle may be intentional; Horner is, after all, making up the whole story.
2. I.e., his purported impotence.
3. Won.
4. Reveals.
5. Cheats, swindlers.
6. Unduly ceremonious, stiff.

QUACK: His wife and sister.

SIR JASPAR: My coach breaking just now before your door, sir, I look upon as an occasional[7] reprimand to me, sir, for not kissing your hands, sir, since your coming out of France, sir; and so my disaster, sir, has been my good fortune, sir; and this is my wife, and sister, sir.

HORNER: What then, sir?

SIR JASPAR: My lady, and sister, sir.—Wife, this is Master Horner.

LADY FIDGET: Master Horner, husband!

SIR JASPAR: My lady, my Lady Fidget, sir.

HORNER: So, sir.

SIR JASPAR: Won't you be acquainted with her, sir? [Aside.] So the report is true, I find, by his coldness or aversion to the sex; but I'll play the wag with him.—Pray salute my wife, my lady, sir.

HORNER: I will kiss no man's wife, sir, for him, sir; I have taken my eternal leave, sir, of the sex already, sir.

SIR JASPAR [aside]: Hah, hah, hah! I'll plague him yet.—Not know my wife, sir?

HORNER: I do know your wife, sir; she's a woman, sir, and consequently a monster, sir, a greater monster than a husband, sir.

SIR JASPAR: A husband! How, sir?

HORNER [makes horns[8]]: So, sir; but I make no more cuckolds, sir.

SIR JASPAR: Hah, hah, hah! Mercury, Mercury![9]

LADY FIDGET: Pray, Sir Jaspar, let us be gone from this rude fellow.

DAINTY: Who, by his breeding, would think he had ever been in France?

LADY FIDGET: Foh, he's but too much a French fellow,[1] such as hate women of quality and virtue for their love to their husbands, Sir Jaspar; a woman is hated by 'em as much for loving her husband as for loving their money. But pray, let's be gone.

HORNER: You do well, madam, for I have nothing that you came for; I have brought over not so much as a bawdy picture, new postures,[2] nor the second part of the École des Filles,[3] nor—

QUACK [apart to Horner]: Hold, for shame, sir! What d'ye mean? You'll ruin yourself forever with the sex—

SIR JASPAR: Hah, hah, hah, he hates women perfectly, I find.

DAINTY: What a pity 'tis he should.

LADY FIDGET: Ay, he's a base, rude fellow for't; but affectation makes not a woman more odious to them than virtue.

HORNER: Because your virtue is your greatest affectation madam.

LADY FIDGET: How, you saucy fellow! Would you wrong my honor?

HORNER: If I could.

LADY FIDGET: How d'ye mean, sir?

SIR JASPAR: Hah, hah, hah! No, he can't wrong your ladyship's honor, upon my honor; he, poor man—hark you in your ear—a mere eunuch.

LADY FIDGET: O filthy French beast, foh, foh! Why do we stay? Let's be gone; I can't endure the sight of him.

7. Opportune.
8. With forefingers on the forehead, the cuckold sign.
9. Both the messenger-god, whose winged hat Horner's "horns" may call to mind, and the chemical often used in treating syphilis.

1. Fop.
2. Pornographic engravings.
3. A pornographic dialogue between a virgin and an experienced woman (1655); Pepys called it "the most bawdy, lewd book that I ever saw."

SIR JASPAR: Stay but till the chairs[4] come; they'll be here presently.

LADY FIDGET: No, no.

SIR JASPAR: Nor can I stay longer. 'Tis—let me see, a quarter and a half quarter of a minute past eleven; the Council[5] will be sat, I must away. Business must be preferred always before love and ceremony with the wise, Mr. Horner.

HORNER: And the impotent, Sir Jaspar.

SIR JASPAR: Ay, ay, the impotent, Master Horner, hah, ha, ha!

LADY FIDGET: What, leave us with a filthy man alone in his lodgings?

SIR JASPAR: He's an innocent man now, you know. Pray stay, I'll hasten the chairs to you.—Mr. Horner, your servant; I should be glad to see you at my house. Pray come and dine with me, and play at cards with my wife after dinner; you are fit for women at that game yet, hah, ha! [Aside.] 'Tis as much a husband's prudence to provide innocent diversion for a wife as to hinder her unlawful pleasures, and he had better employ her than let her employ herself.—Farewell.   [Exit Sir Jaspar.]

HORNER: Your servant, Sir Jaspar.

LADY FIDGET: I will not stay with him, foh!

HORNER: Nay, madam, I beseech you stay, if it be but to see I can be as civil to ladies yet as they would desire.

LADY FIDGET: No, no, foh, you cannot be civil to ladies.

DAINTY: You as civil as ladies would desire?

LADY FIDGET: No, no, no, foh, foh, foh!

[Exeunt Lady Fidget and Dainty.]

QUACK: Now, I think, I, or you yourself rather, have done your business[6] with the women.

HORNER: Thou art an ass. Don't you see already, upon the report and my carriage,[7] this grave man of business leaves his wife in my lodgings, invites me to his house and wife, who before would not be acquainted with me out of jealousy?

QUACK: Nay, by this means you may be the more acquainted with the husbands, but the less with the wives.

HORNER: Let me alone; if I can but abuse the husbands, I'll soon disabuse the wives. Stay—I'll reckon you up the advantages I am like to have by my stratagem: first, I shall be rid of all my old acquaintances, the most insatiable sorts of duns,[8] that invade our lodgings in a morning. And next to the pleasure of making a new mistress is that of being rid of an old one; and of all old debts, love, when it comes to be so, is paid the most unwillingly.

QUACK: Well, you may be so rid of your old acquaintances; but how will you get any new ones?

HORNER: Doctor, thou wilt never make a good chemist, thou art so incredulous and impatient. Ask but all the young fellows of the town if they do not lose more time, like huntsmen, in starting the game than in running it down; one knows not where to find 'em, who will or will not. Women of quality are so civil, you can hardly distinguish love from good breeding and a man is often mistaken; but now I can be sure, she that shows an aversion to me loves the sport, as those women that are gone, whom I warrant to be right.[9] And then the next thing is, your women of

---

4. Sedan chairs, in which two bearers carried a single passenger.
5. Privy Council.
6. Spoiled your reputation.

7. Conduct.
8. Persistent creditors.
9. Ripe for play, promiscuous.

honor, as you call 'em, are only chary[1] of their reputations, not their persons, and 'tis scandal they would avoid, not men. Now may I have, by the reputation of an eunuch, the privileges of one and be seen in a lady's chamber in a morning as early as her husband, kiss virgins before their parents or lovers and may be, in short, the *passe partout*[2] of the town. Now, doctor.

QUACK: Nay, now you shall be the doctor; and your process is so new that we do not know but it may succeed.

HORNER: Not so new neither; *probatum est,*[3] doctor.

QUACK: Well, I wish you luck and many patients whilst I go to mine. [*Exit Quack.*]
    [*Enter Harcourt and Dorilant to Horner.*]

HARCOURT: Come, your appearance at the play yesterday has, I hope, hardened you for the future against the women's contempt and the men's raillery and now you'll abroad as you were wont.

HORNER: Did I not bear it bravely?

DORILANT: With a most theatrical impudence; nay, more than the orange-wenches show there or a drunken vizard-mask[4] or a great-bellied actress; nay, or the most impudent of creatures, an ill poet; or what is yet more impudent, a secondhand critic.

HORNER: But what say the ladies? Have they no pity?

HARCOURT: What ladies? The vizard-masks, you know, never pity a man when all's gone, though in their service.

DORILANT: And for the women in the boxes, you'd never pity them when 'twas in your power.

HARCOURT: They say, 'tis pity, but all that deal with common women should be served so.

DORILANT: Nay, I dare swear, they won't admit you to play at cards with them, go to plays with 'em, or do the little duties which other shadows of men are wont to do for 'em.

HORNER: Who do you call shadows of men?

DORILANT: Half-men.

HORNER: What, boys?

DORILANT: Ay, your old boys, old *beaux garçons,*[5] who, like superannuated[6] stallions, are suffered to run, feed and whinny with the mares as long as they live, though they can do nothing else.

HORNER: Well, a pox on love and wenching! Women serve but to keep a man from better company; though I can't enjoy them, I shall you the more. Good fellowship and friendship are lasting, rational and manly pleasures.

HARCOURT: For all that, give me some of those pleasures you call effeminate too; they help to relish one another.

HORNER: They disturb one another.

HARCOURT: No, mistresses are like books. If you pore upon them too much, they doze[7] you and make you unfit for company; but if used discreetly, you are the fitter for conversation by 'em.

---

1. Careful, wary.
2. One who may go anywhere.
3. "It has been proved or tested," a phrase used in prescriptions.
4. A prostitute; many of them wore masks, as emblems of

their trade.
5. Old gallants.
6. Old and infirm.
7. Stupefy.

DORILANT: A mistress should be like a little country retreat near the town, not to dwell in constantly, but only for a night and away, to taste the town the better when a man returns.

HORNER: I tell you, 'tis as hard to be a good fellow, a good friend and a lover of women, as 'tis to be a good fellow, a good friend and a lover of money. You cannot follow both, then choose your side. Wine gives you liberty, love takes it away.

DORILANT: Gad, he's in the right on't.

HORNER: Wine gives you joy; love, grief and tortures, besides the chirurgeon's. Wine makes us witty; love, only sots. Wine makes us sleep; love breaks it.

DORILANT: By the world, he has reason,[8] Harcourt.

HORNER: Wine makes—

DORILANT: Ay, wine makes us—makes us princes; love makes us beggars, poor rogues, egad—and wine—

HORNER: So, there's one converted.—No, no, love and wine, oil and vinegar.

HARCOURT: I grant it; love will still be uppermost.

HORNER: Come, for my part I will have only those glorious, manly pleasures of being very drunk and very slovenly. [Enter Boy.]

BOY: Mr. Sparkish is below, sir.   [Exit.]

HARCOURT: What, my dear friend! A rogue that is fond of me only, I think, for abusing him.

DORILANT: No, he can no more think the men laugh at him than that women jilt[9] him, his opinion of himself is so good.

HORNER: Well, there's another pleasure by drinking I thought not of: I shall lose his acquaintance, because he cannot drink; and you know 'tis a very hard thing to be rid of him, for he's one of those nauseous offerers at wit, who, like the worst fiddlers, run themselves into all companies.

HARCOURT: One that, by being in the company of men of sense, would pass for one.

HORNER: And may so to the short-sighted world, as a false jewel amongst true ones is not discerned at a distance. His company is as troublesome to us as a cuckold's when you have a mind to his wife's.

HARCOURT: No, the rogue will not let us enjoy one another, but ravishes our conversation, though he signifies no more to't than Sir Martin Mar-all's[1] gaping and awkward thrumming upon the lute does to his man's voice and music.

DORILANT: And to pass for a wit in town shows himself a fool every night to us that are guilty of the plot.

HORNER: Such wits as he are, to a company of reasonable men, like rooks[2] to the gamesters, who only fill a room[3] at the table, but are so far from contributing to the play that they only serve to spoil the fancy of those that do.

DORILANT: Nay, they are used like rooks too, snubbed, checked and abused; yet the rogues will hang on.

HORNER: A pox on 'em, and all that force nature and would be still what she forbids 'em! Affectation is her greatest monster.

---

8. Speaks truth (French *il a raison:* "he is right").
9. Reject.
1. Foolish title character of Dryden's comedy (1667) who lip-synchs and fake-strums a serenade to his mistress while his "man" (servant), hidden, actually performs the

song. When his servant finishes playing, Sir Martin fails to quit miming. Harcourt regards Sparkish as such another empty fraud.
2. Here, simpletons, fools.
3. Space.

HARCOURT: Most men are the contraries to that they would seem. Your bully, you see, is a coward with a long sword; the little, humbly fawning physician, with his ebony cane, is he that destroys men.

DORILANT: The usurer, a poor rogue possessed of moldy bonds and mortgages, and we they call spendthrifts are only wealthy, who lay out his money upon daily new purchases of pleasure.

HORNER: Ay, your arrantest cheat is your trustee or executor; your jealous man, the greatest cuckold; your churchman, the greatest atheist; and your noisy, pert rogue of a wit, the greatest fop, dullest ass and worst company, as you shall see: for here he comes.

[Enter Sparkish to them.]

SPARKISH: How is't, sparks,[4] how is't? Well, faith, Harry, I must rally[5] thee a little, ha, ha, ha, upon the report in town of thee, ha, ha, ha, I can't hold i'faith; shall I speak?

HORNER: Yes, but you'll be so bitter then.

SPARKISH: Honest Dick and Frank here shall answer for me, I will not be extreme bitter, by the universe.

HARCOURT: We will be bound in ten thousand pound bond, he shall not be bitter at all.

DORILANT: Nor sharp, nor sweet.

HORNER: What, not downright insipid?

SPARKISH: Nay then, since you are so brisk and provoke me, take what follows. You must know, I was discoursing and rallying with some ladies yesterday, and they happened to talk of the fine new signs[6] in town.

HORNER: Very fine ladies, I believe.

SPARKISH: Said I, "I know where the best new sign is." "Where?" says one of the ladies. "In Covent Garden,"[7] I replied. Said another, "In what street?" "In Russell Street," answered I. "Lord," says another, "I'm sure there was ne'er a fine new sign there yesterday." "Yes, but there was," said I again, "and it came out of France and has been there a fortnight."

DORILANT: A pox, I can hear no more, prithee.

HORNER: No, hear him out; let him tune his crowd[8] a while.

HARCOURT: The worst music, the greatest preparation.

SPARKISH: Nay, faith, I'll make you laugh. "It cannot be," says a third lady. "Yes, yes," quoth I again. Says a fourth lady—

HORNER: Look to't, we'll have no more ladies.

SPARKISH: No—then mark, mark, now. Said I to the fourth, "Did you never see Mr. Horner? He lodges in Russell Street, and he's a sign of a man, you know, since he came out of France." Heh, hah, he!

HORNER: But the devil take me, if thine be the sign of a jest.

SPARKISH: With that they all fell a-laughing, till they bepissed themselves. What, but it does not move you, methinks? Well, I see one had as good go to law without a witness as break a jest without a laugher on one's side. Come, come, sparks, but where do we dine? I have left at Whitehall an earl to dine with you.

---

4. Fashionable young men; the term is usually derogatory, but Sparkish speaks it in fellowship.
5. Mock, tease.
6. Indicating the business of a shop.

7. The most fashionable area of London, teeming with theaters, taverns, and shops.
8. Fiddle.

DORILANT: Why, I thought thou hadst loved a man with a title better than a suit with a French trimming to't.

HARCOURT: Go, to him again.

SPARKISH: No, sir, a wit to me is the greatest title in the world.

HORNER: But go dine with your earl, sir; he may be exceptious.[9] We are your friends and will not take it ill to be left, I do assure you.

HARCOURT: Nay, faith, he shall go to him.

SPARKISH: Nay, pray, gentlemen.

DORILANT: We'll thrust you out, if you wo'not. What, disappoint anybody for us?

SPARKISH: Nay, dear gentlemen, hear me.

HORNER: No, no, sir, by no means; pray go, sir.

SPARKISH: Why, dear rogues—

DORILANT: No, no.

[They all thrust him out of the room.]

ALL: Ha, ha, ha!

[Sparkish returns.]

SPARKISH: But, sparks, pray hear me. What, d'ye think I'll eat then with gay, shallow fops and silent coxcombs? I think wit as necessary at dinner as a glass of good wine, and that's the reason I never have any stomach when I eat alone.—Come, but where do we dine?

HORNER: Even where you will.

SPARKISH: At Chateline's?[1]

DORILANT: Yes, if you will.

SPARKISH: Or at the Cock?[2]

DORILANT: Yes, if you please.

SPARKISH: Or at the Dog and Partridge?[3]

HORNER: Ay, if you have a mind to't, for we shall dine at neither.

SPARKISH: Pshaw, with your fooling we shall lose the new play; and I would no more miss seeing a new play the first day than I would miss setting in the wits' row. Therefore I'll go fetch my mistress and away.

[Exit Sparkish. Manent[4] Horner, Harcourt, Dorilant. Enter to them Mr. Pinchwife.]

HORNER: Who have we here? Pinchwife?

PINCHWIFE: Gentlemen, your humble servant.

HORNER: Well, Jack, by the long absence from the town, the grumness of thy countenance and the slovenliness of thy habit, I should give thee joy, should I not, of marriage?

PINCHWIFE [aside]: Death! Does he know I'm married too? I thought to have concealed it from him at least.—My long stay in the country will excuse my dress and I have a suit of law, that brings me up to town, that puts me out of humor, besides, I must give Sparkish tomorrow five thousand pound[5] to lie with my sister.

HORNER: Nay, you country gentlemen, rather than not purchase, will buy anything; and he is a cracked title,[6] if we may quibble. Well, but am I to give thee joy? I heard thou wert married.

9. Peevish.
1. A famous French ordinary, or restaurant, in Covent Garden.
2. Probably the Cock Tavern in Bow Street, where Wycherley himself spent time.
3. A tavern in Fleet Street; the least fashionable of the

places Sparkish suggests.
4. Remain.
5. As a dowry.
6. I.e., Sparkish owns shoddy property, has a weak claim to it, and is himself a bad bargain.

PINCHWIFE: What then?

HORNER: Why, the next thing that is to be heard is thou'rt a cuckold.

PINCHWIFE [aside]: Insupportable name!

HORNER: But I did not expect marriage from such a whoremaster[7] as you, one that knew the town so much and women so well.

PINCHWIFE: Why, I have married no London wife.

HORNER: Pshaw, that's all one; that grave circumspection in marrying a country wife is like refusing a deceitful, pampered Smithfield jade[8] to go and be cheated by a friend in the country.

PINCHWIFE [aside]: A pox on him and his simile.—At least we are a little surer of the breed there, know what her keeping has been, whether foiled[9] or unsound.

HORNER: Come, come, I have known a clap[1] gotten in Wales; and there are cozens,[2] justices, clerks and chaplains in the country, I won't say coachmen. But she's handsome and young?

PINCHWIFE [aside]: I'll answer as I should do.—No, no, she has no beauty but her youth; no attraction but her modesty; wholesome, homely and house-wifely; that's all.

DORILANT: He talks as like a grazier[3] as he looks.

PINCHWIFE: She's too awkward, ill-favored and silly to bring to town.

HARCOURT: Then methinks you should bring her, to be taught breeding.

PINCHWIFE: To be taught! No, sir! I thank you. Good wives and private soldiers should be ignorant. [Aside.] I'll keep her from your instructions, I warrant you.

HARCOURT [aside]: The rogue is as jealous as if his wife were not ignorant.

HORNER: Why, if she be ill-favoured, there will be less danger here for you than by leaving her in the country; we have such variety of dainties that we are seldom hungry.

DORILANT: But they have always coarse, constant, swingeing stomachs[4] in the country.

HARCOURT: Foul feeders indeed.

DORILANT: And your hospitality is great there.

HARCOURT: Open house, every man's welcome.

PINCHWIFE: So, so, gentlemen.

HORNER: But, prithee, why wouldst thou marry her? If she be ugly, ill-bred and silly, she must be rich then.

PINCHWIFE: As rich as if she brought me twenty thousand pound out of this town, for she'll be as sure not to spend her moderate portion as a London baggage would be to spend hers, let it be what it would; so 'tis all one. Then, because she's ugly, she's the likelier to be my own; and being ill-bred, she'll have conversation; and since silly and innocent, will not know the difference betwixt a man of one-and-twenty and one of forty.

HORNER: None—to my knowledge; but if she be silly, she'll expect as much from a man of forty-nine as from him of one-and-twenty. But methinks wit is more necessary than beauty, and I think no young woman ugly that has it, and no handsome woman agreeable without it.

---

7. A man who consorts with whores and is given to lechery.
8. Broken-down horse bought at Smithfield Market, where the sellers were often swindlers; here a metaphor for disreputable women purchased at far too high a price.
9. With reference to a horse, injured; to a woman, deflowered.
1. Gonorrhea.
2. Cheaters.
3. One who feeds cattle for market.
4. Immense appetites.

PINCHWIFE: 'Tis my maxim, he's a fool that marries, but he's a greater that does not marry a fool. What is wit in a wife good for, but to make a man a cuckold?

HORNER: Yes, to keep it from his knowledge.

PINCHWIFE: A fool cannot contrive to make her husband a cuckold.

HORNER: No, but she'll club[5] with a man that can; and what is worse, if she cannot make her husband a cuckold, she'll make him jealous and pass for one, and then 'tis all one.

PINCHWIFE: Well, well, I'll take care for one, my wife shall make me no cuckold, though she had your help, Mr. Horner; I understand the town, sir.

DORILANT [aside]: His help!

HARCOURT [aside]: He's come newly to town, it seems, and has not heard how things are with him.

HORNER: But tell me, has marriage cured thee of whoring, which it seldom does?

HARCOURT: 'Tis more than age can do.

HORNER: No, the word is, I'll marry and live honest; but a marriage vow is like a penitent gamester's oath and entering into bonds and penalties to stint himself to such a particular small sum at play for the future, which makes him but the more eager and, not being able to hold out, loses his money again and his forfeit to boot.

DORILANT: Ay, ay, a gamester will be a gamester whilst his money lasts, and a whoremaster whilst his vigor.

HARCOURT: Nay, I have known 'em, when they are broke and can lose no more, keep a-fumbling with the box[6] in their hands to fool with only and hinder other gamesters.

DORILANT: That had wherewithal to make lusty stakes.

PINCHWIFE: Well, gentlemen, you may laugh at me, but you shall never lie with my wife; I know the town.

HORNER: But prithee, was not the way you were in better? Is not keeping better than marriage?

PINCHWIFE: A pox on't! The jades would jilt me; I could never keep a whore to myself.

HORNER: So, then you only married to keep a whore to yourself. Well, but let me tell you, women, as you say, are like soldiers, made constant and loyal by good pay rather than by oaths and covenants. Therefore I'd advise my friends to keep rather than marry, since too, I find, by your example, it does not serve one's turn, for I saw you yesterday in the eighteen-penny place[7] with a pretty country wench.

PINCHWIFE [aside]: How the devil! Did he see my wife then? I sat there that she might not be seen. But she shall never go to a play again.

HORNER: What, dost thou blush at nine-and-forty, for having been seen with a wench?

DORILANT: No, faith, I warrant 'twas his wife, which he seated there out of sight, for he's a cunning rogue and understands the town.

HARCOURT: He blushes. Then 'twas his wife, for men are now more ashamed to be seen with them in public than with a wench.

PINCHWIFE [aside]: Hell and damnation! I'm undone, since Horner has seen her and they know 'twas she.

---

5. Associate.
6. For throwing dice in gaming; also slang for vagina. Parallels between gambling and sex recur throughout the play.

7. The middle gallery of the playhouse occupied by (among others) clerks, merchants, and prostitutes.

HORNER: But prithee, was it thy wife? She was exceedingly pretty; I was in love with her at that distance.

PINCHWIFE: You are like never to be nearer to her. Your servant, gentlemen.
[Offers to go.]

HORNER: Nay, prithee stay.

PINCHWIFE: I cannot, I will not.

HORNER: Come, you shall dine with us.

PINCHWIFE: I have dined already.

HORNER: Come, I know thou hast not. I'll treat thee, dear rogue; thou shalt spend none of thy Hampshire[8] money today.

PINCHWIFE [aside]: Treat me! So, he uses me already like his cuckold.

HORNER: Nay, you shall not go.

PINCHWIFE: I must, I have business at home.   [Exit Pinchwife.]

HARCOURT: To beat his wife; he's as jealous of her as a Cheapside[9] husband of a Covent Garden wife.

HORNER: Why, 'tis as hard to find an old whoremaster without jealousy and the gout, as a young one without fear or the pox.

As gout in age from pox in youth proceeds,
So wenching past, then jealousy succeeds,
The worst disease that love and wenching breeds.

[Exeunt.]

ACT 2

Scene 1

[Mrs. Margery Pinchwife and Alithea. Mr. Pinchwife peeping behind at the door.]

MRS. PINCHWIFE: Pray, sister, where are the best fields and woods to walk in, in London?

ALITHEA: A pretty question! Why, sister, Mulberry Garden and St. James's Park[1] and, for close walks, the New Exchange.[2]

MRS. PINCHWIFE: Pray, sister, tell me why my husband looks so grum[3] here in town and keeps me up so close and will not let me go a-walking, nor let me wear my best gown yesterday.

ALITHEA: Oh, he's jealous, sister.

MRS. PINCHWIFE: Jealous? What's that?

ALITHEA: He's afraid you should love another man.

MRS. PINCHWIFE: How should he be afraid of my loving another man, when he will not let me see any but himself?

ALITHEA: Did he not carry you yesterday to a play?

MRS. PINCHWIFE: Ay, but we sat amongst ugly people; he would not let me come near the gentry, who sat under us, so that I could not see 'em. He told me none but naughty women sat there, whom they toused and moused.[4] But I would have ventured for all that.

ALITHEA: But how did you like the play?

---

8. The rural county in south-central England where Pinchwife now lives.
9. City-merchant (Cheapside was a center of finance).
1. Popular places for gathering, strolling and savoring sights, talk, and entertainment.

2. This elegant arcade, with its covered ("close") walkways, served as the center for fashionable London shopping. The second scene in Act 3 takes place there.
3. Gloomy, surly.
4. Pulled about good-naturedly, but roughly.

MRS. PINCHWIFE: Indeed, I was a-weary of the play, but I liked hugeously the actors; they are the goodliest, properest men, sister!

ALITHEA: O, but you must not like the actors, sister.

MRS. PINCHWIFE: Ay, how should I help it, sister? Pray, sister, when my husband comes in, will you ask leave for me to go a-walking?

ALITHEA [aside]: A-walking, hah, ha! Lord, a country gentlewoman's leisure is the drudgery of a foot-post;[5] and she requires as much airing as her husband's horses.

　　[Enter Mr. Pinchwife to them.]

But here comes your husband; I'll ask, though I'm sure he'll not grant it.

MRS. PINCHWIFE: He says he won't let me go abroad for fear of catching the pox.

ALITHEA: Fie! The smallpox you should say.

MRS. PINCHWIFE: O my dear, dear bud, welcome home! Why dost thou look so fropish? Who has nangered[6] thee?

PINCHWIFE: You're a fool.

　　[Mrs. Pinchwife goes aside and cries.]

ALITHEA: Faith, so she is, for crying for no fault, poor tender creature!

PINCHWIFE: What, you would have her as impudent as yourself, as arrant a jill-flirt, a gadder, a magpie[7] and, to say all, a mere notorious town-woman?

ALITHEA: Brother, you are my only censurer; and the honor of your family shall sooner suffer in your wife there than in me, though I take the innocent liberty of the town.

PINCHWIFE: Hark you, mistress, do not talk so before my wife. The innocent liberty of the town!

ALITHEA: Why, pray, who boasts of any intrigue with me? What lampoon[8] has made my name notorious? What ill women frequent my lodgings? I keep no company with any women of scandalous reputations.

PINCHWIFE: No, you keep the men of scandalous reputations company.

ALITHEA: Where? Would you not have me civil? Answer 'em in a box at the plays? In the drawing room at Whitehall? In St. James's Park? Mulberry Gardens? Or—

PINCHWIFE: Hold, hold! Do not teach my wife where the men are to be found! I believe she's the worse for your town documents[9] already. I bid you keep her in ignorance, as I do.

MRS. PINCHWIFE: Indeed, be not angry with her, bud; she will tell me nothing of the town, though I ask her a thousand times a day.

PINCHWIFE: Then you are very inquisitive to know, I find!

MRS. PINCHWIFE: Not I, indeed, dear; I hate London. Our place-house[1] in the country is worth a thousand of't; would I were there again!

PINCHWIFE: So you shall, I warrant. But were you not talking of plays and players when I came in? [To Alithea.] You are her encourager in such discourses.

MRS. PINCHWIFE: No, indeed, dear; she chid me just now for liking the player-men.

PINCHWIFE [aside]: Nay, if she be so innocent as to own to me her liking them, there is no hurt in't.—Come, my poor rogue, but thou lik'st none better than me?

MRS. PINCHWIFE: Yes, indeed, but I do; the playermen are finer folks.

---

5. A walking message-carrier.
6. Baby-talk: *fropish*, irritable; *nangered*: angered.
7. A wanton girl, a rover, a chatterer.

8. Scurrilous satire.
9. Teachings about fashionable life.
1. Grand home.

PINCHWIFE: But you love none better than me?

MRS. PINCHWIFE: You are mine own dear bud, and I know you; I hate a stranger.

PINCHWIFE: Ay, my dear, you must love me only and not be like the naughty town-women, who only hate their husbands and love every man else, love plays, visits, fine coaches, fine clothes, fiddles, balls, treats, and so lead a wicked town-life.

MRS. PINCHWIFE: Nay, if to enjoy all these things be a town-life, London is not so bad a place, dear.

PINCHWIFE: How! If you love me, you must hate London.

ALITHEA [aside]: The fool has forbid me discovering to her the pleasures of the town and he is now setting her agog upon them himself.

MRS. PINCHWIFE: But, husband, do the town-women love the playermen too?

PINCHWIFE: Yes, I warrant you.

MRS. PINCHWIFE: Ay, I warrant you.

PINCHWIFE: Why, you do not, I hope?

MRS. PINCHWIFE: No, no, bud; but why have we no playermen in the country?

PINCHWIFE: Ha—Mrs. Minx, ask me no more to go to a play.

MRS. PINCHWIFE: Nay, why, love? I did not care for going; but when you forbid me, you make me, as 'twere, desire it.

ALITHEA [aside]: So 'twill be in other things, I warrant.

MRS. PINCHWIFE: Pray let me go to a play, dear.

PINCHWIFE: Hold your peace, I wo'not.

MRS. PINCHWIFE: Why, love?

PINCHWIFE: Why, I'll tell you.

ALITHEA [aside]: Nay, if he tell her, she'll give him more cause to forbid her that place.

MRS. PINCHWIFE: Pray, why, dear?

PINCHWIFE: First, you like the actors and the gallants may like you.

MRS. PINCHWIFE: What, a homely country girl? No, bud, nobody will like me.

PINCHWIFE: I tell you, yes, they may.

MRS. PINCHWIFE: No, no, you jest—I won't believe you, I will go.

PINCHWIFE: I tell you then that one of the lewdest fellows in town, who saw you there, told me he was in love with you.

MRS. PINCHWIFE: Indeed! Who, who, pray, who was't?

PINCHWIFE [aside]: I've gone too far and slipped before I was aware. How over-joyed she is!

MRS. PINCHWIFE: Was it any Hampshire gallant, any of our neighbors? I promise you, I am beholding to him.

PINCHWIFE: I promise you, you lie, for he would but ruin you, as he has done hundreds. He has no other love for women but that; such as he look upon women, like basilisks,[2] but to destroy 'em.

MRS. PINCHWIFE: Ay, but if he loves me, why should he ruin me? Answer me to that. Methinks he should not; I would do him no harm.

ALITHEA: Hah, ha, ha!

PINCHWIFE: 'Tis very well; but I'll keep him from doing you any harm, or me either.

　　[Enter Sparkish and Harcourt.]

---

2. Mythical reptiles whose gaze dealt death.

But here comes company; get you in, get you in.

MRS. PINCHWIFE: But pray, husband, is he a pretty gentleman that loves me?

PINCHWIFE: In, baggage, in. [*Thrusts her in, shuts the door.*] What, all the lewd libertines of the town brought to my lodging by this easy coxcomb! 'Sdeath, I'll not suffer it.

SPARKISH: Here, Harcourt, do you approve my choice? [*To Alithea.*] Dear little rogue, I told you I'd bring you acquainted with all my friends, the wits, and—[*Harcourt salutes her.*]

PINCHWIFE [*aside*]: Ay, they shall know her, as well as you yourself will, I warrant you.

SPARKISH: This is one of those, my pretty rogue, that are to dance at your wedding tomorrow; and him you must bid welcome ever to what you and I have.

PINCHWIFE [*aside*]: Monstrous!

SPARKISH: Harcourt, how dost thou like her, faith?—Nay, dear, do not look down; I should hate to have a wife of mine out of countenance at anything.

PINCHWIFE [*aside*]: Wonderful!

SPARKISH: Tell me, I say, Harcourt, how dost thou like her? Thou hast stared upon her enough to resolve me.

HARCOURT: So infinitely well that I could wish I had a mistress too, that might differ from her in nothing but her love and engagement to you.

ALITHEA: Sir, Master Sparkish has often told me that his acquaintance were all wits and railleurs[3] and now I find it.

SPARKISH: No, by the universe, madam, he does not rally now; you may believe him. I do assure you, he is the honestest, worthiest, true-hearted gentleman—a man of such perfect honor, he would say nothing to a lady he does not mean.

PINCHWIFE [*aside*]: Praising another man to his mistress!

HARCOURT: Sir, you are so beyond expectation obliging that—

SPARKISH: Nay, egad, I am sure you do admire her extremely; I see't in your eyes.—He does admire you, madam.—By the world, don't you?

HARCOURT: Yes, above the world, or the most glorious part of it, her whole sex; and till now I never thought I should have envied you, or any man about to marry, but you have the best excuse for marriage I ever knew.

ALITHEA: Nay, now, sir, I'm satisfied you are of the society of the wits and railleurs, since you cannot spare your friend, even when he is but too civil to you; but the surest sign is since you are an enemy to marriage, for that, I hear, you hate as much as business or bad wine.

HARCOURT: Truly, madam, I never was an enemy to marriage till now, because marriage was never an enemy to me before.

ALITHEA: But why, sir, is marriage an enemy to you now? Because it robs you of your friend here? For you look upon a friend married as one gone into a monastery, that is dead to the world.

HARCOURT: 'Tis indeed because you marry him; I see, madam, you can guess my meaning. I do confess heartily and openly, I wish it were in my power to break the match; by heavens I would.

SPARKISH: Poor Frank!

ALITHEA: Would you be so unkind to me?

3. Mockers, banterers.

HARCOURT: No, no, 'tis not because I would be unkind to you.

SPARKISH: Poor Frank! No, gad, 'tis only his kindness to me.

PINCHWIFE [aside]: Great kindness to you indeed! Insensible fop, let a man make love to his wife to his face!

SPARKISH: Come, dear Frank, for all my wife there that shall be, thou shalt enjoy me sometimes, dear rogue. By my honor, we men of wit condole for our deceased brother in marriage as much as for one dead in earnest. I think that was prettily said of me, ha, Harcourt? But come, Frank, be not melancholy for me.

HARCOURT: No, I assure you I am not melancholy for you.

SPARKISH: Prithee, Frank, dost think my wife that shall be there a fine person?

HARCOURT: I could gaze upon her till I became as blind as you are.

SPARKISH: How, as I am? How?

HARCOURT: Because you are a lover and true lovers are blind, stock blind.[4]

SPARKISH: True, true; but by the world, she has wit too, as well as beauty. Go, go with her into a corner and try if she has wit; talk to her anything; she's bashful before me.

HARCOURT: Indeed, if a woman wants[5] wit in a corner, she has it nowhere.

ALITHEA [aside to Sparkish]: Sir, you dispose of me a little before your time—

SPARKISH: Nay, nay, madam, let me have an earnest[6] of your obedience, or—go, go, madam—

[Harcourt courts Alithea aside.]

PINCHWIFE: How, sir! If you are not concerned for the honor of a wife, I am for that of a sister; he shall not debauch her. Be a pander[7] to your own wife, bring men to her, let 'em make love before your face, thrust 'em into a corner together, then leave 'em in private! Is this your town wit and conduct?

SPARKISH: Hah, ha, ha, a silly wise rogue would make one laugh more than a stark fool, hah, ha! I shall burst. Nay, you shall not disturb 'em; I'll vex thee, by the world. [Struggles with Pinchwife to keep him from Harcourt and Alithea.]

ALITHEA: The writings are drawn, sir, settlements made; 'tis too late, sir, and past all revocation.

HARCOURT: Then so is my death.

ALITHEA: I would not be unjust to him.

HARCOURT: Then why to me so?

ALITHEA: I have no obligation to you.

HARCOURT: My love.

ALITHEA: I had his before.

HARCOURT: You never had it; he wants, you see, jealousy, the only infallible sign of it.

ALITHEA: Love proceeds from esteem; he cannot distrust my virtue. Besides, he loves me, or he would not marry me.

HARCOURT: Marrying you is no more sign of his love than bribing your woman, that he may marry you, is a sign of his generosity. Marriage is rather a sign of interest than love, and he that marries a fortune covets a mistress, not loves her. But if you take marriage for a sign of love, take it from me immediately.

ALITHEA: No, now you have put a scruple in my head; but, in short, sir, to end our dispute, I must marry him; my reputation would suffer in the world else.

4. As blind as any lifeless object.
5. Lacks.

6. Foretaste, pledge.
7. Pimp, procurer.

HARCOURT: No, if you do marry him, with your pardon, madam, your reputation suffers in the world and you would be thought in necessity for a cloak.[8]

ALITHEA: Nay, now you are rude, sir.—Mr. Sparkish, pray come hither, your friend here is very troublesome, and very loving.

HARCOURT [aside to Alithea]: Hold, hold!—

PINCHWIFE: D'ye hear that?

SPARKISH: Why, d'ye think I'll seem to be jealous, like a country bumpkin?

PINCHWIFE: No, rather be a cuckold, like a credulous cit.[9]

HARCOURT: Madam, you would not have been so little generous as to have told him.

ALITHEA: Yes, since you could be so little generous as to wrong him.

HARCOURT: Wrong him! No man can do't, he's beneath an injury; a bubble,[1] a coward, a senseless idiot, a wretch so contemptible to all the world but you that—

ALITHEA: Hold, do not rail at him, for since he is like to be my husband, I am resolved to like him. Nay, I think I am obliged to tell him you are not his friend.— Master Sparkish, Master Sparkish.

SPARKISH: What, what?—Now, dear rogue, has not she wit?

HARCOURT [speaks surlily]: Not so much as I thought and hoped she had.

ALITHEA: Mr. Sparkish, do you bring people to rail at you?

HARCOURT: Madam—

SPARKISH: How! No, but if he does rail at me, 'tis but in jest, I warrant; what we wits do for one another and never take any notice of it.

ALITHEA: He spoke so scurrilously of you, I had no patience to hear him; besides, he has been making love to me.

HARCOURT [aside]: True, damned, telltale woman!

SPARKISH: Pshaw, to show his parts[2]—we wits rail and make love often but to show our parts; as we have no affections, so we have no malice. We—

ALITHEA: He said you were a wretch, below an injury.

SPARKISH: Pshaw!

HARCOURT [aside]: Damned, senseless, impudent, virtuous jade! Well, since she won't let me have her, she'll do as good, she'll make me hate her.

ALITHEA: A common bubble.

SPARKISH: Pshaw!

ALITHEA: A coward.

SPARKISH: Pshaw, pshaw!

ALITHEA: A senseless, driveling idiot.

SPARKISH: How! Did he disparage my parts? Nay, then my honor's concerned; I can't put up that, sir, by the world. Brother, help me to kill him. [Aside.] I may draw now, since we have the odds of him. 'This a good occasion, too, before my mistress—[Offers to draw.]

ALITHEA: Hold, hold!

SPARKISH: What, what?

ALITHEA [aside]: I must not let 'em kill the gentleman neither, for his kindness to me; I am so far from hating him that I wish my gallant had his person and understanding.—Nay, if my honor—

SPARKISH: I'll be thy death.

---

8. I.e., to hide your secrets: perhaps pregnancy or love affairs.

9. "A pert low townsman, a pragmatical trader" (John-

son's *Dictionary*); contemptuous abbreviation of "citizen."

1. Dupe.

2. Abilities, talents.

ALITHEA: Hold, hold! Indeed, to tell the truth, the gentleman said after all that what he spoke was but out of friendship to you.

SPARKISH: How! say I am—I am a fool, that is, no wit, out of friendship to me?

ALITHEA: Yes, to try whether I was concerned enough for you and made love to me only to be satisfied of my virtue, for your sake.

HARCOURT [aside]: Kind, however—

SPARKISH: Nay, if it were so, my dear rogue, I ask thee pardon; but why would not you tell me so, faith?

HARCOURT: Because I did not think on't, faith.

SPARKISH: Come, Horner does not come, Harcourt, let's be gone to the new play.—Come, madam.

ALITHEA: I will not go if you intend to leave me alone in the box and run into the pit, as you use to do.

SPARKISH: Pshaw! I'll leave Harcourt with you in the box to entertain you, and that's as good; if I sat in the box, I should be thought no judge but of trimmings.[3]— Come away, Harcourt, lead her down.   [Exeunt Sparkish, Harcourt and Alithea.]

PINCHWIFE: Well, go thy ways, for the flower of the true town fops, such as spend their estates before they come to 'em and are cuckolds before they're married. But let me go look to my own freehold.—How!—

[Enter Lady Fidget, Mrs. Dainty Fidget and Mrs. Squeamish.]

LADY FIDGET: Your servant, sir; where is your lady? We are come to wait upon her to the new play.

PINCHWIFE: New play!

LADY FIDGET: And my husband will wait upon you presently.

PINCHWIFE [aside]: Damn your civility.—Madam, by no means; I will not see Sir Jaspar here till I have waited upon him at home; nor shall my wife see you till she has waited upon your ladyship at your lodgings.

LADY FIDGET: Now we are here, sir—

PINCHWIFE: No, madam.

DAINTY: Pray, let us see her.

SQUEAMISH: We will not stir till we see her.

PINCHWIFE [aside]: A pox on you all! [Goes to the door, and returns.]—She has locked the door and is gone abroad.

LADY FIDGET: No, you have locked the door and she's within.

DAINTY: They told us below she was here.

PINCHWIFE [aside]: Will nothing do?—Well, it must out then. To tell you the truth, ladies, which I was afraid to let you know before, lest it might endanger your lives, my wife has just now the smallpox come out upon her. Do not be frightened but pray, be gone, ladies; you shall not stay here in danger of your lives. Pray get you gone, ladies.

LADY FIDGET: No, no, we have all had 'em.

SQUEAMISH: Alack, alack.

DAINTY: Come, come, we must see how it goes with her; I understand the disease.

LADY FIDGET: Come.

PINCHWIFE [aside]: Well, there is no being too hard for[4] women at their own weapon, lying; therefore I'll quit the field.   [Exit Pinchwife.]

---

3. Clothes, fashions. The "wits," who came to criticize the play, customarily occupied not the boxes but the "pit."

4. Too clever for.

SQUEAMISH: Here's an example of jealousy.

LADY FIDGET: Indeed, as the world goes, I wonder there are no more jealous, since wives are so neglected.

DAINTY: Pshaw, as the world goes, to what end should they be jealous?

LADY FIDGET: Foh, 'tis a nasty world.

SQUEAMISH: That men of parts, great acquaintance and quality should take up with and spend themselves and fortunes in keeping little playhouse creatures, foh!

LADY FIDGET: Nay, that women of understanding, great acquaintance and good quality should fall a-keeping too of little creatures, foh!

SQUEAMISH: Why, 'tis the men of quality's fault; they never visit women of honor and reputation, as they used to do and have not so much as common civility for ladies of our rank, but use us with the same indifferency and ill-breeding as if we were all married to 'em.

LADY FIDGET: She says true; 'tis an arrant shame women of quality should be so slighted. Methinks birth, birth should go for something. I have known men admired, courted, and followed for their titles only.

SQUEAMISH: Ay, one would think men of honor should not love, no more than marry, out of their own rank.

DAINTY: Fie, fie upon 'em! They are come to think crossbreeding for themselves best, as well as for their dogs and horses.

LADY FIDGET: They are dogs and horses for't.

SQUEAMISH: One would think, if not for love, for vanity a little.

DAINTY: Nay, they do satisfy their vanity upon us sometimes and are kind to us in their report, tell all the world they lie with us.

LADY FIDGET: Damned rascals! That we should be only wronged by 'em! To report a man has had a person, when he has not had a person, is the greatest wrong in the whole world that can be done to a person.

SQUEAMISH: Well, 'tis an arrant shame noble persons should be so wronged and neglected.

LADY FIDGET: But still 'tis an arranter shame for a noble person to neglect her own honor and defame her own noble person with little inconsiderable fellows, foh!

DAINTY: I suppose the crime against our honor is the same with a man of quality as with another.

LADY FIDGET: How! No, sure, the man of quality is likest one's husband and therefore the fault should be the less.

DAINTY: But then the pleasure should be the less.

LADY FIDGET: Fie, fie, fie, for shame, sister! Whither shall we ramble? Be continent[5] in your discourse, or I shall hate you.

DAINTY: Besides, an intrigue is so much the more notorious for the man's quality.

SQUEAMISH: 'Tis true, nobody takes notice of a private man and therefore with him 'tis more secret, and the crime's the less when 'tis not known.

LADY FIDGET: You say true; i'faith, I think you are in the right on't. 'Tis not an injury to a husband till it be an injury to our honors; so that a woman of honor loses no honor with a private person; and to say truth—

DAINTY [apart to Squeamish]: So, the little fellow is grown a private person—with her—

5. Restrained.

LADY FIDGET: But still my dear, dear honor.

[*Enter Sir Jaspar, Horner, Dorilant.*]

SIR JASPAR: Ay, my dear, dear of honor, thou hast still so much honor in thy mouth—

HORNER [*aside*]: That she has none elsewhere.

LADY FIDGET: Oh, what d'ye mean to bring in these upon us?

DAINTY: Foh, these are as bad as wits.

SQUEAMISH: Foh!

LADY FIDGET: Let us leave the room.

SIR JASPAR: Stay, stay; faith, to tell you the naked truth—

LADY FIDGET: Fie, Sir Jaspar, do not use that word "naked."

SIR JASPAR: Well, well, in short, I have business at Whitehall and cannot go to the play with you, therefore would have you go—

LADY FIDGET: With those two to a play?

SIR JASPAR: No, not with t'other but with Mr. Horner; there can be no more scandal to go with him than with Mr. Tattle or Master Limberham.[6]

LADY FIDGET: With that nasty fellow! No—no!

SIR JASPAR: Nay, prithee, dear, hear me. [*Whispers to Lady Fidget.*]

HORNER: Ladies—

[*Horner, Dorilant drawing near Squeamish and Dainty.*]

DAINTY: Stand off.

SQUEAMISH: Do not approach us.

DAINTY: You herd with the wits, you are obscenity all over.

SQUEAMISH: And I would as soon look upon a picture of Adam and Eve, without fig leaves, as any of you, if I could help it; therefore keep off and do not make us sick.

DORILANT: What a devil are these?

HORNER: Why, these are pretenders to honor, as critics to wit, only by censuring others; and as every raw, peevish, out-of-humored, affected, dull, tea-drinking, arithmetical[7] fop sets up for a wit by railing at men of sense, so these for honor by railing at the Court and ladies of as great honor as quality.

SIR JASPAR: Come, Mr. Horner, I must desire you to go with these ladies to the play, sir.

HORNER: I, sir!

SIR JASPAR: Ay, ay, come, sir.

HORNER: I must beg your pardon, sir, and theirs; I will not be seen in women's company in public again for the world.

SIR JASPAR: Ha, ha, strange aversion!

SQUEAMISH: No, he's for women's company in private.

SIR JASPAR: He—poor man—he! Hah, ha, ha!

DAINTY: 'Tis a greater shame amongst lewd fellows to be seen in virtuous women's company than for the women to be seen with them.

HORNER: Indeed, madam, the time was I only hated virtuous women, but now I hate the other too; I beg your pardon, ladies.

LADY FIDGET: You are very obliging, sir, because we would not be troubled with you.

6. I.e., Horner and Dorilant.   7. Precise, fussy.

SIR JASPAR: In sober sadness, he shall go.

DORILANT: Nay, if he wo'not, I am ready to wait upon the ladies; and I think I am the fitter man.

SIR JASPAR: You, sir, no, I thank you for that—Master Horner is a privileged man amongst the virtuous ladies; 'twill be a great while before you are so; heh, he, he! He's my wife's gallant, heh, he, he! No, pray withdraw, sir, for as I take it, the virtuous ladies have no business with you.

DORILANT: And I am sure he can have none with them. 'Tis strange a man can't come amongst virtuous women now but upon the same terms as men are admitted into the Great Turk's seraglio;[8] but heavens keep me from being an ombre[9] player with 'em! But where is Pinchwife?   [Exit Dorilant.]

SIR JASPAR: Come, come, man; what, avoid the sweet society of womankind? that sweet, soft, gentle, tame, noble creature, woman, made for man's companion—

HORNER: So is that soft, gentle, tame and more noble creature a spaniel, and has all their tricks: can fawn, lie down, suffer beating and fawn the more; barks at your friends when they come to see you; makes your bed hard; gives you fleas, and the mange sometimes. And all the difference is, the spaniel's the more faithful animal and fawns but upon one master.

SIR JASPAR: Heh, he, he!

SQUEAMISH: Oh, the rude beast!

DAINTY: Insolent brute!

LADY FIDGET: Brute! Stinking, mortified, rotten French wether,[1] to dare—

SIR JASPAR: Hold, an't please your ladyship.—For shame, Master Horner, your mother was a woman. [Aside.] Now shall I never reconcile 'em. [Aside to Lady Fidget.] Hark you, madam, take my advice in your anger. You know you often want one to make up your drolling[2] pack of ombre players; and you may cheat him easily, for he's an ill gamester and consequently loves play. Besides, you know, you have but two old civil gentlemen, with stinking breaths too, to wait upon you abroad; take in the third into your service. The other are but crazy; and a lady should have a supernumerary gentleman-usher,[3] as a supernumerary coach-horse, lest sometimes you should be forced to stay at home.

LADY FIDGET: But are you sure he loves play and has money?

SIR JASPAR: He loves play as much as you and has money as much as I.

LADY FIDGET: Then I am contented to make him pay for his scurrility; money makes up in a measure all other wants in men. [Aside.] Those whom we cannot make hold for gallants, we make fine.[4]

SIR JASPAR [aside]: So, so; now to mollify, to wheedle him.—Master Horner, will you never keep civil company? Methinks 'tis time now, since you are only fit for them. Come, come, man, you must e'en fall to visiting our wives, eating at our tables, drinking tea with our virtuous relations after dinner, dealing cards to 'em, reading plays and gazettes[5] to 'em, picking fleas out of their shocks[6] for 'em, collecting receipts,[7] new songs, women, pages and footmen for 'em.

HORNER: I hope they'll afford me better employment, sir.

---

8. The Sultan's harem.
9. Three-person card game (with a pun on *hombre*: man).
1. Castrated ram.
2. Jesting, silly.
3. Extra attendant, servant.

4. Compensate, especially by way of money.
5. Newspapers.
6. Poodles.
7. Recipes.

SIR JASPAR: Heh, he, he! 'Tis fit you know your work before you come into your place; and since you are unprovided of a lady to flatter and a good house to eat at, pray frequent mine and call my wife mistress and she shall call you gallant, according to the custom.

HORNER: Who, I?

SIR JASPAR: Faith, thou shalt for my sake; come, for my sake only.

HORNER: For your sake—

SIR JASPAR [to Lady Fidget]: Come, come, here's a gamester for you; let him be a little familiar sometimes. Nay, what if a little rude? Gamesters may be rude with ladies, you know.

LADY FIDGET: Yes, losing gamesters have a privilege with women.

HORNER: I always thought the contrary, that the winning gamester had most privilege with women, for when you have lost your money to a man, you'll lose anything you have, all you have, they say, and he may use you as he pleases.

SIR JASPAR: Heh, he, he! Well, win or lose, you shall have your liberty with her.

LADY FIDGET: As he behaves himself; and for your sake I'll give him admittance and freedom.

HORNER: All sorts of freedom, madam?

SIR JASPAR: Ay, ay, ay, all sorts of freedom thou canst take, and so go to her, begin thy new employment; wheedle[8] her, jest with her and be better acquainted one with another.

HORNER [aside]: I think I know her already, therefore may venture with her, my secret for hers.

    [Horner and Lady Fidget whisper.]

SIR JASPAR: Sister, cuz, I have provided an innocent playfellow for you there.

DAINTY: Who, he!

SQUEAMISH: There's a playfellow indeed!

SIR JASPAR: Yes, sure; what, he is good enough to play at cards, blindman's buff,[9] or the fool with sometimes.

SQUEAMISH: Foh, we'll have no such playfellows.

DAINTY: No, sir, you shan't choose playfellows for us, we thank you.

SIR JASPAR: Nay, pray hear me. [Whispering to them.]

LADY FIDGET [aside to Horner]: But, poor gentleman, could you be so generous, so truly a man of honor, as for the sakes of us women of honor, to cause yourself to be reported no man? No man! And to suffer yourself the greatest shame that could fall upon a man, that none might fall upon us women by your conversation? But indeed, sir, as perfectly, perfectly the same man as before your going into France, sir? As perfectly, perfectly, sir?

HORNER: As perfectly, perfectly, madam. Nay, I scorn you should take my word; I desire to be tried only, madam.

LADY FIDGET: Well, that's spoken again like a man of honor; all men of honor desire to come to the test. But, indeed, generally you men report such things of yourselves, one does not know how or whom to believe and it is come to that pass we dare not take your words, no more than your tailors,[1] without some staid servant of yours be bound with you. But I have so strong a faith in your honor, dear, dear, noble sir, that I'd forfeit mine for yours at any time, dear sir.

---

8. Entice.

9. Game in which a blindfolded player is pushed about as he guesses other players' identities.

1. Tailors often went unpaid by their customers, and so had reason to mistrust them.

HORNER: No, madam, you should not need to forfeit it for me; I have given you security already to save you harmless, my late reputation being so well known in the world, madam.

LADY FIDGET: But if upon any future falling out or upon a suspicion of my taking the trust out of your hands to employ some other, you yourself should betray your trust, dear sir? I mean, if you'll give me leave to speak obscenely, you might tell, dear sir.

HORNER: If I did, nobody would believe me; the reputation of impotency is as hardly recovered again in the world as that of cowardice, dear madam.

LADY FIDGET: Nay then, as one may say, you may do your worst, dear, dear sir.

SIR JASPAR: Come, is your ladyship reconciled to him yet? Have you agreed on matters? For I must be gone to Whitehall.

LADY FIDGET: Why, indeed, Sir Jaspar, Master Horner is a thousand, thousand times a better man than I thought him. Cousin Squeamish, Sister Dainty, I can name him now; truly, not long ago, you know, I thought his very name obscenity and I would as soon have lain with him as have named him.

SIR JASPAR: Very likely, poor madam.

DAINTY: I believe it.

SQUEAMISH: No doubt on't.

SIR JASPAR: Well, well—that your ladyship is as virtuous as any she, I know, and him all the town knows—heh, he, he! Therefore, now you like him, get you gone to your business together; go, go to your business, I say, pleasure, whilst I go to my pleasure, business.

LADY FIDGET: Come then, dear gallant.

HORNER: Come away, my dearest mistress.

SIR JASPAR: So, so. Why, 'tis as I'd have it.   [Exit Sir Jaspar.]

HORNER: And as I'd have it.

LADY FIDGET: Who for his business from his wife will run,
    Takes the best care to have her business done.

[Exeunt omnes.]

ACT 3

Scene 1

[Alithea and Mrs. Pinchwife.]

ALITHEA: Sister, what ails you? You are grown melancholy.

MRS. PINCHWIFE: Would it not make anyone melancholy to see you go every day fluttering about abroad, whilst I must stay at home like a poor, lonely, sullen bird in a cage?

ALITHEA: Ay, sister, but you came young and just from the nest to your cage, so that I thought you liked it and could be as cheerful in't as others that took their flight themselves early and are hopping abroad in the open air.

MRS. PINCHWIFE: Nay, I confess I was quiet enough till my husband told me what pure[1] lives the London ladies live abroad, with their dancing, meetings and junketings,[2] and dressed every day in their best gowns, and, I warrant you, play at ninepins[3] every day of the week, so they do.

---

1. Splendid.
2. Merrymakings.

3. A game like bowling, more common in the country than in London high society.

[Enter Mr. Pinchwife.]

PINCHWIFE: Come, what's here to do? You are putting the town pleasures in her head and setting her a-longing.

ALITHEA: Yes, after ninepins; you suffer none to give her those longings, you mean, but yourself.

PINCHWIFE: I tell her of the vanities of the town like a confessor.

ALITHEA: A confessor! Just such a confessor as he that, by forbidding a silly ostler to grease the horse's teeth,[4] taught him to do't.

PINCHWIFE: Come, Mistress Flippant, good precepts are lost when bad examples are still before us; the liberty you take abroad makes her hanker after it, and out of humor at home, poor wretch! She desired not to come to London; I would bring her.

ALITHEA: Very well.

PINCHWIFE: She has been this week in town and never desired, till this afternoon, to go abroad.

ALITHEA: Was she not at a play yesterday?

PINCHWIFE: Yes, but she ne'er asked me; I was myself the cause of her going.

ALITHEA: Then, if she ask you again, you are the cause of her asking, and not my example.

PINCHWIFE: Well, tomorrow night I shall be rid of you and the next day, before 'tis light, she and I'll be rid of the town, and my dreadful apprehensions. *[To Mrs. Pinchwife.]* Come, be not melancholy, for thou shalt go into the country after tomorrow, dearest.

ALITHEA: Great comfort!

MRS. PINCHWIFE: Pish, what d'ye tell me of the country for?

PINCHWIFE: How's this! What, pish at the country!

MRS. PINCHWIFE: Let me alone, I am not well.

PINCHWIFE: Oh, if that be all—what ails my dearest?

MRS. PINCHWIFE: Truly I don't know; but I have not been well since you told me there was a gallant at the play in love with me.

PINCHWIFE: Ha—

ALITHEA: That's by my example too!

PINCHWIFE: Nay, if you are not well, but are so concerned because a lewd fellow chanced to lie and say he liked you, you'll make me sick too.

MRS. PINCHWIFE: Of what sickness?

PINCHWIFE: O, of that which is worse than the plague, jealousy.

MRS. PINCHWIFE: Pish, you jeer! I'm sure there's no such disease in our receipt-book[5] at home.

PINCHWIFE: No, thou never met'st with it, poor innocent. *[Aside.]* Well, if thou cuckold me, 'twill be my own fault—for cuckolds and bastards are generally makers of their own fortune.

MRS. PINCHWIFE: Well, but pray, bud, let's to go a play tonight.

PINCHWIFE: 'Tis just done, she comes from it. But why are you so eager to see a play?

MRS. PINCHWIFE: Faith, dear, not that I care one pin for their talk there; but I like to look upon the playermen and would see, if I could, the gallant you say loves me; that's all, dear bud.

4. The groomsmen ("ostlers") at inns reputedly played this lucrative trick: they would grease the horse's teeth to discourage its eating, but charge the owner nonetheless for the uneaten feed.
5. Book of medical recipes.

PINCHWIFE: Is that all, dear bud?

ALITHEA: This proceeds from my example.

MRS. PINCHWIFE: But if the play be done, let's go abroad, however, dear bud.

PINCHWIFE: Come, have a little patience and thou shalt go into the country on Friday.

MRS. PINCHWIFE: Therefore I would see first some sights, to tell my neighbors of. Nay, I will go abroad, that's once.[6]

ALITHEA: I'm the cause of this desire too.

PINCHWIFE: But now I think on't, who was the cause of Horner's coming to my lodging today? That was you.

ALITHEA: No, you, because you would not let him see your handsome wife out of your lodging.

MRS. PINCHWIFE: Why, O Lord! Did the gentleman come hither to see me indeed?

PINCHWIFE: No, no.—You are not cause of that damned question too, Mistress Alithea? [Aside.] Well, she's in the right of it. He is in love with my wife—and comes after her—'tis so—but I'll nip his love in the bud, lest he should follow us into the country and break his chariot-wheel near our house on purpose for an excuse to come to't. But I think I know the town.

MRS. PINCHWIFE: Come, pray, bud, let's go abroad before 'tis late, for I will go, that's flat and plain.

PINCHWIFE [aside]: So! the obstinacy already of a town-wife, and I must, whilst she's here, humor her like one.—Sister, how shall we do, that she may not be seen or known?

ALITHEA: Let her put on her mask.

PINCHWIFE: Pshaw, a mask makes people but the more inquisitive and is as ridiculous a disguise as a stage-beard; her shape, stature, habit will be known and if we should meet with Horner, he would be sure to take acquaintance with us, must wish her joy, kiss her, talk to her, leer upon her, and the devil and all. No, I'll not use her to a mask, 'tis dangerous, for masks have made more cuckolds than the best faces that ever were known.

ALITHEA: How will you do then?

MRS. PINCHWIFE: Nay, shall we go? The Exchange will be shut, and I have a mind to see that.

PINCHWIFE: So—I have it—I'll dress her up in the suit we are to carry down to her brother, little Sir James; nay, I understand the town tricks. Come, let's go dress her. A mask! No—a woman masked, like a covered dish, gives a man curiosity and appetite, when, it may be, uncovered, 'twould turn his stomach; no, no.

ALITHEA: Indeed your comparison is something a greasy[7] one. But I had a gentle gallant used to say, "A beauty masked, like the sun in eclipse, gathers together more gazers than if it shined out."

[Exeunt.]

Scene 2

[The scene changes to the New Exchange. Enter Horner, Harcourt, Dorilant.]

DORILANT: Engaged to women, and not sup with us?

HORNER: Ay, a pox on 'em all!

---

6. I.e., That's that.

7. Filthy or obscene.

HARCOURT: You were much a more reasonable man in the morning and had as noble resolutions against 'em as a widower of a week's liberty.

DORILANT: Did I ever think to see you keep company with women in vain?

HORNER: In vain! No—'tis, since I can't love 'em, to be revenged on 'em.

HARCOURT: Now your sting is gone, you looked in the box amongst all those women, like a drone in the hive, all upon you, shoved and ill-used by 'em all, and thrust from one side to t'other.

DORILANT: Yet he must be buzzing amongst 'em still, like other old beetle-headed,[8] liquorish[9] drones. Avoid 'em, and hate 'em as they hate you.

HORNER: Because I do hate 'em, and would hate 'em yet more, I'll frequent 'em; you may see by marriage, nothing makes a man hate a woman more than her constant conversation. In short, I converse with 'em, as you do with rich fools, to laugh at 'em and use 'em ill.

DORILANT: But I would no more sup with women, unless I could lie with 'em, than sup with a rich coxcomb, unless I could cheat him.

HORNER: Yes, I have known thee sup with a fool for his drinking; if he could set out your hand[1] that way only, you were satisfied, and if he were a wine-swallowing mouth 'twas enough.

HARCOURT: Yes, a man drinks often with a fool, as he tosses with a marker,[2] only to keep his hand in ure.[3] But do the ladies drink?

HORNER: Yes, sir, and I shall have the pleasure at least of laying 'em flat with a bottle, and bring as much scandal that way upon 'em as formerly t'other.

HARCOURT: Perhaps you may prove as weak a brother amongst 'em that way as t'other.

DORILANT: Foh, drinking with women is as unnatural as scolding with 'em; but 'tis a pleasure of decayed fornicators, and the basest way of quenching love.

HARCOURT: Nay, 'tis drowning love instead of quenching it. But leave us for civil women too!

DORILANT: Ay, when he can't be the better for 'em. We hardly pardon a man that leaves his friend for a wench, and that's a pretty lawful call.

HORNER: Faith, I would not leave you for 'em, if they would not drink.

DORILANT: Who would disappoint his company at Lewis's[4] for a gossiping?

HARCOURT: Foh, wine and women, good apart, together as nauseous as sack and sugar.[5] But hark you, sir, before you go, a little of your advice; an old maimed general, when unfit for action, is fittest for counsel. I have other designs upon women than eating and drinking with them. I am in love with Sparkish's mistress, whom he is to marry tomorrow. Now how shall I get her?

[Enter Sparkish, looking about.]

HORNER: Why, here comes one will help you to her.

HARCOURT: He! He, I tell you, is my rival, and will hinder my love.

HORNER: No, a foolish rival and a jealous husband assist their rival's designs, for they are sure to make their women hate them, which is the first step to their love for another man.

HARCOURT: But I cannot come near his mistress but in his company.

8. Stupid.
9. Lecherous.
1. Provide you with food and drink.
2. Plays dice with a score-keeper.

3. In practice.
4. A London restaurant.
5. Sack, white wine from Spain or the Canary Islands, was often drunk with sugar.

HORNER: Still the better for you, for fools are most easily cheated when they themselves are accessories; and he is to be bubbled[6] of his mistress, as of his money, the common mistress, by keeping him company.

SPARKISH: Who is that, that is to be bubbled? Faith, let me snack,[7] I han't met with a bubble since Christmas. Gad, I think bubbles are like their brother woodcocks,[8] go out with the cold weather.

HARCOURT [apart to Horner]: A pox! He did not hear all, I hope.

SPARKISH: Come, you bubbling rogues you, where do we sup?—Oh, Harcourt, my mistress tells me you have been making fierce love to her all the play long, hah, ha! But I—

HARCOURT: I make love to her?

SPARKISH: Nay, I forgive thee, for I think I know thee, and I know her, but I am sure I know myself.

HARCOURT: Did she tell you so? I see all women are like these of the Exchange, who, to enhance the price of their commodities, report to their fond customers offers which were never made 'em.

HORNER: Ay, women are as apt to tell before the intrigue as men after it, and so show themselves the vainer sex. But hast thou a mistress, Sparkish? 'Tis as hard for me to believe it as that thou ever hadst a bubble, as you bragged just now.

SPARKISH: Oh, your servant, sir; are you at your raillery, sir? But we were some of us beforehand with you today at the play. The wits were something bold with you, sir; did you not hear us laugh?

HORNER: Yes, but I thought you had gone to plays to laugh at the poet's wit, not at your own.

SPARKISH: Your servant, sir; no, I thank you. Gad, I go to a play as to a country treat;[9] I carry my own wine to one and my own wit to t'other, or else I'm sure I should not be merry at either. And the reason why we are so often louder than the players is because we think we speak more wit and so become the poet's rivals in his audience. For to tell you the truth, we hate the silly rogues, nay, so much that we find fault even with their bawdy upon the stage, whilst we talk nothing else in the pit as loud.

HORNER: But why shouldst thou hate the silly poets? Thou hast too much wit to be one, and they, like whores, are only hated by each other—and thou dost scorn writing, I'm sure.

SPARKISH: Yes, I'd have you to know I scorn writing; but women, women, that make men do all foolish things, make 'em write songs too. Everybody does it. 'Tis even as common with lovers as playing with fans; and you can no more help rhyming to your Phyllis[1] than drinking to your Phyllis.

HARCOURT: Nay, poetry in love is no more to be avoided than jealousy.

DORILANT: But the poets damned your songs, did they?

SPARKISH: Damn the poets! They turned 'em into burlesque, as they call it. That burlesque[2] is a hocus-pocus trick they have got, which, by virtue of *hictius doctius*,[3] *topsy-turvy*, they make a wise and witty man in the world a fool upon the stage, you know not how; and 'tis therefore I hate 'em too, for I know not but it may be

---

6. Cheated, fooled.
7. Have a share.
8. Migratory birds; also fools.
9. Reception.

1. I.e., "sweetheart"; beloved women were often so named in pastoral poetry.
2. I.e., they wrote parodies of Sparkish's songs
3. Like hocus pocus.

my own case, for they'll put a man into a play for looking asquint.[4] Their predecessors were contented to make serving-men only their stage-fools, but these
rogues must have gentlemen, with a pox to 'em, nay, knights; and, indeed, you
shall hardly see a fool upon the stage but he's a knight and, to tell you the truth,
they have kept me these six years from being a knight in earnest, for fear of being
knighted in a play, and dubbed a fool.

DORILANT: Blame 'em not; they must follow their copy,[5] the age.

HARCOURT: But why shouldst thou be afraid of being in a play, who expose yourself every day in the play-houses, and as public places?

HORNER: 'Tis but being on the stage, instead of standing on a bench in the pit.

DORILANT: Don't you give money to painters to draw you like? And are you afraid
of your pictures at length in a playhouse, where all your mistresses may see you?

SPARKISH: A pox! Painters don't draw the smallpox or pimples in one's face.
Come, damn all your silly authors whatever, all books and booksellers, by the
world, and all readers, courteous or uncourteous.

HARCOURT: But who comes here, Sparkish?

[Enter Mr. Pinchwife and his wife in man's clothes, Alithea, Lucy her maid.]

SPARKISH: Oh, hide me! There's my mistress too. [Sparkish hides himself behind
Harcourt.]

HARCOURT: She sees you.

SPARKISH: But I will not see her. 'Tis time to go to Whitehall and I must not fail
the drawing room.

HARCOURT: Pray, first carry me, and reconcile me to her.

SPARKISH: Another time; faith, the King will have supped.

HARCOURT: Not with the worse stomach for thy absence; thou art one of those
fools that think their attendance at the King's meals as necessary as his physicians', when you are more troublesome to him than his doctors, or his dogs.

SPARKISH: Pshaw, I know my interest, sir. Prithee hide me.

HORNER: Your servant, Pinchwife.—What, he knows us not!

PINCHWIFE [to his wife aside]: Come along.

MRS. PINCHWIFE: Pray, have you any ballads? Give me sixpenny worth.

CLASP: We have no ballads.

MRS. PINCHWIFE: Then give me Covent Garden Drollery,[6] and a play or two—Oh,
here's Tarugo's Wiles, and The Slighted Maiden;[7] I'll have them.

PINCHWIFE [apart to her]: No, plays are not for your reading. Come along; will you
discover yourself?

HORNER: Who is that pretty youth with him, Sparkish?

SPARKISH: I believe his wife's brother, because he's something like her, but I never saw her but once.

HORNER: Extremely handsome; I have seen a face like it too. Let us follow 'em.

[Exeunt Pinchwife, Mrs. Pinchwife, Alithea, Lucy; Horner, Dorilant following them.]

HARCOURT: Come, Sparkish, your mistress saw you and will be angry you go not
to her. Besides, I would fain be reconciled to her, which none but you can do,
dear friend.

---

4. I.e., they'll make him a comic character in a play,
mocking even the tiniest fault.
5. The original from which a copy is made.
6. A collection of songs, prologues, epilogues, and poetry
by various authors, including Wycherley, believed to

have been edited by Aphra Behn (1672).
7. Two theatrical "oldies," no longer current: a comedy
by Thomas St. Serfe (1668) and a tragicomedy by Robert
Stapleton (1663).

SPARKISH: Well, that's a better reason, dear friend, I would not go near her now, for hers or my own sake, but I can deny you nothing, for though I have known thee a great while, never go,[8] if I do not love thee as well as a new acquaintance.

HARCOURT: I am obliged to you indeed, dear friend. I would be well with her, only to be well with thee still, for these ties to wives usually dissolve all ties to friends. I would be contented she should enjoy you a-nights, but I would have you to myself a-days, as I have had, dear friend.

SPARKISH: And thou shalt enjoy me a-days, dear, dear friend, never stir, and I'll be divorced from her sooner than from thee. Come along.

HARCOURT [aside]: So, we are hard put to't when we make our rival our procurer; but neither she nor her brother would let me come near her now. When all's done, a rival is the best cloak to steal to a mistress under, without suspicion, and when we have once got to her as we desire, we throw him off like other cloaks.

[Exit Sparkish, and Harcourt following him. Re-enter Mr. Pinchwife, Mrs. Pinchwife in man's clothes.]

PINCHWIFE [to Alithea (off-stage)]: Sister, if you will not go, we must leave you. [Aside.] The fool her gallant and she will muster up all the young saunterers of this place, and they will leave their dear seamstresses to follow us. What a swarm of cuckolds and cuckold-makers are here!—Come, let's be gone, Mistress Margery.

MRS. PINCHWIFE: Don't you believe that; I ha'n't half my bellyful of sights yet.

PINCHWIFE: Then walk this way.

MRS. PINCHWIFE: Lord, what a power of brave signs are here! Stay—the Bull's-Head, the Ram's-Head and the Stag's-Head, dear—

PINCHWIFE: Nay, if every husband's proper sign[9] here were visible, they would be all alike.

MRS. PINCHWIFE: What d'ye mean by that, bud?

PINCHWIFE: 'Tis no matter—no matter, bud.

MRS. PINCHWIFE: Pray tell me; nay, I will know.

PINCHWIFE: They would be all bulls', stags', and rams' heads.

[Exeunt Mr. Pinchwife, Mrs. Pinchwife. Re-enter Sparkish, Harcourt, Alithea, Lucy, at t'other door.]

SPARKISH: Come, dear madam, for my sake you shall be reconciled to him.

ALITHEA: For your sake I hate him.

HARCOURT: That's something too cruel, madam, to hate me for his sake.

SPARKISH: Ay indeed, madam, too, too cruel to me, to hate my friend for my sake.

ALITHEA: I hate him because he is your enemy; and you ought to hate him too, for making love to me, if you love me.

SPARKISH: That's a good one! I hate a man for loving you! If he did love you, 'tis but what he can't help and 'tis your fault, not his, if he admires you. I hate a man for being of my opinion! I'll ne'er do't by the world.

ALITHEA: Is it for your honor or mine, to suffer a man to make love to me, who am to marry you tomorrow?

SPARKISH: Is it for your honor or mine, to have me jealous? That he makes love to you is a sign you are handsome and that I am not jealous is a sign you are virtuous. That, I think, is for your honor.

ALITHEA: But 'tis your honor too I am concerned for.

8. Worry not.   9. I.e., a cuckold's horns.

HARCOURT: But why, dearest madam, will you be more concerned for his honor than he is himself? Let his honor alone, for my sake and his. He, he has no honor—

SPARKISH: How's that?

HARCOURT: But what my dear friend can guard himself.

SPARKISH: O ho—that's right again.

HARCOURT: Your care of his honor argues his neglect of it, which is no honor to my dear friend here; therefore once more, let his honor go which way it will, dear madam.

SPARKISH: Ay, ay, were it for my honor to marry a woman whose virtue I suspected and could not trust her in a friend's hands?

ALITHEA: Are you not afraid to lose me?

HARCOURT: He afraid to lose you, madam! No, no—you may see how the most estimable and most glorious creature in the world is valued by him. Will you not see it?

SPARKISH: Right, honest Frank, I have that noble value for her that I cannot be jealous of her.

ALITHEA: You mistake him, he means you care not for me, nor who has me.

SPARKISH: Lord, madam, I see you are jealous.[1] Will you wrest a poor man's meaning from his words?

ALITHEA: You astonish me, sir, with your want of jealousy.

SPARKISH: And you make me giddy, madam, with your jealousy and fears and virtue and honor. Gad, I see virtue makes a woman as troublesome as a little reading or learning.

ALITHEA: Monstrous!

LUCY [behind]: Well, to see what easy husbands these women of quality can meet with; a poor chambermaid can never have such lady-like luck. Besides, he's thrown away upon her; she'll make no use of her fortune, her blessing. None to[2] a gentleman for a pure cuckold, for it requires good breeding to be a cuckold.

ALITHEA: I tell you then plainly, he pursues me to marry me.

SPARKISH: Pshaw!

HARCOURT: Come, madam, you see you strive in vain to make him jealous of me; my dear friend is the kindest creature in the world to me.

SPARKISH: Poor fellow.

HARCOURT: But his kindness only is not enough for me, without your favor; your good opinion, dear madam, 'tis that must perfect my happiness. Good gentleman, he believes all I say—would you would do so. Jealous of me! I would not wrong him nor you for the world.

SPARKISH: Look you there; hear him, hear him, and do not walk away so.
      [Alithea walks carelessly to and fro.]

HARCOURT: I love you, madam, so—

SPARKISH: How's that! Nay—now you begin to go too far indeed.

HARCOURT: So much, I confess, I say I love you, that I would not have you miserable and cast yourself away upon so unworthy and inconsiderable a thing as what you see here. [Clapping his hand on his breast, points at Sparkish.]

SPARKISH: No, faith, I believe thou wouldst not; now his meaning is plain. But I knew before thou wouldst not wrong me nor her.

1. Here, vehement, fearful.   2. There's no one like.

HARCOURT: No, no, heavens forbid the glory of her sex should fall so low as into the embraces of such a contemptible wretch, the last of mankind—my dear friend here—I injure him! [*Embracing Sparkish.*]

ALITHEA: Very well.

SPARKISH: No, no, dear friend, I knew it.—Madam, you see he will rather wrong himself than me, in giving himself such names.

ALITHEA: Do not you understand him yet?

SPARKISH: Yes, how modestly he speaks of himself, poor fellow.

ALITHEA: Methinks he speaks impudently of yourself, since—before yourself too; insomuch that I can no longer suffer his scurrilous abusiveness to you, no more than his love to me. [*Offers to go.*]

SPARKISH: Nay, nay, madam, pray stay—his love to you! Lord, madam, he has not spoke yet plain enough?

ALITHEA: Yes, indeed, I should think so.

SPARKISH: Well then, by the world, a man can't speak civilly to a woman now but presently she says he makes love to her. Nay, madam, you shall stay, with your pardon, since you have not yet understood him, till he has made an éclaircisse-ment³ of his love to you, that is, what kind of love it is. [*To Harcourt.*] Answer to thy catechism. Friend, do you love my mistress here?

HARCOURT: Yes, I wish she would not doubt it.

SPARKISH: But how do you love her?

HARCOURT: With all my soul.

ALITHEA: I thank him; methinks he speaks plain enough now.

SPARKISH [*to Alithea*]: You are out still.—But with what kind of love, Harcourt?

HARCOURT: With the best and truest love in the world.

SPARKISH: Look you there then, that is with no matrimonial love, I'm sure.

ALITHEA: How's that? Do you say matrimonial love is not best?

SPARKISH: Gad, I went too far ere I was aware. But speak for thyself, Harcourt; you said you would not wrong me nor her.

HARCOURT: No, no, madam, e'en take him for heaven's sake—

SPARKISH: Look you there, madam.

HARCOURT: Who should in all justice be yours, he that loves you most. [*Claps his hand on his breast.*]

ALITHEA: Look you there, Mr. Sparkish, who's that?

SPARKISH: Who should it be?—Go on, Harcourt.

HARCOURT: Who loves you more than women titles or fortune fools. [*Points at Sparkish.*]

SPARKISH: Look you there, he means me still, for he points at me.

ALITHEA: Ridiculous!

HARCOURT: Who can only match your faith and constancy in love.

SPARKISH: Ay.

HARCOURT: Who knows, if it be possible, how to value so much beauty and virtue.

SPARKISH: Ay.

HARCOURT: Whose love can no more be equaled in the world than that heavenly form of yours.

SPARKISH: No.

---

3. Explanation.

HARCOURT: Who could no more suffer a rival than your absence, and yet could no more suspect your virtue than his own constancy in his love to you.

SPARKISH: No.

HARCOURT: Who, in fine,[4] loves you better than his eyes that first made him love you.

SPARKISH: Ay—nay, madam, faith, you shan't go till—

ALITHEA: Have a care, lest you make me stay too long—

SPARKISH: But till he has saluted you, that I may be assured you are friends, after his honest advice and declaration. Come, pray, madam, be friends with him.

   [Enter Mr. Pinchwife, Mrs. Pinchwife]

ALITHEA: You must pardon me, sir, that I am not yet so obedient to you.

PINCHWIFE: What, invite your wife to kiss men? Monstrous! Are you not ashamed? I will never forgive you.

SPARKISH: Are you not ashamed that I should have more confidence in the chastity of your family than you have? You must not teach me. I am a man of honor, sir, though I am frank[5] and free; I am frank, sir—

PINCHWIFE: Very frank, sir, to share your wife with your friends.

SPARKISH: He is an humble, menial[6] friend, such as reconciles the differences of the marriage bed. You know man and wife do not always agree; I design him for that use, therefore would have him well with my wife.

PINCHWIFE: A menial friend!—you will get a great many menial friends by showing your wife as you do.

SPARKISH: What then? It may be I have a pleasure in't, as I have to show fine clothes at a playhouse the first day and count money before poor rogues.

PINCHWIFE: He that shows his wife or money will be in danger of having them borrowed sometimes.

SPARKISH: I love to be envied and would not marry a wife that I alone could love; loving alone is as dull as eating alone. Is it not a frank age? And I am a frank person. And to tell you the truth, it may be I love to have rivals in a wife; they make her seem to a man still but as a kept mistress. And so good night, for I must to Whitehall.—Madam, I hope you are now reconciled to my friend and so I wish you a good night, madam, and sleep if you can, for tomorrow you know I must visit you early with a canonical gentleman. Good night, dear Harcourt.   [Exit Sparkish.]

HARCOURT: Madam, I hope you will not refuse my visit tomorrow, if it should be earlier, with a canonical gentleman, than Mr. Sparkish's.

PINCHWIFE [coming between Alithea and Harcourt]: This gentlewoman is yet under my care; therefore you must yet forbear your freedom with her, sir.

HARCOURT: Must, sir!

PINCHWIFE: Yes, sir, she is my sister.

HARCOURT: 'Tis well she is, sir—for I must be her servant, sir.—Madam—

PINCHWIFE: Come away, sister; we had been gone, if it had not been for you, and so avoided these lewd rake-hells,[7] who seem to haunt us.

   [Enter Horner, Dorilant to them.]

HORNER: How now, Pinchwife?

PINCHWIFE: Your servant.

---

4. In short.
5. Unreserved, open.

6. Household.
7. Scoundrels.

HORNER: What, I see a little time in the country makes a man turn wild and unsociable and only fit to converse with his horses, dogs and his herds.

PINCHWIFE: I have business, sir, and must mind it; your business is pleasure, therefore you and I must go different ways.

HORNER: Well, you may go on, but this pretty young gentleman—[*Takes hold of Mrs. Pinchwife.*]

HARCOURT: The lady—

DORILANT: And the maid—

HORNER: Shall stay with us, for I suppose their business is the same with ours, pleasure.

PINCHWIFE [*aside*]: 'Sdeath, he know her, she carries it so sillily! Yet if he does not, I should be more silly to discover it first.

ALITHEA: Pray, let us go, sir.

PINCHWIFE: Come, come—

HORNER [*to Mrs. Pinchwife*]: Had you not rather stay with us?—Prithee, Pinchwife, who is this pretty young gentleman?

PINCHWIFE: One to whom I'm a guardian. [*Aside.*] I wish I could keep her out of your hands.

HORNER: Who is he? I never saw anything so pretty in all my life.

PINCHWIFE: Pshaw, do not look upon him so much. He's a poor bashful youth, you'll put him out of countenance.—Come away, brother. [*Offers to take her away.*]

HORNER: Oh, your brother!

PINCHWIFE: Yes, my wife's brother.—Come, come, she'll stay supper for us.

HORNER: I thought so, for he is very like her I saw you at the play with, whom I told you I was in love with.

MRS. PINCHWIFE [*aside*]: O jeminy! Is this he that was in love with me? I am glad on't, I vow, for he's a curious fine gentleman, and I love him already too. [*To Mr. Pinchwife.*] Is this he, bud?

PINCHWIFE [*to his wife.*]: Come away, come away.

HORNER: Why, what haste are you in? Why won't you let me talk with him?

PINCHWIFE: Because you'll debauch him; he's yet young and innocent and I would not have him debauched for anything in the world. [*Aside.*] How she gazes on him! The devil!

HORNER: Harcourt, Dorilant, look you here; this is the likeness of that dowdy[8] he told us of, his wife. Did you ever see a lovelier creature? The rogue has reason to be jealous of his wife since she is like him, for she would make all that see her in love with her.

HARCOURT: And as I remember now, she is as like him here as can be.

DORILANT: She is indeed very pretty, if she be like him.

HORNER: Very pretty? A very pretty commendation! She is a glorious creature, beautiful beyond all things I ever beheld.

PINCHWIFE: So, so.

HARCOURT: More beautiful than a poet's first mistress of imagination.

HORNER: Or another man's last mistress of flesh and blood.

MRS. PINCHWIFE: Nay, now you jeer, sir; pray don't jeer me.

PINCHWIFE: Come, come. [*Aside.*] By heavens, she'll discover herself!

HORNER: I speak of your sister, sir.

8. Shabby, dull woman.

PINCHWIFE: Ay, but saying she was handsome, if like him, made him blush. [*Aside.*] I am upon a rack!

HORNER: Methinks he is so handsome he should not be a man.

PINCHWIFE [*aside*]: Oh, there 'tis out! He has discovered her! I am not able to suffer any longer. [*To his wife.*] Come, come away, I say.

HORNER: Nay, by your leave, sir, he shall not go yet.—[*To them.*] Harcourt, Dorilant, let us torment this jealous rogue a little.

HARCOURT: |
DORILANT: | How?

HORNER: I'll show you.

PINCHWIFE: Come, pray, let him go, I cannot stay fooling any longer. I tell you his sister stays supper for us.

HORNER: Does she? Come then, we'll all go sup with her and thee.

PINCHWIFE: No, now I think on't, having stayed so long for us, I warrant she's gone to bed. [*Aside.*] I wish she and I were well out of their hands.—Come, I must rise early tomorrow, come.

HORNER: Well, then, if she be gone to bed, I wish her and you a good night. But pray, young gentleman, present my humble service to her.

MRS. PINCHWIFE: Thank you heartily, sir.

PINCHWIFE [*aside*]: 'Sdeath! she will discover herself yet in spite of me.—He is something more civil to you, for your kindness to his sister, than I am, it seems.

HORNER: Tell her, dear sweet little gentleman, for all your brother there, that you have revived the love I had for her at first sight in the playhouse.

MRS. PINCHWIFE: But did you love her indeed, and indeed?

PINCHWIFE [*aside*]: So, so.—Away, I say.

HORNER: Nay, stay. Yes, indeed, and indeed, pray do you tell her so, and give her this kiss from me. [*Kisses her.*]

PINCHWIFE [*aside*]: O heavens! What do I suffer! Now 'tis too plain he knows her, and yet—

HORNER: And this, and this—[*Kisses her again.*]

MRS. PINCHWIFE: What do you kiss me for? I am no woman.

PINCHWIFE [*aside*]: So—there, 'tis out.—Come, I cannot, nor will stay any longer.

HORNER: Nay, they shall send your lady a kiss too. Here, Harcourt, Dorilant, will you not? [*They kiss her.*]

PINCHWIFE [*aside*]: How! Do I suffer this? Was I not accusing another just now for this rascally patience, in permitting his wife to be kissed before his face? Ten thousand ulcers gnaw away their lips!—Come, come.

HORNER: Good night, dear little gentleman. Madam, good night. Farewell, Pinchwife. [*Apart to Harcourt and Dorilant.*] Did not I tell you I would raise his jealous gall?   [*Exeunt Horner, Harcourt, and Dorilant.*]

PINCHWIFE: So, they are gone at last; stay, let me see first if the coach be at this door.   [*Exit.*]

[*Horner, Harcourt, Dorilant return.*]

HORNER: What, not gone yet? Will you be sure to do as I desired you, sweet sir?

MRS. PINCHWIFE: Sweet sir, but what will you give me then?

HORNER: Anything. Come away into the next walk.

[*Exit Horner, haling away Mrs. Pinchwife.*]

ALITHEA: Hold, hold! What d'ye do?

LUCY: Stay, stay, hold—

HARCOURT: Hold, madam, hold! Let him present[9] him, he'll come presently. Nay, I will never let you go till you answer my question.

LUCY: For God's sake, sir, I must follow 'em.

DORILANT: No, I have something to present you with too; you shan't follow them.

[*Alithea, Lucy struggling with Harcourt and Dorilant. Pinchwife returns.*]

PINCHWIFE: Where?—how?—what's become of?—gone!—whither?

LUCY: He's only gone with the gentleman, who will give him something, an't please your worship.

PINCHWIFE: Something—give him something, with a pox!—where are they?

ALITHEA: In the next walk only, brother.

PINCHWIFE: Only, only! Where, where?

[*Exit Pinchwife and returns presently, then goes out again.*]

HARCOURT: What's the matter with him? Why so much concerned? But dearest madam—

ALITHEA: Pray let me go, sir; I have said and suffered enough already.

HARCOURT: Then you will not look upon nor pity my sufferings?

ALITHEA: To look upon 'em, when I cannot help 'em, were cruelty, not pity; therefore I will never see you more.

HARCOURT: Let me then, madam, have my privilege of a banished lover, complaining or railing, and giving you but a farewell reason why, if you cannot condescend to marry me, you should not take that wretch, my rival.

ALITHEA: He only, not you, since my honor is engaged so far to him, can give me a reason why I should not marry him; but if he be true and what I think him to me, I must be so to him. Your servant, sir.

HARCOURT: Have women only constancy when 'tis a vice and, like fortune, only true to fools?

DORILANT [*to Lucy, who struggles to get from him*]: Thou shalt not stir, thou robust creature; you see I can deal with you, therefore you should stay the rather, and be kind.

[*Enter Pinchwife.*]

PINCHWIFE: Gone, gone, not to be found! Quite gone! Ten thousand plagues go with 'em! Which way went they?

ALITHEA: But into t'other walk, brother.

LUCY: Their business will be done presently sure, an't please your worship; it can't be long in doing, I'm sure on't.

ALITHEA: Are they not there?

PINCHWIFE: No; you know where they are, you infamous wretch, eternal shame of your family, which you do not dishonor enough yourself, you think, but you must help her to do it too, thou legion of bawds!

ALITHEA: Good brother—

PINCHWIFE: Damned, damned sister!

ALITHEA: Look you here, she's coming.

[*Enter Mrs. Pinchwife in man's clothes, running, with her hat under her arm, full of oranges and dried fruit; Horner following.*]

MRS. PINCHWIFE: O dear bud, look you here what I have got, see!

PINCHWIFE [*aside, rubbing his forehead*]: And what I have got here too, which you can't see.

9. Offer a gift to.

MRS. PINCHWIFE: The fine gentleman has given me better things yet.

PINCHWIFE: Has he so? [*Aside.*] Out of breath and colored! I must hold yet.

HORNER: I have only given your little brother an orange, sir.

PINCHWIFE [*to Horner*]: Thank you, sir. [*Aside.*] You have only squeezed my orange, I suppose, and given it me again; yet I must have a city patience. [*To his wife.*] Come, come away.

MRS. PINCHWIFE: Stay, till I have put up my fine things, bud.

   [*Enter Sir Jaspar Fidget.*]

SIR JASPAR: O Master Horner, come, come, the ladies stay for you; your mistress, my wife, wonders you make not more haste to her.

HORNER: I have stayed this half hour for you here and 'tis your fault I am not now with your wife.

SIR JASPAR: But pray, don't let her know so much; the truth on't is, I was advancing a certain project to his Majesty about—I'll tell you.

HORNER: No, let's go and hear it at your house.—Good night, sweet little gentleman. One kiss more, you'll remember me now, I hope. [*Kisses her.*]

DORILANT: What, Sir Jaspar, will you separate friends? He promised to sup with us; and if you take him to your house, you'll be in danger of our company too.

SIR JASPAR: Alas, gentlemen, my house is not fit for you; there are none but civil women there, which are not fit for your turn. He, you know, can bear with the society of civil women now, ha, ha, ha! Besides, he's one of my family—he's— heh, heh, heh!

DORILANT: What is he?

SIR JASPAR: Faith, my eunuch, since you'll have it, heh, he, he!

                                    [*Exeunt Sir Jaspar Fidget and Horner.*]

DORILANT: I rather wish thou wert his, or my cuckold. Harcourt, what a good cuckold is lost there for want of a man to make him one! Thee and I cannot have Horner's privilege, who can make use of it.

HARCOURT: Ay, to poor Horner 'tis like coming to an estate at threescore, when a man can't be the better for't.

PINCHWIFE: Come.

MRS. PINCHWIFE: Presently, bud.

DORILANT: Come, let us go too. [*To Alithea.*] Madam, your servant. [*To Lucy.*] Good night, strapper.[1]

HARCOURT: Madam, though you will not let me have a good day or night, I wish you one; but dare not name the other half of my wish.

ALITHEA: Good night, sir, forever.

MRS. PINCHWIFE: I don't know where to put this here, dear bud; you shall eat it; nay, you shall have part of the fine gentleman's good things, or treat as you call it, when we come home.

PINCHWIFE: Indeed, I deserve it, since I furnished the best part of it. [*Strikes away the orange.*]

> The gallant treats, presents, and gives the ball
> But 'tis the absent cuckold pays for all.

                                                   [*Exeunt.*]

---

1. Robust woman.

ACT 4

Scene 1

[*In Pinchwife's house in the morning. Lucy, Alithea dressed in new clothes.*]

LUCY: Well—madam, now have I dressed you and set you out with so many ornaments and spent upon you ounces of essence and pulvilio,[1] and all this for no other
purpose but as people adorn and perfume a corpse for a stinking secondhand
grave[2]—such or as bad I think as Master Sparkish's bed.

ALITHEA: Hold your peace.

LUCY: Nay, madam, I will ask you the reason why you would banish poor Master
Harcourt forever from your sight. How could you be so hardhearted?

ALITHEA: 'Twas because I was not hardhearted.

LUCY: No, no, 'twas stark love and kindness, I warrant.

ALITHEA: It was so; I would see him no more because I love him.

LUCY: Hey-day, a very pretty reason!

ALITHEA: You do not understand me.

LUCY: I wish you may yourself.

ALITHEA: I was engaged to marry, you see, another man, whom my justice will not
suffer me to deceive or injure.

LUCY: Can there be a greater cheat or wrong done to a man than to give him your
person without your heart? I should make a conscience of[3] it.

ALITHEA: I'll retrieve it for him after I am married a while.

LUCY: The woman that marries to love better will be as much mistaken as the
wencher that marries to live better. No, madam, marrying to increase love is like
gaming to become rich; alas, you only lose what little stock you had before.

ALITHEA: I find by your rhetoric you have been bribed to betray me.

LUCY: Only by his merit, that has bribed your heart, you see, against your word and
rigid honor. But what a devil is this honor! 'Tis sure a disease in the head, like the
megrim, or falling sickness,[4] that always hurries people away to do themselves
mischief. Men lose their lives by it; women what's dearer to 'em, their love, the
life of life.

ALITHEA: Come, pray talk you no more of honor, nor Master Harcourt. I wish the
other would come to secure my fidelity to him and his right in me.

LUCY: You will marry him then?

ALITHEA: Certainly. I have given him already my word and will my hand too, to
make it good when he comes.

LUCY: Well, I wish I may never stick pin more if he be not an arrant natural to[5]
t'other fine gentleman.

ALITHEA: I own he wants the wit of Harcourt, which I will dispense withal for
another want he has, which is want of jealousy, which men of wit seldom want.

LUCY: Lord, madam, what should you do with a fool to your husband? You intend
to be honest, don't you? Then that husbandly virtue, credulity, is thrown away
upon you.

ALITHEA: He only that could suspect my virtue should have cause to do it; 'tis
Sparkish's confidence in my truth that obliges me to be so faithful to him.

LUCY: You are not sure his opinion may last.

---

1. Perfume and fragrant powder.
2. I.e., a grave newly opened for a second burial.
3. Have scruples about.

4. Migraine headache, or epilepsy.
5. An utter fool in comparison to.

ALITHEA: I am satisfied 'tis impossible for him to be jealous after the proofs I have had of him. Jealousy in a husband—Heaven defend me from it! It begets a thousand plagues to a poor woman, the loss of her honor, her quiet and her—

LUCY: And her pleasure.

ALITHEA: What d'ye mean, impertinent?

LUCY: Liberty is a great pleasure, madam.

ALITHEA: I say, loss of her honor, her quiet, nay, her life sometimes, and what's as bad almost, the loss of this town; that is, she is sent into the country, which is the last ill usage of a husband to a wife, I think.

LUCY [aside]: Oh, does the wind lie there?—Then, of necessity, madam, you think a man must carry his wife into the country, if he be wise. The country is as terrible, I find, to our young English ladies as a monastery to those abroad, and, on my virginity, I think they would rather marry a London jailer than a high sheriff of a county, since neither can stir from his employment. Formerly women of wit married fools for a great estate, a fine seat, or the like, but now 'tis for a pretty seat only in Lincoln's Inn Fields, St James's Fields, or the Pall Mall.[6]

[Enter to them Sparkish and Harcourt dressed like a parson.]

SPARKISH: Madam, your humble servant, a happy day to you, and to us all.

HARCOURT: Amen.

ALITHEA: Who have we here?

SPARKISH: My chaplain, faith. O madam, poor Harcourt remembers his humble service to you and, in obedience to your last commands, refrains coming into your sight.

ALITHEA: Is not that he?

SPARKISH: No, fie, no; but to show that he ne'er intended to hinder our match, has sent his brother here to join our hands. When I get me a wife, I must get her a chaplain, according to the custom; this is his brother, and my chaplain.

ALITHEA: His brother?

LUCY [aside]: And your chaplain, to preach in your pulpit then.

ALITHEA: His brother!

SPARKISH: Nay, I knew you would not believe it.—I told you, sir, she would take you for your brother Frank.

ALITHEA: Believe it!

LUCY [aside]: His brother! hah, ha, he! He has a trick left still, it seems.

SPARKISH: Come, my dearest, pray let us go to church before the canonical hour[7] is past.

ALITHEA: For shame, you are abused still.

SPARKISH: By the world, 'tis strange now you are so incredulous.

ALITHEA: 'Tis strange you are so credulous.

SPARKISH: Dearest of my life, hear me. I tell you this is Ned Harcourt of Cambridge; by the world, you see he has a sneaking college look. 'Tis true he's something like his brother Frank and they differ from each other no more than in their age, for they were twins.

LUCY: Hah, ha, he!

ALITHEA: Your servant, sir; I cannot be so deceived, though you are. But come, let's hear; how do you know what you affirm so confidently?

---

6. Fashionable residential areas of London, distinguished by their famous inhabitants and expensive shops, as well as their grand houses.

7. Church law permitted the marriage ceremony only in the morning; it could be performed at any time between 8 A.M. and noon.

SPARKISH: Why, I'll tell you all. Frank Harcourt coming to me this morning, to wish me joy and present his service to you, I asked him if he could help me to a parson, whereupon he told me he had a brother in town who was in orders and he went straight away and sent him you see there to me.

ALITHEA: Yes, Frank goes and puts on a black coat, then tells you he is Ned; that's all you have for't.

SPARKISH: Pshaw, pshaw, I tell you by the same token, the midwife put her garter about Frank's neck to know 'em asunder, they were so like.

ALITHEA: Frank tells you this too.

SPARKISH: Ay, and Ned there too; nay, they are both in a story.

ALITHEA: So, so; very foolish!

SPARKISH: Lord, if you won't believe one, you had best try him by your chambermaid there, for chambermaids must needs know chaplains from other men, they are so used to 'em.

LUCY: Let's see; nay, I'll be sworn he has the canonical smirk and the filthy, clammy palm of a chaplain.

ALITHEA: Well, most reverend doctor, pray let us make an end of this fooling.

HARCOURT: With all my soul, divine, heavenly creature, when you please.

ALITHEA: He speaks like a chaplain indeed.

SPARKISH: Why, was there not "soul," "divine," "heavenly," in what he said?

ALITHEA: Once more, most impertinent black coat, cease your persecution and let us have a conclusion of this ridiculous love.

HARCOURT [aside]: I had forgot. I must suit my style to my coat, or I wear it in vain.

ALITHEA: I have no more patience left; let us make once an end of this troublesome love, I say.

HARCOURT: So be it, seraphic lady, when your honor shall think it meet and convenient so to do.

SPARKISH: Gad, I'm sure none but a chaplain could speak so, I think.

ALITHEA: Let me tell you, sir, this dull trick will not serve your turn; though you delay our marriage, you shall not hinder it.

HARCOURT: Far be it from me, munificent patroness, to delay your marriage. I desire nothing more than to marry you presently, which I might do, if you yourself would, for my noble, good-natured and thrice generous patron here would not hinder it.

SPARKISH: No, poor man, not I, faith.

HARCOURT: And now, madam, let me tell you plainly, nobody else shall marry you; by heavens, I'll die first, for I'm sure I should die[8] after it.

LUCY [aside]: How his love has made him forget his function, as I have seen it in real parsons!

ALITHEA: That was spoken like a chaplain too! Now you understand him, I hope.

SPARKISH: Poor man, he takes it heinously to be refused. I can't blame him; 'tis putting an indignity upon him not to be suffered. But you'll pardon me, madam, it shan't be, he shall marry us. Come away, pray, madam.

LUCY [aside]: Hah, ha, he! More ado! 'Tis late.

ALITHEA: Invincible stupidity! I tell you he would marry me as your rival, not as your chaplain.

---

8. Harcourt plays on literal death and sexual "death": orgasm.

SPARKISH [*pulling her away*]: Come, come, madam.

LUCY: Ay, pray, madam, do not refuse this reverend divine the honor and satisfaction of marrying you, for I dare say he has set his heart upon't, good doctor.

ALITHEA: What can you hope or design by this?

HARCOURT [*aside*]: I could answer her, a reprieve for a day only often revokes a hasty doom; at worst, if she will not take mercy on me and let me marry her, I have at least the lover's second pleasure, hindering my rival's enjoyment, though but for a time.

SPARKISH: Come, madam, 'tis e'en twelve o'clock, and my mother charged me never to be married out of the canonical hours. Come, come. Lord, here's such a deal of modesty, I warrant, the first day.

LUCY: Yes, an't please your worship, married women show all their modesty the first day, because married men show all their love the first day.

[*Exeunt Sparkish, Alithea, Harcourt, and Lucy.*]

Scene 2

[*The scene changes to a bedchamber, where appear Pinchwife, Mrs. Pinchwife.*]

PINCHWIFE: Come, tell me, I say.

MRS. PINCHWIFE: Lord, ha'n't I told it an hundred times over?

PINCHWIFE [*aside*]: I would try if, in the repetition of the ungrateful[9] tale, I could find her altering it in the least circumstance, for if her story be false, she is so too.—Come, how was't, baggage?

MRS. PINCHWIFE: Lord, what pleasure you take to hear it, sure!

PINCHWIFE: No, you take more in telling it, I find; but speak, how was't?

MRS. PINCHWIFE: He carried me up into the house next to the Exchange.

PINCHWIFE: So, and you two were only in the room.

MRS. PINCHWIFE: Yes, for he sent away a youth that was there, for some dried fruit and China oranges.[1]

PINCHWIFE: Did he so? Damn him for it—and for—

MRS. PINCHWIFE: But presently came up the gentle-woman of the house.

PINCHWIFE: O, 'twas well she did; but what did he do whilst the fruit came?

MRS. PINCHWIFE: He kissed me an hundred times and told me he fancied he kissed my fine sister, meaning me, you know, whom he said he loved with all his soul and bid me be sure to tell her so and to desire her to be at her window by eleven of the clock this morning and he would walk under it at that time.

PINCHWIFE [*aside*]: And he was as good as his word, very punctual—a pox reward him for't.

MRS. PINCHWIFE: Well, and he said if you were not within, he would come up to her, meaning me, you know, bud, still.

PINCHWIFE [*aside*]: So—he knew her certainly; but for this confession, I am obliged to her simplicity.—But what, you stood very still when he kissed you?

MRS. PINCHWIFE: Yes, I warrant you; would you have had me discovered myself?

PINCHWIFE: But you told me he did some beastliness to you, as you called it; what was't?

MRS. PINCHWIFE: Why, he put—

---

9. Unpleasant.   1. Sweet oranges, regarded in the seventeenth century as an exotic delicacy.

PINCHWIFE: What?

MRS. PINCHWIFE: Why, he put the tip of his tongue between my lips and so moused[2] me—and I said, I'd bite it.

PINCHWIFE: An eternal canker seize it, for[3] a dog!

MRS. PINCHWIFE: Nay, you need not be so angry with him neither, for to say truth, he has the sweetest breath I ever knew.

PINCHWIFE: The devil!—you were satisfied with it then, and would do it again.

MRS. PINCHWIFE: Not unless he should force me.

PINCHWIFE: Force you, changeling![4] I tell you no woman can be forced.

MRS. PINCHWIFE: Yes, but she may, sure, by such a one as he, for he's a proper, goodly strong man; 'tis hard, let me tell you, to resist him.

PINCHWIFE: So, 'tis plain she loves him, yet she has not love enough to make her conceal it from me; but the sight of him will increase her aversion for me and love for him and that love instruct her how to deceive me and satisfy him, all idiot as she is. Love! 'Twas he gave women first their craft, their art of deluding; out of nature's hands they came plain, open, silly and fit for slaves, as she and Heaven intended 'em; but damned love—well—I must strangle that little monster[5] whilst I can deal with him.—Go fetch pen, ink and paper out of the next room.

MRS. PINCHWIFE: Yes, bud.   [Exit Mrs. Pinchwife.]

PINCHWIFE [aside]: Why should women have more invention in love than men? It can only be because they have more desires, more soliciting passions, more lust, and more of the devil. [Mrs. Pinchwife returns.] Come, minx, sit down and write.

MRS. PINCHWIFE: Ay, dear bud, but I can't do't very well.

PINCHWIFE: I wish you could not at all.

MRS. PINCHWIFE: But what should I write for?

PINCHWIFE: I'll have you write a letter to your lover.

MRS. PINCHWIFE: O Lord, to the fine gentleman a letter!

PINCHWIFE: Yes, to the fine gentleman.

MRS. PINCHWIFE: Lord, you do but jeer; sure, you jest.

PINCHWIFE: I am not so merry. Come, write as I bid you.

MRS. PINCHWIFE: What, do you think I am a fool?

PINCHWIFE [aside]: She's afraid I would not dictate any love to him, therefore she's unwilling.—But you had best begin.

MRS. PINCHWIFE: Indeed, and indeed, but I won't, so I won't.

PINCHWIFE: Why?

MRS. PINCHWIFE: Because he's in town; you may send for him if you will.

PINCHWIFE: Very well, you would have him brought to you; is it come to this? I say, take the pen and write, or you'll provoke me.

MRS. PINCHWIFE: Lord, what d'ye make a fool of me for? Don't I know that letters are never writ but from the country to London and from London into the country? Now he's in town and I am in town too; therefore I can't write to him, you know.

PINCHWIFE [aside]: So, I am glad it is no worse; she is innocent enough yet.—Yes, you may, when your husband bids you, write letters to people that are in town.

MRS. PINCHWIFE: O, may I so? Then I'm satisfied.

PINCHWIFE: Come, begin.—[Dictates.] "Sir"—

2. A variation on "muzzled": kissed deeply.

3. I.e., for acting like.

4. Fool.

5. Cupid.

MRS. PINCHWIFE: Shan't I say, "Dear Sir"? You know one says always something more than bare "Sir."

PINCHWIFE: Write as I bid you, or I will write "whore" with this penknife in your face.

MRS. PINCHWIFE: Nay, good bud—[*She writes.*] "Sir"—

PINCHWIFE: "Though I suffered last night your nauseous, loathed kisses and embraces"—Write.

MRS. PINCHWIFE: Nay, why should I say so? You know I told you he had a sweet breath.

PINCHWIFE: Write.

MRS. PINCHWIFE: Let me but put out "loathed."

PINCHWIFE: Write, I say.

MRS. PINCHWIFE: Well then. [*Writes.*]

PINCHWIFE: Let's see, what have you writ? [*Takes the paper and reads.*] "Though I suffered last night your kisses and embraces"—Thou impudent creature, where is "nauseous" and "loathed"?

MRS. PINCHWIFE: I can't abide to write such filthy words.

PINCHWIFE: Once more write as I'd have you, and question it not, or I will spoil thy writing with this. [*Holds up the penknife.*] I will stab out those eyes that cause my mischief.

MRS. PINCHWIFE: O Lord, I will!

PINCHWIFE: So—so—let's see now! [*Reads.*] "Though I suffered last night your nauseous, loathed kisses and embraces"—go on—"yet I would not have you presume that you shall ever repeat them"—So—[*She writes.*]

MRS. PINCHWIFE: I have writ it.

PINCHWIFE: On then.—"I then concealed myself from your knowledge to avoid your insolencies"—[*She writes.*]

MRS. PINCHWIFE: So—

PINCHWIFE: "The same reason, now I am out of your hands"—[*She writes.*]

MRS. PINCHWIFE: So—

PINCHWIFE: "Makes me own to you my unfortunate, though innocent, frolic, of being in man's clothes"—[*She writes.*]

MRS. PINCHWIFE: So—

PINCHWIFE: "That you may for evermore cease to pursue her, who hates and detests you"—[*She writes on.*]

MRS. PINCHWIFE: So—h—[*Sighs.*]

PINCHWIFE: What, do you sigh?—"detests you—as much as she loves her husband and her honour."

MRS. PINCHWIFE: I vow, husband, he'll ne'er believe I should write such a letter.

PINCHWIFE: What, he'd expect a kinder from you? Come, now your name only.

MRS. PINCHWIFE: What, shan't I say, "Your most faithful, humble servant till death"?

PINCHWIFE: No, tormenting fiend! [*Aside.*] Her style, I find, would be very soft.— Come, wrap it up now, whilst I go fetch wax and a candle, and write on the backside, "For Mr. Horner."   [*Exit Pinchwife.*]

MRS. PINCHWIFE: "For Mr. Horner."—So, I am glad he has told me his name. Dear Mr. Horner! But why should I send thee such a letter that will vex thee and make thee angry with me?—Well, I will not send it—Ay, but then my husband will kill me—for I see plainly he won't let me love Mr. Horner—but what care I for my husband?—I won't, so I won't send poor Mr. Horner such a letter—But then my husband—But oh—What if I writ at bottom, my husband made me write it?—Ay, but then my husband would see't—Can one have no shift?[6] Ah, a London woman would have had a hundred presently. Stay—what if I should write a letter, and wrap it up like this, and write upon't too? Ay, but then my husband would see't—I don't know what to do—But yet y'vads[7] I'll try, so I will—for I will not send this letter to poor Mr. Horner, come what will on't.

   [*She writes, and repeats what she hath writ.*]

"Dear, sweet Mr. Horner"—so—"my husband would have me send you a base, rude, unmannerly letter—but I won't"—so—"and would have me forbid you loving me—but I won't"—so—"and would have me say to you, I hate you, poor Mr. Horner—but I won't tell a lie for him"—there—"for I'm sure if you and I were in the country at cards together"—so—"I could not help treading on your toe under the table"—so—"or rubbing knees with you and staring in your face till you saw me"—very well—"and then looking down and blushing for an hour together"—so—"but I must make haste before my husband comes; and now he has taught me to write letters, you shall have longer ones from me, who am, Dear, dear, poor, dear Mr. Horner, Your most humble friend, and servant to command till death, Margery Pinchwife." Stay, I must give him a hint at bottom—so—now wrap it up just like t'other—so—now write, "For Mr. Horner"—But, oh now, what shall I do with it? For here comes my husband.

   [*Enter Pinchwife.*]

PINCHWIFE [*aside*]: I have been detained by a sparkish coxcomb, who pretended a visit to me; but I fear 'twas to my wife.—What, have you done?

MRS. PINCHWIFE: Ay, ay, bud, just now.

PINCHWIFE: Let's see't. What d'ye tremble for? What, you would not have it go?

MRS. PINCHWIFE: Here. [*Aside.*] No, I must not give him that; so I had been served if I had given him this.

PINCHWIFE [*He opens, and reads the first letter*]: Come, where's the wax and seal?

MRS. PINCHWIFE [*aside*]: Lord, what shall I do now? Nay, then, I have it.—Pray let me see't. Lord, you think me so arrant a fool I cannot seal a letter. I will do't, so I will. [*Snatches the letter from him, changes it for the other, seals it and delivers it to him.*]

PINCHWIFE: Nay, I believe you will learn that, and other things too, which I would not have you.

MRS. PINCHWIFE: So, han't I done it curiously?[8] [*Aside.*] I think I have; there's my letter going to Mr. Horner, since he'll needs have me send letters to folks.

PINCHWIFE: 'Tis very well; but I warrant you would not have it go now?

MRS. PINCHWIFE: Yes, indeed, but I would, bud, now.

PINCHWIFE: Well, you are a good girl then. Come, let me lock you up in your chamber, till I come back, and be sure you come not within three strides of the window when I am gone, for I have a spy in the street. [*Exit Mrs. Pinchwife. Pinchwife locks the door.*] At least, 'tis fit she think so. If we do not cheat women, they'll cheat us, and fraud may be justly used with secret enemies, of which a wife is the most dangerous, and he that has a handsome one to keep, and a frontier town,

6. Expedient; trick.
7. In faith.

8. Adroitly; cleverly.

must provide against treachery rather than open force. Now I have secured all within, I'll deal with the foe without with false intelligence. [*Holds up the letter. Exit Pinchwife.*]

Scene 3

[*The scene changes to Horner's lodging. Quack and Horner.*]

QUACK: Well, sir, how fadges[9] the new design? Have you not the luck of all your brother projectors,[1] to deceive only yourself at last?

HORNER: No, good domine[2] doctor, I deceive you, it seems, and others too, for the grave matrons and old, rigid husbands think me as unfit for love as they are but their wives, sisters and daughters know some of 'em better things already.

QUACK: Already!

HORNER: Already, I say. Last night I was drunk with half a dozen of your civil persons, as you call 'em, and people of honor, and so was made free of their society and dressing-rooms forever hereafter, and am already come to the privileges of sleeping upon their pallets,[3] warming smocks,[4] tying shoes and garters, and the like, doctor, already, already, doctor.

QUACK: You have made use of your time, sir.

HORNER: I tell thee, I am now no more interruption to 'em when they sing or talk bawdy than a little squab[5] French page who speaks no English.

QUACK: But do civil persons and women of honor drink and sing bawdy songs?

HORNER: O, amongst friends, amongst friends. For your bigots in honor are just like those in religion; they fear the eye of the world more than the eye of Heaven and think there is no virtue but railing at vice and no sin but giving scandal. They rail at a poor, little, kept player and keep themselves some young, modest pulpit comedian[6] to be privy to their sins in their closets, not to tell 'em of them in their chapels.

QUACK: Nay, the truth on't is, priests among the women now have quite got the better of us lay confessors, physicians.

HORNER: And they are rather their patients, but—[*Enter Lady Fidget, looking about her.*] Now we talk of women of honor, here comes one. Step behind the screen there and but observe if I have not particular privileges with the women of reputation already, doctor, already.

[*Quack steps behind screen.*]

LADY FIDGET: Well, Horner, am not I a woman of honor? You see I'm as good as my word.

HORNER: And you shall see, madam, I'll not be behindhand with you in honor and I'll be as good as my word too, if you please but to withdraw into the next room.

LADY FIDGET: But first, my dear sir, you must promise to have a care of my dear honor.

HORNER: If you talk a word more of your honor, you'll make me incapable to wrong it. To talk of honor in the mysteries of love is like talking of heaven or the deity in an operation of witchcraft, just when you are employing the devil; it makes the charm impotent.

9. Progresses.
1. Designers, schemers.
2. Master.
3. Mattresses.

4. I.e., their underwear (which the wealthy wanted warmed before worn).
5. Short and stout.
6. Household chaplain.

LADY FIDGET: Nay, fie, let us not be smooty.[7] But you talk of mysteries and bewitching to me; I don't understand you.

HORNER: I tell you, madam, the word "money" in a mistress's mouth, at such a nick of time, is not a more disheartening sound to a younger brother[8] than that of "honor" to an eager lover like myself.

LADY FIDGET: But you can't blame a lady of my reputation to be chary.

HORNER: Chary! I have been chary of it already, by the report I have caused of myself.

LADY FIDGET: Ay, but if you should ever let other women know that dear secret, it would come out. Nay, you must have a great care of your conduct, for my acquaintance are so censorious (oh, 'tis a wicked, censorious world, Mr. Horner!), I say, are so censorious and detracting that perhaps they'll talk, to the prejudice of my honor, though you should not let them know the dear secret.

HORNER: Nay, madam, rather than they shall prejudice your honor, I'll prejudice theirs, and, to serve you, I'll lie with 'em all, make the secret their own, and then they'll keep it. I am a Machiavel in love, madam.

LADY FIDGET: Oh, no, sir, not that way.

HORNER: Nay, the devil take me if censorious women are to be silenced any other way.

LADY FIDGET: A secret is better kept, I hope, by a single person than a multitude; therefore pray do not trust anybody else with it, dear, dear Mr. Horner. [*Embracing him.*]

[*Enter Sir Jaspar Fidget.*]

SIR JASPAR: How now!

LADY FIDGET [*aside*]: Oh, my husband—prevented—and what's almost as bad, found with my arms about another man—that will appear too much—what shall I say?—Sir Jaspar, come hither, I am trying if Mr. Horner were ticklish, and he's as ticklish as can be; I love to torment the confounded toad. Let you and I tickle him.

SIR JASPAR: No, your ladyship will tickle him better without me, I suppose. But is this your buying china? I thought you had been at the china house.[9]

HORNER [*aside*]: China house! That's my cue, I must take it.—A pox, can't you keep your impertinent wives at home? Some men are troubled with the husbands, but I with the wives. But I'd have you to know, since I cannot be your journey-man[1] by night, I will not be your drudge by day, to squire your wife about and be your man of straw, or scarecrow, only to pies and jays,[2] that would be nibbling at your forbidden fruit; I shall be shortly the hackney gentleman-usher[3] of the town.

SIR JASPAR [*aside*]: Heh, heh, he! Poor fellow, he's in the right on't, faith; to squire women about for other folks is as ungrateful an employment as to tell[4] money for other folks.—Heh, he, he! Ben't angry, Horner—

LADY FIDGET: No, 'tis I have more reason to be angry, who am left by you to go abroad indecently alone; or, what is more indecent, to pin myself upon such ill-bred people of your acquaintance as this is.

SIR JASPAR: Nay, prithee, what has he done?

---

7. Smutty.
8. Because the eldest son inherited the estate, younger brothers typically lacked cash.
9. China shop, sometimes used by lovers as a secret meeting place.

1. One who works for another.
2. Crafty fellows and fools.
3. Hired escort.
4. Count.

LADY FIDGET: Nay, he has done nothing.

SIR JASPAR: But what d'ye take ill, if he has done nothing?

LADY FIDGET: Hah, hah, hah! Faith, I can't but laugh, however; why d'ye think the unmannerly toad would not come down to me to the coach? I was fain to come up to fetch him, or go without him, which I was resolved not to do, for he knows china very well and has himself very good, but will not let me see it lest I should beg some. But I will find it out and have what I came for yet.

[*Exit Lady Fidget and locks the door, followed by Horner to the door.*]

HORNER [*apart to Lady Fidget*]: Lock the door, madam.—So, she has got into my chamber, and locked me out. Oh, the impertinency of womankind! Well, Sir Jaspar, plain-dealing is a jewel; if ever you suffer your wife to trouble me again here, she shall carry you home a pair of horns, by my Lord Mayor she shall; though I cannot furnish you myself, you are sure, yet I'll find a way.

SIR JASPAR [*aside*]: Hah, ha, he! At my first coming in and finding her arms about him, tickling him it seems, I was half jealous, but now I see my folly.—Heh, he, he! Poor Horner.

HORNER: Nay, though you laugh now, 'twill be my turn ere long. Oh, women, more impertinent, more cunning and more mischievous than their monkeys,[5] and to me almost as ugly! Now is she throwing my things about and rifling all I have, but I'll get into her the back way and so rifle her for it.

SIR JASPAR: Hah, ha, ha, poor angry Horner.

HORNER: Stay here a little; I'll ferret her out to you presently, I warrant.

[*Exit Horner at t'other door.*]

SIR JASPAR: Wife! My Lady Fidget! Wife! He is coming into you the back way.
[*Sir Jaspar calls through the door to his wife; she answers from within.*]

LADY FIDGET: Let him come, and welcome, which way he will.

SIR JASPAR: He'll catch you and use you roughly and be too strong for you.

LADY FIDGET: Don't you trouble yourself; let him if he can.

QUACK [*behind*]: This indeed I could not have believed from him, nor any but my own eyes.

[*Enter Mrs. Squeamish.*]

SQUEAMISH: Where's this woman-hater, this toad, this ugly, greasy, dirty sloven?

SIR JASPAR [*aside*]: So, the women all will have him ugly; methinks he is a comely person, but his wants make his form contemptible to 'em and 'tis e'en as my wife said yesterday, talking of him, that a proper handsome eunuch was as ridiculous a thing as a gigantic coward.

SQUEAMISH: Sir Jaspar, your servant. Where is the odious beast?

SIR JASPAR: He's within in his chamber, with my wife; she's playing the wag with him.

SQUEAMISH: Is she so? And he's a clownish beast, he'll give her no quarter;[6] he'll play the wag with her again, let me tell you. Come, let's go help her.—What, the door's locked?

SIR JASPAR: Ay, my wife locked it.

SQUEAMISH: Did she so? Let us break it open then.

SIR JASPAR: No, no, he'll do her no hurt.

SQUEAMISH: No. [*Aside.*]But is there no other way to get in to 'em? Whither goes this? I will disturb 'em. [*Exit Squeamish at another door.*]

---

5. Which ladies sometimes kept as pets.   6. No mercy.

OLD LADY SQUEAMISH: Where is this harlotry, this impudent baggage, this rambling tomrig?[7] O Sir Jaspar, I'm glad to see you here. Did you not see my vild[8] grandchild come in hither just now?

SIR JASPAR: Yes.

OLD LADY SQUEAMISH: Ay, but where is she then? Where is she? Lord, Sir Jaspar, I have e'en rattled myself to pieces in pursuit of her. But can you tell what she makes here? They say below, no woman lodges here.

SIR JASPAR: No.

OLD LADY SQUEAMISH: No! What does she here then? Say, if it be not a woman's lodging, what makes she here? But are you sure no woman lodges here?

SIR JASPAR: No, nor no man neither; this is Mr. Horner's lodging.

OLD LADY SQUEAMISH: Is it so, are you sure?

SIR JASPAR: Yes, yes.

OLD LADY SQUEAMISH: So then there's no hurt in't, I hope. But where is he?

SIR JASPAR: He's in the next room with my wife.

OLD LADY SQUEAMISH: Nay, if you trust him with your wife, I may with my Biddy.[9] They say he's a merry harmless man now, e'en as harmless a man as ever came out of Italy with a good voice,[1] and as pretty harmless company for a lady as a snake without his teeth.

SIR JASPAR: Ay, ay, poor man.

[Enter Mrs. Squeamish.]

SQUEAMISH: I can't find 'em.—Oh, are you here, Grandmother? I followed, you must know, my Lady Fidget hither; 'tis the prettiest lodging and I have been staring on the prettiest pictures.

[Enter Lady Fidget with a piece of china in her hand, and Horner following.]

LADY FIDGET: And I have been toiling and moiling[2] for the prettiest piece of china, my dear.

HORNER: Nay, she has been too hard for me, do what I could.

SQUEAMISH: O Lord, I'll have some china too. Good Mr. Horner, don't think to give other people china and me none; come in with me too.

HORNER: Upon my honor, I have none left now.

SQUEAMISH: Nay, nay, I have known you deny your china before now, but you shan't put me off so. Come—

HORNER: This lady had the last there.

LADY FIDGET: Yes, indeed, madam, to my certain knowledge he has no more left.

SQUEAMISH: O, but it may be he may have some you could not find.

LADY FIDGET: What, d'ye think if he had had any left, I would not have had it too? For we women of quality never think we have china enough.

HORNER: Do not take it ill. I cannot make china for you all, but I will have a rollwagon[3] for you too, another time.

SQUEAMISH: Thank you, dear toad.

LADY FIDGET [to Horner aside]: What do you mean by that promise?

HORNER [apart to Lady Fidget]: Alas, she has an innocent, literal understanding.

7. Strumpet.
8. Vile.
9. Abbreviation of Bridget; also, a general term for a young woman.
1. I.e., as a castrato, a male singer castrated in boyhood so as to preserve his soprano voice.
2. Working hard.
3. A cylindrical vase; here (of course) with phallic connotations.

OLD LADY SQUEAMISH: Poor Mr. Horner, he has enough to do to please you all, I see.

HORNER: Ay, madam, you see how they use me.

OLD LADY SQUEAMISH: Poor gentleman, I pity you.

HORNER: I thank you, madam. I could never find pity but from such reverend ladies as you are; the young ones will never spare a man.

SQUEAMISH: Come, come, beast, and go dine with us, for we shall want a man at ombre after dinner.

HORNER: That's all their use of me, madam, you see.

SQUEAMISH: Come, sloven, I'll lead you, to be sure of you: [*Pulls him by the cravat.*]

OLD LADY SQUEAMISH: Alas, poor man, how she tugs him! Kiss, kiss her; that's the way to make such nice[4] women quiet.

HORNER: No, madam, that remedy is worse than the torment; they know I dare suffer anything rather than do it.

OLD LADY SQUEAMISH: Prithee, kiss her and I'll give you her picture in little,[5] that you admired so last night; prithee do.

HORNER: Well, nothing but that could bribe me; I love a woman only in effigy and good painting, as much as I hate them. I'll do't, for I could adore the devil well painted. [*Kisses Mrs. Squeamish.*]

SQUEAMISH: Foh, you filthy toad! Nay, now I've done jesting.

OLD LADY SQUEAMISH: Ha, ha, ha, I told you so.

SQUEAMISH: Foh, a kiss of his—

SIR JASPAR: Has no more hurt in't than one of my spaniel's.

SQUEAMISH: Nor no more good neither.

QUACK [*behind*]: I will now believe anything he tells me.

[*Enter Mr. Pinchwife.*]

LADY FIDGET: O Lord, here's a man! Sir Jaspar, my mask, my mask! I would not be seen here for the world.

SIR JASPAR: What, not when I am with you?

LADY FIDGET: No, no, my honor—let's be gone.

SQUEAMISH: Oh, Grandmother, let us be gone; make haste, make haste, I know not how he may censure us.

LADY FIDGET: Be found in the lodging of anything like a man! Away!

[*Exeunt Sir Jaspar, Lady Fidget, Old Lady Squeamish, Mrs. Squeamish.*]

QUACK [*behind*]: What's here? Another cuckold? He looks like one, and none else sure have any business with him.

HORNER: Well, what brings my dear friend hither?

PINCHWIFE: Your impertinency.

HORNER: My impertinency!—Why, you gentlemen that have got handsome wives think you have a privilege of saying anything to your friends and are as brutish as if you were our creditors.

PINCHWIFE: No, sir, I'll ne'er trust you any way.

HORNER: But why not, dear Jack? Why diffide[6] in me thou knowest so well?

PINCHWIFE: Because I do know you so well.

HORNER: Han't I been always thy friend, honest Jack, always ready to serve thee, in love or battle, before thou wert married, and am so still?

PINCHWIFE: I believe so; you would be my second now indeed.

---

4. Fastidious; also, in an older sense, wanton.
5. Miniature.

6. Distrust.

HORNER: Well then, dear Jack, why so unkind, so grum, so strange to me? Come, prithee kiss me, dear rogue. Gad, I was always, I say, and am still as much thy servant as—

PINCHWIFE: As I am yours, sir. What, you would send a kiss to my wife, is that it?

HORNER: So, there 'tis—a man can't show his friendship to a married man but presently he talks of his wife to you. Prithee, let thy wife alone and let thee and I be all one, as we were wont. What, thou art as shy of my kindness as a Lombard Street[7] alderman of a courtier's civility at Locket's.[8]

PINCHWIFE: But you are overkind to me, as kind as if I were your cuckold already; yet I must confess you ought to be kind and civil to me, since I am so kind, so civil to you, as to bring you this. Look you there, sir. [*Delivers him a letter.*]

HORNER: What is't?

PINCHWIFE: Only a love-letter, sir.

HORNER: From whom?—how! this is from your wife—hum—and hum—[*Reads.*]

PINCHWIFE: Even from my wife, sir. Am I not wondrous kind and civil to you now too? [*Aside.*] But you'll not think her so.

HORNER [*aside*]: Ha, is this a trick of his or hers?

PINCHWIFE: The gentleman's surprised, I find. What, you expected a kinder letter?

HORNER: No, faith, not I, how could I?

PINCHWIFE: Yes, yes, I'm sure you did; a man so well made as you are must needs be disappointed if the women declare not their passion at first sight or opportunity.

HORNER [*aside*]: But what should this mean? Stay, the postscript. [*Reads aside.*] "Be sure you love me, whatsoever my husband says to the contrary, and let him not see this, lest he should come home and pinch me, or kill my squirrel.[9]" [*Aside.*] It seems he knows not what the letter contains.

PINCHWIFE: Come, ne'er wonder at it so much.

HORNER: Faith, I can't help it.

PINCHWIFE: Now, I think, I have deserved your infinite friendship and kindness and have showed myself sufficiently an obliging kind friend and husband; am I not so, to bring a letter from my wife to her gallant?

HORNER: Ay, the devil take me, art thou the most obliging, kind friend and husband in the world, ha, ha!

PINCHWIFE: Well, you may be merry, sir; but in short I must tell you, sir, my honor will suffer no jesting.

HORNER: What dost thou mean?

PINCHWIFE: Does the letter want a comment? Then know, sir, though I have been so civil a husband as to bring you a letter from my wife, to let you kiss and court her to my face, I will not be a cuckold, sir, I will not.

HORNER: Thou art mad with jealousy. I never saw thy wife in my life but at the play yesterday, and I know not if it were she or no. I court her, kiss her!

PINCHWIFE: I will not be a cuckold, I say; there will be danger in making me a cuckold.

HORNER: Why, wert thou not well cured of thy last clap?

PINCHWIFE: I wear a sword.

HORNER: It should be taken from thee lest thou shouldst do thyself a mischief with it; thou art mad, man.

---

7. Banking center of London
8. In Charing Cross, a celebrated restaurant and popular

post-theater meeting place.
9. A fashionable pet.

2338   William Wycherley

PINCHWIFE: As mad as I am, and as merry as you are, I must have more reason from you ere we part. I say again, though you kissed and courted last night my wife in man's clothes, as she confesses in her letter—

HORNER [aside]: Ha!

PINCHWIFE: Both she and I say, you must not design it again, for you have mistaken your woman, as you have done your man.

HORNER [aside]: Oh—I understand something now.—Was that thy wife? Why wouldst thou not tell me 'twas she? Faith, my freedom with her was your fault, not mine.

PINCHWIFE [aside]: Faith, so 'twas.

HORNER: Fie, I'd never do't to a woman before her husband's face, sure.

PINCHWIFE: But I had rather you should do't to my wife before my face than behind my back, and that you shall never do.

HORNER: No—you will hinder me.

PINCHWIFE: If I would not hinder you, you see by her letter, she would.

HORNER: Well, I must e'en acquiesce then and be contented with what she writes.

PINCHWIFE: I'll assure you 'twas voluntarily writ; I had no hand in't, you may believe me.

HORNER: I do believe thee, faith.

PINCHWIFE: And believe her too, for she's an innocent creature, has no dissembling in her; and so fare you well, sir.

HORNER: Pray, however, present my humble service to her and tell her I will obey her letter to a tittle and fulfill her desires, be what they will, or with what difficulty soever I do't, and you shall be no more jealous of me, I warrant her and you.

PINCHWIFE: Well, then, fare you well, and play with any man's honor but mine, kiss any man's wife but mine, and welcome. [Exit Mr. Pinchwife.]

HORNER: Ha, ha, ha, doctor.

QUACK: It seems he has not heard the report of you, or does not believe it.

HORNER: Ha, ha! Now, doctor, what think you?

QUACK: Pray let's see the letter—hum—[Reads the letter.] "for—dear—love you—"

HORNER: I wonder how she could contrive it! What say'st thou to't? 'Tis an original.

QUACK: So are your cuckolds, too, originals, for they are like no other common cuckolds, and I will henceforth believe it not impossible for you to cuckold the Grand Signior[1] amidst his guards of eunuchs, that I say.

HORNER: And I say for the letter, 'tis the first love-letter that ever was without flames, darts, fates, destinies, lying and dissembling in't.

[Enter Sparkish, pulling in Mr. Pinchwife.]

SPARKISH: Come back, you are a pretty brother-in-law, neither go to church, nor to dinner with your sister bride!

PINCHWIFE: My sister denies her marriage and you see is gone away from you dissatisfied.

SPARKISH: Pshaw, upon a foolish scruple, that our parson was not in lawful orders and did not say all the Common Prayer; but 'tis her modesty only, I believe. But let women be never so modest the first day, they'll be sure to come to themselves by night, and I shall have enough of her then. In the meantime, Harry Horner, you must dine with me; I keep my wedding at my aunt's in the Piazza.[2]

---

1. Sultan of Turkey, whose eunuchs guarded his harem.   2. An elegant arcade near Covent Garden; Act 5, Scene 3 is set there.

HORNER: Thy wedding! What stale maid has lived to despair of a husband, or what young one of a gallant?

SPARKISH: Oh, your servant, sir—this gentleman's sister then—no stale maid.

HORNER: I'm sorry for't.

PINCHWIFE [aside]: How comes he so concerned for her?

SPARKISH: You sorry for't? Why, do you know any ill by her?

HORNER: No, I know none but by thee; 'tis for her sake, not yours, and another man's sake that might have hoped, I thought.

SPARKISH: Another man, another man! What is his name?

HORNER: Nay, since 'tis past he shall be nameless. [Aside.] Poor Harcourt, I am sorry thou hast missed her.

PINCHWIFE [aside]: He seems to be much troubled at the match.

SPARKISH: Prithee tell me—nay, you shan't go, brother.

PINCHWIFE: I must of necessity, but I'll come to you to dinner.   [Exit Pinchwife.]

SPARKISH: But, Harry, what, have I a rival in my wife already? But with all my heart, for he may be of use to me hereafter, for though my hunger is now my sauce and I can fall on heartily without, but the time will come when a rival will be as good sauce for a married man to a wife as an orange to veal.

HORNER: O thou damned rogue! Thou hast set my teeth on edge with thy orange.

SPARKISH: Then let's to dinner—there I was with[3] you again. Come.

HORNER: But who dines with thee?

SPARKISH: My friends and relations, my brother Pinchwife, you see, of your acquaintance.

HORNER: And his wife?

SPARKISH: No, gad, he'll ne'er let her come amongst us good fellows. Your stingy country coxcomb keeps his wife from friends, as he does his little firkin[4] of ale for his own drinking, and a gentleman can't get a smack[5] on't; but his servants, when his back is turned, broach[6] it at their pleasures and dust it away,[7] ha, ha, ha! Gad, I am witty, I think, considering I was married today, by the world. But come—

HORNER: No, I will not dine with you, unless you can fetch her too.

SPARKISH: Pshaw, what pleasure canst thou have with women now, Harry?

HORNER: My eyes are not gone; I love a good prospect yet and will not dine with you unless she does too. Go fetch her, therefore, but do not tell her husband 'tis for my sake.

SPARKISH: Well, I'll try what I can do. In the mean-time come away to my aunt's lodging; 'tis in the way to Pinchwife's.

HORNER: The poor woman has called for aid and stretched forth her hand, doctor; I cannot but help her over the pale[8] out of the briars.

[Exeunt Sparkish, Horner, Quack.]

Scene 4

[The scene changes to Pinchwife's house. Mrs. Pinchwife alone, leaning on her elbow. A table, pen, ink and paper.]

MRS. PINCHWIFE: Well, 'tis e'en so, I have got the London disease they call love; I am sick of my husband and for my gallant. I have heard this distemper[9] called a

3. Caught.
4. Small cask.
5. Taste.
6. Tap.

7. Finish it off.
8. Fence; here, figuratively, the constraints of marital fidelity.
9. Disease.

fever, but methinks 'tis liker an ague, for when I think of my husband, I tremble and am in a cold sweat and have inclinations to vomit but when I think of my gallant, dear Mr. Horner, my hot fit comes and I am all in a fever, indeed, and as in other fevers my own chamber is tedious to me and I would fain be removed to his and then methinks I should be well. Ah, poor Mr. Horner! Well, I cannot, will not stay here; therefore I'd make an end of my letter to him, which shall be a finer letter than my last, because I have studied it like anything. O, sick, sick! [*Takes the pen and writes.*]

[*Enter Mr. Pinchwife, who, seeing her writing, steals softly behind her and, looking over her shoulder, snatches the paper from her.*]

PINCHWIFE: What, writing more letters?

MRS. PINCHWIFE: O Lord, bud, why d'ye fright me so?

[*She offers to run out; he stops her and reads.*]

PINCHWIFE: How's this! Nay, you shall not stir, madam. "Dear, dear, dear Mr. Horner"—very well—I have taught you to write letters to good purpose—but let's see't. "First, I am to beg your pardon for my boldness in writing to you, which I'd have you to know I would not have done had not you said first you loved me so extremely, which if you do, you will never suffer me to lie in the arms of another man, whom I loathe, nauseate and detest."—Now you can write these filthy words. But what follows?—"Therefore I hope you will speedily find some way to free me from this unfortunate match, which was never, I assure you, of my choice, but I'm afraid 'tis already too far gone. However, if you love me, as I do you, you will try what you can do, but you must help me away before tomorrow, or else, alas, I shall be forever out of your reach, for I can defer no longer our—our" [*The letter concludes.*]—What is to follow "our"?—Speak, what? Our journey into the country, I suppose—Oh, woman, damned woman and love, damned love, their old tempter! For this is one of his miracles; in a moment he can make all those blind that could see and those see that were blind, those dumb that could speak and those prattle who were dumb before; nay, what is more than all, make these dough-baked,[1] senseless, indocile animals, women, too hard for us, their politic[2] lords and rulers, in a moment. But make an end of your letter and then I'll make an end of you thus, and all my plagues together. [*Draws his sword.*]

MRS. PINCHWIFE: O Lord, O Lord, you are such a passionate man, bud!

[*Enter Sparkish.*]

SPARKISH: How now, what's here to do?

PINCHWIFE: This fool here now!

SPARKISH: What, drawn upon your wife? You should never do that but at night in the dark, when you can't hurt her. This is my sister-in-law, is it not? [*Pulls aside her handkerchief.*] Ay, faith, e'en our country Margery; one may know her. Come, she and you must go dine with me; dinner's ready, come. But where's my wife? Is she not come home yet? Where is she?

PINCHWIFE: Making you a cuckold; 'tis that they all do, as soon as they can.

SPARKISH: What, the wedding day? No, a wife that designs to make a cully[3] of her husband will be sure to let him win the first stake of love, by the world. But come, they stay dinner for us. Come, I'll lead down our Margery.

PINCHWIFE: No—sir, go, we'll follow you.

SPARKISH: I will not wag[4] without you.

---

1. Half-baked, feeble-minded.
2. Sagacious, judicious.

3. Dupe, gull.
4. Stir.

PINCHWIFE [aside]: This coxcomb is a sensible[5] torment to me amidst the greatest in the world.

SPARKISH: Come, come, Madam Margery.

PINCHWIFE: No, I'll lead her my way. What, would you treat your friends with mine, for want of your own wife? [Leads her to t'other door and locks her in and returns. Aside.] I am contented my rage should take breath.

SPARKISH [aside]: I told Horner this.

PINCHWIFE: Come now.

SPARKISH: Lord, how shy[6] you are of your wife! But let me tell you, brother, we men of wit have amongst us a saying that cuckolding, like the smallpox, comes with a fear, and you may keep your wife as much as you will out of danger of infection but if her constitution incline her to't, she'll have it sooner or later, by the world, say they.

PINCHWIFE [aside]: What a thing is a cuckold, that every fool can make him ridiculous!—Well, sir—but let me advise you, now you are come to be concerned, because you suspect the danger, not to neglect the means to prevent it, especially when the greatest share of the malady will light upon your own head, for—

Hows'e'er the kind wife's belly comes to swell,
The husband breeds for her[7] and first is ill.

[Exeunt Pinchwife and Sparkish.]

ACT 5

Scene 1

[Mr. Pinchwife's house. Enter Mr. Pinchwife and Mrs. Pinchwife. A table and candle.]

PINCHWIFE: Come, take the pen and make an end of the letter, just as you intended; if you are false in a tittle, I shall soon perceive it and punish you with this as you deserve. [Lays his hand on his sword.] Write what was to follow—let's see— "You must make haste and help me away before tomorrow, or else I shall be forever out of your reach, for I can defer no longer our—" What follows "our"?

MRS. PINCHWIFE: Must all out then, bud? [Mrs. Pinchwife takes the pen and writes.] Look you there then.

PINCHWIFE: Let's see—"For I can defer no longer our—wedding—Your slighted Alithea."—What's the meaning of this? My sister's name to't. Speak, unriddle!

MRS. PINCHWIFE: Yes, indeed, bud.

PINCHWIFE: But why her name to't? Speak—speak, I say!

MRS. PINCHWIFE: Ay, but you'll tell her then again; if you would not tell her again—

PINCHWIFE: I will not—I am stunned, my head turns round. Speak.

MRS. PINCHWIFE: Won't you tell her, indeed, and indeed?

PINCHWIFE: No, speak, I say.

MRS. PINCHWIFE: She'll be angry with me, but I had rather she should be angry with me than you, bud; and to tell you the truth, 'twas she made me write the letter and taught me what I should write.

---

5. Keenly felt.
6. Distrustful.

7. Grows cuckold's horns in consequence of her behavior.

PINCHWIFE [*aside*]: Ha! I thought the style was somewhat better than her own.—
But how could she come to you to teach you, since I had locked you up alone?

MRS. PINCHWIFE: O, through the keyhole, bud.

PINCHWIFE: But why should she make you write a letter for her to him, since she
can write herself?

MRS. PINCHWIFE: Why, she said because—for I was unwilling to do it.

PINCHWIFE: Because what—because?

MRS. PINCHWIFE: Because, lest Mr. Horner should be cruel and refuse her or
vain afterwards and show the letter, she might disown it, the hand not being hers.

PINCHWIFE [*aside*]: How's this? Ha!—then I think I shall come to myself again.
This changeling could not invent this lie; but if she could, why should she? She
might think I should soon discover it—stay—now I think on't too, Horner said he
was sorry she had married Sparkish, and her disowning her marriage to me makes
me think she has evaded it for Horner's sake. Yet why should she take this course?
But men in love are fools; women may well be so.—But hark you, madam, your
sister went out in the morning and I have not seen her within since.

MRS. PINCHWIFE: Alackaday, she has been crying all day above, it seems, in a
corner.

PINCHWIFE: Where is she? Let me speak with her.

MRS. PINCHWIFE [*aside*]: O Lord, then he'll discover all!—Pray hold, bud. What,
d'ye mean to discover me? She'll know I have told you then. Pray, bud, let me talk
with her first.

PINCHWIFE: I must speak with her, to know whether Horner ever made her any
promise and whether she be married to Sparkish or no.

MRS. PINCHWIFE: Pray, dear bud, don't, till I have spoken with her and told her
that I have told you all, for she'll kill me else.

PINCHWIFE: Go then, and bid her come out to me.

MRS. PINCHWIFE: Yes, yes, bud.

PINCHWIFE: Let me see—

MRS. PINCHWIFE [*aside*]: I'll go, but she is not within to come to him. I have just
got time to know of Lucy her maid, who first set me on work, what lie I shall tell
next, for I am e'en at my wit's end.   [*Exit Mrs. Pinchwife.*]

PINCHWIFE: Well, I resolve it; Horner shall have her. I'd rather give him my sister
than lend him my wife and such an alliance will prevent his pretensions to my
wife, sure. I'll make him of kin to her and then he won't care for her.

[*Mrs. Pinchwife returns.*]

MRS. PINCHWIFE: O Lord, bud, I told you what anger you would make me with
my sister.

PINCHWIFE: Won't she come hither?

MRS. PINCHWIFE: No, no, alackaday, she's ashamed to look you in the face, and
she says, if you go in to her, she'll run away downstairs and shamefully go herself to
Mr. Horner, who has promised her marriage, she says, and she will have no other,
so she won't—

PINCHWIFE: Did he so—promise her marriage—then she shall have no other. Go
tell her so, and if she will come and discourse with me a little concerning the
means, I will about it immediately. Go.   [*Exit Mrs. Pinchwife.*]
His estate is equal to Sparkish's, and his extraction as much better than his as his
parts are; but my chief reason is, I'd rather be of kin to him by the name of brother-in-law than that of cuckold.

[*Enter Mrs. Pinchwife.*]

Well, what says she now?

MRS. PINCHWIFE: Why, she says she would only have you lead her to Horner's lodging—with whom she first will discourse the matter before she talk with you, which yet she cannot do, for alack, poor creature, she says she can't so much as look you in the face, therefore she'll come to you in a mask, and you must excuse her if she make you no answer to any question of yours, till you have brought her to Mr. Horner, and if you will not chide her, nor question her, she'll come out to you immediately.

PINCHWIFE: Let her come. I will not speak a word to her, nor require a word from her.

MRS. PINCHWIFE: Oh, I forgot; besides, she says, she cannot look you in the face though through a mask, therefore would desire you to put out the candle.

PINCHWIFE: I agree to all; let her make haste—there, 'tis out. [*Puts out the candle.*]

[*Exit Mrs. Pinchwife.*]

My case is something better. I'd rather fight with Horner for not lying with my sister than for lying with my wife, and of the two I had rather find my sister too forward than my wife; I expected no other from her free education, as she calls it, and her passion for the town. Well—wife and sister are names which make us expect love and duty, pleasure and comfort, but we find 'em plagues and torments, and are equally, though differently, troublesome to their keeper, for we have as much ado to get people to lie with our sisters as to keep 'em frm lying with our wives.

[*Enter Mrs. Pinchwife masked and in hoods and scarves, and a nightgown[1] and petticoat of Alithea's, in the dark.*]

What, are you come, sister? Let us go then—but first let me lock up my wife.— Mrs. Margery, where are you?

MRS. PINCHWIFE: Here, bud.

PINCHWIFE: Come hither, that I may lock you up; get you in. [*Locks the door.*] Come, sister, where are you now?

[*Mrs. Pinchwife gives him her hand but, when he lets her go, she steals softly on t'other side of him, and is led away by him for his sister Alithea.*]

Scene 2

[*The scene changes to Horner's lodging. Quack, Horner.*]

QUACK: What, all alone? Not so much as one of your cuckolds here, nor one of their wives! They use to take their turns with you, as if they were to watch you.

HORNER: Yes, it often happens that a cuckold is but his wife's spy and is more upon family duty when he is with her gallant abroad, hindering his pleasure, than when he is at home with her, playing the gallant. But the hardest duty a married woman imposes upon a lover is keeping her husband company always.

QUACK: And his fondness wearies you almost as soon as hers.

HORNER: A pox, keeping a cuckold company, after you have had his wife, is as tiresome as the company of a country squire to a witty fellow of the town, when he has got all his money.

QUACK: And as at first a man makes a friend of the husband to get the wife, so at last you are fain to fall out with the wife to be rid of the husband.

1. A loose gown, usually (but not exclusively) worn at night.

HORNER: Ay, most cuckold-makers are true courtiers; when once a poor man has cracked[2] his credit for 'em, they can't abide to come near him.

QUACK: But at first, to draw him in, are so sweet, so kind, so dear, just as you are to Pinchwife. But what becomes of that intrigue with his wife?

HORNER: A pox, he's as surly as an alderman that has been bit[3] and, since he's so coy, his wife's kindness is in vain, for she's a silly innocent.

QUACK: Did she not send you a letter by him?

HORNER: Yes, but that's a riddle I have not yet solved. Allow the poor creature to be willing, she is silly too, and he keeps her up so close—

QUACK: Yes, so close that he makes her but the more willing and adds but revenge to her love, which two, when met, seldom fail of satisfying each other one way or other.

HORNER: What, here's the man we are talking of, I think.

[*Enter Mr. Pinchwife, leading in his wife masked, muffled, and in her sister's gown.*]
Pshaw!

QUACK: Bringing his wife to you is the next thing to bringing a love-letter from her.

HORNER: What means this?

PINCHWIFE: The last time, you know, sir, I brought you a love-letter; now, you see, a mistress. I think you'll say I am a civil man to you.

HORNER: Ay, the devil take me, will I say thou art the civilest man I ever met with, and I have known some! I fancy I understand thee now better than I did the letter. But hark thee, in thy ear—

PINCHWIFE: What?

HORNER: Nothing but the usual question, man: is she sound,[4] on thy word?

PINCHWIFE: What, you take her for a wench and me for a pimp?

HORNER: Pshaw, wench and pimp, paw[5] words. I know thou art an honest fellow and hast a great acquaintance among the ladies and perhaps hast made love for me rather than let me make love to thy wife—

PINCHWIFE: Come, sir, in short, I am for no fooling.

HORNER: Nor I neither; therefore, prithee, let's see her face presently. Make her show, man. Art thou sure I don't know her?

PINCHWIFE: I am sure you do know her.

HORNER: A pox, why dost thou bring her to me then?

PINCHWIFE: Because she's a relation of mine.

HORNER: Is she, faith, man? Then thou art still more civil and obliging, dear rogue.

PINCHWIFE: Who desired me to bring her to you.

HORNER: Then she is obliging, dear rogue.

PINCHWIFE: You'll make her welcome for my sake, I hope.

HORNER: I hope she is handsome enough to make herself welcome. Prithee, let her unmask.

PINCHWIFE: Do you speak to her; she would never be ruled by me.

HORNER: Madam—

[*Mrs. Pinchwife whispers to Horner.*]
She says she must speak with me in private. Withdraw, prithee.

PINCHWIFE [*aside*]: She's unwilling, it seems, I should know all her undecent conduct in this business.—Well then, I'll leave you together and hope when I am gone you'll agree; if not, you and I shan't agree, sir.

---

2. Ruined.
3. A city official who's been tricked.

4. Free from venereal disease.
5. Naughty.

SPARKISH: Indeed, she would needs have it that 'twas Harcourt himself in a parson's habit that married us, but I'm sure he told me 'twas his brother Ned.

PINCHWIFE: Oh, there 'tis out, and you were deceived, not she, for you are such a frank person—but I must be gone. You'll find her at Mr. Horner's; go and believe your eyes. [Exit Mr. Pinchwife.]

SPARKISH: Nay, I'll to her and call her as many crocodiles, sirens, harpies and other heathenish names as a poet would do a mistress who had refused to hear his suit, nay more, his verses on her.—But stay, is not that she following a torch at t'other end of the Piazza? And from Horner's certainly—'tis so.

[Enter Alithea, following a torch,[7] and Lucy behind.]

You are well met, madam, though you don't think so. What, you have made a short visit to Mr. Horner, but I suppose you'll return to him presently; by that time the parson can be with him.

ALITHEA: Mr. Horner, and the parson, sir!

SPARKISH: Come, madam, no more dissembling, no more jilting, for I am no more a frank person.

ALITHEA: How's this?

LUCY [aside]: So, 'twill work, I see.

SPARKISH: Could you find out no easy country fool to abuse? None but me, a gentleman of wit and pleasure about the town? But it was your pride to be too hard for a man of parts, unworthy false woman, false as a friend that lends a man money to lose, false as dice who undo those that trust all they have to 'em.

LUCY [aside]: He has been a great bubble by his similes, as they say.

ALITHEA: You have been too merry, sir, at your wedding dinner, sure.

SPARKISH: What, d'ye mock me too?

ALITHEA: Or you have been deluded.

SPARKISH: By you.

ALITHEA: Let me understand you.

SPARKISH: Have you the confidence—I should call it something else, since you know your guilt—to stand my just reproaches? You did not write an impudent letter to Mr. Horner, who I find now has clubbed with you in deluding me with his aversion for women, that I might not, forsooth, suspect him for my rival.

LUCY [aside]: D'ye think the gentleman can be jealous now, madam?

ALITHEA: I write a letter to Mr. Horner!

SPARKISH: Nay, madam, do not deny it; your brother showed it me just now and told me likewise he left you at Horner's lodging to fetch a parson to marry you to him, and I wish you joy, madam, joy, joy, and to him too, much joy, and to myself more joy for not marrying you.

ALITHEA [aside]: So, I find my brother would break off the match, and I can consent to't, since I see this gentleman can be made jealous.—O Lucy, by his rude usage and jealousy, he makes me almost afraid I am married to him. Art thou sure 'twas Harcourt himself and no parson that married us?

SPARKISH: No, madam, I thank you. I suppose that was a contrivance too of Mr. Horner's and yours, to make Harcourt play the parson; but I would as little as you have him one now, no, not for the world, for shall I tell you another truth? I never had any passion for you till now, for now I hate you. 'Tis true I might have married your portion, as other men of parts of the town do sometimes, and so your servant,

7. A boy carrying a torch.

HORNER [aside]: What means the fool?—If she and I agree, 'tis no matter what you and I do.

[Whispers to Mrs. Pinchwife, who makes signs with her hand for him (Pinchwife) to be gone.]

PINCHWIFE: In the meantime, I'll fetch a parson and find out Sparkish and disabuse him. You would have me fetch a parson, would you not? Well then—now I think I am rid of her, and shall have no more trouble with her. Our sisters and daughters, like usurers' money, are safest when put out; but our wives, like their writings,[6] never safe but in our closets under lock and key.   [Exit Mr. Pinchwife.]
     [Enter Boy.]

BOY: Sir Jaspar Fidget, sir, is coming up.   [Exit.]

HORNER: Here's the trouble of a cuckold, now, we are talking of. A pox on him! Has he not enough to do to hinder his wife's sport but he must other women's too?—Step in here, madam.   [Exit Mrs. Pinchwife.]
     [Enter Sir Jaspar.]

SIR JASPAR: My best and dearest friend.

HORNER [aside to Quack]: The old style, doctor.—Well, be short, for I am busy. What would your impertinent wife have now?

SIR JASPAR: Well guessed, i'faith, for I do come from her.

HORNER: To invite me to supper. Tell her I can't come; go.

SIR JASPAR: Nay, now you are out, faith, for my lady and the whole knot of the virtuous gang, as they call themselves, are resolved upon a frolic of coming to you tonight in a masquerade and are all dressed already.

HORNER: I shan't be at home.

SIR JASPAR [aside]: Lord, how churlish he is to women!—Nay, prithee don't disappoint 'em; they'll think 'tis my fault. Prithee don't. I'll send in the banquet and the fiddles. But make no noise on't, for the poor virtuous rogues would not have it known for the world that they go a-masquerading, and they would come to no man's ball but yours.

HORNER: Well, well—get you gone and tell 'em, if they come, 'twill be at the peril of their honor and yours.

SIR JASPAR: Heh, he, he!—we'll trust you for that; farewell.   [Exit Sir Jaspar.]

HORNER: Doctor, anon you too shall be my guest, But now I'm going to a private feast.

                                                                          [Exeunt.]

Scene 3

[The scene changes to the Piazza of Covent Garden. Sparkish, Pinchwife.]

SPARKISH [with the letter in his hand]: But who would have thought a woman could have been false to me? By the world, I could not have thought it.

PINCHWIFE: You were for giving and taking liberty; she has taken it only, sir, now you find in that letter. You are a frank person and so is she you see there.

SPARKISH: Nay, if this be her hand—for I never saw it.

PINCHWIFE: 'Tis no matter whether that be her hand or no; I am sure this hand, at her desire, led her to Mr. Horner, with whom I left her just now, to go fetch a parson to 'em, at their desire too, to deprive you of her forever, for it seems yours was but a mock marriage.

6. Legal and financial documents.

and to show my unconcernedness, I'll come to your wedding and resign you with as much joy as I would a stale wench to a new cully, nay, with as much joy as I would after the first night, if I had been married to you. There's for you, and so your servant, servant. [Exit Sparkish.]

ALITHEA: How was I deceived in a man!

LUCY: You'll believe, then, a fool may be made jealous now? For that easiness in him that suffers him to be led by a wife will likewise permit him to be persuaded against her by others.

ALITHEA: But marry Mr. Horner! My brother does not intend it, sure; if I thought he did, I would take thy advice and Mr. Harcourt for my husband. And now I wish that if there be any over-wise woman of the town who, like me, would marry a fool for fortune, liberty or title; first, that her husband may love play and be a cully to all the town but her and suffer none but fortune to be mistress of his purse; then, if for liberty, that he may send her into the country under the conduct of some housewifely mother-in-law, and, if for title, may the world give 'em none but that of cuckold.

LUCY: And for her greater curse, madam, may he not deserve it.

ALITHEA: Away, impertinent!—Is not this my old Lady Lanterlu's?[8]

LUCY: Yes, madam. [Aside.] And here I hope we shall find Mr. Harcourt.

[Exeunt Alithea, Lucy.]

Scene 4

[The scene changes again to Horner's lodging. Horner, Lady Fidget, Mrs. Dainty Fidget, Mrs. Squeamish. A table, banquet, and bottles.]

HORNER [aside]: A pox! They are come too soon—before I have sent back my new— mistress. All I have now to do is to lock her in, that they may not see her.

LADY FIDGET: That we may be sure of our welcome, we have brought our entertainment with us and are resolved to treat thee, dear toad.

DAINTY: And that we may be merry to purpose, have left Sir Jaspar and my old Lady Squeamish quarrelling at home at backgammon.

SQUEAMISH: Therefore let us make use of our time, lest they should chance to interrupt us.

LADY FIDGET: Let us sit then.

HORNER: First, that you may be private, let me lock this door and that, and I'll wait upon you presently.

LADY FIDGET: No, sir, shut 'em only and your lips forever, for we must trust you as much as our women.

HORNER: You know all vanity's killed in me; I have no occasion for talking.

LADY FIDGET: Now, ladies, supposing we had drank each of us our two bottles, let us speak the truth of our hearts.

DAINTY:
SQUEAMISH: } Agreed.

LADY FIDGET: By this brimmer,[9] for truth is nowhere else to be found. [Aside to Horner.] Not in thy heart, false man!

HORNER [aside to Lady Fidget]: You have found me a true man, I'm sure.

LADY FIDGET [aside to Horner]: Not every way.—But let us sit and be merry. [Lady Fidget sings.]

8. The lady is comically named after a popular card game, "loo" for short.   9. Brimming cup.

1

Why should our damned tyrants oblige us to live
On the pittance of pleasure which they only give?
We must not rejoice
With wine and with noise.
5   In vain we must wake in a dull bed alone,
Whilst to our warm rival, the bottle, they're gone.
They lay aside charms
And take up these arms.[1]

2

'Tis wine only gives 'em their courage and wit;
10   Because we live sober, to men we submit.
If for beauties you'd pass,
Take a lick of the glass;
'Twill mend your complexions and, when they are gone,
The best red we have is the red of the grape.
15   Then, sisters, lay't on,
And damn a good shape.

DAINTY: Dear brimmer! Well, in token of our openness and plain-dealing, let us throw our masks over our heads.

HORNER: So, 'twill come to the glasses anon.

SQUEAMISH: Lovely brimmer! Let me enjoy him first.

LADY FIDGET: No, I never part with a gallant till I've tried him. Dear brimmer, that mak'st our husbands shortsighted.

DAINTY: And our bashful gallants bold.

SQUEAMISH: And for want of a gallant, the butler lovely in our eyes.—Drink, eunuch.

LADY FIDGET: Drink, thou representative of a husband. Damn a husband!

DAINTY: And, as it were a husband, an old keeper.

SQUEAMISH: And an old grandmother.

HORNER: And an English bawd and a French chirurgeon.[2]

LADY FIDGET: Ay, we have all reason to curse 'em.

HORNER: For my sake, ladies?

LADY FIDGET: No, for our own, for the first spoils all young gallants' industry.

DAINTY: And the other's art makes 'em bold only with common women.

SQUEAMISH: And rather run the hazard of the vile distemper amongst them than of a denial amongst us.

DAINTY: The filthy toads choose mistresses now as they do stuffs,[3] for having been fancied and worn by others.[4]

SQUEAMISH: For being common and cheap.

LADY FIDGET: Whilst women of quality, like the richest stuffs, lie untumbled and unasked for.

HORNER: Ay, neat and cheap and new often they think best.

DAINTY: No, sir, the beasts will be known by a mistress longer than by a suit.

1. I.e., the glasses.
2. The supposed causes of Horner's fictitious plight (see Act 1, scene 1, page 2291).
3. Garments.
4. Second-hand trade was commonplace in Restoration England.

SQUEAMISH: And 'tis not for cheapness neither.

LADY FIDGET: No, for the vain fops will take up druggets[5] and embroider 'em. But I wonder at the depraved appetites of witty men; they use to be out of the common road and hate imitation. Pray tell me, beast, when you were a man, why you rather chose to club with a multitude in a common house[6] for an entertainment than to be the only guest at a good table!

HORNER: Why, faith, ceremony and expectation are unsufferable to those that are sharp bent;[7] people always eat with the best stomach at an ordinary, where every man is snatching for the best bit.

LADY FIDGET: Though he get a cut over the fingers.—But I have heard people eat most heartily of another man's meat, that is, what they do not pay for.

HORNER: When they are sure of their welcome and freedom, for ceremony in love and eating is as ridiculous as in fighting; falling on briskly is all should be done in those occasions.

LADY FIDGET: Well, then, let me tell you, sir, there is nowhere more freedom than in our houses and we take freedom from a young person as a sign of good breeding, and a person may be as free as he pleases with us, as frolic, as gamesome, as wild as he will.

HORNER: Han't I heard you all declaim against wild men?

LADY FIDGET: Yes, but for all that, we think wildness in a man as desirable a quality as in a duck or rabbit; a tame man, foh!

HORNER: I know not, but your reputations frightened me, as much as your faces invited me.

LADY FIDGET: Our reputation! Lord, why should you not think that we women make use of our reputation, as you men of yours, only to deceive the world with less suspicion? Our virtue is like the statesman's religion, the Quaker's word, the gamester's oath and the great man's honor—but to cheat those that trust us.

SQUEAMISH: And that demureness, coyness and modesty that you see in our faces in the boxes at plays is as much a sign of a kind woman as a vizard-mask in the pit.

DAINTY: For, I assure you, women are least masked when they have the velvet vizard on.

LADY FIDGET: You would have found us modest women in our denials only.

SQUEAMISH: Our bashfulness is only the reflection of the men's.

DAINTY: We blush when they are shamefaced.

HORNER: I beg your pardon, ladies; I was deceived in you devilishly. But why that mighty pretense to honor?

LADY FIDGET: We have told you. But sometimes 'twas for the same reason you men pretend business often, to avoid ill company, to enjoy the better and more privately those you love.

HORNER: But why would you ne'er give a friend a wink then?

LADY FIDGET: Faith, your reputation frightened us as much as ours did you, you were so notoriously lewd.

HORNER: And you so seemingly honest.

LADY FIDGET: Was that all that deterred you?

HORNER: And so expensive—you allow freedom, you say—

LADY FIDGET: Ay, ay.

---

5. Cheap woolen fabric.   7. Hungry.
6. A restaurant or brothel.

HORNER: That I was afraid of losing my little money, as well as my little time, both which my other pleasures required.

LADY FIDGET: Money, foh! You talk like a little fellow now; do such as we expect money?

HORNER: I beg your pardon, madam; I must confess, I have heard that great ladies, like great merchants, set but the higher prizes[8] upon what they have, because they are not in necessity of taking the first offer.

DAINTY: Such as we make sale of our hearts?

SQUEAMISH: We bribed for our love? Foh!

HORNER: With your pardon, ladies, I know, like great men in offices, you seem to exact flattery and attendance only from your followers; but you have receivers[9] about you and such fees to pay, a man is afraid to pass your grants.[1] Besides, we must let you win at cards, or we lose your hearts, and if you make an assignation, 'tis at a goldsmith's, jeweller's or china house, where, for your honor you deposit to him, he must pawn his to the punctual cit, and so paying for what you take up, pays for what he takes up.[2]

DAINTY: Would you not have us assured of our gallant's love?

SQUEAMISH: For love is better known by liberality than by jealousy.

LADY FIDGET: For one may be dissembled, the other not. [Aside.] But my jealousy can be no longer dissembled, and they are telling ripe.[3]—Come, here's to our gallants in waiting, whom we must name, and I'll begin. This is my false rogue. [Claps him on the back.]

SQUEAMISH: How!

HORNER: So all will out now.

SQUEAMISH [aside to Horner]: Did you not tell me, 'twas for my sake only you reported yourself no man?

DAINTY [aside to Horner]: Oh, wretch! Did you not swear to me, 'twas for my love and honor you passed for that thing you do?

HORNER: So, so.

LADY FIDGET: Come, speak, ladies; this is my false villain.

SQUEAMISH: And mine too.

DAINTY: And mine.

HORNER: Well then, you are all three my false rogues too, and there's an end on't.

LADY FIDGET: Well then, there's no remedy; sister sharers, let us not fall out, but have a care of our honor. Though we get no presents, no jewels of him, we are savers of our honor, the jewel of most value and use, which shines yet to the world unsuspected, though it be counterfeit.

HORNER: Nay, and is e'en as good as if it were true, provided the world think so, for honor, like beauty now, only depends on the opinion of others.

LADY FIDGET: Well, Harry Common, I hope you can be true to three. Swear—but 'tis to no purpose to require your oath, for you are as often forsworn as you swear to new women.

HORNER: Come, faith, madam, let us e'en pardon one another, for all the difference I find betwixt we men and you women, we forswear ourselves at the beginning of an amour, you as long as it lasts.

8. Prices.
9. Collectors.
1. Accept your favors (because in the end they are so expensive).
2. I.e., you arrange to meet your lover at an expensive

shop, where he in effect pays for your favors by purchasing for you the shopkeeper's ("punctual cit's") costly merchandise.
3. Ripe for the telling.

[*Enter Sir Jaspar Fidget and Old Lady Squeamish.*]

SIR JASPAR: Oh, my Lady Fidget, was this your cunning, to come to Mr. Horner without me? But you have been nowhere else, I hope.

LADY FIDGET: No, Sir Jaspar.

OLD LADY SQUEAMISH: And you came straight hither, Biddy?

SQUEAMISH: Yes, indeed, Lady Grandmother.

SIR JASPAR: 'Tis well, 'tis well; I knew when once they were thoroughly acquainted with poor Horner, they'd ne'er be from him. You may let her masquerade it with my wife and Horner and I warrant her reputation safe.

[*Enter Boy.*]

BOY: Oh, sir, here's the gentleman come whom you bid me not suffer to come up without giving you notice, with a lady too, and other gentlemen—

HORNER: Do you all go in there, whilst I send 'em away, and, boy, do you desire 'em to stay below till I come, which shall be immediately.

[*Exeunt Sir Jaspar, Old Lady Squeamish, Lady Fidget, Mrs. Dainty, Squeamish.*]

BOY: Yes, sir.   [*Exit.*]

[*Exit Horner at t'other door and returns with Mrs. Pinchwife.*]

HORNER: You would not take my advice to be gone home before your husband came back; he'll now discover all. Yet pray, my dearest, be persuaded to go home and leave the rest to my management. I'll let you down the back way.

MRS. PINCHWIFE: I don't know the way home, so I don't.

HORNER: My man shall wait upon you.

MRS. PINCHWIFE: No, don't you believe that I'll go at all. What, are you weary of me already?

HORNER: No, my life, 'tis that I may love you long, 'tis to secure my love, and your reputation with your husband; he'll never receive you again else.

MRS. PINCHWIFE: What care I? D'ye think to frighten me with that? I don't intend to go to him again; you shall be my husband now.

HORNER: I cannot be your husband, dearest, since you are married to him.

MRS. PINCHWIFE: Oh, would you make me believe that? Don't I see every day, at London here, women leave their first husbands and go and live with other men as their wives? Pish, pshaw, you'd make me angry, but that I love you so mainly.[4]

HORNER: So, they are coming up—in again, in, I hear 'em.

[*Exit Mrs. Pinchwife.*]

Well, a silly mistress is like a weak place, soon got, soon lost, a man has scarce time for plunder; she betrays her husband first to her gallant and then her gallant to her husband.

[*Enter Pinchwife, Alithea, Harcourt, Sparkish, Lucy and a Parson.*]

PINCHWIFE: Come, madam, 'tis not the sudden change of your dress, the confidence of your asseverations and your false witness there, shall persuade me I did not bring you hither just now; here's my witness, who cannot deny it, since you must be confronted.—Mr. Horner, did not I bring this lady to you just now?

HORNER [*aside*]: Now must I wrong one woman for another's sake, but that's no new thing with me, for in these cases I am still on the criminal's side, against the innocent.

ALITHEA: Pray, speak, sir.

4. Mightily.

HORNER [*aside*]: It must be so—I must be impudent and try my luck; impudence uses to be too hard for truth.

PINCHWIFE: What, you are studying an evasion or excuse for her. Speak, sir.

HORNER: No, faith, I am something backward only to speak in women's affairs or disputes.

PINCHWIFE: She bids you speak.

ALITHEA: Ay, pray, sir, do; pray satisfy him.

HORNER: Then truly, you did bring that lady to me just now.

PINCHWIFE: O ho!

ALITHEA: How, sir!

HARCOURT: How, Horner!

ALITHEA: What mean you, sir? I always took you for a man of honor.

HORNER [*aside*]: Ay, so much a man of honor that I must save my mistress, I thank you, come what will on't.

SPARKISH: So, if I had had her, she'd have made me believe the moon had been made of a Christmas pie.

LUCY [*aside*]: Now could I speak, if I durst, and solve the riddle, who am the author of it.

ALITHEA: O unfortunate woman! A combination against my honor, which most concerns me now, because you share in my disgrace, sir, and it is your censure, which I must now suffer, that troubles me, not theirs.

HARCOURT: Madam, then have no trouble, you shall now see 'tis possible for me to love too, without being jealous; I will not only believe your innocence myself, but make all the world believe it. [*Apart to Horner.*] Horner, I must now be concerned for this lady's honor.

HORNER: And I must be concerned for a lady's honor too.

HARCOURT: This lady has her honor and I will protect it.

HORNER: My lady has not her honor but has given it me to keep and I will preserve it.

HARCOURT: I understand you not.

HORNER: I would not have you.

MRS. PINCHWIFE [*peeping in behind*]: What's the matter with 'em all?

PINCHWIFE: Come, come, Mr. Horner, no more disputing. Here's the parson; I brought him not in vain.

HARCOURT: No, sir, I'll employ him, if this lady please.

PINCHWIFE: How! What d'ye mean?

SPARKISH: Ay, what does he mean?

HORNER: Why, I have resigned your sister to him; he has my consent.

PINCHWIFE: But he has not mine, sir; a woman's injured honor, no more than a man's, can be repaired or satisfied by any but him that first wronged it; and you shall marry her presently, or—[*Lays his hand on his sword.*]
    [*Enter to them Mrs. Pinchwife.*]

MRS. PINCHWIFE [*aside*]: O Lord, they'll kill poor Mr. Horner! Besides, he shan't marry her whilst I stand by and look on; I'll not lose my second husband so.

PINCHWIFE: What do I see?

ALITHEA: My sister in my clothes!

SPARKISH: Ha!

MRS. PINCHWIFE [*to Mr. Pinchwife*]: Nay, pray now don't quarrel about finding work for the parson; he shall marry me to Mr. Horner, for now, I believe, you have enough of me.

HORNER: Damned, damned, loving changeling!

MRS. PINCHWIFE: Pray, sister, pardon me for telling so many lies of you.

HARCOURT: I suppose the riddle is plain now.

LUCY: No, that must be my work. Good sir, hear me.

[Kneels to Mr. Pinchwife, who stands doggedly, with his hat over his eyes.]

PINCHWIFE: I will never hear woman again, but make 'em all silent, thus—[Offers to draw upon his wife.]

HORNER: No, that must not be.

PINCHWIFE: You then shall go first; 'tis all one to me [Offers to draw on Horner; stopped by Harcourt.]

HARCOURT: Hold!

[Enter Sir Jaspar Fidget, Lady Fidget, Old Lady Squeamish, Mrs. Dainty Fidget, Mrs. Squeamish.]

SIR JASPAR: What's the matter, what's the matter, pray, what's the matter, sir? I beseech you communicate, sir.

PINCHWIFE: Why, my wife has communicated[5], sir, as your wife may have done too, sir, if she knows him, sir.

SIR JASPAR: Pshaw, with him? Ha, ha, he!

PINCHWIFE: D'ye mock me, sir? A cuckold is a kind of a wild beast; have a care, sir.

SIR JASPAR: No, sure, you mock me, sir—he cuckold you! It can't be, ha, ha, he! Why, I tell you, sir—[Offers to whisper.]

PINCHWIFE: I tell you again, he has whored my wife, and yours too, if he knows her, and all the women he comes near; 'tis not his dissembling, his hypocrisy can wheedle me.

SIR JASPAR: How! does he dissemble? Is he a hypocrite? Nay, then—how—wife—sister, is he an hypocrite?

OLD LADY SQUEAMISH: An hypocrite, a dissembler! Speak, young harlotry, speak, how?

SIR JASPAR: Nay, then—O, my head too!—O thou libidinous lady!

OLD LADY SQUEAMISH: O thou harloting harlotry! Hast thou done't then?

SIR JASPAR: Speak, good Horner, art thou a dissembler, a rogue? Hast thou—

HORNER: Soh—

LUCY [apart to Horner]: I'll fetch you off, and her too, if she will but hold her tongue.

HORNER [apart to Lucy]: Canst thou? I'll give thee—

LUCY [to Mr. Pinchwife]: Pray have but patience to hear me, sir, who am the unfortunate cause of all this confusion. Your wife is innocent, I only culpable, for I put her upon telling you all these lies concerning my mistress, in order to the breaking off the match between Mr. Sparkish and her, to make way for Mr. Harcourt.

SPARKISH: Did you so, eternal rotten tooth? Then, it seems, my mistress was not false to me, I was only deceived by you.—Brother that should have been, now man of conduct, who is a frank person now? To bring your wife to her lover—ha!

LUCY: I assure you, sir, she came not to Mr. Horner out of love, for she loves him no more—

MRS. PINCHWIFE: Hold, I told lies for you, but you shall tell none for me, for I do love Mr. Horner with all my soul, and nobody shall say me nay. Pray, don't you go to make poor Mr. Horner believe to the contrary; 'tis spitefully done of you, I'm sure.

5. Fornicated.

HORNER [*aside to Mrs. Pinchwife*]: Peace, dear idiot.

MRS. PINCHWIFE: Nay, I will not peace.

PINCHWIFE: Not till I make you.
  [*Enter Dorilant, Quack.*]

DORILANT: Horner, your servant; I am the doctor's guest, he must excuse our intrusion.

QUACK: But what's the matter, gentlemen? For heaven's sake, what's the matter?

HORNER: Oh, 'tis well you are come. 'Tis a censorious world we live in; you may have brought me a reprieve, or else I had died for a crime I never committed, and these innocent ladies had suffered with me. Therefore pray satisfy these worthy, honorable, jealous gentlemen—that—[*Whispers.*]

QUACK: O, I understand you; is that all? [*Whispers to Sir Jaspar.*] Sir Jaspar, by heavens and upon the word of a physician, sir—

SIR JASPAR: Nay, I do believe you truly.—Pardon me, my virtuous lady and dear of honor.

OLD LADY SQUEAMISH: What, then all's right again?

SIR JASPAR: Ay, ay, and now let us satisfy him too.
  [*They whisper with Mr. Pinchwife.*]

PINCHWIFE: An eunuch! Pray, no fooling with me.

QUACK: I'll bring half the chirurgeons in town to swear it.

PINCHWIFE: They!—they'll swear a man that bled to death through his wounds died of an apoplexy.[6]

QUACK: Pray hear me, sir—why, all the town has heard the report of him.

PINCHWIFE: But does all the town believe it?

QUACK: Pray inquire a little, and first of all these.

PINCHWIFE: I'm sure when I left the town he was the lewdest fellow in't.

QUACK: I tell you, sir, he has been in France since; pray, ask but these ladies and gentlemen, your friend Mr. Dorilant.—Gentlemen and ladies, han't you all heard the late sad report of poor Mr. Horner?

ALL THE LADIES: Ay, ay, ay.

DORILANT: Why, thou jealous fool, dost thou doubt it? He's an arrant French capon.[7]

MRS. PINCHWIFE: 'Tis false, sir, you shall not disparage poor Mr. Horner, for to my certain knowledge—

LUCY: Oh, hold!

SQUEAMISH [*aside to Lucy*]: Stop her mouth!

LADY FIDGET [*to Pinchwife*]: Upon my honor, sir, 'tis as true—

DAINTY: D'ye think we would have been seen in his company?

SQUEAMISH: Trust our unspotted reputations with him!

LADY FIDGET [*aside to Horner*]: This you get, and we too, by trusting your secret to a fool.

HORNER: Peace, madam. [*Aside to Quack.*] Well, doctor, is not this a good design, that carries a man on unsuspected and brings him off safe?

PINCHWIFE [*aside*]: Well, if this were true, but my wife—[*Dorilant whispers with Mrs. Pinchwife.*]

6. A convenient fiction since dueling was now illegal   7. Eunuch.
(1679).

ALITHEA: Come, brother, your wife is yet innocent, you see; but have a care of too strong an imagination, lest like an overconcerned, timorous gamester, by fancying an unlucky cast, it should come. Women and fortune are truest still to those that trust 'em.

LUCY: And any wild thing grows but the more fierce and hungry for being kept up and more dangerous to the keeper.

ALITHEA: There's doctrine for all husbands, Mr. Harcourt.

HARCOURT: I edify, madam, so much that I am impatient till I am one.

DORILANT: And I edify so much by example I will never be one.

SPARKISH: And because I will not disparage my parts I'll ne'er be one.

HORNER: And I, alas, can't be one.

PINCHWIFE: But I must be one—against my will, to a country wife, with a country murrain[8] to me.

MRS. PINCHWIFE [aside]: And I must be a country wife still too, I find, for I can't, like a city one, be rid of my musty husband and do what I list.

HORNER: Now, sir, I must pronounce your wife innocent, though I blush whilst I do it, and I am the only man by her now exposed to shame, which I will straight drown in wine, as you shall your suspicion, and the ladies' troubles we'll divert with a ballet.—Doctor, where are your maskers?

LUCY: Indeed, she's innocent, sir, I am her witness; and her end of coming out was but to see her sister's wedding and what she has said to your face of her love to Mr. Horner was but the usual innocent revenge on a husband's jealousy—was it not, madam? Speak.

MRS. PINCHWIFE [aside to Lucy and Horner]: Since you'll have me tell more lies—Yes, indeed, bud.

PINCHWIFE: For my own sake fain I would all believe; Cuckolds, like lovers, should themselves deceive.
But—[Sighs.]

> His honor is least safe, too late I find,
> Who trusts it with a foolish wife or friend.

[A Dance of Cuckolds.[9]]

HORNER: Vain fops but court and dress and keep a puther,[1]
         To pass for women's men with one another,
5   But he who aims by women to be priz'd,
         First by the men, you see, must be despis'd.

EPILOGUE, SPOKEN BY MRS. KNEPP[2]

Now, you the vigorous,[3] who daily here
O'er vizard-mask in public domineer,
And what you'd do to her if in place where,
Nay, have the confidence to cry, "Come out,"
5   Yet when she says "Lead on," you are not stout,
But to your well-dressed brother straight turn round

---

8. Pestilence.
9. This dance was performed to the then-familiar tune called "Cuckolds All [in] a Row."
1. Make a fuss.
2. Elizabeth Knepp, actress and singer, created the role of

Lady Fidget. Pepys held her in high regard; see page 2103.
3. The epilogue derisively addresses two categories of males who, unlike Horner, pretend to sexual potency: the young (lines 1–13) and the old (14–17).

And cry, "Pox on her, Ned, she can't be sound,"
Then slink away, a fresh one to engage,
With so much seeming heat and loving rage, ⎫
10   You'd frighten listening actress on the stage, ⎭
Till she at last has seen you huffing come ⎫
And talk of keeping in the tiring-room, ⎬
Yet cannot be provok'd to lead her home. ⎭
Next, you Falstaffs[4] of fifty, who beset
15   Your buckram[5] maidenheads, which your friends get,
And while to them you of achievements boast,
They share the booty and laugh at your cost.
In fine, you essenced boys, both old and young,
Who would be thought so eager, brisk and strong,
20   Yet do the ladies, not their husbands, wrong,
Whose purses for your manhood make excuse,
And keep your Flanders mares[6] for show, not use:
Encourag'd by our woman's man today,
A Horner's part may vainly think to play
25   And may intrigues so bashfully disown
That they may doubted be by few or none,[7]
May kiss the cards at picquet, ombre, loo,[8]
And so be thought to kiss the lady too;
But, gallants, have a care, faith, what you do.
30   The world, which to no man his due will give,
You by experience know you can deceive
And men may still believe you vigorous,
But then we women—there's no cozening[9] us.

1675   1675

* ≡◈≡ *

Mary Astell
1666–1731

The pioneering feminist Mary Astell was born in Newcastle to a merchant who dealt in coal, and she was tutored early by an uncle who immersed himself in literature and philosophy. From him she absorbed a lifelong affinity for the ideas of the Cambridge Platonists, who held that reason was the sole route to truth and to the proper love of God; out of this conviction she developed her defiant argument that, despite centuries of cultural practice to the contrary, women's powers of reason were as worth cultivating as men's. At age twenty Astell moved to London, where eight years later she published the book that made her fame. In *A Serious Proposal to the Ladies* (1694), Astell argued for the founding of an all-female academy, where unmarried women might develop their reason, deepen their knowledge, and nurture their faith free from the distractions imposed by social conventions. Astell's idea for such a school

4. I.e., you who resemble the immense, aged, comic liar Shakespeare created in *Henry IV.*
5. A stiff fabric. Falstaff at one point pretends to have killed some "rogues in buckram suits" during a robbery (*1 Henry IV* 2.4). In truth he killed no one, and his younger accomplices made off with the loot.
6. Costly coach horses; here a metaphor for kept mistress-es or prostitutes.
7. I.e., Horner's example may encourage "you" fakers to reverse tactics, and to seek a rake's reputation by feigning "bashfulness."
8. Card games; kissing the cards was a way of flirting with fellow-players.
9. Fooling.

exerted a lasting influence: Daniel Defoe enthusiastically revived it in his *Essay upon Projects* (1697), Samuel Johnson wove it into his philosophical tale *Rasselas* (1759), and Sarah Scott made it the premise of her feminist novel *Millenium Hall* (1762). More important, perhaps, was the *Proposal*'s immediate effect on contemporary women writers and thinkers (Ladies Mary Chudleigh and Mary Wortley Montagu among them), who found in it a template and an endorsement for their own most cherished pursuits and for their sense of possibilities.

Dwelling abstemiously in the Thames-side town of Chelsea, Astell began to enjoy the consequences of celebrity. She received tributes and visits from admiring readers, and she assembled a circle of women like herself—well-educated, pious, unmarried—whose friendships she deeply valued and with whose help she later founded a charity school for girls. Still, the *Proposal* itself was never implemented in her time, in part because the imagined academy for women sounded too much like a Catholic convent to find ready acceptance in Protestant England, and in part because the argument's point—that women could find intellectual, moral, and spiritual self-sufficiency outside marriage—was so unsettling as to rouse energetic opposition.

Astell pushed the argument further in *Some Reflections upon Marriage* (1700), a hundred-page tract written, she reported, in the white heat of an angry and inspired afternoon. Starting from a conservative premise—that as the monarch rightfully possesses absolute authority over the state, so does the husband over his wife—Astell develops a breathtakingly skeptical line of inquiry: why, then, would a woman wish to enter into so self-immolating a contract as marriage in the first place? The question ultimately brings her back to the theme of the *Serious Proposal*: the importance for women of a good education, one that will enable them to see their choices clearly, to make those choices discerningly, and to lead, whether married or not, a Christian life grounded in the cultivation of their own intellect and faith (though Astell strongly implies that within marriage female virtue will produce a grim martyrdom; outside marriage, a richer fulfillment). In limning the alternatives, Astell deploys the directness, the sarcasm, and the urgency that made her famous in her own day and again in ours. She was, as her biographer Ruth Perry notes, "probably the first person to consider the rights and duties of women as a political question"; the prose in which she couched the question gave it an often hypnotic pugnacity.

from Some Reflections upon Marriage

But how can a man respect his wife when he has a contemptible opinion of her and her sex? When from his own elevation he looks down on them as void of understanding, and full of ignorance and passion, so that folly and a woman are equivalent terms with him? Can he think there is any gratitude due to her whose utmost services he exacts as strict duty? Because she was made to be a slave to his will, and has no higher end than to serve and obey him? Perhaps we arrogate too much to ourselves when we say this material world was made for our sakes; that its glorious maker has given us the use of it is certain, but when we suppose that over which we have dominion to be made purely for our sakes, we draw a false conclusion, as he who should say the people were made for the prince who is set over them, would be thought to be out of his senses as well as his politics. Yet even allowing that He who made everything in number, weight and measure, who never acts but for some great and glorious end, an end agreeable to His majesty, allowing that He created such a number of rational spirits merely to serve their fellow creatures, yet how are these lords and masters helped by the contempt they show of their poor humble vassals? Is it not rather an hindrance to that service they expect, as being undeniable and constant proof how unworthy they are to receive it?

None of God's creatures absolutely considered are in their own nature contemptible; the meanest fly, the poorest insect has its use and virtue. Contempt is scarce a human passion; one may venture to say it was not in innocent man, for till sin came into the world, there was nothing in it to be condemned. But pride, which makes everything serve its purposes, wrested this passion from its only use, so that instead of being an antidote against sin, it is become a grand promoter of it, nothing making us more worthy of that contempt we show, than when (poor, weak, dependent creatures as we are!) we look down with scorn and disdain on others.

There is not a surer sign of a noble mind, a mind very far advanced towards perfection, than the being able to bear contempt and an unjust treatment from one's superiors evenly and patiently. For inward worth and real excellency are the true ground of superiority, and one person is not in reality better than another, but as he is more wise and good. But this world being a place of trial and governed by general laws, just retributions being reserved for hereafter, respect and obedience many times become due for order's sake to those who don't otherwise deserve them. Now though humility keeps us from over-valuing ourselves or viewing our merit through a false and magnifying medium, yet it does not put out our eyes; it does not, it ought not to deprive us of that pleasing sentiment which attends our acting as we ought to act, which is as it were a foretaste of heaven, our present reward for doing what is just and fit. And when a superior does a mean and unjust thing, as all contempt of one's neighbor is, and yet this does not provoke his inferiors to refuse that observance which their stations in the world require, they cannot but have an inward sense of their own real superiority, the other having no pretense to it, at the same time that they pay him an outward respect and deference, which is such a flagrant testimony of the sincerest love of order as proves their souls to be of the highest and noblest rank.

A man therefore for his own sake, and to give evidence that he has a right to those prerogatives he assumes, should treat women with a little more humanity and regard than is usually paid them. Your whiffling wits may scoff at them, and what then? It matters not, for they rally[1] everything though ever so sacred, and rail at the women commonly in very good company. Religion, its priests, and these its most constant and regular professors, are the usual subjects of their manly, mannerly, and surprising jests. Surprising indeed! not for the newness of the thought, the brightness of the fancy, or nobleness of expression, but for the good assurance with which such threadbare jests are again and again repeated. But that your grave dons, your learned men, and which is more your men of sense as they would be thought, should stoop so low as to make invectives against the women, forget themselves so much as to jest with their slaves, who have neither liberty nor ingenuity to make reprisals! that they should waste their time and debase their good sense which fits them for the most weighty affairs, such as are suitable to their profound wisdoms and exalted understandings! to render those poor wretches more ridiculous and odious who are already in their opinion sufficiently contemptible, and find no better exercise of their wit and satire than such as are not worth their pains, though it were possible to reform them—this, this indeed may justly be wondered at!

I know not whether or no women are allowed to have souls. If they have, perhaps it is not prudent to provoke them too much, lest silly as they are, they at last recriminate, and then what polite and well-bred gentleman, though himself is concerned, can forbear taking that lawful pleasure which all who understand raillery must taste, when they find his jests who insolently began to peck at his neighbor, returned with interest upon his own head? And indeed men are too humane, too wise to venture at it did they not hope for this effect, and expect the pleasure of finding their wit turn to such account; for if it be

---

1. Mock.

lawful to reveal a secret, this is without doubt the whole design of those fine discourses which have been made against the women from our great forefathers to this present time. Generous man has too much bravery, he is too just and too good to assault a defenseless enemy, and if he did inveigh against the women it was only to do them service. For since neither his care of their education, his hearty endeavors to improve their minds, his wholesome precepts, nor great example could do them good, as his last and kindest essay he resolved to try what contempt would do, and chose rather to expose himself by a seeming want of justice, equity, ingenuity, and good nature, than suffer women to remain such vain and insignificant creatures as they have hitherto been reckoned. And truly women are some degrees beneath what I have thus far thought them, if they do not make the best use of his kindness, improve themselves, and like Christians return it.

Let us see then what is their part, what must they do to make the matrimonial yoke tolerable to themselves as well as pleasing to their lords and masters? That the world is an empty and deceitful thing, that those enjoyments which appear so desirable at a distance, which raised our hopes and expectations to such a mighty pitch, which we so passionately coveted and so eagerly pursued, vanish at our first approach, leaving nothing behind them but the folly of delusion, and the pain of disappointed hopes, is a common outcry; and yet as common as it is, though we complain of being deceived this instant, we do not fail of contributing to the cheat the very next. Though in reality it is not the world that abuses us, 'tis we abuse ourselves, it is not the emptiness of that, but our own false judgments, our unreasonable desires and expectations that torment us; for he who exerts his whole strength to lift a straw, ought not to complain of the burden but of his own disproportionate endeavor which gives him the pain he feels. The world affords us all that pleasure a sound judgment can expect from it, and answers all those ends and purposes for which it was designed. Let us expect no more than is reasonable, and then we shall not fail of our expectations.

It is even so in the case before us: a woman who has been taught to think marriage her only preferment, the sum-total of her endeavors, the completion of all her hopes, that which must settle and make her happy in this world, and very few, in their youth especially, carry a thought steadily to a greater distance; she who has seen a lover dying at her feet, and can't therefore imagine that he who professes to receive all his happiness from her can have any other design or desire than to please her; whose eyes have been dazzled with all the glitter and pomp of a wedding, and who hears of nothing but joy and congratulation; who is transported with the pleasure of being out of pupillage, and mistress not only of herself but of a family too; she who is either so simple or so vain as to take her lover at his word either as to the praises he gave her, or the promises he made for himself. In sum, she whose expectation has been raised by courtship, by all the fine things that her lover, her governess, and domestic flatterers say, will find a terrible disappointment when the hurry is over, and when she comes calmly to consider her condition, and views it no more under a false appearance, but as it truly is.

I doubt in such a view it will not appear over-desirable if she regards only the present state of things. Hereafter may make amends for what she must be prepared to suffer here; then will be her reward, this is her time of trial, the season of exercising and improving her virtues. A woman that is not mistress of her passions, that cannot patiently submit even when reason suffers with her, who does not practice passive obedience[2] to the utmost, will never be acceptable to such an absolute sovereign as a

---

2. The term denoted the Tory policy of obeying Whig monarchs and of refraining from rebellion despite their "usurpation" of the Stuart throne, on the principle that rebellion itself would run contrary to divine and human law.

husband. Wisdom ought to govern without contradiction, but strength however will be obeyed. There are but few of those wise persons who can be content to be made yet wiser by contradiction; the most will have their will, and it is right because it is theirs. Such is the vanity of human nature that nothing pleases like an entire subjection; what imperfections won't a man overlook where this is not wanting! Though we live like brutes, we would have incense offered us that is only due to heaven itself, would have an absolute and blind obedience paid us by all over whom we pretend authority. We were not made to idolize one another, yet the whole strain of courtship is little less than rank idolatry. But does a man intend to give and not receive his share in this religious worship? No such matter; pride and vanity and self-love have their designs, and if the lover is so condescending as to set a pattern in the time of his addresses, he is so just as to expect his wife should strictly copy after it all the rest of her life.

But how can a woman scruple entire subjection, how can she forbear to admire the worth and excellency of the superior sex, if she at all considers it? Have not all the great actions that have been performed in the world been done by them? Have not they founded empires and overturned them? Do not they make laws and continually repeal them and amend them? Their vast minds lay kingdoms waste; no bounds or measures can be prescribed to their desires. War and peace depend on them, they form cabals[3] and have the wisdom and courage to get over all these rubs[4] which may lie in the way of their desired grandeur. What is it they cannot do? They make worlds and ruin them, form systems of universal nature and dispute eternally about them, their pen gives worth to the most trifling controversy, nor can a fray be inconsiderable if they have drawn their swords in't. All that the wise man pronounces is an oracle, and every word the witty speaks a jest. It is a woman's happiness to hear, admire, and praise them, especially if a little ill-nature keeps them at anytime from bestowing due applause on each other. And if she aspires no further she is thought to be in her proper sphere of action; she is as wise and as good as can be expected from her.

She then who marries ought to lay it down for an indisputable maxim, that her husband must govern absolutely and entirely, and that she has nothing else to do but to please and obey. She must not attempt to divide his authority, or so much as dispute it (to struggle with her yoke will only make it gall the more) but must believe him wise and good and in all respects the best, at least he must be so to her. She who can't do this is no way fit to be a wife; she may set up for that peculiar coronet the ancient fathers talked of, but is not qualified to receive that great reward,[5] which attends the eminent exercise of humility and self-denial, patience and resignation—the duties that a wife is called to.

But some refractory woman perhaps will say how can this be? Is it possible for her to believe him wise and good who by a thousand demonstrations convinces her and all the world of the contrary? Did the bare name of husband confer sense on a man, and the mere being in authority infallibly qualify him for government, much might be done. But since a wise man and a husband are not terms convertible, and how loath soever one is to own it, matter of fact won't allow us to deny that the head many times stands in need of the inferior's brains to manage it, she must beg leave to be excused from such high thoughts of her sovereign, and if she submits to his power, it is not so much reason as necessity that compels her.

---

3. Small, secretive groups formed to wield power.
4. Obstacles.
5. Salvation. The "peculiar coronet" is that of martyr-
dom, often imaged as a crown in the writings of early Christian theologians.

Now of how little force soever this objection may be in other respects, methinks it is strong enough to prove the necessity of a good education, and that men never mistake their true interest more than when they endeavor to keep women in ignorance. Could they indeed deprive them of their natural good sense at the same time they deny them the due improvement of it, they might compass their end; otherwise natural sense unassisted may run into a false track, and serve only to punish him justly, who would not allow it to be useful to himself or others. If man's authority be justly established, the more sense a woman has the more reason she will find to submit to it; if according to the tradition of our fathers (who having had *possession* of the pen, thought they had also the best *right* to it), women's understanding is but small, and men's partiality adds no weight to the observation, ought not the more care to be taken to improve them? How it agrees with the justice of men we inquire not, but certainly Heaven is abundantly more equitable than to enjoin women the hardest task and give them the least strength to perform it. And if men, learned, wise, and discreet as they are, who have as is said all the advantages of nature, and without controversy have or may have all the assistance of art, are so far from acquitting themselves as they ought, from living according to that reason and excellent understanding they so much boast of, can it be expected that a woman who is reckoned silly enough in herself, at least comparatively, and whom men take care to make yet more so, can it be expected that she should constantly perform so difficult a duty as entire subjection, to which corrupt nature is so averse?

If the great and wise Cato,[6] a *man*, a man of no ordinary firmness and strength of mind, a man who was esteemed as an oracle, and by the philosophers and great men of his nation equaled even to the gods themselves; if he with all his stoical principles was not able to bear the sight of a triumphant conqueror (who perhaps would have insulted and perhaps would not), but out of a cowardly fear of an insult, ran to death to secure him from it; can it be thought that an ignorant weak woman should have patience to bear a continual outrage and insolence all the days of her life? Unless you will suppose her a very ass, but then remember what the Italians say, to quote them once more, since being very husbands they may be presumed to have some authority in this case: *L'asino pur pigro, stimulato tira quelche calcio*; an ass though slow if provoked will kick.

We never see or perhaps make sport with the ill effects of a bad education, till it come to touch us home in the ill conduct of a sister, a daughter, or wife. Then the women must be blamed, their folly is exclaimed against, when all this while it was the wise man's fault who did not set a better guard on those who according to him stand in so much need of one. A young gentleman, as a celebrated author tells us, ought above all things to be acquainted with the state of the world, the ways and humors, the follies, the cheats, the faults of the age he is fallen into; he should by degrees be informed of the vice of fashion, and warned of the application and design of those who will make it their business to corrupt him, should be told the arts they use and the trains they lay, be prepared to be shocked by some and caressed by others; warned who are like to oppose, who to mislead; who to undermine and who to serve him. He should be instructed how to know and distinguish them, where he should let them see, and when dissemble the knowledge of them and their aims and workings.

---

6. Cato of Utica (95–46 B.C.), Stoic Roman senator and commander, whose devotion to the ideal of a Republic prompted him to commit suicide rather than accede to the growing power of Julius Caesar; his death was traditionally represented as heroic.

Our author is much in the right, and not to disparage any other accomplishments which are useful in their kind, this will turn to more account than any language or philosophy, art or science, or any other piece of good-breeding and fine education that can be taught him, which are no otherwise excellent than as they contribute to this, as this does above all things to the making him a wise, virtuous, and useful man.

And it is not less necessary that a young lady should receive the like instructions; whether or no her temptations be fewer, her reputation and honor however are to be more nicely preserved; they may be ruined by a little ignorance or indiscretion, and then though she has kept her innocence, and so is secured as to the next world, yet she is in a great measure lost to this. A woman cannot be too watchful, too apprehensive of her danger, nor keep at too great a distance from it, since man, whose wisdom and ingenuity is so much superior to hers, condescends for his interest sometimes, and sometimes by way of diversion, to lay snares for her. For though men are virtuous, philosophers and politicians in comparison of the ignorant and illiterate women, yet they don't all pretend to be saints, and 'tis no great matter to them if women, who were born to be their slaves, be now and then ruined for their entertainment.

But according to the rate that young women are educated; according to the way their time is spent; they are destined to folly and impertinence, to say no worse, and which is yet more inhuman, they are blamed for that ill conduct they are not suffered to avoid, and reproached for those faults they are in a manner forced into; so that if heaven has bestowed any sense on them, no other use is made of it than to leave them without excuse. So much and no more of the world is shown them, as serves to weaken and corrupt their minds, to give them wrong notions, and busy them in mean pursuits; to disturb, not to regulate their passions, to make them timorous and dependent, and in a word, fit for nothing else but to act a farce for the diversion of their governors.

Even men themselves improve no otherwise than according to the aim they take, and the end they propose; and he whose designs are but little and mean, will be the same himself. Though ambition, as 'tis usually understood, is a foolish, not to say a base and pitiful vice, yet the aspirings of the soul after true glory are so much its nature, that it seems to have forgot itself and to degenerate, if it can forbear; and perhaps the great secret of education lies in affecting the soul with a lively sense of what is truly its perfection, and exciting the most ardent desires after it.

But, alas! what poor woman is ever taught that she should have a higher design than to get her a husband? Heaven will fall in of course; and if she make but an obedient and dutiful wife, she cannot miss of it. A husband indeed is thought by both sexes so very valuable, that scarce a man who can keep himself clean and make a bow, but thinks he is good enough to pretend to any woman, no matter for the difference of birth or fortune, a *husband* is such a wonder-working name as to make an equality, or something more, whenever it is pronounced. * * *

To wind up this matter, if a woman were duly principled and taught to know the world, especially the true sentiments that men have of her, and the traps they lay for her under so many gilded compliments, and such a seemingly great respect, that disgrace would be prevented which is brought upon too many families, women would marry more discreetly, and demean[7] themselves better in a married state than some people say they do. The foundation indeed ought to be laid deep and strong: she

7. Behave (though the meaning "to lower herself" was also current).

should be made a good Christian, and understand why she is so, and then she will be everything else that is good. Men need keep no spies on a woman's conduct, need have no fear of her virtue, or so much as of her prudence and caution, were but a due sense of true honor and virtue awakened in her, were her reason excited and prepared to consider the sophistry of those temptations which would persuade her from her duty, and were she put in a way to know that it is both her wisdom and interest to observe it. She would then duly examine and weigh all the circumstances, the good and evil of a married state, and not be surprised with unforeseen inconveniences, and either never consent to be a wife, or make a good one when she does. This would show her what human nature *is*, as well as what it *ought* to be, and teach her not only what she may justly expect, but what she must be content with; would enable her to cure some faults, and patiently to suffer what she cannot cure.

Indeed nothing can assure obedience, and render it what it ought to be, but the confidence of duty, the paying it for God's sake. Superiors don't rightly understand their own interest when they attempt to put out their subjects' eyes to keep them obedient. A blind obedience is what a rational creature should never pay, nor would such an one receive it did he rightly understand its nature. For human actions are no otherwise valuable than as they are conformable to reason, but blind obedience is an obeying *without reason*, for ought we know, *against it*. God himself does not require our obedience at this rate; He lays before us the goodness and reasonableness of His laws, and were there anything in them whose equity we could not readily comprehend, yet we have this clear and sufficient reason on which to found our obedience, that nothing but what's just and fit can be enjoined by a just, a wise, and gracious God. But this is a reason will never hold in respect of men's commands unless they can prove themselves infallible, and consequently impeccable too.

It is therefore very much a man's interest that women should be good Christians, in this as in every other instance; he who does his duty finds his own account[8] in it. Duty and true interest are one and the same thing, and he who thinks otherwise is to be pitied for being so much in the wrong; but what can be more the duty of the head, than to instruct and improve those who are under government? She will freely leave him the quiet dominion of this world whose thoughts and expectations are placed on the next. A prospect of heaven, and that only, will cure that ambition which all generous minds are filled with, not by taking it away but by placing it on a right object. She will discern a time when her sex shall be no bar to the best employments, the highest honor; a time when that distinction, now so much used to her prejudice, shall be no more, but provided she is not wanting to herself, her soul shall shine as bright as the greatest hero's. This is a true, and indeed the only consolation, this makes her a sufficient compensation for all the neglect and contempt the ill-grounded customs of the world throw on her, for all the injuries brutal power may do her, and is a sufficient cordial to support her spirits, be her lot in this world what it may.

But some sage persons may perhaps object that were women allowed to improve themselves, and not amongst other discouragements driven back by those wise jests and scoffs that are put upon a woman of sense or learning, a philosophical lady as she is called by way of ridicule, they would be too wise and too good for the men. I grant it, for vicious and foolish men. Nor is it to be wondered that he is afraid he should not be able to govern them were their understandings improved, who is resolved not

8. I.e., is amply compensated.

to take too much pains with his own. But these 'tis to be hoped are no very considerable number, the foolish at least; and therefore this is so far from being an argument against their improvement, that it is a strong one for it, if we do but suppose the men to be as capable of improvement as the women, but much more if according to tradition we believe they have greater capacities. This, if anything, would stir them up to be what they ought, not permit them to waste their time and abuse their faculties in the service of their irregular appetites and unreasonable desires, and to let poor contemptible women who have been their slaves excel them in all that is truly excellent. This would make them blush at employing an immoral mind no better than in making provision for the flesh to fulfill the lusts thereof, since women by a wiser conduct have brought themselves to such a reach of thought, to such exactness of judgment, such clearness and strength of reasoning, such purity and elevation of mind, such command of their passions, such regularity of will and affection, and in a word to such a pitch of perfection as the human soul is capable of attaining even in this life by the grace of God, such true wisdom, such real greatness, as though it does not qualify them to make a noise in this world, to found or overturn empires, yet it qualifies them for what is infinitely better, a kingdom that cannot be moved, an incorruptible crown of glory.

Besides, it were ridiculous to suppose that a woman, were she ever so much improved, could come near the topping genius of men, and therefore why should they envy or discourage her? Strength of mind goes along with strength of body, and 'tis only for some odd accidents which philosophers have not yet thought worthwhile to inquire into, that the sturdiest porter is not the wisest man. As therefore the men have the power in their hands, so there's no dispute of their having the brains to manage it. There is no such thing as good judgment and sense upon earth, if it is not to be found among them. Do not they generally speaking do all the great actions and considerable business of this world, and leave that of the next to the women? Their subtlety in forming cabals and laying deep designs, their courage and conduct in breaking through all ties sacred and civil to effect them, not only advances them to the post of honor and keeps them securely in it for twenty or thirty years, but gets them a name, and conveys it down to posterity for some hundreds, and who would look any further? Justice and injustice are administered by their hands; courts and schools are filled with these sages; 'tis men who dispute for truth as well as men who argue against it; histories are writ by them, they recount each others' great exploits, and have always done so. All famous arts have their original from men, even from the invention of guns to the mystery of good eating. And to show that nothing is beneath their care, any more than above their reach, they have brought *gaming*[9] to an art and science, and a more profitable and honorable one too, than any of those that used to be called *liberal*. Indeed what is it they can't perform, when they attempt it? This strength of their brains shall be every whit as conspicuous at their cups as in a Senate house, and when they please they can make it pass for as sure a mark of wisdom to drink deep as to reason profoundly; a greater proof of courage and consequently of understanding to dare the vengeance of heaven itself than to stand the raillery of some of the worst of their fellow creatures!

Again, it may be said, if a wife's case be as it is here represented, it is not good for a woman to marry, and so there's an end of human race. But this is no fair consequence, for all that can justly be inferred from hence is that a woman has no mighty

9. Gambling.

obligations to the man who makes love to her, she has no reason to be fond of being a wife, or to reckon it a piece of preferment when she is taken to be a man's upper-servant; it is no advantage to her in this world, if rightly managed it may prove one as to the next. For she who marries purely to do good, to educate souls for heaven, who can be so truly mortified as to lay aside her own will and desires, to pay such an entire submission for life, to one whom she cannot be sure will always deserve it, does certainly perform a more heroic action than all the famous masculine heroes can boast of; she suffers a continual martyrdom to bring glory to God and benefit to mankind, which consideration indeed may carry her though all difficulties, I know not what else can, and engage her to love him who proves perhaps so much more worse than a brute, as to make this condition yet more grievous than it needed to be. She has need of a strong reason, of a truly Christian and well-tempered spirit, of all the assistance the best education can give her, and ought to have some good assistance of her own firmness and virtue, who ventures on such a trial; and for this reason 'tis less to be wondered at that women marry off in haste, for perhaps if they took time to consider and reflect upon it, they seldom would.

To conclude, perhaps I've said more than most men will thank me for; I cannot help it, for how much soever I may be their friend and humble servant, I am more a friend to truth. Truth is strong, and some time or other will prevail; nor is it for their honor, and therefore one would think not for their interest, to be partial to themselves and unjust to others. They may fancy I have made some discoveries which like *arcana imperii*[1] ought to be kept secret, but in good earnest I do them more honor than to suppose their lawful prerogatives need any mean arts to support them. If they have usurped, I love justice too much to wish success and continuance to usurpations, which though submitted to out of prudence and for quietness' sake, yet leave everybody free to regain their lawful right whenever they have power and opportunity. I don't say that tyranny *ought*, but we find in *fact*, that it provokes the oppressed to throw off even a lawful yoke that fits too heavy. And if he who is freely elected, after all his fair promises and the fine hopes he raised, proves a tyrant, the consideration that he was one's own choice will not render more submissive and patient, but I fear more refractory. For though it is very unreasonable, yet we see 'tis the course of the world not only to return injury for injury, but crime for crime; both parties indeed are guilty, but the aggressors have a double guilt; they have not only their own, but their neighbor's ruin to answer for.

As to the female reader, I hope she will allow I've endeavored to do her justice, nor betrayed her cause as her advocates usually do, under pretense of defending it: a practice too mean for any to be guilty of who have the least sense of honor, and who do any more than merely pretend to it. I think I have held the balance even, and not being conscious of partiality I ask no pardon for it. To plead for the oppressed and to defend the weak seemed to me a generous undertaking; for though it may be secure, 'tis not always honorable to run over to the strongest party. And if she infers from what has been said that marriage is a very happy state for men, if they think fit to make it so; that they govern the world, they have prescription on their side, women are too weak to dispute it with them, therefore they, as all other governors, are most, if not only, accountable for what's amiss. For whether other governments in their original were or were not conferred according to the merit of the person, yet certainly in this case Heaven would not have allotted the man to govern, but because he was best qualified for it. So far I agree with him. But if she goes on to infer, that

---

1. The secrets of power.

therefore he has not these qualifications, where is his right? If he misemploys, does he not abuse it? And if he abuses, according to modern deduction, he forfeits it; I must leave her there. A peaceable woman indeed will not carry it so far, she will neither question her husband's right nor his fitness to govern, but how? Not as an absolute lord and master, with an arbitrary and tyrannical sway, but as reason governs and conducts a man, by proposing what is just and fit. And the man who acts according to that wisdom he assumes, who would have that superiority he pretends to acknowledged just, will receive no injury by anything that has been offered here. A woman will value him the more who is so wise and good, when she discerns how much he excels the rest of his noble sex; the less he requires, the more will he merit that esteem and deference, which those who are so forward to exact seem conscious they don't deserve. So then the man's prerogative is not at all infringed, whilst the woman's privileges are secured; and if any woman think herself injured, she has a remedy in reserve which few men will envy or endeavor to rob her of, the exercise and improvement of her virtue here, and the reward of it hereafter.

1700   1700

Daniel Defoe
1660–1731

At the age of fifty-two, Daniel Defoe summed up his life in a couplet:

> No man has tasted differing fortunes more,
> And thirteen times I have been rich or poor.

Vicissitude marked his career until the very end, and money, though a constant preoccupation, was not the only medium of change. Deeply engaged in politics, and phenomenally skilled at promoting causes with his pen, Defoe switched allegiances several times among the most conspicuous factions of his day. What's more, since he was prized by each side in turn for his efficiency as a secret agent, his political work often required him to present himself—in person and in print—as someone or something he was not, to incur hostilities from the very factions he was secretly working to support. His accomplishments, late in life, as a pioneer of English fiction partly originate in the fictions he manipulated as a consummate political journalist and spy obliged to "taste" in imagination and performance the "differing fortunes" of the person he pretended, for one purpose or another, to be. Out of all these oscillations—financial, political, imaginative—came one of the most prolific and inventive careers in British literature.

Defoe was born in the City of London in the year of the Restoration to a family whose fortunes were on the rise. His father James Foe manufactured and sold candles, and over the ensuing decades attained positions of increasing eminence in his trade (Defoe himself later added the French prefix to his family surname). Under the influence of their pastor, the Foes left the Church of England to become Dissenters, at a time when to do so was to incur certain exclusion—from attending universities, from holding public office—and possible persecution (violence, imprisonment). At around the age of ten, shortly after his mother's early death, Defoe began a decade in the schools of the Dissenters. The curriculum, underplaying the Greek and Latin of conventional Anglican education, focused instead on new science and philosophy, on clear argument and public speaking, as well as on two forms of thought and composition that cultivated the student's ability to imagine "differing fortunes": prose impersonation, where the student was asked to "play" a given figure (for example, a secretary of state) in a particular situation, and to write a letter or give a speech suitable to the occasion; and casuistry, a kind of moral and theological game of "What if?": if I were to find myself in such and such a predicament, such a dilemma, what should I do? The question recurs, explicitly and implicitly, throughout Defoe's prose.

As Defoe entered his twenties, the question became personally pressing. Many of his class-mates were preparing for the ministry; he opted instead to enter his father's world of trade, though with a taste for range and risk that his prudent forebear had never displayed. Defoe dealt at one time or another in men's clothing, tobacco, wine; opened and operated a brick and tile factory, and invested capital so audaciously and ill-advisedly that in 1692 he was forced to declare bankruptcy, having incurred the enormous debt of £17,000. "The God that gave me brains will give me bread," Defoe remarked at one point, with characteristic confidence in both the deity and himself. From his late thirties onward, he used those brains to earn bread, for himself and his large family, by writing. He worked with astonishing speed and efficiency, pro-ducing by his life's end more than 500 separate works, as well as several periodical series that he wrote (at the rate of two or three essays a week) over the course of many years. Nonetheless, he never quite escaped the financial distresses that had first pushed him into print.

His pen's other impetus was politics. As a Whig and a Dissenter eager to end the reign of the Catholic James II, Defoe had fought as soldier in the abortive Monmouth Rebellion of 1685, and in 1688 celebrated the advent of the Glorious Revolution and William III. He served his new king as secret agent and as author, publishing the phenomenally popular poem *The True-Born Englishman* (1701), whose title sarcastically identifies those "natives" hostile to William on the grounds of his foreign birth (the poem argues, among other things, that their own lineage is far more complex and corrupt than they admit). Defoe's powers as a political advocate were now near full stride, and his knack for irony soon brought him trouble. In his par-odic pamphlet *The Shortest Way with Dissenters*, published anonymously in 1702 at the height of Tory hopes for a new assault on Nonconformists, Defoe impersonates a rabid Tory eager to mete out extravagant punishments on the Nonconformists (to whom Defoe himself had felt a life-long loyalty and tenderness). Neither faction appreciated the joke. After four months in hiding, Defoe was arrested, convicted of libel, and sentenced to prison and to three separate sessions in the pillory, where the crowds (to his surprise) celebrated him as a hero, pelting him with fresh flowers rather than rotten vegetables. The episode initiated a sea change in his affiliations. Dis-illusioned with Whigs and Dissenters, Defoe secretly aligned himself with the ambitious Tory politician Robert Harley, who in an inspired move had arranged to pay some of Defoe's fines and debts after his release from jail. Commissioned by Harley to create and manage a kind of personal secret service, Defoe traveled extensively, often under assumed names, advocating Tory causes (most notably the Union with Scotland) and reporting on the opposition; he also wrote the widely read *Review* (1704—1713), a thrice-weekly periodical essay intricately calcu-lated to further Harley's interests. After the fall of the Tories, the intricacy deepened. Under threat of punishment by the new Whig government, Defoe agreed to work as double agent for *them*, by moving among Tory journalists and contributing to Tory papers, but in such ways as to undermine the Tory cause. For the seasoned ironist and impersonator this was irony enough: having worked brilliantly for years to devise Tory propaganda, he was now at pains to dilute it.

At the age of fifty-nine, Defoe hit upon a new way to make impersonation pay. His book *The Strange, Surprising Adventures of Robinson Crusoe* (1719) was the first in a series of long fic-tions that present themselves as historical fact, as the written reminiscences of people who had actually lived the extraordinary experiences they relate, in books that often bear their fictive names as titles: *Captain Singleton* (1720); *Moll Flanders* (1722); *Colonel Jack* (1722); *Roxana* (1724). In creating these memoirists, Defoe drew on his decades as a journalist. He saturated his stories with particulars (clothing, furniture, tools); his memoirists write a prose that often reads like talk—digressive, fervent, improvisatory. By such strategies he made his tales persua-sive. As a genre, the novel has no one inventor, because it absorbs so much (and so variously) from other kinds of texts: newspapers, essays, diaries, financial accounts, religious devotions, conduct manuals. Defoe, though, was perhaps the most astute early orchestrator of such absorptions. Having written in most of his culture's modes, he melded them into a form of fiction that still seems (in keeping with the genre's name) new.

Vicissitude persisted. Having written his last long fiction (*Roxana*) in 1724, Defoe turned his hand to another project. In his *Tour through the Whole Island of Great Britain* (three volumes, 1724–1726), and in other late works, he celebrated British trade as a source of present prosperity and a seedbed of future empire. He died while hiding out from his creditors in the neighborhood of his birth, once again on the run from debt and cut off from his contentious family. The ending feels emblematic. In many ways the most communicative of writers, Defoe often used his powers to study solitude. "Between me and thee there is a great gulf fixed," remarks Robinson Crusoe on his island, quoting scripture: "thee" is the whole world, from which he finds himself definitively sundered. But the phrase might be invoked by almost any speaker in Defoe—characters talking to characters, ghosts to the living, narrators to readers— as they survey the landscape of their own isolation, even in crowded cities. Defoe devoted his writing life to mapping these "great gulfs," to chronicling the energies—political, social, and commercial—by which the mortals of his time and place tried to bridge them, and to seeking out the work of God and Providence in all these prolific, troubled transactions.

A TRUE RELATION   A *True Relation* was long thought to be Defoe's earliest foray into fiction; it was then discovered to have a firm basis in fact. The original pamphlet was published anonymously; Defoe was not identified as author until 1790. For most of the nineteenth century it was assumed that he had made up the entire story, possibly as publicity for Charles Drelincourt's *Defense against the Fears of Death*, the book that Mrs. Veal repeatedly recommends to her friend Mrs. Bargrave. Shortly after the *Apparition's* first appearance as a pamphlet, in fact, Defoe's text and Drelincourt's were combined into a single, popular volume which went through many printings. In 1895 the Defoe scholar George Aitken published the first independent evidence for the authenticity of the story, if not of the ghost: a Latin memorandum from 1714 recording an interview with the actual Mrs. Bargrave, who adhered (and added) to her narrative nearly a decade after it took place. Other contemporary accounts of her and her story have since been discovered. Defoe, then, was practicing not fiction but journalism, sifting, selecting, and arranging testimony then in circulation, presenting it in the voice of Mrs. Bargrave's "intimate friend," the "very intelligent" Justice of the Peace who professes himself very "affected" by his interview with her (his own status, as historical person or fabricated narrator, has never been established). Mingling "matter of fact" (a recurrent phrase) with matters of mystery, Defoe here manages (as Leslie Stephen once remarked) to embody "in a few lines all the essential particularities of his art."

Following the *Relation* are portions of three parallel contemporary accounts, in different social and intellectual registers: one from a Canterbury woman writing to appease her aunt; another from an informant writing to satisfy the curiosity of one of the chief scientists of the time; and finally, the memorandum which first suggested that Defoe's *Relation* was in some sense *True*.

A True Relation of the Apparition of One Mrs. Veal
the Next Day after Her Death
to One Mrs. Bargrave at Canterbury
the 8th of September, 1705

The Preface

This relation is matter of fact, and attended with such circumstances as may induce any reasonable man to believe it. It was sent by a gentleman, a Justice of Peace at Maidstone in Kent and a very intelligent person, to his friend in London, as it is here worded. Which discourse is attested by a very sober and understanding gentle-woman, a kinswoman of the said gentleman's, who lives in Canterbury within a few doors of the house in which the within named Mrs. Bargrave lives; who believes his kinswoman to be of so discerning a spirit, as not to be put upon by any fallacy. And who positively assured him that the whole matter, as it is here related and laid down, is what is really true, and what she herself had in the same words (as near as may be) from Mrs. Bargrave's own mouth, who she knows had no reason to invent and pub-lish such a story, nor any design to forge and tell a lie, being a woman of much hon-esty and virtue, and her whole life a course as it were of piety. The use which we ought to make of it is to consider that there is a life to come after this, and a just God who will retribute to everyone according to the deeds done in the body; and there-fore, to reflect upon our past course of life we have led in the world, that our time is short and uncertain, and that if we would escape the punishment of the ungodly and receive the reward of the righteous, which is the laying hold of eternal life, we ought for the time to come to turn to God by a speedy repentance, ceasing to do evil and learning to do well: to seek after God early, if happily he may be found of us, and lead such lives for the future as may be well pleasing in his sight.

A Relation of the Apparition of Mrs. Veal

This thing is so rare in all its circumstances, and on so good authority, that my reading and conversation has not given me anything like it; it is fit to gratify the most ingenious and serious inquirer. Mrs. Bargrave is the person to whom Mrs. Veal appeared after her death. She is my intimate friend, and I can avouch for her reputa-tion for these last fifteen or sixteen years on my own knowledge; and I can confirm the good character she had from her youth, to the time of my acquaintance. Though since this relation she is calumniated by some people that are friends to the brother of Mrs. Veal who appeared, who think the relation of this appearance to be a reflection,[1] and endeavor what they can to blast Mrs. Bargrave's reputation and to laugh the story out of countenance. But the circumstances thereof, and the cheerful disposition of Mrs. Bargrave, notwithstanding the unheard of ill usage of a very wicked husband, there is not the least sign of dejection in her face; nor did I ever hear her let fall a desponding or murmuring expression; nay, not when actually under her husband's barbarity, which I have been witness to, and several other persons of undoubted reputation.[2]

Now you must know that Mrs. Veal was a maiden gentlewoman[3] of about thirty years of age, and for some years last past had been troubled with fits, which were per-ceived coming on her by her leaving off from her discourse very abruptly to some impertinence.[4] She was maintained by an only brother, and kept his house in Dover. She was a very pious woman, and her brother a very sober man to all appearance. But now he does all he can to null or quash the story. Mrs. Veal was intimately acquainted with Mrs. Bargrave from her childhood. Mrs. Veal's circumstances were then mean; her father did not take care of his children as he ought, so that they were exposed to hardships. And Mrs. Bargrave in those days had as unkind a father, though she wanted for neither food nor clothing, while Mrs. Veal wanted for both. So that it was in the power of Mrs. Bargrave to be very much her friend in several instances, which mightily endeared Mrs. Veal; insomuch that she would often say, "Mrs. Bargrave, you are not

---

1. I.e., injurious to the family's reputation.
2. The sentence is grammatically incomplete (Defoe sup-plies no verb for the initial subject "the circumstances").

3. "Mrs." (pronounced "Mistress") designated any adult woman, married or unmarried.
4. Irrelevance; digression.

only the best, but the only friend I have in the world, and no circumstances of life shall ever dissolve my friendship." They would often condole each other's adverse fortunes, and read together *Drelincourt upon Death*[5] and other good books. And so like two Christian friends they comforted each other under their sorrow.

Sometime after, Mr. Veal's friends got him a place in the custom house at Dover, which occasioned Mrs. Veal by little and little to fall off from her intimacy with Mrs. Bargrave, though there was never any such thing as a quarrel; but an indifferency came on by degrees, till at last Mrs. Bargrave had not seen her in two years and a half; though above a twelve month of the time Mrs. Bargrave had been absent from Dover, and this last half year has been in Canterbury about two months of the time, dwelling in a house of her own.

In this house, on the eighth of September last, viz. 1705, she was sitting alone in the forenoon, thinking over her unfortunate life and arguing herself into a due resignation to Providence, though her condition seemed hard. And said she, "I have been provided for hitherto, and doubt not but I shall be still, and am well satisfied that my afflictions shall end when it is most fit for me." And then took up her sewing work, which she had no sooner done but she hears a knocking at the door. She went to see who it was there, and this proved to be Mrs. Veal, her old friend, who was in a riding habit. At that moment of time, the clock struck twelve at noon.

"Madam," says Mrs. Bargrave, "I am surprised to see you, you have been so long a stranger," but told her she was glad to see her and offered to salute[6] her, which Mrs. Veal complied with till their lips almost touched, and then Mrs. Veal drew her hand cross her own eyes and said, "I am not very well," and so waived it. She told Mrs. Bargrave she was going a journey, and had a great mind to see her first. "But," says Mrs. Bargrave, "how came you to take a journey alone? I am amazed at it, because I know you have so fond a brother." "O!" says Mrs. Veal, "I gave my brother the slip and came away, because I had so great a mind to see you before I took my journey." So Mrs. Bargrave went in with her, into another room within the first, and Mrs. Veal sat herself down in an elbow-chair, in which Mrs. Bargrave was sitting when she heard Mrs. Veal knock. Then says Mrs. Veal, "My dear friend, I am come to renew our old friendship again, and to beg your pardon for my breach of it, and if you can forgive me you are one of the best of women." "O!" says Mrs. Bargrave, "don't mention such a thing. I have not had an uneasy thought about it; I can easily forgive it." "What did you think of me?" says Mrs. Veal. Says Mrs. Bargrave, "I thought you were like the rest of the world, and that prosperity had made you forget yourself and me." Then Mrs. Veal reminded Mrs. Bargrave of the many friendly offices she did her in former days, and much of the conversation they had with each other in the time of their adversity: what books they read, and what comfort in particular they received from *Drelincourt's Book of Death*, which was the best, she said, on that subject ever wrote. She also mentioned Dr. Sherlock,[7] and two Dutch books which were translated, wrote upon death, and several others. But Drelincourt, she said, had the clearest notions of death and of the future state of any who have handled that subject. Then she asked Mrs. Bargrave whether she had Drelincourt. She said, "Yes." Says Mrs.

5. I.e., *The Christian's Defense against the Fears of Death*, by Charles Drelincourt, a French Protestant pastor and prolific devotional writer who published the book in 1651; the first English translation appeared in 1675.

6. Kiss.

7. William Sherlock, Protestant divine and author of the widely read *Practical Discourse upon Death* (1689).

Veal, "Fetch it," and so Mrs. Bargrave goes upstairs and brings it down. Says Mrs. Veal, "Dear Mrs. Bargrave, if the eyes of our faith were as open as the eyes of our body, we should see numbers of angels about us for our guard. The notions we have of Heaven now are nothing like what it is, as Drelincourt says. Therefore be comforted under your afflictions, and believe that the Almighty has a particular regard to you, and that your afflictions are marks of God's favor. And when they have done the business they were sent for, they shall be removed from you. And believe me, my dear friend, believe what I say to you, one minute of future happiness will infinitely reward you for all your sufferings. For I can never believe" (and claps her hand upon her knee, with a great deal of earnestness, which indeed ran through all her discourse) "that ever God will suffer you to spend all your days in this afflicted state. But be assured that your afflictions shall leave you, or you them, in a short time." She spake in that pathetical and heavenly manner, that Mrs. Bargrave wept several times, she was so deeply affected with it. Then Mrs. Veal mentioned Dr. Horneck's *Ascetic*,[8] at the end of which he gives an account of the lives of the primitive Christians. Their pattern she recommended to our imitation, and said their conversation was not like this of our age. "For now" (says she) "there is nothing but frothy vain discourse, which is far different from theirs. Theirs was to edification, and to build one another up in the faith. So that they were not as we are, nor are we as they are. But," said she, "we might do as they did. There was a hearty friendship among them, but where is it now to be found?" Says Mrs. Bargrave, " 'Tis hard indeed to find a true friend in these days." Says Mrs. Veal, "Mr. Norris[9] has a fine copy of verses called *Friendship in Perfection*, which I wonderfully admire. Have you seen the book?" says Mrs. Veal. "No," says Mrs. Bargrave, "but I have the verses of my own writing out." "Have you?" says Mrs. Veal, "then fetch them." Which she did from above stairs, and offered them to Mrs. Veal to read, who refused, and waived the thing, saying holding down her head would make it ache, and then desired Mrs. Bargrave to read them to her, which she did. As they were admiring friendship, Mrs. Veal said, "Dear Mrs. Bargrave, I shall love you forever. In the verses, there is twice used the word Elysium. Ah!" says Mrs. Veal, "these poets have such names for heaven." She would often draw her hand cross her own eyes, and say, "Mrs. Bargrave, don't you think I am mightily impaired by my fits?" "No," says Mrs. Bargrave, "I think you look as well as ever I knew you."

After all this discourse, which the apparition put in words much finer than Mrs. Bargrave said she could pretend to, and was much more than she can remember (for it cannot be thought that an hour and three quarters' conversation could all be retained, though the main of it she thinks she does). She said to Mrs. Bargrave she would have her write a letter to her brother, and tell him she would have him give rings to such and such, and that there was a purse of gold in her cabinet, and that she would have two broad pieces given to her cousin Watson. Talking at this rate, Mrs. Bargrave thought that a fit was coming upon her,[1] and so placed herself in a chair just before her knees, to keep her from falling to the ground if her fits should occasion it; for the elbow chair she thought would keep her from falling on either side. And to divert Mrs. Veal, as she thought, she took hold of her gown sleeve several times, and commended it. Mrs. Veal told her it was a scoured[2] silk, and newly made up. But for all this Mrs.

---

8. Anthony Horneck, clergyman and author of *The Happy Ascetic* (1681).
9. John Norris, a clergyman, philosopher, and poet.

1. I.e., Mrs. Veal.
2. Polished; cleaned with detergent.

Veal persisted in her request, and told Mrs. Bargrave she must not deny her. And she would have her tell her brother all their conversation, when she had an opportunity. "Dear Mrs. Veal," says Mrs. Bargrave, "this seems so impertinent that I cannot tell how to comply with it; and what a mortifying story will our conversation be to a young gentleman?" "Well," says Mrs. Veal, "I must not be denied." "Why," says Mrs. Bargrave, " 'tis much better methinks to do it yourself." "No," says Mrs. Veal, "though it seems impertinent to you now, you will see more reason for it hereafter." Mrs. Bargrave then, to satisfy her importunity, was going to fetch a pen and ink; but Mrs. Veal said, "Let it alone now, and do it when I am gone; but you must be sure to do it." Which was one of the last things she enjoined her at parting; and so she promised her.

Then Mrs. Veal asked for Mrs. Bargrave's daughter. She said she was not at home. "But if you have a mind to see her," says Mrs. Bargrave, "I'll send for her." "Do," says Mrs. Veal. On which she left her, and went to a neighbor's to send for her. And by the time Mrs. Bargrave was returning, Mrs. Veal was got without the door in the street, in the face of the beast-market on a Saturday (which is market day), and stood ready to part as soon as Mrs. Bargrave came to her. She asked her why she was in such haste. She said she must be going, though perhaps she might not go her journey till Monday. And told Mrs. Bargrave she hoped she should see her again at her cousin Watson's before she went whither she was a-going. Then she said she would take her leave of her, and walked from Mrs. Bargrave in her view till a turning interrupted the sight of her, which was three quarters after one in the afternoon.

Mrs. Veal died the 7th of September at 12 o'clock at noon, of her fits, and had not above four hours' senses before her death, in which time she received the sacrament. The next day after Mrs. Veal's appearing being Sunday, Mrs. Bargrave was mightily indisposed with a cold and a sore throat, that she could not go out that day. But on Monday morning she sends a person to Captain Watson's to know if Mrs. Veal were there. They wondered at Mrs. Bargrave's inquiry, and sent her word that she was not there, nor was she expected. At this answer Mrs. Bargrave told the maid she had certainly mistook the name, or made some blunder. And though she was ill, she put on her hood and went herself to Captain Watson's, though she knew none of the family, to see if Mrs. Veal was there or not. They said they wondered at her asking, for that she had not been in town; they were sure, if she had, she would have been there. Says Mrs. Bargrave, "I am sure she was with me on Saturday almost two hours." They said it was impossible, for they must have seen her if she had. In comes Captain Watson, while they were in dispute, and said that Mrs. Veal was certainly dead, and her escutcheons were making.[3] This strangely surprised Mrs. Bargrave, who went to the person immediately who had the care of them, and found it true. Then she related the whole story to Captain Watson's family, and what gown she had on, and how striped. And that Mrs. Veal told her it was scoured. Then Mrs. Watson cried out, "You have seen her indeed, for none knew but Mrs. Veal and myself that the gown was scoured." And Mrs. Watson owned that she described the gown exactly; "for," said she, "I helped her to make it up." This, Mrs. Watson blazed all about the town, and avouched the demonstration of the truth of Mrs. Bargrave's seeing Mrs. Veal's apparition. And Captain Watson carried two gentlemen immediately to Mrs. Bargrave's house, to hear the relation from her own mouth. And then it spread so fast that gentlemen and persons of quality, the judicious and skeptical part of the world, flocked in upon her, which at last became such a task that she was forced to go

3. Funeral ornaments were being prepared.

out of the way. For they were, in general, extremely satisfied of the truth of the thing, and plainly saw that Mrs. Bargrave was no hypochondriac, for she always appears with such a cheerful air and pleasing mien that she has gained the favor and esteem of all the gentry. And it's thought a great favor if they can but get the relation from her own mouth. I should have told you before that Mrs. Veal told Mrs. Bargrave that her sister and brother-in-law were just come down from London to see her. Says Mrs. Bargrave, "How came you to order matters so strangely?" "It could not be helped," said Mrs. Veal. And her sister and brother did come to see her, and entered the town of Dover just as Mrs. Veal was expiring. Mrs. Bargrave asked her whether she would drink some tea. Says Mrs. Veal, "I do not care if I do. But I'll warrant this mad fellow" (meaning Mrs. Bargrave's husband) "has broke all your trinkets." "But," says Mrs. Bargrave, "I'll get something to drink in for all that." But Mrs. Veal waived it, and said, "It is no matter, let it alone," and so it passed.

All the time I sat with Mrs. Bargrave, which was some hours, she recollected fresh sayings of Mrs. Veal. And one material thing more she told Mrs. Bargrave, that old Mr. Breton allowed Mrs. Veal ten pounds a year, which was a secret, and unknown to Mrs. Bargrave till Mrs. Veal told it her. Mrs. Bargrave never varies in her story, which puzzles those who doubt of the truth, or are unwilling to believe it. A servant in a neighbor's yard adjoining to Mrs. Bargrave's house heard her talking to somebody an hour of the time Mrs. Veal was with her. Mrs. Bargrave went out to her next neighbors the very moment she parted with Mrs. Veal, and told her what ravishing conversation she had with an old friend, and told the whole of it. *Drelincourt's Book of Death* is, since this happened, bought up strangely. And it is to be observed that notwithstanding all this trouble and fatigue Mrs. Bargrave has undergone upon this account, she never took the value of a farthing, nor suffered her daughter to take anything of anybody, and therefore can have no interest in telling the story.

But Mr. Veal does what he can to stifle the matter, and said he would see Mrs. Bargrave. But yet it is certain matter fact that he has been at Captain Watson's since the death of his sister, and yet never went near Mrs. Bargrave. And some of his friends report her to be a great liar, and that she knew of Mr. Breton's ten pounds a year. But the person who pretends to say so has the reputation of a notorious liar among persons which I know to be of undoubted repute. Now Mr. Veal is more a gentleman than to say she lies, but says a bad husband has crazed her. But she needs only to present herself, and it will effectually confute that pretense. Mr. Veal says he asked his sister on her deathbed whether she had a mind to dispose of anything, and she said, "No." Now, what the things which Mrs. Veal's apparition would have disposed of were so trifling, and nothing of justice aimed at in their disposal, that the design of it appears to me to be only in order to make Mrs. Bargrave, so to demonstrate the truth of her appearance as to satisfy the world of the reality thereof, as to what she had seen and heard, and to secure her reputation among the reasonable and understanding part of mankind. And then again, Mr. Veal owns that there was a purse of gold; but it was not found in her cabinet, but in a comb box. This looks improbable, for that Mrs. Watson owned that Mrs. Veal was so very careful of the key of her cabinet that she would trust nobody with it. And if so, no doubt she would not trust her gold out of it. And Mrs. Veal's often drawing her hand over her eyes, and asking Mrs. Bargrave whether her fits had not impaired her, looks to me as if she did it on purpose to remind Mrs. Bargrave of her fits, to prepare her not to think it strange that she should put her upon writing to her brother to dispose of rings and gold, which looked so much like a dying person's bequest. And it took accordingly with Mrs. Bargrave, as the effect of her fits coming upon her, and was one of the many instances of her wonderful love to her, and care of her, that she should not be affrighted. Which indeed appears in her whole management; particularly in her coming to her in the daytime, waiving the salutation, and when she was alone; and then the manner of her parting, to prevent a second attempt to salute her.

Now, why Mr. Veal should think this relation a reflection (as 'tis plain he does by his endeavoring to stifle it), I can't imagine, because the generality believe her to be a good spirit, her discourse was so heavenly. Her two great errands were to comfort Mrs. Bargrave in her affliction and to ask her forgiveness for her breach of friendship, and with a pious discourse to encourage her. So that after all, to suppose that Mrs. Bargrave could hatch such an invention as this from Friday noon till Saturday noon (supposing that she knew of Mrs. Veal's death the very first moment) without jumbling circumstances, and without any interest too—she must be more witty, fortunate, and wicked too than any indifferent person, I dare say, will allow. I asked Mrs. Bargrave several times if she was sure she felt the gown. She answered modestly, "If my senses be to be relied on, I am sure of it." I asked her if she heard a sound when she clapped her hand upon her knee. She said she did not remember she did. And she said, "She appeared to be as much a substance as I did, who talked with her. And I may," said she, "be as soon persuaded that your apparition is talking to me now, as that I did not really see her. For I was under no manner of fear; I received her as a friend, and parted with her as such. I would not," says she, "give one farthing to make anyone believe it. I have no interest in it; nothing but trouble is entailed upon me for a long time for aught that I know. And had it not come to light by accident, it would never have been made public." But now, she says, she will make her own private use of it, and keep herself out of the way as much as she can. And so she has done since. She says she had a gentleman who came thirty miles to her to hear the relation, and that she had told it to a room full of people at a time. Several particular gentlemen have had the story from Mrs. Bargrave's own mouth.

This thing has very much affected me, and I am as well satisfied as I am of the best grounded matter of fact. And why should we dispute matter of fact, because we cannot solve things of which we can have no certain or demonstrative notions, seems strange to me. Mrs. Bargrave's authority and sincerity alone would have been undoubted in any other case.

COMPANION READINGS
L. Lukyn: Letter to her Aunt

[Canterbury, 9 October 1705]

Honored Aunt,

You may very well complain of our negligence in not writing to you, but hope you have a better opinion of me than to think I have quite forgot I have such a relation as an aunt, and to show that I have not, do write, though I have very little to say, without I tell you a long story of an apparition that appeared to one Mrs. Bargrove here at Canterbury at noonday. What I sent[1] you I had from Mrs. Bargrove herself. Last Saturday, was five or six weeks ago, Mrs. Bargrove was in a low room in her

---

1. Send.

own house, and somebody knocked at the door, and it was one Mrs. Veal of Dover, who she was very intimately acquainted with when she lived at Dover, but had not seen her these two years and a half, for so long Mrs. B. has lived in Canterbury. This gentlewoman was much overjoyed at the sight of Mrs. Veal, and went to salute her, but she rushed by her and sat herself down in a great armed chair, and fell into discourse of several things that had happened when they lived together at Dover. Mrs. B. asked Mrs. Veal if she would drink any coffee or tea. She told her that if she talked of eating or drinking she would be gone. That Mrs. Veal was subject to fits and was never trusted alone anywhere without a servant with her, for which reason Mrs. B. asked her how she ventured to come alone. She told her she gave them the slip, for she had a mind to see her alone. She told Mrs. B. she was going a long journey, and she was minded to tell her some things before she went. She desired Mrs. B. if she should die to tell her brother that she would have Mrs. Margaret Watson have a suit of mourning, if not her best gown and petticoat and several other things she had in a cabinet. Captain Watson is this Mrs. Veal's uncle. Mrs. Veal told Mrs. B. that her brother and sister Hazelwood were coming to Dover, but they would not come till she was gone her journey, and it was true as she said, for when they came into Dover, the bell was ringing for her; she was just dead. That was the day after she died, she appeared to Mrs. B. She desired Mrs. B. to write down what she said but Mrs. B. [said] 'twas more proper for her to write it. She told her no, she was not well and could not. But Mrs. B. there lay a book in the room where they were which had like to have thrown down;[2] Mrs. Veal asked her what book it was. She told her it was somebody's consolations against the fears of death (but I have forgot the man's name that writ it). Says Mrs. Veal, "The things of the other world are not as we here think them." She says, "You know that book tells us so." And upon that they had a great deal of very heavenly talk. Mrs. B. said Mrs. Veal did not care she should look her in the face, but would rub her hand over it. She asked Mrs. B. if she did not think her fits had mightily impaired her. She told her she thought she looked a little pale, and Mrs. B. says she had the strangest blackness about her eyes she ever saw. She stayed two hours and at last seemed uneasy to be gone, and did rise up two or three times and sit down again. She desired she might see Mrs. B.'s little girl who boards with Mrs. Frances Casibon. She went to the next door to get somebody to send for the child, and when she came again Mrs. Veal was in the street as far from Mrs. B.'s door as from our house to Mr. Oughton's. So Mrs. B. went after her, and asked her if she would not stay and see the child. She told her no, she could not stay; she was going to her Uncle Watson's, and would have had Mrs. B. agone[3] with her. But she could not then but promised to come to her the next day. And so she had, but she has so sad a husband, and he came home in a cross drunkenness and shut her out of doors, and made her lay in a wet wash-house[4] all night, which hindered her going to Captain Watson's. But a[5] Monday morning she sent there to know if Mrs. Veal was gone her journey. Mrs. Watson wondered what the woman meant; there had been no Mrs. Veal. So when the messenger came to Mrs. B. she fancies she had mistook the message, and so Mrs. B. went herself to Mrs. Watson's, and while they were disputing the matter there came in news of the death of Mrs. Veal, which Mrs. B. and all present were very much surprised at as much a[6] more as she.

2. Perhaps "had been dropped there."
3. Go.
4. A shed used for laundry.
5. On.
6. Or.

Mrs. Veal lay but a day ill; she was taken a-Wednesday and died a-Friday. I have writ you a long epistle and think it high time to conclude with all the duty, love, and service from whom it's due, dear aunt.

Your dutiful niece,
Lukyn

Stephen Gray: Letter to John Flamsteed[1]

Canterbury, November 15, 1705

Reverend Sir,

Yours of the third instant[2] I have received and have according to the utmost of my ability endeavored to fulfill your request. I have not only made inquiry into Mrs. Bargrave's character from persons which were most likely to give a just account of her, but have been and conversed with her myself, so that if I have not answered your queries concerning her to your satisfaction you will impute it to my weakness and not to a want of will to serve you. For indeed my temper is very averse to conversation, yet I must strive what I can to overcome my inclinations when they are any wise obstructive to the obedience due to your commands.

Sir, I have taken the account I have had of Mrs. Bargrave's character from persons that are esteemed qualified in all things as you direct,[3] from those that have known her conversation, both when she lived at Dover and here in Canterbury, as well of the clergy as others, and all give her the character of a religious, discreet, witty, and well-accomplished gentlewoman. She was bred up in the Church of England; her father, who was Mr. Lodowick, was in his lifetime minister of the church at Dover, and she is seen often to frequent the divine service of the church. And as she herself told me, she was once beaten by her husband for being so silly (as he called it) as to receive the sacrament. This in answer to your first query. As to your second, I cannot find but she is a serious person not given to anything of levity. * * * 'Tis now become difficult to get an account of Mrs. Bargrave's relation of her conversation with Mrs. Veal. Mr. Veal, her brother at Dover, and his relations and friends that live here at Canterbury, being willing to have it forgotten, do all they can to stifle it. But I, happening to go to a gentleman's house whose wife I had heard was well acquainted with Mrs. Bargrave at a time when she was there, I acquainted him with the design of my coming. He so far interceded for me that I were the next day sent for to hear Mrs. Bargrave relate her whole story. But I must own that her narrative of it was so very long, and my memory so weak, that I began to despair of giving you a tolerable account of it, had I not been assisted with a copy of it as it was written by an ingenious gentleman who had it from her own mouth before several gentlemen. And as far as I can remember, 'tis very agreeable to what I heard her say.

Mrs. Bargrave, the wife of Mr. Bargrave, an attorney, who formerly lived in Dover, now in Canterbury, had when in Dover contracted a very intimate friendship with one Mrs. Veal, a maiden gentlewoman. But upon Mrs. Bargrave's coming to Canterbury, their friendly conversation had been discontinued for some time. Mrs.

---

1. John Flamsteed (1646–1719) was the astronomer-royal, charged with producing newly precise charts of the heavens. His informant Stephen Gray may be the person of the same name (d. 1736) who later distinguished himself as a very early student of electricity.

2. November 3.

3. Flamsteed's "direction" possesses Royal Society resonance, prizing the testimony of those best "qualified" (by intelligence, reputation, rank) to assess the evidence.

Veal died Friday, September 7th, at Dover, but visited Mrs. Bargrave on Saturday the 8th. She conversed with her two hours, viz. from 12 till 2 in the afternoon. Mrs. Bargrave in the forenoon had been weeping and bewailing herself upon the account of her afflicted condition, but had pretty well composed herself when about 12 o'clock she heard somebody knock at the door. Being alone, she went to the door herself to see who it was, and found it to be Mrs. Veal, her former friend, in a traveling habit. Being very joyful to see her, asked her how she came to find her out in that old hole. To whom Mrs. Veal replied that she would find her out wherever she was. Then Mrs. B. told her she was glad to see her, but wondered she came alone; she, being subject to fits, used not to go but with somebody to attend her. She replied that she had given her friends at her Uncle Watson's the slip. Then Mrs. Bargrave asked her to come in, and offered to salute her, upon which she sat herself down in a chair, saying she was very weary. Then Mrs. Bargrave sat down beside her and told Mrs. Veal she had been in a sad humor just before she came in. "Yes," said Mrs. Veal, "I perceived it by your eyes. Is it no better with you and your husband than it used to be?" To which Mrs. Bargrave replying, "No," Mrs. Veal thereupon undertook to comfort her by giving her hope that in a little time it would be otherwise, and then fell into some religious discourses and exhortations. And seeing a book lie in the window, asked Mrs. Bargrave what book it was. She said it was a book they two had taken great delight in reading in at Dover; it was Drelincourt's discourse *Against the Fear of Death*. Mrs. Veal replied it was an excellent book and full of truth. Mrs. Bargrave answered she preferred it to any she had seen on that subject. "Yes," said Mrs. Veal, "but death and eternity are much other things than the world takes them to be." Mrs. Bargrave, being much pleased with her friend's conversation, began a discourse on friendship and some things past, of the cause of the decay of it in them, and asked her if she had read any of Mr. Norris his works. Mrs. Veal replied she had read some of his letters of divine love. Mrs. Bargrave asked her if she had read a copy of verses of his on friendship. Mrs. Veal said no, and asked Mrs. Bargrave if she had that book, who said no, but she had written them out in another book and would fetch them down and show them to her if she pleased. To which she consented, and Mrs. Bargrave fetched them and offered them to her to read, but she refused, saying she could not read them, but desired Mrs. Bargrave to read them. Which she did, and seemed much affected with them, but told Mrs. Bargrave that friendship was much better and more perfect in the other world than in this. And in discourse she spent some time, to Mrs. Bargrave's great satisfaction. Mrs. Bargrave asked Mrs. Veal if she would drink any tea. To which she replied, "Now but if I would you have no fire to make it." To which she replied that she would soon have her fire. "Nay," said Mrs. Veal, "if you talk of drinking I am gone." Mrs. Veal, perceiving Mrs. Bargrave to look pretty earnestly upon her, endeavored to cover her face with her hand, and asked Mrs. Bargrave if her fits have not somewhat altered her. Mrs. Bargrave, being fearful of discouraging her, endeavored to mitigate.[4] Then Mrs. Veal made as if she was rising to be gone, but sat down again and told Mrs. Bargrave she had almost forgot a main thing she came to her about; and that was that she being to go a journey would desire her to tell her brother some things from her. "What," said Mrs. Bargrave, "you are going your old journey," meaning to Bath or Wells, where she knew she was wont frequently to go. To which Mrs. Veal made little or no reply, but went on to tell Mrs. Bargrave what

---

4. To reassure her.

she would have her tell her brother about a tombstone, saying her brother said he would have a tombstone made for her mother but had not done it, so she would now have him make one large enough to contain them both. And told her some things she had in her cabinet, and of a suit of clothes which she would have given to her cousin, Mrs. Margaret Watson, with some other things which Mrs. Bargrave will relate to none but Mrs. Veal's brother. Mrs. Bargrave thought this might be the effect of her head's being disturbed by some approaching fit that was coming upon her, went to divert her by some discourse about her gown, taking it in her hand, saying, "This is very pretty stuff, madam." Mrs. Veal replied, "It is an old gown I have had scoured and newly made up, but you do this to divert me. But I will not be diverted." Then Mrs. Bargrave would have fetched a pen and ink, that Mrs. Veal might have written what she would have her brother know, but she said she could not write then. Mrs. Bargrave asked her why she did not tell her brother before she came out of Dover, or tell her Uncle Watson now, as one that would sooner be believed. She replied no, and would not be satisfied without a promise from her to do it, which, after some reluctancy, she did. Then Mrs. Veal asked Mrs. Bargrave if she knew her sister who married a clergyman, Mr.————, that lives somewhere in Southwark. Mrs. Bargrave said it was about 20 years ago since she saw her at Dover. "Yes," says Mrs. Veal, "'tis above 25 years since," and told her that her sister, brother, and children were now coming to Dover, "and all things were provided for them just as I were going my journey." Then Mrs. Bargrave asked Mrs. Veal if she would see her little girl, who was at school, but she would send for her if she pleased, and went out of the door to see for a neighbor to call her. But looking back, saw Mrs. Veal was come to the door. Then said Mrs. Bargrave, "Then you will be going?" "Yes," says Mrs. Veal, "I cannot stay." Says Mrs. Bargrave, "I hope you do not go out of town tonight." "No," says Mrs. Veal, "I am going to my uncle Captain Watson's, and shall be there till Monday morning." And asked Mrs. Bargrave if she would not go with her. She said no, she could not go with her, because her husband was not at home, but would come tomorrow and see her before she went her journey; but would walk a little way with her. Which she did, and then they parted. And Mrs. Bargrave saw Mrs. Veal going towards Captain Watson's house for several rods,[5] and then before she went into her own house stepped into a neighbor's, who asked her what made her look so cheerful. Mrs. Bargrave replied that she had had two hours' conversation with an old friend of hers which was come to renew her friendship. Next day in the evening she went to Captain Watson's to inquire for Mrs. Veal, but they said she had not been there. When she came home, her husband told her that her old friend Mrs. Veal was dead. She said nothing to him till next morning; then asked him how he knew it, telling him what had happened. Being greatly surprised, went again to Captain Watson's and described her gown, which Mrs. Watson's daughter knew to be one which Mrs. Veal was wont to wear. But this not satisfying her, she went to the party that brought the news to Canterbury, who told her that Mrs. Veal died on Friday in the afternoon, and that her brother and sister was coming into Dover as the bell was ringing for her. There is this further observable, that the next neighbor's maid, as she was at work in the yard, heard somebody talking very pleasantly with Mrs. Bargrave, and when she came in told her Mrs. so, who said Mrs. Bargrave's husband does not use to be[6] so pleasant with her. Upon which the maid said no, that it was both women's voices she heard, but was not near enough to distinguish their words.

5. A rod is 16.5 feet.   6. Is not ordinarily.

This, Sir, is the substance of Mrs. Bargrave's relation. Most of the sober men of our city do believe it, but there are some that do not. Their chief objections are that Mrs. Bargrave mentions some things in the cabinet that Mr. Veal, when he opened it, could not find there, though he opened it in the presence of several persons whom he called as witnesses. And 'tis likewise said that nobody saw Mrs. Bargrave in the street at that time when she says she walked with her Mrs. Veal. And it's reported of Mrs. Bargrave that she is wont to report the houses wherein she has lived to be haunted, as you have heard. How far this is true, you have heard, in part already heard, but I have received a fuller information of this chatter than Mrs. Veal's[7] modesty would permit her to give me, though consonant enough to what she told me. Mr. Bargrave one day rode a-hunting with some gentlemen. And when they had done, towards night went to a public house about nine miles from Canterbury, where he got drunk and lay there not only that night but some days after. His wife, hearing where he was, went after him, to see if she could get him home (for she is very careful of him, notwithstanding his severity to her). It happened she came at a time when her husband was in the company of a whore. They were, it seems, together in the house of ease.[8] Mrs. Bargrave, when she came in, asked for her husband. They told her he was without in the garden, whither she went. The whore, it seems, saw her, and for fear of being discovered fled immediately; and before she was got over the wall Mrs. Bargrave saw her, and, when her husband came to her, told him that she had seen somewhat getting over the wall which she thought was an apparition. Which he seemed willing to believe, being glad of the opportunity of so pretty a delusion to conceal his roguery. And this Mr. Bargrave has been heard to relate himself long before the apparition of Mrs. Veal to Mrs. Bargrave. Upon the whole consideration of all circumstances, I cannot say those that do not believe Mrs. Bargrave's relation to be true are altogether without reason. Yet I think the arguments for the truth of it are of much greater validity than those against it, and am inclined to believe that Mrs. Bargrave did really converse with the apparition of her deceased friend; but shall leave you, Sir, to consider and weigh the arguments for the credibility or incredibility of it and to determine as you in your incomparably more mature judgment shall think fit to. I asked Mrs. Bargrave if she were willing to take her oath of her relation of this her conversation with Mrs. Veal. She answered, "Not without the consent of Mr. Veal," and that it should be before the Archbishop of Canterbury and some others of the chief ministers of state. Then I told her it would as soon be credited if it were given before two Justices of the Peace. She replied she did not care whether it were believed or not; she knew it to be true, and her word was as good as her oath. And added that it was no article of our faith; we may be saved without it. Besides, those that will not believe the Scriptures will not believe her upon her oath, and that she has no advantage by it, but a great deal of trouble, by multitudes of people coming to her or sending for her almost daily, so that she has had little rest since.

Sir, this is all that I can collect that may either confirm or contradict the credibility of Mrs. Veal's apparition to Mrs. Bargrave. I could have wished the task had been on others that was more capable of it, and then you might have had a more satisfactory account than I fear this will be to you.

This time of the year we are in the greatest hurry of our business, so that I have very little time, and am so fatigued that I can make but few astronomical observations. I do now and then get time to make a few hasty observations of the spots in the sun, and shall observe some of the eclipses of Jupiter's satellites that happen in conve-

---

7. A slip for "Mrs. Bargrave."   8. The outhouse.

nient times; but I will assure you, Sir, tis not without some regret that I must tell you I am afraid I shall not have so many as you may expect, and therefore would not have you so far depend on my observations as not to get what you can observed by others. Though I shall endeavor to serve you in all things to the very extremity of my power.

Sir, your most humble servant,
Stephen Gray

An Interview with Mrs. Bargrave[1]

On May 21, 1714, I asked Mrs. Bargrave whether the matters contained in this narrative are true. To which she replied that she had neither written the printed narrative nor published it, nor did she know the editor;[2] all things contained in it, however, were true as regards the event itself or matters of importance; but one or two circumstances relating to the affair were not described with perfect accuracy by the editor. The editor, no doubt, learned all particulars by word of mouth from Mrs. Bargrave,[3] and then published them without her knowledge. Whatever is changed for the better in this copy[4] is derived from Mrs. Bargrave herself.

Something was also mentioned in this conversation of the former times when the Dissenters were persecuted by King Charles II. At which says Mrs. Veal, "People should not persecute one another whilst they all are upon the road to eternity."

❦

from A Journal of the Plague Year
Being Observations or Memorials of the Most Remarkable Occurrences, as Well Public as Private, Which Happened in London during the Last Great Visitation in 1665[1]

[AT THE BURIAL PIT]

I went all the first part of the time freely about the streets, though not so freely as to run myself into apparent danger, except when they dug the great pit in the churchyard of our parish of Aldgate; a terrible pit it was, and I could not resist my curiosity to go and see it. As near as I may judge, it was about 40 foot in length, and about 15 or 16 foot broad; and at the time I first looked at it, about nine foot deep; but it was said they dug it near 20 foot deep afterwards, in one part of it, till they could go no deeper for the water: for they had, it seems, dug several large pits before this, for though the plague was long a-coming to our parish, yet when it did come, there was no parish in or about London where it raged with such violence as in the two parishes of Aldgate and Whitechapel.

---

1. This account was found written in Latin in a copy of the fourth edition of Defoe's *A True Relation.* The writer has not been identified; it is presented in the translation by George Aitken, the scholar who discovered and published it in his edition of *The Romances and Narratives of Daniel Defoe* (1895) 15.xix.
2. Defoe (whose identity as author/"editor" of the narrative was not yet known).
3. The writer here appears either to forget or to disbelieve Mrs. Bargrave's assertion in the previous sentence.
4. I.e., the fourth edition, in a copy of which these memoranda are inscribed.
1. In the early 1720s, London found itself once again

threatened with the prospect of bubonic plague. Defoe responded with two long pieces of prose: a manual of preventive measures called *Due Preparations for the Plague* (1720), and a historical fiction thoroughly researched and deeply grounded in historical facts. The text's purported narrator—already dead by the time his book is published—presents himself as recasting in retrospect the journal entries he wrote during that terrible year, in the hope that they may benefit future generations. Designated only by his initials, "H. F.," he is probably modeled in part on the author's uncle Henry Foe, who like "H. F." was a London saddler who lived in the parish of Aldgate.

I say they had dug several pits in another ground, when the distemper began to spread in our parish, and especially when the dead carts began to go about, which was not in our parish till the beginning of August. Into these pits they had put perhaps 50 or 60 bodies each; then they made larger holes, wherein they buried all that the cart brought in a week, which by the middle to the end of August, came to from 200 to 400 a week; and they could not well dig them larger, because of the order of the magistrates, confining them to leave no bodies within six foot of the surface; and the water coming on, at about 17 or 18 foot, they could not well, I say, put more in one pit; but now at the beginning of September, the plague raging in a dreadful manner, and the number of burials in our parish increasing to more than was ever buried in any parish about London of no larger extent, they ordered this dreadful gulf to be dug; for such it was, rather than a pit.

They had supposed this pit would have supplied them for a month or more, when they dug it, and some blamed the church wardens for suffering such a frightful thing, telling them they were making preparations to bury the whole parish, and the like; but time made it appear, the church wardens knew the condition of the parish better than they did; for the pit being finished the 4th of September, I think, they began to bury in it the 6th, and by the 20th, which was just two weeks, they had thrown into it 1,114 bodies, when they were obliged to fill it up, the bodies being then come to lie within six foot of the surface: I doubt not but there may be some ancient persons alive in the parish, who can justify the fact of this, and are able to show even in what part of the churchyard the pit lay, better than I can; the mark of it also was many years to be seen in the churchyard on the surface lying in length, parallel with the passage which goes by the west wall of the churchyard, out of Houndsditch, and turns east again into Whitechapel, coming out near the Three Nuns Inn.

It was about the 10th of September, that my curiosity led, or rather drove me to go and see this pit again, when there had been near 400 people buried in it; and I was not content to see it in the daytime, as I had done before; for then there would have been nothing to have been seen but the loose earth; for all the bodies that were thrown in were immediately covered with earth, by those they called the buriers, which at other times were called bearers;[2] but I resolved to go in the night and see some of them thrown in.

There was a strict order to prevent people coming to those pits, and that was only to prevent infection: but after some time, that order was more necessary, for people that were infected, and near their end, and delirious also, would run to those pits wrapped in blankets or rugs and throw themselves in and, as they said, bury themselves: I cannot say that the officers suffered any willingly to lie there; but I have heard that in a great pit in Finsbury, in the parish of Cripplegate, it lying open then to the fields (for it was not then walled about) came and threw themselves in, and expired there, before they threw any earth upon them; and that when they came to bury others, and found them there, they were quite dead, though not cold.

This may serve a little to describe the dreadful condition of that day, though it is impossible to say anything that is able to give a true idea of it to those who did not see it, other than this; that it was indeed very, very, very dreadful, and such as no tongue can express.

2. H. F. combines two categories: the buriers put the dead bodies into the pits, arranging them in order to conserve space, and covering them with lime in order to quicken decomposition. The bearers, by contrast, handled bodies living and dead: during the day they delivered the infected to the plague-hospitals; by night they collected corpses for the pits.

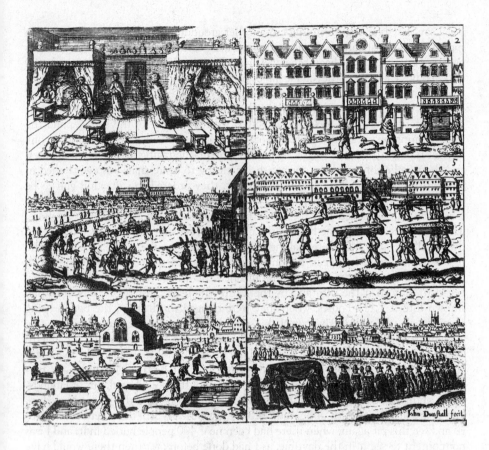

I got admittance into the churchyard by being acquainted with the sexton[3] who attended, who though he did not refuse me at all, yet earnestly persuaded me not to go; telling me very seriously, for he was a good religious and sensible man, that it was indeed their business and duty to venture, and to run all hazards; and that in it they might hope to be preserved; but that I had no apparent call to it, but my own curiosity, which, he said, he believed I would not pretend was sufficient to justify my running that hazard. I told him I had been pressed in my mind to go, and that perhaps it might be an instructing sight that might not be without its uses. "Nay," says the good man, "if you will venture upon that score, 'Name of God go in; for depend upon it, 'twill be a sermon to you, it may be, the best that ever you heard in your life. 'Tis a speaking sight," says he, "and has a voice with it, and a loud one, to call us all to repentance." And with that he opened the door and said, "Go, if you will."

His discourse had shocked my resolution a little, and I stood wavering for a good while; but just at that interval I saw two links[4] come over from the end of the Minories,[5] and heard the bellman,[6] and then appeared a dead cart, as they called it, coming over the streets so I could no longer resist my desire of seeing it, and went in: there was nobody, as I could perceive at first, in the churchyard or going into it,

---

3. Caretaker of the church and graveyard.
4. I.e., boys carrying torches ("links"), who for a fee led people through the streets at night.
5. A street.

6. In ordinary times, the bellman announced the time and weather as he made his way through the streets at night; in plague time, he rang his bell to alert people that the cart burying the dead was approaching.

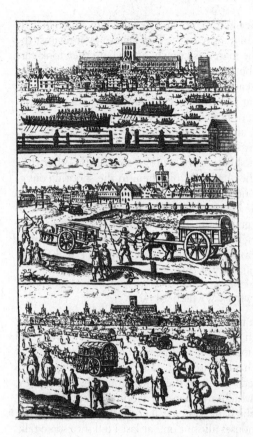

John Dunstall, *Scenes from the Plague in London*, 1665. The sequence tracks the course of corpses, from death within the city to burial in the plague-pits outside the city's walls.

but the buriers and the fellow that drove the cart, or rather led the horse and cart; but when they came up to the pit, they saw a man go to and again, muffled up in a brown cloak and making motions with his hands, under his cloak, as if he was in a great agony; and the buriers immediately gathered about him, supposing he was one of those poor delirious or desperate creatures that used to pretend,[7] as I have said, to bury themselves. He said nothing as he walked about, but two or three times groaned very deeply, and loud, and sighed as he would break his heart.

When the buriers came up to him they soon found he was neither a person infected and desperate, as I have observed above, or a person distempered in mind, but one oppressed with a dreadful weight of grief indeed, having his wife and several of his children, all in the cart that was just come in with him, and he followed in an agony and excess of sorrow. He mourned heartily, as it was easy to see, but with a kind of masculine grief that could not give itself vent by tears, and calmly desiring the buriers to let him alone, said he would only see the bodies thrown in, and go away, so they left importuning him; but no sooner was the cart turned round, and the bodies shot into the pit promiscuously, which was a surprise to him, for he at least expected they would have been decently laid in, though indeed he was afterwards convinced that was impractible; I say, no sooner did he see the sight, but he cried out aloud unable to contain himself; I could not hear what he said, but he went backward two or three

7. Attempt.

steps, and fell down in a swoon: the buriers ran to him and took him up, and in a little while he came to himself, and they led him away to the Pye Tavern over-against the end of Houndsditch, where, it seems, the man was known, and where they took care of him. He looked into the pit again, as he went away, but the buriers had covered the bodies so immediately with throwing in earth that, though there was light enough, for there were lanterns and candles in them placed all night round the sides of the pit, upon the heaps of earth, seven or eight, or perhaps more, yet nothing could be seen.

This was a mournful scene indeed, and affected me almost as much as the rest; but the other was awful, and full of terror. The cart had in it sixteen or seventeen bodies; some were wrapped up in linen sheets, some in rugs, some little other than naked, or so loose that what covering they had fell from them in the shooting out of the cart, and they fell quite naked among the rest; but the matter was not much to them, or the indecency much to anyone else, seeing they were all dead, and were to be huddled together into the common grave of mankind, as we may call it, for here was no difference made, but poor and rich went together; there was no other way of burials, neither was it possible there should, for coffins were not to be had for the prodigious numbers that fell in such a calamity as this.

[ENCOUNTER WITH A WATERMAN]

Much about the same time I walked out into the fields towards Bow; for I had a great mind to see how things were managed in the river, and among the ships; and as I had some concern in shipping, I had a notion that it had been one of the best ways of securing oneself from the infection to have retired into a ship, and musing how to satisfy my curiosity in that point, I turned away over the fields, from Bow to Bromley, and down to Blackwall, to the Stairs, which are there for landing or taking water.[1]

Here I saw a poor man walking on the bank, or seawall, as they call it, by himself. I walked a while also about, seeing the houses all shut up;[2] at last I fell into some talk, at a distance, with this poor man; first I asked him, how people did thereabouts? "Alas, Sir!" says he, "almost all desolate; all dead or sick: here are very few families in this part, or in that village," pointing at Poplar, "where half of them are not dead already, and the rest sick." Then he pointed to one house. "There they are all dead," said he, "and the house stands open; nobody dares go into it. A poor thief," says he, "ventured in to steal something, but he paid dear for his theft; for he was carried to the churchyard too last night." Then he pointed to several other houses. "There," says he, "they are all dead; the man and his wife, and five children. There," says he, "they are shut up; you see a watchman at the door," and so of other houses. "Why," says I, "What do you here all alone?" "Why," says he, "I am a poor desolate man; it has pleased God I am not yet visited,[3] though my family is, and one of my children dead." "How do you mean then," said I, "that you are not visited?" "Why," says he, "that's my house," pointing to a very little low boarded house, "and there my poor wife and two children live," said he, "if they may be said to live; for my wife and one of the children are visited, but I do not come at them." And with that word I saw the tears run very plentifully down his face; and so they did down mine too, I assure you.

But said I, "Why do you not come at them? How can you abandon your own flesh, and blood?" "Oh, Sir!" says he, "the Lord forbid; I do not abandon them; I work for them as much as I am able, and blessed be the Lord, I keep them from want," and

1. H. F.'s walk takes him to the bank of the river Thames.
2. By London ordinances, all houses in which an inhabitant had become infected were "shut up," with the surviving residents confined inside.
3. Infected.

with that I observed, he lifted up his eyes to Heaven, with a countenance that presently told me, I had happened on a man that was no hypocrite, but a serious, religious good man, and his ejaculation was an expression of thankfulness, that in such a condition as he was in, he should be able to say his family did not want. "Well," says I, "honest man, that is a great mercy as things go now with the poor: but how do you live then, and how are you kept from the dreadful calamity that is now upon us all?" "Why Sir," says he, "I am a waterman,[4] and there's my boat," says he, "and the boat serves me for a house; I work in it in the day, and I sleep in it in the night; and what I get, I lay down upon that stone," says he, showing me a broad stone on the other side of the street, a good way from his house, "and then," says he, "I halloo, and call to them till I make them hear; and they come and fetch it."

"Well friend," says I, "but how can you get any money as a waterman? Does anybody go by water these times?" "Yes Sir," says he, "in the way I am employed there does. Do you see there," says he, "five ships lie at anchor," pointing down the river, a good way below the town, "and do you see," says he, "eight or ten ships lie at the chain, there, and at anchor yonder," pointing above the town. "All those ships have families on board, of their merchants and owners, and such like, who have locked themselves up, and live on board, close shut in, for fear of the infection; and I tend on them to fetch things for them, carry letters, and do what is absolutely necessary, that they may not be obliged to come on shore; and every night I fasten my boat on board one of the ship's boats, and there I sleep by myself, and blessed be God, I am preserved hitherto."

"Well," said I, "friend, but will they let you come on board, after you have been on shore here, when this is such a terrible place, and so infected as it is?"

"Why, as to that," said he, "I very seldom go up the ship side, but deliver what I bring to their boat, or lie by the side, and they hoist it on board; if I did, I think they are in no danger from me, for I never go into any house on shore, or touch anybody, no, not of my own family; but I fetch provisions for them."

"Nay," says I, "but that may be worse, for you must have those provisions of somebody or other; and since all this part of the town is so infected, it is dangerous so much as to speak with anybody; for this village," said I, "is as it were, the beginning of London, though it be at some distance from it."

"That is true," added he, "but you do not understand me right, I do not buy provisions for them here; I row up to Greenwich and buy fresh meat there, and sometimes I row down the river to Woolwich and buy there; then I go to single farm houses on the Kentish side, where I am known, and buy fowls and eggs and butter, and bring to the ships, as they direct me, sometimes one, sometimes the other; I seldom come on shore here; and I came now only to call to my wife, and hear how my little family do, and give them a little money, which I received last night."

"Poor man!" said I, "and how much hast thou gotten for them?"

"I have gotten four shillings," said he, "which is a great sum, as things go now with poor men; but they have given me a bag of bread too, and a salt fish and some flesh; so all helps out."

"Well," said I, "and have you given it them yet?"

"No," said he, "but I have called, and my wife has answered, that she cannot come out yet, but in half an hour she hopes to come, and I am waiting for her: poor woman!" says he, "she is brought sadly down; she has a swelling, and it is broke, and I hope she will recover;[5] but I fear the child will die; but *it is the Lord*!"—Here he stopped, and wept very much.

4. Ferryman.
5. The plague afflicted its victims with painful swellings ("buboes"); if the swelling broke open, it was thought to presage recovery.

"Well, honest friend," said I, "thou hast a sure comforter, if thou hast brought thyself to be resigned to the will of God; He is dealing with us all in judgment."

"Oh, Sir," says he, "it is infinite mercy, if any of us are spared; and who am I to repine!"

"Sayest thou so," said I, "and how much less is my faith than thine?" And here my heart smote me, suggesting how much better this poor man's foundation was, on which he stayed in the danger, than mine; that he had nowhere to fly; that he had a family to bind him to attendance, which I had not; and mine was mere presumption, his a true dependence, and a courage resting on God: and yet, that he used all possible caution for his safety.

I turned a little way from the man, while these thoughts engaged me, for indeed, I could no more refrain from tears than he.

At length, after some farther talk, the poor woman opened the door, and called, "Robert, Robert." He answered and bid her stay a few moments, and he would come; so he ran down the common stairs to his boat, and fetched up a sack in which was the provisions he had brought from the ships; and when he returned, he hallooed again; then he went to the great stone which he showed me, and emptied the sack, and laid all out, everything by themselves, and then retired; and his wife came with a little boy to fetch them away; and he called, and said, such a captain had sent such a thing, and such a captain such a thing, and at the end adds, "God has sent it all, give thanks to Him." When the poor woman had taken up all, she was so weak, she could not carry it at once in, *though the weight was not much neither*; so she left the biscuit which was in a little bag and left a little boy to watch it till she came again.

"Well, but," says I to him, "did you leave her the four shillings too, which you said was your week's pay?"

"YES, YES," says he, "you shall hear her own it." So he calls again, "Rachel, Rachel,"[6] which it seems was her name, "did you take up the money?" "YES," said she. "How much was it?" said he. "Four shillings and a groat," said she. "Well, well," says he, "the Lord keep you all"; and so he turned to go away.

As I could not refrain contributing tears to this man's story, so neither could I refrain my charity for his assistance; so I called him. "Hark thee friend," said I, "come hither; for I believe thou art in health, that I may venture thee." So I pulled out my hand, which was in my pocket before. "Here," says I, "go and call thy Rachel once more, and give her a little more comfort from me. God will never forsake a family that trust in him as thou dost." So I gave him four other shillings, and bade him go lay them on the stone and call his wife.

I have not words to express the poor man's thankfulness, neither could he express it himself, but by tears running down his face; he called his wife, and told her God had moved the heart of a stranger, upon hearing their condition, to give them all that money; and a great deal more such as that he said to her. The woman too made signs of the like thankfulness, as well to Heaven, as to me, and joyfully picked it up; and I parted with no money all that year that I thought better bestowed.

1722

6. The name evokes Jeremiah 31.15: "Rachel weeping for her children refused to be comforted."

⇒⊱ PERSPECTIVES ⊰⇐
Reading Papers

Shakespeare never read a newspaper. In the early seventeenth century, the news was purveyed irregularly and improvisatorily. A breaking story or a sensational event might prompt a spate of ballads, broadsides, and bulletins, which would then abate until the next big thing hove into view. The news periodical, nascent on the Continent during Shakespeare's lifetime, arrived in England in 1620 in the form of English-language news sheets dispatched from Amsterdam. London publishers quickly took up the enterprise, to their considerable profit. Shakespeare's caustic contemporary Ben Jonson lived to witness their innovation; he promptly forecast an imminent glut of cheap and worthless information—fearing, with reason, that the new medium would supplant the theater as the public's favored oracle.

Even Jonson, though, could not have foreseen the quantities of print that would pour from presses decades later during the Civil Wars, when the instability of authority allowed innumerable newsbooks to appear, supporting every party in the conflict. During the Interregnum and Restoration, government tried through strict licensing laws to limit the flow and narrow the range of newsprint, but whenever those laws lapsed, innovations abounded: the first daily reports on proceedings in the House of Commons (1680), the first English newspaper outside London (1701), the first daily newspaper (1702), the first weekly journals (1713), melding the news with a miscellany of other departments. At the centennial of Shakespeare's death, London was producing some sixteen newspapers; a century later Britain possessed more than 350, in addition to legions of other periodicals purveying opinion and advice. The newspaper, the periodical essay, and the magazine had become confirmed habits in the lives of almost everyone who could read, and even of many who could not, since the papers were often read aloud, their contents discussed and debated, in public gathering places and household circles.

The periodical was a creature of the seventeenth century and a staple of the eighteenth. It punctuated the calendar with a new print pulse, and imparted to its readership a new sense of moving together in synchrony, in a rhythm that paradoxically combined the solitary and the social, the private and the public. The "mass ceremony" of reading the newspaper is generally performed (as the historian Benedict Anderson has observed) in "privacy, in the lair of the skull. Yet each communicant is well aware that the ceremony he performs is being replicated simultaneously by thousands (or millions) of others, of whose existence he is confident, yet of whose identity he has not the slightest notion." The periodical press, then, gave its readers a new way of seeing the world, and of seeing themselves in the world, as private beings and public entities; it prompted them (in Anderson's phrase) to imagine themselves as a community.

Monarchs and politicians tried hard to control the press, to dictate its views and to contain its criticisms, but in Britain the phenomenon proved too large for such arrant limitation. The news sheets and the essays helped create a new arena of political thought and action, separate from the older power centers of Court and Parliament, a public sphere of newly engaged readers who increasingly valued and deployed their own capacity to form collective opinions, and who increasingly expected their opinions to affect events. The freedom and copiousness of the press became a national boast, and abetted Britons in a conviction they were already cultivating: that they were participants in an ongoing narrative of commerce and taste, politeness, politics, and empire, protagonists in a story with numberless installments and no foreseeable end, unfolding at the center of the world.

Each newspaper in this section is introduced at its first appearance.

→ ⊨◊⊨ →

News and Comment

If the seventeenth century gave birth to the seething enterprise of print journalism, it also ushered in still-lingering distinctions and confusions as to what newspapers ought to be, and do. Most papers proudly declared their objectivity, yet at the same time they plainly manifested their partisan sympathies in their reportage and their prose. The division between news and opinion was rarely sharp, but in the early 1700s, opinion found fuller expression in periodicals like Defoe's *Review* (which more or less took for granted that readers had gathered their news elsewhere, and offered instead a running commentary on events), and in weekly journals like the *Craftsman*, which included ordinary news but which began each number with a long, fervently partisan political essay. Such essays anticipated the op-ed pages of today's newspapers, the closing meditations of news broadcasters.

MERCURIUS PUBLICUS (1660–1663)   During the Civil Wars, journalism gave voice to different factions; afterwards, it became the instrument of consolidated power. During the Interregnum, Cromwell controlled the news through his chief journalist Marchamont Nedham; strict licensing laws ensured that Nedham's *Public Intelligencer* (published every Monday) and *Mercurius Politicus* (every Thursday) were virtually the sole print sources for fresh information. (Mercury, the speedy messenger-god, remained throughout the century the favorite titular deity of the English press; more than a hundred periodicals bore his name). In 1660 the chief architects of the Restoration dismissed Nedham and supplanted him with their own advocate, Henry Muddiman (1629–1692). Taking over Nedham's newsbooks (now pointedly renamed the *Kingdom's Intelligencer* and *Mercurius Publicus*), Muddiman denounced the old regime and heralded the new with the zeal that would maintain him for nearly three decades, despite stiff competition from rival newsmen, as a favored journalist with the House of Stuart, right up to its fall from power in the 1688 Revolution.

from Mercurius Publicus
24–31 January 1661

[ANNIVERSARY OF THE REGICIDE]

London
    This day January 30 (we need say no more but name the day of the month) was doubly observed, not only by a solemn fast, sermons, and prayers at every parish church, for the precious blood of our late pious sovereign King Charles the First, of ever glorious memory; but also by public dragging of those odious carcasses of Oliver Cromwell, Henry Ireton, and John Bradshaw to Tyburn.[1] On Monday night Cromwell and Ireton in two several carts were drawn to Holborn from Westminster, after they were digged up on Saturday last, and the next morning Bradshaw; today they were drawn upon sledges to Tyburn, all the way (as before from Westminster) the outcry of the people went along with them. When these their carcasses were at Tyburn, they were pulled out of their coffins and hanged at the several angles of the triple tree,[2] where they hung till the sun was set; after which they were taken down,

---

1. Ireton (1611–1651) and Bradshaw (1602–1659) had played key roles in the trial, condemnation, and execution of Charles I. Tyburn had been for nearly three centuries the site for the public execution of common criminals (Charles had been dispatched on the grounds of the royal palace at Whitehall).
2. Tyburn's notorious "triangular gallows," whose three long horizontal beams could support as many as 21 hangings at a time.

their heads cut off, and their loathsome trunks thrown into a deep hole under the gallows. And now we cannot forget how at Cambridge when Cromwell first set up for a rebel, he rode under the gallows where, his horse just curvetting,[3] threw his cursed Highness out of the saddle just under the gallows (as if he had been turned off[4] the ladder), the spectators then observing the place, and rather presaging the present work of this day, than the monstrous villainies of this day twelve years.[5] But he is now again thrown under the gallows (never more to be digged up) and there we leave him.

LONDON GAZETTE (1665–PRESENT) New media are often modeled on old. In its first decades, English print journalism took the shape of a newsbook (actually a pamphlet) because that was a format with which printers and consumers had been long familiar. The *London Gazette* was something visibly different: the first news*paper*, a single sheet printed in double columns. Containment was the paper's whole point, not only in format but in content. Published twice weekly, "by authority" (as it proclaimed on its masthead), it remained for thirteen years the only printed news source the English were legally permitted to read, and it presented only that news which its government masters deemed fit for wide publication: full accounts of Continental politics, carefully trimmed treatments of domestic doings, all couched in a dry prose that deliberately eschewed the popular (and sometimes rabble-rousing) effects of the paper's midcentury forebears. The *Gazette* broke briefly from its self-constraints in the number for 10 September 1666, when the Great Fire of London had forced the printer to set up his press in the open air, and the correspondents reported very local events with considerable accuracy and unaccustomed fervor.

from **The London Gazette**
10 September 1666

[THE FIRE OF LONDON[1]]

Whitehall, September 8
The ordinary course of this paper having been interrupted by a sad and lamentable accident of fire lately happened in the City of London, it hath been thought fit for satisfying the minds of so many of His Majesty's good subjects, who must needs be concerned for the issue of so great an accident, to give this short, but true account of it.

On the second instant[2] at one of the clock in the morning there happened to break out a sad and deplorable fire, in Pudding Lane near New Fish Street, which falling out at that hour of the night, and in a quarter of the town so close-built with wooden pitched[3] houses, spread itself so far before day, and with such distraction to the inhabitants and neighbors, that care was not taken for the timely preventing the further diffusion of it by pulling down houses, as ought to have been; so that this lamentable fire in a short time became too big to be mastered by any engines or working near it. It fell out most unhappily too, that a violent easterly wind fomented it, and kept it burning all that day, and the night following spreading itself up to Gracechurch Street, and downwards from Cannon Street to the waterside as far as the Three Cranes in the Vintry.

---

3. Leaping, frisking.
4. Dropped from.
5. Ago. I.e., they foresaw that he would eventually be hung, but not that he would accomplish the regicide of 30 January 1649.

1. Compare the accounts of Pepys (page 2096) and Evelyn (page 2100)
2. 2 September.
3. Covered with pitch (distilled tar) in order to keep out water.

The people in all parts about it distracted by the vastness of it, and their particular care to carry away their goods, many attempts were made to prevent the spreading of it, by pulling down houses, and making great intervals, but all in vain, the fire seizing upon the timber and rubbish, and so continuing itself, even through those spaces, and raging in a bright flame all Monday and Tuesday, notwithstanding His Majesty's own, and his Royal Highness's[4] indefatigable and personal pains to apply all possible remedies to prevent it, calling upon and helping the people with their Guards;[5] and a great number of nobility and gentry unweariedly assisting therein, for which they were requited with a thousand blessings from the poor distressed people. * * *

And we cannot but observe, to the confutation of all His Majesty's enemies, who endeavor to persuade the world abroad of great parties and disaffection at home against His Majesty's government, that a greater instance of the affections of this City could never be given than hath been now given in this sad and deplorable accident, when if at any time disorder might have been expected from the losses, distraction, and almost desperation of some persons in their private fortunes, thousands of people not having had habitations to cover them. And yet in all this time it hath been so far from any appearance of designs or attempts against His Majesty's government, that His Majesty and his royal brother, out of their care to stop and prevent the fire, frequently exposing their persons with very small attendance in all parts of the town, sometimes even to be intermixed with those who labored in the business, yet nevertheless there hath not been observed so much as a murmuring word to fall from any, but on the contrary, even those persons whose losses rendered their conditions most desperate, and to be fit objects of other prayers, beholding those frequent instances of His Majesty's care of this people, forgot their own misery, and filled the streets with their prayers for His Majesty, whose trouble they seemed to compassionate before their own.

THE DAILY COURANT (1702–1735)   The *Daily Courant's* title announced its innovation. Its editor-publisher, Samuel Buckley (d. 1741), was the first in England to put out a paper every day (except for Sunday, which had no paper of its own until the 1770s); before now, papers had appeared thrice weekly at most. In his opening number, Buckley made clear both his dependence on "foreign prints" (newspapers from the Continent) and his distrust of them; his faith in his readers' capacity to winnow bias and interpret information; and his perhaps defensive condescension to his journalistic rivals as he embarked on the audacious enterprise of a daily paper.

from **The Daily Courant No. 1**
Wednesday, 11 March 1702
[EDITORIAL POLICY]

It will be found from the foreign prints, which from time to time, as occasion offers, will be mentioned in this paper, that the author has taken care to be duly furnished with all that comes from abroad in any language. And for an assurance that he will not, under pretense of having private intelligence, impose any additions of feigned circumstances to an action, but give his extracts fairly and impartially, at the beginning of each article he will quote the foreign paper from whence 'tis taken, that the

4. The King's brother James, Duke of York.   5. The royal brothers deployed their soldiers to aid the fire's victims.

public, seeing from what country a piece of news comes with the allowance of that government, may be better able to judge of the credibility and fairness of the relation. Nor will he take upon him to give any comments or conjectures of his own, but will relate only matter of fact, supposing other people to have sense enough to make reflections for themselves.

The *Courant* (as the title shows) will be published daily, being designed to give all the material[1] news as soon as every post arrives; and is confined to half the compass,[2] to save the public at least half the impertinences[3] of ordinary newspapers.

A REVIEW OF THE STATE OF THE BRITISH NATION (1704–1713)   Of the periodical commentators on the news, none was more formidable than Daniel Defoe, who single-handedly wrote his *Review* twice and sometimes thrice a week for nine years. The paper changed its name, its format, and its ostensible focus several times during its long run, but its general purposes remained the same throughout. Defoe wrote to celebrate trade, and to propose strategies for its improvement; to teach a rigorous piety and morality to a readership he saw as lax; and to advance by adroit advocacy the favorite programs of the paper's secret sponsor, Secretary of State Robert Harley (1661–1724). One of these was the Treaty of Union, whereby Scotland would merge under a single government with England and Wales to form the new national entity of Great Britain. Advocates of the measure construed it as a fair exchange, providing expanded trade for Scotland, enhanced security for England. In support of the cause, Defoe not only wrote copiously (pamphlets and essays as well as *Reviews*), he also persuaded Harley to send him to Scotland (where the prospect of Union was far from popular) to serve as chief strategist and propagandist. There, he argued energetically and successfully for passage of the treaty, while keeping his affiliation with Harley a close secret. When the Treaty of Union was ratified, the *Review* indulged in a moment of exultation, in the characteristic voice its creator had devised during his sustained periodic enterprise: that of a writer enmeshed in actual and volatile circumstance, deeply engaged with the politics, conduct, and commerce of the real world, sometimes embattled, often exasperated, occasionally exhausted, but ultimately indefatigable.

For more about Defoe, see his principal listing on page 2366.

Daniel Defoe: *from* A Review of the State of the British Nation, Vol. 4, No. 21
Saturday, 29 March 1707

[THE NEW UNION]

I have a long time dwelt on the subject of a Union; I have happily seen it transacted in the kingdom of Scotland; I have seen it carried on there through innumerable oppositions, both public and private, peaceable and unpeaceable; I have seen it perfected there, and ratified, sent up to England, debated, opposed, and at last passed in both houses, and having obtained the royal assent, I have the pleasure, just while I am writing these lines, to hear the guns proclaiming the happy conjunction from Edinburgh Castle. And though it brings an unsatisfying childish custom in play, and exposes me to a vain and truly ridiculous saying in England, "as the fool thinks, etc.," yet 'tis impossible to put the lively sound of the cannon just now firing into any other note to my ear than the articulate expression of Union, Union. Strange power of

---

1. Relevant.
2. Space. Most newspapers printed on both sides of the sheet. At first, Buckley printed on only one side, unsure
that his sources would supply him with enough matter to fill two sides daily (they soon did).
3. Irrelevancies; filler.

imagination, strange incoherence of circumstances that fills the mind so with the thing that it makes even the thunder of warlike engines cry peace; and what is made to divide and destroy, speaks out the language of this glorious conjunction!

I have hardly room to introduce the various contemplations of the consequences of this mighty transaction; 'tis a sea of universal improvement, every day it discovers new mines of treasure, and when I launch out in the bark of my own imagination, I every minute discover new success, new advantages, and the approaching happiness of both kingdoms. Nor am I an idle spectator here; I have told Scotland of improvements in trade, wealth, and shipping that shall accrue to them on the happy conclusion of this affair, and I am pleased double with this, that I am like to be one of the first men that shall give them the pleasure of the experiment. I have told them of the improvement of their coal trade, and 'tis their own fault if they do not particularly engage 20 or 25 sail of ships immediately from England on that work. I have told them of the improvement of their salt, and I am now contracting for English merchants for Scots salt to the value of about ten thousand pounds per annum. I have told them of linen manufactures, and I have now above 100 poor families at work, by my procuring and direction, for the making such sorts of linen, and in such manner as never was made here before, and as no person in the trade will believe could be made here, till they see it.

This has been my employment in Scotland, and this my endeavor to do that nation service, and convince them by the practice that what I have said of the Union has more weight in it than some have endeavored to persuade them. Those that have charged me with missions and commissions from neither they nor I know who, shall blush at their rashness, and be ashamed for reflecting on a man come hither on purpose to do them good.[1] Have I had a hand in the Union, have I been maltreated by the tongues of the violent, threatened to be murdered, and insulted, because I have pleaded for it and pressed you to it—gentlemen, in Scotland, I refer you to Her Majesty's speech; there's my claim, and you do me too much honor to entitle me to a share in what Her Majesty says shall be their due that have done so. Hearken to the words of your sovereign: "I make no doubt but it will be remembered and spoke of hereafter to the honor of those that have been instrumental to bring it to such an happy conclusion." (Queen's Speech to the Parliament, 6 March 1707.)

Pray, gentlemen, have a care how you charge me with having any hand in bringing forward this matter *to such an happy conclusion*, lest you build that monument upon me which Her Majesty has foretold, and honor the man you would debase. I plead no merit, I do not raise the value of what I have done; and I know some that are gone to London to solicit the reward of what they have had no hand in—I might have said, are gone to claim the merit of what I have been the single author of—but as this has been the constant way of the world with me, so I have no repinings on that account. Nor am I pleading any other merit than that I may have it wrote on my grave that I did my duty in promoting the Union, and consequently the happiness of these nations. ✳ ✳ ✳

THE CRAFTSMAN (1726–1750)   From 1721 to 1742, Sir Robert Walpole served George I and George II as First Lord of the Treasury, and, in effect, as prime minister. Walpole refined

---

1. In both England and Scotland, Defoe had been accused (with reason) of conducting a kind of espionage on behalf of Harley and the Union.

the techniques of earlier ministers. He used his control of the royal purse to build up a following in the House of Commons by means of pensions and lucrative government positions as reward for loyal service; he sought to shape public opinion by imposing strict libel laws against his critics, and by controlling prominent papers (the *London Journal*, the *Free Briton*, and others, as well as the government's long-running *London Gazette*) through adroitly managed patronage. He also enriched himself in the process, building a stately mansion at Houghton, and becoming an avid collector of art. Such brazen abuse of power prompted a two-party coalition in Parliament consisting of members opposed to Walpole's policies.

Many journals and periodicals contributed to the opposition to Walpole, but none was as feared or as popular as the *Craftsman*. In part, this was because no other journal could boast as compelling an array of writing talent. Edited by Nicholas Amhurst (1697–1742), an expelled student and hack writer from Oxford University, the journal derived its political philosophy and character from two politicians: William Pulteney (later Earl of Bath) and Henry St. John (Viscount Bolingbroke). As the respective leaders of the Whig and Tory factions of the Walpole opposition, Pulteney (1684–1764) and Bolingbroke (1678–1751) were in a unique position to coordinate parliamentary attacks on Walpole, as well as to generate public support for their criticisms of the ministry. Thus, from its first appearance in December 1726, the journal dedicated itself to exposing the "mystery of state-craft" in Walpole's ministry, a ministry which it regarded as the "grand fountain of corruption."

Hampered by the libel laws from attacking Walpole outright, the authors of the *Craftsman*, writing under the pseudonym "Caleb D'Anvers," pioneered new techniques of innuendo and allusion that allowed them to attack the ministry without actually breaking the law and incurring its penalties. The following number, for example, pretends to mediate an argument that took place at a party attended by Caleb D'Anvers. It takes advantage of the English interest in "prodigies"—monstrous births, strange apparitions, and vampires—to generate a stinging attack on Walpole as the great "bloodsucker." In so doing, this particular number of the *Craftsman* relies heavily on the pun implicit in the phrase "body politic."

from The Craftsman No. 307
Saturday, 20 May 1732

[VAMPIRES IN BRITAIN]

Non missura cutem, nisi plena cruoris hirudo.[1]

One evening last week I called to see a friend, and met a company of gentlemen and ladies engaged in a dispute about prodigies, occasioned by a very remarkable event which hath lately happened in Hungary. The account of this affair, as it is given in the *London Journal* of March the 11th, is of so extraordinary a nature, that it will be difficult to give my readers any just conception of it, without quoting it at large.

Extract of a private letter from Vienna:

> We have received certain advice of a sort of prodigy lately discovered in Hungary, at a place called Heyducken, situate on the other side of the Tibiscus, or Teys; namely, of dead bodies sucking, as it were, the blood of the living; for the latter visibly dry up, while the former are filled with blood. The fact at first sight seems to be impossible and even ridiculous; but the following is a true copy of a relation attested by unexceptionable witnesses, and sent to the imperial council of war.

1. "A leech that will not let the skin go, unless gorged with blood" (Horace, *Ars Poetica* 476), referring to mad poets who insist on reading their worthless verses to everyone.

Medreyga in Hungary, Jan. 7, 1732.

Upon a current report, that in the village of Medreyga certain dead bodies (called here Vampyres) had killed several persons, by sucking out all their blood, the present inquiry was made by the honorable commander in chief; and Capt. Goschutz of the company of Stallater, the Hadnagi Bariacrar, and the senior Heyduke of the village were severally examined; who unanimously declared that about five years ago a certain Heyduke, named Arnold Paul, was killed by the overturning of a cartload of hay, who in his lifetime was often heard to say, he had been tormented near Caschaw, and upon the borders of Turkish Serbia, by a vampyre; and that to extricate himself, he had eaten some of the earth of the vampyres' graves, and rubbed himself with their blood.

That 20 or 30 days after the decease of the said Arnold Paul, several persons complained that they were tormented, and that, in short, he had taken away the lives of four persons. In order, therefore, to put a stop to such a calamity, the inhabitants of the place, after having consulted their Hadnagi, caused the body of the said Arnold Paul to be taken up, 40 days after he had been dead, and found the same to be fresh and free from all manner of corruption; that he bled at the nose, mouth and ears, as pure and florid blood as was ever seen; and that his shroud and winding sheet were all over bloody; and lastly his finger and toe nails were fallen off, and new ones grown in their room.

As they observed from all these circumstances that he was a vampyre, they according to custom drove a stake through his heart; at which he gave a horrid groan, and lost a great deal of blood. Afterwards they burnt his body to ashes the same day, and threw them into his grave.

These good men say farther that all such as have been tormented or killed by the vampyres become vampyres when they are dead; and therefore they served several other dead bodies as they had done Arnold Paul's, for tormenting the living.

    Signed,

Batruer, first lieutenant of the regiment of Alexander.

Flickhenger, surgeon major to the regiment of Furstemburch.

—three other surgeons.

Gurschitz, Captain at Stallath.

I shall now proceed to give my readers the substance of our conversation upon this extraordinary narrative.

The brunt of the dispute, upon my entering the room, lay between a grave doctor of physic and a beautiful young lady, who was a great admirer of strange and wonderful occurrences. The doctor endeavored to ridicule such romantic stories, by treating them as the common artifices of newswriters to fill up their papers at a dead season, for want of other intelligence. The young lady confessed, with a good deal of modesty and candor, that she believed such things were frequently done; but still insisted on the truth of this relation, which stood attested by such unexceptionable witnesses. She observed that the time, the place, and the names of the persons concerned in this affair were particularly mentioned; that an authentic account of it appears to have been transmitted to the court of Vienna, signed by no less than six persons; four of whom were surgeons, and the other two officers of the army; that such gentlemen must be supposed to have too much skill to be imposed upon themselves in such a matter, and too much honor to impose upon others. To this the doctor replied, with some disdain, that all the surgeons and soldiers in the universe should never make him believe that a dead body, whose animal powers were totally extinguished, could torment the living, by sucking their blood, or performing any other active and operative functions. He added, that it was contrary to all the principles of philosophy, as well as the laws of nature; and, in my opinion, urged the point somewhat too far against a young, female opponent; who, by the color in her cheeks, appeared to be a little nettled and, with a scornful smile, returned; "Well, well, doctor, you may say what you please; but as wise as you pretend to be now, it is not long ago that you endeavored to make us believe a fact equally ridiculous and absurd. Surely, doctor," said she, "you cannot have forgot the famous Rabbit-Woman of Godalmin."[2]—The smartness of this reply produced an hearty laugh on the lady's side, and put the doctor somewhat out of countenance. Then turning to me with an air of triumph and satisfaction, "I am sure," said she, "Mr. D'Anvers, that you are of my opinion, and believe there may be such things as vampyres."—A man, who hath any degree of complaisance, is loath to contradict a pretty girl, who forestalls his judgment in so agreeable a manner. I desired therefore to read over the account very attentively before I gave my opinion upon it; and, clapping on my political spectacles, I soon discovered a secret meaning in it, which I was in hopes would moderate the dispute. I perceived the whole company waited with impatience for my answer; so that having unsaddled my nose, and composed my muscles into a becoming gravity for such an occasion, I delivered myself to them in the following manner.

Gentlemen and ladies,
I think this dispute may be easily compromised without any reproach, or disgrace to either side. I must agree with the learned doctor that an inanimate corpse cannot possibly perform any vital functions; and yet I am firmly persuaded, with the young lady, that there are vampyres, or dead bodies, which afflict and torment the living. In order to explain myself the more clearly on this head, I must desire you to reflect that the account, now before us, comes from the eastern part of the world, which hath always been remarkable for writing in the allegorical style.[3] Besides, it deserves our consideration that the states of Hungary are, at present, under the subjection of the Turks, or the Germans, and governed by them with a pretty hard rein; which obliges them to couch all their complaints under types, figures, and parables. I believe you will make no doubt that this relation of the vampyres is a piece of that kind, and contains a secret satire upon the administration of those countries, when you consider the following particulars.
You see that the method, by which these vampyres are said to torment and kill the living, is by sucking out all their blood; and what, I pray, is a more common phrase for a ravenous minister, even in this part of the world, than a leech, or a bloodsucker, who preys upon human gore, and fattens himself upon the vitals of his country?
Now, if you admit of this interpretation, which I think far from being strained, the whole mystery of the vampyres will unfold itself of course; for a plundering minister carries his oppressions beyond the grave, and continues to torment those whom he leaves behind him by anticipating the public revenues, and entailing a perpetuity of taxes and gabels[4] upon the people, which must drain the body politic by degrees of all its blood and spirit.

2. Mary Tofts, of Godalming in Surrey, reportedly gave birth to a litter of rabbits in the winter of 1726. For a time, this famous fraud deceived many physicians.
3. "Eastern," or Oriental, tales included a wide variety of fables, tall tales, mythical representations, and stories of wonder. Samuel Johnson's Rasselas (1759) is perhaps the most famous example of this broad genre.
4. A form of interest or rent due on land.

It is farther said, in the narrative, that all such as have been tormented, or killed by the vampyres, become vampyres, when they are dead.—This likewise is perfectly agreeable to my system; for those persons who groan under the burdens of such a minister are often obliged to sell or mortgage their estates, and therefore may be said, in a proper sense, to torment their unhappy posterity in the same manner.

Whether this Arnold Paul, or Paul Arnold, mentioned in the narrative, was a person in any office, or employment in the administration, which gave him a power of oppressing the people, either as a tax-layer or a tax-gatherer, I am not able to determine without farther inquiry. He is said, indeed, to have been a Heyduke, which I take to be a character of some consequence in those countries; but, perhaps, he might have been employed only as a ministerial tool, or instrument of oppression, under some great bloodsucker of state. For my own part, I am inclined to this opinion; because it is said that he had killed only four persons; whereas if he had been a vampyre of any considerable rank, we should in all probability have heard of his thousands and his ten thousands.[5] * * *

Having finished my speech, which was honored with the strictest attention, I was very much pleased to find it produce the desired effect, by putting an end to the dispute, which occasioned it. The doctor only nodded his head and told me, with a smile, that I had a political turn for every thing. The young lady expressed her satisfaction in the most obliging terms, and was pleased to say that my solution of this prodigy would make a very good *Craftsman*. She was immediately seconded by the whole company, who pressed me with so much importunity to print it in my next paper, that I could not in good manners refuse their request; and I hope my loving readers will excuse me, on that account, for troubling them this week with a loose, unpremeditated piece of conversation.

Having afterwards smoked my pipe, and spent the evening very agreeably, I took my leave at eleven o'clock, which hath been, for many years, my constant hour. The young lady followed me to the door, and, pulling me by the sleeve, "Pray, Mr. D'Anvers," said she, "don't forget the paper upon the vampyres."

━━◄✦►━━

Periodical Personae

In print journalism it was primarily the news that sold the paper; in the periodical essay it was the voice: the idiosyncratic mix of assertion and deference, comedy and charisma, with which author addressed audience. Political writers had long known the advantages of using a mask or *persona*— a pen name, a fictitious character—as a means of both concealing their identity and expanding the appeal of their controversial arguments. In the early 1700s, the inventors of the periodical essay extended the tactic of the fictitious self into new territory. While collaborating on *The Tatler and The Spectator*, Richard Steele and Joseph Addison devised strategies for making the unreal author a real arbitrator in the culture, a teacher of taste and conduct, manners and morality, someone whom readers found it pleasurable to learn from, to identify with, even to "believe in," despite (and because of) his comically exaggerated quirks, his patent nonexistence. Working behind their carefully crafted masks, Addison and Steele sold so many papers and impressed so many readers that their mark became indelible. For the rest of the century, the periodical essayist's first task was to devise a persona unusual enough to define the paper, and engaging enough to sustain it.

5. An allusion to Saul, who had "slain his thousands," and David, "his ten thousands" (1 Samuel 21.11). D'Anvers goes on to explain that certain private citizens ("sharpers, usurers, stock-jobbers") pursue an economic vampirism as skillfully as do the public officials.

THE TATLER (1709–1711)   At age thirty-five, after a checkered career as soldier, poet, playwright, popular moralist, and Whig propagandist, Captain Richard Steele (1672–1729) was appointed editor of the *London Gazette*, the government's long-running newspaper. Evidently even this task did not sufficiently absorb his energies. Two years later, while still supervising the *Gazette*, he launched *The Tatler*, a periodical of his own that outstripped all its predecessors in commercial success and enduring appeal. It appeared three times a week, ran for two years and 271 numbers, spawned many imitators, and continued to sell (in a four-volume collected edition) for the rest of the century. The *Tatler's* appeal derived in large measure from its putative author, Isaac Bickerstaff, Esquire, whose name Steele had borrowed from one of Swift's satires, but whose character he elaborated into that of a genial, perceptive, and comically self-congratulatory old man. The paper's commodious structure mirrored the gregariousness of its "author." Bickerstaff datelined his dispatches from the coffeehouses around London where papers were distributed, read, and discussed; he included letters (fictitious and authentic) from readers all over the country. The *Tatler's* audience thus found itself absorbed into the paper several ways: they were its constant topic, they sometimes supplied its text, they constituted both its origin and its end point, and they gave it their unprecedented devotion. Steele soon made further discoveries of form under the influence of his school friend Joseph Addison (1672–1729), whom he had brought in (so one contemporary put it) as his "great and constant assistant." Addison and Steele found that Bickerstaff's private musings, dispatched "From my Own Apartment," were the most pleasing items of all, and so they often devoted whole papers to reprinting what their character was pleased to call his "lucubrations" (meditations by candlelight, late at night). John Gay summed up the strategy's success. Coffeehouse owners, Gay reported, "began to be sensible that the Esquire's lucubrations alone had brought them more customers than all their other newspapers put together." Bickerstaff's other "departments" diminished or disappeared, and "the Esquire's lucubrations," now running the full length of the paper, created the format and the fashion for the periodical essay, a unified piece on a single topic as opposed to the fragmentary "miscellany" from which Steele had started. By the time he stopped *The Tatler* (probably because of political pressures following the Whigs' fall from power), he and Addison had devised means and achieved ends with which they would experiment anew in the *Spectator:* ways of creating community shot through with solitude, of mixing sociability and meditation, morality and mirth.

Richard Steele: *from* Tatler No. 1
Tuesday, 12 April 1709

[INTRODUCING MR. BICKERSTAFF]

Quicquid agunt homines nostri farrago libelli.[1]

Though the other papers which are published for the use of the good people of England have certainly very wholesome effects, and are laudable in their particular kinds, they do not seem to come up to the main design of such narrations, which, I humbly presume, should be principally intended for the use of politic persons, who are so public-spirited as to neglect their own affairs to look into transactions of state. Now these gentlemen, for the most part, being persons of strong zeal and weak intellects,[2] it is both a charitable and necessary work to offer something whereby such worthy and well-affected members of the commonwealth may be instructed, after their reading,

1. "Whatever people do [will furnish] the variety of our little book" (Juvenal, *Satires* 1.85–86); or (in the freer and more apt 18th-century translation by Thomas Percy) "Whate'er men do, or say, or think, or dream, / Our motley paper seizes for its theme."

2. Bickerstaff mocks that category of men known as the "coffeehouse politicians," who spent long hours together discussing news. For a more-sustained satire of them, see *Tatler* No. 155 (pages 2405–06).

what to think: which shall be the end and purpose of this my paper, wherein I shall from time to time report and consider all matters of what kind soever that shall occur to me, and publish such my advices and reflections every Tuesday, Thursday, and Saturday in the week, for the convenience of the post.[3] I resolve also to have something which may be of entertainment to the fair sex, in honor of whom I have invented the title of this paper. I therefore earnestly desire all persons, without distinction, to take it in for the present *gratis*,[4] and hereafter at the price of one penny, forbidding all hawkers to take more for it at their peril. And I desire all persons to consider, that I am at a very great charge for proper materials for this work, as well as that before I resolved upon it, I had settled a correspondence in all parts of the known and knowing world. And forasmuch as this globe is not trodden upon by mere drudges of business only, but that men of spirit and genius are justly to be esteemed as considerable agents in it, we shall not upon a dearth of news present you with musty foreign edicts, or dull proclamations, but shall divide our relations of the passages which occur in action or discourse throughout this town, as well as elsewhere, under such dates of places as may prepare you for the matter you are to expect, in the following manner.

All accounts of gallantry,[5] pleasure, and entertainment shall be under the article of White's Chocolate House; poetry, under that of Will's Coffeehouse; learning, under the title of Grecian; foreign and domestic news you will have from St. James's Coffeehouse; and what else I have to offer on any other subject, shall be dated from my own apartment.[6]

I once more desire my reader to consider, that as I cannot keep an ingenious man to go daily to Will's, under two-pence each day merely for his charges; to White's, under sixpence; nor to the Grecian, without allowing him some Plain Spanish,[7] to be as able as others at the learned table; and that a good observer cannot speak with even Kidney[8] at St. James's without clean linen. I say, these considerations will, I hope, make all persons willing to comply with my humble request (when my *gratis* stock is exhausted) of a penny apiece; especially since they are sure of some proper amusement, and that it is impossible for me to want means to entertain 'em, having, besides the force of my own parts, the power of divination, and that I can, by casting a figure, tell you all that will happen before it comes to pass.[9]

But this last faculty I shall use very sparingly, and speak but of few things 'till they are passed, for fear of divulging matters which may offend our superiors.[1] * * *

From my own apartment

I am sorry I am obliged to trouble the public with so much discourse, upon a matter which I at the very first mentioned as a trifle, *viz.* the death of Mr. Partridge, under

---

3. These were the days on which the postal system carried mail from London to the provinces.
4. Steele distributed his first four numbers free, as a way of attracting readers.
5. Flirtation and self-display.
6. Steele exploits associations between topic and venue long familiar to his readers. Each of the coffeehouses he names catered to a clientele "specializing" in the pursuits he names. A journalist himself, Steele parodies the newspaper format that headed each item by the name of its (usually foreign) city of origin.
7. A kind of snuff, used as a stimulant to induce sneezing.
8. A waiter.
9. To "cast a figure" is to work out a horoscope, an ability

that the *Tatler*'s first readers would readily associate with the character "Isaac Bickerstaff." Jonathan Swift had originally created the character (in a series of pamphlets in 1708) as a way of satirizing the fashion for astrological almanacs, which purported to foretell the important events of the coming year. In Swift's first pamphlet, the fictitious astrologer Isaac Bickerstaff forecast the imminent death of the real (and very successful) astrologer John Partridge; in the second pamphlet, Bickerstaff declared blithely that his prophecy had come to pass. Partridge's subsequent, frantic protestations added relish to the joke.
1. Bickerstaff proceeds to supply first dispatches from White's, Will's, and St. James's coffeehouses.

whose name there is an almanac come out for the year 1709.[2] In one page of which, it is asserted by the said John Partridge, that he is still living, and not only so, but that he was also living some time before, and even at the instant when I writ of his death. I have in another place, and in a paper by itself, sufficiently convinced this man that he is dead, and if he has any shame, I don't doubt but that by this time he owns it to all his acquaintance: for though the legs and arms, and whole body, of that man may still appear and perform their animal functions; yet since, as I have elsewhere observed, his art is gone, the man is gone. I am, as I said, concerned that this little matter should make so much noise; but since I am engaged, I take myself obliged in honor to go on in my lucubrations, and by the help of these arts of which I am master, as well as my skill in astrological speculations, I shall, as I see occasion, proceed to confute other dead men, who pretend to be in being, that they are actually deceased. I therefore give all men fair warning to mend their manners, for I shall from time to time print bills of mortality; and I beg the pardon of all such who shall be named therein, if they who are good for nothing shall find themselves in the number of the deceased.

THE SPECTATOR (1711–1713)   In the weeks of the *Spectator*'s first appearance, readers marveled at both its contents and its pace. "We had at first . . . no manner of notion," the wit John Gay reported from London, "how a diurnal paper could be continued in the spirit and style of our present *Spectators*; but to our no small surprise we find them still rising upon us, and can only wonder from whence so prodigious a run of wit and learning can proceed." It proceeded (as Gay guessed) from the minds and pens of the same two writers who had shut down the *Tatler* just a few months before. For their second periodical collaboration, Addison and Steele considerably upped the ante. Not only did they undertake to publish a new number every day (something no essayist had hitherto attempted), they also devised a new persona, intricately linked with their triumphant earlier creation Isaac Bickerstaff. Where the *Tatler* had begun in gregariousness and modulated towards solitude (at "my own apartment"), the new paper started from an even farther remove, in the eccentric silence of Mr. Spectator, who declares at the outset that he has not spoken "three sentences together" since birth. Mr. Spectator carries his "own apartment"—his state of psychological apartness—with him, not at his residence but in his head; "the working of my own mind," he announces early on, "is the chief entertainment of my life."

In his focused interiority, Mr. Spectator played out the principles of psychology that John Locke had propounded, but his extreme self-possession turned out to possess enormous rhetorical impact and commercial cachet as well. More than any other periodical persona, Mr. Spectator managed to embody and to allegorize the operations of the paper he inhabited. Like the paper he was everywhere, at once silent and articulate, fictitious in substance but impressive in effect, observant and absorbent of the culture, able to move into his readers' minds by the mysterious osmosis of reading itself, and to remain there, a disembodied monitor with a rapidly growing portfolio of daily essays. An anonymous pamphleteer reproached Mr. Spectator for the presumptuous "tyranny" of his surveillance, but the paper's tactics of reform remained in power for most of the century. It was read (and imitated) on the Continent, in the American colonies, and in remoter outposts like Sumatra, from whence a British trader wrote home to his daughter in London, admonishing her "to study the *Spectators*, especially those which relate to religion and domestic life. Next to the Bible you cannot read any writings so much to your purpose for the improvement of your mind and the conduct of your actions." The *Spectator*, Gay noted soon after the paper's debut, "is in everyone's hands, and a constant topic for our morning conversation at tea tables and coffeehouses." More than sixty years later, the Scots rhetorician Hugh Blair could only echo and elaborate on Gay's phrasing, in accordance

2. In the 1709 issue of his annual almanac *Merlinus Liberatus*, Partridge had insisted that he was "still alive."

with the paper's now long-established place in the British canon: "The *Spectator* . . . is a book which is in the hands of everyone, and which cannot be praised too highly. The good sense, and good writing, the useful morality, and the admirable vein of humor which abound in it, render it one of those standard books which have done the greatest honor to the English nation."

Joseph Addison: *from* Spectator No. 1
Thursday, 1 March 1711

[INTRODUCING MR. SPECTATOR]

Non fumum ex fulgore, sed ex fumo dare lucem
Cogitat, ut speciosa debinc miracula promat.[1]

I have observed, that a reader seldom peruses a book with pleasure 'till he knows whether the writer of it be a black or a fair man,[2] of a mild or choleric disposition, married or a bachelor, with other particulars of the like nature, that conduce very much to the right understanding of an author. To gratify this curiosity, which is so natural to a reader, I design this paper, and my next, as prefatory discourses to my following writings, and shall give some account in them of the several persons that are engaged in this work. As the chief trouble of compiling, digesting, and correcting will fall to my share, I must do myself the justice to open the work with my own history.

I was born to a small hereditary estate, which, according to the tradition of the village where it lies, was bounded by the same hedges and ditches in William the Conqueror's time[3] that it is at present, and has been delivered down from father to son whole and entire, without the loss or acquisition of a single field or meadow, during the space of six hundred years. There runs a story in the family, that when my mother was gone with child of me about three months, she dreamt that she was brought to bed of[4] a judge. Whether this might proceed from a lawsuit which was then depending in the family, or my father's being a justice of the peace, I cannot determine; for I am not so vain as to think it presaged any dignity that I should arrive at in my future life, though that was the interpretation which the neighborhood put upon it. The gravity of my behavior at my very first appearance in the world, and all the time that I sucked, seemed to favor my mother's dream: for, as she has often told me, I threw away my rattle before I was two months old, and would not make use of my coral[5] 'till they had taken away the bells from it.

As for the rest of my infancy, there being nothing in it remarkable, I shall pass it over in silence. I find that, during my nonage,[6] I had the reputation of a very sullen youth, but was always a favorite of my schoolmaster, who used to say, *that my parts were solid and would wear well.* I had not been long at the university before I distinguished myself by a most profound silence: for during the space of eight years, excepting in the public exercises of the college, I scarce uttered the quantity of an hundred words; and indeed do not remember that I ever spoke three sentences together in my whole life. Whilst I was in this learned body I applied myself with so much diligence

1. "He intends to produce not smoke from fire, but light from smoke, so that he may then put forth striking and amazing things" (Horace, *Ars Poetica* 143–44).
2. Of dark or light complexion.
3. The late 11th century, when William ruled as king of England.
4. Had given birth to. The silence of judges was proverbial.
5. Another sound maker for infants.
6. Childhood.

to my studies that there are very few celebrated books, either in the learned or the modern tongues, which I am not acquainted with.

Upon the death of my father I was resolved to travel into foreign countries, and therefore left the university, with the character[7] of an odd unaccountable fellow that had a great deal of learning, if I would but show it. An insatiable thirst after knowledge carried me into all the countries of Europe, in which there was anything new or strange to be seen; nay, to such a degree was my curiosity raised, that having read the controversies of some great men concerning the antiquities of Egypt, I made a voyage to Grand Cairo, on purpose to take the measure of a pyramid; and as soon as I had set myself right in that particular, returned to my native country with great satisfaction.

I have passed my latter years in this city, where I am frequently seen in most public places, though there are not above half a dozen of my select friends that know me; of whom my next paper shall give a more particular account. There is no place of general resort, wherein I do not often make my appearance.[8] Sometimes I am seen thrusting my head into a round of politicians at Will's, and listening with great attention to the narratives that are made in those little circular audiences. Sometimes I smoke a pipe at Child's; and whilst I seem attentive to nothing but the *Post-Man*,[9] overhear the conversation of every table in the room. I appear on Sunday nights at St. James's Coffeehouse, and sometimes join the little committee of politics in the inner-room, as one who comes there to hear and improve. My face is likewise very well known at the Grecian, the Cocoa Tree, and in the theaters both of Drury Lane, and the Haymarket. I have been taken for a merchant upon the Exchange[1] for above these ten years, and sometimes pass for a Jew in the assembly of stock-jobbers at Jonathan's.[2] In short, wherever I see a cluster of people I always mix with them, though I never open my lips but in my own club.

Thus I live in the world, rather as a spectator of mankind than as one of the species; by which means I have made myself a speculative statesman, soldier, merchant, and artisan, without ever meddling with any practical part in life. I am very well versed in the theory of an husband or a father, and can discern the errors in the economy, business, and diversion of others, better than those who are engaged in them; as standers-by discover blots,[3] which are apt to escape those who are in the game. I never espoused any party with violence, and am resolved to observe an exact neutrality between the Whigs and Tories,[4] unless I shall be forced to declare myself by the hostilities of either side. In short, I have acted in all the parts of my life as a looker-on, which is the character I intend to preserve in this paper.

I have given the reader just so much of my history and character as to let him see I am not altogether unqualified for the business I have undertaken. As for other particulars in my life and adventures, I shall insert them in following papers as I shall see occasion. In the mean time, when I consider how much I have seen, read, and heard, I begin to blame my own taciturnity; and since I have neither time nor inclination to

7. Reputation.

8. With a conspicuous openness to all parties and pursuits, Mr. Spectator distributes his visitations among some of London's favorite meeting places, including ones popular with Whigs (St. James's), Tories (the Cocoa Tree), authors (Child's), lawyers (the Grecian), and the news-obsessives he calls "politicians" (Will's).

9. A thrice-weekly newspaper, favored by Whigs.

1. The Royal Exchange was a large building containing many shops and serving as a meeting place for merchants. (For Addison's paean to the place, see *Spectator* No. 69,

page 2410).

2. Jonathan's coffeehouse, near the Royal Exchange, was a principal meeting place of merchants and stockbrokers ("stock-jobbers").

3. In backgammon, a blot is a piece whose position puts it at risk of being taken.

4. Addison and Steele maintained "neutrality" more strictly in the *Spectator* than they had in the *Tatler*, which had incurred much controversy by its Whig partisanship.

communicate the fullness of my heart in speech, I am resolved to do it in writing; and to print my self out, if possible, before I die. I have been often told by my friends that it is pity so many useful discoveries which I have made should be in the possession of a silent man. For this reason therefore, I shall publish a sheet-full of thoughts every morning, for the benefit of my contemporaries; and if I can any way contribute to the diversion or improvement of the country in which I live, I shall leave it, when I am summoned out of it, with the secret satisfaction of thinking that I have not lived in vain. * * *

THE FEMALE SPECTATOR (APRIL 1744–MAY 1746)   *The Female Spectator* was the first periodical written by a woman for women. Its author, Eliza Haywood (c. 1693–1756), had been an actress, a playwright, and the writer of some sixty romances, novels, and other narratives, many of them scandalous and some of them wildly successful. In the mid-1740s, after a long eclipse prompted in part by Alexander Pope's derision of her in the *Dunciad*, Haywood emerged in a new guise: no longer a purveyor of exotic thrills, she set up instead as a teacher of morality. *The Female Spectator* differed from its namesake in calendar (monthly rather than daily) and format: a pamphlet and not a sheet, each number presented an essay focused on a single topic with several illustrative fictional stories interspersed. The biggest difference, though, was in the new paper's point of view. Mr. Spectator had observed, described, and instructed "the fair sex" from without, as supremely self-confident male mentor. Haywood offered instead a running report from the interior of women's lives. Her vantage point proved popular. *The Female Spectator* continued to sell, in a four-volume collected edition, for more than two decades after its periodical run had ceased.

from Female Spectator Vol. 1, No. 1
[THE AUTHOR'S INTENT]

It is very much by the choice we make of subjects for our entertainment that the refined taste distinguishes itself from the vulgar and more gross. Reading is universally allowed to be one of the most improving as well as agreeable amusements; but then to render it so, one should, among the number of books which are perpetually issuing from the press, endeavor to single out such as promise to be most conducive to those ends. In order to be as little deceived as possible, I, for my own part, love to get as well acquainted as I can with an author, before I run the risk of losing my time in perusing his work; and as I doubt not but most people are of this way of thinking, I shall, in imitation of my learned brother of ever precious memory,[1] give some account of what I am, and those concerned with me in this undertaking; and likewise of the chief intent of the lucubrations[2] hereafter communicated, that the reader, on casting his eye over the four or five first pages, may judge how far the book may or may not be qualified to entertain him, and either accept or throw it aside as he thinks proper. And here I promise that in the pictures I shall give of myself and associates, I will draw no flattering lines, assume no perfection that we are not in reality possessed of, nor attempt to shadow over any defect with an artificial gloss.

As a proof of my sincerity, I shall in the first place assure him that for my own part I never was a beauty, and am now very far from being young (a confession he will

---

1. Addison and Steele's Mr. Spectator.   Isaac Bickerstaff's catchword for his essays in the *Tatler*.
2. Writings by candlelight; Haywood pointedly picks up

find few of my sex ready to make). I shall also acknowledge that I have run through as many scenes of vanity and folly as the greatest coquette of them all. Dress, equipage,[3] and flattery were the idols of my heart. I should have thought that day lost which did not present me with some new opportunity of showing myself. My life, for some years, was a continued round of what I then called pleasure, and my whole time engrossed by a hurry of promiscuous diversions. But whatever inconveniences such a manner of conduct has brought upon myself, I have this consolation, to think that the public may reap some benefit from it. The company I kept was not, indeed, always so well chosen as it ought to have been, for the sake of my own interest or reputation; but then it was general, and by consequence furnished me not only with the knowledge of many occurrences, which otherwise I had been ignorant of, but also enabled me, when the too great vivacity of my nature became tempered with reflection, to see into the secret springs which gave rise to the actions I had either heard or been witness of—to judge of the various passions of the human mind, and distinguish those imperceptible degrees by which they become masters of the heart, and attain the dominion over reason. A thousand odd adventures, which at the time they happened made slight impression on me, and seemed to dwell no longer on my mind than the wonder they occasioned, now rise fresh to my remembrance, with this advantage, that the mystery I then, for want of attention, imagined they contained, is entirely vanished, and I find it easy to account for the cause by the consequence.

With this experience, added to a genius[4] tolerably extensive, and an education more liberal than is ordinarily allowed to persons of my sex, I flattered myself that it might be in my power to be in some measure both useful and entertaining to the public; and this thought was so soothing to those remains of vanity not yet wholly extinguished in me, that I resolved to pursue it, and immediately began to consider by what method I should be most likely to succeed. To confine myself to any one subject, I knew could please but one kind of taste, and my ambition was to be as universally read as possible. From my observations of human nature, I found that curiosity had more or less a share in every breast; and my business, therefore, was to hit this reigning humor in such a manner as that the gratification it should receive from being made acquainted with other people's affairs should at the same time teach every one to regulate their own.

Having agreed within myself on this important point, I commenced author, by setting down many things which, being pleasing to myself, I imagined would be so to others; but on examining them the next day, I found an infinite deficiency both in matter and style, and that there was an absolute necessity for me to call in to my assistance such of my acquaintance as were qualified for that purpose. The first that occurred to me, I shall distinguish by the name of Mira, a lady descended from a family to which wit seems hereditary, married to a gentleman every way worthy of so excellent a wife, and with whom she lives in so perfect a harmony, that having nothing to ruffle the composure of her soul, or disturb those sparkling ideas she received from nature and education, left me no room to doubt if what she favored me with would be acceptable to the public. The next is a widow of quality, who not having buried her vivacity in the tomb of her lord, continues to make one in all the modish diversions of the times, so far, I mean, as she finds them consistent with innocence and honor; and as she is far from having the least austerity in her behavior, nor is

---

3. Fancy carriages, servants, and furniture.   4. Talent, ability.

rigid to the failings she is wholly free from herself, those of her acquaintance who had been less circumspect scruple not to make her the confidante of secrets they conceal from all the world beside. The third is the daughter of a wealthy merchant, charming as an angel, but endued with so many accomplishments that to those who know her truly, her beauty is the least distinguished part of her. This fine young creature I shall call Euphrosyne, since she has all the cheerfulness and sweetness ascribed to that goddess.[5]

These three approved my design, assured me of all the help they could afford, and soon gave a proof of it in bringing their several essays; but as the reader, provided the entertainment be agreeable, will not be interested from which quarter it comes, whatever productions I shall be favored with from these ladies, or any others I may hereafter correspond with, will be exhibited under the general title of *The Female Spectator*, and how many contributors soever there may happen to be to the work, they are to be considered only as several members of one body, of which I am the mouth. * * *

Richard Steele: *from* Tatler No. 18
21 May 1709

[THE NEWS WRITERS IN DANGER[1]]
St. James's Coffeehouse, May 20.

* * * It being therefore visible, that our society[2] will be greater sufferers by the peace than the soldiery itself; insomuch, that the *Daily Courant* is in danger of being broken, my friend Dyer of being reformed,[3] and the very best of the whole band of being reduced to half-pay; might I presume to offer anything in the behalf of my distressed brethren, I would humbly move, that an appendix of proper apartments furnished with pen, ink, and paper, and other necessaries of life should be added to the Hospital of Chelsea,[4] for the relief of such decayed news writers as have served their country in the wars; and that for their exercise, they should compile the annals of their brother-veterans, who have been engaged in the same service, and are still obliged to do duty after the same manner.

I cannot be thought to speak this out of an eye to any private interest; for, as my chief scenes of action are coffeehouses, playhouses, and my own apartment, I am in no need of camps, fortifications, and fields of battle, to support me; I don't call out for heroes and generals to my assistance. Though the officers are broken, and the armies disbanded, I shall still be safe as long as there are men or women, or politicians, or lovers, or poets, or nymphs, or swains, or cits,[5] or courtiers, in being.

---

5. Euphrosyne is one of the three Graces, sister goddesses in Greek mythology who possess (and bestow) the gift of beauty.
1. Papers often defined themselves by contrasting their methods and achievements with those of their rivals. For the essayists, the newspapers afforded the readiest foil. Steele was a seasoned journalist, but he and Addison devised many ways of mocking the vacuity of the newsmongers, and of flattering those readers who preferred essays to mere journalism. In this early *Tatler*, Bickerstaff announces that England will soon be victorious in its for-

eign wars, observes that "the approach of peace strikes a panic through our armies," who will have nowhere left to fight, and worries that peace will prove even more costly to the journalists, who will have nothing left to write about.
2. I.e., the "brotherhood" of news writers.
3. John Dyer's fervently Tory newsletter often denounced the Whigs for (among other things) mismanaging the wars abroad.
4. Where disabled soldiers were given care and lodging.
5. City dwellers, tradespeople.

Joseph Addison: *from* Tatler No. 155
Thursday, 6 April 1710
[THE POLITICAL UPHOLSTERER]

—Aliena negotia curat
Excussus propriis.[1]

From My Own Apartment, April 5

There lived some years since within my neighborhood a very grave person, an upholsterer, who seemed a man of more than ordinary application to business. He was a very early riser, and was often abroad two or three hours before any of his neighbors. He had a particular carefulness in the knitting of his brows, and a kind of impatience in all his motions, that plainly discovered he was always intent on matters of importance. Upon my enquiry into his life and conversation, I found him to be the greatest newsmonger in our quarter;[2] that he rose before day to read the *Post-Man;*[3] and that he would take two or three turns to the other end of the town before his neighbors were up, to see if there were any Dutch mails[4] come in. He had a wife and several children; but was much more inquisitive to know what passed in Poland than in his own family, and was in greater pain and anxiety of mind for King Augustus's[5] welfare than that of his nearest relations. He looked extremely thin in a dearth of news, and never enjoyed himself in a westerly wind.[6] This indefatigable kind of life was the ruin of his shop; for about the time that his favorite prince left the crown of Poland, he broke and disappeared.

This man and his affairs had been long out of my mind, till about three days ago, as I was walking in St. James's Park, I heard somebody at a distance hemming after me: and who should it be but my old neighbor the upholsterer? I saw he was reduced to extreme poverty, by certain shabby superfluities in his dress: for notwithstanding that it was a very sultry day for the time of the year, he wore a loose great coat and a muff, with a long campaign-wig out of curl;[7] to which he had added the ornament of a pair of black garters buckled under the knee. Upon his coming up to me, I was going to inquire into his present circumstances; but was prevented by his asking me, with a whisper, whether the last letters brought any accounts that one might rely upon from Bender?[8] I told him, none that I heard of; and asked him, whether he had yet married his eldest daughter? He told me, No. But pray, says he, tell me sincerely, what are your thoughts of the King of Sweden? For though his wife and children were starving, I found his chief concern at present was for this great monarch. I told him, that I looked upon him as one of the first heroes of the age. But pray, says he, do you think there is anything in the story of his wound? And finding me surprised at the

---

1. "He minds others' concerns, since he has lost his own" (Horace, *Satires* 2.3.19–20).
2. "Monger" not because he sells news but because he tells it, to anyone who will listen; Addison's news-addicted upholsterer became one of the *Tatler's* most popular comic creations, reappearing in several later numbers.
3. The leading Whig newspaper (1695–1730).
4. Mailboats from the Netherlands, bringing fresh news.
5. Frederick Augustus I of Poland, whose loss and recovery of power had filled the papers for several years.

6. Which prevented the arrival of the "Dutch mails."
7. A "campaign wig" was used when traveling and was remarkable for its decorative curls (here flattened and disordered).
8. A town in modern Bessarabia, where Charles XII of Sweden (1682–1718) had sought refuge after a long string of military victories and a final catastrophic defeat (see Samuel Johnson, *The Vanity of Human Wishes*, lines 191–222, pages 2726–27).

question, Nay, says he, I only propose it to you. I answered, that I thought there was no reason to doubt of it. But why in the heel, says he, more than in any other part of the body? Because, says I, the bullet chanced to light there. * * *

We were now got to the upper end of the Mall,[9] where were three or four very odd fellows sitting together upon the bench. These I found were all of them politicians, who used to sun themselves in that place every day about dinner time.[1] * * *

I at length took my leave of the company, and was going away; but had not been gone thirty yards before the upholsterer hemmed again after me. Upon his advancing towards me, with a whisper, I expected to hear some secret piece of news, which he had not thought fit to communicate to the bench; but instead of that, he desired me in my ear to lend him half a crown. In compassion to so needy a statesman, and to dissipate the confusion I found he was in, I told him, if he pleased, I would give him five shillings, to receive five pounds of him when the Great Turk was driven out of Constantinople; which he very readily accepted, but not before he had laid down to me the impossibility of such an event, as the affairs of Europe now stand.

This paper I design for the particular benefit of those worthy citizens who live more in a coffeehouse than in their shops, and whose thoughts are so taken up with the affairs of the Allies, that they forget their customers.

from Joseph Addison: Spectator No. 10
Monday, 12 March 1711

[THE SPECTATOR AND ITS READERS[1]]

Non aliter quam qui adverso vix flumine lembum
Remigiis subigit: si brachia forte remisit,
Atque illum in praeceps prono rapit alveus amni.[2]

It is with much satisfaction that I hear this great city inquiring day by day after these my papers, and receiving my morning lectures with a becoming seriousness and attention. My publisher tells me, that there are already three thousand of them distributed every day: so that if I allow twenty readers to every paper, which I look upon as a modest computation, I may reckon about three-score thousand disciples in London and Westminster, who I hope will take care to distinguish themselves from the thoughtless herd of their ignorant and inattentive brethren. Since I have raised to myself so great an audience, I shall spare no pains to make their instruction agreeable, and their diversion useful. For which reasons I shall endeavor to enliven morality with wit, and to temper wit with morality, that my readers may, if possible, both ways find their account in the speculation of the day. And to the end that their virtue and discretion may not be short transient intermitting starts of thought, I have resolved to refresh their memories from day to day, till I have recovered them out of that desperate state of vice and folly into which the age is fallen. The mind that lies

---

9. The public walk in St. James's Park, near the royal residence.
1. Bickerstaff proceeds to eavesdrop, astonished, on the conversation of these news-obsessives.
1. The *Spectator* bore a close resemblance to the *Daily Courant:* both papers were a single sheet produced by the same printer (Samuel Buckley) for the same price (a penny), and both appeared every day except Sunday. In

this number, Addison elaborates on the ways in which his new essay—less than two weeks old and already very successful—is not a newspaper.
2. "As if one, whose oars can scarce force his skiff against the stream, should by chance slacken his arms, and lo! headlong down the current the channel sweeps it away" (Virgil, *Georgics* 1.201–3).

fallow but a single day sprouts up in follies that are only to be killed by a constant and assiduous culture. It was said of Socrates, that he brought philosophy down from heaven, to inhabit among men;[3] and I shall be ambitious to have it said of me, that I have brought philosophy out of closets and libraries, schools and colleges, to dwell in clubs and assemblies, at tea tables, and in coffeehouses.

I would therefore in a very particular manner recommend these my speculations to all well-regulated families, that set apart an hour in every morning for tea and bread and butter; and would earnestly advise them for their good to order this paper to be punctually served up, and to be looked upon as a part of the tea equipage.

Sir Francis Bacon observes that a well-written book, compared with its rivals and antagonists, is like Moses's serpent, that immediately swallowed up and devoured those of the Egyptians.[4] I shall not be so vain as to think that where the *Spectator* appears, the other public prints will vanish; but shall leave it to my readers' consideration whether, is it not much better to be let into the knowledge of oneself, than to hear what passes in Muscovy[5] or Poland; and to amuse ourselves with such writings as tend to the wearing out of ignorance, passion, and prejudice, than such as naturally conduce to inflame hatreds and make enmities irreconcilable?

In the next place, I would recommend this paper to the daily perusal of those gentlemen whom I cannot but consider as my good brothers and allies, I mean the fraternity of spectators who live in the world without having anything to do in it; and either by the affluence of their fortunes, or laziness of their dispositions, have no other business with the rest of mankind but to look upon them. Under this class of men are comprehended all contemplative tradesmen, titular physicians, Fellows of the Royal Society,[6] Templers[7] that are not given to be contentious, and statesmen that are out of business. In short, everyone that considers the world as a theater, and desires to form a right judgment of those who are the actors on it.

There is another set of men that I must likewise lay a claim to, whom I have lately called the Blanks of society, as being altogether unfurnished with ideas, till the business and conversation of the day has supplied them. I have often considered these poor souls with an eye of great commiseration, when I have heard them asking the first man they have met with, whether there was any news stirring? and by that means gathering together materials for thinking. These needy persons do not know what to talk of, till about twelve a clock in the morning; for by that time they are pretty good judges of the weather, know which way the wind sits, and whether the Dutch mail[8] be come in. As they lie at the mercy of the first man they meet, and are grave or impertinent all the day long, according to the notions which they have imbibed in the morning, I would earnestly entreat them not to stir out of their chambers till they have read this paper, and do promise them that I will daily instill into them such sound and wholesome sentiments as shall have a good effect on their conversation for the ensuing twelve hours.

But there are none to whom this paper will be more useful than to the female world. I have often thought there has not been sufficient pains taken in finding out proper employments and diversions for the fair ones. Their amusements seem contrived for them rather as they are women, than as they are reasonable creatures; and

---

3. Addison paraphrases a remark by the Roman orator Cicero (*Tusculan Disputations* 5.4.10).
4. Bacon makes this point in his *Advancement of Learning* (2.14), alluding to Exodus 7.10–12
5. A territory in west-central Russia (Moscow was its capital).
6. The London group chartered in the 1660s for the advancement of scientific inquiry.
7. Lawyers.
8. The boat bearing letters and newspapers from Holland.

are more adapted to the sex, than to the species. The toilet[9] is their great scene of business, and the right adjusting of their hair the principal employment of their lives. The sorting of a suit of ribbons is reckoned a very good morning's work; and if they make an excursion to a mercer's[1] or a toy shop,[2] so great a fatigue makes them unfit for anything else all the day after. Their more serious occupations are sewing and embroidery, and their greatest drudgery the preparation of jellies and sweetmeats. This, I say, is the state of ordinary women; though I know there are multitudes of those of a more elevated life and conversation, that move in an exalted sphere of knowledge and virtue, that join all the beauties of the mind to the ornaments of dress, and inspire a kind of awe and respect, as well as love, into their male beholders. I hope to increase the number of these by publishing this daily paper, which I shall always endeavor to make an innocent if not an improving entertainment, and by that means at least divert the minds of my female readers from greater trifles. At the same time, as I would fain give some finishing touches to those which are already the most beautiful pieces in human nature, I shall endeavor to point out all those imperfections that are the blemishes, as well as those virtues which are the embellishments, of the sex. In the meanwhile I hope these my gentle readers, who have so much time on their hands, will not grudge throwing away a quarter of an hour in a day on this paper, since they may do it without any hindrance to business.

I know several of my friends and well-wishers are in great pain for me, lest I should not be able to keep up the spirit of a paper which I oblige myself to furnish every day: but to make them easy in this particular, I will promise them faithfully to give it over as soon as I grow dull. This I know will be matter of great raillery to the small wits; who will frequently put me in mind of my promise, desire me to keep my word, assure me that it is high time to give over, with many other little pleasantries of the like nature, which men of a little smart genius cannot forbear throwing out against their best friends, when they have such a handle given them of being witty. But let them remember, that I do hereby enter my caveat against this piece of raillery.

Getting, Spending, Speculating

The periodical essay was one commodity among many, in an economy whose energies were evident almost everywhere: in shops stocked with new (often exotic) goods; at outposts in remote countries where trade was gradually being transmuted into empire; at London banks, where the apparatus of transaction (loans, bills, draughts) was rapidly being refined; in nearby coffeehouses, where the agents and accumulators of wealth paused during busy days to absorb substances imported from abroad (coffee, tobacco, chocolate) as well as that home-crafted item of consumption, the periodical essay itself. The essayists often construed their audience as though it consisted *primarily* of merchants, shopkeepers, and customers—of people profoundly concerned with the course of commerce, whatever their gender or occupation. Defoe, Addison, and Steele all wrote to celebrate trade (its new profusions and possibilities), but also to regularize it, to render it respectable, to reconcile it with notions of human excellence originating in an earlier culture centered on aristocracy. The *Review*, the *Tatler*, and the *Spectator* all undertook (as the historian J. G. A. Pocock has elegantly argued) to redefine the idea of

---

9. Dressing tables.
1. Fabric sellers.

2. Where they might buy ornamental accessories—fans, silks, ribbons, laces—as well as playthings.

The *Gentleman's Magazine*:

St JOHN's GATE.

Lond Gazette
Lond Journ
Fog's Journ.
Appleber's : :
Read'g : : : :
Craftsman :
D. Spectator
Lit Courier of
Grubstreet
Bpp-Docra
Daily-Post
D. Abbertiser
St James's Eb.
Whitehall Eb
Lond. Ebeig
Weekly Mile
General Ebe.
Old Whig
D. Gazetter
Lon. D. Post
Com. Sense

York Mews
Dublin 5 : :
Edinburgh 2
Bristol : : : : :
Nushwich 2
Exeter 2 : :
Worcester
Northampton
Gloucester : :
Stamford : :
Nottingham
Burp Journ.
Chester ditto
Derby ditto
Ipswich do.
Reading do.
Leeds Merc:
Newcastle d
Canterbury
Durham
Kendal
Boston : : ¶
Barbados :
Jamaica &c

For JANUARY, 1738.

CONTAINING,

/More in Quantity, and greater Variety, than any Book of the kind and Price/.

I. ORIGINAL ESSAYS, Moral : The Character of a *Good Man*, by a late illustrious Lady. Of the Magistrate's Right to punish ⷮ Death. Prescience consistent with Liberty. Whether Heaven and Hell be Local.

II. —— PHILOLOGICAL : Essay on Tragedy, with *Horace's* four Rules for ꝗ Drama. Answers to Biblical Questions.

III. —— MATHEMATICS: A new Astronomical Equation, discover'd by Mr *Facio*. A Method to find the Longitude and Latitude at Sea.

IV. —— THE Lady's Adventure, and Love Letters from a Protestant Gent. to a Catholic Lady.

V. ESSAYS from the Weekly Papers. *The Literary Courier of Grub-street.* Characters of News-Papers. Advice to Ladies on their Return to *London.* Zenger's Tryal for printing a Libel. Rules

of Physiognomy in chusing Husbands. The Widow describ'd. The Character of a Prince Royal, *&c.*

VI. POETRY. A Poem, inscrib'd to the *Dublin* Society, by Mr *Arbuckle.* Ode on the Death of P. *George* of *Denmark,* by the celebrated Mr *Aisop.* Prologue to *Venice preserv'd,* by a Person of Quality. The Blind Boy, with the Musick correct. Songs, Epigrams, Ænigmas, &c.

VII. HISTORICAL. The King's Speech; Addresses of the Lords and Commons. The Secrets of Free-Masonry.

VIII. LISTS of Births, Mariages, and Deaths, *&c.*

IX. FOREIGN AFFAIRS.   Match of Don *Carlos* with the Princess Royal of *Poland,* &c. Caution to Mariners.

X. Price of Stocks. Bill of Mortality.

XI. Register of Books.

XII. TABLE of Contents.

By *SYLVANUS URBAN,* Gent.

LONDON: Printed by E. CAVE at St JOHN's GATE, and Sold by the Booksellers of Town and Country ; of whom may be had any former Month.

Where the *Review, Tatler,* and *Spectator* defined themselves *against* their print contemporaries, other periodicals took a different tack. With so much information, instruction, and entertainment flowing from so many sources, a desire developed for a digest that might organize it all. No one catered more adroitly to this new market than did Edward Cave, founder and editor of *Gentleman's Magazine,* a monthly pamphlet whose title coined a pivotal new term for print. "Magazine" meant a military storehouse of provisions and artillery; the *Gentleman's Magazine* promised an intellectual storehouse similarly well stocked. Cave promised "more in quantity, and greater variety, than any book of the kind and price." He delivered on the promise by publishing extracts and abstracts from many periodicals, but he soon cultivated a stable of his own writers (including the young Samuel Johnson) who furnished his readers with an ever-widening range of fresh materials: biographies, poetry, parliamentary debates. The *Magazine's* logo presents it as a compendium of other papers, but Cave had in fact produced a true original, "one of the most successful and lucrative pamphlets" (wrote Johnson, whose observation still holds true) "which literary history has upon record." The title page depicts the 200-year-old gatehouse where the *Gentleman's Magazine* was composed, printed, and sold (the building's fortress-like appearance may entail a visual pun, conjuring up the military meaning of "magazine"). The building is flanked by the names of papers that the *Magazine* has incorporated, one way or another, into its own pages (London papers on the left, provincial and foreign ones on the right). The fictitious name "Sylvanus Urban" conjures up both countryside (*sylvanus,* "wooded") and city; as the bottom lines make clear, Cave aimed his appeal at audiences in both domains.

"virtue," to shift its focus of application from the classically defined obligations of the hereditary landowner to the prudent calculation of the urban merchant, alert to realities and proba-
bilities in an economy awash with speculation and controlled by credit, where "what one
owned was promises": promises by entrepreneurs in search of capital; by stock-jobbers selling
hopes of future prosperity; by the government whose operations depended on intricately structured loans from its own citizens. One central concern of the periodicals was how to commute
promise into actual prosperity, rather than mere air.

In the selections in this section, Addison rejoices in the commercial and cultural confluence at the Royal Exchange (London's shopping center). In a more sentimental vein, Steele
tracks the consequences of foreign trade in the lives and feelings of two lovers. Defoe, by contrast, is harder-headed, more closely analytic. Unlike the authors of the *Spectator*, he had spent
years in business, making and losing fortunes. Surveying the shops of London, Defoe declares
(as in virtually every *Review*) his passion for trade, but he asks what prospects the *present* patterns of consumption actually hold forth.

Joseph Addison: Spectator No. 69
Saturday, 19 May 1711

[ROYAL EXCHANGE[1]]

Hic segetes, illic veniunt felicius uvae:
Arborei foetus alibi, atque injussa virescunt
Gramina. Nonne vides, croceos ut Tmolus odores,
India mittit ebur, molles sua thura Sabaei?
At Chalybes nudi ferrum, virosaque Pontus
Castorea, Eliadum palmas Epirus equarum?
Continuo has leges aeternaque foedera certis
Imposuit Natura locis . . . [2]

There is no place in the town which I so much love to frequent as the Royal
Exchange. It gives me a secret satisfaction, and in some measure gratifies my vanity,
as I am an Englishman, to see so rich an assembly of countrymen and foreigners consulting together upon the private business of mankind, and making this metropolis a
kind of emporium for the whole earth. I must confess I look upon high-change[3] to be
a great council, in which all considerable nations have their representatives. Factors[4]
in the trading world are what ambassadors are in the politic world; they negotiate
affairs, conclude treaties, and maintain a good correspondence between those
wealthy societies of men that are divided from one another by seas and oceans, or
live on the different extremities of a continent. I have often been pleased to hear disputes adjusted between an inhabitant of Japan and an alderman of London, or to see

1. The Exchange, a quadrangle of arcades and shops surrounding a huge courtyard, had functioned as a crucial
site of London commerce since its creation in 1570.
Destroyed in the Great Fire, it was rebuilt from a new
design in 1669. The illustration on page 2411 depicts
both the original building by Thomas Gresham (upper
right corner) and the later structure with its more intricate, Baroque ornamentation. Statues of English kings
occupy the second-floor arches. At the center of the
courtyard, the statue of Charles II in the garb of a Roman
emperor enacts that favored comparison (echoed by
Addison in his essay's epigraph from Virgil) between contemporary Britain and the ancient Roman Empire.
2. "Corn grows more plentifully here, grapes there. In

other places grow trees laden with fruit, and grasses
unbidden. Do you not see how Tmolus sends us its saffron
perfumes; India her ivory; the soft Sabaens their frankin-
cense; but the naked Chalybes send us iron, the Pontus
pungent beaver-oil, and Epirus prize-winning Olympic
horses? These perpetual laws and eternal covenants
Nature has imposed on certain places" (Virgil, *Georgics*
1.54–61).
3. In addition to housing shops, the Exchange was a central meeting place for international merchants, who frequently closed deals in the courtyard. "High change" was
that period when trading was at its peak.
4. Commercial agents.

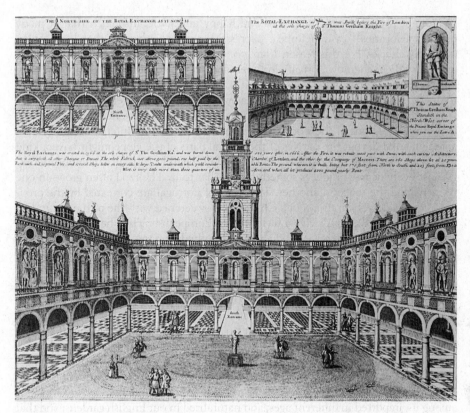

Sutton Nicholls, *The Royal Exchange*, 1712

a subject of the Great Mogul[5] entering into a league with one of the Czar of Muscovy.[6] I am infinitely delighted in mixing with these several ministers of commerce, as they are distinguished by their different walks and different languages. Sometimes I am jostled among a body of Armenians: sometimes I am lost in a crowd of Jews, and sometimes make one in a group of Dutchmen. I am a Dane, Swede, or Frenchman at different times, or rather fancy myself like the old philosopher,[7] who upon being asked what countryman he was, replied that he was a citizen of the world.

Though I very frequently visit this busy multitude of people, I am known to nobody there but my friend, Sir Andrew,[8] who often smiles upon me as he sees me bustling in the crowd, but at the same time connives at my presence without taking any further notice of me. There is indeed a merchant of Egypt, who just knows me by sight, having formerly remitted me some money to Grand Cairo;[9] but as I am not versed in the modern Coptic, our conferences go no further than a bow and a grimace.[1]

This grand scene of business gives me an infinite variety of solid and substantial entertainments. As I am a great lover of mankind, my heart naturally overflows with

5. The Indian emperor.
6. A territory in west-central Russia (Moscow was its capital).
7. Diogenes the Cynic, credited for developing the concept of "cosmopolitanism" (citizenship in the universe), in which all beings are parts of a single whole.

8. Sir Andrew Freeport, a member of Mr. Spectator's club: Whig merchant and ardent advocate (as his name implies) of free trade.
9. Where Mr. Spectator spent some time as a young man (see *Spectator* No. 1, page 2400).
1. The word denoted an expression of politeness.

pleasure at the sight of a prosperous and happy multitude, insomuch that at many public solemnities I cannot forbear expressing my joy with tears that have stolen down my cheeks. For this reason I am wonderfully delighted to see such a body of men thriving in their own private fortunes, and at the same time promoting the public stock; or in other words, raising estates for their own families, by bringing into their country whatever is wanting, and carrying out of it whatever is superfluous.

Nature seems to have taken a particular care to disseminate her blessings among the different regions of the world, with an eye to this mutual intercourse and traffic among mankind, that the natives of the several parts of the globe might have a kind of dependence upon one another, and be united together by their common interest. Almost every degree produces something peculiar to it. The food often grows in one country, and the sauce in another. The fruits of Portugal are corrected by the products of Barbados; the infusion of a China plant sweetened with the pith of an Indian cane; the Philippic islands give a flavor to our European bowls. The single dress of a woman of quality is often the product of an hundred climates. The muff and the fan come together from the different ends of the Earth. The scarf is sent from the torrid zone, and the tippet from beneath the pole. The brocade petticoat rises out of the mines of Peru, and the diamond necklace out of the bowels of Indostan.

If we consider our own country in its natural prospect, without any of the benefits and advantages of commerce, what a barren uncomfortable spot of earth falls to our share! Natural historians tell us that no fruit grows originally among us, besides hips and haws, acorns and pig-nuts, with other delicacies of the like nature; that our climate of itself, and without the assistances of art, can make no further advances towards a plum than to a sloe,[2] and carries an apple to no greater a perfection than a crab;[3] that our melons, our peaches, our figs, our apricots, and cherries, are strangers among us, imported in different ages, and naturalized in our English gardens; and that they would all degenerate and fall away into the trash of our own country, if they were wholly neglected by the planter, and left to the mercy of our sun and soil. Nor has traffic more enriched our vegetable world, than it has improved the whole face of nature among us. Our ships are laden with the harvest of every climate; our tables are stored with spices, and oils, and wines; our rooms are filled with pyramids of China, and adorned with the workmanship of Japan; our morning's draught[4] comes to us from the remotest corners of the earth; we repair our bodies by the drugs of America, and repose ourselves under Indian canopies. My friend Sir Andrew calls the vineyards of France our gardens; the Spice Islands[5] our hotbeds; the Persians our silk weavers, and the Chinese our potters. Nature indeed furnishes us with the bare necessaries of life, but traffic gives us a great variety of what is useful, and at the same time supplies us with everything that is convenient and ornamental. Nor is it the least part of this our happiness, that whilst we enjoy the remotest products of the north and south, we are free from those extremities of weather which give them birth; that our eyes are refreshed with the green fields of Britain, at the same time that our palates are feasted with fruits that rise between the tropics.

For these reasons there are not more useful members in a commonwealth than merchants. They knit mankind together in a mutual intercourse of good offices, distribute the gifts of nature, find work for the poor, add wealth to the rich, and mag-

---

2. The berry of the blackthorn.
3. Crabapple.

4. Drink.
5. A cluster of islands in modern Indonesia.

nificence to the great. Our English merchant converts the tin of his own country into gold, and exchanges his wool for rubies. The Mahometans are clothed in our British manufacture, and the inhabitants of the frozen zone warmed with the fleeces of our sheep.

When I have been upon the 'Change, I have often fancied one of our old kings[6] standing in person, where he is represented in effigy, and looking down upon the wealthy concourse of people with which that place is every day filled. In this case, how would he be surprised to hear all the languages of Europe spoken in this little spot of his former dominions, and to see so many private men, who in his time would have been the vassals of some powerful baron, negotiating like princes for greater sums of money than were formerly to be met with in the Royal Treasury! Trade, without enlarging the British territories, has given us a kind of additional empire: it has multiplied the number of the rich, made our landed estates infinitely more valuable than they were formerly, and added to them an accession of other estates as valuable as the lands themselves.

Richard Steele: Spectator No. 11
Tuesday, 13 March 1711

[INKLE AND YARICO[1]]

Dat veniam corvis, vexat censura columbas.[2]

Arietta is visited by all persons of both sexes who have any pretense to wit and gallantry. She is in that time of life which is neither affected with the follies of youth or infirmities of age; and her conversation is so mixed with gaiety and prudence that she is agreeable both to the young and the old. Her behavior is very frank, without being in the least blameable; and as she is out of the tract of any amorous or ambitious pursuits of her own, her visitants entertain her with accounts of themselves very freely, whether they concern their passions or their interests. I made her a visit this afternoon, having been formerly introduced to the honor of her acquaintance by my friend Will. Honeycomb,[3] who has prevailed upon her to admit me sometimes into her assembly, as a civil, inoffensive man. I found her accompanied with one person only, a commonplace talker who, upon my entrance, rose, and after a very slight civility sat down again; then turning to Arietta, pursued his discourse, which I found was upon the old topic of constancy in love. He went on with great facility in repeating what he talks every day of his life; and with the ornaments of insignificant laughs and gestures, enforced his arguments by quotations out of plays and songs, which allude to the perjuries of the fair, and the general levity[4] of women. Methought he strove to shine more than ordinarily in his talkative way, that he might insult my silence, and distinguish himself before a woman of Arietta's taste and understanding.

6. As depicted in the statues on the second story (see illustration on page 2411).

1. Steele here elaborates on a 60-year-old traveler's tale, in such a way as to combine two of the *Spectator*'s central concerns: the transactions of love and power between men and women, and the impact of commerce on human conduct.

2. "Their verdict goes easy on the raven, but is severe on the dove" (Juvenal, *Satires* 2.63). The speaker, a woman, is complaining of how leniently men assess themselves, and how harshly they criticize women.

3. An aged member of Mr. Spectator's club, proud of his long-ago days as a Restoration rake, and still deeply interested in matters of the heart.

4. Lightness, fickleness.

She had often an inclination to interrupt him, but could find no opportunity, 'till the larum[5] ceased of itself; which it did not 'till he had repeated and murdered the celebrated story of the Ephesian matron.[6]

Arietta seemed to regard this piece of raillery as an outrage done to her sex, as indeed I have always observed that women, whether out of a nicer[7] regard to their honor, or what other reason I cannot tell, are more sensibly touched with those general aspersions which are cast upon their sex, than men are by what is said of theirs.

When she had a little recovered herself from the serious anger she was in, she replied in the following manner.

"Sir, when I consider, how perfectly new all you have said on this subject is, and that the story you have given us is not quite two thousand years old, I cannot but think it a piece of presumption to dispute with you: but your quotations put me in mind of the fable of the lion and the man.[8] The man, walking with that noble animal, showed him, in the ostentation of human superiority, a sign of a man killing a lion. Upon which the lion said very justly, 'We lions are none of us painters, else we could show a hundred men killed by lions, for one lion killed by a man.' You men are writers, and can represent us women as unbecoming as you please in your works, while we are unable to return the injury. You have twice or thrice observed in your discourse that hypocrisy is the very foundation of our education; and that an ability to dissemble our affections is a professed part of our breeding. These, and such other reflections, are sprinkled up and down the writings of all ages, by authors who leave behind them memorials of their resentment against the scorn of particular women, in invectives against the whole sex. Such a writer, I doubt not, was the celebrated Petronius, who invented the pleasant aggravations of the frailty of the Ephesian lady; but when we consider this question between the sexes, which has been either a point of dispute or raillery ever since there were men and women, let us take facts from plain people, and from such as have not either ambition or capacity to embellish their narrations with any beauties of imagination. I was the other day amusing myself with Ligon's *Account of Barbados*; and, in answer to your well-wrought tale, I will give you (as it dwells upon my memory) out of that honest traveler, in his fifty-fifth page, the History of Inkle and Yarico.[9]

"Mr. Thomas Inkle[1] of London, aged 20 years, embarked in the Downs[2] on the good ship called the Achilles, bound for the West Indies, on the 16th of June 1647, in order to improve his fortune by trade and merchandise. Our adventurer was the third son of an eminent citizen, who had taken particular care to instill into his mind an early love of gain, by making him a perfect master of numbers, and consequently giving him a quick view of loss and advantage, and preventing the natural impulses of his passions, by prepossession towards his interests. With a mind thus turned, young Inkle had a person every way agreeable, a ruddy vigor in his countenance, strength in his limbs, with ringlets of fair hair loosely flowing on his shoulders. It happened, in the course of the voyage, that the Achilles, in some distress, put into a creek on the main of America, in search of provisions. The youth, who is the hero of my story, among others, went ashore on this occasion. From their first landing they

---

5. The long-ringing alarm bell (of his talk).
6. The Roman story (told in Petronius's *Satyricon*, pt. 2) of a widow who, while mourning at the tomb of her newly deceased husband, succumbs to the attractions of a soldier standing nearby, and makes love with him on her husband's tomb.
7. More precise.
8. In Aesop's *Fables* (No. 219).

9. Richard Ligon's *True and Exact History of the Island of Barbados* (1657) includes a paragraph on a slave named Yarico and her misadventures in love, which Steele elaborates into the tale that follows.
1. Steele invents the name for this character; it means (perhaps prophetically) "linen tape," a common commodity.
2. A harbor on the southeastern coast of England.

were observed by a party of Indians, who hid themselves in the woods for that purpose. The English unadvisedly marched a great distance from the shore into the
country, and were intercepted by the natives, who slew the greatest number of them.
Our adventurer escaped among others, by flying into a forest. Upon his coming into a
remote and pathless part of the wood, he threw himself, tired and breathless, on a little hillock, when an Indian maid rushed from a thicket behind him. After the first
surprise, they appeared mutually agreeable to each other. If the European was highly
charmed with the limbs, features, and wild graces of the naked American, the American was no less taken with the dress, complexion, and shape of an European, covered from head to foot. The Indian grew immediately enamored of him, and consequently solicitous for his preservation. She therefore conveyed him to a cave, where
she gave him a delicious repast of fruits, and led him to a stream to slake his thirst. In
the midst of these good offices, she would sometimes play with his hair, and delight
in the opposition of its color to that of her fingers; then open his bosom, then laugh
at him for covering it. She was, it seems, a person of distinction, for she every day
came to him in a different dress, of the most beautiful shells, bugles, and bredes.[3] She
likewise brought him a great many spoils, which her other lovers had presented to
her; so that his cave was richly adorned with all the spotted skins of beasts, and most
parti-colored feathers of fowls, which that world afforded. To make his confinement
more tolerable, she would carry him in the dusk of the evening, or by the favor of
moonlight, to unfrequented groves and solitudes, and show him where to lie down in
safety, and sleep amidst the falls of waters, and melody of nightingales. Her part was
to watch and hold him in her arms, for fear of her countrymen, and wake him on
occasions to consult his safety. In this manner did the lovers pass away their time, till
they had learned a language of their own, in which the voyager communicated to his
mistress, how happy he should be to have her in his country, where she should be
clothed in such silks as his waistcoat was made of, and be carried in houses drawn by
horses, without being exposed to wind or weather. All this he promised her the
enjoyment of, without such fears and alarms as they were there tormented with. In
this tender correspondence these lovers lived for several months, when Yarico,
instructed by her lover, discovered a vessel on the coast, to which she made signals,
and in the night, with the utmost joy and satisfaction accompanied him to a ship's
crew of his countrymen, bound for Barbados. When a vessel from the main arrives in
that island, it seems the planters come down to the shore, where there is an immediate market of the Indians and other slaves, as with us of horses and oxen.

　　"To be short, Mr. Thomas Inkle, now coming into English territories, began seriously to reflect upon his loss of time, and to weigh with himself how many days'
interest of his money he had lost during his stay with Yarico. This thought made the
young man very pensive, and careful what account he should be able to give his
friends of his voyage. Upon which considerations, the prudent and frugal young man
sold Yarico to a Barbadian merchant; notwithstanding that the poor girl, to incline
him to commiserate her condition, told him that she was with child by him; but he
only made use of that information, to rise in his demands upon the purchaser."

　　I was so touched with this story, (which I think should be always a counterpart
to the Ephesian matron) that I left the room with tears in my eyes; which a woman of
Arietta's good sense did, I am sure, take for greater applause, than any compliments I
could make her.

3. Tube-shaped glass beads and braiding.

Daniel Defoe: *from* A Review of the State of the British Nation, Vol. 1, No. 43

Thursday, 8 January 1713

[WEAK FOUNDATIONS]

The subject of trade which I am now entered upon has this one excellency in it, for the benefit of the author, that really it can never be exhausted. * * * I remember some time ago I gave you a hint about the mighty alteration in the face of trade in this city; I cannot but touch it again on this occasion, because it relates to what I am upon. Let any man who remembers the glorious state of our trade about thirty or forty years past view but the streets of this opulent city and even the Exchange of London—nay, even our courts of law. It must of necessity put him in mind of Ezra 3.12, where the ancient men who had seen the old temple wept when they saw the weak foundations of the new.

However, to go on as I began and examine our new increase of commerce which we so must boast of: let me note a little to you with what mighty advantages the chasms, gaps, and breaches of our trade are filled up of late, and let us see it, I say, in the streets. Here, in the room of a trifling banker, or goldsmith, we are supplied with a most eminent brandy shop (Cheapside). There in the room of ditto you have a flaming shop[1] for white tea pots and luted earthen mugs (Cornhill), the most excellent offspring of that most valuable manufacture of earthenware. It is impossible that coffee, tea, and chocolate can be so advanced in their consumption without an eminent increase of those trades that attend them; whence we see the most noble shops in the city taken up with the valuable utensils of the tea table. The china warehouses are little marts within themselves (and by the way, are newly become markets of clandestine trade, of which I shall say more very quickly), and the eminent corner houses in the chief streets of London are chosen out by the town tinkers to furnish us with tea kettles and chocolate pots—vide Catherine Street and Bedford Buildings. Two thousand pound is reckoned a small stock in copper pots and lacquered kettles, and the very fitting up one of these brazen people's shops with fine sashes,[2] etc., to set forth his ware, costs above 500£ sterling, which is more by half than the best draper or mercer's shop in London requires.

This certainly shows the increase of our trade. Brass locks for our chambers and parlors, brass knockers for our doors, and the like add to the luster of those shops, of which hereafter. And the same sash works, only finer and larger, are now used to range[3] your brass and copper, that the goldsmiths had always to set out their less valuable silver and gold plate. From hence, be pleased to look upon the druggists of the town who are the merchants of these things. Bucklers-Bury and Little Lombard Street were the places which a few years ago held the whole number, a very few excepted, of that difficult nice employment, whose number is now spread over the whole town and with the most capital stocks, whose whole employ is the furnishing us by wholesale and retail with these most valuable of all drugs, coffee, tea, and chocolate—the general furniture of a druggist's shop being now three bales of coffee, twelve boxes of chocolate, six large canisters of tea, and an hundred and fifty empty gilded boxes. In like manner the rest of the town—how gloriously it is supplied! How do pastry cooks and periwig makers, brandy shops and toy shops, succeed linen drapers, mercers, upholsterers, and the like. A hundred pounds to rent for a house to sell jellies and apple pies; two hundred pounds to fit up a brandy shop, and afterwards not a hundred pound stock to put into it. These I can show many instances of.

---

1. A shop with a kiln for making earthenware.
2. Windows made up of two sliding frames (common now, new and fancy at this time).
3. Display.

Look, gentlemen, upon the particular parts of your town, formerly eminent for the best of tradesmen! View the famous churchyard of St. Paul's where so many aldermen and lord mayors have been raised by the trade of broadcloth and mere woolen manufactures,[4] and on whose trades so many families of poor always depended, that Sir William Turner used to say his shop alone employed 50,000 poor people! What succeeds him? A most noble, and to be sure, a much more valuable vintner's warehouse, *Anglice*,[5] a tavern, more vulgarly a bawdyhouse. And the next draper's shop, a coffee house; what takes up the whole row there? and supplies the place of eighteen or nineteen topping drapers? Who can but observe it! Cane chair makers, gilders of leather, looking-glass shops, and peddlers or toy shops—manifold improvements of trade! and an eminent instance of the growth of our manufactures! * * *

Advertisements from the *Spectator*[1]

At the Lace Chamber on Ludgate Hill, kept by Mary Parsons, is a great quantity of Flanders lace, lately come over, to be sold off at great pennyworths[2] by wholesale or retail. She bought them there herself. [No. 200; Friday, 19 October 1711]

This day is published *The Court and City Vagaries*, being some late (and real) intrigues of several gentlemen and ladies. Written by one of the fair sex, price 6d. Sold by J. Baker in Paternoster Row. [No. 255; Saturday, 22 December 1711]

The famous Italian water, for dying red and gray hairs of the head and eyebrows into a lasting brown or black; at 1, 2, or 4s. the bottle, with printed directions for the use of it. To be had at Mrs. Hannam's toyshop, at the sign of the Three Angels near the Half-Moon Tavern in Cheapside. [Vol. 8, No. 634; Friday, 17 December 1714]

The ladies that called at Mr. Charles Lillie's at the corner of Beauford Buildings,[3] in a hackney coach on Wednesday night, the 6th of this instant, about 10 o'clock, are desired to let him know where to direct to them, he being now able to give a particular account of what they enquired after. [No. 305; Tuesday, 19 February 1712]

⊷ ⋈⋈ ⊷

A Bubbler's Medley

In a culture preoccupied with commerce, sensational economic developments not only filled the columns of the regular newspapers and periodical essays; they also produced reams of "occasional" print—satires and songs, broadsides and commentaries catering to readers tremulously concerned about the fate of their nation's fortunes and their own. In the early eighteenth century, no such event worried more readers, and produced more print, than the South Sea Bubble, an investment scheme whose origin was intricate and outcome catastrophic. (For a picture of the profusion, see the frontispiece to this section opposite page 2061).

The wars Britain fought during William III's and Anne's reigns had a lingering effect. In order to finance expensive military ventures on the Continent, the British relied on a complex

---

4. The trade in textiles had provided the foundation for many family fortunes and (hence) political careers.
5. In English.
1. Periodicals did not merely comment on commerce, they participated in it, earning much of their revenue from the advertisements that they printed at the conclusion of their main editorial matter.

2. At a terrific bargain.
3. Charles Lillie, a close associate of Addison's and Steele's, owned a perfume shop in the Strand. He had been one of the publishers and distributors of the *Tatler*, and sold the *Spectator* at his shop, where he also accepted advertisements for inclusion in the paper.

system of annuities, lotteries, and loans. Of these methods, the annuities caused the most strain in subsequent years. This was because the holders of the annuities had loaned the government money at a time of great crisis and were guaranteed a fixed income for the rest of their lives as well as their children's lives. The interest on these loans varied from 7 percent to 9 percent. Moreover, these particular loans often were irredeemable, that is, the principal could not be paid off without the holder's consent.

In the fall of 1719, the South Sea Company, a concern holding monopoly rights to trade in South America and the Pacific, offered to take over the government's burdensome debt (about £51,000,000). Its plan was as follows: the company would assume the national debt and receive interest at the rate of 5 percent till 1727, when the rate would fall to 4 percent. For this right, it would pay the government a one-time fee of £7,567,000. The company hoped to persuade annuitants to exchange their annuities for stock. The only way the company could make money from this scheme was if its stock rapidly inflated in value. With the connivance of the government and a series of public relations moves designed to foster confidence, the company's stock rose steadily throughout the spring of 1720, hitting a high of 1000 (from a starting point near 100).

The whole scheme oddly mirrored the rise and fall of a similar plan in France in 1719. John Law (1671–1729), a Scottish emigrant and financier, had begun his rise to economic preeminence in 1715. By 1719, he controlled the finances of France, and attempted to incorporate the national debt of France into a trading company known as the Mississippi Company. By a similar inflation of company stock, he managed for a time to redeem much of the national debt, but by March 1720—at the same moment that Britain's plan was being put into operation—his scheme fell apart and he was discredited.

Despite the obvious warnings Law's failure presented, the rise of South Sea stock touched off an investment mania. Companies came into being overnight, often with little more than a name and a crazy idea to recommend them, and were bought into by investors hungry to reap the seemingly endless profit promised by speculating. The government attempted (with little success) to limit the more scandalous of these companies in June, but the speculative fever continued unabated. By the fall of 1720, stocks of all kinds had begun to fall. Fortunes on paper disappeared overnight, and people suffered disastrous losses. Popular resentment threatened to overthrow the government. Sir Robert Walpole (1676–1745), an early opponent of the scheme, came to the rescue of the government, proposing a series of measures to restore public credit and stabilize the financing of the national debt. Many of the South Sea directors had their assets seized, but several of the worst malefactors, including Secretary of State Charles Spencer, Third Earl of Sunderland, were screened from retribution (though Sunderland did lose office). From this crisis one can date the ascendancy of Walpole, which continued until 1742.

The Bubble ruined numberless investors and sold a lot of papers. Popular feeling about the crisis exploded in pamphlets, poems, plays, broadsides, and prose satires. The texts gathered here represent a cross-section of genres and a miscellany of reactions to the expansion and the explosion of the South Sea Bubble.

from Historical Register for the Year 1720[1]

His Lordship was backed by the Duke of W_____n,[2] who endeavored chiefly to evince, "that the South Sea Project might prove of infinite disadvantage to the nation; first, as it gave foreigners an opportunity to double and treble the vast sums

1. The *Historical Register* was a periodical publication that described recent proceedings in the House of Lords and the House of Commons, as well as foreign negotiations, treaties, etc. This excerpt summarizes some speeches delivered in April 1720, for and against the South Sea plan.

2. Philip, first Duke of Wharton: famous libertine, staunch opponent of the South Sea scheme, author of the anti-Walpole journal *The True Briton* (1723–1724) following that minister's ascent in 1721, and, in his final years, a Jacobite.

they had in our public funds, which could not but tempt them to withdraw their capital stock, with their immense gains, to other countries, which might drain Great Britain of a considerable part of its gold and silver. Secondly, that the artificial and prodigious rise of the South Sea stock was a dangerous bait, which might decoy many unwary people to their ruin, and allure them by false prospect of gain, to part with what they had got by their labor and industry, to purchase imaginary riches. And, in the third place, that the addition of above thirty millions new capital, would give such a vast power to the South Sea company, as might endanger the liberties of the nation, and, in time, subvert our excellent constitution; since by their extensive interest they might influence most, if not all, the elections of the members, and consequently overrule the resolutions of the House of Commons." Earl C___per[3] spoke also against the bill, and said "that like the Trojan Horse, it was ushered in, and received with great pomp and acclamations of joy; but was contrived for treachery and destruction." His lordship urged in particular, "that in all public bargains, it is a duty incumbent on them who are entrusted with the administration, to take care that the same be more advantageous to the state than to private persons; but that a quite contrary method seemed to have been followed in the contract made with the South Sea Company." * * *

But the Earl of S_____d[4] answered most of their objections; and, among other things, said, "that they who encouraged and countenanced the scheme of the South Sea company, had nothing in their view, but the easing the nation of part of that heavy load of debt it labors under. That on the other hand, the managers of that company had, undoubtedly, a prospect of private gain, either to themselves, or to their corporation; but that, when that scheme was accepted, neither the one nor the other could foresee that the stocks would have risen to the price they were now advanced. That if they had continued as they were at that time, the public would have had the far greater share of the advantage accruing from that scheme; and if the stocks were kept up to the price they had been raised to, which was not unlikely, it was but reasonable that the South Sea company should enjoy the profits procured to it by the wise management and industry of its directors, which would enable it both to make large dividends among its members, and thereby to compass the ends intended by this scheme." After this the question for committing the bill being put, it was carried in the affirmative, by a majority of 83 voices to 17.

Anne Finch: A Song on the South Sea[1]

Ombre and basset[2] laid aside,
  New games employ the fair;
And brokers all those hours divide
  Which lovers used to share.

3. William, first Earl of Cowper, served George I as Chancellor from 1714 to 1718, when he resigned over the ministry's religious policy but remained on good terms with the court. As an outsider to the Stanhope-Sunderland ministry in good standing with the king, his words against the scheme carried weight.
4. Charles Spencer, third Earl of Sunderland; junior partner in Stanhope's ministry (1718–1721), Secretary of State for the north, and chief ministerial proponent of the South Sea scheme.
1. This poem by Anne Finch, Countess of Winchilsea

(1661–1720) appeared posthumously in 1724 (for other poems by Finch, see pages 2226–30). Since she died in August 1720, she must have written the poem during the height of the Bubble mania. The poem reflects a fact sometimes obscured by all the pamphleteering and satire surrounding the scheme: namely, that it enabled women, for the first time in English history, to indulge in financial speculation and trade at a level nearly equal with men.
2. Popular card games.

5   The court, the park, the foreign song
          And harlequin's grimace,[3]
      Forlorn; amidst the city throng
          Behold each blooming face.

      With Jews and Gentiles undismayed
10   Young tender virgins mix,
      Of whiskers nor of beards afraid,
          Nor all the cozening tricks.

      Bright jewels, polished once to deck
          The fair one's rising breast,
15   Or sparkle round her ivory neck,
          Lie pawned in iron chest.

      The gayer passions of the mind
          How avarice controls!
      Even love does now no longer find
20   A place in female souls.

Thomas D'Urfey: The Hubble Bubbles

[A BALLAD TO THE TUNE OF "OVER THE HILLS AND FAR AWAY"[1]]

      Ye circum, and uncircumcised,[2]
      Come hear my song and be advised.
      Sell all your lands, sell all your flocks,
      Put your money in the stocks,
5   Hubble bubble, bubble hubble now's in play,
      Come buy our hubble bubble whilst may;
      For there's hubble bubble, bubble hubble, night and day,
          At Jonathan's and Garraway.[3]

      Come all who would by fishing gain,[4]
10   Venture like gamesters on the main,°   the ocean
      Whate'er you lose projectors[5] get,
      For you're the gudgeons[6] in the net.
      Hubble bubble, bubble hubble . . .

      Come all ye nymphs of gay desire,
15   Insure your house and selves from fire.[7]
      A house insured brings better rent.
      Come then insure your tenement.
      Hubble bubble, bubble hubble . . .

---

3. Either the popular masquerade costume (at least one writer praised the Bubble of 1720 for putting a temporary end to licentious masquerades) or a reference to the vogue for harlequin plays on stage in London.
1. Printed ballads, providing commentary on the news set to familiar tunes, remained a popular commodity from the Elizabethan era well into the 18th century. The playwright and poet, Thomas D'Urfey (1653–1723) produced many of them.
2. I.e., Jews and gentiles.
3. Two coffeehouses located in Exchange Alley, where shares and stocks were often traded.
4. This stanza alludes to one of the many new companies that sprung up in the wake of the South Sea stock rise; specifically, one of several fishing companies offering stock in 1720.
5. The devisers of the investment scheme.
6. A kind of fish; the word was often applied to gullible people.
7. Among the new companies in 1720 were those offering insurance on anything from houses to horses.

A bubble is blown up with air,
20   In which fine prospects do appear.
The Bubble breaks, the prospect's lost.
Yet must some bubble° pay the cost,   *fool*
Hubble bubble, bubble hubble . . .

1720

Thomas Read: *from* The Weekly Journal
Saturday, 24 September 1720[1]

Mr. Journalman,

I am a farmer in this neighborhood, and by my industry have scraped about £700 together. Not long ago a gentleman of a small estate offered me his sister in wedlock, and she having the name of a good huswife, while she kept her brother's house, I courted, and married her. 'Tis now about five years since, and I am father by her of a boy and girl, and we have lived as contented and happily together, though I say it, as ever a couple in Essex. But a plague of all chances, within this three or four months some of her relations, who used frequently before to walk over afoot to see us, have come a-visiting in their chariots and berlins, fine equipage and liveries,[2] so that they have set my poor wife, one of the best wives in the world before, so agog, that nothing would serve her but must up to town, and try my fortune in the South Sea, where I might get, she said, more by one lucky hit, than by following my plough all my life. I drove her off as long as I could. "Prithee, Honey," said I, "consider that we thrive in the world already, we live contented, which is a kingdom in itself, and bustle and noise is what I hate dreadfully. I am going to put what little money I have upon a mortgage, and that will be gathering with my other honest-got means, till I may be able to purchase the farm I now rent." But all this availed nothing, she said; she had rather see me taken quite off my slavery, and as they had a topping uncle in the South Sea, who had helped other relations, I should venture. I carried up a letter to him, he called me cousin very kindly, subscribed £500 for me, and bought me 100 capital, so that in the compass of a month or six week, I have lost above one half of what I was worth.[3] I was for selling out in time, crying the first loss was the best; but I am still teased to death to venture at all. These disputes are grown up into a family quarrel, and we who never had any words in our lives before, are every day at daggers drawing. So that in short I have even agreed to let her go to town, and manage stocks there, whilst I take care of my stock at home, and we shall see in the end, which of us shall come to the best market, I at Rumford or she in Change Alley. In the meantime I wish Sir, for we usually read your journal at home, that you would put in a word or two between us, which may be of service.

I am your humble servant
and constant reader,
William Wheatsheaf

---

1. Thomas Read's *Weekly Journal* advertised itself as "Being the Freshest Advices Foreign or Domestick" and largely lived up to its billing. Following the foreign notices (this particular number carried information from Malaga, Madrid, Genoa, Vienna, Copenhagen, Stockholm, Geneva, and The Hague), the journal would recount the activities of English lords, gentlemen, and, in 1720, businessmen. Each number also included letters purportedly written by readers on a wide variety of topics.

Toward the end of 1720, more and more of these letters included tales of woe. "William Wheatsheaf's" letter from Rumford is just such a cautionary story, and demonstrates how deeply Bubble mania penetrated English society.
2. All four terms refer to fancy carriages.
3. This indicates that Wheatsheaf bought his £100 worth of South Sea stock when it was at 500, that is, at half its highest value (£1000) and falling fast.

Nicholas Amhurst: *from* The Craftsman No. 47
Saturday, 27 May 1727

[USBECK TO RICA AT ISPAHAN[1]]

Among the Christians, with whom I reside, there are a peculiar sort called stock-job-bers. * * * [They] grow rich very unaccountably, not by traffic, not by arts, or science, or industry, or labor, or mechanics, or navigation, or warfare, or any other business of use or advantage to mankind; but, I will tell thee, Rica, their commerce is lying, political lying; and though each man knows the other to deal in this commodity, yet no one day passes, in which some of these strange fellows do not grow rich, and others are undone, as they out-lie one another, or as the lie of the one gains more credit than that of another. They call the chief nominal commodity which they deal in *South Sea stock;* this is worth more or less in idea only, as the lie of the day takes or does not take. Thou wilt think I rave, that I talk idly, when I tell thee here are many people, whom I have conversed with and who appear in other particulars to be men of reason, and yet, on the first mention of these syllables *South Sea stock,* lose at once all reflection and comparison. They told me that in the year 1720, they carried this ideal value of their stock so high, that what, in the beginning of the year, was not valued above 1000 piasters, mounted to more than 10,000 in less than the space of seven moons; that is, every man had agreed to call himself exceeding rich. At that time indeed the malady was almost epidemical, and the few among the people who retained their reason and their original substance, and would not agree to call it more than what it was intrinsically worth, were grown by the madness of their countrymen very poor on the sudden, and found themselves at once from a plentiful substance, on the point of wanting the common necessaries of life. So dangerous is it for a man to keep his understanding in a general frenzy! But at last, as I have said, at the close of six or seven moons, the people awoke from their golden dreams, and a little time after condescended to call their estates by their real values; though some of them are still as mad as ever. * * *

Women and Men, Manners and Marriage

When Isaac Bickerstaff, in his first *Tatler,* undertook to teach his readers "what to think," politics was apparently what he most expected them to think about. Soon, though, he found a second focus: that cluster of questions today grouped under the rubric "gender." Bickerstaff, his imitators, and his successors strove constantly to instruct men and women as to who they were, what they should become, how they differed from each other, how they ought to interact, and how they might most happily merge in love and marriage. The *Tatler,* the *Review,* and the *Spectator* all urged men to supplant aggression with morality and grace; women to cultivate sound sense over mere caprice; and both sexes to ground their marriages in reciprocity, love, and reason, rather than financial gain or impulsive passion.

The essayists' instruction, though, was far from even-handed. "I will not meddle with the *Spectator,*" Jonathan Swift wrote scornfully to Stella in 1711. "Let him *fair-sex* it to the world's end." Addison and Steele had used that phrase obsessively to describe, address, and instruct their

---

1. For the *Craftsman,* see page 2392. In this particular "letter," the *Craftsman* borrows the form and parodic strategies of Charles-Louis Montesquieu's hugely successful *Persian Letters* (1721), in which Usbek, a traveler from Persia, moves through Europe, reporting home on the customs of the various peoples encountered. The *Craftsman* letter suggests how, with the passage of time, many English people came to the whimsical conclusion that the South Sea obsession was a form of temporary mass insanity.

female readers; it had by now become a kind of shorthand for a variable blend of courtesy and condescension endemic to the periodicals, almost all of which were written by men and directed at an audience in which males possessed a barely questioned sway. Nonetheless, women had for more than a decade occupied an important (albeit elusive) place in the periodical scheme of things, as purchasers, as readers, as participants. In the early 1690s, when John Dunton launched the first "question and answer" periodical, he quickly discovered that queries submitted by women were abundant, popular, and profitable. In the wake of his *Athenian Mercury*, almost all important periodicals devised strategies for incorporating "the fair sex" into their texts and even into their titles: Mr. Spectator sketched lines of identification between his silent, self-contained conduct and the proper demeanor of the women whom he proposed to instruct; the *Tatler* proposed to "honor" (but also mocked) its female audience by its choice of title; many periodicals bore titles pitched even more explicitly at women: the *Female Tatler*, the *Ladies' Almanac*, the *Ladies' Magazine*, etc.

Such "inclusion" entailed obvious control. If the periodicals took up women's questions, they almost invariably supplied men's answers (even the *Ladies'* titles were mostly run by men). Eliza Haywood's *Female Spectator*, written not only for women but by a woman, offered something different. Far more fascinated with women's predicaments than with men's opinions, it helped foster a tradition of women's writing that grew richer and more various (encompassing novels and tracts as well as periodicals) as the century progressed.

Richard Steele: *from* Tatler No. 25
Tuesday, 7 June 1709

[DUELLISTS]

White's Chocolate-house, June 6

A letter from a young lady, written in the most passionate terms (wherein she laments the misfortune of a gentleman, her lover, who was lately wounded in a duel) has turned my thoughts to that subject, and inclined me to examine into the causes which precipitate men into so fatal a folly. And as it has been proposed to treat of subjects of gallantry[1] in the article from hence,[2] and no one point in nature is more proper to be considered by the company who frequent this place, than that of duels, it is worth our consideration to examine into this chimerical groundless humor, and to lay every other thought aside, till we have stripped it of all its false pretenses to credit and reputation amongst men.

But I must confess, when I consider what I am going about, and run over in my imagination all the endless crowd of men of honor who will be offended at such a discourse, I am undertaking, methinks, a work worthy an invulnerable hero in Romance, rather than a private gentleman with a single rapier. But as I am pretty well acquainted by great opportunities with the nature of man, and know of a truth, that all men fight *against their will*, the danger vanishes, and resolution rises upon this subject. For this reason I shall talk very freely on a custom which all men wish exploded, though no man has courage enough to resist it.

But there is one unintelligible word which I fear will extremely perplex my dissertation, and I confess to you I find very hard to explain, which is, the term *satisfaction*. An honest country gentleman had the misfortune to fall into company with two or three modern men of honor, where he happened to be very ill treated; and one of the company being conscious of his offense, sends a note to him in the morning, and tells him, he was ready to give him satisfaction. This is fine doing (says the plain fel-

---

1. Social conduct, particularly that having to do with   2. From White's.
courtship and self-display.

low): last night he sent me away cursedly out of humor, and this morning he fancies it would be a satisfaction to be run through the body.

As the matter at present stands, it is not to do handsome actions denominates a man of honor; it is enough if he dares to defend ill ones. Thus you often see a common sharper[3] in competition with a gentleman of the first rank; though all mankind is convinced, that a fighting gamester is only a pickpocket with the courage of an highwayman. One cannot with any patience reflect on the unaccountable jumble of persons and things in this town and nation, which occasions very frequently, that a brave man falls by a hand below that of the common hangman, and yet his executioner escapes the clutches of the hangman for doing it. I shall therefore hereafter consider, how the bravest men in other ages and nations have behaved themselves upon such incidents as we decide by combat; and show, from their practice, that this resentment neither has its foundation from true reason, or solid fame; but is an imposture, made up of cowardice, falsehood, and want of understanding. For this work, a good history of quarrels would be very edifying to the public, and I apply myself to the town for particulars and circumstances within their knowledge, which may serve to embellish the dissertation with proper cuts. Most of the quarrels I have ever known, have proceeded from some valiant coxcomb's persisting in the wrong, to defend some prevailing folly, and preserve himself from the ingenuity of owning a mistake.

By this means it is called, "giving a man satisfaction," to urge your offense against him with your sword; which puts me in mind of Peter's order to the keeper, in *The Tale of a Tub:* "If you neglect to do all this, damn you and your generation forever; and so we bid you heartily farewell."[4] If the contradiction in the very terms of one of our challenges were as well explained, and turned into downright English, would it not run after this manner?

> Sir,
>
> Your extraordinary behavior last night, and the liberty you were pleased to take with me, makes me this morning give you this, to tell you, because you are an ill-bred puppy, I will meet you in Hyde Park an hour hence; and because you want both breeding and humanity, I desire you would come with a pistol in your hand, on horseback, and endeavor to shoot me through the head, to teach you more manners. If you fail of doing me this pleasure, I shall say, you are a rascal on every post in town: and so, Sir, if you will not injure me more, I shall never forgive what you have done already. Pray Sir, do not fail of getting everything ready, and you will infinitely oblige,
>
> Sir,
> Your most obedient
> humble servant, &c.

Daniel Defoe: *from* A Review of the State of the British Nation, Vol. 9, No. 34

Saturday, 29 November 1712

[A DUELLIST'S CONSCIENCE]

I have in one *Review* lately taken the liberty to mention that so exploded, rejected thing called peace among ourselves. I confess I see no room to expect good usage

---

3. Trickster.   Swift's intricate satire *A Tale of a Tub* (1704), sec. 4.
4. Steele paraphrases this fervent curse from Jonathan

among you when I touch so ungrateful a subject, but I look for all sides to fall upon me as upon one prompting them to what they are resolved against.

I look upon the present feuds and outrageous party quarrelling which we are all embarked in to be the worst war we could ever engage in; and I think it was never so lively represented as by the late wretched unhappy duel between the Lord M[ohu]n and Duke H[amilto]n, wherein, both enraged, both desperately bent to ruin and destroy one another, both draw their swords in an unjust, needless, and dishonorable quarrel, and both die in the engagement.[1] I call the quarrel unjust and dishonorable not as to the cause of quarrel, which I have nothing to do with, but as to the manner of duelling, which I undertake to be unjust and dishonorable, because illegal and unchristian. * * *

I cannot but observe * * * what some public papers pretend about His Grace Duke H[amilto]n, viz., that he spent all the night before the action in his closet, retired pensive; and, says another author, in his devotion. I have nothing to say to the fact in this, for I do not believe it to be true. But for the sake of the surviving part of mankind, let us speak to this ridiculous newsmonger a little. Pray, sir, what devotion could you rationally suppose the Duke to be passing the time in? I cannot but think His Grace was a better Christian, at least I am sure he knew better, than to be praying to God for success upon what he was going about. Let all the men in England but tell me, what could the Duke say? Could anything of a Christian bring him in saying thus, with his eyes up to heaven: "Lord, thou knowest I will affront thy justice tomorrow by taking my cause into my own hand, and executing that vengeance which thou hast forbid me, and reserved to thyself. Lord, give me thy blessing to this wicked and willful action, and grant me success that I may kill my enemy, and become a murderer of my neighbor, etc." If he could not say this, let anyone tell me what he could pray. Can they think he would say thus? "Lord, I am going to commit a most grievous wickedness, and I am resolved to do it in spite of its being abhorred and forbidden by thee. But I WILL do it; however, I desire thou wilt pardon the sin and assist me to increase it by my murdering my adversary." This must be the devotion, the wretched devotion of such a retreat, and for that reason I will not so far affront the memory of Duke H[amilto]n to say he employed that time in devotion. If I might guess at the perturbation of thoughts which took up those few, or such unhappy hours; I say, if I may guess at them *by my own unhappy experience*, and may appeal to others who know what it is, I am of the opinion such times are taken up in the rolling of the passions, the boiling of the blood, the furious agitation of the animal spirits moved by the violence of the provocation. If conscience presumes to give a pinch in the dark, or put in a word, the inflamed organ answers: "Come what will, I cannot go back, I cannot live; I had better be run a thousand times through the body, I can die but once; but to bear this, is to be stabbed every day, to be insulted at the corner of every street, be posted, caned, and the Devil; I cannot bear it, I cannot help it." If the mind retreats a little and looks in through a very, very little bit, it occurs thus: "You are mad, you give up your reason, you are a murderer if you fall not in the action, you are a lost man forever. You know it is not a lawful action." All this is stopped thus: "What! Can I bear to be called COWARD! Had I not better be out of the world! I cannot go off, I must do it, all is at stake, I must, I cannot go from it, die or be damned, or anything is all one, I must do it." And so in the morning away he goes to be undone;

---

1. The duel, between James Douglas, Duke of Hamilton (1658–1712), and Charles Mohun (1675?–1712), had taken place two weeks earlier, on November 15.

goes to lay in a store for repentance; goes to take away his neighbor's life, and lay at stake his own, and sometimes, as in this case, to lose both.

Those people who would send the late Duke to his closet to prayers to prepare for his next day's work, I believe know little what fighting a duel is, or what temper the mind is in when such an appointment is upon their hands; I rather believe His Grace was fighting with my Lord M[ohu]n all night; many a silent pass was made that night in imagination, I doubt not; not that I believe the Duke was weak enough to act by himself the postures or motions of fighting; but I believe it was impossible to suppose that a mind possessed with such views and such resolutions as he then had could refrain from fixing the ideas of the action itself in its thoughts.

But to talk of devotion, let that jest be laid by. I can take upon me to say, God hears no such prayers, nor can any man who is in his right senses have the face to look up to his Maker in such a case as that was.

THE ATHENIAN MERCURY (1691–1697)   In *The Athenian Mercury* (initially titled the *Athenian Gazette*, until the *London Gazette* clamped down), the eccentric and ingenious entrepreneur John Dunton (1659–1732) performed a bold and experiment in interactive media. "All persons whatever," announced the paper's first number, "may be resolved *gratis* in any question that their own satisfaction or curiosity shall prompt them to, if they send [in] their questions by a penny-post letter." Inquiring readers, Dunton promised, would soon see their questions in print, accompanied by knowledgable and thoughtful answers from a society of "Athenians"—actually a quartet of learned but not particularly eminent men (including the editor himself), whose identities Dunton both cloaked and burnished by that elegant cover name, which connoted both ancient wisdom and university education. The paper succeeded so well that he promptly expanded his operation, adding more "members" to the Athenian Society (including Daniel Defoe) and pages to the publication in order to absorb the multitude of questions that kept pouring in. The paper prided itself on its range of topics, but announced in its eighteenth number a particular area of specialization: "Whereas the questions we receive from the *fair sex* are both *pressing* and *numerous*, we being willing to oblige 'em, as knowing they have a very *strong party* in the world, resolve to set apart the first Tuesday in every month on purpose to satisfy questions of that nature"; the recurrent special issue proved so popular that it was soon appearing biweekly, then weekly. Its pages included questions from both men and women on those subjects construed as particularly "feminine" (love, courtship, marriage); the letters often took the form of short but expressive autobiographies—a mode Steele, Addison, and numberless others imitated and developed during the following decades. Dunton claimed to have conceived his "question project" (as he affectionately termed it) in the course of an afternoon's walk. Its influence has lasted centuries, and is still plain to see in columns of advice and information. Dunton taught the periodical press an irresistibly simple and enduringly successful way of mirroring its readers, making them part of (and hence committed to) the papers they read.

from The Athenian Mercury[1]

QUEST. Whether it is lawful for a man to beat his wife?

ANSW. The affirmative would be very disobliging to that sex, without adding any more to it. Therefore we ought to be as cautious and tender as may be in asserting such an ill-natured position. We allow a wife to be[2] naturalized into, and part of her husband, and yet nature sometimes wars against part of itself, in ejecting by

1. The following questions and answers are taken from Vol. 1, Nos. 1 and 2 (1691); Vol. 2, No. 15 (1691); and   Vol. 14, No. 23 (1694).
2. Agree that a wife is.

sweat, urine, etc. what otherwise would be destructive to its very frame; nay, sometimes there is occasion of greater violence, as lancing,[3] burning, dismembering, etc., which the patient submits to as his interest. Now if a man may thus cruelly treat himself, and be an accessory to his own torture, he may legally chastise his wife, who is no nearer to him than he is to himself, but yet (for I am not covetous of the fate of Orpheus[4]) as none but doctors are proper judges of seasonable violences to nature, so there are but few husbands that know how to correct a wife. To do it in a passion, and pretend justice, is ridiculous, because that passion incapacitates the judgment from its office; and to do it when one is pleased is a harder task; so that we conclude, as the legality is unquestionable, so the time and measure are generally too critical[5] for a calculation. When a wife goes astray, it is safe to use a sympathetic remedy, as the rebuke of a kiss; the antipathetic[6] may prove worse than the disease.

QUEST. Whether since it is your opinion that if a man be a discreet and prudent man, he may correct the misbehavior of his wife by beating, *vice versa*, a wife being so qualified, and having a sot to her husband, whether she may not (if able) beat her husband?

ANSW. The power was at first vested in man specifically,[7] without provisions, distinctions, or limitations of sot, foolish, weak, etc. Therefore these altering not his species by consequence, cannot annul his prerogative.

QUEST. Whether it be lawful for a young lady to pray for a husband, and if lawful, in what form?

ANSW. He must renounce humanity, and confess himself a sort of an aggressor upon the privileges of nature, that would not make it as immortal as possible, which is only honorably effected by marriage, whereby we survive in our children. Misery without a friend to bear a part is very afflicting, and happiness without communication is tedious, and (as Seneca[8] has observed) sometimes inclines us to make a voluntary choice of misery for novelty. We should be vagrant sort of animals without marriage, as if nature were ashamed of our converse. We should contribute to the destruction of states, condemn the wisdom of the first Institutor and censure the edicts of such commonwealths who have upon very good grounds discountenanced and punished celibacy. Nay, supposing all the miseries that marriage-haters suggest should fall upon us, it is our own fault, if with Socrates we don't learn more by a scolding wife than by all the precepts of philosophers.[9]

Now if it be lawful to marry, it is lawful for ladies to pray for good husbands, if they find their inclination, concerns in the world, or other motives (which they are to be judges of) consistent with the ends of such society. As to the form of prayer required, they may, if they please, use the following, if they are not better furnished already:

From a profane libertine, from one affectedly pious, from a profuse almoner,[1] from an uncharitable wretch, from a wavering religioso,[2] and an injudicious zealot—deliver me!

---

3. Pricking, for medical purposes.
4. The musician of Greek myth, torn apart by raging women, votaries of Bacchus.
5. Complicated.
6. Remedy.
7. Refers to God's "curse" upon Eve for eating the forbidden fruit: "Thy desire shall be to thy husband, and he

shall rule over thee" (Genesis 3.12).
8. Stoic philosopher and tragic playwright.
9. A misogynist tradition held that the philosopher Socrates's wife Xanthippe berated him constantly, and thereby taught him skill in argument.
1. Charity-giver.
2. One who changes his faith.

From one of a starched gravity, or of ridiculous levity, from an ambitious states-man, from a restless projector,[3] from one that loves anything besides me, but what is very just and honorable—deliver me!

From an ecstasied poet, from a modern wit, from a base coward and a rash fool, from a pad[4] and a pauper—deliver me!

From a Venus's darling, from a Bacchus's proselyte,[5] from a traveling half,[6] from a domestic animal, from all masculine plagues not yet recounted—deliver me!

Give me one whose love has more of judgment than passion, who is master of himself, or at least an indefatigable scholar in such a study, who has an equal flame, that as two tallies[7] we may appear more perfect by union.

Give me one of as genteel an education as a little expense of time will permit, with an indifferent fortune, rather independent of the servile fate of palaces, and yet one whose retirement is not so much from the public as into himself. One (if possible) above all flattery and affronts, and yet as careful in preventing the injury as able to repair it. One, the beauty of whose mind exceeds that of his face, yet not deformed so as to be distinguishable from others even unto a ridicule.

Give me one that has learnt to live much in a little time, one that is no great familiar in converse with the world, nor no little one with himself. One (if two such happinesses may be granted at one time to our sex) who with these uncom-mon endowments of mind may (naturally) have a sweet, mild, easy disposition, or at least one who by his practice and frequent habit has made himself so before he is made mine. But as the master-perfection and chiefest draught,[8] let him be truly virtuous and pious; that is to say, let me be truly happy in my choice. * * *

QUEST. It was my fortune about four years since to be for some time in a family,[9] and a son of the family addressed himself to me. I told him his parents would not like it, my fortune being much inferior to his, and that I feared he would incur his father's displeasure, if he knew he loved me. He said he loved no woman upon the earth but me, and assured me it was for my sake he rejected a very advantageous match that was offered him at that time. All his actions persuaded me his intentions were real. I found myself inclinable to love him. He urged me to make him a promise, that then he would be contented to live so until it should please God to take his good father, who, if he could possibly, he would not disoblige. Now I do love him not for his estate, I take God to witness; for if he had not six pence in the world I could love him as I do, which is far beyond what I am able to say. There was a mutual vow made between us; we called God to witness. He added that if ever he falsified the least tittle of what he had promised, that God's just curse might light on him. Gentlemen, he is twelve years older than I. He is a scholar, and very well qualified. And to show you it was not done rashly, since we were parted (which was as soon as they had any suspicion of our love), he has repeated the same promises in several letters to me. Some time before I went from him, I was told he was married to a gentlewoman that he had a child by. I told him of it; he protested it was false, and that the child was not his, nor did he ever converse with the per-son since; it was at least twelve years ago that the child was born. He invited me lately to see his house, where I observed some of the goods marked with the gen-

---

3. Scientist; deviser of grand plans and schemes.
4. Thief.
5. From a rake, from a drunk.
6. Perhaps suggesting a passive, mute companion.
7. A "tally" was originally a tool used to record a debt or payment. A wooden rod, notched several times crosswise

(to indicate the amount of money transferred) was then cut lengthwise. Creditor and debtor each retained one of the halves, whose "match" with each other constituted legal proof of the transaction.
8. I.e., feature of the portrait.
9. As a servant ("family" meant "household").

tlewoman's name. It made me very uneasy. He quickly found the reason, and assured me there was nothing at all in it; but I since found a letter that came with those goods from that very person. At the reading it I thought I should have died, and I have scarce been myself ever since. She tells him she loves him before her life, and subscribes herself thus, "No more at present from your truest of lovers," and the two first letters of her own name to it. I showed him the letter, and then he said it was things he took for a debt of a relation of hers. Gentlemen, pray, as soon as you can possible, advise me in this thing, for there's not one creature upon the earth that knows it; nor can I confide in any person to ask their advice.

ANSW. We'd not willingly either injure an innocent gentleman, nor mislead you who desire our advice. But if the letter you found was worded as you relate it, his excuse is too weak to clear him. For the writer of it must at least be more than an ordinary friend or acquaintance; and he a very ill man to endeavor to deceive you both, which we should think would go a good way towards taking off your love from him, and settling it on a more worthy object, that neither will nor can deceive or abuse you.

Richard Steele: *from* Tatler No. 104

Thursday, 8 December 1709

[JENNY DISTAFF NEWLY MARRIED[1]]

—*Garrit aniles*
Ex re Fabellas.—[2]

From My Own Apartment, December 7

My brother[3] Tranquillus being gone out of town for some days, my sister Jenny sent me word she would come and dine with me, and therefore desired me to have no other company. I took care accordingly, and was not a little pleased to see her enter the room with a decent and matronlike behavior, which I thought very much became her. I saw she had a great deal to say to me, and easily discovered in her eyes, and the air of her countenance, that she had abundance of satisfaction in her heart, which she longed to communicate. However, I was resolved to let her break into her discourse her own way, and reduced her to a thousand little devices and intimations to bring me to the mention of her husband. But finding I was resolved not to name him, she began of her own accord; my husband (said she) gives his humble service to you: to which I only answered, I hope he is well; and without waiting for a reply, fell into other subjects. She at last was out of all patience, and said (with a smile and manner that I thought had more beauty and spirit than I had ever observed before in her) I did not think, Brother, you had been so ill-natured. You have seen ever since I came in, that I had a mind to talk of my husband, and you won't be so kind as to give me an occasion. I did not know (said I) but it might be a disagreeable subject to you. You do not take me for so old-fashioned a fellow as to think of entertaining a young lady with the discourse of her husband. I know, nothing is more acceptable than to speak of one who is to be so; but to speak of one who is so! Indeed, Jenny, I am a better bred man than you think me. She showed a little dislike at my raillery; and by her bridling

---

1. Jenny Distaff is Isaac Bickerstaff's half-sister. In some earlier *Tatlers* (Nos. 10 and 33), she appeared as an essayist in her own right, composing pieces for the paper whenever her brother was out of town. In more recent numbers (75, 79), Bickerstaff had told the story of arranging her marriage to "Tranquillus" ("the calm one"),

which he described as "a domestic affair of great importance, . . . no less than the disposal of my sister Jenny for life."
2. "He tells an old wives' tale very pertinently" (Horace, *Satires* 2.6.77–78).
3. Brother-in-law.

up, I perceived she expected to be treated hereafter not as Jenny Distaff, but Mrs. Tranquillus. I was very well pleased with this change in her humor; and upon talking with her on several subjects, I could not but fancy that I saw a great deal of her husband's way and manner in her remarks, her phrases, the tone of her voice, and the very air of her countenance. This gave me an unspeakable satisfaction, not only because I had found her an husband, from whom she could learn many things that were laudable, but also because I looked upon her imitation of him as an infallible sign that she entirely loved him. This is an observation that I never knew fail, though I do not remember that any other has made it. The natural shyness of her sex hindered her from telling me the greatness of her own passion; but I easily collected it, from the representation she gave me of his. I have everything, says she, in Tranquillus that I can wish for; and enjoy in him (what indeed you have told me were to be met with in a good husband) the fondness of a lover, the tenderness of a parent, and the intimacy of a friend. It transported me to see her eyes swimming in tears of affection when she spoke. And is there not, Dear Sister, said I, more pleasure in the possession of such a man, than in all the little impertinencies[4] of balls, assemblies, and equipage, which it cost me so much pains to make you condemn? She answered, smiling, Tranquillus has made me a sincere convert in a few weeks, though I am afraid you could not have done it in your whole life. To tell you truly, I have only one fear hanging upon me, which is apt to give me trouble in the midst of all my satisfactions: I am afraid, you must know, that I shall not always make the same amiable appearance in his eye that I do at present. You know, Brother Bickerstaff, that you have the reputation of a conjurer; and if you have any one secret in your art to make your sister always beautiful, I should be happier than if I were mistress of all the worlds you have shown me in a starry night. Jenny (said I) without having recourse to magic, I shall give you one plain rule, that will not fail of making you always amiable to a man who has so great a passion for you, and is of so equal and reasonable a temper as Tranquillus. Endeavor to please, and you must please; be always in the same disposition as you are when you ask for this secret, and, you may take my word, you will never want it. An inviolable fidelity, good humor, and complacency of temper, outlive all the charms of a fine face, and make the decays of it invisible.

We discoursed very long upon this head, which was equally agreeable to us both; for I must confess, (as I tenderly love her) I take as much pleasure in giving her instructions for her welfare, as she herself does in receiving them. * * *

Joseph Addison: Spectator No. 128
Friday, 27 July 1711

[VARIETY OF TEMPER[1]]

. . . Concordia discors.[2]

Women in their nature are much more gay and joyous than men; whether it be that their blood is more refined, their fibers more delicate, and their animal spirits more light and volatile; or whether, as some have imagined, there may not be a kind of sex

---

4. Irrelevancies, distractions.
1. Lady Mary Wortley Montagu praised this essay in a letter written to her husband shortly after it appeared: "One of the *Spectators* is very just, that says a man ought always

to be on his guard against spleen and too severe a philosophy; a woman against levity and coquetry."
2. "Discordant concord" (i.e., harmony arising from difference; Lucan, *Pharsalia* 1.98).

in the very soul,[3] I shall not pretend to determine. As vivacity is the gift of women, gravity is that of men. They should each of them therefore keep a watch upon the particular bias which nature has fixed in their minds, that it may not draw too much, and lead them out of the paths of reason. This will certainly happen, if the one in every word and action affects the character of being rigid and severe, and the other of being brisk and airy. Men should beware of being captivated by a kind of savage philosophy, women by a thoughtless gallantry. Where these precautions are not observed, the man often degenerates into a cynic, the woman into a coquette; the man grows sullen and morose, the woman impertinent and fantastical.[4]

By what I have said we may conclude, men and women were made as counterparts to one another, that the pains and anxieties of the husband might be relieved by the sprightliness and good humor of the wife. When these are rightly tempered, care and cheerfulness go hand in hand; and the family, like a ship that is duly trimmed, wants neither sail nor ballast.

Natural historians observe (for whilst I am in the country I must fetch my allusions from thence[5]) that only the male birds have voices; that their songs begin a little before feeding-time, and end a little after; that whilst the hen is covering her eggs, the male generally takes his stand upon a neighboring bough within her hearing; and by that means amuses and diverts her with his songs during the whole time of her sitting.

This contract among birds lasts no longer than till a brood of young ones arises from it; so that in the feathered kind, the cares and fatigues of the married state, if I may so call it, lie principally upon the female. On the contrary, as in our species the man and woman are joined together for life, and the main burden rests upon the former, nature has given all the little arts of soothing and blandishment to the female, that she may cheer and animate her companion in a constant and assiduous application to the making a provision for his family, and the educating of their common children. This however is not to be taken so strictly, as if the same duties were not often reciprocal, and incumbent on both parties; but only to set forth what seems to have been the general intention of Nature, in the different inclinations and endowments which are bestowed on the different sexes.

But whatever was the reason that man and woman were made with this variety of temper, if we observe the conduct of the fair sex, we find that they choose rather to associate themselves with a person who resembles them in that light and volatile humor which is natural to them, than to such as are qualified to moderate and counterbalance it. It has been an old complaint, that the coxcomb carries it[6] with them before the man of sense. When we see a fellow loud and talkative, full of insipid life and laughter, we may venture to pronounce him a female favorite. Noise and flutter are such accomplishments as they cannot withstand. To be short, the passion of an ordinary woman for a man, is nothing else but self-love diverted upon another object: she would have the lover a woman in every thing but the sex. I do not know a finer piece of satire on this part of womankind than those lines of Mr. Dryden,

> Our thoughtless sex is caught by outward form
> And empty noise, and loves itself in man.[7]

---

3. In *Tatler* No. 172, Steele had asserted that "there is a sort of sex in souls" (i.e., an essential difference between men and women).
4. Irrelevant in her talk, preposterous in her thought.
5. Mr. Spectator is visiting the country estate of his friend and club fellow, Sir Roger de Coverley.
6. Succeeds.
7. From John Dryden's tragedy *Oedipus* (1.1).

This is a source of infinite calamities to the sex, as it frequently joins them to men who in their own thoughts are as fine creatures as themselves; or if they chance to be good-humored, serve only to dissipate their fortunes, inflame their follies, and aggravate their indiscretions.

The same female levity is no less fatal to them after marriage than before. It represents to their imaginations the faithful prudent husband as an honest tractable and domestic animal, and turns their thoughts upon the fine gay gentleman that laughs, sings, and dresses so much more agreeably.

As this irregular vivacity of temper leads astray the hearts of ordinary women in the choice of their lovers and the treatment of their husbands, it operates with the same pernicious influence towards their children, who are taught to accomplish themselves in all those sublime perfections that appear captivating in the eye of their mother. She admires in her son what she loved in her gallant; and by that means contributes all she can to perpetuate herself in a worthless progeny.

The younger Faustina[8] was a lively instance of this sort of women. Notwithstanding she was married to Marcus Aurelius, one of the greatest, wisest, and best of the Roman emperors, she thought a common gladiator much the prettier gentleman; and had taken such care to accomplish[9] her son Commodus according to her own notions of a fine man, that when he ascended the throne of his father, he became the most foolish and abandoned tyrant that was ever placed at the head of the Roman Empire, signalizing himself in nothing but the fighting of prizes, and knocking out men's brains. As he had no taste of true glory, we see him in several medals and statues which are still extant of him, equipped like an Hercules with a club and a lion's skin.

I have been led into this speculation by the characters I have heard of a country gentleman and his lady, who do not live many miles from Sir Roger. The wife is an old coquette, that is always hankering after the diversions of the town; the husband is a morose rustic, that frowns and frets at the name of it; the wife is overrun with affectation, the husband sunk into brutality. The lady cannot bear the noise of the larks and nightingales, hates your tedious summer days, and is sick at the sight of shady woods and purling streams; the husband wonders how any one can be pleased with the fooleries of plays and operas, and rails from morning to night at essenced[1] fops and tawdry courtiers. The children are educated in these different notions of their parents. The sons follow the father about his grounds, while the daughters read volumes of love letters and romances to their mother. By this means it comes to pass, that the girls look upon their father as a clown, and the boys think their mother no better than she should be.

How different are the lives of Aristus and Aspatia? The innocent vivacity of the one is tempered and composed by the cheerful gravity of the other. The wife grows wise by the discourses of the husband, and the husband good-humored by the conversations of the wife. Aristus would not be so amiable were it not for his Aspatia, nor Aspatia so much to be esteemed were it not for her Aristus. Their virtues are blended in their children, and diffuse through the whole family a perpetual spirit of benevolence, complacency, and satisfaction.

---

8. Annia Galeria Faustina (d. A.D. 175), wife of Marcus   9. Educate.
Aurelius (A.D. 121–180), cherished by her husband but   1. Perfumed.
dispraised by ancient writers as an unfaithful wife.

Eliza Haywood: *from* The Female Spectator, Vol. 1, No. 1
April 1744
[SEOMANTHE'S ELOPEMENT[1]]

Seomanthe, to her misfortune, was brought up under the tuition of her aunt Negratia,[2] a woman extremely sour by nature, but rendered yet more so by age and infirmity. Past all the joys of life herself, she looked with a malicious eye on every one who partook of them, censured the most innocent diversions in the severest manner, and the least complaisance between persons of different sexes was, with her, scandalous to the last degree. Her character was so well known that none but prudes, whose deformity was an antidote to desire (worn-out, superannuated rakes, who had outlived all sense of pleasure) and canting zealots,[3] whose bread depended on their hypocrisy, frequented her house. To this sort of company was the young, beautiful, and naturally gay Seomanthe condemned. She heard nothing but railing against that way of life she knew was enjoyed by others of equal rank and fortune with herself, and which she had too much good sense to look upon as criminal. She thought people might be perfectly innocent, yet indulge themselves in sometimes going to a play or opera; nor could be brought to believe the court such a bugbear[4] as she was told it was: a laced coat and a toupee wig had double charms for her, as they were every day so much preached against; and she never saw a coach pass, wherein were gentlemen and ladies, but she wished to be among them, or a well-dressed beau, with whom she did not languish to be acquainted.

At length her desires were fulfilled. Close as she was kept, the report that Negratia had a young lady in her house, who was mistress of a large fortune on the day of marriage, reached the ears of one of those harpies who purchase to themselves a wretched sustenance, by decoying the unwary into everlasting ruin. This creature, who had been employed by one so far a gentleman as to be bred to no business, and whose whole estate was laid out on his back,[5] in hopes of appearing charming in the eyes of some moneyed woman, too truly guessed she had found in Seomanthe what she sought. She came to the house under the pretense of offering some lace, holland,[6] and fine tea, extraordinary cheap. Negratia being what is called a good housewife, and a great lover of bargains, readily admitted her; and while she was examining some of the goods at a small distance off, the artful woman put a letter into Seomanthe's hand, telling her it came from the finest gentleman in the world, who she was sure would die, if she did not favor him with an answer. The young lady took it, blushed, and put it in her bosom, but had not time to make any reply to the woman, Negratia that instant coming towards them. As nobody understood her business better, she managed it so that she was ordered to come again the next day, when she said she should have greater variety to show their ladyships. While she was packing up her bundles, she winked on Seomanthe, and at the same time gave her the most beseeching look; the meaning of which, young and unexperienced as she was, the destined victim but too well comprehended, and was, perhaps, no less impatient for the success of an adventure, the beginning of which afforded her infinite satisfaction.

---

1. Haywood tells this story to illustrate her point that it is sometimes wrong to blame young women for marrying unwisely; parents and other authorities "are sometimes, by an over-caution, guilty of forcing them into things, which otherwise would be far distant from their thoughts."

2. The name means "unpleasing."
3. People pretending to fanatic piety.
4. Danger (with the illusory connotation of "boogeyman").
5. Spent on clothing.
6. Imported fabric.

She ran immediately to her chamber, shut herself in, and broke open her billet,[7] which she found stuffed with flames, darts, wounds, love, and death; the highest encomiums on her beauty, and the most vehement imprecations of not outliving his hope of obtaining her favor—expressions which would have excited only the laughter of a woman who knew the world, but drew tears into the eyes of the innocent Seomanthe. She imagined he had seen her either at church or looking out of the window, for she was permitted to show herself in no other place; and doubted not but all he had wrote to her of his love and despair, was no less true than what she had heard delivered from the pulpit. She looked upon herself as too much obliged by the passion he had for her, not to write an answer full of complaisance, and very dexterously gave it to the woman, on her coming the next day.

On the ensuing Sunday she saw a strange gentleman in the next pew to her; by the glances he stole at her every time he could do it without being taken notice of, she fancied him the person who had declared himself her lover, and was convinced her conjecture had not deceived her, when being kneeled down at her devotions, he found means, while everyone had their fans before their faces, to drop a letter on the bench she leaned upon. She was not so much taken up with the business she was employed about, as not to see it immediately, and throwing her handkerchief over it, clapped it into her pocket. The looks that passed between them afterwards, during the time of divine service, confirmed her in the opinion that he was no less charmed with her than he said he was; and him, that the sight of him had not destroyed the impression his letter by the old woman had made on her.

Both thought they had reason to be highly satisfied with this interview; but poor Seomanthe was up to the head and ears in love. The person of the man was agreeable enough, and, compared to those Negratia had suffered her to converse with, angelic. The prepossession she had for him, at least, rendered him so in her eyes, and she thought every moment an age till she got home to read this second billet, the contents of which were of the same nature with the former, only a postscript added, entreating she would contrive some means to let him entertain her with his passion, by word of mouth. He mentioned the woman who sold the things, and by whose means he at first made a discovery of it,[8] and gave the directions where she lived; begged a meeting there, if possible; at least an answer, whether he might be so happy or not; which, he told her, he would wait for himself early the next morning under her window, if she would be so good as to throw it out.

She sighed at reading it; thought her fate very hard that it was not in her power to comply with the first part of his request, but hesitated not in the least if she ought to grant the other. She snatched the first opportunity she could lay hold on to prepare a letter, in which she let him know how impossible it was for her to come out; but expressed such a regret at not being able to do so, as showed it would be no difficult matter to prevail on her to run the greatest lengths.

By the help of his adviser, he carried on a correspondence with her, which ended in her consenting to quit Negratia forever, and put herself under his protection. In fine, she packed up all her clothes and jewels, threw the former from the window to the woman, who stood ready to receive them on an appointed night; and having put the other into her pocket, exchanged one scene of hypocrisy for another, and flew from a life irksome for the present, to enter into one of lasting misery.

---

7. Letter.   8. I.e., had revealed his passion.

Early in the morning they were married, and it is possible passed some days in the usual transports of a bridal state. But when their place of abode was discovered by the friends and kindred of Seomanthe, who, distracted at her elopement, had searched the whole town, in how wretched a manner was she found! The villain had drawn her whole fortune out of the bank, robbed her of all her jewels and the best of her apparel, had shipped everything off, and was himself embarked she knew not to what place. The people of the house where they lodged, perceiving him, whom they expected to have been their paymaster, gone, seized on the few trifles he had left behind, as satisfaction for the rent, and were going to turn the unfortunate Seomanthe out of doors.

Not the sight of her distress, nor the lamentations she made, which were pitiful enough to have softened the most rugged hearts, had any effect on that of Negratia, who thought no punishment too severe for a person who had deceived her caution. But some others were of a more compassionate disposition. They took her home with them, and comforted her as well as they were able. She still lives with them a dependent on their courtesy, which she is obliged to purchase the continuance of, by rendering herself subservient to all their humors.[9] No news is yet arrived what course her wicked husband took; but it is supposed he is retired either to France or Holland, being almost as much in debt here, as all he wronged Seomanthe of would discharge; so that there is little probability of his ever returning, or if he did, that it would be at all to the satisfaction of his unhappy wife.

I was going on to recite some other instances of the mischiefs, which, for the most part, are the consequence of laying young people under too great a restraint, when Mira[1] came in, and seeing what I was about, took the pen out of my hand, and told me I had already said enough; if I proceeded to expatiate any farther on that head, I should be in danger of being understood to countenance an extreme on the other side,[2] which was much more frequently fatal to our sex.

I yielded to her superior judgment, and needed but few arguments to be convinced, that if unbridled youth were indulged in all the liberties it would take, we should scarce see anything but unhappy objects before maturity arrived.

Eliza Haywood: *from* The Female Spectator, Vol. 2, No. 10
February 1745

[WOMEN'S EDUCATION]

We[1] were beginning to lament the misfortunes our sex frequently fall into through the want of those improvements we are doubtless capable of, when a letter, left for us at our publisher's, was brought in which happened to be on that subject, and cannot anywhere be more properly inserted than in this place.

To the Female Spectator

Ladies,
    Permit me to thank you for the kind and generous task you have undertaken in endeavoring to improve the minds and manners of our unthinking sex. It is the noblest act of charity you could exercise in an age like ours, where the sense of good and evil is

---

9. Whims, moods.
1. One of the Female Spectator's collaborators.

2. I.e., in favor of leniency.
1. The Female Spectator and her collaborators.

almost extinguished, and people desire to appear more vicious than they really are, that so they may be less unfashionable. This humor, which is too prevalent in the female sex, is the true occasion of the many evils and dangers to which they are daily exposed. No wonder the men of sense disregard us! and the dissolute triumph over that virtue they ought to protect!

Yet I think it would be cruel to charge the ladies with all the errors they commit; it is most commonly the fault of a wrong education, which makes them frequently do amiss, while they think they act not only innocently but uprightly. It is therefore only the men—and the men of understanding, too—who, in effect, merit the blame of this, and are answerable for all the misconduct we are guilty of. Why do they call us silly women, and not endeavor to make us otherwise? God and Nature has endued them with means, and custom has established them in the power of rendering our minds such as they ought to be. How highly ungenerous is it then to give us a wrong turn, and then despise us for it!

The Mahometans indeed enslave their women, but then they teach them to believe their inferiority will extend to eternity. But our case is even worse than this; for while we live in a free country, and are assured from our excellent Christian principles that we are capable of those refined pleasures which last to immortality, our minds, our better parts, are wholly left uncultivated, and, like a rich soil neglected, bring forth nothing but noxious weeds.

There are, undoubtedly, no sexes in souls; and we are as able to receive and practice the impressions, not only of virtue and religion, but also of those sciences which the men engross to themselves, as they can be. Surely our bodies were not formed by the great Creator out of the finest mold, that our souls might be neglected like the coarsest of the clay?

O! would too imperious and too tenacious man be so just to the world as to be more careful of the education of those females to whom they are parents or guardians! Would they convince them in their infancy, that dress and show are not the essentials of a fine lady, and that true beauty is seated in the mind; how soon should we see our sex retrieve the many virtues which false taste has buried in oblivion! Strange infatuation! to refuse us what would so much contribute to their own felicity! Would not themselves reap the benefit of our amendment? Should we not be more obedient daughters, more faithful wives, more tender mothers, more sincere friends, and more valuable in every other station of life?

But, I find, I have let my pen run a much greater length than I at first intended. If I have said anything worthy your notice, or what you think the truth of the case, I hope you will mention this subject in some of your future essays; or if you find I have any way erred in my judgment, to set me right will be the greatest favor you can confer on,

Ladies,
Your constant reader,
And humble servant,
CLEORA

Hampton Court,
January 12, 1744–45

After thanking this lady for the favor of her obliging letter, we think it our duty to congratulate her on being one of those happy few who have been blessed with that sort of education which she so pathetically laments the want of in the greatest part of our sex.

Those men are certainly guilty of a great deal of injustice who think that all the learning becoming in a woman is confined to the management of her family; that is, to give orders concerning the table, take care of her children in their infancy, and observe that her servants do not neglect their business. All this, no doubt, is very necessary; but would it not be better if she performs those duties more through principle than custom? And will she be less punctual in her observance of them after she becomes a wife, for being perfectly convinced, before she is so, of the reasonableness of them, and why they are expected from her?

Many women have not been inspired with the least notion of even those requisites in a wife, and when they become so, continue the same loitering, lolloping, idle creatures they were before; and then the men are ready enough to condemn those who had the care of their education. * * *

⇒✦ END OF PERSPECTIVES: READING PAPERS ✦⇐

━━✦✦✦✦━━

Jonathan Swift
1667-1745

Arguably the greatest prose satirist in the history of English literature, Jonathan Swift was born in Dublin, the only son of English parents, seven months after his father died. In his infancy he was kidnapped by his nurse and did not see his mother for three years. With the future dramatist William Congreve he attended the Kilkenny School (Ireland's best), and in 1682 he began six years of study at Trinity College, Dublin. He received his B.A. degree in 1686. From 1689, Swift served as secretary to Sir William Temple (1628–1699), a retired diplomat whose father had befriended Swift's family. Swift worked at Temple's estate at Moor Park in Surrey for most of the next ten years. It was at Moor Park that Swift first experienced the vertigo, nausea, and hearing impairment of Ménière's syndrome, a disturbance of the inner ear that would plague him for the rest of his life and sometimes wrongly led him (and others) to question his mental stability. While working for Temple, Swift also wrote his first poems, undistinguished compositions that do not presage the literary acclaim that was to come.

Not content with his station in life, Swift took an M.A. degree from Oxford University in 1692; three years later, he was ordained a priest in the (Anglican) Church of Ireland and appointed to the undesirable prebendary of Kilroot, where he found the local Presbyterians unsympathetic and the salary meager. Added to professional discontent was personal disappointment: Swift was rejected in his marriage proposal to Jane "Varina" Waring, the daughter of an Anglican clergyman. Swift returned to Moor Park in 1696, and, after Temple died in 1699, held a series of ecclesiastical posts in Ireland, none of which fulfilled his ambition for an important position in England. In 1702 he was made Doctor of Divinity by his alma mater, Trinity College, Dublin.

While at Moor Park, Swift began to tutor an eight-year-old girl, Esther "Stella" Johnson, daughter of Sir William's late steward. Though she was nearly fourteen years Swift's junior, "Stella" would in time become his beloved companion and his most trusted friend. When she was eighteen, Swift described her as "one of the most beautiful, graceful, and agreeable young women in London." In 1701, at Swift's request, Stella and Sir William's spinster cousin, Rebecca Dingley, moved to Dublin, where they remained for the rest of their lives. Swift and Stella met regularly, but never alone. Although there has been much debate about the nature of their relationship, it is clear that Swift and Stella loved, trusted, and valued each other, whether or not they were ever secretly married (the evidence suggests they were not). Swift's *Journal to Stella* (composed 1710 to 1713) and the series of poems he composed for her birthdays reveal a playful intimacy and affection not seen in his more public writings.

Moor Park not only led him to Stella but was also the cradle of Swift's first major literary work: *A Tale of a Tub* (composed 1697 to 1698, published 1704), a brilliant satire on "corruptions in religion and learning," published with *The Battle of the Books*, Swift's mock-epic salvo in the debate between the Ancients and the Moderns. Like most of his subsequent works, *A Tale of a Tub* did not appear under Swift's name, though its ironic treatment of the church subsequently damaged his prospects for ecclesiastical preferment when his authorship became widely known.

In the first decade of the new century Swift placed his hopes for preferment with the Whigs, then in power, and became associated with the Whig writers Joseph Addison and Richard Steele, founder of the *Tatler*, a London periodical in which two of Swift's important early poems, *A Description of the Morning* (1709) and *A Description of a City Shower* (1710), first appeared. Swift's career as a political polemicist began when he rose to the defense of three Whig lords facing impeachment with his allegorical *Discourse of the Contests and Dissentions between the Nobles and Commons in Athens and Rome* (1701). His *Bickerstaff Papers* (1708–1709), witty parodies of the cobbler-turned-astrologer John Partridge, occasioned much laughter regardless of party allegiances. More important, Swift began to write a series of pamphlets on church affairs, including his ironical *Argument against Abolishing Christianity* (1708) and *A Letter . . . Concerning the Sacramental Test* (1709), which damaged his relationship with the Whigs.

While in London as an emissary for the Irish clergy in 1708, Swift met Esther "Vanessa" Vanhomrigh (pronounced "Vanummry") and, as with "Stella," acted as her mentor. Although his feelings for this attractive young woman (twenty-one years younger than he) clearly became more than paternal, Swift was eventually put off by her declaration of "inexpressible passion" and wrote *Cadenus and Vanessa* (composed 1713, published 1726) to cool the relationship.

Vehemently disagreeing with the Whig policies supporting the Dissenters (Protestants who were not members of the established church) because he feared they would weaken the Anglican church, Swift shifted his allegiance to the Tories in 1710 and soon became their principal spokesman and propagandist, taking charge of their weekly periodical the *Examiner* (1710–1711) and producing a series of highly effective political pamphlets, such as *The Conduct of the Allies* (1712), which called for an end to the War of Spanish Succession (1701–1713). Swift's years in London from 1710 to 1714, when he was an important lobbyist for the Church of Ireland and an influential agent of the Tory government, were the most exciting of his life.

In 1713 Swift was installed as Dean of Saint Patrick's Cathedral, Dublin—a prestigious appointment, but far short of the English bishopric he felt he deserved. Returning quickly to London, Swift became a vital presence in the Scriblerus Club—with Alexander Pope, John Arbuthnot, John Gay, Thomas Parnell, and Robert Harley, Earl of Oxford—which met in 1714. The influence of this group, with its love of parody, literary hoaxes, and the ridicule of false learning, is evident in *Gulliver's Travels*. Upon the death of Queen Anne in 1714 and the resultant fall of the Tory Ministry, Swift's hopes for further advancement were dashed, and he took up permanent residence in Ireland, where he conscientiously carried out his duties as Dean.

When Swift successfully defended Irish interests by writing *The Drapier's Letters* (1724–1725)—attacking a government plan to impose a new coin, "Wood's halfpence," that would devalue Ireland's currency and seriously damage the economy—he became a national hero. Thereafter, the people lit bonfires on his birthday and hailed him as a champion of Irish liberty, though he never ceased to regard Ireland as the land of his exile. From Dublin, he corresponded with Pope, Gay, Arbuthnot, and Henry St. John, Lord Bolingbroke; he enjoyed a long visit with his friends in England in 1726. While there, he encouraged Gay's *The Beggar's Opera* and Pope's *The Dunciad*, and arranged for the publication of his own masterpiece, *Gulliver's Travels* (1726).

When the death of George I the following year briefly created hopes of unseating "Prime Minister" Robert Walpole, Swift paid his final visit to England, where he assisted Pope in editing their joint *Miscellanies* in three volumes (1727, 1728, 1732). The years that followed in Dublin saw the production of many of Swift's finest poems, including *The Lady's Dressing Room* (1732), *A Beautiful Young Nymph Going to Bed* (1734), and *Verses on the Death of Dr. Swift* (composed 1731–1732, published 1739), his most celebrated poem. Swift continued to champion the cause of Irish political and economic freedom; with his like-minded friend Thomas

Sheridan, he conducted a weekly periodical, the *Intelligencer* (1728). In 1729, he published his most famous essay, *A Modest Proposal*. Some years later, he supervised the publication of the first four volumes of his *Works* (1735) by the Dublin publisher George Faulkener.

When Swift reached his early seventies, his infirmities made him incapable of carrying out his clerical duties at Saint Patrick's; at seventy-five, he was found "of unsound mind and memory," and guardians were appointed to manage his affairs. In addition to ongoing debilities from Ménière's syndrome, he suffered from arteriosclerosis, aphasia, memory loss, and other diseases of old age; he was not insane, however, as many of his contemporaries believed. A devoted clergyman, Swift practiced the Christian charity he preached, giving more than half of his income to the needy; the founding of Ireland's first mental hospital through a generous provision in his will was the most famous of Swift's many benefactions.

Voltaire hailed Swift as the "English Rabelais," while Henry Fielding lauded him as the "English Lucian." Although the more delicate sensibilities of the nineteenth century eschewed his writings for their coarseness and truculence, twentieth-century readers have prized Swift's work for its intelligence, wit, and inventiveness. A committed champion of social justice and an untiring enemy of pride, Swift was a brilliant satirist in part because he was a thoroughgoing humanist.

A DESCRIPTION OF THE MORNING   Introducing this poem in the ninth number of his new periodical, the *Tatler* (for 30 April 1709), Richard Steele wrote that Swift, "has . . . run into a way [of writing] perfectly new, and described things exactly as they happen." *A Description of the Morning* is an early and important example of the "town eclogue," or urban pastoral, a poetic style further popularized by John Gay's *Trivia, or The Art of Walking the Streets of London* (1716). Traditionally, the eclogue—Virgil's bucolic poems are the most famous example—has no appreciable action or characterization, but depends on the thorough and evocative depiction of a pastoral scene. Swift's *Morning* imitates the conventions of pastoral description, not to portray the idealized natural harmony of Arcadia but rather to present the reality of social disorder masquerading under the appearance of order as day breaks over London. Remarkably, Alexander Pope's *Pastorals*, his first published poems, went on sale in the same week that Swift's pioneering mock-pastoral appeared, though the two future friends would not meet for several years.

A Description of the Morning

	Now hardly° here and there a hackney coach[1]	*harshly*
	Appearing, showed the ruddy morn's approach.	
	Now Betty[2] from her master's bed has flown,	
	And softly stole to discompose her own.	
5	The slipshod 'prentice from his master's door	
	Had pared° the dirt, and sprinkled round the floor.[3]	*reduced*
	Now Moll had whirled her mop with dexterous airs,	
	Prepared to scrub the entry and the stairs.	
	The youth with broomy stumps began to trace	
10	The kennel edge, where wheels had worn the place.[4]	
	The smallcoal man was heard with cadence deep;[5]	
	Till drowned in shriller notes of chimney sweep.	
	Duns° at his Lordship's gate began to meet;	*creditors*

1. A hired coach, drawn by two horses and seating six people; here, equated with the chariot of Phoebus Apollo, Greek god of the sun.
2. Like "Moll" (line 7), a typical maidservant's name.
3. Fresh sawdust was used to absorb mud.
4. Scavenging in the gutters (kennels) "to find old nails"

[Swift's note] was common.
5. Small pieces of coal or charcoal used to light fires; like many other products and services, they were sold by street vendors who advertised, or "cried," their wares by calling or singing as they walked the streets. The smallcoal man has a deep voice; sweeps were always small boys.

And brickdust⁶ Moll had screamed through half a street.
15 The turnkey now his flock returning sees,
Duly let out a-nights to steal for fees.⁷
The watchful bailiffs take their silent stands;
And schoolboys lag with satchels in their hands.⁸

1709   1709

A DESCRIPTION OF A CITY SHOWER   "They say 'tis the best thing I ever writ, and I think
so too," boasted Swift of his *Description of a City Shower* in 1710. It was first published in the
Tatler, No. 238, on 17 October 1710, soon after its composition. Swift's closely observed rendering of London street life playfully mocks the English imitators of Virgil, especially John
Dryden and his celebrated translation, *The Works of Virgil* (1697). We see, for example, Swift's
mock-heroic effects based on Virgil's *Aeneid* (29–19 B.C.), most notably in comparing the tim-
orous "beau" trapped in his sedan chair to the fierce Greek warriors hiding inside the Trojan
Horse, and in calling to mind the storm that led to Queen Dido's seduction and eventual ruin
(Dryden's translation 4.231–238). More important, just as Swift invoked the mock-pastoral in
A Description of the Morning, so too does he create a mock-georgic mode in his *City Shower*.
The division of the poem into portents, preliminaries, and deluge closely parallels the tempest
scene in Virgil's *Georgics* (36–29 B.C.; bk. 1, 431–458, 483–538 in Dryden), so that Swift uses
structural and verbal elements from a classical poem extolling the virtues of agriculture and
rural life to depict the teeming diversity of the contemporary urban scene.

A Description of a City Shower

Careful observers may foretell the hour
(By sure prognostics) when to dread a shower.
While rain depends,° the pensive cat gives o'er   *is impending*
Her frolics, and pursues her tail no more.
5   Returning home at night you find the sink¹
Strike your offended sense with double stink.
If you be wise, then go not far to dine,
You spend in coach-hire more than save in wine.
A coming shower your shooting corns² presage,
10 Old aches³ throb, your hollow tooth will rage:
Sauntering in coffee-house is Dulman seen;
He damns the climate, and complains of spleen.⁴

    Meanwhile the South,° rising with dabbled° wings,   *south wind / muddy*
    A sable cloud athwart the welkin° flings;   *sky*
15 That swilled more liquor than it could contain,
And like a drunkard gives it up again.
Brisk Susan whips her linen from the rope,⁵

6. An abrasive, used for cleaning or for sharpening
knives.
7. As prisoners had to pay the jailer for food and for other
comforts, the jailer has let them out overnight to steal.
8. Cf. the second "age of man" in Shakespeare's *As You
Like It*: "Then the whining schoolboy, with his satchel /
And shining morning face, creeping like snail / Unwillingly to school" (2.7.145–47).
1. Sewer. The poem is built upon Swift's experiences in
London: on November 8, 1710, Swift wrote to his
beloved Stella (Esther Johnson) that "I will give ten

shillings a week for my lodging; for I am almost stunk out
of this with the sink, and it helps me to verses in my
Shower." The parsimonious Swift normally spent around
half this amount for lodgings.
2. The shooting pain in your corns.
3. Pronounced "aitches."
4. Dulman (a descriptive name) complains of melancholy
or depression, then attributed to the spleen.
5. The typically named maid brings in her washing from
the line.

	While the first drizzling shower is borne aslope:°	*at a slant*
	Such is that sprinkling which some careless quean°	*hussy*
20	Flirts° on you from her mop, but not so clean:	*flicks*
	You fly, invoke the gods; then turning, stop	
	To rail; she singing, still whirls on her mop.	
	Nor yet the dust had shunned th' unequal strife,	
	But aided by the wind, fought still for life;	
25	And wafted with its foe by violent gust,	
	'Twas doubtful which was rain, and which was dust.⁶	
	Ah! Where must needy poet seek for aid,	
	When dust and rain at once his coat invade?	
	Sole coat, where dust cemented by the rain	
30	Erects the nap, and leaves a cloudy stain.	
	Now in contiguous drops the flood comes down,	
	Threatening with deluge this devoted° town.	*doomed*
	To shops in crowds the daggled° females fly,	*muddied*
	Pretend to cheapen° goods, but nothing buy.	*bargain for*
35	The Templer spruce,⁷ while every spout's abroach,⁸	
	Stays till 'tis fair, yet seems to call a coach.	
	The tucked-up seamstress walks with hasty strides,	
	While streams run down her oiled umbrella's sides.	
	Here various kinds by various fortunes led,	
40	Commence acquaintance underneath a shed.°	*shelter*
	Triumphant Tories, and desponding Whigs,⁹	
	Forget their feuds, and join to save their wigs.	
	Boxed° in a chair¹ the beau impatient sits,	*confined*
	While spouts run clattering o'er the roof by fits;	
45	And ever and anon with frightful din	
	The leather sounds; he trembles from within.	
	So when Troy chairmen bore the wooden steed,	
	Pregnant with Greeks, impatient to be freed;	
	(Those bully Greeks, who, as the moderns do,	
50	Instead of paying chairmen, run them through²)	
	Laocoon struck the outside with his spear,	
	And each imprisoned hero quaked for fear.³	

	Now from all parts the swelling kennels⁴ flow,	
	And bear their trophies with them as they go:	
55	Filths of all hues and odors, seem to tell	
	What streets they sailed from, by the sight and smell.	
	They, as each torrent drives with rapid force	
	From Smithfield, or St. Pulchre's shape their course;⁵	
	And in huge confluent join at Snow Hill ridge,	

---

6. Swift here parallels a line from Samuel Garth's popular satirical poem, *The Dispensary* (1699): "'Tis doubtful which is sea, and which is sky" (5.176).
7. Well-dressed lawyer.
8. Drainpipe pouring water.
9. 1710, the year this poem was written, was the first year of the Tory ministry under Queen Anne.
1. A sedan chair, carried by two men; this one has a leather roof.

2. With their swords.
3. When the Trojans carried the Greek's wooden horse into Troy, thinking that the opposing army had given up their siege, the priest Laocoon was suspicious, and struck the horse. See *Aeneid* 2.50–53.
4. Gutters, which were also open sewers.
5. Respectively, the cattle market and the parish west of the Newgate prison.

60   Fall from the conduit prone to Holborn Bridge.[6]
    Sweepings from butchers' stalls, dung, guts, and blood, ⎫
    Drowned puppies, stinking sprats,° all drenched in mud, ⎬   *small fish*
    Dead cats and turnip tops come tumbling down the flood.[7] ⎭

1710   1710

STELLA'S BIRTHDAY   Between 1719 and 1727 Swift wrote seven birthday poems to "Stella," his
dear Esther Johnson. The two reprinted here are his first and last. Swift's earliest use of the name
"Stella" in verse was in the first of this series of celebratory verses, which play on the obligation of
the Poet Laureate to write an official "birthday ode" for the monarch every year. Placing himself
in the role of her laureate, Swift may have chosen the name "Stella" to highlight the difference
between his own uncontrived expressions of affection and those of the courtly Sir Philip Sidney in
Astrophil and Stella (1591). Like Shakespeare's Sonnet 130 ("My mistress' eyes are nothing like the
sun"), Swift's first poem on Stella's birthday violates the traditions of the conventional love lyric
by calling attention to his beloved's considerable weight and age, only to suggest that his admiration of her lies in her deeper virtues. In his last birthday poem, Swift attempts to escape from the
prospect of Stella's impending death, first by humor and then by the power of reason; when these
fail, he tenderly acknowledges how much she means to him. Swift was to sail for England less than
a month after he gave those verses to her—both knew that they might never see each other again.
Though more formal than the *Journal to Stella*, Swift's birthday verses were written primarily for
Stella's enjoyment and for the entertainment of their small circle of intimate friends. Despite the
private nature of these poems, Swift nevertheless authorized their publication in the third and last
volume of the Pope-Swift *Miscellanies*, which appeared in March 1728.

Stella's Birthday, 1719
Written in the Year 1718/9[1]

    Stella this day is thirty-four,[2]
    (We shan't dispute a year or more):
    However, Stella, be not troubled,
    Although thy size and years are doubled,
5   Since first I saw thee at sixteen,[3]
    The brightest virgin on the green.[4]
    So little is thy form° declined;   *figure*
    Made up° so largely in thy mind.   *compensated*

       Oh, would it please the gods to *split*
10   Thy beauty, size, and years, and wit,
    No age could furnish out a pair

6. Snow Hill ridge extended down to Holborn Bridge, which spanned Fleet ditch, used as an open sewer; from 1343, local butchers had been given permission to dump entrails in the Fleet.
7. These last three lines were intended against the licentious manner of modern poets, in making three rhymes together, which they call *Triplets*; and the last of the three was two, or sometimes more syllables longer, called an *Alexandrian*. These *Triplets* and *Alexandrians* were brought in by Dryden, and other poets in the reign of Charles II. They were the mere effect of haste, idleness, and want of money, and have been wholly avoided by the best poets since these verses were written [Swift's note].
1. Until the calendar was reformed in 1751, the new year legally began on the Feast of the Annunciation (some-

times called "Lady Day") on March 25th, though January 1st was also commonly recognized as the start of the new year. Therefore, to avoid confusion, it was a widely accepted practice to write dates between January 1 and March 24 according to both methods of reckoning: 1718/19. Since Swift's poem was composed in February or March, we would say it was written in 1719.
2. Stella (Esther Johnson) actually celebrated her thirty-eighth birthday on 13 March 1719.
3. Swift first met Stella when she was eight years old; he may have "seen" her only when she grew from child to woman.
4. The village green, or common land, here implies a pastoral simplicity that suggests the natural innocence of their relationship.

Of nymphs so graceful, wise, and fair:
With half the luster of your eyes,
With half your wit, your years, and size:
15   And then before it grew too late,
How should I beg of gentle fate,
(That either nymph might have her swain),
To split my worship too in twain.

1719   1728

Stella's Birthday, 1727

This day, whate'er the fates decree,
Shall still be kept with joy by me:
This day then, let us not be told,
That you are sick, and I grown old,
5   Nor think on our approaching ills,
And talk of spectacles and pills.
Tomorrow will be time enough
To hear such mortifying stuff.[1]
Yet, since from reason may be brought
10   A better and more pleasing thought,
Which can in spite of all decays,
Support a few remaining days:
From not the gravest of divines,°   *clergymen*
Accept for once some serious lines.

15   Although we now can form no more
Long schemes of life, as heretofore;
Yet you, while time is running fast,
Can look with joy on what is past.

       Were future happiness and pain[2]
20   A mere contrivance of the brain,
As atheists argue, to entice
And fit their proselytes° for vice   *converts*
(The only comfort they propose,
To have companions in their woes);
25   Grant this the case, yet sure 'tis hard,
That virtue, styled its own reward,
And by all sages understood
To be the chief of human good,
Should acting, die, nor leave behind
30   Some lasting pleasure in the mind;
Which by remembrance will assuage
Grief, sickness, poverty, and age;
And strongly shoot a radiant dart
To shine through life's declining part.

35   Say, Stella, feel you no content,
Reflecting on a life well spent?

---

1. Both humbling and leading to death. Stella died less than a year later.   2. I.e., heaven and hell.

Your skillful hand employed to save
Despairing wretches from the grave;[3]
And then supporting with your store,
40 Those whom you dragged from death before
(So Providence on mortals waits,
Preserving what it first creates);
Your generous boldness to defend
An innocent and absent friend;
45 That courage which can make you just,
To merit humbled in the dust;
The detestation you express
For vice in all its glittering dress;
That patience under torturing pain,
50 Where stubborn Stoics would complain.

        Shall these like empty shadows pass,
Or forms reflected from a glass?
Or mere chimeras° in the mind,   *imaginary creatures or notions*
That fly and leave no marks behind?
55 Does not the body thrive and grow
By food of twenty years ago?
And had it not been still supplied,
It must a thousand times have died.
Then, who with reason can maintain
60 That no effects of food remain?
And is not virtue in mankind
The nutriment that feeds the mind?
Upheld by each good action past,
And still continued by the last:
65 Then who with reason can pretend,
That all effects of virtue end?

        Believe me, Stella, when you show
That true contempt for things below,
Nor prize your life for other ends
70 Than merely to oblige your friends;
Your former actions claim their part,
And join to fortify your heart.
For Virtue in her daily race,
Like Janus[4] bears a double face;
75 Looks back with joy where she has gone,
And therefore goes with courage on.
She at your sickly couch will wait,
And guide you to a better state.

        O then, whatever Heaven intends,
80 Take pity on your pitying friends;
Nor let your ills affect your mind,
To fancy they can be unkind.

3. Swift often praised Stella's charity, not only for nursing him in his bouts of illness, but also for attending to the poor in her neighborhood.

4. The god of doorways and of the rising and setting sun, whose two-faced head looks forward and backward, and after whom the month of January is named.

Me, surely me, you ought to spare,
Who gladly would your sufferings share;
85   Or give my scrap of life to you,
And think it far beneath your due;
You, to whose care so oft I owe
That I'm alive to tell you so.

1727   1728

THE LADY'S DRESSING ROOM   The first of Swift's so-called scatological poems, which
have attracted much critical attention and amateur psychoanalysis, these verses enjoyed considerable popularity in Swift's lifetime, though some contemporaries condemned them as "deficient in point of delicacy, even to the highest degree." One of Swift's friends recorded in her
memoirs that *The Lady's Dressing Room* made her mother "instantly" lose her lunch. Sir Walter Scott found in this poem (and other pieces by Swift) "the marks of an incipient disorder of
the mind, which induced the author to dwell on degrading and disgusting subjects." If Pope's
The Rape of the Lock describes Belinda at the "altar" of her dressing table undergoing "the sacred rites of pride" as she and her maid apply all manner of cosmetics to make her a beautiful
"goddess" and arm her for the battle of the sexes, then *The Lady's Dressing Room* reveals the
coarse realities of Celia's embodiment—a humorous and disturbing corrective to the pretense
and false appearances on which her glorification depends. Although Swift assails the social
and literary conventions that celebrate women for their superficial qualities, there is also a
misogynistic quality to the poem, which may be attributable to his anger and disappointment
over his beloved Stella's death in January 1728. Nevertheless, Strephon is ridiculed for being
so naively idealistic about his lover and so easily deceived by appearances; once his secret investigations free him from his illusions, Strephon's permanent revulsion and rejection of all
women show his inability to follow a middle course by appreciating women in their complex
reality.

The Lady's Dressing Room

Five hours (and who can do it less in?)
By haughty Celia spent in dressing;
The goddess from her chamber issues,
Arrayed in lace, brocade, and tissues:
5   Strephon,[1] who found the room was void,
And Betty[2] otherwise employed,
Stole in, and took a strict survey,
Of all the litter as it lay:
Whereof, to make the matter clear,
10   An *inventory* follows here.

And first, a dirty smock appeared,
Beneath the arm-pits well besmeared;
Strephon, the rogue, displayed it wide,
And turned it round on every side.
15   In such a case few words are best,
And Strephon bids us guess the rest;
But swears how damnably the men lie,
In calling Celia sweet and cleanly.

---

1. Strephon and Celia are names usually associated with   2. A typical maidservant's name.
pastoral poetry, and are therefore used mockingly here.

    Now listen while he next produces

20   The various combs for various uses,

    Filled up with dirt so closely fixed,

    No brush could force a way betwixt;

    A paste of composition rare,

    Sweat, dandruff, powder, lead,[3] and hair,

25   A forehead cloth with oil upon't

    To smooth the wrinkles on her front;

    Here alum flour[4] to stop the steams,

    Exhaled from sour, unsavory streams;

    There night-gloves made of Tripsy's[5] hide,

30   Bequeathed by Tripsy when she died;

    With puppy water,[6] beauty's help,

    Distilled from Tripsy's darling whelp.

    Here gallipots° and vials placed,   *ointment jars*

    Some filled with washes, some with paste;

35   Some with pomatum,° paints, and slops,   *hair ointment*

    And ointments good for scabby chops.°   *lips or cheeks*

    Hard° by a filthy basin stands,   *close*

    Fouled with the scouring of her hands;

    The basin takes whatever comes,

40   The scrapings of her teeth and gums,

    A nasty compound of all hues,

    For here she spits, and here she spews.

    But oh! it turned poor Strephon's bowels,

    When he beheld and smelt the towels;

45   Begummed, bemattered, and beslimed;

    With dirt, and sweat, and ear-wax grimed.

    No object Strephon's eye escapes,

    Here, petticoats in frowzy° heaps;   *unkempt*

    Nor be the handkerchiefs forgot,

50   All varnished o'er with snuff[7] and snot.

    The stockings why should I expose,

    Stained with the moisture of her toes;

    Or greasy coifs and pinners° reeking,   *night caps*

    Which Celia slept at least a week in?

55   A pair of tweezers next he found

    To pluck her brows in arches round,

    Or hairs that sink the forehead low,

    Or on her chin like bristles grow.

    The virtues we must not let pass

60   Of Celia's magnifying glass;

    When frighted Strephon cast his eye on't,

---

3. White lead face paint, used to whiten the skin.
4. Powdered alum used like modern antiperspirant.
5. Celia's lapdog; no fashionable lady was without such a pet.
6. A recipe for this cosmetic, made from the innards of a pig or a fat puppy, was given in the "Fop's Dictionary" in

Mundus Muliebris [Womanly Make-up]: *Or, the Ladies' Dressing Room Unlocked* (1690), which Swift also used for other terms.
7. Powdered tobacco, sniffed by fashionable men and women alike.

It showed the visage of a giant:[8]
A glass that can to sight disclose
The smallest worm in Celia's nose,
65   And faithfully direct her nail
To squeeze it out from head to tail;
For catch it nicely by the head,
It must come out alive or dead.

Why, Strephon, will you tell the rest?
70   And must you needs describe the chest?
That careless wench! no creature warn her
To move it out from yonder corner,
But leave it standing full in sight,
For you to exercise your spite!
75   In vain the workman showed his wit
With rings and hinges counterfeit
To make it seem in this disguise
A cabinet to vulgar eyes;
Which Strephon ventured to look in,
80   Resolved to go through *thick and thin*;
He lifts the lid: there need no more,
He smelt it all the time before.

As, from within Pandora's box,
When Epimethus oped the locks,
85   A sudden universal crew
Of human evils upward flew;[9]
He still was comforted to find
That hope at last remained behind.

So, Strephon, lifting up the lid
90   To view what in the chest was hid,
The vapors flew from out the vent,
But Strephon cautious never meant
The bottom of the pan to grope,
And foul his hands in search of hope.

95   O! ne'er may such a vile machine°   construction
Be once in Celia's chamber seen!
O! may she better learn to keep
"Those secrets of the hoary deep."[1]

As mutton cutlets, prime of meat,
100 Which though with art you salt and beat
As laws of cookery require,
And roast them at the clearest fire;
If from adown the hopeful chops

8. Cf. *Gulliver's Travels*, Part 2, "A Voyage to Brobding-
nag," ch. 1: "This made me reflect upon the fair skins of
our *English* ladies, who appear so beautiful to us, only
because they are of our own size, and their defects not to
be seen but through magnifying glass, where we find by
experiment that the smoothest and whitest skins look
rough and coarse, and ill colored."

9. In Greek mythology, Epimethus, acting against advice,
opened the box Jove had given his wife Pandora, and all
the evils and vices of the world flew out, leaving only
hope in the box.
1. Quoting Milton's *Paradise Lost* 2.891, in which Sin is
unleashing the chaotic forces of her infernal realm.

The fat upon a cinder drops,
105   To stinking smoke it turns the flame
Poisoning the flesh from whence it came;
And up exhales a greasy stench
For which you curse the careless wench:
So things which must not be expressed,
110   When *plumped°* into the reeking chest,   dropped
Send up an excremental smell
To taint the parts from which they fell:
The petticoats and gown perfume,
And waft a stink round every room.

115   Thus finishing his grand survey,
The swain disgusted slunk away,
Repeating in his amorous fits,
"Oh! Celia, Celia, Celia shits!"

        But Vengeance, goddess never sleeping,
120   Soon punished Strephon for his peeping.
His foul imagination links
Each dame he sees with all her stinks:
And if unsavory odors fly,
Conceives a lady standing by:
125   All women his description fits,
And both ideas jump° like wits   join together
By vicious fancy coupled fast,
And still appearing in contrast.

        I pity wretched Strephon, blind
130   To all the charms of womankind;
Should I the queen of love refuse,
Because she rose from stinking ooze?[2]
To him that looks behind the scene,
Statira's but some pocky quean.[3]

135   When Celia in her glory shows,
If Strephon would but stop his nose,
Who now so impiously blasphemes
Her ointments, daubs, and paints and creams;
Her washes, slops, and every clout,[4]
140   With which she makes so foul a rout;[5]
He soon would learn to think like me,
And bless his ravished eyes to see
Such order from confusion sprung,
Such gaudy *tulips* raised from *dung*.

c. 1730   1732

---

2. Venus, Roman goddess of sexual love and physical
beauty, rose from the sea.
3. One of the heroines of Nathaniel Lee's highly popular
tragedy *The Rival Queens* (1677); Swift's common slat-
tern (quean) has had either smallpox or venereal disease.

4. Washes were either treated water used for the complexion or stale urine used as a detergent; clouts were
rags.
5. Both of her skin and, presumably, of the men.

VERSES ON THE DEATH OF DR. SWIFT "I have been several months writing near five hundred lines on a pleasant subject," wrote Swift to his friend John Gay in December 1731, "only to tell what my friends and enemies will say on me after I am dead." Swift completed what was to become his most celebrated poem by adding explanatory notes in the early months of 1732. It seems that Swift intended the *Verses* to be published after his death but showed the poem in manuscript to various friends. When the reputation of his *Verses* spread, Swift used the opportunity to publish a different autobiographical poem, *The Life and Genuine Character of Dr. Swift* (1733), which would satisfy public demand and make the eventual appearance of the *Verses* all the more surprising. Six years later, believing they were doing their friend a service, Alexander Pope and William King (1685–1763) published a version of the poem in which they edited out some of Swift's most self-aggrandizing and controversial lines. Swift was "much dissatisfied" with this London edition and responded by supervising the speedy publication of an unexpurgated text of the work in Dublin, though even he had the prudence to leave blank spaces for some of the names in his poem. Among the most controversial elements in the *Verses* were its direct attack on Prime Minister Robert Walpole and his government; the unflattering depiction of the court and singling out of Lady Suffolk and Queen Caroline for ridicule; and Swift's praise of Bolingbroke and Pulteney, leading opposition politicians. Swift's jaunty tetrameter carries an admixture of self-fashioning for posterity and moral instruction, a spirited apologia for his life and writings, and an idealized account of the principles by which he strove to live. *Verses on the Death of Dr. Swift* reveals its subject as a champion of liberty and embattled self-promoter, a humanistic preacher and an unsparing satirist.

Verses on the Death of Dr. Swift, D.S.P.D.[1]
Occasioned by Reading a Maxim in Rochefoucauld

Dans l'adversité de nos meilleurs amis nous trouvons quelque chose, qui ne nous deplaist pas.[2]

"In the adversity of our best friends, we find something that doth not displease us."

As Rochefoucauld his maxims drew
From Nature, I believe 'em true:
They argue° no corrupted mind   suggest
In him; the fault is in mankind.

5   This maxim more than all the rest
Is thought too base for human breast;
"In all distresses of our friends
We first consult our private ends,
While Nature kindly bent to ease us,
10   Points out some circumstance to please us."

If this perhaps your patience move°   strains
Let reason and experience prove.

We all behold with envious eyes,
Our equal raised above our size;
15   Who would not at a crowded show,

---

1. Dean of St. Patrick's, Dublin.
2. François, duc de La Rochefoucauld, *Réflexions ou Sen-* *tences et Maximes Morales* ("Reflections or Moral Aphorisms and Maxims," 1665).

Stand high himself, keep others low?
I love my friend as well as you,
But would not have him stop my view;
Then let me have the higher post;
20   I ask but for an inch at most.

If in a battle you should find,
One, whom you love of all mankind,
Had some heroic action done,
A champion killed, or trophy won;
25   Rather than thus be overtopped,
Would you not wish his laurels[3] cropped?

Dear honest Ned is in the gout,[4]
Lies racked with pain, and you without:[5]
How patiently you hear him groan!
30   How glad the case is not your own!

What poet would not grieve to see,
His brethren write as well as he?
But rather than they should excel,
He'd wish his rivals all in Hell.

35   Her end when emulation misses,
She turns to envy, stings, and hisses:
The strongest friendship yields to pride,
Unless the odds be on our side.

Vain humankind! Fantastic race!
40   Thy various follies, who can trace?
Self-love, ambition, envy, pride,
Their empire in our hearts divide:
Give others riches, power, and station,
'Tis all on me a usurpation.
45   I have no title to aspire;
Yet, when you sink, I seem the higher.
In Pope,[6] I cannot read a line,
But with a sigh, I wish it mine:
When he can in one couplet fix
50   More sense than I can do in six:
It gives me such a jealous fit,
I cry, "Pox take him, and his wit."

Why must I be outdone by Gay,[7]
In my own humorous, biting way?

55   Arbuthnot[8] is no more my friend,
Who dares to irony pretend;

---

3. In ancient times, laurel wreaths were given to poets, athletes, and war heroes to signify their preeminence.
4. A disease characterized by an inflammation of small joints, especially in the feet and hands.
5. Outside his room.
6. Alexander Pope, poet, satirist, and friend of Swift.

7. John Gay, poet and playwright, author of The Beggar's Opera (1728), friend of Swift, Pope, and Arbuthnot.
8. John Arbuthnot (1667–1735), physician to Queen Anne and member of Scriblerus Club along with Swift, Pope, and Gay; he was the principal author of Memoirs of . . . Martinus Scriblerus (1741).

Which I was born to introduce,
Refined it first, and showed its use.

St. John, as well as Pulteney[9] knows,
60 That I had some repute for prose;
And till they drove me out of date,
Could maul a minister of state:
If they have mortified my pride,
And made me throw my pen aside;
65 If with such talents Heaven hath blest 'em,
Have I not reason to detest 'em?

To all my foes, dear fortune, send
Thy gifts, but never to my friend:
I tamely can endure the first,
70 But, this with envy makes me burst.

Thus much may serve by way of proem,°   *preface*
Proceed we therefore to our poem.

The time is not remote, when I
Must by the course of nature die:
75 When I foresee my special friends,
Will try to find their private ends:
Though it is hardly understood,[1]
Which way my death can do them good;
Yet, thus methinks, I hear 'em speak;
80 "See, how the Dean begins to break:°   *weaken*
Poor gentleman, he droops apace,°   *quickly*
You plainly find it in his face:
That old vertigo in his head
Will never leave him, till he's dead:
85 Besides, his memory decays,
He recollects not what he says;
He cannot call his friends to mind;
Forgets the place where last he dined:
Plies you with stories o'er and o'er,
90 He told them fifty times before.
How does he fancy we can sit
To hear his out-of-fashioned wit?
But he takes up with younger folks,
Who for his wine will bear his jokes:
95 Faith,° he must make his stories shorter,   *in truth*
Or change his comrades once a quarter:
In half the time, he talks them round;[2]
There must another set be found.

"For poetry, he's past his prime,
100 He takes an hour to find a rhyme:

---

9. Henry St. John Bolingbroke (1678–1751) and William
Pulteney; both politicians—one a Tory, the other a
Whig—were united in their opposition to Robert Wal-
pole. See Swift's notes to lines 194 and 196.

1. Hard to understand.
2. Runs through his stock of stories and has to begin
again.

His fire° is out, his wit decayed,   *creative fire*
His fancy sunk, his muse a jade.³
I'd have him throw away his pen;
But there's no talking to some men."

105   And then their tenderness appears,
By adding largely to my years:
"He's older than he would be reckoned,
And well remembers Charles the Second."⁴

     "He hardly° drinks a pint of wine;   *barely*
110 And that, I doubt,° is no good sign.   *suspect*
His stomach° too begins to fail: *appetite*
Last year we thought him strong and hale;
But now, he's quite another thing;
I wish he may hold out till spring."

115   Then hug themselves, and reason thus:
"It is not yet so bad with us."

     In such a case they talk in tropes,°   *figuratively*
And by their fears express their hopes:
Some great misfortune to portend,°   *predict*
120 No enemy can match a friend;
With all the kindness they profess,
The merit of a lucky guess
(When daily "Howd'y's"⁵ come of course,°   *routinely*
And servants answer: "Worse and worse")
125 Would please 'em better than to tell
That, God be praised, the Dean is well.
Then he who prophesied the best,
Approves° his foresight to the rest,   *confirms*
"You know, I always feared the worst,
130 And often told you so at first":
He'd rather choose that I should die
Than his prediction prove a lie.
No one foretells I shall recover;
But, all agree to give me over.°   *give up hope*

135   Yet should some neighbor feel a pain
Just in the parts where I complain;
How many a message would he send?
What hearty prayers that I should mend?
Inquire what regimen⁶ I kept;
140 What gave me ease, and how I slept?
And more lament, when I was dead,
Than all the snivellers round my bed.

     My good companions, never fear,
For though you may mistake a year;

3. The poet's muse—his inspiration (always female)—is here a worn-out horse or a disreputable or shrewish woman.

4. King Charles II died in 1685, when Swift was 18.
5. How does [is] he?
6. Prescribed pattern of living, exercising, and eating.

145 Though your prognostics run too fast,
 They must be verified at last.

  "Behold the fatal day arrive!
 How is the Dean? He's just alive.
 Now the departing prayer is read:
150 He hardly breathes. The Dean is dead.
 Before the passing bell[7] begun,
 The news through half the town has run.
 O, may we all for death prepare!
 What has he left? And who's his heir?
155 I know no more than what the news is,
 'Tis all bequeathed to public uses.[8]
 To public use! A perfect whim!
 What had the public done for him?
 Mere envy, avarice, and pride!
160 He gave it all.—But first he died.
 And had the Dean, in all the nation,
 No worthy friend, no poor relation?
 So ready to do strangers good,
 Forgetting his own flesh and blood?"

165 Now Grub Street wits[9] are all employed;
 With elegies, the town is cloyed:
 Some paragraph in every paper,
 To curse the Dean, or bless the Drapier.[1]

  The doctors tender of their fame,
170 Wisely on me lay all the blame:
 "We must confess his case was nice,°   *difficult*
 But he would never take advice;
 Had he been ruled, for aught appears,
 He might have lived these twenty years:
175 For when we opened him we found
 That all his vital parts were sound."

  From Dublin soon to London spread,[2]
 'Tis told at court, the Dean is dead.

  Kind Lady Suffolk[3] in the spleen,[4]
180 Runs laughing up to tell the Queen.
 The Queen, so gracious, mild, and good,

---

7. Death bell, rung to obtain prayers for the passing soul.
8. In fact, when Swift died he left a number of small personal bequests in addition to his large gifts to public charities.
9. Hack writers, paid to produce (often libelous) materials for London journals.
1. The Author imagines, that the Scribblers of the prevailing Party, which he always opposed, will libel him after his Death; but that others will remember him with gratitude, who consider the service he had done to Ireland, under the name of M. B. Drapier [Swift's note, referring to *The Drapier's Letters* (1724–1725), a series of essays he wrote to defend Ireland from the British government's plan to impose a new coin, "Wood's halfpence,"

that would have devastated Ireland's economy].
2. The Dean supposeth himself to die in Ireland [Swift's note]; he did.
3. Mrs. Howard, afterwards Countess of Suffolk, then of the Bedchamber to the Queen, professed much friendship for the Dean. The Queen, then Princess, sent a dozen times to the Dean (then in London) with her command to attend her; which at last he did, by advice of all his friends. She often sent for him afterwards, and always treated him very graciously. He taxed her with a present worth ten pounds, which she promised before he should return to Ireland, but on his taking leave, the medals were not ready" [Swift's note].
4. The 18th-century equivalent of "depression."

Cries, "Is he gone? 'Tis time he should.
He's dead you say, why let him rot;
I'm glad the medals were forgot.[5]

185 I promised them, I own;° but when?   admit
I only was a princess then;
But now as consort of the King,
You know 'tis quite a different thing."

Now, Chartres[6] at Sir Robert's levee,[7]
190 Tells, with a sneer, the tidings heavy:
"Why, is he dead without his shoes?"[8]
(Cries Bob)[9] "I'm sorry for the news;
Oh, were the wretch but living still,
And in his place my good friend Will;[1]
195 Or had a miter° on his head,   bishop's hat
Provided Bolingbroke[2] were dead."

Now Curll his shop from rubbish drains:
Three genuine tomes of Swift's remains.[3]
And then to make them pass the glibber,°   sell better
200 Revised by Tibbalds, Moore, and Cibber.[4]
He'll treat me as he does my betters:
Publish my will, my life, my letters,[5]
Revive the libels born to die;
Which Pope must bear, as well as I.

205 Here shift the scene, to represent
How those I love, my death lament.
Poor Pope will grieve a month; and Gay
A week; and Arbuthnot a day.

---

5. The medals were to be sent to the Dean in four months, but she forgot them, or thought them too dear [expensive]. The Dean, being in Ireland, sent Mrs. Howard a piece of Indian plaid made in that kingdom [Ireland]: which the Queen seeing took from her, and wore it herself, and sent to the Dean for as much as would clothe herself and her children, desiring he would send charge of it. He did the former. It cost thirty-five pounds, but he said he would have nothing except the medals. He was the summer following in England, was treated as usual, and she being then Queen, the Dean was promised a settlement in England, but returned as he went, and, instead of favor or medals, hath been ever since under her Majesty's displeasure [Swift's note].
6. Chartres is a most infamous, vile scoundrel, grown from a foot-boy, or worse, to a prodigious fortune [Swift's note]. Francis Charteris was convicted of rape, and pardoned by the prime minister, Robert Walpole, in 1730.
7. A morning audience held in the bedchamber of a person of distinction before or after rising.
8. I.e., in his bed, rather than meeting a violent death or being hanged.
9. Sir Robert Walpole, Chief Minister of State, treated the Dean, in 1726, with great distinction, invited him to dinner at Chelsea, with the Dean's friends chosen on purpose; appointed an hour to talk with him of Ireland, to which kingdom and people the Dean found him no great friend. . . . The Dean would see him no more [Swift's note].
1. Mr. William Pulteney, from being Mr. Walpole's inti-

mate friend, detesting his Administration, opposed his measures, and joined with my Lord Bolingbroke, to represent his conduct in an excellent paper, called the Craftsman, which is still continued [Swift's note].
2. Henry St. John, Lord Viscount Bolingbroke, Secretary of State to Queen Anne of blessed memory. He is reckoned the most universal genius in Europe; Walpole dreading his abilities, treated him most injuriously, working with King George, who forgot his promise of restoring the said Lord, upon the restless importunity of Walpole [Swift's note].
3. Edmund Curll hath been the most infamous bookseller of any age or country: his character in part may be found in Mr. Pope's Dunciad. He published three volumes all charged on [i.e., attributed to] the Dean, who never writ three pages of them: he hath used many of the Dean's friends in almost as vile a manner [Swift's note].
4. Three stupid verse writers in London, the last to the shame of the Court, and the highest disgrace to wit and learning, was made Laureate [Swift's note]. Lewis Theobald (1688–1744), Shakespearean scholar and poet; James Moore Smythe (1702–1734), playwright whom Pope accused of plagiarism; Colley Cibber (1671–1757), actor and playwright. All three men are satirized in Pope's Dunciad.
5. Curll is notoriously infamous for publishing the lives, letters, and last Wills and Testaments of the nobility and ministers of State, as well as of all the rogues who are hanged at Tyburn [Swift's note].

St. John himself will scarce forbear
210 To bite his pen, and drop a tear.
The rest will give a shrug and cry
"I'm sorry; but we all must die."
Indifference clad in wisdom's guise
All fortitude of mind supplies:
215 For how can stony bowels melt,[6]
In those who never pity felt;
When *we* are lashed, *they* kiss the rod,[7]
Resigning to the will of God.

The fools, my juniors by a year,
220 Are tortured with suspense and fear—
Who wisely thought my age a screen,
When death approached, to stand between:
The screen removed, their hearts are trembling,
They mourn for me without dissembling.

225 My female friends, whose tender hearts
Have better learnt to act their parts,
Receive the news in doleful dumps,
"The Dean is dead (*and what is trumps?*),
Then Lord have mercy on his soul.
230 (*Ladies, I'll venture for the vole.*[8])
Six deans they say must bear the pall.
(*I wish I knew which king to call.*)"
"Madam, your husband will attend
The funeral of so good a friend."
235 "No madam, 'tis a shocking sight,
And he's engaged tomorrow night!
My Lady Club would take it ill,
If he should fail her at quadrille.
He loved the Dean. (*I lead a heart.*)
240 But dearest friends, they say, must part.
His time was come, he ran his race;
We hope he's in a better place."

Why do we grieve that friends should die?
No loss more easy to supply.
245 One year is past; a different scene;
No further mention of the Dean;
Who now, alas, no more is missed
Than if he never did exist.
Where's now this fav'rite of Apollo?[9]
250 Departed; and his works must follow:
Must undergo the common fate;
His kind of wit is out of date.
Some country squire to Lintot[1] goes,

6. I.e., how can one feel compassion.
7. Accept chastisement submissively; kissing a monarch's scepter or a state official's staff was a ritual of submission to authority.
8. All the tricks in the highly popular four-handed card game, quadrille.
9. Patron of poets.
1. Bernard Lintot (1675–1736), London publisher of Pope, Gay, and Steele, among others.

Inquires for Swift in verse and prose:
255   Says Lintot, "I have heard the name:
He died a year ago." "The same."
He searcheth all his shop in vain;
"Sir, you may find them in Duck Lane:[2]
I sent them with a load of books
260   Last Monday to the pastry-cook's.[3]
To fancy they could live a year!
I find you're but a stranger here.
The Dean was famous in his time
And had a kind of knack at rhyme:
265   His way of writing now is past;
The town hath got a better taste:
I keep no antiquated stuff;
But, spick and span I have enough.
Pray, do but give me leave to show 'em;
270   Here's Colley Cibber's birthday poem.[4]
This ode you never yet have seen
By Stephen Duck,[5] upon the Queen.
Then, here's a letter finely penned,
Against the *Craftsman*[6] and his friend;
275   It clearly shows that all reflection
On ministers, is disaffection.
Next, here's Sir Robert's vindication,[7]
And Mr Henley's last oration:[8]
The hawkers° have not got 'em yet,   *street sellers*
280   Your Honor please to buy a set?

"Here's Woolston's tracts,[9] the twelfth edition;
'Tis read by every politician:
The country members,[1] when in town,
To all their boroughs send them down:
285   You never met a thing so smart;
The courtiers have them all by heart:
Those maids of honor (who can read)
Are taught to use them for their creed.
The reverend author's good intention

---

2. A place in London where old [i.e., remaindered] books are sold [Swift's note].
3. Wastepaper from unsold books was used to line baking tins. Cf. Dryden's *Mac Flecknoe* (1682), who notes similar uses for old texts: "Martyrs of pies, and relics of the bum" (line 101).
4. The Poet Laureate was required to write an ode for the monarch's birthday each year. Cibber's appointment as Laureate in 1730 was based on politics, not literary merit.
5. Stephen Duck (1705–1756), known as "the thresher poet," was a laborer whose poetry won him Queen Caroline's favor; Swift made fun of him in *On Stephen Duck, the Thresher, and Favorite Poet, A Quibbling Epigram* (1730).
6. From 1726, the principal periodical written in opposition to Robert Walpole's government. Its title was meant to indicate that Walpole was "a man of craft" (i.e., scheming and deceptive).

7. Walpole hires a set of Party scribblers, who do nothing else but write in his defense [Swift's note].
8. John Henley (1692–1756), known as "Orator Henley" for the Oratory he founded where "at set times, he delivereth strange speeches compiled by himself and his associates. . . . He is an absolute dunce, but generally reputed crazy" [Swift's note].
9. Woolston was a clergyman, but for want of bread, hath in several treatises, in the most blasphemous manner, attempted to turn our Savior and his miracles into ridicule. He is much caressed by many great courtiers, and by all the infidels, and his books read generally by the Court ladies [Swift's note]. Swift appears to conflate the identities of two contemporary clergymen: Thomas Woolston (1670–1733), a notorious Deist, and William Woollaston (1660–1724).
1. Members of Parliament from rural boroughs.

290 Hath been rewarded with a pension:
 He doth an honor to his gown,
 By bravely running priestcraft down:
 He shows, as sure as God's in Gloucester,[2]
 That Jesus was a grand impostor:
295 That all his miracles were cheats,
 Performed as jugglers do their feats;
 The church had never such a writer:
 A shame he hath not got a miter!"

  Suppose me dead; and then suppose
300 A club assembled at the Rose;[3]
 Where from discourse of this and that,
 I grow the subject of their chat:
 And while they toss my name about,
 With favor some, and some without;
305 One quite indifferent in the cause
 My character impartial draws:

  "The Dean, if we believe report,
 Was never ill received at court;
 As for his works in verse and prose,
310 I own myself no judge of those:
 Nor can I tell what critics thought 'em;
 But this I know, all people bought 'em;
 As with a moral view designed
 To cure the vices of mankind:
315 His vein, ironically grave,
 Exposed the fool, and lashed the knave:
 To steal a hint was never known,
 But what he writ was all his own.[4]

  "He never thought an honor done him,
320 Because a duke was proud to own him:
 Would rather slip aside, and choose
 To talk with wits in dirty shoes:
 Despised the fools with stars and garters,[5]
 So often seen caressing Chartres:
325 He never courted men in station,
 Nor persons had in admiration;°   *was in awe of*
 Of no man's greatness was afraid,
 Because he sought for no man's aid.
 Though trusted long in great affairs,
330 He gave himself no haughty airs;
 Without regarding private ends,
 Spent all his credit for his friends,
 And only chose the wise and good;

2. A proverb derived from the number of monasteries there once were in that county.
3. The Rose Tavern, near Drury Lane Theatre, and therefore popular with playgoers.
4. Swift is here having fun with the reader, since this line claiming Swift's originality is stolen from Sir John Denham's elegy *On Mr. Abraham Cowley:* "To him no author was unknown / Yet what he wrote was all his own."
5. Worn by Knights of the Garter.

No flatt'rers; no allies in blood;°   *relatives*
335 But succored virtue in distress,
And seldom failed of good success;
As numbers in their hearts must own,
Who, but for him, had been unknown.

"With princes kept a due decorum,
340 But never stood in awe before 'em:
And to her Majesty, God bless her,
Would speak as free as to her dresser,[6]
She thought it his peculiar whim,
Nor took it ill as come from him.
345 He followed David's lesson just,
"In princes never put thy trust."[7]
And, would you make him truly sour,
Provoke him with a slave in power:
The Irish senate, if you named,
350 With what impatience he declaimed!
Fair LIBERTY was all his cry;
For her he stood prepared to die;
For her he boldly stood alone;
For her he oft exposed his own.
355 Two kingdoms, just as factions led,
Had set a price upon his head;
But not a traitor could be found,
To sell him for six hundred pound.[8]

"Had he but spared his tongue and pen,
360 He might have rose like other men:
But power was never in his thought,
And wealth he valued not a groat;
Ingratitude he often found,
And pitied those who meant the wound;
365 But kept the tenor° of his mind,   *prevailing course*
To merit well of humankind;
Nor made a sacrifice of those
Who still° were true, to please his foes.   *always*
He labored many a fruitless hour
370 To reconcile his friends in power;
Saw mischief by a faction brewing,
While they pursued each other's ruin.
But finding vain was all his care,
He left the Court in mere° despair.[9]   *total*

375 "And, oh! how short are human schemes!
Here ended all our golden dreams.

---

6. Queen Caroline and Lady Suffolk, one of the Ladies of Her Majesty's bedchamber.
7. Psalm 146.3.
8. Two rewards of £300 each were offered in 1713 and 1724 for the revelation of the author of *The Public Spirit of the Whigs* and *The Drapier's Fourth Letter*, respectively, "but in neither kingdoms was the Dean discovered"
[Swift's note].
9. Under Queen Anne's Tory ministry, Swift tried to resolve differences between the Chancellor, Simon Harcourt (1661–1727), Lord Bolingbroke, and the Earl of Oxford, but was unsuccessful, and left London shortly before the collapse of their government.

What St. John's skill in state affairs,
What Ormonde's valor,[1] Oxford's cares,
To save their sinking country lent,
380 Was all destroyed by one event.
Too soon that precious life was ended,[2]
On which alone our weal° depended.   well-being
When up a dangerous faction starts,[3]
With wrath and vengeance in their hearts:
385 By solemn league and covenant bound,[4]
To ruin, slaughter, and confound;
To turn religion to a fable,
And make the government a Babel:
Pervert the law, disgrace the gown,
390 Corrupt the senate, rob the crown;
To sacrifice old England's glory,
And make her infamous in story.
When such a tempest shook the land,
How could unguarded virtue stand?

395   "With horror, grief, despair the Dean
Beheld the dire destructive scene:
His friends in exile, or the Tower,[5]
Himself within the frown of power;
Pursued by base, envenomed pens,[6]
400 Far to the land of slaves and fens;°   Ireland
A servile race in folly nursed,
Who truckle° most, when treated worst.   cringe obsequiously

         "By innocence and resolution,
He bore continual persecution;
405 While numbers to preferment[7] rose;
Whose merits were, to be his foes.
When, ev'n his own familiar° friends   close
Intent upon their private ends,
Like renegadoes now he feels,
410 Against him lifting up their heels.[8]

         "The Dean did by his pen defeat
An infamous, destructive cheat,[9]
Taught fools their interest to know,

1. James Butler (1665–1745), second Earl of Ormonde, succeeded Marlborough as commander in chief of the allied forces in 1712.
2. In the height of the quarrel between the ministers, the Queen [Anne] died [Swift's note].
3. When Queen Anne died, the Whigs were restored to power, "which they exercised with the utmost rage and revenge" [Swift's note]. Swift initially feared for his own safety, and considered emigrating to the island of Guernsey.
4. Alluding to the establishment of Scottish Presbyterianism in 1643, which Swift (as an Anglican) regretted.
5. The Tower of London, where convicted (or suspected) traitors were held.
6. Upon the Queen's death, the Dean returned to live in Dublin . . . numberless libels were writ against him in England, as a Jacobite; he was insulted in the street, and at nights was forced to be attended by his servants armed [Swift's note].
7. Places at the Court or in the church hierarchy, especially bishoprics.
8. From Psalm 41.9: "Yea, mine own familiar friend, in whom I trusted, which did eat of my bread, hath lifted up his heel against me."
9. One Wood, a Hardware-man from England, had a patent for coining copper halfpence in Ireland, to the sum of £108,000, which in the consequence, must leave the kingdom without gold or silver [Swift's note]. Swift responded with The Drapier's Letters (1724–1725).

And gave them arms to ward the blow.°   *defend themselves*
415 Envy hath owned it was his doing
To save that helpless land from ruin,
While they who at the steerage[1] stood,
And reaped the profit, sought his blood.

"To save them from their evil fate,
420 In him was held a crime of state.
A wicked monster on the bench,[2]
Whose fury blood could never quench;
As vile and profligate a villain,
As modern Scroggs, or old Tresilian;[3]
425 Who long all justice had discarded,
Nor feared he God, nor man regarded;[4]
Vowed on the Dean his rage to vent,
And make him of his zeal repent;
But heaven his innocence defends,
430 The grateful people stand his friends;
Not strains of law, nor judges' frown,
Nor topics° brought to please the crown,   *charges*
Nor witness hired, nor jury picked,
Prevail to bring him in convict.

435 "In exile[5] with a steady heart,
He spent his life's declining part;
Where folly, pride, and faction sway,
Remote from St. John, Pope, and Gay.

"His friendship there to few confined,
440 Were always of the middling kind:[6]
No fools of rank, a mongrel breed,
Who fain would pass for lords indeed:
Where titles give no right or power,
And peerage is a withered flower,[7]
445 He would have held it a disgrace,
If such a wretch had known his face.
On rural squires, that kingdom's bane,
He vented oft his wrath in vain:
Biennial squires,[8] to market brought,

1. The helm (of the ship of state).
2. One Whitshed was then Chief Justice: he had some years before prosecuted a printer for a pamphlet writ by the Dean, to persuade the people of Ireland to wear their own manufactures.... He sat as Judge afterwards on the trial of the printer of the Drapier's Fourth Letter; but the Jury, against all he could say or swear, threw out the Bill [Swift's note].
3. Scroggs was Chief Justice under King Charles the Second: his judgment always varied in State trials, according to directions from the [royal] Court. Tresilian was a wicked Judge, hanged above three hundred years ago [Swift's note].
4. Cf. Luke 18.2: "There was in a city a judge, which feared not God, neither regarded man."
5. In Ireland, which he had reason to call a place of exile;

to which country nothing could have driven him, but the Queen's death, who had determined to fix him in England [Swift's note].
6. The Dean was not acquainted with one single Lord spiritual or temporal. He only conversed with private gentlemen of the clergy or laity, and but a small number of either [Swift's note]; not entirely true.
7. The peers of Ireland lost a great part of their jurisdiction by one single Act [of 1720], and tamely submitted to this infamous mark of slavery without the least resentment, or remonstrance [Swift's note].
8. The Parliament (as they call it) in Ireland meet but once in two years; and after giving five times more than they can afford, return home to reimburse themselves by all country jobs and oppressions, of which some few only are here mentioned [Swift's note].

450   Who sell their souls and votes for naught;
              The nation stripped, go joyful back,
              To rob the church, their tenants rack,[9]
              Go snacks° with thieves and rapparees,[1]   *divide the spoils*
              And keep the peace,[2] to pick up fees:
455   In every job[3] to have a share,
              A jail or barrack[4] to repair;
              And turn the tax for public roads
              Commodious to their own abodes.[5]

                "Perhaps I may allow the Dean
460   Had too much satire in his vein;
              And seemed determined not to starve it,
              Because no age could more deserve it.
              Yet, malice never was his aim;
              He lashed the vice but spared the name.[6]
465   No individual could resent,
              Where thousands equally were meant.
              His satire points at no defect,
              But what all mortals may correct;
              For he abhorred that senseless tribe,
470   Who call it humor when they jibe;
              He spared a hump or crooked nose,
              Whose owners set not up for beaux.
              True, genuine dullness moved his pity,
              Unless it offered to be witty.
475   Those who their ignorance confessed,
              He ne'er offended with a jest;
              But laughed to hear an idiot quote,
              A verse from Horace, learned by rote.

                "He knew an hundred pleasant stories,
480   With all the turns of Whigs and Tories:
              Was cheerful to his dying day,
              And friends would let him have his way.

                "He gave the little wealth he had
              To build a house for fools and mad:[7]
485   And showed by one satiric touch,
              No nation wanted it so much:
              That kingdom he hath left his debtor,
              I wish it soon may have a better."

1731–1732   1739

---

9. I.e., torture by extortionate rent; "rack-rent" was an excessive rent nearly equal to the full value of the land.
1. The highwaymen in Ireland are, since the late wars there, usually called rapparees, which was a name given to those Irish soldiers who in small parties used, at that time, to plunder the Protestants [Swift's note].
2. Act as magistrates.
3. Implying a business racket.
4. The army in Ireland is lodged in barracks, the building and repairing whereof, and other charges, have cost a prodigious sum to that unhappy kingdom [Swift's note].
5. There were complaints that the new system of public turnpike roads, then being established in England and in Ireland, was manipulated by estate owners so that the roads ran directly to their own properties.
6. Swift is being ironic, since the poem explicitly identifies many targets of his satire.
7. In his will, Swift made a large bequest to build a mental institution (the first in Ireland), St. Patrick's Hospital, which was opened in 1757.

JOURNAL TO STELLA   In 1710, Swift was sent from Dublin to London by his patron, Archbishop King, with an important commission—to petition the Queen's Bounty (via the government and the Court) for the remission of the Irish "first fruits," the British monarch's tax on the revenues of clergymen in the Church of Ireland. Swift saw the campaign to repeal the "first fruits"—and his contribution to its success—as his passport to fame and preferment. Though Swift did not yet realize it, these were to be the greatest years of his career, a time when he routinely mixed with the most powerful men of his day, when he was courted for his considerable influence, and when he established himself as the most brilliant and successful of the Tory pamphleteers. He was heavily involved in the intricacies of party politics on his country's behalf and for his own advancement; his prospects for success on both fronts were highly promising. Swift never intended to publish the diary-like letters he wrote to his beloved Esther Johnson and her companion, Rebecca Dingley, during the first three years of his extended sojourn in London from 1710 to 1714. He wrote them, as Virginia Woolf keenly observed in *The Common Reader,* because "the reserved, the powerful, the admired, have the most need of such a refuge." After Esther Johnson's death in 1728, Swift preserved this highly personal "journal" probably both for sentimental reasons and for its historical importance, since it provided a unique insider's view of political affairs and Court intrigues—in addition to social gossip and immediate reactions to important public events—in the final years of Queen Anne's reign. Some of these letters were published in the 1750s and 1760s, in collections of Swift's correspondence and works; the entire sequence first appeared, as *Dr. Swift's Journal to Stella,* in 1784.

from Journal to Stella

from *Letter 10*

[SATURDAY]   London, Nov. 25, 1710
I'll tell you something that's plaguy[1] silly: I had forgot to say on the 23d in my last, where I dined, and because I had done it constantly, I thought it was a great omission, and was going to interline it;[2] but at last the silliness of it made me cry, "Pshaw," and I let it alone. I was today to see the Parliament meet; but only saw a great crowd: and Ford[3] and I went to see the tombs at Westminster,[4] and sauntered so long I was forced to go to an eating house for my dinner. Bromley is chosen speaker,[5] *nemine contradicente:*[6] Do you understand those two words? And Pompey, Colonel Hill's[7] black, designs to stand speaker for the footmen.[8] I am engaged to use my interest for him, and have spoken to Patrick[9] to get him some votes. We are now all impatient for the Queen's speech, what she will say about removing the ministry, &c.[1] I have got a cold, and I don't know how; but got it I have, and am hoarse: I don't know whether it will grow better or worse. What's that to you? I won't answer your letter

---

1. Annoyingly, exceedingly.
2. Write it in between the lines he had already written.
3. Charles Ford (1682–1741), an Anglo-Irish friend of Swift's living in London, with whom he corresponded (on and off) for nearly 30 years.
4. Royalty and other members of the aristocracy were buried at Westminster Abbey.
5. William Bromley (1664–1732), high churchman and Member of Parliament for Oxford University from 1702, was chosen speaker of the House of Commons on this day.
6. Nobody voting against.
7. John Hill (d. 1735), major general; like his sister Mrs. Masham, Hill was a favorite of Queen Anne.

8. The footmen to Members of Parliament sometimes held their own unofficial "parliament" and debated the issues of the day while their masters were legislating inside the House.
9. Swift's manservant.
1. Following the trial of the high churchman Dr. Henry Sacheverell (c. 1674–1724) in 1710 for a contentious sermon he had given, there was such strong feeling against the Whig Ministry's apparent oppression of the established Church that the Queen dismissed the Ministry, dissolving Parliament on 21 September 1710. When the new Parliament opened in November, a Tory administration was given control of the government.

to-night. I'll keep you a little longer in suspense: I can't send it. Your mother's cakes are very good, and one of them serves me for a breakfast, and so I'll go sleep like a good boy.

26. I have got a cruel cold, and stayed within all this day in my nightgown, and dined on six pennyworth of victuals, and read and writ, and was denied to everybody.[2] Dr. Raymond[3] called often, and I was denied; and at last, when I was weary, I let him come up, and asked him, without consequence, "How Patrick denied me, and whether he had the art of it?" So by this means he shall be used to have me denied to him;[4] otherwise he would be a plaguy trouble and hindrance to me: he has sat with me two hours, and drank a pint of ale cost me five pence, and smoked his pipe, and 'tis now past eleven that he is just gone. Well, my eighth is with you now, young women, and your seventh to me is somewhere in a postboy's bag; and so go to your gang of Deans, and Stoytes, and Walls, and lose your money;[5] go, sauce-boxes, and so goodnight and be happy, dear rogues. Oh, but your box was sent to Dr. Hawkshaw by Sterne, and you will have it with Hawkshaw, and spectacles, &c. &c.

27.[6] To-day Mr. Harley[7] met me in the court of requests,[8] and whispered me to dine with him. At dinner I told him what those bishops had done, and the difficulty I was under.[9] He bid me never trouble myself; he would tell the Duke of Ormonde the business was done, and that he need not concern himself about it. So now I am easy, and they may hang themselves for a parcel of insolent ungrateful rascals. I suppose I told you in my last, how they sent an address to the Duke of Ormonde, and a letter to Southwell, to call on me for the papers, after the thing was over, but they had not received my letter; though the Archbishop might, by what I writ to him, have expected it would be done. Well, there's an end of that; and in a little time the Queen will send them notice, &c. And so the methods will be settled; and then I shall think of returning, although the baseness of those bishops makes me love Ireland less than I did.

28. Lord Halifax[1] sent to invite me to dinner, where I stayed till six, and crossed him in all his Whig talk, and made him often come over to me.[2] I know he makes court to the new men, although he affects to talk like a Whig. I had a letter today from the Bishop of Clogher;[3] but I writ to him lately, that I would obey his commands to the Duke of Ormonde. He says I bid him read the *London Shaver*, and that you both swore

2. I.e., visitors were not allowed to see him.
3. Rev. Anthony Raymond (c. 1675–1726), rector of Trim, and neighbor of Swift's.
4. I.e., Swift let Raymond know that he would not always be admitted on demand.
5. Stella played cards—and often gambled for small stakes—with a circle of friends, including Dean Sterne, Alderman Stoyte, his wife and her sister, and Archdeacon Walls and his wife.
6. Parliament was formally opened by the queen on this day (Swift does not mention it).
7. Swift cultivated friendships with Robert Harley (1661–1724), first Earl of Oxford, and Henry St. John, first Viscount Bolingbroke (1678–1751), as it became clear that they would rule the new Tory Ministry, in the hope, no doubt, of various favors.
8. A court of equity, actually abolished in 1641; it seems the room at Whitehall retained its name long after losing its function.
9. Swift was concerned to receive due recognition for his part in the success of the "first fruits" scheme: Harley had by this time told Swift that the Queen had accepted his proposal, but enjoined him to secrecy until it could be

made public. While Harley eventually allowed Swift to report some limited success to Archbishop King, the politician procrastinated on making the matter more widely known. The Queen, meanwhile, appointed a new Governor of Ireland (Ormonde), and the Irish bishops who had commissioned Swift naturally felt it would be politically expedient to hand Swift's petition over to the Secretary of State for Ireland, Edward Southwell, especially since they still saw Swift as a Whig. When the letter patent was eventually granted, in July 1711 (though dated 17 February 1711), no mention of Swift was made.
1. Charles Montague, Earl of Halifax (1661–1715), a senior Whig statesman; on 2 October 1710, Swift noted in the *Journal* that he had refused to join Halifax in toasting the revival of Whig fortunes: "I told him he was the only Whig in England I loved."
2. I.e., Swift argued against Halifax, and persuaded him to his point of view.
3. St. George Ashe (c. 1658–1718), successively Bishop of Cloyne, of Clogher, and of Derry, and Swift's tutor at Trinity College, Dublin; obviously he was writing to Swift about the "first fruits" question.

it was *Shaver,* and not *Shower.*[4] You all lie, and you are puppies, and can't read Presto's hand.[5] The Bishop is out entirely in his conjectures of my share in the *Tatlers.*[6]—I have other things to mind, and of much greater importance,[7] else I have little to do to be acquainted with a new ministry, who consider me a little more than Irish bishops do.

29. Now for your saucy good dear letter: let me see, what does it say? Come then. I dined today with Ford, and went home early; he debauched me to his chamber again with a bottle of wine till twelve: so goodnight. I can't write an answer now, you rogues.

30. Today I have been visiting, which I had long neglected; and I dined with Mrs. Barton[8] alone; and sauntered at the coffeehouse till past eight, and have been busy till eleven, and now I'll answer your letter, sauce-box. Well, let me see now again. My wax candle's almost out, but however I'll begin. Well then, don't be so tedious, Mr. Presto; what can you say to MD's letter?[9] Make haste, have done with your preambles—Why, I say I am glad you are so often abroad; your mother thinks it is want of exercise hurts you, and so do I. (She called here tonight, but I was not within, that's by the bye.) Sure you don't deceive me, Stella, when you say you are in better health than you were these three weeks; for Dr. Raymond told me yesterday, that Smyth[1] of the Blind Quay had been telling Mr. Leigh, that he left you extremely ill; and in short, spoke so, that he almost put poor Leigh into tears, and would have made me run distracted; though your letter is dated the 11th instant, and I saw Smyth in the city above a fortnight ago, as I passed by in a coach. Pray, pray, don't write, Stella, until you are mighty, mighty, mighty, mighty well in your eyes, and are sure it won't do you the least hurt. Or come, I'll tell you what; you, mistress Stella, shall write your share at five or six sittings, one sitting a day; and then comes Dingley all together, and then Stella a little crumb towards the end, to let us see she remembers Presto; and then conclude with something handsome and genteel, as your most humblecumdumble, or, &c. O Lord! does Patrick write word of my not coming till *spring?* Insolent man! he know my secrets? No; as my Lord Mayor said, No; if I thought my shirt knew, &c.[2] Faith, I will come as soon as it is any way proper for me to come; but, to say the truth, I am at present a little involved with the present ministry in some certain things (which I tell you as a secret) and soon as ever I can clear my hands, I will stay no longer: for I hope the first-fruit business will be soon over in all its forms. But, to say the truth, the present ministry have a difficult task, and want me, &c. Perhaps they may be just as grateful as others: but, according to the best judgment I have, they are pursuing the true interest of the public; and therefore I am glad to contribute what is in my power. For God's sake, not a word of this to any alive.—Your chancellor?[3] Why, madam, I can tell you he has been dead this fort-

4. Stella and Mrs. Dingley have persuaded the bishop that he should read "shaver" for "shower" in Swift's *Description of a City Shower;* the verses first appeared in the *Tatler,* No. 238 (17 October 1710). Swift was extremely proud of this poem; he mentions it in several letters to Stella.

5. After the Duchess of Shrewsbury called him "Dr. Presto" (a pun on "Swift"), Swift adopted this name throughout his *Journal.*

6. The *Tatler,* founded by Swift's sometime friend Richard Steele, ran from 12 April 1709 to 2 January 1711; Swift contributed to several early numbers.

7. At the request of Harley, Swift took control of the *Examiner,* a weekly Tory periodical founded by Bolingbroke in August 1710, between November 1710 and June 1711 (Nos. 14–46).

8. Catherine Barton (1679–1740), niece of Sir Isaac Newton, and a noted beauty who, despite her Whig affiliations and argumentative ability, remained one of Swift's favorites.

9. MD/Md (my dears?) refers to both Esther Johnson and Rebecca Dingley, though Swift is chiefly directing his thoughts to Esther.

1. "Smyth" may be John Smith, one of Swift's booksellers.

2. Patrick is not as close to Swift as his shirt, and even his shirt does not know.

3. Richard Freeman, a Whig, appointed Lord Chancellor of Ireland in 1707, apparently on the basis of his politics, not his abilities.

night. Faith, I could hardly forbear our little language about a nasty dead chancellor, as you may see by the blot.[4] Ploughing? A pox plough them; they'll plough me to nothing. But have you got your money, both the ten pounds? How durst he pay you the second so soon? Pray be good huswives.—Aye, well, and Joe;[5] why, I had a letter lately from Joe, desiring I would take some care of their poor town, who, he says, will lose their liberties. To which I desired Dr. Raymond would return answer; that the town had behaved themselves so ill to me, so little regarded the advice I gave them, and disagreed so much among themselves, that I was resolved never to have more to do with them; but that whatever personal kindness I could do to Joe, should be done. Pray, when you happen to see Joe, tell him this, lest Raymond should have blundered or forgotten.—Poor Mrs. Wesley—Why these poligyes[6] for being abroad?[7] Why should you be at home at all, until Stella is quite well?—So, here is mistress Stella again with her two eggs, &c. My *Shower* admired with you; why, the Bishop of Clogher says, he has seen something of mine of the same sort, better than the *Shower*. I suppose he means *The Morning*;[8] but it is not half so good. I want your judgment of things, and not your country's. How does MD like it? and do they taste it *all*? &c.[9] I am glad Dean Bolton has paid the twenty pounds.[1] Why should not I chide the Bishop of Clogher for writing to the Archbishop of Cashel, without sending the letter first to me?[2] It does not signify a ——; for he has no credit at court. Stuff—they are all puppies. I'll break your head in good earnest, young woman, for your nasty jest about Mrs. Barton. Unlucky sluttikin, what a word is there? Faith, I was thinking yesterday, when I was with her, whether she could break them or no,[3] and it quite spoiled my imagination. Mrs. Walls, does Stella win as she pretends? No indeed, *doctor*; she loses always, and will play so *ventursomely*, how can she win? See here now; an't you an impudent lying slut? Do, open Domville's[4] letter; what does it signify, if you have a mind? Yes, faith, you write smartly with your eyes shut; all was well but the w. See how I can do it; *Madam Stella, your humble servant.*[5] O, but one may look whether one goes crooked or no, and so write on. I'll tell you what you may do; you may write with your eyes half shut, just as when one is going to sleep: I have done so for two or three lines now; 'tis but just seeing enough to go straight.—Now, madam Dingley, I think I bid you tell Mr. Walls, that in case there be occasion, I will serve his friend as far as I can; but I hope there will be none.[6] Yet I believe you will have a

4. To make this intelligible, it is necessary to observe, that the words "this fortnight" in the preceding sentence, were first written in what he calls their little language, and afterwards scratched out and written plain. It must be confessed this little language, which passed current between Swift and Stella, had occasioned infinite trouble in the revisal of theses papers [Deane Swift's note]. In 1768, Deane Swift (1706–1783), the son of Swift's cousin and a favorite relation of Jonathan Swift, published a selection of his famous relation's correspondence with his own annotations, including some of the letters to Esther Johnson and Rebecca Dingley that comprise the *Journal*.
5. Joseph Beaumont (d. 1731), a linen draper from Trim and Swift's business agent.
6. Apologies.
7. Leaving the house.
8. *A Description of the Morning*, which appeared in the *Tatler*, No. 9 (30 April 1709).
9. I.e., do they understand and appreciate it?
1. John Bolton (c. 1656–1724), Dean of Derry.
2. William Palliser (1646–1726), Archbishop of Cashel

since 1694, and a signatory of Swift's commission to petition on behalf of the Irish "first fruits" proposal.
3. This jest is lost, whatever it was, for want of MD's letter [Deane Swift's note].
4. William Domville (born c. 1686), Irishman living in London, and grandson of the attorney general, whom Swift called "perfectly as fine a gentleman as I know" (*Journal*, 27 November 1711).
5. Here he writ with his eyes shut, and the writing is somewhat crooked, although as well in other respects as if his eyes had been open [Deane Swift's note]. Swift had expressed concern about Stella straining her eyes in an earlier letter (7), and suggested that "if you will write, shut your eyes, and write just a line, and no more."
6. Rev. Thomas Wall's friend was Captain John Pratt (born c. 1670), Deputy Vice-Treasurer of Ireland and younger brother of Benjamin Pratt, Provost of Trinity College, Dublin; his place in Parliament was in jeopardy. He later embezzled large sums of Swift's (and Ireland's) cash.

new Parliament; but I care not whether you have or no a better.[7] You are mistaken in all your conjectures about the *Tatlers*. I have given him one or two hints, and you have heard me talk about the *Shilling*.[8] Faith, these answering letters are very long ones: you have taken up almost the room of a week in journals; and I'll tell you what, I saw fellows wearing crosses today,[9] and I wondered what was the matter; but just this minute I recollect it is little Presto's birthday;[1] and I was resolved these three days to remember it when it came, but could not. Pray, drink my health today at dinner; do, you rogues. Do you like *Sid Hamet's Rod?*[2] Do you understand it all? Well, now at last I have done with your letter, and so I'll lay me down to sleep, and about fair maids; and I hope merry maids all. * * *

                                                                      1768

A MODEST PROPOSAL   In a letter written to Alexander Pope in August 1729, Swift described the condition of Ireland: "There have been three terrible years' dearth of corn [i.e., wheat], and every place strewn with beggars, but dearths are common in better climates, and our evils lie much deeper. Imagine a nation the two-thirds of whose revenues are spent out of it, and who are not permitted [by Britain] to trade with the other third, and where the pride of the women will not suffer them to wear their own manufactures even where they excel what come from abroad." Two months later, Swift published what is today his most famous political essay: *A Modest Proposal*. Swift had previously written a dozen or more tracts to help free Ireland from its desperate social, economic, and political plight. In *A Modest Proposal*, however, Swift wielded two favorite weapons from his armory of satirical techniques—irony and parody—with devastating effect. In creating a persona who combines a mixture of calculating rationality and misplaced compassion but does not comprehend the enormity of his plan, Swift aims his satire not only at the political arithmeticians (forerunners of today's social engineers and economic planners) and the exploitative and predatory absentee landlords living in England but at the Irish people as well. Believing Ireland to be its own worst enemy, Swift delineates a program of commercial cannibalism that institutionalizes the country's own self-destructive tendencies. Preserving a nation through the consumption of its children is self-defeating, however demographically logical, because it undermines the understanding of humanity upon which civil society depends. Swift thus highlights the futility of financial improvement unaccompanied by social and moral reform.

A Modest Proposal

FOR PREVENTING THE CHILDREN OF POOR PEOPLE IN IRELAND
FROM BEING A BURDEN TO THEIR PARENTS OR COUNTRY,
AND FOR MAKING THEM BENEFICIAL TO THE PUBLIC

It is a melancholy object to those who walk through this great town,[1] or travel in the country, when they see the streets, the roads, and cabin doors crowded with beggars of the female sex, followed by three, four, or six children, *all in rags*, and importuning every passenger[2] for an alms. These mothers, instead of being able to work for their honest livelihood, are forced to employ all their time in strolling,[3] to beg sustenance for their helpless infants, who, as they grow up, either turn thieves for want of work,

---

7. The Irish House of Commons was adjourned on 28 August 1710 and reassembled on 9 July 1711.
8. Discussion of John Philips's *The Splendid Shilling* (1701) appeared in the *Tatler*, No. 249 (11 November 1710).
9. For St. Andrew's Day.
1. I.e., his own birthday.

2. Swift's *The Virtues of Sid Hamet the Magician's Rod* (1710), a satire on Sidney Godolphin.
1. Dublin.
2. Passerby.
3. Wandering aimlessly.

or leave their dear native country to fight for the Pretender in Spain,[4] or sell themselves to the Barbados.[5]

I think it is agreed by all parties that this prodigious number of children, in the arms, or on the backs, or at the heels of their mothers, and frequently of their fathers, is in the present deplorable state of the kingdom a very great additional grievance; and therefore whoever could find out a fair, cheap, and easy method of making these children sound, useful members of the commonwealth would deserve so well of the public, as to have his statue set up for a preserver of the nation.

But my intention is very far from being confined to provide only for the children of professed beggars; it is of a much greater extent, and shall take in the whole number of infants at a certain age who are born of parents in effect as little able to support them as those who demand our charity in the streets.

As to my own part, having turned my thoughts for many years upon this important subject, and maturely weighed the several schemes of other projectors,[6] I have always found them grossly mistaken in their computation. It is true a child just dropped from its dam may be supported by her milk for a solar year with little other nourishment, at most not above the value of two shillings, which the mother may certainly get, or the value in scraps, by her lawful occupation of begging, and it is exactly at one year old that I propose to provide for them, in such a manner as instead of being a charge upon their parents or the parish, or wanting food and raiment for the rest of their lives, they shall, on the contrary, contribute to the feeding and partly to the clothing of many thousands.

There is likewise another great advantage in my scheme, that it will prevent those voluntary abortions, and that horrid practice of women murdering their bastard children, alas, too frequent among us, sacrificing the poor innocent babes, I doubt[7] more to avoid the expense than the shame, which would move tears and pity in the most savage and inhuman breast.

The number of souls in this kingdom being usually reckoned one million and a half, of these I calculate there may be about two hundred thousand couple whose wives are breeders, from which number I subtract thirty thousand couple who are able to maintain their own children, although I apprehend there cannot be so many under the present distresses of the kingdom; but this being granted, there will remain an hundred and seventy thousand breeders. I again subtract fifty thousand for those women who miscarry, or whose children die by accident or disease within the year.[8] There only remain a hundred and twenty thousand children of poor parents annually born: the question therefore is how this number shall be reared and provided for, which, as I have already said, under the present situation of affairs, is utterly impossible by all the methods hitherto proposed: for we can neither employ them in handicraft, or agriculture; we neither build houses (I mean in the country) nor cultivate land;[9] they can very seldom pick up a livelihood by stealing till they arrive at six years old, except where they are of towardly parts,[1] although, I confess they learn the rudiments much earlier, during which time they can however be properly looked upon only as *probationers*, as I have

---

4. Catholic Ireland was loyal to the Pretender, James Francis Edward Stuart (1688–1766), son of James II, who was deposed from the English throne in 1688 because of his Catholicism. Religious ties also made the Irish ideal recruits for France and Spain in their wars against England.
5. The impoverished Irish emigrated to the West Indies in large numbers, buying their passage by selling their labor in advance to the sugar plantations.

6. Devisers of new "projects," usually of doubtful value.
7. Believe.
8. It is telling that Swift here projects an infant mortality rate of approximately 30 percent in a child's first year.
9. The vast estates of English absentee landlords, and British retention of Irish land for grazing sheep, rather than agriculture, contributed to Ireland's poverty.
1. Precocious.

been informed by a principal gentleman in the County of Cavan, who protested to me, that he never knew above one or two instances under the age of six, even in a part of the kingdom so renowned for the quickest proficiency in that art.

I am assured by our merchants that a boy or a girl, before twelve years old, is no salable commodity, and even when they come to this age, they will not yield above three pounds, or three pounds and half-a-crown at most on the Exchange,[2] which cannot turn to account[3] either to the parents or kingdom, the charge of nutriment and rags having been at least four times that value.

I shall now therefore humbly propose my own thoughts, which I hope will not be liable to the least objection.

I have been assured by a very knowing American[4] of my acquaintance in London, that a young healthy child well nursed is at a year old a most delicious, nourishing, and wholesome food, whether stewed, roasted, baked, or boiled, and I make no doubt that it will equally serve in a fricassee or ragout.[5]

I do therefore humbly offer it to public consideration, that of the hundred and twenty thousand children already computed, twenty thousand may be reserved for breed, whereof only one fourth part to be males, which is more than we allow to sheep, black cattle, or swine, and my reason is that these children are seldom the fruits of marriage, a circumstance not much regarded by our savages, therefore one male will be sufficient to serve four females. That the remaining hundred thousand may at a year old be offered in sale to the persons of quality and fortune through the kingdom, always advising the mother to let them suck plentifully in the last month, so as to render them plump, and fat for a good table. A child will make two dishes at an entertainment for friends, and when the family dines alone, the fore or hind quarter will make a reasonable dish, and seasoned with a little pepper or salt will be very good boiled on the fourth day, especially in winter.

I have reckoned upon a medium, that a child just born will weigh 12 pounds, and in a solar year if tolerably nursed increaseth to 28 pounds.

I grant this food will be somewhat dear,[6] and therefore very proper for landlords, who, as they have already devoured most of the parents, seem to have the best title to the children.

Infants' flesh will be in season throughout the year, but more plentiful in March, and a little before and after, for we are told by a grave author,[7] an eminent French physician, that fish being a prolific diet,[8] there are more children born in Roman Catholic countries about nine months after Lent than at any other season; therefore reckoning a year after Lent, the markets will be more glutted than usual, because the number of Popish infants is at least three to one in this kingdom, and therefore it will have one other collateral advantage by lessening the number of Papists among us.

I have already computed the charge of nursing a beggar's child (in which list I reckon all cottagers,[9] laborers, and four-fifths of the farmers) to be about two shillings *per annum*, rags included, and I believe no gentleman would repine to give ten shillings for the carcass of a good fat child, which, as I have said, will make four dishes of excellent nutritive meat, when he hath only some particular friend or his own family to dine with him. Thus the Squire will learn to be a good landlord and grow

---

2. At the market.
3. Be of value.
4. Some of the British believed that the harsh living conditions in America made the colonists adopt "savage" practices.
5. A fricassee is meat stewed in gravy, a ragout is a highly seasoned French stew; such foreign dishes were becoming

increasingly popular with fashionable Britons.
6. Both expensive and, of course, beloved.
7. The satirist François Rabelais, in *Gargantua and Pantagruel* (1532–1564), Book 5, ch. 29.
8. One increasing fertility.
9. Tenant farmers.

popular among his tenants, the mother will have eight shillings net profit, and be fit for work till she produces another child.

Those who are more thrifty (as I must confess the times require) may flay the carcass, the skin of which, artificially[1] dressed, will make admirable gloves for ladies and summer boots for fine gentlemen.

As to our City of Dublin, shambles[2] may be appointed for this purpose in the most convenient parts of it, and butchers we may be assured will not be wanting, although I rather recommend buying the children alive and dressing them hot from the knife,[3] as we do roasting pigs.

A very worthy person, a true lover of his country, and whose virtues I highly esteem, was lately pleased, in discoursing on this matter, to offer a refinement upon my scheme. He said that many gentlemen of this kingdom, having of late destroyed their deer, he conceived that the want of venison might be well supplied by the bodies of young lads and maidens, not exceeding fourteen years of age nor under twelve, so great a number of both sexes in every country being now ready to starve for want of work and service;[4] and these to be disposed of by their parents if alive, or otherwise by their nearest relations. But with due deference to so excellent a friend and so deserving a patriot, I cannot be altogether in his sentiments; for as to the males, my American acquaintance assured me from frequent experience that their flesh was generally tough and lean, like that of our schoolboys, by continual exercise, and their taste disagreeable, and to fatten them would not answer the charge. Then as to the females, it would, I think with humble submission, be a loss to the public, because they soon would become breeders themselves; and besides, it is not improbable that some scrupulous people might be apt to censure such a practice (although indeed very unjustly) as a little bordering upon cruelty which, I confess, hath always been with me the strongest objection against any project, however so well intended.

But in order to justify my friend, he confessed that this expedient was put into his head by the famous Psalmanazar,[5] a native of the island Formosa, who came from thence to London above twenty years ago, and in conversation told my friend that in his country when any young person happened to be put to death, the executioner sold the carcass to persons of quality as a prime dainty, and that, in his time, the body of a plump girl of fifteen, who was crucified for an attempt to poison the emperor, was sold to his Imperial Majesty's Prime Minister of State[6] and other great Mandarins of the Court, in joints from the gibbet,[7] at four hundred crowns. Neither indeed can I deny that if the same use were made of several plump young girls in this town, who, without one single groat[8] to their fortunes, cannot stir abroad without a chair,[9] and appear at the playhouse and assemblies[1] in foreign fineries which they never will pay for, the kingdom would not be the worse.

Some persons of a desponding spirit are in great concern about that vast number of poor people who are aged, diseased, or maimed, and I have been desired to employ my thoughts what course may be taken to ease the nation of so grievous an encumbrance. But I am not in the least pain upon that matter, because it is very well known that they are every day dying, and rotting, by cold, and famine, and filth, and vermin,

---

1. Skillfully.
2. Places where meat is slaughtered and sold.
3. Skinning and gutting them immediately after killing.
4. Positions as servants.
5. George Psalmanazar, a Frenchman who pretended to be from Formosa (now Taiwan), wrote a book about its customs, the Historical and Geographical Description of For-

mosa (1704), which was quickly exposed as fraudulent.
6. A reference to Robert Walpole.
7. Gallows.
8. Silver coin (issued 1351–1662) equal to four pennies.
9. A sedan chair, carried by two men.
1. Social gatherings.

as fast as can be reasonably expected. And as to the younger laborers they are now in almost as hopeful a condition. They cannot get work, and consequently pine away for want of nourishment, to a degree that if at any time they are accidentally hired to common labor, they have not strength to perform it; and thus the country and themselves are in a fair way of being soon delivered from the evils to come.

I have too long digressed, and therefore shall return to my subject. I think the advantages by the proposal which I have made are obvious and many, as well as of the highest importance.

For first, as I have already observed, it would greatly lessen the number of Papists, with whom we are yearly overrun, being the principal breeders of the nation as well as our most dangerous enemies, and who stay at home on purpose with a design to deliver the kingdom to the Pretender, hoping to take their advantage by the absence of so many good Protestants, who have chosen rather to leave their country than stay at home, and pay tithes against their conscience, to an Episcopal curate.[2]

Secondly, the poorer tenants will have something valuable of their own, which by law may be made liable to distress,[3] and help to pay their landlords rent, their corn and cattle being already seized, and *money a thing unknown*.

Thirdly, whereas the maintenance of a hundred thousand children from two years old and upwards cannot be computed at less than ten shillings a piece *per annum*, the nation's stock will be thereby increased fifty thousand pounds *per annum*, besides the profit of a new dish introduced to the tables of all gentlemen of fortune in the kingdom who have any refinement in taste, and the money will circulate among ourselves, the goods being entirely of our own growth and manufacture.

Fourthly, the constant breeders, besides the gain of eight shillings sterling *per annum* by the sale of their children, will be rid of the charge of maintaining them after the first year.

Fifthly, this food would likewise bring great custom to taverns, where the vintners will certainly be so prudent as to procure the best receipts[4] for dressing it to perfection, and consequently have their houses frequented by all the fine gentlemen, who justly value themselves upon their knowledge in good eating; and a skillful cook who understands how to oblige his guests will contrive to make it as expensive as they please.

Sixthly, this would be a great inducement to marriage, which all wise nations have either encouraged by rewards or enforced by laws and penalties. It would increase the care and tenderness of mothers toward their children, when they were sure of a settlement for life to the poor babes, provided in some sort by the public to their annual profit instead of expense. We should see an honest emulation[5] among the married women, which of them could bring the fattest child to the market; men would become as fond of their wives, during the time of their pregnancy, as they are now of their mares in foal, their cows in calf, or sows when they are ready to farrow,[6] nor offer to beat or kick them (as it is too frequent a practice) for fear of a miscarriage.

Many other advantages might be enumerated: for instance, the addition of some thousand carcasses in our exportation of barreled beef;[7] the propagation of swine's flesh, and improvement in the art of making good bacon, so much wanted among us by the great destruction of pigs, too frequent at our tables, which are no way comparable

---

2. The tithes, or ecclesiastical taxes, that supported the Church were avoided by the many "good" Protestants who absented themselves from Ireland on the grounds— spurious, Swift implies—of "conscience."
3. Seizure for debt.

4. Recipes.
5. Competition.
6. Give birth.
7. Pickled beef.

in taste or magnificence to a well-grown, fat yearling child, which roasted whole will make a considerable figure at a Lord Mayor's feast or any other public entertainment. But this and many others I omit, being studious of brevity.

Supposing that one thousand families in this city would be constant customers for infants' flesh, besides others who might have it at merry-meetings, particularly weddings and christenings, I compute that Dublin would take off annually about twenty thousand carcasses, and the rest of the kingdom (where probably they will be sold somewhat cheaper) the remaining eighty thousand.

I can think of no one objection that will possibly be raised against this proposal, unless it should be urged that the number of people will be thereby much lessened in the kingdom. This I freely own, and was indeed one principal design in offering it to the world. I desire the reader will observe that I calculate my remedy *for this one individual Kingdom of Ireland, and for no other that ever was, is, or, I think, ever can be upon earth. Therefore let no man talk to me of other expedients:*[8] *Of taxing our absentees at five shillings a pound; of using neither clothes nor household furniture, except what is of our own growth and manufacture; of utterly rejecting the materials and instruments that promote foreign luxury; of curing the expensiveness of pride, vanity, idleness, and gaming in our women; of introducing a vein of parsimony, prudence, and temperance; of learning to love our country, wherein we differ even from* LAPLANDERS, *and the inhabitants of* TOPINAMBOO;[9] *of quitting our animosities and factions, nor act any longer like the Jews, who were murdering one another at the very moment their city was taken;*[1] *of being a little cautious not to sell our country and consciences for nothing; of teaching landlords to have at least one degree of mercy toward their tenants. Lastly, of putting a spirit of honesty, industry, and skill into our shopkeepers, who, if a resolution could now be taken to buy our native goods, would immediately unite to cheat and exact upon us in the price, the measure, and the goodness, nor could ever yet be brought to make one fair proposal of just dealing, though often and earnestly invited to it.*

Therefore I repeat, let no man talk to me of these and the like expedients till he hath at least some glimpse of hope that there will ever be some hearty and sincere attempt to put them in practice.

But as to myself, having been wearied out for many years with offering vain, idle, visionary thoughts, and at length utterly despairing of success, I fortunately fell upon this proposal, which as it is wholly new, so it hath something solid and real, of no expense and little trouble, full in our own power, and whereby we can incur no danger in *disobliging* ENGLAND. For this kind of commodity will not bear exportation, the flesh being of too tender a consistence, to admit a long continuance in salt, *although perhaps I could name a country*[2] *which would be glad to eat up our whole nation without it.*

After all I am not so violently bent upon my own opinion as to reject any offer proposed by wise men, which shall be found equally innocent, cheap, easy, and effectual. But before something of that kind shall be advanced in contradiction to my scheme and offering a better, I desire the author or authors will be pleased maturely to consider two points. First, as things now stand, how they will be able to find food and raiment for an hundred thousand useless mouths and backs. And secondly, there

---

8. The kind of proposals Swift himself had made in earnest for remedying the poverty of Ireland; his *Proposal for the Universal Use of Irish Manufacture in Cloaths and Furniture . . . Utterly Rejecting and Renouncing Everything Wearable that Comes from England* (1720) is a typical example.
9. The inhabitants of the most hostile environments—

the frozen north or the Brazilian jungle—love their countries more than the Irish.
1. According to one historian, when Jerusalem was besieged and captured by the Emperor Titus in A.D. 70, factional fighting inside the city contributed to its destruction.
2. England.

being a round million of creatures in human figure throughout this kingdom whose whole subsistence put into a common stock would leave them in debt two millions of pounds sterling; adding those who are beggars by profession to the bulk of farmers, cottagers, and laborers with their wives and children, who are beggars in effect; I desire those politicians who dislike my overture, and may perhaps be so bold to attempt an answer, that they will first ask the parents of these mortals whether they would not at this day think it a great happiness to have been sold for food at a year old, in the manner I prescribe, and thereby have avoided such a perpetual scene of misfortunes as they have since gone through, by the oppression of landlords, the impossibility of paying rent without money or trade, the want of common sustenance, with neither house nor clothes to cover them from the inclemencies of the weather, and the most inevitable prospect of entailing[3] the like or greater miseries upon their breed forever.

I profess in the sincerity of my heart that I have not the least personal interest in endeavoring to promote this necessary work, having no other motive than the *public good of my country, by advancing our trade, providing for infants, relieving the poor, and giving some pleasure to the rich.* I have no children by which I can propose to get a single penny; the youngest being nine years old, and my wife past child-bearing.

1729   1729

◈

COMPANION READING

William Petty: from *Political Arithmetic*[1]

from *Chapter 4. How to enable the people of England and Ireland to spend 5 millions worth of commodities more than now; and how to raise the present value of the lands and goods of Ireland from 2 to 3.*

This is to be done: 1. By bringing one million of the present 1,300 thousand of the people out of Ireland into England, though at the expense of a million of money. 2. That the remaining three hundred thousand left behind be all herdsmen and dairy women, servants to the owners of the lands and stock transplanted into England, all aged between 16 and 60 years, and to quit all other trades, but that of cattle, and to import nothing but salt and tobacco. Neglecting all housing, but what is fittest for these 300 thousand people, and this trade, though to the loss of 2 millions-worth of houses. Now if a million of people be worth 70 pounds per head one with another, the whole are worth 70 millions; then the said people, reckoned as money at 5 percent interest, will yield 3 millions and a half per annum. 3. And if Ireland send into

---

3. Bequeathing.
1. William Petty (1623–1687) represents the type of Englishman Swift had in mind in his implicit criticism of English rapaciousness in Ireland in A Modest Proposal. Petty, the son of a London clothier and weaver, was an extraordinary scholar and anatomist, and a charter member of the Royal Society. Appointed physician-general to the parliamentary army in Ireland in 1652, he obtained considerable property holdings in Ireland through his additional task of surveying lands forfeited by Roman Catholics. His newfound fortune enabled him to devote

his attention to his economic writings and to the Royal Society in London, though he was less than solicitous of his tenants in Ireland. Swift's friendship with Petty's children, Lord Shelburne and Lady Kerry, did not prevent him parodying Petty's *Political Arithmetic* (1691) in *A Modest Proposal*. Petty's suggestion that Ireland be turned into one huge farm to supply England by removing all the Irish was only one of many "political arithmetic" projects published during the Restoration and 18th century, reflecting English interest in "scientific" programs for social "improvement."

England 1 million and a half worth of effects (receiving nothing back), then England will be enriched from Ireland, and otherwise, 5 millions per annum more than now, which, at 20 year's purchase, is worth one hundred millions of pounds sterling, as was propounded. * * *

POSTSCRIPT

If in this jealous age this essay should be taxed of an evil design to waste and dispeople Ireland, we say that the author of it intends not to be *Felo de se*,[2] and propound something quite contrary, by saying it is naturally possible in about 25 years to double the inhabitants of Great Britain and Ireland and make the people full as many as the territory of those kingdoms can with tolerable labor afford a competent livelihood unto, which I prove thus, (viz.)

1. The sixth part of the people are teeming women[3] of between 18 and 44 years old.
2. It is found by observation that but 1/3 part or between 30 and 40 of the teeming women are married.
3. That a teeming woman, at a medium, bears a child every two years and a half.
4. That in mankind at London, there are 14 males for 13 females, and because males are prolific[4] 40 years, and females but 25, there are in effect 560 males for 325 females.
5. That out of the mass of mankind there dies one out of 30 per annum.
6. That at Paris, where the christenings and the births are the same in number, the christenings are above 18,000 per annum, and consequently the births at London, which far exceed the christenings there, cannot be less than 19,000 where the burials are above 23,000.

AS FOR EXAMPLE

Of 600 people, the sixth part (viz. 100) are teeming women, which (if they were all married) might bear 40 children per annum (viz.) 20 more than do die out of 600, at the rate of one out of 30; and consequently in 16 years the increase will be 320, making the whole 920. And by the same reason, in the next 9 years, the said 920 will be 280 more, in all 1,200, viz. double of the original number of 600.

Upon these principles, if there be about 19,000 births per annum at London, the number of the married teeming women must be above 38,000; and of the whole stock of the teeming women must be above 114,000, and of the whole people six times as many viz. 684,000; which agrees well enough with 696,000, which they have been elsewhere computed to be.

To conclude it is naturally possible, that all teeming women may be married, since there are in effect 560 males to 325 females; and since Great Britain and Ireland can with moderate labor, food, and other necessaries to near double the present people or to about 20 millions of heads, as shall when occasion requires it, be demonstrated. * * *

1691

---

2. Suicidal; literally, "felon of (one)self."
3. Women capable of breeding.

4. Capable of procreation.

—•— ≡◆≡ —•—

Alexander Pope
1688–1744

"The life of a wit is a warfare upon earth; and the present spirit of the learned world is such, that to serve it . . . one must have the constancy of a martyr, and a resolution to suffer for its sake." Though still in his twenties when he wrote these words, Alexander Pope knew from painful experience their bitter truth. As a Roman Catholic, he could not vote, inherit or purchase land, attend a "public" school or a university, live within ten miles of London, hold public office, or openly practice his religion. He was obliged to pay double taxes. Such civil disenfranchisement barred him from receiving the literary patronage most talented writers depended upon for their livelihood. No wonder Pope wrote of "certain laws, by suff'rers thought unjust," by which he was "denied all posts of profit or of trust" (*Imitations of Horace, Epistle* 2.2.60–61). Despite whatever patriotism or loyalty to their country they may have felt, Catholics were widely regarded as alien and seditious. Pope's resentment of this attitude is evident in the *Epistle to Bathurst* (1733) when he calls the London Monument, which bears an inscription blaming the Great Fire of 1666 on a Papist conspiracy to destroy the capital, "a tall bully" who "lies."

Religion was not Pope's greatest impediment to success, however. When he was twelve, he contracted tuberculosis of the spine (Pott's disease), a condition that stunted his growth and left him humpbacked and deformed. At four feet six inches, he could not sit at an ordinary table with other adults unless his seat was raised. His constitution was so weakened that he frequently suffered from migraine headaches, asthma, nausea, and fevers. For much of his life, he could not hold his body upright without the help of stays, and he was unable to bathe, dress or undress, rise or go to bed by himself. Pope summarized his condition most succinctly in *An Epistle to Dr. Arbuthnot* (1735), when he wrote of "this long disease, my life."

Pope was born in London in 1688, the only child of his parents' marriage. Pope's *Epistle to Dr. Arbuthnot* includes a tribute to his father's equanimity and goodness; his mother is praised as "a noble wife." At the age of nine, Pope was sent to a school for Catholic boys but was expelled in his first year for writing a satire on his schoolmaster—a sign of things to come. When he was twelve, his family moved from the environs of London to Binfield, in the royal forest of Windsor; the effect of Windsor's "green retreats" on Pope's youthful imagination is apparent in the *Pastorals* (1709) and in *Windsor-Forest* (1713). At Binfield, he began to teach himself Greek and Latin with great determination, though the rigors of his studies made his sickness worse. Refusing to yield to his infirmity, he began, at fifteen, to journey into London to learn French and Italian. Pope spoke of these adolescent years as his "great reading period" when he "went through all the best critics, almost all the English, French, and Latin poets of any name . . . [and] Homer and some other of the Greek poets in the original." During this time Pope met his great friend John Caryll, at whose request he would write *The Rape of the Lock*, and Martha Blount, who was to become his lifelong intimate companion and to whom he addressed *Of the Characters of Women: An Epistle to a Lady* (1735).

Pope claimed that "as yet a child . . . I lisp'd in numbers [i.e., meter]." Certainly he was a precocious poet and his early efforts were encouraged by many, including the playwrights William Wycherley and William Congreve, to whom Pope dedicated his *Iliad* (1715–1720). If Pope had encouraging friends, he soon had detracting enemies as well. His first publication, the *Pastorals* (1709), occasioned a rivalry between Pope's Tory supporters and the Whig partisans of Ambrose Philips, whose *Pastorals* appeared in the same volume. Pope's next important poem, *An Essay on Criticism* (1711), brought a barrage of vituperative abuse from the critic John Dennis, who called Pope "a hunch-backed toad" and argued that his deformity was merely the outward sign of mental and moral ugliness. Undaunted, Pope continued to publish: the *Messiah* (1712), *The Rape of the Lock* (1712, substantially enlarged in 1714), *Windsor-Forest*

(1713), and *The Temple of Fame* (1715). With the publication of his *Works* (1717), Pope had proved himself master of a dazzling repertoire of poetic modes: pastoral and georgic, didactic, eclogue, mock-epic, allegorical dream-vision, heroic, and elegiac. No other living poet could display such dazzling versatility and comprehensive control.

There was still another area, however, in which Pope was proving the breathtaking range of his poetic gifts. Between 1713 and 1726, Pope devoted much of his creative energy to translating Homer's epics, the *Iliad* and the *Odyssey*, into heroic couplets. "Pope's Homer" not only won for him financial independence so that he could "live and thrive, / Indebted to no Prince or Peer alive" (*Imitations of Horace*, Epistle 2.2), it also confirmed his reputation as the presiding poetic genius of his time. While he was working on the *Odyssey*, Pope produced a six-volume edition of Shakespeare's works (1725), which, though it contained some valuable insights, was very much an amateur effort. When Lewis Theobald, the leading Shakespeare scholar of the time, rather pedantically highlighted Pope's many editorial shortcomings in *Shakespeare Restored, or, a Specimen of the Many Errors Committed . . . by Mr. Pope* (1726), Pope's revenge was not far off: two years later, he published *The Dunciad*, a savagely satirical assault on Pope's critics and the bankrupt cultural values they embodied.

In the seventeen years between Dennis's attack and the publication of *The Dunciad*, Pope's appearance, talent, and character had been assailed in print more than fifty times. His enemies accused him of being obscene, seditious, duplicitous, venal, vain, blasphemous, libelous, ignorant, and a bad poet. Theobald's rebuke was the last straw, perhaps because it was the most justified. Pope's style of comic social criticism owed much to his membership in the Scriblerus Club with John Gay, Jonathan Swift, Dr. John Arbuthnot, Thomas Parnell, and Robert Harley, Earl of Oxford. The Scriblerians originally planned to produce a series entitled *The Works of the Unlearned*; although the group regularly met only for a short while in 1714, its members remained in contact. In addition to *The Dunciad*, the fruit of their exchanges may be seen in Swift's *Gulliver's Travels* (1726), Gay's *The Beggar's Opera* (1728), Pope's *Peri Bathous: Or, the Art of Sinking in Poetry* (1728), and Arbuthnot's and Pope's *Memoirs of the Extraordinary Life, Works, and Discoveries of Martinus Scriblerus* (1741).

An *Essay on Man* (1733–1734) showcased Pope's talent for philosophical poetry. This work and four *Moral Essays* (1731–1735) were originally intended to form part of a long poetic sequence on the nature of humankind that Pope had hoped would be his greatest work, though the project was abandoned. Between 1733 and 1738, Pope published more than a dozen *Imitations of Horace*. In these loose adaptations of Horace's epistles and satires, Pope invested his modern social criticism with the classical authority of a revered Roman poet. The *Moral Essays*, or "Epistles to Several Persons" as Pope called them, also show Pope assuming the mantle of Horace by using the familiar epistle as a vehicle for social commentary. Pope's Horatian poems are his most mature, elegant, and self-assured works.

In 1737, he published an authorized version of his letters, which he doctored to improve his reputation. His last years were a time of retirement at his villa at Twickenham, famous for its grotto of "Friendship and Liberty" and for the five-acre landscape garden Pope had designed. In *The New Dunciad* (1742), Pope shifted his attack from hack writers and low culture to all forms of hypocrisy and pretense. It was his final triumph. He worked with William Warburton on a new edition of his *Works* (1751), even as his many illnesses became still more overwhelming. Though he was a self-confessed "fool to Fame" (*Arbuthnot*), he told those gathered around his deathbed: "There is nothing that is meritorious but virtue and friendship." He was, as his enemies claimed, bellicose, self-indulgent, and self-aggrandizing. He was morally and physically courageous and had a great gift for friendship. Although it is no longer fashionable to call the first half of the eighteenth century the "Age of Pope," many of his contemporaries saw him as the predominant literary genius of his time. Today, most literary historians agree that the greatest English poet between John Milton and William Wordsworth was Alexander Pope.

AN ESSAY ON CRITICISM   Pope was only twenty-one years old when he wrote *An Essay on Criticism*, which was published anonymously in 1711. This aesthetic manifesto in heroic couplets is written in the tradition of Horace's *Ars Poetica* (c. 19 B.C.), Boileau's *Art poétique* (1674), and other verse essays delineating poetic principles and practices. Pope's chief contributions to the genre are his ringing epigrams and the playful ease with which he satirizes contemporary critics who lack genuine poetic understanding. *The Essay on Criticism* is divided into three parts: the first examines the rules of taste, their relationship to Nature, and the authority of classical authors. The second (lines 201–559) considers the impediments preventing the attainment of the classical ideals outlined in part one. In the third part, Pope proposes an aesthetic and moral reformation to restore wit, sense, and taste to their former glory. While acknowledging the importance of precepts, Pope asserts the primacy of poetic genius and the power of imagination.

An Essay on Criticism

'Tis hard to say, if greater want of skill
Appear in writing or in judging ill;
But, of the two, less dangerous is th' offense,
To tire our patience, than mislead our sense:°   judgment
5 Some few in that, but numbers err in this,
Ten censure wrong for one who writes amiss;
A fool might once himself alone expose,
Now one in verse makes many more in prose.[1]
'Tis with our judgments as our watches, none
10 Go just alike, yet each believes his own.
In poets as true genius is but rare,
True taste as seldom is the critic's share;
Both must alike from Heav'n derive their light,
These born to judge, as well as those to write.
15 Let such teach others who themselves excel,
And censure freely who have written well.
Authors are partial to their wit,[2] 'tis true,
But are not critics to their judgment too?
Yet if we look more closely, we shall find
20 Most have the seeds of judgment in their mind;
Nature affords at least a glimm'ring light;
The lines, though touched but faintly, are drawn right.
But as the slightest sketch, if justly traced, ⎤
Is by ill coloring but the more disgraced, ⎬
25 So by false learning is good sense defaced; ⎦
Some are bewildered in the maze of Schools,[3]
And some made coxcombs[4] Nature meant but fools.
In search of wit these lose their common sense,
And then turn critics in their own defense.
30 Each burns alike, who can, or cannot write,
Or° with a rival's or an eunuch's spite.[5]   either
All fools have still° an itching to deride,[6]   continually

---

1. I.e., many bad critics respond to one bad poet.
2. Both their writings and their (fancied) ability to write well.
3. Schools of criticism.

4. Conceited show-offs.
5. I.e., they either seek to compete or, knowing themselves sterile, criticize out of envy.
6. The fool's perpetual itching suggests disease.

And fain° would be upon the laughing side: *gladly*
If Maevius scribble in Apollo's spite,[7]
35   There are, who judge still worse than he can write.
  Some have at first for wits,° then poets past,   *intellectuals*
Turned critics next, and proved plain fools at last;
Some neither can for wits nor critics pass,
As heavy mules are neither horse nor ass.
40   Those half-learned witlings, num'rous in our isle,
As half-formed insects on the banks of Nile;
Unfinished things, one knows not what to call,
Their generation's so equivocal:[8]
To tell° 'em, would a hundred tongues require,   *count*
45   Or one vain wit's, that might a hundred tire.
  But you who seek to give and merit° fame,   *deserve*
And justly bear a critic's noble name,
Be sure yourself and your own reach° to know,   *ability*
How far your genius, taste, and learning go;
50   Launch not beyond your depth, but be discrete,
And mark° that point where sense and dullness meet.   *note*
  Nature to all things fixed the limits fit,
And wisely curbed proud man's pretending° wit: *aspiring*
As on the land while here the ocean gains,
55   In other parts it leaves wide sandy plains;
Thus in the soul while memory prevails,
The solid power of understanding fails;
Where beams of warm imagination play,
The memory's soft figures melt away.
60   One science only will one genius fit;[9]
So vast is Art, so narrow human wit;°   *understanding*
Not only bounded to peculiar° arts,   *particular*
But oft in those, confined to single parts.
Like kings we lose the conquests gained before,
65   By vain ambition still to make them more:
Each might his several province well command,
Would all but stoop to what they understand.
  First follow NATURE, and your judgment frame
By her just standard, which is still° the same: *always*
70   Unerring Nature, still divinely bright,
One clear, unchanged, and universal light,
Life, force, and beauty, must to all impart,
At once the source, and end, and test of art.
Art from that fund each just supply provides,
75   Works without show,[1] and without pomp presides:
In some fair body thus th' informing soul[2]
With spirits feeds, with vigor fills the whole,
Each motion guides, and every nerve sustains;

---

7. Maevius, a third-rate Roman poet, is set against Apollo, patron of good poetry.
8. Like the generation of insects on the banks of the Nile, thought to occur spontaneously, through the action of sun on mud.
9. The artist can hope only to succeed in one subject area or object of study.
1. The suggestion that art should mask its presence came from Horace.
2. The force that animates.

Itself unseen, but in th' effects, remains.
80 Some, to whom Heav'n in wit has been profuse,
    Want° as much more, to turn it to its use;   *need*
    For wit and judgment often are at strife,
    Though meant each other's aid, like man and wife.
    'Tis more to guide than spur the Muse's steed;[3]
85 Restrain his fury, than provoke his speed;
    The winged courser,° like a gen'rous horse,   *swift horse*
    Shows most true mettle° when you check his course.   *spirit*
        Those RULES of old discovered, not devised,
    Are Nature still, but Nature *methodized*;
90 Nature, like Liberty, is but restrained
    By the same laws which first herself ordained.
        Hear how learn'd Greece her useful rules indites,°   *composes*
    When to repress, and when indulge our flights:
    High on Parnassus'[4] top her sons she showed,
95 And pointed out° those arduous paths they trod,   *appointed*
    Held from afar, aloft, th' immortal prize,
    And urged the rest by equal steps to rise;
    Just precepts thus from great examples giv'n,
    She drew from them what they derived from Heav'n.
100 The gen'rous critic fanned the poet's fire,
    And taught the world, with reason to admire.
    Then criticism the Muse's handmaid proved,
    To dress her charms,[5] and make her more beloved;
    But following wits from that intention strayed;
105 Who could not win the mistress, wooed the maid;
    Against the poets their own arms they turned,
    Sure to hate most the men from whom they learned.
    So modern 'pothecaries,° taught the art   *druggists*
    By doctors' bills° to play the doctor's part,   *prescriptions*
110 Bold in the practice of mistaken° rules,   *misunderstood*
    Prescribe, apply, and call their masters fools.
    Some on the leaves of ancient authors prey,[6]
    Nor time nor moths e'er spoiled so much as they:
    Some dryly plain, without invention's° aid,   *imagination's*
115 Write dull receipts° how poems may be made: *recipes*
    These leave the sense, their learning to display,
    And those explain the meaning quite away.
        You then whose judgment the right course would steer,
    Know well each ANCIENT'S proper character,[7]
120 His fable,° subject, scope° in every page,   *plot / intention*
    Religion, country, genius of his age:
    Without all these at once before your eyes,
    Cavil° you may, but never criticize.   *quibble*
    Be Homer's works your study, and delight,
125 Read them by day, and meditate by night,

---

3. Pegasus, the winged horse.
4. Mount Parnassus in Greece was sacred to the Muses.
5. Both dress and address, i.e., both interpret and adjust.
6. Textual commentators, depicted as literal bookworms

in continuation of the earlier insect metaphor.
7. An interest in the historical method in criticism was
on the rise.

Thence form your judgment, thence your maxims bring,
And trace the Muses upward to their spring;
Still with itself compared, his text peruse;
And let your comment be the Mantuan Muse.[8]
130   When first young Maro° in his boundless mind   *Virgil*
A work t' outlast immortal Rome designed,
Perhaps he seemed° above the critic's law,   *thought himself*
And but from Nature's fountains scorned to draw:
But when t' examine every part he came,
135   Nature and Homer were, he found, the same:
Convinced, amazed, he checks the bold design, ⎫
And rules as strict his labored work confine, ⎬
As if the Stagyrite[9] o'erlooked each line. ⎭
Learn hence for ancient rules a just esteem;
140   To copy Nature is to copy them.
Some beauties yet, no precepts can declare,[1]
For there's a happiness as well as care.
Music resembles poetry, in each ⎫
Are nameless graces which no methods teach, ⎬
145   And which a master-hand alone can reach. ⎭
If, where the rules not far enough extend,
(Since rules were made but to promote their end)
Some lucky license° answers to the full   *deviation*
Th' intent proposed, that license is a rule.
150   Thus Pegasus, a nearer way to take,
May boldly deviate from the common track.
Great wits sometimes may gloriously offend,
And rise to faults true critics dare not mend;
From vulgar bounds with brave disorder part,
155   And snatch a grace beyond the reach of Art,
Which, without passing through the judgment, gains
The heart, and all its end at once attains.
In prospects,[2] thus, some objects please our eyes, ⎫
Which out of Nature's common order rise, ⎬
160   The shapeless rock, or hanging precipice. ⎭
But though the Ancients thus their rules invade,
(As kings dispense with laws themselves have made)
Moderns, beware! Or if you must offend
Against the precept, ne'er transgress its end,
165   Let it be seldom, and compelled by need,
And have, at least, their precedent to plead.
The critic else proceeds without remorse,
Seizes your fame, and puts his laws in force.
I know there are, to whose presumptuous thoughts
170   Those freer beauties, ev'n in them, seem faults:[3]

---

8. Virgil (born near Mantua) and his *Aeneid,* which took Homer's epics as models and was the best commentary on them.
9. Aristotle, whose *Poetics* provided the basis for later rules on poetry and epic writing.
1. Pope's belief that true poetic genius consisted not of rigid adherence to rules but of "brave disorder" and "grace

beyond the reach of art" had earlier been expressed in the treatise *On the Sublime,* attributed to the Greek rhetorician Longinus (210?–273).
2. Views of an extensive landscape.
3. I.e., there are critics to whom even the Ancients' occasional "glorious offense" is unforgivable.

Some figures[4] monstrous and misshaped appear,
Considered singly, or beheld too near,
Which, but proportioned to their light, or place,
Due distance reconciles to form and grace.
175 A prudent chief not always must display
His pow'rs in equal ranks, and fair array,
But with th' occasion and the place comply,
Conceal his force, nay seem sometimes to fly.
Those oft are stratagems which errors seem,
180 Nor is it Homer nods, but we that dream.
      Still green with bays[5] each ancient altar[6] stands,
Above the reach of sacrilegious hands,
Secure from flames, from envy's fiercer rage,
Destructive war, and all-involving age.
185 See, from each clime the learn'd their incense bring;
Hear, in all tongues consenting paeans° ring!   *songs of praise*
In praise so just, let every voice be joined,
And fill the gen'ral chorus of mankind!
Hail bards triumphant! born in happier days;
190 Immortal heirs of universal praise!
Whose honors with increase of Ages grow,
As streams roll down, enlarging as they flow!
Nations unborn your mighty names shall sound,
And worlds applaud that must not yet be found!
195 Oh may some spark of your celestial fire
The last, the meanest of your sons inspire,[7]
(That on weak wings, from far, pursues your flights;
Glows while he reads, but trembles as he writes)
To teach vain wits° a science little known,   *would-be critics*
200 T' admire superior sense, and doubt their own!

      Of all the causes which conspire to blind
Man's erring judgment, and misguide the mind,
What the weak head with strongest bias[8] rules,
Is pride, the never-failing vice of fools.
205 Whatever Nature has in worth denied,
She gives in large recruits° of needful° pride;   *supplies / needed*
For as in bodies, thus in souls, we find
What wants° in blood and spirits, swelled with wind;   *is lacking*
Pride, where wit fails, steps in to our defense,
210 And fills up all the mighty void of sense!
If once right reason drives that cloud away,
Truth breaks upon us with resistless day;
Trust not yourself; but your defects to know,
Make use of every friend—and every foe.
215   A little learning is a dang'rous thing;
Drink deep, or taste not the Pierian spring:[9]

---

4. Both figures in the landscape and rhetorical figures or
literary style.
5. Laurels, used to crown both poets and military heroes.
6. The works of each ancient author.
7. Pope himself, who follows tradition in writing about

writing.
8. Not only prejudice but a kind of bowling ball. (In
bowls, the bias ball is one weighted to roll obliquely.)
9. Hippocrene, the stream associated with the Muses.

There shallow draughts[1] intoxicate the brain,
And drinking largely sobers us again.
Fired at first sight with what the Muse imparts,
220   In fearless youth we tempt° the heights of Arts,   *attempt*
While from the bounded° level of our mind,   *limited*
Short views we take, nor see the lengths behind,
But more advanced, behold with strange surprise
New, distant scenes of endless science[2] rise!
225   So pleased at first, the towering Alps we try,
Mount o'er the vales, and seem to tread the sky;
Th' eternal snows appear already past,
And the first clouds and mountains seem the last:
But those attained, we tremble to survey
230   The growing labors of the lengthened way,
Th' increasing prospect tires our wandering eyes,
Hills peep o'er hills, and Alps on Alps arise!
        A perfect judge will read each work of wit
With the same spirit that its author writ,
235   Survey the whole, nor seek slight faults to find,
Where Nature moves, and rapture warms the mind;
Nor lose, for that malignant dull delight,
The gen'rous pleasure to be charmed with wit.
But in such lays° as neither ebb, nor flow,   *poems*
240   Correctly cold, and regularly low,
That shunning faults, one quiet tenor° keep;   *tone*
We cannot blame indeed—but we may sleep.
In wit, as Nature, what affects our hearts
Is not th' exactness of peculiar° parts;   *particular*
245   'Tis not a lip, or eye, we beauty call,
But the joint force and full result of all.
Thus when we view some well-proportioned dome,[3]
(The world's just wonder, and even thine O Rome!)
No single parts unequally surprise;
250   All comes united to th' admiring eyes;
No monstrous height, or breadth, or length appear;
The whole at once is bold, and regular.°   *well-proportioned*
        Whoever thinks a faultless piece to see,
Thinks what ne'er was, nor is, nor e'er shall be.
255   In every work regard the writer's end,
Since none can compass° more than they intend;   *encompass*
And if the means be just, the conduct° true,   *execution*
Applause, in spite of trivial faults, is due.
As men of breeding,[4] sometimes men of wit,
260   T' avoid great errors, must the less commit,
Neglect the rules each verbal critic lays,[5]
For not to know some trifles, is a praise.
Most critics, fond of some subservient art,

---

1. I.e., drinking small amounts.
2. Knowledge, subjects requiring study.
3. Any large and stately building, but those of a classical design are particularly implied.

4. Good breeding (in both birth and upbringing).
5. Lays down. A verbal critic is one concerned with linguistic detail rather than literary whole.

Still make the whole depend upon a part,
265 They talk of principles, but notions° prize,   *prejudices*
And all to one loved folly sacrifice.
    Once on a time, La Mancha's Knight,[6] they say,
A certain bard encountering on the way,
Discoursed in terms as just, with looks as sage,
270 As e'er could Dennis,[7] of the Grecian stage;
Concluding all were desp'rate sots and fools,
Who durst depart from Aristotle's rules.
Our author, happy in a judge so nice,
Produced his play, and begged the Knight's advice,
275 Made him observe the subject and the plot,
The manners, passions, unities,[8] what not?
All which, exact to rule were brought about,
Were but a combat in the lists[9] left out.
"What! leave the combat out?" exclaims the Knight;
280 Yes, or we must renounce the Stagyrite.°   *Aristotle*
"Not so by Heav'n" (he answers in a rage)
"Knights, squires, and steeds, must enter on the stage."
So vast a throng the stage can ne'er contain.
"Then build a new, or act it in a plain."
285   Thus critics, of less judgment than caprice,
Curious,° not knowing, not exact, but nice,°   *picky / fussy*
Form short ideas; and offend in arts
(As most in manners) by a love to parts.[1]
Some to conceit[2] alone their taste confine,
290 And glitt'ring thoughts struck out at every line;
Pleased with a work where nothing's just or fit;
One glaring chaos and wild heap of wit:
Poets like painters, thus, unskilled to trace
The naked Nature and the living grace,
295 With gold and jewels cover every part,
And hide with ornaments their want° of art.   *lack*
True wit is Nature to advantage dressed,
What oft was thought, but ne'er so well expressed,
Something, whose truth convinced at sight we find,
300 That gives us back the image of our mind:
As shades° more sweetly recommend the light,   *shadows*
So modest plainness sets off sprightly wit:
For works may have more wit than does 'em good,
As bodies perish through excess of blood.[3]
305   Others for language all their care express,
And value books, as women men, for dress:
Their praise is still—The style is excellent:

---

6. Don Quixote, Cervantes's foolish knight errant. This episode comes from part two of *Don Quixote* (1615), bk. 3, ch. 10.
7. John Dennis (1657–1734), an eminent critic but not one in Pope's favor.
8. The three unities of plot (one story), time (one day), and place (one location) were thought to have been the

Greek playwrights' structuring principles, recommended by Aristotle.
9. The field of combat in medieval jousting tournaments.
1. Individual talents.
2. Extravagant use of metaphor.
3. Apoplexy, it was thought, was caused by such an excess.

    The sense, they humbly take upon content.°   *trust*
    Words are like leaves; and where they most abound,
310   Much fruit of sense beneath is rarely found.
    False eloquence, like the prismatic glass,
    Its gaudy colors spreads on every place;
    The face of Nature we no more survey,°   *observe*
    All glares alike, without distinction gay:
315   But true expression, like th' unchanging sun, ⎤
    Clears, and improves whate'er it shines upon, ⎬
    It gilds all objects, but it alters none. ⎦
    Expression is the dress of thought,[4] and still
    Appears more decent° as more suitable;   *correct*
320   A vile conceit° in pompous words expressed,   *idea*
    Is like a clown° in regal purple dressed;   *peasant*
    For different styles with different subjects sort,°   *belong*
    As several garbs with Country, Town, and Court.[5]
    Some by old words to fame have made pretense;[6]
325   Ancients in phrase, mere Moderns in their sense!
    Such labored nothings, in so strange a style,
    Amaze the unlearn'd, and make the learned smile.
    Unlucky, as Fungoso in the play,[7] ⎤
    These sparks[8] with awkward vanity display ⎬
330   What the fine gentleman wore yesterday! ⎦
    And but so mimic ancient wits at best,
    As apes our grandsires in their doublets[9] dressed.
    In words, as fashions, the same rule will hold;
    Alike fantastic, if too new, or old;
335   Be not the first by whom the new are tried,
    Nor yet the last to lay the old aside.
        But most by numbers[1] judge a poet's song,
    And smooth or rough, with them, is right or wrong;
    In the bright Muse though thousand charms conspire,°   *work together*
340   Her voice is all these tuneful fools admire,
    Who haunt Parnassus but to please their ear, ⎤
    Not mend their minds; as some to church repair, ⎬
    Not for the doctrine, but the music there. ⎦
    These equal syllables alone require,
345   Though oft the ear the open vowels tire,[2]
    While expletives their feeble aid do join,
    And ten low words oft creep in one dull line,
    While they ring round the same unvaried chimes,
    With sure returns of still expected rhymes.
350   Where-e'er you find the cooling western breeze,

4. It was generally held that a person's appearance reflected his or her inner self.
5. As various styles of dress suit country, mercantile, and courtly life.
6. Made a claim. Deliberately archaic language was used by Spenser and by a number of his 18th-century imitators.
7. In Ben Jonson's *Every Man Out of His Humor* (1599), this student lagged behind the fashions.
8. Hot-blooded young men, aspiring to fame and romantic conquest.
9. Close-fitting garment for the upper body.
1. Meter of verse, patterns of sound.
2. This line, like the couplets that follow, illustrates the fault it criticizes.

In the next line, it whispers through the trees;
If crystal streams with pleasing murmurs creep,
The reader's threatened (not in vain) with sleep.
Then, at the last, and only couplet fraught
355   With some unmeaning thing they call a thought,
A needless Alexandrine[3] ends the song,
That like a wounded snake, drags its slow length along.
Leave such to tune their own dull rhymes, and know
What's roundly smooth, or languishingly slow;
360   And praise the easy vigor of a line,
Where Denham's strength, and Waller's sweetness join.[4]
True ease in writing comes from art, not chance,
As those move easiest who have learned to dance.
'Tis not enough no harshness gives offense,
365   The sound must seem an echo to the sense.[5]
Soft is the strain when Zephyr° gently blows,   *the west wind*
And the smooth stream in smoother numbers flows;
But when loud surges lash the sounding shore,
The hoarse, rough verse should like the torrent roar.
370   When Ajax[6] strives, some rock's vast weight to throw,
The line too labors, and the words move slow;
Not so, when swift Camilla[7] scours the plain,
Flies o'er th' unbending corn, and skims along the main.°   *sea*
Hear how Timotheus'[8] varied lays surprise,
375   And bid alternate passions fall and rise!
While, at each change, the son of Lybian Jove[9]
Now burns with glory, and then melts with love;
Now his fierce eyes with sparkling fury glow;
Now sighs steal out, and tears begin to flow:
380   Persians and Greeks like turns of nature[1] found,
And the world's victor stood subdued by sound!
The pow'rs of music all our hearts allow;°   *admit to*
And what Timotheus was, is Dryden now.

Avoid extremes; and shun the fault of such,
385   Who still are pleased too little, or too much.
At every trifle scorn to take offense,
That always shows great pride, or little sense;
Those heads as stomachs are not sure the best
Which nauseate° all, and nothing can digest.   *feel sick at*
390   Yet let not each gay turn° thy rapture move,   *phrase*
For fools admire,[2] but men of sense approve;
As things seem large which we through mists descry,°   *see*
Dullness is ever apt to magnify.

---

3. The 12 syllables and six stresses of an Alexandrine are illustrated in the next line.
4. Pope follows Dryden in his stylistic characterization of John Denham (1615–1669) and Edmund Waller (1606–1687), two poets greatly respected by writers of the early 18th century, especially for their work in heroic couplets.
5. The following nine lines exemplify the rule laid down here.

6. The fabulously strong Greek hero in Homer's *Iliad*.
7. An Amazon warrior in Virgil's *Aeneid*.
8. Musician to Alexander the Great, as portrayed in Dryden's *Alexander's Feast* (1697).
9. Alexander the Great.
1. Similar changes of emotion.
2. Wonder at the poetry, while "men of sense" deliberate before reaching favorable judgment.

Some foreign writers, some our own despise;
395 The Ancients only, or the Moderns prize:
(Thus wit, like faith, by each man is applied
To one small sect, and all are damned beside.)
Meanly they seek the blessing to confine,
And force that sun but on a part to shine;
400 Which not alone the southern wit sublimes,°   exalts
But ripens spirits in cold northern climes;
Which from the first has shone on Ages past,
Enlights the present, and shall warm the last:
(Though each may feel increases and decays,
405 And see now clearer and now darker days)
Regard not then if wit be old or new,
But blame the false, and value still the true.
    Some ne'er advance a judgment of their own,
But catch the spreading notion° of the Town;[3]   fashion
410 They reason and conclude by precedent,
And own° stale nonsense which they ne'er invent.   express
Some judge of authors' names, not works, and then
Nor° praise nor blame the writings, but the men.   neither
Of all this servile herd the worst is he
415 That in proud dullness joins with Quality,[4]
A constant critic at the great man's board,[5]
To fetch and carry nonsense for my Lord.
What woeful stuff this madrigal would be,
In some starved Hackney sonneteer,[6] or me?
420 But let a Lord once own[7] the happy lines,
How the wit brightens! How the style refines!
Before his sacred name flies every fault,
And each exalted stanza teems with thought!
    The vulgar thus through imitation err;
425 As oft the learned by being singular;
So much they scorn the crowd, that if the throng
By chance go right, they purposely go wrong;
So Schismatics[8] the plain believers quit,
And are but damned for having too much wit.
430   Some praise at morning what they blame at night;
But always think the last° opinion right.   latest
A Muse by these is like a mistress used,
This hour she's idolized, the next abused,
While their weak heads, like towns unfortified,
435 'Twixt sense and nonsense daily change their side.
Ask them the cause; they're "wiser still," they say;
And still tomorrow's wiser than today.
We think our fathers fools, so wise we grow;

3. The fashionable members of the city; the term was commonly used for fashionable London society.
4. The nobility, people of quality.
5. Dining table; i.e., he always eats there.
6. Like the horses from Hackney, in Middlesex, this poet's services are readily for hire. The designation "son-

neteer" indicates one who writes poor poetry. Pope, who made a point of refusing to sell his services, includes himself here perhaps because of his youth when the Essay was written.
7. Own up to, admit that they are his.
8. Religious sectarians.

Our wiser sons, no doubt, will think us so.
440   Once School-Divines[9] this zealous Isle o'erspread;
Who knew most sentences[1] was deepest read;
Faith, gospel, all, seemed made to be disputed,
And none had sense enough to be confuted.°   disproved
Scotists and Thomists,[2] now, in peace remain,
445   Amidst their kindred cobwebs in Duck Lane.[3]
If faith itself has diff'rent dresses worn,
What wonder modes in wit should take their turn?
Oft, leaving what is natural and fit,
The current folly proves the ready wit,[4]
450   And authors think their reputation safe,
Which lives as long as fools are pleased to laugh.
    Some valuing those of their own side,[5] or mind,
Still make themselves the measure of mankind;
Fondly we think we honor merit then,
455   When we but praise ourselves in other men.
Parties in wit attend on those of state,
And public faction doubles private hate.
Pride, malice, folly, against Dryden rose,
In various shapes of parsons, critics, beaus;[6]
460   But sense survived, when merry jests were past;
For rising merit will buoy up at last.
Might he return, and bless once more our eyes,
New Blackmores and new Milbourns must arise;
Nay should great Homer lift his awful head,
465   Zoilus[7] again would start up from the dead.
Envy will merit as its shade° pursue,   shadow
But like a shadow, proves the substance true;
For envied wit, like Sol° eclipsed, makes known   the sun
Th' opposing body's grossness,° not its own.   ponderousness
470   When first that sun too powerful beams displays,
It draws up vapors which obscure its rays;
But ev'n those clouds at last adorn its way,
Reflect new glories, and augment the day.
    Be thou the first true merit to befriend;
475   His praise is lost, who stays till all commend;
Short is the date,° alas, of modern rhymes;   life
And 'tis but just to let 'em live betimes.°   awhile
No longer now that Golden Age appears,
When Patriarch-Wits survived a thousand years;
480   Now length of fame (our second life) is lost,

9. Theologians who followed the highly formal Scholastic method.
1. The *sententiae*, or sayings of the Church Fathers, presented and explained for the student in works like Peter Lombard's *Book of Sentences* (1148–1151).
2. The schools of medieval philosophy formed by followers of Duns Scotus and Thomas Aquinas.
3. A street in London where old and secondhand books were sold.
4. Current folly allows ready wit to show itself.
5. Political persuasion.

6. The parsons: Jeremy Collier, *A Short View of the Profaneness and Immorality of the English Stage* (1698); Luke Milbourne, *Notes on Dryden's Virgil* (1698). The critics: Thomas Shadwell (1642?–1692); Elkanah Settle (1648–1724); Gerard Langbaine (1656–1692), *An Account of the English Dramatic Poets*; Richard Blackmore (1654–1729). Among the beaus: George Villiers, Second Duke of Buckingham, who co-authored *The Rehearsal* (1671); John Wilmot, Second Earl of Rochester, *An Allusion to Horace: The 10th Satyr of the 1st Book* (1680).
7. A critic of Homer's, of the 4th century B.C.

And bare threescore is all ev'n that can boast:
Our sons their fathers' failing language see,
And such as Chaucer⁸ is, shall Dryden be.
So when the faithful pencil has designed
485   Some bright idea of the master's mind,
Where a new world leaps out at his command,
And ready Nature waits upon his hand;
When the ripe colors soften and unite,
And sweetly melt into just shade and light,
490   When mellowing years their full perfection give,
And each bold figure just begins to live;
The treach'rous colors the fair art betray,
And all the bright creation fades away!
    Unhappy wit, like most mistaken° things,   misunderstood
495   Atones not for that envy which it brings.
In youth alone its empty praise we boast,
But soon the short-lived vanity is lost!
Like some fair flow'r the early spring supplies,
That gaily blooms, but ev'n in blooming dies.
500   What is this wit which must our cares employ?
The owner's wife, that other men enjoy,
Then most our trouble still when most admired,
And still the more we give, the more required;
Whose fame with pains we guard, but lose with ease,
505   Sure some to vex, but never all to please;
'Tis what the vicious° fear, the virtuous shun;   wicked
By fools 'tis hated, and by knaves undone!
    If wit so much from ign'rance undergo,
Ah, let not learning too commence° its foe!   start to be
510   Of old, those met rewards who could excel,
And such were praised who but endeavored well:
Though triumphs were to gen'rals only due,
Crowns were reserved to grace the soldiers too.⁹
Now, they who reached Parnassus' lofty crown,
515   Employ their plans to spurn some others down;
And while self-love each jealous writer rules,
Contending wits become the sport of fools:
But still the worst with most regret commend,
For each ill author is as bad a friend.
520   To what base ends, and by what abject ways,
Are mortals urged through sacred° lust of praise!   accursed
Ah, ne'er so dire a thirst of glory boast,
Nor in the critic let the man be lost!
Good nature and good sense must ever join;
525   To err is human; to forgive, divine.
    But if in noble minds some dregs remain,
Not yet purged off, of spleen° and sour disdain,   bad temper

8. Chaucer was admired but seen as quaint and arcane, his language unintelligible. It was common to complain of the transience of the English language at this time.
9. Soldiers who had distinguished themselves in the field received crowns. Unlike those soldiers rewarded for assisting one another, the poets in the following lines achieve their crowns, then turn on their fellow writers.

Discharge that rage on more provoking crimes,

Nor fear a dearth in these flagitious° times.   *corrupt*

530 No pardon vile obscenity should find,

Though wit and art conspire to move your mind;

But dullness with obscenity must prove

As shameful sure as impotence in love.

In the fat Age of pleasure, wealth, and ease,

535 Sprung the rank weed, and thrived with large increase;

When love was all an easy monarch's[1] care;

Seldom at council, never in a war:[2]

Jilts ruled the State, and statesmen farces writ;[3]

Nay wits had pensions,° and young Lords had wit: *government salaries*

540 The fair sat panting at a courtier's play,

And not a Mask[4] went unimproved away:

The modest fan was lifted up no more,

And virgins smiled at what they blushed before—

The following license of a foreign reign[5]

545 Did all the dregs of bold Socinus[6] drain;

Then unbelieving priests reformed the nation,

And taught more pleasant methods of salvation;

Where Heav'ns free subjects might their rights dispute,

Lest God himself should seem too absolute.

550 Pulpits their sacred satire learned to spare,

And vice admired° to find a flatt'rer there!   *was surprised*

Encouraged thus, wit's Titans[7] braved the skies,

And the press groaned with licensed blasphemies[8]—

These monsters, critics! with your darts engage,

555 Here point your thunder, and exhaust your rage!

Yet shun their fault, who, scandalously nice,°   *fastidious*

Will needs mistake an author into vice;

All seems infected that th' infected spy,°   *see*

As all looks yellow to the jaundiced eye.

560   LEARN then what MORALS critics ought to show,

For 'tis but half a judge's task, to know.

'Tis not enough, taste, judgment, learning, join;

In all you speak, let truth and candor shine;

That not alone what to your sense is due,

565 All may allow; but seek your friendship too.

    Be silent always when you doubt your sense;

And speak, though sure, with seeming diffidence:

Some positive persisting fops we know,

Who, if once wrong, will needs be always so;

1. Charles II (1630–1685). Ease was a much-prized social grace in the late 17th and early 18th centuries.
2. Charles had commanded an army defeated at the Battle of Worcester in 1651.
3. "Jilts" were whores, a reference to Charles's many mistresses. The statesmen were the Duke of Buckingham, *The Rehearsal* (1671); Sir Charles Sedley, *The Mulberry Garden* (1668); Sir George Etherege (1634–1691), a number of plays.
4. Masks were initially worn by noblewomen attending plays, but the potential for concealment meant that they came to be particularly associated with prostitutes.

5. That of William III (1650–1702), from the Netherlands, who introduced policies of increased religious toleration.
6. Laelius Socinus (1525–1562) and Faustus Socinus (1539–1604), two Italian theologians who sponsored various heresies, including denying the divinity of Christ.
7. This reference compares the deistic writers to the classical giants, the Titans, who attempted to conquer heaven, and were severely punished as a result.
8. The Licensing Act lapsed in 1663, allowing books to be published that Pope and others found blasphemous.

570 But you, with pleasure own your errors past,
     And make each day a critic on° the last.   *assessment of*
        'Tis not enough your counsel still be true;
     Blunt truths more mischief than nice° falsehoods do.   *delicate*
     Men must be taught as if you taught them not;
575 And things unknown proposed as things forgot:
     Without good breeding, truth is disapproved;
     That only makes superior sense belov'd.
        Be niggards of advice on no pretense;⁹
     For the worse avarice is that of sense:
580 With mean complacence ne'er betray your trust,¹
     Nor be so civil as to prove unjust;
     Fear not the anger of the wise to raise;
     Those best can bear reproof, who merit praise.
        'Twere well, might critics still this freedom take;
585 But Appius² reddens at each word you speak,
     And stares, tremendous!³ with a threatening eye,
     Like some fierce tyrant in old tapestry!
     Fear most to tax an honorable fool,
     Whose right it is, uncensured to be dull;
590 Such without wit are poets when they please,
     As without learning they can take degrees.⁴
     Leave dang'rous truths to unsuccessful satires,
     And flattery to fulsome dedicators,
     Whom, when they praise, the world believes no more,
595 Than when they promise to give scribbling o'er.
     'Tis best sometimes your censure to restrain,
     And charitably let the dull be vain:
     Your silence there is better than your spite,
     For who can rail so long as they can write?
600 Still humming on, their drowsy course they keep,
     And lashed so long, like tops,° are lashed asleep.   *spinning tops*
     False steps but help them to renew the race,
     As after stumbling, jades° will mend their pace.   *ruined horses*
     What crowds of these, impenitently bold,
605 In sounds and jingling syllables grown old,
     Still run on poets in a raging vein,
     Ev'n to the dregs and squeezings of the brain;
     Strain out the last, dull droppings of their sense,
     And rhyme with all the rage of impotence!
610   Such shameless bards we have; and yet 'tis true,
     There are as mad, abandoned critics too.
     The bookful blockhead, ignorantly read,
     With loads of learned lumber in his head,
     With his own tongue still edifies his ears,
615 And always listening to himself appears.
     All books he reads, and all he reads assails,

9. Do not withhold your advice however good your reasons.
1. Do not avoid your duty to give judgment by being servile or polite.
2. Dennis; the hero of his tragedy, *Appius and Virginia*
(1705), was also sensitive to criticism.
3. Staring and use of the adjective "tremendous" were both characteristic of Dennis.
4. Privy Councilors, bishops, and peers could obtain academic degrees without fulfilling normal requirements.

From Dryden's Fables down to Durfey's Tales.[5]
With him, most authors steal their works, or buy;
Garth did not write his own Dispensary.[6]
620   Name a new play, and he's the poet's friend,
Nay showed his faults—but when would poets mend?
No place so sacred from such fops is barred,
Nor is Paul's church more safe than Paul's churchyard:[7]
Nay, fly to altars; there they'll talk you dead;
625   For fools rush in where angels fear to tread.
Distrustful sense with modest caution speaks; ⎫
It still looks home, and short excursions makes; ⎬
But rattling nonsense in full volleys breaks; ⎭
And never shocked, and never turned aside,
630   Bursts out, resistless, with a thundering tide!
      But where's the man, who counsel can bestow,
Still pleased to teach, and yet not proud to know?°   of knowing
Unbiased, or° by favor or by spite;   either
Not dully prepossessed, nor blindly right;
635   Though learn'd, well-bred; and though well-bred, sincere;
Modestly bold, and humanly severe?
Who to a friend his faults can freely show,
And gladly praise the merit of a foe?
Blest with a taste exact, yet unconfined;
640   A knowledge both of books and humankind;
Generous converse;[8] a soul exempt from pride;
And love to praise, with reason on his side?
      Such once were critics, such the happy few,
Athens and Rome in better Ages knew.
645   The mighty Stagyrite° first left the shore,   Aristotle
Spread all his sails, and durst the deeps explore;
He steered securely, and discovered far,
Led by the light of the Maeonian star.°   Homer
Poets, a race long unconfined and free,
650   Still fond and proud of savage liberty,
Received his laws,[9] and stood convinced 'twas fit
Who conquered Nature,[1] should preside o'er wit.
      Horace still charms with graceful negligence,
And without method talks us into sense,
655   Will like a friend familiarly convey
The truest notions in the easiest way.
He, who supreme in judgment, as in wit,
Might boldly censure, as he boldly writ,
Yet judged with coolness though he sung with fire;
660   His precepts teach but what his works inspire.

5. Dryden, *Fables Ancient and Modern* (1700); Thomas
D'Urfey, *Tales Tragical and Comical* (1704). D'Urfey, a
popular playwright and singer, is best known for the ballad collection *Pills to Purge Melancholy*, to which his
name was attached.
6. The report that Pope's friend Samuel Garth had plagiarized his popular mock-heroic work *The Dispensary*

(1699) was, according to William Warburton, "a common slander at that time."
7. Booksellers kept stalls in St. Paul's churchyard.
8. Good conversation and well-mannered behavior.
9. Aristotle's *Poetics* set rules for poetic composition.
1. Aristotle was also noted for his study of the physical
world.

Our critics take a contrary extreme,
They judge with fury, but they write with phlegm:[2]
Nor suffers Horace more in wrong translations
By wits, than critics in as wrong quotations.
665   See Dionysius[3] Homer's thoughts refine,
And call new beauties forth from ev'ry line!
    Fancy and art in gay Petronius[4] please,
The Scholar's learning, with the courtier's ease.
    In grave Quintilian's copious work[5] we find
670 The justest rules, and clearest method joined;
Thus useful arms in magazines we place,
All ranged in order, and disposed with grace,
But less to please the eye, than arm the hand,
Still fit for use, and ready at command.
675   Thee, bold Longinus![6] all the Nine° inspire,   *the Muses*
And bless their critic with a poet's fire.
And ardent judge, who zealous in his trust,
With warmth gives sentence, yet is always just;
Whose own example strengthens all his laws,
680 And is himself that great sublime he draws.
    Thus long succeeding critics justly reigned,
License repressed, and useful laws ordained;
Learning and Rome alike in Empire grew,
And Arts still followed where her eagles[7] flew;
685 From the same foes, at last, both felt their doom,
And the same Age saw learning fall, and Rome.
With tyranny, then superstition joined,
As that the body, this enslaved the mind;
Much was believed, but little understood,
690 And to be dull was construed to be good;
A second deluge learning thus o'er-run,
And the monks finished what the Goths begun.
    At length, Erasmus, that great, injured name,
(The glory of the priesthood, and the shame!)[8]
695 Stemmed the wild torrent of a barb'rous age,
And drove those holy vandals off the stage.
    But see! each Muse, in Leo's[9] golden days,
Starts from her trance, and trims her withered bays!
Rome's ancient Genius,° o'er its ruins spread,   *guardian spirit*
700 Shakes off the dust, and rears his rev'rend head!
Then Sculpture and her sister Arts revive;
Stones leaped to form, and rocks began to live;

2. Under the humoral understanding of the body, an excess of phlegm caused disease, and so the term came to mean coolness, dullness, or apathy.
3. Dionysius of Halicarnassus, a Roman critic contemporary with Horace.
4. Petronius Arbiter (d. A.D. 66) judged on matters of taste in Nero's court.
5. Quintilian (c. 35–c. 99 A.D.) was a Latin rhetorician, whose *Institutio Oratoria* Pope knew well.
6. Longinus (210?–273) was a Greek rhetorician, to whom was attributed the enormously influential treatise *On the Sublime*.
7. The emblem of the Roman Empire.
8. Erasmus (c. 1466–1536), the Dutch humanist who influenced the course of the Reformation; the "glory of the priesthood" because of his learning, Erasmus was its "shame" both because he criticized priests and because he was persecuted for his outspokenness.
9. Pope Leo X (1475–1521), patron of letters and arts.

With sweeter notes each rising temple rung;
A Raphael painted, and a Vida sung![1]
705   Immortal Vida! on whose honored brow
The Poet's bays and critic's ivy[2] grow:
Cremona now shall ever boast thy name,
As next in place to Mantua, next in fame![3]
    But soon by impious arms from Latium[4] chased,
710   Their ancient bounds the banished Muses passed;
Thence Arts o'er all the northern world advance;
But critic Learning flourished most in France.
The rules, a nation born to serve,[5] obeys,
And Boileau[6] still in right of Horace sways.
715   But we, brave Britons, foreign laws despised,
And kept unconquered, and uncivilized,
Fierce for the liberties of wit, and bold,
We still defied the Romans, as of old.
Yet some there were, among the sounder few
720   Of those who less presumed, and better knew,
Who durst° assert the juster ancient cause,   *dared to*
And here restored wit's fundamental laws.
Such was the Muse, whose rules and practice tell,
Nature's chief Master-piece is writing well.[7]
725   Such was Roscommon[8]—not more learn'd than good,
With manners gen'rous as his noble blood;
To him the wit of Greece and Rome was known,
And ev'ry author's merit, but his own.
Such late was Walsh,[9]—the Muse's judge and friend,
730   Who justly knew° to blame or to commend;   *knew when to*
To failings mild, but zealous for desert;
The clearest head, and the sincerest heart.
This humble praise, lamented shade!° receive,   *spirit*
This praise at least a grateful Muse may give!
735   The Muse, whose early voice you taught to sing,
Prescribed her heights, and pruned° her tender wing,   *groomed*
(Her guide now lost) no more attempts to rise,
But in low numbers° short excursions tries: *lowly verses*
Content, if hence th' unlearn'd their wants° may view,   *lacks*
740   The learn'd reflect on what before they knew:
Careless of censure, nor too fond of fame,
Still pleased to praise, yet not afraid to blame,
Averse alike to flatter, or offend,
Not free from faults, nor yet too vain to mend.

c. 1709   1711

1. Raphael (1483–1520) was considered the greatest of painters; Girolamo Vida (c. 1485–1566), Italian poet.
2. Ivy was associated with poets (and with Bacchus), but also with learning.
3. Cremona and Mantua were the birthplaces of Vida and Virgil, respectively.
4. Italy; Rome was conquered by the Holy Roman Empire in 1527.
5. A reference to the despotic reign of Louis XIV.

6. Nicolas Boileau-Despréaux (1636–1711) wrote much that was praised in England.
7. This line is quoted from the then well-known *Essay on Poetry* (1682) by John Sheffield, third Earl of Mulgrave and later first Duke of Buckingham.
8. Wentworth Dillon (c. 1630–1685), fourth Earl of Roscommon; poet, critic, didactic writer.
9. William Walsh (1663–1708), friend and mentor of Pope.

WINDSOR-FOREST "Mr. Pope has published a fine poem called Windsor Forest," wrote Jonathan Swift to his beloved Stella; "read it," he urged her in a letter sent just two days after the poem went on sale. Pope wrote *Windsor-Forest* in two distinct stages: the first part (lines 1–290) was composed in 1704–1705, but the remaining lines celebrating the imminent Peace of Utrecht (1713) that formally ended the long War of Spanish Succession were penned in late 1712 and early 1713. The Peace—a great triumph for the ruling Tory party and the last Stuart monarch, Queen Anne—recognized Great Britain as the world's leading naval power and greatly augmented its colonial and commercial empire at the expense of Spain and France. It would be wrong, however, to imagine that *Windsor-Forest* is half pastoral idyll and half Tory political propaganda; it is, rather, a thoroughgoing synthesis of the topographical, the moral, and the political. Pope's sources for *Windsor-Forest* include Virgil's *Eclogues* and *Georgics*, Ovid's *Metamorphoses*, the Bible, Spenser's *Faerie Queene*, Milton's *Paradise Lost*, Edmund Waller's *On St. James's Park* (1661), and Thomas Otway's *Windsor Castle* (1685). It is, however, Pope's comment on "the distinguishing excellence" of John Denham's *Cooper's Hill* (1642) that best explains Pope's own imaginative procedure in *Windsor-Forest*: "the descriptions of places, and images raised by the poet, are still [i.e., continually] tending to some hint, or leading into some reflection, upon moral life or political institution" (*Iliad* 16.466n). Windsor was the ideal setting for a political poem in which landscape evoked England's proud heritage: from William the Conqueror, who first established a royal residence at Windsor, to "great ANNA" (line 327), who made Windsor Castle her chief residence and frequently rode and hunted in the forest, this was a place suffused with English history. From this enclave of natural beauty and political tradition—the home of monarchs and the haven of Muses— Pope's myth-making genius created a triumphant vision of peace and prosperity, the dawning of a Golden Age.

Windsor-Forest
To the Right Honorable George Lord Lansdowne[1]

Non injussa cano: te nostrae, Vare, myricae
Te nemus omne canet; nec Phoebo gratior ulla est
Quam sibi quae Vari praescripsit pagina nomen.[2]

Thy forests, Windsor! and thy green retreats,
At once the monarch's and the Muse's seats,[3]
Invite my lays.° Be present, sylvan maids![4]   *prompt my poetry*
Unlock your springs, and open all your shades.
5   Granville commands: Your aid O Muses bring!
What Muse for Granville can refuse to sing?
The groves of Eden, vanished now so long,
Live in description, and look green in song:[5]
These, were my breast inspired with equal flame,
10   Like them in beauty, should be like in fame.

1. George Granville (1667–1735), Baron Lansdowne, was himself a poet and playwright. A Tory politician close to Queen Anne, he became Secretary of War in 1710 and so was partly responsible both for British victory and for the peace that followed. Lord Lansdowne greatly admired Pope's poetry and encouraged him to publish a poem on the Peace.
2. Adapted from Virgil's sixth *Eclogue*, lines 9–12, in which the poet dedicates his pastoral poem to his friend Varus (like Lansdowne a prominent military figure): "I do not sing without purpose: our tamarisks, Varus, every grove will sing of you; nor is any page more pleasing to Apollo than one that begins with the name of Varus."
3. Windsor Forest, seat (country home) of Britain's monarchs since Norman times (and even fabled to be the site of the legendary King Arthur's court), in Pope's view was also home to the Muses because the 17th-century poets Sir John Denham and Abraham Cowley had lived nearby.
4. Dryads and naiads, spirits of the trees and water.
5. The Garden of Eden in Genesis was made "green in song" in Milton's (relatively) recent *Paradise Lost*.

Here hills and vales, the woodland and the plain,
Here earth and water seem to strive again,
Not chaos-like together crushed and bruised,
But as the world, harmoniously confused:
15 Where order in variety we see,
And where, though all things differ, all agree.
Here waving groves a checkered scene display,
And part admit and part exclude the day;
As some coy nymph her lover's warm address
20 Nor° quite indulges, nor can quite repress.   *neither*
There, interspersed in lawns° and opening glades,   *clearings*
Thin trees arise that shun each other's shades.
Here in full light the russet plains extend;
There wrapped in clouds the blueish hills ascend:
25 Ev'n the wild heath displays her purple dyes,[6]
And 'midst the desert° fruitful fields arise,   *uncultivated land*
That crowned with tufted trees[7] and springing corn,
Like verdant isles the sable waste adorn.
Let India boast her plants, nor envy we
30 The weeping amber or the balmy tree,
While by our oaks the precious loads are born,[8]
And realms commanded which those trees adorn.
Not proud Olympus[9] yields a nobler sight,
Though gods assembled grace his tow'ring height,
35 Than what more humble mountains offer here,
Where, in their blessings, all those gods appear.
See Pan with flocks, and fruits Pomona crowned,
Here blushing Flora[1] paints th' enameled ground,[2]
Here Ceres' gifts° in waving prospect stand,   *grain crops*
40 And nodding tempt the joyful reaper's hand,
Rich Industry sits smiling on the plains,
And Peace and Plenty tell, a STUART reigns.[3]
    Not thus the land appeared in ages past,[4]
A dreary desert and a gloomy waste,
45 To savage beasts and savage laws a prey,[5]
And kings more furious and severe than they:
Who claimed the skies, dispeopled° air and floods,   *depopulated*
The lonely lords of empty wilds and woods.
Cities laid waste, they stormed the dens and caves,
50 (For wiser brutes were backward° to be slaves.)   *unwilling*
What could be free, when lawless beasts obeyed,

6. Heather's purple blooms cover open moorland in late summer.
7. A cluster of trees; Pope borrowed the phrase from Milton's *L'Allegro* (1632).
8. British ships made of oak allowed Britain both to conquer distant countries and to carry goods from them.
9. The mountain home of the Greek gods.
1. Three deities of natural abundance: Pan presides over shepherds and sheep; Pomona over fruits; Flora over flowers.
2. The enameling of metal to allow for over-layers of intricate painted designs was commonly used as a metaphor for nature.
3. Queen Anne (reigned 1702–1714), last of the Stuart monarchs.
4. Pope's history of the landscape begins with William the Conqueror's creation of the New Forest as a hunting ground reserved for royalty and chronicles the disastrous impact of this appropriation on his successors and the ordinary people.
5. The Forest Laws had imposed harsh penalties on those caught stealing the king's game.

And ev'n the elements[6] a tyrant swayed?
In vain kind seasons swelled the teeming grain,
Soft show'rs distilled, and suns grew warm in vain;
55   The swain with tears his frustrate labor yields,
And famished dies amidst his ripened fields.[7]
What wonder then, a beast or subject slain
Were equal crimes in a despotic reign;
Both doomed alike for sportive tyrants bled,
60   But while the subject starved, the beast was fed.
Proud Nimrod[8] first the bloody chase began,
A mighty hunter, and his prey was man.
Our haughty Norman boasts that barb'rous name,
And makes his trembling slaves the royal game.
65   The fields are ravished from th' industrious swains,
From men their cities, and from gods their fanes:[9]
The leveled towns with weeds lie covered o'er,
The hollow winds through naked temples roar;
Round broken columns clasping ivy twined;
70   O'er heaps of ruin stalked the stately hind;°   *female deer*
The fox obscene° to gaping tombs retires,   *loathsome*
And savage howlings till the sacred quires.[1]
Awed by his nobles, by his commons° cursed,   *commoners*
The oppressor ruled tyrannic where he durst,
75   Stretched o'er the poor, and church, his iron rod,
And served alike his vassals and his God.
Whom ev'n the Saxon spared, and bloody Dane,
The wanton victims of his sport remain.
But see the man who spacious regions gave
80   A waste for beasts, himself denied a grave![2]
Stretched on the lawn his second hope[3] survey,
At once the chaser and at once the prey.
Lo Rufus, tugging at the deadly dart,
Bleeds in the forest, like a wounded hart.[4]
85   Succeeding monarchs heard the subjects' cries,
Nor saw displeased the peaceful cottage rise.
Then gath'ring flocks on unknown° mountains fed,   *unfamiliar*
O'er sandy wilds were yellow harvests spread,
The forests wondered at th' unusual grain,
90   And secret transport touched the conscious swain.[5]

---

6. Through controlling the animals, they effectively controlled their "elements."

7. Because the produce is being cultivated for the game animals, and not for humans.

8. In Genesis 10.9, Nimrod is described as a mighty hunter, but he was also seen as a tyrant, as he founded the kingdoms of Babylon and Assyria.

9. Temples; William I destroyed many villages and churches in creating the New Forest. He was sharply criticized for demolishing God's houses to make dens for wild beasts.

1. Choir stalls; Pope deliberately uses archaic spelling. His description of "quires," "broken columns," and "temples" also suggests grander buildings than the parish churches of this time, calling to mind the destruction of the abbeys during the Reformation.

2. Apparently, at William I's funeral, a knight had tried to stop the King from being buried in land he claimed to own. Pope suggests that this incident and the several royal deaths related to hunting in the forest (depicted in the following four lines) were divine vengeance.

3. Richard, second son of William the Conqueror [Pope's note].

4. William Rufus was accidentally killed by a friend's arrow while out hunting; a hart is a male deer.

5. Joy moves the peasant, well aware of what he has gained; this is a fairly new use of this sense of "conscious."

Fair Liberty, Britannia's goddess, rears
Her cheerful head, and leads the golden years.
    Ye vig'rous swains! while youth ferments your blood,[6]
And purer spirits swell the sprightly flood,
95   Now range the hills, the gameful woods beset,
Wind° the shrill horn, or spread the waving net.   *blow*
When milder Autumn Summer's heat succeeds,
And in the new-shorn field the partridge feeds,
Before his lord the ready spaniel bounds,
100   Panting with hope, he tries the furrowed grounds,
But when the tainted[7] gales the game betray,
Couched close[8] he lies, and meditates the prey;
Secure they trust th' unfaithful field, beset,
Till hov'ring o'er 'em sweeps the swelling net.
105   Thus (if small things we may with great compare)
When Albion° sends her eager sons to war,   *England*
Some thoughtless town, with ease and plenty blessed,
Near, and more near, the closing lines invest;°   *surround*
Sudden they seize th' amazed, defenseless prize,
110   And high in air Britannia's standard flies.
    See! from the brake° the whirring pheasant springs,   *bushes*
And mounts exulting on triumphant wings;
Short is his joy! he feels the fiery wound,
Flutters in blood, and panting beats the ground.
115   Ah! what avail his glossy, varying dyes,
His purple crest, and scarlet-circled eyes,
The vivid green his shining plumes unfold;
His painted wings, and breast that flames with gold?
    Nor yet, when moist Arcturus[9] clouds the sky,
120   The woods and fields their pleasing toils deny.
To plains with well-breathed beagles we repair,
And trace the mazes of the circling hare.
(Beasts, urged by us, their fellow beasts pursue,
And learn of Man each other to undo.)
125   With slaught'ring guns th' unwearied fowler roves,
When frosts have whitened all the naked groves;
Where doves in flocks the leafless trees o'ershade,
And lonely woodcocks haunt the watry glade.
He lifts the tube, and levels with his eye;
130   Straight° a short thunder breaks the frozen sky.   *immediately*
Oft, as in airy rings they skim the heath,
The clam'rous lapwings feel the leaden death:
Oft as the mounting larks their notes prepare,
They fall, and leave their little lives in air.
135   In genial Spring, beneath the quiv'ring shade
Where cooling vapors breathe along the mead,
The patient fisher takes his silent stand

---

6. The blood is quickened by the animal spirits supposed
to move in it.
7. With the animal's scent.
8. Crouching close to the ground.

9. One of the stars in the Great Bear constellation; in
antiquity, its rise with the sun in September was associated with bad weather.

Intent, his angle trembling in his hand;
With looks unmoved, he hopes the scaly breed,
140 And eyes the dancing cork and bending reed.
Our plenteous streams a various race supply;
The bright-eyed perch with fins of Tyrian° dye,   *purple*
The silver eel, in shining volumes° rolled,   *coils*
The yellow carp, in scales bedropped with gold,
145 Swift trouts, diversified with crimson stains,
And pikes, the tyrants of the watry plains.
    Now Cancer glows with Phoebus' fiery car;[1]
The youth rush eager to the sylvan war;
Swarm o'er the lawns, the forest walks surround,
150 Rouse° the fleet hart, and cheer the opening° hound.   *flush out / baying*
Th' impatient courser° pants in ev'ry vein,   *fast horse*
And pawing, seems to beat the distant plain,
Hills, vales, and floods appear already crossed,
And ere he starts, a thousand steps are lost.
155 See! the bold youth strain up the threatening steep,
Rush through the thickets, down the valleys sweep,
Hang o'er their coursers' heads with eager speed,
And earth rolls back beneath the flying steed.
Let old Arcadia boast her ample plain,
160 Th' immortal Huntress, and her virgin train;
Nor envy, Windsor! since thy shades have seen
As bright a goddess, and as chaste a Queen;
Whose care, like hers, protects the sylvan reign,[2]
The earth's fair light, and empress of the main.[3]
165   Here too, 'tis sung, of old Diana strayed,
And Cynthus' top[4] forsook for Windsor shade;
Here was she seen o'er airy wastes to rove,
Seek the clear spring, or haunt the pathless grove;
Here armed with silver bows, in early dawn,
170 Her buskined° virgins traced the dewy lawn.   *boot-wearing*
    Above the rest a rural nymph was famed,
Thy offspring, Thames! the fair Lodona named
(Lodona's fate, in long oblivion cast,
The Muse shall sing, and what she sings shall last),
175 Scarce could the goddess from her nymph be known,
But by the crescent° and the golden zone,°   *moon / belt*
She scorned the praise of beauty, and the care;
A belt her waist, a fillet° binds her hair,   *headband*
A painted quiver on her shoulder sounds,
180 And with her dart the flying deer she wounds.
It chanced, as eager of the chase the maid
Beyond the forest's verdant limits strayed,
Pan saw and loved, and burning with desire

---

1. The sun (Phoebus's chariot) enters the constellation of Cancer, the crab, on June 22.
2. Queen Anne is compared both to the "immortal Huntress" Diana, goddess of chastity, and to Anne's illustrious forebear, the "virgin queen" Elizabeth I.

3. Like Diana, the moon goddess, who governed the tides, Britannia ruled the seas.
4. The mountain on which Diana was said to have been born.

Pursued her flight; her flight increased his fire.
185 Not half so swift the trembling doves can fly,
When the fierce eagle cleaves the liquid° sky;   *transparent*
Not half so swiftly the fierce eagle moves,
When through the clouds he drives the trembling doves;
As from the god she flew with furious pace,
190 Or as the god, more furious, urged the chase.
Now fainting, sinking, pale, the nymph appears;
Now close behind his sounding steps she hears;
And now his shadow reached her as she run,
(His shadow lengthened by the setting sun)
195 And now his shorter breath with sultry air
Pants on her neck, and fans her parting hair.
In vain on Father Thames she calls for aid,
Nor could Diana help her injured maid.
Faint, breathless, thus she prayed, nor prayed in vain:
200 "Ah Cynthia! ah—though banished from thy train,
Let me, O let me, to the shades repair,
My native shades—there weep, and murmur there."
She said, and melting as in tears she lay,
In a soft, silver stream dissolved away.
205 The silver stream her virgin coldness keeps,
Forever murmurs, and forever weeps;
Still bears the name the hapless virgin bore,[5]
And bathes the forest where she ranged before.
In her chaste current oft the goddess laves,°   *bathes*
210 And with celestial tears augments the waves.
Oft in her glass the musing shepherd spies
The headlong mountains and the downward skies,
The watry landscape of the pendant[6] woods,
And absent° trees that tremble in the floods;   *illusory*
215 In the clear azure gleam the flocks are seen,
And floating forests paint the waves with green.
Through the fair scene roll slow the lingering streams,
Then foaming pour along, and rush into the Thames.
      Thou too, great father° of the British floods!   *the Thames*
220 With joyful pride survey'st our lofty woods,
Where tow'ring oaks their growing honors rear,
And future navies on thy shores appear.
Not Neptune's self from all his streams receives
A wealthier tribute, than to thine he gives.
225 No seas so rich, so gay no banks appear,
No lake so gentle, and no spring so clear.
Nor Po so swells the fabling poets' lays,[7]
While led along the skies his current strays,
As thine, which visits Windsor's famed abodes,
230 To grace the mansion of our earthly gods.

---

5. I.e., Loddon, a river that runs through Windsor Forest
and into the Thames.
6. Hanging; the woods both hang over the stream and, in
the stream's reflection, appear to stand upside down.

7. Both Virgil and Ovid compared the Po, a river in Italy,
to the winding constellation Eridanus, named for a river
in Greek mythology.

Nor all his stars above a luster show,
Like the bright beauties on thy banks below;
Where Jove, subdued by mortal passion still,
Might change Olympus for a nobler hill.
235 Happy the man whom this bright court approves,
His sov'reign favors, and his country loves;
Happy next him who to these shades retires,
Whom Nature charms, and whom the Muse inspires,
Whom humbler joys of home-felt quiet please,
240 Successive study, exercise and ease.
He gathers health from herbs the forest yields,
And of their fragrant physic° spoils° the fields: *medicines / despoils*
With chemic art[8] exalts° the min'ral pow'rs,   *distills*
And draws° the aromatic souls of flow'rs.   *extracts*
245 Now marks the course of rolling orbs on high;
O'er figured worlds[9] now travels with his eye.
Of ancient writ unlocks the learned store,
Consults the dead, and lives past ages o'er.
Or wand'ring thoughtful in the silent wood,
250 Attends the duties of the wise and good,
T' observe a mean,[1] be to himself a friend,
To follow Nature, and regard his end.
Or looks on Heav'n with more than mortal eyes,
Bids his free soul expatiate in the skies,
255 Amid her kindred stars familiar roam,
Survey the region, and confess her home!
Such was the life great Scipio[2] once admired,
Thus Atticus,[3] and Trumbull[4] thus retired.
  Ye sacred Nine![5] that all my soul possess,
260 Whose Raptures fire me, and whose visions bless,
Bear me, oh bear me to sequestered scenes,
The bow'ry mazes and surrounding greens;
To Thames's banks which fragrant breezes fill,
Or where ye Muses sport on Cooper's Hill.
265 (On Cooper's Hill eternal wreaths shall grow,[6]
While lasts the mountain, or while Thames shall flow)
I seem through consecrated walks to rove,
I hear soft music die along the grove;
Led by the sound I roam from shade to shade,
270 By god-like poets venerable made:
Here his first lays majestic Denham sung;[7]

---

8. The skills of the chemist.
9. The earth or possibly the zodiac portrayed on a globe.
1. To maintain a steady, balanced course through life; according to Aristotle, wisdom lay in following the "golden mean," or middle way.
2. Scipio Africanus, the Roman general who defeated Hannibal and the Carthaginians in 202 B.C. but declined political office, choosing eventually to retire to the country.
3. Titus Pomponius (109–32 B.C.), despite his friendship and correspondence with Cicero, refused to become involved in politics; he was called Atticus because he spent much time studying in Athens, which lies in the region of Attica.
4. Sir William Trumbull (1639–1716), Pope's elderly friend.
5. The Nine Muses, daughters of Mnemosyne (goddess of memory) and Zeus, each of whom presided over a different art or science.
6. Because commemorated in Sir John Denham's poem *Cooper's Hill* (1642).
7. Denham, described as "majestic" because of the (then unusual) style of the couplets in *Cooper's Hill*, lived near Windsor before the Civil War.

There the last numbers flowed from Cowley's tongue.[8]
O early lost![9] what tears the river shed
When the sad pomp along his banks was led?
275   His drooping swans on ev'ry note expire,
And on his willows[1] hung each Muse's lyre.
      Since Fate relentless stopped their heav'nly voice,
No more the forests ring, or groves rejoice;
Who now shall charm the shades where Cowley strung
280   His living harp, and lofty Denham sung?
But hark! the groves rejoice, the forest rings!
Are these revived? Or is it Granville sings?
      'Tis yours, my Lord, to bless our soft retreats,
And call the Muses to their ancient seats,
285   To paint anew the flow'ry sylvan scenes,
To crown the forests with immortal greens,
Make Windsor hills in lofty numbers rise,
And lift her turrets nearer to the skies;
To sing those honors you deserve to wear,
290   And add new luster to her silver star.[2]
      Here noble Surrey[3] felt the sacred rage,
Surrey, the Granville of a former age:
Matchless his pen, victorious was his lance;
Bold in the lists, and graceful in the dance:
295   In the same shades the Cupids tuned his lyre,
To the same notes of love, and soft desire:
Fair Geraldine,[4] bright object of his vow,
Then filled the groves, as heav'nly Myra[5] now.
      Oh wouldst thou sing what heroes Windsor bore,
300   What kings first breathed upon her winding shore,[6]
Or raise old warriors whose adored remains
In weeping vaults[7] her hallowed earth contains!
With Edward's[8] acts adorn the shining page,
Stretch his long triumphs down through ev'ry age,
305   Draw monarchs chained, and Cressi's glorious field,[9]
The lilies[1] blazing on the regal shield.
Then, from her roofs when Verrio's colors fall,
And leave inanimate the naked wall;[2]
Still in thy song should vanquished France appear,
310   And bleed forever under Britain's spear.

---

8. Mr. [Abraham] Cowley died at Chertsey, on the borders of the Forest, and as from thence conveyed to Westminster [Pope's note], where he was buried in state.
9. Cowley died at age 49.
1. Emblems of sorrow.
2. The star worn by members inducted into the highly prestigious Order of the Garter, founded by Edward III in Windsor Castle's Chapel of St. George.
3. Henry Howard, Earl of Surrey, one of the first refiners of the English poetry; famous in the time of Henry VIIIth for his sonnets, the scene of many of which is laid at Windsor [Pope's note].
4. Lady Elizabeth Fitzgerald (1528?–1589) to whom Surrey was thought to have directed his love poems.
5. The poetic name Granville used for his female addressee.

6. Suggesting the etymological meaning of "Windsor."
7. Because of the seepage of water through the walls; similar natural phenomena explain the conceits in lines 307 and 313.
8. Edward III, born here [Pope's note].
9. The village in northern France where Edward III defeated the French; English triumph over the French (and other nations) was the theme of many of these paintings.
1. Emblem of France, but added to the English crest of arms.
2. In ceiling paintings at Windsor Castle, the artist Antonio Verrio (1639–1707) had depicted the surrender of France in 1356 to Edward the Black Prince, son of Edward III; the paintings were now starting to disintegrate.

Let softer strains ill-fated Henry[3] mourn,
And palms eternal flourish round his urn.
Here o'er the martyr-king the marble weeps,
And fast beside him, once-feared Edward[4] sleeps;
315   Whom not th' extended Albion could contain,
From old Belerium[5] to the northern main,
The grave unites; where ev'n the great find rest,
And blended lie th' oppressor and th' oppressed!
    Make sacred Charles's tomb forever known,[6]
320   (Obscure the place, and uninscribed the stone)
Oh fact° accursed! What tears has Albion shed,   *deed*
Heav'ns! what new wounds, and how her old have bled?
She saw her sons with purple deaths[7] expire,
Her sacred domes° involved in rolling fire,   *stately buildings*
325   A dreadful series of intestine wars,[8]
Inglorious triumphs, and dishonest° scars.   *shameful*
At length great ANNA° said—"Let discord cease!"   *Queen Anne*
She said, the world obeyed, and all was peace!
    In that blessed moment, from his oozy bed
330   Old Father Thames advanced his rev'rend head.
His tresses dropped with dews, and o'er the stream
His shining horns[9] diffused a golden gleam:
Graved on his urn appeared the moon, that guides
His swelling waters, and alternate tides;
335   The figured streams in waves of silver rolled,
And on their banks Augusta° rose in gold.[1]   *London*
Around his throne the sea-born brothers[2] stood,
Who swell with tributary urns his flood.
First the famed authors of his ancient name,
340   The winding Isis and the fruitful Thame:[3]
The Kennet swift, for silver eels renowned;
The Loddon slow, with verdant alders crowned:
Cole, whose dark streams his flow'ry islands lave;
And chalky Wey, that rolls a milky wave:
345   The blue, transparent Vandalis° appears;   *the Wandle*
The gulphy Lee his sedgy tresses rears:
And sullen Mole, that hides his diving flood;
And silent Darent, stained with Danish blood.[4]
    High in the midst, upon his urn reclined,

3. Henry VI, murdered in 1471, was looked upon by some in northern Britain (where he lived for some time as a fugitive) as a saint; the "palms" in line 32 are emblems of martyrdom.
4. Edward IV, responsible for Henry VI's murder, was buried in St. George's Chapel, Windsor, where Henry was later re-interred.
5. Land's End in Cornwall, the south-westernmost point in England.
6. Charles I, executed by the Puritans in 1649 and consequently considered by many a Christian and political martyr, was buried in St. George's Chapel without any service; his tomb remained unidentified until 1813.
7. Death from the Great Plague in 1665; this event, like the Great Fire of London (1666) and the 1688 Revolution alluded to in the following lines, was viewed by many as a result of God's wrath, possibly (as Pope here implies) visited on the nation as a result of Charles I's murder.
8. The civil wars during the reigns of Charles I, Cromwell (in Ireland), James II, and William III (in Ireland).
9. River gods often had bulls' horns, representing their strength, noisiness, and importance for agriculture.
1. A reference to Dryden's description of London's rebuilding after the Great Fire (in brick and white Portland stone) in *Annus Mirabilis* (1667), to which work the rest of this poem is indebted.
2. According to myth, all rivers were children of the sea gods Oceanus and Thethys.
3. The Thames was seen as the son of the Thame and the Isis rivers.
4. The Danes were defeated at Otford, on the Darent, in 1016.

350 (His sea-green mantle waving with the wind)
     The god appeared; he turned his azure eyes
     Where Windsor domes and pompous turrets rise,
     Then bowed and spoke; the winds forget to roar,
     And the hushed waves glide softly to the shore.
355   Hail sacred peace!⁵ hail long-expected days,
     That Thames's glory to the stars shall raise!
     Though Tiber's streams immortal Rome behold,
     Though foaming Hermus⁶ swells with tides of gold,
     From Heav'n itself though sev'nfold Nilus⁷ flows,
360 And harvests on a hundred realms bestows;
     These now no more shall be the Muse's themes,
     Lost in my fame, as in the sea their streams.
     Let Volga's banks⁸ with iron squadrons° shine,   cavalry
     And groves of lances glitter on the Rhine,
365 Let barb'rous Ganges⁹ arm a servile train;
     Be mine the blessings of a peaceful reign.
     No more my sons shall dye with British blood
     Red Iber's¹ sands, or Ister's² foaming flood;
     Safe on my shore each unmolested swain
370 Shall tend the flocks, or reap the bearded grain;
     The shady empire shall retain no trace
     Of war or blood, but in the sylvan chase,
     The trumpets sleep, while cheerful horns are blown,
     And arms employed on birds and beasts alone.
375 Behold! th' ascending villas³ on my side
     Project long shadows o'er the crystal tide.
     Behold! Augusta's glitt'ring spires increase,
     And temples rise,⁴ the beauteous works of peace.
     I see, I see where two fair cities⁵ bend
380 Their ample bow,° a new Whitehall⁶ ascend!   riverbend
     There mighty nations shall inquire their doom,⁷
     The world's great oracle in times to come;
     There kings shall sue, and suppliant states be seen
     Once more to bend before a British QUEEN.
385   Thy trees, fair Windsor! now shall leave their woods,
     And half thy forests rush into my floods,
     Bear Britain's thunder, and her cross⁸ display,
     To the bright regions of the rising day;

5. The war of the Spanish Succession had begun in 1701; peace treaties were signed at London in 1711, and at Utrecht in 1713.
6. An Italian river distinguished by Virgil.
7. Because of its delta, Ovid called the Nile *septemfluus*.
8. An allusion to the defeat of Charles XII of Sweden by the Russians in 1709 (though the battle did not take place near the Volga).
9. Alluding to the Mogul Emperor Aurangzeb's recent wars in India.
1. The Ebro in Spain, where the Allies had gained victory in 1710.
2. The Danube, where Marlborough achieved his famous victory at Blenheim in 1704.
3. Many new private country homes were being built along the Thames up from London at this time.
4. The fifty new churches [Pope's note], built on the queen's orders to meet the requirements of a growing London.
5. London and Westminster, separated by the Thames, were still distinct cities at this time.
6. There were plans afoot to rebuild the palace of Whitehall, which had largely burnt down in the fires of 1691 and 1697.
7. Fate or destiny. In lines 381–422 Pope makes extensive use of Isaiah 60, which forecasts Zion's future glory.
8. St. George's cross which, with the cross of St. Andrew, made the new Union flag of Great Britain; Pope may also allude to recent British missionary work overseas.

	Tempt° icy seas, where scarce the waters roll,	*attempt*
390	Where clearer flames glow round the frozen pole;	
	Or under southern skies exalt° their sails,	*raise*
	Led by new stars, and born by spicy gales!	
	For me the balm[9] shall bleed, and amber flow,	
	The coral redden, and the ruby glow,	
395	The pearly shell its lucid globe infold,	
	And Phoebus warm the ripening ore to gold.[1]	
	The time shall come, when free as seas or wind	
	Unbounded Thames[2] shall flow for all mankind,	
	Whole nations enter with each swelling tide,	
400	And seas but join the regions they divide;	
	Earth's distant ends our glory shall behold,	
	And the new world launch forth to seek the old.	
	Then ships of uncouth form shall stem the tide,	
	And feathered people crowd my wealthy side,[3]	
405	And naked youths and painted chiefs admire	
	Our speech, our color, and our strange attire!	
	Oh stretch thy reign, fair Peace! from shore to shore,	
	Till conquest cease, and slav'ry be no more:	
	Till the freed[4] Indians in their native groves	
410	Reap their own fruits and woo their sable loves,	
	Peru once more a race of kings behold,	
	And other Mexicos be roofed with gold.	
	Exiled by thee from earth to deepest hell,	
	In brazen bonds shall barb'rous Discord dwell:	
415	Gigantic Pride, pale Terror, gloomy Care,	
	And mad Ambition, shall attend her there.	
	There purple Vengeance bathed in gore retires,	
	Her weapons blunted, and extinct her fires:	
	There hateful Envy her own snakes shall feel,	
420	And Persecution mourn her broken wheel:[5]	
	There Faction roar, Rebellion bite her chain,	
	And gasping Furies thirst for blood in vain.	
	Here cease thy flight, nor with unhallowed lays	
	Touch the fair fame of Albion's golden days.	
425	The thoughts of gods let Granville's verse recite,	
	And bring the scenes of opening fate to light.	
	My humble Muse, in unambitious strains,	
	Paints the green forests and the flow'ry plains,	
	Where Peace descending bids her olives spring,	
430	And scatters blessings from her dove-like wing.	
	Ev'n I more sweetly pass my careless days,	
	Pleased in the silent shade with empty praise;	
	Enough for me, that to the list'ning swains	
	First in these fields I sung the sylvan strains.	

1704–13   1713

---

9. Tree sap, often having soothing or healing properties.
1. Phoebus Apollo, god of the sun and patron of poets, was commonly believed to ripen metal into gold with his rays.
2. A wish that London may be made a FREE PORT [Pope's note]; many merchants proposed that customs duties be abolished to make Britain more open to international trade.
3. Four Iroquois Indian chiefs visited England in 1710, causing a sensation.
4. From Spanish oppression.
5. An instrument of torture.

THE RAPE OF THE LOCK   "New things are made familiar, and familiar things are made new," wrote Samuel Johnson about the most accomplished poem of Pope's younger years. "The whole detail of a female day is brought before us invested with so much art of decoration that, though nothing is disguised, everything is striking."

Only a poet with formidable imaginative powers could have made a great mock-heroic poem out of such unpromising materials. When Robert, Lord Petre, cut a love-lock from the head of Arabella Fermor without her permission, the two young people, both in their early twenties, quarreled bitterly. Their families, leading members of the Roman Catholic gentry once on the friendliest terms, became seriously estranged. Pope's friend John Caryll, who saw himself as a mediator among the group, asked him "to write a poem to make a jest of it, and laugh them together."

Pope's first effort was a poem in two cantos, *The Rape of the Locke*, printed in 1712 with some of his other pieces and the work of other poets. Two years later, Pope separately published *The Rape of the Lock*, enlarged to five cantos by the addition of the "machinery" of the sylphs and gnomes, and by the game of Ombre. The poem reached its final form in 1717 when Pope added the moralizing declamation of Clarissa (5.7–35), a parody of the speech of Sarpedon to Glaucus in the *Iliad*. The mock-epic tenor of the five-canto poem was clearly influenced by Pope's translation of the *Iliad*, his main project while most of *The Rape of the Lock* was being composed. Other influences were Homer's *Odyssey*, Virgil's *Aeneid*, Milton's *Paradise Lost*, and Boileau's *Le Lutrin* (1674, 1683), a mock-heroic satire on clerical infighting over the placement of a lectern. Yoking together the mundanely trivial and the mythically heroic as he follows the course of Belinda's day, Pope produced a vivid, yet affectionate, mockery of the fashions and sexual mores common in his own social circle.

The arming of the champion for war became the application of Belinda's (i.e., Arabella's) make-up for the battle of the sexes; the larger-than-life gods of classical mythology became miniature cartoon-like sylphs; Aeneas' voyage up the Tiber became Belinda's progress up the Thames; the depiction of Achilles' shield became the description of Belinda's petticoat; the test of single combat became the game of cards; the hero's journey to the underworld became the gnome's adventure in the Cave of Spleen; and the rape of Helen that started the Trojan War became the "rape" (stealing) of Belinda's hair that began an unpleasant social squabble. All the trappings of classical epic are here: the divine messenger appearing to the hero in a dream, the sacrifice to the gods, the inspirational speech to the troops before battle, the epic feast, the violent melee, and the final triumphant apotheosis. Throughout the poem, the enormous distance between the trivial *matter* and the heroic *manner* produces brilliantly comic results.

The Rape of the Lock

An Heroi-Comical Poem in Five Cantos

Nolueram, Belinda, tuos violare capillos,
Sed juvat hoc precibus me tribuisse tuis.

Martial[1]

To Mrs. Arabella Fermor
       Madam,
       It will be in vain to deny that I have some regard for this piece, since I dedicate it to you. Yet you may bear me witness, it was intended only to divert a few young ladies, who have good sense and good humor enough, to laugh not only at their sex's little unguarded follies, but at their own.[2] But as it was communicated with the air of

1. "I did not wish, [Belinda,] to violate your locks, but I rejoice to have yielded this to your wishes" (Martial, *Epigrams* 12.84). Pope has substituted "Belinda" for Martial's "Polytimus."
2. I.e., at their own individual follies as well.

a secret, it soon found its way into the world. An imperfect copy having been offered to a bookseller, you had the good nature for my sake to consent to the publication of one more correct; this I was forced to before I had executed half my design, for the *machinery* was entirely wanting to complete it.

The *machinery*, Madam, is a term invented by the critics, to signify that part which the deities, angels, or demons, are made to act in a poem; for the ancient poets are in one respect like many modern ladies: let an action be never so trivial in itself, they always make it appear of the utmost importance. These machines I determined to raise on a very new and odd foundation, the Rosicrucian[3] doctrine of spirits.

I know how disagreeable it is to make use of hard words before a lady; but 'tis so much the concern of a poet to have his works understood, and particularly by your sex, that you must give me leave to explain two or three difficult terms.

The Rosicrucians are a people I must bring you acquainted with. The best account I know of them is in a French book called *Le Comte de Gabalis*,[4] which both in its title and size is so like a novel, that many of the fair sex have read it for one by mistake. According to these gentlemen, the four elements are inhabited by spirits, which they call Sylphs, Gnomes, Nymphs, and Salamanders.[5] The Gnomes, or Demons of Earth, delight in mischief; but the Sylphs, whose habitation is in the air, are the best-conditioned[6] creatures imaginable. For they say, any mortals may enjoy the most intimate familiarities with these gentle spirits, upon a condition very easy to all true adepts, an inviolate preservation of chastity.

As to the following cantos, all the passages of them are as fabulous,[7] as the vision at the beginning, or the transformation at the end (except the loss of your hair, which I always mention with reverence). The human persons are as fictitious as the airy ones; and the character of Belinda, as it is now managed, resembles you in nothing but in beauty.

If this poem had as many graces as there are in your person, or in your mind, yet I could never hope it should pass through the world half so uncensured as you have done. But let its fortune be what it will, mine is happy enough, to have given me this occasion of assuring you that I am, with the truest esteem,

Madam,

Your most obedient

humble servant.

A. Pope

CANTO 1

What dire offense from am'rous causes springs,
What mighty contests rise from trivial things,
I sing[8]—This verse to Caryll, Muse! is due;
This, ev'n Belinda may vouchsafe to view:
5   Slight is the subject, but not so the praise,
If she inspire, and he approve my lays.°   *verses*
Say what strange motive, Goddess!° could compel   *his Muse*

---

3. A secret society of the 17th and 18th centuries, devoted to the study of ancient religious, philosophical, and mystical doctrines.
4. Written in 1670 by the Abbé de Monfaucon de Villars, its approach to Rosicrucian philosophy was lighthearted. It was printed in duodecimo, a small "pocketbook" size common to many inexpensive novels.

5. Elemental spirits living in fire.
6. Best natured, having the best character.
7. Fictional.
8. Pope begins with the ancient epic formula of "proposition" of the work as a whole, and "invocation" of the gods' assistance, continuing with the traditional epic questions.

A well-bred lord t' assault a gentle belle?
Oh say what stranger cause, yet unexplored,
10   Could make a gentle belle reject a lord?
In tasks so bold, can little men engage,
And in soft bosoms dwells such mighty rage?
    Sol through white curtains shot a tim'rous ray,
And op'd those eyes that must eclipse the day;
15   Now lapdogs[9] give themselves the rousing shake,
And sleepless lovers, just at twelve, awake:
Thrice rung the bell, the slipper knocked the ground,[1]
And the pressed watch returned a silver sound.[2]
Belinda still her downy pillow pressed,
20   Her guardian Sylph prolonged the balmy rest.
'Twas he had summoned to her silent bed
The morning dream that hovered o'er her head.
A youth more glitt'ring than a birthnight beau,[3]
(That ev'n in slumber caused her cheek to glow)
25   Seemed to her ear his winning lips to lay,
And thus in whispers said, or seemed to say:[4]
    "Fairest of mortals, thou distinguished care
Of thousand bright inhabitants of air!
If e'er one vision touched thy infant thought,
30   Of all the nurse and all the priest have taught,[5]
Of airy elves by moonlight shadows seen,
The silver token, and the circled green,[6]
Or virgins visited by angel pow'rs,[7]
With golden crowns and wreaths of heav'nly flow'rs,
35   Hear and believe! thy own importance know,
Nor bound thy narrow views to things below.
Some secret truths from learned pride concealed,
To maids alone and children are revealed:
What though no credit doubting wits may give?[8]
40   The fair and innocent shall still believe.
Know then, unnumbered spirits round thee fly,
The light militia of the lower sky;
These, though unseen, are ever on the wing,
Hang o'er the box, and hover round the ring.[9]
45   Think what an equipage[1] thou hast in air,
And view with scorn two pages and a chair.[2]
As now your own, our beings were of old,
And once enclosed in woman's beauteous mold;
Thence, by a soft transition, we repair

---

9. Small dogs imported from Asia were highly fashionable ladies' pets at this time.
1. Belinda rings the bell and then finally bangs her slipper on the floor to call her maid.
2. The popular "pressed watch" chimed the hour and quarter hours when its stem was pressed, saving its owner from striking a match to see the time.
3. On a royal birthday, courtiers' clothes were particularly extravagant.
4. His whispering recalls the serpent's temptation of Eve in Milton.

5. The nurse and priest were seen as two standard sources of superstition.
6. Withered circles in the grass and silver coins were supposed to be signs of fairies' presence.
7. Belinda is reminded of the many virgin saints, and particularly the Annunciation to the Virgin Mary.
8. Religious skepticism was on the increase.
9. The theater box and the equally fashionable drive round Hyde Park.
1. Carriage, horses, and attendants.
2. A sedan chair, carried by two chairmen.

50 From earthly vehicles[3] to these of air.
Think not, when woman's transient breath is fled,
That all her vanities at once are dead:
Succeeding vanities she still regards,
And though she plays no more, o'erlooks the cards.
55 Her joy in gilded chariots, when alive,
And love of Ombre,[4] after death survive.
For when the fair in all their pride expire,
To their first elements[5] their souls retire:
The sprites of fiery termagants° in flame   *scolding women*
60 Mount up, and take a salamander's name.
Soft yielding minds to water glide away,
And sip with Nymphs, their elemental tea.
The graver prude sinks downward to a Gnome,
In search of mischief still on earth to roam.
65 The light coquettes in Sylphs aloft repair,
And sport and flutter in the fields of air.
   "Know farther yet; whoever fair and chaste
Rejects mankind, is by some Sylph embraced:
For spirits, freed from mortal laws, with ease
70 Assume what sexes and what shapes they please.[6]
What guards the purity of melting maids,[7]
In courtly balls, and midnight masquerades,
Safe from the treach'rous friend, the daring spark,[8]
The glance by day, the whisper in the dark;
75 When kind occasion prompts their warm desires,
When music softens, and when dancing fires?
'Tis but their Sylph, the wise celestials know,
Though *Honor* is the word with men below.
   "Some nymphs there are, too conscious of their face,
80 For life predestined to the Gnomes' embrace.
These swell their prospects and exalt their pride,
When offers are disdained, and love denied.
Then gay ideas crowd the vacant brain;
While peers° and dukes, and all their sweeping train,   *aristocrats*
85 And garters, stars, and coronets[9] appear,
And in soft sounds, 'your Grace'[1] salutes their ear.
'Tis these that early taint the female soul,
Instruct the eyes of young coquettes to roll,
Teach infant cheeks a bidden° blush to know,   *deliberate*
90 And little hearts to flutter at a beau.
   "Oft when the world imagine women stray,
The Sylphs through mystic mazes guide their way,

---

3. Both the carriage, and the physical body.
4. Ombre (pronounced Omber) was an elaborate card game, introduced into England in the 17th century and highly fashionable in the early 18th century. Given the general tenor of the poem, Pope may also be punning on the origin of the word "Ombre," from the Spanish *hombre*, meaning "man."
5. The four elements of fire, water, earth, and air were thought to make up all things; so an individual's charac-

ter was determined by whichever element dominated his or her soul.
6. Cf. *Paradise Lost*, "For spirits when they please / Can either sex assume, or both" (1.423–24).
7. I.e., the chastity of weakening virgins.
8. A bold, brash, and showy young man.
9. Emblems of noble rank.
1. Form of address for a duke or a duchess.

Through all the giddy circle they pursue,

And old impertinence° expel by new.   *frivolity*

95   What tender maid but must a victim fall

To one man's treat, but for another's ball?

When Florio speaks, what virgin could withstand,

If gentle Damon did not squeeze her hand?

With varying vanities, from ev'ry part,

100   They shift the moving toy shop[2] of their heart;

Where wigs with wigs, with sword knots sword knots strive,[3]

Beaus banish beaus, and coaches coaches drive.[4]

This erring mortals levity may call,

Oh blind to truth! the Sylphs contrive it all.

105   "Of these am I, who thy protection claim,

A watchful sprite, and Ariel is my name.

Late, as I ranged the crystal wilds of air,

In the clear mirror of thy ruling star

I saw, alas! some dread event impend,

110   Ere to the main° this morning sun descend.   *sea*

But Heav'n reveals not what, or how, or where:

Warned by thy Sylph, oh pious maid beware!

This to disclose is all thy guardian can.

Beware of all, but most beware of man!"

115   He said; when Shock,[5] who thought she slept too long,

Leapt up, and waked his mistress with his tongue.

'Twas then Belinda! if report say true,

Thy eyes first opened on a *billet-doux*;°   *love letter*

Wounds, charms, and ardors, were no sooner read,

120   But all the vision vanished from thy head.

      And now, unveiled, the toilet° stands displayed,   *dressing table*

Each silver vase in mystic order laid.

First, robed in white, the nymph intent adores

With head uncovered, the cosmetic pow'rs.

125   A heav'nly image[6] in the glass appears,

To that she bends, to that her eyes she rears;°   *raises*

Th' inferior priestess,[7] at her altar's side,

Trembling, begins the sacred rites of pride.

Unnumbered treasures ope at once, and here

130   The various off'rings of the world appear;

From each she nicely culls with curious° toil,   *careful*

And decks the goddess with the glitt'ring spoil.

This casket India's glowing gems unlocks,

And all Arabia° breathes from yonder box.   *eastern perfume*

135   The tortoise here and elephant unite,

Transformed to combs, the speckled and the white.[8]

Here files of pins extend their shining rows,

---

2. Where toys and trinkets are sold; "moving" here means easily changed, unstable.

3. Most men wore wigs in public; formally dressed men tied ribbons to the hilt of their swords.

4. In word order and versification, these two lines mimic both Homer's and Ovid's description of heroic combat.

5. The shock or shough, a long-haired Icelandic poodle, fashionable as a lapdog.

6. I.e., Belinda herself.

7. Belinda's maid, Betty.

8. Tortoise-shell and ivory.

Puffs, powders, patches, Bibles,[9] *billet-doux.*
Now awful° beauty puts on all its arms;   *awe-inspiring*
140   The fair each moment rises in her charms,
Repairs her smiles, awakens ev'ry grace,
And calls forth all the wonders of her face;
Sees by degrees a purer blush[1] arise,
And keener lightnings[2] quicken in her eyes.
145   The busy Sylphs surround their darling care;
These set the head, and those divide the hair,
Some fold the sleeve, whilst others plait the gown;
And Betty's praised for labors not her own.

CANTO 2

Not with more glories, in th' ethereal plain,°   *sky*
The sun first rises o'er the purpled main,
Than issuing forth, the rival of his beams
Launched on the bosom of the silver Thames.[1]
5   Fair nymphs, and well-dressed youths around her shone,
But ev'ry eye was fixed on her alone.
On her white breast a sparkling cross she wore,
Which Jews might kiss, and infidels adore.[2]
Her lively looks a sprightly mind disclose,
10   Quick as her eyes, and as unfixed as those:
Favors to none, to all she smiles extends,
Oft she rejects, but never once offends.
Bright as the sun, her eyes the gazers strike,
And, like the sun, they shine on all alike.
15   Yet graceful ease, and sweetness void of pride,
Might hide her faults, if belles had faults to hide:
If to her share some female errors fall,
Look on her face, and you'll forget 'em all.
     This nymph, to the destruction of mankind,
20   Nourished two locks which graceful hung behind
In equal curls, and well conspired to deck
With shining ringlets the smooth iv'ry neck.
Love in these labyrinths his slaves detains,
And mighty hearts are held in slender chains.
25   With hairy springes° we the birds betray,   *noose traps*
Slight lines° of hair surprise the finny prey,   *fishing lines*
Fair tresses man's imperial race ensnare,
And beauty draws us with a single hair.
     Th' adventurous Baron[3] the bright locks admired,
30   He saw, he wished, and to the prize aspired:
Resolved to win, he meditates the way,

9. Patches were small beauty spots of black silk, pasted onto the face to make the skin appear whiter. It was fashionable to own Bibles in very small format.
1. The even, artificial blush of rouge.
2. Caused by drops of belladonna (deadly nightshade), which dilates the pupils.
1. Belinda takes a boat from London to Hampton Court,

avoiding the dirt and squalor of the streets; her voyage compares with Aeneas's up the Tiber (*Aeneid* 7), or, alternatively, Cleopatra's up the Nile (*Antony and Cleopatra* 2.2).
2. Kissing the cross was the sign of religious conversion.
3. Robert, Lord Petre (1690–1713), responsible for the original incident.

By force to ravish, or by fraud betray;
For when success a lover's toil attends,
Few ask, if fraud or force attained his ends.
35   For this, ere Phoebus rose, he had implored
Propitious Heav'n, and ev'ry pow'r adored,°   *worshipped*
But chiefly Love—to Love an altar built,
Of twelve vast French romances, neatly gilt.
There lay three garters, half a pair of gloves;
40   And all the trophies of his former loves.
With tender *billet-doux* he lights the pyre,
And breathes three am'rous sighs to raise the fire.
Then prostrate falls, and begs with ardent eyes
Soon to obtain, and long possess the prize:
45   The pow'rs gave ear, and granted half his pray'r,
The rest the winds dispersed in empty air.[4]
        But now secure the painted vessel glides,
The sunbeams trembling on the floating tides,
While melting music steals upon the sky,
50   And softened sounds along the waters die.
Smooth flow the waves, the zephyrs° gently play,   *breezes*
Belinda smiled, and all the world was gay.
All but the Sylph—with careful° thoughts oppressed,   *worried*
Th' impending woe sat heavy on his breast.
55   He summons strait his denizens[5] of air;
The lucid squadrons round the sails repair:
Soft o'er the shrouds° aerial whispers breathe,   *ropes*
That seemed but zephyrs to the train beneath.
Some to the sun their insect wings unfold,
60   Waft on the breeze, or sink in clouds of gold.
Transparent forms, too fine for mortal sight,
Their fluid bodies half dissolved in light,
Loose to the wind their airy garments flew,
Thin glitt'ring textures of the filmy dew;
65   Dipped in the richest tincture of the skies,
Where light disports in ever-mingling dyes,
While ev'ry beam new transient colors flings,
Colors that change whene'er they wave their wings.
Amid the circle, on the gilded mast,
70   Superior by the head, was Ariel placed;[6]
His purple pinions opening to the sun,
He raised his azure wand, and thus begun:
        "Ye Sylphs and Sylphids,° to your chief give ear,   *female Sylphs*
Fays, Fairies, Genii, Elves, and Demons hear!
75   Ye know the spheres and various tasks assigned,
By laws eternal to th' aerial kind.
Some in the fields of purest ether[7] play,
And bask and whiten in the blaze of day.

---

4. Cf. *The Aeneid* 2.794–95, which Dryden translated:
"Apollo heard, and granting half his pray'r, / Shuffled in
winds the rest, and toss'd in empty air."

5. Naturalized foreigner.
6. Heroes of epics were typically taller than their men.
7. Air beyond the moon.

Some guide the course of wandering orbs° on high,   *comets*
80   Or roll the planets through the boundless sky.
Some less refined, beneath the moon's pale light
Pursue the stars that shoot athwart the night,
Or suck the mists in grosser° air below,   *heavier*
Or dip their pinions in the painted bow,°   *rainbow*
85   Or brew fierce tempests on the wintry main,
Or o'er the glebe° distill the kindly rain.   *farmland*
Others on earth o'er human race preside,
Watch all their ways, and all their actions guide:
Of these the chief the care of nations own,
90   And guard with arms divine the British throne.
    "Our humbler province is to tend the fair,
Not a less pleasing, though less glorious care.
To save the powder from too rude° a gale,   *rough*
Nor let th' imprisoned essences° exhale,   *perfumes*
95   To draw fresh colors from the vernal flow'rs,
To steal from rainbows ere they drop in show'rs
A brighter wash;[8] to curl their waving hairs,
Assist their blushes, and inspire their airs;
Nay oft, in dreams, invention we bestow,
100   To change a flounce, or add a furbelow.°   *fringe*
    "This day, black omens threat the brightest fair
That e'er deserved a watchful spirit's care;
Some dire disaster, or° by force or sleight,°   *either / trick*
But what, or where, the fates have wrapped in night.
105   Whether the nymph shall break Diana's law,°   *virginity*
Or some frail China jar receive a flaw,
Or stain her honor, or her new brocade,
Forget her pray'rs, or miss a masquerade,
Or lose her heart, or necklace, at a ball;
110   Or whether Heav'n has doomed that Shock must fall.
Haste then ye spirits! to your charge° repair;   *duty*
The flutt'ring fan be Zephyretta's care;
The drops° to thee, Brillante, we consign;   *earrings*
And, Momentilla, let the watch be thine;
115   Do thou, Crispissa,[9] tend her fav'rite lock;
Ariel himself shall be the guard of Shock.
    "To fifty chosen Sylphs, of special note,
We trust th' important charge, the petticoat:
Oft have we known that sev'nfold fence[1] to fail,
120   Though stiff with hoops, and armed with ribs of whale.
Form a strong line about the silver bound,
And guard the wide circumference around.
    "Whatever spirit, careless of his charge,
His post neglects, or leaves the fair at large,
125   Shall feel sharp vengeance soon o'ertake his sins,

---

8. A cosmetic rinse.
9. The Latin *crispere* means "to curl."
1. Serving Belinda like the epic warrior's shield, her petti-

coat has seven layers bound together with a silver band
(cf. *Iliad* 18 or *Aeneid* 8).

Be stopped in vials, or transfixed with pins;
Or plunged in lakes of bitter washes lie,
Or wedged whole ages in a bodkin's[2] eye:
Gums and pomatums° shall his flight restrain,   *ointments*
130   While clogged he beats his silken wings in vain;
Or alum styptics[3] with contracting power
Shrink his thin essence like a rivelled° flower.   *shriveled*
Or as Ixion[4] fixed, the wretch shall feel
The giddy motion of the whirling mill,[5]
135   In fumes of burning chocolate shall glow,
And tremble at the sea that froths below!"
    He spoke; the spirits from the sails descend;
Some, orb in orb, around the nymph extend,
Some thrid° the mazy ringlets of her hair,   *slid through*
140   Some hang upon the pendants of her ear;
With beating hearts the dire event they wait,
Anxious, and trembling for the birth of fate.

CANTO 3

Close by those meads forever crowned with flow'rs,
Where Thames with pride surveys his rising tow'rs,
There stands a structure of majestic frame,
Which from the neighb'ring Hampton takes its name.[1]
5   Here Britain's statesmen oft the fall foredoom
Of foreign tyrants, and of nymphs at home;
Here thou, great Anna! whom three realms obey,[2]
Dost sometimes counsel take—and sometimes tea.
    Hither the heroes and the nymphs resort,
10   To taste awhile the pleasures of a court;
In various talk th' instructive hours they passed,
Who gave the ball, or paid the visit last:
One speaks the glory of the British Queen,
And one describes a charming Indian screen;
15   A third interprets motions, looks, and eyes;
At ev'ry word a reputation dies.
Snuff, or the fan, supply each pause of chat,
With singing, laughing, ogling, and all that.
    Meanwhile declining from the noon of day,
20   The sun obliquely shoots his burning ray;
The hungry judges soon the sentence sign,
And wretches hang that jurymen may dine;
The merchant from th' Exchange° returns in peace,   *market*
And the long labors of the toilette cease—
25   Belinda now, whom thirst of fame invites,

2. Blunt, thick needle; the Sylph, like the camel in Matthew 19.24, has difficulty getting through. Pope later plays on the various meanings of "bodkin," which also include a hair ornament and a dagger.
3. Astringents that stopped bleeding.
4. Having tried the chastity of Hera, Ixion was punished by being tied to a revolving wheel of fire.

5. An instrument for grinding cocoa beans.
1. Hampton Court, about 15 miles upriver from London, was built in the 16th century by Cardinal Wolsey, and by Queen Anne's day was associated with wits as well as with statesmen.
2. The English Crown still maintained its ancient claim to rule France as well as Great Britain and Ireland.

Burns to encounter two advent'rous knights,
At Ombre[3] singly to decide their doom;
And swells her breast with conquests yet to come.
Straight the three bands prepare in arms to join,
30   Each band the number of the Sacred Nine.[4]
Soon as she spreads her hand, th' aerial guard
Descend, and sit on each important card:
First Ariel perched upon a Matador,[5]
Then each, according to the rank they bore;
35   For Sylphs, yet mindful of their ancient race,
Are, as when women, wondrous fond of place.°   rank
        Behold, four kings in majesty revered,
With hoary whiskers[6] and a forky beard;
And four fair queens whose hands sustain° a flow'r,   hold
40   Th' expressive emblem of their softer pow'r;
Four knaves in garbs succinct,° a trusty band,   girded up
Caps on their heads, and halberds in their hand;
And particolored troops, a shining train,
Draw forth to combat on the velvet plain.[7]
45   The skillful nymph reviews her force with care;
"Let spades be trumps!" she said, and trumps they were.[8]
        Now move to war her sable Matadors,
In show like leaders of the swarthy moors.
Spadillio first, unconquerable lord!
50   Led off two captive trumps, and swept the board.
As many more Manillio forced to yield,
And marched a victor from the verdant field.
Him Basto followed, but his fate more hard
Gained but one trump and one plebeian card.
55   With his broad saber next, a chief in years,
The hoary majesty of spades appears;
Puts forth one manly leg, to sight revealed;
The rest his many-colored robe concealed.
The rebel knave who dares his prince engage,
60   Proves the just victim of his royal rage.
Ev'n mighty Pam[9] that kings and queens o'erthrew,
And mowed down armies in the fights of Lu,
Sad chance of war! now, destitute of aid,
Falls undistinguished by the victor spade!
65   Thus far both armies to Belinda yield;
Now to the Baron fate inclines the field.
His warlike amazon her host invades,
Th' imperial consort of the crown of spades.

3. A card game played with 40 cards, similar to modern bridge: three players hold nine cards each and bid for tricks, with the highest bidder becoming the "ombre" (man) and choosing trumps.
4. Pope links the nine Muses to the nine cards each player holds.
5. The Matadores are the three cards of highest value; Belinda holds all three: when trumps are black, they are the Spadillio (ace of spades), Manillio (deuce of spades), and Basto (ace of clubs).

6. Gray mustache. The royal figures on the cards now conduct a mock-epic review of their forces, and the whole game is described as an epic battle, with the characters appearing as on the cards.
7. The green velvet card table.
8. Cf. Genesis 1.3, "Then God said, 'Let there be light'; and there was light."
9. The knave or jack of clubs, which took precedence over all trumps in the game of Lu, or Loo.

The club's black tyrant first her victim died,
70 Spite of his haughty mien and barb'rous pride:
What boots the regal circle on his head,
His giant limbs in state unwieldy spread?
That long behind he trails his pompous robe,
And of all monarchs only grasps the globe?
75   The Baron now his diamonds pours apace;
Th' embroidered king who shows but half his face,
And his refulgent queen, with pow'rs combined,
Of broken troops an easy conquest find.
Clubs, diamonds, hearts, in wild disorder seen,
80 With throngs promiscuous strew the level green.
Thus when dispersed a routed army runs,
Of Asia's troops and Afric's sable sons,
With like confusion different nations fly,
Of various habit and of various dye,
85 The pierced battalions disunited fall,
In heaps on heaps; one fate o'erwhelms them all.
        The knave of diamonds tries his wily arts,
And wins (oh shameful chance!) the queen of hearts.
At this, the blood the virgin's cheek forsook,
90 A livid paleness spreads o'er all her look;
She sees, and trembles at th' approaching ill,
Just in the jaws of ruin, and codille.[1]
And now (as oft in some distempered state)
On one nice trick[2] depends the gen'ral fate.
95 An ace of hearts steps forth: the king[3] unseen
Lurked in her hand, and mourned his captive queen.
He springs to vengeance with an eager pace,
And falls like thunder on the prostrate ace.
The nymph exulting fills with shouts the sky,
100 The walls, the woods, and long canals reply.
        Oh thoughtless mortals! ever blind to fate,
Too soon dejected, and too soon elate!
Sudden these honors shall be snatched away,
And cursed forever this victorious day.
105   For lo! the board with cups and spoons is crowned,
The berries crackle, and the Mill turns round.[4]
On shining altars of Japan[5] they raise
The silver lamp; the fiery spirits blaze.
From silver spouts the grateful° liquors glide,   *pleasing*
110 While China's earth receives the smoking tide.
At once they gratify their scent and taste,
And frequent cups prolong the rich repast.
Straight° hover round the fair her airy band;   *immediately*
Some, as she sipped, the fuming liquor fanned,
115 Some o'er her lap their careful plumes displayed,

1. Literally "elbow": the defeat suffered by the ombre if
another player wins more tricks.
2. Trick applies in both its technical and general senses as
Belinda makes this careful maneuver.

3. The King of Hearts.
4. Grinding coffee beans.
5. Lacquered tables ("Japan" was a type of varnish originating in that country).

Trembling, and conscious of the rich brocade.
Coffee (which makes the politician wise,
And see through all things with his half-shut eyes)
Sent up in vapors[6] to the Baron's brain
120   New stratagems, the radiant lock to gain.
Ah cease rash youth! desist ere 'tis too late,
Fear the just gods, and think of Scylla's fate![7]
Changed to a bird, and sent to flit in air,
She dearly pays for Nisus' injured hair!
125   But when to mischief mortals bend their will,
How soon they find fit instruments of ill!
Just then, Clarissa drew with tempting grace
A two-edged weapon from her shining case;
So ladies in romance assist their knight,
130   Present the spear, and arm him for the fight.
He takes the gift with rev'rence, and extends
The little engine° on his fingers' ends,   *instrument*
This just behind Belinda's neck he spread,
As o'er the fragrant steams she bends her head:
135   Swift to the lock a thousand sprites repair,
A thousand wings, by turns, blow back the hair,
And thrice they twitched the diamond in her ear,
Thrice she looked back, and thrice the foe drew near.
Just in that instant, anxious Ariel sought
140   The close recesses of the virgin's thought;
As on the nosegay in her breast reclined,
He watched th' ideas rising in her mind,
Sudden he viewed, in spite of all her art,
An earthly lover° lurking at her heart.   *Lord Petre*
145   Amazed, confused, he found his pow'r expired,
Resigned to fate, and with a sigh retired.
        The peer now spreads the glitt'ring forfex° wide,   *scissors*
T' enclose the lock; now joins it, to divide.
Ev'n then, before the fatal engine closed,
150   A wretched Sylph too fondly interposed;
Fate urged the shears, and cut the Sylph in twain
(But airy substance soon unites again)[8]
The meeting points the sacred hair dissever
From the fair head, forever and forever!
155   Then flashed the living lightning from her eyes,
And screams of horror rend th' affrighted skies.
Not louder shrieks to pitying Heav'n are cast,
When husbands or when lapdogs breathe their last,
Or when rich china vessels, fall'n from high,
160   In glitt'ring dust and painted fragments lie!
        Let wreaths of triumph now my temples twine,

6. Both steam and vain imaginations.
7. Scylla plucked purple hair from the head of her father,
King Nisus, to offer to her lover, Minos, so destroying her
father's power. Minos rejected her impiety, and Scylla
was transformed into a bird.

8. Milton lib. 6 [Pope's note], citing *Paradise Lost*
6.329–31, "The girding sword with discontinuous
wound / Passed through him, but the ethereal substance
closed / Not long divisible. . . ."

(The victor cried) the glorious prize is mine!
While fish in streams, or birds delight in air,
Or in a coach and six⁹ the British fair,
165 As long as *Atalantis*¹ shall be read,
Or the small pillow grace a lady's bed,²
While visits shall be paid on solemn days,
When numerous wax lights³ in bright order blaze,
While nymphs take treats, or assignations give,
170 So long my honor, name, and praise shall live!
    What time would spare, from steel receives its date,°   *end*
And monuments, like men, submit to fate!
Steel could the labor of the gods destroy,
And strike to dust th' imperial tow'rs of Troy;⁴
175 Steel could the works of mortal pride confound,
And hew triumphal arches to the ground.
What wonder then, fair nymph! thy hairs should feel
The conqu'ring force of unresisted steel?

CANTO 4

But anxious cares the pensive nymph oppressed,
And secret passions labored in her breast.
Not youthful kings in battle seized alive,
Not scornful virgins who their charms survive,
5 Not ardent lovers robbed of all their bliss,
Not ancient ladies when refused a kiss,
Not tyrants fierce that unrepenting die,
Not Cynthia when her manteau's° pinned awry,   *gown's*
E'er felt such rage, resentment, and despair,
10 As thou, sad virgin! for thy ravished hair.
    For, that sad moment, when the Sylphs withdrew,
And Ariel weeping from Belinda flew,
Umbriel, a dusky melancholy sprite
As ever sullied the fair face of light,
15 Down to the central earth, his proper scene,
Repaired to search the gloomy Cave of Spleen.¹
    Swift on his sooty pinions flits the Gnome,
And in a vapor² reached the dismal dome.
No cheerful breeze this sullen region knows,
20 The dreaded east³ is all the wind that blows.
Here, in a grotto, sheltered close from air,
And screened in shades° from day's detested glare,   *shadows*
She sighs forever on her pensive bed,

9. A carriage drawn by six horses; a symbol of wealth and prestige.
1. The scandalous *Atalantis: Secret Memoirs and Manners of Several Persons of Quality* (1709), by Mary Delarivière Manley.
2. Said to be a place where ladies hid romance novels and other contraband.
3. Candles made of wax, rather than the cheaper tallow. Evening social visits were an essential part of the fashionable woman's routine.

4. Even Troy, fabled to have been built by Apollo and Poseidon, was destroyed by arms.
1. Named after the bodily organ, "spleen" was the current name for the fashionable affliction of melancholy or ill-humor. Umbriel's descent into the womb-like Cave of Spleen suggests the epic commonplace of the journey to the underworld.
2. "The spleen" was also called "the vapors."
3. The east wind was supposed to induce fits of spleen.

Pain at her side, and Megrim° at her head.   *migraine*
25   Two handmaids wait the throne: alike in place,
        But diff'ring far in figure and in face.
        Here stood Ill-Nature like an ancient maid,
        Her wrinkled form in black and white arrayed;
        With store of pray'rs, for mornings, nights, and noons,
30   Her hand is filled; her bosom with lampoons.
            There Affectation with a sickly mien
        Shows in her cheek the roses of eighteen,
        Practiced to lisp, and hang the head aside,
        Faints into airs, and languishes with pride;
35   On the rich quilt sinks with becoming woe,
        Wrapped in a gown, for sickness, and for show.
        The fair ones feel such maladies as these,
        When each new nightdress gives a new disease.
            A constant vapor o'er the palace flies;
40   Strange phantoms rising as the mists arise;
        Dreadful, as hermit's dreams in haunted shades,
        Or bright as visions of expiring maids.[4]
        Now glaring fiends, and snakes on rolling spires,°   *coils*
        Pale specters, gaping tombs, and purple fires:
45   Now lakes of liquid gold, Elysian scenes,[5]
        And crystal domes, and angels in machines.
            Unnumbered throngs on ev'ry side are seen
        Of bodies changed to various forms by Spleen.[6]
        Here living teapots stand, one arm held out,
50   One bent; the handle this, and that the spout:
        A pipkin[7] there like Homer's tripod walks;
        Here sighs a jar, and there a goose pie[8] talks;
        Men prove with child, as pow'rful fancy works,
        And maids, turned bottles, call aloud for corks.
55   Safe passed the Gnome through this fantastic band,
        A branch of healing spleenwort[9] in his hand.
        Then thus addressed the pow'r—"Hail, wayward Queen!
        Who rule the sex to fifty from fifteen,
        Parent of vapors and of female wit,
60   Who give th' hysteric or poetic fit,
        On various tempers act by various ways,
        Make some take physic,° others scribble plays;[1]   *medicine*
        Who cause the proud their visits to delay,
        And send the godly in a pet° to pray.   *ill-humor*
65   A nymph there is that all thy pow'r disdains,
        And thousands more in equal mirth maintains.
        But oh! if e'er thy Gnome could spoil a grace,
        Or raise a pimple on a beauteous face,

---

4. Religious visions of hell and heaven.
5. Elysium was the classical paradise, but this also recalls contemporary theater, which made much of scenic spectacle and the use of machinery.
6. Hallucinations similar to those described in the following lines were common to those afflicted with spleen.
7. Small pot or pan. Hephaistos's "walking" tripods are described in the *Iliad* 18.439ff.
8. Alludes to a real fact, a Lady of distinction imagin'd herself in this condition [Pope's note].
9. Pope changes the golden bough that protected Aeneas on his trip through the underworld into an herb that was supposed to be good for the spleen.
1. Melancholy was associated with artistic creativity.

	Like citron-waters° matrons' cheeks inflame,	*flavored brandy*
70	Or change complexions at a losing game;	
	If e'er with airy horns[2] I planted heads,	
	Or rumpled petticoats, or tumbled beds,	
	Or caused suspicion when no soul was rude,	
	Or discomposed the headdress of a prude,	
75	Or e'er to costive° lapdog gave disease,	*constipated*
	Which not the tears of brightest eyes could ease:	
	Hear me, and touch Belinda with chagrin;	
	That single act gives half the world the spleen."	
	The goddess with a discontented air	
80	Seems to reject him, though she grants his pray'r.	
	A wondrous bag with both her hands she binds,	
	Like that where once Ulysses held the winds;[3]	
	There she collects the force of female lungs,	
	Sighs, sobs, and passions, and the war of tongues.	
85	A vial next she fills with fainting fears,	
	Soft sorrows, melting griefs, and flowing tears.	
	The Gnome rejoicing bears her gifts away,	
	Spreads his black wings, and slowly mounts to day.	
	Sunk in Thalestris'[4] arms the nymph he found,	
90	Her eyes dejected and her hair unbound.	
	Full o'er their heads the swelling bag he rent,	
	And all the furies issued at the vent.	
	Belinda burns with more than mortal ire,	
	And fierce Thalestris fans the rising fire.	
95	"O wretched maid!" she spread her hands, and cried,	
	(While Hampton's echoes "Wretched maid!" replied)	
	"Was it for this you took such constant care	
	The bodkin, comb, and essence to prepare;	
	For this your locks in paper durance° bound,	*curling papers*
100	For this with tort'ring irons wreathed around?	
	For this with fillets[5] strained your tender head,	
	And bravely bore the double loads of lead?°	*wire supports*
	Gods! shall the ravisher display your hair,	
	While the fops envy, and the ladies stare!	
105	Honor forbid! at whose unrivaled shrine	
	Ease, pleasure, virtue, all, our sex resign.	
	Methinks already I your tears survey,	
	Already hear the horrid things they say,	
	Already see you a degraded toast,[6]	
110	And all your honor in a whisper lost!	
	How shall I, then, your helpless fame defend?	
	'Twill then be infamy to seem your friend!	
	And shall this prize, th' inestimable prize,	

2. A sign that a husband had been cuckolded.

3. Given to him by the wind god Aeolus (*Odyssey* 10.19ff.).

4. A queen of the Amazons; here Mrs. Morley, Arabella's second cousin.

5. Headbands, with reference to priestesses in the *Aeneid*.

6. A woman whose toast is often drunk, and who by implication is all too well known to her (male) toasters: (cf. Canto 5.10, and Fielding's *Tom Jones*, where Sophia is not pleased by reports that she has been Tom's toast, bk. 13, ch. 11).

Exposed through crystal to the gazing eyes,
115 And heightened by the diamond's circling rays,
On that rapacious hand forever blaze?[7]
Sooner shall grass in Hyde Park Circus grow,[8]
And wits take lodgings in the sound of Bow;[9]
Sooner let earth, air, sea, to Chaos fall,
120 Men, monkeys, lapdogs, parrots, perish all!"
     She said; then raging to Sir Plume[1] repairs,
And bids her beau demand the precious hairs:
(Sir Plume, of amber snuffbox justly vain,
And the nice conduct of a clouded cane[2])
125 With earnest eyes, and round unthinking face,
He first the snuffbox opened, then the case,
And thus broke out—"My Lord, why, what the devil?
Z—ds![3] damn the lock! 'fore Gad, you must be civil!
Plague on't! 'tis past a jest—nay prithee, Pox!
130 Give her the hair"—he spoke, and rapped his box.
     "It grieves me much" (replied the Peer again)
"Who speaks so well should ever speak in vain.
But by this lock, this sacred lock I swear
(Which never more shall join its parted hair,
135 Which never more its honors shall renew,
Clipped from the lovely head where late it grew)
That while my nostrils draw the vital air,
This hand which won it shall forever wear."
He spoke, and speaking, in proud triumph spread
140 The long-contended honors[4] of her head.
     But Umbriel, hateful Gnome! forbears not so;
He breaks the vial whence the sorrows flow.
Then see! the nymph in beauteous grief appears,
Her eyes half-languishing, half-drowned in tears;
145 On her heaved bosom hung her drooping head,
Which, with a sigh, she raised; and thus she said:
     "Forever cursed be this detested day,[5]
Which snatched my best, my fav'rite curl away!
Happy! ah ten times happy, had I been,
150 If Hampton Court these eyes had never seen!
Yet am not I the first mistaken maid,
By love of courts to num'rous ills betrayed.
Oh had I rather unadmired remained
In some lone isle, or distant northern land;
155 Where the gilt chariot never marks the way,
Where none learn Ombre, none e'er taste bohea!°   tea
There kept my charms concealed from mortal eye,
Like roses that in deserts bloom and die.

7. I.e., mounted in a ring.
8. The fashion for driving coaches around Hyde Park prevented grass from growing there.
9. A commercial area around St. Mary-le-Bow, and not at all fashionable.
1. Sir George Browne, cousin of Arabella's mother.

2. Skilled use of a cane with a head of dark polished stone.
3. Zounds, a corruption of "God's wounds," a mild oath.
4. Her beautiful hair.
5. Echoing Achilles' lament for his slain friend Patroclus (*Iliad* 18.107ff.).

What moved my mind with youthful lords to roam?
160 O had I stayed, and said my pray'rs at home!
'Twas this, the morning omens seemed to tell;
Thrice from my trembling hand the patch box fell;
The tott'ring china shook without a wind,
Nay, Poll° sat mute, and Shock was most unkind!   *her parrot*
165 A Sylph too warned me of the threats of fate,
In mystic visions, now believed too late!
See the poor remnants of these slighted hairs!
My hands shall rend what ev'n thy rapine spares:
These, in two sable ringlets taught to break,°   *divide*
170 Once gave new beauties to the snowy neck.
The sister lock now sits uncouth, alone,
And in its fellow's fate foresees its own;
Uncurled it hangs, the fatal shears demands;
And tempts once more thy sacrilegious hands.
175 Oh hadst thou, cruel! been content to seize
Hairs less in sight, or any hairs but these!"

CANTO 5

She said: the pitying audience melt in tears,
But Fate and Jove had stopped the Baron's ears.
In vain Thalestris with reproach assails,
For who can move when fair Belinda fails?
5   Not half so fixed the Trojan[1] could remain,
While Anna begged and Dido raged in vain.
Then grave Clarissa[2] graceful waved her fan;
Silence ensued, and thus the nymph began.
   "Say, why are beauties praised and honored most,
10   The wise man's passion, and the vain man's toast?
Why decked with all that land and sea afford,
Why angels called, and angel-like adored?
Why round our coaches crowd the white-gloved beaus,
Why bows the side box from its inmost rows?[3]
15   How vain are all these glories, all our pains,
Unless good sense preserve what beauty gains:
That men may say when we the front box grace,
Behold the first in virtue as in face!
Oh! if to dance all night, and dress all day,
20   Charmed the smallpox,[4] or chased old age away;
Who would not scorn what housewife's cares produce,
Or who would learn one earthly thing of use?
To patch, nay ogle, might become a saint,
Nor could it sure be such a sin to paint.

---

1. Aeneas, fixed on his decision to leave Carthage and abandon Dido despite her pleas and those of her sister Anna (*Aeneid* 4.269–449).
2. A new character introduced . . . to open more clearly the moral of the poem, in a parody of the speech of Sarpedon to Glaucus in Homer [Pope's note in the 1717 edition]. Sarpedon's speech (*Iliad* 12) is a famous reflec-

tion on glory: see page 2524 for Pope's translation of the speech.
3. At the theater, gentlemen sat in the side boxes, ladies in the front boxes facing the stage.
4. A common disease, which frequently left permanent facial scars.

25   But since, alas! frail beauty must decay,
      Curled or uncurled, since locks will turn to gray,
      Since painted or not painted, all shall fade,
      And she who scorns a man, must die a maid;
      What then remains, but well our pow'r to use,
30   And keep good humor still whate'er we lose?
      And trust me, dear! good humor can prevail,
      When airs, and flights, and screams, and scolding fail.
      Beauties in vain their pretty eyes may roll;
      Charms strike the sight, but merit wins the soul."
35   So spoke the dame, but no applause ensued;
      Belinda frowned, Thalestris called her prude.
      "To arms, to arms!" the fierce virago⁵ cries,
      And swift as lightning to the combat flies.
      All side in parties, and begin th' attack;
40   Fans clap, silks rustle, and tough whalebones crack;
      Heroes' and heroines' shouts confus'dly rise,
      And bass and treble voices strike the skies.
      No common weapons in their hands are found,
      Like gods they fight, nor dread a mortal wound.
45   So when bold Homer makes the gods engage,
      And heav'nly breasts with human passions rage;
      'Gainst Pallas,° Mars; Latona,⁶ Hermes arms;   *Athena*
      And all Olympus rings with loud alarms.
      Jove's thunder roars, Heav'n trembles all around;
50   Blue Neptune storms, the bellowing deeps resound;
      Earth shakes her nodding tow'rs, the ground gives way;
      And the pale ghosts start at the flash of day!
          Triumphant Umbriel on a sconce's⁷ height
      Clapped his glad wings, and sat to view the fight:
55   Propped on their bodkin spears, the sprites survey
      The growing combat, or assist the fray.
          While through the press enraged Thalestris flies,
      And scatters deaths around from both her eyes,
      A beau and witling° perished in the throng,   *little wit*
60   One died in metaphor, and one in song.
      "O cruel Nymph! a living death I bear,"
      Cried Dapperwit, and sunk beside his chair.
      A mournful glance Sir Fopling upwards cast,
      "Those eyes are made so killing"⁸—was his last:
65   Thus on Meander's flow'ry margin lies
      Th' expiring swan, and as he sings he dies.⁹
          When bold Sir Plume had drawn Clarissa down,
      Chloe stepped in, and killed him with a frown;
      She smiled to see the doughty hero slain,
70   But at her smile the beau revived again.

5. Woman who behaves like a man.
6. Mother of Diana and Apollo.
7. Candlestick attached to the wall.
8. A line from Giovanni Bononcini's opera, *Camilla*
(1696), which at this time was popular in London.
9. Meander: a river in Asia Minor. Swans were popularly believed to sing only on their death. This simile refers to Ovid's *Heroides* 7, a lament from Dido to Aeneas.

Now Jove suspends his golden scales in air,[1]
Weighs the men's wits against the lady's hair;
The doubtful beam long nods from side to side;
At length the wits mount up, the hairs subside.
75   See fierce Belinda on the Baron flies,
With more than usual lightning in her eyes;
Nor feared the chief th' unequal fight to try,
Who sought no more than on his foe to die.[2]
But this bold lord, with manly strength indued,
80   She with one finger and a thumb subdued:
Just where the breath of life his nostrils drew,
A charge of snuff the wily virgin threw;
The Gnomes direct, to ev'ry atom just,
The pungent grains of titillating dust.
85   Sudden, with starting tears each eye o'erflows,
And the high dome re-echoes to his nose.[3]
        "Now meet thy fate," incensed Belinda cried,
And drew a deadly bodkin from her side.
(The same, his ancient personage to deck,
90   Her great-great-grandsire wore about his neck
In three seal rings; which after, melted down,
Formed a vast buckle for his widow's gown:
Her infant grandame's° whistle next it grew,   grandmother's
The bells she jingled, and the whistle blew;
95   Then in a bodkin[4] graced her mother's hairs,
Which long she wore, and now Belinda wears.)
        "Boast not my fall" (he cried) "insulting foe!
Thou by some other shalt be laid as low.
Nor think, to die dejects my lofty mind;
100   All that I dread is leaving you behind!
Rather than so, ah let me still survive,
And burn in Cupid's flames—but burn alive."
        "Restore the lock!" she cries; and all around
"Restore the lock!" the vaulted roofs rebound.
105   Not fierce Othello in so loud a strain
Roared for the handkerchief that caused his pain.
But see how oft ambitious aims are crossed,
And chiefs contend 'till all the prize is lost!
The lock, obtained with guilt, and kept with pain,
110   In ev'ry place is sought, but sought in vain:
With such a prize no mortal must be blest,
So Heav'n decrees! with Heav'n who can contest?
        Some thought it mounted to the lunar sphere,[5]
Since all things lost on earth are treasured there.
115   There heroes' wits are kept in ponderous vases,
And beaus' in snuffboxes and tweezer cases.
There broken vows and deathbed alms are found,

1. To determine victory in battle; a convention found in
both Homer and Virgil.
2. A standard metaphor for sexual climax.
3. Cf. his boast, 4.133–38.
4. A decorative pin, shaped like a dagger.
5. Cf. Ariosto's Orlando Furioso (1516–1532), in which
Orlando's lost wits are sought on the moon. See also Paradise Lost 3.444ff.

And lovers' hearts with ends of riband bound;
The courtier's promises, and sick man's pray'rs,
120   The smiles of harlots, and the tears of heirs,
Cages for gnats, and chains to yoke a flea;
Dried butterflies, and tomes of casuistry.[6]
    But trust the Muse—she saw it upward rise,
Though marked by none but quick poetic eyes:
125   (So Rome's great founder to the heav'ns withdrew,
To Proculus alone confessed in view.[7])
A sudden star, it shot through liquid air,
And drew behind a radiant trail of hair.
Not Berenice's locks first rose so bright,[8]
130   The heav'ns bespangling with disheveled light.
The Sylphs behold it kindling as it flies,
And pleased pursue its progress through the skies.
    This the beau monde shall from the Mall[9] survey,
And hail with music its propitious ray.
135   This, the blest lover shall for Venus° take,   *the planet*
And send up vows from Rosamonda's Lake.[1]
This Partridge[2] soon shall view in cloudless skies,
When next he looks through Galileo's eyes;[3]
And hence th' egregious wizard shall foredoom
140   The fate of Louis, and the fall of Rome.
    Then cease, bright nymph! to mourn thy ravished hair
Which adds new glory to the shining sphere!
Not all the tresses that fair head can boast
Shall draw such envy as the lock you lost.
145   For, after all the murders of your eye,
When, after millions slain, yourself shall die;
When those fair suns[4] shall set, as set they must,
And all those tresses shall be laid in dust;
This lock, the Muse shall consecrate to fame,
150   And mid'st the stars inscribe Belinda's name!
1711–1717   1712; 1714; 1717

THE ILIAD   "In the beginning of my translating the *Iliad* I wished anybody would hang me, a hundred times," Pope confided to his friend Joseph Spence, "it sat so heavily on my mind at first that I often used to dream of it, and so do sometimes still." Pope spent nearly seven years (1713–1720) translating the *Iliad* and writing critical notes to accompany his text. His work was an outstanding commercial and literary success; for his labors Pope made about £5,000, more than a hundred times the annual earnings of a skilled craftsman or a shop owner in Pope's day. Samuel Johnson called Pope's *Iliad* "the noblest version [translation] of poetry which the world has ever seen"; Samuel Taylor Coleridge said Pope's poem was "an astonishing product of matchless talent and ingenuity."

6. Subtle reasoning (often used of arguments justifying immoral conduct).
7. When Romulus was killed mysteriously, Proculus soothed popular grief by asserting that he had been taken up to heaven.
8. The Egyptian queen Berenice made an offering of her hair after her husband returned victorious from the wars; when it disappeared from the temple, the court astronomer claimed it had been made into a new constel-

lation.
9. A fashionable walk in St. James's Park.
1. Where lovers met in St. James's Park.
2. John Partridge was a ridiculous star-gazer, who in his almanacs every year, never failed to predict the downfall of the Pope and the King of France, then at war with the English [Pope's note].
3. I.e., a telescope.
4. I.e., her eyes.

Pope's *Preface* to the translation is an important statement of his poetic values and his ideas on translation. A sample of the translation itself follows, taken from Book 12. In the passage, Sarpedon, king of the Lycians who were allied with the Trojans against the Greeks, exhorts his lieutenant Glaucus to fight bravely. This was the first passage of the *Iliad* that Pope published; it appeared in 1709 with the *Pastorals* as the *Episode of Sarpedon*. Eight years later, Pope's final addition to *The Rape of the Lock* (1717) was a parody of the warrior's famous speech, spoken by Clarissa at the beginning of Canto 5. Pope's own comment reveals his thoughts about Sarpedon's great exhortation: "In former times, kings were looked upon as the generals of armies, who to return the honors that were done to them, were obliged to expose themselves first in battle, and be an example to their soldiers. Upon this Sarpedon grounds his discourse, which is full of generosity and nobleness. We are, says he, honored like gods, and what can be more unjust than not to behave ourselves like men? He ought to be superior in virtue, who is superior in dignity. What strength is there and what greatness in that thought! It includes justice, gratitude, and magnanimity: justice, in that he scorns to enjoy what he does not merit; gratitude, because he would endeavor to recompense his obligations to his subjects; and magnanimity, because he despises death, and thinks of nothing but glory."

from The Iliad

from Preface

[ON TRANSLATION]

Having now spoken of the beauties and defects of the original, it remains to treat of the translation, with the same view to the chief characteristic. As far as that is seen in the main parts of the poem, such as the fable, manners, and sentiments, no translator can prejudice it but by willful omissions or contractions. As it also breaks out in every particular image, description, and simile, whoever lessens or too much softens those takes off from this chief character. It is the first grand duty of an interpreter to give his author entire and unmaimed; and for the rest, the diction and versification only are his proper province, since these must be his own, but the others he is to take as he finds them.

It should then be considered what methods may afford some equivalent in our language for the graces of these in the Greek. It is certain no literal translation can be just to an excellent original in a superior language, but it is a great mistake to imagine (as many have done) that a rash paraphrase can make amends for this general defect, which is no less in danger to lose the spirit of an Ancient, by deviating into the modern manners of expression. If there be sometimes a *darkness*, there is often a *light* in antiquity which nothing better preserves than a version almost literal. I know no liberties one ought to take, but those which are necessary for transfusing the spirit of the original, and supporting the poetical style of the translation; and I will venture to say, there have not been more men misled in former times by a servile dull adherence to the letter, than have been deluded in ours by a chimerical[1] insolent hope of raising and improving their author. It is not to be doubted that the *fire* of the poem is what a translator should principally regard, as it is most likely to expire in his managing; however, it is his safest way to be content with preserving this to his utmost in the whole, without endeavoring to be more than he finds his author is in any particular place. 'Tis a great secret in writing to know when to be plain, and when poetical and figurative, and it is what Homer will teach us if we will but follow

1. Fanciful.

modestly in his footsteps. Where his diction is bold and lofty, let us raise ours as high as we can; but where his is plain and humble, we ought not to be deterred from imitating him by the fear of incurring the censure of a mere English critic. Nothing that belongs to Homer seems to have been more commonly mistaken than the just pitch of his style: some of his translators having swelled into fustian[2] in a proud confidence of the sublime; others sunk into flatness in a cold and timorous notion of simplicity. Methinks I see these different followers of Homer, some sweating and straining after him by violent leaps and bounds (the certain signs of false mettle), others slowly and servilely creeping in his train, while the poet himself is all the time proceeding with an unaffected and equal[3] majesty before them. However, of the two extremes one could sooner pardon frenzy than frigidity: no author is to be envied for such commendations as he may gain by that character of style which his friends must agree together to call simplicity, and the rest of the world will call dullness. There is a graceful and dignified simplicity, as well as a bald and sordid one, which differ as much from each other as the air of a plain man from that of a sloven: 'tis one thing to be tricked up,[4] and another not to be dressed at all. Simplicity is the mean between ostentation and rusticity.

This pure and noble simplicity is nowhere in such perfection as in the Scripture and our author. One may affirm with all respect to the inspired writings, that the divine spirit made use of no other words but what were intelligible and common to men at that time, and in that part of the world; and as Homer is the author nearest to those, his style must of course bear a greater resemblance to the sacred books than that of any other writer. This consideration (together with what has been observed of the parity of some of his thoughts) may, methinks, induce a translator on the one hand to give in to several of those general phrases and manners of expression, which have attained a veneration even in our language from being used in the Old Testament, as on the other, to avoid those which have been appropriated to the divinity, and in a manner consigned to mystery and religion.

For a farther preservation of this air of simplicity, a particular care should be taken to express with all plainness those moral sentences and proverbial speeches which are so numerous in this poet. They have something venerable, and as I may say oracular, in that unadorned gravity and shortness with which they are delivered, a grace which would be utterly lost by endeavoring to give them what we call a more ingenious (that is a more modern) turn in the paraphrase.

Perhaps the mixture of some Graecisms and old words after the manner of Milton, if done without too much affectation, might not have an ill effect in a version of this particular work, which most of any other seems to require a venerable antique cast. But certainly the use of modern terms of war and government, such as platoon, campaign, junto, or the like (into which some of his translators have fallen) cannot be allowable; those only excepted, without which it is impossible to treat the subjects in any living language.

* * *

It only remains to speak of the versification. Homer (as has been said) is perpetually applying the sound to the sense, and varying it on every new subject. This is indeed one of the most exquisite beauties of poetry, and attainable by very few: I know only of Homer eminent for it in the Greek, and Virgil in Latin. I am sensible

2. Bombast; high-flown language.
3. Consistent.
4. Overdressed.

it is what may sometimes happen by chance, when a writer is warm, and fully possessed of his image: however it may be reasonably believed they designed this, in whose verse it so manifestly appears in a superior degree to all others. Few readers have the ear to be judges of it, but those who have will see I have endeavored at this beauty.

Upon the whole, I must confess myself utterly incapable of doing justice to Homer. I attempt him in no other hope but that which one may entertain without much vanity, of giving a more tolerable copy of him than any entire translation in verse has yet done.

* * *

1715   1715

from *Book 12*

[SARPEDON'S SPEECH]

Resolved alike, divine Sarpedon[1] glows
With gen'rous rage that drives him on the foes.
He views the tow'rs, and meditates° their fall,   plans
To sure destruction dooms th' aspiring° wall;   high
5   Then casting on his friend an ardent look,
Fir'd with the thirst of glory, thus he spoke.
"Why boast we, Glaucus! our extended reign,
Where Xanthus' streams[2] enrich the Lycian plain,
Our num'rous herds that range the fruitful field,
10   And hills where vines their purple harvest yield,
Our foaming bowls with purer nectar[3] crowned,
Our feasts enhanced with music's sprightly° sound?   lively
Why on those shores° are we with joy surveyed,°   of Greece / observed
Admired as heroes, and as gods obeyed?
15   Unless great acts superior merit prove,
And vindicate the bount'ous pow'rs above.[4]
'Tis ours, the dignity they give, to grace;
The first in valor, as the first in place.[5]
That when with wond'ring eyes our martial bands
20   Behold our deeds transcending our commands,[6]
Such, they may cry, deserve the sov'reign state,°   role
Whom those that envy, dare not imitate!
Could all our care elude the gloomy° grave,[7]   dark
Which claims no less the fearful than the brave,

---

1. Sarpedon's father was Zeus, the supreme Olympian deity; his mother was Laodemia, a mortal.
2. The Xanthus is the principal river flowing through Lycia, a mountainous country in southwestern Asia Minor.
3. Perhaps mead, which is made from fermented honey, but probably any drink.
4. I.e., the gods' blessings on us.
5. I.e., we must justify our position of authority over the people (which the gods have bestowed) through valor.
6. I.e., we set an example for our troops, rather than commanding from the rear.
7. There is not a more forcible argument than this, to

make all men condemn dangers, and seek glory by brave actions. Immortality with eternal youth is certainly preferable to glory purchased with the loss of life; but glory is certainly better than an ignominious life, which at last, though perhaps late, must end. It is ordained that all men shall die, nor can our escaping danger secure us immortality; it can only give us a longer continuance in disgrace, and even that continuance will be but short, though the infamy everlasting. This is incontestable, and whoever weighs his actions in these scales, can never hesitate in his choice; but what is most remarkable is that Homer does not put this in the mouth of an ordinary person, but ascribes it to the son of Jupiter [Pope's note].

25   For lust of fame I should not vainly dare
        In fighting fields, nor urge thy soul to war.
        But since, alas! ignoble age must come,
        Disease, and death's inexorable doom;°   *fate*
        The life which others pay, let us bestow,
30   And give to Fame what we to Nature owe;
        Brave though we fall, and honored if we live,
        Or° let us glory gain, or glory give!"   *either*
          He said;° his words the list'ning chief inspire   *spoke*
        With equal warmth, and rouse the warrior's fire;
35   The troops pursue their leaders with delight,
        Rush to the foe, and claim the promised fight.
c. 1707   1709

ELOISA TO ABELARD   Peter Abelard (1079–1142), a great French philosopher and theologian, was tutor to the young Heloise (Eloisa). They fell in love, had a son, and secretly married. When the affair became known, Heloise was forced to enter a convent and Abelard was castrated by a gang of thugs hired by Heloise's enraged uncle. Abelard became a Benedictine monk, founding the monastery of the Paraclete, or Holy Spirit. After many years of living respectable and successful lives devoted to God, the two former lovers exchanged a series of epistles in Latin. These austere letters were made more romantic and psychologically complex when they were loosely translated into French in the later seventeenth century. In 1713 Pope's friend John Hughes translated the silently "improved" French version into English; this became the source for Pope's poem, which he chose to conclude his 1717 *Works*. Modeled upon Ovid's *Heroides*, *Eloisa to Abelard* is a "heroic epistle", a dramatic expression of a lover's feelings in a verse letter addressed to an absent loved one. Alternately erotic and pious, gothic and tender, Pope's intensely passionate and penetratingly psychological portrait of Eloisa's conflicting feelings was one of his most widely admired works, particularly among eighteenth-century women readers.

Eloisa to Abelard
The Argument

Abelard and Eloisa flourished in the twelfth century; they were two of the most distinguished persons of their age in learning and beauty, but for nothing more famous than for their unfortunate passion. After a long course of calamities, they retired each to a several[1] convent, and consecrated the remainder of their days to religion. It was many years after this separation, that a letter of Abelard's to a friend which contained the history of his misfortune, fell into the hands of Eloisa. This awakening all her tenderness, occasioned those celebrated letters (out of which the following is partly extracted) which give so lively a picture of the struggles of grace and nature, virtue and passion.

        In these deep solitudes and awful° cells,   *awe-inspiring*
        Where heav'nly-pensive, contemplation dwells,
        And ever-musing melancholy reigns;
        What means this tumult in a vestal's[2] veins?
5   Why rove my thoughts beyond this last retreat?
        Why feels my heart its long-forgotten heat?

1. Different.
2. Virgin bound to the service of the Roman goddess Ves-   ta. As a nun Eloisa, like the vestals, was now set aside for service to the divine.

Yet, yet[3] I love!—From Abelard it came,
And Eloisa yet must kiss the name.
   Dear fatal name! rest ever unrevealed,
10   Nor pass these lips in holy silence sealed.
Hide it, my heart, within that close disguise,
Where, mixed with God's, his loved idea° lies.   *image*
Oh write it not, my hand—the name appears
Already written—wash it out, my tears!
15   In vain lost Eloisa weeps and prays,
Her heart still dictates, and her hand obeys.
   Relentless walls! whose darksome round contains
Repentant sighs, and voluntary pains;
Ye rugged rocks! which holy knees have worn;
20   Ye grots° and caverns shagged with horrid° thorn!   *grottos / bristling*
Shrines! where their vigils pale-eyed virgins keep,
And pitying saints, whose statues learn to weep![4]
Though cold like you, unmoved, and silent grown,
I have not yet forgot myself to stone.[5]
25   All is not Heav'n's while Abelard has part,
Still rebel nature holds out half my heart;
Nor pray'rs nor fast its stubborn pulse restrain,
Nor tears, for ages, taught to flow in vain.
   Soon as thy letters trembling I unclose,
30   That well-known name awakens all my woes.
Oh name forever sad! forever dear!
Still breathed in sighs, still ushered with a tear.
I tremble too where'er my own I find,
Some dire misfortune follows close behind.
35   Line after line my gushing eyes o'erflow,
Led through a sad variety of woe:
Now warm in love, now with'ring in thy bloom,
Lost in a convent's° solitary gloom!   *monastery's*
There stern religion quenched th' unwilling flame,
40   There died the best of passions, love and fame.
   Yet write, or write me all, that I may join
Griefs to thy griefs, and echo sighs to thine.
Nor foes nor fortune take this pow'r away.
And is my Abelard less kind than they?
45   Tears still are mine, and those I need not spare,
Love but demands what else were shed in pray'r;
No happier task these faded eyes pursue,
To read and weep is all they now can do.
   Then share thy pain, allow that sad relief;
50   Ah more than share it! give me all thy grief.
Heav'n first taught letters for some wretch's aid,
Some banished lover, or some captive maid;
They live, they speak, they breathe what love inspires,

---

3. In the sense of both "but" and "still."
4. Through condensation that ran down the statues.
5. This metaphor comes from Hughes's translation of the *Letters of Abelard and Heloise*: "O Vows! O Convent! I

have not lost my humanity under your inexorable discipline! You have not made me marble by changing my habit" (129). See also Milton, *Il Penseroso*, line 42, page 1816.

Warm from the soul, and faithful to its fires,
55   The virgin's wish without her fears impart,
Excuse[6] the blush, and pour out all the heart,
Speed the soft intercourse from soul to soul,
And waft a sigh from Indus[7] to the Pole.

    Thou know'st how guiltless first I met thy flame,
60   When love approached me under friendship's name;
My fancy formed thee of angelic kind,
Some emanation of th' all-beauteous Mind.°   God
Those smiling eyes, attemp'ring° ev'ry ray,   softening
Shone sweetly lambent° with celestial day: radiant
65   Guiltless I gazed; Heav'n listened while you sung;
And truths divine came mended from that tongue.[8]
From lips like those what precept failed to move?
Too soon they taught me 'twas no sin to love.
Back through the paths of pleasing sense I ran,
70   Nor wished an angel whom I loved a man.[9]
Dim and remote the joys of saints I see,
Nor envy them, that Heav'n I lose for thee.

    How oft, when pressed to marriage, have I said,
Curse on all laws but those which love has made!
75   Love, free as air, at sight of human ties
Spreads his light wings, and in a moment flies.
Let wealth, let honor, wait the wedded dame,
August her deed, and sacred be her fame;
Before true passion all those views remove,°   disperse
80   Fame, wealth, and honor! what are you to love?
The jealous god,° when we profane his fires,   Cupid
Those restless passions in revenge inspires;
And bids them make mistaken mortals groan,
Who seek in love for ought but love alone.
85   Should at my feet the world's great master fall,
Himself, his throne, his world, I'd scorn 'em all:
Not Caesar's empress would I deign to prove;
No, make me mistress to the man I love;
If there be yet another name more free,
90   More fond° than mistress, make me that to thee!   beloved
Oh happy state! when souls each other draw,
When love is liberty, and nature, law:
All then is full, possessing, and possessed,
No craving void left aching in the breast:
95   Ev'n thought meets thought ere from the lips it part,
And each warm wish springs mutual from the heart.
This sure is bliss (if bliss on earth there be)
And once the lot of Abelard and me.

    Alas how changed! what sudden horrors rise!
100   A naked lover bound and bleeding lies!

6. Release from the need for.
7. A southern constellation far distant from the northern
Polestar.
8. He was her preceptor in philosophy and divinity

[Pope's note].
9. Having thought you an angel, I now return to my
senses, and happily accept you as human.

Where, where was Eloise? her voice, her hand,
Her poniard, had opposed the dire command.
Barbarian stay! that bloody stroke restrain;
The crime was common, common be the pain.[1]
105   I can no more; by shame, by rage suppressed,
Let tears and burning blushes speak the rest.
    Canst thou forget that sad, that solemn day,
When victims at yon altar's foot we lay?
Canst thou forget what tears that moment fell,
110   When, warm in youth, I bade the world farewell?
As with cold lips I kissed the sacred veil,
The shrines all trembled, and the lamps grew pale:
Heav'n scarce believed the conquest it surveyed,
And saints with wonder heard the vows I made.
115   Yet then, to those dread altars as I drew,
Not on the Cross my eyes were fixed, but you;
Not grace, or zeal, love only was my call,
And if I lose thy love, I lose my all.
Come! with thy looks, thy words, relieve my woe;
120   Those still at least are left thee to bestow.
Still on that breast enamored let me lie,
Still drink delicious poison from thy eye,
Pant on thy lip, and to thy heart be pressed;
Give all thou canst—and let me dream the rest.
125   Ah no! instruct me other joys to prize,
With other beauties charm my partial° eyes,   *fondly biased*
Full in my view set all the bright abode,
And make my soul quit Abelard for God.
    Ah think at least thy flock deserves thy care,
130   Plants of thy hand, and children of thy pray'r.
From the false world in early youth they fled,
By thee to mountains, wilds, and deserts led.
You raised these hallowed walls;[2] the desert smiled,
And paradise was opened in the wild.
135   No weeping orphan saw his father's stores
Our shrines irradiate, or emblaze the floors;[3]
No silver saints, by dying misers giv'n,
Here bribed the rage of ill-requited Heav'n:
But such plain roofs as piety could raise,
140   And only vocal with the Maker's[4] praise.
In these lone walls (their day's eternal bound)
These moss-grown domes° with spiry turrets crowned,   *buildings*
Where awful arches make a noon-day night,
And the dim windows shed a solemn light;
145   Thy eyes diffused a reconciling ray,
And gleams of glory brightened all the day.
But now no face divine contentment wears,

---

1. The crime was shared, so also should have been the penalty.
2. He founded the monastery [Pope's note].
3. "Irradiate" and "emblaze," meaning "adorn gloriously,"

both come from Milton.
4. The satirical tone of the previous lines prompts us to ask whether the "Maker" is God or Abelard.

'Tis all blank sadness, or continual tears.
See how the force of others' pray'rs I try
150   (Oh pious fraud of am'rous charity!)
But why should I on others' pray'rs depend?
Come thou, my father, brother,[5] husband, friend!
Ah let thy handmaid, sister, daughter, move,
And, all those tender names in one, thy love!
155   The darksome pines that o'er yon rocks reclined
Wave high, and murmur to the hollow wind,
The wandering streams that shine between the hills,
The grots that echo to the tinkling rills,
The dying gales that pant upon the trees,
160   The lakes that quiver to the curling breeze;
No more these scenes my meditation aid,
Or lull to rest the visionary maid:[6]
But o'er the twilight groves, and dusky caves,
Long-sounding isles, and intermingled graves,
165   Black Melancholy sits, and round her throws
A death-like silence, and a dread repose:
Her gloomy presence saddens all the scene,
Shades ev'ry flow'r, and darkens ev'ry green,
Deepens the murmur of the falling floods,
170   And breathes a browner horror on the woods.
        Yet here forever, ever must I stay;
Sad proof how well a lover can obey!
Death, only death, can break the lasting chain;
And here ev'n then, shall my cold dust remain,
175   Here all its frailties, all its flames resign,
And wait, till 'tis no sin to mix with thine.
        Ah wretch! believed the spouse of God in vain,
Confessed within the slave of love and man.
Assist me Heav'n! but whence arose that pray'r?
180   Sprung it from piety, or from despair?
Ev'n here, where frozen chastity retires,
Love finds an altar for forbidden fires.
I ought to grieve, but cannot what I ought;
I mourn the lover, not lament the fault;
185   I view my crime, but kindle at the view,
Repent old pleasures, and solicit new:
Now turned to Heav'n, I weep my past offense,
Now think of thee, and curse my innocence.[7]
Of all affliction taught a lover yet,
190   'Tis sure the hardest science° to forget!   knowledge
How shall I lose the sin, yet keep the sense,
And love th' offender, yet detest th' offense?
How the dear object from the crime remove,

5. "Father" and "brother" in the ecclesiastical, as well as emotional, sense. This also applies for "handmaid," "sister," and "daughter" in the following line.
6. One prone to visions.
7. Cf. Letters of Abelard and Heloise: "Among those who are wedded to God I serve a man. . . . I am here, I confess, a sinner, but one who far from weeping for her sins, weeps only for her lover. . . . Every object brings to my mind what I ought to forget. . . . Even into the holy places before the altar I carry with me the memory of our guilty loves" (trans. Hughes, 120–24).

Or how distinguish penitence from love?
195   Unequal task! a passion to resign,
For hearts so touched, so pierced, so lost as mine.
Ere such a soul regains its peaceful state,
How often must it love, how often hate!
How often, hope, despair, resent, regret,
200   Conceal, disdain—do all things but forget.
But let Heav'n seize it, all at once 'tis fir'd,
Not° touched, but rapt, not wakened, but inspired!   *not only*
Oh come! oh teach me nature to subdue,
Renounce my love, my life, myself—and you.
205   Fill my fond heart with God alone, for he
Alone can rival, can succeed to thee.
      How happy is the blameless vestal's lot!
The world forgetting, by the world forgot.
Eternal sunshine of the spotless mind!
210   Each pray'r accepted, and each wish resigned;
Labor and rest, that equal periods keep;
"Obedient slumbers that can wake and weep";[8]
Desires composed, affections ever ev'n,
Tears that delight, and sighs that waft to Heav'n.
215   Grace shines around her with serenest beams,
And whisp'ring angels prompt her golden dreams.
For her th' unfading rose of Eden blooms,
And wings of seraphs shed divine perfumes;
For her the Spouse° prepares the bridal ring,   *Christ*
220   For her white virgins hymenaeals° sing;   *wedding songs*
To sounds of heav'nly harps, she dies away,
And melts in visions of eternal day.
      Far other dreams my erring soul employ,
Far other raptures, of unholy joy:
225   When at the close of each sad, sorrowing day,
Fancy restores what vengeance snatched away,
Then conscience sleeps, and leaving nature free,
All my loose soul unbounded springs to thee.
O cursed, dear horrors of all-conscious° night!   *all-knowing*
230   How glowing guilt exalts the keen delight!
Provoking demons all restraint remove,
And stir within me ev'ry source of love.
I hear thee, view thee, gaze o'er all thy charms,
And round thy phantom glue my clasping arms.
235   I wake—no more I hear, no more I view,
The phantom flies me, as unkind as you,
I call aloud; it hears not what I say;
I stretch my empty arms; it glides away:
To dream once more I close my willing eyes;
240   Ye soft illusions, dear deceits, arise!
Alas no more!—methinks we wandering go
Through dreary wastes, and weep each other's woe;

8. Line 16 from *Description of a Religious House*, by Richard Crashaw (1612–1649).

Where round some mold'ring tow'r pale ivy creeps,
And low-browed rocks hang nodding o'er the deeps.
245   Sudden you mount! you beckon from the skies;
Clouds interpose, waves roar, and winds arise.
I shriek, start up, the same sad prospect find,
And wake to all the griefs I left behind.[9]
    For thee the fates, severely kind, ordain
250   A cool suspense from pleasure and from pain;
Thy life a long, dead calm of fixed repose;
No pulse that riots, and no blood that glows.
Still as the sea, ere winds were taught to blow,
Or moving spirit bade the waters flow;
255   Soft as the slumbers of a saint forgiv'n,
And mild as opening gleams of promised Heav'n.
    Come Abelard! for what hast thou to dread?
The torch of Venus burns not for the dead;
Nature stands checked; religion disapproves;
260   Ev'n thou art cold—yet Eloisa loves.
Ah hopeless, lasting flames! like those that burn
To light the dead, and warm th' unfruitful urn.[1]
    What scenes appear where'er I turn my view!
The dear ideas, where I fly, pursue,
265   Rise in the grove, before the altar rise,
Stain all my soul, and wanton in my eyes!
I waste the matin[2] lamp in sighs for thee,
Thy image steals between my God and me,
Thy voice I seem in ev'ry hymn to hear,
270   With ev'ry bead I drop too soft a tear.[3]
When from the censer clouds of fragrance roll,
And swelling organs lift the rising soul;
One thought of thee puts all the pomp to flight,
Priests, tapers, temples, swim before my sight:
275   In seas of flame my plunging soul is drowned,
While altars blaze, and angels tremble round.
    While prostrate here in humble grief I lie,
Kind, virtuous drops just gath'ring in my eye,
While praying, trembling, in the dust I roll,
280   And dawning grace is opening on my soul:
Come, thou dar'st, all charming as thou art!
Oppose thyself to Heav'n; dispute° my heart;   compete for
Come, with one glance of those deluding eyes,
Blot out each bright idea of the skies.
285   Take back that grace, those sorrows, and those tears,
Take back my fruitless penitence and pray'rs,
Snatch me, just mounting, from the blest abode,
Assist the fiends and tear me from my God!
    No, fly me, fly me! far as Pole from Pole;
290   Rise Alps between us! and whole oceans roll!

---

9. Cf. Pope's comic *Epistle to Miss Blount*.
1. The Romans attempted to supply tombs with inextin-
guishable fires.

2. Morning; Matins are the psalms sung at dawn.
3. Tears of love, not repentance.

Ah come not, write not, think not once of me,
Nor share one pang of all I felt for thee.
Thy oaths I quit,° thy memory resign,   *absolve*
Forget, renounce me, hate whate'er was mine.
295 Fair eyes, and tempting looks (which yet I view!)
Long loved, adored ideas! all adieu!
O grace serene! oh virtue heav'nly fair!
Divine oblivion of low-thoughted care!
Fresh blooming hope, gay daughter of the sky!
300 And faith, our early immortality!⁴
Enter each mild, each amicable guest;
Receive, and wrap me in eternal rest!
      See in her cell sad Eloisa spread,
Propped on some tomb, a neighbor of the dead!
305 In each low wind methinks a spirit calls,
And more than echoes talk along the walls.
Here, as I watched the dying lamps around,
From yonder shrine I heard a hollow sound.
"Come, sister come!" (it said, or seemed to say)
310 "Thy place is here, sad sister come away!
Once like thy self, I trembled, wept, and prayed,
Love's victim then, though now a sainted maid:
But all is calm in this eternal sleep;
Here grief forgets to groan, and love to weep,
315 Ev'n superstition loses ev'ry fear:
For God, not man, absolves our frailties here."
      I come, I come! prepare your roseate bow'rs,
Celestial palms, and ever-blooming flow'rs.
Thither, where sinners may have rest, I go,
320 Where flames refined in breasts seraphic glow.
Thou, Abelard! the last sad office pay,
And smooth my passage to the realms of day:
See my lips tremble, and my eyeballs roll,
Suck my last breath, and catch my flying soul!
325 Ah no—in sacred vestments may'st thou stand,
The hallowed taper trembling in thy hand,
Present the Cross before my lifted eye,
Teach me at once, and learn of° me to die.   *from*
Ah then, thy once-loved Eloisa see!
330 It will be then no crime to gaze on me.
See from my cheek the transient roses fly!
See the last sparkle languish in my eye!
Till ev'ry motion, pulse, and breath, be o'er;
And ev'n my Abelard be loved no more.
335 O death all-eloquent! you only prove
What dust we dote on, when 'tis man we love.
      Then too, when fate shall thy fair frame destroy,
(That cause of all my guilt, and all my joy)
In trance ecstatic may thy pangs be drowned,

4. Faith seen as a foretaste of immortality.

340   Bright clouds descend, and angels watch thee round,
      From opening skies may streaming glories shine,
      And saints embrace thee with a love like mine.
          May one kind grave unite each hapless name,[5]
      And graft my love immortal on thy fame.
345   Then, ages hence, when all my woes are o'er,
      When this rebellious heart shall beat no more;
      If ever chance two wandering lovers brings
      To Paraclete's white walls, and silver springs,
      O'er the pale marble shall they join their heads,
350   And drink the falling tears each other sheds,
      Then sadly say, with mutual pity moved,
      Oh may we never love as these have loved!
      From the full choir when loud Hosanna's rise,
      And swell the pomp of dreadful sacrifice,[6]
355   Amid that scene, if some relenting eye
      Glance on the stone where our cold relics lie,
      Devotion's self shall steal a thought from Heav'n,
      One human tear shall drop, and be forgiv'n.
      And sure if fate some future bard[7] shall join
360   In sad similitude of griefs to mine,
      Condemned whole years in absence to deplore,
      And image charms he must behold no more,
      Such if there be, who loves so long, so well;
      Let him our sad, our tender story tell;
365   The well-sung woes will soothe my pensive ghost;
      He best can paint 'em, who shall feel 'em most.

c. 1716   1717

EPISTLE TO BURLINGTON   For years Pope planned to write a magnum opus, a "system of ethics in the Horatian way." Though this ambitious project was never completed, some of its parts were written, including a set of four verse letters that were intended to conclude the work. Pope himself called the poems *Epistles to Several Persons*; a later editor dubbed them *Moral Essays*. Each work is a familiar letter in verse addressed to someone he knew well and admired. Richard Boyle, third Earl of Burlington (1695–1753), was a connoisseur and patron of the arts, and a capable architect who became a highly influential arbiter of polite taste in English building and landscape design. When first published in 1731, the poem declared on its title page that it was "occasioned by [Burlington's] publishing Palladio's designs of the baths, arches, theaters etc. of Ancient Rome." Burlington was partly responsible for leading an English revival of architecture modeled upon the designs of Andrea Palladio (1508–1580), and his house at Chiswick was a masterful example of the Palladian style. Pope contrasts Burlington's wise and discerning stewardship with the foolish prodigality of "Lord Timon," an emblem of bad taste and extravagant wastefulness. Though there has been much debate about the identity of Lord Timon and the real-life model for his gaudy estate, Timon (and his infamous villa) are most probably composite sketches of, among others, the Duke of Chandos (at Cannons), the Duke of Devonshire (at Chatsworth), and Robert Walpole (at Houghton)—all known for lavish displays of wealth more redolent of vulgar ostentation than aesthetic acumen.

---

5. Abelard and Eloisa were interred in the same grave, or in monuments adjoining, in the Monastery of the Paraclete [Pope's note].
6. The Mass, in which Christ's saving sacrifice is ritually reenacted.
7. Pope himself; he probably refers to Lady Mary Wortley Montagu, then traveling in the Middle East, with whom he later quarreled and became estranged.

Epistle 4. To Richard Boyle, Earl of Burlington

Argument

Of the use of riches. The vanity of expense in people of wealth and quality. The abuse of the word "taste," verse 13. That the first principle and foundation in this as in everything else is good sense, v. 40. The chief proof of it is to follow Nature, even in works of mere luxury and elegance. Instanced in architecture and gardening, where all must be adapted to the genius[1] and use of the place, and the beauties not forced into it, but resulting from it, v. 50. How men are disappointed in their most expensive undertakings, for want of this true foundation, without which nothing can please long, if at all, and the best examples and rules will but be perverted into something burdensome or ridiculous, v. 65, etc. to 92. A description of the false taste of magnificence, the first grand error of which is to imagine that greatness consists in the *size* and *dimension*,[2] instead of the *proportion* and *harmony* of the whole, v. 97, and the second, either in joining together parts incoherent, or too minutely resembling, or in the repetition of the same too frequently, v. 105, etc. A word or two of false taste in books, in music, in painting, even in preaching and prayer, and lastly in entertainments, v. 133, etc. Yet PROVIDENCE is justified in giving wealth to be squandered in this manner, since it is dispersed to the poor and laborious part of mankind, v. 169. [Recurring to what is laid down in the first book, Ep. 2[3] and in the Epistle preceding this, v. 159, etc.[4]] What are the proper objects of magnificence, and a proper field for the expense[5] of great men, v. 177, etc., and finally, the great and public works which become a prince, v. 191, to the end.

'Tis strange, the miser should his cares employ,
To gain those riches he can ne'er enjoy:
Is it less strange, the prodigal should waste
His wealth, to purchase what he ne'er can taste?
5   Not for himself he sees, or hears, or eats;
Artists must choose his pictures, music, meats:
He buys for Topham[6] drawings and designs,
For Pembroke[7] statues, dirty gods,[8] and coins;
Rare monkish manuscripts for Hearne[9] alone,
10   And books for Mead, and butterflies for Sloane.[1]
Think we all these are for himself? no more
Than his fine wife, alas! or finer whore.
    For what has Virro[2] painted, built, and planted?
Only to show, how many tastes he wanted.
15   What brought Sir Visto's[3] ill got wealth to waste?
Some demon whispered, "Visto! have a taste."

1. Character.
2. Extent.
3. Epistle 2 of Pope's *Essay on Man*.
4. Epistle 3, to Allen Lord Bathurst (1685–1775), *Of the Use of Riches*. Epistle 4 to Burlington was also sometimes given this subtitle.
5. Expenditure.
6. Richard Topham (d. 1735), who was a "gentleman famous for a judicious collection of drawings" [Pope's note].
7. Thomas Herbert, eighth Earl of Pembroke (1656–1733).

8. Renaissance pseudo-antiquities.
9. Thomas Hearne (1678–1735), eminent medievalist.
1. Richard Mead (1673–1754) and Sir Hans Sloane (1660–1753), both eminent physicians; the former had a library of around 30,000 books, while the latter had "the finest collection in Europe of natural curiosities" [Pope's note].
2. The wealthy but despicable patron in Juvenal's Fifth Satire.
3. Vista: long, narrow view between rows of trees.

Heav'n visits with a taste the wealthy fool,
And needs no rod but Ripley with a rule.⁴
See! sportive fate, to punish awkward pride,
20   Bids Bubo⁵ build, and sends him such a guide:
A standing sermon,⁶ at each year's expense,
That never coxcomb⁷ reached magnificence!
     You⁸ show us Rome was glorious, not profuse,
And pompous buildings once were things of use.
25   Yet shall (my Lord) your just, your noble rules
Fill half the land with imitating fools;
Who random drawings from your sheets shall take,
And of one beauty many blunders make;
Load some vain church with old theatric state,⁹
30   Turn arcs of triumph to a garden gate;
Reverse your ornaments, and hang them all
On some patched dog hole eked° with ends of wall,   added to
Then clap four slices of pilaster¹ on't,
That, laced with bits of rustic,² makes a front.
35   Or call the winds through long arcades to roar,
Proud to catch cold at a venetian door,³
Conscious they act a true Palladian part,
And if they starve,⁴ they starve by rules of art.
     Oft have you hinted to your brother peer,
40   A certain truth, which many buy too dear:
Something there is more needful than expense,
And something previous ev'n to taste—'tis sense:
Good sense, which only is the gift of Heav'n,
And though no science, fairly worth the sev'n:⁵
45   A light, which in yourself you must perceive;
Jones and Le Nôtre⁶ have it not to give.
     To build, to plant, whatever you intend,
To rear the column, or the arch to bend,
To swell the terrace, or to sink the grot;⁷
50   In all, let Nature never be forgot.
But treat the goddess like a modest fair,
Nor° overdress, nor leave her wholly bare;   neither
Let not each beauty ev'rywhere be spied,
Where half the skill is decently° to hide.   suitably
55   He gains all points, who pleasingly confounds,

---

4. Thomas Ripley (d. 1758), "a carpenter employed by a First Minister [Robert Walpole], who raised him into an architect without any genius in the art" [Pope's note]; he worked on Walpole's hall at Houghton. His carpenter's "rule," or ruler, is also a principle which, if misapplied, would become a rod for the foolish Visto's back.

5. George Bubb Dodington (1691–1762); his mansion at Eastbury, Dorset, designed by Sir John Vanbrugh (whose work Pope disliked), cost £140,000 to complete. "Bubo" is Latin for "owl."

6. The building silently instructs the viewer in gaudy taste.

7. Conceited fool.

8. Burlington, then publishing Palladio's *Antiquities of Rome*, and *The Designs of Inigo Jones*.

9. Design details from classical Roman amphitheaters.

1. Column joined to a wall.

2. A roughened, stonelike surface. The "front" is the entrance to the building.

3. The key unit of Palladio's design: a door with an arched top, framed by two smaller rectangular openings.

4. Because of the cost of the building and the impractical way in which it is laid out.

5. The seven fields of knowledge since medieval times were grammar, rhetoric, logic (the Trivium), arithmetic, geometry, astronomy, and music (the Quadrivium).

6. Inigo Jones (1573–1652), the architect; André Le Nôtre (1613–1700), great French garden designer.

7. Grotto: an artificial cavern.

Surprises, varies, and conceals the bounds.
   Consult the genius of the place[8] in all;
That tells the waters or° to rise, or fall,   *either*
Or helps th' ambitious hill the heav'n to scale,
60   Or scoops in circling theaters° the vale,   *amphitheaters*
Calls in the country, catches opening glades,
Joins willing woods, and varies shades from shades,
Now breaks or now directs, th' intending lines;[9]
Paints as you plant, and, as you work, designs.
65   Still follow sense, of ev'ry art the soul,
Parts answ'ring parts shall slide into a whole,
Spontaneous beauties all around advance,
Start ev'n from difficulty, strike from chance;
Nature shall join you, Time shall make it grow
70   A Work to wonder at—perhaps a Stowe.[1]
      Without it, proud Versailles![2] thy glory falls;
And Nero's terraces desert their walls:[3]
The vast parterres° a thousand hands shall make,   *terraces*
Lo! COBHAM comes, and floats° them with a lake: *floods*
75   Or cut wide views through mountains to the plain,
You'll wish your hill or sheltered seat again.
Ev'n in an ornament its place remark,°   *consider*
Nor in an Hermitage set Dr. Clarke.[4]
      Behold Villario's ten years' toil complete;
80   His quincunx darkens, his espaliers meet,[5]
The wood supports the plain, the parts unite,
And strength of shade contends with strength of light;
A waving glow his bloomy beds display,
Blushing in bright diversities of day,
85   With silver-quiv'ring rills meandered o'er—
Enjoy them, you! Villario can no more;
Tir'd of the scene parterres and fountains yield,
He finds at last he better likes a field.
      Through his young woods how pleased Sabinus strayed,
90   Or sat delighted in the thick'ning shade
With annual joy the red'ning shoots to greet,
Or see the stretching branches long to meet!
His Son's fine taste an op'ner vista loves,
Foe to the dryads° of his father's groves,   *wood nymphs*
95   One boundless green, or flourished carpet views,[6]
With all the mournful family of yews;[7]
The thriving plants ignoble broomsticks made,

8. Both the classical guardian spirit and the character of the particular setting.
9. Lines that direct the viewer's eye.
1. The seat and gardens of Richard Temple, Viscount Cobham (1675–1749), highly praised in its day.
2. Louis XIV's palace, which had the most celebrated gardens in Europe until the advent of landscape gardening.
3. The Golden House of Nero, in Rome.
4. Samuel Clarke (1675–1729) was a distinguished philosopher and theologian. Queen Caroline's ornamental and frivolous "hermitage" in Richmond Park con-

tained a bust of Clarke, among others.
5. Quincunx: group of five trees; espaliers: trees trained on latticework, against walls.
6. The two extremes in parterres, which are equally faulty [Pope's note], the "boundless green" being a virtual field, while the "flourished carpet" is overladen with ornamental flowerbeds.
7. Trees usually planted in cemeteries; Pope's objection is that these evergreens are favored to the exclusion of "the nobler forest trees," now used for brooms.

Now sweep those alleys they were born to shade.
   At Timon's villa let us pass a day,
100   Where all cry out, "What sums are thrown away!"
So proud, so grand, of that stupendous air,
Soft and agreeable come never there.
Greatness, with Timon, dwells in such a draught
As brings all Brobdignag[8] before your thought.
105   To compass this, his building is a town,
His pond an ocean, his parterre a down:[9]
Who but must laugh, the master when he sees,
A puny insect, shiv'ring at a breeze!
Lo, what huge heaps of littleness around!
110   The whole, a labored quarry above ground.
Two cupids squirt before: a lake behind
Improves the keenness of the northern wind.[1]
His gardens next your admiration call,
On ev'ry side you look, behold the wall!
115   No pleasing intricacies intervene,
No artful wildness to perplex the scene;
Grove nods at grove, each alley has a brother,
And half the platform just reflects the other.
The suff'ring eye inverted Nature sees,
120   Trees cut to statues,[2] statues thick as trees,
With here a fountain, never to be played,
And there a summerhouse, that knows no shade;
Here Amphitrite[3] sails through myrtle[4] bow'rs;
There gladiators fight, or die, in flow'rs;
125   Unwatered see the drooping sea-horse mourn,
And swallows roost in Nilus' dusty urn.[5]
   My Lord advances with majestic mien,
Smit° with the mighty pleasure, to be seen: *struck*
But soft—by regular approach—not yet—
130   First through the length of yon hot terrace sweat,
And when up ten steep slopes you've dragged your thighs,
Just at his study door he'll bless your eyes.
   His study! with what authors is it stored?
In books, not authors, curious is my Lord;[6]
135   To all their dated backs[7] he turns you round,
These Aldus printed, those Du Suëil has bound.[8]
Lo some are vellum,° and the rest as good   *parchment*
For all his Lordship knows, but they are wood.
For Locke or Milton 'tis in vain to look,
140   These shelves admit not any modern book.

---

8. The land of giants in Swift's *Gulliver's Travels*, filled with items too large to be used by normal humans.
9. Open uplands of southern England.
1. I.e., the landscaping has worsened, rather than mitigated, natural problems.
2. Cut into ornamental shapes.
3. A sea nymph, Poseidon's wife.
4. Myrtle was associated with Venus, goddess of love.
5. The river god's urn should obviously be pouring water.

6. I.e., he is fussy about having books to decorate his shelves but does not care what the books contain.
7. Many delight chiefly in the elegance of the print or the binding [Pope's note]: some collected rare editions with "dated backs" stamped in gold, others, books in languages they could not read, while some simply painted books onto the upper shelves.
8. Aldus Manutius (1450–1515), Venetian printer; Augustin Desueil (1673–1746), Parisian bookbinder.

And now the chapel's silver bell you hear,
That summons you to all the pride of pray'r:
Light quirks of music, broken and uneven,
Make the soul dance upon a jig to Heaven.
145   On painted ceilings you devoutly stare,
Where sprawl the saints of Verrio or Laguerre,[9]
On gilded clouds in fair expansion lie,
And bring all paradise before your eye.
To rest, the cushion and soft dean invite,
150   Who never mentions Hell to ears polite.[1]
But hark! the chiming clocks to dinner call;
A hundred footsteps scrape the marble hall:
The rich buffet well-colored serpents grace,
And gaping Tritons[2] spew to wash your face.[3]
155   Is this a dinner? this a genial° room?   °welcoming
No, 'tis a temple, and a hecatomb.°   °ritual sacrifice
A solemn sacrifice, performed in state,
You drink by measure, and to minutes eat.
So quick retires each flying course, you'd swear
160   Sancho's dread doctor and his wand were there.[4]
Between each act the trembling salvers ring,
From soup to sweet-wine, and God bless the King.[5]
In plenty starving, tantalized in state,
And complaisantly helped to all I hate,
165   Treated, caressed, and tir'd, I take my leave,
Sick of his civil pride from morn to eve;
I curse such lavish cost, and little skill,
And swear no day was ever passed so ill.
Yet hence the poor are clothed, the hungry fed;
170   Health to himself, and to his infants bread
The lab'rer bears: what his hard heart denies,
His charitable vanity supplies.
Another age shall see the golden ear
Imbrown the slope, and nod on the parterre,
175   Deep harvests bury all his pride has planned,
And laughing Ceres[6] reassume the land.
Who then shall grace, or who improve the soil?
Who plants like BATHURST,[7] or who builds like BOYLE.[8]
'Tis use alone that sanctifies expense,
180   And splendor borrows all her rays from sense.
His Father's acres who enjoys in peace,

---

9. Antonio Verrio (1639–1707) and Louis Laguerre (1663–1721) had painted many ceilings in castles and stately homes.
1. This is a fact: a reverend Dean preaching at Court, threatened the sinner with punishment in "a place he thought it not decent to name in so polite an assembly" [Pope's note].
2. Half human, half fish.
3. Taxes the incongruity of ornaments . . . where an open mouth ejects the water into a fountain, or where shocking images of serpents, etc. are introduced into grottos or

buffets [Pope's note].
4. In Cervante's Don Quixote Vol. 2, bk. 3, ch. 15, a doctor whisks food away before Sancho can eat it. The similarity to pantomime's conjuring tricks is reinforced by the equation of courses with "acts" in line 161.
5. Soup begins the meal, port wine ends it, with the traditional toast to the king.
6. Roman goddess of agriculture.
7. Allen, Lord Bathurst, to whom Epistle 3, Of the Use of Riches, is addressed.
8. Richard Boyle, Lord Burlington.

Or makes his neighbors glad, if he increase;
Whose cheerful tenants bless their yearly toil,
Yet to their Lord owe more than to the soil;
185   Whose ample lawns are not ashamed to feed
The milky heifer and deserving steed;
Whose rising forests, not for pride or show,
But future buildings, future navies grow:
Let his plantations stretch from down to down,
190   First shade a country, and then raise a town.
        You too proceed! make falling arts your care,
Erect new wonders, and the old repair,
Jones and Palladio to themselves restore,
And be whate'er Vitruvius⁹ was before:
195   Till kings call forth th' ideas of your mind,
Proud to accomplish what such hands designed,
Bid harbors open, public ways extend,
Bid temples,¹ worthier of the God, ascend;
Bid the broad arch the dang'rous flood contain,
200   The mole projected break the roaring main;²
Back to his bounds their subject sea command,
And roll obedient rivers through the land;
These honors, peace to happy Britain brings,
These are imperial works, and worthy kings.
1730–1731   1731

from An Essay on Man

*In Four Epistles to Henry St. John, Lord Bolingbroke*¹
Epistle 1

TO THE READER

As the epistolary way of writing hath prevailed much of late, we have ventured to publish this piece composed some time since, and whose author chose this manner, notwithstanding his subject was high and of dignity, because of its being mixed with argument which of its nature approacheth to prose. This,² which we first give the reader, treats of the Nature and State of MAN, with respect to the UNIVERSAL SYSTEM;³ the rest will treat of him with respect to his OWN SYSTEM, as an individual, and as a member of society, under one or other of which heads all ethics are included.

---

9. Marcus Vitruvius Pollio (1st century B.C.), whose book on architecture was highly influential.
1. This poem was published in the year 1732, when some of the new-built churches, by the Act of Queen Anne, were ready to fall, being founded in boggy land . . . others were vilely executed [i.e., built; Pope's note].
2. Burlington eventually helped oversee the building of Westminster Bridge over the Thames, the design of which had originally been left to "the carpenter [Ripley] who would have made it a wooden one" [Pope's note].
1. "I believe," wrote Pope to his friend John Caryll, "that there is not in the whole course of the Scripture any precept so often and so strongly inculcated, as the trust and eternal dependence we ought to repose in that Supreme Being who is our constant preserver and benefactor."

This is the theme of Pope's didactic and exhortatory *Essay on Man*, whose four epistles were published anonymously over eleven months in 1733–1734. For Pope, "to reason right is to submit" (line 164), not least because humankind occupies a middle ground—between angels and beasts—in a divinely ordered universe. Pope had intended the *Essay on Man* and the four *Moral Essays* (1731–1735) to be the first and last parts of a great poetic sequence on the nature of humankind, though he never completed the project. The *Essay* is addressed to Henry St. John, first Viscount Bolingbroke (1678–1751), a leading Tory statesman and political writer whom Pope described as "my guide, philosopher, and friend."
2. I.e., the first Epistle.
3. I.e., within the cosmic order, ordained by God.

As he imitates no man, so he would be thought to vie with no man in these Epistles, particularly with the noted author of two lately published;[4] but this he may most surely say: that the matter of them is such as is of importance to all in general, and of offense to none in particular.

THE DESIGN

Having proposed to write some pieces on human life and manners, such as (to use my lord Bacon's expression) "come home to men's business and bosoms,"[5] I thought it more satisfactory to begin with considering Man in the abstract, his Nature and his State, since, to prove any moral duty, to enforce any moral precept, or to examine the perfection or imperfection of any creature whatsoever, it is necessary first to know what condition and relation it is placed in, and what is the proper end and purpose of its being.

The science[6] of human nature is, like all other sciences, reduced to a few clear points: there are not many *certain truths* in this world. It is therefore in the anatomy of the mind as in that of the body: more good will accrue to mankind by attending to the large, open, and perceptible parts, than by studying too much such finer nerves and vessels, the conformations and uses of which will forever escape our observation. The disputes are all upon these last, and, I will venture to say, they have less sharpened the wits than the hearts of men against each other, and have diminished the practice more than advanced the theory of morality. If I could flatter myself that this Essay has any merit, it is in steering betwixt the extremes of doctrines seemingly opposite, in passing over terms utterly unintelligible, and in forming a temperate yet not inconsistent, and a short yet not imperfect system of ethics.

This I might have done in prose, but I chose verse, and even rhyme, for two reasons. The one will appear obvious: that principles, maxims, or precepts so written, both strike the reader more strongly at first, and are more easily retained by him afterwards. The other may seem odd, but is true: I found I could express them more shortly this way than in prose itself; and nothing is more certain, than that much of the force as well as grace of arguments or instructions depends on their conciseness. I was unable to treat this part of my subject more in detail without becoming dry and tedious, or more poetically, without sacrificing perspicuity to ornament, without wandering from the precision, or breaking the chain of reasoning. If any man can unite all these without diminution of any of them, I freely confess he will compass a thing above my capacity.

What is now published, is only to be considered as a general map of MAN, marking out no more than the greater parts, their extent, their limits, and their connection, but leaving the particular to be more fully delineated in the charts which are to follow. Consequently, these Epistles in their progress (if I have health and leisure to make any progress) will be less dry, and more susceptible of poetical ornament. I am here only opening the fountains, and clearing the passage. To deduce the rivers, to follow them in their course, and to observe their effects, may be a task more agreeable.

4. I.e., Pope himself, whose *Epistle to Bathurst* (1733) and the first *Imitation of Horace* (1733) had recently been published. The *Essay on Man* was published anonymously; Pope uses his little address to the reader both to advertise his own work and to confuse his enemies about the identity of the poem's author.
5. From Bacon's Dedicatory Epistle in the collected edition of the *Essays* (1625).
6. Knowledge.

ARGUMENT

Of the Nature and State of Man, with respect to the UNIVERSE.

Of Man in the abstract.—I. That we can judge only with regard to our own system, being ignorant of the relations of systems and things, verses 17, etc. II. That Man is not to be deemed imperfect, but a being suited to his place and rank in the creation, agreeable to the general order of things, and conformable to ends and relations to him unknown, ver. 35, etc. III. That it is partly upon his ignorance of future events, and partly upon the hope of a future state, that all his happiness in the present depends, ver. 77, etc. IV. The pride of aiming at more knowledge, and pretending to more perfection, the cause of man's error and misery. The impiety of putting himself in the place of God, and judging of the fitness or unfitness, perfection or imperfection, justice or injustice of his dispensations, Ver. 113, etc. V. The absurdity of conceiting himself the final cause of the creation, or expecting that perfection in the *moral* world, which is not in the *natural*, Ver. 131, etc. VI. The unreasonableness of his complaints against Providence, while on the one hand he demands the perfections of the angels, and on the other the bodily qualifications of the brutes; though, to possess any of the sensitive faculties in a higher degree, would render him miserable, Ver. 173, etc. VII. That throughout the whole visible world, an universal order and gradation in the sensual and mental faculties is observed, which causes a subordination of creature to creature, and of all creatures to Man. The gradations of sense, instinct, thought, reflection, reason; that reason alone countervails all the other faculties, Ver. 207. VIII. How much farther this order and subordination of living creatures may extend, above and below us; were any part of which broken, not that part only, but the whole connected creation must be destroyed. Ver. 233. IX. The extravagance, madness, and pride of such a desire, Ver. 259. X. The consequence of all the absolute submission due to providence, both as to our present and future state, Ver. 281, etc. to the end.

	Awake, my ST. JOHN! leave all meaner° things	base
	To low ambition, and the pride of kings.	
	Let us (since life can little more supply	
	Than just to look about us and to die)	
5	Expatiate free[7] o'er all this scene of man;	
	A mighty maze! but not without a plan;	
	A wild, where weeds and flow'rs promiscuous° shoot,	*randomly mixed*
	Or garden, tempting with forbidden fruit.	
	Together let us beat[8] this ample field,	
10	Try what the open, what the covert yield;	
	The latent tracts, the giddy heights explore	
	Of all who blindly creep, or sightless soar;[9]	
	Eye nature's walks,° shoot folly as it flies,	*behaviors*
	And catch the manners living as they rise;	
15	Laugh where we must, be candid° where we can;	*generous*
	But vindicate the ways of God to Man.[1]	

---

7. Wander or speak unrestrainedly.
8. "Beat," "open," "covert" are all hunting terms: Pope imagines them to be searching out game by walking back and forth across open and wooded land.
9. There is a middle way appropriate to man between ignorance and presumption.

1. Cf. *Paradise Lost*, 1.24–26: "That to the highth of this great argument / I may assert eternal providence, / And justify the ways of God to men." Pope's mention of the "garden, tempting with forbidden fruit" (line 8) also calls to mind the opening lines of Milton's epic.

1. Say first, of God above, or Man below,
What can we reason, but from what we know?
Of Man what see we, but his station here,
20 From which to reason, or to which refer?
Through worlds unnumbered though the God be known,
'Tis ours to trace him only in our own.
He, who through vast immensity can pierce,
See worlds on worlds compose one universe,
25 Observe how system into system runs,
What other planets circle other suns,
What varied being peoples° ev'ry star,   *inhabits*
May tell why Heav'n has made us as we are.
But of this frame the bearings, and the ties,
30 The strong connections, nice dependencies,
Gradations just,² has thy° pervading soul   *the reader's*
Looked through? or can a part contain the whole?
    Is the great chain,³ that draws all to agree,
And drawn supports, upheld by God, or thee?

35   2. Presumptuous Man! the reason wouldst thou find,
Why formed so weak, so little, and so blind!
First, if thou canst, the harder reason guess,
Why formed no weaker, blinder, and no less!
Ask of thy mother earth, why oaks are made
40 Taller or stronger than the weeds they shade?
Or ask of yonder argent fields above,
Why Jove's satellites⁴ are less than Jove?
    Of systems possible, if 'tis confest
That wisdom infinite must form the best,
45 Where all must full or not coherent be,⁵
And all that rises, rise in due degree;
Then, in the scale of reas'ning life, 'tis plain
There must be, somewhere, such a rank as Man;
And all the question (wrangle e'er so long)
50 Is only this, if God has placed him wrong?
    Respecting Man, whatever wrong we call,
May, must be right, as relative to all.
In human works, though labored on with pain,
A thousand movements scarce one purpose gain;
55 In God's, one single can its end produce;
Yet serves to second too some other use.
So Man, who here seems principal alone,
Perhaps acts second to some sphere unknown,
Touches some wheel, or verges to some goal;
60 'Tis but a part we see, and not a whole.
    When the proud steed shall know why Man restrains
His fiery course, or drives him o'er the plains;

2. "Connections," "dependencies," and "gradations" were
key terms of the new sciences.
3. The Great Chain of Being linked all levels of creation,
at the same time maintaining a fixed hierarchy.

4. Jupiter's moons. "Satellites" here has four syllables.
5. The Great Chain of Being could not be broken at any
point.

When the dull ox, why now he breaks the clod,
Is now a victim, and now Egypt's god:[6]
65   Then shall Man's pride and dullness comprehend
His actions', passions', being's, use and end;
Why doing, suff'ring, checked, impelled; and why
This hour a slave, the next a deity.

    Then say not Man's imperfect, Heav'n in fault;
70   Say rather, Man's as perfect as he ought;
His knowledge measured to his state and place,
His time a moment, and a point his space.
If to be perfect in a certain sphere,°   *area of influence*
What matter, soon or late, or here or there?
75   The blest today is as completely so,
As who began a thousand years ago.

    3. Heav'n from all creatures hides the book of fate,
All but the page prescribed, their present state;
From brutes what men, from men what spirits° know: *angels*
80   Or who could suffer being here below?
The lamb thy riot° dooms to bleed today,   *extravagance*
Had he thy reason, would he skip and play?
Pleased to the last, he crops the flow'ry food,
And licks the hand just raised to shed his blood.
85   Oh blindness to the future! kindly giv'n,
That each may fill the circle marked by Heav'n;
Who sees with equal eye, as God of all,
A hero perish, or a sparrow fall,
Atoms or systems° into ruin hurled,   *solar systems*
90   And now a bubble burst, and now a world.
    Hope humbly then; with trembling pinions soar;
Wait the great teacher death, and God adore!
What future bliss, he gives not thee to know,
But gives that hope to be thy blessing now.
95   Hope springs eternal in the human breast:
Man never *is*, but always to *be* blest:
The soul, uneasy and confined from home,[7]
Rests and expatiates in a life to come.
    Lo! the poor Indian, whose untutored mind
100   Sees God in clouds, or hears him in the wind;
His soul proud science never taught to stray
Far as the solar walk, or milky way;
Yet simple nature to his hope has giv'n,
Behind the cloud-topped hill, an humbler Heav'n;
105   Some safer world in depth of woods embraced,
Some happier island in the watry waste,
Where slaves once more their native land behold,
No fiends torment, no Christians thirst for gold![8]
To be, contents his natural desire,

---

6. Apis, sacred bull of Memphis.
7. Away from its heavenly origin.

8. The Christian is meant to "thirst for God" (Psalm 42.2).

110   He asks no angel's wing, no seraph's fire;[9]
    But thinks, admitted to that equal sky,
    His faithful dog shall bear him company.

      4. Go, wiser thou! and in thy scale of sense
    Weigh thy opinion against providence;
115   Call imperfection what thou fancy'st such,
    Say, here he gives too little, there too much;
    Destroy all creatures for thy sport or gust,°   *appetite*
    Yet cry, If Man's unhappy, God's unjust;
    If Man alone engross not Heav'n's high care,
120   Alone made perfect here, immortal there:
    Snatch from his hand the balance and the rod,
    Rejudge his justice, be the God of God!
      In pride, in reas'ning pride, our error lies;
    All quit their sphere, and rush into the skies.
125   Pride still is aiming at the blest abodes,
    Men would be angels, angels would be gods.
    Aspiring to be gods, if angels fell,
    Aspiring to be angels, men rebel;
    And who but wishes to invert the laws
130   Of ORDER, sins against th' Eternal Cause.

      5. Ask for what end th' heav'nly bodies shine,
    Earth for whose use? Pride answers, " 'Tis for mine:
    For me kind Nature wakes her genial° pow'r,   *generating*
    Suckles each herb, and spreads out ev'ry flow'r;
135   Annual for me, the grape, the rose renew
    The juice nectareous, and the balmy dew;
    For me, the mine a thousand treasures brings;
    For me, health gushes from a thousand springs;
    Seas roll to waft me, suns to light me rise;
140   My foot-stool earth, my canopy the skies."
      But errs not Nature from this gracious end,
    From burning suns when livid deaths descend,
    When earthquakes swallow, or when tempests sweep
    Towns to one grave, whole nations to the deep?
145   "No" ('tis replied) "the first Almighty cause[1]
    Acts not by partial, but by gen'ral laws;
    Th' exceptions few; some change since all began,
    And what created perfect?"—Why then Man?
    If the great end be human happiness,
150   Then Nature deviates; and can Man do less?
    As much that end a constant course requires
    Of show'rs and sunshine, as of Man's desires;
    As much eternal springs and cloudless skies,
    As men for ever temp'rate, calm, and wise.
155   If plagues or earthquakes break not Heav'n's design,
    Why then a Borgia, or a Catiline?[2]

---

9. Seraphs were traditionally thought of as fiery.
1. God the Creator.
2. Cesare Borgia (1476–1507), an Italian duke from a

notoriously ruthless family. Lucius Sergius Catiline (d. 62
B.C.) plotted unsuccessfully against the Roman state.

Who knows but he, whose hand the light'ning forms,
Who heaves old ocean, and who wings the storms,
Pours fierce ambition in a Caesar's mind,
160   Or turns young Ammon[3] loose to scourge mankind?
From pride, from pride, our very reas'ning springs;
Account for moral as for nat'ral things:
Why charge we Heav'n in those, in these acquit?
In both, to reason right is to submit.
165   Better for us, perhaps, it might appear,
Were there all harmony, all virtue here;
That never air or ocean felt the wind;
That never passion discomposed the mind:
But all subsists by elemental strife;
170   And passions are the elements of life.
The gen'ral ORDER, since the whole began,
Is kept in Nature, and is kept in Man.

6. What would this Man? Now upward will he soar,
And little less than angel, would be more;
175   Now looking downwards, just as grieved appears
To want the strength of bulls, the fur of bears.
Made for his use all creatures if he call,
Say what their use, had he the pow'rs of all?
Nature to these, without profusion kind,
180   The proper organs, proper pow'rs assigned;
Each seeming want compensated of course,[4]
Here with degrees of swiftness, there of force;
All in exact proportion to the state;
Nothing to add, and nothing to abate.
185   Each beast, each insect, happy in its own;
Is Heav'n unkind to Man, and Man alone?
Shall he alone, whom rational we call,
Be pleased with nothing, if not blessed with all?
        The bliss of Man (could pride that blessing find)
190   Is not to act or think beyond mankind;
No pow'rs of body or of soul to share,
But what his nature and his state can bear.
Why has not Man a microscopic eye?
For this plain reason, Man is not a fly.
195   Say what the use, were finer optics giv'n,
T' inspect a mite, not comprehend the Heav'n?[5]
Or touch, if tremblingly alive all o'er,
To smart and agonize at ev'ry pore?
Or quick effluvia[6] darting through the brain,
200   Die of a rose in aromatic pain?
If Nature thundered in his op'ning ears,
And stunned him with the music of the spheres,

3. Alexander the Great, King of Macedonia (336–323
B.C.) and conqueror of Asia Minor, Syria, Egypt, Babylo-
nia, and Persia.
4. As is fitting, in the normal course of events.
5. It was commonly believed that man alone of all the
animals was able to look up to Heaven.
6. Epicurus (c. 340–270 B.C.) and others believed that
sensations reached the brain from the pores via streams of
invisible particles.

How would he wish that Heav'n had left him still
The whisp'ring zephyr,° and the purling rill?   *breeze*
205 Who finds not providence all good and wise,
Alike in what it gives, and what denies?

     7. Far as creation's ample range extends,
The scale of sensual, mental pow'rs ascends:
Mark how it mounts, to Man's imperial race,
210 From the green myriads in the peopled grass:
What modes of sight betwixt each wide extreme,
The mole's dim curtain, and the lynx's beam:
Of smell, the headlong lioness[7] between,
And hound sagacious on the tainted[8] green:
215 Of hearing, from the life that fills the flood,
To that which warbles through the vernal wood:
The spider's touch, how exquisitely fine!
Feels at each thread, and lives along the line:
In the nice bee, what sense so subtly true
220 From pois'nous herbs extracts the healing dew:[9]
How instinct varies in the grov'ling swine,
Compared, half-reas'ning elephant, with thine:
'Twixt that, and reason, what a nice barrier;[1]
Forever sep'rate, yet forever near!
225 Remembrance and reflection how allied;
What thin partitions sense from thought divide:
And middle natures, how they long to join,
Yet never pass th' insuperable line!
Without this just gradation, could they be
230 Subjected these to those, or all to thee?
The pow'rs of all subdued by thee alone,
Is not thy reason all these pow'rs in one?

     8. See, through this air, this ocean, and this earth,
All matter quick,° and bursting into birth.   *living*
235 Above, how high progressive life may go!
Around, how wide! how deep extend below!
Vast chain of being, which from God began,
Natures ethereal, human, angel, Man,
Beast, bird, fish, insect! what no eye can see,
240 No glass° can reach! from infinite to thee,   *magnifying glass*
From thee to nothing!—On superior pow'rs
Were we to press, inferior might on ours:
Or in the full creation leave a void,
Where, one step broken, the great scale's destroyed:
245 From nature's chain whatever link you strike,
Tenth or ten thousandth, breaks the chain alike.

---

7. Lions were, according to Pope, believed to hunt "by
the ear, and not by the nostril."
8. Sagacious: of acute perception; tainted: i.e., with the
smell of the hunted animal.

9. Honey had been thought to fall on flowers as dew and
was used for medicinal purposes.
1. Fine distinction. "Barrier" is pronounced "bar-REAR."

And if each system in gradation roll,
Alike essential to th' amazing whole;
The least confusion but in one, not all
250   That system only, but the whole must fall.
Let earth unbalanced from her orbit fly,[2]
Planets and suns run lawless through the sky,
Let ruling angels from their spheres be hurled,[3]
Being on being wrecked, and world on world,
255   Heav'n's whole foundations to their center nod,
And Nature tremble to the throne of God:
All this dread ORDER break—for whom? for thee?
Vile worm!—oh madness, pride, impiety!

    9. What if the foot, ordained the dust to tread,
260   Or hand to toil, aspired to be the head?
What if the head, the eye, or ear repined
To serve mere engines to the ruling mind?
Just as absurd for any part to claim
To be another, in this gen'ral frame:
265   Just as absurd, to mourn the tasks or pains
The great directing MIND of ALL ordains.
    All are but parts of one stupendous whole,
Whose body, Nature is, and God the soul;
That, changed through all, and yet in all the same,
270   Great in the earth, as in th' ethereal frame,
Warms in the sun, refreshes in the breeze,
Glows in the stars, and blossoms in the trees,
Lives through all life, extends through all extent,
Spreads undivided, operates unspent,
275   Breathes in our soul, informs° our mortal part,   *permeates*
As full, as perfect, in a hair as heart;
As full, as perfect, in vile Man that mourns,
As the rapt seraph that adores and burns;
To him no high, no low, no great, no small;
280   He fills, he bounds, connects, and equals all.

    10. Cease then, nor ORDER imperfection name:[4]
Our proper bliss depends on what we blame.
Know thy own point: This kind, this due degree
Of blindness, weakness, Heav'n bestows on thee.
285   Submit—In this, or any other sphere,
Secure to be as blest as thou canst bear:
Safe in the hand of one disposing Pow'r,
Or° in the natal, or the mortal hour.   *either*
All nature is but art, unknown to thee;
290   All chance, direction, which thou canst not see;
All discord, harmony, not understood;[5]

---

2. Cf. *Paradise Lost* 7.242, where "Earth, self-balanced, on her center hung."
3. According to Thomas Aquinas (c. 1225–1274), a sign of the end of the world.

4. I.e., do not call order imperfection.
5. Here, as earlier in the poem, Pope invokes the Horatian principle of *concordia discors* (Horace, *Epistles* 1.12.19), a harmony of opposites.

All partial evil, universal good:[6]
And, spite of pride, in erring reason's spite,
One truth is clear, "Whatever IS, is RIGHT."

1733

AN EPISTLE FROM MR. POPE, TO DR. ARBUTHNOT   The *Epistle to Dr. Arbuthnot*, perhaps the most relaxed and engaging of all Pope's verse letters, is addressed to John Arbuthnot (1667–1735), who was physician to Queen Anne, a close friend of Pope and Swift, a valued member of the Scriblerus Club, and principal author of the *Memoirs of the Extraordinary Life, Works, and Discoveries of Martinus Scriblerus*, published with Pope's *Works* in 1741. Samuel Johnson described Arbuthnot as "the most universal genius," for he was a fine satirist, a skillful physician, an amateur mathematician, and a capable poet. Pope's epistle is an apology both for himself and for the satirist's art, written against those who had attacked his "person, morals, and family." He asserts the social role of the poet, includes moving autobiographical passages, and powerfully assails his enemies. This Horatian epistle, to the friend whose satires had delighted Pope and whose care had helped preserve and prolong Pope's own frail health, was published just seven weeks before the doctor died.

An Epistle from Mr. Pope, to Dr. Arbuthnot

*Neque sermonibus vulgi dederis te, nec in Praemiis humanis spem
posueris rerum tuarum: suis te oportet illecebris ipsa virtus trahat
ad verum decus. Quid de te alii loquantur, ipsi videant, sed
loquentur tamen.*[1]

Tully

Advertisement

This paper is a sort of Bill of Complaint, begun many years since, and drawn up by snatches, as the several occasions offered. I had no thoughts of publishing it, till it pleased some persons of rank and fortune [the authors of *Verses to the Imitator of Horace*, and of an *Epistle to a Doctor of Divinity from a Nobleman at Hampton Court*][2] to attack in a very extraordinary manner, not only my writings (of which being public the public judge) but my person, morals, and family, whereof to those who know me not, a truer information may be requisite. Being divided between the necessity to say something of myself, and my own laziness to undertake so awkward a task, I thought it the shortest way to put the last hand to this Epistle. If it have anything pleasing, it will be that by which I am most desirous to please, the *truth* and the *sentiment;* and if anything offensive, it will be only to those I am least sorry to offend, the *vicious* or the *ungenerous.*

Many will know their own pictures in it, there being not a circumstance but what is true; but I have, for the most part spared their *names,* and they may escape being laughed at, if they please.

I would have some of them know, it was owing to the request of the learned and candid friend to whom it is inscribed, that I make not as free use of theirs as they have done of mine. However, I shall have this advantage, and honor, on my side,

6. In a letter to John Caryll in 1718, Pope wrote that "true piety would make us know, that all misfortunes may as well be blessings."
1. You will not give yourself up to the flattery of the vulgar, nor hope for success in your affairs from mortal

hands; virtue herself will lead to true honor; see that you follow her guidance. What others see fit to say of you let them say (Cicero, *De Re Publica* 6.23).
2. Lady Mary Wortley Montagu (1689–1762) and John Hervey (1696–1743), Baron Hervey of Ickworth.

that whereas by their proceeding, any abuse may be directed at any man, no injury can possibly be done by mine, since a nameless character can never be found out, but by its *truth* and *likeness*.[3]

Shut, shut the door, good John![4] fatigued I said,
Tie up the knocker, say I'm sick, I'm dead,
The Dog-star[5] rages! nay 'tis past a doubt,
All Bedlam, or Parnassus,[6] is let out:
5   Fire in each eye, and papers in each hand,
They rave, recite, and madden[7] round the land.
    What walls can guard me, or what shades can hide?
They pierce my thickets, through my grot[8] they glide,
By land, by water,[9] they renew the charge,
10   They stop the chariot, and they board the barge.
No place is sacred, not the church is free,
Ev'n Sunday shines no Sabbath-day to me:
Then from the Mint[1] walks forth the man of rhyme,
Happy! to catch me, just at dinner time.
15   Is here a parson, much bemused in beer,[2]
A maudlin poetess, a rhyming peer,
A clerk, foredoomed his father's soul to cross,
Who pens a stanza when he should engross?°   *copy documents*
Is there, who locked from ink and paper, scrawls
20   With desp'rate charcoal round his darkened walls?
All fly to Twit'nam,° and in humble strain   *Twickenham*
Apply to me, to keep them mad or vain.
Arthur,[3] whose giddy son neglects the laws,
Imputes to me and my damned works the cause:
25   Poor Cornus° sees his frantic wife elope,   *cuckold*
And curses wit, and poetry, and Pope.[4]
    Friend to my life, (which did not you prolong,
The world had wanted many an idle Song)
What drop or nostrum° can this plague remove?   *medicines*
30   Or which must end me, a fool's wrath or love?
A dire dilemma! either way I'm sped,°   *hurried toward death*
If foes, they write, if friends, they read me dead.
Seized and tied down to judge, how wretched I!
Who can't be silent, and who will not lie;
35   To laugh were want of goodness and of grace,
And to be grave exceeds all pow'r of face.
I sit with sad civility, I read

---

3. I.e., its similarity to the original.
4. Pope's servant, John Serle.
5. Sirius, which appears in the heat of summer; Pope was finishing the poem in August 1734. The late summer was also the time for reciting poetry in classical Rome.
6. Bedlam (Bethlehem Hospital) was a London "lunatic" asylum; Parnassus was the mountain of the Muses.
7. A word Pope invented.
8. Pope's artificial grotto or cavern, his retreat, at Twickenham.
9. Pope's house at Twickenham was on the river Thames,

and could be reached by boat from London.
1. Debtors were safe from the law in Southwark, London; on Sunday there were no arrests anywhere.
2. Laurence Eusden (1688–1730), Poet Laureate and parson given to drink.
3. Arthur Moore; his son James Moore-Smythe had plagiarized from Pope's works.
4. Both the Pope and the author: as a nation, the British were preoccupied with the threat of Roman Catholicism without (from France and Spain) and within (from Catholics like Pope).

With honest anguish, and an aching head;
And drop at last, but in unwilling ears,
40   This saving counsel, "Keep your piece nine years."[5]
        Nine years! cries he, who high in Drury Lane[6]
Lulled by soft zephyrs° through the broken pane,   *breezes*
Rhymes ere he wakes, and prints before term ends,[7]
Obliged by hunger and request of friends:[8]
45   "The piece you think is incorrect: why take it,
I'm all submission, what you'd have it, make it."
        Three things another's modest wishes bound,°   *encompass*
My friendship, and a prologue,[9] and ten pound.
        Pitholeon[1] sends to me: "You know his Grace,
50   I want a patron; ask him for a place."°   *paid position*
Pitholeon libeled me—"but here's a letter
Informs you, sir, 'twas when he knew no better.
Dare you refuse him? Curll[2] invites to dine,
He'll write a Journal, or he'll turn divine."[3]
55   Bless me! a packet.—" 'Tis a stranger sues,
A virgin tragedy, an orphan Muse."
If I dislike it, "Furies, death and rage!"
If I approve, "Commend it to the stage."
There (thank my stars) my whole commission ends,
60   The play'rs and I are, luckily, no friends.
Fired that the house° reject him, " 'Sdeath I'll print it   *theater*
And shame the fools—your int'rest, sir, with Lintot."[4]
Lintot, dull rogue! will think your price too much.
"Not Sir, if you revise it, and retouch."
65   All my demurs but double his attacks,
At last he whispers "Do, and we go snacks."[5]
Glad of a quarrel, straight° I clap the door,   *immediately*
Sir, let me see your works and you no more.
        'Tis sung, when Midas' ears began to spring,[6]
70   (Midas, a sacred person and a King),
His very Minister who spied them first,
(Some say his Queen) was forced to speak, or burst.
And is not mine, my friend, a sorer case,
When every coxcomb° perks° them in my face?   *fool / shoves*
75   "Good friend forbear! you deal in dang'rous things,
I'd never name Queens, Ministers, or Kings;
Keep close to ears,° and those let asses prick,[7]   *whisper it*
'Tis nothing"—Nothing? if they bite and kick?

---

5. Horace's advice to a poet eager to publish (*Ars Poetica* 386–89).
6. A bad neighborhood where writers lived in garrets.
7. Law court terms were the preferred publishing seasons.
8. It is the second reason, rather than the first, that the aspiring poet gives in his prefaces.
9. To a play of his: a good way to show the public who your friends were.
1. The name taken from a foolish Poet at Rhodes [Pope's note].
2. Edmund Curll (1675–1747), a publisher notorious for commissioning hacks to write libelous journals, full of

"news and scandal."
3. Pope may have meant Leonard Welsted (1688–1747), who was planning a religious work.
4. Bernard Lintot (1675–1736), who published for Pope.
5. Share the profits.
6. King Midas grew ass's ears when he preferred Pan to Apollo in their music contest. One of those closest to him whispered the story to the earth, and it was in turn told by the reeds. Pope was also referring to that contemporary artistic dunce King George II, his wife Queen Caroline, and first minister Robert Walpole.
7. Presumably, their ears, as well as the poet.

Out with it, Dunciad! let the secret pass,
80   That secret to each fool, that he's an ass:
The truth once told (and wherefore should we lie?),
The Queen of Midas slept, and so may I.
    You think this cruel? take it for a rule,
No creature smarts so little as a fool.
85   Let peals of laughter, Codrus![8] round thee break,
Thou unconcerned canst hear the mighty crack.[9]
Pit, box and gall'ry in convulsions hurled,
Thou stand'st unshook amidst a bursting world.
Who shames a scribbler? break one cobweb through,
90   He spins the slight, self-pleasing thread anew;
Destroy his fib, or sophistry; in vain,
The creature's at his dirty work again;
Throned in the center of his thin designs;
Proud of a vast extent of flimsy lines.
95   Whom have I hurt? has poet yet, or peer,
Lost the arched eyebrow, or Parnassian sneer?
And has not Colley[1] still his Lord, and whore?
His butchers Henley, his Freemasons Moore?[2]
Does not one table Bavius[3] still admit?
100   Still to one bishop Philips[4] seem a wit?
Still Sappho[5]—"Hold! for God's sake—you'll offend:
No names—be calm—learn prudence of a friend:
I too could write, and I am twice as tall,
But foes like these!"—One flatt'rer's worse than all;
105   Of all mad creatures, if the learn'd are right,
It is the slaver kills, and not the bite.
A fool quite angry is quite innocent;
Alas! 'tis ten times worse when they *repent*.

    One dedicates, in high heroic prose,
110   And ridicules beyond a hundred foes;
One from all Grub Street[6] will my fame defend,
And, more abusive, calls himself my friend.
This prints my letters,[7] that expects a bribe,
And others roar aloud, "Subscribe, subscribe."
115   There are, who to my person pay their court,
I cough like Horace, and though lean, am short,
Ammon's great son[8] one shoulder had too high,
Such Ovid's nose, and "Sir! you have an eye—"

---

8. A poet, perhaps fictional, ridiculed by Virgil and Juvenal.
9. "Mighty crack" was a phrase used by Addison to describe the collapse of the world; Pope showed how inadequate he thought it both in *Peri Bathous* and here, where it signals the failure of a play.
1. Colley Cibber (1671–1757), actor, playwright, Poet Laureate; he replaced Lewis Theobald as the "hero" of *The Dunciad*, from where the "Parnassian sneer" comes.
2. John "Orator" Henley (1692–1756), a popular and unusual preacher, had set up an "oratory" in Newport Market, one of London's principal meat markets, causing enemies to claim that his audiences consisted only of ignorant butchers. James Moore-Smythe was a Freemason.
3. A bad poet who had attacked Virgil and Horace.
4. Ambrose Philips (c. 1675–1749), poet and secretary to the Bishop of Armagh.
5. Lady Mary Wortley Montagu, whom Pope had attacked previously under the name of this Greek lyric poet; from Arbuthnot's interjection, Pope seems to be implying that she was under Walpole's protection.
6. Home of literary hacks.
7. Forged or stolen (as Curll had in 1726).
8. Alexander the Great.

Go on, obliging creatures, make me see
120   All that disgraced my betters, met in me:
Say for my comfort, languishing in bed,
"Just so immortal Maro° held his head:"   *Virgil*
And when I die, be sure you let me know
Great Homer died three thousand years ago.

125   Why did I write? what sin to me unknown
Dipped me in ink, my parents', or my own?
As yet a child, nor yet a fool to fame,
I lisped in numbers,° for the numbers came.   *verse, meter*
I left no calling for this idle trade,
130   No duty broke, no father disobeyed.
The Muse but served to ease some friend, not wife,
To help me through this long disease, my life,
To second, Arbuthnot! thy art and care,
And teach the being you preserved to bear.

135   But why then publish? Granville⁹ the polite,
And knowing Walsh, would tell me I could write;
Well-natured Garth inflamed with early praise,
And Congreve loved, and Swift endured my lays;
The courtly Talbot, Somers, Sheffield read,
140   Ev'n mitered Rochester would nod the head,
And St. John's self (great Dryden's friends before)
With open arms received one poet more.
Happy my studies, when by these approved!
Happier their author, when by these beloved!
145   From these the world will judge of men and books,
Not from the Burnets, Oldmixons, and Cookes.¹
    Soft were my numbers, who could take offense
While pure description held the place of sense?
Like gentle Fanny's² was my flow'ry theme,
150   A painted mistress, or a purling stream.
Yet then did Gildon³ draw his venal quill;
I wished the man a dinner, and sat still:
Yet then did Dennis rave in furious fret;⁴
I never answered, I was not in debt:
155   If want provoked, or madness made them print,
I waged no war with Bedlam or the Mint.
        Did some more sober critic come abroad?
If wrong, I smiled; if right, I kissed the rod.⁵

---

9. Pope associates himself (and Dryden) with a number of important figures, friends, and patrons: George Granville, Baron Lansdowne (1666–1735); William Walsh (1663–1708); Sir Samuel Garth (1661–1719); William Congreve; Jonathan Swift; Charles Talbot, Duke of Shrewsbury (1660–1718); John Lord Somers (1651–1721); Francis Atterbury, Bishop of Rochester (1662–1732); Henry St. John, Viscount Bolingbroke (1678–1751).
1. Thomas Burnet, John Oldmixon, and Thomas Cooke: "authors of secret and scandalous history" [Pope's note]; Pope is comparing the greatness of his friends with the

small-mindedness of those who attacked him.
2. Lord Hervey, court Vice Chamberlain, whom Pope thought effeminate, and later satirizes as Sporus (lines 305ff.).
3. Charles Gildon (1665–1724) had attacked *The Rape of the Lock*. Pope insinuates that Gildon writes to keep poverty at bay.
4. John Dennis (1657–1734), had attacked Pope; both, Gildon and Dennis, Pope thought, had acted at the instigation of Addison.
5. Accepted their criticism; kissing a monarch's scepter or an official's staff was a ritual of submission to authority.

Pains, reading, study, are their just pretense,
160   And all they want is spirit, taste, and sense.
Commas and points they set exactly right,
And 'twere a sin to rob them of their mite.
Yet ne'er one sprig of laurel graced these ribalds,[6]
From slashing Bentley down to piddling Tibalds.[7]
165   Each wight who reads not, and but scans and spells,
Each word-catcher that lives on syllables,
Ev'n such small critics some regard may claim,
Preserved in Milton's or in Shakespeare's name.
Pretty! in amber to observe the forms
170   Of hairs, or straws, or dirt, or grubs, or worms;
The things, we know, are neither rich nor rare,
But wonder how the devil they got there?
        Were others angry? I excused them too;
Well might they rage; I gave them but their due.
175   A man's true merit 'tis not hard to find,
But each man's secret standard in his mind,
That casting-weight[8] pride adds to emptiness,
This, who can gratify? for who can *guess*?
The Bard[9] whom pilf'red pastorals renown,
180   Who turns a Persian tale for half a crown,[1]
Just writes to make his barrenness appear,
And strains from hard-bound brains eight lines a year:
He, who still wanting though he lives on theft,
Steals much, spends little, yet has nothing left:
185   And he, who now to sense, now nonsense leaning,
Means not, but blunders round about a meaning:
And he, whose fustian's° so sublimely bad,   *bombastic style*
It is not poetry, but prose run mad:
All these, my modest satire bad translate,
190   And owned, that nine such poets made a Tate.[2]
How did they fume, and stamp, and roar, and chafe?
And swear, not Addison himself was safe.
        Peace to all such! but were there one[3] whose fires
True genius kindles, and fair fame inspires,
195   Blest with each talent and each art to please,
And born to write, converse, and live with ease:
Should such a man, too fond to rule° alone,   *of ruling*
Bear, like the Turk, no brother near the throne,[4]
View him with scornful, yet with jealous eyes,
200   And hate for arts that caused himself to rise;

6. Laurel: the poet's crown; ribalds: foolish jesters.
7. Richard Bentley (1662–1742), a classical scholar of great learning and bad temper, earned ridicule for his "corrected" edition of *Paradise Lost* (1732), while Lewis Theobald (1688–1744), sometime "hero" of *The Dunciad*, criticized Pope's edition of Shakespeare in his *Shakespeare Restored* (1726).
8. The weight that tips the balance.
9. Ambrose Philips wrote pastoral poems in imitation of Spenser and translated a book of *Persian Tales*. The fact that, in 1709, his pastorals were published in the same volume as Pope's occasioned a rivalry between the two poets.
1. A standard prostitute's charge.
2. Nahum Tate (1652–1715), playwright and poet.
3. Joseph Addison, here portrayed as Atticus, friend of Cicero, Pope respected Addison's abilities as a writer but did not like him or his politics.
4. Turkish rulers killed close relatives who might be potential rivals.

Damn with faint praise,[5] assent with civil leer,
And without sneering, teach the rest to sneer;
Willing to wound, and yet afraid to strike,
Just hint a fault, and hesitate dislike;
205 Alike reserved to blame, or to commend,
A tim'rous foe, and a suspicious friend,
Dreading ev'n fools, by flatterers besieged,
And so obliging that he ne'er obliged;
Like Cato, give his little Senate laws,[6]
210 And sit attentive to his own applause;
While wits and templars° ev'ry sentence raise,   young lawyers
And wonder with a foolish face of praise.
Who but must laugh, if such a man there be?
Who would not weep, if Atticus were he!
215   What though my name stood rubric on the walls?
Or plastered posts, with claps in capitals?[7]
Or smoking forth, a hundred hawkers[8] load,
On wings of winds came flying all abroad?
I sought no homage from the race that write;
220 I kept, like Asian monarchs, from their sight:
Poems I heeded (now berhymed so long)
No more than thou, great George! a birthday song.[9]
I ne'er with wits or witlings passed my days,
To spread about the itch of verse and praise;
225 Nor like a puppy daggled° through the town,   wandered
To fetch and carry singsong up and down;
Nor at rehearsals sweat, and mouthed, and cried,
With handkerchief and orange[1] at my side:
But sick of fops, and poetry, and prate,
230 To Bufo left the whole Castalian State.[2]
     Proud, as Apollo on his forked hill,
Sat full-blown Bufo, puffed by ev'ry quill;
Fed with soft dedication all day long,
Horace and he went hand in hand in song.[3]
235 His library (where busts of poets dead
And a true Pindar stood without a head)[4]
Received of wits an undistinguished race,
Who first his judgment asked, and then a place:
Much they extolled his pictures, much his seat,°   estate
240 And flattered ev'ry day, and some days eat:
Till grown more frugal in his riper days,

5. Cf. William Wycherley's prologue to The Plain Dealer (1677): "And, with faint praises, one another damn."
6. Pope's prologue to Addison's play Cato (1713) included a version of this line. Now Pope turns the tables, and the noble Roman senator becomes the petty Addison, the senate, his coffeehouse clique.
7. Red lettering, or rubric, was often used by Lintot, Pope's publisher; "claps" were placards, pasted up around the city by booksellers.
8. Hawking by street criers was another way to publicize new works.
9. The Poet Laureate's official ode to the king.

1. Sold in the theaters for eating or throwing.
2. Poetry is the "Castalian State," named for the spring sacred to the Muses on Parnassus (the "forked hill"); it is left to "Bufo," a patron whose name derives from the Latin for toad and who was probably George Bubb Dodington (1691–1762).
3. Dodington, a patron of literature, had been given the place of Maecenas, patron of Virgil and Horace, in a recent translation from Horace's Odes.
4. In Peri Bathous (1728), Pope ridiculed those antiquaries who exhibited headless statues, claiming they were busts of great poets.

He paid some bards with port, and some with praise,
To some a dry rehearsal was assigned,
And others (harder still) he paid in kind.[5]
245   Dryden alone (what wonder?) came not nigh,
Dryden alone escaped this judging eye:
But still the great have kindness in reserve,
He helped to bury whom he helped to starve.[6]
    May some choice patron bless each gray goose quill!
250   May ev'ry Bavius have his Bufo still!
So, when a statesman wants a day's defense,
Or envy holds a whole week's war with sense,
Or simple pride for flatt'ry makes demands;
May dunce by dunce be whistled off my hands!
255   Blest be the Great! for those they take away,
And those they left me—For they left me Gay,[7]
Left me to see neglected genius bloom,
Neglected die! and tell it on his tomb;
Of all thy blameless life the sole return
260   My verse, and Queensb'ry[8] weeping o'er thy urn!
Oh let me live my own! and die so too!
("To live and die is all I have to do"):[9]
Maintain a poet's dignity and ease,
And see what friends, and read what books I please.
265   Above a patron, though I condescend
Sometimes to call a minister my friend:
I was not born for courts or great affairs,
I pay my debts, believe, and say my pray'rs,
Can sleep without a poem in my head,
270   Nor know, if Dennis be alive or dead.
    Why am I asked, what next shall see the light?
Heav'ns! was I born for nothing but to write?
Has life no joys for me? or (to be grave)
Have I no friend to serve, no soul to save?
275   "I found him close with Swift"—"Indeed? no doubt"
(Cries prating Balbus[1]) "something will come out."
'Tis all in vain, deny it as I will.
"No, such a genius never can lie still,"
And then for mine obligingly mistakes
280   The first lampoon Sir Will. or Bubo[2] makes.
Poor guiltless I! and can I choose but smile,
When ev'ry coxcomb knows me by my *style?*
    Cursed be the verse, how well soe'er it flow,
That tends to make one worthy man my foe,
285   Give virtue scandal, innocence a fear,
Or from the soft-eyed virgin steal a tear!

---

5. I.e., he read or gave them his own poetry.
6. Mr. Dryden, after having liv'd in exigencies, had a magnificent funeral bestow'd upon him by the contributions of several persons of quality [Pope's note].
7. John Gay, poet, playwright, and friend of Pope; it was apparently his failure to win patronage that prompted him to write *The Beggar's Opera* (1728).

8. The Duke and Duchess of Queensberry were Gay's patrons.
9. Slightly adapted from *Of Prudence* (1668) by Sir John Denham.
1. A Roman lawyer.
2. Sir William Yonge (d. 1755) and Dodington.

But he, who hurts a harmless neighbor's peace,
Insults fall'n worth, or beauty in distress,
Who loves a lie, lame slander helps about,
290　Who writes a libel, or who copies out:
That fop whose pride affects a patron's name,
Yet absent, wounds an author's honest fame;
Who can your merit selfishly approve,
And show the sense of it, without the love;
295　Who has the vanity to call you friend,
Yet wants the honor injured to defend;[3]
Who tells whate'er you think, whate'er you say,
And, if he lie not, must at least betray:
Who to the Dean and silver bell can swear,
300　And sees at Cannons what was never there:[4]
Who reads but with a lust to misapply,
Make satire a lampoon, and fiction, lie.
A lash like mine no honest man shall dread,
But all such babbling blockheads in his stead.
305　　　Let Sporus[5] tremble—"What? that thing of silk,
Sporus, that mere white curd of ass's milk?
Satire or sense alas! can Sporus feel?
Who breaks a butterfly upon a wheel?"[6]
Yet let me flap this bug with gilded wings,
310　This painted child of dirt that stinks and stings;
Whose buzz the witty and the fair annoys,
Yet wit ne'er tastes, and beauty ne'er enjoys,
So well-bred spaniels civilly delight
In mumbling of the game they dare not bite.
315　Eternal smiles his emptiness betray,
As shallow streams run dimpling all the way.
Whether in florid impotence he speaks,
And, as the prompter breathes, the puppet squeaks;
Or at the ear of Eve,[7] familiar toad,
320　Half froth, half venom, spits himself abroad,
In puns, or politics, or tales, or lies,
Or spite, or smut, or rhymes, or blasphemies.
His wit all seesaw between that and this,
Now high, now low, now master up, now miss,
325　And he himself one vile antithesis.
Amphibious Thing! that acting either part,
The trifling head, or the corrupted heart!
Fop at the toilet,[8] flatt'rer at the board,°　　　　*dining table*
Now trips a Lady, and now struts a Lord.
330　Eve's tempter thus the Rabbins° have expressed,　　*Jewish scholars*
A cherub's face, a reptile all the rest;

---

3. I.e., lacks the honor when you are injured to defend
you.
4. I.e., who misapplies satirical references in Pope's *Epistle
to Burlington.* Pope was upset by the willful misreading of
"Timon's villa" in the poem as Cannons, estate of the
Duke of Chandos.
5. A boy, Nero's favorite sexual partner; here, Lord Her-

vey, confidante of Queen Caroline.
6. The rack, an instrument of torture.
7. In the fourth book of Milton [*Paradise Lost* 4.800] the
devil is represented in this posture [Pope's note]. "Eve" is
Queen Caroline, with whom Hervey is both familiar and
a familiar (a witch's pet).
8. Dressing table.

Beauty that shocks you, parts that none will trust,
Wit that can creep, and pride that licks the dust.
      Not fortune's worshipper, nor fashion's fool,
335 Not lucre's madman, nor ambition's tool,
Not proud, nor servile, be one poet's praise
That, if he pleased, he pleased by manly ways;
That flatt'ry, ev'n to kings, he held a shame,
And thought a lie in verse or prose the same:
340 That not in fancy's maze he wandered long,
But stooped° to truth, and moralized his song: *pounced upon*
That not for fame, but virtue's better end,
He stood° the furious foe, the timid friend,   *withstood*
The damning critic, half-approving wit,
345 The coxcomb hit, or fearing to be hit;
Laughed at the loss of friends he never had,
The dull, the proud, the wicked, and the mad;
The distant threats of vengeance on his head,
The blow unfelt, the tear he never shed;⁹
350 The tale revived, the lie so oft o'erthrown;
Th' imputed trash, and dullness not his own;
The morals blackened when the writings 'scape;
The libeled person, and the pictured shape;¹
Abuse on all he loved, or loved him, spread,
355 A friend in exile, or a father, dead;
The whisper that to greatness still too near,
Perhaps, yet vibrates on his Sovereign's ear—
Welcome for thee, fair virtue! all the past:
For thee, fair virtue! welcome ev'n the last!
360   "But why insult the poor, affront the great?"
A knave's a knave, to me, in ev'ry state,
Alike my scorn, if he succeed or fail,
Sporus at court, or Japhet² in a jail,
A hireling scribbler, or a hireling peer,
365 Knight of the post³ corrupt, or of the shire,
If on a pillory, or near a throne,
He gain his prince's ear, or lose his own.
      Yet soft by nature, more a dupe than wit,
Sappho⁴ can tell you how this man was bit°   *deceived*
370 This dreaded sat'rist Dennis will confess
Foe to his pride, but friend to his distress:⁵
So humble, he has knocked at Tibbald's door,
Has drunk with Cibber, nay has rhymed for Moore.⁶
Full ten years slandered, did he once reply?
375 Three thousand suns went down on Welsted's lie:
To please a mistress, one aspersed his life;

9. A *Pop upon Pope* (1728) tried to humiliate Pope by pretending he had been whipped.
1. Pope was frequently vilified in print by his enemies. His deformity and Roman Catholicism were often mocked—he was even caricatured as a hunchbacked ape wearing the papal crown.
2. Japhet Crook, a forger.

3. A person who supported himself by giving false evidence.
4. Lady Mary Wortley Montagu hurt Pope, who had been very close to her, by switching loyalties to Hervey.
5. In Dennis's old age, Pope had publicly supported his work.
6. Or rather, Moore-Smythe plagiarized from him.

He lashed him not, but let her be his wife:
Let Budgell[7] charge low Grubstreet on his quill,
And write whate'er he pleased, except his will;
380 Let the two Curlls[8] of town and court, abuse
His father, mother, body, soul, and Muse.
Yet why? that father held it for a rule
It was a sin to call our neighbor fool,
That harmless mother thought no wife a whore,—
385 Hear this! and spare his family, James Moore!
Unspotted names! and memorable long,
If there be force in virtue, or in song.
        Of gentle blood (part shed in honor's cause,
While yet in Britain honor had applause)
390 Each parent sprung—"What Fortune, pray?"—Their own,
And better got than Bestia's[9] from the throne.
Born to no pride, inheriting no strife,
Nor marrying discord in a noble wife,
Stranger to civil and religious rage,
395 The good man walked innoxious through his Age.
No courts he saw, no suits would ever try,
Nor dared an oath, nor hazarded a lie:[1]
Unlearn'd, he knew no schoolman's subtle art,
No language, but the language of the heart.
400 By nature honest, by experience wise,
Healthy by temp'rance and by exercise:
His life, though long, to sickness past unknown,
His death was instant, and without a groan.
Oh grant me thus to live, and thus to die!
405 Who sprung from kings shall know less joy than I.
        O Friend!° may each domestic bliss be thine!   Arbuthnot
Be no unpleasing melancholy mine:
Me, let the tender office long engage
To rock the cradle of reposing age,
410 With lenient arts extend a mother's breath,[2]
Make languor smile, and smooth the bed of death,
Explore the thought, explain the asking eye,
And keep a while one parent from the sky!
On cares like these if length of days attend,
415 May Heav'n, to bless those days, preserve my friend,
Preserve him social, cheerful, and serene,
And just as rich as when he served a Queen![3]
Whether that blessing be denied, or giv'n,
Thus far was right, the rest belongs to Heav'n.

1731–1734   1735

---

7. Eustace Budgell (1686–1737); the *Grub Street Journal* accused him of forging the will of Dr. Matthew Tindal to make himself inheritor.
8. Pope uses Edmund Curll's name as a derogatory epithet for Hervey. Curll, an unscrupulous publisher, is attacked in *The Dunciad* and in Swift's *Verses on the Death of Dr. Swift*.
9. A Roman consul who accepted bribes for peace, sug-

gesting the Duke of Marlborough's rewards from Queen Anne.
1. Pope's father refused to take oaths against the Pope, which would have helped him avoid anti-Catholic measures.
2. Pope's mother died two years before the poem was published, but he retained these lines, written in 1731.
3. Arbuthnot had been physician to Queen Anne.

THE DUNCIAD   Encouraged by Jonathan Swift, who spent some months with him at Twickenham in 1726, Pope produced two satires against "Dulness," bad writing, and the stupidity of "Dunces." *Peri Bathous, or the Art of Sinking in Poetry,* a prose treatise about how to write bad poetry, illustrated with many examples from Pope's contemporaries, was first published in 1728. Just two months later there appeared Pope's comic masterpiece, *The Dunciad,* in three books. Pope's pseudo-scholarly edition, *The Dunciad Variorum* (1729), intensified his attack on the hack writers of Grub Street and the proliferation of popular culture. In *The New Dunciad* (1742), the focus of Pope's contempt expanded from Grub Street to the pretentious, the ponderous, and the pedantic in its many forms. In 1743 Pope issued *The Dunciad in Four Books,* incorporating *The New Dunciad* as Book 4 of the poem, adding further mock-scholarly trappings, and transferring the conclusion of the three-book *Dunciad* to the end of Book 4; the "hero" of Books 1–3, Lewis Theobald (1688–1744), a minor writer and editor of Shakespeare, is replaced by the self-aggrandizing playwright and Poet Laureate Colly Cibber (1671–1757). In Book 4, the hero does nothing, and the climax of the poem is the goddess Dulness's infectious yawn, which sends all the world into darkness and primeval chaos. For the reader, the actions of Dulness and her sychophants engender not sleep, but laughter.

from **The Dunciad**

from Book the Fourth

ARGUMENT

The poet being, in this book, to declare the completion of the prophecies mentioned at the end of the former,[1] makes a new invocation, as the greater poets are wont, when some high and worthy matter is to be sung. He shows the Goddess coming in her majesty, to destroy *Order* and *Science,*[2] and to substitute the *Kingdom of the Dull* upon earth. How she leads captive the Sciences, and silenceth the Muses; and what they be who succeed in their stead. All her children, by a wonderful attraction, are drawn about her, and bear along with them divers others, who promote her empire by connivance, weak resistance, or discouragement of arts, such as half-wits, tasteless admirers, vain pretenders, the flatterers of dunces, or the patrons of them. All these crowd round her; one of them offering to approach her, is driven back by a rival, but she commends and encourages both. The first who speak in form[3] are the geniuses[4] of the schools, who assure her of their care to advance her cause, by confining youth to words, and keeping them out of the way of real knowledge. Their address, and her gracious answer, with her charge[5] to them and the universities. The universities appear by their proper deputies, and assure her that the same method is observed in the progress of education; the speech of Aristarchus[6] on this subject. They are driven off by a band of young gentlemen returned from travel with their tutors, one of whom delivers to the Goddess, in a polite oration, an account of the whole conduct and fruits of their travels, presenting to her at the same time a young nobleman perfectly accomplished. She receives him graciously, and indues him with the happy quality of *want of shame.* She sees loitering about her a number of indolent persons abandoning

---

1. Book 3 of *The Dunciad* concludes with an oracle foretelling that the goddess Dulness and hers sons shall triumph in the theaters, the court, and the universities.
2. Knowledge.
3. Formally.
4. Guardian deities.
5. Commission, instruction of duties.

6. Aristarchus of Samothrace (c. 217–145 B.C.), a scholar who "corrected" the poems of Homer; he represents a severe and short-sighted critic. In a preface added to *The Dunciad in Four Books* (1743), he is named "Richard Aristarchus" and clearly represents Richard Bentley, the scholar and critic who, in 1732, published a disastrous "corrected" version of Milton's *Paradise Lost.*

all business and duty, and dying with laziness; to these approaches the antiquary Annius,[7] entreating her to make them virtuosos,[8] and assign them over to him. But Mummius,[9] another antiquary, complaining of his fraudulent proceeding, she finds a method to reconcile their difference. Then enter a troop of people fantastically adorned, offering her strange and exotic presents. Amongst them, one stands forth and demands justice on another, who had deprived him of one of the greatest curiosities in Nature; but he justifies himself so well, that the Goddess gives them both her approbation. She recommends to them to find proper employment for the indolents before-mentioned, in the study of butterflies, shells, birds' nests, moss, etc. but with particular caution not to proceed beyond trifles, to any useful or extensive views of Nature, or of the Author of Nature. Against the last of these apprehensions, she is secured by a hearty address from the Minute Philosophers and Freethinkers,[1] one of whom speaks in the name of the rest. The youth thus instructed and principled are delivered to her in a body, by the hands of Silenus, and then admitted to taste the cup of the Magus her high priest, which causes a total oblivion of all obligations, divine, civil, moral, or rational. To these her adepts she sends priests, attendants, and comforters, of various kinds; confers on them Orders and Degrees; and then dismissing them with a speech, confirming to each his privileges[2] and telling what she expects from each, concludes with a yawn of extraordinary virtue,[3] the progress and effects whereof on all orders of men, and the consummation of all, in the restoration of night and chaos, conclude the poem.

[THE GODDESS COMING IN HER MAJESTY]

> Yet, yet a moment, one dim ray of light
> Indulge, dread chaos, and eternal night!
> Of darkness visible[4] so much be lent,
> As half[5] to show, half veil the deep intent.
> 5 Ye pow'rs! whose mysteries restored I sing,
> To whom Time bears me on his rapid wing,
> Suspend a while your force inertly strong,
> Then take at once the poet and the song.
>   Now flamed the Dog-star's unpropitious ray,[6]
> 10 Smote ev'ry brain, and withered ev'ry bay;[7]
> Sick was the sun, the owl forsook his bow'r,
> The moon-struck prophet felt the madding hour:
> Then rose the seed of chaos, and of night,
> To blot out order, and extinguish light,
> 15 Of dull and venal a new world to mold,
> And bring Saturnian days[8] of lead and gold.

7. A monk, famous for his forgeries.
8. Men knowledgeable in trivial subjects or antique curiosities.
9. A Roman general, who burned Corinth.
1. Petty philosophers and those who rejected orthodox religious dogma in favor of rational inquiry.
2. From this point, the rest of the Argument was added in 1743, describing the new ending added at the same time.
3. Power.
4. Cf. Milton's description of Hell in *Paradise Lost* 1.62–65: "yet from those flames / No light, but rather darkness visible / Served only to discover sights of woe, / Regions of sorrow."

5. This is a great propriety, for a dull poet can never express himself otherwise than by halves or imperfectly [Pope's note].
6. Sirius, the Dog-star, is most visible at the end of summer, the time at which poetry recitals used to take place in classical Rome.
7. The laurel leaves symbolic of poetic success.
8. Saturn's many associations are played on here: Saturnalia was the Roman festival of misrule; while the age of Saturn was the Golden Age, Saturn also symbolized lead, these two metals respectively representing venality (corruption) and dullness.

She mounts the throne: her head a cloud concealed,
In broad effulgence all below revealed[9]
('Tis thus aspiring Dulness ever shines)
20 Soft on her lap her laureate son reclines.
     Beneath her footstool, Science groans in chains,
And Wit dreads exile, penalties, and pains.
There foamed rebellious Logic, gagged and bound,
There, stripped, fair Rhet'ric languished on the ground;
25 His blunted arms by Sophistry are born,[1]
And shameless Billingsgate her robes adorn.
Morality, by her false guardians drawn,
Chicane in furs, and Casuistry in lawn,[2]
Gasps, as they straiten° at each end the cord,   *tighten*
30 And dies, when Dulness gives her Page[3] the word.

[THE GENIUSES OF THE SCHOOLS]

135   Now crowds on crowds around the Goddess press,
Each eager to present the first address.[4]
Dunce scorning dunce beholds the next advance,
But fop shows fop superior complaisance.
When lo! a specter[5] rose, whose index hand
140 Held forth the virtue of the dreadful wand;
His beavered brow° a birchen garland wears,   *beaver hat*
Dropping with infant's blood, and mother's tears.[6]
O'er ev'ry vein a shudd'ring horror runs;
Eton and Winton[7] shake through all their sons.
145 All flesh is humbled, Westminster's bold race[8]
Shrink, and confess the genius° of the place: *guardian deity*
The pale boy-senator[9] yet tingling stands,
And holds his breeches close with both his hands.
     Then thus: "Since man from beast by words is known,
150 Words are man's province, words we teach alone.
When reason doubtful, like the Samian letter,[1]
Points him two ways, the narrower is the better.
Placed at the door of learning, youth to guide,
We never suffer it to stand too wide.
155 To ask, to guess, to know, as they commence,
As fancy opens the quick springs of sense,
We ply the memory, we load the brain,
Bind rebel wit, and double chain on chain,

---

9. Pope glosses this line: "The higher you climb, the more you show your arse."
1. The quibbling reasoning of Sophistry replaces Logic, while Billingsgate (the slang of fish sellers) replaces Rhetoric.
2. Legal trickery wears a judge's ermine robes, while the moral quibbler wears a bishop's fine linen.
3. Sir Francis Page, the "hanging judge," is linked with "Mutes or Pages" given the task of "strangling state criminals in Turkey" [Pope's note].
4. Written congratulations.
5. Dr. Richard Busby (1605–1695), headmaster of Westminster School, famed for instilling discipline as well as learning: the "dreadful wand" is his birch cane.
6. Cf. *Paradise Lost* 1.392–93. "First Moloch, horrid king besmeared with blood / Of human sacrifice, and parents' tears." In the Ancient Near East, the cult of Moloch practiced child sacrifice.
7. Eton and Winchester, two schools influenced by Busby.
8. The many graduates of the top schools who went on to be parliamentarians (at Westminster).
9. Young member of Parliament.
1. The letter "Y," emblem of the choice between the paths of virtue and vice.

Confine the thought, to exercise the breath;[2]
160   And keep them in the pale of words[3] till death.
Whate'er the talents, or howe'er designed,
We hang one jingling padlock on the mind:[4]
A poet the first day, he dips his quill;
And what the last? a very poet still.
165   Pity! the charm works only in our wall,
Lost, lost too soon in yonder House or Hall."[5]

[YOUNG GENTLEMEN RETURNED FROM TRAVEL]

275   In flowed at once a gay embroidered race,
And titt'ring pushed the pedants off the place:
Some would have spoken, but the voice was drowned
By the French horn, or by the op'ning° hound.   baying
The first came forwards, with as easy mien,
280   As if he saw St. James's° and the Queen.   the palace
When thus th' attendant orator[6] begun.
"Receive, great Empress! thy accomplished son:
Thine from the birth, and sacred° from the rod,   spared
A dauntless infant! never scared with God.
285   The sire saw, one by one, his virtues wake:
The mother begged the blessing of a rake.[7]
Thou gav'st that ripeness, which so soon began,
And ceased so soon, he ne'er was boy, nor man.
Through school and college, thy kind cloud o'ercast,
290   Safe and unseen the young Aeneas past:[8]
Thence bursting glorious, all at once let down,°   released
Stunned with his giddy larum° half the town.   noise
Intrepid then, o'er seas and lands he flew:
Europe he saw, and Europe saw him too.
295   There all thy gifts and graces we display,
Thou, only thou, directing all our way!
To where the Seine, obsequious as she runs,
Pours at great Bourbon's feet her silken sons;[9]
Or Tiber, now no longer Roman, rolls,
300   Vain of Italian arts, Italian souls:[1]
To happy convents, bosomed deep in vines,
Where slumber abbots, purple as their wines:
To isles of fragrance, lily-silvered vales,
Diffusing languor in the panting gales:°   light winds
305   To lands of singing, or of dancing slaves,

2. By obliging them to get the classic poets by heart, which furnishes them with endless matter for conversation, and verbal amusement for their whole lives [Pope's note].
3. I.e., within the boundaries of pedantic learning.
4. For youth being used like packhorses and beaten on under a heavy load of words, lest they should tire, their instructors contrive to make the words jingle in rhyme and meter [Pope's note].
5. They can no longer compose once they leave the school for the parliamentary or legal professions, in the House of Commons or Westminster Hall.

6. The "lac'd governor from France" who had entered earlier with "whore" and "pupil" (line 272).
7. She hoped he would become a rake (an arrogant young libertine).
8. Aeneas was hidden in a cloud by Venus when entering Carthage.
9. Bourbon: Louis XIV, so absolute a monarch that even the rivers are "obsequious" (servile).
1. The poetic and martial might of the Roman Empire had degenerated into the effeminacy and shallowness of the Italian states.

Love-whisp'ring woods, and lute-resounding waves.
But chief her shrine where naked Venus keeps,
And cupids ride the Lion of the Deeps;[2]
Where, eased of fleets, the Adriatic main°   *sea*
310 Wafts the smooth eunuch and enamored swain.
Led by my hand, he sauntered Europe round,
And gathered ev'ry vice on Christian ground;
Saw ev'ry court, heard ev'ry king declare
His royal sense, of op'ra's or the fair;[3]
315 The stews° and palace equally explored,   *brothels*
Intrigued with glory, and with spirit whored;
Tried all *hors d'oeuvres,* all *liqueurs* defined,
Judicious drank, and greatly-daring dined;
Dropped the dull lumber of the Latin store,[4]
320 Spoiled his own language, and acquired no more;
All classic learning lost on classic ground;
And last turned *Air,* the echo of a sound![5]
See now, half-cured, and perfectly well-bred,
With nothing but a solo in his head;
325 As much estate, and principle, and wit,
As Jansen, Fleetwood, Cibber[6] shall think fit;
Stol'n from a duel, followed by a nun,
And, if a borough choose him, not undone;[7]
See, to my country happy I restore
330 This glorious youth, and add one Venus[8] more.
Her too receive (for her my soul adores)
So may the sons of sons of sons of whores
Prop thine, O Empress! like each neighbor throne,
And make a long posterity thy own."
335   Pleased, she accepts the hero, and the dame,
Wraps in her veil, and frees from sense of shame.

[THE MINUTE PHILOSOPHERS AND THE CONSUMMATION OF ALL]

Then thick as locusts black'ning all the ground,
A tribe, with weeds and shells fantastic crowned,
Each with some wond'rous gift approached the Pow'r,
400 A nest, a toad, a fungus, or a flow'r.
But far the foremost, two, with earnest zeal,
And aspect ardent to the throne appeal.
The first thus opened: "Hear thy suppliant's call,
Great Queen, and common mother of us all!
405 Fair from its humble bed I reared this flow'r,[9]

2. The winged lion of Venice, a city-state known previously for its naval and trading might, known now as "the brothel of Europe."

3. Britain's king, George II, was notorious for his interest in women and song.

4. His classical learning.

5. Yet less a body than Echo itself; for Echo reflects sense or words at least, this gentleman only airs and tunes [Pope's note].

6. Three very eminent persons, all managers of plays [the first at gambling, the latter two in the theater], who, though not [school] governors by profession, had, each in his way, concerned themselves in the education of youth . . . [Pope's note].

7. If elected to Parliament, he could not be arrested for debt.

8. A prostitute he brings back with him.

9. The attempt to produce the perfect carnation was a contemporary obsession among amateur scientists (or "virtuosi") and compulsive gardeners.

Suckled, and cheered, with air, and sun, and show'r,
Soft on the paper ruff its leaves I spread,
Bright with the gilded button tipped its head,
Then throned in glass, and named it CAROLINE:[1]
410   Each maid cried, charming! and each youth, divine!
Did Nature's pencil ever blend such rays,
Such varied light in one promiscuous blaze?
Now prostrate! dead! behold that Caroline:
No maid cries, charming! and no youth, divine!
415   And lo the wretch! whose vile, whose insect lust
Laid this gay daughter of the spring in dust.
Oh punish him, or to th' Elysian shades[2]
Dismiss my soul, where no carnation fades."[3]
      He ceased, and wept. With innocence of mien,
420   Th' accused stood forth, and thus addressed the Queen.
      "Of all th' enameled race,° whose silv'ry wing   *butterflies*
Waves to the tepid zephyrs° of the spring,   *breezes*
Or swims along the fluid atmosphere,
Once brightest shined this child of heat and air.
425   I saw, and started from its vernal bow'r
The rising game,[4] and chased from flow'r to flow'r.
It fled, I followed; now in hope, now pain;
It stopped, I stopped; it moved, I moved again.[5]
At last it fixed, 'twas on what plant it pleased,
430   And where it fixed, the beauteous bird° I seized: *winged thing*
Rose or carnation was below by care;
I meddle, Goddess! only in my sphere.
I tell the naked fact without disguise,
And to excuse it need but show the prize;
435   Whose spoils this paper[6] offers to your eye,
Fair ev'n in death! this peerless *butterfly*."
      "My sons!" (she answered) "both have done your parts:
Live happy both, and long promote our arts.
But hear a mother, when she recommends
440   To your fraternal care, our sleeping friends.[7]
The common soul, of heav'n's more frugal make,
Serves but to keep fools pert, and knaves awake:
A drowsy watchman, that just gives a knock,
And breaks our rest, to tell us what's a clock.
445   Yet by some object every brain is stirred;
The dull may waken to a hummingbird;
The most recluse, discreetly opened find
Congenial matter in the cockle kind;

---

1. Queen Caroline, wife of George II, patron of gardeners and artists. Pope relates that "one ambitious Gardner at Hammersmith . . . caused his favorite [bloom] to be painted on his sign, with this inscription, 'This is My Queen Caroline'."
2. The classical paradise.
3. Cf. 1 Peter 1.4: for the believer, there is "an inheritance incorruptible, and undefiled, and that fadeth not away, reserved in heaven."

4. As would a hunter of bigger game.
5. Pope here alludes to *Paradise Lost* 4.462–63, in which Eve becomes fascinated with her own reflection, a passage that in turn alludes to the story of Narcissus in Ovid's *Metamorphoses*. Pope thus obliquely comments on the insubstantial character and self-absorption of the butterfly hunter.
6. On which the butterfly is mounted.
7. The other inhabitants of Dulness's court.

The mind, in metaphysics at a loss,
450 May wander in a wilderness of moss;[8]
The head that turns° at superlunar things,   *turns away*
Poised with a tail, may steer on Wilkins' wings,[9]
    "O! would the sons of men once think their eyes
And reason giv'n them but to study *flies?*
455 See Nature in some partial narrow shape,
And let the author of the whole escape:
Learn but to trifle; or, who most observe,
To wonder at their maker, not to serve."
    "Be that my task" (replies a gloomy clerk,[1]
460 Sworn foe to myst'ry,[2] yet divinely dark;
Whose pious hope aspires to see the day
When moral evidence[3] shall quite decay,
And damns implicit faith, and holy lies,
Prompt to impose, and fond to dogmatize):
465 "Let others creep by timid steps, and slow,
On plain experience lay foundations low,
By common sense to common knowledge bred,
And last, to Nature's cause through Nature led.
All-seeing in thy mists, we want no guide,
470 Mother of arrogance, and source of pride!
We nobly take the high priori road,[4]
And reason downward, till we doubt of God:
Make Nature still encroach upon his plan;
And shove him off as far as e'er we can:
475 Thrust some mechanic cause into his place;
Or bind in matter, or diffuse in space.[5]
Or, at one bound o'er-leaping all his laws,
Make God man's image, man, the final cause,[6]
Find virtue local, all relation scorn,[7]
480 See all in *Self*, and but for self be born:
Of nought so certain as our *Reason* still,
Of nought so doubtful as of *Soul* and *Will*.
Oh hide the God still more! and make us see
Such as Lucretius[8] drew, a God like thee:
485 Wrapped up in self, a God without a thought,
Regardless of our merit or default.
Or that bright image to our fancy draw,

---

8. Of which the naturalists count above three hundred species [Pope's note].

9. John Wilkins (1614–1672), bishop and first secretary of the Royal Society; he "entertain'd the extravagant hope of a possibility to fly to the Moon; which has put some volatile geniuses upon making wings for that purpose" [Pope's note].

1. Pope may be punning on the word clerk (pronounced "clark" and meaning one in holy orders) to refer to Samuel Clarke (1675–1729), an Anglican theologian who could not accept the mystery of the Trinity (though otherwise he was orthodox). Pope sees him as an exponent of rational theology: it is his religious skepticism that makes him "gloomy."

2. Religious mystery requiring faith.

3. Evidence able to be assessed by reason or common sense.

4. Arguing *a priori*, from a prior or assumed truth: here, a conception of God that will not stand up to testing in the real, natural world, which instead takes over his role.

5. The first of these follies is that of Descartes; the second of Hobbes; the third of some succeeding philosophers [Pope's note].

6. Human pride in being God's final, perfect creation leads man to put his desires over God's plan.

7. Without God's absolute order, moral relativism rules relations between cultures and individuals.

8. Materialist Roman philosopher, 1st century B.C.; the next two lines are adapted from his *De Rerum Natura* 2.646ff.

Which Theocles[9] in raptured vision saw,
While through poetic scenes the genius roves,
490 Or wanders wild in academic groves;
That NATURE our society adores,
Where Tindal dictates, and Silenus snores."[1]
    Roused at his name, up rose the bousy° sire,   *drowsy*
And shook from out his pipe the seeds of fire;[2]
495 Then snapped his box,° and stroked his belly down: *snuffbox*
Rosy and rev'rend, though without a gown,[3]
Bland and familiar to the throne he came,
Led up the youth, and called the Goddess "Dame."
Then thus. "From priestcraft happily set free,
500 Lo! ev'ry finished son returns to thee:
First slave to words, then vassal to a name,[4]
Then dupe to party; child and man the same;
Bounded by nature, narrowed still by art,
A trifling head, and a contracted heart.
505 Thus bred, thus taught, how many have I seen,
Smiling on all, and smiled on by a Queen.
Marked out for honors, honored for their birth,
To thee the most rebellious things on earth:
Now to thy gentle shadow all are shrunk,
510 All melted down, in pension, or in punk![5]
So K * so B * * sneaked into the grave,[6]
A monarch's half, and half a harlot's slave.
Poor W * * nipped in folly's broadest bloom,[7]
Who praises now? his chaplain on his tomb.
515 Then take them all, oh take them to thy breast!
Thy magus,[8] Goddess! shall perform the rest."
    With that, a WIZARD OLD his cup extends;
Which who so tastes, forgets his former friends,
Sire, ancestors, himself. One casts his eyes
520 Up to a star, and like Endymion dies:[9]
A feather shooting from another's head,
Extracts his brain, and principle is fled,
Lost is his God, his country, ev'rything;

9. A philosopher featured in Shaftesbury's *The Moralists* (1709), who here worships his "genius," nature.
1. Matthew Tindal (1657–1733), a famous deist (i.e., one who bases belief in God solely upon reason, rejecting revelation). Silenus: "an Epicurean philosopher [who] sings the principles of that philosophy in his drink" [Pope's note], associated with Thomas Gordon, Commissioner of the Wine for Walpole's government.
2. In Epicurean language, atoms.
3. Silenus wears no priest's gown because he is usually naked.
4. A recapitulation of the whole course of modern education described in this book, which confines youth to the study of words only in schools, subjects them to the authority of systems in the universities, and deludes them with the names of party distinctions in the world. All equally concurring to narrow the understanding, and establish slavery and error in literature, philosophy, and politics. The whole finished in modern free-thinking; the completion of whatever is vain, wrong, and destructive to the happiness of mankind, as it establishes self-love for the sole principle of action [Pope's note].
5. Paid to keep quiet by Walpole's government, or interested only in whoring.
6. Possibly the Duke of Kent and Earl of Berkeley, both honored as Knights of the Garter, though Pope's joke here is that these "honor'd" men cannot be identified with certainty.
7. Possibly the dissolute young Earl of Warwick, though the obscurity of the reference is again part of Pope's point.
8. The high priest or wizard of the goddess Dulness may be Walpole.
9. The star and feather were insignia of Knights of the Garter; the star was also worn by Knights of the Bath. Loved by the Moon, Endymion was kept in endless slumber by her.

And nothing left but homage to a king!
525　The vulgar herd turn off to roll with hogs,[1]
　　To run with horses, or to hunt with dogs;
　　But, sad example! never to escape
　　Their infamy, still keep the human shape.
　　　But she, good Goddess, sent to ev'ry child
530　Firm impudence, or stupefaction mild;
　　And straight succeeded, leaving shame no room,
　　Cibberian forehead, or Cimmerian gloom.[2]
　　　Kind self-conceit to some her glass° applies,　　　　　　*mirror*
　　Which no one looks in with another's eyes:
535　But as the flatt'rer or dependant paint,
　　Beholds himself a patriot, chief, or saint.
　　　On others int'rest her gay liv'ry° flings,　　　*servants' uniform*
　　Int'rest, that waves on party-colored[3] wings:
　　Turned to the sun, she casts a thousand dyes,
540　And, as she turns, the colors fall or rise.
　　　Others the Siren Sisters[4] warble round,
　　And empty heads console with empty sound.
　　No more, alas! the voice of fame they hear,
　　The balm of Dulness trickling in their ear.
545　Great C * *, H * *, P * *, R * *, K *,[5]
　　Why all your toils? your sons have learned to sing.
　　How quick ambition hastes to ridicule!
　　The sire is made a peer, the son a fool.
　　　On some, a priest succinct in amice white[6]
550　Attends; all flesh is nothing in his sight!
　　Beeves, at his touch, at once to jelly turn,[7]
　　And the huge boar is shrunk into an urn:
　　The board with specious miracles he loads,
　　Turns hares to larks, and pigeons into toads.
555　Another (for in all what one can shine?)
　　Explains the *seve* and *verdeur* of the vine.[8]
　　What cannot copious sacrifice atone?[9]
　　Thy truffles, Perigord! thy hams, Bayonne!
　　With French libation, and Italian strain,
560　Wash Bladen white, and expiate Hays's stain.
　　Knight lifts the head,[1] for what are crowds undone
　　To three essential partridges in one?[2]

---

1. The wizard's cup has the transformative powers of the witch Circe; but while she changed men to beasts and left them their minds, here the minds are changed while the bodies remain human.
2. The Cimmerians lived in Homer's far-western land of darkness, where Odysseus entered the underworld.
3. Meaning both multicolored, and colored according to party political allegiance.
4. Italian opera singers.
5. Although possible identifications have been made for these men, Pope's joke is that their sons, despite having the advantages of birth, earned no place for themselves in history, causing the "great" family names to fall into obscurity.
6. The priest's amice (a linen vestment) becomes the cook's apron.
7. The chef performs priestly miracles, turning beef to jelly and carving meat into odd shapes.
8. Different qualities of wine.
9. French regional foods are sacrificed to the goddess, accompanied by Italian singing.
1. Bladen and Hays were gamblers; Robert Knight, cashier of the South Sea Company, fled England when the company collapsed in 1720, leaving many ruined. All three "lived with the utmost magnificence at Paris, and kept open tables, frequented by persons of the first quality of England, and even by Princes of the blood of France" [Pope's note].
2. Two partridges were used to make the sauce for the third; alluding to the mystery of the Trinity.

Gone ev'ry blush, and silent all reproach,
Contending princes mount them in their coach.
565   Next bidding all draw near on bended knees,
The Queen confers her *Titles* and *Degrees*.
Her children first of more distinguished sort,
Who study Shakespeare at the Inns of Court,[3]
Impale a glowworm, or vertù[4] profess,
570   Shine in the dignity of F. R. S.[5]
Some, deep Freemasons,[6] join the silent race
Worthy to fill Pythagoras's place:
Some botanists, or florists at the least,
Or issue members of an annual feast.
575   Nor past the meanest unregarded, one
Rose a Gregorian, one a Gormogon.[7]
The last, not least in honor or applause,
Isis and Cam made Doctors of her Laws.[8]
     Then blessing all, "Go children of my care!
580   To practice now from theory repair.
All my commands are easy, short, and full:
My sons! be proud, be selfish, and be dull.
Guard my prerogative, assert my throne:
This nod confirms each privilege your own.
585   The cap and switch[9] be sacred to his Grace;
With staff and pumps[1] the Marquis lead the race;
From stage to stage the licensed Earl may run,[2]
Paired with his fellow charioteer the sun;
The learned Baron butterflies design,°   sketch
590   Or draw to silk arachne's subtle line;[3]
The Judge to dance his brother Sergeant[4] call;
The Senator at cricket urge the ball;
The Bishop stow (pontific luxury!)
An hundred souls of turkeys in a pie;[5]
595   The sturdy Squire to Gallic masters stoop,[6]
And drown his lands and manors in a soup.
Others import yet nobler arts from France,
Teach kings to fiddle, and make Senates dance.[7]
Perhaps more high some daring son[8] may soar,
600   Proud to my list to add one monarch more;
And nobly conscious, princes are but things

---

3. When they should be studying law.
4. An interest in antiquities and artistic curios; hence
"virtuoso."
5. Fellow of the Royal Society, as many noble virtuosos
were.
6. Where taciturnity is the only essential qualification, as
it was one of the chief of the disciples of Pythagoras
[Pope's note]. The Freemasons were often deists and freethinkers, who adapted religious rituals in meetings devoted to secular fellowship and philsophical inquiry.
7. Societies founded in ridicule of the Freemasons.
8. Oxford and Cambridge gave honorary degrees.
9. Jockeys' equipment, awarded here to followers of racing.
1. These footman's items were popular with young gen-

tlemen.
2. The Earl of Salisbury had a license to drive a stage-
coach.
3. Making stockings out of spider's webs had been
attempted.
4. The barrister; the call of sergeants involved pompous,
dancelike ceremony.
5. As did the Bishop of Durham.
6. Even the traditionally conservative country Squires
bowed to French fashions, like eating soup.
7. After their prince [Pope's note], as Lilliputian courtiers
had to in *Gulliver's Travels* 1.3.
8. Walpole, whose unprecedented post of "first minister"
gave him virtual control of the country from 1721 till he
was ousted in 1742.

Born for first ministers, as slaves for kings,
Tyrant supreme! shall three estates command,[9]
And MAKE ONE MIGHTY DUNCIAD OF THE LAND!"

605   More she had spoke, but yawned—all nature nods:
What Mortal can resist the yawn of gods?[1]
Churches and chapels instantly it reached;
(St. James's first, for leaden Gilbert[2] preached)
Then catched the schools; the Hall scarce kept awake;

610   The Convocation[3] gaped, but could not speak:
Lost was the nation's sense,[4] nor could be found,
While the long solemn unison went round:
Wide, and more wide, it spread o'er all the realm;
Ev'n Palinurus[5] nodded at the helm:

615   The vapor mild o'er each committee crept;
Unfinished treaties in each office slept;
And chiefless armies dozed out the campaign;
And navies yawned for orders on the main.[6]
O Muse! relate (for you can tell alone,

620   Wits have short memories, and dunces none)
Relate, who first, who last resigned to rest;
Whose heads she partly, whose completely blest;
What charms could faction, what ambition dull,
The venal quiet, and entrance the dull;

625   'Till drowned was sense, and shame, and right, and wrong—
O sing, and hush the nations with thy song![7]

* *

In vain, in vain,—the all-composing hour
Resistless falls: The Muse obeys the pow'r.
She comes! she comes! the sable throne behold

630   Of Night Primaeval, and of Chaos old!
Before her, Fancy's gilded clouds decay,
And all its varying rainbows die away.
Wit shoots in vain its momentary fires,
The meteor drops, and in a flash expires.

635   As one by one, at dread Medea's strain,[8]
The sick'ning stars fade off th' ethereal plain;
As Argus' eyes by Hermes' wand oppressed,[9]
Closed one by one to everlasting rest;
Thus at her felt approach, and secret might,

640   Art after Art goes out, and all is night.

9. The three estates of nobility, clergy, and commoners, all of which Walpole controlled by various means.
1. This verse is truly Homerical, as is the conclusion of the Action, where the great Mother composes all, in the same manner at the period of the Odyssey [Pope's note].
2. Dr. John Gilbert, Dean of Exeter.
3. Assembly of the clergy.
4. The House of Commons, "justly called the sense of the nation" [Pope's note].
5. Aeneas's helmsman, who falls asleep and drowns; here Robert Walpole, steering the state aimlessly.
6. The sea; referring to governmental delays during the war with Spain.
7. To this couplet, which concluded The New Dunciad

(1742), Pope added a final note: "It is impossible to lament sufficiently the loss of the rest of this poem, just at the opening of so fair a scene as the invocation seems to promise. It is to be hoped however that the poet completed it, and that it will not be lost to posterity. . . ." The 30 lines of the poem which follow were moved from the ending of the three-book Dunciad (1728) to The Dunciad, In Four Books (1743).
8. In Seneca's play Medea, the witch attempts to revenge herself for Jason's desertion by causing stars to fall and the sun to halt in its course.
9. Argus had a hundred eyes, enabling him to guard Io against Jupiter's advances. Jupiter, however, sent Mercury (Hermes) to charm Argus to sleep and kill him.

See skulking Truth to her old cavern fled,
Mountains of casuistry° heaped o'er her head!   *false reasoning*
Philosophy, that leaned on Heav'n before,
Shrinks to her second cause,[1] and is no more.
645   Physic of Metaphysic begs defense,
And Metaphysic calls for aid on Sense![2]
See Mystery to Mathematics fly![3]
In vain! they gaze, turn giddy, rave, and die.
Religion blushing veils her sacred fires,
650   And unawares Morality expires.
Nor public flame, nor private, dares to shine;
Nor human spark is left, nor glimpse divine!
Lo! thy dread empire, CHAOS! is restored;
Light dies before thy uncreating word:[4]
655   Thy hand, great Anarch![5] lets the curtain fall;
And Universal Darkness buries All.

c. 1741   1742

————— ❦ —————

Lady Mary Wortley Montagu
1689–1762

In learning, literature, and travel, Lady Mary Wortley Montagu outdistanced almost all of her contemporaries. Born Mary Pierrepont, she acquired her title at age one (when her father became an earl), lost her mother at age three, and immersed herself throughout her youth in the Roman classics, fervently pursuing a plan of self-education at odds with the conventional domesticating agenda (dancing, drawing, social graces) laid out for young women of her rank. For a time in her teens she aspired to implement the idea set forth by the feminist Mary Astell, of founding a convent consecrated to women's learning. In 1712 she married, against her father's wishes, a Whig Member of Parliament named Edward Wortley Montagu, after conducting with him a wary, carefully reasoned courtship mostly by means of letters. When he was appointed Ambassador to Turkey four years later, she accompanied him, and was fascinated by what she saw: by the Turkish practice of inoculating against smallpox, which (having survived the disease herself) she successfully championed in England at her return; by the gaps and continuities between British and Turkish culture, on which she reported eloquently in missives home. Her *Turkish Embassy Letters*, which she compiled from her writings during this sojourn for publication after her death, remain the foundation of her fame.

Her life as a writer yielded other riches, just now beginning to be explored. She wrote essays, including a *Spectator* for Addison and Steele and a later periodical series of her own (1737–1738). She produced short fiction and a comedy but worked more steadily at verse, collaborating with Alexander Pope on some poems and combating him in others, after

---

1. The world is now explained by natural causes.
2. Natural science turns to theoretical philosophy, which in turn looks back to empiricism.
3. Divine revelation is threatened by "certain defenders of religion [who] attempted to show that the mysteries of religion may be mathematically demonstrated" [Pope's

note].
4. Reversing the order of the creation of the world in Genesis, and restoring chaos.
5. A ruler with no political authority; one who promotes disorder and confusion.

their friendship had disintegrated into a round of bitter, witty recriminations. Most plentifully she wrote letters, sharp and searching, adroitly tailored to please her wide array of correspondents.

Montagu's spate of accomplishment made her alert to the constrictions of gender. "There is hardly a character in the world," she wrote at age twenty, "more liable to universal ridicule than that of a Learned Woman." Women, she counseled, should know much but hide their knowledge, lest they lose out on the comforts of love, marriage, and social ease. Deeply attentive to the burdens imposed on women and the tactics available to them, Montagu's idiosyncratic feminism earned esteem from her predecessor Astell, and from many who came after.

Idiosyncrasy exacted costs, in the form of that "ridicule" she had early anticipated, and in the breakdown of important relationships. Her marriage failed, as did a passionate love affair (again largely epistolary) with the bisexual Italian writer Francesco Algarotti. Montagu lived her last twenty-five years mostly in Italy. In retrospect, her self-removal looks like part of a lifelong strategy. Montagu had always held it crucial to keep some distance from her culture's assumptions in order to see them clearly, to critique them, to change or expunge their operations in herself and in the world. The title she chose for her periodical series, *The Nonsense of Common Sense*, encapsulates her lifelong conviction. By the eccentricity of her self-education, the remoteness of her travels and her residences, the originality of her thought and conduct, the amused acerbity of her style, Montagu kept her distance and found her voice.

from The Turkish Embassy Letters[1]
To Lady ———[2]
[ON THE TURKISH BATHS]

Adrianople, 1 April 1717

I am now got into a new world where everything I see appears to me a change of scene, and I write to your Ladyship with some content of mind, hoping at least that you will find the charm of novelty in my letters and no longer reproach me that I tell you nothing extraordinary. I won't trouble you with a relation of our tedious journey, but I must not omit what I saw remarkable at Sophia, one of the most beautiful towns in the Turkish Empire and famous for its hot baths that are resorted to both for diversion and health. I stopped here one day on purpose to see them. Designing to go incognito, I hired a Turkish coach. These *voitures* are not at all like ours, but much more convenient for the country, the heat being so great that glasses[3] would be very troublesome. They are made a good deal in the manner of the Dutch coaches, having wooden lattices painted and gilded, the inside being painted with baskets and nosegays of flowers, intermixed commonly with little poetical mottoes. They are covered all over with scarlet cloth, lined with silk and very often richly embroidered and

1. The text of the *Turkish Embassy Letters* comes not from the actual letters Montagu sent while on her travels but from two manuscript books in which she combined portions of her letters and travel journals with new prose to produce a hybrid account of the trip, which she intended for posthumous publication. In 1724 Montagu lent the volumes to Mary Astell, who inscribed into the second a preface addressed to future readers: ". . . I confess I am malicious enough to desire that the world should see to how much better purpose the *ladies* travel than their *lords*, and that whilst it is surfeited with male travels [i.e.,

travel-books], all in the same tone and stuffed with the same trifles, a *lady* has the skill to strike out a new path and to embellish a worn out subject with variety of fresh and elegant entertainment . . . Let us freely own the superiority of this sublime genius as I do in sincerity of my soul, pleased that a *woman* triumphs, and proud to follow in her train."
2. In the manuscript, Montagu supplies no name for this person, who may be a fictive "recipient."
3. Glass windows (which the Turkish coaches lacked).

fringed. This covering entirely hides the persons in them, but may be thrown back at pleasure and the ladies peep through the lattices. They hold four people very conveniently, seated on cushions, but not raised.

In one of these covered wagons I went to the bagnio[4] about ten o'clock. It was already full of women. It is built of stone in the shape of a dome with no windows but in the roof, which gives light enough. There was five of these domes joined together, the outmost being less than the rest and serving only as a hall where the porteress stood at the door. Ladies of quality generally give this woman the value of a crown or ten shillings, and I did not forget that ceremony. The next room is a very large one, paved with marble, and all round it raised two sofas of marble, one above another. There were four fountains of cold water in this room, falling first into marble basins and then running on the floor in little channels made for that purpose, which carried the streams into the next room, something less than this, with the same sort of marble sofas, but so hot with steams of sulphur proceeding from the baths joining to it, 'twas impossible to stay there with one's clothes on. The two other domes were the hot baths, one of which had cocks of cold water turning into it to temper it to what degree of warmth the bathers have a mind to.

I was in my traveling habit, which is a riding dress, and certainly appeared very extraordinary to them, yet there was not one of 'em that showed the least surprise or impertinent curiosity, but received me with all the obliging civility possible. I know of no European court where the ladies would have behaved themselves in so polite a manner to a stranger.

I believe in the whole there were two hundred women, and yet none of those disdainful smiles or satiric whispers that never fail in our asemblies when anybody appears that is not dressed exactly in fashion. They repeated over and over to me, *uzelle, pek uzelle*, which is nothing but "charming, very charming." The first sofas were covered with cushioned and rich carpets, on which sat the ladies, and on the second their slaves behind 'em, but without any distinction of rank by their dress, all being in the state of nature, that is, in plain English, stark naked, without any beauty or defect concealed, yet there was not the least wanton smile or immodest gesture amongst 'em. They walked and moved with the same majestic grace which Milton describes of our "general mother."[5] There were many amongst them as exactly proportioned as ever any goddess was drawn by the pencil of Guido or Titian,[6] and most of their skins shiningly white, only adorned by their beautiful hair divided into many tresses hanging on their shoulders, braided either with pearl or riband,[7] perfectly representing the figures of the Graces.[8] I was here convinced of the truth of a reflection that I had often made, that if 'twas the fashion to go naked, the face would be hardly observed. I perceived that the ladies with the finest skins and most delicate shapes had the greatest share of my admiration, though their faces were sometimes less beautiful than those of their companions. To tell you the truth, I had wickedness enough to wish secretly that Mr. Gervase could have been there invisible.[9] I fancy it would have very much improved his art to see so many fine women naked in different pos-

4. The bath.
5. Eve (*Paradise Lost* 4.304–18).
6. Artists of the Italian Renaissance.
7. Ribbon.
8. Resembling the three sister divinities who (in Greek mythology) embody and endow grace and beauty.
9. Charles Jervas (c. 1675–1739), a successful portraitist

who had once painted Montagu as a shepherdess. The French painter Jean Auguste Dominique Ingres (1780–1867) later took up the hint implicit in Montagu's "fancy" here. Having transcribed portions of this letter from a French edition (1805), he made use of Montagu's descriptions in his painting *Le Bain Turc* (The Turkish Bath, 1862).

tures, some in conversation, some working, others drinking coffee or sherbet, and many negligently lying on their cushions while their slaves (generally pretty girls of seventeen or eighteen) were employed in braiding their hair in several pretty manners. In short, 'tis the women's coffee-house, where all the news of the town is told, scandal invented, etc. They generally take this diversion once a week, and stay there at least four or five hours without getting cold by immediate coming out of the hot bath into the cool room, which was very surprising to me. The lady that seemed the most considerable among them entreated me to sit by her and would fain have undressed me for the bath. I excused myself with some difficulty, they being all so earnest in persuading me. I was at last forced to open my skirt and show them my stays,[1] which satisfied them very well, for I saw they believed I was so locked up in that machine that it was not in my own power to open it, which contrivance they attributed to my husband. I was charmed with their civility and beauty, and should have been very glad to pass more time with them, but Mr. W[2] resolving to pursue his journey the next morning early, I was in haste to see the ruins of Justinian's church,[3] which did not afford me so agreeable a prospect as I had left, being little more than a heap of stones.

Adieu, Madam. I am sure I have now entertained you with an account of such a sight as you never saw in your life and that no book of travels could inform you of. 'Tis no less than death for a man to be found in one of those places.

To Lady Mar[1]

[ON TURKISH DRESS]

Adrianople, 1 April 1717

I wish to God (dear Sister) that you was as regular in letting me have the pleasure of knowing what passes on your side of the globe as I am careful in endeavoring to amuse you by the account of all I see that I think you care to hear of. You content yourself with telling me over and over that the town is very dull. It may possibly be dull to you when every day does not present you with something new, but for me that am in arrear at least two months' news, all that seems very stale with you would be fresh and sweet here; pray let me into more particulars. I will try to awaken your gratitude by giving you a full and true relation of the novelties of this place, none of which would surprise you more than a sight of my person as I am now in my Turkish habit, though I believe you would be of my opinion that 'tis admirably becoming. I intend to send you my picture; in the meantime accept of it here.

The first piece of my dress is a pair of drawers, very full, that reach to my shoes and conceal the legs more modestly than your petticoats. They are of a thin rose-color damask brocaded with silver flowers, my shoes of white kid leather embroidered with gold. Over this hangs my smock of a fine white silk gauze edged with embroidery. This smock has wide sleeves hanging half way down the arm and is closed at the neck with a diamond button, but the shape and color of the bosom very well to be distinguished through it. The *antery* is a waistcoat[2] made close to the shape, of white and gold damask, with very long sleeves falling back and fringed with deep gold fringe, and should have diamond or pearl buttons. My caftan, of the same stuff with

1. A tightly laced undergarment, stiffened with whalebone, extending from breast to thigh.
2. Her husband, Edward Wortley Montagu.
3. The Church of St. Sofia, built during the reign of the Byzantine Emperor Justinian (483–565).
1. Montagu's sister Frances (1690–1761), who had married the Earl of Mar.
2. A vest.

my drawers, is a robe exactly fitted to my shape and reaching to my feet, with very long straight falling sleeves. Over this is the girdle of about four fingers broad, which all that can afford have entirely of diamonds or other precious stones. Those that will not be at that expense have it of exquisite embroidery on satin, but it must be fastened before with a clasp of diamonds. The *curdée* is a loose robe they throw off or put on according to the weather, being of a rich brocade (mine is green and gold) either lined with ermine or sables; the sleeves reach very little below the shoulders. The headdress is composed of a cap called *talpock*, which is in winter of fine velvet embroidered with pearls or diamonds and in summer of a light shining silver stuff. This is fixed on one side of the head, hanging a little way down with a gold tassel and bound on either with a circle of diamonds (as I have seen several) or a rich embroidered handkerchief. On the other side of the head the hair is laid flat, and here the ladies are at liberty to show their fancies, some putting flowers, others a plume of heron's feathers, and, in short, what they please, but the most general fashion is a large bouquet of jewels made like natural flowers, that is, the buds of pearl, the roses of different colored rubies, the jasmines of diamonds, jonquils of topazes, etc., so well set and enameled 'tis hard to imagine anything of that kind so beautiful. The hair hangs at its full length behind, divided into tresses braided with pearl or riband, which is always in great quantity.

I never saw in my life so many fine heads of hair. I have counted 110 of these tresses of one lady's, all natural; but it must be owned that every beauty is more common here than with us. 'Tis surprising to see a young woman that is not very handsome. They have naturally the most beautiful complexions in the world and generally large black eyes. I can assure you with great truth that the Court of England (though I believe it the fairest in Christendom) cannot show so many beauties as are under our protection here. They generally shape their eyebrows, and the Greeks and Turks have a custom of putting round their eyes on the inside a black tincture that, at a distance or by candlelight, adds very much to the blackness of them. I fancy many of our ladies would be overjoyed to know this secret, but 'tis too visible by day. They dye their nails rose color; I own I cannot enough accustom myself to this fashion to find any beauty in it.

As to their morality or good conduct, I can say like Arlequin, 'tis just as 'tis with you,[3] and the Turkish ladies don't commit one sin the less for not being Christians. Now I am a little acquainted with their ways, I cannot forbear admiring either the exemplary discretion or extreme stupidity of all the writers that have given accounts of 'em.[4] 'Tis very easy to see they have more liberty than we have, no woman of what rank soever being permitted to go in the streets without two muslins, one that covers her face all but her eyes and another that hides the whole dress of her head and hangs half way down her back; and their shapes are wholly concealed by a thing they call a *ferigée*, which no woman of any sort appears without. This has straight sleeves that reaches to their fingers' ends and it laps all round 'em, not unlike a riding hood. In winter 'tis of cloth, and in summer, plain stuff or silk. You may guess how effectually this disguises them, that there is no distinguishing the great lady from her slave, and 'tis impossible for the most jealous husband to know his wife when he meets her, and no man dare either touch or follow a woman in the street.

3. A paraphrase (and misattribution) of a line from Aphra Behn's comedy *The Emperor of the Moon* (1687): the prankster Harlequin, pretending to be an ambassador from the moon, describes the corrupt social customs of his world to a gullible listener, who repeatedly exclaims

that morality there is "just as 'tis here" (3.2).
4. Many (though not all) writers on Turkey had emphasized the strict confinement and chastity of the women there.

This perpetual masquerade gives them entire liberty of following their inclinations without danger of discovery. The most usual method of intrigue is to send an appointment to the lover to meet the lady at a Jew's shop,[5] which are as notoriously convenient as our Indian houses,[6] and yet even those that don't make that use of 'em do not scruple to go to buy pennorths and tumble over[7] rich goods, which are chiefly to be found amongst that sort of people.[8] The great ladies seldom let their gallants[9] know who they are, and 'tis so difficult to find it out that they can very seldom guess at her name they have corresponded with above half a year together. You may easily imagine the number of faithful wives very small in a country where they have nothing to fear from their lovers' indiscretion, since we see so many that have the courage to expose themselves to that in this world and all the threatened punishment of the next, which is never preached to the Turkish damsels. Neither have they much to apprehend from the resentment of their husbands, those ladies that are rich having all their money in their own hands, which they take with 'em upon a divorce with an addition which he is obliged to give 'em. Upon the whole, I look upon the Turkish women as the only free people in the Empire. The very *Divan*[1] pays a respect to 'em, and the *Grand Signor* himself, when a *Bassa*[2] is executed, never violates the privileges of the harem (or women's apartment), which remains unsearched entire to the widow. They are queens of their slaves, which the husband has no permission so much as to look upon, except it be an old woman or two that his lady chooses. 'Tis true their law permits them four wives, but there is no instance of a man of quality that makes use of this liberty, or of a woman of rank that would suffer it. When a husband happens to be inconstant (as those things will happen) he keeps his mistress in a house apart and visits her as privately as he can, just as 'tis with you. Amongst all the great men here I only know the *Tefterdar* (i.e. treasurer) that keeps a number of she slaves for his own use (that is, on his own side of the house, for a slave once given to serve a lady is entirely at her disposal) and he is spoke of as a libertine, or what we should call a rake, and his wife won't see him, though she continues to live in his house.

Thus you see, dear Sister, the manners of mankind do not differ so widely as our voyage writers would make us believe. Perhaps it would be more entertaining to add a few surprising customs of my own invention, but nothing seems to me so agreeable as truth, and I believe nothing so acceptable to you. I conclude with repeating the great truth of my being, dear Sister, etc.

Letter to Lady Bute[1]
[ON HER GRANDDAUGHTER]

28 January 1753

Dear Child,

You have given me a great deal of satisfaction by your account of your eldest daughter. I am particularly pleased to hear she is a good arithmetician; it is the best proof of understanding. The knowledge of numbers is one of the chief distinctions

5. Jewish women sometimes helped arrange these assignations; being permitted to enter the harems, they could transmit secret messages.
6. London shops selling goods imported from India.
7. Penny-worths: good bargains; tumble over: browse through.
8. Jews.

9. Lovers.
1. A governmental official.
2. *Pasha*: a high official.
1. Montagu's only daughter, Mary (1718–1794), had in 1736 married John Stuart, third Earl of Bute. At the time this letter was written, Montagu had been long separated from her husband and was living in Italy.

between us and brutes. If there is anything in blood, you may reasonably expect your children should be endowed with an uncommon share of good sense. Mr. Wortley's[2] family and mine have both produced some of the greatest men that have been born in England. I mean Admiral Sandwich,[3] and my great grandfather who was distinguished by the name of Wise William.[4] I have heard Lord Bute's father mentioned as an extraordinary genius (though he had not many opportunities of showing it), and his uncle the present Duke of Argyll has one of the best heads I ever knew.

I will therefore speak to you as supposing Lady Mary not only capable but desirous of learning. In that case, by all means let her be indulged in it. You will tell me, I did not make it a part of your education. Your prospect was very different from hers, as you had no defect either in mind or person to hinder, and much in your circumstances to attract, the highest offers. It seemed your business to learn how to live in the world, as it is hers to know how to be easy out of it. It is the common error of builders and parents to follow some plan they think beautiful (and perhaps is so) without considering that nothing is beautiful that is misplaced. Hence we see so many edifices raised that the raisers can never inhabit, being too large for their fortunes. Vistas are laid open over barren heaths, and apartments contrived for a coolness very agreeable in Italy but killing in the north of Britain. Thus every woman endeavors to breed her daughter a fine lady, qualifying her for a station in which she will never appear, and at the same time incapacitating her for that retirement to which she is destined. Learning (if she has a real taste for it) will not only make her contented but happy in it. No entertainment is so cheap as reading, nor any pleasure so lasting. She will not want new fashions nor regret the loss of expensive diversions or variety of company if she can be amused with an author in her closet. To render this amusement extensive, she should be permitted to learn the languages. I have heard it lamented that boys lose so many years in mere learning of words. This is no objection to a girl, whose time is not so precious. She cannot advance herself in any profession, and has therefore more hours to spare; and as you say her memory is good, she will be very agreeably employed this way.

There are two cautions to be given on this subject: first, not to think herself learned when she can read Latin or even Greek. Languages are more properly to be called vehicles of learning than learning itself, as may be observed in many schoolmasters, who though perhaps critics in grammar are the most ignorant fellows upon earth. True knowledge consists in knowing things, not words. I would wish her no farther a linguist than to enable her to read books in their originals, that are often corrupted and always injured by translations. Two hours' application every morning will bring this about much sooner than you can imagine, and she will have leisure enough beside to run over the English poetry, which is a more important part of a woman's education than it is generally supposed. Many a young damsel has been ruined by a fine copy of verses, which she would have laughed at if she had known it had been stolen from Mr. Waller.[5] I remember when I was a girl I saved one of my companions from destruction, who communicated to me an epistle she was quite charmed with. As she had a natural good taste, she observed the lines were not so smooth as Prior's[6] or Pope's, but had more thought and spirit than any of theirs. She

---

2. Her estranged husband, Edward Wortley Montagu.
3. Edward Montagu (1625–1672), first Earl of Sandwich (and Samuel Pepys's patron), was Wortley's grandfather.
4. The Hon. William Pierrepont (1608–1678) was a prominent politician.

5. Edmund Waller (1606–1687), love poet frequently quoted (or plagiarized) by amorous wooers.
6. Matthew Prior (1664–1721), like Alexander Pope a celebrated poet.

was wonderfully delighted with such a demonstration of her lover's sense and passion, and not a little pleased with her own charms, that had force enough to inspire such elegancies. In the midst of this triumph, I showed her they were taken from Randolph's poems,[7] and the unfortunate transcriber was dismissed with the scorn he deserved. To say truth, the poor plagiary was very unlucky to fall into my hands; that author, being no longer in fashion, would have escaped anyone of less universal reading than myself. You should encourage your daughter to talk over with you what she reads, and as you are very capable of distinguishing, take care she does not mistake pert folly for wit and humor, or rhyme for poetry, which are the common errors of young people, and have a train of ill consequences.

The second caution to be given her (and which is most absolutely necessary) is to conceal whatever learning she attains, with as much solicitude as she would hide crookedness or lameness. The parade of it can only serve to draw on her the envy, and consequently the most inveterate hatred, of all he and she fools, which will certainly be at least three parts in four of all her acquaintance. The use of knowledge in our sex (beside the amusement of solitude) is to moderate the passions and learn to be contented with a small expense, which are the certain effects of a studious life and, it may be, preferable even to that fame which men have engrossed to themselves and will not suffer us to share. You will tell me I have not observed this rule myself, but you are mistaken; it is only inevitable accident that has given me any reputation that way. I have always carefully avoided it, and ever thought it a misfortune.

The explanation of this paragraph would occasion a long digression, which I will not trouble you with, it being my present design only to say what I think useful for the instruction of my granddaughter, which I have much at heart. If she has the same inclination (I should say passion) for learning that I was born with, history, geography, and philosophy will furnish her with materials to pass away cheerfully a longer life than is allotted to mortals. I believe there are few heads capable of making Sir I. Newton's[8] calculations, but the result of them is not difficult to be understood by a moderate capacity. Do not fear this should make her affect the character of Lady ——, or Lady ——, or Mrs.——.[9] Those women are ridiculous, not because they have learning but because they have it not. One thinks herself a complete historian after reading Eachard's *Roman History*,[1] another a profound philosopher having got by heart some of Pope's unintelligible essays,[2] and a third an able divine on the strength of Whitfield's sermons.[3] Thus you hear them screaming politics and controversy. It is a saying of Thucydides, ignorance is bold, and knowledge reserved.[4] Indeed it is impossible to be far advanced in it without being more humbled by a conviction of human ignorance than elated by learning.

At the same time I recommend books, I neither exclude work nor drawing. I think it as scandalous for a woman not to know how to use a needle, as for a man not to know how to use a sword. I was once extreme fond of my pencil, and it was a great mortification to me when my father turned off[5] my master, having made a considerable progress for the short time I learnt. My over eagerness in the pursuit of it had

7. The minor writer Thomas Randolph (1605–1635), whose collected *Poems* were published in 1638.
8. Isaac Newton, mathematician and scientist, author of *Principia Mathematica* (1687).
9. The names, which Montagu omitted in her manuscript, have not been recovered.
1. Lawrence Echard, *The Roman History* (1695–1698).
2. Probably his *Essay on Man* (1733–1734) in four epis-

tles, published long after the friendship between him and Montagu had ended.
3. George Whitfield (1714–1770), Methodist preacher.
4. Thucydides (c. 460–c. 399 B.C.), Greek historian of the Peloponnesian War; Montagu paraphrases his assertion that "boldness means ignorance and reflection brings hesitation" (*History* 2.40.3).
5. Dismissed.

brought a weakness on my eyes that made it necessary to leave it off, and all the advantage I got was the improvement of my hand. I see by hers that practice will make her a ready writer. She may attain it by serving you for a secretary when your health or affairs make it troublesome to you to write yourself, and custom will make it an agreeable amusement to her. She cannot have too many for that station of life which will probably be her fate. The ultimate end of your education was to make you a good wife (and I have the comfort to hear that you are one); hers ought to be, to make her happy in a virgin state. I will not say it is happier, but it is undoubtedly safer than any marriage. In a lottery where there is (at the lowest computation) ten thousand blanks to a prize, it is the most prudent choice not to venture.

I have always been so thoroughly persuaded of this truth that, notwithstanding the flattering views I had for you (as I never intended you a sacrifice to my vanity), I thought I owed you the justice to lay before you all the hazards attending matrimony. You may recollect I did so in the strongest manner. Perhaps you may have more success in the instructing your daughter. She has so much company at home she will not need seeking it abroad, and will more readily take the notions you think fit to give her. As you were alone in my family, it would have been thought a great cruelty to suffer you no companions of your own age, especially having so many near relations, and I do not wonder their opinions influenced yours. I was not sorry to see you not determined on a single life, knowing it was not your father's intention, and contented myself with endeavoring to make your home so easy that you might not be in haste to leave it.

I am afraid you will think this a very long and insignificant letter. I hope the kindness of the design will excuse it, being willing to give you every proof in my power that I am your most affectionate Mother,

M. Wortley.

Epistle from Mrs. Yonge to Her Husband[1]

    Think not this paper comes with vain pretense
    To move your pity, or to mourn th' offense.
    Too well I know that hard obdurate heart;
    No soft'ning mercy there will take my part,
5   Nor can a woman's arguments prevail,
    When even your patron's wise example fails,[2]
    But this last privilege I still retain,
    Th' oppressed and injured always may complain.
        Too, too severely laws of honor bind
10   The weak submissive sex of womankind.
    If sighs have gained or force compelled our hand,
    Deceived by art, or urged by stern command,
    Whatever motive binds the fatal tie,
    The judging world expects our constancy.
15   Just Heaven! (for sure in heaven does justice reign
    Though tricks below that sacred name profane)
    To you appealing I submit my cause

1. In 1724 the heiress Mary Yonge became embroiled in a highly publicized divorce from her notorious, womanizing husband William, who accused her (accurately) of adultery committed during the couple's separation. Public sympathy was on her side, but the king approved a divorce that allowed her husband to retain most of her fortune. Montagu's poem remained in manuscript throughout her life.
2. I.e., Robert Walpole's. William Yonge was a devoted adherent of the powerful minister, who carried on open adulteries himself but also (unlike Yonge) permitted them to his wife.

Nor fear a judgment from impartial laws.
All bargains but conditional are made;
20   The purchase void, the creditor unpaid,
Defrauded servants are from service free;
A wounded slave regains his liberty.
For wives ill used no remedy remains,
To daily racks condemned, and to eternal chains.
25   From whence is this unjust distinction grown?
Are we not formed with passions like your own?
Nature with equal fire our souls endued,
Our minds as haughty, and as warm our blood;
O're the wide world your pleasures you pursue,⎫
30   The change is justified by something new;   ⎬
But we must sigh in silence—and be true.   ⎭
Our sex's weakness you expose and blame
(Of every prattling fop the common theme),
Yet from this weakness you suppose is due
35   Sublimer virtue than your Cato[3] knew.
Had Heaven designed us trials so severe,
It would have formed our tempers then to bear.
And I have borne (O what have I not borne!)
The pang of jealousy, th' insults of scorn.
40   Wearied at length, I from your sight remove,
And place my future hopes in secret love.
In the gay bloom of glowing youth retired,
I quit the woman's joy to be admired,
With that small pension your hard heart allows,
45   Renounce your fortune, and release your vows.
To custom (though unjust) so much is due;
I hide my frailty from the public view.
My conscience clear, yet sensible of shame,
My life I hazard, to preserve my fame.
50   And I prefer this low inglorious state,   ⎫
To vile dependence on the thing I hate—   ⎬
But you pursue me to this last retreat.   ⎭
Dragged into light, my tender crime is shown
And every circumstance of fondness known.
55   Beneath the shelter of the law you stand,
And urge my ruin with a cruel hand.
While to my fault thus rigidly severe,
Tamely submissive to the man you fear.
This wretched outcast, this abandoned wife,
60   Has yet this joy to sweeten shameful life,
By your mean conduct, infamously loose,
You are at once my accuser, and excuse.
Let me be damned by the censorious prude
(Stupidly dull, or spiritually lewd),
65   My hapless case will surely pity find

---

3. Marcus Porcius Cato of Utica (95–46 B.C.), champion of the Roman Republic, whose name had become a byword for integrity.

From every just and reasonable mind,
When to the final sentence I submit;
The lips condemn me, but their souls acquit.
   No more my husband, to your pleasures go,
70 The sweets of your recovered freedom know;
Go; court the brittle friendship of the great,
Smile at his board, or at his levée[4] wait
And when dismissed, to Madam's toilet° fly,   *dressing room*
More than her chambermaids, or glasses,° lie,   *mirrors*
75 Tell her how young she looks, how heavenly fair,
Admire the lilies and the roses there;
Your high ambition may be gratified,
Some cousin of her own be made your bride,
And you the father of a glorious race
80 Endowed with Ch——l's strength and Low——r's face.[5]
1724   1972

The Lover: A Ballad

1

At length, by so much importunity pressed,
Take (Molly[1]) at once the inside of my breast;
This stupid indifference so often you blame
Is not owing to nature, to fear, or to shame;
5 I am not as cold as a virgin in lead,
Nor is Sunday's sermon so strong in my head;
I know but too well how time flies along,
That we live but few years and yet fewer are young.

2

But I hate to be cheated, and never will buy
10 Long years of repentance for moments of joy.
Oh was there a man (but where shall I find
Good sense, and good nature so equally joined?)
Would value his pleasure, contribute to mine,
Not meanly would boast, nor lewdly design,
15 Not over severe, yet not stupidly vain,
For I would have the power though not give the pain.

3

No pedant yet learned, not rakehelly gay
Or laughing because he has nothing to say,
To all my whole sex obliging and free,
20 Yet never be fond of any but me.
In public preserve the decorums are just
And show in his eyes he is true to his trust,
Then rarely approach, and respectfully bow,
Yet not fulsomely pert, nor yet foppishly low.

---

4. Social assemblies at the homes of the "great," often crowded with petitioners, opportunists, and sycophants.
5. The line implies that the adulterous William Yonge will himself be supplanted in his next wife's bed by fel-
low-libertines: Charles Churchill (c. 1679–1745) and Antony Lowther (d. 1741).
1. Probably Maria ("Molly") Skerrett (1702–1738), Montagu's friend and Robert Walpole's mistress.

4

25 But when the long hours of public are past
    And we meet with champagne and a chicken at last,
    May every fond pleasure that hour endear,
    Be banished afar both discretion and fear,
    Forgetting or scorning the airs of the crowd
30 He may cease to be formal, and I to be proud,
    Till lost in the joy, we confess that we live
    And he may be rude, and yet I may forgive.

5

    And that my delight may be solidly fixed
    Let the friend and the lover be handsomely mixed,
35 In whose tender bosom my soul might confide,
    Whose kindness can soothe me, whose counsel could guide;
    From such a dear lover as here I describe
    No danger should fright me, no millions should bribe,
    But till this astonishing creature I know
40 As I long have lived chaste I will keep myself so.

6

    I never will share with the wanton coquette,
    Or be caught by a vain affectation of wit.
    The toasters and songsters may try all their art
    But never shall enter the pass of my heart;
45 I loathe the lewd rake, the dressed fopling despise,
    Before such pursuers the nice virgin flies;
    And as Ovid has sweetly in parables told
    We harden like trees, and like rivers are cold.[2]

c. 1721–1725   1747

The Reasons that Induced Dr. S. to write a Poem called *The Lady's Dressing Room*[1]

    The Doctor in a clean starched band,
    His golden snuff box in his hand,
    With care his diamond ring displays
    And artful shows its various rays,
5   While grave he stalks down —— street
    His dearest Betty —— to meet.[2]
       Long had he waited for this hour,
    Nor gained admittance to the bower,
    Had joked and punned, and swore and writ,
10 Tried all his gallantry and wit,[3]
    Had told her oft what part he bore

---

2. In his *Metamorphoses*, Ovid tells stories of virgins who are transformed into a laurel tree (Daphne) or a fountain (Arethusa), rather than succumb to the importunities of a pursuing god (1.452–567; 5.572–641).

1. For Jonathan Swift's poem, see page 2445. In her riposte, Montagu mimics Swift's iambic tetrameter and other mannerisms.

2. In Swift's poem, Betty is the maid's name, Celia, the mistress's.

3. Montagu echoes Swift's poem *Cadenus and Vanessa*, where the clumsy lover "Had sighed and languished, vowed, and writ, / For pastime, or to show his wit" (542–43).

In Oxford's schemes in days of yore,[4]
But bawdy,° politics, nor satire   *obscenity*
Could move this dull hard hearted creature.
15 Jenny her maid could taste° a rhyme   *enjoy*
And, grieved to see him lose his time,
Had kindly whispered in his ear,
"For twice two pound you enter here;
My lady vows without that sum
20 It is in vain you write or come."
    The destined offering now he brought,
And in a paradise of thought,
With a low bow approached the dame,
Who smiling heard him preach his flame.
25 His gold she takes (such proofs as these
Convince most unbelieving shes)
And in her trunk rose up to lock it
(Too wise to trust it in her pocket)
And then, returned with blushing grace,
30 Expects the doctor's warm embrace.
    But now this is the proper place
Where morals stare me in the face,
And for the sake of fine expression
I'm forced to make a small digression.
35 Alas for wretched humankind,
With learning mad, with wisdom blind!
The ox thinks he's for saddle fit
(As long ago friend Horace writ[5])
And men their talents still mistaking,
40 The stutterer fancies his is speaking.
With admiration oft we see
Hard features heightened by toupée,
The beau affects° the politician,   *pretends to be*
Wit is the citizen's ambition,
45 Poor Pope philosophy displays on
With so much rhyme and little reason,
And though he argues ne'er so long
That all is right, his head is wrong.[6]
    None strive to know their proper merit
50 But strain for wisdom, beauty, spirit,
And lose the praise that is their due
While they've th' impossible in view.
So have I seen the injudicious heir
To add one window the whole house impair.
55   Instinct the hound does better teach,
Who never undertook to preach;
The frighted hare from dogs does run

4. Swift had collaborated closely in the political schemes
of Robert Harley, first Earl of Oxford (1661–1724).
5. "The ox desires the saddle" (Horace, *Epistles* 1.14.43).

6. Montagu ridicules Pope's conclusion to An *Essay on
Man:* "Whatever IS, is RIGHT." See page 2550.

But not attempts to bear a gun.
Here many noble thoughts occur
60 But I prolixity abhor,
And will pursue th' instructive tale
To show the wise in some things fail.
    The reverend lover with surprise ⎫
Peeps in her bubbies, and her eyes, ⎬
65 And kisses both, and tries—and tries. ⎭
The evening in this hellish play,
Beside his guineas thrown away,
Provoked the priest to that degree
He swore, "The fault is not in me.
70 Your damned close stool° so near my nose,   *chamber pot*
Your dirty smock, and stinking toes
Would make a Hercules as tame
As any beau that you can name."
    The nymph grown furious roared, "By God
75 The blame lies all in sixty odd,"[7]
And scornful pointing to the door
Cried, "Fumbler, see my face no more."
"With all my heart I'll go away,
But nothing done, I'll nothing pay.
80 Give back the money." "How," cried she,
"Would you palm such a cheat on me!
For poor four pound to roar and bellow—
Why sure you want some new Prunella?"[8]
"I'll be revenged, you saucy quean"°   *whore*
85 (Replies the disappointed Dean)
"I'll so describe your dressing room
The very Irish shall not come."
She answered short, "I'm glad you'll write.
You'll furnish paper when I shite."[9]

1734

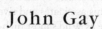

John Gay
1685–1732

John Gay was born to hardworking, pious tradespeople in Barnstaple, a busy port town in southwestern England. Educated well but orphaned early, he moved at age eighteen to London, where he tried trade for a time, gave it up for literature, and made himself a master of the mock, at a moment when the mock mattered most.

---

7. I.e., Swift's impotence derives not from her odors but from his age (65 at the time the poem was written).
8. "Prunella" is both a fabric used in clergy vestments (Swift was a clergyman), and the name of the promiscu-

ous, low-born heroine in Richard Estcourt's comic interlude *Prunella* (1708).
9. Compare line 118 of Swift's poem, page 2448.

In the early eighteenth century, the "mock" was not just a gesture of derision but an intricate art form, in which scenes of contemporary life, appropriated from streets, stables, salons, and other ordinary sites, were represented in grand styles first crafted for the actions of ancient heroes. In his mock-pastoral *Description of a City Shower* (1709), for example, Swift depicted the muddy chaos of an urban rainstorm in the language Virgil had devised to render the rural delights of a Golden Age; in his mock-epic *Rape of the Lock* (1712), Pope portrayed the trivial agitations of London beaux and belles in formulations absorbed from Homer. Befriended by Pope and Swift, Gay became perhaps the most supple and assiduous practitioner in their mock-heroic vein. In his early successes, he showed himself adept at devising new combinations of mode and topic, new ways of savoring both high styles and low subjects even while making fun of them. In *The Shepherd's Week* (1714), he took on both Virgil's idealism and also the ungainly "realism" attempted by some of that Roman poet's eighteenth-century imitators. He endowed his shepherds with preposterously "rustic" names (Bumkinet, Hobnelia, Bowzybeus) and a ludicrously hybrid language, alternately high-flying and homespun. But he gave them also a grace and good nature that survive the mock. The poem's closing image of a drunken swain sleeping out the sunset ("ruddy, like his face, the sun descends") reads like the poet's own benediction. In his next big work, *Trivia, or the Art of Walking the Streets of London* (1716), Gay's grandiloquent Virgilian instruction makes city walking seem not just a "trivial" chore but an "art," comic, challenging, alternately appalling and attractive.

Gay built his life as he made his art, by improvising. He earned money by his plays and poems; he lost money in that evanescent investment scheme the South Sea Bubble; he served as Commissioner of Lotteries, and as secretary, steward, and companion to several members of the nobility; and he sought for years to secure steady patronage at court, by means of flattering verse and ingratiating conduct. His frustration peaked when he published a virtuosic set of *Fables* (1727) for the four-year-old Prince William and received as reward a royal appointment as attendant to the prince's two-year-old sister. The aristocrats he courted valued him for his compliant temper and beguiling company, but they patronized him in both senses of the word.

Gay refused the royal appointment, staking his hopes instead on his new project for the stage, *The Beggar's Opera* (1728). The initial notion for the piece had come from Swift, who suggested a "Newgate pastoral"—that is, a mixture in which the "whores and thieves" who inhabited Newgate prison and its neighborhood would supplant the nymphs and shepherds frolicking on Arcadian hillsides. Swift's hint is an ordinary mock recipe: two worlds collide, one real, one fictitious. Gay built from it an intricate hall of mirrors, where many more worlds met. For his thieves he drew on two real-life models, recently executed: Jonathan Wild and Jack Sheppard. Wild had run a large criminal organization that profited him two ways: he collected money from the resale of goods stolen by his subordinates; and he collected rewards from the government for turning in his associates and rivals whenever they became too troublesome. Sheppard had acquired fame as Wild's most high-spirited and elusive prey; a brilliant thief in his own right, he had often managed to escape the prisons and predicaments into which Wild had betrayed him. In *The Beggar's Opera*, Gay resurrects the two late criminals as Mr. Peachum, who like Wild manages a lucrative double life, and Captain Macheath, who like Sheppard proves susceptible of capture and gifted at escape. Here the worlds begin to multiply. Developing a comparison then current in the political press, Gay made his criminals conjure up the most powerful politician alive: Robert Walpole, the Whig prime minister who ran his political machine (so the *Opera* insists) with the efficiency of Peachum and the self-indulgence of Macheath.

The Beggar's Opera mixed low with high in form as well as content. Like "Newgate pastoral," the phrase "beggar's opera" fuses opposites. Italian opera was the most expensive, exotic, and fashionable entertainment in London. Gay's theatrical game was to replay opera's intricacies using beggars' means. He supplanted the elaborate arias of foreign composers with the simpler tunes of British street songs; he replaced the original words to those tunes with new lyrics that voiced his characters' strong emotions; he even re-enacted a recent, much-publicized rivalry between two high-paid prima donnas, at war for the allegiance of their audience, in the contest he stages between Peachum's daughter Polly and the jailer's daughter Lucy Lockit for the devotion of fickle Captain Macheath. On Gay's stage, worlds converge with a density even Swift could not have foreseen. Opera house and street corner; Whitehall and Newgate; art and commerce; politics, business, and crime: all of these turn out to operate on the same principles of self-interest.

Reading the new piece before its premiere, Gay's well-wishers hedged their bets as to its success. "It would either take greatly," the playwright William Congreve predicted, "or be damned confoundedly." In the event, it did both. The triumph of the opening night is the stuff of theatrical legend, but it provoked a counter-chorus of condemnation from critics who saw the play as endangering opera, glorifying thieves, traducing government. Amid the debate, the play enjoyed a long run, entrancing an audience made up of the very people it mocked (including Walpole himself, who reportedly conducted an extra chorus of the play's most satiric song, "When you censure the age"). *The Beggar's Opera* offered theatergoers simple pleasures (deft performances, comic reversals, well-loved tunes) and intricate ones too: the often ironic play of Gay's new lyrics against the original words that the auditors had already in their heads; the debunking of love and marriage in sharp dialogue and the glorifying of it in sentimental song; the volatile charisma of the mock-hero Macheath, who for many observers came to seem utterly heroic by evening's end; the arresting alchemy by which Gay transmuted (as the Romantic essayist William Hazlitt later expressed it) "this motley group" of "highwaymen, turnkeys, their mistresses, wives, or daughters . . . into a set of fine gentlemen and ladies, satirists and philosophers." In his painting of the opening night (Color Plate 27), William Hogarth suggests how these transformations came to include the spectators as well. Occupying the sides of the stage, an audience of aristocrats, politicians, and theater people (Gay himself among them) observe the play in progress; they are encompassed by the same prison walls wherein Macheath and his pursuers play out their intricate transactions, in which everything and everyone—goods, votes, spouses—had become commodities, items of exchange, reckoned in account books as profit and as loss.

The Beggar's Opera brought Gay prosperity and celebrity but not security. Walpole evicted him from his subsidized lodgings and banned production of the *Opera*'s much-anticipated sequel *Polly*. When Gay died less than five years after his fabled first night, however, he was buried with elaborate ceremony in the Poet's Corner of Westminster Abbey. Friends commended the appropriateness of the site but marveled at the incongruity of the pomp. Incongruity, though, had been Gay's stock in trade, and nowhere more so than in his greatest hit. Its long run continues in theaters around the world. It spawned numberless short-lived imitations in its own time and a more durable descendant in the twentieth century: *Die Dreigroschenoper* (*The Threepenny Opera*, 1928), in which Bertolt Brecht and Kurt Weill adapted Gay's characters, plot, and critique of commerce to produce their own dark and gleeful Marxist assault on contemporary capitalism. By routes less direct, Gay's work has infused both the modern musical theater (which continues to combine operatic and popular modes) and pop culture in general—where, for example, Brecht and Weill's sardonic "Ballad of Mack the Knife" became a pop hit of the early 1960s. *The Beggar's Opera* grabbed attention first—and sustains it still—for the ironic dexterity with which it mixed things up, in full mock mode.

The Beggar's Opera

Nos haec novimus esse nihil.[1]

Dramatis Personae[2]

Men

PEACHUM
LOCKIT
MACHEATH
FILCH
JEMMY TWITCHER ⎫
CROOK-FINGERED JACK ⎪
WAT DREARY ⎪
ROBIN OF BAGSHOT ⎪
NIMMING NED ⎬ *Macheath's Gang*
HARRY PADINGTON ⎪
MATT OF THE MINT ⎪
BEN BUDGE ⎭
BEGGAR
PLAYER
CONSTABLES, DRAWER, TURNKEY, ETC.

Women

MRS. PEACHUM
POLLY PEACHUM
LUCY LOCKIT
DIANA TRAPES
MRS. COAXER ⎫
DOLLY TRULL ⎪
MRS. VIXEN ⎪
BETTY DOXY ⎬ *Women of the Town*
JENNY DIVER ⎪
MRS. SLAMMEKIN ⎪
SUKY TAWDRY ⎪
MOLLY BRAZEN ⎭

INTRODUCTION

[Beggar, Player]

BEGGAR: If poverty be a title[3] to poetry, I am sure nobody can dispute mine. I own
myself of the Company of Beggars; and I make one at their weekly festivals at St.
Giles's.[4] I have a small yearly salary for my catches,[5] and am welcome to a mock
laureate dinner there whenever I please, which is more than most poets can say.

---

1. We know these things to be nothing (Martial, *Epigrams*
13.2.8).
2. Many of these names reflect the characters' low-life
habits: to "peach" is to inform on, to filch is to steal,
twitchers are pickpockets, nimmers are thieves, and trulls
and doxies are prostitutes.
3. Deed of ownership.

4. An almshouse near the parish of St. Giles, patron saint
of lepers and beggars.
5. Rounds, songs for two or more voices in which each
voice starts the same melody at a different time. The form
was very popular; enthusiasts assembled in "catch clubs"
for whole evenings of singing.

PLAYER: As we live by the Muses, 'tis but gratitude in us to encourage poetical merit wherever we find it. The Muses, contrary to all other ladies, pay no distinction to dress, and never partially[6] mistake the pertness of embroidery for wit, nor the modesty of want for dullness. Be the author who he will, we push his play as far as it will go. So (though you are in want) I wish you success heartily.

BEGGAR: This piece I own was originally writ for the celebrating the marriage of James Chanter and Moll Lay, two most excellent ballad singers. I have introduced the similes that are in all your celebrated operas: the swallow, the moth, the bee, the ship, the flower, etc. Besides, I have a prison scene which the ladies always reckon charmingly pathetic. As to the parts, I have observed such a nice impartiality to our two ladies, that it is impossible for either of them to take offense.[7] I hope I may be forgiven, that I have not made my opera throughout unnatural, like those in vogue; for I have no recitative.[8] Excepting this, as I have consented to have neither prologue nor epilogue, it must be allowed an opera in all its forms. The piece indeed hath been heretofore frequently represented by ourselves in our great room at St. Giles's, so that I cannot too often acknowledge your charity in bringing it now on the stage.

PLAYER: But I see 'tis time for us to withdraw; the actors are preparing to begin. Play away the overture.   [*Exeunt.*]

ACT 1

Scene 1. Peachum's House

[*Peachum sitting at a table with a large book of accounts before him.*]

Air 1. An old woman clothed in gray, etc.[9]

Through all the employments of life
  Each neighbor abuses his brother;
Whore and rogue they call husband and wife:
  All professions be-rogue one another.
The priest calls the lawyer a cheat,
  The lawyer be-knaves the divine;
And the statesman, because he's so great,[1]
  Thinks his trade as honest as mine.

A lawyer is an honest employment, so is mine. Like me too he acts in a double capacity, both against rogues and for 'em; for 'tis but fitting that we should protect and encourage cheats, since we live by them.

Scene 2

[*Peachum, Filch*]

FILCH: Sir, Black Moll hath sent word her trial comes on in the afternoon, and she hopes you will order matters so as to bring her off.

---

6. In a prejudiced way.
7. The Beggar alludes to recent rivalries between leading ladies in Italian operas.
8. Sung speech, an operatic convention. The Beggar promises that here, by contrast, dialogue will be spoken naturally.

9. I.e., this air is to be sung to the familiar ballad tune, *An Old Woman Clothed in Gray.*
1. The word "great" was often attached to the Whig Prime Minister Robert Walpole, whom Gay's Tory party opposed vigorously in the 1720s and 1730s.

PEACHUM: Why, she may plead her belly at worst;[2] to my knowledge she hath taken care of that security. But as the wench is very active and industrious, you may satisfy her that I'll soften the evidence.

FILCH: Tom Gagg, Sir, is found guilty.

PEACHUM: A lazy dog! When I took him the time before, I told him what he would come to if he did not mend his hand. This is death without reprieve. I may venture to book him.[3] [Writes.] For Tom Gagg, forty pounds. Let Betty Sly know that I'll save her from transportation,[4] for I can get more by her staying in England.

FILCH: Betty hath brought more goods into our lock to-year than any five of the gang; and in truth, 'tis a pity to lose so good a customer.

PEACHUM: If none of the gang take her off, she may, in the common course of business, live a twelve-month longer. I love to let women scape. A good sportsman always lets the hen partridges fly, because the breed of the game depends upon them. Besides, here the law allows us no reward; there is nothing to be got by the death of woman—except our wives.[5]

FILCH: Without dispute, she is a fine woman! 'Twas to her I was obliged for my education, and (to say a bold word) she hath trained up more young fellows to the business than the gaming-table.

PEACHUM: Truly, Filch, thy observation is right. We and the surgeons[6] are more beholden to women than all the professions besides.

Air 2. The bonny gray-eyed morn, etc.

FILCH: 'Tis woman that seduces all mankind,
         By her we first were taught the wheedling arts:
    Her very eyes can cheat; when most she's kind,
         She tricks us of our money with our hearts.
    For her, like wolves by night we roam for prey,
         And practice ev'ry fraud to bribe her charms;
    For suits of love, like law, are won by pay,
         And beauty must be fee'd into our arms.

PEACHUM: But make haste to Newgate,[7] boy, and let my friends know what I intend; for I love to make them easy one way or other.

FILCH: When a gentleman is long kept in suspense, penitence may break his spirit ever after. Besides, certainty gives a man a good air upon his trial, and makes him risk another without fear or scruple. But I'll away, for 'tis a pleasure to be the messenger of comfort to friends in affliction.

Scene 3

[Peachum]

But 'tis now high time to look about me for a decent execution against next Sessions.[8] I hate a lazy rogue, by whom one can get nothing 'till he is hanged. A register of the gang, [reading] Crook-fingered Jack. A year and a half in the service; Let me see how much the stock owes to his industry; one, two, three, four, five

2. A pregnant woman could not be hanged.
3. I.e., enter in the books the reward for "peaching" him.
4. Convicts were often transported to the colonies.
5. Husbands inherited their wives' property.

6. Who treat venereal diseases.
7. London's main prison.
8. Of the criminal court.

gold watches, and seven silver ones. A mighty clean-handed fellow! Sixteen snuff-boxes, five of them of true gold. Six dozen of handkerchiefs, four silver-hilted swords, half a dozen of shirts, three tie-perriwigs, and a piece of broad cloth. Considering these are only the fruits of his leisure hours, I don't know a prettier fellow, for no man alive hath a more engaging presence of mind upon the road. Wat Dreary, alias Brown Will, an irregular dog, who hath an underhand way of disposing of his goods. I'll try him[9] only for a Sessions or two longer upon his good behavior. Harry Padington, a poor petty-larceny rascal, without the least genius; that fellow, though he were to live these six months, will never come to the gallows with any credit. Slippery Sam; he goes off the next Sessions, for the villain hath the impudence to have views of following his trade as a tailor, which he calls an honest employment. Mat of the Mint; lifted[1] not above a month ago, a promising sturdy fellow, and diligent in his way; somewhat too bold and hasty, and may raise good contributions on[2] the public, if he does not cut himself short by murder. Tom Tipple, a guzzling soaking sot, who is always too drunk to stand himself, or to make others stand. A cart[3] is absolutely necessary for him. Robin of Bagshot, alias Gorgon, alias Bluff Bob, alias Carbuncle, alias Bob Booty.[4]

Scene 4

[Peachum, Mrs. Peachum]

MRS. PEACHUM: What of Bob Booty, husband? I hope nothing bad hath betided him. You know, my dear, he's a favorite customer of mine. 'Twas he made me a present of this ring.

PEACHUM: I have set his name down in the blacklist, that's all, my dear; he spends his life among women, and as soon as his money is gone, one or other of the ladies will hang him for the reward, and there's forty pound lost to us forever.

MRS. PEACHUM: You know, my dear, I never meddle in matters of death; I always leave those affairs to you. Women indeed are bitter bad judges in these cases, for they are so partial to the brave that they think every man handsome who is going to the camp[5] or the gallows.

Air 3. Cold and raw, etc.

If any wench Venus's girdle wear,
    Though she be never so ugly;
Lilies and roses will quickly appear,
    And her face look wond'rous smugly.
Beneath the left ear so fit but a cord
    (A rope so charming a zone[6] is!),
The youth in his cart hath the air of a lord,
    And we cry, There dies an Adonis!

But really, husband, you should not be too hardhearted, for you never had a finer, braver set of men than at present. We have not had a murder among them all, these seven months. And truly, my dear, that is a great blessing.

9. Keep him on.
1. Enlisted.
2. From.
3. A condemned prisoner rode in a cart to his execution.

4. All names referring to the prime minister, Robert Walpole.
5. To war.
6. Belt.

PEACHUM: What a dickens is the woman always a whimpering about murder for? No gentleman is ever looked upon the worse for killing a man in his own defense; and if business cannot be carried on without it, what would you have a gentleman do?

MRS. PEACHUM: If I am in the wrong, my dear, you must excuse me, for nobody can help the frailty of an over-scrupulous conscience.

PEACHUM: Murder is as fashionable a crime as a man can be guilty of. How many fine gentlemen have we in Newgate every year, purely upon that article! If they have wherewithal to persuade the jury to bring it in[7] manslaughter, what are they the worse for it? So, my dear, have done upon this subject. Was Captain Macheath here this morning, for the bank-notes[8] he left with you last week?

MRS. PEACHUM: Yes, my dear; and though the bank hath stopped payment, he was so cheerful and so agreeable! Sure there is not a finer gentleman upon the road than the Captain! If he comes from Bagshot[9] at any reasonable hour he hath promised to make one this evening with Polly and me, and Bob Booty, at a party of quadrille.[1] Pray, my dear, is the Captain rich?

PEACHUM: The Captain keeps too good company ever to grow rich. Marybone and the chocolate-houses[2] are his undoing. The man that proposes to get money by "play" should have the education of a fine gentleman, and be trained up to it from his youth.

MRS. PEACHUM: Really, I am sorry upon Polly's account the Captain hath not more discretion. What business hath he to keep company with lords and gentlemen? He should leave them to prey upon one another.

PEACHUM: Upon Polly's account! What, a plague, does the woman mean? Upon Polly's account!

MRS. PEACHUM: Captain Macheath is very fond of the girl.

PEACHUM: And what then?

MRS. PEACHUM: If I have any skill in the ways of women, I am sure Polly thinks him a very pretty man.

PEACHUM: And what then? You would not be so mad to have the wench marry him! Gamesters and highwaymen are generally very good to their whores, but they are very devils to their wives.

MRS. PEACHUM: But if Polly should be in love, how should we help her, or how can she help herself? Poor girl, I am in the utmost concern about her.

Air 4. Why is your faithful slave disdained? etc.

If love the virgin's heart invade,
How, like a moth, the simple maid
    Still plays about the flame!
If soon she be not made a wife;
Her honor's singed, and then for life,
    She's—what I dare not name.

PEACHUM: Look ye, wife. A handsome wench in our way of business is as profitable as at the bar of a Temple coffeehouse, who looks upon it as her livelihood to grant every liberty but one. You see I would indulge the girl as far as prudently we

7. Reduce it to.
8. Bankers' checks.
9. Bagshot Heath, west of London, where many highway-

men plied their trade.
1. A fashionable card game for four.
2. Both sites of gambling.

can. In anything, but marriage! After that, my dear, how shall we be safe? Are we not then in her husband's power? For a husband hath the absolute power over all a wife's secrets but her own. If the girl had the discretion of a court lady, who can have a dozen young fellows at her ear without complying with one, I should not matter it; but Polly is tinder, and a spark will at once set her on a flame. Married! If the wench does not know her own profit, sure she knows her own pleasure better than to make herself a property! My daughter to me should be, like a court lady to a minister of state, a key to the whole gang. Married! If the affair is not already done, I'll terrify her from it, by the example of our neighbors.

MRS. PEACHUM: Mayhap, my dear, you may injure the girl. She loves to imitate the fine ladies, and she may only allow the Captain liberties in the view of interest.[3]

PEACHUM: But 'tis your duty, my dear, to warn the girl against her ruin, and to instruct her how to make the most of her beauty. I'll go to her this moment, and sift[4] her. In the meantime, wife, rip out the coronets and marks[5] of these dozen of cambric handkerchiefs, for I can dispose of them this afternoon to a chap in the city.

Scene 5

[Mrs. Peachum]

Never was a man more out of the way[6] in an argument than my husband! Why must our Polly, forsooth, differ from her sex, and love only her husband? And why must Polly's marriage, contrary to all observation, make her the less followed by other men? All men are thieves in love, and like a woman the better for being another's property.

Air 5. Of all the simple things we do, etc.

A maid is like the golden oar,[7]
Which hath guineas intrinsical in't,
    Whose worth is never known, before
    It is tried and imprest[8] in the Mint.
    A wife's like a guinea in gold,
    Stamped with the name of her spouse;
    Now here, now there; is bought, or is sold;
    And is current in every house.

Scene 6

[Mrs. Peachum, Filch]

MRS. PEACHUM: Come hither Filch. I am as fond of this child, as though my mind misgave me[9] he were my own. He hath as fine a hand at picking a pocket as a woman, and is as nimble fingered as a juggler. If an unlucky Session does not cut the rope of thy life, I pronounce, boy, thou wilt be a great man[1] in history. Where was your post last night, my boy?

---

3. Self-interest, profit.
4. Question.
5. The embroidered marks of the handkerchiefs' aristocratic owners.
6. In the wrong.

7. Ore.
8. Smelted and stamped.
9. Suspected.
1. Another jab at the prime minister, Robert Walpole.

FILCH: I plyed at the opera, Madam; and considering 'twas neither dark nor rainy, so that there was no great hurry in getting chairs and coaches, made a tolerable hand on't. These seven handkerchiefs, Madam.

MRS. PEACHUM: Colored ones, I see. They are of sure sale from our warehouse at Redriff among the seamen.

FILCH: And this snuffbox.

MRS. PEACHUM: Set in gold! A pretty encouragement this to a young beginner.

FILCH: I had a fair tug at a charming gold watch. Pox take the tailors for making the fobs[2] so deep and narrow! It stuck by the way, and I was forced to make my escape under a coach. Really, Madam, I fear I shall be cut off in the flower of my youth, so that every now and then (since I was pumped[3]) I have thoughts of taking up[4] and going to sea.

MRS. PEACHUM: You should go to Hockley in the Hole,[5] and to Marybone, child, to learn valor. These are the schools that have bred so many brave men. I thought, boy, by this time, thou hadst lost fear as well as shame. Poor lad! How little does he know as yet of the Old Baily![6] For the first fact I'll insure thee from being hanged; and going to sea, Filch, will come time enough upon a sentence of transportation. But now, since you have nothing better to do, ev'n go to your book, and learn your catechism;[7] for really a man makes but an ill figure in the ordinary's paper,[8] who cannot give a satisfactory answer to his questions. But, hark you, my lad. Don't tell me a lie; for you know I hate a liar. Do you know of anything that hath passed between Captain Macheath and our Polly?

FILCH: I beg you, Madam, don't ask me; for I must either tell a lie to you or to Miss Polly; for I promised her I would not tell.

MRS. PEACHUM: But when the honor of our family is concerned—

FILCH: I shall lead a sad life with Miss Polly, if ever she come to know that I told you. Besides, I would not willingly forfeit my own honor by betraying anybody.

MRS. PEACHUM: Yonder comes my husband and Polly. Come Filch, you shall go with me into my own room, and tell me the whole story. I'll give thee a glass of a most delicious cordial that I keep for my own drinking.

Scene 7

[Peachum, Polly]

POLLY: I know as well as any of the fine ladies how to make the most of myself and of my man too. A woman knows how to be mercenary, though she hath never been in a court or at an assembly.[9] We have it in our natures, Papa. If I allow Captain Macheath some trifling liberties, I have this watch and other visible marks of his favor to show for it. A girl who cannot grant some things, and refuse what is most material, will make but a poor hand of her beauty, and soon be thrown upon the common.

Air 6. What shall I do to show how much I love her, etc.

Virgins are like the fair flower in its luster,
    Which in the garden enamels the ground;

2. Watch-pockets.
3. Half-drowned under a pump (a punishment for pickpockets).
4. Reforming.
5. A site of boxing and bear-baiting.

6. London's main trial court.
7. Religious instruction.
8. The chaplain of Newgate (the Ordinary) often published the confessions of recently executed prisoners.
9. A fashionable social gathering.

Near it the bees in play flutter and cluster,
And gaudy butterflies frolic around.
But, when once plucked, 'tis no longer alluring,
To Covent Garden[1] 'tis sent (as yet sweet),
There fades, and shrinks, and grows past all enduring,
Rots, stinks, and dies, and is trod under feet.

PEACHUM: You know, Polly, I am not against your toying and trifling with a customer in the way of business, or to get out a secret, or so. But if I find out that you have played the fool and are married, you jade you, I'll cut your throat, hussy. Now you know my mind.

Scene 8

[Peachum, Polly, Mrs. Peachum]

Air 7. Oh London is a fine town

[Mrs. Peachum, in a very great passion.]

Our Polly is a sad slut! nor heeds what we have taught her.
I wonder any man alive will ever rear a daughter!
For she must have both hoods and gowns, and hoops to swell her pride,
With scarves and stays,[2] and gloves and lace; and she will have men beside;
And when she's dressed with care and cost, all tempting, fine and gay,
As men should serve a cowcumber,[3] she flings herself away.
Our Polly is a sad slut, etc.

You baggage! You hussy! You inconsiderate jade! Had you been hanged, it would not have vexed me, for that might have been your misfortune; but to do such a mad thing by choice! The wench is married, husband.

PEACHUM: Married! The Captain is a bold man, and will risk anything for money; to be sure he believes her a fortune. Do you think your mother and I should have lived comfortably so long together, if ever we had been married? Baggage!

MRS. PEACHUM: I knew she was always a proud slut; and now the wench hath played the fool and married, because forsooth she would do like the gentry. Can you support the expense of a husband, hussy, in gaming, drinking, and whoring? Have you money enough to carry on the daily quarrels of man and wife about who shall squander most? There are not many husbands and wives who can bear the charges[4] of plaguing one another in a handsome way. If you must be married, could you introduce nobody into our family but a highwayman? Why, thou foolish jade, thou wilt be as ill-used, and as much neglected, as if thou hadst married a lord!

PEACHUM: Let not your anger, my dear, break through the rules of decency, for the Captain looks upon himself in the military capacity, as a gentleman by his profession. Besides what he hath already, I know he is in a fair way of getting, or of dying;[5] and both these ways, let me tell you, are most excellent chances for a wife. Tell me hussy, are you ruined or no?

MRS. PEACHUM: With Polly's fortune, she might very well have gone off to a person of distinction. Yes, that you might, you pouting slut!

---

1. A London market for flowers, fruits, and vegetables; also a haunt of prostitutes.
2. Corsets.
3. A (worthless) cucumber.
4. Expense.
5. He is likely to make more or to die trying.

PEACHUM: What, is the wench dumb? Speak, or I'll make you plead by squeezing out an answer from you.[6] Are you really bound wife to him, or are you only upon liking? [*Pinches her.*]

POLLY: Oh! [*Screaming.*]

MRS. PEACHUM: How the mother is to be pitied who hath handsome daughters! Locks, bolts, bars, and lectures of morality are nothing to them. They break through them all. They have as much pleasure in cheating a father and mother, as in cheating at cards.

PEACHUM: Why, Polly, I shall soon know if you are married, by Macheath's keeping from[7] our house.

Air 8. Grim king of the ghosts, etc.

POLLY: *Can love be controlled by advice?*
         Will Cupid our mothers obey?
     Though my heart were as frozen as ice,
         At his flame 'twould have melted away.

     When he kissed me so closely he pressed,
         'Twas so sweet that I must have complied;
     So I thought it both safest and best
         To marry, for fear you should chide.

MRS. PEACHUM: Then all the hopes of our family are gone forever and ever!

PEACHUM: And Macheath may hang his father and mother-in-law, in hope to get into their daughter's fortune.

POLLY: I did not marry him (as 'tis the fashion) coolly and deliberately for honor and money. But, I love him.

MRS. PEACHUM: Love him! worse and worse! I thought the girl had been better bred. Oh husband, husband! Her folly makes me mad! My head swims! I'm distracted! I can't support myself—Oh! [*Faints.*]

PEACHUM: See, wench, to what a condition you have reduced your poor mother! A glass of cordial, this instant. How the poor woman takes it to heart!

[*Polly goes out, and returns with it.*]

Ah, hussy, now this is the only comfort your mother has left!

POLLY: Give her another glass, Sir; my mama drinks double the quantity whenever she is out of order. This, you see, fetches[8] her.

MRS. PEACHUM: The girl shows such a readiness, and so much concern, that I could almost find in my heart to forgive her.

Air 9. O Jenny, O Jenny, where hast thou been

     O Polly, you might have toyed and kissed.
     By keeping men off, you keep them on.

POLLY: *But he so teased me,*
         And he so pleased me,
     What I did, you must have done.

---

6. Confessions were sometimes extracted by pressing with weights.
7. Staying away from.
8. Revives.

The Beggar's Opera, Act 1   2597

MRS. PEACHUM: Not with a highwayman.—You sorry slut!

PEACHUM: A word with you, wife. 'Tis no new thing for a wench to take man
without consent of parents. You know 'tis the frailty of woman, my dear.

MRS. PEACHUM: Yes, indeed, the sex is frail. But the first time a woman is frail,
she should be somewhat nice[9] methinks, for then or never is the time to make her
fortune. After that, she hath nothing to do but guard herself from being found out,
and she may do what she pleases.

PEACHUM: Make yourself a little easy; I have a thought shall soon set all matters
again to rights. Why so melancholy, Polly? Since what is done cannot be undone,
we must all endeavor to make the best of it.

MRS. PEACHUM: Well, Polly, as far as one woman can forgive another, I forgive
thee. Your father is too fond of you, hussy.

POLLY: Then all my sorrows are at an end.

MRS. PEACHUM: A mighty likely speech in troth, for a wench who is just married!

Air 10. Thomas, I cannot, etc.

POLLY: *I, like a ship in storms, was tossed;*
Yet afraid to put into land;
For seized in the port the vessel's lost,
Whose treasure is contraband.
The waves are laid,[1]
My duty's paid.
O joy beyond expression!
Thus, safe a-shore,
I ask no more,
My all is in my possession.

PEACHUM: I hear customers in t'other room; Go, talk with 'em, Polly; but come to
us again, as soon as they are gone. But, hark ye, child, if 'tis the gentleman who
was here yesterday about the repeating-watch,[2] say you believe we can't get intelligence of it till tomorrow. For I lent it to Suky Straddle, to make a figure with it
tonight at a tavern in Drury Lane.[3] If t'other gentleman calls for the silver-hilted
sword; you know beetle-browed Jemmy hath it on, and he doth not come from
Tunbridge till Tuesday night; so that it cannot be had till then.

Scene 9

[Peachum, Mrs. Peachum]

PEACHUM: Dear wife, be a little pacified. Don't let your passion run away with
your senses. Polly, I grant you, hath done a rash thing.

MRS. PEACHUM: If she had had only an intrigue with the fellow, why the very
best families have excused and huddled up a frailty of that sort. 'Tis marriage, husband, that makes it a blemish.

PEACHUM: But money, wife, is the true fuller's earth[4] for reputations, there is not a
spot or a stain but what it can take out. A rich rogue nowadays is fit company for
any gentleman; and the world, my dear, hath not such a contempt for roguery as
you imagine. I tell you, wife, I can make this match turn to our advantage.

9. Careful, fastidious.
1. Have subsided.
2. An especially valuable timepiece: it announced the
current hour and quarter-hour by a series of bells that
rang at the push of a button.
3. Another haunt of prostitutes; also the location of the
rival theater.
4. A mineral used as a cleaning solvent.

MRS. PEACHUM: I am very sensible,[5] husband, that Captain Macheath is worth money, but I am in doubt whether he hath not two or three wives already, and then if he should die in a Session or two, Polly's dower would come into dispute.

PEACHUM: That, indeed, is a point which ought to be considered.

Air 11. A soldier and a sailor

A fox may steal your hens, Sir,
A whore your health and pence, Sir,
Your daughter rob your chest, Sir,
Your wife may steal your rest, Sir,
   A thief your goods and plate.[6]
But this is all but picking,
With rest, pence, chest, and chicken;
It ever was decreed, Sir,
If lawyer's hand is fee'd, Sir,
   He steals your whole estate.

The lawyers are bitter enemies to those in our way.[7] They *don't care*[8] that anybody should get a clandestine livelihood but themselves.

Scene 10

[*Mrs. Peachum, Peachum, Polly*]

POLLY: 'Twas only Nimming Ned. He brought in a damask window curtain, a hoop petticoat, a pair of silver candlesticks, a periwig, and one silk stocking from the fire that happened last night.

PEACHUM: There is not a fellow that is cleverer in his way, and saves more goods out of the fire than Ned. But now, Polly, to your affair; for matters must not be left as they are. You are married then, it seems?

POLLY: Yes, Sir.

PEACHUM: And how do you propose to live, child?

POLLY: Like other women, Sir, upon the industry of my husband.

MRS. PEACHUM: What, is the wench turned fool? A highwayman's wife, like a soldier's, hath as little of his pay as of his company.

PEACHUM: And had not you the common views of a gentlewoman in your marriage, Polly?

POLLY: I don't know what you mean, Sir.

PEACHUM: Of a jointure,[9] and of being a widow.

POLLY: But I love him, Sir: how then could I have thoughts of parting with him?

PEACHUM: Parting with him! Why, that is the whole scheme and intention of all marriage articles. The comfortable estate of widowhood is the only hope that keeps up a wife's spirits. Where is the woman who would scruple to be a wife, if she had it in her power to be a widow whenever she pleased? If you have any views of this sort, Polly, I shall think the match not so very unreasonable.

POLLY: How I dread to hear your advice! Yet I must beg you to explain yourself.

PEACHUM: Secure what he hath got, have him peached the next Sessions, and then at once you are made a rich widow.

---

5. Well aware.
6. Utensils plated with silver or gold.
7. In our line of work.

8. Want.
9. "Estate settled on a wife to be enjoyed after her husband's decease" (Johnson's *Dictionary*).

POLLY: What, murder the man I love! The blood runs cold at my heart with the very thought of it.

PEACHUM: Fie, Polly! What hath murder to do in the affair? Since the thing sooner or later must happen, I dare say, the Captain himself would like that we should get the reward for his death sooner than a stranger. Why, Polly, the Captain knows, that as 'tis his employment to rob, so 'tis ours to take robbers; every man in his business. So that there is no malice in the case.

MRS. PEACHUM: Ay, husband, now you have nicked the matter. To have him peached is the only thing could ever make me forgive her.

Air 12. Now ponder well, ye parents dear

POLLY: *Oh, ponder well! be not severe;*
So save a wretched wife!
For on the rope that hangs my dear
Depends poor Polly's life.

MRS. PEACHUM: But your duty to your parents, hussy, obliges you to hang him. What would many a wife give for such an opportunity!

POLLY: What is a jointure, what is widowhood to me? I know my heart. I cannot survive him.

Air 13. Le printemps rappelle aux armes[1]

The turtle[2] thus with plaintive crying,
Her lover dying,
The turtle thus with plaintive crying,
Laments her dove.
Down she drops quite spent with sighing,
Paired in death, as paired in love.

Thus, Sir, it will happen to your poor Polly.

MRS. PEACHUM: What, is the fool in love in earnest then? I hate thee for being particular.[3] Why, wench, thou art a shame to thy very sex.

POLLY: But hear me, Mother. If you ever loved—

MRS. PEACHUM: Those cursed playbooks she reads have been her ruin. One word more, hussy, and I shall knock your brains out, if you have any.

PEACHUM: Keep out of the way, Polly, for fear of mischief, and consider of what is proposed to you.

MRS. PEACHUM: Away, hussy. Hang your husband, and be dutiful.

Scene 11

[Mrs. Peachum, Peachum]

[Polly listening.]

MRS. PEACHUM: The thing, husband, must and shall be done. For the sake of intelligence[4] we must take other measures, and have him peached the next Session without her consent. If she will not know her duty, we know ours.

---

1. Spring calls to arms.
2. Turtledove.
3. Odd, exceptional.

4. "Account of things distant or secret" (Johnson's *Dictionary*).

PEACHUM: But really, my dear, it grieves one's heart to take off a great man. When I consider his personal bravery, his fine stratagem, how much we have already got by him, and how much more we may get, methinks I can't find in my heart to have a hand in his death. I wish you could have made Polly undertake it.

MRS. PEACHUM: But in a case of necessity—our own lives are in danger.

PEACHUM: Then, indeed, we must comply with the customs of the world, and make gratitude give way to interest. He shall be taken off.

MRS. PEACHUM: I'll undertake to manage Polly.

PEACHUM: And I'll prepare matters for the Old Baily.

Scene 12

[Polly]

Now I'm a wretch, indeed. Methinks I see him already in the cart, sweeter and more lovely than the nosegay[5] in his hand! I hear the crowd extolling his resolution and intrepidity! What volleys of sighs are sent from the windows of Holborn,[6] that so comely a youth should be brought to disgrace! I see him at the tree![7] The whole circle are in tears! Even butchers weep! Jack Ketch[8] himself hesitates to perform his duty, and would be glad to lose his fee, by a reprieve. What then will become of Polly! As yet I may inform him of their design, and aid him in his escape. It shall be so. But then he flies, absents himself, and I bar myself from his dear dear conversation! That too will distract me.[9] If he keep out of the way, my Papa and Mama may in time relent, and we may be happy. If he stays, he is hanged, and then he is lost forever! He intended to lie concealed in my room, 'till the dusk of the evening: If they are abroad, I'll this instant let him out, lest some accident should prevent him. [Exit, and returns.]

Scene 13

[Polly, Macheath]

Air 14. Pretty Parrot, say—

MACHEATH: Pretty Polly, say,
               When I was away,
               Did your fancy never stray
                   To some newer lover?
POLLY: Without disguise,
               Heaving sighs,
               Doting eyes,
               My constant heart discover.[1]
                   Fondly let me loll!
MACHEATH: O pretty, pretty Poll.

POLLY: And are you as fond as ever, my dear?

MACHEATH: Suspect my honor, my courage, suspect anything but my love. May my pistols miss fire, and my mare slip her shoulder while I am pursued, if I ever forsake thee!

---

5. Bouquet, often carried by condemned prisoners.
6. The road from Newgate to Tyburn, where criminals were hanged.
7. The gallows ("Tyburn tree").

8. England's most famous hangman (d. 1686); thereafter, any hangman.
9. Make me crazy.
1. Reveal, uncover.

POLLY: Nay, my dear, I have no reason to doubt you, for I find in the romance you lent me, none of the great heroes were ever false in love.

Air 15. Pray, fair one, be kind

MACHEATH: *My heart was so free,*
　　　　　　It roved like the bee,
　　　　'Till Polly my passion requited;
　　　　　I sipped each flower,
　　　　　I changed ev'ry hour,
　　　But here ev'ry flower is united.

POLLY: Were you sentenced to transportation, sure, my dear, you could not leave me behind you—could you?

MACHEATH: Is there any power, any force that could tear me from thee? You might sooner tear a pension out of the hands of a courtier, a fee from a lawyer, a pretty woman from a looking glass, or any woman from quadrille. But to tear me from thee is impossible!

Air 16. Over the hills and far away

　　Were I laid on Greenland's coast,
　　　　And in my arms embraced my lass;
　　Warm amidst eternal frost,
　　　　Too soon the half year's night² would pass.

POLLY: *Were I sold on Indian soil,*
　　　　Soon as the burning day was closed,
　　I could mock the sultry toil,
　　　　When on my charmer's breast reposed.
MACHEATH: *And I would love you all the day,*
POLLY: 　　　　　*Every night would kiss and play,*
MACHEATH: *If with me you'd fondly stray*
POLLY: 　　　　　*Over the hills and far away.*

POLLY: Yes, I would go with thee. But oh!—how shall I speak it? I must be torn from thee. We must part.
MACHEATH: How! Part!
POLLY: We must, we must. My Papa and Mama are set against thy life. They now, even now are in search after thee. They are preparing evidence against thee. Thy life depends upon a moment.

Air 17. Gin thou wert mine awn thing—

　　O what pain it is to part!
　　　Can I leave thee, can I leave thee?
　　O what pain it is to part!
　　　Can thy Polly ever leave thee?
　　But lest death my love should thwart,
　　　And bring thee to the fatal cart,

---

2. The long dark winter of the polar regions.

> *Thus I tear thee from my bleeding heart!*
> *Fly hence, and let me leave thee.*

One kiss and then—one kiss—begone—farewell.

MACHEATH: My hand, my heart, my dear, is so riveted to thine, that I cannot unloose my hold.

POLLY: But my Papa may intercept thee, and then I should lose the very glimmering of hope. A few weeks, perhaps, may reconcile us all. Shall thy Polly hear from thee?

MACHEATH: Must I then go?

POLLY: And will not absence change your love?

MACHEATH: If you doubt it, let me stay—and be hanged.

POLLY: O how I fear! How I tremble! Go—but when safety will give you leave, you will be sure to see me again; for 'till then Polly is wretched.

Air 18. O the broom, etc.

[*Parting, and looking back at each other with fondness; he at one door, she at the other.*]

MACHEATH: *The miser thus a shilling sees,*
> *Which he's obliged to pay,*
> *With sighs resigns it by degrees,*
> *And fears 'tis gone for aye.*[3]

POLLY: *The boy, thus, when his sparrow's flown,*
> *The bird in silence eyes;*
> *But soon as out of sight 'tis gone,*
> *Whines, whimpers, sobs, and cries.*

ACT 2

Scene 1. A Tavern near Newgate

[*Jemmy Twitcher, Crook-fingered Jack, Wat Dreary, Robin of Bagshot, Nimming Ned, Henry Padington, Matt of the Mint, Ben Budge, and the rest of the gang, at the table, with wine, brandy, and tobacco.*]

BEN: But prithee, Matt, what is become of thy brother Tom? I have not seen him since my return from transportation.

MATT: Poor brother Tom had an accident this time twelvemonth, and so clever a made fellow he was, that I could not save him from those fleaing[1] rascals the surgeons; and now, poor man, he is among the otamys[2] at Surgeon's Hall.

BEN: So it seems, his time was come.

JEMMY: But the present time is ours, and nobody alive hath more. Why are the laws leveled at us? Are we more dishonest than the rest of mankind? What we win, gentlemen, is our own by the law of arms, and the right of conquest.

CROOK-FINGERED JACK: Where shall we find such another set of practical philosophers, who to a man are above the fear of death?

WAT: Sound men, and true!

ROBIN: Of tried courage, and indefatigable industry!

3. Forever.
1. Flaying, robbing.

2. Skeletons (from "anatomies"). The corpses of executed criminals were often used in medical studies.

NED: Who is there here that would not die for his friend?

HARRY: Who is there here that would betray him for his interest?

MATT: Show me a gang of courtiers that can say as much.

BEN: We are for a just partition of the world, for every man hath a right to enjoy life.

MATT: We retrench[3] the superfluities of mankind. The world is avaricious, and I hate avarice. A covetous fellow, like a jackdaw, steals what he was never made to enjoy, for the sake of hiding it. These are the robbers of mankind, for money was made for the free-hearted and generous, and where is the injury of taking from another, what he hath not the heart to make use of?

JEMMY: Our several stations[4] for the day are fixed. Good luck attend us all. Fill the glasses.

Air 19. Fill ev'ry glass, etc.

MATT: *Fill ev'ry glass, for wine inspires us,*
> *And fires us*
With courage, love, and joy.
Women and wine should life employ.
Is there aught else on earth desirous?

CHORUS: *Fill ev'ry glass, etc.*

Scene 2

[To them enter Macheath]

MACHEATH: Gentlemen, well met. My heart hath been with you this hour; but an unexpected affair hath detained me. No ceremony, I beg you.

MATT: We were just breaking up to go upon duty. Am I to have the honor of taking the air with you, Sir, this evening upon the heath? I drink a dram now and then with the stage-coachmen in the way of friendship and intelligence; and I know that about this time there will be passengers upon the Western Road,[5] who are worth speaking with.

MACHEATH: I was to have been of that party—but—

MATT: But what, Sir?

MACHEATH: Is there any man who suspects my courage?

MATT: We have all been witnesses of it.

MACHEATH: My honor and truth to the gang?

MATT: I'll be answerable for it.

MACHEATH: In the division of our booty, have I ever shown the least marks of avarice or injustice?

MATT: By these questions something seems to have ruffled you. Are any of us suspected?

MACHEATH: I have a fixed confidence, gentlemen, in you all, as men of honor, and as such I value and respect you. Peachum is a man that is useful to us.

MATT: Is he about to play us any foul play? I'll shoot him through the head.

MACHEATH: I beg you, gentlemen, act with conduct and discretion. A pistol is your last resort.

MATT: He knows nothing of this meeting.

---

3. Cut back, economize.
4. Our respective jobs.

5. Through Bagshot Heath, west of London.

MACHEATH: Business cannot go on without him. He is a man who knows the world, and is a necessary agent to us. We have had a slight difference, and till it is accommodated I shall be obliged to keep out of his way. Any private dispute of mine shall be of no ill consequence to my friends. You must continue to act under his direction, for the moment we break loose from him, our gang is ruined.

MATT: As a bawd[6] to a whore, I grant you, he is to us of great convenience.

MACHEATH: Make him believe I have quitted the gang, which I can never do but with life.[7] At our private quarters I will continue to meet you. A week or so will probably reconcile us.

MATT: Your instructions shall be observed. 'Tis now high time for us to repair to our several duties; so till the evening at our quarters in Moor-fields[8] we bid you farewell.

MACHEATH: I shall wish myself with you. Success attend you. [Sits down melancholy at the table.]

Air 20. March in Rinaldo, with drums and trumpets

MATT: *Let us take the road.*
  Hark! I hear the sound of coaches!
  The hour of attack approaches,
To your arms, brave boys, and load.
  See the ball I hold!
  Let the chemists[9] toil like asses,
  Our fire their fire surpasses,
  And turns all our lead to gold.

[The gang, ranged in the front of the stage, load their pistols, and stick them under their girdles,[1] then go off singing the first part in chorus.]

Scene 3

[Macheath, Drawer[2]]

MACHEATH: What a fool is a fond wench! Polly is most confoundedly bit.[3] I love the sex. And a man who loves money might as well be contented with one guinea, as I with one woman. The town perhaps hath been as much obliged to me, for recruiting it with free-hearted ladies, as to any recruiting officer in the army. If it were not for us and the other gentlemen of the sword, Drury Lane would be uninhabited.

Air 21. Would you have a young virgin, etc.

If the heart of a man is depressed with cares,
The mist is dispelled when a woman appears;
Like the notes of a fiddle, she sweetly, sweetly
Raises the spirits, and charms our ears,
  Roses and lilies her cheeks disclose,

---

6. Pimp.
7. I.e., I will quit the gang only when I quit my life.
8. Just outside the old City wall.
9. Alchemists, who sought to turn base metals into gold.

1. Belts.
2. Bartender.
3. Ensnared.

But her ripe lips are more sweet than those.
    Press her,
    Caress her
    With blisses,
    Her kisses
Dissolve us in pleasure, and soft repose.

I must have women. There is nothing unbends[4] the mind like them. Money is not
so strong a cordial for the time. Drawer! [Enter Drawer.] Is the porter gone for all
the ladies, according to my directions?

DRAWER: I expect him back every minute. But you know, Sir, you sent him as far
as Hockley in the Hole, for three of the ladies, for one in Vinegar Yard, and for
the rest of them somewhere about Lewkner's Lane.[5] Sure some of them are below,
for I hear the bar bell. As they come I will show them up. Coming, coming!

Scene 4

[Macheath, Mrs. Coaxer, Dolly Trull, Mrs. Vixen, Betty Doxy, Jenny Diver,
Mrs. Slammekin, Suky Tawdry, and Molly Brazen]

MACHEATH: Dear Mrs. Coaxer, you are welcome. You look charmingly today. I
hope you don't want the repairs of quality, and lay on paint.[6]—Dolly Trull! Kiss
me, you slut; are you as amorous as ever, hussy? You are always so taken up with
stealing hearts, that you don't allow yourself time to steal anything else. Ah Dolly,
thou wilt ever be a coquette!—Mrs. Vixen, I'm yours, I always loved a woman of
wit and spirit; they make charming mistresses, but plaguy wives.—Betty Doxy!
Come hither, hussy. Do you drink as hard as ever? You had better stick to good
wholesome beer; for in troth, Betty, strong waters[7] will in time ruin your constitution. You should leave those to your betters.—What! And my pretty Jenny Diver
too! As prim and demure as ever! There is not any prude, though ever so high
bred, hath a more sanctified look, with a more mischievous heart. Ah! Thou art a
dear artful hypocrite.—Mrs. Slammekin! As careless and genteel as ever! All you
fine ladies, who know your own beauty, affect an undress.—But see, here's Suky
Tawdry come to contradict what I was saying. Everything she gets one way she
lays out upon her back. Why, Suky, you must keep at least a dozen tallymen.[8]—
Molly Brazen! [She kisses him.] That's well done. I love a free-hearted wench.
Thou hast a most agreeable assurance, girl, and art as willing as a turtle. But hark!
I hear music. The harper is at the door. "If music be the food of love, play on."[9] Ere
you seat yourselves, ladies, what think you of a dance? Come in. [Enter Harper.]
Play the French tune, that Mrs. Slammekin was so fond of.

[A dance á la ronde[1] in the French manner; near the end of it this song and chorus.]

Air 22. Cotillon

Youth's the season made for joys,
    Love is then our duty,
She alone who that employs,
    Well deserves her beauty.

4. Relaxes.
5. Both in Drury Lane.
6. I hope you do not need to paint your face as women of
quality do.
7. Hard liquor.
8. Merchants who provide goods on credit.
9. The opening line of Shakespeare's Twelfth Night.
1. A circular dance.

> Let's be gay,
> While we may,
> Beauty's a flower, despised in decay.
> Youth's the season etc.
>
> Let us drink and sport today,
> Ours is not tomorrow.
> Love with youth flies swift away,
> Age is nought but sorrow.
> Dance and sing,
> Time's on the wing,
> Life never knows the return of spring.

CHORUS: *Let us drink, etc.*

MACHEATH: Now, pray ladies, take your places. Here fellow. [*Pays the Harper.*] Bid the Drawer bring us more wine. [*Exit Harper.*] If any of the ladies choose gin, I hope they will be so free to call for it.

JENNY: You look as if you meant me. Wine is strong enough for me. Indeed, Sir, I never drink strong waters, but when I have the cholic.

MACHEATH: Just the excuse of the fine ladies! Why, a lady of quality is never without the cholic. I hope, Mrs. Coaxer, you have had good success of late in your visits among the mercers.[2]

COAXER: We have so many interlopers—yet with industry, one may still have a little picking. I carried a silver-flowered lutestring, and a piece of black padesoy[3] to Mr. Peachum's lock but last week.

VIXEN: There's Molly Brazen hath the ogle of a rattlesnake. She riveted a linen-draper's eye so fast upon her, that he was nicked[4] of three pieces of cambric before he could look off.

BRAZEN: Oh dear, Madam! But sure nothing can come up to your handling of laces! And then you have such a sweet deluding tongue! To cheat a man is nothing; but the woman must have fine parts indeed who cheats a woman!

VIXEN: Lace, Madam, lies in a small compass, and is of easy conveyance. But you are apt, Madam, to think too well of your friends.

COAXER: If any woman hath more art than another, to be sure, 'tis Jenny Diver. Though her fellow be never so agreeable, she can pick his pocket as coolly, as if money were her only pleasure. Now that is a command of the passions uncommon in a woman!

JENNY: I never go to the tavern with a man, but in the view of business. I have other hours, and other sort of men for my pleasure. But had I your address,[5] Madam—

MACHEATH: Have done with your compliments, ladies; and drink about: You are not so fond of me, Jenny, as you use to be.

JENNY: 'Tis not convenient, Sir, to show my fondness among so many rivals. 'Tis your own choice, and not the warmth of my inclination that will determine you.[6]

Air 23. All in a misty morning, etc.

> Before the barn door crowing,
> The cock by hens attended,

---

2. Dealers in textiles.
3. Types of silk fabric.
4. Robbed.

5. Polished manner.
6. Make up your mind.

His eyes around him throwing,
  Stands for a while suspended.
Then one he singles from the crew,
  And cheers the happy hen;
With how do you do, and how do you do,
  And how do you do again.

MACHEATH: Ah Jenny! Thou art a dear slut.

TRULL: Pray, Madam, were you ever in keeping?[7]

TAWDRY: I hope, Madam, I ha'n't been so long upon the town, but I have met with some good fortunes as well as my neighbors.

TRULL: Pardon me, Madam, I meant no harm by the question; 'twas only in the way of conversation.

TAWDRY: Indeed, Madam, if I had not been a fool, I might have lived very hand-somely with my last friend. But upon his missing five guineas, he turned me off. Now I never suspected he had counted them.

SLAMMEKIN: Who do you look upon, Madam, as your best sort of keepers?

TRULL: That, Madam, is thereafter as they be.[8]

SLAMMEKIN: I, Madam, was once kept by a Jew; and bating[9] their religion, to women they are a good sort of people.

TAWDRY: Now for my part, I own I like an old fellow: for we always make them pay for what they can't do.

VIXEN: A spruce prentice, let me tell you, ladies, is no ill thing, they bleed[1] freely. I have sent at least two or three dozen of them in my time to the plantations.[2]

JENNY: But to be sure, Sir, with so much good fortune as you have had upon the road, you must be grown immensely rich.

MACHEATH: The road, indeed, hath done me justice, but the gaming table hath been my ruin.

Air 24. When once I lay with another man's wife, etc.

JENNY: The gamesters and lawyers are jugglers[3] alike,
    If they meddle your all is in danger.
  Like gypsies, if once they can finger a souse,[4]
  Your pockets they pick, and they pilfer your house,
    And give your estate to a stranger.

A man of courage should never put anything to the risk, but his life. These are the tools of a man of honor. Cards and dice are only fit for cowardly cheats, who prey upon their friends. [She takes up his pistol. Tawdry takes up the other.]

TAWDRY: This, Sir, is fitter for your hand. Besides your loss of money, 'tis a loss to the ladies. Gaming takes you off from women. How fond could I be of you! But before company, 'tis ill bred.

MACHEATH: Wanton hussies!

JENNY: I must and will have a kiss to give my wine a zest.

---

7. A kept mistress of a wealthy gentleman.
8. It depends how they treat me.
9. Apart from.
1. Spend.

2. I.e., incited them to steal and thereby caused them to be transported to the colonies.
3. Sleight-of-hand artists.
4. Get their hands on a sou (a French penny).

[*They take him about the neck, and make signs to Peachum and the constables, who rush in upon him.*]

Scene 5

[*To them, Peachum and constables*]

PEACHUM: I seize you, Sir, as my prisoner.

MACHEATH: Was this well done, Jenny? Women are decoy ducks; who can trust them! Beasts, jades, jilts, harpies, furies, whores!

PEACHUM: Your case, Mr. Macheath is not particular. The greatest heroes have been ruined by women. But, to do them justice, I must own they are a pretty sort of creatures, if we could trust them. You must now, Sir, take your leave of the ladies, and if they have a mind to make you a visit, they will be sure to find you at home. The gentleman, ladies, lodges in Newgate. Constables, wait upon the Captain to his lodgings.

Air 25. When first I laid siege to my Chloris, etc.

MACHEATH: *At the tree I shall suffer with pleasure,*
   At the tree I shall suffer with pleasure,
      Let me go where I will,
      In all kinds of ill,
   I shall find no such furies as these are.

PEACHUM: Ladies, I'll take care the reckoning shall be discharged.[5]

[*Exit Macheath, guarded with Peachum and constables.*]

Scene 6

[*The women remain*]

VIXEN: Look ye, Mrs. Jenny, though Mr. Peachum may have made a private bargain with you and Suky Tawdry for betraying the Captain, as we were all assisting, we ought all to share alike.

COAXER: I think, Mr. Peachum, after so long an acquaintance, might have trusted me as well as Jenny Diver.

SLAMMEKIN: I am sure at least three men of his hanging, and in a year's time too (if he did me justice) should be set down to my account.[6]

TRULL: Mrs. Slammekin, that is not fair. For you know one of them was taken in bed with me.

JENNY: As far as a bowl of punch or a treat, I believe Mrs. Suky will join with me. As for anything else, ladies, you cannot in conscience expect it.

SLAMMEKIN: Dear Madam—

TRULL: I would not for the world—

SLAMMEKIN: 'Tis impossible for me—

TRULL: As I hope to be saved, Madam—

SLAMMEKIN: Nay, then I must stay here all night—

TRULL: Since you command me.   [*Exit with great ceremony.*]

---

5. The bill shall be paid.

6. I.e., I deserve the credit for at least three men that Peachum has had hanged.

Scene 7. Newgate

[Lockit, Turnkeys,[7] Macheath, Constables]

LOCKIT: Noble Captain, you are welcome. You have not been a lodger of mine this year and half. You know the custom, Sir. Garnish,[8] Captain, garnish. Hand me down those fetters there.

MACHEATH: Those, Mr. Lockit, seem to be the heaviest of the whole set. With your leave, I should like the further pair better.

LOCKIT: Look ye, Captain, we know what is fittest for our prisoners. When a gentleman uses me with civility, I always do the best I can to please him. Hand them down I say. We have them of all prices, from one guinea to ten, and 'tis fitting every gentleman should please himself.

MACHEATH: I understand you, Sir. *[Gives money.]* The fees here are so many, and so exorbitant, that few fortunes can bear the expense of getting off[9] handsomely, or of dying like a gentleman.

LOCKIT: Those, I see, will fit the Captain better. Take down the further pair. Do but examine them, Sir. Never was better work. How genteelly they are made! They will sit as easy as a glove, and the nicest[1] man in England might not be ashamed to wear them. *[He puts on the chains.]* If I had the best gentleman in the land in my custody I could not equip him more handsomely. And so, Sir, I now leave you to your private meditations.

Scene 8

[Macheath]

Air 26. Courtiers, courtiers think it no harm, etc.

Man may escape from rope and gun;
Nay, some have outlived the doctor's pill:
Who takes a woman must be undone,
    That basilisk[2] is sure to kill.
The fly that sips treacle is lost in the sweets,
So he that tastes woman, woman, woman,
    He that tastes woman, ruin meets.

To what a woeful plight have I brought myself! Here must I (all day long, 'till I am hanged) be confined to hear the reproaches of a wench who lays her ruin at my door. I am in the custody of her father, and to be sure if he knows of the matter, I shall have a fine time on't betwixt this[3] and my execution. But I promised the wench marriage. What signifies a promise to a woman? Does not man in marriage itself promise a hundred things that he never means to perform? Do all we can, women will believe us; for they look upon a promise as an excuse for following their own inclinations. But here comes Lucy, and I cannot get from her. Would I were deaf!

7. Jailers.
8. Pay the jailer the customary bribe.
9. Escaping punishment.
1. Most discerning.

2. Mythical serpent which killed by its breath or its glance.
3. This moment.

Scene 9

[Macheath, Lucy]

LUCY: You base man you, how can you look me in the face after what hath passed between us? See here, perfidious wretch, how I am forced to bear about the load of infamy you have laid upon me.[4] O Macheath! Thou hast robbed me of my quiet. To see thee tortured would give me pleasure.

Air 27. A lovely lass to a friar came, etc.

Thus when a good housewife sees a rat
    In her trap in the morning taken,
With pleasure her heart goes pit a pat,
    In revenge for her loss of bacon.
      Then she throws him
        To the dog or cat,
To be worried, crushed, and shaken.

MACHEATH: Have you no bowels,[5] no tenderness, my dear Lucy, to see a husband in these circumstances?
LUCY: A husband!
MACHEATH: In every respect but the form, and that, my dear, may be said over us at any time. Friends should not insist upon ceremonies. From a man of honor, his word is as good as his bond.
LUCY: 'Tis the pleasure of all you fine men to insult the women you have ruined.

Air 28. 'Twas when the sea was roaring, etc.

How cruel are the traitors,
    Who lie and swear in jest,
To cheat unguarded creatures
    Of virtue, fame, and rest!
Whoever steals a shilling,
    Through shame the guilt conceals:
In love the perjured villain
    With boasts the theft reveals.

MACHEATH: The very first opportunity, my dear (have but patience), you shall be my wife in whatever manner you please.
LUCY: Insinuating monster! And so you think I know nothing of the affair of Miss Polly Peachum. I could tear thy eyes out!
HEATH: Sure Lucy, you can't be such a fool as to be jealous of Polly!
LUCY: Are you not married to her, you brute you?
MACHEATH: Married! Very good. The wench gives it out only to vex thee, and to ruin me in thy good opinion. 'Tis true, I go to the house; I chat with the girl, I kiss her, I say a thousand things to her (as all gentlemen do) that mean nothing, to divert myself; and now the silly jade hath set it about that I am married to her, to let me know what she would be at. Indeed, my dear Lucy, these violent passions may be of ill consequence to a woman in your condition.

---

4. I.e., she is pregnant.   5. The bodily seat of tenderness, pity.

LUCY: Come, come, Captain, for all your assurance, you know that Miss Polly hath put it out of your power to do me the justice you promised me.

MACHEATH: A jealous woman believes everything her passion suggests. To convince you of my sincerity, if we can find the ordinary,[6] I shall have no scruples of making you my wife; and I know the consequence of having two at a time.

LUCY: That you are only to be hanged, and so get rid of them both.

MACHEATH: I am ready, my dear Lucy, to give you satisfaction—if you think there is any in marriage. What can a man of honor say more?

LUCY: So then it seems, you are not married to Miss Polly.

MACHEATH: You know, Lucy, the girl is prodigiously conceited. No man can say a civil thing to her, but (like other fine ladies) her vanity makes her think he's her own for ever and ever.

Air 29. The sun had loosed his weary teams, etc.

> The first time at the lookingglass
>   The mother sets her daughter,
> The image strikes the smiling lass
>   With self-love ever after.
> Each time she looks, she, fonder grown,
>   Thinks ev'ry charm grows stronger.
> But alas, vain maid, all eyes but your own
>   Can see you are not younger.

When women consider their own beauties, they are all alike unreasonable in their demands; for they expect their lovers should like them as long as they like themselves.

LUCY: Yonder is my father—perhaps this way we may light upon the ordinary, who shall try if you will be as good as your word. For I long to be made an honest woman.

Scene 10

[Peachum, Lockit with an account book]

LOCKIT: In this last affair, Brother Peachum, we are agreed. You have consented to go halves in Macheath.

PEACHUM: We shall never fall out about an execution. But as to that article, pray how stands our last year's account?

LOCKIT: If you will run your eye over it, you'll find 'tis fair and clearly stated.

PEACHUM: This long arrear[7] of the government is very hard upon us! Can it be expected that we should hang our acquaintance for nothing, when our betters will hardly save theirs without being paid for it. Unless the people in employment pay better, I promise them for the future, I shall let other rogues live besides their own.

LOCKIT: Perhaps, Brother, they are afraid these matters may be carried too far. We are treated too by them with contempt, as if our profession was not reputable.

PEACHUM: In one respect indeed, our employment may be reckoned dishonest, because like great statesmen, we encourage those who betray their friends.

LOCKIT: Such language, Brother, anywhere else, might turn to your prejudice.[8] Learn to be more guarded, I beg you.

---

6. The prison chaplain.
7. Lateness in the payment of debts.

8. Be used against you.

Air 30. How happy are we, etc.

When you censure the age,
Be cautious and sage,
Lest the courtiers offended should be:
   If you mention vice or bribe,
   'Tis so pat[9] to all the tribe;
Each cries, "That was leveled at me!"

PEACHUM: Here's poor Ned Clincher's name, I see. Sure, Brother Lockit, there was a little unfair proceeding in Ned's case: for he told me in the condemned hold,[1] that for value received, you had promised him a Session or two longer without molestation.

LOCKIT: Mr. Peachum, this is the first time my honor was ever called in question.

PEACHUM: Business is at an end if once we act dishonorably.

LOCKIT: Who accuses me?

PEACHUM: You are warm,[2] Brother.

LOCKIT: He that attacks my honor, attacks my livelihood. And this usage, Sir, is not to be borne.

PEACHUM: Since you provoke me to speak, I must tell you too, that Mrs. Coaxer charges you with defrauding her of her information money[3] for the apprehending of curl-pated Hugh. Indeed, indeed, Brother, we must punctually pay our spies, or we shall have no information.

LOCKIT: Is this language to me, Sirrah, who have saved you from the gallows, Sirrah!
                                                  [*Collaring each other.*]

PEACHUM: If I am hanged, it shall be for ridding the world of an arrant rascal.

LOCKIT: This hand shall do the office of the halter[4] you deserve, and throttle you—you dog!—

PEACHUM: Brother, Brother, we are both in the wrong. We shall be both losers in the dispute—for you know we have it in our power to hang each other. You should not be so passionate.

LOCKIT: Nor you so provoking.

PEACHUM: 'Tis our mutual interest; 'tis for the interest of the world we should agree. If I said anything, Brother, to the prejudice of your character, I ask pardon.

LOCKIT: Brother Peachum, I can forgive as well as resent. Give me your hand. Suspicion does not become a friend.

PEACHUM: I only meant to give you occasion to justify yourself. But I must now step home, for I expect the gentleman about this snuffbox that Filch nimmed two nights ago in the park. I appointed him at this hour.

Scene 11

[*Lockit, Lucy*]

LOCKIT: Whence come you, hussy?

LUCY: My tears might answer that question.

LOCKIT: You have then been whimpering and fondling, like a spaniel, over the fellow that hath abused you.

9. Suitable.
1. Death row.
2. Angry.

3. Reward for informing on someone.
4. Noose.

LUCY: One can't help love; one can't cure it. 'Tis not in my power to obey you, and hate him.

LOCKIT: Learn to bear your husband's death like a reasonable woman. 'Tis not the fashion, nowadays, so much as to affect sorrow upon these occasions. No woman would ever marry, if she had not the chance of mortality for a release. Act like a woman of spirit, hussy, and thank your father for what he is doing.

Air 31. Of a noble race was Shenkin

LUCY: *Is then his fate decreed, Sir?*
    Such a man can I think of quitting?
    When first we met, so moves me yet,
    O see how my heart is splitting!

LOCKIT: Look ye, Lucy, there is no saving him. So, I think, you must do like other widows: buy yourself weeds,[5] and be cheerful.

Air 32

    You'll think ere many days ensue
      This sentence not severe;
    I hang your husband, child, 'tis true,
      But with him hang your care.
      Twang dang dillo dee.

Like a good wife, go moan over your dying husband. That, child, is your duty. Consider, girl, you can't have the man and the money too—so make yourself as easy as you can, by getting all you can from him.

Scene 12

[Lucy, Macheath]

LUCY: Though the ordinary was out of the way today, I hope, my dear, you will, upon the first opportunity, quiet my scruples. Oh, Sir! My father's hard heart is not to be softened, and I am in the utmost despair.

MACHEATH: But if I could raise a small sum—would not twenty guineas, think you, move him? Of all the arguments in the way of business, the perquisite[6] is the most prevailing. Your father's perquisites for the escape of prisoners must amount to a considerable sum in the year. Money well timed, and properly applied, will do anything.

Air 33. London ladies

    If you at an office solicit your due,[7]
      And would not have matters neglected;
    You must quicken the clerk with the perquisite too,
      To do what his duty directed.
    Or would you the frowns of a lady prevent,
      She too has this palpable failing,
    The perquisite softens her into consent;
      That reason with all is prevailing.

---

5. A widow's mourning clothes.   7. Seek what is due to you.
6. Tip.

LUCY: What love or money can do shall be done: for all my comfort depends upon your safety.

Scene 13

[Lucy, Macheath, Polly]

POLLY: Where is my dear husband? Was a rope ever intended for this neck! O let me throw my arms about it, and throttle thee with love! Why dost thou turn away from me? 'Tis thy Polly. 'Tis thy wife.

MACHEATH: Was ever such an unfortunate rascal as I am!

LUCY: Was there ever such another villain!

POLLY: O Macheath! Was it for this we parted? Taken! Imprisoned! Tried! Hanged! Cruel reflection! I'll stay with thee 'till death. No force shall tear thy dear wife from thee now. What means my love? Not one kind word! Not one kind look! Think what thy Polly suffers to see thee in this condition.

Air 34. All in the downs, etc.

Thus when the swallow, seeking prey,
  Within the sash[8] is closely pent,
His comfort, with bemoaning lay,[9]
  Without sits pining for th' event.
Her chatt'ring lovers all around her skim;
She heeds them not (poor bird!) her soul's with him.

MACHEATH: I must disown her. [Aside.] The wench is distracted.

LUCY: Am I then bilked of my virtue? Can I have no reparation? Sure men were born to lie, and women to believe them! O villain! Villain!

POLLY: Am I not thy wife? Thy neglect of me, thy aversion to me too severely proves it. Look on me. Tell me, am I not thy wife?

LUCY: Perfidious wretch!

POLLY: Barbarous husband!

LUCY: Hadst thou been hanged five months ago, I had been happy.

POLLY: And I too. If you had been kind to me 'till death, it would not have vexed me. And that's no very unreasonable request (though from a wife) to a man who hath not above seven or eight days to live.

LUCY: Art thou then married to another? Hast thou two wives, monster?

MACHEATH: If women's tongues can cease for an answer—hear me.

LUCY: I won't. Flesh and blood can't bear my usage.

POLLY: Shall I not claim my own? Justice bids me speak.

Air 35. Have you heard of a frolicsome ditty, etc.

MACHEATH: *How happy could I be with either,*
  Were t'other dear charmer away!
But while you thus tease me together,
  To neither a word will I say;
  But tol de rol, etc.

---

8. Window frame.   9. Plaintive song.

POLLY: Sure, my dear, there ought to be some preference shown to a wife! At least she may claim the appearance of it. He must be distracted with his misfortunes, or he could not use me thus!

LUCY: O villain, villain! Thou hast deceived me. I could even inform against thee with pleasure. Not a prude wishes more heartily to have facts against her intimate acquaintance, than I now wish to have facts against thee. I would have her satisfaction, and they should all out.

Air 36. Irish trot

POLLY: *I'm bubbled.*[1]
LUCY: *I'm bubbled.*
POLLY: *Oh how I am troubled!*
LUCY: *Bamboozled, and bit!*
POLLY: *My distresses are doubled.*
LUCY: *When you come to the tree, should the hangman refuse,*
        These fingers, with pleasure, could fasten the noose.
POLLY: *I'm bubbled, etc.*

MACHEATH: Be pacified, my dear Lucy. This is all a fetch[2] of Polly's, to make me desperate with[3] you in case I get off. If I am hanged, she would fain[4] the credit of being thought my widow. Really, Polly, this is no time for a dispute of this sort; for whenever you are talking of marriage, I am thinking of hanging.

POLLY: And hast thou the heart to persist in disowning me?

MACHEATH: And hast thou the heart to persist in persuading me that I am married? Why, Polly, dost thou seek to aggravate my misfortunes?

LUCY: Really, Miss Peachum, you but expose yourself. Besides, 'tis barbarous in you to worry a gentleman in his circumstances.

Air 37

POLLY: *Cease your funning;*
      Force or cunning
  Never shall my heart trapan.[5]
    All these sallies
    Are but malice
  To seduce my constant man.
    'Tis most certain,
    By their flirting
  Women oft, have envy shown;
    Pleased, to ruin
    Others' wooing;
  Never happy in their own!

POLLY: Decency, Madam, methinks might teach you to behave yourself with some reserve with the husband, while his wife is present.

MACHEATH: But seriously, Polly, this is carrying the joke a little too far.

---

1. Cheated, fooled.
2. Trick.
3. Ruin my hopes of having.
4. Would like.
5. Esnare.

LUCY: If you are determined, Madam, to raise a disturbance in the prison, I shall be obliged to send for the turnkey to show you the door. I am sorry, Madam, you force me to be so ill-bred.

POLLY: Give me leave to tell you, Madam. These forward airs don't become you in the least, Madam. And my duty, Madam, obliges me to stay with my husband, Madam.

Air 38. Good-morrow, gossip Joan

LUCY: *Why how now, Madam Flirt?*
    If you thus must chatter;
    And are for flinging dirt,
      Let's try who best can spatter;
    Madam Flirt!

POLLY: *Why how now, saucy jade;*
    Sure the wench is tipsy!

[*To him.*]   *How can you see me made*
    The scoff of such a gypsy?

[*To her.*]   *Saucy jade!*

Scene 14
[*Lucy, Macheath, Polly, Peachum*]

PEACHUM: Where's my wench? Ah, hussy! Hussy! Come you home, you slut; and when your fellow is hanged, hang yourself, to make your family some amends.

POLLY: Dear, dear father, do not tear me from him—I must speak; I have more to say to him. Oh! Twist thy fetters about me, that he may not haul me from thee!

PEACHUM: Sure all women are alike! If ever they commit the folly, they are sure to commit another by exposing themselves. Away—not a word more. You are my prisoner now, hussy.

Air 39. Irish howl

POLLY: *No power on earth can e'er divide*
The knot that sacred love hath tied.
When parents draw against our mind,[6]
The true-love's knot they faster bind.
    Oh, oh ray, oh Amborah, oh, oh, etc.

                         [*Holding Macheath, Peachum pulling her.*]

Scene 15
[*Lucy, Macheath*]

MACHEATH: I am naturally compassionate, wife, so that I could not use the wench as she deserved, which made you at first suspect there was something in what she said.

LUCY: Indeed, my dear, I was strangely puzzled.

MACHEATH: If that had been the case, her father would never have brought me into this circumstance. No, Lucy, I had rather die than be false to thee.

---

6. Pull against our wishes.

LUCY: How happy am I, if you say this from your heart! For I love thee so, that I could sooner bear to see thee hanged than in the arms of another.

MACHEATH: But couldst thou bear to see me hanged?

LUCY: O, Macheath, I can never live to see that day.

MACHEATH: You see, Lucy, in the account of love you are in my debt, and you must now be convinced, that I rather choose to die than be another's. Make me, if possible, love thee more, and let me owe my life to thee. If you refuse to assist me, Peachum and your father will immediately put me beyond all means of escape.

LUCY: My father, I know, hath been drinking hard with the prisoners, and I fancy he is now taking his nap in his own room. If I can procure the keys, shall I go off with thee, my dear?

MACHEATH: If we are together, 'twill be impossible to lie concealed. As soon as the search begins to be a little cool, I will send to thee. 'Till then my heart is thy prisoner.

LUCY: Come then, my dear husband, owe thy life to me, and though you love me not, be grateful. But that Polly runs in my head strangely.

MACHEATH: A moment of time may make us unhappy forever.

Air 40. The lass of Patie's mill, etc.

LUCY: *I like the fox shall grieve,*
    Whose mate hath left her side.
Whom hounds, from morn to eve,
    Chase o'er the country wide.
Where can my lover hide?
    Where cheat the weary pack?
If love be not his guide,
    He never will come back!

ACT 3

Scene 1. Newgate

[Lockit, Lucy]

LOCKIT: To be sure, wench, you must have been aiding and abetting to help him to this escape.

LUCY: Sir, here hath been Peachum and his daughter Polly, and to be sure they know the ways of Newgate as well as if they had been born and bred in the place all their lives. Why must all your suspicion light upon me?

LOCKIT: Lucy, Lucy, I will have none of these shuffling answers.

LUCY: Well then, if I know anything of him I wish I may be burnt!

LOCKIT: Keep your temper, Lucy, or I shall pronounce you guilty.

LUCY: Keep yours, Sir, I do wish I may be burned. I do—and what can I say more to convince you?

LOCKIT: Did he tip handsomely? How much did he come down with? Come hussy, don't cheat your father; and I shall not be angry with you. Perhaps you have made a better bargain with him than I could have done. How much, my good girl?

LUCY: You know, Sir, I am fond of him, and would have given money to have kept him with me.

LOCKIT: Ah, Lucy! Thy education might have put thee more upon thy guard; for a girl in the bar of an alehouse is always besieged.

LUCY: Dear Sir, mention not my education—for 'twas to that I owe my ruin.

Air 41. If love's a sweet passion, etc.

When young at the bar you first taught me to score,[1]
And bid me be free of my lips, and no more;
I was kissed by the parson, the squire, and the sot.
When the guest was departed, the kiss was forgot.
But his kiss was so sweet, and so closely he pressed,
That I languished and pined till I granted the rest.

If you can forgive me, Sir, I will make a fair confession, for to be sure he hath been a most barbarous villain to me.

LOCKIT: And so you have let him escape, hussy? Have you?

LUCY: When a woman loves, a kind look, a tender word can persuade her to anything, and I could ask no other bribe.

LOCKIT: Thou wilt always be a vulgar[2] slut, Lucy. If you would not be looked upon as a fool, you should never do anything but upon the foot of[3] interest. Those that act otherwise are their own bubbles.[4]

LUCY: But love, Sir, is a misfortune that may happen to the most discreet woman, and in love we are all fools alike. Notwithstanding all he swore, I am now fully convinced that Polly Peachum is actually his wife. Did I let him escape (fool that I was!) to go to her? Polly will wheedle herself into his money, and then Peachum will hang him, and cheat us both.

LOCKIT: So I am to be ruined, because, forsooth, you must be in love! A very pretty excuse!

LUCY: I could murder that impudent happy strumpet. I gave him his life, and that creature enjoys the sweets of it. Ungrateful Macheath!

Air 42. South Sea ballad

My love is all madness and folly,
Alone I lie,
Toss, tumble, and cry,
What a happy creature is Polly!
Was e'er such a wretch as I!
With rage I redden like scarlet,
That my dear inconstant varlet,
Stark blind to my charms,
Is lost in the arms
Of that jilt, that inveigling harlot!
Stark blind to my charms,
Is lost in the arms
Of that jilt, that inveigling harlot!
This, this my resentment alarms.

LOCKIT: And so, after all this mischief, I must stay here to be entertained with your caterwauling, Mistress Puss! Out of my sight, wanton strumpet! You shall fast and mortify yourself into reason, with now and then a little handsome discipline[5] to bring you to your senses. Go.

1. Tally, keep an account.
2. Common.
3. For the sake of.

4. Cheat themselves.
5. A beating.

Scene 2

[Lockit]

LOCKIT: Peachum then intends to outwit me in this affair; but I'll be even with him. The dog is leaky in his liquor,[6] so I'll ply him that way, get the secret from him, and turn this affair to my own advantage. Lions, wolves, and vultures don't live together in herds, droves, or flocks. Of all animals of prey, man is the only sociable one. Every one of us preys upon his neighbor, and yet we herd together. Peachum is my companion, my friend. According to the custom of the world, indeed, he may quote thousands of precedents for cheating me. And shall not I make use of the privilege of friendship to make him a return?

Air 43. Packington's Pound

Thus gamesters united in friendship are found,
Though they know that their industry all is a cheat;
They flock to their prey at the dicebox's sound,
And join to promote one another's deceit.
    But if by mishap
    They fail of a chap,[7]
To keep in their hands, they each other entrap.
Like pikes, lank with hunger, who miss of their ends,[8]
They bite their companions, and prey on their friends.

Now, Peachum, you and I, like honest tradesmen, are to have a fair trial which of us two can overreach the other.—Lucy! [Enter Lucy.] Are there any of Peachum's people now in the house?

LUCY: Filch, Sir, is drinking a quartern[9] of strong waters in the next room with Black Moll.

LOCKIT: Bid him come to me.

Scene 3

[Lockit, Filch]

LOCKIT: Why, boy, thou lookest as if thou wert half starved, like a shotten herring.[1]

FILCH: One had need have the constitution of a horse to go through the business. Since the favorite child-getter[2] was disabled by a mishap, I have picked up a little money by helping the ladies to a pregnancy against their being called down to sentence. But if a man cannot get an honest livelihood any easier way, I am sure, 'tis what I can't undertake for another Session.

LOCKIT: Truly, if that great man should tip off,[3] 'twould be an irreparable loss. The vigor and prowess of a knight-errant never saved half the ladies in distress that he hath done. But, boy, can'st thou tell me where thy master is to be found?

FILCH: At his lock,[4] Sir, at the Crooked Billet.

LOCKIT: Very well. I have nothing more with you.

[Exit Filch.]

---

6. Talkative when drunk.
7. Cannot get a customer (prey).
8. Fail to catch their prey.
9. Quarter-pint.
1. A herring that has spawned.

2. Begetter (i.e., Macheath).
3. Die.
4. A cant word signifying a warehouse where stolen goods are deposited [Gay's note].

I'll go to him there, for I have many important affairs to settle with him; and in the way of those transactions, I'll artfully get into his secret. So that Macheath shall not remain a day longer out of my clutches.

Scene 4. A Gaming House

[*Macheath in a fine tarnished coat, Ben Budge, Matt of the Mint*]

MACHEATH: I am sorry, gentlemen, the road was so barren of money. When my friends are in difficulties, I am always glad that my fortune can be serviceable to them. [*Gives them money.*] You see, gentlemen, I am not a mere Court friend, who professes everything and will do nothing.

Air 44. Lillibullero

The modes of the Court so common are grown,
  That a true friend can hardly be met;
Friendship for interest is but a loan,
  Which they let out for what they can get.
    'Tis true, you find
    Some friends so kind,
Who will give you good counsel themselves to defend.
    In sorrowful ditty,
    They promise, they pity,
But shift you[5] for money, from friend to friend.

But we, gentlemen, have still honor enough to break through the corruptions of the world. And while I can serve you, you may command me.

BEN: It grieves my heart that so generous a man should be involved in such difficulties, as oblige him to live with such ill company, and herd with gamesters.

MATT: See the partiality of mankind! One man may steal a horse, better than another look over a hedge.[6] Of all mechanics,[7] of all servile handicraftsmen, a gamester is the vilest. But yet, as many of the quality[8] are of the profession, he is admitted amongst the politest company. I wonder we are not more respected.

MACHEATH: There will be deep play tonight at Marybone, and consequently money may be picked up upon the road. Meet me there, and I'll give you the hint who is worth setting.[9]

MATT: The fellow with a brown coat with a narrow gold binding, I am told, is never without money.

MACHEATH: What do you mean, Matt? Sure you will not think of meddling with him! He's a good honest kind of a fellow, and one of us.

BEN: To be sure, Sir, we will put ourselves under your direction.

MACHEATH: Have an eye upon the moneylenders. A rouleau,[1] or two, would prove a pretty sort of an expedition. I hate extortion.

MATT: Those rouleaus are very pretty things. I hate your bank bills. There is such a hazard in putting them off.[2]

---

5. Put you off.
6. I.e., one man is permitted to steal a horse, though another is not permitted even to look at one; proverbial.
7. Tradesmen.

8. The people of quality (gentry).
9. Setting upon, robbing.
1. A packet of gold coins.
2. Getting rid of them, passing them off.

MACHEATH: There is a certain man of distinction, who in his time hath nicked me out of a great deal of the ready. He is in my cash,[3] Ben; I'll point him out to you this evening, and you shall draw upon him for the debt. The company are met; I hear the dicebox in the other room. So, gentlemen, your servant. You'll meet me at Marybone.

Scene 5. Peachum's Lock

[*A table with wine, brandy, pipes, and tobacco.*
Peachum, Lockit]

LOCKIT: The coronation account,[4] Brother Peachum, is of so intricate a nature, that I believe it will never be settled.

PEACHUM: It consists indeed of a great variety of articles. It was worth to our people, in fees of different kinds, above ten installments.[5] This is part of the account, Brother, that lies open before us.

LOCKIT: A lady's tail[6] of rich brocade—that, I see, is disposed of.

PEACHUM: To Mrs. Diana Trapes, the tallywoman,[7] and she will make a good hand[8] on't in shoes and slippers, to trick out young ladies, upon their going into keeping.

LOCKIT: But I don't see any article of the jewels.

PEACHUM: Those are so well known, that they must be sent abroad. You'll find them entered under the article of exportation. As for the snuffboxes, watches, swords, etc., I thought it best to enter them under their several heads.

LOCKIT: Seven and twenty women's pockets[9] complete; with the several things therein contained; all sealed, numbered, and entered.

PEACHUM: But, Brother, it is impossible for us now to enter upon this affair. We should have the whole day before us. Besides, the account of the last half year's plate is in a book by itself, which lies at the other office.

LOCKIT: Bring us then more liquor. Today shall be for pleasure, tomorrow for business. Ah, Brother, those daughters of ours are two slippery hussies. Keep a watchful eye upon Polly, and Macheath in a day or two shall be our own again.

Air 45. Down in the north country, etc.

LOCKIT: *What gudgeons[1] are we men!*
Ev'ry woman's easy prey.
Though we have felt the hook, again
We bite and they betray.
The bird that hath been trapped,
When he hears his calling mate,
To her he flies, again he's clapped
Within the wiry grate.

---

3. Owes me money.
4. A manuscript inventory of items stolen during the coronation of George II; Peachum "keeps books" like an ordinary businessman.
5. I.e., the thieves have found a single coronation more than ten times as profitable as the annual installment of the new Lord Mayor.
6. Train (of a woman's dress).

7. One who provides goods on credit.
8. Profit.
9. A pocket was a detachable bag worn outside the woman's dress.
1. "A small fish . . . easily caught, and therefore made a proverbial name for a man easily cheated" (Johnson's *Dictionary*).

PEACHUM: But what signifies catching the bird, if your daughter Lucy will set open the door of the cage?

LOCKIT: If men were answerable for the follies and frailties of their wives and daughters, no friends could keep a good correspondence together for two days. This is unkind of you, Brother; for among good friends, what they say or do goes for nothing.

[*Enter a servant.*]

SERVANT: Sir, here's Mrs. Diana Trapes wants to speak with you.

PEACHUM: Shall we admit her, Brother Lockit?

LOCKIT: By all means. She's a good customer, and a fine-spoken woman. And a woman who drinks and talks so freely will enliven the conversation.

PEACHUM: Desire her to walk in.

[*Exit servant.*]

Scene 6

[*Peachum, Lockit, Mrs. Trapes*]

PEACHUM: Dear Mrs. Dye, your servant. One may know by your kiss, that your gin is excellent.

TRAPES: I was always very curious[2] in my liquors.

LOCKIT: There is no perfumed breath like it. I have been long acquainted with the flavor of those lips. Han't I, Mrs. Dye?

TRAPES: Fill it up. I take as large draughts of liquor, as I did of love. I hate a flincher in either.

Air 46. A shepherd kept sheep, etc.

In the days of my youth I could bill like a dove, fa, la, la, etc.
Like a sparrow at all times was ready for love, fa, la, la, etc.
The life of all mortals in kissing should pass,
Lip to lip while we're young—then the lip to the glass, fa, la, etc.

But now, Mr. Peachum, to our business. If you have blacks[3] of any kind, brought in of late: mantoes,[4] velvet scarves, petticoats—let it be what it will—I am your chap, for all my ladies are very fond of mourning.

PEACHUM: Why, look ye, Mrs. Dye, you deal so hard with us, that we can afford to give the gentlemen, who venture their lives for the goods, little or nothing.

TRAPES: The hard times oblige me to go very near[5] in my dealing. To be sure, of late years I have been a great sufferer by the Parliament. Three thousand pounds would hardly make me amends. The act for destroying the Mint[6] was a severe cut upon our business. 'Till then, if a customer[7] stepped out of the way, we knew where to have her. No doubt you know Mrs. Coaxer. There's a wench now (till today) with a good suit of clothes of mine upon her back, and I could never set eyes upon her for three months together. Since the act too against imprisonment

2. Fastidious.
3. Black clothing.
4. Loose robes (French: *manteaux*).
5. To pay as little as possible.
6. The Mint was a safe haven for debtors, and hence a

gathering place for disreputable characters. The Act (10 October 1723) made it much harder to feign bankruptcy, and thereby to take refuge in the Mint.
7. Prostitute.

for small sums,[8] my loss there too hath been very considerable, and it must be so, when a lady can borrow a handsome petticoat, or a clean gown, and I not have the least hank[9] upon her! And, o' my conscience, now-a-days most ladies take a delight in cheating, when they can do it with safety.

PEACHUM: Madam, you had a handsome gold watch of us t'other day for seven guineas. Considering we must have our profit, to a gentleman upon the road, a gold watch will be scarce worth the taking.

TRAPES: Consider, Mr. Peachum, that watch was remarkable, and not of very safe sale. If you have any black velvet scarves—they are a handsome winter wear; and take with most gentlemen who deal with my customers. 'Tis I that put the ladies upon a good foot. 'Tis not youth or beauty that fixes their price. The gentlemen always pay according to their dress, from half a crown to two guineas; and yet those hussies make nothing of bilking of me. Then too, allowing for accidents. I have eleven fine customers now down under the surgeon's hands[1]—what with fees and other expenses, there are great goings-out, and no comings-in, and not a farthing to pay for at least a month's clothing. We run great risks—great risks indeed.

PEACHUM: As I remember, you said something just now of Mrs. Coaxer.

TRAPES: Yes, Sir. To be sure I stripped her of a suit of my own clothes about two hours ago; and have left her as she should be, in her shift, with a lover of hers at my house. She called him upstairs, as he was going to Marybone in a hackney coach. And I hope, for her own sake and mine, she will persuade the Captain to redeem[2] her, for the Captain is very generous to the ladies.

LOCKIT: What Captain?

TRAPES: He thought I did not know him. An intimate acquaintance of yours, Mr. Peachum—only Captain Macheath—as fine as a lord.

PEACHUM: Tomorrow, dear Mrs. Dye, you shall set your own price upon any of the goods you like. We have at least half a dozen velvet scarves, and all at your service. Will you give me leave to make you a present of this suit of nightclothes for your own wearing? But are you sure it is Captain Macheath?

TRAPES: Though he thinks I have forgot him, nobody knows him better. I have taken a great deal of the Captain's money in my time at second hand, for he always loved to have his ladies well dressed.

PEACHUM: Mr. Lockit and I have a little business with the Captain—you understand me—and we will satisfy you for Mrs. Coaxer's debt.

LOCKIT: Depend upon it. We will deal like men of honor.

TRAPES: I don't inquire after your affairs—so whatever happens, I wash my hands on't. It hath always been my maxim, that one friend should assist another. But if you please, I'll take one of the scarves home with me. 'Tis always good to have something in hand.

Scene 7. Newgate

[Lucy]

LUCY: Jealousy, rage, love, and fear are at once tearing me to pieces. How I am weather-beaten and shattered with distresses!

---

8. "An Act to Prevent Frivolous and Vexatious Arrests" (24 June 1726); "small sums" meant ten pounds if a Superior court matter, or 40 shillings if an Inferior.
9. Hold.

1. For treatment of venereal disease.
2. I.e., will help her to buy back (as at a pawn shop) her "suit of . . . clothes."

Air 47. One evening, having lost my way, etc.

I'm like a skiff on the ocean tossed,
  Now high, now low, with each billow born,
With her rudder broke, and her anchor lost,
  Deserted and all forlorn.
While thus I lie rolling and tossing all night,
That Polly lies sporting on seas of delight!
  Revenge, revenge, revenge,
Shall appease my restless sprite.

I have the ratsbane[3] ready. I run no risk; for I can lay her death upon the gin, and so many die of that naturally that I shall never be called in question. But say I were to be hanged—I never could be hanged for anything that would give me greater comfort than the poisoning that slut.

[*Enter Filch.*]

FILCH: Madam, here's our Miss Polly come to wait upon you.
LUCY: Show her in.

Scene 8

[*Lucy, Polly*]

LUCY: Dear Madam, your servant. I hope you will pardon my passion, when I was so happy to see you last. I was so overrun with the spleen,[4] that I was perfectly out of myself. And really when one hath the spleen, everything is to be excused by a friend.

Air 48. Now Roger, I'll tell thee, because thou'rt my son

When a wife's in her pout,
  (As she's sometimes, no doubt)
The good husband as meek as a lamb,
  Her vapors to still,
  First grants her her will,
And the quieting draught is a dram.[5]
Poor man! And the quieting draught is a dram.

I wish all our quarrels might have so comfortable a reconciliation.
POLLY: I have no excuse for my own behavior, Madam, but my misfortunes. And really, Madam, I suffer too upon your account.
LUCY: But, Miss Polly, in the way of friendship, will you give me leave to propose a glass of cordial to you?
POLLY: Strong waters are apt to give me the headache. I hope, Madam, you will excuse me.
LUCY: Not the greatest lady in the land could have better in her closet, for her own private drinking. You seem mighty low in spirits, my dear.

---

3. Rat poison.
4. Generally, ill temper; more specifically, a fashionable disease resembling hypochondria, also known as "the vapors."
5. A shot of alcohol.

POLLY: I am sorry, Madam, my health will not allow me to accept of your offer. I should not have left you in the rude manner I did when we met last, Madam, had not my Papa hauled me away so unexpectedly. I was indeed somewhat provoked, and perhaps might use some expressions that were disrespectful. But really, Madam, the Captain treated me with so much contempt and cruelty, that I deserved your pity, rather than your resentment.

LUCY: But since his escape, no doubt all matters are made up again. Ah Polly! Polly! 'Tis I am the unhappy wife; and he loves you as if you were only his mistress.

POLLY: Sure, Madam, you cannot think me so happy as to be the object of your jealousy. A man is always afraid of a woman who loves him too well—so that I must expect to be neglected and avoided.

LUCY: Then our cases, my dear Polly, are exactly alike. Both of us indeed have been too fond.

Air 49. O Bessy Bell

POLLY: *A curse attends that woman's love,*
Who always would be pleasing.
LUCY: *The pertness of the billing dove,*
Like tickling, is but teasing.
POLLY: *What then in love can woman do?*
LUCY: *If we grow fond they shun us.*
POLLY: *And when we fly them, they pursue.*
LUCY: *But leave us when they've won us.*

LUCY: Love is so very whimsical in both sexes, that it is impossible to be lasting. But my heart is particular,[6] and contradicts my own observation.

POLLY: But really, Mistress Lucy, by his last behavior, I think I ought to envy you. When I was forced from him, he did not show the least tenderness. But perhaps, he hath a heart not capable of it.

Air 50. Would fate to me Belinda give

Among the men, coquettes we find,
Who court by turns all womankind;
And we grant all their hearts desired,
When they are flattered, and admired.

The coquettes of both sexes are self-lovers, and that is a love no other whatever can dispossess. I fear, my dear Lucy, our husband is one of those.

LUCY: Away with these melancholy reflections; indeed, my dear Polly, we are both of us a cup too low.[7] Let me prevail upon you, to accept of my offer.

Air 51. Come, sweet lass, etc.

Come, sweet lass,
Let's banish sorrow
Till tomorrow;
Come, sweet lass,

6. In two senses: (1) preoccupied with one person (Macheath), and therefore (2) idiosyncratic—an exception to the rule she has just pronounced.
7. I.e., needing a drink.

> Let's take a chirping[8] glass.
>> Wine can clear
>> The vapors of despair;
>> And make us light as air;
>> Then drink, and banish care.

I can't bear, child, to see you in such low spirits. And I must persuade you to what I know will do you good. [*Aside.*] I shall now soon be even with the hypocritical strumpet.   [*Exit.*]

Scene 9.

[*Polly*]

All this wheedling of Lucy cannot be for nothing. At this time too! When I know she hates me! The dissembling of a woman is always the forerunner of mischief. By pouring strong waters down my throat, she thinks to pump some secrets out of me. I'll be upon my guard, and won't taste a drop of her liquor, I'm resolved.

Scene 10

[*Lucy, with strong waters; Polly*]

LUCY: Come, Miss Polly.

POLLY: Indeed, child, you have given yourself trouble to no purpose. You must, my dear, excuse me.

LUCY: Really, Miss Polly, you are so squeamishly affected about taking a cup of strong waters as a lady before company. I vow, Polly, I shall take it monstrously ill if you refuse me. Brandy and men (though women love them never so well)[9] are always taken by us with some reluctance—unless 'tis in private.

POLLY: I protest, Madam, it goes against me. What do I see! Macheath again in custody! Now every glimmering of happiness is lost. [*Drops the glass of liquor on the ground.*]

LUCY [*Aside*]: Since things are thus, I'm glad the wench hath escaped: for by this event, 'tis plain, she was not happy enough to deserve to be poisoned.

Scene 11

[*Lockit, Macheath, Peachum, Lucy, Polly*]

LOCKIT: Set your heart to rest, Captain. You have neither the chance of love or money for another escape, for you are ordered to be called down upon your trial immediately.

PEACHUM: Away, hussies! This is not a time for a man to be hampered with his wives. You see, the gentleman is in chains already.

LUCY: O husband, husband, my heart longed to see thee; but to see thee thus distracts me!

POLLY: Will not my dear husband look upon his Polly? Why hadst thou not flown to me for protection? With me thou hadst been safe.

8. Cheering.   9. However much women may love them.

Air 52. The last time I went o'er the moor

POLLY: *Hither, dear husband, turn your eyes.*
LUCY: *Bestow one glance to cheer me.*
POLLY: *Think with that look, thy Polly dies.*
LUCY: *O shun me not—but hear me.*
POLLY: *'Tis Polly sues.*
LUCY: *'Tis Lucy speaks.*
POLLY: *Is thus true love requited?*
LUCY: *My heart is bursting.*
POLLY: *Mine too breaks.*
LUCY: *Must I—*
POLLY: *Must I be slighted?*

MACHEATH: What would you have me say, ladies? You see, this affair will soon be at an end, without my disobliging either of you.

PEACHUM: But the settling this point, Captain, might prevent a lawsuit between your two widows.

Air 53. Tom Tinker's my true love

MACHEATH: *Which way shall I turn me? How can I decide?*
Wives, the day of our death, are as fond as a bride.
One wife is too much for most husbands to hear,
But two at a time there's no mortal can bear.
This way, and that way, and which way I will,
What would comfort the one, t'other wife would take ill.

POLLY: But if his own misfortunes have made him insensible to mine—A father sure will be more compassionate. Dear, dear Sir, sink[1] the material evidence, and bring him off at his trial. Polly upon her knees begs it of you.

Air 54. I am a poor shepherd undone

When my hero in court appears,
    And stands arraigned for his life;
Then think of poor Polly's tears;
    For Ah! Poor Polly's his wife.
Like the sailor he holds up his hand,
    Distressed on the dashing wave.
To die a dry death at land,
    Is as bad as a wat'ry grave.
And alas, poor Polly!
Alack, and well-a-day!
Before I was in love,
    Oh! Every month was May.

LUCY: If Peachum's heart is hardened, sure you, Sir, will have more compassion on a daughter. I know the evidence is in your power. How then can you be a tyrant to me? [*Kneeling.*]

1. Suppress.

Air 55. Ianthe the lovely, etc.

When he holds up his hand arraigned for his life,
O think of your daughter, and think I'm his wife!
What are cannons, or bombs, or clashing of swords?
For death is more certain by witness's words.
Then nail up their lips; that dread thunder allay;
And each month of my life will hereafter be May.

LOCKIT: Macheath's time is come, Lucy. We know our own affairs, therefore let us
have no more whimpering or whining.

Air 56. A cobbler there was, etc.

Ourselves, like the great, to secure a retreat,
When matters require it, must give up our gang:
    And good reason why,
    Or, instead of the fry,[2]
    Ev'n Peachum and I,
Like poor petty rascals, might hang, hang;
Like poor petty rascals, might hang.

PEACHUM: Set your heart at rest, Polly. Your husband is to die today. Therefore, if
you are not already provided, 'tis high time to look about for another. There's
comfort for you, you slut.

LOCKIT: We are ready, Sir, to conduct you to the Old Bailey.

Air 57. Bonny Dundee

MACHEATH: The charge is prepared; the lawyers are met,
    The judges all ranged (a terrible show!).
    I go undismayed, for death is a debt—
    A debt on demand—so take what I owe.
    Then farewell my love. Dear charmers, adieu.
    Contented I die—'tis the better for you.
    Here ends all dispute the rest of our lives,
    For this way at once I please all my wives.

Now, gentlemen, I am ready to attend you.

Scene 12

[Lucy, Polly, Filch]

POLLY: Follow them, Filch, to the court. And when the trial is over, bring me a particular account of his behavior, and of everything that happened. You'll find me
here with Miss Lucy. [Exit Filch.] But why is all this music?

LUCY: The prisoners, whose trials are put off till next Session, are diverting themselves.

POLLY: Sure there is nothing so charming as music! I'm fond of it to distraction! But
alas! Now, all mirth seems an insult upon my affliction. Let us retire, my dear Lucy,
and indulge our sorrows. The noisy crew, you see, are coming upon us.   [Exit.]

---

2. Small fish.

[*A dance of prisoners in chains, etc.*]

Scene 13. The Condemned Hold

[*Macheath, in a melancholy posture*]

Air 58. Happy Groves

O cruel, cruel, cruel case!
Must I suffer this disgrace?

Air 59. Of all the girls that are so smart

Of all the friends in time of grief,
When threatening death looks grimmer,
Not one so sure can bring relief,
As this best friend, a brimmer.³   [*Drinks.*]

Air 60. Britons strike home

Since I must swing, I scorn, I scorn to wince or whine.   [*Rises.*]

Air 61. Chevy Chase

But now again my spirits sink;
I'll raise them high with wine.   [*Drinks a glass of wine.*]

Air 62. To old Sir Simon the king

But valor the stronger grows,
The stronger liquor we're drinking.
And how can we feel our woes,
When we've lost the trouble of thinking?   [*Drinks.*]

Air 63. Joy to great Caesar

If thus—A man can die
Much bolder with brandy.   [*Pours out a bumper of brandy.*]

Air 64. There was an old woman

So I drink off this bumper. And now I can stand the test.
And my comrades shall see, that I die as brave as the best. [*Drinks.*]

Air 65. Did you ever hear of a gallant sailor

But can I leave my pretty hussies,
Without one tear, or tender sigh?

Air 66. Why are mine eyes still flowing

Their eyes, their lips, their busses⁴
Recall my love—Ah must I die?

3. A cup filled to the brim.   4. Kisses.

Air 67. Green Sleeves

Since laws were made for ev'ry degree,
To curb vice in others, as well as me,
I wonder we ha'n't better company,
    Upon Tyburn tree!
But gold from law can take out the sting;
And if rich men like us were to swing,
'Twould thin the land, such numbers to string
    Upon Tyburn tree!

JAILER: Some friends of yours, Captain, desire to be admitted. I leave you together.

Scene 14

[Macheath, Ben Budge, Matt of the Mint]

MACHEATH: For my having broke[5] prison, you see, gentlemen, I am ordered immediate execution. The sheriff's officers, I believe, are now at the door. That Jemmy Twitcher should peach me, I own surprised me! 'Tis a plain proof that the world is all alike, and that even our gang can no more trust one another than other people. Therefore, I beg you, gentlemen, look well to yourselves, for in all probability you may live some months longer.

MATT: We are heartily sorry, Captain, for your misfortune. But 'tis what we must all come to.

MACHEATH: Peachum and Lockit, you know, are infamous scoundrels. Their lives are as much in your power, as yours are in theirs. Remember your dying friend. 'Tis my last request. Bring those villains to the gallows before you, and I am satisfied.

MATT: We'll do't.

JAILER: Miss Polly and Miss Lucy entreat a word with you.

MACHEATH: Gentlemen, adieu.

Scene 15

[Lucy, Macheath, Polly]

MACHEATH: My dear Lucy—my dear Polly—whatsoever hath passed between us is now at an end. If you are fond of marrying again, the best advice I can give you is to ship yourselves off for the West Indies, where you'll have a fair chance of getting a husband apiece; or by good luck, two or three, as you like best.

POLLY: How can I support this sight!

LUCY: There is nothing moves one so much as a great man in distress.

Air 68. All you that must take a leap, etc.

LUCY: *Would I might be hanged!*
POLLY: *And I would so too!*
LUCY: *To be hanged with you.*
POLLY: *My dear, with you.*
MACHEATH: *O leave me to thought! I fear! I doubt!*
    I tremble! I droop! See, my courage is out.   [*Turns up the empty bottle.*]

5. Broken out of.

POLLY: *No token of love?*

MACHEATH: *See, my courage is out.*   [*Turns up the empty pot.*]

LUCY: *No token of love?*

POLLY: *Adieu!*

LUCY: *Farewell!*

MACHEATH: *But hark! I hear the toll of the bell.*

CHORUS: *Tol de rol lol, etc.*

JAILER: Four women more, Captain, with a child a-piece! See, here they come.
[*Enter women and children.*]

MACHEATH: What—four wives more! This is too much. Here—tell the sheriff's officers I am ready.

[*Exit Macheath guarded.*]

Scene 16

[*To them, enter Player and Beggar*]

PLAYER: But, honest friend, I hope you don't intend that Macheath shall be really executed.

BEGGAR: Most certainly, Sir. To make the piece perfect, I was for doing strict poetical justice. Macheath is to be hanged; and for the other personages of the drama, the audience must have supposed they were all either hanged or transported.

PLAYER: Why then, friend, this is a downright deep tragedy. The catastrophe is manifestly wrong, for an opera must end happily.

BEGGAR: Your objection, Sir, is very just; and is easily removed. For you must allow, that in this kind of drama, 'tis no matter how absurdly things are brought about. So—you rabble there—run and cry a reprieve—let the prisoner be brought back to his wives in triumph.

PLAYER: All this we must do, to comply with the taste of the town.[6]

BEGGAR: Through the whole piece you may observe such a similitude of manners in high and low life, that it is difficult to determine whether (in the fashionable vices) the fine gentlemen imitate the gentlemen of the road, or the gentlemen of the road the fine gentlemen. Had the play remained, as I at first intended, it would have carried a most excellent moral. 'Twould have shown that the lower sort of people have their vices in a degree as well as the rich, and that they are punished for them.

Scene 17

[*To them, Macheath with rabble, etc.*]

MACHEATH: So, it seems, I am not left to my choice, but must have a wife at last. Look ye, my dears, we will have no controversy now. Let us give this day to mirth, and I am sure she who thinks herself my wife will testify her joy by a dance.

ALL: Come, a dance, a dance.

MACHEATH: Ladies, I hope you will give me leave to present a partner to each of you. And (if I may without offense) for this time, I take Polly for mine. [*To Polly.*] And for life, you slut, for we were really married. As for the rest—But at present keep your own secret.

6. The fashionable audience.

A Dance

Air 69. Lumps of pudding, etc.

Thus I stand like the Turk, with his doxies around;[7]
From all sides their glances his passion confound;
For black, brown, and fair, his inconstancy burns,
And the different beauties subdue him by turns:
Each calls forth her charms, to provoke his desires:
Though willing to all; with but one he retires.
But think of this maxim, and put off your sorrow,
The wretch of today, may be happy tomorrow.

CHORUS: *But think of this maxim, etc.*

FINIS.

1727   1728

❋ "THE BEGGAR'S OPERA" AND ITS TIME ❋

Influences and Impact

Attending performances of *The Beggar's Opera* in 1728, audiences encountered elements intensely familiar and newly mixed: old tunes supplied with new words; Newgate prison (notorious for its filth and depravity) reimagined as a site of revels, dancing, and amorous dalliance; and two famous criminals—Jonathan Wild and Jack Sheppard—reconceived as comic singers, fuddled tacticians, and intrafamilial contenders, indeed as those stock antagonists the huffy father and the sleek son-in-law.

The mix of elements proved potent long beyond the first production; the play was revived in London at least once a year for more than a century and a half. Gay's songs, scenes, and above all his central character Macheath became cultural icons, habitually referred and resorted to by many different admirers for many different purposes. The selections that follow trace some of the influences the *Opera* absorbed, and some of those it disseminated.

Thomas D'Urfey[1]
from *Wit and Mirth: or, Pills to Purge Melancholy*
WHY IS YOUR FAITHFUL SLAVE DISDAINED?[2]

Why is your faithful slave disdained?
By gentle arts my heart you gained!
    Oh, keep it by the same!
For ever shall my passion last,
5   If you will make me once possessed
    Of what I dare not name.

---

7. Like a Sultan in a harem.
1. In 1719, at the close of his checkered career as playwright, court poet, ballad-maker, and singer, Thomas D'Urfey (1653–1723) compiled his own edition of *Wit and Mirth*, a song anthology that had appeared, in various versions and with considerable success, over the preceding 20 years. D'Urfey's popular collection provided Gay

with his principal source for both the melodies and the lyric memories by which he proposed to beguile his audience. Many of Gay's new texts push playfully and pointedly against D'Urfey's originals, reversing genders and subverting sentiments.
2. Compare *The Beggar's Opera*, Air 4: "If love the virgin's heart invade" (page 2592).

Though charming are your wit and face,
'Tis not alone to hear and gaze
    That will suffice my flame;
10 Love's infancy on hopes may live,
But you to mine full grown must give
    Of what I dare not name.

When I behold your lips, your eyes,
Those snowy breasts that fall and rise,
15   Fanning my raging flame;
That shape so made to be embraced,
What would I give I might but taste
    Of what I dare not name!

In courts I never wish to rise,
20 Both wealth and honor I despise,
    And that vain breath called fame;
By love I hope no crowns to gain.
'Tis something more I would obtain:
    'Tis what I dare not name.

What Shall I Do to Show How Much I Love Her?[1]

What shall I do to show how much I love her?
    How many millions of sighs can suffice?
That which wins other hearts ne'er can move her,
    Those common methods of love she'll despise.
5 I will love more than man e'er loved before me,
    Gaze on her all the day, and melt all the night,
'Till for her own sake at last she'll implore me,
    To love her less to preserve our delight.

Since gods themselves could not ever[2] be loving,
10   Men must have breathing recruits[3] for new joys;
I wish my soul could be ever improving,
    Though eager love, more than sorrow, destroys.
In fair Aurelia's arms leave me expiring,
    To be embalmed with the sweets of her breath.
15 To the last moment I'll still be desiring;
    Never had hero so glorious a death.[4]

Would Ye Have a Young Virgin?[1]

Would ye have a young virgin of fifteen years?
You must tickle her fancy with *sweets* and *dears*,
Ever toying, and playing, and sweetly, sweetly,
Wittily, prettily, talk her down.
5 Chase her, and praise her, if fair or brown,
        Soothe her and smoothe her,
        And tease her, and please her,
And touch but her smicket[2], and all's your own.

1. Compare Air 6: "Virgins are like the fair flower in its luster" (page 2594).
2. Always.
3. I.e., pauses to catch their breath.

4. With the familiar pun on "death" as sexual fulfillment.
1. Compare Air 21: "If the heart of a man is depressed with cares" (page 2604).
2. Petticoat; undergarment.

Do ye fancy a widow well known in a man?[3]
10   With a front of assurance come boldly on.
Let her rest not an hour, but briskly, briskly,
Put her in mind how her time steals on.
Rattle and prattle although she frown,
Rouse her and touse her from morn to noon,
15   Show her some hour y'are able to grapple,
Then get but her writings[4] and all's your own.

Do ye fancy a punk[5] of a humor free,
That's kept by a fumbler of quality?[6]
You must rail at her keeper, and tell her, tell her
20   Pleasure's best charm is variety.
Swear her much fairer than all the town,
Try her, and ply her when Cully's[7] gone,
        Dog her, and jog[8] her,
        And meet her, and treat her,
25   And kiss with two guineas,[9] and all's your own.

LUMPS OF PUDDING[1]

When I was in the low country,[2]
When I was in the low country,
What slices of pudding[3] and pieces of bread
My mother gave me when I was in need.

5   My mother she killed a good fat hog,
She made such puddings would choke a dog;
And I shall ne'er forget till I dee[4]
What lumps of pudding my mother gave me.

She hung them up upon a pin,
10   The fat run out and the maggots crept in;
If you won't believe me you may go and see
What lumps of pudding my mother gave me.

And every day my mother would cry
Come stuff your belly, girl, until you die;
15   'Twould make you laugh if you were to see
What lumps of pudding my mother gave me.

I no sooner at night was got into bed,
But she all in kindness would come with speed;
She gave me such parcels I thought I should dee,
20   With eating of pudding my mother gave me.

---

3. I.e., experienced with men.
4. I.e., legal documents transferring her wealth.
5. Whore; prostitute.
6. I.e., an inept, wealthy (and probably older) lover.
7. I.e., her duped lover.
8. Push; pressure.
9. A guinea was a coin worth one shilling and one pound.

1. Compare Air 69: "Thus I stand like a Turk, with his doxies around" (page 2632).
2. A low-lying region, close to sea level.
3. The word referred to many different kinds of recipes, meat as well as dairy, savory as well as sweet.
4. Die.

At last I rambled abroad and then
I met in my frolic an honest man.
Quoth he, "My dear Phillis I'll give unto thee
Such pudding you never did see."

25   Said I, "Honest man, I thank thee most kind."
And as he told me indeed I did find;
He gave me a lump which did so agree,
One bit was worth all my mother gave me.

                                                          1719

Daniel Defoe[1]
from *The True and Genuine Account of the Life and Actions of the Late Jonathan Wild*[2]
[PREFACE]

The several absurd and ridiculous accounts which have been published, notwith-standing early and seasonable caution given, of the life and conduct of this famous, or if you please, infamous creature, JONATHAN WILD, make a short preface to this account absolutely necessary.

It is something strange, that a man's life should be made a kind of a romance[3] before his face, and while he was upon the spot to contradict it; or, that the world should be so fond of a formal chimney-corner tale,[4] that they had rather a story should be made merry than true. The author of this short but exact account of Mr. Wild assures the world, that the greatest part of all that has hitherto appeared of this kind has been evidently invented and framed out of the heads of the scribbling authors, merely to get a penny, without regard to truth of fact, or even to probability, or with-out making any conscience of their imposing on the credulous world.

Nay, so little ground has there been for them, that except there was such a man as JONATHAN WILD, that he was born at Wolverhampton, lived in the Old Bailey, was called a thief-catcher, and was hanged at Tyburn, there is not one story printed of him that can be called truth, or that is not mingled up with so much falsehood and fable as to smother and drown that little truth which is at the bot-tom of it.

The following tract does not indeed make a jest of his story as they do, or pre-sent his history, which indeed is a tragedy of itself, in a style of mockery and ridicule, but in a method agreeable to the fact. They that had rather have a false-hood to laugh at, than a true account of things to inform them, had best buy the fiction, and leave the history to those who know how to distinguish good from evil.

---

1. For Defoe, see pages 2366–86. This brief account of Wild's life appeared in June 1725, less than a month after his execution. The attribution to Defoe is plausible on grounds of style but unsupported by external evidence, and has been questioned.
2. Wild (c. 1682–1725) attained an unprecedented mix of celebrity and notoriety by organizing crime more effi-ciently, more ruthlessly, and more profitably than any predecessor in the London underworld. His tactics for reaping gain from both robbers and their victims supplied much of the basis for Peachum's operations in *The Beg-gar's Opera*. (In the wake of the play's success one news-paper reported, albeit unreliably, that Wild and Gay had once actually met, and that the thief-taker had instructed the playwright in "all the knavish offices and intrigues of the thieving trade.") In the selections here, Defoe assess-es Wild's impact, details his methods, and reports his exe-cution, attending all the while to the new workings of publicity, the play of popular genres (romance, history, tragedy) around the core of facts.
3. "A tale of wild adventures in war and love" (Johnson's *Dictionary*).
4. The kind of story told at hearthside: joke, fairy tale, folktale, etc.

[TACTICS]

* * * [Wild's] method was this: When a purchase was made,[1] Jonathan inquired first where it was gotten, what house had been robbed, or who had lost the goods; and having learnt that, his next business was to have the goods deposited in proper places, always avoiding the receiving them himself, or bringing himself into any jeopardy as to the law. Then he found out proper instruments to employ to go to the persons who had been robbed, and tell them that if they could describe what they had lost, they believed they could help them to them again; for that[2] there was a parcel of stolen goods stopped by an honest broker, to whom they were offered to be sold, and if their goods were among them they might have them again for a small matter of expense.

The people who had been robbed, it may be supposed, were always willing enough to hear of their goods again, and very thankful to the discoverer, and so readily gave an account of the things they had lost, with such proper descriptions of them as were needful. The next day they should be told there was such or such part of their goods stopped among other goods, which it was supposed were stolen from other people, and so upon assurance given on both sides to make no inquiry into the particular circumstances of stopping the goods, and a consideration to the person who went between, for helping the loser to his goods again, the things were restored, and the person received abundance of thanks and acknowledgments for their honesty and kindness. And this part always fell to Jonathan, or his mistress Milliner,[3] or perhaps both, who always pretended they got nothing for their pains but the satisfaction of having helped the people to recover their own again, which was taken by a company of rogues; professing their sorrow that they had not had the good luck at the same time to detect the rogues that took them, and bring them to the punishment they deserved.

On the other hand, they acted as safe a part with the thief also; for, rating and reproving the rogue for his villainy, they would pretend to bring them to an honest restoring the goods again, taking a reasonable consideration for their honesty, and so bring them to lodge them in such a place as should be directed. And sometimes, as I have been told, he has officiously caused the thief or thieves to be taken with the goods upon them, when he has not been able to bring them to comply, and so has made himself both thief and chapman,[4] as the proverb says; getting a reward for the discovery, and bringing the poor wretch to the gallows too, and this only because he could not make his market of him to his mind.[5] * * *

It must be confessed, Jonathan Wild played a sure game in all this; and therefore it is not to be wondered at that he went on for so many years without any disaster. Nay, he acquired a strange and, indeed, unusual reputation, for a mighty honest man; till his success hardened him to put on a face of public service in it, and for that purpose to profess an open and bare correspondence among the gang of thieves. By which his house became an office of intelligence for inquiries of that kind, as if all stolen goods had been deposited with him, in order to be restored. But even this good character of his, as it did not last long, so neither did it come all at once; and some tell us (how true it is, I will not affirm) that he was obliged to give up every now and then one or two of his clients to the gallows, to support his rising reputation. In which cases, he never failed to proclaim his own credit in bringing offenders to justice, and in delivering his country from

---

1. Robbery was committed.
2. Because.
3. Mary Milliner, a brothel-keeper, was Wild's lover and

accomplice.
4. Purchaser.
5. I.e., draw a satisfactory profit from his thievery.

such dangerous people. Some have gone so far as to tell us the very particulars which recommended any of the gangs to him for a sacrifice, and to divide them into classes: For example, (1) such as having committed the secret of a fact[6] to him yet would not submit their purchase to his disposal. Or (2), would not accept reasonable terms of composition for restoring the goods: Or (3), used any threatening speeches against their comrades. These he would immediately cause to be apprehended, he knowing both their haunts, and where the goods were deposited; and in such cases, none so vigilant in the discovery, or so eager in apprehending the thief. And, generally speaking, he had his ways and means to bring in others of the gang to come in and confess, that they might impeach the person so intended to be given up to justice. * * *

[EXECUTION][1]

We come now to his behavior after this condemnation, and at the place of execution; at which last place he indeed scarce said a word to God or man, being either dozed with the liquid laudanum[2] which he had taken, or demented and confused by the horror of what was before him, and the reflection of what was within him. Nor even before he took the dose of laudanum was he in any suitable manner sensible of his condition, or concerned about it; very little sign appeared of his having the least hope concerning his future state. But as he lived hardened, he seemed to die stupid. He declined coming to the chapel, either to the sermon or prayers, pleading his lameness by the gout, but chiefly the crowds and disorders of the people discomposing or disordering him. In the condemned hold, or place where malefactors are kept after their sentence, they had prayers as usual; and he seemed to join with them in a kind of form, but little or nothing of the penitence of a criminal, in view of death, appeared upon him. His principal inquiries seemed to be about what kind of state was to be expected after death, and how the invisible world was to be described; but nothing of the most certain judgment which is there to be expected, righteous and terrible, according to the deeds done in the body, or of a savior to whom to have recourse, as the slayer in the old law had to the city of refuge, to save him from the avenger of blood. As his time shortened he seemed more and more confused, and then began to entertain discourses of the lawfulness of dismissing ourselves out of the present misery after the example of the ancient Romans,[3] which, as he said, was then esteemed as an act of bravery and gallantry, and recorded to their honor.

This kind of discourse was indeed sufficient to have caused the keepers to have had an eye to him, so as to prevent any violence he might offer to himself, and they did watch him as narrowly as they could. However, he so far deceived them, as that the day before his execution he found means to have a small bottle with the liquid laudanum conveyed to him unseen, of which he took so large a quantity, that it was soon perceived by the change it made upon him, for he was so drowsy that he could not hold up his head, or keep open his eyes, at the time of reading the prayers. Upon this two of his fellow prisoners endeavored to rouse him (not suspecting that he had taken enough to hurt him), and taking him by the hands, they persuaded him to stand up, and walk a little about the room, which he could not do without help because of

---

6. Crime; robbery.
1. In 1725, Wild's long series of successes came to an end, when he was forced to stand trial under a new law (nicknamed the "Jonathan Wild Act") that made it a capital crime to accept money for the recovery of stolen proper-

ty. Former associates, disenchanted by his treacheries, testified against him.
2. A solution containing opium.
3. I.e., of committing suicide, a practice regarded in Rome as an honorable response to failure or disgrace.

his gout.[4] This walking, though it did a little waken him, had several other operations at the same time. For first it changed his countenance, turning it to be exceeding pale, then it put him into a violent sweat, which made them apprehend he would faint, upon which they offered to give him something to keep up his spirits, but he refused it, telling them he was very sick; soon after which he vomited very violently, and this in all probability prolonged his life for the execution, for by their stirring him, and making him vomit, he brought up the greatest part of the laudanum which he had taken, before it had been long enough in his stomach to mix with the animal spirits or blood, which if it had done but one hour more, he would certainly have taken his last sleep in the prison. But nature, having thus discharged itself of the load, he revived again, and though still dozed and insensible of what he said or did, yet he was able to walk about, speak, and act sufficiently for the part that remained to him, namely, for the last scene of his life at the gallows.

Accordingly, on Monday the 24th of May, he was conveyed in a cart to Tyburn, and though it was apparent he was still under the operation of the laudanum, and that which was left in his stomach had so far seized upon his spirits as to make him almost stupid, yet it began to go off, and nature getting the mastery of it, he began to be more sensible of what he was going about; but the scene was then short, and he had little to do but to stand up in the cart, and, the needful apparatus being made, be turned off with the rest, which was done about 3 o'clock in the afternoon. The rudeness of the mob to him, both at his first going into the cart, and all the way from thence to the place of execution, is not to be expressed, and shows how notorious his life had been, and what impression his known villainies had made on the minds of the people. For, contrary to the general behavior of the street in such cases, instead of compassionate expressions, and a general cast of pity, which ordinarily sits on the countenances of the people, when they see the miserable objects of justice go to their execution; here was nothing to be heard but cursings and execrations. Abhorring the crimes and the very name of the man, throwing stones and dirt at him all the way, and even at the place of execution; the other malefactors being all ready to be turned off, but the hangman giving him leave to take his own time, and he continuing setting down in the cart, the mob impatient, and fearing a reprieve, though they had no occasion for it, called furiously upon the hangman to dispatch him, and at last threatened to tear him to pieces, if he did not tie him up immediately.

In short there was a kind of an universal rage against him, which nothing but his death could satisfy, or put an end to, and if a reprieve had come, it would have, 'twas thought, been difficult for the officers to have brought him back again without his receiving some mischief, if not his death's wound, from the rabble. So detestable had he made himself by his notorious crimes, and to such a height were his wicked practices come.

Thus ended the tragedy, and thus was a life of horrid and inimitable wickedness finished at the gallows, the very same place where, according to some, above 120 miserable creatures had been hanged whose blood in great measure may be said to lie at his door, either in their being first brought into the thieving trade, or led on in it by his encouragement and assistance; and many of them at last betrayed and brought to justice by his means, upon which worst sort of murder he valued himself, and would have had it passed for merit, even with the government itself.

1725

---

4. A disease, common at the time, entailing painful inflammation of the joints in hands and feet.

Henry Fielding [1]
from *The Life of Mr. Jonathan Wild the Great*
["An Adventure Where Wild, in the Division of the Booty,
Exhibits an Astonishing Instance of Greatness"]

Mr. Wild and Mr. Bagshot[2] went together to the tavern, where Mr. Bagshot (generously, as he thought) offered to share the booty, and, having divided the money into two unequal heaps, and added a golden snuff-box[3] to the lesser heap, he desired Mr. Wild to take his choice.

Mr. Wild immediately conveyed the larger share of the ready into his pocket, according to an excellent maxim of his: "First secure what share you can before you wrangle for the rest"; and then, turning to his companion, he asked him with a stern countenance whether he intended to keep all that sum to himself? Mr. Bagshot answered, with some surprise, that he thought Mr. Wild had no reason to complain; for it was surely fair, at least on his part, to content himself with an equal share of the booty, who had taken the whole. "I grant you took it," replied Wild; "but, pray, who proposed or counseled the taking it? Can you say that you have done more than executed my scheme? and might not I, if I had pleased, have employed another, since you well know there was not a gentleman in the room but would have taken the money if he had known how, conveniently and safely, to do it?" "That is very true," returned Bagshot, "but did not I execute the scheme, did not I run the whole risk? Should not I have suffered the whole punishment if I had been taken, and is not the laborer worthy of his hire?"[4] "Doubtless," says Jonathan, "he is so, and your hire I shall not refuse you, which is all that the laborer is entitled to or ever enjoys. I remember when I was at school to have heard some verses which for the excellence of their doctrine made an impression on me, purporting that the birds of the air and the beasts of the field work not for themselves.[5] It is true, the farmer allows fodder to his oxen and pasture to his sheep; but it is for his own service, not theirs. In the same manner the ploughman, the shepherd, the weaver, the builder, and the soldier work not for themselves but others; they are contented with a poor pittance (the laborer's hire), and permit us, the GREAT, to enjoy the fruits of their labors. Aristotle, as my master told us, hath plainly proved, in the first book of his politics, that the low, mean, useful part of mankind are born slaves to the wills of their superiors, and are indeed as much their property as the cattle.[6] It is well said of us, the higher order of mortals, that we are born only to devour the fruits of the earth; and it may be as well said of the lower class, that they are born only to produce them for us. Is not the battle gained by the sweat and danger of the common soldier? Are not the honor and

---

1. Over the course of a short life, Henry Fielding (1707–1754) sustained several brilliant careers, as playwright, journalist, polemicist, novelist, lawyer, magistrate. *Jonathan Wild* combines components of many of them. By the time it appeared, in 1743, Walpole had been stripped of power for one year and Wild had been dead for almost twenty. But Fielding, like Gay and others before him, pointedly conflates the politician and the criminal. The epithet "the great man," which Fielding applies to Wild on nearly every page, had in real life adhered to Walpole throughout his tenure as prime minister. By such echoes and displacements, Fielding anatomizes with sometimes heavy irony the ways in which a powerfully seductive leader can persuade his followers to collude in their own exploitation.
2. Fielding borrowed the name of Wild's accomplice from Gay's *Opera:* Peachum, combing his catalogue of criminals eligible for the gallows, mentions one "Robin

Bagshot, alias Gorgon, alias Bluff Bob, alias Carbuncle, alias Bob Booty" (1.3). All those aliases riff wittily on the reputation and nicknames of Robert Walpole—though in Fielding's anecdote it is Wild, and not Bagshot, who will expound Walpole's methods. At this juncture in the story, Bagshot, acting on Wild's instructions, has just robbed a rich gambler at gunpoint.
3. Snuff was powdered tobacco, enjoyed as a stimulant and sneeze-inducer; the pocket-cases in which it was carried were often ornate and expensive.
4. I.e., his wages (Bagshot echoes Luke 10.7).
5. Wild, trumping one scriptural quotation with another, here echoes Matthew 6.26.
6. "For that [person who] can foresee by the exercise of mind is by nature intended to be lord and master, and that which can with its body give effect to such foresight is a subject, and by nature a slave; hence master and slave have the same interest" (Aristotle, *Politics* 1.2).

fruits of the victory the general's who laid the scheme? Is not the house built by the labor of the carpenter and the bricklayer? Is it not built for the profit of the architect and for the use of the inhabitant, who could not easily have placed one brick upon another? Is not the cloth or the silk wrought into its form and variegated with all the beauty of colors by those who are forced to content themselves with the coarsest and vilest part of their work, while the profit and enjoyment of their labors fall to the share of others? Cast your eye abroad, and see who is it lives in the most magnificent buildings, feasts his palate with the most luxurious dainties, his eyes with the most beautiful sculptures and delicate paintings, and clothes himself in the finest and richest apparel; and tell me if all these do not fall to his lot who had not any the least share in producing all these conveniences, nor the least ability so to do? Why then should the state of a prig[7] differ from all others? Or why should you, who are the laborer only, the executor of my scheme, expect a share in the profit? Be advised, therefore; deliver the whole booty to me, and trust to my bounty for your reward." Mr Bagshot was some time silent, and looked like a man thunderstruck, but at last, recovering himself from his surprise, he thus began: "If you think, Mr. Wild, by the force of your arguments, to get the money out of my pocket, you are greatly mistaken. What is all this stuff to me? D—n me, I am a man of honor, and, though I can't talk as well as you, by G— you shall not make a fool of me; and if you take me for one, I must tell you, you are a rascal." At which words he laid his hand to his pistol. Wild, perceiving the little success the great strength of his arguments had met with, and the hasty temper of his friend, gave over his design for the present, and told Bagshot he was only in jest. But this coolness with which he treated the other's flame had rather the effect of oil than of water. Bagshot replied in a rage: "D—n me, I don't like such jests; I see you are a pitiful rascal and a scoundrel." Wild, with a philosophy worthy of great admiration, returned: "As for your abuse, I have no regard to it; but, to convince you I am not afraid of you, let us lay the whole booty on the table, and let the conqueror take it all." And having so said, he drew out his shining hanger,[8] whose glittering so dazzled the eyes of Bagshot, that, in a tone entirely altered, he said: "No! he was contented with what he had already; that it was mighty ridiculous in them to quarrel among themselves; that they had common enemies enough abroad, against whom they should unite their common force; that if he had mistaken Wild he was sorry for it; and that as for a jest, he could take a jest as well as another." Wild, who had a wonderful knack of discovering and applying the passions of men, beginning now to have a little insight into his friend, and to conceive what arguments would make the quickest impression on him, cried out in a loud voice: "That he had bullied him into drawing his hanger, and, since it was out, he would not put it up without satisfaction." "What satisfaction would you have?" answered the other. "Your money or your blood," said Wild. "Why, look ye, Mr. Wild," said Bagshot, "if you want to borrow a little of my part, since I know you to be a man of honor, I don't care if I lend you; for, though I am not afraid of any man living, yet rather than break with a friend, and as it may be necessary for your occasions—" Wild, who often declared that he looked upon borrowing to be as good a way of taking as any, and, as he called it, the genteelest kind of sneaking-budge,[9] putting up his hanger, and shaking his friend by the hand, told him he had hit the nail on the head; it was really his present necessity only that prevailed with him against his will, for that his honor was concerned to pay a considerable sum the next morning. Upon which, contenting himself with one half of Bagshot's share, so that he had three parts in four of the whole, he took leave of his companion and retired to rest.

7. Thief.
8. A short sword.

9. Robbing-scheme; scam.

["THE MASTER OF THE SHOW"]

* * * The stage of the world differs from that in Drury Lane[1] principally in this—that whereas, on the latter, the hero or chief figure is almost continually before your eyes, while the under-actors are not seen above once in an evening; now, on the former, the hero or great man is always behind the curtain, and seldom or never appears or doth anything in his own person. He doth indeed, in this GRAND DRAMA, rather perform the part of the prompter, and doth instruct the well-drest figures, who are strutting in public on the stage, what to say and do. To say the truth, a puppet-show will illustrate our meaning better, where it is the master of the show (the great man) who dances and moves everything, whether it be the King of Muscovy[2] or whatever other potentate *alias* puppet which we behold on the stage; but he himself keeps wisely out of sight: for, should he once appear, the whole motion would be at an end. Not that any one is ignorant of his being there, or supposes that the puppets are not mere sticks of wood, and he himself the sole mover; but as this (though every one knows it) doth not appear visibly, i.e., to their eyes, no one is ashamed of consenting to be imposed upon; of helping on the drama, by calling the several sticks or puppets by the names which the master hath allotted to them, and by assigning to each the character which the great man is pleased they shall move in, or rather in which he himself is pleased to move them.

It would be to suppose thee, gentle reader, one of very little knowledge in this world, to imagine thou hast never seen some of these puppet-shows which are so frequently acted on the great stage; but though thou shouldst have resided all thy days in those remote parts of this island which great men seldom visit, yet, if thou hast any penetration, thou must have had some occasions to admire both the solemnity of countenance in the actor and the gravity in the spectator, while some of those farces are carried on which are acted almost daily in every village in the kingdom. He must have a very despicable opinion of mankind indeed who can conceive them to be imposed on as often as they appear to be so. The truth is, they are in the same situation with the readers of romances;[3] who, though they know the whole to be one entire fiction, nevertheless agree to be deceived; and, as these find amusement, so do the others find ease and convenience in this concurrence. * * *

1743

from *A Narrative of All the Robberies, Escapes, &c. of John Sheppard*[1]
[ON THIEF-CATCHING]

I have often lamented the scandalous practice of thief-catching, as it is called, and the public manner of offering rewards for stolen goods, in defiance of two several acts of parliament—the thief-catchers living sumptuously, and keeping public offices of intelligence. These who forfeit their lives every day they breathe,[2] and deserve the

1. Drury Lane was the site and name of one of the two foremost playhouses in London; several of Fielding's own comedies had been produced there.
2. A powerful principality in Russia (Moscow was its capital).
3. The term was applied loosely and variously to novels and other, more fantastical prose fictions.
1. John Sheppard (1702–1724), widely and familiarly known as Jack, was an accomplished thief, a promiscuous seducer, the greatest escape artist of his time, and the chief inspiration behind Gay's Macheath. Jonathan Wild, goaded by Sheppard's audacity, celebrity, and independence, tried time and again to have him caught and

hung, but Sheppard repeatedly broke out of the most elaborate confinements the Newgate specialists could devise for him. During his last imprisonment, his jailers charged sightseers special admission for the privilege of simply looking at the doomed but dapper convict. By this time, Sheppard's popularity was sufficient to turn the tables: the public, favoring him, began to revile his nemesis Wild. The present *Narrative*, purportedly an autobiography, went on sale the day after Sheppard's execution. It was for a long time attributed to Defoe, but is probably the work of some less eminent ghostwriter.
2. I.e., they commit crimes deserving such forfeiture.

gallows as richly as any of the thieves, send us as their representatives to Tyburn,[3] once a month. Thus they hang by proxy, while we do it fairly in person.

I never corresponded with any of them. I was indeed twice at a thief-catcher's *levée*,[4] and must confess the man treated me civilly. He complimented me on my successes, said he heard that I had both an hand and head admirably well turned to *business*, and that I and my friends *should be always welcome to him*. But caring not for his acquaintance, I never troubled him, nor had we any dealings together.

[THE GREAT ESCAPE]

As my last escape from Newgate out of the strong room called the Castle[1] has made a greater noise in the world than any other action of my life, I shall relate every minute circumstance thereof as far as I am able to remember, intending thereby to satisfy the curious and do justice to the innocent. * * *

* * * As near as can be remembered, just before three in the afternoon I went to work, taking off first my handcuffs;[2] next with main strength I twisted a small iron link of the chain between my legs asunder, and the broken pieces proved extreme useful to me in my design. The fett-locks[3] I drew up to the calves of my legs, taking off before that my stockings, and with my garters made them firm to my body, to prevent their shackling.[4] I then proceeded to make a hole in the chimney of the Castle about three foot wide, and six foot high from the floor, and with the help of the broken links aforesaid wrenched an iron bar out of the chimney, of about two feet and a half in length, and an inch square: a most notable implement. I immediately entered the Red Room directly over the Castle, where some of the Preston rebels[5] had been kept a long time agone. And, as the keepers say, the door had not been unlocked for seven years; but I intended not to be seven years in opening it, though they had. I went to work upon the nut of the lock, and with little difficulty got it off, and made the door fly before me. In this room I found a large nail, which proved of great use in my farther progress. The door of the entry between the Red Room and the Chapel proved an hard task, it being a laborious piece of work; for here I was forced to break away the wall, and dislodge the bolt which was fastened on the other side. This occasioned much noise, and I was very fearful of being heard by the Master-side debtors.[6] Being got to the Chapel, I climbed over the iron spikes, and with ease broke one of them off for my further purposes, and opened the door on the inside. The door going out of the Chapel to the leads,[7] I stripped the nut from off the lock, as I had done before from that of the Red Room, and then got into the entry between the Chapel and the leads; and came to another strong door, which being fastened by a very strong lock, there I had like to have stopped, and it being full dark, my spirits began to fail me, as greatly doubting of succeeding. But cheering up, I wrought on with great diligence, and in less than half an hour, with the main help of the nail from the Red Room, and the spike from the Chapel, wrenched the box off, and so made the door my humble servant.

1724

---

3. The site of public executions, which were regarded also as edifying public entertainments. A crowd of about 200,000 saw Sheppard die there.
4. A social gathering, customarily held before noon; "the concourse of those who crowd round a man of power in a morning" (Johnson's *Dictionary*).
1. The prison's most formidable cell, where Sheppard was secured "with my legs chained together, loaded with heavy irons, and stapled down to the floor."
2. Sheppard has earlier discovered that he can remove these with his teeth.

3. The shackles around his feet.
4. I.e., to prevent their falling back down to his feet and encumbering him.
5. Prisoners taken during the failed Jacobite uprising at Preston, November 1715.
6. I.e., convicts (mostly debtors) confined in Newgate's Master's Ward, where the wealthiest prisoners could purchase the most comfortable accommodations.
7. I.e., the prison roof, made of lead tiles, across which Sheppard will eventually make his escape from Newgate to the rooftop of a neighboring house.

John Thurmond

from *Harlequin Sheppard*[1]

[SHEPPARD RECAPTURED][2]

The scene changes to Clare Market,[3] and discovers[4] a butcher's shop. SHEPPARD comes in very merry, and goes to purchase some of the meat. While he is employed with the butcher, an alehouse boy[5] comes in, with pots over his shoulder and, discovering SHEPPARD, retires. SHEPPARD and the butcher go off together.

The scene changes to a room in an alehouse. FRISKY MOLL[6] enters, and seems to be pleased,[7] as having heard of SHEPPARD's escape. SHEPPARD comes in, and discovering himself to her, she's mightily rejoiced. They drink together, and after some time dance. While they are in high mirth, the alehouse boy appears with the constable and others, and seize SHEPPARD. FRISKY MOLL makes resistance, but they carry him off. And the entertainment concludes with

A CANTING SONG[8]

Sung by FRISKY MOLL

From prigs that snaffle the prancers strong[9]
   To you of the Peter lay,[1]
I pray now listen a while to my song,
   How my boman he hicked away.[2]

5   He broke through all rubs in the whitt,[3]
   And chived his darbies in twain;[4]
But filing of a rumbo ken,[5]
   My boman is snabbled again.[6]

I, Frisky Moll, with my rum coll,[7]
10   Would grub in a bowzing ken;[8]
But ere for the scran he had tipped the cole,[9]
   The harman,[1] he came in.

---

1. The word "harlequin" in a play's title promised a pantomime, a short show with music and songs but no dialogue, presented at the playhouses as part of an evening's entertainment. *Harlequin Sheppard*, purporting to display Sheppard's celebrated escape and ultimate capture, was performed at the Theater Royal in Drury Lane 12 days after his execution. Since it was booed off the stage on its first night (28 November 1724), the audience may not have witnessed its final scene, reprinted here.
2. After his famous escape from the Castle on 15 October 1724, Sheppard remained free for two weeks; on 31 October he was recognized and arrested in Drury Lane, not far from the playhouse where *Harlequin Sheppard* appeared a month later.
3. A market specializing in butchers' shops; Sheppard's mother and several of his mistress/accomplices lived nearby.
4. Reveals.
5. I.e., tavern-servant.
6. A woman named "Moll Frisky" figures in several accounts of Sheppard's last days. Notorious as a ladies' man, Sheppard had earlier been betrayed back into custody by a longtime lover called Edgworth Bess.
7. The word "seems" does not imply falsity or connivance on Moll's part; it is instead a conventional pantomime stage direction, instructing the actor to display the specified emotion.
8. Cant is jargon, here the specialized slang of London's underworld. For more than a century, writers of criminal literature had managed to please an enormous readership by deploying and explaining this "secret" language. In its original edition, *Harlequin Sheppard* included footnotes for all the cant terms in this song; those glosses appear in quotation marks in the notes that follow here.
9. "Gentlemen of the pad"; i.e., horse-stealers. Prigs: thieves; snaffle: bridle; prancers: horses; pad: path, road.
1. "Those that break shop-glasses [i.e., windows], or cut portmanteaus [i.e., large, well-packed pieces of luggage] behind coaches." Lay: trick, scam.
2. "Her rogue had got away."
3. Rubs: obstacles; whitt: "Newgate, or any other prison."
4. "Sawed his chains in two."
5. "Robbing a pawnbroker's shop." Sheppard had in fact committed such a crime shortly after his great escape.
6. "Taken again."
7. "Clever thief."
8. "Would eat in an alehouse."
9. "Before the reckoning [i.e., tavern bill] was paid"; cole: cash.
1. "Constable."

A famble, a tattle, and two pops,[2]
    Had my boman when he was ta'en;
15   But had he not bowzed in the diddle-shops,[3]
    He'd still been in Drury Lane.

1724

Charlotte Charke[1]

from *A Narrative of the Life of Mrs. Charlotte Charke*

[A MACHEATH "PERFORMED IN CHARACTER"]

We waited in court, expecting every moment to be called upon, and dismissed with a slight reprimand. But alas! 'twas not so easy as we thought, for we were beckoned to the other end of the court, and told, that the keeper of the prison insisted on our going to jail, only for a show, and to say we had been under lock and key. An honor, I confess, I was not in the least ambitious of; and for the show, I thought 'twould never be over, for it lasted from nine in the morning 'til the same hour of the next; and had it not been for the generous and friendly assistance of the before-mentioned gentleman,[2] I believe would have held out 'til *Doomsday* with me, for another day must have absolutely put an end to my life. * * *

The evening wore apace, and the clock struck eight, the dreadful signal for the gates to be locked up for the night.

I offered half a guinea apiece for beds,[3] but was denied them; and, if I had not fortunately been acquainted with the turnkey, who was a very good-natured fellow, we must have been turned into a place to lie upon the bare ground, and have mixed among the felons, whose chains were rattling all night long, and made the most hideous noise I ever heard, there being upwards of two hundred men and boys under the different sentences of death and transportation.

Their rags and misery gave me so shocking an idea, I begged the man, in pity, to hang us all three, rather than put us among such a dreadful crew. The very stench of them would have been a sufficient remedy against any future ills that could have happened to me; but those dreadful apprehensions were soon ended, by the young fellow who was our warder for the night, making interest with a couple of shoemakers, who were imprisoned in the women's condemned-hole; which, till they came, had not been occupied for a considerable time.

These two persons were confined, one for debt, the other for having left his family, with a design to impose his wife and children on the parish.[4]

Extremely glad were we to be admitted into the dismal cell; which, though the walls and flooring were formed of flint, at that time I was proud of entering, as the men were neat, and their bed (which my companions only took part of) entirely clean.

---

2. "A ring, a watch, and a pair of pistols."
3. "Gevena-shops," i.e., gin-shops, taverns.
1. Charlotte Charke (1713–1760) was a strolling player, an actor who spent much of her life traveling and performing with makeshift companies in English provincial towns. Her distinction derived in part from her lineage (her father was Colley Cibber, one of the central figures in the London theater early in the eighteenth century); in part from her gift for cross-dressing, for assuming masculine roles and costume both onstage and off (she "passed" as a man for long periods of her life); but most of all from her autobiography, in which she proclaims her

aspirations, disappointments, and eccentricities with hypnotic fervor. In the excerpt here, she tells of being arrested and briefly confined in a local jail, along with a few of her fellow actors, on false charges whose chief purpose was to force the players to buy back their freedom by paying off the authorities.
2. A benefactor who later came to the players' rescue.
3. In prisons at this period, even the most basic comforts were obtainable only by bribery; compare Lockit's enthusiasm for "garnish" (payment; *Beggar's Opera* 2.7).
4. The parish, or local governing body, was obliged to support all legal residents who were thus abandoned.

The two gentlemen of the craft had, the day we were brought in, furnished themselves with each a skin, for under-leathers; which, being hollow, one within the other, I chose for my dormitory,[5] and having a pair of boots on and a great coat, rolled into my leathern couch, secure from every evil that might occur from such a place, except a cold, which I got, occasioned by the dampness of my bedchamber.

As we were not there for any crime, *but that committed by those who informed against us*, I had the good fortune to prevail on my friend the turnkey to permit me to send for candles and some good liquor, to reward our kind hosts, and preserve us from the dreadful apprehensions of getting each an ague[6] in our petrified apartment.

I continued, for the most part of the night, very low spirited and in very ill humor, 'til I was roused by the drollery of one Mr. Maxfield, my fellow-sufferer, a good-natured man, and of an odd turn of humor; who would not let me indulge my melancholy, which he saw had strongly possessed me, and insisted, as he had often seen me exhibit Captain Macheath in a sham-prison, I should, as I was then actually in the condemned-hold, sing all the bead-roll of songs in the last act,[7] that he might have the pleasure of saying, I had once performed IN CHARACTER.

1755

James Boswell
from *London Journal*[1]
[ENTRIES ON MACHEATH]

TUESDAY 3 MAY 1763.[2] * * * I thought I should see prisoners of one kind or other, so went to Newgate. I stepped into a sort of court before the cells. They are surely most dismal places. There are three rows of 'em, four in a row, all above each other. They have double iron windows, and within these, strong iron rails; and in these dark mansions are the unhappy criminals confined. I did not go in, but stood in the court, where were a number of strange blackguard beings with sad countenances, most of them being friends and acquaintances of those under sentence of death. Mr. Rice the broker was confined in another part of the house. In the cells were Paul Lewis for robbery and Hannah Diego for theft. I saw them pass by to chapel. The woman was a big unconcerned being. Paul, who had been in the sea-service and was called Captain, was a genteel, spirited young fellow. He was just a Macheath. He was dressed in a white coat and blue silk vest and silver, with his hair neatly queued[3] and a silver-laced hat, smartly cocked. An acquaintance asked him how he was. He said, "Very well"; quite resigned. Poor fellow! I really took a great concern for him, and wished to relieve him. He walked firmly and with a good air, with his chains rattling upon him, to the chapel.[4] * * *

THURSDAY 19 MAY 1763. * * * I then sallied forth to the Piazzas in rich flow of animal spirits and burning with fierce desire. I met two very pretty little girls who asked me to take them with me. "My dear girls," said I, "I am a poor fellow. I can give you no money. But if you choose to have a glass of wine and my company and let us be gay and obliging to each other without money, I am your man." They agreed with great good humor. So back to the Shakespeare[5] I went. "Waiter," said I, "I have got

5. Bed; sleeping-place.
6. A cold.
7. I.e., the medley of tunes Macheath sings "in a melancholy posture" as he contemplates his imminent execution (*Beggar's Opera* 3.13, page 2629).
1. For James Boswell, see pages 2826–27. As a young man, Boswell played Macheath in an amateur household production of *The Beggar's Opera*. As the following excerpts from his journals suggest, he remained preoccu-

pied with the character and the play throughout his life.
2. At this point, Boswell is 22 years old, living in London at a deliberate distance from his family in Scotland, trying to choose a career and a destiny, and sightseeing and journal-writing all the while.
3. I.e., arranged in a braided ponytail.
4. Like Macheath and other Newgate convicts in *The Beggar's Opera* (3.12–15).

here a couple of human beings; I don't know how they'll do." "I'll look, your Honor," cried he, and with inimitable effrontery stared them in the face and then cried, "They'll do very well." "What," said I, "are they good fellow-creatures? Bring them up, then." We were shown into a good room and had a bottle of sherry before us in a minute. I surveyed my seraglio[6] and found them both good subjects for amorous play. I toyed with them and drank about and sung *Youth's the Season*[7] and thought myself Captain Macheath; and then I solaced my existence with them, one after the other, according to their seniority. I was quite *raised*, as the phrase is: thought I was in a London tavern, the Shakespeare's Head, enjoying high debauchery after my sober winter. I parted with my ladies politely and came home in a glow of spirits.

WEDNESDAY 15 FEBRUARY 1775.[8] * * * Drank tea first at home, then at Captain Schaw's; went with him and Mrs. Schaw to *The Beggar's Opera*, performed by desire of several ladies of quality. There was an elegant audience. Digges[9] looked and sung as well as ever. I was quite in London.[1] A girl from Ireland who played Polly, by the name of Mistress Ramsay, pleased me very well. Only her notes were sometimes not sweet enough, but like the cry of a peacock. I sat between Lady Betty Cochrane and Mrs. Schaw in one of the rows of the pit taken by Lady Dundonald. I was cheerful and happy, having no pretensions, being very well established as an agreeable companion, and being a married man. Life is like a road, the first part of which is a hill. A man must for a while be constantly pulling that he may get forward, and not run back. When he has got beyond the steep, and on smooth ground—that is, when his character is fixed—he goes on smoothly upon level ground. I could not help indulging Asiatic ideas as I viewed such a number of pretty women some of them young gay creatures with their hair dressed with flowers.[2] But thoughts of mortality and change came upon me, and then I was glad to feel indifference.

END OF "THE BEGGAR'S OPERA," INFLUENCES AND IMPACT

William Hogarth
1697–1764

"I had naturally a good eye," William Hogarth remembered near his life's end. "Shows of all sorts gave me uncommon pleasure when an infant." The "shows" (spectacles) that filled his eye in the turbulent London neighborhood of Smithfield where he grew up suffused his art for life: the antics of actors and the raucousness of audiences at Bartholomew Fair; the chicanery

5. I.e., the Shakespeare's Head tavern in Covent Garden, an area teeming with brothels and gambling houses.
6. Harem. Compare Macheath's final song: "Thus I stand like the Turk, with his doxies around" (3.17).
7. The song accompanies Macheath's dance among his "free-hearted ladies" (2.4).
8. Boswell is now married with two daughters, living in Edinburgh and working as a lawyer.
9. West Digges, eminent Edinburgh actor, whose performances as Macheath had entranced Boswell since boyhood.

1. I.e., transported in mind and memory by several means: by the setting of the *Opera*; by the echoes of London theatrical life; by the recollection of his former Macheath-like "high debauchery" in the city, and of his youthful idolatry of Digges.
2. Perhaps an echo of Macheath's amorous line "But here ev'ry flower is united" (1.13). The song mingles memories of promiscuity with pledges of fidelity; the line reappears throughout Boswell's journals. By "Asiatic ideas," Boswell means both Old Testament polygamy and fantasies of the harem.

and pathos of prostitutes and thieves; the casual injustice of constables and magistrates. Above all, he watched his father fail. Richard Hogarth, a classical scholar, spent four years as a prisoner for debt, when his coffeehouse (catering to learned men and specializing in Latin conversation) failed to cover its own expenses. The debtor's family was effectually imprisoned too, and Hogarth, in his early teens during the ordeal, never forgot. "The emphasis throughout his work" (notes his biographer Ronald Paulson) "is on prisons, real and metaphorical. Even when he is not dealing with people who are in a prison . . . he portrays rooms that are more like prison cells than boudoirs or parlors."

At age seventeen, Hogarth was apprenticed to a silver engraver, ornamenting platters, rings, tableware, and the like. Finding the work dull, he switched to copper engraving, the technique by which book illustrators and printmakers created and reproduced their pictures. Late in his twenties he commenced his career as painter. His first great successes combined both craft and art. Hogarth produced the series of six pictures that make up *A Harlot's Progress* first as a set of paintings in oil, then as a sequence of copper engravings aimed at wider distribution. If *A Harlot's Progress* launched his popularity, *A Rake's Progress* (engraved in 1735 from canvases painted the year before) clinched his reputation as Britain's most masterly, mocking delineator of contemporary vice and folly. Though he continued for a while to nurture conventional ambitions as a painter of portraits and historical subjects catering to aristocratic tastes, Hogarth came gradually to recognize the originality, force, and commercial viability of his satrical engravings. As he later expressed it (in his own idiosyncratic syntax), he had discovered a style pitched between "the sublime and the grotesque," and had devised "a more new way of proceeding, viz. painting and engraving modern moral subjects, a field unbroke up in any country or any age. . . . Provided I could strike the passions, and by small sums from many, by means of prints which I could engrave from my pictures myself, I could secure my property to myself." Hogarth managed to "strike the passions" both ways: by depicting them vividly in the countenance of his characters, and by igniting them in his audience. He also managed, better than any predecessor, to "secure his property to himself." He petitioned Parliament to pass the Engraver's Copyright Act (often called "Hogarth's Act"), which protected printmakers from the then rampant piratical reproduction of their work, and which thereby (in Hogarth's proud words) "made prints a considerable article and trade in this country, there being more business of that kind done in this town than in Paris or anywhere else." The engravings of *A Rake's Progress* were first published, pointedly, the day after Hogarth's Act became the law of the land.

Early in his career, Hogarth had been praised as a "Shakespeare in painting," and admirers noted repeatedly the literary force of his graphic art; only he, wrote one, could "teach pictures to speak and to think." Hogarth had appropriated the very idea of an instructive moral "progress" from John Bunyan's phenomenally popular religious narrative *Pilgrim's Progress*, but he made the journey at once darker and more satiric. Bunyan's Mr. Christian progresses through Vanity Fair and other dangers toward the Celestial City; Hogarth's protagonists remain mired within the Vanity Fair of contemporary London; their "progress" takes them downward to degradation and death. His art also helped shape a newer form of narrative, the novel. Like the novel, Hogarth's sequences abound in suggestive subplots, telling asides, and startling revelations, played out in the tiniest details carefully placed. Novelists as different from one another as Samuel Richardson, Henry Fielding, and Laurence Sterne valued him as a friend, sought him as a collaborator, and embraced him as a past master in their own moral and narrative mode. "I almost dare affirm," wrote Fielding, "that those two works of his, which he calls *The Rake's* and *The Harlot's Progress*, are calculated more to serve the cause of virtue, and for the preservation of mankind, than all the folios of morality which have ever been written."

A Rake's Progress

Plate 1   Tom Rakewell's father (depicted in the portrait above the mantle) has recently died. The old man was miserly: he wore a coat and fur hat indoors so as not to incur the costs of a fire; he saved broken junk (in the open chest); he nearly starved his housecat (lower left). The young man is profligate: he has torn open doors and cabinets in search of sequestered wealth; he is being measured for new and ostentatious clothes; he is trying to pay off the raging mother of Sarah Young, the weeping woman (at right) whom he has made pregnant.

Plate 2   Nearly unrecognizable in his new elegance, Rakewell (the tallest figure in the picture) surrounds himself with instructors and tradespeople eager to sell their services. In the foreground (from left to right) are a composer, a fencing master, a dance teacher (with fiddle), a hired killer (in black; the note in Tom's hand, from "William Stab," vouches for the assassin as "a man of honor"); a huntsman (with horn); and a jockey, whose trophy cup bears the suggestive name of the winning horse: "Silly Tom." The two moping Englishmen at the back may be miffed to find themselves supplanted by the fashionable foreigners in front of them. The painting above the mantle depicts the Judgment of Paris, that indolent princeling whose unrestrained desires precipitated the catastrophe of the Trojan War.

Plate 3   Rakewell (sprawled at left) has bought himself an orgy. All the Roman portraits in the upper right corner have been defaced, except that of the emperor Nero, who looks out over the havoc like some patron saint of vandalism (his reputed incendarism is re-enacted by the woman standing at the back near the shattered mirror, holding a candle flame to the map of the world). One prostitute caresses Tom while conveying away his watch; in the foreground opposite, a woman disrobes in preparation for an obscene dance that will likely involve the reflective platter and large candle held by the cross-eyed lackey in the doorway. Admonitions to the orgiasts lie at hand, in the form of the chicken's carcass (lower right corner), stripped and forked; and in the person of the ballad singer, tattered, pregnant, and ignored, whose song bears the telling title "Black Joke."

Plate 4   Carried in his sedan chair to a night of gaming at White's Chocolate House and gambling club (rear left), Tom is stopped by a bailiff who serves him with a notice of arrest for debt. He receives aid not from the revellers in the distance but from Sarah Young, the abandoned lover whose mother he tried to buy off in Plate 1. Reversing that gesture, she seeks to secure his release by offering the money she has earned by making ribbons and caps (sample wares hang at her side). On a ladder a lamplighter, distracted by the goings-on, carelessly (and emblematically) spills his flammable fluid onto Rakewell's head. Hogarth reworked this picture more often than any other in the series. In this late version, a lightning bolt aims pointedly at the gambling house, upper left, while at the lower right, a group of urchins in the open air has made an early start at playing comparably dangerous games.

Plate 5   Intent on wealth, not the love Sarah offers, Rakewell weds an old woman in a dim, disintegrating church where light and faith are in scant supply. On the left, the Poor's Box," receptacle of charity, has long been shut (a cobweb covers its lid); on the right wall, the table of commandments is cracked. The one-eyed bride appears to wink at the grim parson; Rakewell proffers her the ring while eying her maid. On the floor, a canine couple parodies the human ceremony; in the back, a woman with churchkeys flailing tries to prevent the intrusion of Sarah Young, holding the child Rakewell has sired. Sarah's mother does vigorous but unavailing battle.

Plate 6   During a night of gambling, Rakewell has evidently lost the fortune he acquired by his calculating marriage. Wigless, frantic, he falls to one knee and curses his lot; his rage is replicated (as were his nuptials) by a dog on the floor to his right. The croupier at rear center, carrying the candles, echoes the "world-burning" woman in Plate 3. This time, though, the building is actually on fire. The lantern-bearing watchman at left has come to give warning. Most of the gamblers are too immersed in their own operations to notice either Rakewell's anguish or their own danger.

Plate 7   In the wake of his losses, Rakewell has at last been imprisoned for debt, unable to pay the "garnish" (or customary bribe) that the jailer behind him expects, or even the cost of a beer. The note on the table—"I have read your play and find it will not do"—rejects his last poor, literary attempt at solvency. His wife rails, Sarah faints, his daughter tugs at Sarah's skirts, and his cellmates embody futilities even more preposterous than his own playwriting. The impoverished man at left has devised "a new scheme for paying the debts of the nation." The man seated at the stove is an alchemist, vainly trying to transmute base metals into gold; before his imprisonment, he also built himself a pair of wings (upper left), but they, like Rakewell's upward aspirations, have produced only debt and confinement, not flight and freedom.

Plate 8   Rakewell has been moved from debtor's prison to Bethlehem Royal Hospital (better known as Bedlam), London's asylum for the insane. Grinning outright for the first time in the series, Tom claws at his head while guards restrain him. Sarah Young, weeping, has come to give him comfort. The other two women are here to amuse themselves (at the cost of two pence per visit, Bedlam had become one of London's most popular entertainments). Some inmates display lunatic religious zeal; others have gone mad in pursuit of science. The man drawing the world on the wall seeks a solution to the longitude, the navigational problem that had obsessed Britons for many decades. Behind the open door of the central cell, a naked madman sits and thinks he's king. In this final revision of the plate (1763), Hogarth has superimposed upon the longitudinist's globe an emblem of Britannia, as though empire and madhouse were now one.

≈ PERSPECTIVES ≈

Mind and God

Nature, and Nature's Laws lay hid in Night.
God said, *Let Newton be!* and All was *Light.*

So wrote Alexander Pope, capturing in a couplet the awe with which many of his contemporaries regarded the accomplishments of Isaac Newton. The lines, intended for Newton's tomb, compass his whole career. Pope's last word evokes one of the scientist's early breakthroughs: the discovery that sunlight, for all its seeming "whiteness," teemed with colors, whose operations could be mathematically described. Later, in his masterwork *Naturalis Philosophiae Principia Mathematica* (The Mathematical Principles of Natural Philosophy, 1687), Newton had expounded "Nature's Laws" on a scale and with a precision heretofore unmatched, pinpointing, in compact mathematical formulas, the laws governing gravity and motion, both on earth and throughout the heavens. In Pope's replaying of Genesis, Newton himself becomes a principle, not merely the interpreter of Creation but virtually synonomous with it: God's luminous word, from which revelation follows. For numberless admirers, the name of Newton figured forth not only the intricate simplicities of "Nature's Laws," but also the astonishing, hitherto unsuspected capacity of the human mind to shed light upon the works of God.

The human mind itself promptly became the object of new investigation, Newtonian in its ambitions and its methods. Two years after the *Principia* appeared, John Locke published his *Essay Concerning Human Understanding* (1689), a work comparably influential, in which he sought answers to key questions of epistemology: what do we know? and by what means do we come to know it? Locke, like Newton, brought luster to the scientific approach championed by the Royal Society (of which both men were members): empiricism, the conviction that truth could be attained solely through experiment and experience. The intimate interplay of those two crucial elements is nicely registered in Albert Einstein's account of the way that Newton did his work: "The conceptions which he used to reduce the material of experience to order seemed to flow spontaneously from experience itself, from the beautiful experiments which he ranged in order like playthings and describes with an affectionate wealth of detail." Locke imported empiricism from the physical sciences into the realms of philosophy and psychology. Striving to found a science of mind, to make sense of the running encounter between the material world and human perception, Locke and his successors found in experience both a method for investigating epistemological problems and the core of their solution: for these thinkers, experience is how we know, it is what we know, and it is how we can learn more about the processes of our knowing. The human mind is intrinsically (though not methodically) empiricist in its ways of gathering its "wealth of detail" about the world.

Under the mind's new scrutinies, God's place and primacy fell open to new questions. Empiricism itself was seen to cut two ways. On the one hand, as Newton and the vast majority of his followers delightedly proclaimed, experimental observation was revealing a universal architecture so exquisite as to prove both the existence and the matchless artistry of God the architect; this route from reason to religious faith became known as the "argument from design." On the other hand, discovery was beginning to conjure up alternative possibilities unsettling to faith: of a God not wholly supreme but subject to nature's inexorable laws; or of laws so efficiently self-sustaining that they needed no God to enforce them. In some of its modes, empiricism itself could be seen to imperil faith, since direct experience or demonstration of the divine proved elusive in a science that limited itself to the observation of material, mechanical causes and effects. For Newton, Locke, and countless other inquirers, empiricism promised to explain the ways of God; but they had begun a process which, in other hands, might threaten to explain God away.

The clash between science and theology gathered force in the mid-nineteenth century, when discoveries in geology (the age of the Earth) and biology (evolution) rendered Scripture strongly suspect. But contention between faith and science was manifest much earlier. At the start of the nineteenth century, William Blake briefly sketched the lines of struggle in his private notebook. "Newton's particles of light," he wrote

> Are sands upon the Red sea shore,
> Where Israel's tents do shine so bright.

Against the arrogance of inquiry, Blake insists upon humility and awe; biblical revelation trumps all the small advancements of human knowledge. Pope had gestured in this direction some seven decades earlier. He suggested, in his *Essay on Man*, that for "superior beings" (angels, God), the sight of Newton unfolding "all Nature's law" might provide the same kind of amazement and amusement that we mortals derive from the antics of a performing ape—a creature who knows more than we might expect, but far less than we ourselves. So great (Pope argues) is the difference between human and divine capacities. Throughout the eighteenth century, in works suffused by the concepts of Newton and of Locke, the relations between mind and God were brilliantly explicated and newly contested, as poets and philosophers undertook, from varying vantages and factions, to sing God's praise, to parse his ways, to work toward him by reason or (in rare instances) to reason him out of existence altogether.

⇥◆⇤

Isaac Newton
1642–1727

Albert Einstein summed up Newton's abilities as follows: "In one person, he combined the experimenter, the theorist, the mechanic, and, not least, the artist in exposition." Einstein praises magnificently, and omits much. Newton also combined in his one person a supreme mathematician, an obsessive alchemist, a forceful administrator, and (perhaps most important, in his own view) an ardent theologian, eager to discover and expound the place of God in his creation. His voluminous, unorthodox writings on the subject remained unpublished in his lifetime. By denying the full divinity of Christ, Newton accorded God *more* authority than did conventional Anglicanism. His views, if known, would have toppled him from the public eminences he enjoyed: as Lucasian Professor of Mathematics at Cambridge, as Master of the Mint in London, as President of the Royal Society. Still, Newton's first admirers found in his scientific work exhilarating support for a more mainstream theology: the strongest foundation yet for the argument from design. It was the business of natural philosophy, Newton repeatedly insisted, "to deduce causes from effects, until we come to the First Cause, which is certainly not mechanical." Newton's own scientific revelations gave rise to a passionate interest in "natural religion"—a faith in God's existence and benevolence, grounded in the orderliness and beauty of the natural world. One of that faith's adherents was the ambitious young classicist and clergyman Richard Bentley (1662–1742), who, having been commissioned to deliver a series of lectures defending Christianity against atheism, found in Newton's recently published *Principia* abundant new evidence for his own arguments about the divine "origin and frame of the universe." While preparing his lectures for the press, Bentley sent Newton a set of questions, in order to make sure that he was correctly understanding and deploying the *Principia*. Newton's four replies (the first is excerpted here) map the convergence that interests him most, between the discoveries of science and the majesty of God.

from **Letter to Richard Bentley**

10 December 1692

Sir,

When I wrote my treatise about our system, I had an eye upon such principles as might work with considering men for the belief of a Deity, and nothing can rejoice me more than to find it useful for that purpose. But if I have done the public any service this way, 'tis due to nothing but industry and a patient thought.

As to your first query, it seems to me, that if the matter of our sun and planets and all the matter in the universe was evenly scattered throughout all the heavens, and every particle had an innate gravity towards all the rest,[1] and the whole space throughout which this matter was scattered was but finite, the matter on the outside of this space would by its gravity tend towards all the matter on the inside, and by consequence fall down to the middle of the whole space, and there compose one great spherical mass. But if the matter was evenly diffused through an infinite space, it would never convene into one mass, but some of it convene into one mass and some into another so as to make an infinite number of great masses scattered at great distances from one to another throughout all that infinite space. And thus might the sun and fixed stars be formed, supposing the matter were of a lucid[2] nature. But how the matter should divide itself into two sorts, and that part of it which is fit to compose a shining body should fall down into one mass and make a sun, and the rest which is fit to compose an opaque body should coalesce not into one great body like the shining matter but into many little ones; or, if the sun was at first an opaque body like the planets, or the planets lucid bodies like the sun, how he alone should be changed into a shining body whilst all they continue opaque, or all they be changed into opaque ones whilst he remains unchanged, I do not think explicable by mere natural causes but am forced to ascribe it to the counsel[3] and contrivance of a voluntary agent. The same power, whether natural or supernatural, which placed the sun in the center of the orbs[4] of the six primary planets, placed Saturn in the center of the orbs of his five secondary planets,[5] and Jupiter in the center of the orbs of his four secondary ones, and the Earth in the center of the moon's orb; and therefore, had this cause been a blind one without contrivance and design, the sun would have been a body of the same kind with Saturn, Jupiter and the Earth; that is without light and heat. Why there is one body in our system qualified to give light and heat to all the rest I know no reason but because the author of the system thought it convenient, and why there is but one body of this kind I know no reason but because one was sufficient to warm and enlighten all the rest. For the Cartesian hypothesis[6] of suns losing their light and then turning into comets and comets into planets can have no place in my system and is plainly erroneous, because it's certain that comets as often as they appear to us descend into the system of our planets lower than the orb of Jupiter and sometimes lower than the orbs of Venus and Mercury, and yet never stay here but always return from the sun with the same degrees of motion by which they approached him.

---

1. Newton did not endorse this premise. "You sometimes speak," he wrote Bentley in his second letter, "of gravity as essential and inherent to matter: pray do not ascribe that notion to me, for the cause of gravity is what I do not pretend to know."
2. Light-producing.
3. Deliberate design.

4. Orbits.
5. I.e., Saturn's moons; Newton states the numbers of planets and their moons then known.
6. A theory put forth by the French mathematician and philosopher René Descartes (1596–1650) in his highly influential treatises on physics, which Newton's *Principia* had challenged.

To your second query I answer that the motions which the planets now have could not spring from any natural cause alone but were impressed by an intelligent agent. For since comets descend into the region of our planets and here move all manner of ways, going sometimes the same way with the planets, sometimes the contrary way, and sometimes in cross ways in planes inclined to the plane of the ecliptic at all kinds of angles, it's plain that there is no natural cause which could determine all the planets both primary and secondary to move the same way and in the same plane without any considerable variation.[7] This must have been the effect of counsel. Nor is there any natural cause which could give the planets those just degrees of velocity in proportion to their distances from the sun and other central bodies about which they move and to the quantity of matter contained in those bodies, which were requisite to make them move in concentric orbs about those bodies. Had the planets been as swift as comets in proportion to their distances from the sun (as they would have been, had their motions been caused by their gravity, whereby the matter at the first formation of the planets might fall from the remotest regions towards the sun), they would not move in concentric orbs but in such eccentric ones as the comets move in. Were all the planets as swift as Mercury or as slow as Saturn or his satellites, or were their several velocities otherwise much greater or less than they are (as they might have been had they arose from any other cause than their gravity), or had their distances from the centers about which they move been greater or less than they are with the same velocities; or had the quantity of matter in the sun or in Saturn, Jupiter, and the Earth and by consequence their gravitating power been greater or less than it is, the primary planets could not have revolved about the sun nor the secondary ones about Saturn, Jupiter and the Earth in concentric circles as they do, but would have moved in hyperbolas or parabolas or in ellipses very eccentric. To make this system therefore, with all its motions, required a cause which understood and compared together the quantities of matter in the several bodies of the sun and planets and the gravitating powers resulting from thence, the several distances of the primary planets from the sun and secondary ones from Saturn, Jupiter, and the Earth, and the velocities with which these planets could revolve at those distances about those quantities of matter in the central bodies. And to compare and adjust all these things together in so great a variety of bodies argues that cause to be not blind and fortuitous, but very well skilled in mechanics and geometry.

To your third query I answer that it may be represented that the sun may, by heating those planets most which are nearest to him, cause them to be better concocted[8] and more condensed by concoction. But when I consider that our Earth is much more heated in its bowels below the upper crust by subterraneous fermentations of mineral bodies than by the sun, I see not why the interior parts of Jupiter and Saturn might not be as much heated, concocted, and coagulated by those fermentations as our Earth is, and therefore this various density should have some other cause than the various distances of the planets from the sun; and I am confirmed in this opinion by considering that the planets of Jupiter and Saturn, as they are rarer[9] than

7. Newton oversimplifies: the planes of the planets actually incline to each other by as much as five degrees. Newton's arguments in this letter, suggests his biographer Richard Westfall, "reveal above all a determination to find God in nature," even to impose God upon nature. All the phenomena that Newton here attributes to the intervention of divine "counsel" and "skill" were explained scientifically over the course of the next century by physicists applying and extending Newton's own

system, so that (as the most brilliant of the extenders, Pierre Simon Laplace, is said to have remarked to Napoleon) the hypothesis of divine intervention was no longer necessary.
8. Purified by heat (and hence made denser by the absence of the extraneous matter that the heat has annihilated).
9. Less dense.

the rest, so they are vastly greater and contain a far greater quantity of matter and have many satellites about them, which qualifications surely arose not from their being placed at so great a distance from the sun, but were rather the cause why the Creator placed them at that great distance. For by their gravitating powers they disturb one another's motions very sensibly, as I find by some late observations of Mr. Flamsteed,[1] and had they been placed much nearer to the sun and to one another they would by the same powers have caused a considerable disturbance in the whole system. * * *

Lastly, I see nothing extraordinary in the inclination of the Earth's axis for proving a Deity unless you will urge it as a contrivance for winter and summer and for making the Earth habitable towards the poles, and that the diurnal rotations of the sun and planets, as they could hardly arise from any cause purely mechanical, so by being determined all the same way with the annual and menstrual[2] motions they seem to make up that harmony in the system which (as I explained above) was the effect of choice rather than of chance.

There is yet another argument for a Deity which I take to be a very strong one, but till the principles on which 'tis grounded be better received I think it more advisable to let it sleep. I am

Your most humble servant to command
IS. NEWTON

+ ≡◊≡ +

John Locke
1632–1704

In the preface to his *Essay Concerning Human Understanding*, Locke depicts "the incomparable Mr. Newton" as one of the "master builders" of the new science, and himself as a mere "under-laborer," busy "clearing the ground a little, and removing some of the rubbish that lies in the way to knowledge." The eighteenth century, though, tended to venerate the two thinkers equally, Newton as master explicator of the cosmos, Locke as master inquirer into the mind. Starting from the claim that "simple ideas," acquired early, constituted the building blocks of thought, Locke constructed a system of the mind of comparable in intricacy with Newton's universe, but of greater idiosyncrasy (since the content of consciousness differed from person to person, and indeed determined individual identity). Part of Locke's appeal lay in the comparative accessibility of his empiricism. His experiments, unlike Newton's, required neither telescope nor prism, calculus nor genius: readers could perform them (as Locke repeatedly suggested) in the laboratories of their minds, using their own perceptions and memories as raw material. More than any other text, Locke's *Essay* spurred that fascination with the first person which suffuses so much eighteenth-century writing: autobiographies, essays, diaries, travel journals, philosophic treatises, novels. Locke described the workings of the mind so persuasively that in effect he changed them too, prompting an analytic self-consciousness that had not obtained in the same kind and to the same degree before his book appeared.

1. John Flamsteed (1646–1719), astronomer and director of the Royal Greenwich Observatory, had recently supplied Newton with these data; the two men later quarrelled bitterly over Flamsteed's reluctance to make available the immense, precise, and urgently needed records of his celestial observations.
2. Monthly.

from An Essay Concerning Human Understanding
[On Ideas[1]]

Every man being conscious to himself that he thinks, and that which his mind is employed about whilst thinking being the *ideas* that are there, 'tis past doubt, that men have in their minds several *ideas*, such as are those expressed by the words *whiteness, hardness, sweetness, thinking, motion, man, elephant, army, drunkenness*, and others. It is in the first place then to be inquired, how he comes by them? I know it is a received doctrine, that men have native *ideas* and original characters[2] stamped upon their minds, in their very first being. This opinion I have at large examined already, and I suppose what I have said in the foregoing book[3] will be much more easily admitted, when I have shown whence the understanding may get all the *ideas* it has, and by what ways and degrees they may come into the mind; for which I shall appeal to everyone's own observation and experience.

Let us then suppose the mind to be, as we say, white paper, void of all characters, without any *ideas*. How comes it to be furnished? Whence comes it by that vast store, which the busy and boundless fancy of man has painted on it, with an almost endless variety? Whence has it all the materials of reason and knowledge? To this I answer, in one word, from *experience*. In that, all our knowledge is founded, and from that it ultimately derives itself. Our observation employed either about *external, sensible objects, or about the internal operations of our minds, perceived and reflected on by ourselves, is that which supplies our understandings with all the materials of thinking*. These two are the fountains of knowledge, from whence all the *ideas* we have, or can naturally have, do spring.

First, *our senses*, conversant about particular sensible objects, do *convey into the mind*, several distinct *perceptions* of things, according to those various ways, wherein those objects do affect them; and thus we come by those *ideas* we have of *yellow, white, heat, cold, soft, hard, bitter, sweet*, and all those which we call sensible qualities, which when I say the senses convey into the mind, I mean, they from external objects convey into the mind what produces there those *perceptions*. This great source of most of the *ideas* we have, depending wholly upon our senses and derived by them to the understanding, I call SENSATION.

Secondly, the other fountain from which experience furnisheth the understanding with *ideas* is the *perception of the operations of our own minds* within us, as it is employed about the *ideas* it has got; which operations, when the soul comes to reflect on, and consider, do furnish the understanding with another set of *ideas*, which could not be had from things without; and such are *perception, thinking, doubting, believing, reasoning, knowing, willing*, and all the different actings of our own minds; which we being conscious of, and observing in ourselves, do from these receive into our understandings, as distinct *ideas*, as we do from bodies affecting our senses. This source of *ideas* every man has wholly in himself. And though it be not sense, as having nothing to do with external objects, yet it is very like it, and might properly enough be called *internal sense*. But as I call the other *sensation*, so I call this REFLECTION, the *ideas* it affords being such only, as the mind gets by reflecting on its own operations within itself. By REFLECTION then, in the following part of this discourse, I would be under-

---

1. All selections are from Book 2, "Of Ideas"; chapter and section numbers follow each section, in brackets. Most of Locke's italics have been retained.

2. Inscriptions.
3. In which Locke denied the existence of "innate principles," received by the soul "in its very first being" (1.2.1).

stood to mean, that notice which the mind takes of its own operations, and the manner of them, by reason whereof there come to be *ideas* of these operations in the understanding. These two, I say, *viz.* external, material things, as the objects of SENSATION, and the operations of our own minds within, as the objects of REFLECTION, are, to me, the only originals,[4] from whence all our *ideas* take their beginnings. The term *operations* here I use in a large sense, as comprehending not barely the actions of the mind about its *ideas*, but some sort of passions arising sometimes from them, such as is the satisfaction or uneasiness arising from any thought.

The understanding seems to me not to have the least glimmering of any *ideas*, which it doth not receive from one of these two. *External objects furnish the mind with the ideas of sensible qualities*, which are all those different perceptions they produce in us; and the *mind furnishes the understanding with* ideas *of its own operations*.

These, when we have taken a full survey of them, and their several modes, combinations, and relations, we shall find to contain all our whole stock of *ideas*; and that we have nothing in our minds which did not come in one of these two ways. Let anyone examine his own thoughts, and thoroughly search into his understanding, and then let him tell me, whether all the original *ideas* he has there are any other than of the objects of his *senses*, or of the operations of his mind, considered as objects of his *reflection*; and how great a mass of knowledge soever he imagines to be lodged there, he will, upon taking a strict view, see that he has *not any idea in his mind, but what one of these two have imprinted*; though, perhaps, with infinite variety compounded and enlarged by the understanding, as we shall see hereafter.

He that attentively considers the state of a *child*, at his first coming into the world, will have little reason to think him stored with plenty of *ideas*, that are to be the matter of his future knowledge. 'Tis by degrees he comes to be furnished with them. And though the *ideas* of obvious and familiar qualities imprint themselves before the memory begins to keep a register of time and order, yet 'tis often so late, before some unusual qualities come in the way, that there are few men that cannot recollect the beginning of their acquaintance with them; and if it were worthwhile, no doubt a child might be so ordered as to have but a very few, even of the ordinary *ideas*, till he were grown up to a man. But all that are born into the world being surrounded with bodies that perpetually and diversely affect them, variety of *ideas*, whether care be taken about it or no, are imprinted on the minds of children. *Light* and *colors* are busy at hand everywhere, when the eye is but open; *sounds* and some *tangible qualities* fail not to solicit their proper senses, and force an entrance to the mind; but yet, I think, it will be granted easily, that if a child were kept in a place where he never saw any other but black and white till he were a man, he would have no more *ideas* of scarlet or green, than he that from his childhood never tasted an oyster, or a pineapple, has of those particular relishes.

Men then come to be furnished with fewer or more simple *ideas* from without, according as the *objects* they converse with[5] afford greater or less variety; and from the operation of their minds within, according as they more or less *reflect* on them. For, though he that contemplates the operations of his mind cannot but have plain and clear *ideas* of them; yet unless he turn his thoughts that way, and considers them *attentively*, he will no more have clear and distinct *ideas* of all the *operations of his mind*, and all that may be observed therein, than he will have all the particular *ideas* of any landscape, or of the parts and motions of a clock, who will not turn his eyes to

---

4. Origins.   5. Encounter.

it, and with attention heed all the parts of it. The picture or clock may be so placed that they may come in his way every day; but yet he will have but a confused *idea* of all the parts they are made up of, till he *applies himself with attention*, to consider them each in particular. [1.1–7]

* * *

But to return to the matter in hand, the *ideas* we have of substances, and the ways we come by them; I say *our specific* ideas *of substances* are nothing else but *a collection of a certain number of simple ideas, considered as united in one thing*. These *ideas* of substances, though they are commonly called simple apprehensions, and the names of them simple terms, yet in effect, are complex and compounded. Thus the *idea* which an *Englishman* signifies by the name *swan* is white color, long neck, red beak, black legs, and whole feet, and all these of a certain size, with a power of swimming in the water, and making a certain kind of noise, and, perhaps, to a man who has long observed those kind of birds, some other properties, which all terminate in sensible simple *ideas*, all united in one common subject.

Besides the complex *ideas* we have of material sensible substances, of which I have last spoken, by the simple *ideas* we have taken from those operations of our own minds, which we experiment[6] daily in ourselves, as thinking, understanding, willing, knowing, and power of beginning motion, etc. co-existing in some substance, we are able to frame *the complex* idea *of an immaterial spirit*. And thus by putting together the *ideas* of thinking, perceiving, liberty, and power of moving themselves and other things, we have as clear a perception and notion of immaterial substances, as we have of material. For putting together the *ideas* of thinking and willing, or the power of moving or quieting corporeal motion, joined to substance, of which we have no distinct *idea*, we have the *idea* of an immaterial spirit; and by putting together the *ideas* of coherent solid parts, and a power of being moved, joined with substance, of which likewise we have no positive *idea*, we have the *idea* of matter. The one is as clear and distinct an *idea*, as the other: the *idea* of thinking, and moving a body, being as clear and distinct *ideas*, as the *ideas* of extension, solidity, and being moved. [23.14–15]

* * *

If we examine the *idea* we have of the incomprehensible Supreme Being, we shall find that we come by it the same way; and that the complex *ideas* we have both of God, and separate spirits, are made up of the simple *ideas* we receive from *reflection*; *v.g.* having, from what we experiment in ourselves, got the *ideas* of existence and duration; of knowledge and power; of pleasure and happiness; and of several other qualities and powers, which it is better to have than to be without; when we would frame an *idea* the most suitable we can to the Supreme Being, we enlarge every one of these with our *idea* of infinity; and so putting them together, make our complex *idea of God*. For that the mind has such a power of enlarging some of its *ideas*, received from sensation and reflection, has been already showed. [23.33]

[On Identity]

Personal identity consists, not in the identity of substance, but, as I have said, in the identity of *consciousness*, wherein, if Socrates and the present Mayor of Queenborough agree, they are the same person. If the same Socrates waking and sleeping do not partake of the same *consciousness*, Socrates waking and sleeping is not the same person. And to punish Socrates waking, for what sleeping Socrates thought, and

---

6. Experience.

waking Socrates was never conscious of, would be no more of right, than to punish one twin for what his brother-twin did, whereof he knew nothing, because their outsides were so like that they could not be distinguished; for such twins have been seen.

But yet possibly it will still be objected, suppose I wholly lose the memory of some parts of my life, beyond a possibility of retrieving them, so that perhaps I shall never be conscious of them again; yet am I not the same person that did those actions, had those thoughts, that I was once conscious of, though I have now forgot them? To which I answer, that we must here take notice what the word *I* is applied to, which in this case is the man only. And the same man being presumed to be the same person, *I* is easily here supposed to stand also for the same person. But if it be possible for the same man to have distinct incommunicable consciousness at different times, it is past doubt the same man would at different times make different persons; which, we see, is the sense of mankind in the solemnest declaration of their opinions, human laws not punishing the *mad man* for the *sober man's* actions, nor the *sober man* for what the *mad man* did, thereby making them two persons; which is somewhat explained by our way of speaking in *English*, when we say such an one *is not himself*, or is *besides himself*; in which phrases it is insinuated, as if those who now, or, at least, first used them, thought, that *self* was changed, the *self* same person was no longer in that man.

But yet 'tis hard to conceive that Socrates the same individual man should be two persons. To help us a little in this, we must consider what is meant by *Socrates*, or the same individual *man*.

First, it must be either the same individual, immaterial, thinking substance: in short, the same numerical soul, and nothing else.

Secondly, or the same animal,[7] without any regard to an immaterial soul.

Thirdly, or the same immaterial spirit united to the same animal.

Now take which of these suppositions you please, it is impossible to make personal identity to consist in anything but consciousness, or reach any farther than that does.

For by the first of them, it must be allowed possible that a man born of different women, and in distant times, may be the same man. A way of speaking, which whoever admits, must allow it possible for the same man to be two distinct persons, as any two that have lived in different ages without the knowledge of one another's thoughts.

By the second and third, Socrates in this life, and after it, cannot be the same man any way, but by the same consciousness; and so making *human identity* to consist in the same thing wherein we place *personal identity*, there will be no difficulty to allow the same man to be the same person. But then they who place *human identity* in consciousness only, and not in something else, must consider how they will make the infant Socrates the same man with Socrates after the resurrection. But whatsoever to some men makes a *man*, and consequently the same individual man, wherein perhaps few are agreed, personal identity can by us be placed in nothing but consciousness (which is that alone which makes what we call *self*) without involving us in great absurdities.

But is not a man drunk and sober the same person? Why else is he punished for the fact[8] he commits when drunk, though he be never afterwards conscious of it? Just as much the same person, as a man that walks, and does other things in his sleep, is

7. Physical, living body.   8. Deed.

the same person, and is answerable for any mischief he shall do in it. Human laws punish both with a justice suitable to their way of knowledge: because in these cases, they cannot distinguish certainly what is real, what counterfeit; and so the ignorance in drunkeness or sleep is not admitted as a plea. For though punishment be annexed to personality, and personality to consciousness, and the drunkard perhaps be not conscious of what he did, yet human judicatures justly punish him; because the fact is proved against him, but what of consciousness cannot be proved for him. But in the great day,[9] wherein the secrets of all hearts shall be laid open, it may be reasonable to think, no one shall be made to answer for what he knows nothing of; but shall receive his doom, his conscience accusing or excusing him. [27.19–22]

1671–1689   1689

+→ ⇥◆⇤ +→

Isaac Watts
1674–1748

"As his mind was capacious, his curiosity excursive, and his industry continual," wrote Samuel Johnson in praise of the dissenting minister Isaac Watts, "his writings are very numerous." Watts produced books of poetry, logic, theology, philosophy, and science, but the writings that have mattered most are the hymns and psalm translations (about seven hundred in all) that he began composing in his early twenties. In his philosophical writings, Watts worked hard to absorb the innovations of Newton's physics and Locke's psychology; in his hymns, an older structure of piety prevails. One of empiricism's chief effects was to entangle truth with time, to make knowledge a consequence of *process* (a series of experiments, a sequence of ideas). In Watts's hymns, truth is eternal; the mind's chief tasks are to register God's greatness and to praise it aright. The singing of hymns, and of psalms awkwardly translated from the Hebrew, had been a practice of long standing in Protestant congregations. Watts brought to these forms a new clarity and grace, in verses he carefully crafted, week after week, for the immediate use and pleasure of his congregants. He sought (he once explained) to achieve an "ease of numbers [i.e., meter] and smoothness of sound, and . . . to make the sense plain and obvious." In print, the simplicity of his style gradually won a wider attention, extending far beyond local circles of dissent. As the religious historian and poet Donald Davie has pointed out, Watts's hymns and psalms probably touched more minds (and certainly resounded in more throats) over the course of the eighteenth century than any of the texts we now deem greater hits: *Gulliver's Travels*, Johnson's *Dictionary*, Thomson's *Seasons*. In his lifetime and for more than a century after, Watts was reckoned the English, Christian successor to that ancient king of Israel traditionally credited with creating the Psalms. "Were David to speak English," Watts's brother once remarked to him, "he would choose to make use of your style."

A Prospect of Heaven Makes Death Easy[1]

There is a land of pure delight
        Where saints immortal reign;
Infinite day excludes the night,
        And pleasures banish pain.

5   There everlasting spring abides,
        And never-withering flowers:

---

9. I.e., Judgment Day.   1. From *Hymns and Spiritual Songs* (1707).

Death like a narrow sea divides
    This heav'nly land from ours.

Sweet fields beyond the swelling flood
10   Stand dressed in living green:
So to the Jews old Canaan stood,
    While Jordan rolled between.[2]

But timorous mortals start° and shrink   *tremble*
    To cross this narrow sea,
15 And linger shivering on the brink,
    And fear to launch away.

O! could we make our doubts remove,°   *withdraw*
    Those gloomy doubts that rise,
And see the Canaan that we love,
20   With unbeclouded eyes:

Could we but climb where Moses stood,[3]
    And view the landskip° o'er,   *landscape*
Not Jordan's stream, nor death's cold flood
    Should fright us from the shore.

1707

The Hurry of the Spirits, in a Fever and Nervous Disorders[1]

My frame of nature is a ruffled sea,
And my disease the tempest. Nature feels
A strange commotion to her inmost center;
The throne of reason shakes. "Be still, my thoughts;
5 Peace and be still." In vain my reason gives
The peaceful word, my spirit strives in vain
To calm the tumult and command my thoughts.
This flesh, this circling blood, these brutal powers
Made to obey, turn rebels to the mind,
10 Nor hear its laws. The engine° rules the man.   *body*
Unhappy change! When nature's meaner springs,
Fired to impetuous ferments, break all order;
When little restless atoms rise and reign
Tyrants in sovereign uproar, and impose
15 Ideas on the mind; confused ideas
Of non-existents and impossibles,
Who can describe them? Fragments of old dreams,
Borrowed from midnight, torn from fairy fields
And fairy skies, and regions of the dead,
20 Abrupt, ill-sorted. O 'tis all confusion!
If I but close my eyes, strange images

2. In Joshua 3, the children of Israel, at the end of their 40-year journey in the desert, see the promised land of Canaan across the River Jordan.
3. Having led the Israelites to the end of their desert journey, Moses on his last day of life climbed the mountain of Nebo, and surveyed the entire promised land (Deuteronomy 34.1–4).
1. Not a hymn but an autobiographical poem, the first in a sequence entitled *Thoughts and Meditations in a Long Sickness, 1712 and 1713*, published decades later in Watts' *Reliquiae Juveniles* (writings in youth).

In thousand forms and thousand colors rise,
Stars, rainbows, moons, green dragons, bears and ghosts,
An endless medley rush upon the stage
25   And dance and riot wild in reason's court
Above control. I'm in a raging storm,
Where seas and skies are blended, while my soul
Like some light worthless chip of floating cork
Is tossed from wave to wave: now overwhelmed
30   With breaking floods, I drown, and seem to lose
All being; now high-mounted on the ridge
Of tall foaming surge, I'm all at once
Caught up into the storm, and ride the wind,
The whistling wind; unmanageable steed,
35   And feeble rider! Hurried many a league
Over the rising hills of roaring brine,
Through airy wilds unknown, with dreadful speed
And infinite surprise, till some few minutes
Have spent the blast, and then perhaps I drop
40   Near to the peaceful coast. Some friendly billow
Lodges me on the beach, and I find rest.
Short rest I find; for the next rolling wave
Snatches me back again; then ebbing far
Sets me adrift, and I am borne off to sea,
45   Helpless, amidst the bluster of the winds,
Beyond the ken of shore.

Ah, when will these tumultuous scenes be gone?
When shall this weary spirit, tossed with tempests,
Harassed and broken, reach the ports of rest,
50   And hold it firm? When shall this wayward flesh
With all th' irregular springs of vital movement
Ungovernable, return to sacred order,
And pay their duties to the ruling mind?

1712   1734

Against Idleness and Mischief[1]

How doth the little busy bee
Improve each shining hour,
And gather honey all the day
From every opening flower!

5   How skillfully she builds her cell!
How neat she spreads the wax!
And labors hard to store it well
With the sweet food she makes.

In works of labor, or of skill,
10   I would be busy too;

---

1. From *Divine Songs Attempted in Easy Language, for the Use of Children*. The poems in this durable little collection were memorized by numberless children in the 18th and 19th centuries, including Lewis Caroll's Alice. Wandering through Wonderland, she is commanded by its inhabitants (as she doubtless was in school) to recite these verses, and discovers to her dismay that the lines come out all wrong.

For Satan finds some mischief still°   *always*
    For idle hands to do.

In books, or work, or healthful play,
    Let my first years be passed.
15   That I may give for every day
    Some good account at last.

                                                  1715

Man Frail, and God Eternal[1]

Our God, our help in ages past,
    Our hope for years to come,
Our shelter from the stormy blast,
    And our eternal home.

5   Under the shadow of thy throne
    Thy saints have dwelt secure.
Sufficient is thine arm alone,
    And our defense is sure.

Before the hills in order stood,
10   Or earth received her frame,
From everlasting thou art God,
    To endless years the same.

Thy word commands our flesh to dust,
    Return, ye sons of men.
15   All nations rose from earth at first,
    And turn to earth again.

A thousand ages in thy sight
    Are like an evening gone;
Short as the watch that ends the night,
20   Before the rising sun.

The busy tribes of flesh and blood
    With all their lives and cares
Are carried downwards by thy flood,
    And lost in following years.

25   Time, like an ever-rolling stream
    Bears all its sons away.
They fly forgotten, as a dream
    Dies at the opening day.

Like flowery fields the nations stand
30   Pleased with the morning light.
The flowers beneath the mower's hand
    Lie withering ere 'tis night.

1. An imitation of Psalm 90, lines 1–6. This and the next poem are from *The Psalms of David Imitated in the Language of the New Testament, and Applied to the Christian State and Worship.* As the title indicates, Watts intended not merely to translate the Psalms, but to recast them. In his preface, he declares himself "the first who hath brought down the royal author [King David] into the common affairs of the Christian life, and let the psalmist of Israel into the Church of Christ, without anything of a Jew about him."

Our God, our help in ages past,
   Our hope for years to come,
35   Be thou our guard while troubles last,
   And our eternal home.

1719

Miracles Attending Israel's Journey[1]

When Israel, freed from Pharaoh's hand,
Left the proud tyrant and his land,
The tribes with cheerful homage own[2]
Their king, and Judah[3] was his throne.

5   Across the deep[4] their journey lay;
The deep divides to make them way.
Jordan beheld their march, and fled
With backward current to his head.[5]

The mountains shook like frighted sheep.
10   Like lambs the little hillocks leap.[6]
Not Sinai[7] on her base could stand,
Conscious of sovereign power at hand.

What power could make the deep divide?
Make Jordan backward roll his tide?
15   Why did ye leap, ye little hills?
And whence the fright that Sinai feels?

Let every mountain, every flood,
Retire, and know th'approaching God,
The king of Israel. See him here.
20   Tremble thou earth, adore, and fear.

He thunders, and all nature mourns.
The rock to standing pool he turns.
Flints spring with fountains at his word,[8]
And fires and seas confess the Lord.

1719

---

1. An imitation of Psalm 114. In 1712, Watts sent a version of this poem to the *Spectator*, where it appeared (No. 461, Tuesday, 19 August 1712) along with a letter from the poet explaining a discovery he had made while translating: "As I was describing the journey of Israel from Egypt, and added the Divine Presence amongst them, I perceived a beauty in the Psalm which was entirely new to me, and which I was going to lose; and that is, that the poet utterly conceals the presence of God in the beginning of it. . . . The reason now seems evident, and this conduct necessary. For if God had appeared before [i.e., at the start of the poem], there could be no wonder why the mountains should leap and the sea retire; therefore that this convulsion of nature may be brought in with due surprise, his name is not mentioned till afterward, and then with a very agreeable turn of thought God is introduced at once in all his majesty."
2. Acknowledged (God as their king).
3. A portion of the land promised by God to the Israelites; here the name is used to designate the entire promised land.
4. The Red Sea, whose miraculous parting made possible the Israelites' escape from Egypt (Exodus 14.21–31).
5. Alludes to a second, similar miracle later in the journey: God makes the waters of the river Jordan "stand upon an heap," so that the Israelites can pass "clean over" dry ground, into the promised land (Joshua 3.14–17).
6. Lines 9–10 may refer (in the original Psalm) to the hills and mountains of the promised land, the dwelling places of local gods who tremble at Israel's advent.
7. The sacred mountain on which Moses received from the Lord the Ten Commandments. At the Lord's approach, "the whole mount quaked greatly" (Exodus 19.18).
8. In the Book of Numbers (20.8–11), God miraculously produces water from rock in order to sustain the Israelites during their journey.

—∙—≋◈≋—∙—

Joseph Addison
1672–1719

The ideas of Newton and Locke became widely known not through their own writings (which were voluminous and often dense), but through various popularizations: lectures, demonstrations, explanatory handbooks, the popular press. One of the chief disseminators was the *Spectator*, the phenomenally successful series of daily essays composed by Joseph Addison and Richard Steele (for more on the *Spectator*, see page 2399). Addison in particular undertook to inculcate the ideas of Newton and Locke, sometimes directly by quotation and commentary, but more often indirectly, by absorption and a kind of tacit transmission. "The working of my own mind," Mr. Spectator announces early on, "is the general entertainment of my life," and he recommends this notably Lockean "entertainment" to his readers too; his own name honors Locke's reckoning of sight as the mind's chief instrument for the gathering of ideas. In the following extract, Addison pays comparably implicit homage to Newton, in an ode that quickly became one of the touchstones of eighteenth-century devotion. Though Addison places his poem in a tradition that combines Aristotle with the Psalms, Newton is powerfully present too, in the depiction of a heaven whose silent motions proclaim to human reason the perfection of God's design.

from Spectator No. 465
Saturday, 23 August 1712[1]

* * * The last method which I shall mention for the giving life to a man's faith is frequent retirement from the world, accompanied with religious meditation. When a man thinks of any thing in the darkness of the night, whatever deep impressions it may make in his mind, they are apt to vanish as soon as the day breaks about him. The light and noise of the day, which are perpetually soliciting his senses and calling off his attention, wear out of his mind the thoughts that imprinted themselves in it with so much strength during the silence and darkness of the night. A man finds the same difference as to himself in a crowd and in a solitude; the mind is stunned and dazzled amidst that variety of objects which press upon her in a great city: she cannot apply herself to the consideration of those things which are of the utmost concern to her. The cares or pleasures of the world strike in with every thought, and a multitude of vicious examples give a kind of justification to our folly. In our retirements everything disposes us to be serious. In courts and cities we are entertained with the works of men, in the country with those of God. One is the province of art, the other of nature. Faith and devotion naturally grow in the mind of every reasonable man, who sees the impressions of divine power and wisdom in every object on which he casts his eye. The Supreme Being has made the best arguments for his own existence, in the formation of the heavens and the earth, and these are arguments which a man of sense cannot forbear attending to, who is out of the noise and hurry of human affairs. Aristotle says,[2] that should a man live under ground, and there converse with works of art and mechanism, and should afterwards be brought up into the open day, and see the several glories of the heaven and earth, he would immediately pronounce them the works of such

---

1. Addison often set Saturdays aside for particularly serious topics, as a way of preparing his readers for the religious solemnities of Sunday (the only day on which the *Spectator* did not appear). He devotes the present paper to

"the proper means of strengthening and confirming" Christian faith.
2. Addison paraphrases lines quoted by Cicero from *De Philosophia*, a work of Aristotle's long lost.

a being as we define God to be. The Psalmist has very beautiful strokes of poetry to this purpose, in that exalted strain, "The heavens declare the glory of God: and the firmament showeth his handiwork. One day telleth another: and one night certifieth another. There is neither speech nor language: but their voices are heard among them. Their sound is gone out into all lands: and their words into the ends of the world."[3] As such a bold and sublime manner of thinking furnishes very noble matter for an ode, the reader may see it wrought into the following one.[4]

1

The spacious firmament on high,
With all the blue ethereal sky,
And spangled heav'ns, a shining frame,
Their great original proclaim:
5   Th' unwearied sun, from day to day,
Does his Creator's power display,
And publishes to every land
The works of an almighty hand.

2

Soon as the evening shades prevail,
10   The moon takes up the wondrous tale,
And nightly to the list'ning earth
Repeats the story of her birth:
Whilst all the stars that round her burn,
And all the planets, in their turn,
15   Confirm the tidings as they roll,
And spread the truth from pole to pole.

3

What though, in solemn silence, all
Move round the dark terrestrial ball?
What though nor real voice nor sound
20   Amid their radiant orbs be found?
In reason's ear they all rejoice,
And utter forth a glorious voice,
For ever singing, as they shine,
"The hand that made us is divine."

George Berkeley
1685–1753

For Locke, "ideas" are formed in the mind out of its ongoing encounter with the very real world outside it, where swans swim and elephants plod. For George Berkeley—clergyman, poet, traveler, and philosopher—ideas are all there is. *Esse est percipi*, he argues throughout his philosophical writings: to be is to be perceived. "All those bodies which compose the mighty frame of the world, have not any subsistence without a mind"—a mind engaged in the act of perceiving them. What, then, accounts for the apparent independence and continuity of real

3. Psalm 19.1–4.
4. Addison may have published this ode partly as a response to Watts's imitation of Psalm 114, which had

appeared in the *Spectator* just four days earlier (see page 2669).

objects (trees, to take one of Berkeley's recurrent examples), which seem to remain in place even when no mortal observes them? Berkeley's answer: one mind *is* perpetually engaged in perceiving them. The mind of God creates the ideas, sustains them, renders them consistent with themselves and independent of our intermittent human perceptions. In Berkeley's argument, this divine activity both constitutes proof of God's existence (since such an "infinite mind" is necessary to explain why the world appears to us as it does), and lies at the core of God's benevolence. Berkeley expounded his theory of "immaterialism" in his *Essay Towards a New Theory of Vision* (1709) and *Treatise Concerning the Principles of Human Knowledge* (1710), before recasting it in the more compact, accessible, and popular format of *Three Dialogues Between Hylas and Philonous*. Philonous ("Lover of mind") voices Berkeley's views, while Hylas ("Wooden") expresses the bemused incredulity with which Berkeley's readers continued to greet the philosopher's radical unmaking and reweaving of the fabric of everyday life. Scoffers tended to overlook the solution Berkeley was proffering to an abiding theological problem. Newton's cosmology had given rise (despite his own piety) to the unsettling image of the Clockmaker God, who having made the universe a perfectly efficient mechanism, could now let it run without further intervention. Newton addressed this problem in part by insisting that God had to intervene at intervals in order to adjust his system. Berkeley's God, by contrast, is no clockmaker at all; having authored the world in the beginning, he continues to make it anew at every moment by the creative act of his continual perception.

from Three Dialogues Between Hylas and Philonous

HYLAS: But do you in earnest think, the real existence of sensible things consists in their being actually perceived? If so, how comes it that all mankind distinguish between them? Ask the first man you meet, and he shall tell you, *to be perceived* is one thing, and *to exist* is another.

PHILONOUS: I am content, Hylas, to appeal to the common sense of the world for the truth of my notion. Ask the gardener why he thinks yonder cherry tree exists in the garden, and he shall tell you, because he sees and feels it; in a word, because he perceives it by his senses. Ask him why he thinks an orange tree not to be there, and he shall tell you, because he does not perceive it. What he perceives by sense, that he terms a real being, and saith it *is*, or *exists*; but that which is not perceivable, the same, he saith, hath no being.

HYLAS: Yes, Philonous, I grant the existence of a sensible thing consists in being perceivable, but not in being actually perceived.

PHILONOUS: And what is perceivable but an idea? And can an idea exist without being actually perceived? These are points long since agreed between us.

HYLAS: But be your opinion never so true, yet surely you will not deny it is shocking, and contrary to the common sense of men. Ask the fellow whether yonder tree hath an existence out of his mind: what answer think you he would make?

PHILONOUS: The same that I should myself, to wit, that it doth exist out of his mind. But then to a Christian it cannot surely be shocking to say, the real tree existing without his mind is truly known and comprehended by (that is, *exists in*) the infinite mind of God. Probably he may not at first glance be aware of the direct and immediate proof there is of this, inasmuch as the very being of a tree, or any other sensible thing, implies a mind wherein it is. But the point itself he cannot deny. The question between the materialists[1] and me is not whether things have a real existence out of the mind of this or that person, but whether

1. Those who assert the existence of matter, independent of perception.

they have an absolute existence, distinct from being perceived by God, and exterior to all minds. This indeed some heathens and philosophers have affirmed, but whoever entertains notions of the Deity suitable to the Holy Scriptures will be of another opinion.

HYLAS: But according to your notions, what difference is there between real things, and chimeras formed by the imagination, or the visions of a dream, since they are all equally in the mind?

PHILONOUS: The ideas formed by the imagination are faint and indistinct; they have besides an entire dependence on the will. But the ideas perceived by sense, that is, real things, are more vivid and clear, and being imprinted on the mind by a spirit distinct from us, have not a like dependence on our will. There is therefore no danger of confounding these with the foregoing: and there is as little of confounding them with the visions of a dream, which are dim, irregular, and confused. And though they should happen to be never so lively and natural, yet by their not being connected, and of a piece with the preceding and subsequent transactions of our lives, they might easily be distinguished from realities. In short, by whatever method you distinguish *things* from *chimeras* on your own scheme, the same, it is evident, will hold also upon mine. For it must be, I presume, by some perceived difference, and I am not for depriving you of any one thing that you perceive.

HYLAS: But still, Philonous, you hold, there is nothing in the world but spirits and ideas. And this, you must needs acknowledge, sounds very oddly.

PHILONOUS: I own the word *idea*, not being commonly used for *thing*, sounds something out of the way. My reason for using it was, because a necessary relation to the mind is understood to be implied by that term; and it is now commonly used by philosophers to denote the immediate objects of the understanding. But however oddly the proposition may sound in words, yet it includes nothing so very strange or shocking in its sense, which in effect amounts to no more than this, to wit, that there are only things perceiving, and things perceived; or that every unthinking being is necessarily, and from the very nature of its existence, perceived by some mind; if not by any finite created mind, yet certainly by the infinite mind of God, in whom "we live, and move, and have our being."[2] Is this as strange as to say, the sensible qualities are not on the objects, or that we cannot be sure of the existence of things, or know anything of their real natures, though we both see and feel them, and perceive them by all our senses?

HYLAS: And in consequence of this, must we not think there are no such things as physical or corporeal causes but that a spirit is the immediate cause of all the phenomena in nature? Can there be anything more extravagant than this?

PHILONOUS: Yes, it is infinitely more extravagant to say, a thing which is inert, operates on the mind, and which is unperceiving, is the cause of our perceptions. Besides, that which to you, I know not for what reason, seems so extravagant, is no more than the Holy Scriptures assert in a hundred places. In them God is represented as the sole and immediate author of all those effects which some heathens and philosophers are wont to ascribe to nature, matter, fate, or the like unthinking principle. This is so much the constant language of Scripture, that it were needless to confirm it by citations. * * *

1713

---

2. Acts 17.28.

→•← ⊨♦⊨ →•←

David Hume
1711–1776

As he lay dying at home in his native city of Edinburgh, David Hume entertained a visitor by conjuring up, with characteristic cheerfulness, a scenario in the afterlife. He imagined himself begging the fatal ferryman Charon for a little more time: "Have a little patience, good Charon, I have been endeavoring to open the eyes of the public. If I live a few years longer, I may have the satisfaction of seeing the downfall of some of the prevailing systems of superstition." The "prevailing system" which Hume had become most notorious for attacking was the Christian religion, whose favorite tenets—providence, miracles, the argument from design, the afterlife itself—he had called into question, with increasing audacity, over the course of his work. But he had also done much damage to newer systems of thought, notably Locke's. Locke had regarded personal identity as coherent and continuous, the consequence of lifelong experiences and ideas accumulated in the memory. Hume, in his early, massive *Treatise of Human Nature* (1739–1740), waived all this away as an arrant fiction—though perhaps a necessary one, since empiricism properly pursued reveals so radical an incoherence in mortal minds that empiricists themselves must intermittently abandon philosophy in order to go about their daily lives. Like many of his empiric predecessors, Hume argued that knowledge of the real world "must be founded entirely on experience"; more than any predecessor he was willing to entertain (and to entertain with) the doubts and demolitions arising from that premise. In his own lifetime, his skepticism did not prove as contagious as he had hoped. The *Treatise*, he recalled wryly, "fell *deadborn from the press*, without reaching such distinction as even to excite a murmur among the zealots." Though his attempt to recast his chief arguments more succinctly in *An Enquiry Concerning Human Understanding* (1748) prompted a somewhat livelier response, he eventually made his fortune not as a philosopher but as author of the highly successful *History of England* (1754–1763). He faced the general indifference or hostility to his arguments as blithely as he later greeted death, continually refining his views and revising his prose. He knew himself out of sync with his times. When, in his fantasy, he forecasts to Charon the imminent downfall of superstition, the ferryman responds, "You loitering rogue, that will not happen these many hundred years. Do you fancy I will grant you a lease for so long a term? Get into the boat this instant, you lazy loitering rogue." More than two hundred years later, the artful mischief of Hume's work has secured him some such lease. His writings, lucid and elusive, forthright and sly, demand (and receive) continual reassessment; his skepticism has proven more powerful than his contemporaries suspected, and he figures as perhaps the wittiest and most self-possessed philosophical troublemaker since Socrates.

from A Treatise of Human Nature
[THE MIND AS THEATER[1]]

There are some philosophers,[2] who imagine we are every moment intimately conscious of what we call our *self*; that we feel its existence and its continuance in existence; and are certain, beyond the evidence of a demonstration, both of its perfect identity and simplicity. The strongest sensation, the most violent passion, say they, instead of distracting us from this view, only fix it the more intensely, and make us consider their influence on *self* either by their pain or pleasure. To attempt a farther

---

1. From Book 1, section 6, "Of Personal Identity."
2. Notably Joseph Butler, an Anglican bishop who argued in *The Analogy of Religion* (1736) that the existence of the self is a truth of which every person is continually (and correctly) certain.

proof of this were to weaken its evidence; since no proof can be derived from any fact, of which we are so intimately conscious; nor is there anything of which we can be certain, if we doubt of this.

Unluckily all these positive assertions are contrary to that very experience which is pleaded for them, nor have we any idea of *self*, after the manner it is here explained. For from what impression could this idea be derived? This question 'tis impossible to answer without a manifest contradiction and absurdity; and yet 'tis a question, which must necessarily be answered, if we would have the idea of self pass for clear and intelligible. It must be some one impression, that gives rise to every real idea. But self or person is not any one impression, but that to which our several impressions and ideas are supposed to have a reference. If any impression gives rise to the idea of self, that impression must continue invariably the same through the whole course of our lives, since self is supposed to exist after that manner. But there is no impression constant and invariable. Pain and pleasure, grief and joy, passions and sensations succeed each other, and never all exist at the same time. It cannot, therefore, be from any of these impressions, or from any other, that the idea of self is derived; and consequently there is no such idea.

But farther, what must become of all our particular perceptions upon this hypothesis? All these are different, and distinguishable, and separable from each other, and may be separately considered, and may exist separately, and have no need of anything to support their existence. After what manner, therefore, do they belong to self; and how are they connected with it? For my part, when I enter most intimately into what I call *myself*, I always stumble on some particular perception or other, of heat or cold, light or shade, love or hatred, pain or pleasure. I never can catch *myself* at any time without a perception, and never can observe anything but the perception. When my perceptions are removed for any time, as by sound sleep, so long am I insensible of *myself*, and may truly be said not to exist. And were all my perceptions removed by death, and could I neither think, nor feel, nor see, nor love, nor hate after the dissolution of my body, I should be entirely annihilated, nor do I conceive what is farther requisite to make me a perfect nonentity. If anyone upon serious and unprejudiced reflection, thinks he has a different notion of *himself*, I must confess I can reason no longer with him. All I can allow him is, that he may be in the right as well as I, and that we are essentially different in this particular. He may, perhaps, perceive something simple and continued, which he calls *himself*; though I am certain there is no such principle in me.

But setting aside some metaphysicians of this kind, I may venture to affirm of the rest of mankind, that they are nothing but a bundle or collection of different perceptions, which succeed each other with an inconceivable rapidity, and are in a perpetual flux and movement. Our eyes cannot turn in their sockets without varying our perceptions. Our thought is still more variable than our sight; and all our other senses and faculties contribute to this change; nor is there any single power of the soul which remains unalterably the same, perhaps for one moment. The mind is a kind of theater, where several perceptions successively make their appearance: pass, re-pass, glide away, and mingle in an infinite variety of postures and situations. There is properly no *simplicity* in it at one time, nor *identity* in different; whatever natural propension we may have to imagine that simplicity and identity. The comparison of the theater must not mislead us. They are the successive perceptions only, that constitute the mind; nor have we the most distant notion of the place where these scenes are represented, or of the materials, of which it is composed. * * *

[PHILOSOPHY AND COMMON LIFE[3]]

But what have I here said, that reflections very refined and metaphysical have little or no influence upon us? This opinion I can scarce forbear retracting, and condemning from my present feeling and experience. The *intense* view of these manifold contradictions and imperfections in human reason has so wrought upon me, and heated my brain, that I am ready to reject all belief and reasoning, and can look upon no opinion even as more probable or likely than another. Where am I, or what? From what causes do I derive my existence, and to what condition shall I return? Whose favor shall I court, and whose anger must I dread? What beings surround me? and on whom have I any influence, or who have any influence on me? I am confounded with all these questions, and begin to fancy myself in the most deplorable condition imaginable, environed with the deepest darkness, and utterly deprived of the use of every member and faculty.

Most fortunately it happens, that since reason is incapable of dispelling these clouds, nature herself suffices to that purpose, and cures me of this philosophical melancholy and delirium, either by relaxing this bent of mind, or by some avocation and lively impression of my senses, which obliterate all these chimeras. I dine, I play a game of backgammon, I converse, and am merry with my friends; and when after three or four hour's amusement, I would return to these speculations, they appear so cold, and strained, and ridiculous, that I cannot find in my heart to enter into them any farther.

Here then I find myself absolutely and necessarily determined to live, and talk, and act like other people in the common affairs of life. But notwithstanding that my natural propensity, and the course of my animal spirits and passions, reduce me to this indolent belief in the general maxims of the world, I still feel such remains of my former disposition, that I am ready to throw all my books and papers into the fire, and resolve never more to renounce the pleasures of life for the sake of reasoning and philosophy. For these are my sentiments in that splenetic[4] humor, which governs me at present. I may, nay I must yield to the current of nature, in submitting to my senses and understanding; and in this blind submission I show most perfectly my skeptical disposition and principles. But does it follow, that I must strive against the current of nature, which leads me to indolence and pleasure; that I must seclude myself, in some measure, from the commerce and society of men, which is so agreeable; and that I must torture my brain with subtleties and sophistries, at the very time that I cannot satisfy myself concerning the reasonableness of so painful an application, nor have any tolerable prospect of arriving by its means at truth and certainty? Under what obligation do I lie of making such an abuse of time? And to what end can it serve either for the service of mankind, or for my own private interest? No: if I must be a fool, as well as those who reason or believe anything *certainly* are, my follies shall at least be natural and agreeable. Where I strive against my inclination, I shall have a good reason for my resistance; and will no more be led a wandering into such dreary solitudes, and rough passages, as I have hitherto met with.

---

3. From Book 1, Section 7: "Conclusion of This Book." The first book of the *Treatise* serves as a long prelude to the whole; in concluding it, Hume considers the "manifest contradictions" between the assumptions on which ordinary peole lead their lives, and the volatile questions raised by "refined reasoning" (rigorous philosophic inquiry). Pinpointing these contradictions in himself, he contemplates the precariousness of his enterprise, and the intricacy of his motives for undertaking it.

4. Depressive, irritable.

There are the sentiments of my spleen[5] and indolence; and indeed I must confess, that philosophy has nothing to oppose to them, and expects a victory more from the returns of a serious good-humored disposition, than from the force of reason and conviction. In all the incidents of life we ought still to preserve our skepticism. If we believe, that fire warms, or water refreshes, 'tis only because it costs us too much pains to think otherwise. Nay if we are philosophers, it ought only to be upon skeptical principles, and from an inclination, which we feel to the employing ourselves after that manner. Where reason is lively, and mixes itself with some propensity, it ought to be assented to. Where it does not, it never can have any title to operate upon us.

At the time, therefore, that I am tired with amusement and company, and have indulged a *reverie* in my chamber, or in a solitary walk by a riverside, I feel my mind all collected within itself, and am naturally *inclined* to carry my view into all those subjects, about which I have met with so many disputes in the course of my reading and conversation.[6] I cannot forbear having a curiosity to be acquainted with the principles of moral good and evil, the nature and foundation of government, and the cause of those several passions and inclinations, which actuate and govern me. I am uneasy to think I approve of one object, and disapprove of another; call one thing beautiful, and another deformed; decide concerning truth and falsehood, reason and folly, without knowing upon what principles I proceed. I am concerned for the condition of the learned world, which lies under such a deplorable ignorance in all these particulars. I feel an ambition to arise in me of contributing to the instruction of mankind, and of acquiring a name by my inventions and discoveries. These sentiments spring up naturally in my present disposition; and should I endeavor to banish them, by attaching myself to any other business or diversion, I *feel* I should be a loser in point of pleasure; and this is the origin of my philosophy.

1734–1737   1739–1740

from An Enquiry Concerning Human Understanding[1]
from *Section 10: Of Miracles*

A miracle is a violation of the laws of nature; and as a firm and unalterable experience has established these laws, the proof against a miracle, from the very nature of the fact, is as entire as any argument from experience can possibly be imagined. Why is it more than probable that all men must die; that lead cannot, of itself, remain suspended in the air; that fire consumes wood, and is extinguished by water; unless it be, that these events are found agreeable to the laws of nature, and there is required a violation of these laws, or in other words, a miracle to prevent them? Nothing is esteemed a miracle, if it ever happen in the common course of nature. It is no miracle that a man, seemingly in good health, should die on a sudden; because such a kind of death, though more unusual than any other, has yet been frequently observed to happen. But it is a miracle that a dead man should come to life; because that has never been observed in any age or country. There must, therefore, be a uniform experience

---

5. Despondency.
6. In the list that follows, Hume names many of the topics he will take up later in the *Treatise.*
1. Hume wrote this essay in the mid–1730s, intending to include it in his *Treatise;* conscious of its volatility, he withheld it for a dozen years, publishing it for the first

time in his *Philosophical Essays Concerning Human Understanding* (1748); ten years later a revised version of the work appeared, under the new title *An Enquiry. . . .* The essay proved at least as explosive as he had anticipated, prompting a spate of refutations; for Samuel Johnson's and James Boswell's views, see page 2846.

against every miraculous event, otherwise the event would not merit that appellation. And as a uniform experience amounts to a proof, there is here a direct and full *proof*, from the nature of the fact, against the existence of any miracle; nor can such a proof be destroyed, or the miracle rendered credible, but by an opposite proof, which is superior.

The plain consequence is (and it is a general maxim worthy of our attention), "That no testimony is sufficient to establish a miracle, unless the testimony be of such a kind, that its falsehood would be more miraculous than the fact which it endeavors to establish; and even in that case there is a mutual destruction of arguments, and the superior only gives us an assurance suitable to that degree of force which remains after deducting the inferior." When anyone tells me, that he saw a dead man restored to life, I immediately consider with myself, whether it be more probable, that this person should either deceive or be deceived, or that the fact, which he relates, should really have happened. I weigh the one miracle against the other; and according to the superiority which I discover, I pronounce my decision, and always reject the greater miracle. If the falsehood of his testimony would be more miraculous than the event which he relates, then, and not till then, can he pretend to command my belief or opinion.

In the foregoing reasoning we have supposed, that the testimony, upon which a miracle is founded, may possibly amount to an entire proof, and that the falsehood of that testimony would be a real prodigy. But it is easy to show that we have been a great deal too liberal in our concession, and that there never was a miraculous event established on so full an evidence.

For *first*, there is not to be found, in all history, any miracle attested by a sufficient number of men, of such unquestioned good sense, education, and learning, as to secure us against all delusion in themselves; of such undoubted integrity, as to place them beyond all suspicion of any design to deceive others; of such credit and reputation in the eyes of mankind, as to have a great deal to lose in case of their being detected in any falsehood; and at the same time, attesting facts performed in such a public manner and in so celebrated a part of the world, as to render the detection unavoidable. All which circumstances are requisite to give us a full assurance in the testimony of men.

Secondly. We may observe in human nature a principle which, if strictly examined, will be found to diminish extremely the assurance which we might, from human testimony, have, in any kind of prodigy. The maxim by which we commonly conduct ourselves in our reasonings is that the objects of which we have no experience resemble those of which we have; that what we have found to be most usual is always most probable; and that where there is an opposition of arguments, we ought to give the preference to such as are founded on the greatest number of past observations. But though, in proceeding by this rule, we readily reject any fact which is unusual and incredible in an ordinary degree; yet in advancing farther, the mind observes not always the same rule; but when anything is affirmed utterly absurd and miraculous, it rather the more readily admits of such a fact, upon account of that very circumstance which ought to destroy all its authority. The passion of *surprise* and *wonder*, arising from miracles, being an agreeable emotion, gives a sensible tendency towards the belief of those events from which it is derived. And this goes so far, that even those who cannot enjoy this pleasure immediately, nor can believe those miraculous events, of which they are informed, yet love to partake of the satisfaction at second-hand or by rebound, and place a pride and delight in exciting the admiration of others.

With what greediness are the miraculous accounts of travelers received, their descriptions of sea and land monsters, their relations of wonderful adventures, strange men, and uncouth manners? But if the spirit of religion join itself to the love of wonder, there is an end of common sense; and human testimony, in these circumstances, loses all pretensions to authority. A religionist may be an enthusiast,[2] and imagine he sees what has no reality. He may know his narrative to be false, and yet persevere in it, with the best intentions in the world, for the sake of promoting so holy a cause; or even where this delusion has not place, vanity, excited by so strong a temptation, operates on him more powerfully than on the rest of mankind in any other circumstances; and self-interest with equal force. His auditors may not have, and commonly have not, sufficient judgment to canvass his evidence. What judgment they have, they renounce by principle, in these sublime and mysterious subjects; or if they were ever so willing to employ it, passion and a heated imagination disturb the regularity of its operations. Their credulity increases his impudence; and his impudence overpowers their credulity. * * *

Thirdly. It forms a strong presumption against all supernatural and miraculous relations, that they are observed chiefly to abound among ignorant and barbarous nations; or if a civilized people has ever given admission to any of them, that people will be found to have received them from ignorant and barbarous ancestors, who transmitted them with that inviolable sanction and authority, which always attend received opinions. When we peruse the first histories of all nations, we are apt to imagine ourselves transported into some new world, where the whole frame of nature is disjointed, and every element performs its operations in a different manner from what it does at present. Battles, revolutions, pestilence, famine, and death are never the effect of those natural causes which we experience. Prodigies, omens, oracles, judgments, quite obscure the few natural events that are intermingled with them. But as the former grow thinner every page, in proportion as we advance nearer the enlightened ages, we soon learn that there is nothing mysterious or supernatural in the case, but that all proceeds from the usual propensity of mankind towards the marvelous, and that, though this inclination may at intervals receive a check from sense and learning, it can never be thoroughly extirpated from human nature. * * *

Upon the whole, then, it appears that no testimony for any kind of miracle has ever amounted to a probability, much less to a proof; and that, even supposing it amounted to a proof, it would be opposed by another proof; derived from the very nature of the fact, which it would endeavor to establish. It is experience only which gives authority to human testimony; and it is the same experience which assures us of the laws of nature. When, therefore, these two kinds of experience are contrary, we have nothing to do but subtract the one from the other, and embrace an opinion, either on one side or the other, with that assurance which arises from the remainder. But according to the principle here explained, this subtraction, with regard to all popular religions, amounts to an entire annihilation; and therefore we may establish it as a maxim, that no human testimony can have such force as to prove a miracle, and make it a just foundation for any such system of religion. * * *

What we have said of miracles may be applied, without any variation, to prophecies; and indeed, all prophecies are real miracles, and as such only can be admitted as proofs of any revelation. If it did not exceed the capacity of human nature to foretell future events, it would be absurd to employ any prophecy as an argument for a divine

---

2. Fanatic.

mission or authority from heaven. So that, upon the whole, we may conclude, that
the *Christian religion* not only was at first attended with miracles, but even at this day
cannot be believed by any reasonable person without one. Mere reason is insufficient
to convince us of its veracity. And whoever is moved by *faith* to assent to it, is conscious of a continued miracle in his own person, which subverts all the principles of
his understanding, and gives him a determination to believe what is most contrary to
custom and experience.

c. 1736   1748

Christopher Smart
1722–1771

"Newton . . . is more of error than of the truth, but I am of the Word of God," wrote Christopher Smart in his astonishing poem *Jubilate Agno* ("Rejoice in the Lamb"). For Smart, as for a
growing number of Christians in the century's second half, the Newtonian "error" consisted in
a commitment to materialist science, to an empiricism that investigated the physical world
and sought its seeming system, rather than submitting to faith in a God who worked by will
and sometimes by miracle, free of any fixed laws of nature. Smart composed *Jubilate Agno* in his
late thirties, while confined in a madhouse; after a brilliant career as a classical scholar at
Cambridge, and an auspicious start in London as a literary adventurer (poet, editor, translator,
essayist), he suffered a derangement whose chief symptom was his compulsion to pray spontaneously in public places (he was too much "of the Word of God" to be socially acceptable).
Released from the asylum after five years, Smart recast much material from the *Jubilate Agno* in
his *Song of David* (1763); following Watts's precedent, he published a translation of the Psalms
(1767) and (while imprisoned for debt at the very end of his life) a book of *Hymns for the
Amusement of Children* (1771). *Jubilate Agno* remained in manuscript and unknown for a century and a half after the poet's death. Smart called it "my Magnificat," *magnificat* being the title
of the liturgical hymn first uttered by the Virgin Mary upon learning that she would conceive
a son: "My Soul doth magnify the Lord" (Luke 1.46–55). Structured like a responsive prayer,
Smart's poem moves rapidly across a wide range of reference, from the scriptural and mystical
to the local and the homely ("God be gracious to Baumgarden"—a London bassoon player).
But Smart returns repeatedly to a preoccupation touched on in the poem's title: to the animal
world as emblem and embodiment of God's grace and greatness (in Smart's time natural history was among the branches of knowledge least touched by the new science, and most inflected
by faith and folklore). In the excerpts that follow, Smart punningly pinpoints the animal
essences of languages ancient and modern, then depicts the feline who kept him company during his years of confinement, singing Jeoffry's praises with such exuberance as to make *magnificat* seem a latent, sacred, and affectionate pun.

from **Jubilate Agno**
[ANIMALS IN LANGUAGE[1]]

625   For the power of some animal is predominant in every language.
         For the power and spirit of a CAT is in the Greek.

---

1. These selections come from Fragment B of Smart's manuscript. Some pages of Smart's manuscript contain long
sequences of lines beginning "Let"; other pages contain lines beginning "For," with clear enough indications that the
"Let" and "For" lines were meant to be dovetailed and read alternately, in the form of responsive prayer. For the two
excerpts printed here, though, lines beginning "Let" have not been found—and may never have been written.

For the sound of a cat is in the most useful preposition κατ' ευχην.[2]

For the pleasantry of a cat at pranks is in the language ten thousand times over.[3]

For JACK UPON PRANCK is in the performance of περι together or separate.[4]

630 For Clapperclaw[5] is in the grappling of the words upon one another in all the modes of versification.

For the sleekness of a Cat is in his αγλαιηφι.[6]

For the Greek is thrown from heaven and falls upon its feet.[7]

For the Greek when distracted from the line is sooner restored to rank and rallied into some form than any other.

For the purring of a Cat is his τρυζει.[8]

635 For his cry is in ουαι,[9] which I am sorry for.

For the Mouse (Mus) prevails in the Latin.[1]

For *Edi-mus, bibi-mus, vivi-mus—ore-mus.*[2]

For the Mouse is a creature of great personal valor.

For—this is a true case—Cat takes female mouse from the company of male—male mouse will not depart, but stands threat'ning and daring.

640 For this is as much as to challenge, if you will let her go, I will engage you, as prodigious a creature as you are.

For the Mouse is of an hospitable disposition.

For bravery and hospitality were said and done by the Romans rather than others.

For two creatures the Bull and the Dog prevail in the English.

For all the words ending in -ble are in the creature. Invisi-ble, Incompre-hensi-ble, ineffa-ble, A-ble.

645 For the Greek and Latin are not dead languages, but taken up and accepted for the sake of him that spoke them.

For can is (*canis*[3]) is cause and effect a dog.

For the English is concise and strong. Dog and Bull again.

For Newton's notion of colors is αλογος,[4] unphilosophical.

[MY CAT JEOFFRY]

695 For I will consider my Cat Jeoffry.

For he is the servant of the Living God duly and daily serving him.

For at the first glance of the glory of God in the East he worships in his way.

For is this done by wreathing his body seven times round with elegant quickness.

For then he leaps up to catch the musk, which is the blessing of God upon his prayer.

700 For he rolls upon prank to work it in.

For having done duty and received blessing he begins to consider himself.

For this he performs in ten degrees.

For first he looks upon his fore-paws to see if they are clean.

For secondly he kicks up behind to clear away there.

2. Greek *kat' euchen:* "according to prayer."
3. The syllable *kat* appears in many word forms.
4. Greek *perikato* means "upside down" (as, probably, does "Jack Upon Pranck").
5. To claw, scratch.
6. *Aglaiefi:* "beauty."
7. Perhaps an allusion to the Greek poetic term *catalexis,* the shortening or omission of a "foot" from a line of verse; the prefix *cata-* means "down."

8. *Truzei:* "murmur."
9. *Ouai:* exclamation of lament ("ah!").
1. Partly because (as Smart illustrates in line 637), the syllable *mus* means "mouse" and is also the suffix for first person plural present-tense conjugations.
2. "We eat, we drink, we live—let us pray."
3. Latin: dog.
4. *Alogos:* literally, "without the Word."

705   For thirdly he works it upon stretch with the fore-paws extended.
     For fourthly he sharpens his paws by wood.
     For fifthly he washes himself.
     For sixthly he rolls upon wash.
     For seventhly he fleas himself, that he may not be interrupted upon the beat.
710   For eighthly he rubs himself against a post.
     For ninthly he looks up for his instructions.
     For tenthly he goes in quest of food.
     For having considered God and himself he will consider his neighbor.
     For if he meets another cat he will kiss her in kindness.
715   For when he takes his prey he plays with it to give it chance.
     For one mouse in seven escapes by his dallying.
     For when his day's work is done his business more properly begins.
     For he keeps the Lord's watch in the night against the adversary.
     For he counteracts the powers of darkness by his electrical skin and glar-
        ing eyes.
720   For he counteracts the Devil, who is death, by brisking about the life.
     For in his morning orisons he loves the sun and the sun loves him.
     For he is of the tribe of Tiger.
     For the Cherub Cat is a term of the Angel Tiger.
     For he has the subtlety and hissing of a serpent, which in goodness he
        suppresses.
725   For he will not do destruction, if he is well-fed, neither will he spit without
        provocation.
     For he purrs in thankfulness, when God tells him he's a good Cat.
     For he is an instrument for the children to learn benevolence upon.
     For every house is incomplete without him and a blessing is lacking in
        the spirit.
     For the Lord commanded Moses concerning the cats at the departure of the
        Children of Israel from Egypt.[5]
730   For every family had one cat at least in the bag.
     For the English Cats are the best in Europe.
     For he is the cleanest in the use of his fore-paws of any quadrupede.
     For the dexterity of his defense is an instance of the love of God to him
        exceedingly.
     For he is the quickest to his mark of any creature.
735   For he is tenacious of his point.
     For he is a mixture of gravity and waggery.
     For he knows that God is his Savior.
     For there is nothing sweeter than his peace when at rest.
     For there is nothing brisker than his life when in motion.
740   For he is of the Lord's poor and so indeed is he called by benevolence per-
        petually—Poor Jeoffry! poor Jeoffry! the rat has bit thy throat.
     For I bless the name of the Lord Jesus that Jeoffry is better.
     For the divine spirit comes about his body to sustain it in complete cat.
     For his tongue is exceeding pure so that it has in purity what it wants in music.
     For he is docile and can learn certain things.
745   For he can set up with gravity which is patience upon approbation.

---

5. "Take your flocks and your herds," says the Egyptian Pharaoh when demanding the Israelites' departure (Exodus 12.32); Smart adds the Lord and the cats.

For he can fetch and carry, which is patience in employment.
For he can jump over a stick which is patience upon proof positive.
For he can spraggle° upon waggle at the word of command.   *sprawl*
For he can jump from an eminence into his master's bosom.
750   For he can catch the cork and toss it again.
For he is hated by the hypocrite and miser.
For the former is afraid of detection.
For the latter refuses the charge.
For he camels his back to bear the first notion of business.
755   For he is good to think on, if a man would express himself neatly.
For he made a great figure in Egypt for his signal services.
For he killed the Ichneumon-rat° very pernicious by land.   *mongoose*
For his ears are so acute that they sting again.
For from this proceeds the passing quickness of his attention.
760   For by stroking of him I have found out electricity.
For I perceived God's light about him both wax and fire.
For the Electrical fire is the spiritual substance, which God sends from
    heaven to sustain the bodies both of man and beast.
For God has blessed him in the variety of his movements.
For, though he cannot fly, he is an excellent clamberer.
765   For his motions upon the face of the earth are more than any other
    quadrupede.
For he can tread to all the measures upon the music.
For he can swim for life.
For he can creep.

c. 1758–1763   1939

William Cowper
1731–1800

Like Christopher Smart, William Cowper suffered madness, loved animals, wrote hymns, and invented capacious new structures for religious verse. But where Smart wrote to celebrate his sure salvation, Cowper wrote out of the certainty that he was damned—unworthy of redemption and predestined for hellfire. The conviction first took hold in 1763, when a paralyzing panic cut him off from impending attachments (to a new job he was about to secure, a beloved woman he was soon to marry) and prompted several attempts at suicide. The course of recovery took him first to an asylum, then through a conversion to Calvinism, then to the household of Mary Unwin, who loved and looked after him for the next four decades, and finally into partnership with Unwin's neighbor, the austere hymn-writer John Newton, with whom Cowper collaborated for years on a new collection of religious song, the *Olney Hymns* (it included, along with several of Cowper's still-sung texts, Newton's perdurable *Amazing Grace*). A second, sharper attack of madness, ten years after the first, deepened Cowper's conviction of his doom but also ushered in years of plentiful poetic composition. Seizing any small occasion (a fish dinner, the death of a pet bird) to produce a short, often comic piece of verse, Cowper wrote poems to hold terror at bay. As his output increased, his ambition did too. *The Task*, a massive mock epic grounded in the comforts of Cowper's rural retirement (sofa, garden, seasons) but ranging satirically over the whole wide world, surprised even its author by its scope and popularity. Spurred by its success, Cowper undertook to translate Homer's epics, hoping to surpass Pope's attempts earlier in the century. In a passage near the midpoint of *The Task* (printed here), Newton appears briefly as the embodiment of Cowper's deepest hope, that the mind might merge with God through a science immersed in faith—"philosophy baptized." In his last, autobiographical poem, *The Cast-away*, Cowper draws a darker picture, of a mind sundered from its maker by distance and despair.

Light Shining out of Darkness[1]

God moves in a mysterious way,
    His wonders to perform;
He plants his footsteps in the sea,
    And rides upon the storm.

5   Deep in unfathomable mines
    Of never-failing skill,
He treasures up his bright designs,
    And works his sov'reign will.

Ye fearful saints[2] fresh courage take,
10   The clouds ye so much dread
Are big with mercy, and shall break
    In blessings on your head.

Judge not the Lord by feeble sense,
    But trust him for his grace;
15   Behind a frowning providence,
    He hides a smiling face.

His purposes will ripen fast,
    Unfolding every hour;
The bud may have a bitter taste,
20   But sweet will be the flower.

Blind unbelief is sure to err,
    And scan his work in vain;
God is his own interpreter,
    And he will make it plain.

c. 1773   1774

from The Task
["PHILOSOPHY BAPTIZED"[1]]

God never meant that man should scale the heav'ns
By strides of human wisdom. In his works
Though wond'rous, he commands us in his word
To seek *him* rather, where his mercy shines.
225   The mind indeed enlightened from above
Views him in all. Ascribes to the grand cause
The grand effect. Acknowledges with joy
His manner, and with rapture tastes his style.
But never yet did philosophic° tube   *scientific*

---

1. Written and first published during the period of Cowper's collaboration with John Newton; later included in their *Olney Hymns* (1779).
2. Cowper addresses those who (according to Calvinist theology) are predestined for salvation.

1. From Book 3, "The Garden" (for more of *The Task*, see pages 2704–07).

230   That brings the planets home into the eye
       Of observation, and discovers, else°   *otherwise*
       Not visible, his family of worlds,
       Discover him that rules them; such a veil
       Hangs over mortal eyes, blind from the birth
235   And dark in things divine. Full often too
       Our wayward intellect, the more we learn
       Of nature, overlooks her author more,
       From instrumental causes proud to draw
       Conclusions retrograde and mad mistake.
240   But if his word once teach us, shoot a ray
       Through all the heart's dark chambers, and reveal
       Truths undiscerned but by that holy light,
       Then all is plain. Philosophy baptized
       In the pure fountain of eternal love
245   Has eyes indeed; and viewing all she sees
       As meant to indicate a God to man,
       Gives *him* his praise, and forfeits not her own.
       Learning has borne such fruit in other days
       On all her branches. Piety has found
250   Friends in the friends of science, and true prayer
       Has flowed from lips wet with Castalian dews.[2]
       Such was thy wisdom, Newton, childlike sage!
       Sagacious reader of the works of God,
       And in his word sagacious. * * *

1783–1785   1785

The Cast-away[1]

    Obscurest night involved° the sky,   *encompassed*
       Th' Atlantic billows roared,
    When such a destined° wretch as I   *doomed*
       Washed headlong from on board
5   Of friends, of hope, of all beret,
       His floating home for ever left.

    No braver chief[2] could Albion° boast   *Britain*
       Than he with whom he went,
    Nor ever ship left Albion's coast
10   With warmer wishes sent.
       He loved them both, but both in vain,
       Nor him beheld, nor her again.

    Not long beneath the whelming brine
       Expert to swim, he lay,

---

2. I.e., from poets (who have drunk of the inspirational Castalian spring on the mountain of the Muses).

1. Cowper based this poem on a mariner's account, in a popular travel book, of having watched helplessly as a shipmate was hurled overboard during a storm: "We were the more grieved at his unhappy fate, as we . . . conceived from the manner in which he swam that he might continue sensible, for a considerable time longer, of the hor-

ror attending his irretrievable situation." Cowper collates the doomed man's situation with his own, which he conceived as also "irretrievable"; the poem, left in manuscript at his death, is his last surviving original poem in English.

2. George Anson, commander of the naval squadron in which the sailor was lost.

15   Nor soon he felt his strength decline
            Or courage die away;
        But waged with Death a lasting strife
        Supported by despair of life.

        He shouted, nor his friends had failed
20   To check the vessel's course,
        But so the furious blast prevailed
            That, pitiless perforce,
        They left their outcast mate behind,
        And scudded still before the wind.

25   Some succor yet they could afford,
            And, such as storms allow,
        The cask, the coop, the floated cord
            Delayed not to bestow;
        But he, they knew, nor ship nor shore,
30   Whate'er they gave, should visit more.

        Nor, cruel as it seemed, could he
            Their haste, himself, condemn,
        Aware that flight, in such a sea,
            Alone could rescue them;
35   Yet bitter felt it still to die
        Deserted, and his friends so nigh.

        He long survives who lives an hour
            In ocean, self-upheld,
        And so long he, with unspent power,
40   His destiny repelled,
        And ever, as the minutes flew,
        Entreated help, or cried, Adieu!

        At length, his transient respite past,
            His comrades, who before
45   Had heard his voice in every blast,
            Could catch the sound no more;
        For then, by toil subdued, he drank
        The stifling wave, and then he sank.

        No poet wept him: but the page
50   Of narrative[3] sincere
        That tells his name, his worth,° his age,   rank
            Is wet with Anson's tear,
        And tears by bards or heroes shed
        Alike immortalize the dead.

55   I therefore purpose not or dream,
            Descanting on his fate,
        To give the melancholy theme
            A more enduring date,

3. The log book of the ship from which he fell.

But misery still delights to trace
60   Its semblance in another's case.

No voice divine the storm allayed,
     No light propitious shone,
When, snatched from all effectual aid,
     We perished, each, alone;
65   But I beneath a rougher sea,
And whelmed in deeper gulphs than he.
1799   1804

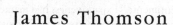

—⟶+ END OF PERSPECTIVES: MIND AND GOD +⟵—

James Thomson
1700–1748

"Nature delights me in every form," James Thomson declared in a letter at age twenty-five. "I am just now painting her in her most lugubrious dress; for my own amusement describing winter as it presents itself." Though he may not have known it yet, he was "just now" embarking on his life's central work. In his long poem *The Seasons* (of which this piece on winter was the earliest installment), Thomson sought to develop a poetic structure capacious enough to compass the varied forms of nature in which he took so much delight.

Thomson wrote his letter in London, where he had recently arrived, to a friend in his native Scotland, where he would never return. The winters he remembered were those of the terrain where he had spent his first fifteen years, in a village near the border with England. When Thomson was seven, geographical proximity became political reality. The Act of Union, energetically endorsed by the poet's Whig neighbors, linked Scotland with England and Wales to form the new entity of Great Britain; that event resonates throughout the poet's life and work, in his depictions of nature (which remain centered in Scotland even as they span the globe), in his passionate advocacy of the politics he'd absorbed in youth, in his celebration of the incipient British empire.

Born to a Presbyterian minister praised for his "diligence," and to a mother noted for her "imagination," "warmth," and enthusiastic piety, Thomson felt toward both parents a lifelong affection. In deference to their wishes, and despite an early inclination to poetry, he initially planned to follow his father into the ministry. But Edinburgh, where he went at age fifteen to study divinity, abounded in literary aspirants, endeavors, publications, and societies. During his ten years there, Thomson gradually found that the attractions of poetry outflanked those of professional piety. Like many ambitious Scotsmen of the time, Thomson headed for London, along the route the Union had made smooth. There, aided and encouraged by new literary friends (Pope and Gay among them), he launched the poem of nature that he describes in his letter home. *Winter* (1726) was followed by *Summer* and *Spring* (both 1727); *The Seasons* (1730) brought the cycle to completion, with the new piece on *Autumn* added to the three earlier sections, now much expanded and revised. The work struck readers and reviewers as something altogether new, and quickly established the poet's fame. The following years produced another long poem, equally ambitious but less successful (*Liberty*, 1735–1736), a series of verse tragedies, and a plenitude of distractions. Thomson engaged exuberantly in politics and in the pleasures of food and drink, cherished his friends, and fell in love with women who did not love him back. The years also brought recurrent returns of *The Seasons*: the poem reappeared, in a greatly enlarged and altered edition, in 1744, and in yet another incarnation two years later. In *The Castle of Indolence* (1748), Thomson produced an allegory, by turns serious and comic, on that very propensity toward imaginative idleness that had both generated his poetry and prevented his producing more. The poem, deeply autobiographical, proved valedictory as well. Four months after its publication the poet died, mourned by his many friends as "our old, tried, amiable, open, and honest-hearted Thomson," and by a wider world of readers as the writer who had newly transmuted nature into language, in the century's single most popular poem.

The Seasons often gave rise to a measure of puzzlement commingled with its popularity. Thomson had set so much going in the poem that familiar conventions of artistic order and containment seemed overthrown. "The great defect of *The Seasons*," Samuel Johnson opined, "is its want of method"—its lack of a self-evident logical structure. Still, reader after reader (including Johnson) discovered that this seeming defect correlated mysteriously with the poem's many pleasures: its comprehensiveness, its range of tones and modes, its contagious "enthusiasm," whereby (in Johnson's account) "our thoughts expand with [Thomson's] imagery and kindle with his sentiments." Expansiveness had marked the poem's making as well as its impact. During two decades of creation and revision, Thomson kept nature at the center of his scrutiny, but made it the repository for his many preoccupations: Whig politics, imperial expansion, ancient history, Christian faith, modern science. The poem links and navigates all these topics not so much by "method" as by the restless motion of the maker's mind. In this innovative arrangement, the physical world becomes a medium of meditation, a mirror of mind and culture, the meeting place where human inquiry most fully encounters divine display, in order to discern and to wonder at the ways of both self and God. Like his idol Isaac Newton, whose discoveries pervade the poem, Thomson was reading and representing God's Book of Nature in new, immensely influential terms. "Enthusiasm" itself means immersion "in the God," possession by the divine. Thomson makes good on the term when he declares at the poem's close that the seasons "are but the varied God," phenomena that mortals must inhabit and observe with deep discernment, proper awe. Thomson's own enthusiasm proved contagious across boundaries of space, time, and medium. His poem was translated and ardently imitated in most of the languages of Europe; the composer Franz Joseph Haydn set its sentiments to music, and draughtsmen depicted its scenes so often that it remained for a hundred years the most illustrated work in English. For writers of many nations and several generations, *The Seasons* served as almost inexhaustible sourcebook, as supplementary Scripture.

from **Winter. A Poem**[1]

[AUTUMN EVENING AND NIGHT]

See! Winter comes, to rule the varied year,
Sullen and sad; with all his rising train,
Vapors, and clouds, and storms. Be these my theme,
These, that exalt the soul to solemn thought,
5   And heavenly musing. Welcome kindred glooms!
Wished, wintery horrors, hail! With frequent foot,
Pleased have I, in my cheerful morn of life,
When nursed by careless solitude I lived,
And sung of Nature with unceasing joy,
10   Pleased have I wandered through your rough domains;
Trod the pure, virgin-snows, myself as pure;

1. This was the earliest version Thomson published; for some of his subsequent revisions, see the selection from *Autumn* on pages 2692–96.

Heard the winds roar, and the big torrent burst;
Or seen the deep-fermenting tempest brewed
In the red evening sky. Thus passed the time
15 Till, through the opening chambers of the south,[2]
Looked out the joyous Spring, looked out, and smiled.

    Thee too, inspirer of the toiling swain!
Fair Autumn, yellow robed! I'll sing of thee,
Of thy last, tempered days and sunny calms;
20 When all the golden hours are on the wing,
Attending thy retreat, and round thy wain,°   *chariot*
Slow-rolling, onward to the southern sky.

    Behold![3] the well-poised hornet, hovering, hangs
With quivering pinions in the genial blaze;
25 Flies off in airy circles; then returns
And hums and dances to the beating ray.
Nor shall the man that, musing, walks alone,
And, heedless, strays within his radiant lists,°   *boundaries*
Go unchastised away. Sometimes a fleece
30 Of clouds, wide-scattering, with a lucid[4] veil,
Soft, shadow o'er th' unruffled face of heaven;
And, through their dewy sluices,° shed the sun,   *floodgates*
With tempered influence down. Then is the time,
For those, whom Wisdom, and whom Nature charm,
35 To steal themselves from the degenerate crowd,
And soar above this little scene of things:
To tread low-thoughted Vice beneath their feet:
To lay their passions in a gentle calm,
And woo lone Quiet, in her silent walks.

40   Now solitary, and in pensive guise,
Oft let me wander o'er the russet mead,°   *meadow*
Or through the pining grove, where scarce is heard
One dying strain, to cheer the woodman's toil.
Sad Philomel,[5] perchance, pours forth her plaint
45 Far through the withering copse.° Meanwhile the leaves,   *woods*
That late the forest clad with lively green,
Nipped by the drizzly night, and sallow-hued,
Fall wavering through the air; or shower amain,°   *fiercely*
Urged by the breeze, that sobs amid the boughs.
50 Then listening hares forsake the rustling woods,
And, starting at the frequent noise, escape
To the rough stubble, and the rushy fen.°   *marsh*
Then woodcocks o'er the fluctuating main
That glimmers to the glimpses of the moon
55 Stretch their long voyage to the woodland glade;
Where, wheeling with uncertain flight, they mock

2. The southern sky, "opening" as clouds dissipate.
3. In *The Seasons*, Thomson transferred this passage (lines 23–79), extensively revised, to *Autumn* (lines 955–1036; see pages 2692–94).
4. The adjective meant both "shining" and "transparent."
5. The nightingale. In Greek myth, the Athenian princess Philomela, raped by her brother-in-law Tereus, is transformed into a bird and nightly laments her fate.

The nimble fowler's° aim. Now Nature droops;   *bird hunter's*
Languish the living herbs, with pale decay:
And all the various family of flowers
60   Their sunny robes resign. The falling fruits,
Through the still night, forsake the parent bough
That in the first gray glances of the dawn,
Looks wild, and wonders at the wintry waste.

          The year, yet pleasing, but declining fast,
65   Soft, o'er the secret soul, in gentle gales,
A philosophic melancholy breathes,
And bears the swelling thought aloft to heaven.
Then forming fancy rouses to conceive,
What never mingled with the vulgar's° dream: *common people's*
70   Then wake the tender pang, the pitying tear,
The sigh for suffering worth, the wish preferred°   *offered up*
For humankind, the joy to see them blessed,
And all the social offspring of the heart!

          Oh! bear me then to high embowering shades;
75   To twilight groves and visionary vales;
To weeping grottos and to hoary caves;
Where angel forms are seen, and voices heard,
Sighed in low whispers that abstract the soul
From outward sense far into worlds remote.

80   Now,[6] when the western sun withdraws the day,
And humid evening, gliding o'er the sky,
In her chill progress checks the straggling beams,
And robs them of their gathered, vapory prey,
Where marshes stagnate, and where rivers wind,
85   Cluster the rolling fogs, and swim along
The dusky-mantled lawn:° then slow descend,   *open ground*
Once more to mingle with their watery friends.
The vivid stars shine out, in radiant files;
And boundless ether[7] glows; till the fair moon
90   Shows her broad visage, in the crimsoned east;
Now, stooping, seems to kiss the passing cloud:
Now, o'er the pure cerulean,[8] rides sublime.
Wide the pale deluge floats, with silver waves,
O'er the skied° mountain, to the low-laid vale;   *sky-high*
95   From the white rocks, with dim reflection, gleams,
And faintly glitters through the waving shades.

          All night, abundant dews, unnoted, fall,
And, at return of morning, silver o'er
The face of Mother Earth; from every branch
100   Depending,° tremble the translucent gems,   *hanging*
And, quivering, seem to fall away, yet cling,

6. In *The Seasons*, this passage (lines 80–103) appeared, revised, in *Autumn* (lines 1082–1102; see page 2695).
7. "An element more fine and subtle than air" (Johnson's *Dictionary*); it was assumed to fill the highest regions above the earth.
8. Deep blue (of the evening sky).

And sparkle in the sun, whose rising eye,
With fogs bedimmed, portends a beauteous day.

* * *

[WINTER NIGHT]

Now, all amid the rigors of the year,
In the wild depth of winter, while without
255   The ceaseless winds blow keen, be my retreat
A rural, sheltered, solitary scene;
Where ruddy fire and beaming tapers join
To chase the cheerless gloom. There let me sit,
And hold high converse with the mighty dead—
260   Sages of ancient time, as gods revered,
As gods beneficent, who blessed mankind
With arts and arms, and humanized a world.
Roused at th' inspiring thought, I throw aside
The long-lived volume[9] and, deep-musing, hail
265   The sacred shades that slowly rising pass
Before my wondering eyes. First Socrates,[1]
Truth's early champion, martyr for his God;
Solon[2] the next, who built his commonweal
On equity's firm base. Lycurgus[3] then,
270   Severely good; and him of rugged Rome,
Numa,[4] who softened her rapacious sons.
Cimon sweet-souled, and Aristides[5] just.
Unconquered Cato,[6] virtuous in extreme;
With that attempered hero,[7] mild and firm,
275   Who wept the brother while the tyrant bled.
Scipio[8] the humane warrior, gently brave,
Fair learning's friend, who early sought the shade,
To dwell, with innocence, and truth, retired.
And, equal to the best, the Theban,[9] he
280   Who, single, raised his country into fame.
Thousands behind, the boast of Greece and Rome,
Whom virtue owns, the tribute of a verse
Demand, but who can count the stars of heaven?
Who sing their influence on this lower world?
285   But see who yonder comes! nor comes alone,

9. Plutarch's Lives: biographies of eminent Greeks and Romans—composed by the Greek historian and philosopher (c. A.D. 46–120).
1. Socrates (469–399 B.C.), Athenian philospher, condemned to death for his teachings.
2. Solon (639–558 B.C.), Athenian statesman who introduced a newly humane system of laws.
3. Legendary Spartan lawgiver.
4. Rome's legendary second king, deemed a better ruler than the founder Romulus because his long reign was peaceful and enlightened.
5. Cimon (c. 510–449 B.C.) and Aristeides (d. 468 B.C.), military leaders and statesmen noted for their victorious strategies in the Persian Wars and for their rectitude in government.

6. Marcus Porcius Cato (96–46 B.C.), Roman champion of republican government; he chose to commit suicide rather than surrender himself to Julius Caesar, whose imperial ambitions he had resisted in the Roman civil wars.
7. Timoleon, a Corinthian who, alarmed at the tyrannical aspirations of his brother Timophanes, conspired in his assassination (365 B.C.), during which he wept for the kin he had helped to kill.
8. Scipio Africanus (236–183 B.C.), charismatic Roman general, conqueror of Spain and defeater of Hannibal.
9. Either Pelopidas (c. 410–364 B.C.) or Epaminondas (d. 362 B.C.), military tacticians who led Thebes to victory over Sparta.

With sober state, and of majestic mien,
The Sister-Muses in his train. 'Tis he!
— Maro![1] the best of poets, and of men!
Great Homer too appears, of daring wing!
290   Parent of song! and equal by this side,
The British Muse,[2] joined hand in hand, they walk,
Darkling,[3] nor miss their way to fame's ascent.

Society divine! Immortal minds!
Still visit thus my nights, for you reserved,
295   And mount my soaring soul to deeds like yours.
Silence! thou lonely power! the door be thine:
See, on the hallowed hour, that none intrude,
Save Lycidas,[4] the friend, with sense refined,
Learning digested well, exalted faith,
300   Unstudied wit, and humor ever gay.

1725–1726   1726

from The Seasons

from *Autumn*

[NIGHTFALL AND NIGHT[1]]

950   But see the fading many-colored woods,
Shade deepening over shade, the country round
Imbrown; a crowded umbrage,° dusk and dun,   *shade*
Of every hue from wan declining green
To sooty dark. These now the lonesome Muse,
955   Low-whispering, lead into their leaf-strewn walks,
And give the season in its latest view.[2]
Meantime,[3] light shadowing all, a sober calm
Fleeces unbound ether; whose least wave
Stands tremulous, uncertain where to turn
960   The gentle current; while, illumined wide,
The dewy-skirted clouds imbibe the sun,
And through their lucid veil his softened force
Shed o'er the peaceful world. Then is the time
For those whom Wisdom and whom Nature charm
965   To steal themselves from the degenerate° crowd,   *unworthy*
And soar above this little scene of things—
To tread low-thoughted Vice beneath their feet,
To soothe the throbbing passions into peace,
And woo lone Quiet in her silent walks.
970   Thus solitary, and in pensive guise,

1. Virgil (Publius Virgilius Maro, 70–19 B.C.), Roman poet, author of the *Aeneid*.
2. John Milton.
3. In the dark (Milton was blind, and Homer was traditionally thought to have been so).
4. Thomson takes the name (and its connotation of learned companion) from Milton's pastoral elegy (1638) lamenting the death of his college friend Edward King.
1. The original version of *Winter* begins with the descrip-

tion of an evening in late autumn; later, Thomson revised this description and transferred it to the section on autumn, which made its first appearance in *The Seasons* (1730). Thomson repeatedly revised the poem in the years that followed; the text here is taken from the last edition he produced (1746).
2. The colors display the very end of autumn.
3. For Thomson's earlier version of this passage (lines 955–1036), see *Winter*, lines 23–79, pages 2689–90.

Oft let me wander o'er the russet mead,
And through the saddened grove, where scarce is heard
One dying strain to cheer the woodman's toil.
Haply some widowed songster pours his plaint
975 Far in faint warblings through the tawny copse;
While congregated thrushes, linnets, larks,
And each wild throat whose artless strains so late
Swelled all the music of the swarming shades,
Robbed of their tuneful souls, now shivering sit
980 On the dead tree, a dull despondent flock,
With not a brightness waving o'er their plumes,
And naught save chattering discord in their note.
Oh, let not, aimed from some inhuman eye,
The gun the music of the coming year
985 Destroy, and harmless, unsuspecting harm,
Lay the weak tribes, a miserable prey!
In mingled murder fluttering on the ground!
     The pale descending year, yet pleasing still,
A gentler mood inspires; for now the leaf
990 Incessant rustles from the mournful grove,
Oft startling such as, studious, walk below,
And slowly circles through the waving air.
But should a quicker breeze amid the boughs
Sob, o'er the sky the leafy deluge streams;
995 Till choked, and matted with the dreary shower,
The forest-walks, at every rising gale,
Roll wide the withered waste, and whistle bleak.
Fled is the blasted verdure of the fields;
And, shrunk into their beds, the flowery race
1000 Their sunny robes resign. Even what remained
Of bolder fruits falls from the naked tree;
And woods, fields, gardens, orchards, all around
The desolated prospect thrills the soul.
     He comes! he comes! in every breeze the power
1005 Of Philosophic Melancholy comes!
His near approach the sudden-starting tear,
The glowing cheek, the mild dejected air,
The softened feature, and the beating heart,
Pierced deep with many a virtuous pang, declare.
1010 O'er all the soul his sacred influence breathes;
Inflames imagination; through the breast
Infuses every tenderness; and far
Beyond dim earth exalts the swelling thought.
Ten thousand thousand fleet° ideas, such   rapid
1015 As never mingled with the vulgar dream,
Crowd fast into the mind's creative eye.
As fast the correspondent passions rise,
As varied, and as high—devotion raised
To rapture, and divine astonishment;
1020 The love of nature unconfined, and, chief,
Of human race; the large ambitious wish,

To make them blest; the sigh for suffering worth,
Lost in obscurity; the noble scorn,
Of tyrant pride; the fearless great resolve;
1025 The wonder which the dying patriot draws,
Inspiring glory through remotest time;
The awakened throb for virtue, and for fame;
The sympathies of love, and friendship dear;
With all the social offspring of the heart.
1030   Oh! bear me then to vast embowering shades,
To twilight groves, and visionary vales!⁴
To weeping grottoes, and prophetic glooms!
Where angel forms athwart the solemn dusk,
Tremendous sweep, or seem to sweep along;
1035 And voices more than human, through the void
Deep-sounding, seize the enthusiastic ear.
    Or is this gloom too much?⁵ Then lead, ye powers,
That o'er the garden and the rural seat
Preside, which shining through the cheerful land
1040 In countless numbers blest Britannia sees;
O lead me to the wide-extended walks,
The fair majestic paradise of Stowe!⁶
Not Persian Cyrus,⁷ on Ionia's shore,
E'er saw such sylvan scenes; such various art
1045 By genius fired, such ardent genius tamed
By cool judicious art; that, in the strife,
All-beauteous Nature fears to be outdone.
And there, O Pitt,⁸ thy country's early boast,
There let me sit beneath the sheltered slopes,
1050 Or in that Temple⁹ where, in future times,
Thou well shalt merit a distinguished name;
And, with thy converse blest, catch the last smiles
Of Autumn beaming o'er the yellow woods.
While there with thee the enchanted round I walk,
1055 The regulated wild, gay Fancy° then   *imagination*
Will tread in thought the groves of Attic land;¹
Will from thy standard taste refine her own,²
Correct her pencil to the purest truth
Of Nature, or, the unimpassioned shades
1060 Forsaking, raise it to the human mind.
O if hereafter she, with juster hand,
Shall draw the tragic scene, instruct her thou,

4. Valleys where I may see visions.
5. Thomson added lines 1036–1081 in his revision of 1744.
6. Stowe, the Buckinghamshire estate of Sir Richard Temple, Viscount Cobham (1669–1749), had been laid out and reworked by a long series of distinguished architects and landscapers; the garden was among the most celebrated of the 18th century (see Pope, *Epistle to Burlington*, lines 57–70, page 2538).
7. Cyrus the Younger (d. 401 B.C.), a Persian prince, designed and planted a famous garden at Sardis (on "Ionia's shore," the coast of Asia Minor).

8. The statesman and orator William Pitt (1708–1778) was esteemed by Thomson and Cobham as a leading voice among those Whigs opposed to the still-dominant party faction led by Robert Walpole; Pitt later became Secretary of State and Prime Minister.
9. The Temple of Virtue in Stowe Gardens [Thomson's note]; this monument to ancient heroes was one of the gardens' most celebrated buildings.
1. Ancient Greece (Attica was the countryside surrounding Athens).
2. Influenced by your standard of taste, Fancy will refine hers.

To mark the varied movements of the heart,
What every decent[3] character requires,
1065 And every passion speaks. O through her strain°   song, style
Breathe thy pathetic eloquence! that molds
Th' attentive senate, charms, persuades, exalts,
Of honest zeal th' indignant lightning throws,
And shakes corruption on her venal throne.
1070 While thus we talk, and through Elysian vales[4]
Delighted rove, perhaps a sigh escapes.
What pity, Cobham, thou thy verdant files
Of ordered trees shouldst here inglorious range,
Instead of squadrons flaming o'er the field,
1075 And long-embattled hosts![5] When the proud foe,
The faithless vain disturber of mankind,
Insulting Gaul, has roused the world to war;
When keen, once more, within their bounds to press[6]
Those polished robbers, those ambitious slaves,
1080 The British youth would hail thy wise command,
They tempered ardor and thy veteran skill.[7]

The western sun withdraws the shortened day;[8]
And humid evening, gliding o'er the sky,
In her chill progress, to the ground condensed
1085 The vapors throws. Where creeping waters ooze,
Where marshes stagnate, and where rivers wind,
Cluster the rolling fogs, and swim along
The dusky-mantled lawn. Meanwhile the moon,
Full-orbed and breaking through the scattered clouds,
1090 Shows her broad visage in the crimsoned east.
Turned to the sun direct, her spotted disk
(Where mountains rise, umbrageous dales descend,
And oceans roll, as optic tube° descries)   telescope
A smaller earth, gives all his blaze again,
1095 Void of its flame, and sheds a softer day.
Now through the passing cloud she seems to stoop,
Now up the pure cerulean rides sublime.
Wide the pale deluge floats, and streaming mild
O'er the skied° mountain to the shadowy vale,   sky-high
1100 While rocks and floods reflect the quivering gleam,
The whole air whitens with a boundless tide
Of silver radiance, trembling round the world.
But when, half-blotted from the sky, her light,
Fainting, permits the starry fires to burn,

---

3. Appropriate (Thomson, who wrote several tragedies, here asks Pitt for guidance in suiting his language to his characers and their emotions).
4. The Elysian Fields at Stowe (named for Elysium, Greek myth's paradise for heroes) were the most wild and natural area of the gardens.
5. Cobham left the Walpole government in 1733; thereafter he worked on his gardens and formed a group of opposition Whigs known as "Cobham's Cubs." Here Thomson wishes that Cobham, an accomplished soldier,

might deploy his gifts as military leader rather than as shaper of landscapes.
6. I.e., contain within their own borders.
7. Thomson here imagines how effective Cobham would be as a leader in the War of the Austrian Succession (1740–1748), England's current conflict with France ("insulting Gaul," "polished robbers," "ambitious slaves").
8. Compare the earlier version of these lines in *Winter* (lines 80–96 on page 2690).

1105 With keener luster through the depth of heaven;
    Or quite extinct her deadened orb appears,
    And scarce appears, of sickly beamless white;
    Oft in this season, silent from the north
    A blaze of meteors shoots⁹—ensweeping first
1110 The lower skies, they all at once converge
    High to the crown of heaven, and all at once
    Relapsing quick as quickly reascend,
    And mix, and thwart,° extinguish, and renew,   *cross*
    All ether coursing in a maze of light.
1115   From look to look, contagious through the crowd,
    The panic runs, and into wondrous shapes
    Th' appearance throws—armies in meet array,
    Thronged with aërial spears, and steeds of fire;
    Till the long lines of full-extended war
1120 In bleeding fight commixed, the sanguine flood
    Rolls a broad slaughter o'er the plains of heaven.
    As thus they scan the visionary scene,
    On all sides swells the superstitious din,
    Incontinent;° and busy frenzy talks   *unrestrained*
1125 Of blood and battle; cities overturned,
    And late at night in swallowing earthquake sunk,
    Or hideous wrapped in fierce ascending flame;
    Of sallow famine, inundation, storm;
    Of pestilence, and every great distress;
1130 Empires subversed, when ruling fate has struck
    The unalterable hour: even Nature's self
    Is deemed to totter on the brink of time.
    Not so the man of philosophic eye,
    And inspect sage;° the waving brightness he   *wise insight*
1135 Curious surveys, inquisitive to know
    The causes, and materials, yet unfixed,¹
    Of this appearance beautiful, and new. * * *

1726–1746   1746

Rule, Britannia¹

When Britain first, at Heaven's command,
    Arose from out the azure main;°   *sea*
This was the charter of the land,
    And guardian angels sung this strain:

9. The aurora borealis, or northern lights.
1. Unaccounted for (by science).
1. Thomson wrote several longer poems of impassioned patriotism (*Britannia*, 1729; *Liberty*, 1735–1736), but his convictions found their most enduring expression in this short piece, first performed as the climactic song of *Alfred*, a patriotic masque on the subject of the Saxon king (848–899). Defeated by the Danes, the monarch receives comfort from a "venerable bard," who expresses with uncanny prescience the 18th-century appetite for naval conquest and expanding empire. The masque was created by Thomson in collaboration with his fellow Scots expatriate David Mallet (?1705–1765) and the composer Thomas Arne (1710–1778), as part of an entertainment commissioned by Frederick, Prince of Wales, to celebrate his daughter's third birthday and the anniversary of his German grandfather's accession to the English throne. Thomson's ode outlasted its occasion, gradually acquiring the status of an alternate national anthem (just behind *God Save the King*). While the Empire endured, Thomson's song proffered for many Britons a stirring account of their national origins, essence, and destiny.

5   "Rule, Britannia, rule the waves;
         "Britons never will be slaves."

    The nations, not so blest as thee,
         Must, in their turns, to tyrants fall:
    While thou shalt flourish great and free,
10   The dread and envy of them all.
              "Rule," etc.

    Still more majestic shalt thou rise,
         More dreadful, from each foreign stroke:
    As the loud blast that tears the skies,
15   Serves but to root thy native oak.
              "Rule," etc.

    Thee haughty tyrants ne'er shall tame:
         All their attempts to bend thee down
    Will but arouse thy generous flame;
20   But work their woe, and thy renown.
              "Rule," etc.

    To thee belongs the rural reign;
         Thy cities shall with commerce shine:
    All thine shall be the subject main,
25   And every shore it circles thine.
              "Rule," etc.

    The Muses, still[2] with freedom found,
         Shall to thy happy coast repair:
    Blest isle! with matchless beauty crowned,
30   And manly hearts to guard the fair.
              "Rule, Britannia, rule the waves;
              "Britons never will be slaves."

1740   1740

❀ "THE SEASONS" AND ITS TIME ❀

Poems of Nightfall and Night

The aubade, or dawn-song, was a favorite form in the Middle Ages and the Renaissance: poets from Chaucer to Donne portrayed lovers entwined abed, lamenting the intrusive rising of the sun. In eighteenth-century England, poets were more preoccupied with the night piece, as a medium not for amorous pairings but for meditative solitude. In a culture marked by the intensified noise, density, and busyness of the cities, privacy was an experience newly construed and prized; in the scene of nightfall (particularly *country* nightfall), poets found an ideal setting for its enactment. Anne Finch opens her *Nocturnal Reverie* with a key line from one of Shakespeare's dialogues between lovers, but she transmutes conversation into soliloquy. William Collins, in his most famous ode, addresses the Evening as a "maid composed," a "nymph reserved," whose quietude facilitates his solitary thought; in his poem on the death of his

2. The word meant both "always" and "as yet."

friend James Thomson, Collins renders his sense of loss by images of encroaching dark. The other selections here come from larger works—Edward Young's *Night Thoughts* and William Cowper's *The Task*—which participate in the tradition that Thomson's *Seasons* had commenced: copious blank-verse description and meditation, produced, expanded, and revised over the course of years, mingling widely various materials and modes in a new, purportedly improvisatory way. "The method pursued," Young explained of his long poem, "was rather *imposed*, by what spontaneously arose in the author's mind on that occasion, than *meditated* or *designed*"; Cowper, more simply, attributed the expansion of *The Task* to the unexpected directions dictated by his own "train of thought." Drawing on darkness as resource and backdrop, Thomson, Young, and Cowper were working toward a new mode: the epic of the solitary mind in action. From them the lines of influence run long and clear, through the Gothic fiction of the late eighteenth century, through Wordsworth's meditative excursions, into the stream of consciousness in Joyce's *Ulysses* and the nocturnal dreamspeak of *Finnegans Wake*.

Anne Finch
A Nocturnal Reverie[1]

In such a night,[2] when every louder wind
Is to its distant cavern safe confined;
And only gentle Zephyr° fans his wings,   *the west wind*
And lonely Philomel,° still waking, sings;   *the nightingale*
5   Or from some tree, famed for the owl's delight,
She, hollowing clear, directs the wanderer right:
In such a night, when passing clouds give place,
Or thinly veil the heavens' mysterious face;
When in some river, overhung with green,
10   The waving moon and trembling leaves are seen;
When freshened grass now bears itself upright,
And makes cool banks to pleasing rest invite,
Whence springs the woodbind, and the bramble-rose,
And where the sleepy cowslip sheltered grows;
15   Whilst now a paler hue the foxglove takes,
Yet checkers still with red the dusky brakes:°   *thickets*
When scattered glow-worms, but in twilight fine,
Show trivial beauties, watch their hour to shine;
Whilst Salisbury[3] stands the test of every light,
20   In perfect charms, and perfect virtue bright;
When odors, which declined repelling day,
Through temperate air uninterrupted stray;
When darkened groves their softest shadows wear,
And falling waters we distinctly hear;
25   When through the gloom more venerable shows
Some ancient fabric,° awful in repose,   *building*
While sunburnt hills their swarthy looks conceal,
And swelling haycocks thicken up the vale;
When the loosed horse now, as his pasture leads,
30   Comes slowly grazing through th' adjoining meads,
Whose stealing pace, and lengthened shade we fear,

---

1. For Anne Finch, see page 2226.
2. Finch takes her opening words from the evocation of night in Shakespeare's *Merchant of Venice* (5.1.1–21), where the lovers Lorenzo and Jessica speak the phrase repeatedly to each other, as they retell old tales of nocturnal passion and betrayal.
3. Anne Tufton, Countess of Salisbury, daughter of one of Finch's close friends.

Till torn up forage in his teeth we hear;
When nibbling sheep at large pursue their food,
And unmolested kine rechew the cud;
35   When curlews cry beneath the village-walls,
And to her straggling brood the partridge calls;
Their short-lived jubilee the creatures keep,
Which but endures, whilst tyrant-man does sleep;
When a sedate content the spirit feels,
40   And no fierce light disturbs, whilst it reveals;
But silent musings urge the mind to seek
Something, too high for syllables to speak;
Till the free soul to a compos'dness charmed,
Finding the elements of rage disarmed,
45   O'er all below a solemn quiet grown,
Joys in th' inferior° world, and thinks it like her own: *lower*
In such a night let me abroad remain,
Till morning breaks, and all's confused again;
Our cares, our toils, our clamors are renewed,
50   Or pleasures, seldom reached, again pursued.

1713

Edward Young[1]

from *The Complaint*

OR NIGHT THOUGHTS ON LIFE, DEATH, AND IMMORTALITY

Tired Nature's sweet restorer, balmy Sleep!
He, like the world, his ready visit pays
Where Fortune smiles; the wretched he forsakes:
Swift on his downy pinion° flies from woe,   *wing*
5   And lights on lids unsullied with a tear.
    From short (as usual) and disturbed repose,
I wake. How happy they, who wake no more!
Yet that were vain, if dreams infest the grave.
I wake, emerging from a sea of dreams
10   Tumultuous; where my wrecked, desponding thought
From wave to wave of fancied misery,
At random drove, her helm of reason lost.
Though now restored, 'tis only change of pain,
(A bitter change!) severer for severe.
15   The day too short for my distress! and Night,
Even in the zenith of her dark domain,
Is sunshine, to the color of my fate.
    Night, sable goddess! from her ebon° throne,   *black*
In rayless majesty, now stretches forth
20   Her leaden scepter o'er a slumb'ring world.

---

1. After a frustrating London career as poet and playwright in frantic pursuit of political advancement, Edward Young (1683–1765) took holy orders, withdrew to a small village, and at age 59 commenced a set of poems that brought him sudden, staggering success. In *The Complaint*, a sequence of nine night pieces (and more than 9,000 lines) published serially over the course of three years, Young mixed morbid melancholy, Gothic dread, and Christian solace. The combination appealed powerfully to a vast number and variety of readers, in Britain and on the Continent. In its meditative blank verse and its capacious, fluid form, *Night Thoughts* was plainly influenced by Thomson's *Seasons*; well into the 19th century, the two works were often packaged (along with *Paradise Lost*) in a single, highly saleable volume. Both poems pervaded the century's consciousness, and later figured as principal forebears of Romantic thought and writing. This excerpt is from *Night 1*.

Silence, how dead! and darkness, how profound!
Nor eye, nor list'ning ear an object finds;
Creation sleeps. 'Tis as° the general pulse   *as if*
Of life stood still, and Nature made a pause;
25 An awful pause! prophetic of her end.
And let her prophecy be soon fulfilled;
Fate! drop the curtain; I can lose no more.
    Silence, and Darkness! Solemn sisters! Twins
From ancient Night, who nurse the tender thought
30 To reason, and on reason build resolve
(That column of true majesty in man),
Assist me: I will thank you in the grave;
The grave, your kingdom. There this frame shall fall
A victim sacred to your dreary shrine.
35 But what are ye? Thou,[2] who didst put to flight
Primeval Silence, when the morning stars,
Exulting, shouted o'er the rising ball;
O Thou! whose word from solid darkness struck
That spark, the sun; strike wisdom from my soul;
40 My soul, which flies to Thee, her trust, her treasure,
As misers to their gold, while others rest.
    Through this opaque of nature, and of soul,
This double night, transmit one pitying ray,
To lighten, and to cheer. O lead my mind,
45 (A mind that fain would wander from its woe)
Lead it through various scenes of life and death;
And from each scene the noblest truths inspire.
Nor less inspire my conduct than my song;
Teach my best reason reason; my best will
Teach rectitude; and fix my firm resolve
50 Wisdom to wed, and pay her long arrear:°   *old debt*
Nor let the phial of thy vengeance, poured
On this devoted head, be poured in vain.
    The bell strikes one. We take no note of time
But from its loss. To give it then a tongue,
55 Is wise in man. As if an angel spoke,
I feel the solemn sound. If heard aright,
It is the knell of my departed hours:
Where are they? With the years beyond the flood.
It is the signal that demands dispatch;
60 How much is to be done? my hopes and fears
Start up alarmed, and o'er life's narrow verge
Look down—on what? A fathomless abyss;
A dread eternity! how surely mine!
And can eternity belong to me,
65 Poor pensioner on the bounties of an hour?
    How poor, how rich, how abject, how august,
How complicate, how wonderful, is man?
How passing wonder He, who made him such!

---

2. Young here shifts addressees, from the plural "ye" (Silence and Darkness) to the singular "Thou" (God, imagined at the moment of Creation).

Who centered in our make such strange extremes?
From different natures marvelously mixed,
70   Connection exquisite of distant worlds!
Distinguished link in being's endless chain!
Midway from nothing to the deity!
A beam ethereal sullied and absorbed!
Though sullied and dishonored, still divine!
75   Dim miniature of greatness absolute!
An heir of glory! a frail child of dust!
Helpless immortal! Insect infinite!
A worm! a God! I tremble at myself,
And in myself am lost! At home a stranger,
80   Thought wanders up and down, surprised, aghast,
And wondering at her own. How reason reels!
O what a miracle to man is man,
Triumphantly distressed! what joy, what dread!
Alternately transported and alarmed!
85   What can preserve my life? or what destroy?
An angel's arm can't snatch me from the grave;
Legions of angels can't confine me there.
      'Tis past conjecture; all things rise in proof:
While o'er my limbs sleep's soft dominion spread,
90   What, though my soul fantastic measures trod
O'er fairy fields; or mourned along the gloom
Of pathless woods; or down the craggy steep
Hurled headlong, swam with pain the mantled pool;
Or scaled the cliff; or danced on hollow winds,
95   With antic shapes, wild natives of the brain?
Her ceaseless flight, though devious, speaks her nature
Of subtler essence than the trodden clod;
Active, aërial, towering, unconfined,
Unfettered with her gross companion's fall.
100   Even silent night proclaims my soul immortal:
Even silent night proclaims eternal day.
For human weal, Heaven husbands all events,
Dull sleep instructs, nor sport vain dreams in vain.

1742   1742, 1750

William Collins [1]
Ode to Evening

If aught of oaten stop,[2] or pastoral song,
May hope, chaste Eve, to soothe thy modest ear,

---

1. As a student at Oxford, William Collins (1721–1759) secured some distinction, published a few poems, and promptly left for London and the life (as his friend Samuel Johnson described it) of "a literary adventurer." While amusing himself at the city's pleasure gardens and play-houses, amid a spritely circle of actors and writers, Collins planned a number of books. He published only one, a small collection entitled *Odes on Several Descriptive and Allegorical Subjects* (1747); its failure to attract notice prompted him to burn the many copies that had gone unsold. In his late twenties, the poet fell prey to a manic depression verging on madness, which disabled him the rest of his life. His odes, neglected in his time, appealed strongly to tastes that came into vogue just after his death: for sentiment and the sublime, for the expression of overpowering emotions, of disruptive experiences, and of visionary intensities beyond the familiar, civic, human scale.

2. If any music played on an oat-reed pipe (Collins uses the pastoral-archaic idiom associated with Spenser and Milton).

Like thy own solemn springs,
Thy springs, and dying gales,
5   O nymph reserved, while now the bright-haired sun
Sits in yon western tent, whose cloudy skirts,
    With brede° ethereal wove,   braid
    O'erhang his wavy bed:
Now air is hushed, save where the weak-eyed bat,
10 With short shrill shriek flits by on leathern wing,
    Or where the beetle winds°   blows
    His small but sullen horn,
As oft he rises 'midst the twilight path,
Against the pilgrim borne in heedless hum:
15   Now teach me, maid composed,
    To breathe some softened strain,°   song
Whose numbers° stealing through thy darkening vale,   verses
May not unseemly with its stillness suit,
    As musing slow, I hail
20   Thy genial loved return!
For when thy folding star arising shows
His paly circlet, at his warning lamp
    The fragrant Hours, and elves
    Who slept in flowers the day,
25 And many a nymph who wreathes her brows with sedge,
And sheds the freshening dew, and lovelier still,
    The pensive Pleasures sweet
    Prepare thy shadowy car.°   chariot
Then lead, calm vot'ress,[3] where some sheety lake
30 Cheers the lone heath, or some time-hallowed pile,°   building
    Or upland fallows[4] gray
    Reflect its last cool gleam.
But when chill blustering winds, or driving rain,
Forbid my willing feet, be mine the hut,
35   That from the mountain's side,
    Views wilds, and swelling floods,
And hamlets brown, and dim-discovered spires,
And hears their simple bell, and marks o'er all
    Thy dewy fingers draw
40   The gradual dusky veil.
While Spring shall pour his showers, as oft he wont,[5]
And bathe thy breathing tresses, meekest Eve!
    While Summer loves to sport,
    Beneath thy lingering light;
45 While sallow Autumn fills thy lap with leaves;
Or Winter, yelling through the troublous air,
    Affrights thy shrinking train,
    And rudely rends thy robes;
So long, sure-found beneath the sylvan shed,
50 Shall Fancy, Friendship, Science, rose-lipped Health,

---

3. "A woman devoted to . . . worship" (Johnson's *Dictio-*   4. Fields ploughed but unplanted.
nary).   5. Is accustomed to do.

Thy gentlest influence own,
And hymn thy favorite name!

1746   1746, 1748

William Collins
Ode Occasioned by the Death of Mr. Thomson

The scene of the following stanzas is supposed to lie on the Thames near Richmond.[1]

Haec tibi semper erunt, et cum solennia vota
reddemus Nymphis, et cum lustrabimus agros.

—— ——*Amavit nos quoque Daphnis.*[2]

1

In yonder grave a Druid[3] lies,
    Where slowly winds the stealing wave!
The year's best sweets shall duteous rise
    To deck its poet's sylvan grave!

2

5   In you deep bed of whispering reeds
    His airy harp[4] shall now be laid,
That he, whose heart in sorrow bleeds,
    May love through life the soothing shade.

3

Then maids and youths shall linger here,
10   And, while its sounds at distance swell,
Shall sadly seem in Pity's ear
    To hear the woodland pilgrim's[5] knell.

4

Remembrance oft shall haunt the shore
    When Thames in summer wreaths is dressed,
15   And oft suspend the dashing oar
    To bid his gentle spirit rest!

5

And oft as Ease and Health retire
    To breezy lawn or forest deep,

---

1. A scenic riverside village nine miles from London's center; Thomson had lived there in his last years, and was buried in the parish churchyard. Collins, who had dwelt there too, in close friendship with Thomson, here invokes the local geography quite specifically. His ode compasses two motions: in space, as the speaker moves past Richmond up the river; in time, as day modulates into night. Collins's poem was praised by a contemporary for the "dirge-like melancholy it breathes, and the warmth of affection that seems to have dictated it"; it has long enjoyed a print intimacy with the poet whom it eulogizes. Thomson's editors have often presented it as a preface to his works; his biographers have reprinted it as a coda to his life, a summation of his worth.
2. "These rites shall be thine forever, both when we pay our yearly vows to the Nymphs, and when we purify our fields ... Daphnis loved us too" (Virgil, *Eclogues* 5.74–75, 52). In the pastoral tradition, the legendary Daphnis is credited as the first shepherd to have made music, the inventor of bucolic song; in Virgil's lines, one of Daphnis's followers mourns his master's "cruel death" and promises perpetual homage.
3. The Druids were the priest-magicians of ancient Britain. In the 18th century they were thought to have possessed extraordinary intimacy with, and power over, the forces of nature.
4. "The harp of Aeolus" [Collins's note], an instrument whose strings make sounds when the breezes play upon them (Aeolus was the mythological Greek monarch of the winds). Thomson, the first to invoke this instrument in English verse, had made it a figure for poetic responsiveness to inspiration; many poets since have taken up the trope.
5. I.e., Thomson's, whose love of forest walks Collins here recalls.

The friend shall view yon whitening spire,[6]
20   And mid the varied landscape weep.

6

But thou, who own'st that earthy bed,
      Ah! what will every dirge avail?
Or tears, which Love and Pity shed
      That mourn beneath the gliding sail![7]

7

25   Yet lives there one, whose heedless eye
      Shall scorn thy pale shrine glimmering near?
With him, sweet bard, may Fancy die,
      And Joy desert the blooming year.

8

But thou, lorn stream,[8] whose sullen tide
30   No sedge-crowned Sisters now attend,
Now waft me from the green hill's side,
      Whose cold turf hides the buried friend!

9

And see, the fairy valleys fade,
      Dun Night has veiled the solemn view![9]
35   —Yet once again, dear parted shade,
      Meek Nature's child, again adieu!

10

The genial meads,° assigned to bless   meadows
      Thy life, shall mourn thy early doom,
Their hinds° and shepherd-girls shall dress   shepherds
40   With simple hands thy rural tomb.

11

Long, long, thy stone and pointed clay[1]
      Shall melt the musing Briton's eyes:
"O! vales and wild woods," shall he say,
      "In yonder grave your Druid lies!"

1748–1749   1749

William Cowper
from *The Task*[1]

from BOOK 4. THE WINTER EVENING
[READING THE NEWSPAPER]

Now stir the fire, and close the shutters fast,
Let fall the curtains, wheel the sofa round,

---

6. Of the parish church where Thomson was buried.
7. Of the boat moving down the Thames (see line 15).
8. The Thames, forlorn because it is no longer inhabited by the leaf-adorned river nymphs ("sedge-crowned Sisters") who dwelt there during Thomson's lifetime.
9. Collins echoes Thomson's *Autumn* lines 950–952 (see page 2692).
1. I.e., the poet's churchyard monument.
1. For William Cowper, see page 2683. As preface to *The Task*, Cowper offered the following brief "history": "A lady, fond of blank verse, demanded a poem of that kind from the author, and gave him the SOFA for a subject. He obeyed; and having much leisure, connected another subject with it; and pursuing the train of thought to

which his situation and turn of mind led him, brought forth at length, instead of the trifle which he at first intended, a serious affair—a volume." The modulation from triviality to seriousness (and back again) is intrinsic not only to the history of the poem but to its substance too. In six epic "Books" bearing markedly domestic titles (*The Sofa, The Time-Piece, The Garden, The Winter Evening, The Winter Morning Walk, The Winter Walk at Noon*), Cowper savors rural pleasures and satirizes the life of cities. Mingling grand diction with cozy fact ("I sing the Sofa," the poem begins), Cowper revels in their seeming disparity, as a resource both for comic self-deprecation and for earnest affirmation. These domestic delights, *The Task* implies, deserve this scale of celebration.

And while the bubbling and loud-hissing urn
Throws up a steamy column, and the cups°   *of tea*
40   That cheer but not inebriate, wait on each,
So let us welcome peaceful evening in.
Not such his ev'ning, who with shining face
Sweats in the crowded theater, and squeezed
And bored with elbow-points through both his sides,
45   Out-scolds the ranting actor on the stage.
Nor his, who patient stands till his feet throb,
And his head thumps, to feed upon the breath
Of patriots[2] bursting with heroic rage,
Or placemen,[3] all tranquillity and smiles.
50   This folio of four pages,° happy work!   *the newspaper*
Which not ev'n critics criticize, that holds
Inquisitive attention while I read,
Fast bound in chains of silence, which the fair,[4]
Though eloquent themselves, yet fear to break,
55   What is it, but a map of busy life,
Its fluctuations and its vast concerns?
Here runs the mountainous and craggy ridge
That tempts ambition. On the summit, see,
The seals of office glitter in his eyes;
60   He climbs, he pants, he grasps them. At his heels,
Close at his heels a demagogue ascends,
And with a dext'rous jerk soon twists him down
And wins them, but to lose them in his turn.
Here rills of oily eloquence in soft
65   Meanders lubricate the course they take;
The modest speaker is ashamed and grieved
T' engross a moment's notice, and yet begs,
Begs a propitious ear for his poor thoughts,
However trivial all that he conceives.
70   Sweet bashfulness! it claims, at last, this praise:
The dearth of information and good sense
That it foretells us, always comes to pass.
Cataracts of declamation thunder here,
There forests of no-meaning spread the page
75   In which all comprehension wanders lost;
While fields of pleasantry amuse us there,
With merry descants° on a nation's woes.   *commentaries*
The rest[5] appears a wilderness of strange
But gay confusion: roses for the cheeks,
80   And lilies for the brows of faded age,
Teeth for the toothless, ringlets for the bald,
Heaven, earth, and ocean plundered of their sweets,
Nectareous essences, Olympian dews,
Sermons and city feasts and favorite airs,[6]
85   Aetherial journies,[7] submarine exploits,[8]

2. Political zealots.
3. Office-holders, bureaucrats.
4. The women of the house.
5. I.e., the newspaper's advertisements.

6. Popular melodies (sold as sheet music).
7. In hot-air balloons; the first flight had taken place in 1783.
8. In diving bells, which had been in use for more than a century.

And Katterfelto[9] with his hair on end
At his own wonders, wond'ring for his bread.
   'Tis pleasant through the loop-holes of retreat
To peep at such a world. To see the stir
90   Of the great Babel[1] and not feel the crowd.
To hear the roar she sends through all her gates
At a safe distance, where the dying sound
Falls a soft murmur on th' uninjured ear.
Thus sitting and surveying thus at ease
95   The globe and its concerns, I seem advanced
To some secure and more than mortal height,
That lib'rates and exempts me from them all.
It turns submitted to my view, turns round
With all its generations; I behold
100 The tumult and am still. The sound of war
Has lost its terrors ere it reaches me;
Grieves but alarms me not. I mourn the pride
And avarice that make man a wolf to man,
Hear the faint echo of those brazen throats
105 By which he speaks the language of his heart,
And sigh, but never tremble at the sound.
He travels and expatiates, as the bee
From flow'r to flow'r, so he from land to land;
The manners, customs, policy of all
110 Pay contribution to the store he gleans,
He sucks intelligence in every clime,
And spreads the honey of his deep research
At his return, a rich repast for me.
He travels and I too. I tread his deck,
115 Ascend his topmast, through his peering eyes
Discover countries, with a kindred heart
Suffer his woes, and share in his escapes,
While fancy, like the finger of a clock,
Runs the great circuit, and is still at home.

[THE INVOCATION]

Come Ev'ning once again,[2] season of peace
Return sweet Ev'ning, and continue long!
245 Methinks I see thee in the streaky west,
With matron-step slow-moving, while the night
Treads on thy sweeping train; one hand employed
In letting fall the curtain of repose
On bird and beast, the other charged for man
250 With sweet oblivion of the cares of day;
Not sumptuously adorned, nor needing aid

9. Gustave Katterfelto, a magician whose performances were advertised under the rubric "Wonders, Wonders, Wonders."
1. The biblical Tower of Babel (Genesis 11.1–9), whose construction God prevented by making the builders speak different languages ("babble"); Cowper here uses

the word for its long-established association with "Babylon," meaning any great city.
2. Cowper's invocation in the ensuing lines echoes both Milton's *Paradise Lost* (4.568–609) and Collins' *Ode to Evening* (page 2701).

Like homely featured Night, of clust'ring gems,
A star or two just twinkling on thy brow
Suffices thee; save that the moon is thine
255 No less than hers, not worn indeed on high
With ostentatious pageantry, but set
With modest grandeur in thy purple zone,°   belt
Resplendent less, but of an ampler round.
Come then, and thou shalt find thy vot'ry° calm   worshipper
260 Or make me so. Composure is thy gift.
And whether I devote thy gentle hours
To books, to music, or the poet's toil,
To weaving nets for bird-alluring fruit;
Or twining silken threads round ivory reels.
265 When they° command whom man was born to please,   women
I slight thee not, but make thee welcome still.
1783–1785   1785

END OF "THE SEASONS" AND POEMS OF NIGHTFALL AND NIGHT

Thomas Gray
1716–1771

Toward the end of his most famous poem, *Elegy Written in a Country Churchyard*, Thomas Gray commends the quietude with which the villagers have led their ordinary lives:

Along the cool sequestered vale of life
They kept the noiseless tenor of their way.

Tenor here means "course," and the line incorporates a notable revision: Gray had originally written "silent tenor," and then written the new adjective "noiseless" above the old, without crossing out "silent." In retrospect, this manuscript moment of alternate possibilities looks emblematic. Sickly, shy, and melancholic, Gray was often drawn toward silence but never settled there. Words—in ancient literature and in modern history, in talk and correspondence with his friends, in the varied idioms of his own compelling poems—exerted too strong a fascination. The fascination started early. At age nine, having weathered a bleak childhood in the troubled London household of his irascible father and doting mother, he entered the privileged precincts of Eton College, where his uncles worked and where he hit upon the satisfactions that would fill his life: passionate reading (in the classics first and foremost) and passionate friendships, with three schoolmates in particular: Richard West, Thomas Ashton, and Horace Walpole, son of the notorious prime minister Robert Walpole. Dubbing themselves the Quadruple Alliance, the four friends piqued themselves on a collective erudition, refinement, and wit that set them off from their contemporaries. The links among them mattered enormously in Gray's life of writing: West inspired his poems; Walpole sponsored their publication; and all Gray's friendships, at Eton and beyond, drew from Gray a steady flow of virtuosic letters, in which the voice of the "Alliance," at once antic and vulnerable, never abated. "His letters," remarked Walpole (whose own letters have evoked similar praise), "were the best I ever saw, and had more novelty and wit." Gray's affections took form and motion partly from their containment. He was homosexual; yet there is no evidence that he ever physically consummated the great passions of his life—for Walpole, for West, and, in his last years, for the young Swiss scion Charles-Victor de Bonstatten.

After nine years at Eton, Gray was admitted to Cambridge. He found university life far less pleasing, with its drudgeries, pressures, and solitudes, but Cambridge ultimately afforded him a few new friendships and a permanent sanctuary. After a Grand Tour of Europe, undertaken in Walpole's company (the two men quarreled en route, after which they were estranged for five years), Gray returned to the university, ostensibly to learn law, but in fact to pursue his own private program of study. He read widely, copiously, and systematically in many subjects (botany, zoology, and music, as well as literature and history), making himself one of the most learned scholars alive, and eventually becoming (in 1768) Regius Professor of Modern History. He never delivered a lecture, and continued to spend much of his time alone reading, but thoroughgoing privacy had long ceased to be an option. In his late thirties, Gray had stumbled, reluctantly, into enormous poetic fame. He had written Latin verse when young; in 1742, the year his beloved West died of tuberculosis, he commenced English poetry in earnest. Some of his labor's early fruits bespeak an insistent sense of loss: a sonnet on West's death (never printed during the poet's lifetime); the *Ode on a Distant Prospect of Eton College*, in which the distance is one of time as well as space; and the *Elegy*, whose completion took five years or more and whose publication in 1751 (a "distress" the poet had hoped to avoid) brought upon Gray an instantaneous, massive, and baffling celebrity. As if in recoil, he veered onto an alternate poetic path, carefully crafting over the ensuing years a set of intricate Pindaric odes, including *The Bard* and *The Progress of Poesy*; the two poems were printed, on Walpole's own press, in 1757. They provoked both admiration, as a new embodiment of poetic sublimity, and derision, as gratuitously labored, showily obscure. In the years following their murky reception, Gray wrote only a few poems and published none. He pursued other studies (including Norse literature); fell in love one final time; and died abruptly, mourned deeply by his friends and widely by a public whose thoughts and feelings about death itself he had done much to shape. In one early version of the *Elegy* the line about silence appears as an admonition addressed by the poet to himself: "Pursue the silent tenor of thy doom." In his letters (published posthumously) and in his poems, Gray worked for that doom a delicate but decisive reversal.

LETTERS
To Horace Walpole, 16 April 1734[1]

I believe by your not making me happy in a longer letter than that I have just received, you had a design to prevent my tiring you with a tedious one; but in revenge for your neglect I'm resolved to send you one five times as long. Sir, do you think that I'll be fobbed off with eleven lines and a half?[2] After waiting this week in continual expectation, and proposing to myself all the pleasure that you, if you would, might give me; Gadsbud! I am provoked into a fermentation! when I see you next, I'll firk you, I'll rattle you with a *certiorari*.[3] Let me tell you, I am at present as full of wrath and choler as—as—you are of wit and good-nature; though I begin to doubt your title to the last of them, since you have balked me in this manner: what an excuse do you make with your Passion-week and fiddle-faddle, as if you could ever be at a loss what to say; why, I that am in the country could give you a full and true account of half a dozen intrigues, between a boar and a sow, people of very good fashion, that come to

1. This is Gray's earliest extant letter, written during Eton College's Easter holidays, when Gray and Walpole were both away from school.
2. Gray echoes Shakespeare's tavern-hostess Mrs. Quickly, complaining that Sir John Falstaff constantly postpones the payment of his debts: "I . . . have been fubbed off, and fubbed off, and fubbed off, . . . that it is a shame

to be thought on." (*2 Henry IV*, 2.1).
3. From William Congreve's comedy *The Double Dealer*, where Sir Paul Plyant, "provoked into a fermentation" by fear of his wife's infidelity, vows vengeance on her wooer: "I'll rattle him up, I warrant you, I'll firk him with a *certiorari*!" (punish with a legal writ establishing his claim) (2.4).

an assignation and squeak like ten masquerades; I have a great mind to make you hear the whole progress of the affair, together with the humors of Miss Pigsnies,[4] the lady's confidante; but you will perhaps think I invent it, and so I shall let it alone. But I wonder you are not ashamed of yourself; in town, and not able to furnish out an epistle as long as a cow's tail! (excuse the rusticity of my simile). In short, I have tried and condemned you in my mind; all that you can allege to save yourself won't do; for I find by your excuses you are brought to your *dernière chemise*;[5] and as you stand guilty, I adjudge you to be drawn to the place of execution, your chamber, where taking pen in hand, you shall write a letter as long as this, to him, who is nothing, when not

Your sincere friend and most devoted humble servant,

T. Gray

To Richard West, December 1736[6]

You must know that I do not take degrees,[7] and, after this term, shall have nothing more of college impertinencies to undergo, which I trust will be some pleasure to you, as it is a great one to me. I have endured lectures daily and hourly since I came last, supported by the hopes of being shortly at full liberty to give myself up to my friends and classical companions,[8] who, poor souls! though I see them fallen into great contempt with most people here, yet I cannot help sticking to them, and out of a spirit of obstinacy (I think) love them the better for it; and indeed what can I do else? Must I plunge into metaphysics? Alas, I cannot see in the dark; nature has not furnished me with the optics of a cat. Must I pore upon mathematics? Alas, I cannot see in too much light; I am no eagle. It is very possible that two and two make four, but I would not give four farthings to demonstrate this ever so clearly; and if these be the profits of life, give me the amusements of it. The people I behold all around me, it seems, know all this and more, and yet I do not know one of them who inspires me with any ambition of being like him. Surely it was of this place, now Cambridge, but formerly known by the name of Babylon, that the prophet spoke when he said, "the wild beasts of the desert shall dwell there, and their houses shall be full of doleful creatures, and owls shall build there, and satyrs shall dance there; their forts and towers shall be a den forever, a joy of wild asses; there shall the great owl make her nest, and lay and hatch and gather under her shadow; it shall be a court of dragons; the screech owl also shall rest there, and find for herself a place of rest."[9] You see here is a pretty collection of desolate animals, which is verified in this town to a tittle, and perhaps it may also allude to your habitation, for you know all types may be taken by abundance of handles;[1] however, I defy your owls to match mine.

If the default of your spirits and nerves be nothing but the effect of the hyp,[2] I have not more to say. We all must submit to that wayward queen; I too in no small degree own her sway,

4. I.e., "Miss Darling" (from Middle English *piggesnye*—"pig's eye"—a term of endearment).
5. Gray echoes the title of Colley Cibber's popular comedy *Love's Last Shift* (French: *La Dernière Chemise de l'Amour*), with a pun on "shift": as petticoat (Fr.: *chemise*) and as stratagem or trick.
6. Gray writes from Peterhouse, Cambridge, to West at Christ Church, Oxford.
7. Having decided (for the time being) to enroll in the legal training program at the Inner Temple, London, with a view to becoming a barrister, Gray no longer needed to obtain a Cambridge degree.
8. I.e., the ancient Greek and Roman authors; the

requirements for his degree had obliged him to neglect these in favor of logic, philosophy ("metaphysics"), and mathematics.
9. Gray quotes passages from Isaiah (chs. 13, 33, and 34), prophesying ruin to sinful cities (Babylon among them).
1. "Types" are biblical motifs, re-echoed through history (animals in ancient Babylon are equated to scholars in present Cambridge); in the religious and allusive 18th century, the ways of applying them (of making them into "handles") were indeed many and varied.
2. Short for *hypochondria*, the standard 18th-century term for melancholy, depression.

I feel her influence while I speak her power.

But if it be a real distemper, pray take more care of your health, if not for your own at least for our sakes, and do not be so soon weary of this little world: I do not know what refined friendships you may have contracted in the other, but pray do not be in a hurry to see your acquaintance above; among your terrestrial familiars, however, though I say it that should not say it, there positively is not one that has a greater esteem for you than

Yours most sincerely, etc.

To Horace Walpole, 12 June 1750[3]

Dear Sir,

As I live in a place where even the ordinary tattle of the town arrives not till it is stale, and which produces no events of its own, you will not desire any excuse from me for writing so seldom, especially as of all people living I know you are the least a friend to letters spun out of one's own brains, with all the toil and constraint that accompanies sentimental productions. I have been here at Stoke a few days (where I shall continue good part of the summer); and having put an end to a thing, whose beginning you have seen long ago, I immediately send it you.[4] You will, I hope, look upon it in the light of a *thing with an end to it;* a merit that most of my writings have wanted,[5] and are like to want, but which this epistle I am determined shall not want, when it tells you that I am ever

Yours,
T. Gray

Not that I have done yet; but who could avoid the temptation of finishing so roundly and so cleverly in the manner of good queen Anne's days?[6] Now I have talked of writings, I have seen a book, which is by this time in the press, against Middleton (though without naming him), by Ashton.[7] As far as I can judge from a very hasty reading, there are things in it new and ingenious, but rather too prolix, and the style here and there savoring too strongly of sermon. I imagine it will do him credit. So much for other people, now to *self* again. You are desired to tell me your opinion, if you can take the pains, of these lines.[8] I am once more

Ever Yours.

To Horace Walpole, 11 February 1751[9]

My dear Sir,

As you have brought me into a little sort of distress, you must assist me, I believe, to get out of it, as well as I can. Yesterday I had the misfortune of receiving a letter from certain gentlemen (as their bookseller expresses it) who have taken the *Maga-*

---

3. Gray writes to Walpole (in London) from Stoke Poges, the village where his mother and aunt (once partners in a London millinery shop) had retired following the death of his father; Gray often paid long visits there.
4. The "thing" is Gray's poem, eventually published as *Elegy Written in a Country Churchyard*. Walpole noted later that he had seen "the twelve or more first lines" of the poem about four years before the date of this letter.
5. Lacked. (Gray and his friends were bemused by his disinclination to complete and publish most of his projects.)
6. Queen Anne's reign (1702–1714) was famed for the letter-writing of witty authors, notably Swift and Pope.

7. In the book, a work of theological controversy, Thomas Ashton, Walpole's and Gray's old comrade in the Quadruple Alliance, had attacked Walpole's late friend Conyers Middleton (1683–1750); Walpole chose to break off relations with Ashton and to "forbid him my house."
8. Walpole admired the poem enormously and promoted it enthusiastically, circulating manuscript copies among his London friends.
9. In this and the following letter, Gray writes from Cambridge to Walpole in London.

zine of Magazines into their hands.[1] They tell me, that an *ingenious* poem, called *Reflections* in a Country Churchyard, has been communicated to them, which they are printing forthwith: that they are informed, that the *excellent* author of it is I by name, and that they beg not only his *indulgence*, but the *honor of his correspondence*, etc. As I am not at all disposed to be either so indulgent, or so correspondent, as they desire, I have but one bad way left to escape the honor they would inflict upon me and am therefore obliged to desire you would make Dodsley print it immediately (which may be done in less than a week's time[2]) from your copy, but without my name, in what form is most convenient for him, but in his best paper and character.[3] He must correct the press himself, and print it without any interval between the stanzas,[4] because the sense is in some places continued beyond them; and the title must be, "Elegy, wrote in a Country Church-yard." If he would add a line or two to say it came into his hands by accident, I should like it better.[5] If you think fit, the 102nd line may be read "Awake, and faithful to her wonted fires," but if this be worse than before, it must go as it was. In the 126th, for *ancient* Thorn, read *aged*.[6]

If you behold the *Mag: of Mag:* in the light that I do, you will not refuse to give yourself this trouble on my account, which you have taken of your own accord before now. Adieu, Sir, I am

Yours ever,

TG

If Dodsley don't do this immediately, he may as well let it alone.[7]

from To Horace Walpole, 20 February 1751

My dear Sir,

You have indeed conducted with great decency my little *misfortune:* you have taken a paternal care of it, and expressed much more kindness than could have been expected from so near a relation. But we are all frail; and I hope to do as much for you another time. Nurse Dodsley has given it a pinch or two in the cradle,[8] that (I doubt) it will bear the marks of as long as it lives. But no matter: we have ourselves suffered under her hands before now; and besides, it will only look the more careless, and by *accident* as it were.[9] I thank you for your advertisement, which saves my honor, and in a manner *bien flatteuse pour moi*,[1] who should be put to it[2] even to make myself a compliment in good English. * * *

I am ever yours,

T. Gray

---

1. Both Walpole and Gray despised the monthly magazines (including this comparative newcomer) as cynically exploitative, gathering any text they could use to their advantage, and printing it (sloppily) without compensating the author. In this case, though, as the letter notes, Walpole is partly (and perhaps deliberately) responsible for Gray's "distress": once the poem started circulating in manuscript, it became inevitable that some editor would get hold of it.
2. The thriving publisher Robert Dodsley (1704–1764) worked even faster than expected, producing a pamphlet edition of the *Elegy* four days after the date of this letter.
3. Typeface.
4. Gray later changed his mind about this, separating each quatrain with space before and after.
5. Walpole devised an "Advertisement," published in the first edition: "The following poem came into my hands by accident, if the general approbation with which this little piece has been spread may be called by so slight a term as accident. It is this approbation which makes it unnecessary for me to make any apology but to the author; as he cannot but feel some satisfaction in having pleased so many readers already, I flatter myself he will forgive my communicating that pleasure to many more."
6. Gray miscounted the poem's lines; the revisions proposed here apply to lines 92 and 116 (Gray later removed the comma after "Awake").
7. Dodsley did it in the nick of time; a day after his edition appeared, the *Magazine of Magazines* published the poem and (unlike Dodsley) named Gray as its author.
8. Misprints.
9. Gray echoes Walpole's "Advertisement" (see note 5).
1. French: very flattering for me.
2. Should find it difficult.

Sonnet on the Death of Mr. Richard West[1]

In vain to me the smiling mornings shine,
And redd'ning Phoebus lifts his golden fire:
The birds in vain their amorous descant join,
Or cheerful fields resume their green attire:
These ears, alas! for other notes repine,   5
A different object do these eyes require.
My lonely anguish melts no heart but mine;
And in my breast the imperfect joys expire.
Yet morning smiles the busy race to cheer,
And new-born pleasure brings to happier men;   10
The fields to all their wonted tribute bear;
To warm their little loves the birds complain.
I fruitless mourn to him that cannot hear,
And weep the more because I weep in vain.

1742   1775

Ode on a Distant Prospect of Eton College[1]

Ye distant spires, ye antique towers,
That crown the wat'ry glade,
Where grateful Science° still adores   knowledge
Her Henry's holy shade;[2]
And ye, that from the stately brow   5
Of Windsor's heights[3] th' expanse below
Of grove, of lawn, of mead survey,
Whose turf, whose shade, whose flowers among
Wanders the hoary Thames along
His silver-winding way.   10

    Ah happy hills, ah, pleasing shade,
Ah, fields beloved in vain,
Where once my careless childhood strayed,
A stranger yet to pain!
I feel the gales, that from ye blow,   15
A momentary bliss bestow,
As waving fresh their gladsome wing,
My weary soul they seem to soothe,
And, redolent of joy and youth,
To breathe a second spring.   20

    Say, Father Thames, for thou hast seen
Full many a sprightly race
Disporting on thy margent° green   margin
The paths of pleasure trace,
Who foremost now delight to cleave   25

1. West had died of tuberculosis on 1 June 1742, at age 25. Gray composed this sonnet the following August, and in the same month wrote the ode that follows.
1. One of England's oldest and most eminent schools for boys (founded 1440); Gray had attended from 1725 to 1734.
2. The ghost ("shade") of Henry VI (1421–1471), the school's founder.
3. The college is located within the borough of Windsor, on the river Thames.

With pliant arm thy glassy wave?
The captive linnet which enthrall?
What idle progeny succeed
To chase the rolling circle's speed,[4]
30   Or urge the flying ball?

    While some on earnest business bent
Their murm'ring labors ply
'Gainst graver hours, that bring constraint
To sweeten liberty:
35   Some bold adventurers disdain
The limits of their little reign,
And unknown regions dare descry:
Still as they run they look behind,
They hear a voice in every wind,
40   And snatch a fearful joy.

    Gay hope is theirs by fancy fed,
Less pleasing when possessed;
The tear forgot as soon as shed,
The sunshine of the breast:
45   Theirs buxom° health of rosy hue,   *lively*
Wild wit, invention ever-new,
And lively cheer of vigor born;
The thoughtless day, the easy night,
The spirits pure, the slumbers light,
50   That fly th' approach of morn.

    Alas, regardless of their doom,
The little victims play!
No sense have they of ills to come,
Nor care beyond today:
55   Yet see how all around 'em wait
The ministers of human fate,
And black Misfortune's baleful train!°   *attendants*
Ah, shew them where in ambush stand
To seize their prey the murth'rous° band!   *murderous*
60   Ah, tell them, they are men!

    These shall the fury Passions tear,
The vultures of the mind,
Disdainful Anger, pallid Fear,
And Shame that skulks behind;
65   Or pining Love shall waste their youth,
Or Jealousy with rankling tooth,
That inly gnaws the secret heart,
And Envy wan, and faded Care,
Grim-visaged comfortless Despair,
70   And Sorrow's piercing dart.

    Ambition this shall tempt to rise,
Then whirl the wretch from high,

---

4. A children's game involving a hoop.

To bitter Scorn a sacrifice,
And grinning Infamy.
75 The stings of Falsehood those shall try,
And hard Unkindness' altered eye,
That mocks the tear it forced to flow;
And keen Remorse with blood defiled,
And moody Madness laughing wild
80 Amid severest woe.

    Lo, in the vale of years beneath
A grisly troop are seen,
The painful family of Death,
More hideous than their Queen:
85 This racks the joints, this fires the veins,
That every laboring sinew strains,
Those in the deeper vitals rage:
Lo, Poverty, to fill the band,
That numbs the soul with icy hand,
90 And slow-consuming Age.

    To each his suff'rings: all are men,
Condemned alike to groan;
The tender for another's pain;
Th' unfeeling for his own.
95 Yet ah! why should they know their fate?
Since sorrow never comes too late,
And happiness too swiftly flies.
Thought would destroy their paradise.
No more; where ignorance is bliss,
100 'Tis folly to be wise.
1742   1747

Ode on the Death of a Favorite Cat, Drowned in a Tub of Gold Fishes[1]

'Twas on a lofty vase's side,
Where China's gayest art had dyed
    The azure flowers, that blow;°   blossom
Demurest of the tabby kind,
5   The pensive Selima reclined,
    Gazed on the lake below.

Her conscious tail her joy declared;
The fair round face, the snowy beard,
    The velvet of her paws,
10 Her coat, that with the tortoise vies,
Her ears of jet, and emerald eyes,
    She saw; and purred applause.

---

1. The cat had belonged to Walpole, who asked Gray to write her an epitaph. Gray sent something more substantial: "There's a poem for you; it is rather too long for an epitaph." Walpole admired the ode so much that he saw to its publication and had the first stanza inscribed on the "tub" itself—actually a china vase, which Walpole enshrined on a pedestal and displayed at his home, Strawberry Hill, where it still stands.

Still had she gazed; but 'midst the tide
Two angel forms were seen to glide,
15 The genii° of the stream: *protective deities*
Their scaly armor's Tyrian hue[2]
Through richest purple to the view
  Betrayed a golden gleam.

The hapless nymph with wonder saw:
20 A whisker first and then a claw,
  With many an ardent wish,
She stretched in vain to reach the prize.
What female heart can gold despise?
  What cat's averse to fish?

25 Presumptuous maid! with looks intent
Again she stretched, again she bent,
  Nor knew the gulf between.
(Malignant Fate sat by and smiled)
The slippery verge her feet beguiled,
30 She tumbled headlong in.

Eight times emerging from the flood
She mewed to ev'ry wat'ry God,
  Some speedy aid to send.
No dolphin came,[3] no Nereid° stirred: *water-nymph*
35 Nor cruel Tom, nor Susan heard.
  A favorite has no friend!

From hence, ye beauties, undeceived,
Know, one false step is ne'er retrieved,
  And be with caution bold.
40 Not all that tempts your wandering eyes
And heedless hearts, is lawful prize;
  Nor all that glisters,° gold.   *glitters*

1747   1748

Elegy Written in a Country Churchyard

The curfew tolls the knell of parting day,
The lowing herd wind slowly o'er the lea,
The plowman homeward plods his weary way,
And leaves the world to darkness and to me.

5 Now fades the glimmering landscape on the sight,
And all the air a solemn stillness holds,
Save where the beetle wheels his droning flight,
And drowsy tinklings lull the distant folds;

Save that from yonder ivy-mantled tower
10 The moping owl does to the moon complain

---

2. A deep purple dye made from mollusks, prized by the ancients as a mark of luxury.

3. As did the dolphin who, in Greek mythology, rescued the drowning poet Arion.

Of such as, wand'ring near her secret bower,
Molest her ancient solitary reign.

Beneath those rugged elms, that yew-tree's shade,
Where heaves the turf in many a mouldering heap,
15   Each in his narrow cell for ever laid,
The rude forefathers of the hamlet sleep.

The breezy call of incense-breathing morn,
The swallow twitt'ring from the straw-built shed,
The cock's shrill clarion, or the echoing horn,
20   No more shall rouse them from their lowly bed.

For them no more the blazing hearth shall burn,
Or busy housewife ply her evening care:
No children run to lisp their sire's return,
Or climb his knees the envied kiss to share.

25   Oft did the harvest to their sickle yield,
Their furrow oft the stubborn glebe° has broke;   *clod of earth*
How jocund did they drive their team afield!
How bowed the woods beneath their sturdy stroke!

Let not Ambition mock their useful toil,
30   Their homely joys, and destiny obscure;
Nor Grandeur hear, with a disdainful smile,
The short and simple annals of the poor.

The boast of heraldry, the pomp of power,
And all that beauty, all that wealth e'er gave,
35   Awaits alike th' inevitable hour.
The paths of glory lead but to the grave.

Nor you, ye Proud, impute to these the fault,
If Mem'ry o'er their tomb no trophies raise,
Where through the long-drawn aisle and fretted vault
40   The pealing anthem swells the note of praise.

Can storied urn or animated bust
Back to its mansion call the fleeting breath?
Can Honor's voice provoke the silent dust,
Or Flatt'ry soothe the dull cold ear of Death?

45   Perhaps in this neglected spot is laid
Some heart once pregnant with celestial fire;
Hands that the rod of empire might have swayed,
Or waked to ecstasy the living lyre.

But Knowledge to their eyes her ample page
50   Rich with the spoils of time did ne'er unroll;
Chill Penury repressed their noble rage,
And froze the genial current of the soul.

Full many a gem of purest ray serene,
The dark unfathomed caves of ocean bear:

55   Full many a flower is born to blush unseen,
        And waste its sweetness on the desert air.

        Some village-Hampden[1] that with dauntless breast
        The little tyrant of his fields withstood;
        Some mute inglorious Milton here may rest,
60   Some Cromwell guiltless of his country's blood.

        Th' applause of listening senates to command,
        The threats of pain and ruin to despise,
        To scatter plenty o'er a smiling land,
        And read their history in a nation's eyes,

65   Their lot forbade: nor circumscribed alone
        Their growing virtues, but their crimes confined;
        Forbade to wade through slaughter to a throne,
        And shut the gates of mercy on mankind,

        The struggling pangs of conscious truth to hide,
70   To quench the blushes of ingenuous shame,
        Or heap the shrine of Luxury and Pride
        With incense kindled at the Muse's flame.[2]

        Far from the madding crowd's ignoble strife,
        Their sober wishes never learned to stray;
75   Along the cool sequestered vale of life
        They kept the noiseless tenor of their way.

        Yet ev'n these bones from insult to protect
        Some frail memorial still erected nigh,
        With uncouth rhymes and shapeless sculpture decked,
80   Implores the passing tribute of a sigh.

        Their name, their years, spelt by th' unlettered muse,
        The place of fame and elegy supply:
        And many a holy text around she strews,
        That teach the rustic moralist to die.

85   For who to dumb Forgetfulness a prey,
        This pleasing anxious being e'er resigned,
        Left the warm precincts of the cheerful day,
        Nor cast one longing ling'ring look behind?

---

1. John Hampden (1594–1643), Parliamentary statesman and general in the Civil Wars, famed for his firm defiance of Charles I.
2. According to Gray's friend William Mason, the poem originally concluded at this juncture with the following four stanzas, preserved in a manuscript at Eton College:

The thoughtless world to majesty may bow
Exalt the brave, and idolize success,
But more to innocence their safety owe
Than power and genius e'er conspired to bless.

And thou, who mindful of the unhonored dead
Dost in these notes their artless tale relate
By night and lonely contemplation led
To linger in the gloomy walks of fate,

Hark how the sacred calm, that broods around
Bids ev'ry fierce tumultuous passion cease
In still small accents whisp'ring from the ground
A grateful earnest of eternal peace.

No more with reason and thyself at strife;
Give anxious cares and endless wishes room
But through the cool sequestered vale of life
Pursue the silent tenor of thy doom.

On some fond breast the parting soul relies,
90   Some pious drops the closing eye requires;
Ev'n from the tomb the voice of nature cries,
Ev'n in our ashes live their wonted fires.

For thee, who mindful of th' unhonored dead
Dost in these lines their artless tale relate;
95   If chance, by lonely Contemplation led,
Some kindred spirit shall inquire thy fate,

Haply some hoary-headed swain may say,
"Oft have we seen him at the peep of dawn
Brushing with hasty steps the dews away
100   To meet the sun upon the upland lawn.

"There at the foot of yonder nodding beech
That wreathes its old fantastic roots so high,
His listless length at noontide would he stretch,
And pore upon the brook that babbles by.

105   "Hard by yon wood, now smiling as in scorn,
Mutt'ring his wayward fancies he would rove,
Now drooping, woeful wan, like one forlorn,
Or crazed with care, or crossed in hopeless love.

"One morn I missed him on the 'customed hill,
110   Along the heath and near his favorite tree;
Another came; nor yet beside the rill,
Nor up the lawn, nor at the wood was he;

"The next with dirges due in sad array
Slow through the church-way path we saw him borne.
115   Approach and read (for thou can'st read) the lay,
Graved on the stone beneath yon aged thorn."

The Epitaph

Here rests his head upon the lap of earth
A youth to fortune and to fame unknown.
Fair Science frowned not on his humble birth,
120   *And Melancholy marked him for her own.*

Large was his bounty, and his soul sincere,
Heaven did a recompense as largely send:
He gave to Mis'ry all he had, a tear,
He gained from Heav'n ('twas all he wished) a friend.

125   *No farther seek his merits to disclose,*
Or draw his frailties from their dread abode,
(There they alike in trembling hope repose)
The bosom of his Father and his God.

Samuel Johnson
1709–1784

Samuel Johnson was born among books—his father sold them, not very successfully, at the family's combined home and shop in the market town of Lichfield. The son went on to create some of the most celebrated books of his age: an entire *Dictionary*, an edition of Shakespeare, a travel book, philosophical fictions, two eminent series of essays, a thick cluster of biographies. Despite his output, Johnson suffered from a chronic sense that he was underusing his talent, and throughout his *oeuvre* he wrote about "human unsuccess" (in W. H. Auden's phrase) with an empathy and acuity that few have matched before or since.

Johnson's struggles began early. An infection in infancy, followed by an attack of scrofula at age two, left his face scarred and his sight and hearing permanently impaired; by the age of eight a nervous disorder, probably Tourette's syndrome, brought on the compulsive gesticulations and intermittent muttering that would afflict him throughout his life, making him appear bizarre or even repellent at first encounter—until (as many testified) the stunning moment when he would begin to speak. His impressiveness had begun early, too. In childhood, the speed with which he acquired knowledge and the force with which he retained it astonished classmates and teachers, and also his parents, whose desire to show off his attainments often made him miserable. Johnson found more congenial mentors in his cousin, the rakish but learned young clergyman Cornelius Ford, at whose home he spent about half a year at age sixteen, and in Gilbert Walmesley, a middle-aged Lichfield lawyer, who welcomed Johnson often to his ample table and to the intelligent, disputatious company there assembled. Under Ford's and Walmesley's influence, Johnson undertook an intense but improvisatory program of reading, mostly in his father's shop. He read with a ferocious concentration that locked the texts into lifelong memory. "In this irregular manner," he later recalled, "I had looked into a great many books, which were not commonly known at the university, where they seldom read any books but what are put into their hands by their tutors; so that when I came to Oxford, Dr. Adams, now master of Pembroke College, told me, I was the best qualified for the university that he had ever known come there."

Despite such qualifications, Johnson's time at Oxford ushered in not triumph but frustration, and an oppressive sense of failure. Though he continued to be admired for his reading, and began to be noted for his writing, Johnson left the university after only thirteen months, "miserably poor" and unable to pay the fees, unbearably depressed and incapable of envisioning a viable future. After a melancholy year at home, during which his father died in debt, Johnson tried his hand at a variety of jobs beneath his earlier expectations: as assistant at a grammar school (he applied for three such positions, secured one, and left it in disgust after six months), and as occasional contributor to *The Birmingham Journal*. At Birmingham, he befriended the merchant Harry Porter and his wife Elizabeth ("Tetty"); she saw past his awkwardness at their first encounter, remarking to her daughter, "This is the most sensible man that I ever saw in my life." In 1735, ten months after her husband's death, she and Johnson married, despite wariness in both families at their difference in age (she was twenty years his senior). The new husband and wife tried to start a country boarding school, but it attracted only a handful of students. Early in 1737, Johnson decided to try something new: the life of a freelance writer in London.

The generic term for such a life was "Grub Street": it identified both an actual London street where some writers lived and plied their trade, and also the painful state of mind in which almost all of them did so, eking out precarious incomes from whatever assignments they could drum up. From the first, Johnson fared a little better than most. He attached himself immediately to Edward Cave, founder of the flourishing *Gentleman's Magazine*, in which Johnson's writing appeared plentifully over the next decade: essays, poems, short biographies, reviews, and voluminous, ingeniously fictionalized reports of debates in Parliament (authentic transcriptions were prohibited by law). The work provided some security but no prosperity: Johnson and his wife lived in poverty for many years. The struggle fueled articulate rage: in his poem *London* (1738), Johnson inveighed against the corruption of Robert Walpole's government and the cruelties of the city. Among his Grub Street colleagues he found a friend who, far more than himself, had made a sense of injury the basis of both life and art. The poet Richard Savage, generous, brilliant, and unstable, believed himself the abandoned offspring of a wealthy countess, and squandered much of his short life in the vain pursuit of recognition and redress. In *The Life of Richard Savage* (1744), published soon after his friend's early death, Johnson for the first time orchestrated many of the elements that would make his own work great: a commitment to biographical precision rather than routine panegyric; an analysis of expectation, self-delusion, and disappointment; a deep sympathy combined with nuanced judgment.

Savage was a memoir of Grub Street, but not yet for Johnson a valedictory. For two more years he continued his life of anonymous publication, narrow income, and declining spirits— "lost," as a friend lamented, "both to himself and the world." Then a new project found him. In 1746, the bookseller Robert Dodsley, struck by the erudition evident in Johnson's unsigned pieces, persuaded him to create a new dictionary of English, and assembled a consortium of publishers to finance (and profit from) the enormous undertaking. Johnson and his wife promptly moved from cramped and squalid quarters to a three-story house complete with a well-lit garret. There, with the help of six part-time assistants, Johnson made his lexicon, compiling word lists, tracking shifts and gradations of meaning, devising definitions, and illustrating them with quotations culled from the authors he most admired. The writer who (as Adam Smith later testified) "knew more books than any man alive" now decanted them discriminatingly into the two folio volumes of his *Dictionary* (1755), so as to make the work not only a standard reference for the language but also a compendium of its literature and its learning. The task took Johnson longer than he had anticipated—seven years, not three—but during this span he had busied himself in other ways as well: publishing *The Vanity of Human Wishes* (1749), a long poem on the pain of disillusion; witnessing the long-postponed production of his tragedy *Irene* (which brought him welcome added income); and composing, twice a week for two years, the periodical essay called *The Rambler* (1750–1752), the most formidable and famous instance of the genre since Addison and Steele had set down the *Spectator* forty years before. Johnson had embarked on the *Dictionary* as a virtual unknown; he emerged from the project with lasting fame and a double measure of celebratory sobriquets: he was widely known as "Dictionary Johnson," and was sometimes referred to simply (without surname) as "the Rambler."

As an epitome of his character the second label was perhaps more apt. A restlessness closely connected with loneliness had marked Johnson's mind since childhood. During the years of the *Dictionary*'s making, the loneliness had deepened. In 1752 Tetty died, and despite the strains in a marriage that had been differently difficult for both of them, Johnson mourned her obsessively for the rest of his days. He also contrived new sources of companionship, at home and in the wider world. He housed under his roof a group of eccentric, often difficult characters, including the ungainly man of medicine Robert Levet; the Jamaican servant Francis Barber; the blind Anna Williams, who waited up late every night to keep him company in his final cup of tea, often after he had spent long hours in more elevated society. He established what amounted to a second residence in the more polished household of the brewer Henry Thrale and his witty wife Hester, who welcomed and pampered not only Johnson but also the accomplished people who now rejoiced to rotate in his orbit: the actor David Garrick (who had been his pupil in the failed school and his companion on the road to London); the painter Joshua Reynolds; the politician and orator Edmund Burke; the writer Oliver Goldsmith; and Johnson's ardent young protégé and future biographer James Boswell. At the Thrales' country seat, and at the London clubs he formed to stave off solitude, Johnson sat surrounded by luminaries, savoring and often dominating the conversation. He talked (as Boswell noted) "for victory," and he generally secured it by a kind of surprise attack, a witty demolition of his companions' most familiar premises and casual assumptions. He won his listeners over by texture as well as text: by the spontaneous clarity and force of his utterance (as lexicographer he had defined every word he spoke); by the depth and energy of his voice.

Writing was by contrast largely solitary. Johnson's work pattern in the decade after the *Dictionary* recapitulated that of the one before: one ambitious, overarching project—this time an edition of all Shakespeare's plays (1765)—punctuated by shorter writings of lasting significance: a new periodical essay called *The Idler* (1758–1760); the philosophical tale *Rasselas, Prince of Abyssinia* (1759). In 1762 Johnson received a royal pension from George III in recognition of the *Dictionary*, assuring him an income of £300 a year for the remainder of his life. The pension brought Johnson a new security, along with the occasional accusation that his subsequent political pamphlets, generally favorable to the regime, amounted to paid propaganda. In fact, Johnson's politics throughout his life correlated fairly well with the views he implicitly espoused in the distinction he once drew for Boswell: "The prejudice of the Tory is for establishment; the prejudice of the Whig is for innovation." Born into a world where Whigs had long prevailed, Johnson early committed himself to Tory ways of thought: he cherished precedent, defended "subordination" (social hierarchy), and opposed Whiggish innovation with seriocomic fervor. What remained most notable about his politics was their compassion. "From first to last," John Wain remarks, Johnson "rooted his life among the poor and outcast"; in his work he argued the causes of prostitutes and slaves, of anyone sunk by the "want of necessaries" into "motionless despondence."

In the wake of his pension, Johnson's writing grew sparser, and markedly more social, compassing gestures to and for people he valued. He continued an ingrained habit of churning out prose for his friends to use under their own names: dictating law briefs for lawyers, composing sermons for preachers. He carried on an abundant and affectionate correspondence with Hester Thrale. With Boswell as companion, he traveled to the Scottish Highlands, and on his return published his account of that gregarious trip, *A Journey to the Western Islands* (1775). His final large work was social in a different sense. He accepted a commission to provide *Prefaces Biographical and Critical* for an anthology of English poets of the past hundred and fifty years. These included predecessors who had influenced him, contemporaries he had known, successors he regarded with admiration or alarm. To write their biographies, to analyze their works, was in a sense to live over his own literary life, and to reenter, at length and for the last time, the world of reading and of writing in which he'd now made his way for almost seven decades.

"Our social comforts drop away," Johnson lamented when his friend Levet died in 1782; his own last years were marred by loss. Successive deaths shrunk his contentious household; his friendship with Hester Thrale disintegrated under the pressure of her passion for a man of whom Johnson disapproved; a stroke temporarily deprived him of speech and ushered in his final difficult illness. At his death, an admirer remarked that Johnson had left "a chasm, which not only nothing can fill up, but which nothing has a tendency to fill up. Johnson is dead. Let us go to the next best:—there is nobody: no man can be said to put you in mind of Johnson." Biographers rushed in to fill the chasm, with the testimony of friends and of detractors, and with transcriptions of the hypnotic talk that many of them (notably Boswell and Thrale) had begun to record decades before. For most of the nineteenth century the fame of Johnson's talk far surpassed that of his writing. In recent decades scholars and readers have redressed the balance, finding in Johnson's prose and verse the richest repositories of his thought. Throughout a life of arduous struggle, prodigious accomplishment, and (in the end) near-matchless celebrity, Johnson wrote most eloquently and most feelingly—even in the *Dictionary*, even in literary criticism—of human vulnerabilities: to hope and disappointment, suffering and loss.

THE VANITY OF HUMAN WISHES   In his *Life of Pope*, Johnson defines the imitation, a poetic form much in vogue during the late seventeenth and early eighteenth centuries, as a "mode . . . in which the ancients are familiarized by adapting their sentiments to modern topics. . . . It is a kind of middle composition between translation and original design, which pleases when the thoughts are unexpectedly applicable and the parallels lucky." *The Vanity of Human Wishes* is Johnson's most sustained and successful endeavor in the mode. In the second century A.D., the Roman poet Juvenal had written an enduring satire on human ambition and failure, drawing vivid instances from history and from contemporary life. Johnson does the same, replacing the Roman's ancient examples with modern ones, supplanting his Stoic "sentiments" with a Christian credo. Johnson produced his imitation quickly, composing the whole of it in his mind before writing any of it down. It was the first work to appear under his own name, after more than a decade of abundant but anonymous publications. Its title and text sound themes that would preoccupy him for the remainder of his writing life: the dangers of desire, the inevitability of disappointment, the necessity of faith. *The Vanity of Human Wishes* is Johnson's signature poem in more ways than one.

The Vanity of Human Wishes
The Tenth Satire of Juvenal Imitated

    Let Observation, with extensive view,
    Survey mankind, from China to Peru;
    Remark each anxious toil, each eager strife,
    And watch the busy scenes of crowded life;
5   Then say how hope and fear, desire and hate,
    O'erspread with snares the clouded maze of fate,
    Where wav'ring man, betrayed by vent'rous pride,
    To tread the dreary paths without a guide,
    As treach'rous phantoms in the mist delude,
10   Shuns fancied ills, or chases airy[1] good;
    How rarely reason guides the stubborn choice,
    Rules the bold hand, or prompts the suppliant voice;
    How nations sink, by darling schemes oppressed,
    When vengeance listens to the fool's request.
15   Fate wings with every wish th' afflictive dart,
    Each gift of nature, and each grace of art,
    With fatal heat impetuous courage glows,
    With fatal sweetness elocution flows,
    Impeachment stops the speaker's pow'rful breath,
20   And restless fire precipitates on death.
       But scarce observed, the knowing and the bold
    Fall in the gen'ral massacre of gold;
    Wide-wasting pest! that rages unconfined,
    And crowds with crimes the records of mankind;
25   For gold his sword the hireling ruffian draws,
    For gold the hireling judge distorts the laws;
    Wealth heaped on wealth, nor truth nor safety buys,
    The dangers gather as the treasures rise.
       Let hist'ry tell where rival kings command,
30   And dubious title shakes the madded land,
    When statutes° glean the refuse of the sword,   *tax laws*
    How much more safe the vassal than the lord;
    Low skulks the hind° beneath the rage of pow'r,   *rural laborer*

---

1. "Wanting reality; having no steady foundation in truth or nature" (Johnson's *Dictionary*).

And leaves the wealthy traitor in the Tow'r,[2]
35   Untouched his cottage, and his slumbers sound,
Though confiscation's vultures hover round.
      The needy traveler, secure and gay,
Walks the wild heath, and sings his toil away.
Does envy seize thee? crush th' upbraiding joy,
40   Increase his riches and his peace destroy;
Now fears in dire vicissitude invade,
The rustling brake° alarms, and quiv'ring shade,   thicket
Nor light nor darkness bring his pain relief,
One shows the plunder, and one hides the thief.
45   Yet still one gen'ral cry the skies assails,
And gain and grandeur load the tainted gales;
Few know the toiling statesman's fear or care,
Th' insidious rival and the gaping heir.
      Once more, Democritus,[3] arise on earth,
50   With cheerful wisdom and instructive mirth,
See motley[4] life in modern trappings dressed,
And feed with varied fools th' eternal jest:
Thou who couldst laugh where want enchained caprice,
Toil crushed conceit, and man was of a piece;
55   Where wealth unloved without a mourner died,
And scarce a sycophant was fed by pride;
Where ne'er was known the form of mock debate,
Or seen a new-made mayor's unwieldy state;
Where change of fav'rites made no change of laws,
60   And senates heard before they judged a cause;
How wouldst thou shake at Britain's modish tribe,
Dart the quick taunt, and edge the piercing gibe?
Attentive truth and nature to descry,°   discern
And pierce each scene with philosophic eye.
65   To thee were solemn toys or empty show,
The robes of pleasure and the veils of woe:
All aid the farce, and all thy mirth maintain,
Whose joys are causeless, or whose griefs are vain.
      Such was the scorn that filled the sage's mind,
70   Renewed at ev'ry glance on humankind;
How just that scorn ere yet thy voice declare,
Search every state, and canvass every prayer.
      Unnumbered suppliants crowd Preferment's gate,
Athirst for wealth, and burning to be great;
75   Delusive Fortune hears th' incessant call,
They mount, they shine, evaporate, and fall.[5]
On every stage the foes of peace attend,
Hate dogs their flight, and insult mocks their end.
Love ends with hope, the sinking statesman's door
80   Pours in the morning worshiper no more;

2. The Tower of London.   4. Multicolored clothes worn by jesters.
3. Ancient Greek philosopher who laughed at the follies   5. The image is that of Fortune's wheel.
of humanity.

For growing names the weekly scribbler lies,
To growing wealth the dedicator flies,
From ev'ry room descends the painted face,
That hung the bright Palladium[6] of the place,
85 And smoked in kitchens, or in auctions sold,
To better features yields the frame of gold;
For now no more we trace in ev'ry line
Heroic worth, benevolence divine:
The form distorted justifies the fall,
90 And detestation rids th' indignant wall.
　　But will not Britain hear the last appeal,
Sign her foes' doom, or guard her fav'rites' zeal?
Through Freedom's sons no more remonstrance rings,
Degrading nobles and controlling kings;
95 Our supple tribes° repress their patriot throats,　　　　　*of voters*
And ask no questions but the price of votes;
With weekly libels and septennial ale,[7]
Their wish is full to riot and to rail.
　　In full-blown dignity, see Wolsey[8] stand,
100 Law in his voice, and fortune in his hand:
To him the church, the realm, their pow'rs consign,
Through him the rays of regal bounty shine,
Turned by his nod the stream of honor flows,
His smile alone security bestows:
105 Still to new heights his restless wishes tow'r,
Claim leads to claim, and pow'r advances pow'r;
Till conquest unresisted ceased to please,
And rights submitted, left him none to seize.
At length his sov'reign frowns—the train of state
110 Mark the keen glance, and watch the sign to hate.
Wheree'er he turns he meets a stranger's eye,
His suppliants scorn him, and his followers fly;
At once is lost the pride of awful state,
The golden canopy, the glitt'ring plate,
115 The regal palace, the luxurious board,
The liv'ried army, and the menial lord.
With age, with cares, with maladies oppressed,
He seeks the refuge of monastic rest.
Grief aids disease, remembered folly stings,
120 And his last sighs reproach the faith of kings.
　　Speak thou, whose thoughts at humble peace repine,
Shall Wolsey's wealth, with Wolsey's end be thine?
Or liv'st thou now, with safer pride content,
The wisest justice on the banks of Trent?[9]
125 For why did Wolsey near the steeps° of fate,　　　　　*precipices*
On weak foundations raise th' enormous weight?
Why but to sink beneath misfortune's blow,

---

6. A statue of Pallas Athena, guardian of Troy.
7. Drink offered to voters as bribes during campaigns for
Parliament, held every seven years.
8. Cardinal Wolsey (1475–1530), Henry VIII's Lord
Chancellor, who was dismissed and imprisoned for failing
to procure the King a divorce from Catherine of Aragon.
9. The river that divides northern from southern England; it is near Lichfield, Johnson's birthplace.

With louder ruin to the gulfs below?
    What gave great Villiers[1] to th' assassin's knife,
130   And fixed disease on Harley's[2] closing life?
What murdered Wentworth, and what exiled Hyde,[3]
By kings protected, and to kings allied?
What but their wish indulged in courts to shine,
And pow'r too great to keep, or to resign?
135   When first the college rolls receive his name,
The young enthusiast[4] quits his ease for fame;
Through all his veins the fever of renown
Burns from the strong contagion of the gown;[5]
O'er Bodley's dome[6] his future labors spread,
140   And Bacon's mansion[7] trembles o'er his head.
Are these thy views? proceed, illustrious youth,
And virtue guard thee to the throne of Truth!
Yet should thy soul indulge the gen'rous heat,
Till captive Science° yields her last retreat;   *knowledge*
145   Should Reason guide thee with her brightest ray,
And pour on misty Doubt resistless day;
Should no false Kindness lure to loose delight,
Nor Praise relax, nor Difficulty fright;
Should tempting Novelty thy cell refrain,
150   And Sloth effuse her opiate fumes in vain;
Should Beauty blunt on fops her fatal dart,
Nor claim the triumph of a lettered heart;
Should no disease thy torpid veins invade,
Nor Melancholy's phantoms haunt thy shade;
155   Yet hope not life from grief or danger free,
Nor think the doom of man reversed for thee:
Deign on the passing world to turn thine eyes,
And pause awhile from letters, to be wise;
There mark what ills the scholar's life assail,
160   Toil, envy, want, the patron,[8] and the jail.
See nations slowly wise, and meanly just,
To buried merit raise the tardy bust.
If dreams yet flatter, once again attend,
Hear Lydiat's life, and Galileo's end.[9]
165   Nor deem, when learning her last prize bestows,
The glitt'ring eminence exempt from foes;
See when the vulgar 'scape, despised or awed,

1. George Villiers (1592–1628), first Duke of Buckingham and a favorite of James I, was stabbed to death.
2. Robert Harley (1661–1724), first Earl of Oxford and leading statesman during the reign of Queen Anne, was impeached when George I succeeded to the throne in 1714.
3. Thomas Wentworth (1593–1641), first Earl of Strafford and adviser to Charles I, was executed at the beginning of the English Civil War. Edward Hyde (1609–1674), first Earl of Clarendon, served Charles II but then fell from favor.
4. "One of hot imagination" (Johnson's *Dictionary*).
5. Scholastic dress (but also a reference to the poisoned garment that killed Hercules).
6. The Bodleian Library, Oxford.
7. "There is a tradition, that the study of friar Bacon [Roger Bacon, a medieval philosopher] built an arch over the bridge, will fall, when a man greater than Bacon shall pass under it" [Johnson's note].
8. Johnson originally wrote "garret," but changed it to "patron" after enduring the neglect of Lord Chesterfield (see his letter to Chesterfield, page 2822).
9. Thomas Lydiat (1572–1646) was a distinguished but impoverished mathematician. The astronomer Galileo Galilei (1564–1642) was silenced by the Inquisition.

Rebellion's vengeful talons seize on Laud.[1]
From meaner minds, though smaller fines content,
170 The plundered palace or sequestered rent;
Marked out by dangerous parts° he meets the shock,   *abilities*
And fatal Learning leads him to the block:
Around his tomb let Art and Genius weep,
But hear his death, ye blockheads, hear and sleep.
175   The festal blazes, the triumphal show,
The ravished standard, and the captive foe,
The senate's thanks, the gazette's pompous tale,
With force resistless o'er the brave prevail.
Such bribes the rapid Greek[2] o'er Asia whirled,
180 For such the steady Romans shook the world;
For such in distant lands the Britons shine,
And stain with blood the Danube or the Rhine;
This pow'r has praise, that virtue scarce can warm,
Till fame supplies the universal charm.
185 Yet Reason frowns on War's unequal game,
Where wasted nations raise a single name,
And mortgaged states their grandsires' wreaths[3] regret,
From age to age in everlasting debt;
Wreaths which at last the dear-bought right convey
190 To rust on medals, or on stones decay.
    On what foundation stands the warrior's pride,
How just his hopes let Swedish Charles[4] decide;
A frame of adamant, a soul of fire,
No dangers fright him, and no labors tire;
195 O'er love, o'er fear, extends his wide domain,
Unconquered lord of pleasure and of pain;
No joys to him pacific scepters yield,
War sounds the trump, he rushes to the field;
Behold surrounding kings their pow'r combine,
200 And one capitulate, and one resign;
Peace courts his hand, but spreads her charms in vain;
"Think nothing gained," he cries, "till nought remain,
On Moscow's walls till Gothic standards fly,
And all be mine beneath the polar sky."
205 The march begins in military state,
And nations on his eye suspended wait;
Stern Famine guards the solitary coast,
And Winter barricades the realms of Frost;
He comes, not want and cold his course delay—
210 Hide, blushing Glory, hide Pultowa's day:
The vanquished hero leaves his broken bands,
And shows his miseries in distant lands;
Condemned a needy supplicant to wait,
While ladies interpose, and slaves debate.

1. William Laud (1572–1645), Archbishop of Canterbury under Charles I, was beheaded by the Parliamentarians.
2. Alexander the Great.
3. Garlands of victory.

4. Charles XII of Sweden, whose precarious military career ended at the Battle of Pultowa (1709). After his defeat by the Russians, Charles attempted to forge an alliance with the Turks.

215   But did not Chance at length her error mend?
          Did no subverted empire mark his end?
          Did rival monarchs give the fatal wound?
          Or hostile millions press him to the ground?
          His fall was destined to a barren strand,
220   A petty fortress, and a dubious hand;[5]
          He left the name, at which the world grew pale,
          To point a moral, or adorn a tale.
              All times their scenes of pompous woes afford,
          From Persia's tyrant[6] to Bavaria's lord.[7]
225   In gay hostility, and barb'rous pride,
          With half mankind embattled at his side,
          Great Xerxes comes to seize the certain prey,
          And starves exhausted regions in his way;
          Attendant Flattery counts his myriads o'er,
230   Till counted myriads soothe his pride no more;
          Fresh praise is tried till madness fires his mind,
          The waves he lashes, and enchains the wind;
          New pow'rs are claimed, new pow'rs are still bestowed,
          Till rude resistance lops the spreading god;
235   The daring Greeks deride the martial show,
          And heap heir valleys with the gaudy foe;
          Th' insulted sea with humbler thoughts he gains,
          A single skiff to speed his ligh remains;
          Th' encumbered oar scarce leaves the dreaded coast
240   Through purple billows and a floating host.
              The bold Bavarian, in a luckless hour,
          Tries the dread summits of Cesarean power,
          With unexpected legions bursts away,
          And sees defenseless realms receive his sway;
245   Short sway! fair Austria spreads her mournful charms,
          The queen, the beauty, sets the world in arms;
          From hill to hill the beacon's rousing blaze
          Spreads wide the hope of plunder and of praise;
          The fierce Croatian, and the wild Hussar,
250   And all the sons of ravage crowd the war;
          The baffled prince in honor's flattering bloom
          Of hasty greatness finds the fatal doom,
          His foes' derision, and his subjects' blame,
          And steals to death from anguish and from shame.
255   Enlarge my life with multitude of days,
          In health, in sickness, thus the suppliant prays;
          Hides from himself his state, and shuns to know,
          That life protracted is protracted woe.
          Time hovers o'er, impatient to destroy,

5. Charles XII of Sweden was thought to have been killed by one of his own officers during a siege of little military consequence.
6. Xerxes (?519–465 B.C.) invaded Greece with a large army and navy. In order to transport his troops, he built a bridge of boats across the Hellespont. When a storm broke up this bridge, Xerxes ordered the wind and water to be punished. The Persian army was defeated at the Battle of Plataea, the navy at the Battle of Salamis.
7. Charles Albert (1697–1745), Elector of Bavaria, was defeated by Empress Maria Theresa, whose army included Austrian colonists from Croatia and Hungarian cavalry called "jussars."

260   And shuts up all the passages of joy:
       In vain their gifts the bounteous seasons pour,
       The fruit autumnal, and the vernal flow'r,
       With listless eyes the dotard views the store,
       He views, and wonders that they please no more;
265   Now pall the tasteless meats, and joyless wines,
       And Luxury° with sighs her slave resigns.   *voluptuousness*
       Approach, ye minstrels, try the soothing strain,
       Diffuse the tuneful lenitives[8] of pain:
       No sounds alas would touch th' impervious ear,
270   Though dancing mountains witnessed Orpheus[9] near;
       Nor lute nor lyre his feeble pow'rs attend,
       Nor sweeter music of a virtuous friend,
       But everlasting dictates crowd his tongue,
       Perversely grave, or positively wrong.
275   The still returning tale, and ling'ring jest,
       Perplex the fawning niece and pampered guest,
       While growing hopes scarce awe the gathering sneer,
       And scarce a legacy can bribe to hear;
       The watchful guests still hint the last° offense,   *latest*
280   The daughter's petulance, the son's expense,
       Improve his heady rage with treach'rous skill,
       And mold his passions till they make his will.
           Unnumbered maladies his joints invade,
       Lay siege to life and press the dire blockade;
285   But unextinguished Avarice still remains,
       And dreaded losses aggravate his pains;
       He turns, with anxious heart and crippled hands,
       His bonds of debt, and mortgages of lands;
       Or views his coffers with suspicious eyes,
290   Unlocks his gold, and counts it till he dies.
           But grant, the virtues of a temp'rate prime
       Bless with an age exempt from scorn or crime;
       An age that melts with unperceived decay,
       And glides in modest innocence away;
295   Whose peaceful day Benevolence endears,
       Whose night congratulating Conscience cheers;
       The gen'ral favorite as the gen'ral friend:
       Such age there is, and who shall wish its end?
           Yet ev'n on this her load Misfortune flings,
300   To press the weary minutes' flagging wings:
       New sorrow rises as the day returns,
       A sister sickens, or a daughter mourns.
       Now kindred Merit fills the sable bier,
       Now lacerated Friendship claims a tear.
305   Year chases year, decay pursues decay,
       Still drops some joy from with'ring life away;
       New forms arise, and different views engage,

---

8. "Anything medicinally applied to ease pain" (John-   9. In Greek mythology, the musician Orpheus charmed
son's *Dictionary*).   wild beasts and moved mountains.

Superfluous lags the vet'ran on the stage,
Till pitying Nature signs the last release,
310   And bids afflicted worth retire to peace.
     But few there are whom hours like these await,
Who set unclouded in the gulfs of fate.
From Lydia's monarch should the search descend,
By Solon cautioned to regard his end,[1]
315   In life's last scene what prodigies surprise,
Fears of the brave, and follies of the wise?
From Marlborough's eyes the streams of dotage flow,[2]
And Swift expires a driveler and a show.[3]
     The teeming mother, anxious for her race,
320   Begs for each birth the fortune of a face:
Yet Vane could tell what ills from beauty spring;
And Sedley cursed the form that pleased a king.[4]
Ye nymphs of rosy lips and radiant eyes,
Whom Pleasure keeps too busy to be wise,
325   Whom Joys with soft varieties invite,
By day the frolic, and the dance by night,
Who frown with vanity, who smile with art,
And ask the latest fashion of the heart,
What care, what rules your heedless charms shall save,
330   Each nymph your rival, and each youth your slave?
Against your fame with fondness hate combines,
The rival batters, and the lover mines.
With distant voice neglected Virtue calls,
Less heard and less, the faint remonstrance falls;
335   Tired with contempt, she quits the slipp'ry reign,
And Pride and Prudence take her seat in vain.
In crowd at once, where none the pass defend,
The harmless Freedom, and the private Friend.
The guardians yield, by force superior plied;
340   By Interest, Prudence; and by Flattery, Pride.
Now beauty falls betrayed, despised, distressed,
And hissing Infamy proclaims the rest.
     Where then shall Hope and Fear their objects find?
Must dull Suspense corrupt the stagnant mind?
345   Must helpless man, in ignorance sedate,°   calm
Roll darkling° down the torrent of his fate?   in the dark
Must no dislike alarm, no wishes rise,
No cries attempt the mercies of the skies?
Inquirer, cease, petitions yet remain,
350   Which Heav'n may hear, nor deem religion vain.
Still raise for good the supplicating voice,
But leave to Heav'n the measure and the choice,

1. Solon, Greek philosopher and legislator, warned the wealthy King Croesus of Lydia that no one should count himself happy until reaching the end of life.
2. John Churchill (1650–1722), first Duke of Marlborough, hero of the War of the Spanish Succession, lived for six years after suffering two paralytic strokes.
3. Jonathan Swift, who declined into senility, was thought to have been exhibited by his servant for money.
4. Anne Vane (1705–1736) was the mistress of the Prince of Wales, Catherine Sedley (1657–1717) of James II.

Safe in his power, whose eyes discern afar
The secret ambush of a specious prayer.
355   Implore his aid, in his decisions rest,
Secure whate'er he gives, he gives the best.
Yet when the sense of sacred presence fires,
And strong devotion to the skies aspires,
Pour forth thy fervors for a healthful mind,
360   Obedient passions, and a will resigned;
For love, which scarce collective man can fill;
For patience sov'reign o'er transmuted ill;
For faith, that panting for a happier seat,
Counts death kind Nature's signal of retreat:
365   These goods for man the laws of Heav'n ordain,
These goods he grants, who grants the power to gain;
With these celestial Wisdom calms the mind,
And makes the happiness she does not find.

1748   1749

A Short Song of Congratulation[1]

Long expected one and twenty
  Ling'ring year at last is flown,
Pomp and pleasure, pride and plenty,
  Great Sir John, are all your own.

5   Loosened from the minor's tether,
  Free to mortgage or to sell,
Wild as wind, and light as feather
  Bid the slaves of thrift farewell.[2]

Call the Bettys, Kates, and Jennys
10   Ev'ry name that laughs at care,
Lavish of your grandsire's guineas,
  Show the spirit of an heir.

All that prey on vice and folly
  Joy to see their quarry fly,
15   Here the gamester light and jolly
  There the lender grave and sly.

Wealth, Sir John, was made to wander,
  Let it wander as it will;
See the jockey, see the pander,
20   Bid them come, and take their fill.

When the bonny blade carouses,
  Pockets full, and spirits high,
What are acres? What are houses?
  Only dirt, or wet or dry.

1. Written for Sir John Lade (1759–1838), the nephew of Johnson's close friend Henry Thrale.
2. Sir John fulfilled Johnson's predictions: he made a scandalous marriage and then squandered his inheritance.

25   If the guardian or the mother
            Tell the woes of willful waste,
        Scorn their counsel and their pother,
            You can hang or drown at last.

1780   1794

On the Death of Dr. Robert Levet[1]

Condemned to Hope's delusive mine,
    As on we toil from day to day,
By sudden blasts, or slow decline,
    Our social comforts drop away.

5   Well tried through many a varying year,
        See Levet to the grave descend;
    Officious,[2] innocent, sincere,
        Of ev'ry friendless name the friend.

    Yet still he fills Affection's eye,
10   Obscurely° wise, and coarsely kind;   *privately*
    Nor, lettered Arrogance, deny
        Thy praise to merit unrefined.

    When fainting Nature called for aid,
        And hov'ring Death prepared the blow,
15 His vig'rous remedy displayed
        The power of art without the show.

    In Misery's darkest caverns known,
        His useful care was ever nigh,
    Where hopeless Anguish poured his groan,
20   And lonely Want retired to die.

    No summons mocked by chill delay,
        No petty gain disdained by pride,
    The modest wants of ev'ry day
        The toil of ev'ry day supplied.

25 His virtues walked their narrow round,
        Nor made a pause, nor left a void;
    And sure th' Eternal Master found
        The single talent well employed.[3]

    The busy day, the peaceful night,
30   Unfelt, uncounted, glided by;
    His frame was firm, his pow'rs were bright,
        Though now his eightieth year was nigh.

---

1. Robert Levet (1705–1782), a friend and dependent of Johnson, had acquired a modicum of medical training while working as a waiter in Paris; he put this training to use by caring for the poorest of the London poor ("Dr." was an honorific title). Many of Johnson's friends wondered why he admired and supported a man whom Boswell described as "an obscure practiser in physick amongst the lower people." Johnson's elegy answers that question.
2. "Kind; doing good offices" (Johnson's *Dictionary*).
3. A reference to Jesus' Parable of the Talents (Matthew 25.14–30), which haunted Johnson throughout his adult life.

Then with no throbbing fiery pain,
No cold gradations of decay,
35   Death broke at once the vital chain,
And freed his soul the nearest way.

1782   1783

THE RAMBLER   In the midst of working on his *Dictionary*, Johnson took on an ambitious additional task: he wrote *The Rambler*, a twice-weekly periodical essay which he sustained for two
full years (1750–1752). The project brought him needed income and also a useful respite from
the strains of lexicography. *The Rambler*'s most famous antecedent was Addison and Steele's
the *Spectator* (1711–1713), and though Johnson would later praise Addison's prose as a "model
of the middle style . . . always equable and always easy," he chose for his own essays a mode
more astringent: a large, often Latinate vocabulary, intricately balanced sentences, a steady
alertness to the human propensity for self-delusion, a willingness to confront rather than ingratiate. Pressures of production could run high (Johnson later claimed that he sometimes wrote
his essay with the printer's messenger standing at his side, waiting to take the text to the
press), and speed of output may have helped shape the results. Many *Ramblers*, with their formidably wrought prose and surprising turns of thought, manage to seem imposing and improvisatory at the same time. Free to choose his topics, working under relentlessly recurrent dead-
lines, Johnson drew on four decades dense with reading and thought, during which (in the
words of his biographer John Hawkins) he had "accumulated a fund of moral science that was
more than sufficient for such an undertaking," and had become "in a very eminent degree
qualified for the office of an instructor of mankind in their greatest and most important concerns." Readers proved eager for the instruction. More than any of his earlier writings, *The
Rambler* established Johnson's style, his substance, and his fame.

Rambler No. 4

[ON FICTION]

Saturday, 31 March 1750

Simul et jucunda et idonea dicere vitae.

Horace, *Ars Poetica* 1.334

And join both profit and delight in one.

Creech

The works of fiction with which the present generation seems more particularly
delighted are such as exhibit life in its true state, diversified only by accidents that
daily happen in the world, and influenced by passions and qualities which are really
to be found in conversing with mankind.

This kind of writing may be termed not improperly the comedy of romance, and
is to be conducted nearly by the rules of comic poetry. Its province is to bring about
natural events by easy means, and to keep up curiosity without the help of wonder: it
is therefore precluded from the machines[1] and expedients of the heroic romance, and
can neither employ giants to snatch away a lady from the nuptial rites, nor knights to
bring her back from captivity; it can neither bewilder its personages in deserts, nor
lodge them in imaginary castles.

---

1. "Supernatural agency in poems" (Johnson's *Dictionary*).

I remember a remark made by Scaliger upon Pontanus,[2] that all his writings are filled with the same images; and that if you take from him his lillies and his roses, his satyrs and his dryads, he will have nothing left that can be called poetry. In like manner, almost all the fictions of the last age will vanish, if you deprive them of a hermit and a wood, a battle and a shipwreck.

Why this wild strain of imagination found reception so long, in polite and learned ages, it is not easy to conceive; but we cannot wonder that, while readers could be procured, the authors were willing to continue it: for when a man had by practice gained some fluency of language, he had no further care than to retire to his closet,[3] let loose his invention, and heat his mind with incredibilities; a book was thus produced without fear of criticism, without the toil of study, without knowledge of nature, or acquaintance with life.

The task of our present writers is very different; it requires, together with that learning which is to be gained from books, that experience which can never be attained by solitary diligence, but must arise from general converse, and accurate observation of the living world. Their performances have, as Horace expresses it, *plus oneris quantum veniae minus*, little indulgence, and therefore more difficulty.[4] They are engaged in portraits of which every one knows the original, and can detect any deviation from exactness of resemblance. Other writings are safe, except from the malice of learning, but these are in danger from every common reader; as the slipper ill executed was censured by a shoemaker who happened to stop in his way at the Venus of Apelles.[5]

But the fear of not being approved as just copiers of human manners, is not the most important concern that an author of this sort ought to have before him. These books are written chiefly to the young, the ignorant, and the idle, to whom they serve as lectures of conduct, and introductions into life. They are the entertainment of minds unfurnished with ideas, and therefore easily susceptible of impressions; not fixed by principles, and therefore easily following the current of fancy; not informed by experience, and consequently open to every false suggestion and partial account.

That the highest degree of reverence should be paid to youth, and that nothing indecent should be suffered to approach their eyes or ears, are precepts extorted by sense and virtue from an ancient writer, by no means eminent for chastity of thought.[6] The same kind, though not the same degree, of caution, is required in every thing which is laid before them, to secure them from unjust prejudices, perverse opinions, and incongruous combinations of images.

In the romances formerly written, every transaction and sentiment was so remote from all that passes among men, that the reader was in very little danger of making any applications to himself; the virtues and crimes were equally beyond his sphere of activity; and he amused himself with heroes and with traitors, deliverers and persecutors, as with beings of another species, whose actions were regulated upon motives of their own, and who had neither faults nor excellencies in common with himself.

But when an adventurer is leveled with the rest of the world, and acts in such scenes of the universal drama, as may be the lot of any other man, young spectators fix their eyes upon him with closer attention, and hope by observing his behavior and success to regulate their own practices, when they shall be engaged in the like part.

---

2. The Renaissance humanist Julius Caesar Scaliger (1484–1558) criticized the poetry of Giovanni Pontano (1426–1503).
3. Study.
4. Horace, *Epistles* 2.1.170.

5. In his *Natural History*, Pliny the Elder tells this story of the famous painter Apelles.
6. Johnson refers to the opening lines of Juvenal's fourteenth satire.

For this reason these familiar histories may perhaps be made of greater use than the solemnities of professed morality, and convey the knowledge of vice and virtue with more efficacy than axioms and definitions. But if the power of example is so great, as to take possession of the memory by a kind of violence, and produce effects almost without the intervention of the will, care ought to be taken that, when the choice is unrestrained, the best examples only should be exhibited; and that which is likely to operate so strongly, should not be mischievous or uncertain in its effects.

The chief advantage which these fictions have over real life is, that their authors are at liberty, though not to invent, yet to select objects, and to cull from the mass of mankind those individuals upon which the attention ought most to be employed; as a diamond, though it cannot be made, may be polished by art, and placed in such a situation as to display that lustre which before was buried among common stones.

It is justly considered as the greatest excellency of art, to imitate nature; but it is necessary to distinguish those parts of nature, which are most proper for imitation: greater care is still required in representing life, which is so often discolored by passion, or deformed by wickedness. If the world be promiscuously[7] described, I cannot see of what use it can be to read the account; or why it may not be as safe to turn the eye immediately upon mankind, as upon a mirror which shows all that presents itself without discrimination.

It is therefore not a sufficient vindication of a character, that it is drawn as it appears, for many characters ought never to be drawn; nor of a narrative, that the train of events is agreeable to observation and experience, for that observation which is called knowledge of the world will be found much more frequently to make men cunning than good. The purpose of these writings is surely not only to show mankind, but to provide that they may be seen hereafter with less hazard; to teach the means of avoiding the snares which are laid by Treachery for Innocence, without infusing any wish for that superiority with which the betrayer flatters his vanity; to give the power of counteracting fraud, without the temptation to practice it; to initiate youth by mock encounters in the art of necessary defense, and to increase prudence without impairing virtue.

Many writers, for the sake of following nature, so mingle good and bad qualities in their principal personages, that they are both equally conspicuous; and as we accompany them through their adventures with delight, and are led by degrees to interest ourselves in their favor, we lose the abhorrence of their faults, because they do not hinder our pleasure, or, perhaps, regard them with some kindness for being united with so much merit.

There have been men indeed splendidly wicked, whose endowments threw a brightness on their crimes, and whom scarce any villainy made perfectly detestable, because they never could be wholly divested of their excellencies; but such have been in all ages the great corrupters of the world, and their resemblance ought no more to be preserved, than the art of murdering without pain.

Some have advanced, without due attention to the consequences of this notion, that certain virtues have their correspondent faults, and therefore that to exhibit either apart is to deviate from probability. Thus men are observed by Swift to be "grateful in the same degree as they are resentful."[8] This principle, with others of the same kind, supposes man to act from a brute impulse, and pursue a certain degree of inclination, without any choice of the object; for otherwise, though it should be

---

7. Indiscriminately.
8. In fact, it was Pope who made this observation, in the   *Miscellanies* he coauthored with Swift.

allowed that gratitude and resentment arise from the same constitution of the passions, it follows not that they will be equally indulged when reason is consulted; yet unless that consequence be admitted, this sagacious maxim becomes an empty sound, without any relation to practice or to life.

Nor is it evident, that even the first motions to these effects are always in the same proportion. For pride, which produces quickness of resentment, will obstruct gratitude, by unwillingness to admit that inferiority which obligation implies; and it is very unlikely that he who cannot think he receives a favor will acknowledge or repay it.

It is of the utmost importance to mankind that positions of this tendency should be laid open and confuted; for while men consider good and evil as springing from the same root, they will spare the one for the sake of the other, and in judging, if not of others at least of themselves, will be apt to estimate their virtues by their vices. To this fatal error all those will contribute, who confound the colors of right and wrong, and instead of helping to settle their boundaries, mix them with so much art, that no common mind is able to disunite them.

In narratives where historical veracity has no place, I cannot discover why there should not be exhibited the most perfect idea of virtue; of virtue not angelical, nor above probability, for what we cannot credit we shall never imitate, but the highest and purest that humanity can reach, which, exercised in such trials as the various revolutions of things shall bring upon it, may, by conquering some calamities, and enduring others, teach us what we may hope, and what we can perform. Vice, for vice is necessary to be shown, should always disgust; nor should the graces of gaiety, or the dignity of courage, be so united with it, as to reconcile it to the mind. Wherever it appears, it should raise hatred by the malignity of its practices, and contempt by the meanness of its stratagems; for while it is supported by either parts[9] or spirit, it will be seldom heartily abhorred. The Roman tyrant was content to be hated, if he was but feared;[1] and there are thousands of the readers of romances willing to be thought wicked, if they may be allowed to be wits. It is therefore to be steadily inculcated, that virtue is the highest proof of understanding, and the only solid basis of greatness; and that vice is the natural consequence of narrow thoughts, that it begins in mistake, and ends in ignominy.

Rambler No. 5
[ON SPRING]

Tuesday, 3 April 1750

Et nunc omnis ager, nunc omnis parturit arbos,
Nunc frondent silvae, nunc formosissimus annus.

Virgil, *Eclogues* 3.56–57

Now every field, now every tree is green;
Now genial nature's fairest face is seen.

Elphinston

---

9. Abilities.

1. The Roman historian Suetonius reports this of the emperor Caligula.

Every man is sufficiently discontented with some circumstances of his present state, to suffer his imagination to range more or less in quest of future happiness, and to fix upon some point of time, in which, by the removal of the inconvenience which now perplexes him, or acquisition of the advantage which he at present wants,[1] he shall find the condition of his life very much improved.

When this time, which is too often expected with great impatience, at last arrives, it generally comes without the blessing for which it was desired; but we solace ourselves with some new prospect, and press forward again with equal eagerness.

It is lucky for a man, in whom this temper prevails, when he turns his hopes upon things wholly out of his own power; since he forbears then to precipitate his affairs, for the sake of the great event that is to complete his felicity, and waits for the blissful hour, with less neglect of the measures necessary to be taken in the mean time.

I have long known a person of this temper, who indulged his dream of happiness with less hurt to himself than such chimerical wishes commonly produce, and adjusted his scheme with such address, that his hopes were in full bloom three parts of the year, and in the other part never wholly blasted. Many, perhaps, would be desirous of learning by what means he procured to himself such a cheap and lasting satisfaction. It was gained by a constant practice of referring the removal of all his uneasiness to the coming of the next spring; if his health was impaired, the spring would restore it; if what he wanted was at a high price, it would fall its value in the spring.

The spring, indeed, did often come without any of these effects, but he was always certain that the next would be more propitious; nor was ever convinced that the present spring would fail him before the middle of summer; for he always talked of the spring as coming 'till it was past, and when it was once past, everyone agreed with him that it was coming.

By long converse with this man, I am, perhaps, brought to feel immoderate pleasure in the contemplation of this delightful season; but I have the satisfaction of finding many, whom it can be no shame to resemble, infected with the same enthusiasm;[2] for there is, I believe, scarce any poet of eminence, who has not left some testimony of his fondness for the flowers, the zephyrs, and the warblers of the spring. Nor has the most luxuriant imagination been able to describe the serenity and happiness of the golden age, otherwise than by giving a perpetual spring, as the highest reward of uncorrupted innocence.

There is, indeed, something inexpressibly pleasing, in the annual renovation of the world, and the new display of the treasures of nature. The cold and darkness of winter, with the naked deformity of every object on which we turn our eyes, make us rejoice at the succeeding season, as well for what we have escaped, as for what we may enjoy; and every budding flower, which a warm situation brings early to our view, is considered by us as a messenger to notify the approach of more joyous days.

The spring affords to a mind, so free from the disturbance of cares or passions as to be vacant to calm amusements, almost every thing that our present state makes us capable of enjoying. The variegated verdure of the fields and woods, the succession of grateful odors, the voice of pleasure pouring out its notes on every side, with the gladness apparently conceived by every animal, from the growth of his food, and the clemency of the weather, throw over the whole earth an air of gaiety, significantly expressed by the smile of nature.

---

1. Lacks.

2. "Elevation of fancy; exaltation of ideas" (Johnson's *Dictionary*).

Yet there are men to whom these scenes are able to give no delight, and who hurry away from all the varieties of rural beauty, to lose their hours, and divert their thoughts by cards, or assemblies, a tavern dinner, or the prattle of the day.

It may be laid down as a position which will seldom deceive, that when a man cannot bear his own company there is something wrong. He must fly from himself, either because he feels a tediousness in life from the equipoise of an empty mind, which, having no tendency to one motion more than another but as it is impelled by some external power, must always have recourse to foreign objects; or he must be afraid of the intrusion of some unpleasing ideas, and, perhaps, is struggling to escape from the remembrance of a loss, the fear of a calamity, or some other thought of greater horror.

Those whom sorrow incapacitates to enjoy the pleasures of contemplation, may properly apply to such diversions, provided they are innocent, as lay strong hold on the attention; and those, whom fear of any future affliction chains down to misery, must endeavor to obviate the danger.

My considerations shall, on this occasion, be turned on such as are burdensome to themselves merely because they want subjects for reflection, and to whom the volume of nature is thrown open, without affording them pleasure or instruction, because they never learned to read the characters.

A French author has advanced this seeming paradox, that "very few men know how to take a walk"; and, indeed, it is true, that few know how to take a walk with a prospect of any other pleasure, than the same company would have afforded them at home.

There are animals that borrow their color from the neighboring body, and, consequently, vary their hue as they happen to change their place. In like manner it ought to be the endeavor of every man to derive his reflections from the objects about him; for it is to no purpose that he alters his position, if his attention continues fixed to the same point. The mind should be kept open to the access of every new idea, and so far disengaged from the predominance of particular thoughts, as easily to accommodate itself to occasional entertainment.

A man that has formed this habit of turning every new object to his entertainment, finds in the productions of nature an inexhaustible stock of materials upon which he can employ himself, without any temptations to envy or malevolence; faults, perhaps, seldom totally avoided by those, whose judgment is much exercised upon the works of art. He has always a certain prospect of discovering new reasons for adoring the sovereign author of the universe, and probable hopes of making some discovery of benefit to others, or of profit to himself. There is no doubt but many vegetables and animals have qualities that might be of great use, to the knowledge of which there is not required much force of penetration, or fatigue of study, but only frequent experiments, and close attention. What is said by the chemists of their darling mercury, is, perhaps, true of every body through the whole creation, that, if a thousand lives should be spent upon it, all its properties would not be found out.

Mankind must necessarily be diversified by various tastes, since life affords and requires such multiplicity of employments, and a nation of naturalists is neither to be hoped, or desired; but it is surely not improper to point out a fresh amusement to those who languish in health, and repine in plenty, for want of some source of diversion that may be less easily exhausted, and to inform the multitudes of both sexes, who are burdened with every new day, that there are many shows which they have not seen.

He that enlarges his curiosity after the works of nature, demonstrably multiplies the inlets to happiness; and, therefore, the younger part of my readers, to whom I dedicate this vernal speculation, must excuse me for calling upon them, to make use at once of the spring of the year, and the spring of life; to acquire, while their minds may be yet impressed with new images, a love of innocent pleasures, and an ardor for useful knowledge; and to remember, that a blighted spring makes a barren year, and that the vernal flowers, however beautiful and gay, are only intended by nature as preparatives to autumnal fruits.

Rambler No. 60

[ON BIOGRAPHY]

Saturday, 13 October 1750

—Quid sit pulchrum, quid turpe, quid utile, quid non,
Plenius et melius Chrysippo et Crantore dicit.

Horace, *Epistles* 1.2.3–4

Whose works the beautiful and base contain;
Of vice and virtue more instructive rules,
Than all the sober sages of the schools.

Francis

All joy or sorrow for the happiness or calamities of others is produced by an act of the imagination, that realizes the event however fictitious, or approximates[1] it however remote, by placing us, for a time, in the condition of him whose fortune we contemplate; so that we feel, while the deception lasts, whatever motions would be excited by the same good or evil happening to ourselves.

Our passions are therefore more strongly moved, in proportion as we can more readily adopt the pains or pleasures proposed to our minds, by recognizing them as once our own, or considering them as naturally incident to our state of life. It is not easy for the most artful writer to give us an interest in happiness or misery, which we think ourselves never likely to feel, and with which we have never yet been made acquainted. Histories of the downfall of kingdoms, and revolutions of empires, are read with great tranquility; the imperial tragedy pleases common auditors only by its pomp of ornament, and grandeur of ideas; and the man whose faculties have been engrossed by business, and whose heart never fluttered but at the rise or fall of stocks, wonders how the attention can be seized, or the affections agitated by a tale of love.

Those parallel circumstances, and kindred images, to which we readily conform our minds, are, above all other writings, to be found in narratives of the lives of particular persons; and therefore no species of writing seems more worthy of cultivation than biography, since none can be more delightful or more useful, none can more certainly enchain the heart by irresistible interest, or more widely diffuse instruction to every diversity of condition.

The general and rapid narratives of history, which involve a thousand fortunes in the business of a day, and complicate innumerable incidents in one great transaction,

---

1. Bring close.

afford few lessons applicable to private life, which derives its comforts and its wretchedness from the right or wrong management of things which nothing but their frequency makes considerable, *parva, si non fiant quotidie,* says Pliny,[2] and which can have no place in those relations which never descend below the consultation of senates, the motions of armies, and the schemes of conspirators.

I have often thought that there has rarely passed a life of which a judicious and faithful narrative would not be useful. For, not only every man has, in the mighty mass of the world, great numbers in the same condition with himself, to whom his mistakes and miscarriages, escapes and expedients, would be of immediate and apparent use; but there is such an uniformity in the state of man, considered apart from adventitious and separable decorations and disguises, that there is scarce any possibility of good or ill, but is common to humankind. A great part of the time of those who are placed at the greatest distance by fortune, or by temper, must unavoidably pass in the same manner; and though, when the claims of nature are satisfied, caprice, and vanity, and accident, begin to produce discriminations and peculiarities, yet the eye is not very heedful, or quick, which cannot discover the same causes still terminating their influence in the same effects, though sometimes accelerated, sometimes retarded, or perplexed by multiplied combinations. We are all prompted by the same motives, all deceived by the same fallacies, all animated by hope, obstructed by danger, entangled by desire, and seduced by pleasure.

It is frequently objected to relations of particular lives, that they are not distinguished by any striking or wonderful vicissitudes. The scholar who passed his life among his books, the merchant who conducted only his own affairs, the priest, whose sphere of action was not extended beyond that of his duty, are considered as no proper objects of public regard, however they might have excelled in their several stations, whatever might have been their learning, integrity, and piety. But this notion arises from false measures of excellence and dignity, and must be eradicated by considering that, in the esteem of uncorrupted reason, what is of most use is of most value.

It is, indeed, not improper to take honest advantages of prejudice, and to gain attention by a celebrated name; but the business of the biographer is often to pass slightly over those performances and incidents, which produce vulgar greatness, to lead the thoughts into domestic privacies, and display the minute details of daily life, where exterior appendages are cast aside, and men excel each other only by prudence and by virtue. The account of Thuanus is, with great propriety, said by its author to have been written, that it might lay open to posterity the private and familiar character of that man, *cujus ingenium et candorem ex ipsius scriptis sunt olim semper miraturi,*[3] whose candor and genius will to the end of time be by his writings preserved in admiration.

There are many invisible circumstances which, whether we read as inquirers after natural or moral knowledge, whether we intend to enlarge our science,[4] or increase our virtue, are more important than public occurrences. Thus Sallust, the great master of nature, has not forgot, in his account of Catiline, to remark that "his walk was now quick, and again slow," as an indication of a mind revolving something with violent commotion.[5] Thus the story of Melancthon[6] affords a striking lecture on the value of time, by informing us, that when he made an appointment, he expected

---

2. "Matters which would be trivial were they not part of a daily routine" (Pliny the Younger, *Epistles* 3.1).
3. Johnson quotes from a commentary affixed by Nicolas Rigault to the *History of His Own Time* by the French historian Jacques-Auguste de Thou (1553–1617). The Latin is translated by the words that follow.

4. Knowledge.
5. Johnson quotes from an account by the Roman historian Sallust of Catiline's conspiracy against Rome.
6. Johnson quotes from a biography of the Protestant theologian Philip Melancthon (1497–1560) by Joachim Camerarius.

not only the hour, but the minute to be fixed, that the day might not run out in the idleness of suspense; and all the plans and enterprises of De Witt are now of less importance to the world, than that part of his personal character which represents him as "careful of his health, and negligent of his life."[7]

But biography has often been allotted to writers who seem very little acquainted with the nature of their task, or very negligent about the performance. They rarely afford any other account than might be collected from public papers, but imagine themselves writing a life when they exhibit a chronological series of actions or preferments; and so little regard the manners or behavior of their heroes, that more knowledge may be gained of a man's real character, by a short conversation with one of his servants, than from a formal and studied narrative, begun with his pedigree, and ended with his funeral.

If now and then they condescend to inform the world of particular facts, they are not always so happy as to select the most important. I know not well what advantage posterity can receive from the only circumstance by which Tickell has distinguished Addison from the rest of mankind, the irregularity of his pulse:[8] nor can I think myself overpaid for the time spent in reading the life of Malherb,[9] by being enabled to relate, after the learned biographer, that Malherb had two predominant opinions; one, that the looseness of a single woman might destroy all her boast of ancient descent; the other, that the French beggars made use very improperly and barbarously of the phrase "noble gentleman," because either word included the sense of both.

There are, indeed, some natural reasons why these narratives are often written by such as were not likely to give much instruction or delight, and why most accounts of particular persons are barren and useless. If a life be delayed till interest and envy are at an end, we may hope for impartiality, but must expect little intelligence; for the incidents which give excellence to biography are of a volatile and evanescent kind, such as soon escape the memory, and are rarely transmitted by tradition. We know how few can portray a living acquaintance, except by his most prominent and observable particularities, and the grosser features of his mind; and it may be easily imagined how much of this little knowledge may be lost in imparting it, and how soon a succession of copies will lose all resemblance of the original.

If the biographer writes from personal knowledge, and makes haste to gratify the public curiosity, there is danger lest his interest, his fear, his gratitude, or his tenderness, overpower his fidelity, and tempt him to conceal, if not to invent. There are many who think it an act of piety to hide the faults or failings of their friends, even when they can no longer suffer by their detection; we therefore see whole ranks of characters adorned with uniform panegyric, and not to be known from one another, but by extrinsic and casual circumstances. "Let me remember," says Hale, "when I find myself inclined to pity a criminal, that there is likewise a pity due to the country."[1] If we owe regard to the memory of the dead, there is yet more respect to be paid to knowledge, to virtue, and to truth.

7. Johnson quotes the essayist Sir William Temple's verdict on the Dutch statesman Jan de Witt (1625–1672).
8. Thomas Tickell prefixed a biography of Joseph Addison to his edition of Addison's *Works* (1721).
9. Johnson refers to the biography of the French poet

Francois de Malherbe (1555–1628) by the Marquis de Racan.
1. Johnson quotes from the biography of Sir Matthew Hale (1609–1676), eminent jurist and religious writer, by Gilbert Burnet.

Rambler No. 170

[ON MISELLA, A PROSTITUTE][1]

Saturday, 2 November 1751

Confiteor; si quid prodest delicta fateri.

Ovid, *Amores* 2.4.3

I grant the charge; forgive the fault confess'd.

TO THE RAMBLER

SIR,

I am one of those beings, from whom many, that melt at the sight of all other misery, think it meritorious to withhold relief; one whom the rigor of virtuous indignation dooms to suffer without complaint, and perish without regard; and whom I myself have formerly insulted in the pride of reputation and security of innocence.

I am of a good family, but my father was burdened with more children than he could decently support. A wealthy relation, as he traveled from London to his country seat, condescending to make him a visit, was touched with compassion of his narrow fortune, and resolved to ease him of part of his charge, by taking the care of a child upon himself. Distress on one side and ambition on the other, were too powerful for parental fondness, and the little family passed in review before him, that he might make his choice. I was then ten years old, and without knowing for what purpose, I was called to my great cousin, endeavored to recommend myself by my best courtesy, sung him my prettiest song, told the last story that I had read, and so much endeared myself by my innocence, that he declared his resolution to adopt me, and to educate me with his own daughters.

My parents felt the common struggles at the thought of parting, and "some natural tears they dropped, but wiped them soon."[2] They considered, not without that false estimation of the value of wealth which poverty long continued always produces, that I was raised to higher rank than they could give me, and to hopes of more ample fortune than they could bequeath. My mother sold some of her ornaments to dress me in such a manner as might secure me from contempt at my first arrival; and when she dismissed me, pressed me to her bosom with an embrace that I still feel, gave me some precepts of piety which, however neglected, I have not forgotten, and uttered prayers for my final happiness, of which I have not yet ceased to hope, that they will at last be granted.

My sisters envied my new finery, and seemed not much to regret our separation; my father conducted me to the stagecoach with a kind of cheerful tenderness; and in a very short time, I was transported to splendid apartments, and a luxurious table, and grew familiar to show, noise and gaiety.

In three years my mother died, having implored a blessing on her family with her last breath. I had little opportunity to indulge a sorrow, which there was none to partake with me, and therefore soon ceased to reflect much upon my loss. My father turned all his care upon his other children, whom some fortunate adventures and unexpected legacies enabled him, when he died four years after my mother, to leave in a condition above their expectations.

---

1. Deriving from Latin, Misella means literally "wretched little one."

2. Milton, *Paradise Lost* 12.645, describing Adam and Eve's emotions on leaving Eden.

I should have shared the increase of his fortune, and had once a portion assigned me in his will; but my cousin assuring him that all care for me was needless, since he had resolved to place me happily in the world, directed him to divide my part amongst my sisters.

Thus I was thrown upon dependence without resource. Being now at an age in which young women are initiated in company, I was no longer to be supported in my former character but at considerable expense; so that partly lest I should waste money, and partly lest my appearance might draw too many compliments and assiduities, I was insensibly degraded from my equality, and enjoyed few privileges above the head servant, but that of receiving no wages.

I felt every indignity, but knew that resentment would precipitate my fall. I therefore endeavored to continue my importance by little services and active officiousness,[3] and for a time preserved myself from neglect, by withdrawing all pretenses to competition, and studying to please rather than to shine. But my interest, notwithstanding this expedient, hourly declined, and my cousin's favorite maid began to exchange repartees with me, and consult me about the alterations of a cast gown.

I was now completely depressed, and though I had seen mankind enough to know the necessity of outward cheerfulness, I often withdrew to my chamber to vent my grief, or turn my condition in my mind, and examine by what means I might escape from perpetual mortification. At last, my schemes and sorrows were interrupted by a sudden change of my relation's behavior, who one day took an occasion when we were left together in a room, to bid me suffer myself no longer to be insulted, but assume the place which he always intended me to hold in the family. He assured me, that his wife's preference of her own daughters should never hurt me; and, accompanying his professions with a purse of gold, ordered me to bespeak a rich suit at the mercer's,[4] and to apply privately to him for money when I wanted it, and insinuate that my other friends supplied me, which he would take care to confirm.

By this stratagem, which I did not then understand, he filled me with tenderness and gratitude, compelled me to repose on him as my only support, and produced a necessity of private conversation. He often appointed interviews at the house of an acquaintance, and sometimes called on me with a coach, and carried me abroad. My sense of his favor, and the desire of retaining it, disposed me to unlimited complaisance, and though I saw his kindness grow every day more fond, I did not suffer any suspicion to enter my thoughts. At last the wretch took advantage of the familiarity which he enjoyed as my relation, and the submission which he exacted as my benefactor, to complete the ruin of an orphan whom his own promises had made indigent, whom his indulgence had melted, and his authority subdued.

I know not why it should afford subject of exultation, to overpower on any terms the resolution, or surprise the caution of a girl; but of all the boasters that deck themselves in the spoils of innocence and beauty, they surely have the least pretensions to triumph, who submit to owe their success to some casual influence. They neither employ the graces of fancy, nor the force of understanding, in their attempts; they cannot please their vanity with the art of their approaches, the delicacy of their adulations, the elegance of their address, or the efficacy of their eloquence; nor applaud themselves as possessed of any qualities, by which affection is attracted. They surmount no obstacles, they defeat no rivals, but attack only those who cannot resist, and are often content to possess the body without any solicitude to gain the heart.

3. Dutiful behavior.   4. Dealer in fabrics.

Many of these despicable wretches does my present acquaintance with infamy and wickedness enable me to number among the heroes of debauchery. Reptiles whom their own servants would have despised, had they not been their servants, and with whom beggary would have disdained intercourse, had she not been allured by hopes of relief. Many of the beings which are now rioting in taverns, or shivering in the streets, have been corrupted not by arts of gallantry which stole gradually upon the affections and laid prudence asleep, but by the fear of losing benefits which were never intended, or of incurring resentment which they could not escape; some have been frighted by masters, and some awed by guardians into ruin.

Our crime had its usual consequence, and he soon perceived that I could not long continue in his family. I was distracted at the thought of the reproach which I now believed inevitable. He comforted me with hopes of eluding all discovery, and often upbraided me with the anxiety, which perhaps none but himself saw in my countenance; but at last mingled his assurances of protection and maintenance with menaces of total desertion, if in the moments of perturbation I should suffer his secret to escape, or endeavor to throw on him any part of my infamy.

Thus passed the dismal hours till my retreat could no longer be delayed. It was pretended that my relations had sent for me to a distant county, and I entered upon a state which shall be described in my next letter.

I am, Sir, &c.
MISELLA

Rambler No. 171
[MISELLA CONTINUES]

Tuesday, 5 November 1751

Taedet coeli convexa tueri.

Virgil, *Aeneid* 4.451

Dark is the sun, and loathsome is the day.

TO THE RAMBLER

SIR,

Misella now sits down to continue her narrative. I am convinced that nothing would more powerfully preserve youth from irregularity, or guard inexperience from seduction, than a just description of the condition into which the wanton plunges herself, and therefore hope that my letter may be a sufficient antidote to my example.

After the distraction, hesitation and delays which the timidity of guilt naturally produces, I was removed to lodgings in a distant part of the town, under one of the characters commonly assumed upon such occasions. Here being, by my circumstances, condemned to solitude, I passed most of my hours in bitterness and anguish. The conversation of the people with whom I was placed, was not at all capable of engaging my attention or dispossessing the reigning ideas. The books which I carried to my retreat were such as heightened my abhorrence of myself; for I was not so far abandoned as to sink voluntarily into corruption, or endeavor to conceal from my own mind the enormity of my crime.

My relation remitted none of his fondness, but visited me so often that I was sometimes afraid lest his assiduity should expose him to suspicion. Whenever he came he found me weeping, and was therefore less delightfully entertained than he expected. After frequent expostulations upon the unreasonableness of my sorrow, and innumerable protestations of everlasting regard, he at last found that I was more affected with the loss of my innocence, than the danger of my fame,[1] and that he might not be disturbed by my remorse, began to lull my conscience with the opiates of irreligion. His arguments were such as my course of life has since exposed me often to the necessity of hearing, vulgar, empty and fallacious; yet they at first confounded me by their novelty, filled me with doubt and perplexity, and interrupted that peace which I began to feel from the sincerity of my repentance, without substituting any other support. I listened a while to his impious gabble, but its influence was soon overpowered by natural reason and early education, and the convictions which this new attempt gave me of his baseness completed my abhorrence. I have heard of barbarians, who, when tempests drive ships upon their coast, decoy them to the rocks that they may plunder their lading, and have always thought that wretches thus merciless in their depredations, ought to be destroyed by a general insurrection of all social beings; yet how light is this guilt to the crime of him, who in the agitations of remorse cuts away the anchor of piety, and when he has drawn aside credulity from the paths of virtue, hides the light of heaven which would direct her to return. I had hitherto considered him as a man equally betrayed with myself by the concurrence of appetite and opportunity; but I now saw with horror that he was contriving to perpetuate his gratification, and was desirous to fit me to his purpose by complete and radical corruption.

To escape, however, was not yet in my power. I could support the expenses of my condition, only by the continuance of his favor. He provided all that was necessary, and in a few weeks, congratulated me upon my escape from the danger which we had both expected with so much anxiety. I then began to remind him of his promise to restore me with my fame uninjured to the world. He promised me in general terms, that nothing should be wanting which his power could add to my happiness, but forbore to release me from my confinement. I knew how much my reception in the world depended upon my speedy return, and was therefore outrageously impatient of his delays, which I now perceived to be only artifices of lewdness. He told me, at last, with an appearance of sorrow, that all hopes of restoration to my former state were forever precluded; that chance had discovered my secret, and malice divulged it; and that nothing now remained, but to seek a retreat more private, where curiosity or hatred could never find us.

The rage, anguish, and resentment, which I felt at this account, are not to be expressed. I was in so much dread of reproach and infamy, which he represented as pursuing me with full cry, that I yielded myself implicitly to his disposal, and was removed with a thousand studied precautions through by-ways and dark passages, to another house, where I harassed him with perpetual solicitations for a small annuity, that might enable me to live in the country with obscurity and innocence.

This demand he at first evaded with ardent professions, but in time appeared offended at my importunity and distrust; and having one day endeavored to soothe me with uncommon expressions of tenderness, when he found my discontent immovable, left me with some inarticulate murmurs of anger. I was pleased that he was at last roused to sensibility, and expecting that at his next visit, he would comply with my request, lived with great tranquility upon the money in my hands, and was

1. Reputation.

so much pleased with this pause of persecution, that I did not reflect how much his absence had exceeded the usual intervals, till I was alarmed with the danger of wanting subsistence. I then suddenly contracted my expenses, but was unwilling to supplicate for assistance. Necessity, however, soon overcame my modesty or my pride, and I applied to him by a letter, but had no answer. I writ in terms more pressing, but without effect. I then sent an agent to inquire after him, who informed me, that he had quitted his house, and was gone with his family to reside for some time upon his estate in Ireland.

However shocked at this abrupt departure, I was yet unwilling to believe that he could wholly abandon me, and therefore by the sale of my clothes I supported myself, expecting that every post would bring me relief. Thus I passed seven months between hope and dejection, in a gradual approach to poverty and distress, emaciated with discontent and bewildered with uncertainty. At last, my landlady, after many hints of the necessity of a new lover, took the opportunity of my absence to search my boxes, and missing some of my apparel, seized the remainder for rent, and led me to the door.

To remonstrate against legal cruelty was vain; to supplicate obdurate brutality was hopeless. I went away I knew not whither, and wandered about without any settled purpose, unacquainted with the usual expedients of misery, unqualified for laborious offices, afraid to meet an eye that had seen me before, and hopeless of relief from those who were strangers to my former condition. Night came on in the midst of my distraction, and I still continued to wander till the menaces of the watch obliged me to shelter myself in a covered passage.

Next day, I procured a lodging in the backward garret of a mean house, and employed my landlady to inquire for a service. My applications were generally rejected for want of a character.[2] At length, I was received at a draper's; but when it was known to my mistress that I had only one gown, and that of silk, she was of opinion, that I looked like a thief, and without warning, hurried me away. I then tried to support myself by my needle, and by my landlady's recommendation, obtained a little work from a shop, and for three weeks lived without repining; but when my punctuality had gained me so much reputation, that I was trusted to make up a head[3] of some value, one of my fellow-lodgers stole the lace, and I was obliged to fly from a prosecution.

Thus driven again into the streets, I lived upon the least that could support me, and at night accommodated myself under penthouses[4] as well as I could. At length I became absolutely penniless; and having strolled all day without sustenance, was at the close of evening accosted by an elderly man, with an invitation to a tavern. I refused him with hesitation; he seized me by the hand, and drew me into a neighboring house, where when he saw my face pale with hunger, and my eyes swelling with tears, he spurned me from him, and bad me cant and whine in some other place; he for his part would take care of his pockets.

I still continued to stand in the way, having scarcely strength to walk farther, when another soon addressed me in the same manner. When he saw the same tokens of calamity, he considered that I might be obtained at a cheap rate, and therefore quickly made overtures, which I had no longer firmness to reject. By this man I was maintained four months in penurious wickedness, and then abandoned to my former condition, from which I was delivered by another keeper.

2. Letter of reference.
3. Headdress.

4. Eaves of houses.

In this abject state I have now passed four years, the drudge of extortion and the sport of drunkenness; sometimes the property of one man, and sometimes the common prey of accidental lewdness; at one time tricked up for sale by the mistress of a brothel, at another begging in the streets to be relieved from hunger by wickedness; without any hope in the day but of finding some whom folly or excess may expose to my allurements, and without any reflections at night, but such as guilt and terror impress upon me.

If those who pass their days in plenty and security, could visit for an hour the dismal receptacles to which the prostitute retires from her nocturnal excursions, and see the wretches that lie crowded together, mad with intemperance, ghastly with famine, nauseous with filth, and noisome with disease; it would not be easy for any degree of abhorrence to harden them against compassion, or to repress the desire which they must immediately feel to rescue such numbers of human beings from a state so dreadful.

It is said that in France they annually evacuate their streets, and ship their prostitutes and vagabonds to their colonies. If the women that infest this city had the same opportunity of escaping from their miseries, I believe very little force would be necessary; for who among them can dread any change? Many of us indeed are wholly unqualified for any but the most servile employments, and those perhaps would require the care of a magistrate to hinder them from following the same practices in another country; but others are only precluded by infamy from reformation, and would gladly be delivered on any terms from the necessity of guilt and the tyranny of chance. No place but a populous city can afford opportunities for open prostitution, and where the eye of justice can attend to individuals, those who cannot be made good may be restrained from mischief. For my part I should exult at the privilege of banishment, and think myself happy in any region that should restore me once again to honesty and peace.

I am, Sir, &c.

MISELLA

Rambler No. 207

[BEGINNINGS, MIDDLES, AND ENDS]

Tuesday, 10 March 1752

Solve senescentem mature sanus equum, ne
Peccet ad extremum ridendus.

Horace, *Epistles* 1.1.8–9

The voice of reason cries with winning force,
Loose from the rapid car your aged horse,
Lest, in the race derided, left behind,
He drag his jaded limbs and burst his wind.

Francis

Such is the emptiness of human enjoyment, that we are always impatient of the present. Attainment is followed by neglect, and possession by disgust; and the malicious remark of the Greek epigrammatist on marriage may be applied to every other course of life, that its two days of happiness are the first and the last.[1]

1. Johnson paraphrases the poet Palladas, whose epigrams appear in the *Greek Anthology* (11.381).

Few moments are more pleasing than those in which the mind is concerting measures for a new undertaking. From the first hint that wakens the fancy, till the hour of actual execution, all is improvement and progress, triumph and felicity. Every hour brings additions to the original scheme, suggests some new expedient to secure success, or discovers consequential advantages not hitherto foreseen. While preparations are made, and materials accumulated, day glides after day through elysian prospects, and the heart dances to the song of hope.

Such is the pleasure of projecting, that many content themselves with a succession of visionary schemes, and wear out their allotted time in the calm amusement of contriving what they never attempt or hope to execute.

Others, not able to feast their imagination with pure ideas, advance somewhat nearer to the grossness of action, with great diligence collect whatever is requisite to their design, and, after a thousand researches and consultations, are snatched away by death, as they stand in procinctu[2] waiting for a proper opportunity to begin.

If there were no other end of life, than to find some adequate solace for every day, I know not whether any condition could be preferred to that of the man who involves himself in his own thoughts, and never suffers experience to show him the vanity of speculation; for no sooner are notions reduced to practice, than tranquility and confidence forsake the breast; every day brings its task, and often without bringing abilities to perform it: difficulties embarrass, uncertainty perplexes, opposition retards, censure exasperates, or neglect depresses. We proceed, because we have begun; we complete our design, that the labor already spent may not be vain: but as expectation gradually dies away, the gay smile of alacrity disappears, we are compelled to implore severer powers, and trust the event to patience and constancy.

When once our labor has begun, the comfort that enables us to endure it is the prospect of its end; for though in every long work there are some joyous intervals of self-applause, when the attention is recreated by unexpected facility, and the imagination soothed by incidental excellencies; yet the toil with which performance struggles after idea, is so irksome and disgusting,[3] and so frequent is the necessity of resting below that perfection which we imagined within our reach, that seldom any man obtains more from his endeavors than a painful conviction of his defects, and a continual resuscitation of desires which he feels himself unable to gratify.

So certainly is weariness the concomitant of our undertakings, that every man, in whatever he is engaged, consoles himself with the hope of change; if he has made his way by assiduity to public employment, he talks among his friends of the delight of retreat; if by the necessity of solitary application he is secluded from the world, he listens with a beating heart to distant noises, longs to mingle with living beings, and resolves to take hereafter his fill of diversions, or display his abilities on the universal theatre, and enjoy the pleasure of distinction and applause.

Every desire, however innocent, grows dangerous, as by long indulgence it becomes ascendant in the mind. When we have been much accustomed to consider any thing as capable of giving happiness, it is not easy to restrain our ardor, or to forbear some precipitation in our advances, and irregularity in our pursuits. He that has cultivated the tree, watched the swelling bud and opening blossom, and pleased himself with computing how much every sun and shower add to its growth, scarcely stays

---

2. Under arms, ready for action.   3. Distasteful.

till the fruit has obtained its maturity, but defeats his own cares by eagerness to reward them. When we have diligently labored for any purpose, we are willing to believe that we have attained it, and, because we have already done much, too suddenly conclude that no more is to be done.

All attraction is increased by the approach of the attracting body. We never find ourselves so desirous to finish, as in the latter part of our work, or so impatient of delay, as when we know that delay cannot be long. This unseasonable importunity of discontent may be partly imputed to languor and weariness, which must always oppress those more whose toil has been longer continued; but the greater part usually proceeds from frequent contemplation of that ease which is now considered as within reach, and which, when it has once flattered our hopes, we cannot suffer to be withheld.

In some of the noblest compositions of wit, the conclusion falls below the vigor and spirit of the first books; and as a genius is not to be degraded by the imputation of human failings, the cause of this declension is commonly sought in the structure of the work, and plausible reasons are given why in the defective part less ornament was necessary, or less could be admitted. But, perhaps, the author would have confessed, that his fancy was tired, and his perseverance broken; that he knew his design to be unfinished, but that, when he saw the end so near, he could no longer refuse to be at rest.

Against the instillations of this frigid opiate, the heart should be secured by all the considerations which once concurred to kindle the ardor of enterprise. Whatever motive first incited action, has still greater force to stimulate perseverance; since he that might have lain still at first in blameless obscurity, cannot afterwards desist but with infamy and reproach. He, whom a doubtful promise of distant good, could encourage to set difficulties at defiance, ought not to remit his vigor, when he has almost obtained his recompense. To faint or loiter, when only the last efforts are required, is to steer the ship through tempests, and abandon it to the winds in sight of land; it is to break the ground and scatter the seed, and at last to neglect the harvest.

The masters of rhetoric direct, that the most forcible arguments be produced in the latter part of an oration, lest they should be effaced or perplexed by supervenient images. This precept may be justly extended to the series of life: nothing is ended with honor, which does not conclude better than it begun. It is not sufficient to maintain the first vigor; for excellence loses its effect upon the mind by custom, as light after a time ceases to dazzle. Admiration must be continued by that novelty which first produced it, and how much soever is given, there must always be reason to imagine that more remains.

We not only are most sensible of the last impressions, but such is the unwillingness of mankind to admit transcendent merit, that, though it be difficult to obliterate the reproach of miscarriages by any subsequent achievement, however illustrious, yet the reputation raised by a long train of success, may be finally ruined by a single failure, for weakness or error will be always remembered by that malice and envy which it gratifies.

For the prevention of that disgrace, which lassitude and negligence may bring at last upon the greatest performances, it is necessary to proportion carefully our labor to our strength. If the design comprises many parts, equally essential, and therefore not to be separated, the only time for caution is before we engage; the powers of the mind must be then impartially estimated, and it must be remembered, that not to complete the plan, is not to have begun it; and, that nothing is done, while any thing is omitted.

But, if the task consists in the repetition of single acts, no one of which derives its efficacy from the rest, it may be attempted with less scruple, because there is always opportunity to retreat with honor. The danger is only lest we expect from the world the indulgence with which most are disposed to treat themselves; and in the hour of listlessness imagine, that the diligence of one day will atone for the idleness of another, and that applause begun by approbation will be continued by habit.

He that is himself weary will soon weary the public. Let him therefore lay down his employment, whatever it be, who can no longer exert his former activity or attention; let him not endeavor to struggle with censure, or obstinately infest the stage till a general hiss commands him to depart.[4]

from A Review of Soame Jenyns' *A Free Inquiry into the Nature and Origin of Evil*[1]

This is a treatise, consisting of six letters, upon a very difficult and important question, which, I am afraid, this author's endeavors will not free from the perplexity which has entangled the speculatists of all ages, and which must always continue while *we see* but *in part*. He calls it a *free* inquiry, and indeed his freedom is, I think, greater than his modesty. Though he is far from the contemptible arrogance or the impious licentiousness of Bolingbroke,[2] yet he decides too easily upon questions out of the reach of human determination, with too little consideration of mortal weakness, and with too much vivacity for the necessary caution. * * *

We are next entertained with Pope's alleviations of those evils which we are doomed to suffer:

Poverty, or the want of riches, is generally compensated by having more hopes and fewer fears, by a greater share of health, and a more exquisite relish of the smallest enjoyments, than those who possess them are usually blessed with. The want of taste and genius, with all the pleasures that arise from them, are commonly recompensed by a more useful kind of common sense, together with a wonderful delight, as well as success, in the busy pursuits of a scrambling world. The sufferings of the sick are greatly relieved by many trifling gratifications imperceptible to others, and sometimes almost repaid by the inconceivable transports occasioned by the return of health and vigor. Folly cannot be very grievous, because imperceptible; and I doubt not but there is some truth in that rant of a mad poet, that there is a pleasure in being mad which none but madmen know. Ignorance, or the want of knowledge and literature, the appointed lot of all born to poverty and the drudgeries of life, is the only opiate capable of infusing that insensibility which can enable them to endure the miseries of the one, and the fatigues of the other. It is a cordial administered by the gracious hand of providence, of which they ought never to be deprived by an ill-judged and improper education. It is the basis of all subordination, the support of society, and the privilege of individuals: and I have ever thought it a most remarkable instance of the divine wisdom that whereas in all animals, whose individuals rise little

4. With his next essay (*Rambler* No. 208), Johnson brought the series to a close.

1. Soame Jenyns (1704–1787), a wealthy dilettante who dabbled in literature, politics, and theology, published his *Free Inquiry* early in 1757; Johnson's review appeared in the *Literary Magazine* a few months later. Much of what Jenyns has to say in his theodicy (or vindication of the justice and goodness of God) is derived from Pope's *Essay on Man* (for Johnson's opinion of the *Essay*, see page 2817). Central to both Pope's poem and Jenyns's treatise

is the doctrine of the Great Chain of Being, which models the universe as a hierarchical scale or continuum. This continuum stretches from God down through angels, humans, animals, and inanimate nature. Like Pope, Jenyns concludes that the cosmos is formed on principles of a "just subordination."

2. Henry St. John (1678–1751), Viscount Bolingbroke, politician and political theorist, whose *Reflections Concerning Innate Moral Principles* Johnson considered dangerous in its deism.

above the rest of their species, knowledge is instinctive, in man, whose individuals are so widely different, it is acquired by education, by which means the prince and the laborer, the philosopher and the peasant, are in some measure fitted for their respective situations.

Much of these positions is perhaps true, and the whole paragraph might well pass without censure, were not objections necessary to the establishment of knowledge. *Poverty* is very gently paraphrased by *want of riches.* In that sense almost every man may in his own opinion be poor. But there is another poverty which is *want of competence,* of all that can soften the miseries of life, of all that diversify attention, or delight imagination. There is yet another poverty which is *want of necessaries,* a species of poverty which no care of the public, no charity of particulars,[3] can preserve many from feeling openly, and many secretly.

That hope and fear are inseparably or very frequently connected with poverty and riches my surveys of life have not informed me. The milder degrees of poverty are sometimes supported by hope, but the more severe often sink down in motionless despondence. Life must be seen before it can be known. This author and Pope perhaps never saw the miseries which they imagine thus easy to be borne. The poor indeed are insensible of many little vexations which sometimes embitter the possessions and pollute the enjoyment of the rich. They are not pained by casual incivility, or mortified by the mutilation of a compliment; but this happiness is like that of a malefactor who ceases to feel the cords that bind him when the pincers are tearing his flesh.

That want of taste for one enjoyment is supplied by the pleasures of some other may be fairly allowed. But the compensations of sickness I have never found near to equivalence, and the transports of recovery only prove the intenseness of the pain.

With folly no man is willing to confess himself very intimately acquainted, and therefore its pains and pleasures are kept secret. But what the author says of its happiness seems applicable only to fatuity, or gross dullness, for that inferiority of understanding which makes one man without any other reason the slave, or tool, or property of another, which makes him sometimes useless, and sometimes ridiculous, is often felt with very quick sensibility. On the happiness of madmen, as the case is not very frequent, it is not necessary to raise a disquisition, but I cannot forbear to observe that I never yet knew disorders of mind increase felicity: every madman is either arrogant and irascible, or gloomy and suspicious, or possessed by some passion or notion destructive to his quiet. He has always discontent in his look, and malignity in his bosom. And, if we had the power of choice, he would soon repent, who should resign his reason to secure his peace.

Concerning the portion of ignorance necessary to make the condition of the lower classes of mankind safe to the public and tolerable to themselves, both morals and policy exact a nicer[4] inquiry than will be very soon or very easily made. There is undoubtedly a degree of knowledge which will direct a man to refer all to providence, and to acquiesce in the condition which omniscient goodness has determined to allot him; to consider this world as a phantom that must soon glide from before his eyes, and the distresses and vexations that encompass him as dust scattered in his path, as a blast that chills him for a moment, and passes off forever.

Such wisdom, arising from the comparison of part with the whole of our existence, those that want[5] it most cannot possibly obtain from philosophy, nor, unless the method of education and the general tenor of life are changed, will very easily receive it from religion. The bulk of mankind is not likely to be very wise or very

3. Particular individuals.   5. Lack.
4. More discriminating.

good: and I know not whether there are not many states of life in which all knowledge less than the highest wisdom will produce discontent and danger. I believe it may be sometimes found that a *little learning* is to a poor man a *dangerous thing*.[6] But such is the condition of humanity that we easily see, or quickly feel the wrong, but cannot always distinguish the right. Whatever knowledge is superfluous, in irremediable poverty, is hurtful, but the difficulty is to determine when poverty is irremediable, and at what point superfluity begins. Gross ignorance every man has found equally dangerous with perverted knowledge. Men left wholly to their appetites and their instincts, with little sense of moral or religious obligation, and with very faint distinctions of right and wrong, can never be safely employed or confidently trusted: they can be honest only by obstinacy, and diligent only by compulsion or caprice. Some instruction, therefore, is necessary, and much, perhaps, may be dangerous.

Though it should be granted that those who are *born to poverty and drudgery* should not be *deprived* by an *improper education* of the *opiate of ignorance*, even this concession will not be of much use to direct our practice, unless it be determined who are those that are *born to poverty*. To entail irreversible poverty upon generation after generation only because the ancestor happened to be poor is in itself cruel, if not unjust, and is wholly contrary to the maxims of a commercial nation, which always suppose and promote a rotation of property, and offer every individual a chance of mending his condition by his diligence. Those who communicate literature to the son of a poor man consider him as one not born to poverty, but to the necessity of deriving a better fortune from himself. In this attempt, as in others, many fail, and many succeed. Those that fail will feel their misery more acutely; but since poverty is now confessed to be such a calamity as cannot be borne without the opiate of insensibility, I hope the happiness of those whom education enables to escape from it may turn the balance against that exacerbation which the others suffer.

I am always afraid of determining on the side of envy or cruelty. The privileges of education may sometimes be improperly bestowed, but I shall always fear to withhold them, lest I should be yielding to the suggestions of pride, while I persuade myself that I am following the maxims of policy; and under the appearance of salutary restraints, should be indulging the lust of dominion, and that malevolence which delights in seeing others depressed.

Pope's doctrine is at last exhibited in a comparison which, like other proofs of the same kind, is better adapted to delight the fancy than convince the reason:

> Thus the universe resembles a large and well-regulated family, in which all the officers and servants, and even the domestic animals, are subservient to each other in a proper subordination: each enjoys the privileges and perquisites peculiar to his place, and at the same time contributes by that just subordination to the magnificence and happiness of the whole.

The magnificence of a house is of use or pleasure to the master, and sometimes to the domestics. But the magnificence of the universe adds nothing to the supreme Being; for any part of its inhabitants with which human knowledge is acquainted, an universe much less spacious or splendid would have been sufficient; and of happiness it does not appear that any is communicated from the beings of a lower world to those of a higher. * * *

Having thus dispatched the consideration of particular evils, he comes at last to a general reason for which *evil* may be said to be *our good*. He is of opinion that there is some inconceivable benefit in pain abstractedly considered; that pain however

---

6. "A little learning is a dangerous thing" (Pope, *Essay on Criticism*, line 215).

inflicted, or wherever felt, communicates some good to the general system of being, and that every animal is some way or other the better for the pain of every other animal. This opinion he carries so far as to suppose that there passes some principle of union through all animal life, as attraction is communicated to all corporeal nature, and that the evils suffered on this globe may by some inconceivable means contribute to the felicity of the inhabitants of the remotest planet.

How the origin of evil is brought nearer to human conception by any *inconceivable* means, I am not able to discover. We believed that the present system of creation was right, though we could not explain the adaptation of one part to the other, or for the whole succession of causes and consequences. Where has this inquirer added to the little knowledge that we had before? He has told us of the benefits of evil, which no man feels, and relations between distant parts of the universe, which he cannot himself conceive. There was enough in this question inconceivable before, and we have little advantage from a new inconceivable solution.

I do not mean to reproach this author for not knowing what is equally hidden from learning and from ignorance. The shame is to impose words for ideas upon ourselves or others. To imagine that we are going forward when we are only turning round. To think that there is any difference between him that gives no reason, and him that gives a reason which by his own confession cannot be conceived.

But that he may not be thought to conceive nothing but things inconceivable, he has at last thought on a way by which human sufferings may produce good effects. He imagines that as we have not only animals for food, but choose some for our diversion, the same privilege may be allowed to some beings above us, *who may deceive, torment, or destroy us for the ends only of their own pleasure or utility*. This he again finds impossible to be conceived, *but that impossibility lessens not the probability of the conjecture, which by analogy is so strongly confirmed*.

I cannot resist the temptation of contemplating this analogy, which I think he might have carried further very much to the advantage of his argument. He might have shown that these *hunters whose game is man* have many sports analogous to our own. As we drown whelps and kittens, they amuse themselves now and then with sinking a ship, and stand round the fields of Blenheim or the walls of Prague,[7] as we encircle a cockpit.[8] As we shoot a bird flying, they take a man in the midst of his business or pleasure, and knock him down with an apoplexy. Some of them, perhaps, are virtuosi, and delight in the operations of an asthma, as a human philosopher[9] in the effects of the air pump.[1] To swell a man with a tympany[2] is as good sport as to blow a frog. Many a merry bout have these frolic beings at the vicissitudes of an ague,[3] and good sport it is to see a man tumble with an epilepsy, and revive and tumble again, and all this he knows not why. As they are wiser and more powerful than we, they have more exquisite diversions, for we have no way of procuring any sport so brisk and so lasting as the paroxysms of the gout and stone,[4] which undoubtedly must make high mirth, especially if the play be a little diversified with the blunders and puzzles of the blind and deaf. We know not how far their sphere of observation may extend. Perhaps now and then a merry being may place himself in such a situation as to enjoy at once all the varieties of an epidemical disease, or amuse his leisure with the tossings and contortions of every possible pain exhibited together.

7. Johnson refers to famous, and famously bloody, battles.
8. The arena in which cocks equipped with spurs fought each other, often to the death.
9. Scientist.
1. A vacuum pump used in experiments concerning air to deprive animals of oxygen.
2. "A kind of obstructed flatulence that swells the body like a drum" (Johnson's *Dictionary*).
3. Fever.
4. Kidney or gall stone.

One sport the merry malice of these beings has found means of enjoying to which we have nothing equal or similar. They now and then catch a mortal proud of his parts,[5] and flattered either by the submission of those who court his kindness, or the notice of those who suffer him to court theirs. A head thus prepared for the reception of false opinions, and the projection of vain designs, they easily fill with idle notions, till in time they make their plaything an author; their first diversion commonly begins with an ode or an epistle, then rises perhaps to a political irony, and is at last brought to its height by a treatise of philosophy. Then begins the poor animal to entangle himself in sophisms, and flounder in absurdity, to talk confidently of the scale of being, and to give solutions which himself confesses impossible to be understood. Sometimes, however, it happens that their pleasure is without much mischief. The author feels no pain, but while they are wondering at the extravagance of his opinion, and pointing him out to one another as a new example of human folly, he is enjoying his own applause, and that of his companions, and perhaps is elevated with the hope of standing at the head of a new sect.

Many of the books which now crowd the world may be justly suspected to be written for the sake of some invisible order of beings, for surely they are of no use to any of the corporeal inhabitants of the world. Of the productions of the last bounteous year, how many can be said to serve any purpose of use or pleasure? The only end of writing is to enable the readers better to enjoy life, or better to endure it; and how will either of those be put more in our power by him who tells us that we are puppets, of which some creature not much wiser than ourselves manages the wires? That a set of beings unseen and unheard are hovering about us, trying experiments upon our sensibility, putting us in agonies to see our limbs quiver, torturing us to madness that they may laugh at our vagaries; sometimes obstructing the bile that they may see how a man looks when he is yellow; sometimes breaking a traveler's bones to try how he will get home; sometimes wasting a man to a skeleton, and sometimes killing him fat for the greater elegance of his hide?

This is an account of natural evil which though, like the rest, not quite new, is very entertaining, though I know not how much it may contribute to patience. The only reason why we should contemplate evil is that we may bear it better; and I am afraid nothing is much more placidly endured for the sake of making others sport. * * *
1757   1757

Idler No. 31[1]

[ON IDLENESS]

Saturday, 18 November 1758

Many moralists have remarked, that pride has of all human vices the widest dominion, appears in the greatest multiplicity of forms, and lies hid under the greatest variety of disguises; of disguises, which, like the moon's "veil of brightness," are both its "luster and its shade,"[2] and betray it to others, though they hide it from ourselves.

---

5. Abilities.

1. *The Idler* (1758–1760) bears a more self-deprecating title than *The Rambler*; other circumstances, too, suggest that Johnson intended a less imposing performance in this series of periodical essay than in its predecessor. The new pieces appeared not twice but once a week, and not as an independent sheet but as a department within a weekly newspaper called *The Universal Chronicle* (which achieved little eminence apart from Johnson's contribu-

tion). The *Idlers* were shorter than the *Ramblers*, and dealt more often in light topics and comic touches. Boswell opined that the second series had "less body and more spirit . . . more variety of real life, and greater facility of language." His judgment is hardly definitive; the comparison has been assayed, with varying results, many times since.

2. Both quotations come from Samuel Butler's poem *Hudibras* (1663–1678) 2.1.905 and 908.

It is not my intention to degrade pride from this pre-eminence of mischief, yet I know not whether idleness may not maintain a very doubtful and obstinate competition.

There are some that profess idleness in its full dignity, who call themselves the Idle, as Busiris in the play "calls himself the Proud";[3] who boast that they do nothing, and thank their stars that they have nothing to do; who sleep every night till they can sleep no longer, and rise only that exercise may enable them to sleep again; who prolong the reign of darkness by double curtains, and never see the sun but to "tell him how they hate his beams";[4] whose whole labor is to vary the postures of indulgence, and whose day differs from their night but as a couch or chair differs from a bed.

These are the true and open votaries of idleness, for whom she weaves the garlands of poppies, and into whose cup she pours the waters of oblivion; who exist in a state of unruffled stupidity,[5] forgetting and forgotten; who have long ceased to live, and at whose death the survivors can only say, that they have ceased to breathe.

But idleness predominates in many lives where it is not suspected, for, being a vice which terminates in itself, it may be enjoyed without injury to others, and is therefore not watched like fraud, which endangers property, or like pride, which naturally seeks its gratifications in another's inferiority. Idleness is a silent and peaceful quality, that neither raises envy by ostentation, nor hatred by opposition; and therefore nobody is busy to censure or detect it.

As pride sometimes is hid under humility, idleness is often covered by turbulence and hurry. He that neglects his known duty and real employment, naturally endeavors to crowd his mind with something that may bar out the remembrance of his own folly, and does any thing but what he ought to do with eager diligence, that he may keep himself in his own favor.

Some are always in a state of preparation, occupied in previous measures, forming plans, accumulating materials, and providing for the main affair. These are certainly under the secret power of idleness. Nothing is to be expected from the workman whose tools are forever to be sought. I was once told by a great master, that no man ever excelled in painting, who was eminently curious[6] about pencils[7] and colors.

There are others to whom idleness dictates another expedient, by which life may be passed unprofitably away without the tediousness of many vacant hours. The art is, to fill the day with petty business, to have always something in hand which may raise curiosity, but not solicitude, and keep the mind in a state of action, but not of labor.

This art has for many years been practiced by my old friend Sober,[8] with wonderful success. Sober is a man of strong desires and quick imagination, so exactly balanced by the love of ease, that they can seldom stimulate him to any difficult undertaking; they have, however, so much power, that they will not suffer him to lie quite at rest, and though they do not make him sufficiently useful to others, they make him at least weary of himself.

Mr. Sober's chief pleasure is conversation; there is no end of his talk or his attention; to speak or to hear is equally pleasing; for he still fancies that he is teaching or learning something, and is free for the time from his own reproaches.

3. *Busiris* (1719) by Edward Young.
4. Milton, *Paradise Lost* 4.37.
5. Stupor.
6. "Difficult to please" (Johnson's *Dictionary*).

7. Brushes.
8. Johnson's friends believed that the portrait of Sober was autobiographical.

But there is one time at night when he must go home, that his friends may sleep; and another time in the morning, when all the world agrees to shut out interruption. These are the moments of which poor Sober trembles at the thought. But the misery of these tiresome intervals, he has many means of alleviating. He has persuaded himself that the manual arts are undeservedly overlooked; he has observed in many trades the effects of close thought, and just ratiocination. From speculation he proceeded to practice, and supplied himself with the tools of a carpenter, with which he mended his coal-box very successfully, and which he still continues to employ, as he finds occasion.

He has attempted at other times the crafts of the shoemaker, tinman, plumber, and potter; in all these arts he has failed, and resolves to qualify himself for them by better information. But his daily amusement is chemistry. He has a small furnace, which he employs in distillation, and which has long been the solace of his life. He draws oils and waters, and essences and spirits, which he knows to be of no use; sits and counts the drops as they come from his retort, and forgets that, while a drop is falling, a moment flies away.

Poor Sober! I have often teased him with reproof, and he has often promised reformation; for no man is so much open to conviction as the idler, but there is none on whom it operates so little. What will be the effect of this paper I know not; perhaps he will read it and laugh, and light the fire in his furnace; but my hope is that he will quit his trifles, and betake himself to rational and useful diligence.

Idler No. 32
[ON SLEEP]

Saturday, 25 November 1758

Among the innumerable mortifications that waylay human arrogance on every side may well be reckoned our ignorance of the most common objects and effects, a defect of which we become more sensible by every attempt to supply it. Vulgar and inactive minds confound familiarity with knowledge, and conceive themselves informed of the whole nature of things when they are shown their form or told their use; but the speculatist, who is not content with superficial views, harasses himself with fruitless curiosity, and still as he inquires more perceives only that he knows less.

Sleep is a state in which a great part of every life is passed. No animal has been yet discovered, whose existence is not varied with intervals of insensibility; and some late philosophers have extended the empire of sleep over the vegetable world.

Yet of this change so frequent, so great, so general, and so necessary, no searcher has yet found either the efficient or final cause; or can tell by what power the mind and body are thus chained down in irresistible stupefaction; or what benefits the animal receives from this alternate suspension of its active powers.

Whatever may be the multiplicity or contrariety of opinions upon this subject, nature has taken sufficient care that theory shall have little influence on practice. The most diligent inquirer is not able long to keep his eyes open; the most eager disputant will begin about midnight to desert his argument, and once in four and twenty hours, the gay and the gloomy, the witty and the dull, the clamorous and the silent, the busy and the idle, are all overpowered by the gentle tyrant, and all lie down in the equality of sleep.

Philosophy has often attempted to repress insolence by asserting that all conditions are leveled by death; a position which, however it may deject the happy, will seldom afford much comfort to the wretched. It is far more pleasing to consider that sleep is equally a leveler with death; that the time is never at a great distance, when the balm of rest shall be effused alike upon every head, when the diversities of life shall stop their operation, and the high and the low shall lie down together.

It is somewhere recorded of Alexander, that in the pride of conquests, and intoxication of flattery, he declared that he only perceived himself to be a man by the necessity of sleep. Whether he considered sleep as necessary to his mind or body it was indeed a sufficient evidence of human infirmity; the body which required such frequency of renovation gave but faint promises of immortality; and the mind which, from time to time, sunk gladly into insensibility had made no very near approaches to the felicity of the supreme and self-sufficient nature.

I know not what can tend more to repress all the passions that disturb the peace of the world than the consideration that there is no height of happiness or honor from which man does not eagerly descend to a state of unconscious repose; that the best condition of life is such that we contentedly quit its good to be disentangled from its evils; that in a few hours splendor fades before the eye and praise itself deadens in the ear; the senses withdraw from their objects, and reason favors the retreat.

What then are the hopes and prospects of covetousness, ambition and rapacity? Let him that desires most have all his desires gratified, he never shall attain a state which he can, for a day and a night, contemplate with satisfaction, or from which, if he had the power of perpetual vigilance, he would not long for periodical separations.

All envy would be extinguished if it were universally known that there are none to be envied, and surely none can be much envied who are not pleased with themselves. There is reason to suspect that the distinctions of mankind have more show than value when it is found that all agree to be weary alike of pleasures and of cares, that the powerful and the weak, the celebrated and obscure, join in one common wish, and implore from nature's hand the nectar of oblivion.

Such is our desire of abstraction from ourselves that very few are satisfied with the quantity of stupefaction which the needs of the body force upon the mind. Alexander himself added intemperance to sleep, and solaced with the fumes of wine the sovereignty of the world. And almost every man has some art by which he steals his thoughts away from his present state.

It is not much of life that is spent in close attention to any important duty. Many hours of every day are suffered to fly away without any traces left upon the intellects. We suffer phantoms to rise up before us, and amuse ourselves with the dance of airy images, which after a time we dismiss forever, and know not how we have been busied.

Many have no happier moments than those that they pass in solitude, abandoned to their own imagination, which sometimes puts sceptres in their hands or mitres on their heads, shifts the scene of pleasure with endless variety, bids all the forms of beauty sparkle before them, and gluts them with every change of visionary luxury.

It is easy in these semi-slumbers to collect all the possibilities of happiness, to alter the course of the sun, to bring back the past, and anticipate the future, to unite all the beauties of all seasons, and all the blessings of all climates, to receive and bestow felicity, and forget that misery is the lot of man. All this is a voluntary dream, a temporary recession from the realities of life to airy fictions; an habitual subjection of reason to fancy.

Others are afraid to be alone, and amuse themselves by a perpetual succession of companions, but the difference is not great; in solitude we have our dreams to ourselves, and in company we agree to dream in concert. The end sought in both is forgetfulness of ourselves.

Idler No. 84

[ON AUTOBIOGRAPHY]

Saturday, 24 November 1759

Biography is, of the various kinds of narrative writing, that which is most eagerly read, and most easily applied to the purposes of life.

In romances, when the wild field of possibility lies open to invention, the incidents may easily be made more numerous, the vicissitudes more sudden, and the events more wonderful; but from the time of life when fancy begins to be overruled by reason and corrected by experience, the most artful tale raises little curiosity when it is known to be false; though it may, perhaps, be sometimes read as a model of a neat or elegant style, not for the sake of knowing what it contains, but how it is written; or those that are weary of themselves, may have recourse to it as a pleasing dream, of which, when they awake, they voluntarily dismiss the images from their minds.

The examples and events of history press, indeed, upon the mind with the weight of truth; but when they are reposited in the memory, they are oftener employed for show than use, and rather diversify conversation than regulate life. Few are engaged in such scenes as give them opportunities of growing wiser by the downfall of statesmen or the defeat of generals. The stratagems of war, and the intrigues of courts, are read by far the greater part of mankind with the same indifference as the adventures of fabled heroes, or the revolutions of a fairy region. Between falsehood and useless truth there is little difference. As gold which he cannot spend will make no man rich, so knowledge which he cannot apply will make no man wise.

The mischievous consequences of vice and folly, of irregular desires and predominant passions, are best discovered by those relations which are leveled with the general surface of life, which tell not how any man became great, but how he was made happy; not how he lost the favor of his prince, but how he became discontented with himself.

Those relations are therefore commonly of most value in which the writer tells his own story. He that recounts the life of another, commonly dwells most upon conspicuous events, lessens the familiarity of his tale to increase its dignity, shows his favorite at a distance decorated and magnified like the ancient actors in their tragic dress, and endeavors to hide the man that he may produce a hero.

But if it be true which was said by a French prince, "that no man was a hero to the servants of his chamber," it is equally true that every man is yet less a hero to himself. He that is most elevated above the crowd by the importance of his employments or the reputation of his genius, feels himself affected by fame or business but as they influence his domestic life. The high and low, as they have the same faculties and the same senses, have no less similitude in their pains and pleasures. The sensations are the same in all, though produced by very different occasions. The prince feels the same pain when an invader seizes a province, as the farmer when a thief drives away his cow. Men thus equal in themselves will appear equal in honest and impartial biography; and those whom fortune or nature place at the greatest distance may afford instruction to each other.

The writer of his own life has at least the first qualification of an historian, the knowledge of the truth; and though it may be plausibly objected that his temptations to disguise it are equal to his opportunities of knowing it, yet I cannot but think that impartiality may be expected with equal confidence from him that relates the passages of his own life, as from him that delivers the transactions of another.

Certainty of knowledge not only excludes mistake but fortifies veracity. What we collect by conjecture, and by conjecture only can one man judge of another's motives or sentiments, is easily modified by fancy or by desire; as objects imperfectly discerned take forms from the hope or fear of the beholder. But that which is fully known cannot be falsified but with reluctance of understanding, and alarm of conscience; of understanding, the lover of truth; of conscience, the sentinel of virtue.

He that writes the life of another is either his friend or his enemy, and wishes either to exalt his praise or aggravate his infamy; many temptations to falsehood will occur in the disguise of passions, too specious[1] to fear much resistance. Love of virtue will animate panegyric, and hatred of wickedness embitter censure. The zeal of gratitude, the ardor of patriotism, fondness for an opinion, or fidelity to a party, may easily overpower the vigilance of a mind habitually well disposed, and prevail over unassisted and unfriended veracity.

But he that speaks of himself has no motive to falsehood or partiality except self-love, by which all have so often been betrayed, that all are on the watch against its artifices. He that writes an apology for[2] a single action, to confute an accusation, or recommend himself to favor, is indeed always to be suspected of favoring his own cause; but he that sits down calmly and voluntarily to review his life for the admonition of posterity, or to amuse himself, and leaves this account unpublished, may be commonly presumed to tell truth, since falsehood cannot appease his own mind, and fame will not be heard beneath the tomb.

Idler No. 97
[ON TRAVEL WRITING]

Saturday, 23 February 1760

It may, I think, be justly observed, that few books disappoint their readers more than the narrations of travelers. One part of mankind is naturally curious to learn the sentiments, manners, and condition of the rest; and every mind that has leisure or power to extend its views, must be desirous of knowing in what proportion Providence has distributed the blessings of nature or the advantages of art, among the several nations of the earth.

This general desire easily procures readers to every book from which it can expect gratification. The adventurer upon unknown coasts, and the describer of distant regions, is always welcomed as a man who has labored for the pleasure of others, and who is able to enlarge our knowledge and rectify our opinions; but when the volume is opened, nothing is found but such general accounts as leave no distinct idea behind them, or such minute enumerations as few can read with either profit or delight.

---

1. "Plausible; superficially, not solidly right" (Johnson's   2. Defense of.
Dictionary).

Every writer of travels should consider that, like all other authors, he undertakes either to instruct or please, or to mingle pleasure with instruction. He that instructs must offer to the mind something to be imitated or something to be avoided; he that pleases must offer new images to his reader, and enable him to form a tacit comparison of his own state with that of others.

The greater part of travelers tell nothing, because their method of traveling supplies them with nothing to be told. He that enters a town at night and surveys it in the morning, and then hastens away to another place, and guesses at the manners of the inhabitants by the entertainment which his inn afforded him, may please himself for a time with a hasty change of scenes, and a confused remembrance of palaces and churches; he may gratify his eye with variety of landscapes; and regale his palate with a succession of vintages; but let him be contented to please himself without endeavor to disturb others. Why should he record excursions by which nothing could be learned, or wish to make a show of knowledge which, without some power of intuition unknown to other mortals, he never could attain.

Of those who crowd the world with their itineraries,[1] some have no other purpose than to describe the face of the country; those who sit idle at home, and are curious to know what is done or suffered in distant countries, may be informed by one of these wanderers, that on a certain day he set out early with the caravan, and in the first hour's march saw, towards the south, a hill covered with trees, then passed over a stream which ran northward with a swift course, but which is probably dry in the summer months; that an hour after he saw something to the right which looked at a distance like a castle with towers, but which he discovered afterwards to be a craggy rock; that he then entered a valley in which he saw several trees tall and flourishing, watered by a rivulet not marked in the maps, of which he was not able to learn the name; that the road afterward grew stony, and the country uneven, where he observed among the hills many hollows worn by torrents, and was told that the road was passable only part of the year: that going on they found the remains of a building, once perhaps a fortress to secure the pass, or to restrain the robbers, of which the present inhabitants can give no other account than that it is haunted by fairies; that they went to dine at the foot of a rock, and traveled the rest of the day along the banks of a river, from which the road turned aside towards evening, and brought them within sight of a village, which was once a considerable town, but which afforded them neither good victuals nor commodious lodging.

Thus he conducts his reader through wet and dry, over rough and smooth, without incidents, without reflection; and, if he obtains his company for another day, will dismiss him again at night equally fatigued with a like succession of rocks and streams, mountains and ruins.

This is the common style of those sons of enterprise, who visit savage countries, and range through solitude and desolation; who pass a desert, and tell that it is sandy; who cross a valley, and find that it is green. There are others of more delicate sensibility, that visit only the realms of elegance and softness; that wander through Italian palaces, and amuse the gentle reader with catalogues of pictures; that hear masses in magnificent churches, and recount the number of the pillars or variegations of the pavement. And there are yet others who, in disdain of trifles, copy inscriptions elegant and rude, ancient and modern; and transcribe into their book

1. Travel books.

the walls of every edifice, sacred or civil. He that reads these books must consider his labor as its own reward; for he will find nothing on which attention can fix, or which memory can retain.

He that would travel for the entertainment of others should remember that the great object of remark is human life. Every nation has something peculiar in its manufactures, its works of genius, its medicines, its agriculture, its customs, and its policy. He only is a useful traveler who brings home something by which his country may be benefited; who procures some supply of want or some mitigation of evil, which may enable his readers to compare their condition with that of others, to improve it whenever it is worse, and whenever it is better to enjoy it.

A DICTIONARY OF THE ENGLISH LANGUAGE　Johnson's *Dictionary* struck its first readers as a nearly superhuman accomplishment; it seems one still. "A dictionary of the English language," observed one early reviewer, had never before "been attempted with the least degree of success"; the closest antecedents to Johnson's project were the national dictionaries of France and Italy, and these had been composed by whole academies of scholars, working collectively over the course of decades. Here, by contrast, was the seven years' labor of a single author (aided only by six part-time amanuenses): 40,000 words defined with unprecedented exactitude, and illustrated with more than 114,000 passages drawn from English prose and poetry of the previous 250 years. Ninety years earlier, members of the newly founded Royal Society for Improving Natural Knowledge had dreamed of such a resource; Johnson produced it by empirical methods much like the ones they promulgated. He spent his first years on the project accumulating data, rereading the English writers he valued most, marking any passage that strikingly illuminated the workings of a particular word. He then worked from this heap of collected evidence to the fine-honed, sharply distinguished conclusions of his definitions. The results have been variously and accurately described as the first standard English dictionary; as one of the final fruits of Renaissance humanism; as a commonplace-book (or database) of important English writing from Sidney to Pope; as a massive map of its author's mind. The key to that map resides in the *Dictionary*'s Preface, where Johnson measures the grandeur of his aspirations against the limitations of his achievement. In this mix of personal memoir and linguistic meditation, lexicography becomes a local instance of the vanity of human wishes. Human language, massive, metamorphic, and intractable, overmatches the human desire to codify and contain it, to fix it once and for all.

from A Dictionary of the English Language
from Preface
[ON METHOD]

It is the fate of those who toil at the lower employments of life to be rather driven by the fear of evil than attracted by the prospect of good; to be exposed to censure, without hope of praise; to be disgraced by miscarriage or punished for neglect, where success would have been without applause and diligence without reward.

Among these unhappy mortals is the writer of dictionaries; whom mankind have considered not as the pupil but the slave of science, the pioneer[1] of literature, doomed only to remove rubbish and clear obstructions from the paths through which learning and genius press forward to conquest and glory, without bestowing a smile

---

1. "One whose business is to level the road, throw up works, or sink mines in military operations" (Johnson's *Dictionary*).

on the humble drudge that facilitates their progress. Every other author may aspire to praise; the lexicographer can only hope to escape reproach, and even this negative recompense has been yet granted to very few.

I have, notwithstanding this discouragement, attempted a dictionary of the English language which, while it was employed in the cultivation of every species of literature, has itself been hitherto neglected; suffered to spread, under the direction of chance, into wild exuberance; resigned to the tyranny of time and fashion; and exposed to the corruptions of ignorance, and caprices of innovation.

When I took the first survey of my undertaking, I found our speech copious without order, and energetic without rules: wherever I turned my view, there was perplexity to be disentangled and confusion to be regulated; choice was to be made out of boundless variety, without any established principle of selection; adulterations were to be detected without a settled test of purity; and modes of expression to be rejected or received without the suffrages[2] of any writers of classical reputation or acknowledged authority.

Having therefore no assistance but from general grammar, I applied myself to the perusal of our writers; and, noting whatever might be of use to ascertain or illustrate any word or phrase, accumulated in time the materials of a dictionary, which, by degrees, I reduced to method, establishing to myself in the progress of the work such rules as experience and analogy suggested to me; experience, which practice and observation were continually increasing; and analogy, which, though in some words obscure, was evident in others.

[ON DEFINITIONS AND EXAMPLES]

That part of my work on which I expect malignity most frequently to fasten is the explanation; in which I cannot hope to satisfy those who are perhaps not inclined to be pleased, since I have not always been able to satisfy myself. To interpret a language by itself is very difficult; many words cannot be explained by synonyms because the idea signified by them has not more than one appellation; nor by paraphrase, because simple ideas cannot be described. When the nature of things is unknown, or the notion unsettled and indefinite, and various in various minds, the words by which such notions are conveyed or such things denoted will be ambiguous and perplexed. And such is the fate of hapless lexicography that not only darkness, but light, impedes and distresses it; things may be not only too little, but too much known, to be happily illustrated. To explain requires the use of terms less abstruse than that which is to be explained, and such terms cannot always be found; for as nothing can be proved but by supposing something intuitively known and evident without proof, so nothing can be defined but by the use of words too plain to admit a definition.

Other words there are, of which the sense is too subtle and evanescent to be fixed in a paraphrase; such are all those which are by the grammarians termed expletives, and, in dead languages, are suffered to pass for empty sounds, of no other use than to fill a verse or to modulate a period,[1] but which are easily perceived in living tongues to have power and emphasis, though it be sometimes such as no other form of expression can convey. * * *

The solution of all difficulties and the supply of all defects must be sought in the examples subjoined to the various senses of each word, and ranged according to the time of their authors.

---

2. Votes, testimonies.   1. Clause or sentence.

When first I collected these authorities, I was desirous that every quotation should be useful to some other end than the illustration of a word; I therefore extracted from philosophers principles of science; from historians remarkable facts; from chemists complete processes; from divines striking exhortations; and from poets beautiful descriptions. Such is design while it is yet at a distance from execution. When the time called upon me to range this accumulation of elegance and wisdom into an alphabetical series, I soon discovered that the bulk of my volumes would fright away the student, and was forced to depart from my scheme of including all that was pleasing or useful in English literature, and reduce my transcripts very often to clusters of words in which scarcely any meaning is retained; thus to the weariness of copying, I was condemned to add the vexation of expunging. Some passages I have yet spared which may relieve the labor of verbal searches, and intersperse with verdure and flowers the dusty deserts of barren philology.

The examples, thus mutilated, are no longer to be considered as conveying the sentiments or doctrine of their authors; the word for the sake of which they are inserted, with all its appendant clauses, has been carefully preserved; but it may sometimes happen, by hasty detruncation, that the general tendency of the sentence may be changed: the divine may desert his tenets, or the philosopher his system.

Some of the examples have been taken from writers who were never mentioned as masters of elegance or models of style; but words must be sought where they are used; and in what pages, eminent for purity, can terms of manufacture or agriculture be found? Many quotations serve no other purpose than that of proving the bare existence of words, and are therefore selected with less scrupulousness than those which are to teach their structures and relations.

My purpose was to admit no testimony of living authors, that I might not be misled by partiality, and that none of my cotemporaries might have reason to complain; nor have I departed from this resolution but when some performance of uncommon excellence excited my veneration, when my memory supplied me, from late books, with an example that was wanting, or when my heart, in the tenderness of friendship, solicited admission for a favorite name.

So far have I been from any care to grace my pages with modern decorations that I have studiously endeavored to collect examples and authorities from the writers before the Restoration, whose works I regard as "the wells of English undefiled,"[2] as the pure sources of genuine diction. Our language, for almost a century, has, by the concurrence of many causes, been gradually departing from its original Teutonic character, and deviating towards a Gallic structure and phraseology, from which it ought to be our endeavor to recall it by making our ancient volumes the groundwork of style, admitting among the additions of later times only such as may supply real deficiencies, such as are readily adopted by the genius[3] of our tongue, and incorporate easily with our native idioms.

But as every language has a time of rudeness[4] antecedent to perfection, as well as of false refinement and declension, I have been cautious lest my zeal for antiquity might drive me into times too remote and crowd my book with words now no longer understood. I have fixed Sidney's work for the boundary beyond which I make few excursions. From the authors which rose in the time of Elizabeth, a speech might be formed adequate to all the purposes of use and elegance. If the language of theology were extracted from

2. Johnson quotes Spenser's praise of Chaucer in *The Faerie Queene* (4.2.2).

3. Native spirit.

4. Barbarism.

Hooker and the translation of the Bible; the terms of natural knowledge[5] from Bacon; the phrases of policy, war, and navigation from Raleigh; the dialect of poetry and fiction from Spenser and Sidney; and the diction of common life from Shakespeare, few ideas would be lost to mankind for want of English words in which they might be expressed.

It is not sufficient that a word is found unless it be so combined as that its meaning is apparently[6] determined by the tract[7] and tenor of the sentence; such passages I have therefore chosen, and when it happened that any author gave a definition of a term or such an explanation as is equivalent to a definition, I have placed his authority as a supplement to my own, without regard to the chronological order that is otherwise observed.

Some words, indeed, stand unsupported by any authority, but they are commonly derivative nouns or adverbs, formed from their primitives by regular and constant analogy, or names of things seldom occurring in books, or words of which I have reason to doubt the existence.

There is more danger of censure from the multiplicity than paucity of examples; authorities will sometimes seem to have been accumulated without necessity or use, and perhaps some will be found which might, without loss, have been omitted. But a work of this kind is not hastily to be charged with superfluities: those quotations which to careless or unskillful perusers appear only to repeat the same sense will often exhibit to a more accurate examiner diversities of signification or, at least, afford different shades of the same meaning: one will show the word applied to persons, another to things; one will express an ill, another a good, and a third a neutral sense; one will prove the expression genuine from an ancient author; another will show it elegant from a modern: a doubtful authority is corroborated by another of more credit; an ambiguous sentence is ascertained by a passage clear and determinate; the word, how often soever repeated, appears with new associates and in different combinations, and every quotation contributes something to the stability or enlargement of the language. * * *

I have sometimes, though rarely, yielded to the temptation of exhibiting a genealogy of sentiments, by showing how one author copied the thoughts and diction of another: such quotations are indeed little more than repetitions which might justly be censured, did they not gratify the mind by affording a kind of intellectual history.

[CONCLUSION]

A large work is difficult because it is large, even though all its parts might singly be performed with facility; where there are many things to be done, each must be allowed its share of time and labor in the proportion only which it bears to the whole; nor can it be expected that the stones which form the dome of a temple should be squared and polished like the diamond of a ring.

Of the event of this work, for which, having labored it with so much application, I cannot but have some degree of parental fondness, it is natural to form conjectures. Those who have been persuaded to think well of my design will require that it should fix our language and put a stop to those alterations which time and chance have hitherto been suffered to make in it without opposition. With this consequence I will confess that I flattered myself for a while; but now begin to fear that I have indulged expectation which neither reason nor experience can justify. When we see men grow

5. Science.
6. Clearly.

7. "Continuity; course; manner of process" (Johnson's *Dictionary*).

old and die at a certain time one after another, from century to century, we laugh at
the elixir that promises to prolong life to a thousand years; and with equal justice
may the lexicographer be derided, who being able to produce no example of a nation
that has preserved their words and phrases from mutability, shall imagine that his
dictionary can embalm his language and secure it from corruption and decay, that it
is in his power to change sublunary nature, and clear the world at once from folly,
vanity, and affectation.

With this hope, however, academies have been instituted to guard the avenues of
their languages, to retain fugitives and repulse intruders; but their vigilance and activity
have hitherto been vain; sounds are too volatile and subtle for legal restraints; to
enchain syllables and to lash the wind are equally the undertakings of pride, unwilling
to measure its desires by its strength. The French language has visibly changed under the
inspection of the Academy,[1] the style of Amelot's translation of Father Paul is observed
by Le Courayer to be *un peu passé;*[2] and no Italian will maintain that the diction of any
modern writer is not perceptibly different from that of Boccace, Machiavel, or Caro.[3]

Total and sudden transformations of a language seldom happen; conquests and
migrations are now very rare; but there are other causes of change which, though slow in
their operation, and invisible in their progress, are perhaps as much superior to human
resistance, as the revolutions of the sky, or intumescence of the tide. Commerce, however necessary, however lucrative, as it depraves the manners, corrupts the language;
they that have frequent intercourse with strangers, to whom they endeavor to accommodate themselves, must in time learn a mingled dialect, like the jargon which serves
the traffickers[4] on the Mediterranean and Indian coasts. This will not always be confined to the exchange, the warehouse, or the port, but will be communicated by degrees
to other ranks of the people, and be at last incorporated with the current speech.

There are likewise internal causes equally forcible. The language most likely to
continue long without alteration would be that of a nation raised a little, and but a
little, above barbarity, secluded from strangers, and totally employed in procuring the
conveniences of life; either without books or, like some of the Mahometan countries,
with very few: men thus busied and unlearned, having only such words as common
use requires, would perhaps long continue to express the same notions by the same
signs. But no such constancy can be expected in a people polished by arts and classed
by subordination, where one part of the community is sustained and accommodated
by the labor of the other. Those who have much leisure to think will always be
enlarging the stock of ideas, and every increase of knowledge, whether real or fancied, will produce new words or combinations of words. When the mind is unchained
from necessity, it will range after convenience; when it is left at large in the fields of
speculation, it will shift opinions; as any custom is disused, the words that expressed
it must perish with it; as any opinion grows popular, it will innovate speech in the
same proportion as it alters practice.

As by the cultivation of various sciences a language is amplified, it will be more furnished with words deflected from their original sense; the geometrician will talk of a
courtier's zenith, or the eccentric[5] virtue of a wild hero, and the physician of sanguine

---

1. The French Academy, founded in 1635, undertook to
preserve the purity of the language.
2. When in the 1730s Le Courayer retranslated Father
Paolo Sarpi's *History of the Council of Trent*, he criticized
his predecessor Amelot's version (1683) as "a little out-
dated."

3. Johnson refers to Giovanni Boccaccio (1313–1375),
author of *The Decameron;* Niccolo Machiavelli
(1469–1527), author of *The Prince;* and Annibale Caro
(1507–1566), author of pastoral romances.
4. Merchants.
5. "Deviating from the center" (Johnson's *Dictionary*).

expectations and phlegmatic delays.[6] Copiousness of speech will give opportunities to capricious choice, by which some words will be preferred and others degraded; vicissitudes of fashion will enforce the use of new or extend the signification of known terms. The tropes of poetry will make hourly encroachments, and the metaphorical will become the current sense: pronunciation will be varied by levity or ignorance, and the pen must at length comply with the tongue; illiterate writers will at one time or other, by public infatuation, rise into renown, who, not knowing the original import of words, will use them with colloquial licentiousness, confound distinction, and forget propriety. As politeness increases, some expressions will be considered as too gross and vulgar for the delicate, others as too formal and ceremonious for the gay and airy; new phrases are therefore adopted, which must for the same reasons be in time dismissed. Swift, in his petty[7] treatise on the English language,[8] allows that new words must sometimes be introduced, but proposes that none should be suffered to become obsolete. But what makes a word obsolete more than general agreement to forbear it? and how shall it be continued when it conveys an offensive idea, or recalled again into the mouths of mankind when it has once become unfamiliar by disuse and unpleasing by unfamiliarity?

There is another cause of alteration more prevalent than any other, which yet in the present state of the world cannot be obviated. A mixture of two languages will produce a third distinct from both, and they will always be mixed where the chief part of education, and the most conspicuous accomplishment, is skill in ancient or in foreign tongues. He that has long cultivated another language will find its words and combinations crowd upon his memory; and haste or negligence, refinement or affectation, will obtrude borrowed terms and exotic expressions.

The great pest of speech is frequency of translation. No book was ever turned from one language into another without imparting something of its native idiom; this is the most mischievous and comprehensive innovation; single words may enter by thousands and the fabric of the tongue continue the same, but new phraseology changes much at once; it alters not the single stones of the building but the order of the columns.[9] If an academy should be established for the cultivation of our style, which I, who can never wish to see dependence multiplied, hope the spirit of English liberty will hinder or destroy, let them, instead of compiling grammars and dictionaries, endeavor, with all their influence, to stop the license of translators, whose idleness and ignorance, if it be suffered to proceed, will reduce us to babble a dialect of France.

If the changes that we fear be thus irresistible, what remains but to acquiesce with silence, as in the other insurmountable distresses of humanity? It remains that we retard what we cannot repel, that we palliate what we cannot cure. Life may be lengthened by care, though death cannot be ultimately defeated: tongues, like governments, have a natural tendency to degeneration; we have long preserved our constitution, let us make some struggles for our language.

In hope of giving longevity to that which its own nature forbids to be immortal, I have devoted this book, the labor of years, to the honor of my country, that we may no longer yield the palm[1] of philology without a contest to the nations of the Continent. The chief glory of every people arises from its authors: whether I shall add anything by my own writings to the reputation of English literature must be left to time:

---

6. "Sanguine" and "phlegmatic" are medical terms relating to the doctrine of the four humors. Those in whom blood predominates are "sanguine" or optimistic, those ruled by phlegm are dull and sluggish.
7. Little.

8. *A Proposal for Correcting, Improving, and Ascertaining the English Tongue* (1712).
9. In classical architecture, the five "orders" are Doric, Ionic, Corinthian, Tuscan, and Composite.
1. Crown (symbol of victory).

much of my life has been lost under the pressures of disease; much has been trifled away; and much has always been spent in provision for the day that was passing over me; but I shall not think my employment useless or ignoble if by my assistance foreign nations and distant ages gain access to the propagators of knowledge, and understand the teachers of truth; if my labors afford light to the repositories of science, and add celebrity to Bacon, to Hooker, to Milton, and to Boyle.

When I am animated by this wish, I look with pleasure on my book, however defective, and deliver it to the world with the spirit of a man that has endeavored well. That it will immediately become popular I have not promised to myself: a few wild blunders and risible absurdities, from which no work of such multiplicity was ever free, may for a time furnish folly with laughter, and harden ignorance in contempt; but useful diligence will at last prevail, and there never can be wanting some who distinguish desert,[2] who will consider that no dictionary of a living tongue ever can be perfect, since while it is hastening to publication some words are budding and some falling away; that a whole life cannot be spent upon syntax and etymology, and that even a whole life would not be sufficient; that he whose design includes whatever language can express, must often speak of what he does not understand; that a writer will sometimes be hurried by eagerness to the end, and sometimes faint with weariness under a task, which Scaliger compares to the labors of the anvil and the mine;[3] that what is obvious is not always known, and what is known is not always present; that sudden fits of inadvertency will surprise vigilance, slight avocations will seduce attention, and casual eclipses of the mind will darken learning; and that the writer shall often in vain trace his memory at the moment of need for that which yesterday he knew with intuitive readiness, and which will come uncalled into his thoughts tomorrow.

In this work, when it shall be found that much is omitted, let it not be forgotten that much likewise is performed; and though no book was ever spared out of tenderness to the author, and the world is little solicitous to know whence proceeded the faults of that which it condemns; yet it may gratify curiosity to inform it, that the *English Dictionary* was written with little assistance of the learned, and without any patronage of the great; not in the soft obscurities of retirement or under the shelter of academic bowers, but amidst inconvenience and distraction, in sickness and in sorrow. It may repress the triumph of malignant criticism to observe that if our language is not here fully displayed, I have only failed in an attempt which no human powers have hitherto completed. If the lexicons of ancient tongues, now immutably fixed and comprised in a few volumes, are yet, after the toil of successive ages, inadequate and delusive; if the aggregated knowledge, and cooperating diligence of the Italian academicians did not secure them from the censure of Beni;[4] if the embodied critics of France, when fifty years had been spent upon their work, were obliged to change its economy and give their second edition another form, I may surely be contented without the praise of perfection, which, if I could obtain, in this gloom of solitude, what would it avail me? I have protracted my work till most of those whom I wished to please have sunk into the grave, and success and miscarriage are empty sounds: I therefore dismiss it with frigid tranquillity, having little to fear or hope from censure or from praise.

2. Merit.
3. Johnson refers to a poem, *Against the Compilers of the Lexicons*, by the great Renaissance scholar Joseph Justus

Scaliger.
4. Paolo Beni criticized the Italian dictionary published in 1612 by the Accademia della Crusca.

FUNK. n.s. A stink. A low word.

FÚNNEL. n.s. [*infundibulum*, Latin; whence *fundible, fundle, funnel.*]

1. An inverted hollow cone with a pipe descending from it, through which liquors are poured into vessels with narrow mouths; a tundish.

> If you pour a glut of water upon a bottle, it receives little of it; but with a *funnel*, and by degrees, you shall fill many of them.
>
> —Ben. Jonson's *Discoveries*

> Some the long *funnel*'s curious mouth extend,
> Through which ingested meats with ease descend.
>
> —Blackmore

> The outward ear or auricula is made hollow, and contracted by degrees, to draw the sound inward, to take in as much as may be of it, as we use a *funnel* to pour liquor into any vessel.
>
> —Ray on the Creation

2. A pipe or passage of communication.

> Towards the middle are two large *funnels*, bored through the roof of the grotto, to let in light or fresh air.
>
> —Addison

FÚTURE n.s. [from the adjective.] Time to come; somewhat to happen hereafter.

> Thy letters have transported me beyond
> This ign'rant present time; and I feel now
> The *future* in the instant.
>
> —Shakespeare, *Macbeth*

> The mind, once jaded by an attempt above its power, either is disabled for the *future*, or else checks at any vigorous undertaking ever after.
>
> —Locke

IMAGINÁTION. n.s. [*imaginatio*, Lat. *imagination*, Fr. from *imagine.*]

1. Fancy; the power of forming ideal pictures; the power of representing things absent to one's self or others.

> *Imagination* I understand to be the representation of an individual thought. *Imagination* is of three kinds: joined with belief of that which is to come; joined with memory of that which is past; and of things present, or as if they were present: for I comprehend in this imagination feigned and at pleasure, as if one should imagine such a man to be in the vestments of a pope, or to have wings.
>
> —Bacon

> Our simple apprehension of corporal objects, if present, is sense; if absent, *imagination*: when we would perceive a material object, our fancies present us with its idea.
>
> —Glanville

---

1. All entries are from the fourth edition of Johnson's *Dictionary* (1773), the last that Johnson prepared. Each entry is presented complete, with etymology, definitions, illustrations.

O whither shall I run, or which way fly
The sight of this so horrid spectacle,
Which erst my eyes beheld, and yet behold!
For dire *imagination* still pursues me.

—Milton

Where beams of warm *imagination* play,
The memory's soft figures melt away.

—Pope

2. Conception; image in the mind; idea.

Sometimes despair darkens all her *imaginations*; sometimes the active passion of love cheers and clears her invention.

—Sidney

Princes have but their titles for their glories,
An outward honor for an inward toil;
And, for unfelt *imaginations*,
They often feel a world of restless cares.

—Shakespeare, *Richard III*

Better I were distract,
So should my thoughts be severed from my griefs;
And woes, by wrong *imaginations*, lose
The knowledge of themselves.

—Shakespeare, *King Lear*

His *imaginations* were often as just as they were bold and strong.

—Dennis

3. Contrivance; scheme.

Thou hast seen all their vengeance, and all their *imaginations* against me.

—Bible (Lamentations 3.60)

4. An unsolid or fanciful opinion.

We are apt to think that space, in itself, is actually boundless; to which *imagination*, the idea of space, of itself leads us.

—Locke

JÚDGMENT. n.s. [*jugement*, Fr.]

1. The power of discerning the relations between one term or one proposition and another.

O *judgment!* thou art fled to brutish beasts,
And men have lost their reason.

—Shakespeare, *Julius Caesar*

The faculty, which God has given man to supply the want of certain knowledge, is *judgment*, whereby the mind takes any proposition to be true or false, without perceiving a demonstrative evidence in the proofs.

—Locke

Judgment is that whereby we join ideas together by affirmation or negation; so, this tree is high.

—Watts

2. Doom; the right or power of passing judgment.

> If my suspect be false, forgive me, God;
> For *judgment* only doth belong to thee.
>
> —Shakespeare, *Henry VI*

3. The act of exercising judicature; judicatory.

> They gave *judgment* upon him.
>
> —Bible (2 Kings)

> When thou, O Lord, shalt stand disclosed
> In majesty severe,
> And sit in *judgment* on my soul,
> O how shall I appear?
>
> —Addison's *Spectator*

4. Determination; decision.

> Where distinctions or identities are purely material, the *judgment* is made by the imagination, otherwise by the understanding.
>
> —Glanville's *Scepsis*

> We shall make a certain *judgment* what kind of dissolution that earth was capable of.
>
> —Burnet's *Theory*

> Reason ought to accompany the exercise of our senses, whenever we would form a just *judgment* of things proposed to our inquiry.
>
> —Watts

5. The quality of distinguishing propriety and impropriety; criticism.

> *Judgment*, a cool and slow faculty, attends not a man in the rapture of poetical composition.
>
> —Dennis

> 'Tis with our *judgments* as our watches, none
> Go just alike; yet each believes his own.
>
> —Pope

6. Opinion; notion.

> I see men's *judgments* are
> A parcel of their fortunes, and things outward
> Draw the inward quality after them,
> To suffer all alike.
>
> —Shakespeare, *Antony and Cleopatra*

> When she did think my master loved her well,
> She, in my *judgment*, was as fair as you.
>
> —Shakespeare

7. Sentence against a criminal.

> When he was brought again to th' bar, to hear
> His knell rung out, his *judgment*, he was stirred
> With agony.
>
> —Shakespeare, *Henry VIII*

> The chief priests informed me, desiring to have *judgment* against him.
>
> —Bible (Acts 25.15)

On Adam last this *judgment* he pronounced.

—Milton

8. Condemnation. This is a theological use.

The *judgment* was by one to condemnation; but the free gift is of many offenses unto justification.

—Bible (Romans 5.16)

The precepts, promises, and threatenings of the Gospel will rise up in *judgment* against us, and the articles of our faith will be so many articles of accusation.

—Tillotson

9. Punishment inflicted by Providence, with reference to some particular crime.

This *judgment* of the heavens that makes us tremble,
Touches us not with pity.

—Shakespeare, *King Lear*

We cannot be guilty of greater uncharitableness, than to interpret afflictions as punishments and *judgments*: it aggravates the evil to him who suffers, when he looks upon himself as the mark of divine vengeance.

—Addison's *Spectator*

10. Distribution of justice.

The Jews made insurrection against Paul, and brought him to the *judgment* seat.

—Bible (Acts 18.12)

Your dishonor
Mangles true *judgment*, and bereaves the state
Of that integrity which should become it.

—Shakespeare, *Coriolanus*

In *judgments* between rich and poor, consider not what the poor man needs, but what is his own.

—Taylor

A bold and wise petitioner goes strait to the throne and *judgment* seat of the monarch.

—Arbuthnot and Pope

11. Judiciary law; statute.

If ye hearken to these *judgments*, and keep and do them, the Lord thy God shall keep unto thee the covenant.

—Bible (Deuteronomy)

12. The last doom.

The dreadful *judgment* day
So dreadful will not be as was his sight.

—Shakespeare, *Henry VI*

KNACK. n.s.

1. A little machine; a petty contrivance; a toy.

> When I was young, I was wont
> To load my she with *knacks*: I would have ransacked
> The peddler's silken treasury, and have poured it
> To her acceptance.
>
> —Shakespeare, *Winter's Tale*

> For thee, fond boy,
> If I may ever know thou dost but sigh
> That thou no more shalt see this *knack*, as never
> I mean thou shalt, we'll bar thee from success.
>
> —Shakespeare

> This cap was moulded on a porringer,
> A velvet dish; fie, fie, 'tis lewd and filthy:
> Why 'tis a cockle, or a walnut shell,
> A *knack*, a toy, a trick, a baby's cap.
>
> —Shakespeare

> But is't not presumption to write verse to you,
> Who make the better poems of the two?
> For all these pretty *knacks* that you compose,
> Alas! what are they but poems in prose!
>
> —Denham

> He expounded both his pockets,
> And found a watch, with rings and lockets;
> A copper-plate, with almanacks
> Engraved upon't, with other *knacks*.
>
> —Hudibras

2. A readiness; an habitual facility; a lucky dexterity.

> I'll teach you the *knacks*
> Of eating of flax,
> And out of their noses
> Draw ribbands and posies.
>
> —Ben. Jonson's *Gypsies*

The *knack* of fast and loose passes with foolish people for a turn of wit; but they are not aware all this while of the desperate consequences of an ill habit.

—L'Estrange

There is a certain *knack* in conversation that gives a good grace by the manner and address.

—L'Estrange

> Knaves, who in full assemblies have the *knack*
> Of turning truth to lies, and white to black.
>
> —Dryden

My author has a great *knack* at remarks: in the end he makes another, about our refining in controversy, and coming nearer and nearer to the church of Rome.

—Atterbury

> The dean was famous in his time,
> And had a kind of *knack* at rhyme.

> —Swift

3. A nice trick.

> For how should equal colors do the *knack*?
> Chameleons who can paint in white and black?

> —Pope

LEXICÓGRAPHER. n.s. [λεξικον and γραφειν; *lexicographe*, Fr.] A writer of dictionaries; a harmless drudge, that busies himself in tracing the original, and detailing the signification of words.

> Commentators and *lexicographers* acquainted with the Syriac language, have given these hints in their writings on scripture.

> —Watt's *Improvement of the Mind*

SÚBSTANCE. n.s. [*substance*, Fr.; *substantia*, Lat.]

1. Being; something existing; something of which we can say that it is.

> Since then the soul works by herself alone,
> Springs not from sense, nor humors well agreeing,
> Her nature is peculiar, and her own;
> She is a *substance*, and a perfect being.

> —Davies

> The strength of gods,
> And this empyreal *substance* cannot fail.

> —Milton

2. That which supports accidents.

> What creatures there inhabit, of what mold,
> And *substance*.

> —Milton

> Every being is considered as subsisting in and by itself, and then it is called a *substance*; or it subsists in and by another, and then it is called a mode or manner of being.

> —Watts

3. The essential part.

> It will serve our turn to comprehend the *substance*, without confining ourselves to scrupulous exactness in form.

> —Digby

> This edition is the same in *substance* with the Latin.

> —Burn

> They are the best epitomes, and let you see with one cast of the eye the *substance* of a hundred pages.

> —Addison

4. Something real, not imaginary; something solid, not empty.

> Shadows tonight
> Have struck more terror to the soul of Richard,
> Than can the *substance* of ten thousand soldiers
> Armed in proof and led by shallow Richmond.
>
> —Shakespeare

> He the future evil shall no less
> In apprehension than in *substance* feel.
>
> —Milton

> Heroic virtue did his actions guide,
> And he the *substance*, not th' appearance chose:
> To rescue one such friend he took more pride,
> Than to destroy whole thousands of such foes.
>
> —Dryden

> God is no longer to be worshipped and believed in as a god foreshowing and assuring by types, but as a god who has performed the *substance* of what he promised.
>
> —Nelson

5. Body; corporeal nature.

> Between the parts of opaque and colored bodies are many spaces, either empty or replenished with mediums of other densities; as water between the tinging corpuscles wherewith any liquor is impregnated, air between the aqueous globules that constitute clouds or mists, and for the most part spaces void of both air and water; but yet perhaps not wholly void of all *substance* between the parts of hard bodies.
>
> —Newton

> The qualities of plants are more various than those of animal *substances*.
>
> —Arbuthnot on Aliments

> There may be a great and constant cough, with an extraordinary discharge of phlegmatic matter, while, notwithstanding, the *substance* of the lungs remains sound.
>
> —Blackmore

6. Wealth; means of life.

> He hath eaten me out of house and home, and hath put all my *substance* into that fat belly of his, but I will have some of it out again.
>
> —Shakespeare, *Henry IV*

> We are destroying many thousand lives, and exhausting our *substance*, but not for our own interest.
>
> —Swift

VACÚITY. n.s. [*vacuitas*; from *vacuus*, Lat. *vacuité*, Fr.]

1. Emptiness; state of being unfilled.

> Hunger is such a state of *vacuity*, as to require a fresh supply of aliment.
>
> —Arbuthnot

2. Space unfilled; space unoccupied.

> In filling up *vacuities*, turning out shadows and ceremonies, by explicit prescription of substantial duties, which those shadows did obscurely represent.
>
> —Hammond's *Fund*

> He, that seat soon failing, meets
> A vast *vacuity*.
>
> —Milton

> Body and space are quite different things, and a *vacuity* is interspersed among the particles of matter.
>
> —Bentley

> God, who alone can answer all our longings, and fill every *vacuity* of our soul, should entirely possess our heart.
>
> —Rogers

> Redeeming still at night these *vacuities* of the day.
>
> —Fell

3. Inanity; want of reality.

> The soul is seen, like other things, in the mirror of its effects: but if they'll run behind the glass to catch at it, their expectations will meet with *vacuity* and emptiness.
>
> —Glanville

THE HISTORY OF RASSELAS, PRINCE OF ABYSSINIA   Johnson wrote *Rasselas* with his customary speed but under particular pressures. He composed the tale probably in late January 1759, possibly (as Boswell reports) during the "evenings of one week." This was the month of his mother's death; he may have made the book in order to help defray expenses and to articulate loss. His friend the painter Sir Joshua Reynolds later praised *Rasselas* for compassing within its few pages as much wisdom as though it had been written "by an angel or some superior being, whose comprehensive faculties could develop and lay open the inmost recesses of the human mind," and who could convey "in a few hours the experience of ages." The experience that *Rasselas* imparts, Johnson had expressed in other forms before. Rasselas is a prince born to a life of ease within the Happy Valley, a sequestered utopia of limitless luxuries; he suffers, though, from an oppressive sense of dissatisfaction, or (in a favorite Johnsonian term) "vacuity." Tantalized by his conviction that true happiness must lie elsewhere, he escapes the valley accompanied by his sister Nekayah and his mentor Imlac, only to find his own propensity for misplaced hopes, unfulfilled plans, and ineffectual wishes mirrored in the unhappy lives of nearly every mortal he meets with. Early in the tale, just before effecting his escape, Rasselas asks Imlac to tell the story of his own life, lived mostly in the larger world. In his reminiscences, Imlac gently sketches the cycles of desire and disillusion that the prince and princess will shortly experience for themselves.

from The History of Rasselas, Prince of Abyssinia
Chapter 8. The History of Imlac

The close of the day is, in the regions of the torrid zone, the only season of diversion and entertainment, and it was therefore mid-night before the music ceased, and the princesses retired. Rasselas then called for his companion and required him to begin the story of his life.

"Sir," said Imlac, "my history will not be long: the life that is devoted to knowledge passes silently away, and is very little diversified by events. To talk in public, to think in solitude, to read and to hear, to inquire, and answer inquiries, is the business of a scholar. He wanders about the world without pomp or terror, and is neither known nor valued but by men like himself.

"I was born in the kingdom of Goiama, at no great distance from the fountain of the Nile. My father was a wealthy merchant, who traded between the inland countries of Africk and the ports of the Red Sea. He was honest, frugal and diligent, but of mean sentiments, and narrow comprehension: he desired only to be rich, and to conceal his riches, lest he should be spoiled[1] by the governors of the province."

"Surely," said the prince, "my father must be negligent of his charge, if any man in his dominions dares take that which belongs to another. Does he not know that kings are accountable for injustice permitted as well as done? If I were emperor, not the meanest of my subjects should be oppressed with impunity. My blood boils when I am told that a merchant durst not enjoy his honest gains for fear of losing them by the rapacity of power. Name the governor who robbed the people, that I may declare his crimes to the emperor."

"Sir," said Imlac, "your ardor is the natural effect of virtue animated by youth: the time will come when you will acquit your father, and perhaps hear with less impatience of the governor. Oppression is, in the Abyssinian dominions, neither frequent nor tolerated; but no form of government has been yet discovered, by which cruelty can be wholly prevented. Subordination supposes power on one part and subjection on the other; and if power be in the hands of men, it will sometimes be abused. The vigilance of the supreme magistrate may do much, but much will still remain undone. He can never know all the crimes that are committed, and can seldom punish all that he knows."

"This," said the prince, "I do not understand, but I had rather hear thee than dispute. Continue thy narration."

"My father," proceeded Imlac, "originally intended that I should have no other education, than such as might qualify me for commerce; and discovering in me great strength of memory, and quickness of apprehension, often declared his hope that I should be some time the richest man in Abyssinia."

"Why," said the prince, "did thy father desire the increase of his wealth, when it was already greater than he durst discover or enjoy? I am unwilling to doubt thy veracity, yet inconsistencies cannot both be true."

"Inconsistencies," answered Imlac, "cannot both be right, but, imputed to man, they may both be true. Yet diversity is not inconsistency. My father might expect a time of greater security. However, some desire is necessary to keep life in motion, and he, whose real wants are supplied, must admit those of fancy."

"This," said the prince, "I can in some measure conceive. I repent that I interrupted thee."

"With this hope," proceeded Imlac, "he sent me to school; but when I had once found the delight of knowledge, and felt the pleasure of intelligence and the pride of invention, I began silently to despise riches, and determined to disappoint the purpose of my father, whose grossness of conception raised my pity. I was twenty years old before his tenderness would expose me to the fatigue of travel, in which time I

1. Plundered.

had been instructed, by successive masters, in all the literature[2] of my native country. As every hour taught me something new, I lived in a continual course of gratifications; but, as I advanced towards manhood, I lost much of the reverence with which I had been used to look on my instructors; because, when the lesson was ended, I did not find them wiser or better than common men.

"At length my father resolved to initiate me in commerce, and, opening one of his subterranean treasuries, counted out ten thousand pieces of gold. 'This, young man,' said he, 'is the stock with which you must negotiate. I began with less than the fifth part, and you see how diligence and parsimony have increased it. This is your own to waste or to improve. If you squander it by negligence or caprice, you must wait for my death before you will be rich: if, in four years, you double your stock, we will thenceforward let subordination cease, and live together as friends and partners; for he shall always be equal with me, who is equally skilled in the art of growing rich.'

"We laid our money upon camels, concealed in bales of cheap goods, and traveled to the shore of the Red Sea. When I cast my eye on the expanse of waters my heart bounded like that of a prisoner escaped. I felt an unextinguishable curiosity kindle in my mind, and resolved to snatch this opportunity of seeing the manners of other nations, and of learning sciences[3] unknown in Abyssinia.

"I remembered that my father had obliged me to the improvement of my stock, not by a promise which I ought not to violate, but by a penalty which I was at liberty to incur, and therefore determined to gratify my predominant desire, and by drinking at the fountains of knowledge, to quench the thirst of curiosity.

"As I was supposed to trade without connection with my father, it was easy for me to become acquainted with the master of a ship, and procure a passage to some other country. I had no motives of choice to regulate my voyage; it was sufficient for me that, wherever I wandered, I should see a country which I had not seen before. I therefore entered a ship bound for Surat, having left a letter for my father declaring my intention.

Chapter 9. The History of Imlac Continued

"When I first entered upon the world of waters, and lost sight of land, I looked round about me with pleasing terror, and thinking my soul enlarged by the boundless prospect, imagined that I could gaze round for ever without satiety; but, in a short time, I grew weary of looking on barren uniformity, where I could only see again what I had already seen. I then descended into the ship, and doubted for a while whether all my future pleasures would not end like this in disgust and disappointment. 'Yet, surely,' said I, 'the ocean and the land are very different; the only variety of water is rest and motion, but the earth has mountains and valleys, deserts and cities: it is inhabited by men of different customs and contrary opinions; and I may hope to find variety in life, though I should miss it in nature.'

"With this thought I quieted my mind, and amused myself during the voyage; sometimes by learning from the sailors the art of navigation, which I have never practiced, and sometimes by forming schemes for my conduct in different situations, in not one of which I have been ever placed.

2. "Learning; skill in letters" (Johnson's *Dictionary*).   3. Modes of knowledge.

"I was almost weary of my naval amusements when we landed safely at Surat. I secured my money, and purchasing some commodities for show, joined myself to a caravan that was passing into the inland country. My companions, for some reason or other, conjecturing that I was rich, and, by my inquiries and admiration,[4] finding that I was ignorant, considered me as a novice whom they had a right to cheat, and who was to learn at the usual expense the art of fraud. They exposed me to the theft of servants, and the exaction of officers, and saw me plundered upon false pretenses, without any advantage to themselves, but that of rejoicing in the superiority of their own knowledge."

"Stop a moment," said the prince. "Is there such depravity in man, as that he should injure another without benefit to himself? I can easily conceive that all are pleased with superiority; but your ignorance was merely accidental, which, being neither your crime nor your folly, could afford them no reason to applaud themselves; and the knowledge which they had, and which you wanted, they might as effectually have shown by warning, as betraying you."

"Pride," said Imlac, "is seldom delicate, it will please itself with very mean advantages; and envy feels not its own happiness, but when it may be compared with the misery of others. They were my enemies because they grieved to think me rich, and my oppressors because they delighted to find me weak."

"Proceed," said the prince. "I doubt not of the facts which you relate, but imagine that you impute them to mistaken motives."

"In this company," said Imlac, "I arrived at Agra, the capital of Indostan, the city in which the great Mogul commonly resides. I applied myself to the language of the country, and in a few months was able to converse with the learned men; some of whom I found morose and reserved, and others easy and communicative; some were unwilling to teach another what they had with difficulty learned themselves; and some showed that the end of their studies was to gain the dignity of instructing.

"To the tutor of the young princes I recommended myself so much, that I was presented to the emperor as a man of uncommon knowledge. The emperor asked me many questions concerning my country and my travels; and though I cannot now recollect any thing that he uttered above the power of a common man, he dismissed me astonished at his wisdom, and enamored of his goodness.

"My credit was now so high, that the merchants, with whom I had traveled, applied to me for recommendations to the ladies of the court. I was surprised at their confidence of solicitation, and gently reproached them with their practices on the road. They heard me with cold indifference, and showed no tokens of shame or sorrow.

"They then urged their request with the offer of a bribe; but what I would not do for kindness I would not do for money; and refused them, not because they had injured me, but because I would not enable them to injure others; for I knew they would have made use of my credit to cheat those who should buy their wares.

"Having resided at Agra, till there was no more to be learned, I traveled into Persia, where I saw many remains of ancient magnificence, and observed many new accommodations[5] of life. The Persians are a nation eminently social, and their assemblies afforded me daily opportunities of remarking characters and manners, and of tracing human nature through all its variations.

4. "Wonder; the act of admiring or wondering" (Johnson's *Dictionary*).

5. "Conveniences, things requisite to ease or refreshment" (Johnson's *Dictionary*).

"From Persia I passed into Arabia, where I saw a nation at once pastoral and warlike; who live without any settled habitation; whose only wealth is their flocks and herds; and who have yet carried on, through all ages, an hereditary war with all mankind, though they neither covet nor envy their possessions.

Chapter 10. Imlac's History Continued. A Dissertation upon Poetry

"Wherever I went, I found that poetry was considered as the highest learning, and regarded with a veneration somewhat approaching to that which man would pay to the angelic nature. And it yet fills me with wonder, that, in almost all countries, the most ancient poets are considered as the best: whether it be that every other kind of knowledge is an acquisition gradually attained, and poetry is a gift conferred at once; or that the first poetry of every nation surprised them as a novelty, and retained the credit by consent which it received by accident at first: or whether, as the province of poetry is to describe nature and passion,[6] which are always the same, the first writers took possession of the most striking objects for description, and the most probable occurrences for fiction, and left nothing to those that followed them, but transcription of the same events, and new combinations of the same images. Whatever be the reason, it is commonly observed that the early writers are in possession of nature, and their followers of art: that the first excel in strength and invention, and the latter in elegance and refinement.

"I was desirous to add my name to this illustrious fraternity. I read all the poets of Persia and Arabia, and was able to repeat by memory the volumes that are suspended in the mosque of Mecca. But I soon found that no man was ever great by imitation. My desire of excellence impelled me to transfer my attention to nature and to life. Nature was to be my subject, and men to be my auditors: I could never describe what I had not seen: I could not hope to move those with delight or terror, whose interests and opinions I did not understand.

"Being now resolved to be a poet, I saw every thing with a new purpose; my sphere of attention was suddenly magnified: no kind of knowledge was to be overlooked. I ranged mountains and deserts for images and resemblances, and pictured upon my mind every tree of the forest and flower of the valley. I observed with equal care the crags of the rock and the pinnacles of the palace. Sometimes I wandered along the mazes of the rivulet, and sometimes watched the changes of the summer clouds. To a poet nothing can be useless. Whatever is beautiful, and whatever is dreadful, must be familiar to his imagination: he must be conversant with all that is awfully[7] vast or elegantly little. The plants of the garden, the animals of the wood, the minerals of the earth, and meteors of the sky, must all concur to store his mind with inexhaustible variety: for every idea is useful for the enforcement or decoration of moral or religious truth; and he who knows most will have most power of diversifying his scenes, and of gratifying his reader with remote allusions and unexpected instruction.

"All the appearances of nature I was therefore careful to study, and every country which I have surveyed has contributed something to my poetical powers."

"In so wide a survey," said the prince, "you must surely have left much unobserved. I have lived, till now, within the circuit of these mountains, and yet cannot walk abroad without the sight of something which I had never beheld before, or never heeded."

6. Nature: "the constitution and appearance of things" (Johnson's *Dictionary*); Passion: "violent commotion of the mind" (Johnson's *Dictionary*).
7. Solemnly.

"The business of a poet," said Imlac, "is to examine, not the individual, but the species; to remark general properties and large appearances: he does not number the streaks of the tulip, or describe the different shades in the verdure of the forest. He is to exhibit in his portraits of nature such prominent and striking features, as recall the original to every mind; and must neglect the minuter discriminations, which one may have remarked, and another have neglected, for those characteristics which are alike obvious to vigilance and carelessness.

"But the knowledge of nature is only half the task of a poet; he must be acquainted likewise with all the modes of life. His character requires that he estimate the happiness and misery of every condition; observe the power of all the passions in all their combinations, and trace the changes of the human mind as they are modified by various institutions and accidental influences of climate or custom, from the sprightliness of infancy to the despondence of decrepitude. He must divest himself of the prejudices of his age or country; he must consider right and wrong in their abstracted and invariable state; he must disregard present laws and opinions, and rise to general and transcendental truths, which will always be the same: he must therefore content himself with the slow progress of his name; condemn the applause of his own time, and commit his claims to the justice of posterity. He must write as the interpreter of nature, and the legislator of mankind, and consider himself as presiding over the thoughts and manners of future generations; as a being superior to time and place.

"His labor is not yet at an end: he must know many languages and many sciences; and, that his style may be worthy of his thoughts, must, by incessant practice, familiarize to himself every delicacy of speech and grace of harmony."

Chapter 11. Imlac's Narrative Continued. A Hint on Pilgrimage

Imlac now felt the enthusiastic[8] fit, and was proceeding to aggrandize his own profession, when the prince cried out, "Enough! Thou hast convinced me, that no human being can ever be a poet. Proceed with thy narration."

"To be a poet," said Imlac, "is indeed very difficult." "So difficult," returned the prince, "that I will at present hear no more of his labors. Tell me whither you went when you had seen Persia."

"From Persia," said the poet, "I traveled through Syria, and for three years resided in Palestine, where I conversed with great numbers of the northern and western nations of Europe; the nations which are now in possession of all power and all knowledge; whose armies are irresistible, and whose fleets command the remotest parts of the globe. When I compared these men with the natives of our own kingdom, and those that surround us, they appeared almost another order of beings. In their countries it is difficult to wish for any thing that may not be obtained: a thousand arts, of which we never heard, are continually laboring for their convenience and pleasure; and whatever their own climate has denied them is supplied by their commerce."

"By what means," said the prince, "are the Europeans thus powerful? or why, since they can so easily visit Asia and Africa for trade or conquest, cannot the Asiatics and Africans invade their coasts, plant colonies in their ports, and give laws to their natural princes? The same wind that carries them back would bring us thither."

8. "Vehemently hot in any cause" (Johnson's *Dictionary*).

"They are more powerful, Sir, than we," answered Imlac, "because they are wiser; knowledge will always predominate over ignorance, as man governs the other animals. But why their knowledge is more than ours, I know not what reason can be given, but the unsearchable will of the Supreme Being."

"When," said the prince with a sigh, "shall I be able to visit Palestine, and mingle with this mighty confluence of nations? Till that happy moment shall arrive, let me fill up the time with such representations as thou canst give me. I am not ignorant of the motive that assembles such numbers in that place, and cannot but consider it as the center of wisdom and piety, to which the best and wisest men of every land must be continually resorting."

"There are some nations," said Imlac, "that send few visitants[9] to Palestine; for many numerous and learned sects in Europe concur to censure pilgrimage as superstitious, or deride it as ridiculous."

"You know," said the prince, "how little my life has made me acquainted with diversity of opinions: it will be too long to hear the arguments on both sides; you, that have considered them, tell me the result."

"Pilgrimage," said Imlac, "like many other acts of piety, may be reasonable or superstitious, according to the principles upon which it is performed. Long journeys in search of truth are not commanded. Truth, such as is necessary to the regulation of life, is always found where it is honestly sought. Change of place is no natural cause of the increase of piety, for it inevitably produces dissipation of mind. Yet, since men go every day to view the fields where great actions have been performed, and return with stronger impressions of the event, curiosity of the same kind may naturally dispose us to view that country whence our religion had its beginning; and I believe no man surveys those awful scenes without some confirmation of holy resolutions. That the Supreme Being may be more easily propitiated in one place than in another, is the dream of idle superstition; but that some places may operate upon our own minds in an uncommon manner, is an opinion which hourly experience will justify. He who supposes that his vices may be more successfully combated in Palestine, will, perhaps, find himself mistaken, yet he may go thither without folly: he who thinks they will be more freely pardoned, dishonors at once his reason and religion."

"These," said the prince, "are European distinctions. I will consider them another time. What have you found to be the effect of knowledge? Are those nations happier than we?"

"There is so much infelicity," said the poet, "in the world, that scarce any man has leisure from his own distresses to estimate the comparative happiness of others. Knowledge is certainly one of the means of pleasure, as is confessed by the natural desire which every mind feels of increasing its ideas. Ignorance is mere privation, by which nothing can be produced: it is a vacuity in which the soul sits motionless and torpid for want of attraction; and, without knowing why, we always rejoice when we learn, and grieve when we forget. I am therefore inclined to conclude that, if nothing counteracts the natural consequence of learning, we grow more happy as our minds take a wider range.

"In enumerating the particular comforts of life we shall find many advantages on the side of the Europeans. They cure wounds and diseases with which we languish and perish. We suffer inclemencies of weather which they can obviate. They have engines for the dispatch of many laborious works, which we must perform by manual industry. There is such communication between distant places, that one friend can

9. Pilgrims.

hardly be said to be absent from another. Their policy removes all public inconveniences: they have roads cut through their mountains, and bridges laid upon their rivers. And, if we descend to the privacies of life, their habitations are more commodious, and their possessions are more secure."

"They are surely happy," said the prince, "who have all these conveniences, of which I envy none so much as the facility with which separated friends interchange their thoughts."

"The Europeans," answered Imlac, "are less unhappy than we, but they are not happy. Human life is every where a state in which much is to be endured, and little to be enjoyed."

Chapter 12. The Story of Imlac Continued

"I am not yet willing," said the prince, "to suppose that happiness is so parsimoniously distributed to mortals; nor can believe but that, if I had the choice of life, I should be able to fill every day with pleasure. I would injure no man, and should provoke no resentment: I would relieve every distress, and should enjoy the benedictions of gratitude. I would choose my friends among the wise, and my wife among the virtuous; and therefore should be in no danger from treachery, or unkindness. My children should, by my care, be learned and pious, and would repay to my age what their childhood had received. What would dare to molest him who might call on every side to thousands enriched by his bounty, or assisted by his power? And why should not life glide quietly away in the soft reciprocation of protection and reverence? All this may be done without the help of European refinements, which appear by their effects to be rather specious[1] than useful. Let us leave them and pursue our journey."

"From Palestine," said Imlac, "I passed through many regions of Asia; in the more civilized kingdoms as a trader, and among the barbarians of the mountains as a pilgrim. At last I began to long for my native country, that I might repose after my travels, and fatigues, in the places where I had spent my earliest years, and gladden my old companions with the recital of my adventures. Often did I figure to myself those, with whom I had sported away the gay hours of dawning life, sitting round me in its evening, wondering at my tales, and listening to my counsels.

"When this thought had taken possession of my mind, I considered every moment as wasted which did not bring me nearer to Abyssinia. I hastened into Egypt, and, notwithstanding my impatience, was detained ten months in the contemplation of its ancient magnificence, and in enquiries after the remains of its ancient learning. I found in Cairo a mixture of all nations; some brought thither by the love of knowledge, some by the hope of gain, and many by the desire of living after their own manner without observation, and of lying hid in the obscurity of multitudes: for, in a city, populous as Cairo, it is possible to obtain at the same time the gratifications of society, and the secrecy of solitude.

"From Cairo I traveled to Suez, and embarked on the Red Sea, passing along the coast till I arrived at the port from which I had departed twenty years before. Here I joined myself to a caravan and re-entered my native country.

"I now expected the caresses of my kinsmen, and the congratulations of my friends, and was not without hope that my father, whatever value he had set upon riches, would own with gladness and pride a son who was able to add to the felicity

1. "Showy; pleasing to the view" (Johnson's *Dictionary*).

and honor of the nation. But I was soon convinced that my thoughts were vain. My father had been dead fourteen years, having divided his wealth among my brothers, who were removed to some other provinces. Of my companions the greater part was in the grave, of the rest some could with difficulty remember me, and some considered me as one corrupted by foreign manners.

"A man used to vicissitudes is not easily dejected. I forgot, after a time, my disappointment, and endeavored to recommend myself to the nobles of the kingdom: they admitted me to their tables, heard my story, and dismissed me. I opened a school, and was prohibited to teach. I then resolved to sit down in the quiet of domestic life, and addressed a lady that was fond of my conversation, but rejected my suit, because my father was a merchant

"Wearied at last with solicitation and repulses, I resolved to hide myself for ever from the world, and depend no longer on the opinion or caprice of others. I waited for the time when the gate of the Happy Valley should open, that I might bid farewell to hope and fear: the day came; my performance was distinguished with favor, and I resigned myself with joy to perpetual confinement."

"Hast thou here found happiness at last?" said Rasselas. "Tell me without reserve; art thou content with thy condition? or, dost thou wish to be again wandering and inquiring? All the inhabitants of this valley celebrate their lot, and, at the annual visit of the emperor, invite others to partake of their felicity."

"Great prince," said Imlac, "I shall speak the truth: I know not one of all your attendants who does not lament the hour when he entered this retreat. I am less unhappy than the rest, because I have a mind replete with images, which I can vary and combine at pleasure. I can amuse my solitude by the renovation of the knowledge which begins to fade from my memory, and by recollection of the accidents of my past life. Yet all this ends in the sorrowful consideration, that my acquirements are now useless, and that none of my pleasures can be again enjoyed. The rest, whose minds have no impression but of the present moment, are either corroded by malignant passions, or sit stupid in the gloom of perpetual vacancy."

"What passions can infest those," said the prince, "who have no rivals? We are in a place where impotence precludes malice, and where all envy is repressed by community of enjoyments."

"There may be community," said Imlac, "of material possessions, but there can never be community of love or of esteem. It must happen that one will please more than another; he that knows himself despised will always be envious; and still more envious and malevolent, if he is condemned to live in the presence of those who despise him. The invitations, by which they allure others to a state which they feel to be wretched, proceed from the natural malignity of hopeless misery. They are weary of themselves, and of each other, and expect to find relief in new companions. They envy the liberty which their folly has forfeited, and would gladly see all mankind imprisoned like themselves.

"From this crime, however, I am wholly free. No man can say that he is wretched by my persuasion. I look with pity on the crowds who are annually soliciting admission to captivity, and wish that it were lawful for me to warn them of their danger."

"My dear Imlac," said the prince, "I will open to thee my whole heart. I have long meditated an escape from the Happy Valley. I have examined the mountains on every side, but find myself insuperably barred: teach me the way to break my prison; thou shalt be the companion of my flight, the guide of my rambles, the partner of my fortune, and my sole director in the *choice of life*."

"Sir," answered the poet, "your escape will be difficult, and, perhaps, you may soon repent your curiosity. The world, which you figure to yourself smooth and quiet as the lake in the valley, you will find a sea foaming with tempests, and boiling with whirlpools: you will be sometimes overwhelmed by the waves of violence, and sometimes dashed against the rocks of treachery. Amidst wrongs and frauds, competitions and anxieties, you will wish a thousand times for these seats of quiet, and willingly quit hope to be free from fear."

"Do not seek to deter me from my purpose," said the prince: "I am impatient to see what thou hast seen; and, since thou art thyself weary of the valley, it is evident, that thy former state was better than this. Whatever be the consequence of my experiment, I am resolved to judge with my own eyes of the various conditions of men, and then to make deliberately my *choice of life.*"

"I am afraid," said Imlac, "you are hindered by stronger restraints than my persuasions; yet, if your determination is fixed, I do not counsel you to despair. Few things are impossible to diligence and skill."

1759   1759

THE PLAYS OF WILLIAM SHAKESPEARE   Johnson first proposed a new edition of Shakespeare's plays, without success, in 1745; he finally published one twenty tears later. In the intervening decades, his work on the *Dictionary* had made him (in Bertrand Bronson's phrase) "the greatest living authority on Shakespeare's diction," and had secured him such fame that the booksellers greeted his renewed Shakespeare proposal with enthusiasm rather than indifference. Even so, he found the work slow going; he promised completion in eighteen months and took nine years. Five major editions had appeared since the start of the century, and Johnson was alert to their many inadequacies. Earlier editors displayed a passion for emendation, for finding "printer's errors" everywhere in the text, and replacing them with overconfident conjectures as to what Shakespeare had really "meant" and wrote. Johnson opted more often to let things be: to take a passage as given, to discover its intention, to explain its success, or to analyze its failure. The same kind of scrutiny suffuses his Preface, in which he investigates how plays really operate upon their audience. In the process, he demolishes the critical criteria by which Shakespeare had long been deemed an inferior crafter of drama (albeit an inimitably inspired poet). Johnson's *Shakespeare* is distinctive for the energy of its thought and of its feeling; for the intensity of its grappling with the impact of tiny passages and of towering genius.

from The Plays of William Shakespeare
from *Preface*

["JUST REPRESENTATIONS OF GENERAL NATURE"]

That praises are without reason lavished on the dead, and that the honors due only to excellence are paid to antiquity, is a complaint likely to be always continued by those who, being able to add nothing to truth, hope for eminence from the heresies of paradox; or those who, being forced by disappointment upon consolatory expedients, are willing to hope from posterity what the present age refuses and flatter themselves that the regard which is yet denied by envy will be at last bestowed by time.

Antiquity, like every other quality that attracts the notice of mankind, has undoubtedly votaries that reverence it not from reason, but from prejudice. Some seem to admire indiscriminately whatever has been long preserved, without considering that time has sometimes cooperated with chance; all perhaps are more willing to honor past than present excellence; and the mind contemplates genius through the shades of age, as the eye surveys the sun through artificial opacity. The great contention of criticism is to find the faults of the moderns and the beauties of the ancients. While an author is yet living, we estimate his powers by his worst performance; and when he is dead, we rate them by his best.

To works, however, of which the excellence is not absolute and definite, but gradual and comparative; to works not raised upon principles demonstrative and scientific but appealing wholly to observation and experience, no other test can be applied than length of duration and continuance of esteem. What mankind have long possessed they have often examined and compared; and if they persist to value the possession, it is because frequent comparisons have confirmed opinion in its favor. As among the works of nature no man can properly call a river deep or a mountain high, without the knowledge of many mountains and many rivers; so, in the productions of genius, nothing can be styled excellent till it has been compared with other works of the same kind. Demonstration immediately displays its power and has nothing to hope or fear from the flux of years; but works tentative and experimental must be estimated by their proportion to the general and collective ability of man, as it is discovered in a long succession of endeavors. Of the first building that was raised, it might be with certainty determined that it was round or square, but whether it was spacious or lofty must have been referred to time. The Pythagorean scale of numbers was at once discovered to be perfect; but the poems of Homer we yet know not to transcend the common limits of human intelligence but by remarking that nation after nation, and century after century, has been able to do little more than transpose his incidents, new-name his characters, and paraphrase his sentiments.

The reverence due to writings that have long subsisted arises, therefore, not from any credulous confidence in the superior wisdom of past ages or gloomy persuasion of the degeneracy of mankind, but is the consequence of acknowledged and indubitable positions that what has been longest known has been most considered, and what is most considered is best understood.

The poet of whose works I have undertaken the revision[1] may now begin to assume the dignity of an ancient and claim the privilege of established fame and prescriptive veneration. He has long outlived his century, the term commonly fixed as the test of literary merit. Whatever advantages he might once derive from personal allusions, local customs, or temporary opinions have for many years been lost; and every topic of merriment or motive of sorrow which the modes of artificial[2] life afforded him now only obscure the scenes which they once illuminated. The effects of favor and competition are at an end; the tradition of his friendships and his enmities have perished; his works support no opinion with arguments nor supply any faction with invectives; they can neither indulge vanity nor gratify malignity, but are read without any other reason than the desire of pleasure and are therefore praised only as pleasure is obtained; yet, thus unassisted by interest or passion, they have passed through variations of taste and changes of manners, and, as they devolved from one generation to another, have received new honors at every transmission.

But because human judgment, though it be gradually gaining upon certainty, never becomes infallible; and approbation, though long continued, may yet be only the approbation of prejudice or fashion; it is proper to inquire by what peculiarities of excellence Shakespeare has gained and kept the favor of his countrymen.

---

1. Edition.   2. "Made by art; not natural" (Johnson's *Dictionary*).

Nothing can please many, and please long, but just representations of general nature. Particular manners can be known to few, and therefore few only can judge how nearly they are copied. The irregular combinations of fanciful invention may delight awhile by that novelty of which the common satiety of life sends us all in quest; but the pleasures of sudden wonder are soon exhausted, and the mind can only repose on the stability of truth.

Shakespeare is, above all writers, at least above all modern writers, the poet of nature, the poet that holds up to his readers a faithful mirror of manners and of life. His characters are not modified by the customs of particular places, unpracticed by the rest of the world; by the peculiarities of studies or professions which can operate but upon small numbers; or by the accidents of transient fashions or temporary opinions: they are the genuine progeny of common humanity, such as the world will always supply, and observation will always find. His persons act and speak by the influence of those general passions and principles by which all minds are agitated and the whole system of life is continued in motion. In the writings of other poets a character is too often an individual; in those of Shakespeare it is commonly a species.

It is from this wide extension of design that so much instruction is derived. It is this which fills the plays of Shakespeare with practical axioms and domestic wisdom. It was said of Euripides that every verse was a precept;[3] and it may be said of Shakespeare that from his works may be collected a system of civil and economical prudence.[4] Yet his real power is not shown in the splendor of particular passages, but by the progress of his fable and the tenor of his dialogue; and he that tries to recommend him by select quotations will succeed like the pedant in Hierocles,[5] who, when he offered his house for sale, carried a brick in his pocket as a specimen.

It will not easily be imagined how much Shakespeare excels in accommodating his sentiments to real life but by comparing him with other authors. It was observed of the ancient schools of declamation that the more diligently they were frequented, the more was the student disqualified for the world, because he found nothing there which he should ever meet in any other place. The same remark may be applied to every stage but that of Shakespeare. The theater, when it is under any other direction, is peopled by such characters as were never seen, conversing in a language which was never heard, upon topics which will never arise in the commerce of mankind. But the dialogue of this author is often so evidently determined by the incident which produces it, and is pursued with so much ease and simplicity, that it seems scarcely to claim the merit of fiction, but to have been gleaned by diligent selection out of common conversation and common occurrences.

Upon every other stage the universal agent is love, by whose power all good and evil is distributed and every action quickened or retarded. To bring a lover, a lady, and a rival into the fable; to entangle them in contradictory obligations, perplex them with oppositions of interest, and harass them with violence of desires inconsistent with each other; to make them meet in rapture and part in agony, to fill their mouths with hyperbolical joy and outrageous sorrow, to distress them as nothing human ever was distressed, to deliver them as nothing human ever was delivered, is the business of a modern dramatist. For this, probability is violated, life is misrepresented, and language is depraved. But love is only one of many passions; and as it has

---

3. This observation was made by Cicero in his *Familiar Letters* (16.8).
4. Public and private duty.

5. The critic Hierocles, writing in the 5th century A.D., tells this story in his commentary on Pythagoras.

no great influence upon the sum of life, it has little operation in the dramas of a poet who caught his ideas from the living world and exhibited only what he saw before him. He knew that any other passion, as it was regular or exorbitant, was a cause of happiness or calamity.

Characters thus ample and general were not easily discriminated and preserved, yet perhaps no poet ever kept his personages more distinct from each other. I will not say with Pope that every speech may be assigned to the proper speaker, because many speeches there are which have nothing characteristical; but, perhaps, though some may be equally adapted to every person, it will be difficult to find any that can be properly transferred from the present possessor to another claimant. The choice is right, when there is reason for choice.

Other dramatists can only gain attention by hyperbolical or aggravated[6] characters, by fabulous and unexampled excellence or depravity, as the writers of barbarous romances invigorated the reader by a giant and a dwarf; and he that should form his expectations of human affairs from the play, or from the tale, would be equally deceived. Shakespeare has no heroes; his scenes are occupied only by men, who act and speak as the reader thinks that he should himself have spoken or acted on the same occasion. Even where the agency is supernatural, the dialogue is level with life. Other writers disguise the most natural passions and most frequent incidents, so that he who contemplates them in the book will not know them in the world. Shakespeare approximates the remote and familiarizes the wonderful; the event which he represents will not happen but, if it were possible, its effects would probably be such as he has assigned; and it may be said that he has not only shown human nature as it acts in real exigences, but as it would be found in trials to which it cannot be exposed.

This, therefore, is the praise of Shakespeare, that his drama is the mirror of life; that he who has mazed his imagination in following the phantoms which other writers raise up before him may here be cured of his delirious ecstasies by reading human sentiments in human language, by scenes from which a hermit may estimate the transactions of the world and a confessor predict the progress of the passions.

[Faults; The Unities]

Shakespeare with his excellencies has likewise faults, and faults sufficient to obscure and overwhelm any other merit. I shall show them in the proportion in which they appear to me, without envious malignity or superstitious veneration. No question can be more innocently discussed than a dead poet's pretensions to renown; and little regard is due to that bigotry which sets candor[1] higher than truth.

His first defect is that to which may be imputed most of the evil in books or in men. He sacrifices virtue to convenience and is so much more careful to please than to instruct that he seems to write without any moral purpose. From his writings indeed a system of social duty may be selected, for he that thinks reasonably must think morally; but his precepts and axioms drop casually from him; he makes no just distribution of good or evil, nor is always careful to show in the virtuous a disapprobation of the wicked; he carries his persons indifferently through right and wrong and at the close dismisses them without further care and leaves their examples to

---

6. Exaggerated.   1. "Sweetness of temper; kindness" (Johnson's *Dictionary*).

operate by chance. This fault the barbarity of his age cannot extenuate; for it is always a writer's duty to make the world better, and justice is a virtue independent on time or place.

The plots are often so loosely formed that a very slight consideration may improve them, and so carelessly pursued that he seems not always to comprehend his own design. He omits opportunities of instructing or delighting which the train of his story seems to force upon him, and apparently rejects those exhibitions which would be more affecting, for the sake of those which are more easy.

It may be observed that in many of his plays the latter part is evidently neglected. When he found himself near the end of his work and in view of his reward, he shortened the labor to snatch the profit. He therefore remits his efforts where he should most vigorously exert them, and his catastrophe is improbably produced or imperfectly represented.

He had no regard to distinction of time or place but gives to one age or nation, without scruple, the customs, institutions, and opinions of another, at the expense not only of likelihood but of possibility. These faults Pope has endeavored, with more zeal than judgment, to transfer to his imagined interpolators. We need not wonder to find Hector quoting Aristotle,[2] when we see the loves of Theseus and Hippolyta combined with the Gothic mythology of fairies.[3] Shakespeare, indeed, was not the only violator of chronology, for in the same age Sidney, who wanted not[4] the advantages of learning, has, in his Arcadia, confounded the pastoral with the feudal times, the days of innocence, quiet, and security, with those of turbulence, violence, and adventure.

In his comic scenes he is seldom very successful when he engages his characters in reciprocations of smartness and contests of sarcasm; their jests are commonly gross and their pleasantry licentious; neither his gentlemen nor his ladies have much delicacy nor are sufficiently distinguished from his clowns by any appearance of refined manners. Whether he represented the real conversation of his time is not easy to determine. The reign of Elizabeth is commonly supposed to have been a time of stateliness, formality, and reserve; yet perhaps the relaxations of that severity were not very elegant. There must, however, have been always some modes of gaiety preferable to others, and a writer ought to choose the best.

In tragedy his performance seems constantly to be worse as his labor is more. The effusions of passion which exigence forces out are for the most part striking and energetic; but whenever he solicits his invention or strains his faculties, the offspring of his throes is tumor, meanness, tediousness, and obscurity.

In narration he affects a disproportionate pomp of diction and a wearisome train of circumlocution and tells the incident imperfectly in many words which might have been more plainly delivered in few. Narration in dramatic poetry is naturally tedious, as it is unanimated and inactive and obstructs the progress of the action; it should therefore always be rapid and enlivened by frequent interruption. Shakespeare found it an encumbrance and, instead of lightening it by brevity, endeavored to recommend it by dignity and splendor.

His declamations or set speeches are commonly cold and weak, for his power was the power of nature; when he endeavored, like other tragic writers, to catch opportunities of amplification and, instead of inquiring what the occasion demanded, to show how much his stores of knowledge could supply, he seldom escapes without the pity or resentment of his reader.

---

2. *Troilus and Cressida* 2.2.166–67.   4. Did not lack.
3. This combination occurs in A *Midsummer Night's Dream*.

It is incident to him to be now and then entangled with an unwieldy senti-ment, which he cannot well express and will not reject; he struggles with it awhile and, if it continues stubborn, comprises it in words such as occur and leaves it to be disentangled and evolved by those who have more leisure to bestow upon it.

Not that always where the language is intricate the thought is subtle, or the image always great where the line is bulky; the equality of words to things is very often neglected, and trivial sentiments and vulgar ideas disappoint the attention to which they are recommended by sonorous epithets and swelling figures.[5]

But the admirers of this great poet have most reason to complain when he approaches nearest to his highest excellence and seems fully resolved to sink them in dejection and mollify them with tender emotions by the fall of greatness, the danger of innocence, or the crosses[6] of love. What he does best, he soon ceases to do. He is not long soft and pathetic without some idle conceit[7] or contemptible equivocation. He no sooner begins to move than he counteracts himself; and terror and pity, as they are rising in the mind, are checked and blasted by sudden frigidity.

A quibble[8] is to Shakespeare what luminous vapors are to the traveler; he follows it at all adventures; it is sure to lead him out of his way and sure to engulf him in the mire. It has some malignant power over his mind, and its fascinations are irresistible. Whatever be the dignity or profundity of his disquisition, whether he be enlarging knowledge or exalting affection, whether he be amusing attention with incidents or enchaining it in suspense, let but a quibble spring up before him and he leaves his work unfinished. A quibble is the golden apple for which he will always turn aside from his career or stoop from his elevation.[9] A quibble, poor and barren as it is, gave him such delight that he was content to purchase it by the sacrifice of reason, propri-ety, and truth. A quibble was to him the fatal Cleopatra for which he lost the world and was content to lose it.

It will be thought strange that in enumerating the defects of this writer I have not yet mentioned his neglect of the unities, his violation of those laws which have been instituted and established by the joint authority of poets and critics.

For his other deviations from the art of writing, I resign him to critical justice without making any other demand in his favor than that which must be indulged to all human excellence: that his virtues be rated with his failings. But from the censure which this irregularity may bring upon him, I shall, with due reverence to that learn-ing which I must oppose, adventure to try how I can defend him.

His histories, being neither tragedies nor comedies, are not subject to any of their laws; nothing more is necessary to all the praise which they expect than that the changes of action be so prepared as to be understood, that the incidents be vari-ous and affecting, and the characters consistent, natural, and distinct. No other unity is intended, and therefore none is to be sought.

In his other works he has well enough preserved the unity of action. He has not, indeed, an intrigue regularly perplexed and regularly unraveled; he does not endeavor to hide his design only to discover it, for this is seldom the order of real events, and Shake-speare is the poet of nature; but his plan has commonly, what Aristotle requires,[1] a begin-ning, a middle, and an end, one event is concatenated with another, and the conclusion

---

5. Figures of speech.
6. Obstacles, vexations.
7. Play on words.
8. Pun.

9. Johnson alludes to the story of the runner Atalanta, who lost a race because she was distracted by golden apples tossed in her path.
1. Aristotle, *Poetics*, ch. 8.

follows by easy consequence. There are perhaps some incidents that might be spared, as in other poets there is much talk that only fills up time upon the stage; but the general system makes gradual advances, and the end of the play is the end of expectation.

To the unities of time and place he has shown no regard; and perhaps a nearer view of the principles on which they stand will diminish their value and withdraw from them the veneration which, from the time of Corneille,[2] they have very generally received, by discovering that they have given more trouble to the poet than pleasure to the auditor.

The necessity of observing the unities of time and place arises from the supposed necessity of making the drama credible. The critics hold it impossible that an action of months or years can be possibly believed to pass in three hours; or that the spectator can suppose himself to sit in the theater while ambassadors go and return between distant kings, while armies are levied and towns besieged, while an exile wanders and returns, or till he whom they saw courting his mistress shall lament the untimely fall of his son. The mind revolts from evident falsehood, and fiction loses its force when it departs from the resemblance of reality.

From the narrow limitation of time necessarily arises the contraction of place. The spectator, who knows that he saw the first act at Alexandria, cannot suppose that he sees the next at Rome, at a distance to which not the dragons of Medea[3] could, in so short a time, have transported him; he knows with certainty that he has not changed his place; and he knows that place cannot change itself; that what was a house cannot become a plain; that what was Thebes can never be Persepolis.

Such is the triumphant language with which a critic exults over the misery of an irregular poet and exults commonly without resistance or reply. It is time, therefore, to tell him by the authority of Shakespeare, that he assumes, as an unquestionable principle, a position which, while his breath is forming it into words, his understanding pronounces to be false. It is false, that any representation is mistaken for reality; that any dramatic fable in its materiality was ever credible, or, for a single moment, was ever credited.

The objection arising from the impossibility of passing the first hour at Alexandria and the next at Rome supposes that when the play opens the spectator really imagines himself at Alexandria and believes that his walk to the theater has been a voyage to Egypt, and that he lives in the days of Antony and Cleopatra. Surely he that imagines this may imagine more. He that can take the stage at one time for the palace of the Ptolemies may take it in half an hour for the promontory of Actium. Delusion, if delusion be admitted, has no certain limitation; if the spectator can be once persuaded that his old acquaintance are Alexander and Caesar, that a room illuminated with candles is the plain of Pharsalia or the bank of Granicus,[4] he is in a state of elevation above the reach of reason or of truth, and from the heights of empyrean poetry may despise the circumscriptions of terrestrial nature. There is no reason why a mind thus wandering in ecstasy should count the clock, or why an hour should not be a century in that calenture[5] of the brains that can make the stage a field.

The truth is that the spectators are always in their senses and know from the first act to the last that the stage is only a stage, and that the players are only players. They come to hear a certain number of lines recited with just gesture and elegant modulation. The lines relate to some action, and an action must be in some place;

2. The French neoclassical dramatist Pierre Corneille published his influential *Essay on the Three Unities* in 1660.
3. After killing her rival and her children, Medea eluded pursuit in a chariot drawn by dragons.
4. Johnson refers to the site of battles fought by Julius Caesar and Alexander the Great.
5. Fever.

but the different actions that complete a story may be in places very remote from each other; and where is the absurdity of allowing that space to represent first Athens and then Sicily which was always known to be neither Sicily nor Athens, but a modern theater?

By supposition, as place is introduced, time may be extended; the time required by the fable elapses for the most part between the acts; for, of so much of the action as is represented, the real and poetical duration is the same. If in the first act preparations for war against Mithridates are represented to be made in Rome, the event of the war may, without absurdity, be represented in the catastrophe as happening in Pontus; we know that there is neither war nor preparation for war; we know that we are neither in Rome nor Pontus; that neither Mithridates nor Lucullus are before us. The drama exhibits successive imitations of successive actions; and why may not the second imitation represent an action that happened years after the first if it be so connected with it that nothing but time can be supposed to intervene? Time is, of all modes of existence, most obsequious to the imagination; a lapse of years is as easily conceived as a passage of hours. In contemplation we easily contract the time of real actions and therefore willingly permit it to be contracted when we only see their imitation.

It will be asked how the drama moves if it is not credited. It is credited with all the credit due to a drama. It is credited, whenever it moves, as a just picture of a real original; as representing to the auditor what he would himself feel if he were to do or suffer what is there feigned to be suffered or to be done. The reflection that strikes the heart is not that the evils before us are real evils, but that they are evils to which we ourselves may be exposed. If there be any fallacy, it is not that we fancy the players, but that we fancy ourselves unhappy for a moment; but we rather lament the possibility than suppose the presence of misery, as a mother weeps over her babe when she remembers that death may take it from her. The delight of tragedy proceeds from our consciousness of fiction; if we thought murders and treasons real, they would please no more.

Imitations produce pain or pleasure not because they are mistaken for realities, but because they bring realities to mind. When the imagination is recreated[6] by a painted landscape, the trees are not supposed capable to give us shade, or the fountains coolness; but we consider how we should be pleased with such fountains playing beside us and such woods waving over us. We are agitated in reading the history of *Henry the Fifth*, yet no man takes his book for the field of Agincourt. A dramatic exhibition is a book recited with concomitants that increase or diminish its effect. Familiar[7] comedy is often more powerful in the theater than on the page; imperial tragedy is always less. The humor of Petruchio[8] may be heightened by grimace; but what voice or what gesture can hope to add dignity or force to the soliloquy of Cato?[9]

A play read affects the mind like a play acted. It is therefore evident that the action is not supposed to be real; and it follows that between the acts a longer or shorter time may be allowed to pass, and that no more account of space or duration is to be taken by the auditor of a drama than by the reader of a narrative, before whom may pass in an hour the life of a hero or the revolutions of an empire.

6. "Delighted, gratified" (Johnson's *Dictionary*).
7. Domestic.
8. The hero of *The Taming of the Shrew*.

9. The protagonist of Addison's tragedy, *Cato* (1713), soliloquizes at the beginning of the final act.

Whether Shakespeare knew the unities and rejected them by design, or deviated from them by happy ignorance, it is, I think, impossible to decide and useless to inquire. We may reasonably suppose that when he rose to notice, he did not want the counsels and admonitions of scholars and critics, and that he at last deliberately persisted in a practice which he might have begun by chance. As nothing is essential to the fable but unity of action, and as the unities of time and place arise evidently from false assumptions, and, by circumscribing the extent of the drama, lessen its variety, I cannot think it much to be lamented that they were not known by him, or not observed; nor, if such another poet could arise, should I very vehemently reproach him that his first act passed at Venice and his next in Cyprus.[1] Such violations of rules merely positive become the comprehensive genius of Shakespeare, and such censures are suitable to the minute and slender criticism of Voltaire:

> Non usque adeo permiscuit imis
> Longus summa dies, ut non, si voce Metelli
> Serventur leges, malint a Caesare tolli.[2]

Yet when I speak thus slightly of dramatic rules, I cannot but recollect how much wit and learning may be produced against me; before such authorities I am afraid to stand, not that I think the present question one of those that are to be decided by mere authority, but because it is to be suspected that these precepts have not been so easily received but for better reasons than I have yet been able to find. The result of my inquiries, in which it would be ludicrous to boast of impartiality, is that the unities of time and place are not essential to a just drama; that, though they may sometimes conduce to pleasure, they are always to be sacrificed to the nobler beauties of variety and instruction; and that a play written with nice observation of critical rules is to be contemplated as an elaborate curiosity, as the product of superfluous and ostentatious art, by which is shown rather what is possible than what is necessary.

He that, without diminution of any other excellence, shall preserve all the unities unbroken deserves the like applause with the architect who shall display all the orders of architecture[3] in a citadel without any deduction from its strength; but the principal beauty of a citadel is to exclude the enemy, and the greatest graces of a play are to copy nature and instruct life. * * *

[SELECTED NOTES ON *OTHELLO*]

OTHELLO: Wherein of antres vast, and deserts idle,
Rough quarries, rocks, and hills, whose heads touch heaven . . . (1.3.141–42)

Whoever ridicules this account of the progress of love,[1] shows his ignorance, not only of history, but of nature and manners. It is no wonder that, in any age, or in any nation, a lady, recluse, timorous, and delicate, should desire to hear of events and scenes which she could never see, and should admire the man who had endured dangers, and performed actions, which, however great, were yet magnified by her timidity.

1. Johnson refers to *Othello*.
2. Johnson quotes from the epic poem *Pharsalia* by Lucan: "Things are not yet so confused that / If the laws were preserved by the voice of Metellus, / They would not prefer to be suppressed by Caesar." Johnson aligns Metellus, a politician of negligible importance, with Voltaire; Caesar correlates with Shakespeare.
3. The five classical styles of architecture.
1. As had Thomas Rymer in his *Short View of Tragedy* (1692).

Every mind is liable to absence and inadvertency, else Pope could never have rejected a word so poetically beautiful.[2] "Idle" is an epithet used to express the infertility of the chaotic state, in the Saxon translation of the Pentateuch.

> DESDEMONA: That I did love the Moor to live with him,
> My downright violence and storm of fortunes
> May trumpet to the world. (1.3.249–51)

There is no need of this emendation.[3] "Violence" is not "violence suffered," but "violence acted." Breach of common rules and obligations. The old quarto has, "scorn" of fortune, which is perhaps the true reading.

> DESDEMONA: I saw Othello's visage in his mind,
> And to his honors and his valiant parts
> Did I my soul and fortunes consecrate. (1.3.253–55)

It must raise no wonder, that I loved a man of an appearance so little engaging; I saw his face only in his mind; the greatness of his character reconciled me to his form.

> OTHELLO: Excellent wretch![4] (3.3.91)

The meaning of the word "wretch," is not generally understood. It is now, in some parts of England, a term of the softest and fondest tenderness. It expresses the utmost degree of amiableness, joined with an idea, which perhaps all tenderness includes, of feebleness, softness, and want of protection. Othello, considering Desdemona as excelling in beauty and virtue, soft and timorous by her sex, and by her situation absolutely in his power, calls her "excellent wretch." It may be expressed: "Dear, harmless, helpless excellence."

> OTHELLO: when I love thee not,
> Chaos is come again. (3.3.91–92)

When my love is for a moment suspended by suspicion, I have nothing in my mind but discord, tumult, perturbation, and confusion.

> IAGO: She did deceive her father, marrying you;
> And when she seemed to shake and fear your looks,
> She loved them most. (3.3.206–8)

This and the following argument of Iago ought to be deeply impressed on every reader. Deceit and falsehood, whatever conveniences they may for a time promise or produce, are, in the sum of life, obstacles to happiness. Those who profit by the cheat, distrust the deceiver, and the act by which kindness was sought, puts an end to confidence.

The same objection may be made with a lower degree of strength against the imprudent generosity of disproportionate marriages. When the first heat of passion is over, it is easily succeeded by suspicion, that the same violence of inclination which caused one irregularity, may stimulate to another; and those who have shown, that their passions are too powerful for their prudence, will, with very slight appearances against them, be censured, as not very likely to restrain them by their virtue.

---

2. In his edition of Shakespeare's works (1725), Alexander Pope had emended "deserts idle" to "deserts wild."
3. A prior editor had emended "violence and storm of fortunes" to "violence to forms, my fortunes."
4. In his edition of Shakespeare's works (1733–1734), Lewis Theobald had emended "wretch" to "wench."

EMILIA: 'Tis not a year or two shows us a man. (3.4.97)

From this line it may be conjectured, that the author intended the action of this play to be considered as longer than is marked by any note of time. Since their arrival at Cyprus, to which they were hurried on their wedding-night, the fable seems to have been in one continual progress, nor can I see any vacuity into which a "year or two," or even a month or two, could be put. On the night of Othello's arrival, a feast was proclaimed; at that feast Cassio was degraded, and immediately applies to Desdemona to get him restored. Iago indeed advises Othello to hold him off a while, but there is no reason to think, that he has been held off long. A little longer interval would increase the probability of the story, though it might violate the rules of the drama. See Act 5, Scene 2

OTHELLO: It is the cause, it is the cause, my soul.
Let me not name it to you, you chaste stars!
It is the cause. (5.2.1–3)

The abruptness of this soliloquy makes it obscure. The meaning I think is this. "I am here," says Othello in his mind, "overwhelmed with horror. What is the reason of this perturbation? Is it want of resolution to do justice? Is it the dread of shedding blood? No; it is not the action that shocks me, but 'it is the cause, it is the cause, my soul; let me not name it to you, ye chaste stars! it is the cause.' "

OTHELLO: This sorrow's heavenly;
It strikes where it doth love. (5.2.21–2)

This tenderness, with which I lament the punishment which justice compels me to inflict, is a holy passion.

I wish these two lines could be honestly ejected. It is the fate of Shakespeare to counteract his own pathos.

OTHELLO: Oh perjured woman! thou dost stone my heart,
And mak'st me call, what I intend to do,
A murder, which I thought a sacrifice. (5.2.67–69)

This line is difficult. "Thou hast hardened my heart, and makest me" kill thee with the rage of a "murderer," when "I thought to have sacrificed" thee to justice with the calmness of a priest striking a victim.

It must not be omitted, that one of the elder quartos reads, "thou dost stone *thy* heart"; which I suspect to be genuine. The meaning then will be, "thou forcest me" to dismiss thee from the world in the state of the "murdered" without preparation for death, "when I intended" that thy punishment should have been "a sacrifice" atoning for thy crime.

I am glad that I have ended my revisal of this dreadful scene. It is not to be endured.

The beauties of this play impress themselves so strongly upon the attention of the reader, that they can draw no aid from critical illustration. The fiery openness of Othello, magnanimous, artless, and credulous, boundless in his confidence, ardent in his affection, inflexible in his resolution, and obdurate in his revenge; the cool malignity of Iago, silent in his resentment, subtle in his designs, and studious at once of his interest and his vengeance; the soft simplicity of Desdemona, confident of merit, and conscious of innocence, her artless perseverance in her suit, and her slowness to suspect that she can be suspected, are such proofs of Shakespeare's skill in human nature, as, I suppose, it is vain to seek in any modern writer. The gradual progress which Iago makes in the Moor's conviction, and the circumstances which he employs to inflame him, are so artfully natural, that, though it will perhaps not be said of him as he says of himself, that he is "a man not easily jealous," yet we cannot but pity him when at last we find him "perplexed in the extreme."

There is always danger lest wickedness conjoined with abilities should steal upon esteem, though it misses of approbation; but the character of Iago is so conducted, that he is from the first scene to the last hated and despised.

Even the inferior characters of this play would be very conspicuous in any other piece, not only for their justness but their strength. Cassio is brave, benevolent, and honest, ruined only by his want of stubbornness to resist an insidious invitation. Roderigo's suspicious credulity, and impatient submission to the cheats which he sees practiced upon him, and which by persuasion he suffers to be repeated, exhibit a strong picture of a weak mind betrayed by unlawful desires, to a false friend; and the virtue of Emilia is such as we often find, worn loosely, but not cast off, easy to commit small crimes, but quickened and alarmed at atrocious villanies.

The scenes from the beginning to the end are busy, varied by happy interchanges, and regularly promoting the progression of the story; and the narrative in the end, though it tells but what is known already, yet is necessary to produce the death of Othello.

Had the scene opened in Cyprus, and the preceding incidents been occasionally related, there had been little wanting to a drama of the most exact and scrupulous regularity.[5]

TRAVEL WRITING   In the late eighteenth century, travel books were among the most popular genres on the market; they appear to have outsold novels many times over. In a 1770 letter to Hester Thrale, Johnson offered a simple explanation for why so many were so bad: "Those whose lot it is to ramble can seldom write, and those who know how to write very seldom ramble." Three years later, a journey with his friend James Boswell, to the Hebridean islands of northwest Scotland, gave Johnson an opportunity to show that he could do both. Writing plentiful notes and letters en route, and a book shortly after his return, Johnson clearly saw himself as participating in his century's new passion for anthropological exploration, transporting hard data from the islands of Scotland as Captain James Cook (for example) was doing from those of the South Pacific. Though the 1707 Act of Union had officially made Scotland one with England in the new national entity Great Britain, it had actually exacerbated difference rather than erased it: in the Jacobite uprisings of the ensuing half century, Scots rebels fiercely resisted assimilation, while English armies and politicians ever more ruthlessly enforced it. Nowhere were the costs of both resistance and defeat so available for scrutiny as in the Hebrides, the home of the Highland clans that had waged the rebellion against huge odds, and were now being systematically stripped of the cultural practices that had set them apart from centuries. In their predicament Johnson found new matter for old preoccupations: in their glorification of their past he saw the persistent human tendency to distract itself with delusion when truth is too hard to bear; in the paucity of natural resources and the disintegration of the culture he found fresh evidence that (in the words of Rasselas) "human life is everywhere a state in which much is to be endured, and little to be enjoyed." For many Scots readers of the Journey, Johnson's interpretation of their culture seemed too narrow to be forgiven. They claimed that as a prejudiced Englishman he had failed to appreciate the fertility of their history, the abundance of their resources, the plenitude of their prospects. What Johnson constructed as empathetic but empiric inquiry, they

5. I.e., according to the rules of the "unities," which Johnson rejects in the Preface.

dismissed as bigoted opacity. The *Journey* excited controversy at its first appearance, and does so still; it remains nonetheless one of the eighteenth century's richest documents of cultural encounter.

Letter to Hester Thrale[1]

Dearest Madam: Skye, Sep. 21, 1773

I am so vexed at the necessity of sending yesterday so short a letter, that I purpose to get a long letter beforehand by writing something every day, which I may the more easily do, as a cold makes me now too deaf to take the usual pleasure in conversation. Lady Macleod[2] is very kind to me, and the place at which we now are is equal in strength of situation, in the wildness of the adjacent country, and in the plenty and elegance of the domestic entertainment, to a castle in gothic romances. The sea with a little island is before us, cascades play within view. Close to the house is the formidable skeleton of an old castle probably Danish; and the whole mass of building stands upon a protuberance of rock, inaccessible till of late but by a pair of stairs on the sea side, and secure in ancient times against any enemy that was likely to invade the kingdom of Skye. Macleod has offered me an island, if it were not too far off I should hardly refuse it; my island would be pleasanter than Brighthelmston,[3] if You and Master[4] could come to it, but I cannot think it pleasant to live quite alone. *Oblitusque meorum, obliviscendus et illis.*[5] That I should be elated by the dominion of an Island to forgetfulness of my friends at Streatham,[6] and I hope never to deserve that they should be willing to forget me.

It has happened that I have been often recognized in my journey where I did not expect it. At Aberdeen I found one of my acquaintance a professor of physic. Turning aside to dine with a country gentleman, I was owned at table by one who had seen me at a philosophical lecture. At Macdonald's[7] I was claimed by a naturalist, who wanders about the Islands to pick up curiosities, and I had once in London attracted the notice of Lady Macleod. I will now go on with my account.

The Highland girl made tea, and looked and talked not inelegantly. Her father was by no means an ignorant or a weak man. There were books in the cottage, among which were some volumes of Prideaux's *Connection*.[8] This man's conversation we were glad of while we stayed. He had been out, as they call it, in forty five,[9] and still retained his old opinions. He was going to America, because his rent was raised beyond what he thought himself able to pay.

At night our beds were made, but we had some difficulty in persuading ourselves to lie down in them, though we had put on our own sheets. At last we ventured, and I slept very soundly, in the vale called Glenmorison amidst the rocks and mountains. Next morning our landlord liked us so well, that he walked some miles with us for our

---

1. Writer, and wife of the prosperous brewer Henry Thrale; she was one of Johnson's dearest friends and favorite correspondents. For more on her life and writings, see page 2858. In this letter Johnson narrates roughly the same stretch of days covered in the selections from Johnson's *Journey* (pages 2799–2808) and Boswell's *Journal* (pages 2828–35).
2. Johnson's hostess at Dunvegan, a Macleod family seat on the island of Skye and the oldest continuously inhabited castle in Scotland.
3. Johnson compares the island of Isa (in the gift of Norman Macleod, chief of the Macleods of Dunvegan) to the Thrales' retreat at the sea resort of Brighton

("Brighthelmston").
4. Johnson's nickname for Hester Thrale's husband Henry.
5. Yet there would I live, forgetting my friends and by them forgotten (Horace, *Epistles* 1.11.8–9).
6. The Thrales' principal residence outside of London.
7. The home of Allan Macdonald at Kingsburgh, where Johnson had stayed before going to Dunvegan.
8. *The Old and New Testaments Connected* (1716–1718) by Humphrey Prideaux.
9. The Jacobite Rebellion of 1745–1746, which ended when the army of Prince Charles Edward Stuart ("Bonnie Prince Charlie") was defeated at the Battle of Culloden.

company through a country so wild and barren that the proprietor does not with all his pressure upon his tenants raise more than four hundred a year from near an hundred square miles, or sixty thousand acres. He let us know that he had forty head of black cattle, an hundred goats, and an hundred sheep upon a farm which he remembered let at five pounds a year, but for which he now paid twenty. He told us some stories of their march into England. At last he left us, and we went forward, winding among mountains sometimes green and sometimes naked, commonly so steep as not easily to be climbed by the greatest vigor and activity. Our way was often crossed by little rivulets, and we were entertained with small streams trickling from the rocks, which after heavy rains must be tremendous torrents.

About noon, we came to a small glen, so they call a valley, which compared with other places appeared rich and fertile. Here our guides desired us to stop that the horses might graze, for the journey was very laborious, and no more grass would be found. We made no difficulty of compliance, and I sat down to make notes on a green bank, with a small stream running at my feet, in the midst of savage solitude, with mountains before me, and on either hand covered with heath. I looked round me, and wondered that I was not more affected, but the mind is not at all times equally ready to be put in motion. If my Mistress, and Master, and Queeney[1] had been there we should have produced some reflections among us either poetical or philosophical, for though *solitude be the nurse of woe*,[2] conversation is often the parent of remarks and discoveries.

In about an hour we remounted, and pursued our journey. The lake by which we had traveled from some time ended in a river, which we passed by a bridge and came to another glen with a collection of huts, called Auknasheals, the huts were generally built of clods of earth held together by the intertexture of vegetable fibers, of which earth there are great levels in Scotland which they call mosses. Moss in Scotland is bog in Ireland, and mosstrooper is bogtrotter. There was however one hut built of loose stones piled up with great thickness into a strong though not solid wall. From this house we obtained some great pails of milk, and having brought bread with us, were very liberally regaled. The inhabitants, a very coarse tribe, ignorant of any language but Earse,[3] gathered so fast about us, that if we had not had Highlanders with us, they might have caused more alarm than pleasure. They are called the clan of Macrae.

We had been told that nothing gratified the Highlanders so much as snuff and tobacco, and had accordingly stowed ourselves with both at Fort Augustus. Boswell opened his treasure and gave them each a piece of tobacco roll. We had more bread than we could eat for the present, and were more liberal than provident. Boswell cut it in slices and gave each of them an opportunity of tasting wheaten bread for the first time. I then got some halfpence for a shilling and made up the deficiencies of Boswell's distribution, who had given some money among the children. We then directed that the mistress of the stone house should be asked what we must pay her, she who perhaps had never sold anything but cattle before, knew not, I believe, well what to ask, and referred herself to us. We obliged her to make some demand, and our Highlanders settled the account with her at a shilling. One of the men advised her, with the cunning that clowns[4] never can be without, to ask more but she said

1. Hester and Henry Thrale, and their eldest daughter Hester Maria, whose family nickname was "Queeney."
2. "The silent heart . . . learns to know / That solitude's the nurse of woe" (Thomas Parnell, *Hymn to Content-*

ment, lines 19, 23–24).
3. The form of Gaelic spoken in Scotland.
4. Yokels.

that a shilling was enough. We gave her half a crown[5] and she offered part of it again. The Macraes were so well pleased with our behavior, that they declared it the best day they had seen since the time of the old Laird of MacLeod, who I suppose, like us, stopped in their valley, as he was travelling to Skye.

We were mentioning this view of the Highlander's life at Macdonald's, and mentioning the Macraes with some degree of pity, when a Highland lady informed us, that we might spare our tenderness, for she doubted not, but the woman who supplied us with milk, was mistress of thirteen or fourteen milch cows.

I cannot forbear to interrupt my narrative. Boswell, with some of his troublesome kindness, has informed this family, and reminded me that the eighteenth of September is my birthday. The return of my birthday, if I remember it, fills me with thoughts which it seems to be the general care of humanity to escape. I can now look back upon threescore and four years, in which little has been done, and little has been enjoyed, a life diversified by misery, spent part in the sluggishness of penury, and part under the violence of pain, in gloomy discontent, or importunate distress. But perhaps I am better than I should have been, if I had been less afflicted. With this I will try to be content.

In proportion as there is less pleasure in retrospective considerations the mind is more disposed to wander forward into futurity, but at sixty four what promises, however liberal, of imaginary good, can futurity venture to make? Yet something will be always promised, and some promises will always be credited. I am hoping, and I am praying that I may live better in the time to come, whether long or short, than I have yet lived, and in the solace of that hope endeavor to repose. Dear Queeney's day is next, I hope, she at sixty four will have less to regret.

I will now complain no more, but tell my Mistress of my travels.

After we left the Macraes, we traveled on through a country like that which we passed in the morning, the highlands are very uniform, for there is little variety in universal barrenness. The rocks however are not all naked, some have grass on their sides, and birches and alders on their tops, and in the valleys are often broad and clear streams which have little depth, and commonly run very quick. The channels are made by the violence of wintry floods, the quickness of the stream is in proportion to the declivity of the descent, and the breadth of the channel makes the water shallow in a dry season.

There are red deer and roebucks in the mountains, but we found only goats in the road, and had very little entertainment as we traveled either for the eye or ear. There are, I fancy, no singing birds in the Highlands.

Towards night we came to a very formidable hill named Ratiken, which we climbed with more difficulty than we had yet experienced, and at last came to Glenelg, a place on the seaside opposite to Skye. We were by this time weary and disgusted, nor was our humor much mended, by an inn, which, though it was built with lime and slate, the Highlander's description of a house which he thinks magnificent, had neither wine, bread, eggs, nor anything that we could eat or drink. When we were taken up stairs, a dirty fellow bounced out of the bed in which one of us was to lie. Boswell blustered, but nothing could he get. At last a gentleman in the neighborhood who heard of our arrival sent us rum and white sugar. Boswell was now provided for in part, and the landlord prepared some mutton chops, which we could not eat, and killed two hens, of which Boswell made his servant broil a limb, with what effect I know not. We had a lemon, and a piece of bread, which supplied me with my supper.

5. A crown was worth five shillings.

When the repast was ended, we began to deliberate upon bed. Mrs. Boswell had warned us that we should *catch something,* and had given us sheets for our security; for Sir Alexander and Lady Macdonald, she said, came back from Skye, so scratching themselves——. I thought sheets a slender defense, against the confederacy with which we were threatened, and by this time our Highlanders had found a place where they could get some hay; I ordered hay to be laid thick upon the bed, and slept upon it in my great coat. Boswell laid sheets upon his hay, and reposed in linen like a gentleman. The horses were turned out to grass, with a man to watch them. The hill Ratiken, and the inn at Glenelg, are the only things of which we, or travelers yet more delicate, could find any pretensions to complain.

Sept. 2. I rose rustling from the hay, and went to tea, which I forget whether we found or brought. We saw the Isle of Skye before us darkening the horizon with its rocky coast. A boat was procured, and we launched into one of the Straits of the Atlantic Ocean. We had a passage of about twelve miles to the point where Sir Alexander resided, having come from his seat in the midland part, to a small house on the shore, as we believe, that he might with less reproach entertain us meanly. If he aspired to meanness[6] his retrograde ambition was completely gratified, but he did not succeed equally in escaping reproach. He had no cook, nor, I suppose, much provision, nor had the Lady the common decencies of her tea table. We picked up our sugar with our fingers. Boswell was very angry, and reproached him with his improper parsimony. I did not much reflect upon the conduct of a man with whom I was not likely to converse as long at any other time.

You will now expect that I should give you some account of the Isle of Skye, of which though I have been twelve days upon it, I have little to say. It is an island perhaps fifty miles long, so much indented by inlets of the sea, that there is no part of it removed from the water more than six miles. No part that I have seen is plain, you are always climbing or descending, and every step is upon rock or mire. A walk upon plowed ground in England is a dance upon carpets, compared to the toilsome drudgery of wandering in Skye. There is neither town nor village in the island, nor have I seen any house but Macleod's, that is not much below your habitation at Brighthelmston. In the mountains there are stags and roebucks, but no hares and few rabbits, nor have I seen any thing that interested me, as zoologist, except an otter, bigger than I thought an otter could have been.

You are perhaps imagining that I am withdrawn from the gay and the busy world into regions of peace and pastoral felicity, and am enjoying the relics of the golden age; that I am surveying Nature's magnificence from a mountain, or remarking her minuter beauties on the flowery bank of a winding rivulet, that I am invigorating myself in the sunshine, or delighting my imagination with being hidden from the invasion of human evils and human passions in the darkness of a thicket, that I am busy in gathering shells and pebbles on the shore, or contemplative on a rock, from which I look upon the water and consider how many waves are rolling between me and Streatham.

The use of traveling is to regulate imagination by reality, and instead of thinking how things may be, to see them as they are. Here are mountains which I should once have climbed, but to climb steeps is now very laborious, and to descend them dangerous, and I am now content with knowing that by a scrambling up a rock, I shall only see other rocks, and a wider circuit of barren desolation. Of streams we have here a sufficient number, but they murmur not upon pebbles but upon rocks; of flowers, if

6. Lack of generosity.

Chloris[7] herself were here, I could present her only with the bloom of heath. Of lawns and thickets, he must read, that would know them, for here is little sun and no shade. On the sea I look from my window, but am not much tempted to the shore for since I came to this island, almost every breath of air has been a storm, and what is worse, a storm with all its severity, but without its magnificence, for the sea is here so broken into channels, that there is not a sufficient volume of water either for lofty surges, or loud roar.

On Sept. 6 we left Macdonald, to visit Raarsa, the island which I have already mentioned. We were to cross part of Skye on horseback, a mode of traveling very uncomfortable, for the road is so narrow, where any road can be found, that only one can go, and so craggy that the attention can never be remitted. It allows therefore neither the gaiety of conversation nor the laxity of solitude, nor has it in itself the amusement of much variety, as it affords only all the possible transpositions of bog, rock, and rivulet. Twelve miles, by computation, make a reasonable journey for a day.

At night we came to a tenant's house of the first rank of tenants where we were entertained better than the landlords. There were books, both English and Latin. Company gathered about us, and we heard some talk of the second sight and some talk of the events of forty five, a year which will not soon be forgotten among the islanders. The next day we were confined by a storm, the company, I think, increased and our entertainment was not only hospitable but elegant. At night, a minister's sister in very fine brocade sung Earse songs. I wished to know the meaning, but the Highlanders are not much used to scholastic questions, and no translation could be obtained.

Next day, Sept. 8, the weather allowed us to depart, a good boat was provided us, and we went to Raarsa, under the conduct of Mr. Malcolm Macleod, a gentleman who conducted Prince Charles through the mountains in his distresses.[8] The prince, he says, was more active than himself, they were at least one night, without any shelter.

The wind blew enough to give the boat a kind of dancing agitation, and in about three or four hours we arrived at Raarsa, where we were met by the Laird and his friends upon the shore. Raarsa, for such is his title, is master of two islands, upon the smaller of which, called Rona, he has only flocks and herds. Rona gives title to his eldest son. The money which he raises by rent from all his dominions, which contain at least fifty thousand acres, is not believed to exceed two hundred and fifty pounds, but as he keeps a large farm in his own hands, he sells every year great numbers of cattle which he adds to his revenue, and, his table is furnished from the farm and from the sea with very little expense, except for those things this country does not produce, and of these he is very liberal. The wine circulates vigorously, and the tea and chocolate[9] and coffee, however they are got are always at hand. I am, Madam, Your most obedient servant,

SAM. JOHNSON

We are this morning trying to get out of Skye.

from **A Journey to the Western Islands of Scotland**
Anoch

Early in the afternoon we came to Anoch, a village in Glenmollison of three huts, one of which is distinguished by a chimney. Here we were to dine and lodge, and were conducted through the first room, that had the chimney, into another lighted

7. Goddess of flowers.
8. After the Battle of Culloden (see note 9 on page 2795), Bonnie Prince Charlie escaped capture with diffi-

culty; his adventures as a fugitive in the Highlands and the Hebrides became legendary.
9. Hot chocolate.

by a small glass window. The landlord attended us with great civility, and told us what he could give us to eat and drink. I found some books on a shelf, among which were a volume or more of Prideaux's *Connection*.

This I mentioned as something unexpected, and perceived that I did not please him: I praised the propriety of his language, and was answered that I need not wonder, for he had learned it by grammar.[1]

By subsequent opportunities of observation, I found that my host's diction had nothing peculiar. Those Highlanders that can speak English, commonly speak it well, with few of the words, and little of the tone by which a Scotchman is distinguished. Their language seems to have been learned in the army or the navy, or by some communication with those who could give them good examples of accent and pronunciation. By their Lowland neighbors they would not willingly be taught; for they have long considered them as a mean and degenerate race. These prejudices are wearing fast away; but so much of them still remains, that when I asked a very learned minister in the islands, which they considered as their most savage clans: "Those," said he, "that live next the Lowlands."

As we came hither early in the day, we had time sufficient to survey the place. The house was built like other huts of loose stones, but the part in which we dined and slept was lined with turf and wattled with twigs, which kept the earth from falling. Near it was a garden of turnips and a field of potatoes. It stands in a glen, or valley, pleasantly watered by a winding river. But this country, however it may delight the gazer or amuse the naturalist, is of no great advantage to its owners. Our landlord told us of a gentleman, who possesses lands, eighteen Scotch miles[2] in length, and three in breadth; a space containing at least a hundred square English miles. He has raised his rents, to the danger of depopulating his farms, and he sells his timber, and by exerting every art of augmentation, has obtained an yearly revenue of four hundred pounds, which for a hundred square miles is three halfpence an acre.

Some time after dinner we were surprised by the entrance of a young woman, not inelegant either in mien or dress, who asked us whether we would have tea. We found that she was the daughter of our host, and desired her to make it. Her conversation, like her appearance, was gentle and pleasing. We knew that the girls of the Highlands are all gentlewomen, and treated her with great respect, which she received as customary and due, and was neither elated by it, nor confused, but repaid my civilities without embarrassment, and told me how much I honored her country by coming to survey it.

She had been at Inverness to gain the common female qualifications, and had, like her father, the English pronunciation. I presented her with a book,[3] which I happened to have about me, and should not be pleased to think that she forgets me.

In the evening the soldiers, whom we had passed on the road, came to spend at our inn the little money that we had given them. They had the true military impatience of coin in their pockets, and had marched at least six miles to find the first place where liquor could be bought. Having never been before in a place so wild and unfrequented, I was glad of their arrival, because I knew that we had made them friends, and to gain

---

1. Through study of Latin grammar.
2. Longer than English miles.
3. A treatise on arithmetic by Edward Cocker. Johnson
later defended his choice to Boswell: "Why, sir, if you are to have but one book with you upon a journey, let it be a book of science. . . . a book of science is inexhaustible."

still more of their good will, we went to them, where they were carousing in the barn, and added something to our former gift. All that we gave was not much, but it detained them in the barn, either merry or quarreling, the whole night, and in the morning they went back to their work, with great indignation at the bad qualities of whiskey.

We had gained so much the favor of our host, that, when we left his house in the morning, he walked by us a great way, and entertained us with conversation both on his own condition, and that of the country. His life seemed to be merely pastoral, except that he differed from some of the ancient Nomads in having a settled dwelling. His wealth consists of one hundred sheep, as many goats, twelve milk-cows, and twenty-eight beeves[4] ready for the drover.

From him we first heard of the general dissatisfaction, which is now driving the Highlanders into the other hemisphere;[5] and when I asked him whether they would stay at home, if they were well treated, he answered with indignation, that no man willingly left his native country. Of the farm, which he himself occupied, the rent had, in twenty-five years, been advanced from five to twenty pounds, which he found himself so little able to pay, that he would be glad to try his fortune in some other place. Yet he owned the reasonableness of raising the Highland rents in a certain degree, and declared himself willing to pay ten pounds for the ground which he had formerly had for five.

Our host having amused us for a time, resigned us to our guides. The journey of this day was long, not that the distance was great, but that the way was difficult. We were now in the bosom of the Highlands, with full leisure to contemplate the appearance and properties of mountainous regions, such as have been, in many countries, the last shelters of national distress, and are everywhere the scenes of adventures, stratagems, surprises and escapes.

Mountainous countries are not passed but with difficulty, not merely from the labor of climbing, for to climb is not always necessary, but because that which is not mountain is commonly bog, through which the way must be picked with caution. Where there are hills, there is much rain, and the torrents pouring down into the intermediate spaces, seldom find so ready an outlet, as not to stagnate, till they have broken the texture of the ground.

Of the hills, which our journey offered to the view on either side, we did not take the height, nor did we see any that astonished us with their loftiness. Towards the summit of one, there was a white spot, which I should have called a naked rock, but the guides, who had better eyes, and were acquainted with the phenomena of the country, declared it to be snow. It had already lasted to the end of August, and was likely to maintain its contest with the sun, till it should be reinforced by winter.

The height of mountains philosophically considered is properly computed from the surface of the next sea; but as it affects the eye or imagination of the passenger, as it makes either a spectacle or an obstruction, it must be reckoned from the place where the rise begins to make a considerable angle with the plain. In extensive continents the land may, by gradual elevation, attain great height, without any other appearance than that of a plane gently inclined, and if a hill placed upon such raised ground be described, as having its altitude equal to the whole space above the sea, the representation will be fallacious.

---

4. Oxen.

5. At this time, increasing numbers of impoverished Scots farmers were emigrating to America.

These mountains may be properly enough measured from the inland base; for it is not much above the sea. As we advanced at evening towards the western coast, I did not observe the declivity to be greater than is necessary for the discharge of the inland waters.

We passed many rivers and rivulets, which commonly ran with a clear shallow stream over a hard pebbly bottom. These channels, which seem so much wider than the water that they convey would naturally require, are formed by the violence of wintry floods, produced by the accumulation of innumerable streams that fall in rainy weather from the hills, and bursting away with resistless impetuosity, make themselves a passage proportionate to their mass.

Such capricious and temporary waters cannot be expected to produce many fish. The rapidity of the wintry deluge sweeps them away, and the scantiness of the summer stream would hardly sustain them above the ground. This is the reason why in fording the northern rivers, no fishes are seen, as in England, wandering in the water.

Of the hills many may be called with Homer's Ida "abundant in springs," but few can deserve the epithet which he bestows upon Pelion by "waving their leaves."[6] They exhibit very little variety; being almost wholly covered with dark heath, and even that seems to be checked in its growth. What is not heath is nakedness, a little diversified by now and then a stream rushing down the steep. An eye accustomed to flowery pastures and waving harvests is astonished and repelled by this wide extent of hopeless sterility. The appearance is that of matter incapable of form or usefulness, dismissed by nature from her care and disinherited of her favors, left in its original elemental state, or quickened only with one sullen power of useless vegetation.

It will very readily occur, that this uniformity of barrenness can afford very little amusement to the traveler; that it is easy to sit at home and conceive rocks and heath, and waterfalls; and that these journeys are useless labors, which neither impregnate the imagination, nor enlarge the understanding. It is true that of far the greater part of things, we must content ourselves with such knowledge as description may exhibit, or analogy supply; but it is true likewise, that these ideas are always incomplete, and that, at least till we have compared them with realities, we do not know them to be just. As we see more, we become possessed of more certainties, and consequently gain more principles of reasoning, and found a wider basis of analogy.

Regions mountainous and wild, thinly inhabited, and little cultivated, make a great part of the earth, and he that has never seen them, must live unacquainted with much of the face of nature, and with one of the great scenes of human existence.

As the day advanced towards noon, we entered a narrow valley not very flowery, but sufficiently verdant. Our guides told us, that the horses could not travel all day without rest or meat, and entreated us to stop here, because no grass would be found in any other place. The request was reasonable and the argument cogent. We therefore willingly dismounted and diverted ourselves as the place gave us opportunity.

I sat down on a bank, such as a writer of romance might have delighted to feign. I had indeed no trees to whisper over my head, but a clear rivulet streamed at my feet. The day was calm, the air soft, and all was rudeness, silence, and solitude. Before me,

---

6. Mount Ida and Mount Pelion are thus described in Homer's *Iliad*.

and on either side, were high hills, which by hindering the eye from ranging, forced the mind to find entertainment for itself. Whether I spent the hour well I know not; for here I first conceived the thought of this narration.

We were in this place at ease and by choice, and had no evils to suffer or to fear; yet the imaginations excited by the view of an unknown and untraveled wilderness are not such as arise in the artificial solitude of parks and gardens: a flattering notion of self-sufficiency, a placid indulgence of voluntary delusions, a secure expansion of the fancy, or a cool concentration of the mental powers. The phantoms which haunt a desert are want, and misery, and danger; the evils of dereliction rush upon the thoughts; man is made unwillingly acquainted with his own weakness, and meditation shows him only how little he can sustain, and how little he can perform. There were no traces of inhabitants, except perhaps a rude pile of clods called a summer hut, in which a herdsman had rested in the favorable seasons. Whoever had been in the place where I then sat, unprovided with provisions and ignorant of the country, might, at least before the roads were made, have wandered among the rocks, till he had perished with hardship, before he could have found either food or shelter. Yet what are these hillocks to the ridges of Taurus, or these spots of wildness to the deserts of America?

It was not long before we were invited to mount, and continued our journey along the side of a lough, kept full by many streams, which with more or less rapidity and noise crossed the road from the hills on the other hand. These currents, in their diminished state, after several dry months, afford, to one who has always lived in level countries, an unusual and delightful spectacle; but in the rainy season, such as every winter may be expected to bring, must precipitate an impetuous and tremendous flood. I suppose the way by which we went is at that time impassable.

Glensheals

The lough at last ended in a river broad and shallow like the rest, but that it may be passed when it is deeper, there is a bridge over it. Beyond it is a valley called Glensheals, inhabited by the clan of Macrae. Here we found a village called Auknasheals, consisting of many huts, perhaps twenty, built all of "dry-stone," that is, stones piled up without mortar.

We had, by the direction of the officers at Fort Augustus, taken bread for ourselves, and tobacco for those Highlanders who might show us any kindness. We were now at a place where we could obtain milk, but must have wanted[7] bread if we had not brought it. The people of this valley did not appear to know any English, and our guides now became doubly necessary as interpreters. A woman, whose hut was distinguished by greater spaciousness and better architecture, brought out some pails of milk. The villagers gathered about us in considerable numbers, I believe without any evil intention, but with a very savage wildness of aspect and manner. When our meal was over, Mr. Boswell sliced the bread, and divided it amongst them, as he supposed them never to have tasted a wheaten loaf before. He then gave them little pieces of twisted tobacco, and among the children we distributed a small handful of half-pence, which they received with great eagerness. Yet I have been since told, that the people of that valley are not indigent; and when we mentioned them afterwards as needy and pitiable, a Highland lady let us know, that we

7. Lacked.

might spare our commiseration; for the dame whose milk we drank had probably more than a dozen milk-cows. She seemed unwilling to take any price, but being pressed to make a demand, at last named a shilling. Honesty is not greater where elegance is less. One of the by-standers, as we were told afterwards, advised her to ask more, but she said a shilling was enough. We gave her half a crown, and I hope got some credit by our behavior; for the company said, if our interpreters did not flatter us, that they had not seen such a day since the old Laird of Macleod passed through their country.

The Macraes, as we heard afterwards in the Hebrides, were originally an indigent and subordinate clan, and having no farms nor stock, were in great numbers servants to the Maclellans, who, in the war of Charles the First, took arms at the call of the heroic Montrose,[8] and were, in one of his battles, almost all destroyed. The women that were left at home, being thus deprived of their husbands, like the Scythian ladies of old, married their servants,[9] and the Macraes became a considerable race.

The Highlands

As we continued our journey, we were at leisure to extend our speculations, and to investigate the reason of those peculiarities by which such rugged regions as these before us are generally distinguished.

Mountainous countries commonly contain the original, at least the oldest race of inhabitants, for they are not easily conquered, because they must be entered by narrow ways, exposed to every power of mischief from those that occupy the heights; and every new ridge is a new fortress, where the defendants have again the same advantages. If the assailants either force the strait, or storm the summit, they gain only so much ground; their enemies are fled to take possession of the next rock, and the pursuers stand at gaze, knowing neither where the ways of escape wind among the steeps, nor where the bog has firmness to sustain them: besides that, mountaineers have an agility in climbing and descending distinct from strength or courage, and attainable only by use.

If the war be not soon concluded, the invaders are dislodged by hunger; for in those anxious and toilsome marches, provisions cannot easily be carried, and are never to be found. The wealth of mountains is cattle, which, while the men stand in the passes, the women drive away. Such lands at last cannot repay the expense of conquest, and therefore perhaps have not been so often invaded by the mere ambition of dominion; as by resentment of robberies and insults, or the desire of enjoying in security the more fruitful provinces.

As mountains are long before they are conquered, they are likewise long before they are civilized. Men are softened by intercourse mutually profitable, and instructed by comparing their own notions with those of others. Thus Caesar found the maritime parts of Britain made less barbarous by their commerce with the Gauls.[1] Into a barren and rough tract no stranger is brought either by the hope of gain or of pleasure. The inhabitants having neither commodities for sale, nor money for purchase, seldom visit more polished places, or if they do visit them, seldom return.

8. James Graham (1612–1650), Marquis of Montrose, fought the Parliamentarians in a doomed attempt to restore the Stuart monarchy.
9. The Greek historian Herodotus tells this story in his *Histories* (4.2).
1. In his *De Bello Gallico* (5.14.1), Julius Caesar describes the civilizing effects of commerce on English ports along the southern coast.

It sometimes happens that by conquest, intermixture, or gradual refinement, the cultivated parts of a country change their language. The mountaineers then become a distinct nation, cut off by dissimilitude of speech from conversation with their neighbors. Thus in Biscay, the original Cantabrian,[2] and in Dalecarlia, the old Swedish still subsists.[3] Thus Wales and the Highlands speak the tongue of the first inhabitants of Britain, while the other parts have received first the Saxon, and in some degree afterwards the French, and then formed a third language between them.

That the primitive manners are continued where the primitive language is spoken, no nation will desire me to suppose, for the manners of mountaineers are commonly savage, but they are rather produced by their situation than derived from their ancestors.

Such seems to be the disposition of man, that whatever makes a distinction produces rivalry. England, before other causes of enmity were found, was disturbed for some centuries by the contests of the northern and southern counties; so that at Oxford, the peace of study could for a long time be preserved only by choosing annually one of the Proctors from each side of the Trent.[4] A tract intersected by many ridges of mountains, naturally divides its inhabitants into petty nations, which are made by a thousand causes enemies to each other. Each will exalt its own chiefs, each will boast the valor of its men, or the beauty of its women, and every claim of superiority irritates competition; injuries will sometimes be done, and be more injuriously defended; retaliation will sometimes be attempted, and the debt exacted with too much interest.

In the Highlands it was a law, that if a robber was sheltered from justice, any man of the same clan might be taken in his place. This was a kind of irregular justice, which, though necessary in savage times, could hardly fail to end in a feud, and a feud once kindled among an idle people with no variety of pursuits to divert their thoughts, burned on for ages either sullenly glowing in secret mischief, or openly blazing into public violence. Of the effects of this violent judicature, there are not wanting memorials. The cave is now to be seen to which one of the Campbells, who had injured the Macdonalds, retired with a body of his own clan. The Macdonalds required the offender, and being refused, made a fire at the mouth of the cave, by which he and his adherents were suffocated together.

Mountaineers are warlike, because by their feuds and competitions they consider themselves as surrounded with enemies, and are always prepared to repel incursions, or to make them. Like the Greeks in their unpolished state, described by Thucydides,[5] the Highlanders, till lately, went always armed, and carried their weapons to visits, and to church.[6]

Mountaineers are thievish, because they are poor, and having neither manufactures nor commerce, can grow richer only by robbery. They regularly plunder their neighbors, for their neighbors are commonly their enemies; and having lost that reverence for property, by which the order of civil life is preserved, soon consider all as enemies, whom they do not reckon as friends, and think themselves licensed to invade whatever they are not obliged to protect.

2. The Romans called the northern province of Spain "Cantabria"; Johnson's name for the same region is "Biscay."
3. Dalecarlia was a province in southern Sweden.
4. A river that forms the traditional boundary between northern and southern England.

5. In his history of the Peloponnesian War (1.6.3).
6. After crushing the Jacobite Rebellion of 1745–1746, the English attempted to stamp out future revolts by enacting a series of repressive laws, one of which forbade Highlanders to carry arms.

By a strict administration of the laws, since the laws have been introduced into the Highlands, this disposition to thievery is very much repressed. Thirty years ago no herd had ever been conducted through the mountains, without paying tribute in the night, to some of the clans; but cattle are now driven, and passengers travel without danger, fear, or molestation.

Among a warlike people, the quality of highest esteem is personal courage, and with the ostentatious display of courage are closely connected promptitude of offense and quickness of resentment. The Highlanders, before they were disarmed, were so addicted to quarrels, that the boys used to follow any public procession or ceremony, however festive, or however solemn, in expectation of the battle, which was sure to happen before the company dispersed.

Mountainous regions are sometimes so remote from the seat of government, and so difficult of access, that they are very little under the influence of the sovereign, or within the reach of national justice. Law is nothing without power; and the sentence of a distant court could not be easily executed, nor perhaps very safely promulgated, among men ignorantly proud and habitually violent, unconnected with the general system, and accustomed to reverence only their own lords. It has therefore been necessary to erect many particular jurisdictions, and commit the punishment of crimes, and the decision of right to the proprietors of the country who could enforce their own decrees. It immediately appears that such judges will be often ignorant, and often partial;[7] but in the immaturity of political establishments no better expedient could be found. As government advances towards perfection, provincial judicature is perhaps in every empire gradually abolished.

Those who had thus the dispensation of law, were by consequence themselves lawless. Their vassals had no shelter from outrages and oppressions; but were condemned to endure, without resistance, the caprices of wantonness, and the rage of cruelty.

In the Highlands, some great lords had an hereditary jurisdiction over counties; and some chieftains over their own lands; till the final conquest of the Highlands afforded an opportunity of crushing all the local courts, and of extending the general benefits of equal law to the low and the high, in the deepest recesses and obscurest corners.

While the chiefs had this resemblance of royalty, they had little inclination to appeal, on any question, to superior judicatures. A claim of lands between two powerful lairds was decided like a contest for dominion between sovereign powers. They drew their forces into the field, and right attended on the strongest. This was, in ruder times, the common practice, which the kings of Scotland could seldom control.

Even so lately as in the last years of King William,[8] a battle was fought at Mull Roy, on a plain a few miles to the south of Inverness, between the clans of Mackintosh and Macdonald of Keppoch. Col. Macdonald, the head of a small clan, refused to pay the dues demanded from him by Mackintosh, as his superior lord. They disdained the interposition of judges and laws, and calling each his followers to maintain the dignity of the clan, fought a formal battle, in which several considerable men fell on the side of Mackintosh, without a complete victory to either. This is said to have been the last open war made between the clans by their own authority.

---

7. Prejudiced.   8. William III ruled from 1689 to 1702.

The Highland lords made treaties, and formed alliances, of which some traces may still be found, and some consequences still remain as lasting evidences of petty regality. The terms of one of these confederacies were, that each should support the other in the right, or in the wrong, except against the king.

The inhabitants of mountains form distinct races, and are careful to preserve their genealogies. Men in a small district necessarily mingle blood by intermarriages, and combine at last into one family, with a common interest in the honor and disgrace of every individual. Then begins that union of affections, and cooperation of endeavors, that constitute a clan. They who consider themselves as ennobled by their family, will think highly of their progenitors, and they who through successive generations live always together in the same place, will preserve local stories and hereditary prejudices. Thus every Highlander can talk of his ancestors, and recount the outrages which they suffered from the wicked inhabitants of the next valley.

Such are the effects of habitation among mountains, and such were the qualities of the Highlanders, while their rocks secluded them from the rest of mankind, and kept them an unaltered and discriminated race. They are now losing their distinction, and hastening to mingle with the general community.

Glenelg

We left Auknasheals and the Macraes in the afternoon, and in the evening came to Ratiken, a high hill on which a road is cut, but so steep and narrow, that it is very difficult. There is now a design of making another way round the bottom. Upon one of the precipices, my horse, weary with the steepness of the rise, staggered a little, and I called in haste to the Highlander to hold him. This was the only moment of my journey, in which I thought myself endangered.

Having surmounted the hill at last, we were told that at Glenelg, on the sea-side, we should come to a house of lime and slate and glass. This image of magnificence raised our expectation. At last we came to our inn weary and peevish, and began to inquire for meat and beds.

Of the provisions the negative catalogue was very copious. Here was no meat, no milk, no bread, no eggs, no wine. We did not express much satisfaction. Here however we were to stay. Whisky we might have, and I believe at last they caught a fowl and killed it. We had some bread, and with that we prepared ourselves to be contented, when we had a very eminent proof of Highland hospitality. Along some miles of the way, in the evening, a gentleman's servant had kept us company on foot with very little notice on our part. He left us near Glenelg, and we thought on him no more till he came to us again, in about two hours, with a present from his master of rum and sugar. The man had mentioned his company, and the gentleman, whose name, I think, is Gordon, well knowing the penury of the place, had this attention to two men, whose names perhaps he had not heard, by whom his kindness was not likely to be ever repaid, and who could be recommended to him only by their necessities.

We were now to examine our lodging. Out of one of the beds, on which we were to repose, started up, at our entrance, a man black as a Cyclops from the forge.[9] Other circumstances of no elegant recital concurred to disgust us. We had

9. In classical literature, the Cyclops were often described as blacksmiths, who forged weapons for the gods in an underground workshop.

been frighted by a lady at Edinburgh, with discouraging representations of Highland lodgings. Sleep, however, was necessary. Our Highlanders had at last found some hay, with which the inn could not supply them. I directed them to bring a bundle into the room, and slept upon it in my riding coat. Mr. Boswell being more delicate, laid himself sheets with hay over and under him, and lay in linen like a gentleman.

from *Skye. Armidel*

In the morning, September the second, we found ourselves on the edge of the sea. Having procured a boat, we dismissed our Highlanders, whom I would recommend to the service of any future travelers, and were ferried over to the Isle of Skye. We landed at Armidel, where we were met on the sands by Sir Alexander Macdonald, who was at that time there with his lady, preparing to leave the island and reside at Edinburgh.

Armidel is a neat house, built where the Macdonalds had once a seat, which was burned in the commotions that followed the Revolution.[1] The walled orchard, which belonged to the former house, still remains. It is well shaded by tall ash trees, of a species, as Mr. Janes the fossilist[2] informed me, uncommonly valuable. This plantation is very properly mentioned by Dr. Campbell, in his new account of the state of Britain,[3] and deserves attention; because it proves that the present nakedness of the Hebrides is not wholly the fault of Nature. * * *

1773–1774   1775

LIVES OF THE POETS   In March 1777, a consortium of booksellers persuaded Johnson to undertake a new endeavor. "I am engaged," he informed Boswell, "to write little Lives and little Prefaces, to a little edition of the English Poets" of the past century and a half. In the end, he produced fifty-two *Prefaces Biographical and Critical*, now better known as *Lives of the Poets*. Some of the lives remained "little" (the booksellers had selected the poets, and Johnson did not consider all of them worthy of sustained attention); but many of them expanded in range and interest far beyond Johnson's initial expectation. As Boswell later observed, Johnson pursued the project "with peculiar delight" because he knew this literary territory so very well. In the longest *Lives* (of Milton, Dryden, Addison, and Pope), Johnson paid complex tribute to the predecessors who had mattered most to him as models in his youth—who had shaped the literary world in which he had now found his own place. The three-part structure in which Johnson cast most of the prefaces was well calculated to display the powers and precepts accumulated over a lifetime. In the first part, an account of the poet's life, he fulfilled his own dictum (in *Rambler* No. 60) that biography is most useful when it deals in the "minute details" and "domestic privacies" of the subject's daily life; in the second part, an assessment of the poet's character, he implemented his own conviction that the biographer (unlike the eulogist) should forgo pure praise in favor of complex truth; in the third section, a critical review of the poet's work, he found full scope for the close analysis of literary cause and effect that had always informed his reading. "The biographical part of literature," he had once remarked, "is what I love the most." The *Lives* were that love's last labor. In them, the fusion of a favorite genre with a deeply familiar subject produced, in John Wain's words, "the greatest masterpiece of English eighteenth-century criticism."

---

1. The "Glorious Revolution" of 1688–1689, when the Stuart monarch James II was replaced by William and Mary.

2. The mineralogist John Jeans.

3. Johnson refers to John Campbell's *Political Survey of Britain* (1774).

from **Lives of the Poets**

from *The Life of Milton*

[ON *PARADISE LOST*]

Whatever be his subject he never fails to fill the imagination. But his images and descriptions of the scenes or operations of nature do not seem to be always copied from original form, nor to have the freshness, raciness,[1] and energy of immediate observation. He saw nature, as Dryden expresses it, "through the spectacles of books"; and on most occasions calls learning to his assistance. The garden of Eden brings to his mind the vale of Enna, where Proserpine was gathering flowers. Satan makes his way through fighting elements, like Argo between the Cyanean rocks, or Ulysses between the two Sicilian whirlpools, when he shunned Charybdis "on the larboard." The mythological allusions have been justly censured, as not being always used with notice of their vanity; but they contribute variety to the narration, and produce an alternate exercise of the memory and the fancy.

His similes are less numerous and more various than those of his predecessors. But he does not confine himself within the limits of rigorous comparison: his great excellence is amplitude, and he expands the adventitious[2] image beyond the dimensions which the occasion required. Thus, comparing the shield of Satan to the orb of the moon, he crowds the imagination with the discovery of the telescope and all the wonders which the telescope discovers.

Of his moral sentiments it is hardly praise to affirm that they excel those of all other poets; for this superiority he was indebted to his acquaintance with the sacred writings. The ancient epic poets, wanting the light of revelation, were very unskillful teachers of virtue: their principal characters may be great, but they are not amiable. The reader may rise from their works with a greater degree of active or passive fortitude, and sometimes of prudence; but he will be able to carry away few precepts of justice, and none of mercy. * * *

In Milton every line breathes sanctity of thought and purity of manners, except when the train of the narration requires the introduction of the rebellious spirits; and even they are compelled to acknowledge their subjection to God in such a manner as excites reverence and confirms piety.

Of human beings there are but two; but those two are the parents of mankind, venerable before their fall for dignity and innocence, and amiable after it for repentance and submission. In their first state their affection is tender without weakness, and their piety sublime without presumption. When they have sinned they show how discord begins in mutual frailty, and how it ought to cease in mutual forbearance; how confidence of the divine favor is forfeited by sin, and how hope of pardon may be obtained by penitence and prayer. A state of innocence we can only conceive, if indeed in our present misery it be possible to conceive it; but the sentiments and worship proper to a fallen and offending being we have all to learn, as we have all to practice.

The poet whatever be done is always great. Our progenitors in their first state conversed with angels; even when folly and sin had degraded them they had not in their humiliation "the port of mean suitors"; and they rise again to reverential regard when we find that their prayers were heard.

---

1. "Strong; flavorous; tasting of the soil" (Johnson's *Dictionary*).   2. Accidental.

As human passions did not enter the world before the Fall, there is in the *Paradise Lost* little opportunity for the pathetic;[3] but what little there is has not been lost. That passion which is peculiar to rational nature, the anguish arising from the consciousness of transgression and the horrors attending the sense of the Divine Displeasure, are very justly described and forcibly impressed. But the passions are moved only on one occasion; sublimity is the general and prevailing quality in this poem—sublimity variously modified, sometimes descriptive, sometimes argumentative.

The defects and faults of *Paradise Lost*, for faults and defects every work of man must have, it is the business of impartial criticism to discover. As in displaying the excellence of Milton I have not made long quotations, because of selecting beauties there had been no end, I shall in the same general manner mention that which seems to deserve censure; for what Englishman can take delight in transcribing passages, which, if they lessen the reputation of Milton, diminish in some degree the honor of our country?

The generality of my scheme does not admit the frequent notice of verbal inaccuracies which Bentley,[4] perhaps better skilled in grammar than in poetry, has often found, though he sometimes made them, and which he imputed to the obtrusions of a reviser whom the author's blindness obliged him to employ. A supposition rash and groundless, if he thought it true; and vile and pernicious, if, as is said, he in private allowed it to be false.

The plan of *Paradise Lost* has this inconvenience, that it comprises neither human actions nor human manners. The man and woman who act and suffer are in a state which no other man or woman can ever know. The reader finds no transaction in which he can be engaged, beholds no condition in which he can by any effort of imagination place himself; he has, therefore, little natural curiosity or sympathy.

We all, indeed, feel the effects of Adam's disobedience; we all sin like Adam, and like him must all bewail our offenses; we have restless and insidious enemies in the fallen angels, and in the blessed spirits we have guardians and friends; in the Redemption of mankind we hope to be included: in the description of heaven and hell we are surely interested, as we are all to reside hereafter either in the regions of horror or of bliss.

But these truths are too important to be new: they have been taught to our infancy; they have mingled with our solitary thoughts and familiar conversation, and are habitually interwoven with the whole texture of life. Being therefore not new they raise no unaccustomed emotion in the mind: what we knew before we cannot learn; what is not unexpected, cannot surprise.

Of the ideas suggested by these awful scenes, from some we recede with reverence, except when stated hours require their association; and from others we shrink with horror, or admit them only as salutary inflictions, as counterpoises to our interests and passions. Such images rather obstruct the career of fancy than incite it.

Pleasure and terror are indeed the genuine sources of poetry; but poetical pleasure must be such as human imagination can at least conceive, and poetical terror such as human strength and fortitude may combat. The good and evil of Eternity are too ponderous for the wings of wit; the mind sinks under them in passive helplessness, content with calm belief and humble adoration.

---

3. "Affecting the passions" (Johnson's *Dictionary*).
4. Richard Bentley, a distinguished classical scholar

whose edition of *Paradise Lost* (1732) incorporates numerous misguided "corrections."

Known truths however may take a different appearance, and be conveyed to the mind by a new train of intermediate images. This Milton has undertaken, and performed with pregnancy and vigor of mind peculiar to himself. Whoever considers the few radical[5] positions which the Scriptures afforded him will wonder by what energetic operations he expanded them to such extent and ramified them to so much variety, restrained as he was by religious reverence from licentiousness of fiction.

Here is a full display of the united force of study and genius; of a great accumulation of materials, with judgment to digest and fancy to combine them: Milton was able to select from nature or from story, from ancient fable or from modern science, whatever could illustrate or adorn his thoughts. An accumulation of knowledge impregnated his mind, fermented by study and exalted by imagination.

It has been therefore said without an indecent hyperbole by one of his encomiasts, that in reading *Paradise Lost* we read a book of universal knowledge.

But original deficience cannot be supplied. The want of human interest is always felt. *Paradise Lost* is one of the books which the reader admires and lays down, and forgets to take up again. None ever wished it longer than it is. Its perusal is a duty rather than a pleasure. We read Milton for instruction, retire harassed and overburdened, and look elsewhere for recreation; we desert our master, and seek for companions.

from *The Life of Pope*

[TRANSLATING THE *ILIAD*]

The next year (1713) produced a bolder attempt, by which profit was sought as well as praise. The poems which he had hitherto written, however they might have diffused his name, had made very little addition to his fortune. The allowance which his father made him, though, proportioned to what he had, it might be liberal, could not be large; his religion hindered him from the occupation of any civil employment,[1] and he complained that he wanted even money to buy books.

He therefore resolved to try how far the favor of the public extended, by soliciting a subscription to a version of the *Iliad*, with large notes.

To print by subscription[2] was, for some time, a practice peculiar to the English. The first considerable work for which this expedient was employed is said to have been Dryden's *Virgil*, and it had been tried again with great success when *The Tatlers* were collected into volumes.

There was reason to believe that Pope's attempt would be successful. He was in the full bloom of reputation, and was personally known to almost all whom dignity of employment or splendor of reputation had made eminent; he conversed indifferently[3] with both parties, and never disturbed the public with his political opinions; and it might be naturally expected, as each faction then boasted its literary zeal, that the great men, who on other occasions practiced all the violence of opposition, would emulate each other in their encouragement of a poet who had delighted all, and by whom none had been offended.

---

5. Original.
1. As a Roman Catholic, Pope was prohibited from holding public office or from entering such professions as the law and medicine.

2. A method of publication in which customers subsidized the cost of printing a book by paying all or part of the price in advance.
3. Impartially.

With those hopes, he offered an English *Iliad* to subscribers, in six volumes in quarto,[4] for six guineas; a sum, according to the value of money at that time, by no means inconsiderable, and greater than I believe to have been ever asked before. His proposal, however, was very favorably received, and the patrons of literature were busy to recommend his undertaking, and promote his interest. Lord Oxford,[5] indeed, lamented that such a genius should be wasted upon a work not original; but proposed no means by which he might live without it. Addison recommended caution and moderation, and advised him not to be content with the praise of half the nation, when he might be universally favored.

The greatness of the design, the popularity of the author, and the attention of the literary world, naturally raised such expectations of the future sale, that the booksellers[6] made their offers with great eagerness; but the highest bidder was Bernard Lintot, who became proprietor on condition of supplying, at his own expense, all the copies which were to be delivered to subscribers, or presented to friends, and paying two hundred pounds for every volume.

Of the quartos it was, I believe, stipulated that none should be printed but for the author, that the subscription might not be depreciated; but Lintot impressed the same pages upon a small folio, and paper perhaps a little thinner; and sold exactly at half the price, for half a guinea each volume, books so little inferior to the quartos, that, by a fraud of trade, those folios, being afterwards shortened by cutting away the top and bottom, were sold as copies printed for the subscribers.

Lintot printed two hundred and fifty on royal paper in folio for two guineas a volume; of the small folio, having printed seventeen hundred and fifty copies of the first volume, he reduced the number in the other volumes to a thousand.

It is unpleasant to relate that the bookseller, after all his hopes and all his liberality, was, by a very unjust and illegal action, defrauded of his profit. An edition of the English *Iliad* was printed in Holland in duodecimo, and imported clandestinely for the gratification of those who were impatient to read what they could not yet afford to buy. This fraud could only be counteracted by an edition equally cheap and more commodious; and Lintot was compelled to contract his folio at once into a duodecimo, and lose the advantage of an intermediate gradation.[7] The notes, which in the Dutch copies were placed at the end of each book, as they had been in the large volumes, were now subjoined to the text in the same page, and are therefore more easily consulted. Of this edition two thousand five hundred were first printed, and five thousand a few weeks afterwards; but indeed great numbers were necessary to produce considerable profit.

Pope, having now emitted his proposals, and engaged not only his own reputation, but in some degree that of his friends who patronized his subscription, began to be frighted at his own undertaking; and finding himself at first embarrassed with difficulties, which retarded and oppressed him, he was for a time timorous and uneasy; had his nights disturbed by dreams of long journeys through unknown ways, and wished, as he said, "that somebody would hang him."

This misery, however, was not of long continuance; he grew by degrees more acquainted with Homer's images and expressions, and practice increased his facility of versification. In a short time he represents himself as dispatching regularly fifty verses a day, which would show him by an easy computation the termination of his labor.

---

4. A book consisting of printed sheets that have been folded twice; typically, a quarto is smaller than a folio, whose sheets have been folded only once.
5. Robert Harley, first Earl of Oxford, was head of the Tory ministry that held power from 1710 to 1714.

6. Publishers.
7. Lintot had to forgo publication in the larger and more profitable quarto or octavo formats for a smaller duodecimo edition. This format was commonly adopted for inexpensive books designed for a popular audience.

His own diffidence was not his only vexation. He that asks a subscription soon finds that he has enemies. All who do not encourage him defame him. He that wants money will rather be thought angry than poor, and he that wishes to save his money conceals his avarice by his malice. Addison had hinted his suspicion that Pope was too much a Tory; and some of the Tories suspected his principles because he had contributed to *The Guardian,* which was carried on by Steele.[8]

To those who censured his politics were added enemies yet more dangerous, who called in question his knowledge of Greek, and his qualifications for a translator of Homer. To these he made no public opposition, but in one of his letters escapes from them as well as he can. At an age like his, for he was not more than twenty-five, with an irregular education, and a course of life of which much seems to have passed in conversation, it is not very likely that he overflowed with Greek. But when he felt himself deficient he sought assistance; and what man of learning would refuse to help him? Minute enquiries into the force of words are less necessary in translating Homer than other poets, because his positions are general, and his representations natural, with very little dependence on local or temporary customs, on those changeable scenes of artificial life, which, by mingling original with accidental notions, and crowding the mind with images which time effaces, produce ambiguity in diction, and obscurity in books. To this open display of unadulterated nature it must be ascribed, that Homer has fewer passages of doubtful meaning than any other poet either in the learned or in modern languages. I have read of a man, who being, by his ignorance of Greek, compelled to gratify his curiosity with the Latin printed on the opposite page, declared that from the rude simplicity of the lines literally rendered, he formed nobler ideas of the Homeric majesty than from the labored elegance of polished versions.

Those literal translations were always at hand, and from them he could easily obtain his author's sense with sufficient certainty; and among the readers of Homer the number is very small of those who find much in the Greek more than in the Latin, except the music of the numbers.[9]

If more help was wanting, he had the poetical translation of Eobanus Hessus, an unwearied writer of Latin verses; he had the French *Homers* of La Valterie and Dacier, and the English of Chapman,[1] Hobbes, and Ogylby. With Chapman, whose work, though now totally neglected, seems to have been popular almost to the end of the last century, he had very frequent consultations, and perhaps never translated any passage till he had read his version, which indeed he has been sometimes suspected of using instead of the original.

Notes were likewise to be provided; for the six volumes would have been very little more than six pamphlets without them. What the mere perusal of the text could suggest, Pope wanted no assistance to collect or methodize; but more was necessary; many pages were to be filled, and learning must supply materials to wit and judgment. Something might be gathered from Dacier;[2] but no man loves to be indebted to his contemporaries, and Dacier was accessible to common readers. Eustathius[3] was therefore necessarily consulted. To read Eustathius, of whose work there was then no Latin version, I suspect Pope, if he had been willing, not to have

---

8. Three months after *The Spectator* was brought to a close, Richard Steele started *The Guardian,* which appeared every weekday for seven months. Unlike its predecessor, this new periodical had a partisan (Whig) political cast.
9. Poetic meter.

1. George Chapman's translation of *The Iliad* appeared in 1611.
2. The annotated French version of the *Iliad* by Anne Dacier (1654–1720) had been translated into English in 1712.
3. A 12-century Byzantine commentator on Homer.

been able; some other was therefore to be found, who had leisure as well as abilities, and he was doubtless most readily employed who would do much work for little money.

The history of the notes has never been traced. Broome, in his preface to his poems, declares himself the commentator "in part upon the *Iliad*"; and it appears from Fenton's letter, preserved in the Museum, that Broome was at first engaged in consulting Eustathius; but that after a time, whatever was the reason, he desisted; another man of Cambridge was then employed, who soon grew weary of the work; and a third, that was recommended by Thirlby, is now discovered to have been Jortin, a man since well known to the learned world, who complained that Pope, having accepted and approved his performance, never testified any curiosity to see him, and who professed to have forgotten the terms on which he worked.[4] The terms which Fenton uses are very mercantile: "I think at first sight that his performance is very commendable, and have sent word for him to finish the 17th book, and to send it with his demands for his trouble. I have here enclosed the specimen; if the rest come before the return, I will keep them till I receive your orders."

Broome then offered his service a second time, which was probably accepted, as they had afterwards a closer correspondence. Parnell[5] contributed the *Life of Homer*, which Pope found so harsh, that he took great pains in correcting it; and by his own diligence, with such help as kindness or money could procure him, in somewhat more than five years he completed his version of the *Iliad*, with the notes. He began it in 1712, his twenty-fifth year, and concluded it in 1718, his thirtieth year.

When we find him translating fifty lines a day, it is natural to suppose that he would have brought his work to a more speedy conclusion. The *Iliad*, containing less than sixteen thousand verses, might have been dispatched in less than three hundred and twenty days by fifty verses in a day. The notes, compiled with the assistance of his mercenaries, could not be supposed to require more time than the text. According to this calculation, the progress of Pope may seem to have been slow; but the distance is commonly very great between actual performances and speculative possibility. It is natural to suppose, that as much as has been done today may be done tomorrow; but on the morrow some difficulty emerges, or some external impediment obstructs. Indolence, interruption, business, and pleasure, all take their turns of retardation; and every long work is lengthened by a thousand causes that can, and ten thousand that cannot, be recounted. Perhaps no extensive and multifarious performance was ever effected within the term originally fixed in the undertaker's mind. He that runs against Time, has an antagonist not subject to casualties.

The encouragement given to this translation, though report seems to have overrated it, was such as the world has not often seen. The subscribers were five hundred and seventy-five. The copies for which subscriptions were given were six hundred and fifty-four; and only six hundred and sixty were printed. For those copies Pope had nothing to pay; he therefore received, including the two hundred pounds a volume, five thousand three hundred and twenty pounds four shillings, without deduction, as the books were supplied by Lintot.

4. Because Pope's knowledge of Greek was uncertain, he depended on others to help him translate Eustathius. These assistants included the scholars William Broome and John Jortin; Jortin had been recommended by his Cambridge tutor, Styan Thirlby. Broome and Elijah Fen-ton went on to assist Pope in his translation of *The Odyssey*.
5. Thomas Parnell (1679–1718), Irish poet and friend of Pope and of Swift.

By the success of his subscription Pope was relieved from those pecuniary distresses with which, notwithstanding his popularity, he had hitherto struggled. Lord Oxford had often lamented his disqualification for public employment, but never proposed a pension. While the translation of Homer was in its progress, Mr. Craggs, then secretary of state, offered to procure him a pension, which, at least during his ministry, might be enjoyed with secrecy. This was not accepted by Pope, who told him, however, that, if he should be pressed with want of money, he would send to him for occasional supplies. Craggs was not long in power, and was never solicited for money by Pope, who disdained to beg what he did not want.

With the product of this subscription, which he had too much discretion to squander, he secured his future life from want, by considerable annuities. The estate of the Duke of Buckingham was found to have been charged with five hundred pounds a year, payable to Pope, which doubtless his translation enabled him to purchase.

It cannot be unwelcome to literary curiosity, that I deduce thus minutely the history of the English *Iliad*. It is certainly the noblest version of poetry which the world has ever seen; and its publication must therefore be considered as one of the great events in the annals of learning.

[POPE AND DRYDEN]

In acquired knowledge the superiority must be allowed to Dryden, whose education was more scholastic, and who before he became an author had been allowed more time for study, with better means of information. His mind has a larger range, and he collects his images and illustrations from a more extensive circumference of science. Dryden knew more of man in his general nature, and Pope in his local manners. The notions of Dryden were formed by comprehensive speculation, and those of Pope by minute attention. There is more dignity in the knowledge of Dryden, and more certainty in that of Pope.

Poetry was not the sole praise of either, for both excelled likewise in prose; but Pope did not borrow his prose from his predecessor. The style of Dryden is capricious and varied, that of Pope is cautious and uniform; Dryden obeys the motions of his own mind, Pope constrains his mind to his own rules of composition. Dryden is sometimes vehement and rapid; Pope is always smooth, uniform, and gentle. Dryden's page is a natural field, rising into inequalities, and diversified by the varied exuberance of abundant vegetation; Pope's is a velvet lawn, shaven by the scythe, and leveled by the roller.

Of genius, that power which constitutes a poet; that quality without which judgment is cold and knowledge is inert; that energy which collects, combines, amplifies, and animates—the superiority must, with some hesitation, be allowed to Dryden. It is not to be inferred that of this poetical vigor Pope had only a little, because Dryden had more, for every other writer since Milton must give place to Pope; and even of Dryden it must be said that if he has brighter paragraphs, he has not better poems. Dryden's performances were always hasty, either excited by some external occasion, or extorted by domestic necessity; he composed without consideration, and published without correction. What his mind could supply at call, or gather in one excursion, was all that he sought, and all that he gave. The dilatory caution of Pope enabled him to condense his sentiments, to multiply his images, and to accumulate all that study might produce, or chance might supply. If the flights of Dryden therefore are higher, Pope continues longer on the wing. If of Dryden's fire the blaze is brighter, of

Pope's the heat is more regular and constant. Dryden often surpasses expectation, and Pope never falls below it. Dryden is read with frequent astonishment, and Pope with perpetual delight.

This parallel will, I hope, when it is well considered, be found just; and if the reader should suspect me, as I suspect myself, of some partial fondness for the memory of Dryden, let him not too hastily condemn me; for meditation and enquiry may, perhaps, show him the reasonableness of my determination.

[ON THE RAPE OF THE LOCK]

To the praises which have been accumulated on *The Rape of the Lock* by readers of every class, from the critic to the waiting-maid, it is difficult to make any addition. Of that which is universally allowed to be the most attractive of all ludicrous compositions, let it rather be now inquired from what sources the power of pleasing is derived.

Dr. Warburton, who excelled in critical perspicacity, has remarked that the preternatural agents are very happily adapted to the purposes of the poem. The heathen deities can no longer gain attention: we should have turned away from a contest between Venus and Diana. The employment of allegorical persons always excites conviction of its own absurdity: they may produce effects, but cannot conduct actions; when the phantom is put in motion, it dissolves; thus Discord may raise a mutiny, but Discord cannot conduct a march, nor besiege a town. Pope brought into view a new race of Beings, with powers and passions proportionate to their operation. The sylphs and gnomes act at the toilet[6] and the tea-table, what more terrific and more powerful phantoms perform on the stormy ocean or the field of battle; they give their proper help, and do their proper mischief. * * *

In this work are exhibited in a very high degree the two most engaging powers of an author: new things are made familiar, and familiar things are made new. A race of aerial people never heard of before is presented to us in a manner so clear and easy, that the reader seeks for no further information, but immediately mingles with his new acquaintance, adopts their interests and attends their pursuits, loves a sylph and detests a gnome.

That familiar things are made new every paragraph will prove. The subject of the poem is an event below the common incidents of common life; nothing real is introduced that is not seen so often as to be no longer regarded, yet the whole detail of a female-day is here brought before us invested with so much art of decoration that, though nothing is disguised, every thing is striking, and we feel all the appetite of curiosity for that from which we have a thousand times turned fastidiously away.

[ON ELOISA TO ABELARD]

The *Epistle of Eloisa to Abelard* is one of the most happy productions of human wit: the subject is so judiciously chosen that it would be difficult, in turning over the annals of the world, to find another which so many circumstances concur to recommend. We regularly interest ourselves most in the fortune of those who most deserve our notice. Abelard and Eloisa were conspicuous in their days for eminence of merit. The heart naturally loves truth. The adventures and misfortunes of this illustrious pair are known from undisputed history. Their fate does not leave the mind in hopeless dejection; for they both found quiet and consolation in retirement and piety. So new and so affecting is their story that it supersedes invention, and imagination ranges at full liberty without straggling into scenes of fable.

6. Dressing table.

The story thus skillfully adopted has been diligently improved. Pope has left nothing behind him which seems more the effect of studious perseverance and laborious revisal. Here is particularly observable the *curiosa felicitas*,[7] a fruitful soil, and careful cultivation. Here is no crudeness of sense, nor asperity of language.

[On An Essay on Man]

The *Essay on Man* was a work of great labor and long consideration, but certainly not the happiest of Pope's performances. The subject is perhaps not very proper for poetry, and the poet was not sufficiently master of his subject; metaphysical morality was to him a new study, he was proud of his acquisitions, and, supposing himself master of great secrets, was in haste to teach what he had not learned. Thus he tells us, in the first Epistle, that from the nature of the Supreme Being may be deduced an order of beings such as mankind, because Infinite Excellence can do only what is best. He finds out that these beings must be "somewhere," and that "all the question is whether man be in a wrong place." Surely if, according to the poet's Leibnitzian reasoning,[8] we may infer that man ought to be only because he is, we may allow that his place is the right place, because he has it. Supreme Wisdom is not less infallible in disposing than in creating. But what is meant by "somewhere" and "place" and "wrong place" it had been vain to ask Pope, who probably had never asked himself.

Having exalted himself into the chair of wisdom he tells us much that every man knows, and much that he does not know himself; that we see but little, and that the order of the universe is beyond our comprehension, and opinion not very uncommon; and that there is a chain of subordinate beings "from infinite to nothing," of which himself and his readers are equally ignorant. But he gives us one comfort which, without his help, he supposes unattainable, in the position "that though we are fools, yet God is wise."

This *Essay* affords an egregious instance of the predominance of genius, the dazzling splendor of imagery, and the seductive powers of eloquence. Never were penury of knowledge and vulgarity of sentiment so happily disguised. The reader feels his mind full, though he learns nothing; and when he meets it in its new array no longer knows the talk of his mother and his nurse. When these wonder-working sounds sink into sense, and the doctrine of the *Essay*, disrobed of its ornaments, is left to the powers of its naked excellence, what shall we discover? That we are, in comparison with our Creator, very weak and ignorant; that we do not uphold the chain of existence; and that we could not make one another with more skill than we are made. We may learn yet more: that the arts of human life were copied from the instinctive operations of other animals; that if the world be made for man, it may be said that man was made for geese. To these profound principles of natural knowledge are added some moral instructions equally new: that self-interest well understood will produce social concord; that men are mutual gainers by mutual benefits; that evil is sometimes balanced by good; that human advantages are unstable and fallacious, of uncertain duration and doubtful effect; that our true honor is not to have a great part, but to act it well; that virtue only is our own; and that happiness is always in our power.

Surely a man of no very comprehensive search may venture to say that he has heard all this before, but it was never till now recommended by such a blaze of embellishment or such sweetness of melody. The vigorous contraction of some

7. Studied inspiration.
8. Johnson believed that Pope had been influenced by the deterministic philosophy of Gottfried Wilhelm von Leibnitz (1646–1716).

thoughts, the luxuriant amplification of others, the incidental illustrations, and sometimes the dignity, sometimes the softness of the verses, enchain philosophy, suspend criticism, and oppress judgment by overpowering pleasure.

This is true of many paragraphs; yet if I had undertaken to exemplify Pope's felicity of composition before a rigid critic I should not select the *Essay on Man,* for it contains more lines unsuccessfully labored, more harshness of diction, more thoughts imperfectly expressed, more levity without elegance, and more heaviness without strength, than will easily be found in all his other works.

from **Annals**[1]

[INFANCY AND CHILDHOOD]

1. 1709–10

Sept. 7,[2] 1709, I was born at Lichfield. My mother had a very difficult and dangerous labor, and was assisted by George Hector, a man-midwife of great reputation. I was born almost dead, and could not cry for some time. When he had me in his arms, he said, "Here is a brave boy."

In a few weeks an inflammation was discovered on my buttock, which was at first, I think, taken for a burn; but soon appeared to be a natural disorder. It swelled, broke, and healed.

My father being that year Sheriff of Lichfield, and to ride the circuit of the County next day, which was a ceremony then performed with great pomp; he was asked by my mother, "Whom he would invite to the Riding?" and answered, "All the town now." He feasted the citizens with uncommon magnificence, and was the last but one that maintained the splendor of the riding.

I was, by my father's persuasion, put to one Marclew, commonly called Bellison, the servant, or wife of a servant of my father, to be nursed in George Lane, where I used to call when I was a bigger boy, and eat fruit in the garden, which was full of trees. Here it was discovered that my eyes were bad; and an issue[3] was cut in my left arm, of which I took no great notice, as I think my mother has told me, having my little hand in a custard. How long this issue was continued I do not remember. I believe it was suffered to dry when I was about six years old.

It is observable, that, having been told of this operation, I always imagined that I remembered it, but I laid the scene in the wrong house. Such confusions of memory I suspect to be common.

My mother visited me every day, and used to go different ways, that her assiduity might not expose her to ridicule; and often left her fan or glove behind her, that she might have a pretense to come back unexpected; but she never discovered any token

1. Johnson often recommended that his friends keep records of their lives—in diaries, in autobiography—but he generally regarded the practice as intrinsically private. Just before his death, he burned two large volumes of his own diaries that Boswell in particular had longed to consult for his planned biography. Boswell never knew about another manuscript, titled *Annals,* which had partly survived the deathbed purge (though Johnson managed to destroy 32 pages of it). This account, of Johnson's early years, was first published in 1805; the original is now lost. Johnson apparently began writing it in his middle fifties, perhaps with the intention of producing a full autobiography, but perhaps also to investigate the origin of condi-

tions of mind and of body that had affected him his whole life.
2. "18, in the present style" (Johnson's note). Britain's shift to the Gregorian calendar in 1752 "advanced" all previous bithdays and other anniversaries by 11 days.
3. An incision designed to drain off the scrofular infection. Johnson assumed that his ailment, which deprived him of all but peripheral vision in one eye, was caused by the scrofula (or tuberculosis of the lymph glands) that left his face and neck permanently scarred. In fact, the eye ailment occurred when he was only a few weeks old, whereas he contracted scrofula when he was two.

of neglect. Dr. Swinfen told me, that the scrofulous sores which afflicted me proceeded from the bad humors[4] of the nurse, whose son had the same distemper, and was likewise short-sighted, but both in a less degree. My mother thought my diseases derived from her family.

In ten weeks I was taken home, a poor, diseased infant, almost blind.

I remember my aunt Nath. Ford told me, when I was about . . . years old, that she would not have picked such a poor creature up in the street.

In . . . 67, when I was at Lichfield, I went to look for my nurse's house; and, inquiring somewhat obscurely, was told "this is the house in which you were nursed." I saw my nurse's son, to whose milk I succeeded, reading a large Bible,[5] which my nurse had bought, as I was then told, some time before her death.

Dr. Swinfen used to say, that he never knew any child reared with so much difficulty.

2. 1710–11

In the second year I know not what happened to me. I believe it was then that my mother carried me to Trysul,[6] to consult Dr. Atwood, an oculist of Worcester. My father and Mrs. Harriots, I think, never had much kindness for each other. She was my mother's relation; and he had none so high to whom he could send any of his family. He saw her seldom himself, and willingly disgusted her, by sending his horses from home on Sunday; which she considered, and with reason, as a breach of duty. My father had much vanity, which his adversity hindered from being fully exerted. I remember that, mentioning her legacy in the humility of distress, he called her *our good Cousin Harriots*. My mother had no value for his relations; those indeed whom we knew of were much lower than hers. This contempt began, I know not on which side, very early: but, as my father was little at home, it had not much effect.

My father and mother had not much happiness from each other. They seldom conversed; for my father could not bear to talk of his affairs; and my mother, being unacquainted with books, cared not to talk of any thing else. Had my mother been more literate, they had been better companions. She might have sometimes introduced her unwelcome topic with more success, if she could have diversified her conversation. Of business she had no distinct conception; and therefore her discourse was composed only of complaint, fear, and suspicion. Neither of them ever tried to calculate the profits of trade, or the expenses of living. My mother concluded that we were poor, because we lost by some of our trades; but the truth was, that my father, having in the early part of his life contracted debts, never had trade sufficient to enable him to pay them, and maintain his family; he got something, but not enough.

It was not till about 1768 that I thought to calculate the returns of my father's trade, and by that estimate his probable profits. This, I believe, my parents never did.

3. 1711–12

This year, in Lent—12, I was taken to London, to be touched for the evil by Queen Anne.[7] My mother was at Nicholson's, the famous bookseller, in Little Britain. My mother, then with child, concealed her pregnancy, that she might not be hindered

---

4. Infectious tendencies (Johnson's nurse was thought to be a carrier of scrofula).
5. He needed a large-print Bible because he was almost blind.

6. Near Wolverhampton, Staffordshire, the home of Mrs. Johnson's first cousin, Elizabeth Harriots.
7. It was widely believed that the monarch had the power to cure scrofula through "the royal touch."

from the journey. I always retained some memory of this journey, though I was then but thirty months old. I remembered a little dark room behind the kitchen, where the jack-weight[8] fell through a hole in the floor, into which I once slipped my leg. I seem to remember, that I played with a string and a bell, which my cousin Isaac Johnson gave me; and that there was a cat with a white collar, and a dog, called Chops, that leaped over a stick: but I know not whether I remember the thing, or the talk of it.

I remember a boy crying at the palace when I went to be touched. Being asked "on which side of the shop was the counter?" I answered, "on the left from the entrance," many years after, and spoke, not by guess, but by memory. We went in the stage-coach, and returned in the wagon, as my mother said, because my cough was violent. The hope of saving a few shillings was no slight motive; for she, not having been accustomed to money, was afraid of such expenses as now seem very small. She sewed two guineas in her petticoat, lest she should be robbed.

We were troublesome to the passengers; but to suffer such inconveniences in the stage-coach was common in those days to persons in much higher rank. I was sick; one woman fondled me, the other was disgusted. She bought me a small silver cup and spoon, marked SAM. I. lest if they had been marked S. I. which was her name, they should, upon her death, have been taken from me. She bought me a speckled linen frock, which I knew afterwards by the name of my London frock. The cup was one of the last pieces of plate which dear Tetty[9] sold in our distress. I have now the spoon. She bought at the same time two teaspoons, and till my manhood she had no more.

My father considered tea as very expensive, and discouraged my mother from keeping company with the neighbors, and from paying visits or receiving them. She lived to say, many years after, that, if the time were to pass again, she would not comply with such unsocial injunctions.

I suppose that in this year I was first informed of a future state. I remember, that being in bed with my mother one morning, I was told by her of the two places to which the inhabitants of this world were received after death; one a fine place filled with happiness, called Heaven; the other a sad place, called Hell. That this account much affected my imagination, I do not remember. When I was risen, my mother bade me repeat what she had told me to Thomas Jackson.[1] When I told this afterwards to my mother, she seemed to wonder that she should begin such talk so late as that the first time could be remembered. * * *

On Saturday, as on Thursday, we were examined. We were sometimes, on one of those days, asked our Catechism,[2] but with no regularity or constancy. G. Hector never had been taught his Catechism.

The progress of examination was this. When we learned *Propria quae Maribus*, we were examined in the Accidence;[3] particularly we formed verbs, that is, went through the same person in all the moods and tenses. This was very difficult to me; and I was once very anxious about the next day, when this exercise was to be performed, in which I had failed till I was discouraged. My mother encouraged me, and I proceeded better. When I told her of my good escape, "We often," said she, dear mother! "come off best, when we are most afraid." She told me that once, when she asked me about forming verbs, I said, "I did not form them in an ugly

---

8. Part of the mechanism that turned the spit upon which meat was roasted.
9. Elizabeth, Johnson's wife ("Tetty" was a provincial diminutive of Elizabeth).
1. A family retainer.

2. The essentials of Christianity set down in question-and-answer form.
3. Johnson refers to sections from William Lily's *Short Introduction of Grammar*, which had served as a basic textbook since the mid-16th century.

shape." "You could not," said she, "speak plain; and I was proud that I had a boy who was forming verbs." These little memorials soothe my mind. Of the parts of Corderius or Aesop,[4] which we learned to repeat, I have not the least recollection, except of a passage in one of the Morals, where it is said of some man, that, when he hated another, he made him rich; this I repeated emphatically in my mother's hearing, who could never conceive that riches could bring any evil. She remarked it, as I expected.

I had the curiosity, two or three years ago, to look over Garretson's *Exercises*, Willymot's *Particles*, and Walker's *Exercises*;[5] and found very few sentences that I should have recollected if I had found them in any other books. That which is read without pleasure is not often recollected nor infixed by conversation, and therefore in a great measure drops from the memory. Thus it happens that those who are taken early from school, commonly lose all that they had learned. * * *

The whole week before we broke up, and the part of the week in which we broke up, were spent wholly, I know not why, in examination; and were therefore easy to both us and the master. The two nights before the vacation were free from exercise.

This was the course of the school, which I remember with pleasure; for I was indulged and caressed by my master, and, I think, really excelled the rest.

I was with Hawkins[6] but two years, and perhaps four months. The time, till I had computed it, appeared much longer by the multitude of novelties which it supplied, and of incidents, then in my thoughts important, it produced. Perhaps it is not possible that any other period can make the same impression on the memory.

10. 1719

In the Spring of 1719, our class consisting of eleven, the number was always fixed in my memory, but one of the names I have forgotten, was removed to the upper school, and put under Holbrooke,[7] a peevish and ill-tempered man. We were removed sooner than had been the custom; for the head-master, intent upon his boarders, left the town-boys long in the lower school. Our removal was caused by a reproof from the town clerk; and Hawkins complained that he had lost half his profit. At this removal I cried. The rest were indifferent. My exercise in Garretson was somewhere about the gerunds. Our places in Aesop and Helvicus I have totally forgotten.

At Whitsuntide[8] Mrs. Longworth brought me a *Hermes Garretsoni*, of which I do not remember that I ever could make much use. It was afterwards lost, or stolen at school. My exercise was then in the end of the syntax. Hermes furnished me with the word *inliciturus*, which I did not understand, but used it.

This task was very troublesome to me; I made all the twenty-five exercises, others made but sixteen. I never showed all mine; five lay long after in a drawer in the shop. I made an exercise in a little time, and showed it my mother; but the task being long upon me, she said, "Though you could make an exercise in so short a time, I thought you would find it difficult to make them all as soon as you should."

This Whitsuntide, I and my brother were sent to pass some time at Birmingham; I believe, a fortnight. Why such boys were sent to trouble other houses, I cannot tell. My mother had some opinion that much improvement was to be had by changing the

---

4. Central to the grammar school curriculum were the fables of Aesop and the dialogues of the Renaissance scholar Mathurin Corderius.
5. Grammatical textbooks.
6. Humphrey Hawkins, a Lichfield schoolmaster.

7. The Reverend Edward Holbrooke, clergyman and schoolmaster.
8. The week beginning on the seventh Sunday after Easter.

mode of life. My uncle Harrison was a widower; and his house was kept by Sally Ford, a young woman of such sweetness of temper, that I used to say she had no fault. We lived most at uncle Ford's, being much caressed by my aunt, a good-natured, coarse woman, easy of converse, but willing to find something to censure in the absent. My uncle Harrison did not much like us, nor did we like him. He was a very mean and vulgar man, drunk every night, but drunk with little drink, very peevish, very proud, very ostentatious, but, luckily, not rich. At my aunt Ford's I eat so much of a boiled leg of mutton, that she used to talk of it. My mother, who had lived in a narrow sphere, and was then affected by little things, told me seriously that it would hardly ever be forgotten. Her mind, I think, was afterwards much enlarged, or greater evils wore out the care of less.

I stayed after the vacation was over some days; and remember, when I wrote home, that I desired the horses to come on Thursday of the first school week; and then, and not till then, they should be welcome to go. I was much pleased with a rattle to my whip, and wrote of it to my mother.

When my father came to fetch us home, he told the ostler,[9] that he had twelve miles home, and two boys under his care. This offended me. He had then a watch, which he returned when he was to pay for it.

In making, I think, the first exercise under Holbrook, I perceived the power of continuity of attention, of application not suffered to wander or to pause. I was writing at the kitchen windows, as I thought, alone, and turning my head saw Sally dancing. I went on without notice, and had finished almost without perceiving that any time had elapsed. This close attention I have seldom in my whole life obtained. * * *

LETTERS

To Lord Chesterfield[1]

My Lord: 7 February 1755

I have been lately informed by the proprietor of *The World* that two papers in which my Dictionary is recommended to the public were written by your Lordship.[2] To be so distinguished is an honor which, being very little accustomed to favors from the great, I know not well how to receive, or in what terms to acknowledge.

When upon some slight encouragement I first visited your Lordship I was overpowered like the rest of mankind by the enchantment of your address, and could not forbear to wish that I might boast myself *le vainqueur du vainqueur de la terre*,[3] that I might obtain that regard for which I saw the world contending; but I found my attendance so little encouraged, that neither pride nor modesty would suffer me to continue it. When I had once adressed your Lordship in public, I had exhausted all the art of pleasing which a retired and uncourtly scholar can possess. I had done all that I could, and no man is well pleased to have his all neglected, be it ever so little.

---

9. Stableman.
1. Philip Dormer Stanhope (1694–1773), fourth Earl of Chesterfield, a politician and man of letters renowned for his elegant manners and his knowledge of the polite world. In 1747 Johnson had dedicated his *Plan of a Dictionary* to Chesterfield but had received neither financial nor moral support from him during the long years of labor

on the *Dictionary*.
2. Chesterfield had contributed two essays to Robert Dodsley's periodical *The World*. In these essays he praised the forthcoming *Dictionary* in such a way as to imply that he had been its enlightened sponsor.
3. "The conqueror of the world's conqueror" (the opening line of the epic *Alaric*, by Georges de Scudéry).

Seven years, my lord, have now passed since I waited in your outward rooms or was repulsed from your door, during which time I have been pushing on my work through difficulties of which it is useless to complain, and have brought it at last to the verge of publication without one act of assistance, one word of encouragement, or one smile of favor. Such treatment I did not expect, for I never had a patron before.

The shepherd in Virgil grew at last acquainted with Love, and found him a native of the rocks.[4] Is not a patron, my lord, one who looks with unconcern on a man struggling for life in the water and when he has reached ground encumbers him with help?[5] The notice which you have been pleased to take of my labors, had it been early, had been kind; but it has been delayed till I am indifferent and cannot enjoy it, till I am solitary and cannot impart it, till I am known and do not want it.

I hope it is no very cynical asperity not to confess obligation where no benefit has been received, or to be unwilling that the public should consider me as owing that to a patron, which providence has enabled me to do for myself.

Having carried on my work thus far with so little obligation to any favorer of learning I shall not be disappointed though I should conclude it, if less be possible, with less, for I have been long wakened from that dream of hope, in which I once boasted myself with so much exultation, my lord, your Lordship's most humble, most obedient servant,

S.J.

To Hester Thrale

Dear Madam: Bolt Court, Fleetstreet, June 19, 1783

I am sitting down in no cheerful solitude to write a narrative which would once have affected you with tenderness and sorrow, but which you will perhaps pass over now with the careless glance of frigid indifference.[1] For this diminution of regard however, I know not whether I ought to blame you, who may have reasons which I cannot know, and I do not blame myself who have for a great part of human life done you what good I could, and have never done you evil.

I had been disordered in the usual way, and had been relieved by the usual methods, by opium and cathartics,[2] but had rather lessened my dose of opium.

On Monday the 16 I sat for my picture,[3] and walked a considerable way with little inconvenience. In the afternoon and evening I felt myself light and easy, and began to plan schemes of life. Thus I went to bed, and in a short time waked and sat up as has been long my custom when I felt a confusion and indistinctness in my head which lasted, I suppose about half a minute. I was alarmed and prayed God, that however he might afflict my body he would spare my understanding. This prayer, that I might try the integrity of my faculties, I made in Latin verse. The lines were not very good, but I knew them not to be very good, I made them easily, and concluded myself to be unimpaired in my faculties.

4. Johnson alludes to a pastoral poem by Virgil (*Eclogue* 8), in which Love is described as coming from a land of "flinty crags."

5. In his *Dictionary*, Johnson defines "patron" as "commonly a wretch who supports with insolence, and is paid with flattery."

1. As she became more and more attached to Gabriel Piozzi, an Italian musician, Hester Thrale (correctly sens-

ing how angry Johnson would be) began to disengage from their close friendship. Though he knew something had gone wrong, Johnson did not learn of the love affair until a year later, when Mrs. Thrale wrote to inform him of her marriage.

2. Purgatives.

3. Johnson's portrait was being painted.

Soon after I perceived that I had suffered a paralytic stroke, and that my speech was taken from me. I had no pain, and so little dejection in this dreadful state that I wondered at my own apathy, and considered that perhaps death itself when it should come, would excite less horror than seems now to attend it.

In order to rouse the vocal organs I took two drams. Wine has been celebrated for the production of eloquence; I put myself into violent motion, and, I think, repeated it. But all was vain; I then went to bed, and, strange as it may seem, I think, slept. When I saw light, it was time to contrive what I should do. Though God stopped my speech he left me my hand, I enjoyed a mercy which was not granted to my Dear Friend Lawrence,[4] who now perhaps overlooks me as I am writing and rejoices that I have what he wanted.[5] My first note was necessarily to my servant, who came in talking, and could not immediately comprehend why he should read what I put into his hands.

I then wrote a card to Mr. Allen,[6] that I might have a discreet friend at hand to act as occasion should require. In penning this note I had some difficulty, my hand, I know not how nor why, made wrong letters. I then wrote to Dr. Taylor[7] to come to me, and bring Dr. Heberden, and I sent to Dr. Brocklesby, who is my neighbor. My physicians are very friendly and very disinterested; and give me great hopes, but you may imagine my situation. I have so far recovered my vocal powers, as to repeat the Lord's Prayer with no very imperfect articulation. My memory, I hope, yet remains as it was. But such an attack produces solicitude for the safety of every faculty.

How this will be received by you, I know not, I hope you will sympathize with me, but perhaps

> My Mistress gracious, mild, and good,
> Cries, Is he dumb? 'tis time he should.[8]

But can this be possible, I hope it cannot. I hope that what, when I could speak, I spoke of You, and to You, will be in a sober and serious hour remembered by You, and surely it cannot be remembered but with some degree of kindness. I have loved You with virtuous affection, I have honored You with sincere esteem. Let not all our endearment be forgotten, but let me have in this great distress your pity and your prayers. You see I yet turn to You with my complaints as a settled and unalienable friend, do not, do not drive me from You, for I have not deserved either neglect or hatred.

To the girls,[9] who do not write often, for Susy has written only once, and Miss Thrale owes me a letter, I earnestly recommend as their guardian and friend, that they remember their Creator in the days of their youth.[1]

I suppose You may wish to know how my disease is treated by the physicians. They put a blister upon my back, and two from my ear to my throat, one on a side. The blister on the back has done little, and those on the throat have not risen. I bullied, and bounced, (it sticks to our last sand)[2] and compelled the apothecary to make his salve according to the Edinburgh dispensatory[3] that it might adhere better. I

4. Johnson's favorite physician, Dr. Thomas Lawrence, had died earlier that month after suffering a stroke.
5. Lacked.
6. Johnson's printer and neighbor, Edmund Allen.
7. The clergyman John Taylor, one of Johnson's oldest and closest friends.
8. Johnson adapts a couplet from Swift's *Verses on the Death of Dr. Swift:* "The Queen, so gracious, mild and good, / Cries, 'Is he gone? 'Tis time he should' " (lines 181–82).
9. Hester Thrale's four surviving daughters: Hester Maria ("Miss Thrale"), Susanna ("Susy"), Sophia, and Cecilia.
1. "Remember now thy Creator in the days of thy youth, while the evil days come not" (Ecclesiastes 12.1).
2. "Time, that on all things lays his lenient hand, / Yet tames not this; it sticks to our last sand" (Pope, *Epistle to Cobham*, lines 224–25).
3. Medical manual.

have two on now of my own prescription. They likewise give me salt of hartshorn, which I take with no great confidence, but am satisfied that what can be done, is done for me.

O God, give me comfort and confidence in Thee, forgive my sins, and if it be thy good pleasure, relieve my diseases for Jesus Christ's sake. Amen.

I am almost ashamed of this querulous letter, but now it is written, let it go. I am Madam, Your most humble servant,

SAM. JOHNSON

To Hester Thrale Piozzi

Madam: July 2, 1784

If I interpret your letter right, You are ignominiously married,[1] if it is yet undone, let us once talk together. If You have abandoned your children and your religion, God forgive your wickedness; if You have forfeited your fame, and your country, may your folly do no further mischief.[2]

If the last act is yet to do, I, who have loved you, esteemed you, reverenced you, and served you, I who long thought You the first of humankind, entreat that before your fate is irrevocable, I may once more see You. I was, I once was, Madam, most truly yours,

SAM. JOHNSON

I will come down if you permit it.

To Hester Thrale Piozzi

Dear Madam: London, July 8, 1784

What You have done, however I may lament it, I have no pretense to resent, as it has not been injurious to me. I therefore breathe out one sigh more of tenderness perhaps useless, but at least sincere.

I wish that God may grant You every blessing, that you may be happy in this world for its short continuance, and eternally happy in a better state. And whatever I can contribute to your happiness, I am very ready to repay for that kindness which soothed twenty years of a life radically wretched.

Do not think slightly of the advice which I now presume to offer. Prevail upon Mr. Piozzi to settle in England. You may live here with more dignity than in Italy, and with more security. Your rank will be higher, and your fortune more under your own eye. I desire not to detail all my reasons; but every argument of prudence and interest is for England, and only some phantoms of imagination seduce you to Italy.

I am afraid, however, that my counsel is vain, yet I have eased my heart by giving it.

When Queen Mary took the resolution of sheltering herself in England, the Archbishop of St. Andrew's attempting to dissuade her,[1] attended on her journey and when they came to the irremeable[2] stream that separated the two kingdoms,

---

1. Hester Thrale had written on June 30 to inform John-son of her marriage to Gabriel Piozzi.
2. Johnson's objections to Gabriel Piozzi include the fact that he is a musician (and therefore socially inferior), a Catholic, and an Italian.
1. Johnson draws on a semifictional account of Mary

Queen of Scots' fateful decision to take refuge in Eng-land. According to this version, she crossed the river on horseback, attended by John Hamilton, Archbishop of St. Andrews.
2. "Admitting no return" (Johnson's *Dictionary*).

walked by her side into the water, in the middle of which he seized her bridle, and with earnestness proportioned to her danger and his own affection, pressed her to return. The Queen went forward.—If the parallel reaches thus far; may it go no further. The tears stand in my eyes.

I am going into Derbyshire,[3] and hope to be followed by your good wishes, for I am with great affection, Your most humble servant,

SAM. JOHNSON

Any letters that come for me hither, will be sent me.

⊷ ⊨◊⊨ ⊶

James Boswell
1740–1795

"I have discovered," James Boswell announced at age twenty-two in the journal he had just commenced, "that we may be in some degree whatever character we choose." The possibilities opened up by this discovery both exhilarated and troubled him. Neither the "choosing" nor the "being" turned out to be as simple as he expected, in part because some alternate choice always beckoned. In the pages of his journal, Boswell performed his excited choices and anxious reconsiderations. The oscillation did much to drive the intricate comedy and intermittent pathos, the energetic posing and fervent self-scrutiny of the diaries he kept all his adult life, and of the published books he crafted from them.

Boswell's parents had chosen their own characters early, and had stuck to them assiduously. His father was a Scots laird—heir to an ancient family and a landed estate—and a distinguished jurist, serving as justice on Scotland's highest courts. His mother was an impassioned Calvinist, who numbered among her many strictures an abhorrence of the theater; the actors' freedom of character-choice, which made the playhouse for her a place of sinful deception, would make it the site of a lifelong enchantment for her son. Boswell's parents had chosen firmly for their first-born too. James was to become, like his father, an eminent lawyer and respectable landowner.

Boswell chafed at the narrowness of the scheme. Struggling (he later recalled) "against paternal affection, ambition, interest," he ran away to London for a short spell at age eighteen and returned there at twenty-two, seeking a commission as a soldier with the king's personal bodyguard, a post that would have secured him lifelong residence in the city, flashy uniforms, and ample opportunities to display himself in them. While Boswell waited for this prospect to materialize (it never did), he found his real calling. He started to keep a copious journal, narrating each day in succession, dispatching the text in weekly packets to his friend John Johnston back home in Scotland. Here too was self-display, intricately contrived. Boswell managed his journal as a kind of manuscript theater—often written as a play text, complete with dialogue and stage directions—for an audience of one (the performance of his journal texts for a wider reading public would later become his literary life's work). London, the theatrical city, teemed with "characters" living and dead, real and fictional, whom Boswell by turns and in combinations strove to "be": Addison, Steele, and their imaginary paragon of self-possession Mr. Spectator; Captain Macheath from *The Beggar's Opera* (on whose adventures Boswell modeled some of his own sexual exploits; see page 2645); the actors Thomas Sheridan and David Garrick; and most important, Garrick's old teacher Samuel Johnson, whose writings had provided Boswell with a model of moral firmness more attractive than his father's, and who befriended the young diarist six months into his London stay.

---

3. The home of John Taylor.

The friendship with Johnson gave Boswell's journal a new purpose (to record the conversations of this dazzling talker) and his life a new direction. Reconciled to his father's plan, Boswell studied law in Holland and, as reward for his painfully diligent endeavors, made the Grand Tour of Europe, where he collected the conversation and the counsel of further celebrities: the French iconoclasts Voltaire and Rousseau, and the Corsican rebel leader Pasquale Paoli, then fighting to free his island from foreign domination. Returning to Scotland in 1766, Boswell took up the life his father had mapped for him, settling in Edinburgh, and becoming (as he haughtily informed his disreputable friend John Wilkes) "a Scottish lawyer, a Scottish laird, and a Scottish married man." In each of these roles, though, he repeatedly broke character. He went down to London almost every spring, ostensibly to cultivate his legal practice but really to renew his old absorptions: in theater, in sexual adventure, in the spellbinding company of Johnson and the group of artists, writers, and thinkers who surrounded him.

Boswell yearned to join their number not merely as admirer but as eminent author, and he soon did. Over the ensuing years, he produced much journalism and some verse, as well as three books in which he explored with increasing audacity the potential of his own diary as a public text—as a vehicle of entertainment, instruction, profit, and fame. He pursued for the journal form a print authority it had not previously possessed, devising ways for it to encroach upon, even to colonize, territory and tasks traditionally reserved to other genres: travel book, "character" sketch, biography. In his first attempt, An Account of Corsica . . . and Memoirs of Pascal Paoli (1769), he recast his original travel journal (rearranging the entries, dropping the dates) to produce a heroic portrait of his friend the liberator. In his second experiment, A Journal of a Tour to the Hebrides with Samuel Johnson (1785), which appeared the year after Johnson's death, the imperative to portraiture was even more pronounced. The public craved accounts of the lost titan, and this time Boswell met that demand a different way. He presented his journal as a journal, with scrupulously dated, plentifully narrated consecutive entries rich in the "minute details of daily life" that Johnson himself had stipulated as the criteria for good biography. The book struck readers as startlingly new. Some mocked it for its minutiae ("How are we all with rapture touched," exclaimed one versifier, "to see / Where, when, and at what hour, you swallowed tea!"), while many praised its veracity and abundance.

There was much more where that came from. In The Life of Samuel Johnson, LL.D. (1791), Boswell deployed the Tour's techniques on a massive scale. Drawing on his diaries, and on years of arduous research among Johnson's many acquaintances, Boswell built a thousand-page biography that is largely a book of talk, of conversations diligently recorded and deftly dramatized, the culmination of the textual theater that Boswell had long practiced in manuscript. Johnson's capacious mind and imposing presence find embodiment in a text dense with accumulated time, told and retold over the span of almost three decades that stretches from Boswell's first Johnsonian journal entry to the biography's publication. Pleased with the book's commercial success, stung by charges that he had been either too partial to Johnson or too critical of him, Boswell worked at two further editions (in which his footnotes swelled with new information and rebuttals). He died at fifty-five, unmade by alcoholism, by venereal disease, and by the violent depressions that accompanied his ongoing uncertainty as to what he might "be" and had become.

His books sustained his fame, though ever since the Life's first appearance, readers have debated the degree of its accuracy and the merits of its portraiture. Two centuries later, Boswell's biography has become a touchstone text for the problem of the "documentary"—the question of how art and "fact" should merge in representations of historical events. Over the past eighty years the debate has been deepened by the unexpected recovery of Boswell's original papers, including the diaries that he drew on and boasted of in his published books. The papers had long been given up for lost, but masses of them had actually been stashed and forgotten by various descendants in odd receptacles (cabinet, croquet box, grain loft) on estates scattered across Scotland and Ireland. The papers' recovery took more than twenty years; the process of their publication continues. Taken together, Boswell's papers and his published works make it possible to trace the intricate course by which the flux of his energetic, agitated life became fixed in text.

from **London Journal**

[A SCOT IN LONDON]

Wednesday, 1 December [1762]. * * * On Tuesday I wanted to have a silver-hilted sword, but upon examining my pockets as I walked up the Strand,[1] I found that I had left the most of my guineas at home and had not enough to pay for it with me. I determined to make a trial of the civility of my fellow-creatures, and what effect my external appearance and address would have. I accordingly went to the shop of Mr. Jefferys, sword-cutter to His Majesty, looked at a number of his swords, and at last picked out a very handsome one at five guineas. "Mr. Jefferys," said I, "I have not money here to pay for it. Will you trust me?" "Upon my word, Sir," said he, "you must excuse me. It is a thing we never do to a stranger." I bowed genteelly and said, "Indeed, Sir, I believe it is not right." However, I stood and looked at him, and he looked at me. "Come, Sir," cried he, "I will trust you." "Sir," said I, "if you had not trusted me, I should not have bought it from you." He asked my name and place of abode, which I told him. I then chose a belt, put the sword on, told him I would call and pay it tomorrow, and walked off. I called this day and paid him. "Mr. Jefferys," said I, "there is your money. You paid me a very great compliment. I am much obliged to you. But pray don't do such a thing again. It is dangerous." "Sir," said he, "we know our men. I would have trusted you with the value of a hundred pounds." This I think was a good adventure and much to my honor. * * *

This afternoon I was surprised with the arrival of Lady Betty Macfarlane, Lady Anne Erskine, Captain Erskine, and Miss Dempster, who were come to the Red Lion Inn at Charing Cross. It seems Lady Betty had written to the laird that if he would not come down, she would come up; and upon his giving her an indolent answer, like a woman of spirit, she put her resolution in practice. I immediately went to them.[2]

To tell the plain truth, I was vexed at their coming. For to see just the plain *hamely*[3] Fife family hurt my grand ideas of London. Besides, I was now upon a plan of studying polite reserved behavior, which is the only way to keep up dignity of character. And as I have a good share of pride, which I think is very proper and even noble, I am hurt with the taunts of ridicule and am unsatisfied if I do not feel myself something of a superior animal. This has always been my favorite idea in my best moments. Indeed, I have been obliged to deviate from it by a variety of circumstances. After my wild expedition to London in the year 1760, after I got rid of the load of serious reflection which then burthened me, by being always in Lord Eglinton's company, very fond of him, and much caressed by him, I became dissipated and thoughtless.[4] When my father forced me down to Scotland, I was at first very low-spirited, although to appearance very high. I afterwards from my natural vivacity endeavored to make myself easy; and like a man who takes to drinking to banish care, I threw myself loose as a heedless, dissipated, rattling fellow who might say or do every ridiculous thing. This made me sought after by everybody for the present hour, but I found myself a very inferior being; and I found many people presuming to treat me as such, which notwithstanding of my appearance of undiscerning gaiety, gave me much pain. I was, in short, a character very different from what God intended me

---

1. A major commercial street in the West End of London.
2. With the exception of Miss Dempster, the sister of his friend George, Boswell refers to the daughters and son of the Fifth Earl of Kellie ("the laird"). The family came from Fife, a county in eastern Scotland.

3. Scots dialect for "homely," home-like.
4. At the age of 18, Boswell had run away to London, where he impulsively converted to Catholicism. The tenth Earl of Eglinton, a charming and generous rake, weaned him from religion by turning him into a libertine.

and I myself chose. I remember my friend Johnston[5] told me one day after my return from London that I had turned out different from what he imagined, as he thought I would resemble Mr. Addison.[6] I laughed and threw out some loud sally of humor, but the observation struck deep. Indeed, I must do myself the justice to say that I always resolved to be such a man whenever my affairs were made easy and I got upon my own footing. For as I despaired of that, I endeavored to lower my views and just to be a good-humored comical being, well liked either as a waiter, a common soldier, a clerk in Jamaica, or some other odd out-of-the-way sphere. Now, when my father at last put me into an independent situation, I felt my mind regain its native dignity. I felt strong dispositions to be a Mr. Addison. Indeed, I had accustomed myself so much to laugh at everything that it required time to render my imagination solid and give me just notions of real life and of religion. But I hoped by degrees to attain to some degree of propriety. Mr. Addison's character in sentiment, mixed with a little of the gaiety of Sir Richard Steele and the manners of Mr. Digges,[7] were the ideas which I aimed to realize.

Indeed, I must say that Digges has more or as much of the deportment of a man of fashion as anybody I ever saw; and he keeps up this so well that he never once lessened upon me even on an intimate acquaintance, although he is now and then somewhat melancholy, under which it is very difficult to preserve dignity; and this I think is particularly to be admired in Mr. Digges. Indeed, he and I never came to familiarity, which is justly said to beget contempt. The great art of living easy and happy in society is to study proper behavior, and even with our most intimate friends to observe politeness; otherwise we will insensibly treat each other with a degree of rudeness, and each will find himself despised in some measure by the other. As I was therefore pursuing this laudable plan, I was vexed at the arrival of the Kellie family, with whom when in Scotland I had been in the greatest familiarity. Had they not come for a twelvemonth, I should have been somewhat established in my address, but as I had been but a fortnight from them, I could not without the appearance of strong affectation appear much different from what they had seen me. I accordingly was very free, but rather more silent, which they imputed to my dullness, and roasted me about London's not being agreeable to me. I bore it pretty well, and left them.

* * *

Wednesday, 15 December [1762]. The enemies of the people of England who would have them considered in the worst light represent them as selfish, beef-eaters, and cruel. In this view I resolved today to be a true-born Old Englishman. I went into the City[8] to Dolly's Steak-house in Paternoster Row and swallowed my dinner by myself to fulfill the charge of selfishness; I had a large fat beefsteak to fulfill the charge of beef-eating; and I went at five o'clock to the Royal Cockpit in St. James's Park and saw cockfighting for about five hours to fulfill the charge of cruelty.

A beefsteak house is a most excellent place to dine at. You come in there to a warm, comfortable, large room, where a number of people are sitting at table. You take whatever place you find empty; call for what you like, which you get well and cleverly dressed. You may either chat or not as you like. Nobody minds you, and you pay very

---

5. John Johnston of Grange, Boswell's close friend, to whom he was sending the journal in weekly installments.
6. Joseph Addison, author, with Sir Richard Steele, of the *Tatler* and *Spectator* papers. Addison was particularly identified with the character of the silent, all-seeing Mr. Spectator.

7. West Digges, an actor in Edinburgh, particularly known for his portrayal of Macheath in *The Beggar's Opera*.
8. The older, eastern half of London, which included the centers of finance, law, and journalism.

reasonably. My dinner (beef, bread and beer and waiter) was only a shilling. The wait-
ers make a great deal of money by these pennies.[9] Indeed, I admire the English for
attending to small sums, as many smalls make a great, according to the proverb.

At five I filled my pockets with gingerbread and apples (quite the method), put on
my old clothes and laced hat, laid by my watch, purse, and pocketbook, and with oaken
stick in my hand sallied to the pit. I was too soon there. So I went into a low inn, sat
down amongst a parcel of arrant blackguards, and drank some beer. The sentry near the
house had been very civil in showing me the way. It was very cold. I bethought myself
of the poor fellow, so I carried out a pint of beer myself to him. He was very thankful
and drank my health cordially. He told me his name was Hobard, that he was a watch-
maker but in distress for debt, and enlisted that his creditors might not touch him.

I then went to the Cockpit, which is a circular room in the middle of which the
cocks fight. It is seated round with rows gradually rising. The pit and the seats are all
covered with mat. The cocks, nicely cut and dressed and armed with silver heels, are
set down and fight with amazing bitterness and resolution. Some of them were quickly dispatched. One pair fought three quarters of an hour. The uproar and noise of betting is prodigious. A great deal of money made a very quick circulation from hand to
hand. There was a number of professed gamblers there. An old cunning dog whose
face I had seen at Newmarket[1] sat by me a while. I told him I knew nothing of the
matter.[2] "Sir," said he, "you have as good a chance as anybody." He thought I would
be a good subject for him. I was young-like. But he found himself balked. I was
shocked to see the distraction and anxiety of the betters. I was sorry for the poor
cocks. I looked round to see if any of the spectators pitied them when mangled and
torn in a most cruel manner, but I could not observe the smallest relenting sign in
any countenance. I was therefore not ill pleased to see them endure mental torment.
Thus did I complete my true English day, and came home pretty much fatigued and
pretty much confounded at the strange turn of this people.

[LOUISA][1]

Wednesday, 12 January [1763]. Louisa and I agreed that at eight at night she would
meet me in the piazzas of Covent Garden.[2] I was quite elevated, and felt myself able
and undaunted to engage in the wars of the Paphian Queen.[3]

I dined at Sheridan's[4] very heartily. He showed to my conviction that Garrick[5]
did not play the great scene in the Second Part of King Henry[6] with propriety. "People," said he, "in this age know when particular lines or even speeches are well spoke;
but they do not study character, which is a matter of the utmost moment, as people of
different characters feel and express their feelings very differently. For want of a
knowledge of this, Mr. Barry[7] acted the distress of Othello, the Moorish warrior
whose stubborn soul was hard to bend, and that of Castalio, the gentle lover who was
all tenderness, in the self-same way. Now Mr. Garrick in that famous scene whines

---

9. The waiter's tip was one of the 12 pence that made up
a shilling.
1. A town in Suffolk famous for horse racing.
2. About betting on cockfighting.
1. An actress at Covent Garden Theatre, whose real
name was Mrs. Lewis.
2. The arcades along the northern perimeter of the
square, designed by Inigo Jones and popularly known as
"piazzas," were a famous trysting place.
3. Venus.

4. Thomas Sheridan, Irish actor and teacher of elocution;
father of Richard Brinsley Sheridan, author of The School
for Scandal.
5. David Garrick (1717–1779), the most celebrated
actor-manager of his age.
6. Shakespeare's 2 Henry IV 4.5.
7. Spranger Barry, a well-known actor who played the
protagonist in Shakespeare's Othello and in Otway's The
Orphan.

most piteously when he ought to upbraid. Shakespeare has discovered[8] there a most intimate knowledge of human nature. He shows you the King worn out with sickness and so weak that he faints. He had usurped the crown by the force of arms and was convinced that it must be held with spirit. He saw his son given up to low debauchery. He was anxious and vexed to think of the anarchy that would ensue at his death. Upon discovering that the Prince had taken the crown from his pillow, and concluding him desirous of his death, he is fired with rage. He starts up. He cries, 'Go chide him hither!' His anger animates him so much that he throws aside his distemper. Nature furnishes all her strength for one last effort. He is for a moment renewed. He is for a moment the spirited Henry the Fourth. He upbraids him with bitter sarcasm and bold figures. And then what a beautiful variety is there, when, upon young Harry's contrition, he falls on his neck and melts into parental tenderness."

I yielded this point to Sheridan candidly. But upon his attacking Garrick as a tragedian in his usual way, I opposed him keenly, and declared he was prejudiced; because the world thought him a good tragic actor. "So do I, Sir," said he; "I think him the best I ever saw." BOSWELL: "Except yourself, Mr. Sheridan. But come, we shall take this for granted. The world then think him near equal or as good as you in what you excel in." SHERIDAN: "Sir, I am not a bit prejudiced. I don't value acting. I shall suppose that I was the greatest actor that ever lived and universally acknowledged so, I would not choose that it should be remembered. I would have it erased out of the anecdotes of my life. Acting is a poor thing in the present state of the stage. For my own part, I engaged in it merely as a step to something greater, a just notion of eloquence." This was in a good measure true. But he certainly talked too extravagantly.

An old Irish maid, or rather an Irish old maid (O most hideous character!) dined with us. She was indeed a terrible Joy.[9] She was a woman of knowledge and criticism and correct taste. But there came to tea a Miss Mowat who played once on the stage here for a winter or two, a lovely girl. Many an amorous glance did I exchange with her. I was this day quite flashy with love. We often addressed our discourse to each other. I hope to see her again; and yet what have I to do with anybody but dear Louisa?

At the appointed hour of eight I went to the piazzas, where I sauntered up and down for a while in a sort of trembling suspense, I knew not why. At last my charming companion appeared, and I immediately conducted her to a hackney coach which I had ready waiting, pulled up the blinds, and away we drove to the destined scene of delight. We contrived to seem as if we had come off a journey, and carried in a bundle our nightclothes, handkerchiefs, and other little things. We also had with us some almond biscuits, or as they call them in London, macaroons, which looked like provision on the road. On our arrival at Hayward's[1] we were shown into the parlor, in the same manner that any decent couple would be. I here thought proper to conceal my own name (which the people of the house had never heard), and assumed the name of Mr. Digges. We were shown up to the very room where he slept. I said my cousin, as I called him, was very well. That Ceres and Bacchus might in moderation lend their assistance to Venus,[2] I ordered a genteel supper and some wine.

Louisa told me she had two aunts who carried her over to France when she was a girl, and that she could once speak French as fluently as English. We talked a little in it, and agreed that we would improve ourselves by reading and speaking it every day.

8. Revealed.
9. Irishwoman.
1. Fleet Street inn, recommended to Boswell by Digges.

2. Deities of grain, wine, and love, respectively. Boswell refers to the proverb, "without Ceres and Bacchus, Venus grows cold."

I asked her if we did not just look like man and wife. "No," said she, "we are too fond for married people." No wonder that she may have a bad idea of that union, considering how bad it was for her. She has contrived a pretty device for a seal.[3] A heart is gently warmed by Cupid's flame, and Hymen[4] comes with his rude torch and extinguishes it. She said she found herself quite in a flutter. "Why, really," said I, "reason sometimes has no power. We have no occasion to be frightened, and yet we are both a little so. Indeed, I preserve a tolerable presence of mind." I rose and kissed her, and conscious that I had no occasion to doubt my qualifications as a gallant,[5] I joked about it: "How curious would it be if I should be so frightened that we should rise as we lay down." She reproved my wanton language by a look of modesty. The bells of St. Bride's church rung their merry chimes hard by. I said that the bells in Cupid's court would be this night set a-ringing for joy at our union.

We supped cheerfully and agreeably and drank a few glasses, and then the maid came and put the sheets, well aired, upon the bed. I now contemplated my fair prize. Louisa is just twenty-four, of a tall rather than short figure, finely made in person, with a handsome face and an enchanting languish in her eyes. She dresses with taste. She has sense, good humour, and vivacity, and looks quite a woman in genteel life. As I mused on this elevating subject, I could not help being somehow pleasingly confounded to think that so fine a woman was at this moment in my possession, that without any motives of interest[6] she had come with me to an inn, agreed to be my intimate companion, as to be my bedfellow all night, and to permit me the full enjoyment of her person.

When the servant left the room, I embraced her warmly and begged that she would not now delay my felicity. She declined to undress before me, and begged I would retire and send her one of the maids. I did so, gravely desiring the girl to go up to Mrs. Digges. I then took a candle in my hand and walked out to the yard. The night was very dark and very cold. I experienced for some minutes the rigors of the season, and called into my mind many terrible ideas of hardships, that I might make a transition from such dreary thoughts to the most gay and delicious feelings. I then caused make a bowl of negus,[7] very rich of the fruit, which I caused be set in the room as a reviving cordial.

I came softly into the room, and in a sweet delirium slipped into bed and was immediately clasped in her snowy arms and pressed to her milk-white bosom. Good heavens, what a loose[8] did we give to amorous dalliance! The friendly curtain of darkness concealed our blushes. In a moment I felt myself animated with the strongest powers of love, and, from my dearest creature's kindness, had a most luscious feast. Proud of my godlike vigor, I soon resumed the noble game. I was in full glow of health. Sobriety had preserved me from effeminacy[9] and weakness, and my bounding blood beat quick and high alarms. A more voluptuous night I never enjoyed. Five times was I fairly lost in supreme rapture. Louisa was madly fond of me; she declared I was a prodigy, and asked me if this was not extraordinary for human nature. I said twice as much might be, but this was not, although in my own mind I was somewhat proud of my performance. She said it was what there was no just reason to be proud of. But I told her I could not help it. She said it was what we had in common with the beasts. I said no. For we had it highly improved by the pleasures of sentiment.[1] I asked her what

---

3. A personal emblem or insignia, which would be impressed on the wax sealing a letter.
4. God of marriage, who traditionally carries a torch.
5. A lover; Boswell jokes that, were he anxious, he might lose his erection, in which case the couple would "rise" from the bed, without consummation.

6. Mercenary motives.
7. A drink of wine and hot water, sweetened and flavored.
8. What freedom.
9. Impotence.
1. Feelings of affection.

she thought enough. She gently chid me for asking such questions, but said two times. I mentioned the Sunday's assignation,[2] when I was in such bad spirits, told her in what agony of mind I was, and asked her if she would not have despised me for my imbecility. She declared she would not, as it was what people had not in their own power.

She often insisted that we should compose ourselves to sleep before I would consent to it. At last I sunk to rest in her arms and she in mine. I found the negus, which had a fine flavor, very refreshing to me. Louisa had an exquisite mixture of delicacy and wantonness that made me enjoy her with more relish. Indeed I could not help roving in fancy to the embraces of some other ladies which my lively imagination strongly pictured. I don't know if that was altogether fair. However, Louisa had all the advantage. She said she was quite fatigued and could neither stir leg nor arm. She begged I would not despise her, and hoped my love would not be altogether transient. I have painted this night as well as I could. The description is faint; but I surely may be styled a Man of Pleasure.

Thursday, 20 January [1763][3] * * * I then went to Louisa. With excellent address did I carry on this interview, as the following scene, I trust, will make appear:

LOUISA: My dear Sir! I hope you are well today.

BOSWELL: Excessively well, I thank you. I hope I find you so.

LOUISA: No, really, Sir. I am distressed with a thousand things. (Cunning jade, her circumstances![4]) I really don't know what to do.

BOSWELL: Do you know that I have been very unhappy since I saw you?

LOUISA: How so, Sir?

BOSWELL: Why, I am afraid that you don't love me so well, nor have not such a regard for me, as I thought you had.

LOUISA: Nay, dear Sir! [Seeming unconcerned.]

BOSWELL: Pray, Madam, have I no reason?

LOUISA: No, indeed, Sir, you have not.

BOSWELL: Have I no reason, Madam? Pray think.

LOUISA: Sir!

BOSWELL: Pray, Madam, in what state of health have you been in for some time?

LOUISA: Sir, you amaze me.

BOSWELL: I have but too strong, too plain reason to doubt of your regard. I have for some days observed the symptoms of disease, but was unwilling to believe you so very ungenerous. But now, Madam, I am thoroughly convinced.

LOUISA: Sir, you have terrified me. I protest I know nothing of the matter.

BOSWELL: Madam, I have had no connection with any woman but you these two months. I was with my surgeon this morning, who declared I had got a strong infection, and that she from whom I had it could not be ignorant of it. Madam, such a thing in this case is worse than from a woman of the town,[5] as from her you may expect it. You have used me very ill. I did not deserve it. You know you said where there was no confidence, there was no breach of trust. But surely I placed some confidence in you. I am sorry that I was mistaken.

2. During an assignation ten days earlier, Boswell had attempted—unsuccessfully—to consummate the relationship.
3. The day before, Boswell had observed in himself the unmistakable signs of venereal disease: "Too, too plain was Signor Gonorrhoea!" He then visited his doctor, who confirmed the diagnosis and asserted "that the woman who gave it me could not but know about it."
4. During the course of the relationship, Louisa had talked often about her debts, and Boswell had made her a loan.
5. Prostitute.

LOUISA: Sir, I will confess to you that about three years ago I was very bad.[6] But for these fifteen months I have been quite well. I appeal to God Almighty that I am speaking true; and for these six months I have had to do with no man but yourself.

BOSWELL: But by G-d, Madam, I have been with none but you, and here am I very bad.

LOUISA: Well, Sir, by the same solemn oath I protest that I was ignorant of it.

BOSWELL: Madam, I wish much to believe you. But I own I cannot upon this occasion believe a miracle.

LOUISA: Sir, I cannot say more to you. But you will leave me in the greatest misery. I shall lose your esteem. I shall be hurt in the opinion of everybody, and in my circumstances.

BOSWELL [to himself]: What the devil does the confounded jilt mean by being hurt in her circumstances? This is the grossest cunning. But I won't take notice of that at all.—Madam, as to the opinion of everybody, you need not be afraid. I was going to joke and say that I never boast of a lady's *favors*. But I give you my word of honor that you shall not be discovered.

LOUISA: Sir, this is being more generous than I could expect.

BOSWELL: I hope, Madam, you will own that since I have been with you I have always behaved like a man of honor.

LOUISA: You have indeed, Sir.

BOSWELL [rising]: Madam, your most obedient servant.

During all this conversation I really behaved with a manly composure and polite dignity that could not fail to inspire an awe, and she was pale as ashes and trembled and faltered. Thrice did she insist on my staying a little longer, as it was probably the last time that I should be with her. She could say nothing to the purpose. And I sat silent. As I was going, said she, "I hope, Sir, you will give me leave to inquire after your health." "Madam," said I, archly, "I fancy it will be needless for some weeks." She again renewed her request. But unwilling to be plagued any more with her, I put her off by saying I might perhaps go to the country, and left her. I was really confounded at her behavior. There is scarcely a possibility that she could be innocent of the crime of horrid imposition. And yet her positive asseverations really stunned me. She is in all probability a most consummate dissembling whore.

Thus ended my intrigue with the fair Louisa, which I flattered myself so much with, and from which I expected at least a winter's safe copulation. It is indeed very hard. I cannot say, like young fellows who get themselves clapped in a bawdy house,[7] that I will take better care again. For I really did take care. However, since I am fairly trapped, let me make the best of it. I have not got it from imprudence. It is merely the chance of war.

I then called at Drury Lane for Mr. Garrick. He was vastly good to me. "Sir," said he, "you will be a very great man. And when you are so, remember the year 1763. I want to contribute my part towards saving you. And pray, will you fix a day when I shall have the pleasure of treating you with tea?" I fixed next day. "Then, Sir," said he, "the cups shall dance and the saucers skip."

What he meant by my being a great man I can understand. For really, to speak seriously, I think there is a blossom about me of something more distinguished than the generality of mankind. But I am much afraid that this blossom will never swell

6. Severely infected.   7. Acquire gonorrhea in a brothel.

into fruit, but will be nipped and destroyed by many a blighting heat and chilling frost. Indeed, I sometimes indulge noble reveries of having a regiment, of getting into Parliament, making a figure, and becoming a man of consequence in the state. But these are checked by dispiriting reflections on my melancholy temper and imbecility of mind. Yet I may probably become sounder and stronger as I grow up. Heaven knows. I am resigned. I trust to Providence. I was quite in raptures with Garrick's kindness—the man whom from a boy I used to adore and look upon as a heathen god—to find him paying me so much respect! How amiable is he in comparison of Sheridan! I was this day with him what the French call un étourdi [a scatterbrain]. I gave free vent to my feelings. Love[8] was by, to whom I cried, "This, Sir, is the real scene." And taking Mr. Garrick cordially by the hand, "Thou greatest of men," said I, "I cannot express how happy you make me." This, upon my soul, was no flattery. He saw it was not. And the dear great man was truly pleased with it. This scene gave me a charming flutter of spirits and dispelled my former gloom. * * *

[FIRST MEETING WITH JOHNSON]

Monday, 16 May [1763]. Temple[1] and his brother breakfasted with me. I went to Love's to try to recover some of the money which he owes me. But, alas, a single guinea was all I could get. He was just going to dinner, so I stayed and eat a bit, though I was angry at myself afterwards. I drank tea at Davies's[2] in Russell Street, and about seven came in the great Mr. Samuel Johnson, whom I have so long wished to see. Mr. Davies introduced me to him. As I knew his mortal antipathy at the Scotch, I cried to Davies, "Don't tell where I come from." However, he said, "From Scotland." "Mr. Johnson," said I, "indeed I come from Scotland, but I cannot help it." "Sir," replied he, "that, I find, is what a very great many of your countrymen cannot help." Mr. Johnson is a man of a most dreadful appearance. He is a very big man, is troubled with sore eyes, the palsy, and the king's evil.[3] He is very slovenly in his dress and speaks with a most uncouth voice. Yet his great knowledge and strength of expression command vast respect and render him very excellent company. He has great humor and is a worthy man. But his dogmatical roughness of manners is disagreeable. I shall mark what I remember of his conversation. * * *

1762–1763   1950

An Account of My Last Interview with David Hume, Esq.

Partly recorded in my Journal, partly enlarged from my memory,
3 March 1777[1]

On Sunday forenoon the 7 of July 1776, being too late for church, I went to see Mr. David Hume, who was returned from London and Bath,[2] just a-dying. I found him alone, in a reclining posture in his drawing room. He was lean, ghastly, and quite of

8. James Love, actor and longtime friend of Boswell.
1. William Johnson Temple, Boswell's most intimate and upstanding friend.
2. Thomas Davies, actor and bookseller.
3. Scrofula, a form of tuberculosis that the king's touch was believed to cure.
1. Boswell was terrified of death, preoccupied with the question of an afterlife, and in doubt as to the sturdiness of his own Christian faith. All these agitations converged at the deathbed of the "infidel" Scots philosopher David

Hume (1711–1776), whom he had known (and intermittently exasperated) for about 15 years. Boswell first wrote this account three weeks after the event, and revisited it twice, altering and expanding it in March of the following year, and adding a postscript ten months later. For David Hume, see Perspectives: Mind and God (page 2674) and the conversations recorded in the *Life of Johnson* (page 2845).
2. To his house in Edinburgh.

an earthy appearance. He was dressed in a suit of gray cloth with white metal buttons, and a kind of scratch wig. He was quite different from the plump figure which he used to present. He had before him Dr. Campbell's *Philosophy of Rhetoric*.[3] He seemed to be placid and even cheerful. He said he was just approaching to his end. I think these were his words. I know not how I contrived to get the subject of immortality introduced. He said he never had entertained any belief in religion since he began to read Locke and Clarke. I asked him if he was not religious when he was young. He said he was, and he used to read *The Whole Duty of Man*;[4] that he made an abstract from the catalogue of vices at the end of it, and examined himself by this, leaving out murder and theft and such vices as he had no chance of committing, having no inclination to commit them. This, he said, was strange work; for instance, to try if, notwithstanding his excelling his schoolfellows, he had no pride or vanity. He smiled in ridicule of this as absurd and contrary to fixed principles and necessary consequences, not adverting that religious discipline does not mean to extinguish, but to moderate, the passions; and certainly an excess of pride or vanity is dangerous and generally hurtful. He then said flatly that the morality of every religion was bad, and, I really thought, was not jocular when he said that when he heard a man was religious, he concluded he was a rascal, though he had known some instances of very good men being religious. This was just an extravagant reverse of the common remark as to infidels.

I had a strong curiosity to be satisfied if he persisted in disbelieving a future state even when he had death before his eyes. I was persuaded from what he now said, and from his manner of saying it, that he did persist. I asked him if it was not possible that there might be a future state. He answered it was possible that a piece of coal put upon the fire would not burn; and he added that it was a most unreasonable fancy that we should exist forever. That immortality, if it were at all, must be general; that a great proportion of the human race has hardly any intellectual qualities; that a great proportion dies in infancy before being possessed of reason; yet all these must be immortal; that a porter who gets drunk by ten o'clock with gin must be immortal; that the trash of every age must be preserved, and that new universes must be created to contain such infinite numbers. This appeared to me an unphilosophical objection, and I said, "Mr. Hume, you know spirit does not take up space."

I may illustrate what he last said by mentioning that in a former conversation with me on this subject he used pretty much the same mode of reasoning, and urged that Wilkes[5] and his mob must be immortal. One night last May as I was coming up King Street, Westminster, I met Wilkes, who carried me into Parliament Street to see a curious procession pass: the funeral of a lamplighter attended by some hundreds of his fraternity with torches. Wilkes, who either is, or affects to be, an infidel, was rattling away, "I think there's an end of that fellow. I think he won't rise again." I very calmly said to him, "You bring into my mind the strongest argument that ever I heard against a future state"; and then told him David Hume's objection that Wilkes and his mob must be immortal. It seemed to make a proper impression, for he grinned abashment, as a Negro grows whiter when he blushes. But to return to my last interview with Mr. Hume.

3. George Campbell (1719–1796), a Scots clergyman, had made his philosophical reputation by a book-length rebuttal to Hume's essay *Of Miracles*, but he cheerfully acknowledged Hume's influence on his thought, and the two men sustained an affectionate relationship. *The Philosophy of Rhetoric*, which would become Campbell's most successful work, was now newly published.
4. A massively popular work of uncertain authorship, first published in 1658, which prescribed a rigorous code of Christian conduct.
5. John Wilkes (1725–1797), radical politician.

I asked him if the thought of annihilation never gave him any uneasiness. He said not the least; no more than the thought that he had not been, as Lucretius observes.[6] "Well," said I, "Mr. Hume, I hope to triumph over you when I meet you in a future state; and remember you are not to pretend that you was joking with all this infidelity." "No, no," said he. "But I shall have been so long there before you come that it will be nothing new." In this style of good humor and levity did I conduct the conversation. Perhaps it was wrong on so awful[7] a subject. But as nobody was present, I thought it could have no bad effect. I however felt a degree of horror, mixed with a sort of wild, strange, hurrying recollection of my excellent mother's pious instructions, of Dr. Johnson's noble lessons, and of my religious sentiments and affections during the course of my life. I was like a man in sudden danger eagerly seeking his defensive arms; and I could not but be assailed by momentary doubts while I had actually before me a man of such strong abilities and extensive inquiry dying in the persuasion of being annihilated. But I maintained my faith. I told him that I believed the Christian religion as I believed history. Said he: "You do not believe it as you believe the Revolution."[8] "Yes," said I; "but the difference is that I am not so much interested in the truth of the Revolution; otherwise I should have anxious doubts concerning it. A man who is in love has doubts of the affection of his mistress, without cause." I mentioned Soame Jenyns's little book in defense of Christianity, which was just published but which I had not yet read.[9] Mr. Hume said, "I am told there is nothing of his usual spirit in it."

He had once said to me, on a forenoon while the sun was shining bright, that he did not wish to be immortal. This was a most wonderful[1] thought. The reason he gave was that he was very well in this state of being, and that the chances were very much against his being so well in another state; and he would rather not be more than be worse. I answered that it was reasonable to hope he would be better; that there would be a progressive improvement. I tried him at this interview with that topic, saying that a future state was surely a pleasing idea. He said no, for that it was always seen through a gloomy medium; there was always a Phlegethon[2] or a hell. "But," said I, "would it not be agreeable to have hopes of seeing our friends again?" and I mentioned three men lately deceased, for whom I knew he had a high value: Ambassador Keith, Lord Alemoor, and Baron Mure. He owned it would be agreeable, but added that none of them entertained such a notion. I believe he said, such a foolish, or such an absurd, notion; for he was indecently[3] and impolitely positive in incredulity. "Yes," said I, "Lord Alemoor was a believer." David acknowledged that *he* had *some* belief.

I somehow or other brought Dr. Johnson's name into our conversation. I had often heard him speak of that great man in a very illiberal manner. He said upon this occasion, "Johnson should be pleased with my *History*."[4] Nettled by Hume's frequent attacks upon my revered friend in former conversations, I told him now that Dr. Johnson did not allow him much credit; for he said, "Sir, the fellow is a Tory by

---

6. Titus Lucretius Carus, Roman philosopher and poet; Hume's observation appears to echo more closely an observation by the Stoic philosopher Seneca: "Death is non-existence. What that may be I already know. What shall be after me is what was before me" (*Epistolae* 54.4).
7. Solemn.
8. The "Glorious Revolution" of 1688–1689, when the Stuart monarch James II was replaced by William and Mary.
9. Soame Jenyns (1704–1787) had published *A View of the Internal Evidence of the Christian Religion;* for Johnson's

review of his earlier *Free Inquiry,* see page 2749.
1. Astonishing.
2. In Greek mythology, a river in Hades.
3. In his first version, Boswell had written the milder "improperly."
4. The six-volume *History of Great Britain* (1754–1762); Hume was now revising it, and had noted that his alterations to the portion on the "two first Stuarts" were "invariably to the Tory side" (the view favored by Johnson).

chance."[5] I am sorry that I mentioned this at such a time. I was off my guard; for the truth is that Mr. Hume's pleasantry was such that there was no solemnity in the scene; and death for the time did not seem dismal. It surprised me to find him talking of different matters with a tranquillity of mind and a clearness of head which few men posses at any time. Two particulars I remember: Smith's *Wealth of Nations*, which he commended much, and Monboddo's *Origin of Language*, which he treated contemptuously.[6] I said, "If I were you, I should regret annihilation. Had I written such an admirable history, I should be sorry to leave it." He said, "I shall leave that history, of which you are pleased to speak so favorably, as perfect as I can."[7] He said, too, that all the great abilities with which men had ever been endowed were relative to this world. He said he became a greater friend to the Stuart family as he advanced in studying for his history; and he hoped he had vindicated the two first of them so effectually that they would never again be attacked.

Mr. Lauder, his surgeon, came in for a little, and Mr. Mure, the Baron's son, for another small interval. He was, as far as I could judge, quite easy with both. He said he had no pain, but was wasting away. I left him with impressions which disturbed me for some time.

(Additions from memory, 22 January 1778) Speaking of his singular notion that men of religion were generally bad men, he said, "One of the men" (or "The man"—I am not sure which) "of the greatest honor that I ever knew is my Lord Marischal,[8] who is a downright atheist. I remember I once hinted something as if I believed in the being of a God, and he would not speak to me for a week." He said this with his usual grunting pleasantry, with that thick breath which fatness had rendered habitual to him, and that smile of simplicity which his good humor constantly produced.

When he spoke against Monboddo, I told him that Monboddo said to me that he believed the abusive criticism upon his book in *The Edinburgh Magazine and Review* was written by Mr. Hume's direction. David seemed irritated, and said, "Does the *scoundrel*" (I am sure either *that* or "*rascal*") "say so?" He then told me that he had observed to one of the Faculty of Advocates that Monboddo was wrong in his observation that————and gave as a proof the line in Milton. When the review came out, he found this very remark in it, and said to that advocate, "Oho! I have discovered you"—reminding him of the circumstance.[9]

It was amazing to find him so keen in such a state. I must add one other circumstance which is material, as it shows that he perhaps was not without some hope of a future state, and that his spirits were supported by a consciousness (or at least a notion) that his conduct had been virtuous. He said, "If there were a future state, Mr. Boswell, I think I could give as good an account of my life as most people."

1776–1778   1970

5. "As being a Scotchman," Johnson had gone on to explain, "but not upon a principle of duty; for he has no principle."

6. *The Wealth of Nations* (1776), by Hume's friend Adam Smith, is the foundation text of modern economics; in *The Origin and Progress of Language* (1773), James Burnett, Lord Monboddo, argued (among other things) that humans and orangutans are of the same species.

7. Once, to entertain Adam Smith, Hume pretended that these revisions might furnish him with an excuse for living longer: " 'Allow me a little time,'" he imagined himself saying to the mythic ferryman who conveyed the dead to Hades, " 'that I may see how the public receives the alterations.' But Charon would answer, 'When you have seen the effect of these, you will be for making other alterations. There will be no end to such excuses; so, honest friend, please step into the boat.' "

8. George Keith, tenth Earl Marischal of Scotland, a renowned Jacobite who as an old man had befriended the young Boswell and accompanied him on the German portion of his Grand Tour.

9. The details of the dispute remain obscure; Boswell never filled in the blank or identified the "line in Milton."

from A Journal of a Tour to the Hebrides with Dr. Samuel Johnson[1]

Tuesday, August 31 [1773] * * * We had tea in the afternoon, and our landlord's daughter, a modest civil girl, very neatly dressed, made it for us. She told us, she had been a year at Inverness, and learned reading and writing, sewing, knotting, working lace, and pastry. Dr. Johnson made her a present of a book which he had bought at Inverness.

The room had some deals laid across the joists,[2] as a kind of ceiling. There were two beds in the room, and a woman's gown was hung on a rope to make a curtain of separation between them. Joseph[3] had sheets, which my wife had sent with us, laid on them. We had much hesitation, whether to undress, or lie down with our clothes on. I said at last, "I'll plunge in! There will be less harbor for vermin about me, when I am stripped!" Dr. Johnson said, he was like one hesitating whether to go into the cold bath. At last he resolved too. I observed he might serve a campaign.[4] JOHNSON: "I could do all that can be done by patience: whether I should have strength enough, I know not." He was in excellent humor. To see the Rambler[5] as I saw him tonight was really an amusement. I yesterday told him I was thinking of writing a poetical letter to him, on his return from Scotland, in the style of Swift's humorous epistle[6] in the character of Mary Gulliver to her husband, Captain Lemuel Gulliver, on his return to England from the country of the Houyhnhums:—

> At early morn I to the market haste,
> Studious in ev'ry thing to please thy taste.
> A curious fowl and sparagrass I chose;
> (For I remember you were fond of those).
> Three shillings cost the first, the last sev'n groats;
> Sullen you turn from both, and call for *oats:*

He laughed, and asked in whose name I would write it. I said, in Mrs. Thrale's.[7] He was angry. "Sir, if you have any sense of decency or delicacy, you won't do that!" BOSWELL: "Then let it be in Cole's, the landlord of the Mitre Tavern; where we have so often sat together." JOHNSON: "Ay, that may do."

After we had offered up our private devotions, and had chatted a little from our beds, Dr. Johnson said, "God bless us both, for Jesus Christ's sake! Good night!" I pronounced "Amen." He fell asleep immediately. I was not so fortunate for a long time. I fancied myself bit by innumerable vermin under the clothes; and that a spider was traveling from the wainscot towards my mouth. At last I fell into insensibility.

Wednesday, September 1. I awaked very early. I began to imagine that the landlord, being about to emigrate, might murder us to get our money, and lay it upon the soldiers in the barn. Such groundless fears will arise in the mind before it has resumed

1. In the fall of 1773, Boswell fulfilled his long-held ambition of accompanying Johnson on a journey through Scotland. Throughout the tour he kept a copious journal, which Johnson read in progress. Eleven years later, in the months following Johnson's death, Boswell revised the journal, with much help from their mutual friend the Shakespearean scholar Edmond Malone, and published it as a "good prelude"—foretaste and trial balloon—for the full *Life* that he and Johnson had long known he would write. For parallel accounts by Johnson of the days that Boswell narrates here, see the selections from his letters to Hester Thrale (page 2795) and his *Journey to the West-*

ern *Islands of Scotland* (page 2799).
2. Planks laid across roof beams.
3. Boswell's servant, Joseph Ritter.
4. A military campaign.
5. The title of Johnson's biweekly periodical essay (1750–1752) had become a kind of shorthand for the author at his most learned and magisterial.
6. This poem was actually written by Alexander Pope. It first appeared in *Several Copies of Verses on Occasion of Mr. Gulliver's Travels* (1727).
7. Johnson's close friend and favorite correspondent.

its vigor after sleep! Dr. Johnson had had the same kind of ideas; for he told me afterwards, that he considered so many soldiers, having seen us, would be witnesses, should any harm be done, and that circumstance, I suppose, he considered as a security. When I got up, I found him sound asleep in his miserable stye,[8] as I may call it, with a colored handkerchief tied round his head. With difficulty could I awaken him. It reminded me of Henry the Fourth's fine soliloquy on sleep; for there was here as uneasy a pallet as the poet's imagination could possibly conceive.[9]

A redcoat of the 15th regiment, whether officer or only sergeant, I could not be sure, came to the house on his way to the mountains to shoot deer, which it seems the Laird of Glenmorison does not hinder anybody to do. Few, indeed, can do them harm. We had him to breakfast with us. We got away about eight. M'Queen[1] walked some miles to give us a convoy. He had, in 1745, joined the Highland army at Fort Augustus, and continued in it till after the battle of Culloden. As he narrated the particulars of that ill-advised but brave attempt,[2] I could not refrain from tears. There is a certain association of ideas in my mind upon that subject, by which I am strongly affected. The very Highland names, or the sound of a bagpipe, will stir my blood, and fill me with a mixture of melancholy and respect for courage; with pity for an unfortunate and superstitious regard for antiquity, and thoughtless inclination for war; in short, with a crowd of sensations with which sober rationality has nothing to do.

We passed through Glensheal, with prodigious mountains on each side. We saw where the battle was fought in the year 1719.[3] Dr. Johnson owned he was now in a scene of as wild nature as he could see; but he corrected me sometimes in my inaccurate observations. "There, (said I) is a mountain like a cone." JOHNSON: "No, Sir. It would be called so in a book; and when a man comes to look at it, he sees it is not so. It is indeed pointed at the top; but one side of it is larger than the other." Another mountain I called immense. JOHNSON: "No; it is no more than a considerable protuberance."

We came to a rich green valley, comparatively speaking, and stopped awhile to let our horses rest and eat grass. We soon afterwards came to Auchnasheal, a kind of rural village, a number of cottages being built together, as we saw all along in the Highlands. We passed many miles this day without seeing a house, but only little summer huts, called *shielings*. Evan Campbell, servant to Mr. Murchison, factor[4] to the Laird of Macleod in Glenelg, ran along with us today. He was a very obliging fellow. At Auchnasheal, we sat down on a green turf seat at the end of a house; they brought us out two wooden dishes of milk, which we tasted. One of them was frothed like a syllabub.[5] I saw a woman preparing it with such a stick as is used for chocolate, and in the same manner. We had a considerable circle about us, men, women, and children, all M'Craas, Lord Seaforth's people. Not one of them could speak English.[6] I observed to Dr. Johnson, it was much the same as being with a tribe of Indians. JOHNSON: "Yes, Sir; but not so terrifying." I gave all who chose it, snuff and tobacco. Governor Trapaud had made us buy a quantity at Fort Augustus, and put them up in

---

8. Pig pen.
9. In Shakespeare's *2 Henry IV*, the wakeful king muses that sleep comes more readily to "the uneasy pallets" of the poor than to the bed of the monarch (3.1.4–31).
1. The keeper of the inn at Glenmoriston.
2. Originating in the Highlands of Scotland, the 1745 rebellion was an unsuccessful attempt to restore "Bonny Prince Charlie" (Charles Stuart, grandson of the deposed James II) to the throne of England and Scotland. The

Jacobite forces were finally subdued at the battle of Culloden, and this defeat (as well as the restrictive measures enforced by the British afterward) meant the end of the old way of life for the once-powerful clans.
3. On 10 June 1719 a combined army of Spaniards and Highlanders was crushed by the British.
4. Estate manager.
5. A drink of milk, curdled, sweetened, and whipped.
6. They spoke Erse, the Gaelic dialect of the Highlands.

small parcels. I also gave each person a bit of wheat bread, which they had never tasted before. I then gave a penny apiece to each child. I told Dr. Johnson of this; upon which he called to Joseph and our guides, for change for a shilling, and declared that he would distribute among the children. Upon this being announced in Erse, there was a great stir; not only did some children come running down from neighboring huts, but I observed one black-haired man, who had been with us all along, had gone off, and returned, bringing a very young child. My fellow traveler then ordered the children to be drawn up in a row; and he dealt about[7] his copper, and made them and their parents all happy. The poor M'Craas,[8] whatever may be their present state, were of considerable estimation in the year 1715, when there was a line in a song,

> And aw[9] the brave M'Craas are coming.

There was great diversity in the faces of the circle around us: some were as black and wild in their appearance as any American savages whatever. One woman was as comely almost as the figure of Sappho,[1] as we see it painted. We asked the old woman, the mistress of the house where we had the milk, (which by the bye, Dr. Johnson told me, for I did not observe it myself, was built not of turf, but of stone) what we should pay. She said, what we pleased. One of our guides asked her in Erse if a shilling was enough. She said, "Yes." But some of the men bade her ask more. This vexed me; because it showed a desire to impose upon strangers, as they knew that even a shilling was high payment. The woman, however, honestly persisted in her first price; so I gave her half a crown. Thus we had one good scene of life uncommon to us. The people were very much pleased, gave us many blessings, and said they had not had such a day since the old Laird of Macleod's time.

Dr. Johnson was much refreshed by this repast. He was pleased when I told him he would make a good chief. He said, "Were I a chief, I would dress my servants better than myself, and knock a fellow down if he looked saucy to a Macdonald in rags: but I would not treat men as brutes. I would let them know why all of my clan were to have attention paid to them. I would tell my upper servants why, and make them tell the others."

We rode on well, till we came to the high mountain called the Rattakin, by which time both Dr. Johnson and the horses were a good deal fatigued. It is a terrible steep to climb, notwithstanding the road is formed slanting along it; however, we made it out. On the top of it we met Captain M'Leod of Balmenoch (a Dutch officer[2] who had come from Skye) riding with his sword slung across him. He asked, "Is this Mr. Boswell?" which was a proof that we were expected. Going down the hill on the other side was no easy task. As Dr. Johnson was a great weight, the two guides agreed that he should ride the horses alternately. Hay's were the two best, and the Doctor would not ride but upon one or other of them, a black or a brown. But as Hay complained much after ascending the Rattakin, the Doctor was prevailed with to mount one of Vass's greys.[3] As he rode upon it downhill, it did not go well; and he grumbled. I walked on a little before, but was excessively entertained with the method taken to keep him in good humor. Hay led the horse's head, talking to Dr. Johnson as much as he could; and (having heard him, in the forenoon, express a pastoral pleasure on seeing the goats browsing) just when the Doctor was uttering his displeasure, the fellow

---

7. Handed out.
8. This clan played an important part in the Jacobite rebellion of 1715.
9. All (in Scots dialect).

1. Ancient Greek poet.
2. A mercenary in the Dutch army.
3. John Hay and Lauchlan Vass were Highland guides employed by Boswell.

cried, with a very Highland accent, "See, such pretty goats!" Then he whistled, *whu!* and made them jump. Little did he conceive what Dr. Johnson was. Here now was a common ignorant Highland clown, imagining that he could divert, as one does a child, *Dr. Samuel Johnson!* The ludicrousness, absurdity, and extraordinary contrast between what the fellow fancied, and the reality, was truly comic.

It grew dusky; and we had a very tedious ride for what was called five miles, but I am sure would measure ten. We had no conversation. I was riding forward to the inn at Glenelg, on the shore opposite to Skye, that I might take proper measures, before Dr. Johnson, who was now advancing in dreary silence, Hay leading his horse, should arrive. Vass also walked by the side of his horse, and Joseph followed behind: as therefore he was thus attended, and seemed to be in deep meditation, I thought there could be no harm in leaving him for a little while. He called me back with a tremendous shout, and was really in a passion with me for leaving him. I told him my intentions, but he was not satisfied, and said, "Do you know, I should as soon have thought of picking a pocket, as doing so?" BOSWELL: "I am diverted with you, Sir." JOHNSON: "Sir, I could never be diverted with incivility. Doing such a thing, makes one lose confidence in him who has done it, as one cannot tell what he may do next." His extraordinary warmth confounded me so much, that I justified myself but lamely to him; yet my intentions were not improper. I wished to get on, to see how we were to be lodged, and how we were to get a boat; all which I thought I could best settle myself, without his having any trouble. To apply his great mind to minute particulars is wrong: it is like taking an immense balance, such as is kept on quays for weighing cargoes of ships, to weigh a guinea. I knew I had neat little scales, which would do better: and that his attention to everything which falls in his way, and his uncommon desire to be always in the right, would make him weigh, if he knew of the particulars: it was right therefore for me to weigh them, and let him have them only in effect. I however continued to ride by him, finding he wished I should do so.

As we passed the barracks at Bernéra, I looked at them wishfully, as soldiers have always everything in the best order: but there was only a sergeant and a few men there. We came on to the inn at Glenelg. There was no provender for our horses; so they were sent to grass,[4] with a man to watch them. A maid showed us up stairs into a room damp and dirty, with bare walls, a variety of bad smells, a coarse black greasy fir table, and forms of the same kind; and out of a wretched bed started a fellow from his sleep, like Edgar in *King Lear*, "Poor Tom's a cold."[5]

This inn was furnished with not a single article that we could either eat or drink; but Mr. Murchison, factor to the Laird of Macleod in Glenelg, sent us a bottle of rum and some sugar, with a polite message to acquaint us that he was very sorry that he did not hear of us till we had passed his house, otherwise he should have insisted on our sleeping there that night; and that, if he were not obliged to set out for Inverness early next morning, he would have waited upon us. Such extraordinary attention from this gentleman, to entire strangers, deserves the most honorable commemoration.

Our bad accommodation here made me uneasy, and almost fretful. Dr. Johnson was calm. I said, he was so from vanity. JOHNSON: "No, Sir, it is from philosophy." It pleased me to see that the Rambler could practice so well his own lessons.

---

4. Graze.

5. The frequent refrain of Edgar (disguised as the beggar Poor Tom) in Shakespeare's *King Lear*.

I resumed the subject of my leaving him on the road, and endeavored to defend it better. He was still violent upon that head, and said, "Sir, had you gone on, I was thinking that I should have returned with you to Edinburgh, and then have parted from you, and never spoken to you more."

I sent for fresh hay, with which we made beds for ourselves, each in a room equally miserable. Like Wolfe, we had a "choice of difficulties."[6] Dr. Johnson made things easier by comparison. At M'Queen's, last night, he observed that few were so well lodged in a ship. Tonight he said, we were better than if we had been upon the hill. He lay down buttoned up in his great coat.[7] I had my sheets spread on the hay, and my clothes and great coat laid over me, by way of blankets.

Thursday, September 2. I had slept ill. Dr. Johnson's anger had affected me much. I considered that, without any bad intention, I might suddenly forfeit his friendship; and was impatient to see him this morning. I told him how uneasy he had made me by what he had said, and reminded him of his own remark at Aberdeen, upon old friendships being hastily broken off. He owned he had spoken to me in passion; that he would not have done what he threatened; and that, if he had, he should have been ten times worse than I; that forming intimacies, would indeed be "limning the water,"[8] were they liable to such sudden dissolution; and he added, "Let's think no more on't." BOSWELL: "Well, then, Sir, I shall be easy. Remember, I am to have fair warning in case of any quarrel. You are never to spring[9] a mine upon me. It was absurd in me to believe you." JOHNSON: "You deserved about as much, as to believe me from night to morning." * * *

1773   1785

from The Life of Samuel Johnson, LL.D.

[INTRODUCTION; BOSWELL'S METHOD]

To write the Life of him who excelled all mankind in writing the lives of others, and who, whether we consider his extraordinary endowments or his various works, has been equaled by few in any age, is an arduous, and may be reckoned in me a presumptuous task.

Had Dr. Johnson written his own life, in conformity with the opinion which he has given, that every man's life may be best written by himself;[1] had he employed in the preservation of his own history, that clearness of narration and elegance of language in which he has embalmed so many eminent persons, the world would probably have had the most perfect example of biography that was ever exhibited. But although he at different times, in a desultory manner, committed to writing many particulars of the progress of his mind and fortunes, he never had preserving diligence enough to form them into a regular composition. Of these memorials a few have been preserved; but the greater part was consigned by him to the flames, a few days before his death.

As I had the honor and happiness of enjoying his friendship for upwards of twenty years; as I had the scheme of writing his life constantly in view; as he was well apprised of this circumstance, and from time to time obligingly satisfied my inquiries,

---

6. General James Wolfe, who died fighting the French in Canada in 1759. Describing his campaign against Quebec, Wolfe wrote, "In this situation there is such a choice of difficulties that I own myself at a loss how to determine."
7. Overcoat.

8. A quotation from an epigram by Francis Bacon: "Who then to frail mortality shall trust, / But limns [paints] the water, or but writes in dust."
9. Explode.
1. In *Idler* No. 84.

by communicating to me the incidents of his early years; as I acquired a facility in recollecting, and was very assiduous in recording, his conversation, of which the extraordinary vigor and vivacity constituted one of the first features of his character; and as I have spared no pains in obtaining materials concerning him, from every quarter where I could discover that they were to be found, and have been favored with the most liberal communications by his friends; I flatter myself that few biographers have entered upon such a work as this with more advantages; independent of literary abilities, in which I am not vain enough to compare myself with some great names who have gone before me in this kind of writing. * * *

Instead of melting down my materials into one mass, and constantly speaking in my own person, by which I might have appeared to have more merit in the execution of the work, I have resolved to adopt and enlarge upon the excellent plan of Mr. Mason, in his Memoirs of Gray.[2] Wherever narrative is necessary to explain, connect, and supply, I furnish it to the best of my abilities; but in the chronological series of Johnson's life, which I trace as distinctly as I can, year by year, I produce, wherever it is in my power, his own minutes,[3] letters, or conversation, being convinced that this mode is more lively, and will make my readers better acquainted with him, than even most of those were who actually knew him, but could know him only partially; whereas there is here an accumulation of intelligence from various points, by which his character is more fully understood and illustrated.

Indeed I cannot conceive a more perfect mode of writing any man's life than not only relating all the most important events of it in their order, but interweaving what he privately wrote, and said, and thought; by which mankind are enabled as it were to see him live, and to "live o'er each scene"[4] with him, as he actually advanced through the several stages of his life. Had his other friends been as diligent and ardent as I was, he might have been almost entirely preserved. As it is, I will venture to say that he will be seen in this work more completely than any man who has ever yet lived.

And he will be seen as he really was; for I profess to write, not his panegyric, which must be all praise, but his Life; which, great and good as he was, must not be supposed to be entirely perfect. To be as he was, is indeed subject of panegyric enough to any man in this state of being; but in every picture there should be shade as well as light, and when I delineate him without reserve, I do what he himself recommended, both by his precept[5] and his example. * * *

What I consider as the peculiar value of the following work is the quantity that it contains of Johnson's conversation; which is universally acknowledged to have been eminently instructive and entertaining; and of which the specimens that I have given upon a former occasion have been received with so much approbation that I have good grounds for supposing that the world will not be indifferent to more ample communications of a similar nature. * * *

I am fully aware of the objections which may be made to the minuteness on some occasions of my detail of Johnson's conversation, and how happily it is adapted for the petty exercise of ridicule, by men of superficial understanding and ludicrous

2. William Mason constructed his Memoirs of Thomas Gray (1775) around a selection of the poet's letters.
3. Memoranda.
4. "To wake the soul by tender strokes of art, / To raise the genius, and to mend the heart, / To make mankind in conscious virtue bold, / Live o'er each scene, and be what

they behold" (lines 1–4 of Pope's prologue to Addison's Cato).
5. Boswell proceeds to quote from Rambler No. 60 (see page 2738) in which Johnson articulates his biographical principles.

fancy;[6] but I remain firm and confident in my opinion, that minute particulars are frequently characteristic,[7] and always amusing, when they relate to a distinguished man. I am therefore exceedingly unwilling that anything, however slight, which my illustrious friend thought it worth his while to express, with any degree of point,[8] should perish. * * *

Of one thing I am certain, that considering how highly the small portion which we have of the table talk and other anecdotes of our celebrated writers[9] is valued, and how earnestly it is regretted that we have not more, I am justified in preserving rather too many of Johnson's sayings than too few; especially as from the diversity of dispositions it cannot be known with certainty beforehand, whether what may seem trifling to some, and perhaps to the collector himself, may not be most agreeable to many; and the greater number that an author can please in any degree, the more pleasure does there arise to a benevolent mind.

To those who are weak enough to think this a degrading task, and the time and labor which have been devoted to it misemployed, I shall content myself with opposing the authority of the greatest man of any age, Julius Caesar, of whom Bacon observes, that "in his book of Apothegms which he collected, we see that he esteemed it more honor to make himself but a pair of tables, to take the wise and pithy words of others, than to have every word of his own to be made an apothegm or an oracle."

Having said thus much by way of introduction, I commit the following pages to the candor of the Public.

[CONVERSATIONS ABOUT HUME]

[21 July 1763] Next morning I found him alone, and have preserved the following fragments of his conversation. Of a gentleman[1] who was mentioned, he said, "I have not met with any man for a long time who has given me such general displeasure. He is totally unfixed in his principles, and wants to puzzle other people." I said his principles had been poisoned by a noted infidel writer,[2] but that he was, nevertheless, a benevolent good man. JOHNSON: "We can have no dependence upon that instinctive, that constitutional goodness which is not founded upon principle. I grant you that such a man may be a very amiable member of society. I can conceive him placed in such a situation that he is not much tempted to deviate from what is right; and as every man prefers virtue, when there is not some strong incitement to transgress its precepts, I can conceive him doing nothing wrong. But if such a man stood in need of money, I should not like to trust him; and I should certainly not trust him with young ladies, for *there* there is always temptation. Hume and other skeptical innovators are vain men, and will gratify themselves at any expense. Truth will not afford sufficient food to their vanity; so they have betaken themselves to error. Truth, Sir, is a cow which will yield such people no more milk, and so they are gone to milk the bull. If I could have allowed myself to gratify my vanity at the expense of truth, what fame might I have acquired. Everything which Hume has advanced against Christianity had passed through my mind long before he wrote. Always remember this,

---

6. Boswell's Hebridean journal had already been parodied in print for its "minuteness" and "detail."
7. Revealing of character.
8. "Remarkable turn of words or thought" (Johnson's *Dictionary*).
9. E.g., Joseph Spence's *Anecdotes, Observations and Char-*

acters of Books and Men, Collected from the Conversation of Mr. Pope, which (though unpublished until 1820) Johnson drew on for his *Life* of Pope.
1. Boswell's friend George Dempster.
2. The skeptical philosopher David Hume.

that after a system is well settled upon positive evidence, a few partial objections ought not to shake it. The human mind is so limited that it cannot take in all the parts of a subject, so that there may be objections raised against anything. There are objections against a *plenum*, and objections against a *vacuum*;[3] yet one of them must certainly be true."

I mentioned Hume's argument against the belief of miracles, that it is more probable that the witnesses to the truth of them are mistaken, or speak falsely, than that the miracles should be true. JOHNSON: "Why, Sir, the great difficulty of proving miracles should make us very cautious in believing them. But let us consider; although God has made Nature to operate by certain fixed laws, yet it is not unreasonable to think that he may suspend those laws, in order to establish a system highly advantageous to mankind. Now the Christian religion is a most beneficial system, as it gives us light and certainty where we were before in darkness and doubt. The miracles which prove it are attested by men who had no interest in deceiving us; but who, on the contrary, were told that they should suffer persecution, and did actually lay down their lives in confirmation of the truth of the facts which they asserted. Indeed, for some centuries the heathens did not pretend to deny the miracles; but said they were performed by the aid of evil spirits. This is a circumstance of great weight. Then, Sir, when we take the proofs derived from prophecies which have been so exactly fulfilled, we have most satisfactory evidence. Supposing a miracle possible, as to which, in my opinion, there can be no doubt, we have as strong evidence for the miracles in support of Christianity, as the nature of the thing admits."

At night Mr. Johnson and I supped in a private room at the Turk's Head coffeehouse, in the Strand. "I encourage this house (said he); for the mistress of it is a good civil woman, and has not much business."

"Sir, I love the acquaintance of young people; because, in the first place, I don't like to think myself growing old. In the next place, young acquaintances must last longest, if they do last; and then, Sir, young men have more virtue than old men; they have more generous sentiments in every respect. I love the young dogs of this age: they have more wit and humor and knowledge of life than we had; but then the dogs are not so good scholars. Sir, in my early years I read very hard. It is a sad reflection, but a true one, that I knew almost as much at eighteen as I do now. My judgment, to be sure, was not so good; but I had all the facts. I remember very well, when I was at Oxford, an old gentleman said to me, 'Young man, ply your book diligently now, and acquire a stock of knowledge; for when years come upon you, you will find that poring upon books will be but an irksome task.'"

* * *

[26 October 1769] When we were alone, I introduced the subject of death, and endeavored to maintain that the fear of it might be got over. I told him that David Hume said to me, he was no more uneasy to think he should *not be* after this life, than that he *had not been* before he began to exist. JOHNSON: "Sir, if he really thinks so, his perceptions are disturbed; he is mad: if he does not think so, he lies. He may tell you, he holds his finger in the flame of a candle, without feeling pain; would you believe him? When he dies, he at least gives up all he has." BOSWELL: "Foote,[4] Sir, told me, that when he was very ill he was not afraid to die." JOHNSON: "It is not true,

3. According to the scientific theory of the *plenum*, all space is full (*plenus*) of matter; the opposing theory postulated that there are parts of space that are empty (*vacuus*) of matter.

4. Samuel Foote (1721–1771), actor, playwright, and theatrical manager.

Sir. Hold a pistol to Foote's breast, or to Hume's breast, and threaten to kill them, and you'll see how they behave." BOSWELL: "But may we not fortify our minds for the approach of death?" Here I am sensible I was in the wrong, to bring before his view what he ever looked upon with horror; for although when in a celestial frame, in his *Vanity of Human Wishes*,[5] he has supposed death to be "kind Nature's signal for retreat," from this state of being to "a happier seat," his thoughts upon this awful change were in general full of dismal apprehensions. His mind resembled the vast amphitheater, the Colosseum at Rome. In the center stood his judgment, which, like a mighty gladiator, combated those apprehensions that, like the wild beasts of the Arena, were all around in cells, ready to be let out upon him. After a conflict, he drove them back into their dens; but not killing them, they were still assailing him. To my question, whether we might not fortify our minds for the approach of death, he answered, in a passion, "No, Sir, let it alone. It matters not how a man dies, but how he lives. The act of dying is not of importance, it lasts so short a time." He added (with an earnest look), "A man knows it must be so, and submits. It will do him no good to whine."

I attempted to continue the conversation. He was so provoked that he said, "Give us no more of this"; and was thrown into such a state of agitation, that he expressed himself in a way that alarmed and distressed me, showed an impatience that I should leave him, and when I was going away, called to me sternly, "Don't let us meet tomorrow."

I went home exceedingly uneasy. All the harsh observations which I had ever heard made upon his character crowded into my mind; and I seemed to myself like the man who had put his head into the lion's mouth a great many times with perfect safety, but at last had it bit off.

[DINNER WITH WILKES]

[May 1776] I am now to record a very curious incident in Dr. Johnson's life, which fell under my own observation; of which *pars magna fui*,[1] and which I am persuaded will, with the liberal-minded, be much to his credit.

My desire of being acquainted with celebrated men of every description had made me, much about the same time, obtain an introduction to Dr. Samuel Johnson and to John Wilkes, Esq.[2] Two men more different could perhaps not be selected out of all mankind. They had even attacked one another with some asperity in their writings; yet I lived in habits of friendship with both. I could fully relish the excellence of each; for I have ever delighted in that intellectual chemistry which can separate good qualities from evil in the same person.

Sir John Pringle,[3] "mine own friend and my Father's friend," between whom and Dr. Johnson I in vain wished to establish an acquaintance, as I respected and lived in intimacy with both of them, observed to me once, very ingeniously, "It is not in friendship as in mathematics, where two things, each equal to a third, are equal between themselves. You agree with Johnson as a middle quality, and you agree with me as a middle quality; but Johnson and I should not agree." Sir John was not sufficiently flexible, so I desisted, knowing, indeed, that the repulsion was equally strong

5. Johnson's imitation of Juvenal's tenth satire, lines 363–64 (see page 2730).

1. "I was no small part." (Virgil, *Aeneid* 2.5).

2. John Wilkes (1727–1797), libertine, satirist, and radical politician, had been expelled from Parliament for blasphemous and seditious libel. Johnson considered Wilkes an unprincipled philanderer and demagogue.

3. John Pringle (1707–1782), distinguished physician and president of the Royal Society. Johnson disliked Pringle's freethinking religious views and his pro-American political convictions.

on the part of Johnson, who, I know not from what cause, unless his being a Scotchman, had formed a very erroneous opinion of Sir John. But I conceived an irresistible wish, if possible, to bring Dr. Johnson and Mr. Wilkes together. How to manage it was a nice[4] and difficult matter.

My worthy booksellers[5] and friends, Messieurs Dilly in the Poultry, at whose hospitable and well-covered table I have seen a greater number of literary men than at any other, except that of Sir Joshua Reynolds, had invited me to meet Mr. Wilkes and some more gentlemen on Wednesday, May 15. "Pray," said I, "let us have Dr. Johnson."—"What, with Mr. Wilkes? not for the world," said Mr. Edward Dilly, "Dr. Johnson would never forgive me."—"Come," said I, "if you'll let me negotiate for you, I will be answerable that all shall go well." DILLY: "Nay, if you will take it upon you, I am sure I shall be very happy to see them both here."

Notwithstanding the high veneration which I entertained for Dr. Johnson, I was sensible that he was sometimes a little actuated by the spirit of contradiction, and by means of that I hoped I should gain my point. I was persuaded that if I had come upon him with a direct proposal, "Sir, will you dine in company with Jack Wilkes?" he would have flown into a passion, and would probably have answered, "Dine with Jack Wilkes, Sir! I'd as soon dine with Jack Ketch."[6] I therefore, while we were sitting quietly by ourselves at his house in an evening, took occasion to open my plan thus:—"Mr. Dilly, Sir, sends his respectful compliments to you, and would be happy if you would do him the honor to dine with him on Wednesday next along with me, as I must soon go to Scotland." JOHNSON: "Sir, I am obliged to Mr. Dilly. I will wait upon him." BOSWELL: "Provided, Sir, I suppose, that the company which he is to have is agreeable to you." JOHNSON: "What do you mean, Sir? What do you take me for? Do you think I am so ignorant of the world, as to imagine that I am to prescribe to a gentleman what company he is to have at his table?" BOSWELL: "I beg your pardon, Sir, for wishing to prevent you from meeting people whom you might not like. Perhaps he may have some of what he calls his patriotic[7] friends with him." JOHNSON: "Well, Sir, and what then? What care I for his patriotic friends? Poh!" BOSWELL: "I should not be surprised to find Jack Wilkes there." JOHNSON: "And if Jack Wilkes should be there, what is that to me, Sir? My dear friend, let us have no more of this. I am sorry to be angry with you; but really it is treating me strangely to talk to me as if I could not meet any company whatever, occasionally." BOSWELL: "Pray forgive me, Sir. I meant well. But you shall meet whoever comes, for me." Thus I secured him, and told Dilly that he would find him very well pleased to be one of his guests on the day appointed.

Upon the much-expected Wednesday, I called on him about half an hour before dinner, as I often did when we were to dine out together, to see that he was ready in time, and to accompany him. I found him buffeting[8] his books, as upon a former occasion, covered with dust and making no preparation for going abroad. "How is this, Sir?" said I. "Don't you recollect that you are to dine at Mr. Dilly's?" JOHNSON: "Sir, I did not think of going to Dilly's: it went out of my head. I have ordered dinner at home with Mrs. Williams."[9] BOSWELL: "But, my dear Sir, you

4. Delicate.
5. Publishers.
6. Famous 17th-century hangman.
7. Those in favor of diminishing the power of the monarch and supporting the rights of the American colonists. Johnson had recently written a political tract

called The Patriot (1774) in which he attacked Wilkes and his supporters.
8. Vigorously cleaning.
9. An elderly blind woman who lived in Johnson's house as one of several dependents.

know you were engaged to Mr. Dilly, and I told him so. He will expect you, and will be much disappointed if you don't come." JOHNSON: "You must talk to Mrs. Williams about this."

Here was a sad dilemma. I feared that what I was so confident I had secured would yet be frustrated. He had accustomed himself to show Mrs. Williams such a degree of humane attention, as frequently imposed some restraint upon him; and I knew that if she should be obstinate, he would not stir. I hastened downstairs to the blind lady's room and told her I was in great uneasiness, for Dr. Johnson had engaged to me to dine this day at Mr. Dilly's, but that he had told me he had forgotten his engagement, and had ordered dinner at home. "Yes, Sir," said she, pretty peevishly, "Dr. Johnson is to dine at home." "Madam," said I "his respect for you is such that I know he will not leave you unless you absolutely desire it. But as you have so much of his company, I hope you will be good enough to forgo it for a day; as Mr. Dilly is a very worthy man, has frequently had agreeable parties at his house for Dr. Johnson, and will be vexed if the Doctor neglects him today. And then, Madam, be pleased to consider my situation; I carried the message, and I assured Mr. Dilly that Dr. Johnson was to come, and no doubt he has made a dinner, and invited a company, and boasted of the honor he expected to have. I shall be quite disgraced if the Doctor is not there." She gradually softened to my solicitations, which were certainly as earnest as most entreaties to ladies upon any occasion, and was graciously pleased to empower me to tell Dr. Johnson, "That all things considered, she thought he should certainly go." I flew back to him, still in dust, and careless of what should be the event,[1] "indifferent in his choice to go or stay";[2] but as soon as I had announced to him Mrs. Williams's consent, he roared, "Frank, a clean shirt," and was very soon dressed. When I had him fairly[3] seated in a hackney coach with me, I exulted as much as a fortune hunter who has got an heiress into a post chaise with him to set out for Gretna Green.[4]

When we entered Mr. Dilly's drawing room, he found himself in the midst of a company he did not know. I kept myself snug and silent, watching how he would conduct himself. I observed him whispering to Mr. Dilly, "Who is that gentleman, Sir?"—"Mr. Arthur Lee."—JOHNSON: "Too, too, too" (under his breath), which was one of his habitual mutterings. Mr. Arthur Lee could not but be very obnoxious to Johnson, for he was not only a *patriot* but an *American*. He was afterwards minister from the United States at the court of Madrid. "And who is the gentleman in lace?"—"Mr. Wilkes, Sir." This information confounded him still more; he had some difficulty to restrain himself, and taking up a book, sat down upon a window seat and read, or at least kept his eye upon it intently for some time, till he composed himself. His feelings, I dare say, were awkward enough. But he no doubt recollected his having rated[5] me for supposing that he could be at all disconcerted by any company, and he, therefore, resolutely set himself to behave quite as an easy man of the world, who could adapt himself at once to the disposition and manners of those whom he might chance to meet.

The cheering sound of "Dinner is upon the table" dissolved his reverie, and we *all* sat down without any symptom of ill humor. There were present, besides Mr. Wilkes, and Mr. Arthur Lee, who was an old companion of mine when he studied

1. Not caring how the matter turned out.
2. Boswell adapts a line from Addison's *Cato:* "Indiff'rent in his choice to sleep or die" (5.1).
3. Securely.
4. A village just across the border in Scotland; it was the common destination of eloping couples, who could thereby bypass the formalities and restrictions of the Anglican Church.
5. Chided.

physics at Edinburgh, Mr. (now Sir John) Miller, Dr. Lettsom, and Mr. Slater, the druggist. Mr. Wilkes placed himself next to Dr. Johnson and behaved to him with so much attention and politeness that he gained upon him insensibly.[6] No man eat[7] more heartily than Johnson, or loved better what was nice and delicate. Mr. Wilkes was very assiduous in helping him to some fine veal. "Pray give me leave, Sir—It is better here—A little of the brown—Some fat, Sir—A little of the stuffing—Some gravy—Let me have the pleasure of giving you some butter—Allow me to recommend a squeeze of this orange, or the lemon, perhaps, may have more zest."—"Sir, Sir, I am obliged to you, Sir," cried Johnson, bowing, and turning his head to him with a look for some time of "surly virtue,"[8] but, in a short while, of complacency.

Foote being mentioned, Johnson said, "He is not a good mimic." One of the company added, "A merry Andrew, a buffoon." JOHNSON: "But he has wit[9] too, and is not deficient in ideas, or in fertility and variety of imagery, and not empty of reading;[1] he has knowledge enough to fill up his part. One species of wit he has in an eminent degree, that of escape. You drive him into a corner with both hands; but he's gone, Sir, when you think you have got him—like an animal that jumps over your head. Then he has a great range for his wit; he never lets truth stand between him and a jest, and he is sometimes mighty coarse. Garrick is under many restraints from which Foote is free." WILKES: "Garrick's wit is more like Lord Chesterfield's." JOHNSON: "The first time I was in company with Foote was at Fitzherbert's.[2] Having no good opinion of the fellow, I was resolved not to be pleased; and it is very difficult to please a man against his will. I went on eating my dinner pretty sullenly, affecting not to mind him. But the dog was so very comical, that I was obliged to lay down my knife and fork, throw myself back upon my chair, and fairly laugh it out. No, Sir, he was irresistible. He upon one occasion experienced, in an extraordinary degree, the efficacy of his powers of entertaining. Among the many and various modes which he tried of getting money, he became a partner with a small-beer brewer, and he was to have a share of the profits for procuring customers among his numerous acquaintance. Fitzherbert was one who took his small beer;[3] but it was so bad that the servants resolved not to drink it. They were at some loss how to notify[4] their resolution, being afraid of offending their master, who they knew liked Foote much as a companion. At last they fixed upon a little black boy, who was rather a favorite, to be their deputy and deliver their remonstrance; and having invested him with the whole authority of the kitchen, he was to inform Mr. Fitzherbert, in all their names, upon a certain day, that they would drink Foote's small beer no longer. On that day Foote happened to dine at Fitzherbert's, and this boy served at table; he was so delighted with Foote's stories, and merriment, and grimace,[5] that when he went downstairs, he told them, 'This is the finest man I have ever seen. I will not deliver your message. I will drink his small beer.' "

Somebody observed that Garrick could not have done this. WILKES: "Garrick would have made the small beer still smaller. He is now leaving the stage; but he will play Scrub[6] all his life." I knew that Johnson would let nobody attack Garrick but himself, as Garrick once said to me, and I had heard him praise his liberality; so to bring out

---

6. Imperceptibly.
7. Ate (pronounced "ett").
8. Boswell quotes from Johnson's poem *London*.
9. Intelligence, cleverness.
1. Devoid of learning.
2. William Fitzherbert (1712–1772), landowner and politician.

3. Weak beer.
4. Express.
5. Exaggerated facial expressions (Foote specialized in caricatures of his contemporaries).
6. A character in George Farquhar's comedy, *The Beaux' Stratagem*.

his commendation of his celebrated pupil, I said, loudly, "I have heard Garrick is liberal." JOHNSON: "Yes, Sir, I know that Garrick has given away more money than any man in England that I am acquainted with, and that not from ostentatious views. Garrick was very poor when he began life; so when he came to have money, he probably was very unskillful in giving away, and saved when he should not. But Garrick began to be liberal as soon as he could; and I am of opinion, the reputation of avarice which he has had, has been very lucky for him and prevented his having many enemies. You despise a man for avarice, but do not hate him. Garrick might have been much better attacked for living with more splendor than is suitable to a player: if they had had the wit to have assaulted him in that quarter, they might have galled him more. But they have kept clamoring about his avarice, which has rescued him from much obloquy and envy."

Talking of the great difficulty of obtaining authentic information for biography, Johnson told us, "When I was a young fellow I wanted to write the *Life of Dryden*, and in order to get materials, I applied to the only two persons then alive who had seen him; these were old Swinney, and old Cibber.[7] Swinney's information was no more than this, "That at Will's coffeehouse Dryden had a particular chair for himself, which was set by the fire in winter, and was then called his winter-chair; and that it was carried out for him to the balcony in summer, and was then called his summer-chair." Cibber could tell no more but "that he remembered him a decent old man, arbiter of critical disputes at Will's." You are to consider that Cibber was then at a great distance from Dryden, had perhaps one leg only in the room, and durst not draw in the other." BOSWELL: "Yet Cibber was a man of observation?" JOHNSON: "I think not." BOSWELL: "You will allow his *Apology* to be well done." JOHNSON: "Very well done, to be sure, Sir. That book is a striking proof of the justice of Pope's remark:

> Each might his several province well command,
> Would all but stoop to what they understand."[8]

BOSWELL: "And his plays are good." JOHNSON: "Yes; but that was his trade; *l'esprit du corps*: he had been all his life among players and play-writers. I wondered that he had so little to say in conversation, for he had kept the best company, and learnt all that can be got by the ear. He abused Pindar[9] to me, and then showed me an ode of his own, with an absurd couplet, making a linnet soar on an eagle's wing. I told him that when the ancients made a simile, they always made it like something real."

Mr. Wilkes remarked, that "among all the bold flights of Shakespeare's imagination, the boldest was making Birnam Wood march to Dunsinane,[1] creating a wood where there never was a shrub; a wood in Scotland! ha! ha! ha!" And he also observed that "the clannish slavery of the Highlands of Scotland was the single exception to Milton's remark[2] of 'The mountain nymph, sweet Liberty,' being worshipped in all hilly countries." "When I was at Inverary," said he, "on a visit to my old friend, Archibald, Duke of Argyle, his dependents congratulated me on being such a favorite of his Grace. I said, 'It is then, gentlemen, truly lucky for me; for if I had displeased the Duke, and he had wished it, there is not a Campbell among you but would have been ready to bring John Wilkes's head to him in a charger. It would have been only

---

7. Owen Mac Swiney and Colley Cibber, actors from the first half of the 18th century. Cibber was also a poet, playwright, and the author of a widely read autobiography (his *Apology*).
8. Pope, *Essay on Criticism*, lines 66–67.
9. Spoke disparagingly of the ancient Greek poet Pindar,

famous for his odes.
1. In Act 5 of *Macbeth*. In his *Journey to the Western Islands* (1775), Johnson had commented repeatedly on the treelessness of Scotland.
2. In his poem *L'Allegro* (36).

Off with his head! So much for Aylesbury.[3]

I was then member[4] for Aylesbury." * * *

Mr. Arthur Lee mentioned some Scotch who had taken possession of a barren part of America, and wondered why they should choose it. JOHNSON: "Why, Sir, all barrenness is comparative. The Scotch would not know it to be barren." BOSWELL: "Come, come, he is flattering the English. You have now been in Scotland, Sir, and say if you did not see meat and drink enough there." JOHNSON: "Why yes, Sir; meat and drink enough to give the inhabitants sufficient strength to run away from home." All these quick and lively sallies were said sportively, quite in jest, and with a smile, which showed that he meant only wit. Upon this topic he and Mr. Wilkes could perfectly assimilate; here was a bond of union between them, and I was conscious that as both of them had visited Caledonia,[5] both were fully satisfied of the strange narrow ignorance of those who imagine that it is a land of famine. But they amused themselves with persevering in the old jokes. When I claimed a superiority for Scotland over England in one respect, that no man can be arrested there for a debt merely because another swears it against him; but there must first be the judgment of a court of law ascertaining its justice; and that a seizure of the person, before judgment is obtained, can take place only if his creditor should swear that he is about to fly from the country, or, as it is technically expressed, is *in meditatione fugae*. WILKES: "That, I should think, may be safely sworn of all the Scotch nation." JOHNSON (to Mr. Wilkes): "You must know, Sir, I lately took my friend Boswell and showed him genuine civilized life in an English provincial town. I turned him loose at Lichfield, my native city, that he might see for once real civility: for you know he lives among savages in Scotland, and among rakes in London." WILKES: "Except when he is with grave, sober, decent people like you and me." JOHNSON (smiling): "And we ashamed of him."

They were quite frank and easy. Johnson told the story of his asking Mrs. Macaulay[6] to allow her footman to sit down with them, to prove the ridiculousness of the argument for the equality of mankind; and he said to me afterwards, with a nod of satisfaction, "You saw Mr. Wilkes acquiesced." Wilkes talked with all imaginable freedom of the ludicrous title given to the Attorney General, *Diabolus Regis*,[7] adding, "I have reason to know something about that officer; for I was prosecuted for a libel."[8] Johnson, who many people would have supposed must have been furiously angry at hearing this talked of so lightly, said not a word. He was now, *indeed*, "a good-humored fellow."

After dinner we had an accession[9] of Mrs. Knowles, the Quaker lady, well known for her various talents, and of Mr. Alderman Lee. Amidst some patriotic groans, somebody (I think the Alderman) said, "Poor old England is lost." JOHNSON: "Sir, it is not so much to be lamented that Old England is lost, as that the Scotch have found it."[1] WILKES : "Had Lord Bute governed Scotland only, I should not have taken the trouble to write his eulogy, and dedicate *Mortimer* to him."[2]

3. Wilkes adapts Colley Cibber's popular version of Shakespeare's *Richard III*, which contains the line, "Off with his head. So much for Buckingham."
4. Of Parliament.
5. Scotland (from the Roman name for North Britain).
6. Catherine Macaulay, author of a controversial *History of England* (1763–1783). In order to test her egalitarian principles, Johnson had proposed that she invite her footman to join them at dinner. "I thus, Sir, showed her the absurdity of the leveling doctrine," he told Boswell. "She has never liked me since."
7. The King's Devil.
8. See n 2, page 2847.
9. I.e., these additional guests arrived: Mary Morris

Knowles (1733–1807), a highly accomplished needlewoman whose "sutile pictures" Johnson praised in a letter to Mrs. Thrale; and William Lee (1739–1795), merchant, diplomat, and the only American ever elected an alderman of London.
1. Soon after succeeding to the throne in 1760, George III made his former tutor, the Scottish Earl of Bute, Prime Minister of Britain. The appointment unleashed a flood of anti-Scottish propaganda.
2. As part of a sustained campaign against Bute's government, Wilkes had chosen to reprint a 1731 play called *The Fall of Mortimer* and had prefaced it with a mock-respectful dedication to the prime minister.

Mr. Wilkes held a candle to show a fine print of a beautiful female figure which hung in the room, and pointed out the elegant contour of the bosom with the finger of an arch connoisseur. He afterwards, in a conversation with me, waggishly insisted that all the time Johnson showed visible signs of a fervent admiration of the corresponding charms of the fair Quaker.

This record, though by no means so perfect as I could wish, will serve to give a notion of a very curious interview, which was not only pleasing at the time, but had the agreeable and benignant effect of reconciling any animosity, and sweetening any acidity, which in the various bustle of political contest, had been produced in the minds of two men, who though widely different, had so many things in common— classical learning, modern literature, wit, and humor, and ready repartee—that it would have been much to be regretted if they had been forever at a distance from each other.

Mr. Burke gave me much credit for this successful *negotiation* and pleasantly said that "there was nothing to equal it in the whole history of the *Corps Diplomatique*."

I attended Dr. Johnson home, and had the satisfaction to hear him tell Mrs. Williams how much he had been pleased with Mr. Wilkes's company, and what an agreeable day he had passed.

[CONVERSATIONS AT STREATHAM AND THE CLUB][1]

[30 March 1778] I mentioned that I had in my possession the Life of Sir Robert Sibbald, the celebrated Scottish antiquary, and founder of the Royal College of Physicians at Edinburgh, in the original manuscript in his own handwriting; and that it was I believed the most natural and candid account of himself that ever was given by any man. As an instance, he tells that the Duke of Perth, then Chancellor of Scotland, pressed him very much to come over to the Roman Catholic faith; that he resisted all his Grace's arguments for a considerable time, till one day he felt himself, as it were, instantaneously convinced, and with tears in his eyes ran into the Duke's arms, and embraced the ancient religion; that he continued very steady in it for some time, and accompanied his Grace to London one winter, and lived in his household; that there he found the rigid fasting prescribed by the church very severe upon him; that this disposed him to reconsider the controversy, and having then seen that he was in the wrong, he returned to Protestantism. I talked of some time or other publishing this curious life. MRS. THRALE: "I think you had as well let alone that publication. To discover[2] such weakness exposes a man when he is gone." JOHNSON: "Nay, it is an honest picture of human nature. How often are the primary motives of our greatest actions as small as Sibbald's, for his re-conversion." MRS. THRALE: "But may they not as well be forgotten?" JOHNSON: "No, Madam, a man loves to review his own mind. That is the use of a diary, or journal." LORD TRIMLESTOWN: "True, Sir. As the ladies love to see themselves in a glass, so a man likes to see himself in his journal." BOSWELL: "A very pretty allusion." JOHNSON: "Yes, indeed." BOSWELL: "And as a lady adjusts her dress before a mirror, a man adjusts his character by looking at his journal." I next year found the very same thought in Atterbury's *Funeral Sermon on Lady Cutts*, where, having mentioned her *Diary*, he says, "In this glass she every day dressed her mind." This is a proof of coincidence, and not of plagiarism; for I had never read that sermon before.

---

1. These were two of Johnson's favorite venues of conversation. Streatham was the country estate of Henry and Hester Thrale, where Johnson and his friends were often guests. The Club was a group of distinguished thinkers, writers, artists, and statesman that met weekly.
2. Reveal.

Next morning, while we were at breakfast, Johnson gave a very earnest recommendation of what he himself practiced with the utmost conscientiousness: I mean a strict attention to truth, even in the most minute particulars. "Accustom your children," said he, "constantly to this; if a thing happened at one window, and they, when relating it, say that it happened at another, do not let it pass, but instantly check them; you do not know where deviation from truth will end." BOSWELL: "It may come to the door: and when once an account is at all varied in one circumstance, it may by degrees be varied so as to be totally different from what really happened." Our lively hostess, whose fancy was impatient of the rein,[3] fidgeted at this, and ventured to say, "Nay, this is too much. If Mr. Johnson should forbid me to drink tea, I would comply, as I should feel the restraint only twice a day; but little variations in narrative must happen a thousand times a day, if one is not perpetually watching." JOHNSON: "Well, Madam, and you *ought* to be perpetually watching. It is more from carelessness about truth than from intentional lying, that there is so much falsehood in the world."

In his review of Dr. Warton's *Essay on the Writings and Genius of Pope*, Johnson has given the following salutary caution upon this subject:

"Nothing but experience could evince[4] the frequency of false information, or enable any man to conceive that so many groundless reports should be propagated, as every man of eminence may hear of himself. Some men relate what they think, as what they know; some men of confused memories and habitual inaccuracy ascribe to one man what belongs to another; and some talk on, without thought or care. A few men are sufficient to broach falsehoods, which are afterwards innocently diffused by successive relaters."

Had he lived to read what Sir John Hawkins and Mrs. Piozzi have related concerning himself[5] how much would he have found his observation illustrated. He was indeed so much impressed with the prevalence of falsehood, voluntary or unintentional, that I never knew any person who upon hearing an extraordinary circumstance told, discovered more of the *incredulus odi*.[6] He would say, with a significant look and decisive tone, "It is not so. Do not tell this again." He inculcated upon all his friends the importance of perpetual vigilance against the slightest degrees of falsehood; the effect of which, as Sir Joshua Reynolds observed to me, has been, that all who were of his *school* are distinguished for a love of truth and accuracy, which they would not have possessed in the same degree, if they had not been acquainted with Johnson.

Talking of ghosts, he said, "It is wonderful that five thousand years have now elapsed since the creation of the world, and still it is undecided whether or not there has ever been an instance of the spirit of any person appearing after death. All argument is against it; but all belief is for it."

He said, "John Wesley's[7] conversation is good, but he is never at leisure. He is always obliged to go at a certain hour. This is very disagreeable to a man who loves to fold his legs and have out his talk, as I do."

On Friday, April 3, I dined with him in London, in a company where were present several eminent men, whom I shall not name, but distinguish their parts in the conversation by different letters.[8]

3. Whose imagination did not like to be restrained.
4. Prove, serve as evidence of.
5. Boswell refers to the two rival biographies, Sir John Hawkins's *Life of Samuel Johnson LL.D.* (1787) and Hester Thrale Piozzi's *Anecdotes of the Late Samuel Johnson LL.D.* (1786).
6. Hostile incredulity.

7. Co-founder (1703–1791) of the Methodist movement.
8. "F" stands for John Fitzpatrick, Earl of Upper Ossory, an Irish nobleman; "E" for Edmund Burke, statesman and political theorist; "R" for Richard Brinsley Sheridan, playwright; "C" for George Fordyce, a chemist; "P" for Sir Joshua Reynolds ("Painter").

F: "I have been looking at this famous antique marble dog of Mr. Jennings, valued at a thousand guineas, said to be Alcibiades's dog."[9] JOHNSON: "His tail then must be docked.[1] That was the mark of Alcibiades's dog." E: "A thousand guineas! The representation of no animal whatever is worth so much. At this rate a dead dog would indeed be better than a living lion." JOHNSON: "Sir, it is not the worth of the thing, but of the skill in forming it which is so highly estimated. Everything that enlarges the sphere of human powers, that shows man he can do what he thought he could not do, is valuable. The first man who balanced a straw upon his nose; Johnson,[2] who rode upon three horses at a time; in short, all such men deserved the applause of mankind, not on account of the use of what they did, but of the dexterity which they exhibited." BOSWELL: "Yet a misapplication of time and assiduity is not to be encouraged. Addison, in one of his *Spectators*, commends the judgment of a king, who, as a suitable reward to a man that by long perseverance had attained to the art of throwing a barleycorn through the eye of a needle, gave him a bushel of barley." JOHNSON: "He must have been a king of Scotland, where barley is scarce." F: "One of the most remarkable antique figures of an animal is the boar at Florence." JOHNSON: "The first boar that is well made in marble should be preserved as a wonder. When men arrive at a facility of making boars well, then the workmanship is not of such value, but they should however be preserved as examples, and as a greater security for the restoration of the art, should it be lost."

E: "We hear prodigious complaints at present of emigration. I am convinced that emigration makes a country more populous." J: "That sounds very much like a paradox." E: "Exportation of men, like exportation of all other commodities, makes more be produced." JOHNSON: "But there would be more people were there not emigration, provided there were food for more." E: "No; leave a few breeders, and you'll have more people than if there were no emigration." JOHNSON: "Nay, Sir, it is plain there will be more people, if there are more breeders. Thirty cows in good pasture will produce more calves than ten cows, provided they have good bulls." E: "There are bulls enough in Ireland."[3] Johnson (smiling): "So, Sir, I should think from your argument." BOSWELL: "You said, exportation of men, like exportation of other commodities, makes more be produced. But a bounty is given to encourage the exportation of corn, and no bounty is given for the exportation of men, though, indeed, those who go, gain by it." R: "But the bounty on the exportation of corn is paid at home." E: "That's the same thing." JOHNSON: "No, Sir." R: "A man who stays at home gains nothing by his neighbors emigrating." BOSWELL: "I can understand that emigration may be the cause that more people may be produced in a country; but the country will not therefore be the more populous, for the people issue from it. It can only be said that there is a flow of people. It is an encouragement to have children, to know that they can get a living by emigration." R: "Yes, if there were an emigration of children under six years of age. But they don't emigrate till they could earn their livelihood in some way at home." C: "It is remarkable that the most unhealthy countries, where there are the most destructive diseases, such as Egypt and Bengal, are the most populous." JOHNSON: "Countries which are the most populous have the most destructive diseases. *That* is the true state of the proposition." C: "Holland is very unhealthy, yet it is

9. A marble statue purchased in Rome by the collector Henry Jennings, it was called after an antique sculpture in the Uffizi, Florence.

1. Clipped.
2. An acrobatic rider (no relation).
3. An "Irish bull" was a foolish blunder.

exceedingly populous." JOHNSON: "I know not that Holland is unhealthy. But its pop-ulousness is owing to an influx of people from all other countries. Disease cannot be the cause of populousness, for it not only carries off a great proportion of the people, but those who are left are weakened and unfit for the purposes of increase."

R: "Mr. E., I don't mean to flatter, but when posterity reads one of your speeches in Parliament, it will be difficult to believe that you took so much pains, knowing with certainty that it could produce no effect, that not one vote would be gained by it." E. "Waiving your compliment to me, I shall say in general, that it is very well worthwhile for a man to take pains to speak well in Parliament. A man, who has van-ity, speaks to display his talents; and if a man speaks well, he gradually establishes a certain reputation and consequence[4] in the general opinion, which sooner or later will have its political reward. Besides, though not one vote is gained, a good speech has its effect. Though an act which has been ably opposed passes into a law, yet in its progress it is modeled, it is softened in such a manner that we see plainly the Minis-ter[5] has been told that the Members attached to him are so sensible of its injustice or absurdity from what they have heard that it must be altered." JOHNSON: "And, Sir, there is a gratification of pride. Though we cannot out-vote them we will out-argue them. They shall not do wrong without its being shown both to themselves and to the world." E: "The House of Commons is a mixed body. (I except the Minority, which I hold to be pure [smiling][6] but I take the whole House.) It is a mass by no means pure; but neither is it wholly corrupt, though there is a large proportion of cor-ruption in it. There are many members who generally go with the Minister, who will not go all lengths. There are many honest well-meaning country gentlemen who are in Parliament only to keep up the consequence of their families. Upon most of these a good speech will have influence." JOHNSON: "We are all more or less governed by interest.[7] But interest will not make us do everything. In a case which admits of doubt, we try to think on the side which is for our interest, and generally bring our-selves to act accordingly. But the subject must admit of diversity of coloring;[8] it must receive a color on that side." *** In the House of Commons there are members enough who will not vote what is grossly unjust or absurd. No, Sir, there must always be right enough, or appearance of right, to keep wrong in countenance." BOSWELL: "There is surely always a majority in Parliament who have places, or who want to have them, and who therefore will be generally ready to support government without requir-ing any pretext." E: "True, Sir; that majority will always follow

Quo clamor vocat et turba faventium."[9]

BOSWELL: "Well now, let us take the common phrase, Place-hunters.[1] I thought they had hunted without regard to anything, just as their huntsmen, the Minister, leads, looking only to the prey." J: "But taking your metaphor, you know that in hunting there are few so desperately keen as to follow without reserve. Some do not choose to leap ditches and hedges and risk their necks, or gallop over steeps, or even to dirty themselves in bogs and mire." BOSWELL: "I am glad there are some good, quiet, moderate political hunters." E: "I believe, in any body of men in England, I should have been in the Minority; I have always been in the Minority." P: "The House of Commons resembles a private company. How seldom is any man convinced

4. Importance, social standing.
5. Prime minister.
6. The party to which Burke belonged was out of power.
7. Self-interest.
8. Legitimately have two sides to it.
9. Amid the plaudits of the noisy crowd (Horace, *Odes* 3.24.46).
1. Those who sought political sinecures ("places").

by another's argument; passion and pride rise against it." R: "What would be the consequence, if a Minister, sure of a majority in the House of Commons, should resolve that there should be no speaking at all upon his side." E: "He must soon go out. That has been tried; but it was found it would not do."

E: "The Irish language is not primitive; it is Teutonic, a mixture of the northern tongues: it has much English in it." JOHNSON: "It may have been radically Teutonic; but English and High Dutch have no similarity to the eye, though radically the same. Once, when looking into Low Dutch, I found, in a whole page, only one word similar to English; *stroem*, like *stream*, and it signified *tide*." E: "I remember having seen a Dutch sonnet, in which I found this word, *roesnopies*. Nobody would at first think that this could be English; but, when we inquire, we find *roes*, rose, and *nopie*, knob; so we have *rosebuds*."

JOHNSON: "I have been reading Thicknesse's travels, which I think are entertaining." BOSWELL: "What, Sir, a good book?" JOHNSON: "Yes, Sir, to read once; I do not say you are to make a study of it and digest it; and I believe it to be a true book in his intention. All travelers generally mean to tell truth; though Thicknesse observes, upon Smollett's account[2] of his alarming a whole town in France by firing a blunderbuss, and frightening a French nobleman till he made him tie on his portmanteau, that he would be loath to say Smollett had told two lies in one page; but he had found the only town in France where these things could have happened. Travelers must often be mistaken. In everything, except where mensuration can be applied, they may honestly differ. There has been, of late, a strange turn in travelers to be displeased."

E: "From the experience which I have had—and I have had a great deal—I have learnt to think *better* of mankind." JOHNSON: "From my experience I have found them worse in commercial dealings, more disposed to cheat, than I had any notion of; but more disposed to do one another good than I had conceived." J: "Less just and more beneficent." JOHNSON: "And really it is wonderful, considering how much attention is necessary for men to take care of themselves, and ward off immediate evils which press upon them, it is wonderful how much they do for others. As it is said of the greatest liar, that he tells more truth than falsehood; so it may be said of the worst man, that he does more good than evil." BOSWELL: "Perhaps from experience men may be found *happier* than we suppose." JOHNSON: "No, Sir; the more we inquire, we shall find men the less happy." P: "As to thinking better or worse of mankind from experience, some cunning people will not be satisfied unless they have put men to the test, as they think. There is a very good story told of Sir Godfrey Kneller, in his character of a justice of the peace. A gentleman brought his servant before him, upon an accusation of having stolen some money from him; but it having come out that he had laid it purposely in the servant's way, in order to try his honesty, Sir Godfrey sent the master to prison." JOHNSON: "To resist temptation once is not a sufficient proof of honesty. If a servant, indeed, were to resist the continued temptation of silver lying in a window, as some people let it lie, when he is sure his master does not know how much there is of it, he would give a strong proof of honesty. But this is a proof to which you have no right to put a man. You know, humanly speaking, there is a certain degree of temptation which will overcome any virtue. Now, in so far as you approach temptation to a man, you do him an injury; and, if he is overcome, you share his guilt." P: "And, when once overcome, it is easier for him

2. Philip Thicknesse, *A Year's Journey through France and Spain* (1777); Tobias Smollett, *Travels in France and Italy* (1766).

to be got the better of again." BOSWELL: "Yes, you are his seducer; you have debauched him. I have known a man resolve to put friendship to the test by asking a friend to lend him money merely with that view, when he did not want it." JOHNSON: "That is very wrong, Sir. Your friend may be a narrow man, and yet have many good qualities: narrowness may be his only fault. Now you are trying his general character as a friend, by one particular singly, in which he happens to be defective, when, in truth, his character is composed of many particulars."

E: "I understand the hogshead[3] of claret, which this society was favored with by our friend the Dean, is nearly out; I think he should be written to, to send another of the same kind. Let the request be made with a happy ambiguity of expression, so that we may have the chance of his sending *it* also as a present." JOHNSON: "I am willing to offer my services as secretary on this occasion." P: "As many as are for Dr. Johnson being secretary hold up your hands.—Carried unanimously." BOSWELL: "He will be our Dictator." JOHNSON: "No, the company is to dictate to me. I am only to write for wine; and I am quite disinterested, as I drink none; I shall not be suspected of having forged the application. I am no more than humble *scribe*." E: "Then you shall *pre-scribe*." BOSWELL: "Very well. The first play of words today." J: "No, no; the *bulls* in Ireland." JOHNSON: "Were I your Dictator you should have no wine. It would be my business *cavere ne quid detrimenti Respublica caperet*,[4] and wine is dangerous. Rome was ruined by luxury" (smiling). E: "If you allow no wine as Dictator, you shall not have me for your master of horse."[5]

1791

————— ✠ —————

Hester Salusbury Thrale Piozzi
1740–1821

Hester Salusbury Thrale Piozzi: the litany of last names tells some of her story. She was born to the Salusburys, an aristocratic and in some branches wealthy Welsh family; both her parents could claim the bloodline, neither of them the wealth. So she was wed at age twenty-three to Henry Thrale, a successful English brewer twelve years her senior, for whom she neither felt nor feigned love. She accepted his proposal in order to secure for her family a large bequest that hinged on her being married. Nonetheless, she threw herself with a will into domestic life at Streatham, Henry's estate six miles outside London. She bore twelve children and mourned eight of them, dead in infancy or childhood. She worked hard helping her husband to advance his endless commercial and political aspirations. And she hosted frequent gatherings of eminent houseguests, with Samuel Johnson the most frequent and most eminent of them all. Johnson had met the Thrales in 1765 and valued them both, Henry for his affability, Hester for her wide curiosity, sharp conversation, and attentive care. For nearly two decades she made Streatham Johnson's second home, and a center of British intellectual life.

Hester Thrale had always read and written plentifully, and in her early twenties had published some short verse in newspapers. During her marriage to Thrale her writing remained mostly a matter of manuscript—occasional poems, innumerable letters, and two sustained

---

3. A large barrel.
4. "To ensure that no harm befall the republic." Johnson quotes from the *Senatus Consultum Ultimum*, a declaration of public emergency by the Roman senate. This dec-

laration suspended ordinary laws and appointed a dictator for the duration of the emergency.
5. Under the emergency decree, the master of the horse served as second in command to the dictator.

autobiographical documents: *The Family Book,* in which she recorded the progress of her off-spring, and *Thraliana,* a text more her own, in which she recorded talk, thought, experience, feeling, "and in fine, every thing that struck me at the time." Johnson had recommended the practice, and her husband had given her the handsomely bound blank books in which to pursue it. In those volumes she detailed (among many other things) her intricate connection and her frequent exasperation with both men.

At Henry's death in 1781, much changed. Helped by Johnson, Hester Thrale managed and then sold the brewery. Despite objections by Johnson, and by almost all her family and friends, she fell deeply in love for the only time in her life, with the Italian musician Gabriel Piozzi. Foreign, Roman Catholic, irascible, and not rich, Piozzi combined traits that alienated virtually everyone in Thrale's once cohesive world. Friends marveled at the sudden prevalence of passion in a woman who had once been, as one of them lamented, "the best mother, the best wife, the best friend, the most amiable member of society. . . . I am myself convinced that the poor woman is mad." So were many others, but in the summer of 1784, the "poor woman" married her beloved and departed with him for Italy, leaving in her wake a cacophony, in gossip and newsprint, of scandal and scorn.

In her new marriage and new country, Hester Piozzi launched her career as published author. She produced *Anecdotes of the Late Samuel Johnson* (1786), culled from *Thraliana;* a collection of Johnson's *Letters* (1788); *Observations and Reflections* (1789), reworked from her journal of a tour through Europe; and *British Synonomy* (1794), an anecdotal survey of the overlapping meanings of English words. Piozzi's books brought her equivocal fame at best, heavily mixed with retrospectives on her history as celebrated hostess and social renegade. She spent her last decades in England, Wales, and (after Piozzi's death) at Bath, where she once reported with amusement that a tourist had "brought his son here, that he might see the *first woman in England.* So I am now grown one of the curiosities of Bath, it seems, and *one of the Antiquities."* Her writing, though, has too much edge to pass as harmless "curiosity." When her *Anecdotes of Johnson* first appeared, Horace Walpole voiced a common complaint: "Her panegyric is loud in praise of her hero; and almost every fact she relates disgraces him." Walpole exaggerates, but the push-pull that he points to is one element that makes her work still fascinating. Again and again she immerses herself energetically in the conventional roles assigned to women ("best mother," "best wife," "best friend"), then steps aside to examine them askance, to question, to debunk, even to renounce them. Vibrating between acquiescence and anger, sentimentality and acerbity, Hester Salusbury Thrale Piozzi struck a note of her own, making for herself an interesting life, and a various and idiosyncratic body of work.

from The Family Book

[ON HER DAUGHTER'S PROGRESS]

Hester Maria Thrale born on the 17th September 1764 at her father's house, Southwark.[1]

This is to serve as a memorandum of her corporeal and mental powers at the age of two years, to which she is arrived this 17 September 1766. She can walk and run alone up and down all smooth places though pretty steep, and though the backstring[2] is still kept on it is no longer of use. She is perfectly healthy, of a lax constitution, and is strong enough to carry a hound-puppy two months old quite across the lawn at Streatham; also to carry a bowl[3] such as are used on bowling greens up the mount to the tubs.[4] She is neither remarkably big nor tall, being just 34 inches high, but eminently pretty. She can speak most words and speak them plain enough too, but is no

---

1. In this borough across the river from London, the Thrales owned a city home adjacent to their brewery.
2. A cord at the back of the pinafore, sometimes held like a leash to keep the infant from harm.
3. A bowling ball.
4. Watering troughs.

great talker. She repeats the Pater Noster,[5] the three Christian virtues[6] and the signs of the zodiac in Watt's verses;[7] she likewise knows them on the globe perfectly well. She can tell all her letters great and small and spell little words as D,o,g, Dog, C,a,t, Cat etc. She knows her nine figures and the simplest combinations of 'em as 3, 4, 34; 6, 8, 68; but none beyond a hundred. She knows all the heathen deities by their attributes and counts 20 without missing one. Signed—H. L. Thrale.

Sponsors[8] to H. M. T.: Mrs. Salusbury, Mrs. Nesbitt, and Sir John Lade.

* * *

Hester Maria Thrale,   London 17 March 1767.

Six months have now elapsed since I wrote down an account of what she could do; the following is for a record of the amazing improvements made in this last half year; her person has however undergone no visible change. She cannot read at all, but knows the compass as perfectly as any mariner upon the seas; is mistress of the solar system, can trace the orbits, and tell the arbitrary marks of the planets as readily as Dr. Bradley.[9] The comets she knows at sight when represented upon paper, and all the chief constellations on the celestial globe. The signs of the zodiac she is thoroughly acquainted with, as also the difference between the ecliptic and equator. She has too by the help of the dissected maps acquired so nice a knowledge of geography as to be well able to describe not only the four quarters of the world, but almost, nay, I do think every nation on the terrestrial globe, and all the principal islands in all parts of the world. These—with the most remarkable seas, gulfs, straits, etc.—she has so full an acquaintance with, that she discovers them colored, or penciled, separate or together in any scale small or great, map or globe. She can repeat likewise the names of all the capital cities in Europe besides those of Persia and India—China I mean; also the 3 Christian virtues in English, the 4 cardinal ones in Latin[1], the 1st page of Lily's Grammar[2] to the bottom, the seven days of the week, the 12 months of the Year, the twos of the multiplication table, the four points of the compass, the four quarters of the world, the Pater Noster, the Nicene Creed and the Decalogue;[3] the responses of the church catechism to the end of the duty to our neighbor, and the names of the richest, wisest, and meekest man, etc. She has also in these last six months learned to distinguish colors, and to name them; as also to tell a little story with some grace and emphasis, as the story of the Fall of Man, of Perseus and Andromeda, of the Judgment of Paris, and two or three more. These are certainly uncommon performances of a baby 2 years and 6 months only; but they are most strictly true. She cannot however read at all. * * *

17 September 1767. A little blue-cover book will now best show the further acquisitions of Hester M. Thrale who has this day completed the second and begun the third[4] year of her life by repeating all the responses in that book by heart—this 17 September 1767 at Brighthelmstone.[5] She is yet a miserable poor speller, and can scarce read a word.

* * *

17 December 1768. Hester Maria Thrale is this day four years and a quarter old. I have made her up a little red book to which I must appeal for her progress in improvements. She went through it this day quite well. The astronomical part is the

---

5. The Lord's Prayer.
6. Faith, hope, and charity (1 Corinthians 13.13).
7. Isaac Watts, poet and hymnist whose *Divine Songs for the Use of Children* (1715) includes a poem on the zodiac.
8. Godparents.
9. James Bradley (1693–1762), eminent astronomer.

1. Prudence, temperance, fortitude, and justice.
2. A Latin textbook.
3. The Ten Commandments.
4. I.e., completed the third and begun the fourth.
5. Brighton, a popular seaside resort, where the Thrales kept a house for use each autumn.

hardest. She can now read tolerably, but not at sight, and has a manner of reading that is perfectly agreeable, free from tone or accent. At 3 years and a half however she wrote some cards to her friends with a print taken from the picture which Zoffany[6] drew of her at 20 months old; but as I lay in[7] soon after, the writing was totally forgotten, and is now all to begin again. She has this day repeated her catechism quite through, her Latin grammar to the end of the 5 declensions, a fable in Phaedrus, an epigram in Martial,[8] the revolutions, diameters, and distance of the planets. She is come vastly forward in sense and expression and once more I appeal to her little red book. With regard to her person, it is accounted exquisitely pretty. Her hair is sandy, her eyes of a very dark blue, and their luster particularly fine; her complexion delicate, and her carriage[9] uncommonly genteel. Her temper is not so good; reserved to all, insolent where she is free, and sullen to those who teach or dress or do anything towards her. Never in a passion, but obstinate to that uncommon degree that no punishment except severe smart[1] can prevail on her to beg pardon if she has offended.

[ON THE DEATH OF HER SON]

[March 1776] On Thursday the 21st they all[1] rose well and lively, and Queeney went with me to fetch her sister from school for a week. She seemed sullen all the way there and back but not sick, so I huffed her and we got home in good time to dress for dinner, when we expected Sir Robert Cotton and the Davenants.[2] Harry however had seen a play of his friend Murphy's[3] advertised, and teased me so to let him see it that I could not resist his importunity, and treated one of our principal clerks to go with him. He came home at 12 o'clock half mad with delight, and in such spirits, health, and happiness that nothing ever exceeded. Queeney however drooped all afternoon, complained of the headache, and Mr. Thrale was so cross at my giving Harry leave to go to the play, instead of showing him to Sir Robert, that I passed an uneasy time of it, and could not enjoy the praises given to Susan, I was so fretted about the two eldest. When Harry came home so happy, however, all was forgotten, and he went to rest in perfect tranquility. Queeney however felt hot, and I was not at all pleased with her, but on Friday morning the boy rose quite cheerful and did our little business with great alacrity. Count Manucci[4] came to breakfast by appointment. We were all to go show him the Tower[5] forsooth, so Queeney made light of her illness and pressed me to take her too. There was one of the ships bound for Boston now in the river with our beer aboard.[6] Harry ran to see the blaze in the morning and coming back to the counting-house, "I see," he says to our first clerk, "I see your porter[7] is good, Mr. Perkins, for it *burns* special well." Well by this time we set out for the Tower, Papa and Manucci and the children and I. Queeney was not half well, but Harry continued in high spirits both among the lions and the arms, repeating passages from the English history, examining the artillery and getting into every mortar[8]

---

6. Johann Zoffany (1733–1810), a portraitist much in demand by royal, aristocratic, and merchant families (see his portrait of Queen Charlotte and her children, Color Plate 22).
7. Gave birth (to her fourth child) and convalesced.
8. Phaedrus translated Aesop's *Fables* from Greek into Latin; Martial was a Roman poet celebrated for his short, witty verses.
9. Bearing
1. I.e., a whipping (with a rod that was kept on the nursery mantle).
1. I.e., the three children now at home: Hester

("Queeney"), Henry (the only son, now nine years old), and Sophy (four); the sister at school was Susan (five).
2. Cousins of Hester Thrale.
3. Arthur Murphy (1727–1805), Irish actor, playwright, and friend of the family.
4. A Florentine nobleman whom the Thrales had first met in Paris.
5. Of London.
6. Carrying a cargo of beer from the Thrale brewery; while in the river, the ship had caught fire.
7. Dark beer.
8. Cannon.

till he was as black as the ground. Count Manucci observed his pranks, and said he must be a soldier with him; but Harry would not fight for the Grand Duke of Tuscany because he was a Papist, and "Look here," said he, showing the instruments of torture to the Count, "what those Spanish Papists intended for us." From the place we drove to Moore's Carpet Manufactory, where the boy was still active, attentive, and lively. But as Queeney's looks betrayed the sickness she would fain have concealed, we drove homewards, taking in our way Brooke's Menagerie, where I just stopped to speak about my peafowl. Here Harry was happy again with a lion intended for a show who was remarkably tame, and a monkey so beautiful and gentle, that I was as much pleased with him as the children. Here we met a Mr. Hervey who took notice of the boy how well he looked. "Yes," said I, "if the dirt were scraped off him." It was now time to get home, and Harry after saying how hungry he was, instantly "pounced" as he called it on a piece of cold mutton and spent the afternoon among us all recounting the pleasures of the day. He went to bed that night as perfectly well as ever I saw man, woman, or child in my life. Queeney however took some rhubarb, and went on drooping and felt feverish. I looked at her two or three times in the night too, and found her hot and feverish, but her dear brother slept as cool and comfortable as possible, and on the morning of the next fatal day, Saturday 23rd of March 1776, he rose in perfect health, went to the baker for his roll and watched the drawing it out of the oven, carried it to Bachelor's Hall, as he called it where the young clerks live down the brewhouse yard; there he got butter, and cooked a merry breakfast among them. After this he returned with two penny cakes he had bought for the little girls, and distributed them between them in his pleasant manner for[9] minuets that he made them dance. I was all this while waiting on Queeney, who seemed far from well, and I was once very impatient at the noise the maids and children made in the nursery, by laughing excessively at his antic tricks. By this time I came down to my dressing room to tutor Sophy till the clock struck ten which is my regular breakfast hour. I had scarce made the tea when Moll came to tell me Queeney was better, and Harry making a figure of 5:10,[1] so we always called his manner of twisting about when anything ailed him. When I got to the nursery, there was Harry crying as if he had been whipped instead of ill, so I reproved him for making such a bustle about nothing, and said, "See how differently your sister behaves," who though in earnest far from well, had begged to make breakfast for Papa and Mr. Baretti,[2] while I was employed above. The next thing I did was to send for Mr. Lawrence of York Buildings, to whom Nurse was always partial.[3] My note expressed to him that both the eldest children were ill, but Hetty worst. Presently, however, finding the boy inclined to vomit, I administered a large wine glass of emetic wine, which however did nothing any way, though he drank small liquids with avidity. And now, seeing his sickness increase, and his countenance begin to alter, I sent out Sam with orders not to come back without some physician—Jebb, Bromfield, Pinkstan, or Lawrence of Essex Street, whichever he could find. In the mean time I plunged Harry into water as hot as could easily be borne, up to his middle, and had just taken him out of the tub and laid him in a warm bed, when Jebb came, and gave him first hot wine, then usquebaugh,[4] then Daffy's Elixir,[5] so fast that it alarmed me, though I had no notion of Death, having seen him so perfectly well at 9 o'clock. He then had poultices made with mustard put to his

9. In exchange for.
1. I.e., bent in half, with knees pulled in to the chest.
2. Giuseppe Baretti (1719–1789), Italian scholar and author, a close friend of Henry Thrale.

3. Herbert Lawrence was a local physician; "Nurse" took care of the Thrale children.
4. Whiskey.
5. A laxative.

feet, and strong broth and wine clysters[6] injected, but we could get no evacuation any way, and the inclination to vomit still continuing, Jebb gave him five grains of ipecacuanha[7] and then drove away to call Heberden's help.[8] The child all this while spoke well and brisk, sat upright to talk with the doctors, and said he had no pain now but his breath was short. This I attributed to the hot things he had taken, and thought Jebb in my heart far more officious than wise. I was however all confusion, distress, and perplexity, and Mr. Thrale bid me not cry so, for I should look like a hag when I went to Court next day. He often saw Harry in the course of the morning, and apprehended no danger at all. No more did Baretti, who said he should be whipped for frighting his mother for nothing. Queeney had for some time been laid down on her own bed, and got up fancying herself better. But soon a universal shriek called us all together to Harry's bedside, where he struggled a moment—thrusting his finger down his throat to excite vomiting—and then, turning to Nurse, said very distinctly, "Don't scream so—I *know* I must die."

This however I did not hear. Lady Lade, who I believe had been here half the morning watching the event, asked me kindly what she should do for me. I replied, "Oh take me these two little girls away—they distract me." She accordingly then carried them off and set 'em safe at Kensington, where they are still. This most dreadful of all our misfortunes, which they say happened about 3 o'clock or 4, on the 23rd day of March 1776, had such an effect on poor Queeney that I expected her to follow him. Jebb however did something for her, and advising speedy change of scene, I rose in the morning of the 30th after a sleepless night, and in a sort of desperation drove away with her to Bath, which little journey did her infinite service. Baretti kindly offered to go with me, so he conducted the troop and diverted Queeney's melancholy with all the tricks he could think on. She is now—though not recovered—yet I hope out of danger (as the phrase is). I saw the little girls at Kensington yesterday as I came home. This is the 9th of April 1776.

[ON HER MARRIAGE AND HOUSEHOLD]

25 September 1778. My eldest daughter Hester Maria was measured, and found of a pleasing and sufficient height. She was this last birthday, 17 September 1778, fourteen years old. She is very pretty still, but is of a pale complection. Her person, mind, and temper have never indeed suffered any considerable changes. Her face and figure are very lovely, her mind very highly cultivated, and her temper haughty and contemptuous. She is blue-eyed, fair-haired, has a good set of teeth, good shape, and the carriage of a girl of fashion. Books are her delight, and she chooses her own studies now for me, who do not interfere much—nor would she suffer[1] me. She is my Mistress completely, but has I think no great influence over her Papa. We kept her birthday merrily, gave old Nurse money, and she treated the servants with a dance. If my Master's mad management does not bereave us all of all our property,[2] she stands foremost now to inherit our possessions, and *mine* thank God are entailed.[3] Little as they are, and greatly as Mr. Thrale despises them, they may become our best friends, and he will take the swiftest methods to make them so, by feeding the brew house with its own flesh till it perishes with a sudden and dreadful ruin.

6. Enemas.
7. A purgative.
8. William Heberden, one of the best physicians in London.
1. Allow.
2. "My Master" is Henry Thrale, who often spent more capital than his brewery could afford, in an obsessive attempt to surpass his competitors.
3. Secured by law to be inherited by her husband and children. She is mistaken here, and later reclaimed the property for herself and her second husband.

* * *

This is the last day of the year 1778. My children are all about me and my house is full of friends. Susan and I read two acts of Molière's *Bourgeois*[4] today. She understands it to a miracle, and translates with some idea even of giving an English turn to the idiom, or an English idiom to the phrase. Sophy reads English narrative to amuse herself perfectly well without any tone or drawl; they both work well, and write very prettily, spelling as exactly as myself. Sue can do sums in the three first rules of arithmetic; pounds, shillings, and pence quite readily, and pretends to tinkle the harpsichord, but I think she has for that affair neither ear nor fingers. Susan's geographical and grammatical knowledge amazes even me, but she never will dance I think. When Sophy gets a good master[5] she will be eminent in that art. Hester is well—and beautiful, Susan is a pretty girl as need be, Cecilia is much liked, and Harriett quite a cherubim. Sophy is much the plainest as to countenance but her form is most complete and her temper enchanting. Hester and Susan are touchy, moody, and capricious.

Mr. Thrale is once more happy in his mind, and at leisure to be so in love with S.S.[6] that it is comical. She is a charming young creature; everybody must love her. We have her, and F. Browne and Murphy and Seward and the Davenants and Johnson here, besides Tom Cotton and occasional comers in.

I think I am again pregnant, I think I am; then let us conclude the old year with humble thanks to almighty God for all his mercies through Jesus Christ our Lord, and most of all for the health of my dear children, and for the boon I hope I have obtained by my prayers and tears—that I shall never follow any more of my offspring to the grave—Amen Lord Jesus!

Amen!

if so—I will not fret about this rival this S.S. no I won't.[7]

1766–1778   1976

from **Thraliana**

[FIRST ENTRIES]

It is many years since Doctor Samuel Johnson advised me to get a little book, and write in it all the little anecdotes which might come to my knowledge, all the observations I might make or hear; all the verses never likely to be published, and in fine every thing which struck me at the time. Mr. Thrale has now treated me with a repository, and provided it with the pompous title of Thraliana.[1] I must endeavor to fill it with nonsense new and old. 15 September 1776.

Bob Lloyd[2] used to say that a parent or other person devoted to the care and instruction of youth, led the life of a finger post, still fixed to one disagreeable spot himself, while his whole business was only to direct others in the way.

An old man's child, says Johnson, leads much the same sort of life as a child's dog, teased like that with fondness through folly, and exhibited like that to every company, through idle and empty vanity.

---

4. The comedy *Le Bourgeois Gentilhomme* (1671) by the French playwright Molière.
5. Teacher.
6. Sophia Streatfield (1754–1835); noted for her beauty and for her accomplished Greek scholarship, she had become a family friend, a godparent to Henrietta, and an obsession of Henry Thrale's.
7. The Family Book ends here.
1. He had given his wife six leather-bound blank volumes, each displaying the "pompous title" on its cover, on a red label stamped with gold lettering.
2. A poet.

I have heard Johnson observe that as education is often compared to agriculture, so it resembles it chiefly in this: that though no one can tell whether the crop may answer the culture,[3] yet if nothing be sowed, we all see that no crop can be obtained.

* * *

[Brighton, July–August 1780] I have picked up Piozzi[4] here, the great Italian singer; he shall teach Hester. She will have some powers in the musical way I believe. Her voice though not strong is sweet and flexible, her taste correct, and her expression pleasing. The other two girls leave me tomorrow; they will do very well; Susan is three parts a Beauty, and quite a Scholar for ten Years old. * * *

I dread the general election more than ever. Mr. Thrale is now well enough to canvass in person, and 'twill kill him.[5] Had it happened when he *could not absolutely* have stirred, we would have done it for him, but now! Well! One should not however anticipate misfortunes, they will come time enough.

* * *

[8 August 1780] Piozzi is become a prodigious favorite with me. He is so intelligent a creature, so discerning, one can't help wishing for his good opinion. His singing surpasses everybody's for taste, tenderness, and true elegance. His hand on the fortepiano too is so soft, so sweet, so delicate, every tone goes to one's heart I think, and fills the mind with emotions one would not be without, though inconvenient enough sometimes. I made him sing yesterday, and though he says his voice is gone, I cannot somehow or other get it out of my ears—odd enough!

These were the Verses he sung to me.

> *Amor—non sò che sia,*
> *Ma sò che è un traditor;*
> *Cosa è la gelosia?*
> *Non l'hò provato ancor.*

> *La donna mi vien detto*
> *Fà molto sospirar;*
> *Ed Io poveretto,*
> *Men' voglio innamorar.*

I instantly translated them for him, and made him sing them in English thus all'Improviso.

> For Love—I can't abide it,
> The treacherous rogue I know;
> Distrust!—I never tried it
> Whether t'would sting or no.

> For Flavia many sighs are,
> Sent up by sad despair.
> And yet poor simple I Sir
> Am hasting to the snare.

---

3. I.e., will prove worth the care expended on it.
4. "He is amazingly like my father" [Thrale's note]. Born near Venice, Gabriel Piozzi (1740–1809) had now lived in England for about four years, giving concerts and teaching voice.
5. Henry Thrale was running for Parliament; he ended up finishing third in a field of three.

[October–November 1780] Here is Sophy Streatfield again, handsomer than ever, and flushed with new conquests: the Bishop of Chester feels her power I am sure. She showed me a letter from him that was as tender, and had all the *tokens* upon it as strong as ever I remember to have seen 'em. I repeated to her out of Pope's Homer. "Very well Sophy," says I,

> "Range undisturbed among the hostile crew,
> But touch not *Hinchliffe*, Hinchliffe is *my* due."[6]

"Miss Streatfield," says my Master, "could have quoted these lines *in the Greek*." His saying so piqued me; and piqued me because it was true. I wish I understood Greek! Mr. Thrale's preference of her to me never vexed me so much as my consciousness— or fear at least—that he had *reason* for his preference. She has ten times my beauty, and five times my scholarship. Wit and knowledge has she none.

How fond some people are of riding in a carriage! Those most I think who had from beginning least chance of keeping one. Johnson dotes on a coach; so do many people indeed. I never get into any vehicle, but for the sake of being conveyed to some place, or some person. The motion is unpleasing to me in itself, and the straitness[7] of the room makes it inconvenient. Conversation too is almost wholly precluded, the grinding of the wheels hinders one from hearing, and the necessity of raising one's voice makes it less comfortable to talk. A book is better than a friend in a carriage—and a carriage is the only place where it is so.

* * *

[10 December 1780] We have got a sort of literary curiosity amongst us; the foul copy of Pope's Homer,[8] with all his old intended verses, sketches, emendations etc. Strange that a man should keep such things! Stranger still that a woman should write such a book as this; put down every occurrence of her life, every emotion of her heart, and call it a *Thraliana* forsooth—but then I mean to destroy it.

All wood and wire behind the scenes[9] sure enough! One sees that Pope labored as hard—

> as if the Stagyrite o'erlooked each line[1]

indeed, and how very little effect those glorious verses at the end of the 8th book of the *Iliad* have upon one, when one sees 'em all in their cradles and clouts;[2] and "light" changed for "bright"—and then the whole altered again, and the line must end with "night"—and Oh Dear! thus—*torturing one poor word a thousand ways*.[3]

Johnson says 'tis pleasant to see the progress of such a mind. True; but 'tis a malicious pleasure, such as men feel when they watch a woman at her toilet[4] and

> see by degrees a purer blush arise, *etc.*[5]

Wood and wire once more! Wood and wire!—

* * *

6. "Rage uncontrolled through all the hostile crew / But touch not Hector; Hector is my due"; Achilles's instructions to Patroclus in Pope's translation of Homer's *Iliad* (16.113). John Hinchliffe was Bishop of Peterborough and a friend of the family.
7. Narrowness
8. The manuscript draft of Pope's translation of the *Iliad* (see page 2523). Johnson was consulting it for his biography of Pope (see page 2811).

9. I.e., backstage at a theater.
1. Pope's *Essay on Criticism* (line 138). The "Stagyrite" is Aristotle, the Greek philosopher Pope here invokes as the ultimate arbiter of literary judgment.
2. Diapers.
3. Dryden, *Mac Flecknoe* (line 208).
4. Dressing table.
5. From Pope's description of Belinda in *The Rape of the Lock* (1.143).

[January 1781] What an odd partiality I have for a rough character! and even for the hard parts of a soft one! Fanny Burney[6] has secured my heart. I now love her with a fond and firm affection, besides my esteem of her parts,[7] and my regard for her father. Her lofty spirit—dear Creature!—has quite subdued mine; and I adore her for the pride which once revolted me. There is no true affection, no friendship in the sneakers and fawners. 'Tis not for obsequious civility that I delight in Johnson or Hinchliffe, Sir Richard Jebb or Piozzi, who has as much spirit *in his way* as the best of them—great solidity of mind too I think, some sarcasm, and wonderful discernment in that rough Italian. I will do him all the service I can.

[10 January 1781] I will now write out the Characters of the people who are intended to have their portraits hung up in the Library here at Streatham.[8] * * *

My own and my eldest daughter's portraits in one picture come next, and are to be placed over the chimney.[9]

> In features so placid, so smooth, so serene,
> What trace of the wit or the Welsh-woman's seen?
> Of the temper sarcastic, the flattering tongue,
> The sentiment right—with th' occasion still wrong.
> What trace of the tender, the rough, the refined,
> The soul in which all contrarieties joined?
> Where though merriment loves over method to rule,
> Religion resides, and the virtues keep school;
> Till when tired we condemn her dogmatical air,
> Like a rocket she rises, and leaves us to stare.
> To such contradictions d'ye wish for a clue?
> Keep vanity still—that vile passion—in view.
> For 'tis thus the slow miner his fortune to make,
> Of arsenic thin scattered pursues the pale track;
> Secure where that poison pollutes the rich ground,
> That it points to the soil where some silver is found.

The portrait of my eldest daughter deserves better lines than these which follow. She is a valuable girl.

> Of a virgin so tender the face or the fame,
> Alike would be injured by praise or by blame.
> To the world's fiery trial too early consigned,
> She soon shall experience it, cruel or kind.
>
> His concern thus the anxious enameller hides,
> And his well finished work to the furnace confides;
> But jocund resumes it secure from decay,
> If the colors stand firm on the dangerous day.

* * *

6. Frances Burney (1752–1840), diarist and novelist. Her first novel, *Evelina, or a Young Lady's Entrance into the World* (1778), brought her to the attention and admiration of the Streatham circle.
7. Intellect.
8. The 13 paintings, by Sir Joshua Reynolds, had been commissioned by Henry Thrale. They depicted his wife, daughter, and distinguished friends, including Johnson, Burke, Baretti, and Reynolds himself. A "character" is a word portrait; Hester Thrale wrote one in verse for each person Reynolds depicted.
9. Her verse self-portrait follows.

One Page more I see ends the 3d Volume of Thraliana! strange farrago as it is of sense, nonsense, public, private follies—but chiefly my own—and *I* the little Hero etc. Well! but who should be the Hero of an *Ana?* Let me vindicate my own vanity if it be with my last pen. This volume will be finished at Streatham and be left there— where I may never more return to dwell!

Mr. Thrale *may* die,[1] and not leave me sufficient to keep Streatham open as it has been kept, and I shall hate to live in it with more thought about expenses than I have done. I *may* indeed be left sole mistress of the brewhouse to manage for my girls, but that I hardly think will be the case; and if not so, why Farewell pretty Streatham, where I have spent many a merry hour, and many a sad one.

My poor little old Aunt at Bath is dying too, and I am dolt enough to be sincerely sorry, the more as her past kindnesses claim that personal attendance from me, which Mr. Thrale will not permit me to pay her—poor, little, old, insipid, useless creature! May God Almighty in his mercy, pity, receive and bless her, as a most inoffensive atom of humanity—for whom his only Son consented to be crucified, and among whose flock she has most innocently fed for sixty or seventy years.—

Here closes the third volume

Streatham
Monday 29 January 1781.

[THE DEATH OF HENRY THRALE; MARRIAGE TO GABRIEL PIOZZI]

[Sunday 18 March 1781] Well! Now I have experienced the delights of a London winter spent in the bosom of flattery, gaiety, and Grosvenor Square. 'Tis a poor thing however, and leaves a void in the mind; but I have had my compting-house[1] duties to attend, my sick Master to watch, my little children to look after—and how much good have I done in any way? Not a scrap as I can see. The pecuniary affairs have gone on perversely: how should they choose when the sole proprietor is incapable of giving orders, yet not so far incapable as to be set aside! Distress, fraud, folly meet me at every turn, and I am not able to fight against them all, though endued with an iron constitution which shakes not by sleepless nights, or days severely fretted. Mr. Thrale talks now of going to Spa and Italy again. How shall we drag him thither? A man who cannot keep awake four hours at a stroke, who can scarce retain the Feces etc. Well! This will indeed be a trial of one's patience; and who must go with us on this expedition? Mr. Johnson! He will indeed be the only happy person of the party. He values nothing under heaven but his own mind, which is a spark *from* Heaven; and *that* will be invigorated by the addition of new ideas. If Mr. Thrale dies on the road, Johnson will console himself by learning *how it is* to travel with a corpse—and after all, such reasoning is the true philosophy—one's heart is a mere encumbrance. Would I could leave mine behind. The children shall go to their sisters at Kensington. Mrs. Cumyns[2] may take care of 'em all. God grant us a happy Meeting! Some *where* and some *time!*

Baretti should attend I think. There is no man who has so much of *every* language, and can manage so well with Johnson, and is so tidy on the road, so active too to obtain good accommodations. He is the man in the world I think whom I most abhor, and who hates, and professes to hate me the most. But what does that signify? He will be careful of Mr. Thrale and Hester whom he *does* love—and he won't strangle me I suppose. It

---

1. He had suffered a series of strokes.
1. Bookkeeping. During her husband's final illness, Thrale was helping to manage the brewery.

2. A childhood friend, who now ran a school which Sophia and Susan Thrale attended.

will be very convenient to have him. Somebody we must have. Croza would court our Daughter, and Piozzi could not talk to Johnson, nor I suppose do one any good, but sing to one—and how should we sing *songs in a strange land?* Baretti must be the man, and I will beg it of him as a favor. Oh the triumph he will have! and the lies that he will tell!

If I die abroad I shall leave all my papers in charge with Fanny Burney. I have at length conquered all her scruples, and won her confidence and her heart. 'Tis the most valuable conquest I ever *did* make, and dearly, very dearly, do I love my little *Tayo,* so the people at Otaheite[3] call a *bosom friend.* She is now satisfied of my affection, and has no reserves, no ill opinion, no further notion I shall insult her sweetness. I now respect her caution, and esteem her above all living women. Mrs. Byron will half break her heart at my going. Mrs. Lambart is going herself.[4]

No danger of all these distresses it seems. Mr. Thrale died on the 4th of April 1781.[5]

* * *

[20 September 1782] Now! That little dear discerning creature Fanny Burney says I'm in love with Piozzi—very likely! He is so amiable, so honorable, so much above his situation by his abilities, that if

> Fate hadn't fast bound her
> With Styx nine times round her
> Sure Music and Love were victorious.[6]

But if he is ever so worthy, ever so lovely, he is *below me* forsooth. In what is he below me? In virtue—I would I were above him. In understanding—I would mine were from this instant under the guardianship of his. In birth—to be sure, he is below me in birth, and so is almost every man I know, or have a chance to know. But he is below me in fortune—is mine sufficient for us both? More than amply so. Does he deserve it by his conduct in which he has always united warm notions of honor with cool attention to economy, the spirit of a gentleman with the talents of a professor? How shall any man deserve fortune if he does not? But I am the guardian of five daughters by Mr. Thrale, and must not disgrace their name and family. Was then the man my mother chose for me of higher extraction than him I have chosen for myself? No. But his fortune was higher. I wanted fortune then perhaps, do I want it now? Not at all. But I am not to think about myself. I married the first time to please my mother, I must marry the second time to please my daughter.[7] I have always sacrificed my own choice to that of others, so I must sacrifice it again. But why? Oh because I am a woman of superior understanding, and must not for the world degrade myself from my situation in life. But if I have superior understanding, let me at least make use of it for once, and rise to the rank of a human being conscious of its own power to discern good from ill. The person who has uniformly acted by the will of others, has hardly that dignity to boast. * * *

[4 November 1782] Sir Richard Musgrave[8] has sent me proposals of marriage from Ireland. His wife is dying at least if not dead, and he is in haste for a better. He will get *me* to be sure!! a likely matter! when my head is full of nothing but my children—my heart of my beloved Piozzi! * * *

---

3. Tahiti, where Burney's brother James had traveled on one of Captain James Cook's expeditions.
4. Sophia Byron and Elizabeth Lambart were Thrale's close friends and frequent correpondents.
5. Thrale set down these two sentences at the center of a blank page.
6. Pope, *Ode for Music, on St. Cecelia's Day* (lines 90–92).

The passage describes Eurydice, momentarily freed from her imprisonment in the underworld by the enchanting music of her lover Orpheus.
7. Queeney, who objected vehemently to the prospect of her mother's marriage to Piozzi.
8. Irish baronet and member of Parliament, whom Thrale had met at Bath in 1776.

[Brighthelmstone, Saturday, 16 November 1782] For him I have been contented to reverse the laws of Nature, and request of my child that concurrence which at my age (and a widow) I am not required either by divine or human institutions to ask even of a parent. The life I gave her she may now more than repay, only by agreeing to what she will with difficulty prevent, and which if she does prevent, will give her lasting remorse—for those who stab *me* shall hear me groan—whereas if she will—but how can she?—gracefully, or even compassionately consent, if she will go abroad with me upon the chance of his death or mine preventing our union, and live with me till she is of age—perhaps there is no heart so callous by avarice, no soul so poisoned by prejudice, no head so feathered by foppery, that will forbear to excuse her when she returns to the rich and the gay, for having saved the life of a mother through compliance extorted by anguish, contrary to the received opinions of the world.

[Brighthelmstone, 19 November 1782] What is above written, though intended only to unload my heart by writing it, I showed in a transport of passion to Queeney and to Burney. Sweet Fanny Burney cried herself half blind over it, said there was no resisting such pathetic eloquence, and that if she was the daughter instead of the friend, she should be even tempted to attend me to the altar. But that while she possessed her reason, nothing should seduce her to approve what reason itself would condemn: that children, religion, situation, country and character—besides the diminution of fortune by the certain loss of £800 a year were too much to sacrifice to any *one* man. If however I were resolved to make the sacrifice, *à la bonne heure!*[9] It was an astonishing proof of an attachment, very difficult for mortal man to repay.

I will talk no more of it.

* * *

[29 January 1783] Adieu to all that's dear, to all that's lovely. I am parted from my Life, my Soul! my Piozzi: *Sposo promesso! Amante adorato! Amico senza equale.*[1] If I can get health and strength to write my story here, 'tis all I wish for now! Oh Misery!

The cold dislike of my eldest daughter I thought might wear away by familiarity with his merit, and that we might live tolerably together or at least part friends, but no. Her aversion increased daily, and she communicated it to the others. They treated *me* insolently, and *him* very strangely—running away whenever he came as if they saw a serpent, and plotting with their governess, a cunning Italian, how to invent lies to make me hate him, and twenty such narrow tricks. By these means the notion of my partiality took air—and whether Miss Thrale sent him word slyly, or not I cannot tell; but on the 25 January 1783 Mr. Crutchley[2] came hither to *conjure* me not to go to Italy: he had heard *such* things he said, and by *means* next to *miraculous.* The next day, Sunday 26, Fanny Burney came, said I must marry him instantly, or give him up; that my reputation would be lost else. I actually groaned with anguish, threw myself on the bed in an agony which my fair daughter beheld with frigid indifference. She had indeed never by one tender word endeavored to dissuade me from the match, but said coldly that if I *would* abandon my children, I *must;* that their father had not deserved such treatment from me; that I should be punished by Piozzi's neglect, for that she knew he hated me, and that I turned out my offspring to chance for his sake like puppies in a pond to swim or drown according as Providence pleased; that for her part she must look herself out a place like the other servants, for my face would she

9. Fine! Good for you! (French.)
1. Promised husband, adored lover, friend without equal.

2. Jeremiah Crutchley, one of the executors of Henry Thrale's will.

never see more. "Nor write to me?" said I. "I shall not Madam," replied she with a cold sneer, "easily find *out your address*, for you are going you know not whither I believe." Susan and Sophy said nothing at all, but they taught the two little ones to cry, "Where are you going Mama? Will you leave us, and die as our poor papa did?" There was no standing *that*, so I wrote my lover word that my mind was all distraction, and bid him come to me the next morning my birthday, 27 January. Mean time I took a vomit, and spent the Sunday night in torture not to be described. My falsehood to my Piozzi, my strong affection for him, the incapacity I felt in myself to resign the man I so adored, the hopes I had so cherished, inclined me strongly to set them all at defiance, and go with him to Church to sanctify the promises I had so often made him, while the idea of abandoning the children of my first husband, who left me so nobly provided for, and who depended on my attachment to his offspring, awakened the voice of conscience, and threw me on my knees to pray for *his* direction who was hereafter to judge my conduct.

His grace illuminated me, his power strengthened me; and I flew to my daughter's bed in the morning and told, told her my resolution to resign my own, my dear, my favorite purposes; and to prefer my children's interest to my love. She questioned my ability to make the sacrifice; said one word from him would undo all my[3] * * *

[27 June 1784] My daughters parted with me at last prettily enough *considering* (as the phrase is). We shall perhaps be still better friends apart than together. Promises of correspondence and kindness were very sweetly reciprocated, and the eldest wished for Piozzi's safe return obligingly.[4]

I fancy two days more will absolutely bring him to Bath—The present moments are critical and dreadful, and would shake stronger nerves than mine. Oh Lord strengthen me to do thy will I pray.

[28 June] I am not *yet sure* of seeing him again—not *sure* he lives, not *sure* he loves me, *yet*. Should any thing happen *now!!* Oh I will not trust myself with such a fancy—it will either kill me, or drive me distracted.

[2 July] The happiest day of my whole life I think. Yes, *quite* the happiest.[5] My Piozzi came home yesterday and dined with me. But my spirits were too much agitated, my heart too much dilated, I was too painfully happy *then*. My sensations are more quiet today, and my felicity less tumultuous. I have spent the night as I ought in prayer and Thanksgiving. Could I have slept, I had not deserved such blessings. May the Almighty but preserve them to me! He lodges at our old house on the South Parade. His companion Mecci[6] is a faithless treacherous fellow—but no matter! 'Tis all over now.

[Bath, 25 July] I am returned from church the happy wife of my lovely, my faithful Piozzi, subject of my prayers, object of my wishes, my sighs, my reverence, my esteem.

His nerves have been horribly shaken, but he lives, he loves me, and will be mine *for ever*. He has sworn it in the face of God and the whole Christian Church: Catholics, Protestants, all are witnesses. May he who has preserved us thus long for each other give us a long life together—and so I hope and trust he will through the merits of Jesus Christ. Amen.

---

3. The remainder of the entry is lost, because the next page is missing. Informed of Thrale's decision, Piozzi left for Italy. Negotiations between mother and daughter continued for another year, until Queeney finally capitulated on the grounds that Thrale's agitation was endangering her health. The daughters were to remain in England, looked after by the trustees of their father's estate;

the mother would reside with her new husband in Italy.
4. He was now returning from Italy to England.
5. For Johnson's admonitory letter on this same date, see page 2825.
6. Francesco Mecci, a teacher of Italian, whom Thrale apparently suspected of trying to prevent the marriage.

[London, 3 September] I have now been six weeks married, and enjoyed greater and longer felicity than I ever yet experienced. To crown all, my dear daughters Susanna and Sophia have spent the day with myself and my amiable husband. We part in peace, and love, and harmony, and tomorrow I set off for the finest country in the world, in company with the most excellent man in it.

Some natural tears they dropped, but wiped 'em soon. Milton.[7]

* * *

[THE DEATH OF JOHNSON]

[Milan, January 1785] The new year is begun. May God prosper it to my husband, my children, and myself. I went to church and prayed most fervently for their happiness.

My Piozzi is not well. He has no disorder though that shortens life, notwithstanding the uneasiness it occasions him. Strong fibers with weak nerves produce all his sufferings, and add to his natural irritability. The constant complaints too which he makes of his health take off from the envy his situation would otherwise provoke, but he is best on a journey. I shall like to go to Venice in the spring—if nothing prevents me, *which I should like still better*. Praying for children is wrong however, and I will do it no more. I used to weary Heaven with requests for pregnancy, and now!! all I begged for are in the grave almost, and those that are left, love not *me*.

I had letters the other day indeed of which I ought not to complain. Susan and Sophy's kindness *should* compensate for the frigidity of their elder sister, and Mr. Cator says all of them are well.

Oh poor Dr. Johnson!!![8]

[25 January 1785] I have recovered myself sufficiently to think what will be the consequence to me of Johnson's death, but must wait the event as all thoughts on the future in this world are vain.

Six people have already undertaken to write his life I hear, of which Sir John Hawkins, Mr. Boswell, Tom Davies, and Dr. Kippis are four. Piozzi says he would have me add to the number, and so I would; but that I think my anecdotes too few, and am afraid of saucy answers if I send to England for others. The saucy answers I should disregard, but my heart is made vulnerable by my late marriage, and I am certain that to spite me, they would insult my husband. Poor Johnson! I see they will leave *nothing untold* that I labored so long to keep secret; and I was so very delicate in trying to conceal his fancied insanity,[9] that I retained no proofs of it—or hardly any—nor ever mentioned it in these books, lest by dying first *they* might be printed and the secret (for such I thought it) discovered.

I used to tell him in jest that his biographers would be at a loss concerning some orange peel he used to keep in his pocket,[1] and many a joke we had about the Lives that would be published. "Rescue me out of all their hands, my dear, and do it *yourself*," said he. "Taylor, Adams, and Hector[2] will furnish you with juvenile anecdotes,

---

7. From the description of Adam and Eve as they prepare to depart from paradise (*Paradise Lost* 12.645).
8. He had died 13 December 1785.
9. Johnson had confided to her more than to others how

deeply and how often he feared the loss of his faculties.
1. He used it as a laxative.
2. Johnson's childhood friends.

and Baretti will give you all the rest that you have not already—for I think Baretti is a liar only when he speaks of himself." "Oh!" said I, "Baretti told me yesterday that you got by heart six pages of Machiavel's *History*[3] once, and repeated 'em thirty years afterwards word for word." "O why this indeed is a *gross* lie," says Johnson. "I never read the book at all." "Baretti too told me of *you*" (said I) "that you once kept sixteen cats in your chamber, and yet they scratched your legs to such a degree, you were forced to use mercurial plasters[4] for some time after." "Why this" (replied Johnson) "is an unprovoked lie indeed. I thought the fellow would not have broken through divine and human laws thus, to make Puss his heroine. But I see I was mistaken."

1776–1808   1951

━━━━━◄◆►━━━━━

Oliver Goldsmith
1730–1774

Goldsmith's cluster of famous friends never tired of describing and diagnosing what they saw as the baffling discrepancy between his success in writing and his oddity in conversation. Samuel Johnson put the problem succinctly: "No man was more foolish when he had not a pen in his hand, or more wise when he had." The actor David Garrick compacted the same paradox into the second line of an imaginary epitaph, composed while its outraged subject was present in the room: "Here lies Nolly Goldsmith, for shortness called Noll, / Who wrote like an angel, and talked like poor Poll"—that is, like a parrot, noisily spouting verbiage mimicked from minds better furnished than his own. Always quick to take offense, Goldsmith took so much at this that he devoted the remaining months of his short life to a *Retaliation* in which he took vengeance, in the form of caustic verse epitaphs, on the many people from whom he thought he had suffered slights.

Goldsmith's awkwardness, competitiveness, and defensiveness arose partly from discomfort as to humble origins and scattershot education. Born in Ireland to an eccentric curate, he had come to London in 1756 after a checkered academic career spent in Dublin, Edinburgh, and on the Continent, half-heartedly pursuing degrees (never obtained) in divinity and medicine. Upon arriving in London, Goldsmith took a series of odd jobs (druggist, physician, schoolteacher) before establishing himself as a reviewer, translator, essayist, and editor. His work brought him to the attention of the eminent, in whose company he launched that precarious social strategy which his closest friend, the painter Joshua Reynolds, later analyzed: "He had a very strong desire, which I believe nobody will think very peculiar, to be liked, to have his company sought after by his friends. To this end, for it was a system, he abandoned his respectable character as a writer or a man of observation to that of a character [in whose presence] nobody was afraid of being humiliated." As Reynolds acknowledges, the "system" often backfired, because Goldsmith wanted desperately to be impressive as well as "liked." Friends found his mystery worth probing because of the almost palpable preponderance of his merits: alongside irascibility, Goldsmith possessed a compelling charm and generosity; and an amazing *feeling* (Reynolds's emphatic term) for what made writing work.

To support spendthrift habits and a love of gambling, Goldsmith undertook much compendious hackwork—*A History of England* (1764); *Roman History* (1769); *Grecian History* (1774); and a *History of the Earth, and Animated Nature* (1774). At the same time, he managed

3. Niccolò Machiavelli's history of Florence, *Storie Fiorentine* (1520–1525).   4. Bandages soaked in mercury.

to score more successes in more genres than almost any of his contemporaries save Johnson: periodical essay (*The Citizen of the World*, 1760–1761); biography (*The Life of Richard Nash*, 1762); novel (*The Vicar of Wakefield*, 1766); stage comedy (*The Good Natured Man*, 1768; *She Stoops to Conquer*, 1773); and poetry (*The Traveller*, 1764; and *The Deserted Village*, 1770). *The Deserted Village* was the work most celebrated in his own lifetime. Two years in the making, the poem recasts an argument Goldsmith had voiced earlier in an essay against the acquisition of rural acreage by merchants who, having acquired their wealth by the commerce of empire and the trade in luxuries, were now bent on converting their new-bought lands from productive communal pasture into pretty pleasure grounds: "In almost every part of the kingdom the laborious husbandman [farmer] has been reduced, and the lands are now either occupied by some general undertaker, or turned into enclosures destined for the purposes of amusement or luxury." Such encroachment, Goldsmith contended, was driving farm families from their villages and annihilating centuries of graceful country tradition. In his poem, Goldsmith mingled nostalgia for a rural past with dread of a commercial future. Contemporary critics promptly ushered *The Deserted Village* into the poetic canon by sundering those elements Goldsmith had worked hard to fuse: they dismissed the poem's economic doctrine and praised its imaginative power. Like the poet's friends, the poem's readers are left to sort out and savor Goldsmith's characteristic complexity: a "sentimental radicalism" (the phrase is John Barrell's) whereby the conservative defense of old values produces a new and volatile empathy with the plight of the poor.

The Deserted Village

TO SIR JOSHUA REYNOLDS[1]

Dear Sir,

I can have no expectations in an address of this kind, either to add to your reputation, or to establish my own. You can gain nothing from my admiration, as I am ignorant of that art in which you are said to excel; and I may lose much by the severity of your judgment, as few have a juster taste in poetry than you. Setting interest therefore aside, to which I never paid much attention, I must be indulged at present in following my affections. The only dedication I ever made was to my brother,[2] because I loved him better than most other men. He is since dead. Permit me to inscribe this poem to you.

How far you may be pleased with the versification and mere mechanical parts of this attempt, I don't pretend to inquire; but I know you will object (and indeed several of our best and wisest friends concur in the opinion) that the depopulation it deplores is nowhere to be seen, and the disorders it laments are only to be found in the poet's own imagination. To this I can scarce make any other answer than that I sincerely believe what I have written; that I have taken all possible pains, in my country excursions, for these four or five years past, to be certain of what I allege; and that all my views and inquiries have led me to believe those miseries real, which I here attempt to display. But this is not the place to enter into an inquiry, whether the country be depopulating, or not; the discussion would take up much room, and I should prove myself, at best, an indifferent politician, to tire the reader with a long preface, when I want his unfatigued attention to a long poem.

In regretting the depopulation of the country, I inveigh against the increase of our luxuries; and here also I expect the shout of modern politicians against me. For

1. Reynolds (1723–1792) was one of England's leading portrait painters and first president of the Royal Academy; his close friendship with Goldsmith had begun in the mid-1760s.

2. Goldsmith had dedicated his previous long poem, *The Traveller* (1764), to his brother Henry, who died in 1768.

twenty or thirty years past, it has been the fashion to consider luxury as one of the greatest national advantages; and all the wisdom of antiquity in that particular, as erroneous.[3] Still however, I must remain a professed ancient on that head, and continue to think those luxuries prejudicial to states, by which so many vices are introduced, and so many kingdoms have been undone. Indeed so much has been poured out of late on the other side of the question, that, merely for the sake of novelty and variety, one would sometimes wish to be in the right.

I am,
Dear Sir,
Your sincere friend,
and ardent admirer,
OLIVER GOLDSMITH.

Sweet Auburn, loveliest village of the plain,[4]
Where health and plenty cheered the laboring swain,
Where smiling spring its earliest visit paid,
And parting summer's lingering blooms delayed:
5   Dear lovely bowers of innocence and ease,
Seats of my youth, when every sport could please,
How often have I loitered o'er thy green,
Where humble happiness endeared each scene;
How often have I paused on every charm,
10   The sheltered cot,° the cultivated farm,   *cottage*
The never-failing brook, the busy mill,
The decent church that topped the neighboring hill,
The hawthorn bush, with seats beneath the shade,
For talking age and whispering lovers made.
15   How often have I blessed the coming day,
When toil remitting lent its turn to play,
And all the village train, from labor free,
Led up their sports beneath the spreading tree,
While many a pastime circled in the shade,
20   The young contending as the old surveyed;
And many a gambol frolicked o'er the ground,
And sleights of art and feats of strength went round.
And still as each repeated pleasure tired,
Succeeding sports the mirthful band inspired;
25   The dancing pair that simply sought renown
By holding out to tire each other down;
The swain mistrustless of his smutted face,
While secret laughter tittered round the place;
The bashful virgin's sidelong looks of love,
30   The matron's glance that would those looks reprove.
These were thy charms, sweet village; sports like these,
With sweet succession, taught even toil to please;
These round thy bowers their cheerful influence shed,
These were thy charms—But all these charms are fled.

---

3. A long line of ancient authors—Horace, Seneca, and Pliny among them—had warned that the traffic in luxuries was sapping Rome's health, and had urged moderation.

4. "Auburn" is fictitious; it may be based in part on the Irish village of Lissoy, Goldsmith's childhood home.

35   Sweet smiling village, loveliest of the lawn,
          Thy sports are fled, and all thy charms withdrawn;
          Amidst thy bowers the tyrant's hand is seen,
          And desolation saddens all thy green:
          One only master grasps the whole domain,
40   And half a tillage⁵ stints° thy smiling plain;   *sets limits to*
          No more thy glassy brook reflects the day,
          But choked with sedges, works its weedy way.
          Along thy glades, a solitary guest,
          The hollow sounding bittern guards its nest;
45   Amidst thy desert walks the lapwing flies,
          And tires their echoes with unvaried cries.
          Sunk are thy bowers, in shapeless ruin all,
          And the long grass o'ertops the mouldering wall,
          And trembling, shrinking from the spoiler's hand,
50   Far, far away thy children leave the land.

          Ill fares the land, to hastening ills a prey,
          Where wealth accumulates and men decay:
          Princes and lords may flourish or may fade;
          A breath can make them, as a breath has made;
55   But a bold peasantry, their country's pride,
          When once destroyed, can never be supplied.

          A time there was, ere England's griefs began,
          When every rood° of ground maintained its man;   *quarter acre*
          For him light labor spread her wholesome store,
60   Just gave what life required, but gave no more:
          His best companions, innocence and health;
          And his best riches, ignorance of wealth.

          But times are altered; trade's unfeeling train
          Usurp the land and dispossess the swain;
65   Along the lawn,° where scattered hamlets rose,   *open countryside*
          Unwieldy wealth and cumbrous pomp repose;
          And every want to opulence allied,
          And every pang that folly pays to pride.
          These gentle hours that plenty bade to bloom,
70   Those calm desires that asked but little room,
          Those healthful sports that graced the peaceful scene,
          Lived in each look, and brightened all the green;
          These far departing seek a kinder shore,
          And rural mirth and manners are no more.

75   Sweet Auburn! parent of the blissful hour,
          Thy glades forlorn confess the tyrant's power.
          Here as I take my solitary rounds,
          Amidst thy tangling walks, and ruined grounds,
          And, many a year elapsed, return to view
80   Where once the cottage stood, the hawthorn grew,

5. Piece of tilled land.

Remembrance wakes with all her busy train,
Swells at my breast, and turns the past to pain.

In all my wanderings round this world of care,
In all my griefs—and God has given my share—
85   I still had hopes my latest hours to crown,
Amidst these humble bowers to lay me down;
To husband out life's taper[6] at the close,
And keep the flame from wasting by repose.
I still had hopes, for pride attends us still,
90   Amidst the swains to show my book-learned skill,
Around my fire an evening group to draw,
And tell of all I felt, and all I saw;
And, as an hare whom hounds and horns pursue,
Pants to the place from whence at first she flew,
95   I still had hopes, my long vexations past,
Here to return—and die at home at last.

O blest retirement, friend to life's decline,
Retreats from care that never must be mine,
How happy he who crowns in shades like these
100   A youth of labor with an age of ease;
Who quits a world where strong temptations try,
And, since 'tis hard to combat, learns to fly.
For him no wretches, born to work and weep,
Explore the mine, or tempt the dangerous deep;
105   No surly porter stands in guilty state
To spurn imploring famine from the gate,
But on he moves to meet his latter end,
Angels around befriending virtue's friend;
Bends to the grave with unperceived decay,
110   While resignation gently slopes the way;
And, all his prospects brightening to the last,
His Heaven commences ere the world be past!

Sweet was the sound when oft at evening's close
Up yonder hill the village murmur rose;
115   There as I passed with careless steps and slow,
The mingling notes came softened from below;
The swain responsive as the milkmaid sung,
The sober herd that lowed to meet their young,
The noisy geese that gabbled o'er the pool,
120   The playful children just let loose from school,
The watchdog's voice that bayed the whispering wind,
And the loud laugh that spoke the vacant° mind,   *carefree*
These all in sweet confusion sought the shade,
And filled each pause the nightingale had made.
125   But now the sounds of population fail,
No cheerful murmurs fluctuate in the gale,
No busy steps the grass-grown footway tread,

6. Candle. "To husband out" means to maintain something thriftily, so that it lasts long.

For all the bloomy flush of life is fled.
All but yon widowed, solitary thing
130   That feebly bends beside the plashy[7] spring;
She, wretched matron, forced, in age, for bread,
To strip the brook with mantling° cresses[8] spread,   *growing*
To pick her wintry faggot° from the thorn,   *firewood*
To seek her nightly shed, and weep till morn;
135   She only left of all the harmless train,
The sad historian of the pensive plain.

Near yonder copse, where once the garden smiled,
And still where many a garden flower grows wild;
There, where a few torn shrubs the place disclose,
140   The village preacher's modest mansion rose.
A man he was, to all the country dear,
And passing rich with forty pounds a year;
Remote from towns he ran his godly race,
Nor e'er had changed, nor wished to change his place;
145   Unpracticed he to fawn, or seek for power,
By doctrines fashioned to the varying hour;
Far other aims his heart had learned to prize,
More skilled to raise the wretched than to rise.
His house was known to all the vagrant train,
150   He chid their wanderings, but relieved their pain;
The long remembered beggar was his guest,
Whose beard descending swept his aged breast;
The ruined spendthrift, now no longer proud,
Claimed kindred there, and had his claims allowed;
155   The broken soldier, kindly bade to stay,
Sat by his fire, and talked the night away;
Wept o'er his wounds, or tales of sorrow done,
Shouldered his crutch, and showed how fields were won.
Pleased with his guests, the good man learned to glow,
160   And quite forgot their vices in their woe;
Careless their merits or their faults to scan,
His pity gave ere charity began.

Thus to relieve the wretched was his pride,
And even his failings leaned to virtue's side;
165   But in his duty prompt at every call,
He watched and wept, he prayed and felt, for all.
And, as a bird each fond endearment tries,
To tempt its new fledged offspring to the skies,
He tried each art, reproved each dull delay,
170   Allured to brighter worlds, and led the way.

Beside the bed where parting life was laid,
And sorrow, guilt, and pain by turns dismayed,
The reverend champion stood. At his control,
Despair and anguish fled the struggling soul;

---

7. Abounding in pools.   8. Leafy, edible plants.

175   Comfort came down the trembling wretch to raise,
    And his last faltering accents whispered praise.

      At church, with meek and unaffected grace,
    His looks adorned the venerable place;
    Truth from his lips prevailed with double sway,
180   And fools, who came to scoff, remained to pray.
    The service past, around the pious man,
    With steady zeal each honest rustic ran;
    Even children followed with endearing wile,
    And plucked his gown, to share the good man's smile.
185   His ready smile a parent's warmth expressed,
    Their welfare pleased him, and their cares distressed;
    To them his heart, his love, his griefs were given,
    But all his serious thoughts had rest in Heaven.
    As some tall cliff that lifts its awful form,
190   Swells from the vale, and midway leaves the storm,
    Though round its breast the rolling clouds are spread,
    Eternal sunshine settles on its head.

      Beside yon straggling fence that skirts the way,
    With blossomed furze° unprofitably gay,   *thorny bushes*
195   There, in his noisy mansion, skilled to rule,
    The village master taught his little school;
    A man severe he was, and stern to view,
    I knew him well, and every truant knew;
    Well had the boding tremblers learned to trace
200   The day's disasters in his morning face;
    Full well they laughed with counterfeited glee,
    At all his jokes, for many a joke had he;
    Full well the busy whisper circling round,
    Conveyed the dismal tidings when he frowned;
205   Yet he was kind, or if severe in aught,
    The love he bore to learning was in fault;
    The village all declared how much he knew;
    'Twas certain he could write, and cipher too;
    Lands he could measure, terms and tides presage,[9]
210   And even the story ran that he could gauge.[1]
    In arguing too, the parson owned° his skill,   *acknowledged*
    For even though vanquished, he could argue still;
    While words of learned length, and thundering sound,
    Amazed the gazing rustics ranged around;
215   And still they gazed, and still the wonder grew,
    That one small head could carry all he knew.

      But past is all his fame. The very spot,
    Where many a time he triumphed, is forgot.
    Near yonder thorn, that lifts its head on high,
220   Where once the signpost caught the passing eye,

9. "Terms" were the days when payments of rents and wages were due; "tides" were holidays like Easter that shifted date from year to year; information on both was readily available in the annual almanacs.
1. Calculate the capacity of barrels and other containers.

Low lies that house where nut-brown draughts° inspired,   *drinks*
Where gray-beard mirth and smiling toil retired,
Where village statesmen talked with looks profound,
And news much older than their ale went round.
225   Imagination fondly stoops to trace
The parlor splendors of that festive place;
The whitewashed wall, the nicely sanded floor,
The varnished clock that clicked behind the door;
The chest contrived a double debt to pay,
230   A bed by night, a chest of drawers by day;
The pictures placed for ornament and use,
The twelve good rules,[2] the royal game of goose;[3]
The hearth, except when winter chilled the day,
With aspen boughs, and flowers, and fennel gay,
235   While broken teacups, wisely kept for show,
Ranged o'er the chimney, glistened in a row.

     Vain transitory splendors! Could not all
Reprieve the tottering mansion from its fall!
Obscure it sinks, nor shall it more impart
240   An hour's importance to the poor man's heart;
Thither no more the peasant shall repair
To sweet oblivion of his daily care;
No more the farmer's news, the barber's tale,
No more the woodman's ballad shall prevail;
245   No more the smith his dusky brow shall clear,
Relax his ponderous strength, and lean to hear;
The host himself no longer shall be found
Careful to see the mantling° bliss go round;   *foaming*
Nor the coy maid, half willing to be pressed,
250   Shall kiss the cup to pass it to the rest.

     Yes! let the rich deride, the proud disdain,
These simple blessings of the lowly train;
To me more dear, congenial to my heart,
One native charm, than all the gloss of art;
255   Spontaneous joys, where nature has its play,
The soul adopts, and owns their first born sway;
Lightly they frolic o'er the vacant mind,
Unenvied, unmolested, unconfined.
But the long pomp, the midnight masquerade,
260   With all the freaks of wanton wealth arrayed,
In these, ere triflers half their wish obtain,
The toiling pleasure sickens into pain;
And, even while fashion's brightest arts decoy,
The heart distrusting asks, if this be joy.

265   Ye friends to truth, ye statesmen, who survey
The rich man's joys increase, the poor's decay,

---

2. This list of simple life lessons ("Keep no bad company"; "Encourage no vice"), supposedly compiled by Charles I, was displayed, beneath a picture of his execution, in many country inns and houses.

3. A game in which dice determine the movement of the pieces across the board.

'Tis yours to judge, how wide the limits stand
Between a splendid and an happy land.
Proud swells the tide with loads of freighted ore,
270 And shouting Folly hails them from her shore;
Hoards, even beyond the miser's wish abound,
And rich men flock from all the world around.
Yet count our gains. This wealth is but a name
That leaves our useful products still the same.
275 Not so the loss. The man of wealth and pride
Takes up a space that many poor supplied;
Space for his lake, his park's extended bounds,
Space for his horses, equipage, and hounds;
The robe that wraps his limbs in silken sloth
280 Has robbed the neighboring fields of half their growth;
His seat, where solitary sports are seen,
Indignant spurns the cottage from the green;
Around the world each needful product flies,
For all the luxuries the world supplies.
285 While thus the land adorned for pleasure all
In barren splendor feebly waits the fall.

As some fair female unadorned and plain,
Secure to please while youth confirms her reign,
Slights every borrowed charm that dress supplies,
290 Nor shares with art the triumph of her eyes;
But when those charms are past, for charms are frail,
When time advances, and when lovers fail,
She then shines forth, solicitous to bless,
In all the glaring impotence of dress.
295 Thus fares the land, by luxury betrayed;
In nature's simplest charms at first arrayed;
But verging to decline, its splendors rise,
Its vistas strike, its palaces surprise;
While scourged by famine from the smiling land,
300 The mournful peasant leads his humble band;
And while he sinks without one arm to save,
The country blooms—a garden, and a grave.

Where then, ah where, shall poverty reside,
To scape the pressure of contiguous pride?
305 If to some common's[4] fenceless limits strayed,
He drives his flock to pick the scanty blade,
Those fenceless fields the sons of wealth divide,
And even the bare-worn common is denied.

If to the city sped—What waits him there?
310 To see profusion that he must not share;
To see ten thousand baneful arts combined
To pamper luxury, and thin mankind;
To see those joys the sons of pleasure know

4. Grazing land once shared by all the villagers.

Extorted from his fellow-creature's woe.
315   Here, while the courtier glitters in brocade,
There the pale artist° plies the sickly trade;   *artisan*
Here, while the proud their long-drawn pomps display,
There the black gibbet glooms beside the way.
The dome° where Pleasure holds her midnight reign,   *lavish house*
320   Here, richly decked, admits the gorgeous train;
Tumultuous grandeur crowds the blazing square,
The rattling chariots clash, the torches glare.
Sure scenes like these no troubles e'er annoy!
Sure these denote one universal joy!
325   Are these thy serious thoughts?—Ah, turn thine eyes
Where the poor houseless shivering female lies.
She once, perhaps, in village plenty blest,
Has wept at tales of innocence distressed;
Her modest looks the cottage might adorn,
330   Sweet as the primrose peeps beneath the thorn;
Now lost to all; her friends, her virtue fled,
Near her betrayer's door she lays her head,
And pinched with cold, and shrinking from the shower,
With heavy heart deplores that luckless hour
335   When idly first, ambitious of the town,
She left her wheel and robes of country brown.

     Do thine, sweet Auburn, thine, the loveliest train,
Do thy fair tribes participate° her pain?   *partake of*
Even now, perhaps, by cold and hunger led,
340   At proud men's doors they ask a little bread!

     Ah, no. To distant climes, a dreary scene,
Where half the convex world intrudes between,
Through torrid tracts with fainting steps they go,
Where wild Altama[5] murmurs to their woe.
345   Far different there from all that charmed before,
The various terrors of that horrid shore;
Those blazing suns that dart a downward ray,
And fiercely shed intolerable day;
Those matted woods where birds forget to sing,
350   But silent bats in drowsy clusters cling,
Those poisonous fields with rank luxuriance crowned,
Where the dark scorpion gathers death around;
Where at each step the stranger fears to wake
The rattling terrors of the vengeful snake;
355   Where crouching tigers wait their hapless prey,
And savage men, more murderous still than they;
While oft in whirls the mad tornado flies,
Mingling the ravaged landscape with the skies.
Far different these from every former scene,
360   The cooling brook, the grassy vested green,
The breezy covert of the warbling grove,
That only sheltered thefts of harmless love.

5. The Altamaha River, in Georgia (then a colony).

Good Heaven! what sorrows gloomed that parting day,
That called them from their native walks away;
365 When the poor exiles, every pleasure past,
Hung round their bowers, and fondly looked their last,
And took a long farewell, and wished in vain
For seats like these beyond the western main;
And shuddering still to face the distant deep,
370 Returned and wept, and still returned to weep.
The good old sire the first prepared to go
To new-found worlds, and wept for others' woe.
But for himself, in conscious virtue brave,
He only wished for worlds beyond the grave.
375 His lovely daughter, lovelier in her tears,
The fond companion of his helpless years,
Silent went next, neglectful of her charms,
And left a lover's for a father's arms.
With louder plaints the mother spoke her woes,
380 And blessed the cot° where every pleasure rose;   cottage
And kissed her thoughtless babes with many a tear,
And clasped them close in sorrow doubly dear;
Whilst her fond husband strove to lend relief
In all the silent manliness of grief.

385   O luxury! Thou curst by Heaven's decree,
How ill exchanged are things like these for thee!
How do thy potions, with insidious joy,
Diffuse their pleasures only to destroy!
Kingdoms, by thee to sickly greatness grown,
390 Boast of a florid vigor not their own;
At every draught more large and large they grow,
A bloated mass of rank unwieldy woe;
Till sapped their strength, and every part unsound,
Down, down they sink, and spread a ruin round.

395   Even now the devastation is begun,
And half the business of destruction done;
Even now, methinks, as pondering here I stand,
I see the rural virtues leave the land.
Down where yon anchoring vessel spreads the sail,
400 That idly waiting flaps with every gale,
Downward they move, a melancholy band,
Pass from the shore, and darken all the strand.
Contented toil, and hospitable care,
And kind connubial tenderness are there;
405 And piety, with wishes placed above,
And steady loyalty, and faithful love:
And thou, sweet Poetry, thou loveliest maid,
Still first to fly where sensual joys invade;
Unfit, in these degenerate times of shame,
410 To catch the heart, or strike for honest fame;
Dear charming nymph, neglected and decried,
My shame in crowds, my solitary pride;
Thou source of all my bliss, and all my woe,

That found'st me poor at first, and keep'st me so;
415   Thou guide by which the nobler arts excel,
Thou nurse of every virtue, fare thee well.
Farewell, and O where'er thy voice be tried,
On Torno's[6] cliffs, or Pambamarca's[7] side,
Whether where equinoctial fervors[8] glow,
420   Or winter wraps the polar world in snow,
Still let thy voice, prevailing over time,
Redress the rigors of the inclement clime;
Aid slighted truth, with thy persuasive strain
Teach erring man to spurn the rage of gain;
425   Teach him that states of native strength possessed,
Though very poor, may still be very blest;
That trade's proud empire hastes to swift decay,
As ocean sweeps the labored mole° away;   breakwater
While self-dependent power can time defy,
430   As rocks resist the billows and the sky.[9]

1770

~~~

COMPANION READINGS
George Crabbe:[1] from *The Village*

The village life, and every care that reigns
O'er youthful peasants and declining swains;
What labor yields, and what, that labor past,
Age, in its hour of languor, finds at last;
5   What forms the real picture of the poor,
Demand a song—the Muse can give no more.

* * *

I grant indeed that fields and flocks have charms
40   For him that grazes or for him that farms;
But when amid such pleasing scenes I trace
The poor laborious natives of the place,
And see the midday sun, with fervid ray,
On their bare heads and dewy temples play;
45   While some, with feebler heads and fainter hearts,
Deplore their fortune, yet sustain their parts,

---

6. The Tornio, a river in Sweden.
7. A mountain in Ecuador.
8. Equatorial heat.
9. Samuel Johnson supplied the poem's last two couplets.
1. Physician, clergyman, poet (1754–1832). Reacting against Goldsmith's poetic nostalgia in *The Deserted Village*, and against the larger tradition of pastoral poetry which conceived the countryside as an Arcadia abounding in simple pleasures, Crabbe tried to depict realistically the benighted lives of the rural poor. Within the long compass of his own lifetime, his work found favor among readers of widely divergent convictions and generations, across the cusp of centuries and revolutions. Johnson, Reynolds, and Burke encouraged him early; Jane Austen reckoned him her favorite poet; Lord Byron praised him as "Nature's sternest painter yet the best." The first three excerpts given here are from Book 1 of *The Village*.

Then shall I dare these real ills to hide
In tinsel trappings of poetic pride?

* * *

Ye gentle souls who dream of rural ease,
Whom the smooth stream and smoother sonnet please;
Go! if the peaceful cot your praises share,
175 Go, look within, and ask if peace be there;
If peace be his—that drooping weary fire,
Or theirs, that offspring round their feeble sire,
Or hers, that matron pale, whose trembling hand
Turns on the wretched hearth th' expiring brand.

* * *

See the stout churl, in drunken fury great,
Strike the bare bosom of his teeming mate![2]
35 His naked vices, rude and unrefined,
Exert their open empire o'er the mind;
But can we less the senseless rage despise,
Because the savage acts without disguise?

* * *

And hark! the riots of the green begin,
That sprang at first from yonder noisy inn;
65 What time° the weekly pay was vanished all,   *once*
And the slow hostess scored the threatening wall;[3]
What time they asked, their friendly feast to close,
A final cup, and that will make them foes;
When blows ensue that break the arm of toil,
70 And rustic battle ends the boobies' broil.

* * *

Yet why, you ask, these humble crimes relate,
Why make the poor as guilty as the great?
90   To show the great, those mightier sons of Pride,
How near in vice the lowest are allied;
Such are their natures and their passions such,
But these disguise too little, those too much:
So shall the man of power and pleasure see
95   In his own slave as vile a wretch as he;
In his luxurious lord the servant find
His own low pleasures and degenerate mind;
And each in all the kindred vices trace
Of a poor, blind, bewildered, erring race;
100   Who, a short time in varied fortune past,
Die, and are equal in the dust at last.

1780–1783   1783

---

2. From Book 2. In this section of *The Village* Crabbe is describing (according to rubrics he published with the poem) "the repose and pleasure of a summer Sabbath, interrupted by intoxication and dispute"; in the next excerpt he proceeds to "the evening riots."

3. At taverns, the running debts of the drinkers were often recorded by means of marks ("scores") on the wall. Compare Goldsmith's description of the village tavern (*Deserted Village* 217–220).

George Crabbe: from *The Parish Register*

The year revolves, and I again explore
The simple annals of my parish poor;[1]
What infant members in my flock appear,
What pairs I blessed in the departed year;
5   And who, of old or young, of nymphs or swains,
Are lost to life, its pleasures and its pains.
        No Muse I ask, before my view to bring
The humble actions of the swains I sing.—
How passed the youthful, how the old their days;
10   Who sank in sloth, and who aspired to praise;
Their tempers, manners, morals, customs, arts,
What parts° they had, and how they employed their parts;   talents
By what elated, soothed, seduced, depressed,
Full well I know—these records give the rest.
15   Is there a place, save one the poet sees,
A land of love, of liberty and ease,
Where labor wearies not, nor cares suppress
Th' eternal flow of rustic happiness;
Where no proud mansion frowns in awful state,
20   Or keeps the sunshine from the cottage gate;
Where young and old, intent on pleasure, throng,
And half man's life is holiday and song?
Vain search for scenes like these! no view appears,
By sighs unruffled or unstained by tears;
25   Since vice the world subdued and waters drowned,
Auburn and Eden can no more be found.
c. 1802–1806   1807

❦

Richard Brinsley Sheridan
1751–1816

For much of the eighteenth century, theatrical fashion favored comedies that made one weep: the reunion between a despairing shepherdess and her long-lost love, for example, might clinch the fifth act of a play riddled with pathetic scenes and heart-throbbing emotion. Contemporary comedy dwelt on the private lives of fairly decent people, who spoke fluently of proper behavior and obsessively of proper morals. Richard Brinsley Sheridan's own mother Frances had written several of these "sentimental" comedies, but when her son became manager of the Drury Lane theatre 1776, his first project was to revive the wicked, witty Restoration comedies of William Congreve. It was a bold move, given the current prudish intolerance of sexual humor. "We dare not propose a peep beyond the ankle at any account," Sheridan wrote his father-in-law, "for the critics in the pit at a new play are much greater prudes than the ladies in the

1. The speaker is a parish priest.

boxes." So Sheridan pruned and trimmed Congreve, subduing his racier puns and cutting whole lines of sexual invitation. In 1777, after presenting three plays by Congreve in six weeks, Sheridan directed the premiere of his own *School for Scandal*. He had let Congreve prepare the ground; he cultivated his own satiric attacks on "sentiment" and "sentimental rogues" from the sharp soil of Restoration wit.

Sheridan was not trying to out-Congreve Congreve. *The School for Scandal* does offer a wholesale attack on hypocritical, honey-sweet morality, but it criticizes too the cruelty that had formed an essential component of Restoration comedy. As the damningly named Lady Sneerwell admits, "there's no possibility of being witty without ill-nature." Restoration heroes were manifestly ill-natured, given to mocking fops, gossips, bawds, and their own lovers. Sheridan's hero Charles is *not* ill-natured but open-hearted (even at times maudlin), and the play endorses his outlook, as Sheridan maps the ways that malice works its own undoing. The playgoers who crowded the 2,000 seats of Drury Lane, unlike their Restoration antecedents a hundred years earlier, came not merely to see vice be witty, but to see witty vice exposed and expunged.

Sheridan's hybrid paid off handsomely. The *Morning Chronicle* reported in 1777 that "the new comedy of *The School for Scandal* is now so much in fashion that it is almost a matter of danger to offer a single objection to it." It was the biggest moneymaker of Sheridan's early years as manager, a post he held from 1776 to 1811. The fact that Sheridan was managing Drury Lane while writing *The School* is tremendously important. Like Shakespeare, Sheridan spun his characters from the talents and attributes of his own actors. Sir Benjamin Backbite, for example, was first played by James William Dodd, an actor who specialized in fops, men about town, empty-headed dandies. He was a wild success as Backbite, "the prince of pink heels, the soul of empty eminence," wrote a contemporary: "As he tottered rather than walked down the stage, in all the protuberance of endless muslin and lace in his cravats and frills, he reminded you of the jutting motion of the pigeon." If Charles and Maria seem a bit chilly, it may be because Sheridan decided he could not give them a love-scene: "the actors who played the parts were not able to do such a scene justice." The comedy is a manager's—a director's—play, one in which the actors may have exerted as much of a shaping influence as did the resonances with the Restoration.

Sheridan's experiment with Congrevian humor and sentimental underpinnings has remained enormously popular, but Drury Lane needed several *Schools* to get itself out of debt, and Sheridan wrote only three more plays. One was *The Critic* (1779), a riotous send-up of theatrical practices and the playgoers who doted on them. His management style was reckless: he borrowed money from the company to support his private extravagance; his leading actors often went unpaid; one of his managers committed suicide in despair over the financial future of the theater. Sheridan bankrupted the Drury Lane and himself. In 1809 the playhouse accidentally burned to the ground. Its manager, calmly observing the catastrophe from a cafe across the way, rebuffed sympathy with a quip: "A man may surely be allowed to take a glass of wine by his own fireside." His remarkable charm had kept him at the helm of Drury Lane for some thirty-five years, despite the various financial crises that marred his tenure.

Beginning in 1780, Sheridan had worked concurrently in another theatrical venue as well: Parliament, to which he was elected despite the lingering suspicion that his driving motives were financial rather than political (members could not be arrested for debt). Despite detraction, he sustained a long and at times highly influential political career. His speeches were considered splendid, sometimes terrifying examples of linguistic ingenuity, in which Sheridan would seize his antagonist's words and twist them to his purposes, ridiculing the opposition mercilessly in the process. As an MP, he was blisteringly eloquent, breathtakingly ill-prepared, and occasionally blind drunk. His charisma could not hold off financial disaster forever. In 1811 he was removed from managership of the Drury Lane, and in 1813, after he lost his seat in Parliament, his extravagances caught up with him. He was briefly imprisoned, and died shortly thereafter, over 5,000 pounds in debt.

The School for Scandal

A Comedy

Dramatis Personae (as acted at Drury Lane Theatre, 8 May 1777)

SIR PETER TEAZLE	SNAKE
SIR OLIVER SURFACE	CARELESS
JOSEPH SURFACE	SIR TOBY BUMPER
CHARLES SURFACE	
CRATREE	LADY TEAZLE
SIR BENJAMIN BACKBITE	MARIA
ROWLEY	LADY SNEERWELL
MOSES	MRS. CANDOUR
TRIP	

PROLOGUE

Spoken by Mr. King.[1]
Written by D. Garrick, Esqr.[2]

A School for Scandal! Tell me, I beseech you,
Needs there a school this modish° art to teach you?   *fashionable*
No need of lessons now, the knowing think:
We might as well be taught to eat and drink.
5   Caused by a dearth of scandal, should the vapors°   *depression*
Distress our fair ones, let 'em read the papers.[3]
Their pow'rful mixtures such disorders hit,°   *exactly suit*
Crave what they will, there's *quantum sufficit*.[4]

"Lud,"[5] cries my Lady Wormwood, who loves tattle,°   *gossip, idle talk*
10 And puts much salt and pepper in her prattle;
Just ris'n at noon, all night at cards when threshing
Strong tea and scandal; "Bless me how refreshing!
Give me the papers, Lisp[6]—how bold, and free—[*Sips.*]
Last night Lord L—[*Sips.*] *was caught with Lady D—*.
15 For aching heads, what charming *sal volatile!*[7] [*Sips.*]
If Mrs. B—will still continue flirting,
We hope she'll draw, or we'll un-draw the curtain.[8]
Fine satire, poz[9]—in public all abuse it—
But by ourselves, [*Sips.*] our praise we can't refuse it.[1]
20 Now Lisp, read you, there at that dash and star."[2] [*Sips.*]
"Yes, ma'am: a Certain Lord had best beware,
Who lives not twenty miles from Grosv'nor Square[3]
For should he Lady W—find willing,

---

1. Thomas King (1730–1805), the comic actor who created the role of Sir Peter Teazle.
2. David Garrick (1717–1779), dramatist, poet, theatrical manager, and the preeminent actor of his day; upon his retirement in 1776, he chose Sheridan to succeed him as manager at the Drury Lane Theatre.
3. I.e., the gossip columns and magazines.
4. More than enough (of scandal).
5. Fashionable slang for "Lord!"
6. A conventional comedy-name for a lady's maid.

7. A solution of ammonium carbonate; the bracing fumes restored one from a faint.
8. She'll stop, or the paper will expose her.
9. Fashionable slang for "positively."
1. I.e., when alone, we can't help admiring it.
2. Newspapers often used dashes and stars (as in the names "Lord L—" and "Lady D—") to disguise (and at the same time insinuate) the identities of the people they discussed, and to protect the papers from legal action.
3. An exclusive neighborhood in London.

Wormwood is bitter." "O, that's me, the villain!
25   Throw it behind the fire, and never more,
Let that vile paper come within my door."
Thus at our friends we laugh, who feel the dart—
To reach our feelings, we ourselves must smart.

Is our young bard[4] so young to think that he
30   Can stop the full spring-tide of calumny—
Knows he the world so little and its trade?
Alas, the devil is sooner raised, than laid.°   suppressed
So strong, so swift, the monster there's no gagging;
Cut scandal's head off, still the tongue is wagging.
35   Proud of your smiles once lavishly bestowed
Again our young Don Quixote[5] takes the road:
To show his gratitude, he draws his pen,
And seeks this hydra,[6] scandal, in its den,
From his fell gripe° the frighted fair° to save   *terrible clutches* / i.e., women
40   Though he should fall—th'attempt must please the brave.
For your applause, all perils he would through,
He'll *fight*, that's *write*, a cavalliero[7] true,
Till ev'ry drop of blood, that's ink, is spilt for you.

ACT 1

Scene 1

[*Lady Sneerwell's house. Lady Sneerwell at the dressing table. Snake drinking chocolate.*]

LADY SNEERWELL: The paragraphs, you say, Mr. Snake, were all inserted?

SNAKE: They were, madam—and as I copied them myself in a feigned hand[1] there can be no suspicion whence they came.

LADY SNEERWELL: Did you circulate the report of Lady Brittle's intrigue with Captain Boastall?

SNAKE: That is in as fine a train[2] as your ladyship could wish. In the common course of things, I think it must reach Mrs. Clackit's[3] ears within four and twenty hours and then, you know, the business is as good as done.

LADY SNEERWELL: Why, truly, Mrs. Clackit has a very pretty talent, and a great deal of industry.

SNAKE: True, madam, and has been tolerably successful in her day. To my knowledge, she has been the cause of six matches being broken off, and three sons being disinherited, of four forced elopements, as many close confinements,[4] nine separate maintenances,[5] and two divorces; nay, I have more than once traced her causing a *Tête-à-Tête* in the *Town and Country Magazine*[6]—when the parties perhaps have never seen each other's faces before in the course of their lives.

---

4. Sheridan (then 26 years old).
5. Don Quixote (here pronounced "Quicksote"), Cervantes' famous hero, wandered the roads looking for monsters to kill; Sheridan's attack on scandal is seen as a similarly fantastic task.
6. A nine-headed monster from Greek legend; for every head cut off, two grew in its place.
7. A cavalier or knight on horseback.
1. Disguised handwriting.

2. Making as good progress.
3. From the French *claqueter*: to chatter.
4. Hidden pregnancies (because the children were illegitimate).
5. The sum a husband paid for a wife's expenses while they live apart.
6. The magazine included a popular gossip column illustrated by engravings of the couples whose putative intrigues the prose exposed.

LADY SNEERWELL: She certainly has talents, but her manner is gross.

SNAKE: 'Tis very true—she generally designs well, has a free tongue and a bold invention, but her coloring is too dark and her outline often extravagant. She wants that delicacy of hint and mellowness of sneer which distinguish your ladyship's scandal.

LADY SNEERWELL: Ah! You are partial, Snake.

SNAKE: Not in the least—everybody allows that Lady Sneerwell can do more with a word or a look than many can with the most labored detail even when they happen to have a little truth on their side to support it.

LADY SNEERWELL: Yes, my dear Snake, and I am no hypocrite to deny the satisfaction I reap from the success of my efforts. Wounded myself in the early part of my life by the envenomed tongue of slander, I confess I have since known no pleasure equal to the reducing others to the level of my own injured reputation.

SNAKE: Nothing can be more natural. But Lady Sneerwell, there is one affair in which you have lately employed me wherein I confess I am at a loss to guess your motives.

LADY SNEERWELL: I conceive you mean with respect to my neighbor Sir Peter Teazle and his family?

SNAKE: I do. Here are two young men, to whom Sir Peter has acted as a kind of guardian since their father's death, the elder possessing the most amiable character and universally well spoken of, the other the most dissipated and extravagant young fellow in the kingdom, without friends or character—the former an avowed admirer of your ladyship and apparently your favorite; the latter attached to Maria, Sir Peter's ward, and confessedly beloved by her. Now on the face of these circumstances, it is utterly unaccountable to me why you, the widow of a city knight,[7] with a good jointure,[8] should not close with[9] the passion of a man of such character and expectations as Mr. Surface—and more so, why you should be so uncommonly earnest to destroy the mutual attachment subsisting between his brother Charles and Maria.

LADY SNEERWELL: Then at once to unravel this mystery, I must inform you that love has no share whatever in the intercourse between Mr. Surface and me.

SNAKE: No!

LADY SNEERWELL: His real attachment is to Maria, or her fortune—but finding in his brother a favored rival, he has been obliged to mask his pretensions[1] and profit by my assistance.

SNAKE: Yet still I am more puzzled why you should interest yourself in his success.

LADY SNEERWELL: Heav'ns! How dull you are! Cannot you surmise the weakness which I hitherto through shame have concealed even from you? Must I confess that Charles—that libertine, that extravagant, that bankrupt in fortune and reputation—that he it is for whom I am thus anxious and malicious, and to gain whom I would sacrifice—everything?

SNAKE: Now, indeed, your conduct appears consistent—but how came you and Mr. Surface so confidential?

LADY SNEERWELL: For our mutual interest. I have found him out a long time since—I know him to be artful, selfish and malicious: in short, a sentimental knave.

---

7. I.e., a London merchant who was subsequently knighted.
8. Income left her by her dead husband.

9. As in "close a bargain," with sexual innuendo.
1. Intentions.

SNAKE: Yet Sir Peter vows he has not his equal in England, and above all he praises him as a man of sentiment.[2]

LADY SNEERWELL: True, and with the assistance of his sentiments and hypocrisy he has brought him entirely into his interest[3] with regard to Maria.

[Enter Servant.]

SERVANT: Mr. Surface.

LADY SNEERWELL: Show him up.

[Exit Servant.]

He generally calls about this time. I don't wonder at people's giving him to me for a lover.

[Enter Surface.]

SURFACE: My dear Lady Sneerwell, how do you do today? Mr. Snake, your most obedient.[4]

LADY SNEERWELL: Snake has just been arraigning[5] me on our mutual attachment, but I have informed him of our real views. You know how useful he has been to us—and believe me, the confidence is not ill placed.

SURFACE: Madam, it is impossible for me to suspect a man of Mr. Snake's sensibility[6] and discernment.

LADY SNEERWELL: Well, well, no compliments now—but tell me when you saw your mistress Maria, or what is more material[7] to me, your brother?

SURFACE: I have not seen either since I left you, but I can inform you that they never meet—some of your stories have taken a good effect on Maria.

LADY SNEERWELL: Ah! My dear Snake, the merit of this belongs to you—but do your brother's distresses increase?

SURFACE: Every hour, I am told. He has had another execution[8] in the house yesterday—in short, his dissipation and extravagance exceed any thing I ever heard of.

LADY SNEERWELL: Poor Charles!

SURFACE: True, madam. Notwithstanding his vices, one can't help feeling for him. Aye, poor Charles! I'm sure I wish it was in my power to be of any essential service to him, for the man who does not share in the distresses of a brother, even though merited by his own misconduct, deserves—

LADY SNEERWELL: O Lud, you are going to be moral and forget that you are among friends.

SURFACE: Egad,[9] that's true. I'll keep that sentiment 'till I see Sir Peter. However, it is certainly a charity to rescue Maria from such a libertine—who if he is to be reclaimed can be so only by a person of your ladyship's superior accomplishments and understanding.

SNAKE: I believe, Lady Sneerwell, here's company coming. I'll go and copy the letter I mentioned to you. Mr. Surface, your most obedient.

[Exit Snake.]

SURFACE: Sir, your very devoted. Lady Sneerwell, I am very sorry you have put any further confidence in that fellow.

LADY SNEERWELL: Why so?

---

2. A "sentiment" was a fervently expressed emotional thought, often taking the form of a brief moral pronouncement on the nature of human life.

3. I.e., has persuaded Sir Peter to help fulfill his desires.

4. Polite greeting, short for "your most obedient servant."

5. Interrogating.

6. Capacity for refined feeling.

7. Important.

8. A formal confiscation of property to cover unpaid debts.

9. A softened oath, akin to "By God."

SURFACE: I have lately detected him in frequent conference with old Rowley, who was formerly my father's steward,[1] and has never, you know, been a friend of mine.

LADY SNEERWELL: And do you think he would betray us?

SURFACE: Nothing more likely: take my word for't, Lady Sneerwell, that fellow hasn't virtue enough to be faithful even to his own villainy. Hah! Maria!

[Enter Maria.]

LADY SNEERWELL: Maria, my dear, how do you do? What's the matter?

MARIA: O, there is that disagreeable lover of mine, Sir Benjamin Backbite, has just called at my guardian's with his odious Uncle Crabtree, so I slipped out and run hither to avoid them.

LADY SNEERWELL: Is that all?

SURFACE: If my brother Charles had been of the party, ma'am, perhaps you would not have been so much alarmed.

LADY SNEERWELL: Nay now, you are severe, for I dare swear the truth of the matter is Maria heard you were here; but my dear, what has Sir Benjamin done that you should avoid him so?

MARIA: Oh, he has done nothing, but 'tis for what he has said—his conversation is a perpetual libel on all his acquaintance.

SURFACE: Aye, and the worst of it is there is no advantage in not knowing him; for he'll abuse a stranger just as soon as his best friend—and his uncle's as bad.

LADY SNEERWELL: Nay, but we should make allowance:[2] Sir Benjamin is a wit and a poet.

MARIA: For my part, I own, madam, wit loses its respect with me when I see it in company with malice. What do you think, Mr. Surface?

SURFACE: Certainly, madam, to smile at the jest which plants a thorn in another's breast is to become a principal in the mischief.[3]

LADY SNEERWELL: Pshaw! There's no possibility of being witty without a little ill nature—the malice of a good thing is the barb that makes it stick. What's your opinion, Mr. Surface?

SURFACE: To be sure, madam, that conversation where the spirit of raillery[4] is suppressed will ever appear tedious and insipid.

LADY SNEERWELL: Well, I'll not debate how far scandal may be allowable—but in a man I am sure it is always contemptible; we have pride, envy, rivalship, and a thousand motives to depreciate each other, but the male-slanderer must have the cowardice of a woman before he can traduce[5] one.

[Enter Servant.]

SERVANT: Madam, Mrs. Candour is below and if your ladyship's at leisure will leave her carriage.

LADY SNEERWELL: Beg her to walk in. Now Maria, however, here is a character to your taste, for though Mrs. Candour is a little talkative, everybody allows her to be the best natured and best sort of woman.

MARIA: Yes, with a very gross affectation of good nature and benevolence, she does more mischief than the direct malice of old Crabtree.

SURFACE: I'faith, 'tis very true, Lady Sneerwell. Whenever I hear the current running against the characters of my friends, I never think them in such danger as when Candour undertakes their defense.

---

1. Estate manager.
2. Excuse him.
3. I.e., to become a major offender oneself.

4. Ridicule.
5. Defame.

LADY SNEERWELL: Hush, here she is.

[*Enter Mrs. Candour.*]

MRS. CANDOUR: My dear Lady Sneerwell, how have you been this century? Mr. Surface, what news do you hear? Though indeed it is no matter, for I think one hears nothing else but scandal.

SURFACE: Just so, indeed, madam.

MRS. CANDOUR: Ah! Maria, child—what, is the whole affair off between you and Charles? His extravagance, I presume—the town talks of nothing else.

MARIA: I am very sorry, ma'am, the town has so little to do.

MRS. CANDOUR: True, true, child, but there is no stopping people's tongues. I own I was hurt to hear it—as indeed I was to learn from the same quarter that your guardian, Sir Peter, and Lady Teazle have not agreed lately so well as could be wished.

MARIA: 'Tis strangely impertinent[6] for people to busy themselves so.

MRS. CANDOUR: Very true, child, but what's to be done? People will talk—there's no preventing it—why, it was but yesterday, I was told that Miss Gadabout had eloped with Sir Filagree Flirt—but Lord! There is no minding what one hears—though to be sure I had this from very good authority.

MARIA: Such reports are highly scandalous.

MRS. CANDOUR: So they are, child—shameful! shameful! But the world is so censorious, no character escapes—Lud now! Who would have suspected your friend Miss Prim of an indiscretion? Yet such is the ill nature of people that they say her uncle stopped her last week, just as she was stepping into the York diligence[7] with her dancing master.

MARIA: I'll answer for't there are no grounds for the report—

MRS. CANDOUR: Oh, no foundation in the world, I dare swear, no more probably than for the story circulated last month—of Mrs. Festino's affair with Colonel Cassino—though to be sure that matter was never rightly cleared up.

SURFACE: The license of invention[8] some people take is monstrous indeed.

MARIA: 'Tis so, but in my opinion those who report such things are equally culpable.[9]

MRS. CANDOUR: To be sure, they are—tale bearers are as bad as the tale makers—'tis an old observation and a very true one; but what's to be done, as I said before? How will you prevent people from talking? Today Mrs. Clackit assured me Mr. and Mrs. Honeymoon were at last become mere man and wife like the rest of their acquaintances—she likewise hinted that a certain widow in the next street had got rid of her dropsy[1] and recovered her shape in a most surprising manner—and at the same time Miss Tattle, who was by, affirmed that Lord Buffalo had discovered his lady at a house of no extraordinary fame[2]—and that Sir Harry Bouquet and Tom Saunter were to measure swords[3] on a similar provocation, but Lord! Do you think I would report these things? No, no, tale bearers, as I said before, are just as bad as tale makers.

SURFACE: Ah! Mrs. Candour, if everybody had your forbearance and good nature!

MRS. CANDOUR: I confess, Mr. Surface, I cannot bear to hear people attacked behind their backs, and when ugly circumstances come out against one's acquaintances I own I always love to think the best—by the by, I hope 'tis not true that your brother is absolutely ruined.

6. Presumptuous.
7. A public stage-coach bound for the city of York.
8. Freedom to invent.
9. At fault.

1. A disease characterized by marked swelling (here, actually a pregnancy).
2. I.e., a house of ill repute, or a whorehouse.
3. Hold a duel.

SURFACE: I am afraid his circumstances are very bad indeed, ma'am.

MRS. CANDOUR: Ah! I heard so—but you must tell him to keep up his spirits—everybody almost is in the same way—Lord Spindle, Sir Thomas Splint, Captain Quinze, and Mr. Nickit⁴—all up,⁵ I hear, within this week! So if Charles is undone he'll find half his acquaintances ruined too—and that, you know, is a consolation.

SURFACE: Doubtless, ma'am, a very great one.

[Enter Servant.]

SERVANT: Mr. Crabtree and Sir Benjamin Backbite.

[Exit Servant.]

LADY SNEERWELL: So! Maria, you see your lover pursues you. Positively, you shan't escape.

[Enter Crabtree and Sir Benjamin Backbite.]

CRABTREE: Lady Sneerwell, I kiss your hands. Mrs. Candour, I don't believe you are acquainted with my nephew, Sir Benjamin Backbite? Egad, ma'am, he has a pretty wit—and is a pretty poet too, isn't he, Lady Sneerwell?

SIR BENJAMIN: O fie, uncle!

CRABTREE: Nay, egad, it's true. I'll back him at a rebus⁶ or a charade⁷ against the best rhymer in the kingdom. Has your ladyship heard the epigram he wrote last week on Lady Frizzle's feather catching fire? Do, Benjamin, repeat it, or the charade you made last night extempore⁸ at Mrs. Drowzy's *conversazione*⁹—come now, your first is the name of a fish, your second a great naval commander, and—

SIR BENJAMIN: Uncle, now prithee—

CRABTREE: I'faith, ma'am, 'twould surprise you to hear how ready he is at these things.

LADY SNEERWELL: I wonder, Sir Benjamin, you never publish anything.

SIR BENJAMIN: To say truth, ma'am, 'tis very vulgar to print, and as my little productions are mostly satires and lampoons on particular people, I find they circulate more by giving copies in confidence to the friends of the parties. However, I have some love elegies which, when favored with this lady's smiles, I mean to give to the public.

CRABTREE: Before heav'n, ma'am, they'll immortalize you—you'll be handed down to posterity like Petrarch's Laura or Waller's Sacharissa.¹

SIR BENJAMIN: Yes, madam, I think you will like them when you shall see them on a beautiful quarto² page where a neat rivulet of text shall murmur through a meadow of margin—'fore Gad, they will be the most elegant things of their kind.

CRABTREE: But, ladies, that's true. Have you heard the news?—

MRS. CANDOUR: What, sir, do you mean the report of—

CRABTREE: No, ma'am, that's not it. Miss Nicely is going to be married to her own footman.

MRS. CANDOUR: Impossible!

---

4. In the dice game called hazard, a "nick" was a winning throw.

5. Bankrupt.

6. A game in which the leader creates a pun for each syllable of a name, word, or phrase to be guessed by the others.

7. A riddle game in which the syllables of each word to be guessed are described enigmatically.

8. On the spur of the moment.

9. A party devoted to elegant conversation about cultural matters.

1. The Renaissance poet Francesco Petrarca (1304–1374) addressed many poems to his beloved Laura; as did the Restoration Edmund Waller (1606–1687) to Lady Dorothy Sidney, whom he dubbed "Sacharissa" ("most sweet").

2. A popular format for printed books, with pages approximately the size of this one, produced by folding a large printer's sheet into quarters.

CRABTREE: Ask Sir Benjamin.

SIR BENJAMIN: 'Tis very true, ma'am. Everything is fixed and the wedding livery bespoke.[3]

CRABTREE: Yes, and they do say there were pressing reasons for't.

LADY SNEERWELL: Why, I have heard something of this before.

MRS. CANDOUR: It can't be—and I wonder any one should believe such a story of so prudent a lady as Miss Nicely.

SIR BENJAMIN: O Lud, ma'am, that's the very reason 'twas believed at once. She has always been so cautious and so reserved that everybody was sure there was some reason for it at bottom.

MRS. CANDOUR: Why, to be sure a tale of scandal is as fatal to the credit of a prudent lady of her stamp[4] as a fever is generally to those of the strongest constitutions, but there is a sort of puny, sickly reputation that is always ailing, yet will outlive the robuster characters of a hundred prudes.

SIR BENJAMIN: True, madam, there are valetudinarians[5] in reputation as well as constitution who, being conscious of their weak part, avoid the least breath of air and supply their want of stamina by care and circumspection.

MRS. CANDOUR: Well, but this may be all a mistake—you know, Sir Benjamin, very trifling circumstances often give rise to the most injurious tales—

CRABTREE: That they do, I'll be sworn, ma'am—did you ever hear how Miss Piper came to lose her lover and her character last summer at Tunbridge?[6] Sir Benjamin, you remember it.

SIR BENJAMIN: O, to be sure, the most whimsical circumstance.

LADY SNEERWELL: How was it, pray?

CRABTREE: Why, one evening at Mrs. Ponto's assembly, the conversation happened to turn on the difficulty of breeding Nova-Scotia sheep in this country. Says a young lady in company, "I have known instances of it, for Miss Letitia Piper, a first cousin of mine, had a Nova-Scotia sheep that produced her twins." "What!" cries the old dowager[7] Lady Dundizzy (who you know is as deaf as a post) "has Miss Piper had twins?" This mistake, as you may imagine, threw the whole company into a fit of laughing; however, 'twas the next morning everywhere reported, and in a few days believed by the whole town, that Miss Letitia Piper had actually been brought to bed of a fine boy and a girl—and in less than a week there were people who could name the father, and the farmhouse where the babies were put out to nurse.

LADY SNEERWELL: Strange indeed!

CRABTREE: Matter of fact, I assure you. O Lud, Mr. Surface, pray, is it true that your uncle Sir Oliver is coming home?

SURFACE: Not that I know of, indeed, sir.

CRABTREE: He has been in the East Indies a long time. You can scarcely remember him, I believe. Sad comfort, whenever he returns, to hear how your brother has gone on.

SURFACE: Charles has been imprudent, sir, to be sure, but I hope no busy people have already prejudiced Sir Oliver against him—he may reform.

---

3. I.e., the wedding clothes are ordered: but since "liveries" generally indicates the uniform of a male servant, the comment is tongue-in-cheek.
4. Type.
5. Sickly people preoccupied with health.
6. Tunbridge Wells, a fashionable resort.
7. A widow whose title derives from her late husband.

SIR BENJAMIN: To be sure, he may—for my part I never believed him to be so utterly void of principle as people say, and though he has lost all his friends, I am told nobody is better spoken of—by the Jews.

CRABTREE: That's true, egad, nephew—if the old Jewry[8] were a ward I believe Charles would be an alderman. No man more popular there—before gad. I hear he pays as many annuities as the Irish Tontine[9] and that whenever he's sick they have prayers for the recovery of his health in the synagogue.

SIR BENJAMIN: Yet no man lives in greater splendor: they tell me when he entertains his friends he can sit down to dinner with a dozen of his own securities,[1] have a score[2] tradesmen waiting in the antechamber[3] and an officer[4] behind every guest's chair.

SURFACE: This may be entertainment to you, gentlemen, but you pay very little regard to the feelings of a brother.

MARIA: Their malice is intolerable. Lady Sneerwell, I must wish you a good morning. I'm not very well.

[Exit Maria.]

MRS. CANDOUR: O dear, she changed color very much!

LADY SNEERWELL: Do, Mrs. Candour, follow her—she may want assistance.

MRS. CANDOUR: That I will, with all my soul, ma'am—poor dear girl, who knows what her situation may be!

[Exit Mrs. Candour.]

LADY SNEERWELL: 'Twas nothing but that she could not bear to hear Charles reflected on, notwithstanding their difference.

SIR BENJAMIN: The young lady's *penchant*[5] is obvious.

CRABTREE: But Benjamin, you mustn't give up the pursuit for that; follow her and put her into good humor. Repeat her some of your own verses. Come, I'll assist you.

SIR BENJAMIN: Mr. Surface, I did not mean to hurt you—but depend upon't, your brother is utterly undone—[Going.]

CRABTREE: O Lud! Aye, undone as ever man was—can't raise a guinea. [Going.]

SIR BENJAMIN: And everything sold, I'm told, that was moveable—[Going.]

CRABTREE: I have seen one that was at his house—not a thing left but some empty bottles that were overlooked, and the family pictures which, I believe, are framed in the wainscot[6]—[Going.]

SIR BENJAMIN: And I'm very sorry to hear also some bad stories against him. [Going.]

CRABTREE: O, he has done many mean[7] things—that's certain!

SIR BENJAMIN: But, however, as he's your brother—[Going.]

CRABTREE: We'll tell you all another opportunity.

[Exeunt Crabtree and Sir Benjamin.]

---

8. The district of London inhabited by Jews.
9. In order to pay off its debts, the Irish government had launched a "tontine," a scheme in which contributors received an annual dividend during their lifetimes, which increased as the number of original contributors was reduced by death. Crabtree's gist here is that the impecunious Charles pays the Jewish moneylenders so much interest that they would (1) elect him to the city council; and (2) fear his disappearance.

1. People who have co-signed his loans.
2. Twenty.
3. Small room leading to the dining room.
4. Bailiff, come to serve notice of a lawsuit for unpaid debt.
5. Partiality.
6. Wall paneling (from which the pictures, built in, could not be removed).
7. Ignoble, dishonorable.

LADY SNEERWELL: Ha, ha! ha! 'Tis very hard for them to leave a subject they have not quite run down.

SURFACE: And I believe the abuse was no more acceptable to your ladyship than to Maria.

LADY SNEERWELL: I doubt her affections are farther engaged than we imagined, but the family are to be here this evening, so you may as well dine where you are and we shall have an opportunity of observing farther. In the meantime, I'll go and plot mischief, and you shall study sentiments.   [*Exeunt.*]

Scene 2

[*Sir Peter's house. Enter Sir Peter.*]

SIR PETER: When an old bachelor takes a young wife—what is he to expect? 'Tis now six months since Lady Teazle made me the happiest of men, and I have been the miserablest dog ever since that ever committed wedlock: we tiffed a little going to church, and came to a quarrel before the bells were done ringing. I was more than once nearly choked with gall[8] during the honeymoon, and had lost all comfort in life before my friends had done wishing me joy—yet I chose with caution: a girl bred wholly in the country, who never knew luxury beyond one silk gown nor dissipation above the annual gala of a race-ball—yet now she plays her part in all the extravagant fopperies[9] of the fashion and the town with as ready a grace as if she had never seen a bush nor a grass plat[1] out of Grosvenor Square! I am sneered at by my old acquaintance, paragraphed in the newspapers. She dissipates my fortune, and contradicts all my humors:[2] yet the worst of it is I doubt[3] I love her or I should never bear all this. However, I'll never be weak enough to own[4] it.

[*Enter Rowley.*]

ROWLEY: Oh, Sir Peter, your servant. How is it with you, sir?

SIR PETER: Very bad, Master Rowley, very bad. I meet with nothing but crosses and vexations.

ROWLEY: What can have happened to trouble you since yesterday?

SIR PETER: A good question to a married man.

ROWLEY: Nay, I'm sure your lady, Sir Peter, can't be the cause of your uneasiness.

SIR PETER: Why, has anyone told you she was dead?

ROWLEY: Come, come, Sir Peter, you love her, notwithstanding your tempers do not exactly agree.

SIR PETER: But the fault is entirely hers, Master Rowley. I am myself the sweetest tempered man alive and hate a teasing temper—and so I tell her, a hundred times a day.

ROWLEY: Indeed!

SIR PETER: Aye, and what is very extraordinary, in all our disputes she is always in the wrong! But Lady Sneerwell and the set she meets at her house encourage the perverseness of her disposition. Then, to complete my vexations, Maria, my ward, whom I ought to have the power of a father over, is determined to turn rebel too

8. Rage.
9. Absurdities.
1. Patch.

2. Whims.
3. I'm afraid.
4. Admit.

and absolutely refuses the man whom I have long resolved on for her husband—
meaning, I suppose, to bestow herself on his profligate brother.

ROWLEY: You know, Sir Peter, I have always taken the liberty to differ with you on
the subject of these two young gentlemen. I only wish you may not be deceived in
your opinion of the elder—for Charles, my life on't, he will retrieve his errors yet.
Their worthy father, once my honored master, was at his years nearly as wild a
spark[5] yet when he died, he did not leave a more benevolent heart to lament his
loss.

SIR PETER: You are wrong, Master Rowley. On their father's death, you know, I
acted as a kind of guardian to them both, 'till their uncle Sir Oliver's eastern liberality gave them an early independence. Of course, no person could have more
opportunities of judging of their hearts, and I was never mistaken in my life.
Joseph is indeed a model for the young men of the age. He is a man of sentiment—and acts up to the sentiments he professes—but for the other, take my
word for't, if he had any grains of virtue by descent,[6] he has dissipated them with
the rest of his inheritance. Ah! My old friend Sir Oliver will be deeply mortified
when he finds how part of his bounty has been misapplied!

ROWLEY: I am sorry to find you so violent against the young man, because this may
be the most critical period of his fortune—I came hither with news that will surprise you.

SIR PETER: What? Let me hear.

ROWLEY: Sir Oliver is arrived and at this moment in town.

SIR PETER: How! You astonish me. I thought you did not expect him this month!

ROWLEY: I did not, but his passage has been remarkably quick.

SIR PETER: Egad, I shall rejoice to see my old friend. 'Tis sixteen years since we
met. We have had many a day together. But does he still enjoin us not to inform
his nephews of his arrival?

ROWLEY: Most strictly—he means before it is known to make some trial of their
dispositions.

SIR PETER: Ah, there needs no art to discover their merits! However, he shall
have his way—but pray, does he know I am married?

ROWLEY: Yes, and will soon wish you joy.

SIR PETER: What, as we drink health to a friend in a consumption. Ah, Oliver
will laugh at me—we used to rail at matrimony together, but he has been steady
to his text.[7] Well, he must be at my house though—I'll instantly give orders for
his reception. But Master Rowley, don't drop a word that Lady Teazle and I ever
disagree.

ROWLEY: By no means.

SIR PETER: For I should never be able to stand Noll's[8] jokes—so I'd have him
think, Lord forgive me, that we are a very happy couple.

ROWLEY: I understand you, but then you must be very careful not to differ while
he's in the house with you.

SIR PETER: Egad, and so we must—and that's impossible. Ah! Master Rowley,
when an old bachelor marries a young wife, he deserves—no, the crime carries the
punishment along with it.   [Exeunt.]

---

5. Amorous, mischief-making man-about-town.   7. Conviction.
6. I.e., inherited from his ancestors.   8. Nickname for "Oliver."

ACT 2

Scene 1

[Sir Peter Teazle's house. Enter Sir Peter and Lady Teazle.]

SIR PETER: Lady Teazle, Lady Teazle, I'll not bear it.

LADY TEAZLE: Sir Peter, Sir Peter, you may bear it or not as you please, but I ought to have my own way in everything, and what's more, I will too. What! Though I was educated in the country, I know very well that women of fashion in London are accountable to nobody after they are married.

SIR PETER: Very well, ma'am, very well! So a husband is to have no influence, no authority?

LADY TEAZLE: Authority! No, to be sure—if you wanted authority over me, you should have adopted me and not married me; I am sure you were old enough.

SIR PETER: Old enough! Aye, there it is. Well, well, Lady Teazle, though my life may be made unhappy by your temper, I'll not be ruined by your extravagance.

LADY TEAZLE: My extravagance! I'm sure I'm not more extravagant than a woman of fashion ought to be.

SIR PETER: No, no, madam, you shall throw away no more sums on such unmeaning luxury—'Slife,[1] to spend as much to furnish your dressing room with flowers in winter as would suffice to turn the Pantheon[2] into a greenhouse and give a *fête-champêtre*[3] at Christmas!

LADY TEAZLE: Lord! Sir Peter, am I to blame because flowers are dear[4] in cold weather? You should find fault with the climate and not with me. For my part, I am sure I wish it was spring all the year round—and that roses grew under one's feet!

SIR PETER: Oons![5] Madam, if you had been born to this, I shouldn't wonder at your talking thus—but you forget what your situation was when I married you.

LADY TEAZLE: No, no, I don't—'twas a very disagreeable one, or I should never have married you.

SIR PETER: Yes, yes, madam, you were then in somewhat an humbler style—the daughter of a plain country squire. Recollect, Lady Teazle, when I saw you first, sitting at your tambor[6] in a pretty figure[7] linen gown with a bunch of keys by your side, your hair combed smooth over a roll,[8] and your apartment hung round with fruits in worsted[9] of your own working—

LADY TEAZLE: O, yes, I remember it very well, and a curious life I led! My daily occupation to inspect the dairy, superintend the poultry, make extracts from the family receipt[1] book and comb my Aunt Deborah's lap-dog.

SIR PETER: Yes, yes, ma'am, 'twas so indeed.

LADY TEAZLE: And then you know my evening amusements: to draw patterns for ruffles which I had not the materials to make—to play Pope Joan[2] with the curate[3]—to read a novel to my aunt—or to be stuck down to an old spinet[4] to strum my father to sleep after a fox chase.

---

1. A euphemistic abbreviation of the oath "on God's life."
2. A fashionable concert hall in London, constructed in imitation of the Pantheon in Rome.
3. French: garden party.
4. Expensive.
5. Euphemistic abbreviation of the oath "by God's wounds."

6. A wooden hoop used for embroidery.
7. Patterned.
8. A pad, used to give height to a hairstyle.
9. Fine woolen yarn used for embroidery.
1. Recipe (for foods or medicines).
2. A card game.
3. Assistant to the parish priest.
4. Small harpsichord.

SIR PETER: I am glad you have so good a memory. Yes, madam, these were the recreations I took you from—but now you must have your coach, *vis-à-vis*,[5] and three powdered footmen before your chair, and in summer a pair of white cats[6] to draw you to Kensington Gardens[7]—no recollection, I suppose, when you were content to ride double behind the butler on a docked[8] coach horse.

LADY TEAZLE: No, I swear I never did that—I deny the butler and the coach horse.

SIR PETER: This, madam, was your situation, and what have I not done for you? I have made you a woman of fashion, of fortune, of rank—in short, I have made you my wife—

LADY TEAZLE: Well then, and there is but one thing more you can make me, to add to the obligation, and that is—

SIR PETER: My widow, I suppose?

LADY TEAZLE: Hem! hem!

SIR PETER: Thank you, madam, but don't flatter yourself, for though your ill conduct may disturb my peace, it shall never break my heart, I promise you; however, I am equally obliged to you for the hint.

LADY TEAZLE: Then why will you endeavor to make yourself so disagreeable to me, and thwart me in every little elegant expense?

SIR PETER: 'Slife, madam, I say: had you any of these elegant expenses when you married me?

LADY TEAZLE: Lud, Sir Peter, would you have me be out of the fashion?

SIR PETER: The fashion indeed! What had you to do with the fashion before you married me?

LADY TEAZLE: For my part, I should think you would like to have your wife thought a woman of taste.

SIR PETER: Aye, there again—taste! Zounds, madam, you had no taste when you married me.

LADY TEAZLE: That's very true indeed, Sir Peter, and after having married you, I am sure I should never pretend to taste again! But now, Sir Peter, if we have finished our daily jangle, I presume I may go to my engagement at Lady Sneerwell's.

SIR PETER: Aye, there's another precious circumstance: a charming set of acquaintance you have made there.

LADY TEAZLE: Nay, Sir Peter, they are people of rank and fortune—and remarkably tenacious of reputation.

SIR PETER: Yes, egad, they are tenacious of reputation with a vengeance, for they don't choose[9] anybody should have a character but themselves—such a crew! Ah! Many a wretch has rid on a hurdle[1] who has done less mischief than those utterers of forged tales, coiners of scandal, and clippers[2] of reputation.

LADY TEAZLE: What, would you restrain the freedom of speech?

SIR PETER: O! They have made you just as bad as any one of the society.

LADY TEAZLE: Why, I believe I do bear a part with a tolerable grace—but I vow I have no malice against the people I abuse: when I say an ill natured thing, 'tis out of pure good humor—and I take it for granted they deal exactly in the same

---

5. A carriage in which two or four people could face each other.
6. Ponies.
7. A fashionable gathering place adjoining Hyde Park.
8. Short-tailed.

9. I.e., choose that.
1. The wooden frame that transported traitors to execution.
2. A coiner counterfeits money; a clipper cuts off a coin's rim in order to resell the metal.

manner with me. But, Sir Peter, you know you promised to come to Lady Sneer-well's too.

SIR PETER: Well, well, I'll call in just to look after my own character.

LADY TEAZLE: Then indeed, you must make haste after me or you'll be too late—so goodby to ye.

[Exit Lady Teazle.]

SIR PETER: So—I have gained much by my intended expostulations[3]—yet with what a charming air she contradicts everything I say, and how pleasingly she shows her contempt of my authority—well, though I can't make her love me, there is a great satisfaction in quarreling with her, and I think she never appears to such advantage as when she's doing everything in her power to plague me. [Exit.]

Scene 2

[Lady Sneerwell's. Lady Sneerwell, Mrs. Candour, Crabtree, Sir Benjamin and Surface.]

LADY SNEERWELL: Nay, positively we will hear it—

SURFACE: Yes, yes, the epigram, by all means.

SIR BENJAMIN: Plague on 't, uncle—'tis mere nonsense.

CRABTREE: No, no, before gad, very clever for an extempore—

SIR BENJAMIN: But, ladies, you should be acquainted with the circumstance. You must know that one day last week, as Lady Betty Curricle[4] was taking the dust in Hyde Park in a sort of duodecimo phaeton,[5] she desired me to write some verses on her ponies, upon which I took out my pocket-book—and in one moment produced the following:

Sure never were seen two such beautiful ponies
Other horses are clowns—and these, macaronies.[6]
Nay, to give 'em this title I'm sure isn't wrong—
Their legs are so slim—and their tails are so long.

CRABTREE: There, ladies, done in the smack of a whip—and on horseback, too.

SURFACE: A very Phoebus[7] mounted—indeed, Sir Benjamin.

SIR BENJAMIN: O, dear sir, trifles—trifles!

[Enter Lady Teazle and Maria.]

MRS. CANDOUR: I must have a copy.

LADY SNEERWELL: Lady Teazle, I hope we shall see Sir Peter.

LADY TEAZLE: I believe he'll wait on your ladyship presently.

LADY SNEERWELL: Maria, my love, you look grave—come, you shall sit down to cards with Mr. Surface.

MARIA: I take very little pleasure in cards; however, I'll do as your ladyship pleases.

LADY TEAZLE: I am surprised Mr. Surface should sit down with her—I thought he would have embraced this opportunity of speaking to me before Sir Peter came.

MRS. CANDOUR [coming forward]: Now, I'll die, but you are so scandalous I'll forswear your society.

3. Friendly protests.
4. A "curricle" is a fast two-wheeled carriage.
5. A "duodecimo phaeton" suggests a very small open carriage (the "duodecimo" was the smallest format for the printed book, one-third the size of the quarto, and suitable for carrying in a pocket).
6. Gaudily dressed young men, so called because of their penchant for Italian fashion.
7. "The bright one": Apollo, the god of poetry and music, was sometimes depicted as driving the chariot that transported the sun across the heavens.

LADY TEAZLE: What's the matter, Mrs. Candour?

MRS. CANDOUR: They'll not allow our friend Miss Vermilion to be handsome.

LADY SNEERWELL: O, surely she's a pretty woman.

CRABTREE: I am very glad you think so, ma'am.

MRS. CANDOUR: She has a charming, fresh color—

LADY TEAZLE: Yes, when it is fresh put on.

MRS. CANDOUR: O fie, I'll swear her color is natural—I have seen it come and go.

LADY TEAZLE: I dare swear you have, ma'am—it goes of a night and comes again in the morning.

MRS. CANDOUR: Ha! ha! ha! How I hate to hear you talk so—but surely now her sister is—or was—very handsome.

CRABTREE: Who, Mrs. Evergreen? O Lud, she's six and fifty if she's an hour.

MRS. CANDOUR: Now positively you wrong her. Fifty-two or fifty-three is the utmost—and I don't think she looks more—

SIR BENJAMIN: Ah, there is no judging by her looks unless one could see her face.

LADY SNEERWELL: Well, well, if Mrs. Evergreen does take some pains to repair the ravages of time, you must allow she effects it with great ingenuity; and surely that's better than the careless manner in which the widow Ochre caulks her wrinkles.

SIR BENJAMIN: Nay, now, Lady Sneerwell—you are severe upon the widow. Come, come, it is not that she paints so ill—but when she has finished her face she joins it on so badly to her neck that she looks like a mended statue, in which the connoisseur sees at once that the head's modern though the trunk's antique.

CRABTREE: Ha! ha! ha! Well said, nephew!

MRS. CANDOUR: Ha! ha! ha! Well, you make me laugh, but I vow I hate you for't—what do you think of Miss Simper?

SIR BENJAMIN: Why, she has very pretty teeth.

LADY TEAZLE: Yes, and on that account, when she is neither speaking nor laughing (which very seldom happens)—she never absolutely shuts her mouth, but leaves it always on a jar,[8] as it were.

MRS. CANDOUR: How can you be so ill-natured?

LADY TEAZLE: Nay, I allow even that's better than the pains Mrs. Prim takes to conceal her losses in front. She draws her mouth 'till it positively resembles the aperture of a poor's-box,[9] and all her words appear to slide out edgeways.

LADY SNEERWELL: Very well, Lady Teazle, I see you can be a little severe—

LADY TEAZLE: In defense of a friend, it is but justice, but here comes Sir Peter to spoil our pleasantry!

[Enter Sir Peter Teazle.]

SIR PETER: Ladies, your most obedient. [Aside.] Mercy on me, here is the whole set! A character dead at every word, I suppose.

MRS. CANDOUR: I am rejoiced you are come, Sir Peter—they have been so censorious,[1] they will allow good qualities to nobody—not even good-nature to our friend Mrs. Pursy.

LADY TEAZLE: What, the fat dowager who was at Mrs. Codille's last night—

MRS. CANDOUR: Nay—her bulk is her misfortune and when she takes such pains to get rid of it, you ought not to reflect on her.

8. Partly open.
9. A church receptacle with a narrow opening for money

donated to the poor.
1. Critical.

LADY SNEERWELL: That's very true, indeed.

LADY TEAZLE: Yes, I know she almost lives on acids and small whey,[2] laces herself by pullies,[3] and often in the hottest noon of summer you may see her on a little squat pony with her hair platted up behind like a drummer's—and puffing round the Ring[4] on a full trot.

MRS. CANDOUR: I thank you, Lady Teazle, for defending her.

SIR PETER: Yes, a good defense truly.

MRS. CANDOUR: But Sir Benjamin is as censorious as Miss Sallow.

CRABTREE: Yes, and she is a curious being to pretend[5] to be censorious—an awkward gawky[6] without any one good point under heaven!

MRS. CANDOUR: Positively, you shall not be so very severe. Miss Sallow is a relation of mine by marriage, and as for her person, great allowance is to be made—for let me tell you, a woman labors under many disadvantages who tries to pass for a girl at six and thirty.

LADY SNEERWELL: Though surely she is handsome still—and for the weakness in her eyes, considering how much she reads by candlelight, it is not to be wondered at.

MRS. CANDOUR: True, and then as to her manner—upon my word I think it is particularly graceful, considering she never had the least education, for you know her mother was a Welsh milliner[7] and her father a sugar-baker[8] at Bristow.

SIR BENJAMIN: Ah! You are both of you too good-natured!

SIR PETER [aside]: Yes, damned good-natured! This their own relation! Mercy on me!

SIR BENJAMIN: And Mrs. Candour is of so moral a turn—she can sit for an hour to hear Lady Stucco[9] talk sentiment.

LADY TEAZLE: Nay, I vow Lady Stucco is very well with the dessert after dinner, for she's just like the French fruit[1] one cracks for mottos—made up of paint and proverb.

MRS. CANDOUR: Well, I never will join in ridiculing a friend—and so I constantly tell my cousin Ogle—and you all know what pretensions she has to be critical in[2] beauty—

CRABTREE: O, to be sure, she has herself the oddest countenance that ever was seen. 'Tis a collection of features from all the different countries of the globe.

SIR BENJAMIN: So she has indeed: an Irish front,

CRABTREE: Caledonian locks[3]—

SIR BENJAMIN: Dutch nose[4]—

CRABTREE: Austrian lip[5]—

SIR BENJAMIN: Complexion of a Spaniard[6]—

CRABTREE: And teeth à la Chinoise[7]—

SIR BENJAMIN: In short, her face resembles a *table d'hôte* at Spaw[8] where no two guests are of a nation—

---

2. I.e., on vinegar and on the watery part of milk.
3. I.e., she uses machinery to tighten her corset strings.
4. A fashionable drive in Hyde Park.
5. Presume.
6. Bungler.
7. Bonnet-maker.
8. Refiner.
9. White plaster used for coating wall surfaces.
1. Sugar candy with a saying inside.

2. I.e., expert in judging.
3. Long, shaggy hair, like that of Scottish Highlanders.
4. A snub nose.
5. A pouty lower lip.
6. Dark skin.
7. Black (because of the Chinese practice of staining the teeth).
8. A common table for guests at the resort in Belgium, famous for its mineral springs.

CRABTREE: Or a congress at the close of a general war—wherein all the members, even to her eyes, appear to have a different interest, and her nose and chin are the only parties likely to join issue.[9]

MRS. CANDOUR: Ha! ha! ha!

SIR PETER [aside]: Mercy on my life! A person they dine with twice a week.

MRS. CANDOUR: Nay, but I vow you shall not carry the laugh off so—for, give me leave to say that Mrs. Ogle—

SIR PETER: Madam, madam, I beg your pardon; there's no stopping these good gentlemen's tongues, but when I tell you, Mrs. Candour, that the lady they are abusing is a particular friend of mine, I hope you'll not take her part.[1]

LADY SNEERWELL: Well said, Sir Peter, but you are a cruel creature—too phlegmatic[2] yourself for a jest and too peevish to allow wit on others.

SIR PETER: Ah! Madam, true wit is more nearly allied to good nature than your ladyship is aware of.

LADY TEAZLE: True, Sir Peter, I believe they are so near akin that they can never be united—

SIR BENJAMIN: Or, rather, madam: suppose them man and wife because one so seldom sees them together.

LADY TEAZLE: But Sir Peter is such an enemy to scandal, I believe he would have it put down by parliament.

SIR PETER: Before Heaven! Madam, if they were to consider the sporting with reputation of as much importance as poaching on manors,[3] and pass an Act for the Preservation of Fame—I believe there are many would thank them for the bill.

LADY SNEERWELL: O Lud! Sir Peter, would you deprive us of our privileges?[4]

SIR PETER: Aye, madam, and then no person should be permitted to kill characters, or run down reputations, but qualified old maids and disappointed widows.

LADY SNEERWELL: Go, you monster—

MRS. CANDOUR: But sure, you would not be quite so severe on those who only report what they hear?

SIR PETER: Yes, madam, I would have law merchant for them too—and in all cases of slander currency, whenever the drawer of the lie was not to be found, the injured party should have a right to come on any of the endorsers.[5]

CRABTREE: Well, for my part, I believe there never was a scandalous tale without some foundation.

LADY SNEERWELL: Come ladies, shall we sit down to cards in the next room?
    [Enter Servant and whispers to Sir Peter.]

SIR PETER: I'll be with them directly! [Aside.] I'll get away unperceived.

LADY SNEERWELL: Sir Peter, you are not leaving us?

SIR PETER: Your ladyship must excuse me—I'm called away by particular business, but I leave my character behind me.

    [Exit Sir Peter.]

SIR BENJAMIN: Well certainly, Lady Teazle, that lord of yours is a strange being— I could tell you some stories of him would make you laugh heartily if he wasn't your husband.

---

9. To come to agreement, to unite.
1. Speak in her defense.
2. Dull, unexcitable.
3. Illegal hunting on country estates.

4. I.e., special rules like the ones that apply to merchants.
5. The metaphor equates spreading gossip with entering into debt; if the incurrer of the debt should fail to pay up, the endorsers may be held responsible.

LADY TEAZLE: O pray, don't mind that. Come, do let's hear 'em.

[*They join the rest of the company, all talking as they are going into the next room.*]

SURFACE [*rising with Maria*]: Maria, I see you have no satisfaction in this society.

MARIA: How is it possible I should? If to raise malicious smiles at the infirmities and misfortunes of those who have never injured us be the province of wit or humor, Heav'n grant me a double portion of dullness.

SURFACE: Yet they appear more ill natured than they are. They have no malice at heart.

MARIA: Then is their conduct still more contemptible, for in my opinion nothing could excuse the intemperance of their tongues but a natural and ungovernable bitterness of mind.

SURFACE: But can you, Maria, feel thus for others and be unkind to me alone—is hope to be denied the tenderest passion?

MARIA: Why will you distress me by renewing this subject?

SURFACE: Ah! Maria, you would not treat me thus and oppose your guardian Sir Peter's wishes—but that I see that profligate Charles is still a favored rival.

MARIA: Ungenerously urged—but whatever my sentiments of that unfortunate young man are, be assured I shall not feel more bound to give him up because his distresses have lost him the regard even of a brother.

[*Lady Teazle returns.*]

SURFACE: Nay but Maria, do not leave me with a frown. By all that's honest, I swear—[*Aside.*] Gad's life here's Lady Teazle—You must not, no you shall not, for though I have the greatest regard for Lady Teazle—

MARIA: Lady Teazle!

SURFACE: Yet were Sir Peter to suspect—

LADY TEAZLE [*coming forward*]: What's this, pray? Do you take her for me? Child, you are wanted in the next room.   [*Exit Maria.*]
What is all this, pray?

SURFACE: O, the most unlucky circumstance in nature. Maria has somehow suspected the tender concern which I have for your happiness and threatened to acquaint Sir Peter with her suspicions—and I was just endeavoring to reason with her when you came.

LADY TEAZLE: Indeed. But you seemed to adopt—a very tender method of reasoning. Do you usually argue on your knees?

SURFACE: O, she's a child, and I thought a little bombast[6]—but Lady Teazle, when are you to give me your judgment on my library, as you promised?

LADY TEAZLE: No, no. I begin to think it would be imprudent—and you know I admit you as a lover no further than fashion requires.

SURFACE: True, a mere platonic cicisbeo[7]—what every London wife is entitled to.

LADY TEAZLE: Certainly, one must not be out of the fashion. However, I have so much of my country prejudices left, that though Sir Peter's ill humor may vex me ever so, it never shall provoke me to—

SURFACE: The only revenge in your power. Well, I applaud your moderation.

LADY TEAZLE: Go—you are an insinuating wretch—but we shall be missed. Let us join the company.

---

6. Extravagant utterance and behavior.   7. I.e., an escort but not a lover.

SURFACE: But we had best not return together.

LADY TEAZLE: Well don't stay, for Maria shan't come to hear any more of your reasoning, I promise you.

[Exit Lady Teazle.]

SURFACE: A curious dilemma, truly, my politics have run me into. I wanted at first only to ingratiate myself with Lady Teazle, that she might not be my enemy with Maria—and I have, I don't know how, become her serious lover. Sincerely, I begin to wish I had never made such a point of gaining so very good a character, for it has led me into so many cursed rogueries that I doubt I shall be exposed at last.

[Exit.]

Scene 3

[Sir Peter's. Enter Sir Oliver and Rowley.]

SIR OLIVER: Ha! ha! ha! And so my old friend is married, hey? A young wife out of the country! Ha! ha! ha! That he should have stood bluff to [8] old bachelor so long and sink into a husband at last!

ROWLEY: But you must not rally[9] him on the subject, Sir Oliver—'tis a tender point, I assure you, though he has been married only seven months.

SIR OLIVER: Then he has been just half a year on the stool of repentance.[1] Poor Peter! But you say he has entirely given up Charles? Never sees him, hey?

ROWLEY: His prejudice against him is astonishing—and I am sure greatly increased by a jealousy of him with Lady Teazle, which he has been industriously led into by a scandalous society in the neighborhood who have contributed not a little to Charles's ill name. Whereas the truth is, I believe, if the lady is partial to either of them his brother is the favorite.

SIR OLIVER: Aye, I know. There are a set of malicious, prating, prudent gossips, both male and female, who murder characters to kill time and will rob a young fellow of his good name before he has years to know the value of it. But I am not to be prejudiced against my nephew by such, I promise you. No! No, if Charles has done nothing false or mean, I shall compound for [2] his extravagance.

ROWLEY: Then, my life on't, you will reclaim him. Ah sir, it gives me new life to find that your heart is not turned against him—and that the son of my good old master has one friend, however, left.

SIR OLIVER: What! Shall I forget, Master Rowley, when I was at his years myself? Egad, my brother and I were neither of us very prudent youths—and yet I believe you have not seen many better men than your old master was.

ROWLEY: Sir, 'tis this reflection gives me assurance that Charles may yet be a credit to his family—but here comes Sir Peter.

SIR OLIVER: Egad, so he does. Mercy on me, he's greatly altered—and seems to have a settled, married look. One may read husband in his face at this distance.

[Enter Sir Peter Teazle.]

SIR PETER: Hah! Sir Oliver, my old friend, welcome to England a thousand times!

SIR OLIVER: Thank you, thank you, Sir Peter and—i'faith[3]—I am as glad to find you well, believe me.

---

8. Stand firm as an.
9. Make fun of.
1. A stool formerly placed in Scottish churches, on which

offenders against chastity made public atonement.
2. Pay the debts incurred by.
3. In faith; truly.

SIR PETER: Ah! 'Tis a long time since we met—sixteen years I doubt, Sir Oliver, and many a cross accident in the time.

SIR OLIVER: Aye, I have had my share, but what, I find you are married—hey, my old boy. Well, well, it can't be helped, and so I wish you joy with all my heart.

SIR PETER: Thank you, thank you, Sir Oliver—yes I have entered into the happy state, but we'll not talk of that now.

SIR OLIVER: True, true, Sir Peter, old friends should not begin on grievances at first meeting—no, no, no.

ROWLEY [to Sir Oliver]: Take care, pray, sir—

SIR OLIVER: Well, so one of my nephews I find is a wild rogue—hey?

SIR PETER: Wild! Ah, my old friend, I grieve for your disappointment there. He's a lost young man indeed; however, his brother will make you amends. Joseph is indeed what a youth should be—everybody in the world speaks well of him.

SIR OLIVER: I am sorry to hear it; he has too good a character to be an honest fellow. Everybody speaks well of him! Pshaw! Then he has bowed as low to knaves and fools as to the honest dignity of genius or virtue.

SIR PETER: What, Sir Oliver, do you blame him for not making enemies?

SIR OLIVER: Yes, if he has merit enough to deserve them.

SIR PETER: Well, well, you'll be convinced when you know him—'tis edification to hear him converse. He professes the noblest sentiments.

SIR OLIVER: Ah, plague on his sentiments. If he salutes me with a scrap of morality in his mouth I shall be sick directly. But, however, don't mistake me, Sir Peter. I don't mean to defend Charles's errors, but before I form my judgment of either of them I intend to make a trial of their hearts—and my friend Rowley and I have planned something for the purpose.

ROWLEY: And Sir Peter shall own he has been for once mistaken.

SIR PETER: O, my life on Joseph's honor!

SIR OLIVER: Well, come give us a bottle of good wine—and we'll drink the lads' healths and tell you our scheme.

SIR PETER: Allons[4] then—

SIR OLIVER: And don't, Sir Peter, be so severe against your old friend's son. Odds my life, I am not sorry that he has run out of the course a little—for my part, I hate to see prudence clinging to the green succors[5] of youth—'tis like ivy round a sapling, and spoils the growth of the tree.   [Exeunt.]

ACT 3

Scene 1

[Sir Peter's. Sir Peter, Sir Oliver, and Rowley.]

SIR PETER: Well then, we will see this fellow first and have our wine afterwards. But how is this, Master Rowley? I don't see the jet[1] of your scheme.

ROWLEY: Why, sir, this Mr. Stanley whom I was speaking of is nearly[2] related to them by their mother. He was once a merchant in Dublin, but has been ruined by a series of undeserved misfortunes. He has applied by letter since his confinement[3] both to Mr. Surface and Charles. From the former, he has received nothing but

4. Let's go (French).
5. Tender shoots (of a growing plant or tree).
1. Point.

2. Closely.
3. I.e., for debt.

evasive promises of future service, while Charles has done all that his extravagance has left him power to do, and he is at this time endeavoring to raise a sum of
money, part of which, in the midst of his own distresses, I know he intends for the
service of poor Stanley.

SIR OLIVER: Ah! He is my brother's son.

SIR PETER: Well, but how is Sir Oliver personally to—

ROWLEY: Why, sir, I will inform Charles and his brother that Stanley has obtained
permission to apply in person to his friends—and as they have neither of them
ever seen him, let Sir Oliver assume his character, and he will have a fair opportunity of judging at least of the benevolence of their dispositions. And believe me,
sir, you will find in the youngest brother one who, in the midst of folly and dissipation, has still, as our immortal bard expresses it—"a tear for pity and a hand
open as day for melting charity."[4]

SIR PETER: Pshaw! What signifies his having an open hand, or purse either, when
he has nothing left to give! Well, well, make the trial if you please—but where is
the fellow whom you brought for Sir Oliver to examine, relative to Charles's
affairs?

ROWLEY: Below, waiting his commands, and no one can give him better intelligence—this, Sir Oliver, is a friendly Jew who, to do him justice, has done everything in his power to bring your nephew to a proper sense of his extravagance.

SIR PETER: Pray, let us have him in.

ROWLEY: Desire Mr. Moses to walk upstairs.

SIR PETER: But why should you suppose he will speak the truth?

ROWLEY: O, I have convinced him that he has no chance of recovering certain
sums advanced to Charles but through the bounty of Sir Oliver, who he knows is
arrived; so that you may depend on his fidelity to his interest.[5] I have also another
evidence in my power, one Snake—whom I have detected in a matter little short
of forgery, and shall shortly produce to remove some of your prejudices, Sir Peter,
relative to Charles and Lady Teazle.

SIR PETER: I have heard too much on that subject.

ROWLEY: Here comes the honest Israelite.

[Enter Moses.]

This is Sir Oliver—

SIR OLIVER: Sir, I understand you have lately had great dealings with my nephew
Charles.

MOSES: Yes, Sir Oliver, I have done all I could for him, but he was ruined before he
came to me for assistance.

SIR OLIVER: That was unlucky, truly—for you have had no opportunity of showing your talents.

MOSES: None at all—I hadn't the pleasure of knowing his distresses 'till he was
some thousands worse than nothing.[6]

SIR OLIVER: Unfortunate indeed! But I suppose you have done all in your power
for him, honest Moses?

MOSES: Yes, he knows that. This very evening I was to have brought him a gentleman from the city who doesn't know him and will, I believe, advance him some
money.

---

4. From Shakespeare's 2 Henry IV 4.4.31–32.   to do so.
5. I.e., Moses will tell the truth because it is to his benefit   6. I.e., in debt.

SIR PETER: What, one Charles has never had money from before?

MOSES: Yes Mr. Premium of Crutched-Friars[7]—formerly a broker.

SIR PETER: Egad, Sir Oliver, a thought strikes me—Charles, you say, doesn't know Mr. Premium?

MOSES: Not at all.

SIR PETER: Now then, Sir Oliver, you may have a better opportunity of satisfying yourself than by an old romancing tale of a poor relation. Go with my friend Moses and represent Mr. Premium, and then I'll answer for't, you will see your nephew in all his glory.

SIR OLIVER: Egad, I like this idea better than the other, and I may visit Joseph afterward as old Stanley.

SIR PETER: True, so you may.

ROWLEY: Well, this is taking Charles rather at a disadvantage to be sure. However, Moses, you understand Sir Peter and will be faithful?

MOSES: You may depend upon me—this is near the time I was to have gone.

SIR OLIVER: I'll accompany you as soon as you please, Moses, but hold, I have forgot one thing—how the plague shall I be able to pass for a Jew?

MOSES: There's no need. The principal[8] is Christian.

SIR OLIVER: Is he? I'm sorry to hear it, but then again—an't I rather too smartly dressed to look like a money-lender?

SIR PETER: Not at all. 'Twould not be out of character if you went in your own carriage—would it, Moses?

MOSES: Not in the least.

SIR OLIVER: Well, but—how must I talk? There's certainly some cant[9] of usury[1]—and mode of treating[2] that I ought to know.

SIR PETER: O, there's not much to learn—the great point, as I take it, is to be exorbitant enough in your demands, hey Moses?

MOSES: Yes, that's a very great point.

SIR OLIVER: I'll answer for't, I'll not be wanting[3] in that—I'll ask him eight or ten per cent on the loan at least.

MOSES: If you ask him no more than that, you'll be discovered immediately.

SIR OLIVER: Hey—what the plague! How much then?

MOSES: That depends upon the circumstances. If he appears not very anxious for the supply, you should require only forty or fifty per cent—but if you find him in great distress and want the monies very bad, you may ask double.

SIR PETER: A good honest trade you're learning, Sir Oliver.

SIR OLIVER: Truly I think so—and not unprofitable.

MOSES: Then, you know, you haven't the monies yourself—but are forced to borrow them for him of a friend.

SIR OLIVER: Oh, I borrow it of a friend, do I?

MOSES: Yes—and your friend is an unconscionable dog—but you can't help it.

SIR OLIVER: My friend is an unconscionable dog, is he?

MOSES: Yes—and he himself hasn't the moneys by him, but is forced to sell stock at a great loss.

---

7. A small street in the commercial center of London.
8. Head of the company (i.e., Mr. Premium).
9. Jargon.
1. Practice of lending money at exorbitant levels of
interest.
2. Way of negotiating.
3. Failing.

SIR OLIVER: He is forced to sell stock, is he, at a great loss is he—well, that's very kind of him.

SIR PETER: I'faith, Sir Oliver, Mr. Premium, I mean, you'll soon be master of the trade—but Moses, wouldn't you have him run out a little against the Annuity Bill?[4] That would be in character, I should think.

MOSES: Very much.

ROWLEY: And lament that a young man now must be at years of discretion before he is suffered to ruin himself?

MOSES: Aye—great pity!

SIR PETER: And abuse the public for allowing merit to an act whose only object is to snatch misfortune and imprudence from the rapacious relief of usury! And give the minor a chance of inheriting his estate, without being undone[5] by coming into possession.

SIR OLIVER: So, so, Moses shall give me further instructions as we go together.

SIR PETER: You will not have much time, for your nephew lives hard[6] by.

SIR OLIVER: O, never fear—my tutor appears so able that though Charles lived in the next street, it must be my own fault if I am not a complete rogue before I turn the corner.

[Exeunt Sir Oliver and Moses.]

SIR PETER: So, now I think Sir Oliver will be convinced. You are partial, Rowley, and would have prepared Charles for the other plot.

ROWLEY: No, upon my word, Sir Peter—

SIR PETER: Well, go bring me this Snake, and I'll hear what he has to say presently.[7] I see Maria, and want to speak with her—

[Exit Rowley.]

I should be glad to be convinced my suspicions of Lady Teazle and Charles were unjust. I have never yet opened my mind on this subject to my friend Joseph—I'm determined I will do it. He will give me his opinion sincerely.

[Enter Maria.]

So, child, has Mr. Surface returned with you?

MARIA: No, sir. He was engaged.

SIR PETER: Well, Maria, do you not reflect the more you converse with that amiable young man, what return[8] his partiality for you deserves?

MARIA: Indeed, Sir Peter, your frequent importunity[9] on this subject distresses me extremely—you compel me to declare that I know no man who has ever paid me a particular attention whom I would not prefer to Mr. Surface.

SIR PETER: So! Here's perverseness! No, no, Maria, 'tis Charles only whom you would prefer—'tis evident his vices and follies have won your heart.

MARIA: This is unkind, sir—you know I have obeyed you in neither seeing nor corresponding with him. I have heard enough to convince me that he is unworthy my regard. Yet I cannot think it culpable, if while my understanding severely condemns his vices, my heart suggests some pity for his distresses.

---

4. A law that protected minors from obtaining a life annuity (in which, in return for a loan, the debtor makes yearly payments for the rest of his life); it would become law in May 1777, the same month as the play's first performance.
5. Ruined (because he ran up huge debts which will have

to be paid out of his inheritance).
6. Near.
7. Soon; forthwith.
8. Recompense.
9. Inquiry.

SIR PETER: Well, well, pity him as much as you please, but give your heart and hand to a worthier object.

MARIA: Never to his brother.

SIR PETER: Go—perverse and obstinate! But take care, madam, you have never yet known what the authority of a guardian is—don't compel me to inform you of it.

MARIA: I can only say you shall not have just reason—'tis true by my father's will I am for a short period bound to regard you as his substitute, but must cease to think you so, when you would compel me to be miserable.

[Exit Maria.]

SIR PETER: Was ever man so crossed as I am! Everything conspiring to fret me! I hadn't been involved in matrimony a fortnight before her father—a hale and hearty man—died on purpose, I believe, for the pleasure of plaguing me with the care of his daughter. But here comes my helpmate! She appears in great good humor. How happy I should be if I could tease her into loving me though but a little.

LADY TEAZLE: Lud! Sir Peter, I hope you haven't been quarreling with Maria. It isn't using me well to be ill-humored when I am not by!

SIR PETER: Ah! Lady Teazle, you might have the power to make me good-humored at all times.

LADY TEAZLE: I am sure I wish I had, for I want you to be in charming sweet temper at this moment—do be good-humored now—and let me have two hundred pounds, will you?

SIR PETER: Two hundred pounds! What an't I to be in a good humor without paying for it? But speak to me thus, and, i'faith, there's nothing I could refuse you. You shall have it, but seal me a bond for the repayment.[1]

LADY TEAZLE: O no—there, my note of hand will do as well.

SIR PETER [kissing her hand]: And you shall no longer reproach me with not giving you an independent settlement—I mean shortly to surprise you. But shall we always live thus—hey?

LADY TEAZLE: If you please—I'm sure I don't care how soon we leave off quarreling, provided you'll own you were tired first.

SIR PETER: Well then, let our future contest be who shall be most obliging.

LADY TEAZLE: I assure you, Sir Peter, good nature becomes you—you look now as you did before we were married! When you used to walk with me under the elms and tell me stories of what a gallant you were in your youth, and chuck me under the chin—you would—and ask me if I thought I could love an old fellow who would deny me nothing—didn't you?

SIR PETER: Yes, yes, and you were as kind and attentive.

LADY TEAZLE: Aye, so I was—and would always take your part when my acquaintance used to abuse you and turn you into ridicule.

SIR PETER: Indeed!

LADY TEAZLE: Aye, and when my cousin Sophy has called you a stiff, peevish old bachelor and laughed at me for thinking of marrying one who might be my father, I have always defended you, and said I didn't think you so ugly by any means, and that I dared say you'd make a very good sort of a husband.

SIR PETER: And you prophesied right—and we shall certainly now be the happiest couple.

1. I.e., give me a kiss.

LADY TEAZLE: And never differ again.

SIR PETER: No, never—though at the same time indeed, my dear Lady Teazle, you must watch your temper very narrowly, for in all our little quarrels, my dear, if you recollect, my love, you always began first.

LADY TEAZLE: I beg your pardon, my dear Sir Peter, indeed, you always gave the provocation.

SIR PETER: Now see, my angel, take care—contradicting isn't the way to keep friends.

LADY TEAZLE: Then don't you begin it, my love!

SIR PETER: There now—you—you are going on—you don't perceive, my life, that you are just doing the very thing which you know always makes me angry.

LADY TEAZLE: Nay, you know if you will be angry without any reason—

SIR PETER: There, now you want to quarrel again.

LADY TEAZLE: No, I am sure I don't, but if you will be so peevish—

SIR PETER: There, now who begins first?

LADY TEAZLE: Why you, to be sure. I said nothing, but there's no bearing your temper.

SIR PETER: No, no, madam, the fault's in your own temper.

LADY TEAZLE: Aye, you are just what my cousin Sophy said you would be.

SIR PETER: Your cousin Sophy is a forward, impertinent gypsy.[2]

LADY TEAZLE: You are a great bear, I'm sure, to abuse my relations.

SIR PETER: Now may all the plagues of marriage be doubled on me if ever I try to be friends with you any more!

LADY TEAZLE: So much the better.

SIR PETER: No, no, madam, 'tis evident you never cared a pin for me—and I was a madman to marry you—a pert rural coquette[3] that had refused half the honest squires[4] in the neighborhood.

LADY TEAZLE: And I am sure I was a fool to marry you—an old, dangling[5] bachelor who was single at fifty, only because he never could meet with anyone who would have him.

SIR PETER: Aye, aye, madam, but you were pleased enough to listen to me—you never had such an offer before.

LADY TEAZLE: No! Didn't I refuse Sir Twivy Tarrier, who everybody said would have been a better match, for his estate is just as good as yours—and he has broke his neck since we have been married!

SIR PETER: I have done with you, madam. You are an unfeeling, ungrateful—but there's an end of everything. I believe you capable of anything that's bad—yes, madam, I now believe the reports relative to you and Charles, madam. Yes, madam, you and Charles are not without grounds—

LADY TEAZLE: Take care, Sir Peter, you had better not insinuate any such thing! I'll not be suspected without cause, I promise you.

SIR PETER: Very well, madam, very well—a separate maintenance as soon as you please. Yes, madam, or a divorce. I'll make an example of myself for the benefit of all old bachelors. Let us separate, madam—

LADY TEAZLE: Agreed, agreed—and now, my dear Sir Peter, we are of a mind once more; we may be the happiest couple, and never differ again, you know. Ha! ha! Well, you are going to be in a passion, I see, and I shall only interrupt you—so, bye-bye!   [Exit.]

---

2. Immodest, intrusive hussy.
3. Flirt.

4. Country gentlemen.
5. Unclaimed.

SIR PETER: Plagues and tortures! Can't I make her angry neither! O, I am the miserablest fellow—but I'll not bear her presuming to keep her temper. No, she may break my heart, but she shan't keep her temper.   [*Exit.*]

Scene 2

[*Charles's house. Enter Trip, Moses, and Sir Oliver.*]

TRIP: Here, Master Moses, if you'll stay a moment, I'll try whether Mr.—what's the gentleman's name?

SIR OLIVER [*aside*]: Mr. Moses—what *is* my name?

MOSES: Mr. Premium.

TRIP: Premium, very well.

                                              [*Exit Trip taking snuff.*]

SIR OLIVER: To judge by the servants, one wouldn't believe the master was ruined—but what, sure this was my brother's house?

MOSES: Yes sir, Mr. Charles bought it of Mr. Joseph with the furniture, pictures, etc. Just as the old gentleman left it. Sir Peter thought it a great piece of extravagance in him!

SIR OLIVER: In my mind, the other's economy in selling it to him was more reprehensible by half.

    [*Re-enter Trip.*]

TRIP: My master says you must wait, gentlemen. He has company and can't speak with you yet.

SIR OLIVER: If he knew who it was wanted to see him, perhaps he wouldn't have sent such a message.

TRIP: Yes, yes, sir, he knows you are here. I didn't forget little Premium—no, no, no.

SIR OLIVER: Very well, and I pray, sir, what may be your name?

TRIP: Trip, sir—my name is Trip, at your service.

SIR OLIVER: Well then, Mr. Trip—you have a pleasant sort of a place[6] here, I guess.

TRIP: Why, yes, here are three or four of us pass our time agreeably enough, but then our wages are sometimes a little in arrear,[7] and not very great either—but fifty pounds a year and find our own bags and bouquets.[8]

SIR OLIVER [*aside*]: Bags and bouquets! Halters and bastinadoes![9]

TRIP: But *à propos*,[1] Moses, have you been able to get me that little bill discounted?[2]

SIR OLIVER: Wants to raise money too! Mercy on me—has his distresses, I warrant, like a lord—and affects[3] creditors and duns![4]

MOSES: 'Twas not to be done, indeed, Mr. Trip. [*Gives the note.*]

TRIP: Good lack, you surprise me—my friend Brush has endorsed[5] it, and I thought when he put his mark on the back of a bill 'twas as good as cash.

MOSES: No, 'twouldn't do.

TRIP: A small sum, but twenty pounds—hearkee,[6] Moses, do you think you couldn't get it me by way of annuity?[7]

---

6. Job.
7. Overdue.
8. I.e., we must furnish our own fashionable accessories (a "bag" was a powdered wig which was rounded off by a silk satchel at the neck).
9. Nooses (for hanging) and clubs (for beating).
1. On the subject.
2. I.e., was Moses able to get him a loan (from which he

would take a commission, or "discount")?
3. Presumes to deal with.
4. Insistent debt-collectors.
5. Co-signed it.
6. Listen.
7. An agreement to make a series of annual payments in return for a loan.

2914   Richard Brinsley Sheridan

SIR OLIVER: An annuity! Ha! ha! ha! A footman raise money by annuity—well done luxury, egad!

MOSES: But you must insure your place.

TRIP: O, with all my heart—I'll insure my place and my life too, if you please.

SIR OLIVER: It's more than I would your neck.

TRIP: But then, Moses, it must be done before this d——d register[8] takes place. One wouldn't like to have one's name made public, you know.

MOSES: No, certainly. But is there nothing you could deposit?

TRIP: Why, nothing capital of my master's wardrobe has dropped lately—but I could give you a mortgage on some of his winter clothes with equity of redemption[9] before November or you shall have the reversion of the French velvet, or a post obit on the blue and silver.[1] These, I should think, Moses—with a few pair of point ruffles[2] as a collateral security[3]—hey my little fellow?

MOSES: Well, well.

  [Bell rings.]

TRIP: Gad, I heard the bell. I believe, gentlemen, I can now introduce you—don't forget the annuity, little Moses; this way, gentlemen, insure my place! You know—

SIR OLIVER: If the man be a shadow of his master, this is the temple of dissipation indeed!   [Exeunt.]

Scene 3

[Charles, Careless, etc., etc., at a table with wine, etc.]

CHARLES: 'Fore heaven, 'tis true. There's the great degeneracy of the age—many of our acquaintance have taste, spirit, and politeness—but plague on't, they won't drink.

CARELESS: It is so, indeed, Charles. They give in to all the substantial luxuries of the table, and abstain from nothing but wine and wit.

CHARLES: O, certainly society suffers by it intolerably—for now instead of the social spirit of raillery that used to mantle over[4] a glass of bright burgundy, their conversation is become just like the spa water they drink, which has all the pertness and flatulence[5] of champagne, without its spirit or flavor.

1ST. GENT: But what are they to do who love play[6] better than wine?

CARELESS: True—there's Harry diets himself for gaming,[7] and is now under a hazard regimen.[8]

CHARLES: Then he'll have the worst of it—what, you wouldn't train a horse for the course by keeping him from corn! For my part, egad, I am now never so successful as when I am a little merry—let me throw on a bottle of champagne, and I never lose—at least I never feel my losses, which is exactly the same thing.

2ND. GENT: Aye—that I believe.

---

8. The pending Annuity Bill required that all such arrangements be publicly registered.
9. I.e., while retaining the right to buy them back by paying off the loan and interest.
1. I.e., ownership of this fancy apparel after it "dies" (i.e., when Charles gives it up; gentlemen sometimes handed down their cast-off clothing to their valets).
2. Long lace fabric worn at the wrists, sold independently of shirts.

3. I.e., as guarantee of payment.
4. Arise from.
5. Gassiness.
6. Gambling.
7. Eats and drinks abstemiously, in hopes of improving his gambling performance.
8. A diet designed to improve his chances at the dice game called hazard.

CHARLES: And then, what man can pretend to be a believer in love who is an abjurer of wine? 'Tis the test by which the lover knows his own heart. Fill a dozen bumpers[9] to a dozen beauties—and she that floats at top is the maid that has bewitched you.

CARELESS: Now then, Charles—be honest and give us your real favorite.

CHARLES: Why, I have withheld her only in compassion to you—if I toast her, you must give a round of her peers,[1] which is impossible on earth!

CARELESS: O, then, we'll find some canonized vestals[2] or heathen goddesses that will do, I warrant.

CHARLES: Here, then—bumpers, you rogues, bumpers! Maria—Maria—[All drink.]

1ST. GENT: Maria who?

CHARLES: O damn the surname! 'Tis too formal to be registered in love's calendar. But now, Sir Toby Bumper, beware—we must have beauty superlative.

CARELESS: Nay, never study,[3] Sir Toby, we'll stand to[4] the toast though your mistress should want an eye—and you know you have a song will excuse you.

SIR TOBY: Egad, so I have—and I'll give him the song instead of the lady.

Song and Chorus[5]

> Here's to the maiden of bashful fifteen
> Here's to the widow of fifty
> Here's to the flaunting, extravagant quean,[6]
> And here's to the housewife that's thrifty.

CHORUS: Let the toast pass—
>   Drink to the lass—
> I'll warrant she'll prove an excuse for the glass!

> Here's to the charmer whose dimples we prize!
> Now to the maid who has none, sir;
> Here's to the girl with a pair of blue eyes,
> And here's to the nymph with but one, sir!

CHORUS: Let the toast pass, etc.

> Here's to the maid with a bosom of snow,
> Now to her that's as brown as a berry:
> Here's to the wife with a face full of woe,
> And now for the damsel that's merry.

CHORUS: Let the toast pass, etc.

>   For let 'em be clumsy or let 'em be slim
>   Young or ancient, I care not a feather:
> So fill a pint bumper quite up to the brim
>   And let us e'en toast 'em together!

CHORUS: Let the toast pass, etc.

ALL: Bravo. Bravo!
     [Enter Trip and whispers to Charles.]

9. Overflowing glasses.
1. Propose toasts to her equals.
2. In ancient Rome, the goddess Vesta was served by virgins sworn to lifelong chastity.
3. Think too hard.

4. Rise and drink.
5. The song echoes "A health to the nut-brown lass," written by Sir John Suckling (1609–1642).
6. Harlot.

CHARLES: Gentlemen, you must excuse me a little—Careless, take the chair,[7] will you?

CARELESS: Nay, prithee, Charles, what now? This is one of your peerless beauties, I suppose, has dropped in by chance.

CHARLES: No, faith—to tell you the truth, 'tis a Jew and a broker who are come by appointment.

CARELESS: O, damn it, let's have the Jew in—

1ST. GENT: Aye, and the broker too, by all means.

2ND. GENT: Yes, yes, the Jew and the broker.

CHARLES: Egad, with all my heart. Trip, bid the gentlemen walk in.—Though there's one of them a stranger, I can tell you.

CARELESS: Charles, let us give them some generous burgundy—and perhaps they'll grow conscientious.

CHARLES: O, hang 'em—no, wine does but draw forth a man's natural qualities and to make them drink would only be to whet their knavery.
    [Enter Trip, Sir Oliver and Moses.]

CHARLES: So, honest Moses, walk in, walk in, pray, Mr. Premium—that's the gentleman's name, isn't it, Moses?

MOSES: Yes, sir.

CHARLES: Set chairs, Trip. Sit down, Mr. Premium. Glasses, Trip. Sit down, Moses. Come, Mr. Premium, I'll give you a sentiment: here's success to usury. Moses, fill the gentleman a bumper.

MOSES: Success to usury!

CARELESS: Right, Moses. Usury is prudence and industry, and deserves to succeed.

SIR OLIVER: Then here is all the success it deserves.

CARELESS: No, no—that won't do, Mr. Premium, you have demurred[8] to the toast, and must drink it in a pint bumper.

1ST. GENT: A pint bumper at least.

MOSES: O pray, sir, consider. Mr. Premium's a gentleman.

CARELESS: And therefore loves good wine.

2ND. GENT: Give Moses a quart glass—this is mutiny, and a high contempt of the chair.

CARELESS: Here—now for't—I'll see justice done to the last drop of my bottle.

SIR OLIVER: Nay, pray gentlemen, I did not expect this usage.

CHARLES: No, hang it, Careless, you shan't: Mr. Premium's a stranger.

SIR OLIVER: Odd! I wish I was well out of this company.

CARELESS: Plague on 'em then, if they won't drink, we'll not sit down with 'em; come Harry, the dice are in the next room; Charles, you'll join us when you have finished your business with these gentlemen—

CHARLES: I will. I will. [Exeunt.] Careless!

CARELESS: Well—

CHARLES: Perhaps I may want you.

CARELESS: O, you know, I am always ready—word, note or bond, 'tis all the same to me.   [Exit.]

MOSES: Sir, this is Mr. Premium, a gentleman of the strictest honor and secrecy— and always performs what he undertakes. Mr. Premium, this is—

---

7. Chairman's seat: i.e., play host.   8. Objected.

CHARLES: Pshaw, have done! Sir, my friend Moses is a very honest fellow, but a little slow at expression; he'll be an hour giving us our titles. Mr. Premium, the plain state of the matter is this: I am an extravagant young fellow, who wants money to borrow, you I take to be a prudent old fellow, who has got money to lend. I am blockhead enough to give fifty per cent, sooner than not have it, and you, I presume, are rogue enough to take a hundred if you could get it. Now, sir, you see we are acquainted at once, and may proceed to business without farther ceremony.

SIR OLIVER: Exceeding frank, upon my word. I see, sir, you are not a man of many compliments.

CHARLES: O no, sir—plain dealing in business I always think best.

SIR OLIVER: Sir, I like you the better for't; however, you are mistaken in one thing—I have no money to lend. But I believe I could procure some of a friend, but then he's an unconscionable dog, isn't he, Moses? And must sell stock to accommodate you—mustn't he, Moses?

MOSES: Yes indeed! You know I always speak the truth, and scorn to tell a lie.

CHARLES: Right! People that expect truth generally do. But these are trifles, Mr. Premium. What—I know money isn't to be bought without paying for't.

SIR OLIVER: Well, but what security could you give—you have no land, I suppose?

CHARLES: Not a mole-hill nor a twig, but what's in beau[9] pots out at the window.

SIR OLIVER: Nor any stock, I presume.

CHARLES: Nothing but livestock—and that's only a few pointers[1] and ponies. But pray, Mr. Premium, are you acquainted at all with any of my connections?

SIR OLIVER: Why, to say truth, I am.

CHARLES: Then you must know that I have a devilish rich uncle in the East Indies—Sir Oliver Surface—from whom I have the greatest expectations.

SIR OLIVER: That you have a wealthy uncle I have heard—but how your expectations will turn out is more, I believe, than you can tell.

CHARLES: O, no, there can be no doubt of it—they tell me I'm a prodigious favorite and that he talks of leaving me everything.

SIR OLIVER: Indeed, this is the first I've heard on't.

CHARLES: Yes, yes, 'tis just so—Moses knows 'tis true, don't you, Moses?

MOSES: O yes, I'll swear to't.

SIR OLIVER: Egad, they'll persuade me presently I'm at Bengal.

CHARLES: Now I propose, Mr. Premium, if it's agreeable to you, to grant you a post obit[2] on Sir Oliver's life, though at the same time the old fellow has been so liberal to me that I give you my word I should be very sorry to hear anything had happened to him.

SIR OLIVER: Not more than I should, I assure you. But the bond you mention happens to be just the worst security you could offer me—for I might live to a hundred and never recover the principal.

CHARLES: O yes, you would—the moment Sir Oliver dies, you know, you'd come on me for the money.

SIR OLIVER: Then I believe I should be the most unwelcome dun you ever had in your life.

CHARLES: What, I suppose you are afraid now that Sir Oliver is too good a life?[3]

---

9. I.e., handsomely decorated.
1. Hunting dogs.
2. I.e., Premium will receive payment on Sir Oliver's

death.
3. I.e., he'll live too long.

SIR OLIVER: No, indeed I am not—though I have heard he is as hale and healthy as any man of his years in Christendom.

CHARLES: There again you are misinformed. No, no, the climate has hurt him considerably—poor uncle Oliver—yes, he breaks apace,[4] I'm told—and so much altered lately that his nearest relations don't know him.

SIR OLIVER: No! Ha! ha! ha! So much altered lately that his relations don't know him, ha! ha! ha! That's droll, egad—ha! ha! ha!

CHARLES: Ha! ha! You're glad to hear that, little Premium.

SIR OLIVER: No, no, I'm not.

CHARLES: Yes, yes, you are—ha! ha! ha!—you know that mends your chance.[5]

SIR OLIVER: But I'm told Sir Oliver is coming over—nay, some say he is actually arrived.

CHARLES: Pshaw! Sure, I must know better than you whether he's come or not. No, no, rely on't, he is at this moment at Calcutta, isn't he Moses?

MOSES: O yes, certainly.

SIR OLIVER: Very true, as you say—you must know better than I; though I have it from pretty good authority—haven't I, Moses?

MOSES: Yes, most undoubted.

SIR OLIVER: But, sir, as I understand you want a few hundreds immediately, is there nothing you would dispose of?

CHARLES: How do you mean?

SIR OLIVER: For instance now, I have heard that your father left behind him a great quantity of massy old plate.[6]

CHARLES: O, Lud, that's gone, long ago—Moses can tell you how better than I can.

SIR OLIVER [aside]: Good lack! All the family race cups and corporation bowls![7]— Then it was also supposed that his library was one of the most valuable and complete—

CHARLES: Yes, yes. So it was—vastly too much so for a private gentleman. For my part, I was always of a communicative disposition, so I thought it a shame to keep so much knowledge to myself.

SIR OLIVER [aside]: Mercy on me! Learning that had run in the family like an heirloom!—Pray, what are become of the books?

CHARLES: You must enquire of the auctioneer, Master Premium, for I don't believe even Moses can direct you there.

MOSES: I never meddle with books.

SIR OLIVER: So, so—nothing of the family property left, I suppose.

CHARLES: Not much indeed, unless you have a mind to the family pictures. I have got a room full of ancestors above, and if you have a taste for old paintings, egad, you shall have 'em a bargain.

SIR OLIVER: Hey! And the devil! Sure you wouldn't sell your forefathers—would you?

CHARLES: Every man of 'em, to the best bidder.

SIR OLIVER: What your great uncles and aunts?

CHARLES: Aye, and my great grandfathers and grandmothers, too.

SIR OLIVER [aside]: Now I give him up!—What the plague, have you no bowels[8] for your own kindred? Odds life, do you take me for Shylock in the play, that you would raise money of me, on your own flesh and blood?[9]

---

4. Is quickly growing decrepit.
5. Improves the likelihood of your getting paid quickly.
6. Heavy, substantial utensils and dishes, generally made of silver.
7. Silver bowls presented as local prizes at races.

8. Compassion, feelings.
9. The play is Shakespeare's The Merchant of Venice; Shylock is the usurer who demands a pound of flesh as security against a loan.

CHARLES: Nay, my little broker, don't be angry. What need you care, if you have your money's worth?

SIR OLIVER: Well, I'll be the purchaser. I think I can dispose of the family—oh, I'll never forgive him this—never!

[Enter Careless.]

CARELESS: Come, Charles—what keeps you?

CHARLES: I can't come yet, i'faith! We are going to have a sale above. Here's little Premium will buy all my ancestors.

CARELESS: Oh, burn your ancestors!

CHARLES: No, he may do that afterward, if he pleases. Stay, Careless, we want you; egad, you shall be auctioneer. So come along with us.

CARELESS: Oh, have with you, if that's the case. I can handle a hammer as well as a dice box!

SIR OLIVER: Oh, the profligates!

CHARLES: Come, Moses—you shall be appraiser if we want one. Gads life, little Premium, you don't seem to like the business.

SIR OLIVER: Oh, yes I do vastly—ha, ha, yes, yes, I think it a rare joke to sell one's family by auction, ha! ha! [Aside.] Oh, the prodigal![1]

CHARLES: To be sure! When a man wants money, where the plague should he get assistance, if he can't make free with his own relations?   [Exeunt.]

ACT 4

Scene 1

[Picture room at Charles's. Enter Charles, Sir Oliver, Moses and Careless.]

CHARLES: Walk in, gentlemen, pray walk in! Here they are, the family of the Surfaces, up to the Conquest.[1]

SIR OLIVER: And, in my opinion, a goodly collection.

CHARLES: Aye, aye, these are done in the true spirit of portrait painting—no volunteer grace or expression[2]—not like the works of your modern Raphael,[3] who gives you the strongest resemblance, yet contrives to make your own portrait independent of you—so that you may sink the original and not hurt the picture. No, no, the merit of these is the inveterate[4] likeness—all stiff and awkward as the originals and like nothing in human nature beside!

SIR OLIVER: Ah! We shall never see such figures of men again.

CHARLES: No, I hope not. You see, Master Premium, what a domestic character I am—here I sit of an evening surrounded by my family. But come, get to your pulpit, Mr. Auctioneer; here's an old gouty[5] chair of my grandfather's will answer the purpose.

CARELESS: Aye, aye, this will do—but Charles, I have ne'er a hammer, and what's an auctioneer without his hammer?

CHARLES: Egad, that's true. What parchment have we here? [Takes down a roll.] Richard, heir to Thomas—our genealogy in full! Here, Careless, you shall have no common bit of mahogany—here's the family tree for you, you rogue—this shall be your hammer, and now you may knock down my ancestors with their own pedigree.

---

1. Reckless spendthrift.

1. I.e., dating back to 1066, when William the Conqueror seized control of England.

2. I.e., the subjects are stiffly arranged, with no spontaneity in stance or face.

3. Sir Joshua Reynolds, who brought vigor and naturalness to English portraiture. "Raphael" refers to the Italian Renaissance painter, Rafaello Sanzio (1483–1520).

4. Deep-rooted.

5. A chair designed for those suffering from gout, a disease that caused inflammation of the joints.

SIR OLIVER: What an unnatural rogue! An *ex post facto*[6] parricide!

CARELESS: Yes, yes, here's a list of your generation, indeed. Faith, Charles—this is the most convenient thing you could have found for the business, for 'twill serve not only as a hammer, but a catalogue into the bargain. But come, begin: a-going, a-going, a-going!

CHARLES: Bravo, Careless! Well, here's my great uncle Sir Richard Raviline,[7] a marvelous good general in his day, I assure you. He served in all the Duke of Marlborough's wars,[8] and got that cut over his eye at the Battle of Malplaquet.[9] What say you, Mr. Premium—look at him—there's a hero for you! Not cut out of his feathers,[1] as your modern, clipped captains are—but enveloped in wig and regimentals,[2] as a general should be. What do you bid?

MOSES: Mr. Premium would have you speak.

CHARLES: Why, then, he shall have him for ten pounds, and I am sure that's not dear for a staff officer.

SIR OLIVER: Heaven deliver me! His famous uncle Richard for ten pounds! Very well, sir—I take him at that.

CHARLES: Careless, knock down my uncle Richard. Here now is a maiden sister of his, my great aunt Deborah, done by Kneller,[3] thought to be in his best manner, and a very formidable likeness. There she is, you see, a shepherdess feeding her flock. You shall have her for five pounds ten—the sheep are worth the money.

SIR OLIVER: Ah! Poor Deborah—a woman who set such a value on herself! Five pound ten! She's mine.

CHARLES: Knock down my aunt Deborah! Here now are two that were a sort of cousins of theirs—you see, Moses, these pictures were done some time ago, when beaux wore wigs, and the ladies wore their own hair.[4]

SIR OLIVER: Yes, truly, headdresses appear to have been a little lower in those days.

CHARLES: Well, take that couple for the same.

MOSES: 'Tis good bargain.

CHARLES: Careless! This now is a grandfather of my mother's, a learned judge, well known on the western circuit.[5] What do you rate him at, Moses?

MOSES: Four guineas.

CHARLES: Four guineas! Gad's life, you don't bid me the price of his wig! Mr. Premium, you have more respect for the woolsack[6]—do let us knock his lordship down at fifteen.

SIR OLIVER: By all means.

CARELESS: Gone.

CHARLES: And there are two brothers of his, William and Walter Blunt, Esquires, both Members of Parliament and noted speakers, and what's very extraordinary, I believe this is the first time they were ever bought and sold.

SIR OLIVER: That's very extraordinary indeed! I'll take them at your own price for the honor of Parliament.

---

6. Retroactive.

7. A "ravelin" is a fortification.

8. John Churchill, Duke of Marlborough (1650–1722) was one of England's greatest generals, fighting successfully against the French from 1702 to 1709.

9. Marlborough's last battle with the French, 11 September 1709.

1. I.e., still wearing the elaborate plumes of old-fashioned military dress.

2. Uniform.

3. Sir Godfrey Kneller (1646–1723), England's leading portraitist during the Restoration.

4. "Beaux" are fops, or dandies: by 1770, men were powdering their own hair instead of wearing wigs, whereas ladies were wearing wigs up to a yard wide, covered with ostrich feathers (a fashion created by the Duchess of Devonshire, the supposed model for Mrs. Teazle).

5. A route traveled by justices who held court at appointed places along the way.

6. The Lord Chancellor's wool-stuffed cushion in the House of Lords, here representative of all judges.

CARELESS: Well said, Little Premium—I'll knock 'em down at forty.

CHARLES: Here's a jolly fellow—I don't know what relation, but he was Mayor of Manchester, take him at eight pounds.

SIR OLIVER: No, no—six will do for the Mayor.

CHARLES: Come, make it guineas and I'll throw you the two aldermen there into the bargain.

SIR OLIVER: They're mine.

CHARLES: Careless—knock down the Mayor and aldermen. But plague on't, we shall be all day retailing in this manner. Do let us deal wholesale—what say you, little Premium: give me three hundred pounds for the rest of the family in the lump.

CARELESS: Aye, aye, that will be the best way.

SIR OLIVER: Well, well, anything to accommodate you; they are mine. But there is one portrait, which you have always passed over—

CARELESS: What, that ill-looking little fellow over the settee?[7]

SIR OLIVER: Yes, sir, I mean that, though I don't think him so ill-looking a little fellow by any means.

CHARLES: What that? Oh, that's my uncle Oliver! 'Twas done before he went to India.

CARELESS: Your Uncle Oliver! Gad! Then you'll never be friends, Charles. That now to me is as stern a looking rogue as ever I saw—an unforgiving eye, and a damned, disinheriting countenance! An inveterate knave, depend on't, don't you think so, little Premium?

SIR OLIVER: Upon my soul, sir, I do not; I think it is as honest a looking face as any in the room—dead or alive. But I suppose your Uncle Oliver goes with the rest of the lumber?

CHARLES: No, hang it, I'll not part with poor Noll—the old fellow has been very good to me, and egad, I'll keep his picture, while I've a room to put it in.

SIR OLIVER [aside]: The rogue's my nephew after all!—But, sir, I have somehow taken a fancy to that picture.

CHARLES: I'm sorry for't, for you certainly will not have it. Oons! Haven't you got enough of 'em?

SIR OLIVER [aside]: I forgive him everything!—But, sir, when I take a whim in my head I don't value money—I'll give as much for that as for all the rest.

CHARLES: Don't tease me, Master Broker, I tell you I'll not part with it. And there's an end on't.

SIR OLIVER [aside]: How like his father the dog is!—Well, well, I have done. [Aside.] I did not perceive it before, but I think I never saw such a resemblance.— Well, sir, here is a draught[8] for your sum.

CHARLES: Why, 'tis for eight hundred pounds!

SIR OLIVER: You will not let Oliver go?

CHARLES: Zounds! No, I tell you once more.

SIR OLIVER: Then never mind the difference; we'll balance another time, but give me your hand on the bargain. You are an honest fellow, Charles—I beg pardon, sir, for being so free. Come Moses.

CHARLES: Egad, this is a whimsical old fellow—but hearkee, Premium, you'll prepare lodgings for these gentlemen.

7. A long upholstered seat.
8. An order for payment of money from the writer's   account; a check.

SIR OLIVER: Yes, yes, I'll send for them in a day or two.

CHARLES: But hold—do now send a genteel[9] conveyance for them, for I assure you they were most of them used to ride in their own carriages.

SIR OLIVER: I will, I will, for all but Oliver.

CHARLES: Aye, all but the little honest nabob.[1]

SIR OLIVER: You're fixed on that—

CHARLES: Peremptorily.[2]

SIR OLIVER: A dear, extravagant rogue! Good day. Come, Moses. Let me hear now who dares call him profligate!

[Exeunt Sir Oliver and Moses.]

CARELESS: Why, this is the oddest genius of the sort[3] I ever saw.

CHARLES: Egad, he's the prince of brokers, I think. I wonder how the devil Moses got acquainted with so honest a fellow. Hah! Here's Rowley. Do, Careless, say I'll join the company in a moment.

CARELESS: I will, but don't now let that old blockhead persuade you to squander any of that money on old, musty debts, or any such nonsense; for tradesmen, Charles, are the most exorbitant[4] fellows!

CHARLES: Very true, and paying them is only encouraging them.

CARELESS: Nothing else.

CHARLES: Aye, aye, never fear.

[Exit Careless.]

So—this was an odd old fellow indeed! Let me see, two thirds of this is mine by right—five hundred and thirty pounds.[5] 'Fore heaven, I find one's ancestors are more valuable relations than I took 'em for! Ladies and gentlemen, your most obedient and very grateful humble servant.

[Enter Rowley.]

Hah! Old Rowley, egad, you are just come in time to take leave of your old acquaintance.

ROWLEY: Yes, I heard they were going—but I wonder you can have such spirits under so many distresses.

CHARLES: Why there's the point—my distresses are so many that I can't afford to part with my spirits, but I shall be rich and splenetic[6] all in good time. However, I suppose you are surprised that I am not more sorrowful at parting with so many near relations. To be sure, 'tis very affecting—but rot 'em, you see they never move a muscle, so why should I?

ROWLEY: There's no making you serious a moment.

CHARLES: Yes, faith: I am so now. Here, my honest Rowley, here, get me this changed, and take a hundred pounds of it immediately to old Stanley.

ROWLEY: A hundred pounds! Consider only—

CHARLES: Gad's life, don't talk about it! Poor Stanley's wants are pressing—and if you don't make haste, we shall have someone call that has a better right to the money.

ROWLEY: Ah! There's the point.—I never will cease dunning you with the old proverb—

---

9. Stylish.

1. A Hindi-derived word meaning a wealthy person, applied particularly to Englishmen who, while serving as officials in India, made huge fortunes.

2. Absolutely.

3. I.e., of his trade.

4. Excessively demanding.

5. Moses will receive one-third as his commission.

6. Irritable.

CHARLES: "Be just before you're generous."[7] Hey!—Why so I would, if I could, but justice is an old, lame, hobbling beldame[8]—and I can't get her to keep pace with generosity, for the soul of me.

ROWLEY: Yet, Charles, believe me, one hour's reflection—

CHARLES: Aye, aye, it's all very true—but hearkee, Rowley, while I have, by heaven, I'll give—so damn your economy[9]—and now for hazard . . .   [Exeunt.]

Scene 2

[The parlor. Enter Sir Oliver and Moses.]

MOSES: Well, sir, I think, as Sir Peter said, you have seen Mr. Charles in high glory—'tis great pity he's so extravagant.

SIR OLIVER: True—but he wouldn't sell my picture.

MOSES: And loves wine and women so much—

SIR OLIVER: But he wouldn't sell my picture.

MOSES: And game so deep[1]—

SIR OLIVER: But he wouldn't sell my picture. O—here's Rowley!

[Enter Rowley.]

ROWLEY: So, Sir Oliver, I find you have made a purchase.

SIR OLIVER: Yes, yes—Our young rake has parted with his ancestors like old tapestry.

ROWLEY: And here has he commissioned me to redeliver you part of the purchase money; I mean though in your necessitous character of old Stanley—

MOSES: Ah! There is the pity of all! He is so damned charitable.

ROWLEY: And I have left a hosier and two tailors in the hall—who I'm sure won't be paid, and this hundred would satisfy 'em!

SIR OLIVER: Well, well, I'll pay his debts—and his benevolences too—but now I am no more a broker and you shall introduce me to the elder brother as old Stanley.

ROWLEY: Not yet awhile. Sir Peter, I know, means to call there about this time.

[Enter Trip.]

TRIP: O gentlemen, I beg pardon for not showing you out—this way. Moses, a word.

[Exeunt Trip and Moses.]

SIR OLIVER: There's a fellow for you—would you believe it! That puppy intercepted the Jew on our coming and wanted to raise money before he got to his master.

ROWLEY: Indeed!

SIR OLIVER: Yes—they are now planning an annuity business. Ah! Master Rowley, in my day servants were content with the follies of their masters when they were worn a little threadbare, but now they have their vices, like their birthday clothes with the gloss on.[2]   [Exeunt.]

Scene 3

[The library in Joseph Surface's house. Surface and Servant.]

SURFACE: No letter from Lady Teazle?

SERVANT: No, sir.

---

7. Paraphrased from the Roman statesman Cicero (106–43 B.C.): "nothing is generous which is not also just" (De Officiis 1.14).
8. Old woman.
9. Stinginess.
1. I.e., gambling for such large amounts of money.
2. Brand-new festive dress, worn in honor of the King's birthday celebration.

SURFACE: I am surprised she hasn't sent, if she is prevented from coming. Sir Peter certainly does not suspect me—yet I wish I may not lose the heiress, through the scrape[3] I have drawn myself in with the wife. However, Charles's imprudence and bad character are great points in my favor.

[Knocking.]

SERVANT: Sir, I believe that must be Lady Teazle.

SURFACE: Hold, see whether it is or not before you go to the door—I have a particular message for you if it should be my brother.

SERVANT: 'Tis her ladyship, sir. She always leaves her chair at the milliner's in the next street.

SURFACE: Stay, stay—draw that screen before the window—that will do. My opposite neighbor is a maiden lady of so curious[4] a temper!

[Servant draws the screen and exits.]

I have a difficult hand to play in this affair. Lady Teazle has lately suspected my views on Maria—but she must by no means be let into that secret, at least not 'till I have her more in my power.

[Enter Lady Teazle.]

LADY TEAZLE: What, sentiment in soliloquy! Have you been very impatient now? O Lud! Don't pretend to look grave—I vow I couldn't come before.

SURFACE: O madam, punctuality is a species of constancy, a very unfashionable quality in a lady.

LADY TEAZLE: Upon my word, you ought to pity me. Do you know that Sir Peter is grown so ill-tempered to me of late!—and so jealous! Of Charles, too, that's the best of the story, isn't it?

SURFACE [aside]: I am glad my scandalous friends keep that up.

LADY TEAZLE: I am sure I wish he would let Maria marry him—and then perhaps he would be convinced—don't you, Mr. Surface?

SURFACE [aside]: Indeed I do not.—O certainly I do, for then my dear Lady Teazle would also be convinced how wrong her suspicions were of my having any design on the silly girl. [Sits.]

LADY TEAZLE: Well, well, I'm inclined to believe you. But isn't it provoking to have the most ill natured things said to one? And there's my friend Lady Sneerwell has circulated I don't know how many scandalous tales of me, and all without any foundation, too—that's what vexes me.

SURFACE: Aye, madam, to be sure that is the provoking circumstance—without foundation! Yes, yes, there's the mortification indeed, for when a slanderous story is believed against one, there certainly is no comfort like the consciousness of having deserved it.

LADY TEAZLE: No, to be sure—then I'd forgive their malice. But to attack me, who am really so innocent, and who never say an ill natured thing of anybody— that is, of any friend! And then Sir Peter too—to have him so peevish and so suspicious when I know the integrity of my own heart—indeed 'tis monstrous.

SURFACE: But my dear Lady Teazle, 'tis your own fault if you suffer it. When a husband entertains a groundless suspicion of his wife, and withdraws his confidence from her, the original compact is broke and she owes it to the honor of her sex to endeavor to outwit him.

LADY TEAZLE: Indeed—so that if he suspects me without cause, it follows that the best way of curing his jealousy is to give him reason for't.

---

3. Predicament.   4. Habitually inquisitive.

SURFACE: Undoubtedly—for your husband should never be deceived in you, and in that case it becomes you to be frail, in compliment to his discernment.

LADY TEAZLE: To be sure, what you say is very reasonable—and when the consciousness of my own innocence—

SURFACE: Ah! My dear madam, there is the great mistake—'tis this very conscious innocence that is of the greatest prejudice to you. What is it makes you negligent of forms, and careless of the world's opinion?—why the consciousness of your innocence. What makes you thoughtless in your conduct and apt to run into a thousand little imprudences?—why the consciousness of your innocence. What makes you impatient of Sir Peter's temper and outrageous at his suspicions?—why the consciousness of your own innocence.

LADY TEAZLE: 'Tis very true.

SURFACE: Now, my dear Lady Teazle, if you would but once make a trifling *faux-pas*,[5] you can't conceive how cautious you would grow, and how ready to humor and agree with your husband.

LADY TEAZLE: Do you think so—

SURFACE: O, I'm sure on't, and then you would find all scandal would cease at once—for, in short, your character at present is like a person in a plethora,[6] absolutely dying of too much health.

LADY TEAZLE: So, so, then I perceive your prescription is that I must sin in my own defense—and part with my virtue to preserve my reputation.

SURFACE: Exactly so, upon my credit, ma'am.

LADY TEAZLE: Well, certainly this is the oddest doctrine—and the newest receipt for avoiding calumny.

SURFACE: An infallible one, believe me. Prudence, like experience, must be paid for.

LADY TEAZLE: Why, if my understanding were once convinced—

SURFACE: O certainly, madam, your understanding should be convinced. Yes, yes—Heav'n forbid I should persuade you to do anything you thought wrong—no, no—I have too much honor to desire it.

LADY TEAZLE: Don't you think we may as well leave honor out of the argument?

SURFACE: Ah, the ill effects of your country education, I see, still remain with you.

LADY TEAZLE: I doubt they do indeed, and I will fairly own to you that if I could be persuaded to do wrong it would be by Sir Peter's ill-usage sooner than your honorable logic after all.

SURFACE: Then by this hand which he is unworthy of—
    [*Enter Servant.*]
'Sdeath,[7] you blockhead, what do you want—

SERVANT: I beg pardon, sir, but I thought you wouldn't choose Sir Peter to come up without announcing him?

SURFACE: Sir Peter! Oons and the devil—

LADY TEAZLE: Sir Peter! O Lud! I'm ruined—I'm ruined—

SERVANT: Sir, 'twasn't I let him in.

LADY TEAZLE: O, I'm undone—what will become of me now, Mr. Logic? O mercy, he's on the stairs. I'll get behind here—and if ever I am so imprudent again—
    [*Goes behind the screen.*]

SURFACE: Give me that book! [*Sits down—Servant pretends to adjust his hair.*]

---

5. False step (French); an action prohibited by social convention.

6. An illness arising from an excess of fluids in the body.
7. Euphemistic abbreviation of "God's death."

[*Enter Sir Peter.*]

SIR PETER: Aye, ever improving himself! Mr. Surface, Mr. Surface!

SURFACE: Oh! My dear Sir Peter, I beg your pardon. [*Gaping*[8] *and throws away the book.*] I have been dozing over a stupid book! Well, I am much obliged to you for this call. You haven't been here, I believe, since I fitted up this room. Books, you know, are the only things I am a coxcomb in[9]—

SIR PETER: 'Tis very neat indeed. Well, well, that's proper—and you make even your screen a source of knowledge—hung, I perceive, with maps.

SURFACE: O yes, I find great use in that screen.

SIR PETER: I dare say you must—certainly when you want to find anything in a hurry.

SURFACE [*aside*]: Aye, or to hide anything in a hurry either.

SIR PETER: Well, I have a little private business—

SURFACE [*to Servant*]: You needn't stay.

SERVANT: No, sir.   [*Exit.*]

SURFACE: Here's a chair, Sir Peter, I beg—

SIR PETER: Well, now we are alone—there *is* a subject, my dear friend, on which I wish to unburden my mind to you, a point of the greatest moment[1] to my peace. In short, my good friend, Lady Teazle's conduct of late has made me extremely unhappy.

SURFACE: Indeed! I'm very sorry to hear it.

SIR PETER: Yes, 'tis but too plain she has not the least regard for me—but what's worse, I have pretty good authority to suspect that she must have formed an attachment to another.

SURFACE: You astonish me.

SIR PETER: Yes, and between ourselves—I think I have discovered the person.

SURFACE: How—you alarm me exceedingly!

SIR PETER: Ah! My dear friend, I knew you would sympathize with me.

SURFACE: Yes, believe me, Sir Peter—such a discovery would hurt me just as much as it would you.

SIR PETER: I am convinced of it. Ah! It is a happiness to have a friend whom one can trust even with one's family secrets—but have you no guess who I mean?

SURFACE: I haven't the most distant idea. It can't be Sir Benjamin Backbite.

SIR PETER: O no! What say you to Charles?

SURFACE: My brother—impossible!

SIR PETER: Ah! My dear friend, the goodness of your own heart misleads you— you judge of others by yourself.

SURFACE: Certainly, Sir Peter, the heart that is conscious of its own integrity is ever slow to credit another's treachery.

SIR PETER: True, but your brother has no sentiment—you never hear him talk so.

SURFACE: Yet I can't but think that Lady Teazle herself has too much principle—

SIR PETER: Aye, but what's her principle against the flattery of a handsome, lively young fellow?

SURFACE: That's very true.

SIR PETER: And then you know the difference of our ages makes it very improbable that she should have a great affection for me—and if she were to be frail, and I were to make it public, why the town would only laugh at me, the foolish old bachelor who had married a girl.

---

8. Yawning.   1. Importance.
9. Vain about (generally used in reference to clothing).

SURFACE: That's true—to be sure, they would laugh.

SIR PETER: Laugh! Aye, and make ballads, and paragraphs, and the devil knows what of me.

SURFACE: No, you must never make it public.

SIR PETER: But, then again, that the nephew of my old friend Sir Oliver should be the person to attempt such a wrong hurts me more nearly—

SURFACE: Aye, there's the point; when ingratitude barbs the dart of injury, the wound has double danger in it.

SIR PETER: Aye, I that was, in a manner, left his guardian—in whose house he had been so often entertained, who never in my life denied him my advice—

SURFACE: O, 'tis not to be credited. There may be a man capable of such baseness to be sure, but for my part, till you can give me positive proofs, I cannot but doubt it. However, if this should be proved on him, he is no longer a brother of mine! I disclaim kindred with him, for the man who can break through the laws of hospitality, and attempt the wife of his friend, deserves to be branded as the pest of society!

SIR PETER: What a difference there is between you—what noble sentiments!

SURFACE: Yet I cannot suspect Lady Teazle's honor—

SIR PETER: I am sure I wish to think well of her—and to remove all ground of quarrel between us. She has lately reproached me more than once with having made no settlement on her, and in our last quarrel she almost hinted that she should not break her heart if I was dead. Now, as we seem to differ in our ideas of expense, I have resolved she shall be her own mistress in that respect for the future—and if I were to die, she shall find that I have not been inattentive to her interest while living. Here, my friend, are the drafts of two deeds[2] which I wish to have your opinion on: by one, she will enjoy eight hundred a year independent while I live, and by the other the bulk of my fortune after my death.

SURFACE: This conduct, Sir Peter, is indeed truly generous! [Aside.] I wish it may not corrupt my pupil.

SIR PETER: Yes, I am determined she shall have no cause to complain—though I would not have her acquainted with the latter instance of my affection yet awhile.

SURFACE [aside]: Nor I—if I could help it.

SIR PETER: And now, my dear friend, if you please, we will talk over the situation of your hopes with Maria.

SURFACE [softly]: No, no, Sir Peter. Another time if you please.

SIR PETER: I am sensibly chagrined[3] at the little progress you seem to make in her affection.

SURFACE [softly]: I beg you will not mention it—what are my disappointments when your happiness is in debate! [Aside.] 'Sdeath! I should be ruined every way.

SIR PETER: And though you are so averse to my acquainting Lady Teazle with your passion, I am sure she's not your enemy in the affair.

SURFACE: Pray, Sir Peter, now oblige me. I am really too much affected by the subject we have been speaking on to bestow a thought on my own concerns. The man who is entrusted with his friend's distresses can never—well, sir?
    [Enter Servant.]

SERVANT: Your brother, sir, is speaking to a gentleman in the street, and says he knows you are within.

SURFACE: 'Sdeath, blockhead—I'm not within. I'm out for the day.

SIR PETER: Stay—hold—a thought has struck me. You shall be at home.

2. Legal documents.   3. Acutely annoyed.

SURFACE: Well, well, let him up. [*Exit Servant.*] He'll interrupt, Sir Peter, however—

SIR PETER: Now my good friend, oblige me, I entreat you. Before Charles comes, let me conceal myself somewhere. Then do you tax him on the point we have been talking on, and his answers may satisfy me at once.

SURFACE: O, fie, Sir Peter! Would you have me join in so mean a trick—to trepan[4] my brother to—

SIR PETER: Nay, you tell me you are sure he is innocent—if so, you do him the greatest service in giving him an opportunity to clear himself, and you will set my heart at rest—come, you shall not refuse me. Here, behind this screen will be [*goes to the screen*]—Hey! What the devil—there seems to be one list'ner here already— I'll swear I saw a petticoat.

SURFACE: Ha! ha! ha! Well, this is ridiculous enough. I'll tell you, Sir Peter, though I hold a man of intrigue to be a most despicable character—yet you know it doesn't follow that one is to be an absolute Joseph[5] either. Hearkee, 'tis a little French milliner—a silly rogue that plagues me—and having some character, on your coming she ran behind the screen.

SIR PETER: Ah! You rogue—but egad, she has overheard all I have been saying of my wife.

SURFACE: O, 'twill never go any further—you may depend on't.

SIR PETER: No! Then, i'faith, let her hear it out. Here's a closet will do as well.

SURFACE: Well, go in then.

SIR PETER: Sly rogue—sly rogue! [*Goes into the closet.*]

SURFACE: A very narrow escape indeed! And a curious situation I'm in!—to part man and wife in this manner.

LADY TEAZLE [*peeping from the screen*]: Couldn't I steal off?

SURFACE: Keep close my angel—

SIR PETER [*peeping out*]: Joseph—tax him home!

SURFACE: Back—my dear friend!

LADY TEAZLE [*peeping*]: Couldn't you lock Sir Peter in?

SURFACE: Be still, my life.

SIR PETER [*peeping*]: You're sure the little milliner won't blab?

SURFACE: In! In! My good Sir Peter—foregad[6]—I wish I had a key to the door. [*Enter Charles.*]

CHARLES SURFACE: Hello! Brother—what has been the matter? Your fellow wouldn't let me up at first—what, have you had a Jew or a wench with you?

SURFACE: Neither, brother, I assure you.

CHARLES SURFACE: But—what has made Sir Peter steal off? I thought he had been with you.

SURFACE: He was, brother—but hearing you were coming he did not choose to stay.

CHARLES SURFACE: What, was the old gentleman afraid I wanted to borrow money of him!

JOSEPH: No, sir, but I am sorry to find, Charles, that you have lately given that worthy man grounds for great uneasiness.

CHARLES SURFACE: Yes, they tell me I do that to a great many worthy men— but how so, pray?

<hr>

4. Trick.
5. The biblical Joseph rebuffed the sexual advances of

Potiphar's wife (Genesis 39.7–20).
6. Abbreviation for "before [in the presence of] God"

JOSEPH: To be plain with you, brother, he thinks you are endeavoring to gain Lady Teazle's affections from him.

CHARLES SURFACE: Who I—O Lud! Not I, upon my word. Ha! ha! ha! So the old fellow has found out that he has got a young wife—has he? Or, what's worse, has her ladyship discovered that she has an old husband?

JOSEPH: This is no subject to jest on, brother. He who can laugh—

CHARLES SURFACE: True, brother, as you were going to say—then seriously, I never had the least idea of what you charge me with, upon my honor.

SURFACE [aloud]: Well, it will give Sir Peter great satisfaction to hear this.

CHARLES SURFACE: To be sure, I once thought the lady seemed to have taken a fancy to me, but upon my soul I never gave her the least encouragement. Besides, you know my attachment to Maria.

SURFACE: But sure, brother, even if Lady Teazle had betrayed the fondest partiality for you—

CHARLES SURFACE: Why, lookee Joseph—I hope I shall never deliberately do a dishonorable action, but if a pretty woman were purposely to throw herself in my way—and that pretty woman married to a man old enough to be her father—

SURFACE: Well!

CHARLES SURFACE: Why, I believe I should be obliged to borrow a little of your morality, that's all. But brother, do you know now that you surprise me exceedingly by naming me with Lady Teazle, for faith, I always understood you were her favorite.

SURFACE: O, for shame, Charles—this retort is foolish.

CHARLES SURFACE: Nay, I swear I have seen you exchange such significant glances—

SURFACE: Nay, nay, sir—this is no jest.

CHARLES SURFACE: Egad, I'm serious. Don't you remember one day when I called here—

SURFACE: Nay, prithee, Charles—

CHARLES SURFACE: And found you together—

SURFACE: Zounds, sir, I insist—

CHARLES SURFACE: And another time when your servant—

SURFACE: Brother, brother, a word with you—[Aside.] Gad, I must stop him—

CHARLES SURFACE: Informed me, I say, that—

SURFACE: Hush! I beg your pardon, but Sir Peter has overheard all we have been saying—I knew you would clear yourself or I should not have consented—

CHARLES SURFACE: How, Sir Peter! Where is he?

SURFACE: Softly. There—[Points to the closet.]

CHARLES SURFACE: O, 'fore Heav'n, I'll have him out! Sir Peter come forth—

SURFACE: No, no—

CHARLES SURFACE: I say, Sir Peter, come into court. [Pulls in Sir Peter.] What, my old guardian—what, turn inquisitor and take evidence incog?[7]

SIR PETER: Give me your hand, Charles. I believe I have suspected you wrongfully, but you mustn't be angry with Joseph—'twas my plan—

CHARLES SURFACE: Indeed!

SIR PETER: But I acquit you. I promise you I don't think near so ill of you as I did—what I have heard has given me great satisfaction.

7. Short for "incognito," or secretly.

CHARLES SURFACE: Egad, then, 'twas lucky you didn't hear any more—[half aside] Wasn't it Joseph?

SIR PETER: Ah! You would have retorted on him—

CHARLES SURFACE: Aye, aye, that was a joke—

SIR PETER: Yes, yes, I know his honor too well.

CHARLES SURFACE: But you might as well have suspected him as me in this matter for all that. [Half aside.] Mightn't he, Joseph?

SIR PETER: Well, well, I believe you—

SURFACE [aside]: Would they were both well out of the room!

[Enter Servant, who whispers to Surface.]

SIR PETER: And in future perhaps we may not be such strangers.

SURFACE: Lady Sneerwell! Stop her by all means—

[Exit Servant.]

Gentlemen, I beg pardon, I must wait on you downstairs. Here is a person come on particular business.

CHARLES SURFACE: Well, you can see him in another room. Sir Peter and I haven't met a long time and I have something to say to him.

SURFACE: They must not be left together. I'll contrive to send Lady Sneerwell away, and return directly. [Aside to him.] Sir Peter, not a word of the French milliner.

[Exit Surface.]

SIR PETER: O, not for the world! Ah, Charles, if you associated more with your brother, one might indeed hope for your reformation. He is a man of sentiment— well! There is nothing in the world so noble as a man of sentiment!

CHARLES SURFACE: Pshaw! He is too moral by half—and so apprehensive of his good name, as he calls it, that I suppose he would as soon let a priest into his house as a girl—

SIR PETER: No, no, come, come—you wrong him. No, no, Joseph is no rake, but he is not such a saint in that respect either—[Aside.] I have a great mind to tell him—we should have a laugh.

CHARLES SURFACE: Oh hang him! He's a very anchorite,[8] a young hermit.

SIR PETER: Hearkee—you must not abuse him. He may chance to hear of it again, I promise you.

CHARLES SURFACE: Why, you won't tell him—

SIR PETER: No, but, this way—egad! I'll tell him!—hearkee! Have you a mind to have a good laugh at Joseph?

CHARLES SURFACE: I should like it of all things.

SIR PETER: Then, i'faith, we will—[Aside.] I'll be quit with him for discovering me—[Whispering.] He had a girl with him when I called.

CHARLES SURFACE: What—Joseph! You jest—

SIR PETER: Hush!—a little French milliner [Whispers] and the best of the jest is, she's in the room now.

CHARLES SURFACE: The devil she is—

SIR PETER: Hush! I tell you—[Points.]

CHARLES SURFACE: Behind the screen. 'Slife, let us unveil her—

SIR PETER: No—no! He's coming—you shan't indeed—

CHARLES SURFACE: O egad! We'll have a peep at the little milliner.

SIR PETER: Not for the world—Joseph will never forgive me.

8. A pious recluse.

CHARLES SURFACE: I'll stand by you—

SIR PETER [*struggling with Charles*]: Odds! Here he is ...

[*Surface enters just as Charles throws down the screen.*]

CHARLES SURFACE: Lady Teazle! By all that's wonderful!

SIR PETER: Lady Teazle! By all that's horrible!

CHARLES SURFACE: Sir Peter—this is one of the smartest French milliners I ever saw! Egad, you seem all to have been diverting yourselves here at hide and seek—and I don't see who is out of the secret! Shall I beg your ladyship to inform me? Not a word! Brother! Will you please to explain this matter? What—morality dumb too? Sir Peter, though I found you in the dark, perhaps you are not so now. All mute! Well, though I can make nothing of the affair, I suppose you perfectly understand one another, so I'll leave you to yourselves. [*Going.*] Brother, *I'm sorry to find you have given that worthy man so much uneasiness!* Sir Peter, *there's nothing in the world so noble as a man of sentiment!*

[*Exit Charles.*]

[*They stand for some time looking at each other.*]

SURFACE: Sir Peter—notwithstanding, I confess, that appearances are against me, if you will afford me your patience, I make no doubt but I shall explain everything to your satisfaction.

SIR PETER: If you please.

SURFACE: The fact is, sir, that Lady Teazle, knowing my pretensions to your ward Maria, I say, sir, Lady Teazle—being apprehensive of the jealousy of your temper, and knowing my friendship to the family—she, sir, I say, called here—in order that I might explain those pretensions, but on your coming—being apprehensive, as I said, of your jealousy, she withdrew—and this, you may depend on't, is the whole truth of the matter.

SIR PETER: A very clear account, upon my word, and I dare swear the lady will vouch for every article of it.

LADY TEAZLE [*coming forward*]: For not one word of it, Sir Peter.

SIR PETER: How! Don't you even think it worth while to agree in the lie?

LADY TEAZLE: There is not one syllable of truth in what that gentleman has told you.

SIR PETER: I believe you, upon my soul, ma'am.

SURFACE [*aside*]: 'Sdeath, madam, will you betray me?

LADY TEAZLE: Good Mr. Hypocrite, by your leave, I will speak for myself.

SIR PETER: Aye, let her alone, sir. You'll find she'll make out a better story than you without prompting.

LADY TEAZLE: Hear me, Sir Peter. I came hither on no matter relating to your ward, and even ignorant of this gentleman's pretensions to her—but I came seduced by his insidious arguments, at least to listen to his pretended passion, if not to sacrifice your honor to his baseness—

SIR PETER: Now I believe the truth is coming indeed.

SURFACE: The woman's mad—

LADY TEAZLE: No, sir. She has recovered her senses, and your own arts have furnished her with the means. Sir Peter, I do not expect you to credit me, but the tenderness you expressed for me when I am sure you could not think I was a witness to it, has penetrated to my heart, and had I left the place without the shame of this discovery, my future life should have spoke the sincerity of my gratitude. As for that smooth-tongued hypocrite, who would have seduced the wife of his too credulous friend, while he affected honorable addresses to his ward, I behold him now in a light so truly despicable that I shall never again respect myself for having listened to him.   [*Exit.*]

SURFACE: Notwithstanding all this, Sir Peter—Heav'n knows—

SIR PETER: That you are a villain! And so I leave you to your conscience.

SURFACE: You are too rash, Sir Peter—you shall hear me! The man who shuts out conviction by refusing to—

SIR PETER: Oh!

[*Exeunt, Surface following and speaking.*]

ACT 5

Scene 1

[*The library. Enter Surface and Servant.*]

SURFACE: Mr. Stanley! Why should you think I would see him? You must know he comes to ask something!

SERVANT: Sir, I should not have let him in but that Mr. Rowley came to the door with him.

SURFACE: Pshaw! Blockhead, to suppose that I should now be in a temper to receive visits from poor relations! Well, why don't you show the fellow up?

SERVANT: I will, sir—why sir—it was not my fault that Sir Peter discovered my lady—

SURFACE: Go, fool! [*Exit Servant.*] Sure, fortune never played a man of my policy[1] such a trick before! My character with Sir Peter! My hopes with Maria! Destroyed in a moment! I'm in a rare humor to listen to other people's distresses; I shan't be able to bestow even a benevolent sentiment on Stanley. So! Here he comes and Rowley with him—I *must* try to recover myself, and put a little charity into my face, however.   [*Exit.*]

[*Enter Sir Oliver and Rowley.*]

SIR OLIVER: What! Does he avoid us? That was he—was it not?

ROWLEY: It was, sir—but I doubt you are come a little too abruptly. His nerves are so weak, that the sight of a poor relation may be too much for him—I should have gone first, to break you to him.

SIR OLIVER: A plague of his nerves—yet this is he whom Sir Peter extolls as a man of the most benevolent way of thinking!

ROWLEY: As to his way of thinking—I can't pretend to decide; for, to do him justice, he appears to have as much speculative benevolence as any private gentleman in the kingdom—though he is seldom so sensual as to indulge himself in the exercise of it.

SIR OLIVER: Yet has a string of charitable sentiments, I suppose, at his finger's ends!

ROWLEY: Or rather, at his tongue's end, Sir Oliver—for I believe there is no sentiment he has more faith in than that "Charity begins at home."

SIR OLIVER: And his, I presume, is of that domestic sort which never stirs abroad at all.

ROWLEY: I doubt you'll find it so—but he's coming. I mustn't seem to interrupt you, and, you know, immediately as you leave him, I come in to announce your arrival in your real character.

1. Cunning.

SIR OLIVER: True—and afterward you'll meet me at Sir Peter's.

ROWLEY: Without losing a moment.

[Exit Rowley.]

SIR OLIVER: So—I don't like the complaisance[2] of his features.

[Re-enter Surface.]

SURFACE: Sir, I beg you ten thousand pardons for keeping you a moment waiting. Mr. Stanley, I presume.

SIR OLIVER: At your service.

SURFACE: Sir, I beg you will do me the honor to sit down; I entreat you, sir.

SIR OLIVER: Dear sir, there's no occasion.—[Aside.] Too civil by half!

SURFACE: I have not the pleasure of knowing you, Mr. Stanley, but I am extremely happy to see you look so well. You were nearly related to my mother, I think, Mr. Stanley.

SIR OLIVER: I was, sir, so nearly that my present poverty, I fear, may do discredit to her wealthy children—else I should not have presumed to trouble you.

SURFACE: Dear sir, there needs no apology. He that is in distress, though a stranger, has a right to claim kindred with the wealthy. I am sure I wish I was of that class, and had it in my power to offer you even a small relief.

SIR OLIVER: If your uncle, Sir Oliver, were here, I should have a friend.

SURFACE: I wish he were, sir, with all my heart—you should not want an advocate with him, believe me, sir.

SIR OLIVER: I should not need one—my distresses would recommend me. But I imagined his bounty had enabled you to become the agent of his charity.

SURFACE: My dear sir, you were strangely misinformed. Sir Oliver is a worthy man—a very worthy sort of man—but avarice, Mr. Stanley, is the vice of age. I will tell you, my good sir—in confidence!—what he has done for me has been a mere nothing, though people, I know, have thought otherwise, and for my part I never chose to contradict the report.

SIR OLIVER: What! Has he never transmitted you bullion![3]—rupees!—pagodas![4]

SURFACE: O dear sir, nothing of the kind—no, no—a few presents now and then—China shawls, congo tea,[5] avadavats[6] and Indian crackers[7]—little more, believe me.

SIR OLIVER [aside]: Here's gratitude for twelve thousand pounds! Avadavats and Indian crackers!

SURFACE: Then, my dear sir—you have heard, I doubt not, of the extravagance of my brother. There are very few would credit what I have done for that unfortunate young man!

SIR OLIVER [aside]: Not I for one!

SURFACE: The sums I have lent him! Indeed, I have been exceedingly to blame—it was an amiable weakness! However, I don't pretend to defend it—and now I feel it doubly culpable, since it has deprived me of the power of serving you, Mr. Stanley, as my heart directs.

SIR OLIVER [aside]: Dissembler!—Then, sir, you cannot assist me?

SURFACE: At present it grieves me to say I cannot, but whenever I have the ability you may depend upon hearing from me.

SIR OLIVER: I am extremely sorry.

2. Habitual courtesy, deferential look.
3. Raw gold or silver.
4. Rupees and pagodas are Indian coins.

5. Black tea from China.
6. Small red and black singing birds from India.
7. Firecrackers.

SURFACE: Not more than I am, believe me—to pity without the power to relieve is still more painful than to ask and be denied.

SIR OLIVER: Kind sir, your most obedient, humble servant.

SURFACE: You leave me deeply affected, Mr. Stanley—William, be ready to open the door.

SIR OLIVER: O dear sir—no ceremony.

SURFACE: Your very obedient—

SIR OLIVER: Sir, your most obsequeous—

SURFACE: You may depend upon hearing from me, whenever I can be of service.

SIR OLIVER: Sweet sir, you are too good.

SURFACE: In the mean time, I wish you health and spirits.

SIR OLIVER: Your ever grateful, and perpetual, humble servant.

SURFACE: Sir, yours as sincerely.

SIR OLIVER: Now I am satisfied!   [Exit.]

SURFACE [solus]: This is one bad effect of a good character; it invites applications from the unfortunate, and there needs no small degree of address to gain the reputation of benevolence without incurring the expense. The silver ore of pure charity is an expensive article in the catalogue of a man's good qualities, whereas the sentimental French plate[8] I use instead of it makes just as good a show—and pays no tax. [Enter Rowley.]

ROWLEY: Mr. Surface, your servant. I was apprehensive of interrupting you, though my business demands immediate attention, as this note will inform you.

SURFACE: Always happy to see Mr. Rowley. [Reads.] How! "Oliver—Surface!" My uncle arrived!

ROWLEY: He is indeed; we have just parted—quite well—after a speedy voyage, and impatient to embrace his worthy nephew.

SURFACE: I am astonished! William—stop Mr. Stanley if he's not gone.

ROWLEY: O, he's out of reach, I believe.

SURFACE: Why didn't you let me know this when you came in together?

ROWLEY: I thought you had particular business—but I must be gone to inform your brother, and appoint him here to meet his uncle. He will be with you in a quarter of an hour.

SURFACE: So he says. Well, I am strangely overjoyed at his coming—[Aside.] Never to be sure was anything so damned unlucky!

ROWLEY: You will be delighted to see how well he looks.

SURFACE: O, I'm rejoiced to hear it—[Aside.] Just at this time!

ROWLEY: I'll tell him how impatiently you expect him.

SURFACE: Do, do, pray give my best duty and affection—indeed I cannot express the sensations I feel at the thought of seeing him!

                                                                [Exit Rowley.]

Certainly, his coming just as this time is the cruellest piece of ill fortune!   [Exit.]

                                    Scene 2

[At Sir Peter's. Enter Mrs. Candour and Maid.]

MAID: Indeed, ma'am, my lady will see nobody at present.

MRS. CANDOUR: Did you tell her it was her friend, Mrs. Candour?

---

8. Dishes and utensils coated with (rather than made of) silver.

MAID: Yes, ma'am, but she begs you will excuse her.

MRS. CANDOUR: Do go again—I shall be glad to see her if it be only for a moment, for I am sure she must be in great distress.

[Exit Maid.]

Dear heart, how provoking! I'm not mistress of half the circumstances! We shall have the whole affair in the newspapers with the names of the parties at length before I have dropped the story at a dozen houses.

[Enter Sir Benjamin.]

O dear Sir Benjamin, you have heard, I suppose—

SIR BENJAMIN: Of Lady Teazle and Mr. Surface—

MRS. CANDOUR: And Sir Peter's discovery—

SIR BENJAMIN: O, the strangest piece of business to be sure!

MRS. CANDOUR: Well, I never was so surprised in my life!—I am so sorry for all parties, indeed I am.

SIR BENJAMIN: Now I don't pity Sir Peter at all. He was so extravagantly partial to Mr. Surface—

MRS. CANDOUR: Mr. Surface! Why, 'twas with Charles Lady Teazle was—detected.

SIR BENJAMIN: No such thing—Mr. Surface is the gallant.

MRS. CANDOUR: No, no, Charles is the man—'twas Mr. Surface brought Sir Peter on purpose to discover them.

SIR BENJAMIN: I tell you I have it from one—

MRS. CANDOUR: And I have it from one—

SIR BENJAMIN: Who had it from one who had it—

MRS. CANDOUR: From one immediately—but here's Lady Sneerwell; perhaps she knows the whole affair.

[Enter Lady Sneerwell.]

LADY SNEERWELL: So, my dear Mrs. Candour. Here's a sad affair of our friend Lady Teazle—

MRS. CANDOUR: Aye! My dear friend, who could have thought it?

LADY SNEERWELL: Well, there is no trusting appearances. Though indeed she was always too lively for me.

MRS. CANDOUR: To be sure, her manners were a little too free—but she was very young—

LADY SNEERWELL: And had indeed some good qualities—

MRS. CANDOUR: So she had indeed—but have you heard the particulars?

LADY SNEERWELL: No, but everybody says that Mr. Surface—

SIR BENJAMIN: Aye, there I told you. Mr. Surface was the man.

MRS. CANDOUR: No, no indeed—the assignation[9] was with Charles.

LADY SNEERWELL: With Charles! You alarm me, Mrs. Candour.

MRS. CANDOUR: Yes, yes—he was the lover. Mr. Surface—do him justice—was only the informer.

SIR BENJAMIN: Well, I'll not dispute with you, Mrs. Candour, but be it which it may—I hope that Sir Peter's wound will not—

MRS. CANDOUR: Sir Peter's wound! O Mercy! I didn't hear a word of their fighting—

LADY SNEERWELL: Nor I, a syllable!

SIR BENJAMIN: No—what, no mention of the duel?

9. Illicit lovers' meeting.

MRS. CANDOUR: Not a word—

SIR BENJAMIN: O Lord—yes, yes—they fought before they left the room.

LADY SNEERWELL: Pray let us hear.

MRS. CANDOUR: Aye, do oblige us with the duel.

SIR BENJAMIN: "Sir," says Sir Peter—immediately after the discovery—"you are a most ungrateful fellow."

MRS. CANDOUR: Aye, to Charles—

SIR BENJAMIN: No, no, to Mr. Surface—"a most ungrateful fellow, and old as I am, sir, says he, I insist on immediate satisfaction."

MRS. CANDOUR: Aye, that must have been to Charles, for 'tis very unlikely Mr. Surface should go to fight in his own house.

SIR BENJAMIN: 'Gad's life, ma'am, not at all—giving me immediate satisfaction. On this, madam, Lady Teazle, seeing Sir Peter in such danger, ran out of the room in strong hysterics and Charles after her calling out for hartshorn and water!¹ Then, madam, they began to fight with swords—

  [Enter Crabtree.]

CRABTREE: With pistols, nephew—I have it from undoubted authority.

MRS. CANDOUR: O, Mr. Crabtree, then it is all true.

CRABTREE: Too true indeed, ma'am, and Sir Peter's dangerously wounded—

SIR BENJAMIN: By a thrust in seconde²—quite through his left side.

CRABTREE: By a bullet lodged in the thorax.

MRS. CANDOUR: Mercy on me, poor Sir Peter—

CRABTREE: Yes ma'am, though Charles would have avoided the matter if he could.

MRS. CANDOUR: I knew Charles was the person.

SIR BENJAMIN: O, my uncle, I see, knows nothing of the matter.

CRABTREE: But Sir Peter taxed him with the basest ingratitude—

SIR BENJAMIN: That I told you, you know.

CRABTREE: Do, nephew, let me speak—and insisted on an immediate—

SIR BENJAMIN: Just as I said.

CRABTREE: Odds life, nephew, allow others to know something too! A pair of pistols lay on the bureau, for Mr. Surface, it seems, had come the night before late from Salt Hill where he had been to see the Montem³ with a friend who has a son at Eton, so unluckily the pistols were left charged.

SIR BENJAMIN: I heard nothing of this—

CRABTREE: Sir Peter forced Charles to take one, and they fired—it seems pretty nearly together—Charles's shot took place as I told you, and Sir Peter's missed—but what is very extraordinary, the ball struck against a little bronze Pliny⁴ that stood over the chimney piece—grazed out of the window at a right angle—and wounded the postman, who was just coming to the door with a double letter⁵ from Northamptonshire—

SIR BENJAMIN: My uncle's account is more circumstantial, I must confess—but I believe mine is the true one for all that.

LADY SNEERWELL: I am more interested in this affair than they imagine, and must have better information.

                                                [Exit Lady Sneerwell.]

1. A solution, also known as smelling salts, used to revive someone who has fainted.
2. A thrust downward, delivered under the opponent's blade.
3. An annual procession at Eton College.
4. Pliny the Elder (A.D. 23–79), author of Natural History.
5. A letter written on two sheets of paper, costing double postage.

SIR BENJAMIN [*after a pause looking at each other*]: Ah! Lady Sneerwell's alarm is very easily accounted for—

CRABTREE: Yes, yes, they certainly *do* say—but that's neither here nor there.

MRS. CANDOUR: But pray, where is Sir Peter at present?

CRABTREE: Oh! They brought him home and he is now in the house, though the servants are ordered to deny it.

MRS. CANDOUR: I believe so—and Lady Teazle, I suppose, attending him—

CRABTREE: Yes, yes—I saw one of the faculty[6] enter just before me.

SIR BENJAMIN: Hey, who comes here?

CRABTREE: O this is he, the physician, depend on't.

MRS. CANDOUR: O certainly, it must be the physician, and now we shall know—
    [*Enter Sir Oliver.*]

CRABTREE: Well, Doctor—what hopes?

MRS. CANDOUR: Aye, Doctor, how's your patient?

SIR BENJAMIN: Now, Doctor, isn't it a wound with a small sword?[7]

CRABTREE: A bullet lodged in the thorax—for a hundred!

SIR OLIVER: Doctor! A wound with a small sword! And a bullet in the thorax! Oons, are you mad, good people?

SIR BENJAMIN: Perhaps, sir, you are not a doctor.

SIR OLIVER: Truly, I am to thank you for my degree if I am.

CRABTREE: Only a friend of Sir Peter's, then, I presume; but sir, you must have heard of this accident—

SIR OLIVER: Not a word!

CRABTREE: Not of his being dangerously wounded?

SIR OLIVER: The devil he is!

SIR BENJAMIN: Run through the body—

CRABTREE: Shot in the breast—

SIR BENJAMIN: By one Mr. Surface—

CRABTREE: Aye, the younger.

SIR OLIVER: Hey! What the plague! You seem to differ strangely in your accounts—however, you agree that Sir Peter is dangerously wounded.

SIR BENJAMIN: Oh, yes, we agree there.

CRABTREE: Yes, yes, I believe there can be no doubt of that.

SIR OLIVER: Then, upon my word, for a person in that situation he is the most imprudent man alive—for here he comes, walking as if nothing at all were the matter.
    [*Enter Sir Peter.*]
Odds heart, Sir Peter—you are come in good time, I promise you, for we had just given you over.

SIR BENJAMIN: Egad, uncle, this is the most sudden recovery!

SIR OLIVER: Why, man, what do you do out of bed with a small sword through your body, and a bullet lodged in your thorax!

SIR PETER: A small sword and a bullet—

SIR OLIVER: Aye, these gentlemen would have killed you, without law or physic—and wanted to dub[8] me a doctor—to make me an accomplice.

SIR PETER: Why, what is all this?

---

6. I.e., a doctor.   8. Give me the title of.
7. A light sword or rapier.

SIR BENJAMIN: We rejoice, Sir Peter, that the story of the duel is not true—and are sincerely sorry for your other misfortunes.

SIR PETER [aside]: So, so—all over the town already.

CRABTREE: Though, Sir Peter, you were certainly vastly to blame to marry at all, at your years.

SIR PETER: Sir, what business is that of yours?

MRS. CANDOUR: Though, indeed, as Sir Peter made so good a husband, he's very much to be pitied!

SIR PETER: Plague on your pity, ma'am, I desire none of it.

SIR BENJAMIN: However, Sir Peter, you must not mind the laughing and jests you will meet with on this occasion—

SIR PETER: Sir, I desire to be master in my own house.

CRABTREE: 'Tis no uncommon case, that's one comfort.

SIR PETER: I insist on being left to myself; without ceremony, I insist on your leaving my house directly!

MRS. CANDOUR: Well, well, we are going, and depend on't, we'll make the best report of you we can—

SIR PETER: Leave my house—

CRABTREE: And tell how hardly you have been treated.

SIR PETER: Leave my house.

SIR BENJAMIN: And how patiently you bear it.

SIR PETER: Fiends—Vipers!—Furies! Oh, that their own venom would choke them!

[Exeunt Mrs. Candour, Sir Benjamin, Crabtree.]

SIR OLIVER: They are very provoking, indeed, Sir Peter.
    [Enter Rowley.]

ROWLEY: I heard high words—what has ruffled you, Sir Peter?

SIR PETER: Pshaw, what signifies asking? Do I ever pass a day without my vexations?

SIR OLIVER: Well, I'm not inquisitive—I come only to tell you that I have seen both my nephews in the manner we proposed—

SIR PETER: A precious couple they are!

ROWLEY: Yes, and Sir Oliver is convinced that your judgment was right, Sir Peter.

SIR OLIVER: Yes, I find Joseph is indeed the man, after all.

ROWLEY: Yes, as Sir Peter says, he's a man of sentiment.

SIR OLIVER: And acts up to the sentiments he professes.

ROWLEY: It certainly is edification[9] to hear him talk.

SIR OLIVER: Oh, he's a model for the young men of the age! But how's this, Sir Peter, you don't join in your friend Joseph's praise as I expected.

SIR PETER: Sir Oliver, we live in a damned wicked world, and the fewer we praise the better.

ROWLEY: What, do you say so, Sir Peter—who were never mistaken in your life?

SIR PETER: Pshaw! Plague on you both—I see by your sneering you have heard the whole affair—I shall go mad among you!

ROWLEY: Then to fret you no longer, Sir Peter, we are indeed acquainted with it all. I met Lady Teazle coming from Mr. Surface's—so humbled that she deigned to request me to be her advocate with you.

9. Beneficial morally and spiritually.

SIR PETER: And does Sir Oliver know all too?

SIR OLIVER: Every circumstance!

SIR PETER: What, of the closet—and the screen—hey?

SIR OLIVER: Yes, yes, and the little French milliner—O, I have been vastly diverted with the story—ha! ha!

SIR PETER: 'Twas—very pleasant!

SIR OLIVER: I never laughed more in my life, I assure you, ha! ha!

SIR PETER: O, vastly diverting—ha! ha!

ROWLEY: To be sure Joseph—with his sentiments—ha! ha!

SIR PETER: Yes, yes, his sentiments—ha! ha!—a hypocritical villain!

SIR OLIVER: Aye, and that rogue Charles, to pull Sir Peter out of the closet—ha! ha!

SIR PETER: Ha! ha! 'Twas devilish entertaining to be sure—

SIR OLIVER: Ha! ha! Egad, Sir Peter, I should like to have seen your face when the screen was thrown down, ha! ha!

SIR PETER: Yes, yes, my face when the screen was thrown down, ha! ha! O, I must never show my head again!

SIR OLIVER: But come, come, it isn't fair to laugh at you neither my old friend—though upon my soul I can't help it—

SIR PETER: O pray don't restrain your mirth on my account. It does not hurt me at all—I laugh at the whole affair myself—yes, yes—I think being a standing jest for all one's acquaintances a very happy situation—O yes—and then of a morning to read the paragraphs about Mr. S——, Lady T——, and Sir P—— will be so entertaining!

ROWLEY: Without affectation,[1] Sir Peter, you may despise the ridicule of fools—but I see Lady Teazle going toward the next room. I am sure you must desire a reconciliation as earnestly as she does.

SIR OLIVER: Perhaps my being here prevents her coming to you. Well, I'll leave honest Rowley to mediate between you, but he must bring you all presently to Mr. Surface's, where I am now returning—if not to reclaim a libertine, at least to expose hypocrisy.

SIR PETER: Ah! I'll be present at your discovering yourself there with all my heart—though 'tis a vile unlucky place for discoveries.

ROWLEY: We'll follow.

[Exit Sir Oliver.]

SIR PETER: She is not coming here, you see, Rowley.

ROWLEY: No, but she has left the door of that room open, you perceive. See, she is in tears!

SIR PETER: Certainly a little mortification appears very becoming in a wife—don't you think it will do her good to let her pine a little?

ROWLEY: O, this is ungenerous in you—

SIR PETER: Well, I know not what to think—you remember, Rowley, the letter I found of hers, evidently intended for Charles?

ROWLEY: A mere forgery, Sir Peter, laid in your way on purpose. This is one of the points which I intend Snake shall give you conviction on.

SIR PETER: I wish I were once satisfied of that. She looks this way—what a remarkably elegant turn of the head she has! Rowley, I'll go to her—

ROWLEY: Certainly.

1. Putting on airs.

SIR PETER: Though when it is known that we are reconciled, people will laugh at me ten times more!

ROWLEY: Let them laugh—and retort their malice only by showing them you are happy in spite of it.

SIR PETER: I'faith, so I will—and if I'm not mistaken, we may yet be the happiest couple in the country.

ROWLEY: Nay, Sir Peter, he who once lays aside suspicion—

SIR PETER: Hold, my dear Rowley—if you have any regard for me, never let me hear you utter anything like a sentiment. I have had enough of them to serve me the rest of my life.   [Exeunt.]

Scene 3

[The library in Joseph Surface's house. Surface and Lady Sneerwell.]

LADY SNEERWELL: Impossible! Will not Sir Peter immediately be reconciled to Charles? And of consequence no longer oppose his union with Maria? The thought is distraction to me![2]

SURFACE: Can passion furnish a remedy?

LADY SNEERWELL: No, nor cunning either. O, I was a fool! An idiot—to league[3] with such a blunderer!

SURFACE: Sure, Lady Sneerwell, I am the greatest sufferer—yet you see I bear the accident with calmness.

LADY SNEERWELL: Because the disappointment doesn't reach your heart. Your interest only attached you to Maria. Had you felt for her what I have for that ungrateful libertine, neither your temper nor hypocrisy could prevent your showing the sharpness of your vexation.

SURFACE: But why should your reproaches fall on me for this disappointment?

LADY SNEERWELL: Are not you the cause of it? What had you to do, to bate[4] in your pursuit of Maria to pervert Lady Teazle by the way? Had you not a sufficient field for your roguery in blinding Sir Peter and supplanting your brother? I hate such an avarice of crimes—'tis an unfair monopoly and never prospers.

SURFACE: Well, I admit I have been to blame. I confess I deviated from the direct road of wrong, but I don't think we're so totally defeated neither.

LADY SNEERWELL: No!

SURFACE: You tell me you have made a trial of Snake since we met, and that you still believe him faithful to us—

LADY SNEERWELL: I do believe so.

SURFACE: And that he has undertaken, should it be necessary, to swear and prove that Charles is at this time contracted by vows and honor to your ladyship—which some of his former letters to you will serve to support.

LADY SNEERWELL: This indeed might have assisted—

SURFACE: Come, come, it is not too late yet.

[Knocking.]

But hark! This is probably my uncle, Sir Oliver. Retire to that room—we'll consult farther when he's gone.

LADY SNEERWELL: Well! But if he should find you out too—

SURFACE: O, I have no fear of that—Sir Peter will hold his tongue for his own credit sake, and you may depend on't I shall soon discover Sir Oliver's weak side!

2. I.e., drives me mad.   4. Pause.
3. Join forces.

LADY SNEERWELL: I have no diffidence[5] of your abilities—only be constant to one roguery at a time.   [Exit.]

SURFACE: I will, I will—so, 'tis confounded hard after such bad fortune to be baited[6] by one's confederate in evil. Well, at all events, my character is so much better than Charles's that I certainly—hey! what!—this is not Sir Oliver, but old Stanley again! Plague on't! That he should return to tease me just now! We shall have Sir Oliver come and find him here, and—

    [Enter Sir Oliver.]

    Gad's life, Mr. Stanley—why have you come back to plague me just at this time? You must not stay now, upon my word!

SIR OLIVER: Sir, I hear your uncle Oliver is expected here—and though he has been so penurious[7] to you, I'll try what he'll do for me.

SURFACE: Sir, 'tis impossible for you to stay now, so I must beg—come any other time and I promise you you shall be assisted.

SIR OLIVER: No—Sir Oliver and I must be acquainted.

SURFACE: Zounds, sir, then I insist on your quitting the room directly.

SIR OLIVER: Nay, sir!

SURFACE: Sir—I insist on't. Here, William, show this gentleman out. Since you compel me, sir, not one moment—this is such insolence! [Going to push him out.]

    [Enter Charles.]

CHARLES SURFACE: Heydey! What's the matter now? What the devil, have you got hold of my little broker here! Zounds, brother, don't hurt little Premium. What's the matter, my little fellow?

SURFACE: So! He has been with you too, has he?

CHARLES SURFACE: To be sure he has! Why 'tis as honest a little—but sure, Joseph, you have not been borrowing money too, have you?

SURFACE: Borrowing, no! But brother—you know here we expect Sir Oliver every—

CHARLES SURFACE: O Gad! That's true—Noll mustn't find the little broker here to be sure.

SURFACE: Yet Mr. Stanley insists—

CHARLES SURFACE: Stanley! Why his name's Premium—

SURFACE: No, no, Stanley—

CHARLES SURFACE: No, no, Premium—

SURFACE: Well, no matter which, but—

CHARLES SURFACE: Aye, aye, Stanley or Premium, 'tis the same thing, as you say, for I suppose he goes by half a hundred names—besides A.B.'s at the coffee houses—[8]

    [Knock.]

SURFACE: Death—here's Sir Oliver at the door.

    [Knocking again.]

    Now I beg, Mr. Stanley—

CHARLES SURFACE: Aye, and I beg, Mr. Premium—

SIR OLIVER: Gentlemen—

SURFACE: Sir, by Heav'n you shall go—

CHARLES SURFACE: Aye, out with him certainly.

SIR OLIVER: This violence—

---

5. Lack of confidence in.
6. Harassed.
7. Stingy.

8. Coffee houses accepted mail for certain customers under initials only; money-lenders used this service.

SURFACE: 'Tis your own fault.

CHARLES SURFACE: Out with him to be sure—[*Both forcing Sir Oliver out.*]
  [*Enter Sir Peter, Lady Teazle, Maria, and Rowley.*]

SIR PETER: My old friend Sir Oliver! Hey—what in the name of wonder! Here are dutiful nephews! Assault their uncle at the first visit—

LADY TEAZLE: Indeed, Sir Oliver, 'twas well we came in to rescue you.

ROWLEY: Truly it was, for I perceive, Sir Oliver, the character of old Stanley was no protection to you.

SIR OLIVER: Nor of Premium either. The necessities of the former couldn't extort a shilling from that benevolent gentleman and now—egad!—I stood a chance of faring worse than my ancestors, and being knocked down without being bid for. [*After a pause—Joseph and Charles turning to each other.*]

SURFACE: Charles!

CHARLES SURFACE: Joseph!

SURFACE: 'Tis now complete!

CHARLES SURFACE: Very.

SIR OLIVER: Sir Peter, my friend, and Rowley too—look on that elder nephew of mine. You know what he has already received from my bounty, and you know also how gladly I would have regarded half my fortune as held in trust for him—judge then my disappointment in discovering him to be destitute of truth, charity, and gratitude.

SIR PETER: Sir Oliver, I should be more surprised at this declaration if I had not myself found him selfish, treacherous and hypocritical.

LADY TEAZLE: And if the gentleman pleads not guilty to these, pray let him call *me* to his character.

SIR PETER: Then I believe we need add no more. If he knows himself, he will consider it as the most perfect punishment that he is known by the world.

CHARLES SURFACE [*aside*]: If they talk this way to honesty—what will they say to *me* by and bye!

SIR OLIVER: As for that prodigal—his brother there—

CHARLES SURFACE [*aside*]: Aye, now comes my turn—the damned family pictures will ruin me!

SURFACE: Sir Oliver! Uncle! Will you honor me with a hearing?

CHARLES SURFACE [*aside*]: Now if Joseph would make one of his long speeches, I might recollect myself a little—

SIR OLIVER: I suppose you would undertake to justify yourself entirely.

SURFACE: I trust I could.

SIR OLIVER: Pshaw! Well, sir! And you [*to Charles*] could justify yourself too, I suppose—

CHARLES SURFACE: Not that I know of, Sir Oliver.

SIR OLIVER: What, little Premium has been let too much into the secret, I presume?

CHARLES SURFACE: True, sir, but they were family secrets and should never be mentioned again, you know.

ROWLEY: Come, Sir Oliver, I know you cannot speak of Charles's follies with anger.

SIR OLIVER: Odds heart, no more I can—nor with gravity either. Sir Peter, do you know the rogue bargained with me for all his ancestors—sold me judges and generals by the foot and maiden aunts as cheap as broken china!

CHARLES SURFACE: To be sure, Sir Oliver, I did make a little free with the family canvas, that's the truth on't—my ancestors may certainly rise in evidence against me; there's no denying it—but believe me sincere when I tell you, and upon my soul I would not say it if I was not—that if I do not appear mortified at the exposure of my follies, it is because I feel at this moment the warmest satisfaction in seeing you—my liberal benefactor.

SIR OLIVER: Charles—I believe you. Give me your hand again. The ill-looking little fellow over the settee has made your peace, sirrah![9]

CHARLES SURFACE: Then, sir, my gratitude to the original is still increased.

LADY TEAZLE [pointing to Maria]: Yet I believe, Sir Oliver, here is one whom Charles is still more anxious to be reconciled to.

SIR OLIVER: O, I have heard of his attachment there—and with the young lady's pardon, if I construe right that blush—

SIR PETER: Well, child, speak your sentiments—

MARIA: Sir, I have little to say—but that I shall rejoice to hear that he is happy. For me, whatever claim I had to his affection, I willingly resign it to one who has a better title.

CHARLES SURFACE: How, Maria!

SIR PETER: Heydey—what's the mystery now? While he appeared an incorrigible rake you would give your hand to no one else, and now that he's likely to reform I warrant you won't have him!

MARIA: His own heart—and Lady Sneerwell—know the cause.

CHARLES SURFACE: Lady Sneerwell—

SURFACE: Brother, it is with great concern I am obliged to speak on this point, but my regard to justice compels me. And Lady Sneerwell's injuries can no longer be concealed—[Goes to the door.]

[Enter Lady Sneerwell.]

SIR PETER: So! Another French milliner, egad! He has one in every room in the house, I suppose.

LADY SNEERWELL: Ungrateful Charles! Well may you be surprised and feel for the indelicate situation which your perfidy has forced me into.

CHARLES SURFACE: Pray, uncle, is this another plot of yours? For as I have life I don't understand it.

SURFACE: I believe, sir, there is but the evidence of one person more necessary to make it extremely clear.

SIR PETER: And that person, I imagine, is Mr. Snake. Rowley, you were perfectly right to bring him with us—and pray let him appear.

ROWLEY: Walk in, Mr. Snake.

[Enter Snake.]

I thought his testimony might be wanted; however, it happens unluckily that he comes to confront Lady Sneerwell and not to support her.

LADY SNEERWELL: Villain! Treacherous to me at last! [Aside.] Speak, fellow, have you too conspired against me?

SNAKE: I beg your ladyship ten thousand pardons; you paid me extremely liberally for the lie in question—but I have unfortunately been offered double to speak the truth.

9. Contemptuous or teasing form of "sir."

Richard Brinsley Sheridan

SIR PETER: Plot and counterplot. Egad—I wish your ladyship joy of the success of your negotiation.

LADY SNEERWELL: The torments of shame and disappointment on you all!

LADY TEAZLE: Hold. Lady Sneerwell, before you go, let me thank you for the trouble you and that gentleman have taken in writing letters to me from Charles and answering them yourself—and let me also request you to make my respects to the scandalous college of which you are president, and inform them that Lady Teazle, licentiate,[1] begs leave to return the diploma they granted her—as she leaves off practice and kills characters no longer.

LADY SNEERWELL: You too, madam—provoking—insolent! May your husband live these fifty years! [Exit.]

SIR PETER: Oons, what a fury—

LADY TEAZLE: What a malicious creature it is!

SIR PETER: Hey—not for her last wish?

LADY TEAZLE: O, no—

SIR OLIVER: Well, Sir, and what have you to say now?

SURFACE: Sir, I am so confounded to find that Lady Sneerwell could be guilty of suborning[2] Mr. Snake in this manner to impose on us all, that I know not what to say—however, lest her revengeful spirit should prompt her to injure my brother, I had certainly better follow her directly. [Exit.]

SIR PETER: Moral to the last drop!

SIR OLIVER: Aye and marry her, Joseph, if you can—oil and vinegar, egad! You'll do very well together.

ROWLEY: I believe we have no more occasion for Mr. Snake at present.

SNAKE: Before I go, I beg pardon, once for all, for whatever uneasiness I have been the humble instrument of causing to the parties present.

SIR PETER: Well, well, you have made atonement by a good deed at last.

SNAKE: But I must request of the company that it shall never be known—

SIR PETER: Hey! What the plague—are you ashamed of having done a right thing once in your life?

SNAKE: Ah, sir, consider I live by the badness of my character! I have nothing but my infamy to depend on, and if it were once known that I had been betrayed into an honest action, I should lose every friend I have in the world.

SIR OLIVER: Well, well, we'll not traduce you by saying anything in your praise, never fear.

[Exit Snake.]

SIR PETER: There's a precious rogue—yet that fellow is a writer and a critic!

LADY TEAZLE: See, Sir Oliver, there needs no persuasion now to reconcile your nephew and Maria— [Charles and Maria apart.]

SIR OLIVER: Aye, aye, that's as it should be, and egad, we'll have the wedding tomorrow morning.

CHARLES SURFACE: Thank you, my dear uncle.

SIR PETER: What! You rogue, don't you ask the girl's consent first?

CHARLES SURFACE: O, I have done that a long time—above a minute ago, and she has looked yes.

MARIA: For shame—Charles—I protest, Sir Peter, there has not been a word—

---

1. Holder of a certificate of competence.   2. Bribing.

SIR OLIVER: Well then, the fewer the better—may your love for each other never know abatement.[3]

SIR PETER: And may you live as happily together as Lady Teazle and I—intend to do.

CHARLES SURFACE: Rowley, my old friend—I am sure you congratulate me and I suspect that I owe you much.

SIR OLIVER: You do indeed, Charles.

ROWLEY: If my efforts to serve you had not succeeded, you would have been in my debt for the attempt—but deserve to be happy, and you overpay me.[4]

SIR PETER: Aye, honest Rowley always said you would reform.

CHARLES SURFACE: Why, as to reforming, Sir Peter, I'll make no promises—and that I take to be a proof that I intend to set about it. But here shall be my monitor—my gentle guide. Ah, can I leave the virtuous path those eyes illumine?

> Though thou, dear maid, should'st waive thy beauty's sway,[5]
> Thou still must rule—because I will obey;
> An humbled fugitive from folly view,
> No sanctuary near but love and—YOU.
> [*To the audience.*]
> You can, indeed, each anxious fear remove,
> For even scandal dies if you approve.

EPILOGUE

Written by G. Colman, Esq.[6]
Spoken by Mrs. Abington[7] in the character of Lady Teazle

I, who was late so volatile and gay,
Like a trade-wind must now blow all one way,
Bend all my cares, my studies, and my vows,
To one old rusty weathercock—my spouse!
5 So wills our virtuous bard—the motley Bayes[8]
Of crying epilogues[9] and laughing plays.

Old bachelors, who marry smart young wives,
Learn from our play to regulate your lives!
Each bring his dear to town—all faults upon her—
10 London will prove the very source of honor.
Plunged fairly in, like a cold bath, it serves,
When principles relax, to brace the nerves.
Such is my case—and yet I might deplore
That the gay dream of dissipation's o'er;
15 And say, ye fair, was ever lively wife,
Born with a genius for the highest life

---

3. Decrease.
4. I.e., you would owe me only if I had not been successful in helping you; if you reform, I will receive more than I have earned.
5. I.e., even though you were to give up the power your beauty possesses.
6. George Colman (1732–1794) was a successful comic dramatist and manager of the Haymarket Theatre.
7. Frances Abington (1737–1815), the celebrated comic

actress for whom Sheridan wrote the role of Lady Teazle. She scored a huge success in the part. (For a discussion of her career, see pages 2083–84; for a portrait of her in another role, see Color Plate 23.)
8. Genius skilled in different moods (i.e., tragedy or comedy).
9. Sheridan's epilogue for George Ayscough's *Semiramis* (1776) had been hailed by the *Whitehall Evening-Post* as the best tragic epilogue the reviewer had ever heard.

Like me, untimely blasted in her bloom,
Like me condemned to such a dismal doom?
Save money—when I just knew how to waste it!
20   Leave London—just as I began to taste it!
Must I then watch the early-crowing cock?
The melancholy ticking of a clock?
In the lone rustic hall forever pounded,
With dogs, cats, rats, and squalling brats surrounded?
25   With humble curates can I now retire
(While good Sir Peter boozes with the squire)
And at backgammon mortify my soul,
That pants for loo,[1] or flutters at a vole?[2]
"Seven's the main!"[3]—dear sound that must expire,
30   Lost at hot-cockles[4] round a Christmas fire!
The transient hour of fashion too soon spent,
Farewell the tranquil mind, farewell content![5]
Farewell the plumèd head, the cushioned *tête*,[6]
That takes the cushion from its proper seat!
35   The spirit stirring drum! (card drums[7] I mean—
Spadille, odd trick, pam, basto, king and queen![8])
And you, ye knockers,[9] that with brazen throat
The welcome visitor's approach denote,
Farewell!—all quality of high renown,
40   Pride, pomp, and circumstance of glorious town!
Farewell! Your revels I partake no more,
And Lady Teazle's occupation's o'er!
All this I told our bard—he smiled and said 'twas clear
I ought to play deep tragedy next year.
45   Meanwhile he drew wise morals from his play,
And in these solemn periods[1] stalked away:
"Blessed were the fair like you, her faults who stopped,
And closed her follies when the curtain dropped!
No more in vice or error to engage,
50   Or play the fool at large on life's great stage."

1777

1. A fashionable card game.
2. Winning all the tricks in a deal.
3. A call in the dice game hazard.
4. A rustic game in which one player guesses the names of those who strike him on the back.
5. In this and the ensuing ten lines, Colman parodies the lament in which Shakespeare's Othello, possessed by sudden jealousy and despair, gives over his brilliant military

career (*Othello* 3.3.348–57)
6. A wig, tall and elaborately ornamented.
7. Fashionable private gatherings for playing cards.
8. Nicknames for playing cards: "spadille" is the ace of spades in ombre, and "pam" is the knave of clubs in loo.
9. Door-knockers.
1. Sentences.

POLITICAL AND RELIGIOUS ORDERS

One political order that cannot be ignored by readers of British literature and history is the monarchy, since it provides the terms by which historical periods are even today divided up. Thus much of the nineteenth century is often spoken of as the "Victorian" age or period, after Queen Victoria (reigned 1837–1901), and the writing of the period is given the name Victorian literature. By the same token, writing of the period 1559–1603 is often called "Elizabethan" after Elizabeth I, and that of 1901–1910 "Edwardian" after Edward VII. This system however is based more on convention than logic, since few would call the history (or literature) of late twentieth-century Britain "Elizabethan" any more than they would call the history and literature of the eighteenth century "Georgian," though four king Georges reigned between 1714 and 1820. Where other, better terms exist these are generally adopted.

As these notes suggest, however, it is still common to think of British history in terms of the dates of the reigning monarch, even though the political influence of the monarchy has been strictly limited since the seventeenth century. Thus, where an outstanding political figure has emerged it is he or she who tends to name the period of a decade or longer; for the British, for example, the 1980s was the decade of "Thatcherism" as for Americans it was the period of "Reaganomics." The monarchy, though, still provides a point of common reference and has up to now shown a remarkable historical persistence, transforming itself as occasion dictates to fit new social circumstances. Thus, while most of the other European monarchies disappeared early in the twentieth century, if they had not already done so, the British institution managed to transform itself from imperial monarchy, a role adopted in the nineteenth century, to become the head of a welfare state and member of the European Union. Few of the titles gathered by Queen Victoria, such as Empress of India, remain to Elizabeth II (reigns 1952–), whose responsibilities now extend only to the British Isles with some vestigial role in Australia, Canada, and New Zealand among other places.

The monarchy's political power, like that of the aristocracy, has been successively diminished over the past several centuries, with the result that today both monarch and aristocracy have only formal authority. This withered state of today's institutions, however, should not blind us to the very real power they wielded in earlier centuries. Though the medieval monarch King John had famously been obliged to recognize the rule of law by signing the Magna Carta ("Great Charter") in 1215, thus ending arbitrary rule, the sixteenth- and seventeenth-century English monarchs still officially ruled by "divine right" and were under no obligation to attend to the wishes of Parliament. Charles I in the 1630s reigned mostly without summoning a parliament, and the concept of a "constitutional monarchy," being one whose powers were formally bound by statute, was introduced only when King William agreed to the Declaration of Right in 1689. This document, together with the contemporaneous Bill of Rights, while recognizing that sovereignty still rests in the monarch, formally transferred executive and legislative powers to Parliament. Bills still have to receive Royal Assent, though this was last denied by Queen Anne in 1707; the monarch still holds "prerogative" powers, though these, which include the appointment of certain officials, the dissolution of Parliament and so on, are, in practice wielded by the prime minister. Further information on the political character of various historical periods can be found in the period introductions.

Political power in Britain is thus held by the prime minister and his or her cabinet, members of which are also members of the governing party in the House of Commons. As long as the government is able to command a majority in the House of Commons, sometimes by a coalition of several parties but more usually by the absolute majority of one, it both makes the laws and carries them out. The situation is therefore very different from the American doctrine of the "Separation of Powers," in which Congress is independent of the President and can even be controlled by the opposing party. The British state of affairs has led to the office of prime minister being compared to that of an "elected dictatorship" with surprising frequency over the past several hundred years.

British government is bicameral, having both an upper and a lower house. Unlike other bicameral systems, however, the upper house, the House of Lords, is not elected, its membership being largely hereditary. Membership can come about in four main ways: (1) by birth, (2) by appointment by the current prime minister often in consultation with the Leader of the Opposition, (3) by virtue of holding a senior position in the judiciary, and (4) by being a bishop of the Established Church (the Church of England). In the House of Commons, the lower house, the particular features of the British electoral system have meant that there are never more than two large parties, one of which is in power. These are, together, "Her Majesty's Government and Opposition." Local conditions in Northern Ireland and Scotland have meant that these areas sometimes send members to Parliament in London who are members neither of the Conservative nor of the Labour parties; in general, however, the only other group in the Commons is the small Liberal Party.

Taking these categories in turn, all members of the hereditary aristocracy (the "peerage") have a seat in the House of Lords. The British aristocracy, unlike those of other European countries, was never formally dispossessed of political power (for example by a revolution), and though their influence is now limited, nevertheless all holders of hereditary title—dukes, marquesses, earls, viscounts and barons, in that order of precedence—sit in the Lords. Some continue to do political work and may be members of the Government or of the Opposition, though today it would be considered unusual for a senior member of government to sit in the House of Lords. The presence of the hereditary element in the Lords tends to give the institution a conservative tone, though the presence of the other members ensures this is by no means always the case. Secondly there are "life peers," who are created by the monarch on the prime minister's recommendation under legislation dating from 1958. They are generally individuals who have distinguished themselves in one field or another; retiring senior politicians from the Commons are generally elevated to the Lords, for example, as are some senior civil servants, diplomats, business and trade union leaders, academics, figures in the arts, retiring archbishops, and members of the military. Some of these take on formal political responsibilities and others do not. Finally, senior members of the judiciary sit in the Lords as Law Lords, while senior members of the Church of England hierarchy also sit in the Lords and frequently intervene in political matters. It has been a matter of some controversy whether senior members of other religious denominations, or religions, should also sit in the House of Lords. Within the constitution (by the Parliament Act of 1911 and other acts) the powers of the House of Lords are limited mostly to the amendment and delay of legislation; from time to time the question of its reform or abolition is raised.

In addition, there are minor orders of nobility that should be mentioned. A baronet is a holder of a hereditary title, but he is not a member of the peerage; the style is Sir (followed by his first and last names), Baronet (usually abbreviated as Bart. or Bt.). A knight is a member of one of the various orders of British knighthood, the oldest of which dates back to the Middle Ages (the Order of the Garter), the majority to the eighteenth or nineteenth centuries (the Order of the Thistle, the Bath, Saint Michael, and Saint George, etc.). The title is nonhereditary and is given for various services; it is marked by various initials coming after the name. K.C.B., for example, stands for "Knight Commander of the Bath," and there are many others.

In the House of Commons itself, the outstanding feature is the dominance of the party system. Party labels, such as "Whigs" and "Tories," were first used from the late seventeenth century, when groups of members began to form opposing factions in a Parliament now freed of much of the power of the king. The "Tories," for example, a name now used to refer to the modern Conservative Party, were originally members of that faction that supported James II (exiled in 1689); the word "Tory" comes from the Irish (Gaelic) for outlaw or thief. The "Whigs," on the other hand, supported the constitutional reforms associated with the 1689 Glorious Revolution; the word "whig" is obscurely related to the idea of regicide. The Whig faction largely dominated the political history of the eighteenth century, though the electorate was too small, and politics too controlled by the patronage of the great aristocratic families, for much of a party system to develop. It was only in the middle decades of the nineteenth century that the familiar party system in parliament and the associated electioneering organization in the country at large came into being. The Whigs were replaced by the Liberal Party around the mid-century, as the Liberals were to be replaced by the Labour Party in the early decades of the twentieth century; the Tories had become firm Conservatives by the time of Lord Derby's administrations in the mid-nineteenth century.

The party system has always been fertile ground for a certain amount of parliamentary theater, and it has fostered the emergence of some powerful personalities. Whereas the eighteenth-century Whig prime minister Sir Robert Walpole owed his authority to a mixture of personal patronage and the power made available through the alliances of powerful families, nineteenth-century figures such as Benjamin Disraeli (Conservative prime minister 1868, 1874–1880) and William Ewart Gladstone (Liberal prime minister 1868–1874; 1880–1885; 1885; 1892–1894), were at the apex of their respective party machines. Disraeli, theatrical, personable and with a keen eye for publicity (he was, among other things, a close personal friend of Queen Victoria), formed a great contrast to the massive moral appeals of his parliamentary opponent Gladstone. One earlier figure, William Pitt (1759–1806), prime minister at twenty-four and leader of the country during the French Revolution and earlier Napoleonic wars, stands comparison with these in the historical record; of twentieth-century political figures, David Lloyd-George, Liberal prime minister during World War I, and Winston Churchill, Conservative, during World War II, deserve special mention.

Though political power in the United Kingdom now rests with Parliament at Westminster in London, this has not always been the only case. Wales, which is now formally a principality within the political construction "England and Wales," was conquered by the English toward the end of the thirteenth century—too early for indigenous representative institutions to have fallen into place. Scotland, on the other hand, which from 1603 was linked with England under a joint monarchy but only became part of the same political entity with the Act of Union in 1707, did develop discrete institutions. Recent votes in both Scotland and Wales are leading toward greater local legislative control over domestic issues in both Scotland and Wales. Many Scottish institutions—for example, the legal and educational systems—are substantially different from those of England, which is not true in the case of Wales. The Church of Scotland in particular has no link with the Church of England, having been separately established in 1690 on a Presbyterian basis; this means that authority in the Scottish church is vested in elected pastors and lay elders and not in an ecclesiastical hierarchy of priests and bishops. But the most vexed of the relationships within the union has undoubtedly been that between England and Ireland.

There has been an English presence in Ireland from the Middle Ages on, and this became dominant in the later sixteenth century when English policy was deliberately to conquer and colonize the rest of the country. The consequence of this policy, however, was that an Irish Protestant "Ascendancy" came to rule over a largely dispossessed Catholic Irish peasantry; in 1689 at the Battle of the Boyne this state of affairs was made permanent, as Irish Catholic support for the exiled and Catholic-sympathizing James II was routed by the invading troops of the new Protestant king, William III. An Irish parliament met in Dublin, but this was restricted to Protestants; the Church of Ireland was the established Protestant church in a country where most of the population was Catholic. Irish political representation was shifted to Westminster by Pitt in 1800 under the formal Act of Union with Ireland; the Church of Ireland was disestablished by Gladstone later in the century. In the twentieth century, continuing agitation in the Catholic south of the country first for Home Rule and subsequently for independence from Britain—agitation that had been a feature of almost the whole nineteenth century at greater or lesser levels of intensity—led to the establishment first of the Irish Free State (1922) and later of the Republic (1948). In the Protestant North of the country, a local parliament met from 1922 within the common framework of the United Kingdom, but this was suspended in 1972 and representation returned to Westminster, as renewed violence in the province threatened local institutions. In Northern Ireland several hundred years of conflict between Protestants, who form the majority of the population in the province, and Catholics have led to continuing political problems.

Since the Reformation in the sixteenth century Britain has officially been a Protestant country with a national church headed by the monarch. This "Established Church," the Church of England or Anglican Church, has its own body of doctrine in the Thirty-Nine Articles and elsewhere, its own order of services in the Book of Common Prayer, and its own translation of the Bible (the "Authorized Version"), commissioned by James I (reigned 1603–1625) as Head of the Church. There is an extensive ecclesiastical hierarchy and a worldwide communion that includes the American Episcopalian Church.

The Reformation in England was not an easy business, and it has certain negative consequences even today. Some of these have been touched upon above in the case of Ireland. Those professing Roman Catholicism were excluded from political office and suffered other penalties until 1829, and a Catholic hierarchy parallel to that of the Church of England only came into being in Britain in the later nineteenth century. Though many of the restrictions on Roman Catholics enacted by Act of Parliament at the end of the seventeenth century were considerably softened in the course of the eighteenth, nevertheless they were very real.

English Protestantism, however, is far from being all of a piece. As early as the sixteenth century, many saw the substitution of the King's authority and that of the national ecclesiastical hierarchy for that of the Pope to be no genuine Protestant Reformation, which they thought demanded local autonomy and individual judgment. In the seventeenth century many "dissenting" or "Non-Conformist" Protestant sects thus grew up or gathered strength (many becoming "Puritans"), and these rejected the authority of the national church and its bishops and so the authority of the king. They had a brief moment of freedom during the Civil War and the Commonwealth (1649–1660) following the execution of Charles I, when there was a flowering of sects from Baptists and Quakers, which still exist today, to Ranters, Shakers, Anabaptists, Muggletonians, etc., which in the main do not (except for some sects in the United States). The monarchy and the Church were decisively reestablished in 1660, but subsequent legislation, most importantly the Act of Toleration (1689), suspended laws against dissenters on certain conditions.

Religious dissent or nonconformity remained powerful social movements over the following centuries and received new stimulus from the "New Dissenting" revivalist movements of the eighteenth century (particularly Methodism, though there was also a growth in the Congregationalist and Baptist churches). By the nineteenth century, the social character and geographical pattern of English dissent had been established: religious nonconformity was a feature of the new working classes brought into being by the Industrial Revolution in the towns of the Midlands and North of England. Anglicanism, which was associated with the preindustrial traditional order, was rejected also by many among the rising bourgeoisie and lower middle classes; almost every major English novel of the mid-nineteenth century and beyond is written against a background of religious nonconformity or dissent, which had complex social and political meanings. Nonconformity was also a particular feature of Welsh society.

Under legislation enacted by Edward I in 1290, the Jews were expelled from England, and there were few of them in the country until the end of the seventeenth century, when well-established Jewish communities began to appear in London (the medieval legislation was repealed under the Commonwealth in the 1650s). Restrictions on Jews holding public office continued until the mid-nineteenth century, and at the end of the century large Jewish communities were formed in many English cities by refugees from Central and Eastern European anti-Semitism.

Britain today is a multicultural country and significant proportions of the population, many of whom came to Britain from former British Empire territories, profess Hinduism or Islam, among other religions. The United Kingdom has been a member of the European Union since the early 1970s, and this has further loosened ties between Britain and former empire territories or dominions, many of which are still linked to Britain by virtue of the fact that the British monarch is Head of the "Commonwealth," an organization to which many of them belong. In some cases, the British monarch is also Head of State. Most importantly, however, British membership of the European Union has meant that powers formerly held by the national parliament have been transferred either to the European Parliament in Strasbourg, France, or to the European Commission, the executive agency in Brussels, Belgium, or, in the case of judicial review and appeal, to the European Court of Justice. This process seems set to generate tensions in Britain for some years to come.

David Tresilian

ENGLISH MONARCHS

Before the Norman conquest (1066), these included:

Alfred the Great	871–899
Edmund I	940–946
Ethelred the Unready	948–1016
Edward the Confessor	1042–1066
Harold II	1066

The following monarchs are divided by the dynasty ("House") to which they belong:

Normandy

William I the Conqueror	1066–1087
William II, Rufus	1087–1100
Henry I	1100–1135

Blois

Stephen	1135–1154

Plantagenet

Henry II	1154–1189
Richard I "Coeur de Lion"	1189–1199
John	1199–1216
Henry III	1216–1272
Edward I	1272–1307
Edward II	1307–1327
Edward III	1327–1377
Richard II	1377–1399

Lancaster

Henry IV	1399–1413
Henry V	1413–1422
Henry VI	1422–1471

York

Edward IV	1461–1483
Edward V	1483
Richard III	1483–1485

Tudor

Henry VII	1485–1509
Henry VIII	1509–1547
Edward VI	1547–1553
Mary I	1553–1558
Elizabeth I	1558–1603

Kings of England and of Scotland:

Stuart

James I (James VI of Scotland)	1603–1625
Charles I	1625–1649
Commonwealth (Republic)	
Council of State	1649–1653
Oliver Cromwell, Lord Protector	1653–1658
Richard Cromwell	1658–1660

Stuart

Charles II	1660–1685
James II	1685–1688
(Interregnum 1688–1689)	
William III and Mary II	1685–1701 (Mary dies 1694)
Anne	1702–1714

Hanover

George I	1714–1727
George II	1727–1760
George III	1760–1820
George IV	1820–1830
William IV	1830–1837
Victoria	1837–1901

Saxe-Coburg and Gotha

Edward VII	1901–1910

Windsor

George V	1910–1936
Edward VIII	1936
George VI	1936–1952
Elizabeth II	1952–

MONEY, WEIGHTS, AND MEASURES

The possibility of confusion by the British monetary system has considerably decreased since 1971, when decimalization of the currency took place. There are now 100 pence to a pound (worth about $1.60 in the late 1990s). Prior to this date the currency featured a gallery of other units as well. These coins—shillings, crowns, half-crowns, florins, threepenny-bits, and far-things—were contemporary survivals of the currency's historical development. As such they had a familiar presence in the culture, which was reflected in the slang terms used to refer to them in the spoken language. At least one of these terms, that of a "quid" for a pound, is still in use today.

The old currency divided the pound into 20 shillings, each of which contained 12 pence. There were, therefore, 240 pence in 1 pound. Five shillings made a crown, a half-crown was 2½ shillings, and a florin was 2 shillings; there was also a sixpence, a threepenny-bit, and a far-thing (a quarter of a penny). In slang, a shilling was a "bob," a sixpence a "tanner," and a penny a "copper." Sums were written as, for example, £12. 6s. 6d. or £12/6/6 (12 pounds, 6 shillings, and 6 pence; the "d." stands for "denarius," from the Latin). Figures up to £5 were often expressed in shillings alone: the father of the novelist D. H. Lawrence, for instance, who was a coal miner, was paid around 35 shillings a week at the beginning of the twentieth century—i.e., 1 pound and 15 shillings, or £1/15/–. At this time two gold coins were also still in circula-tion, the sovereign (£1) and the half-sovereign (10s.), which had been the principal coins of the nineteenth century; the largest silver coin was the half-crown (2 / 6). Later all coins were composed either of copper or an alloy of copper and nickel. The guinea was £1/1/– (1 pound and 1 shilling, or 21 shillings); though the actual coin had not been minted since the begin-ning of the nineteenth century, the term was still used well into the twentieth to price luxury items and to pay professional fees.

The number of dollars that a pound could buy has fluctuated with British economic for-tunes. The current figure has been noted above; in 1912 it was about $5.00. To get a sense of how much the pound was worth to those who used it as an everyday index of value, however, we have to look at what it could buy within the system in which it was used. To continue the Lawrence example, a coal miner may have been earning 35 shillings a week in the early years of the twentieth century, but of this he would have to have paid six shillings as rent on the family house; his son, by contrast, could command a figure of £300 as a publisher's advance on his novel The Rainbow (pub. 1915), a sum which alone would have placed him somewhere in the middle class. In A Room of One's Own (1928) Virginia Woolf recommended the figure of £500 a year as necessary if a woman were to write; at today's values this would be worth around £25,000 ($41,000)—considerably more than the pay of, for example, a junior faculty member at a British university, either then or now.

In earlier periods an idea of the worth of the currency, being the relation between wages and prices, can similarly be established by taking samples from across the country at specific dates. Toward the end of the seventeenth century, for example, Poor Law records tell us that a family of five could be considered to subsist on an annual income of £13/14/-, which included £9/14/– spent on food. At the same time an agricultural laborer earned around £15/12/– annu-ally, while at the upper end of the social scale, the aristocracy dramatically recovered and increased their wealth in the period after the restoration of the monarchy in 1660. By 1672 the early industrialist Lord Wharton was realizing an annual profit of £3,200 on his lead mine and smelting plant in the north of England; landed aristocratic families such as the Russells, spon-sors of the 1689 Glorious Revolution and later dukes of Bedford, were already worth £10,000 a year in 1660. Such details allow us to form some idea of the value of the £10 the poet John Milton received for Paradise Lost (pub. 1667), as well as to see the great wealth that went into building the eighteenth-century estates that now dot the English countryside.

By extending the same method to the analysis of wage-values during the Industrial Revolution over a century and a half later, the economic background to incidents of public disorder in the period, such as the 1819 "Peterloo Massacre" in London, can be reconstructed, as can the background to the poems of Wordsworth, for example, many of which concern vagrancy and the lives of the rural poor. Thus the essayist William Cobbett calculated in the 1820s that £1/4/– a week was needed to support a family of five, though actual average earnings were less than half this sum. By contrast, Wordsworth's projection of "a volume which consisting of 160 pages might be sold at 5 shillings" (1806)—part of the negotiations for his *Poems in Two Volumes* (1807)—firmly establishes the book as a luxury item. Jane Austen's contemporaneous novel *Mansfield Park* (1814), which gives many details about the economic affairs of the English rural gentry, suggests that at least £1000 a year is a desirable income.

Today's pound sterling, though still cited on the international exchanges with the dollar, the deutsche mark, and the yen, decisively lost to the dollar after World War I as the central currency in the international system. At present it seems highly likely that, with some other European national currencies, it will shortly cease to exist as the currency unit of the European Union is adopted as a single currency in the constituent countries of the Union.

British weights and measures present less difficulty to American readers since the vast inertia permeating industry and commerce following the separation of the United States from Britain prevented the reform of American weights and measures along metric lines, which had taken place where the monetary system was concerned. Thus the British "Imperial" system, with some minor local differences, was in place in both countries until decimalization of the British system began in stages from the early 1970s on. Today all British weights and measures, with the exception of road signs, which still generally give distances in miles, are metric in order to bring Britain into line with European Union standards. Though it is still possible to hear especially older people measuring area in acres and not in hectares, distances in miles and not in kilometers, or feet and yards and not centimeters and meters, weight in pounds and ounces and not in grams and kilograms, and temperature in Fahrenheit and not in centigrade, etc., it is becoming increasingly uncommon. Measures of distance that might be found in older texts— such as the league (three miles, but never in regular use), the furlong (220 yards), and the ell (45 inches)—are now all obsolete; the only measure still heard in current use is the stone (14 pounds), and this is generally used for body weight.

David Tresilian

LITERARY AND CULTURAL TERMS*

Absolutism. In criticism, the belief in irreducible, unchanging values of form and content that underlie the tastes of individuals and periods and arise from the stability of an absolute hierarchical order.

Accent. Stress or emphasis on a syllable, as opposed to the syllable's length of duration, its quantity. *Metrical accent* denotes the metrical pattern ($\smile$ –) to which writers fit and adjust accented words and rhetorical emphases, keeping the meter as they substitute word-accented feet and tune their rhetoric.

Accentual Verse. Verse with lines established by counting accents only, without regard to the number of unstressed syllables. This was the dominant form of verse in English until the time of Chaucer.

Acrostic. Words arranged, frequently in a poem or puzzle, to disclose a hidden word or message when the correct combination of letters is read in sequence.

Aestheticism. Devotion to beauty. The term applies particularly to a 19th-century literary and artistic movement celebrating beauty as independent from morality, and praising form above content; art for art's sake.

Aesthetics. The study of the beautiful; the branch of philosophy concerned with defining the nature of art and establishing criteria of judgment.

Alexandrine. A six-foot iambic pentameter line.

Allegorical Meaning. A secondary meaning of a narrative in addition to its primary meaning or literal meaning.

Allegory. A story that suggests another story. The first part of this word comes from the Greek *allos*, "other." An allegory is present in literature whenever it is clear that the author is saying, "By this I also mean that." In practice, allegory appears when a progression of events or images suggests a translation of them into conceptual language. Allegory is thus a technique of aligning imaginative constructs, mythological or poetic, with conceptual or moral models. During the Romantic era a distinction arose between allegory and symbol. With Coleridge, symbol took precedence: "an allegory is but a translation of abstract notions into picture-language," but "a symbol always partakes of the reality which it makes intelligible."

Alliteration. "Adding letters" (*Latin ad* + *littera*, "letter"). Two or more words, or accented syllables, chime on the same initial letter (*lost love* alone; *after apple*-picking) or repeat the same consonant.

Alliterative Revival. The outburst of alliterative verse that occurred in the second half of the 14th century in west and northwest England.

Alliterative Verse. Verse using alliteration on stressed syllables for its fundamental structure.

Allusion. A meaningful reference, direct or indirect, as when William Butler Yeats writes, "Another Troy must rise and set," calling to mind the whole tragic history of Troy.

Amplification. A restatement of something more fully and in more detail, especially in oratory, poetry, and music.

Analogy. A comparison between things similar in a number of ways; frequently used to explain the unfamiliar by the familiar.

Anapest. A metrical foot: $\smile\smile$ –.

Anaphora. The technique of beginning successive clauses or lines with the same word.

---

*Adapted from *The Harper Handbook to Literature* by Northrop Frye, Sheridan Baker, George Perkins, and Barbara M. Perkins, 2d edition (Longman, 1997).

Anatomy. Greek for "a cutting up": a dissection, analysis, or systematic study. The term was popular in titles in the 16th and 17th centuries.

Anglo-Norman (Language). The language of upper-class England after the Norman Conquest in 1066.

Anglo-Saxon. The people, culture, and language of three neighboring tribes—Jutes, Angles, and Saxons—who invaded England, beginning in 449, from the lower part of Denmark's Jutland Peninsula. The Angles, settling along the eastern seaboard of central and northern England, developed the first literate culture of any Germanic people. Hence England (Angle-land) became the dominant term.

Antagonist. In Greek drama, the character who opposes the protagonist, or hero: therefore, any character who opposes another. In some works, the antagonist is clearly the villain (Iago in *Othello*), but in strict terminology an antagonist is merely an opponent and may be in the right.

Anthropomorphism. The practice of giving human attributes to animals, plants, rivers, winds, and the like, or to such entities as Grecian urns and abstract ideas.

Antithesis. (1) A direct contrast or opposition. (2) The second phase of dialectical argument, which considers the opposition—the three steps being *thesis, antithesis, synthesis*. (3) A rhetorical figure sharply contrasting ideas in balanced parallel structures.

Aphorism. A pithy saying of known authorship, as distinguished from a folk proverb.

Apology. A justification, as in Sir Philip Sidney's *The Apology for Poetry* (1595).

Apostrophe. (Greek, "a turning away"). An address to an absent or imaginary person, a thing, or a personified abstraction.

Archaism. An archaic or old-fashioned word or expression—for example, *o'er, ere,* or *darkling*.

Archetype. (1) The first of a genre, like Homer's *Iliad*, the first heroic epic. (2) A natural symbol imprinted in human consciousness by experience and literature, like dawn symbolizing hope or an awakening; night, death or repose.

Assonance. Repetition of middle vowel sounds: *fight, hive; pane, make*. Assonance, most effective on stressed syllables, is often found within a line of poetry; less frequently it substitutes for end rhyme.

Aubade. Dawn song, from French *aube*, for dawn. The aubade originated in the Middle Ages as a song sung by a lover greeting the dawn, ordinarily expressing regret that morning means parting.

Avant-Garde. Experimental, innovative, at the forefront of a literary or artistic trend or movement. The term is French for *vanguard*, the advance unit of an army. It frequently suggests a struggle with tradition and convention.

Ballad. A narrative poem in short stanzas, with or without music. The term derives by way of French *ballade* from Latin *ballare*, "to dance," and once meant a simple song of any kind, lyric or narrative, especially one to accompany a dance. As ballads evolved, most lost their association with dance, although they kept their strong rhythms. Modern usage distinguishes three major kinds: the anonymous *traditional ballad* (popular ballad or *folk ballad*), transmitted orally; the *broadside ballad*, printed and sold on single sheets; and the *literary ballad* (or art ballad), a sophisticated imitation of the traditional ballad.

Ballad Stanza. The name for common meter as found in ballads: a quatrain in iambic meter, alternating tetrameter and trimeter lines, usually rhyming *abcb*.

Bard. An ancient Celtic singer of the culture's lore in epic form; a poetic term for any poet.

Baroque. (1) A richly ornamented style in architecture and art. Founded in Rome by Frederigo Barocci about 1550, and characterized by swirling allegorical frescoes on ceilings and walls, it flourished throughout Europe until 1700. (2) A chromatic musical style with strict forms containing similar exuberant ornamentation, flourishing from 1600 to 1750. In literature, Richard Crashaw's bizarre imagery and the conceits and rhythms of John Donne and other metaphysical poets are sometimes called baroque, sometimes mannerist.

Some literary historians designate a Baroque Age from 1580 to 1680, between the Renaissance and the Enlightenment.

Bathos. (1) A sudden slippage from the sublime to the ridiculous. (2) Any anticlimax. (3) Sentimental pathos. (4) Triteness or dullness.

Blank Verse. Unrhymed iambic pentameter. *See also* Meter. In the 1540s Henry Howard, earl of Surrey, seems to have originated it in English as the equivalent of Virgil's unrhymed dactylic hexameter. In *Gorboduc* (1561), Thomas Sackville and Thomas Norton introduced blank verse into the drama, whence it soared with Marlowe and Shakespeare in the 1590s. Milton forged it anew for the epic in *Paradise Lost* (1667).

Bloomsbury Group. An informal social and intellectual group associated with Bloomsbury, a London residential district near the British Museum, from about 1904 until the outbreak of World War II. Virginia Woolf was a principal member. With her husband, Leonard Woolf, she established the Hogarth Press, which published works by many of their friends. The group was loosely knit, but famed, especially in the 1920s, for its exclusiveness, aestheticism, and social and political freethinking.

Broadside. A sheet of paper printed on one side only. Broadsides containing a ballad, a tract, a criminal's gallows speech, a scurrilous satire, and the like were once commonly sold on the streets like newspapers.

Burden. (1) A refrain or set phrase repeated at intervals throughout a song or poem. (2) A bass accompaniment, the "load" carried by the melody, the origin of the term.

Burlesque. (1) A ridicule, especially on the stage, treating the lofty in low style, or the low in grandiose style. (2) A bawdy vaudeville, with obscene clowning and stripteasing.

Caesura. A pause in a metrical line, indicated by punctuation, momentarily suspending the beat (from Latin "a cutting off"). Caesuras are *masculine* at the end of a foot, and *feminine* in mid-foot.

Canon. The writings accepted as forming a part of the Bible, of the works of an author, or of a body of literature. Shakespeare's canon consists of works he wrote, which may be distinguished from works attributed to him but written by others. The word derives from Greek *kanon*, "rod" or "rule," and suggests authority. Canonical authors and texts are those taught most frequently, noncanonical are those rarely taught, and in between are disputed degrees of canonicity for authors considered minor or marginalized.

Canto. A major division in a long poem. The Italian expression is from Latin *cantus*, "song," a section singable in one sitting.

Caricature. Literary cartooning, depicting characters with exaggerated physical traits such as huge noses and bellies, short stature, squints, tics, humped backs, and so forth. Sir Thomas Browne seems to have introduced the term into English in 1682 from the Italian *caricatura*.

Catalog. In literature, an enumeration of ancestors, of ships, of warriors, of a woman's beauties, and the like; a standard feature of the classical epic.

Celtic Revival. In the 18th century, a groundswell of the Romantic movement in discovering the power in ancient, primitive poetry, particularly Welsh and Scottish Gaelic, as distinct from that of the classics.

Chiasmus. A rhetorical balance created by the inversion of one of two parallel phrases or clauses; from the Greek for a "placing crosswise," as in the Greek letter χ (chi).

Chronicle. A kind of history, with the emphasis on *time* (Greek *chronos*). Events are described in order as they occurred. The chronicles of the Middle Ages provided material for later writers and serve now as important sources of knowledge about the period. Raphael Holinshed's *Chronicle* (1577) is especially famous as the immediate source of much of Shakespeare's knowledge of English history.

Chronicle Play. A play dramatizing historical events, as from a chronicle. Chronicle plays tend to stress time order, presenting the reign of a king, for example, with much emphasis on pageantry and little on the unity of action and dramatic conflict necessary for a tragedy.

Classical Literature. (1) The literature of ancient Greece and Rome. (2) Later literature reflecting the qualities of classical Greece or Rome. *See also*, Classicism; Neoclassicism. (3) The classic literature of any time or place, as, for example, classical American literature or classical Japanese literature.

Classicism. A principle in art and conduct reflecting the ethos of ancient Greece and Rome: balance, form, proportion, propriety, dignity, simplicity, objectivity, rationality, restraint, unity rather than diversity. In English literature, classicism emerged with Erasmus (1466–1536) and his fellow humanists. In the Restoration and 18th century, classicism, or neoclassicism, expressed society's deep need for balance and restraint after the shattering Civil War and Puritan commonwealth. Classicism continued in the 19th century, after the Romantic period, particularly in the work of Matthew Arnold. T. E. Hulme, Ezra Pound, and T. S. Eliot expressed it for the 20th century.

Cliché. An overused expression, once clever or metaphorical but now trite and timeworn.

Closed Couplet. The heroic couplet, especially when the thought and grammar are complete in the two iambic pentameter lines.

Closet Drama. A play written for reading in the "closet," or private study. Closet dramas were usually in verse, like Percy Shelley's *Prometheus Unbound* (1820) and Robert Browning's *Pippa Passes* (1841).

Cockney. A native of the East End of central London. The term originally meant "cocks' eggs," a rural term of contempt for city softies and fools. Cockneys are London's ingenious street peddlers, speaking a dialect rich with an inventive rhyming slang, dropping and adding aitches.

Comedy. One of the typical literary structures, originating as a form of drama and later extending into prose fiction and other genres as well. Comedy, as Susanne Langer says, is the image of Fortune; tragedy, the image of Fate. Each sorts out for attention the different facts of life. Comedy sorts its pleasures. It pleases our egos and endows our dreams, stirring at once two opposing impulses, our vindictive lust for superiority and our wishful drive for success and happiness ever after. The dark impulse stirs the pleasure of laughter; the light, the pleasure of wish fulfillment.

Comedy of Humors. Comedy based on the ancient physiological theory that a predominance of one of the body's four fluids (humors) produces a comically unbalanced personality: (1) blood—sanguine, hearty, cheerful, amorous; (2) phlegm—phlegmatic, sluggish; (3) choler (yellow bile)—angry, touchy; (4) black bile—melancholic.

Comedy of Manners. Suave, witty, and risqué, satire of upper-class manners and immorals, particularly that of Restoration masters like George Etherege and William Congreve.

Common Meter. The ballad stanza as found in hymns and other poems: a quatrain (four-line stanza) in iambic meter, alternating tetrameter and trimeter, rhyming *abcb* or *abab*.

Complaint. A lyric poem, popular in the Middle Ages and the Renaissance, complaining of unrequited love, a personal situation, or the state of the world.

Conceit. Any fanciful, ingenious expression or idea, but especially one in the form of an extended metaphor.

Concordia Discors. "Discordant harmony," a phrase expressing for the 18th century the harmonious diversity of nature, a pleasing balance of opposites.

Concrete Poetry. Poetry that attempts a concrete embodiment of its idea, expressing itself physically apart from the meaning of the words. A recent relative of the much older *shaped poem*, the concrete poem places heavy emphasis on the picture and less on the words, so that the visual experience may be more interesting than the linguistic.

Connotation. The ideas, attitudes, or emotions associated with a word in the mind of speaker or listener, writer or reader. It is contrasted with the *denotation*, the thing the word stands for, the dictionary definition, an objective concept without emotional coloring.

Consonance. (1) Repetition of inner or end consonant sounds, as, for example, the r and s sounds from Gerard Manley Hopkins's *God's Grandeur:* "broods with warm breast." (2) In a broader sense, a generally pleasing combination of sounds or ideas; things that sound well together.

Couplet. A pair of rhymed metrical lines, usually in iambic tetrameter or pentameter. Sometimes the two lines are of different length.

Covenanters. Scottish Presbyterians who signed a covenant in 1557 as a "godly band" to stand together to resist the Anglican church and the English establishment.

Cynghanedd. A complex medieval Welsh system of rhyme, alliteration, and consonance, to which Gerard Manley Hopkins alluded to describe his interplay of euphonious sounds, actually to be heard in any rich poet, as in the Welsh Dylan Thomas: "The force that through the green fuse drives the flower / Drives my green age."

Dactyl. A three-syllable metrical foot: $-\smile\smile$. It is the basic foot of dactylic hexameter, the six-foot line of Greek and Roman epic poetry.

Dactylic Hexameter. The classical or heroic line of the epic. A line based on six dactylic feet, with spondees substituted, and always ending $-\smile\smile\ \mid\ --$.

Dead Metaphor. A metaphor accepted without its figurative picture: "a jacket," for the paper around a book, with no mental picture of the human coat that prompted the original metaphor.

Decasyllabic. Having ten syllables. An iambic pentameter line is decasyllabic.

Deconstruction. The critical dissection of a literary text's statements, ambiguities, and structure to expose its hidden contradictions, implications, and fundamental instability of meaning. Jacques Derrida originated deconstruction in *Of Grammatology* (1967) and *Writing and Difference* (1967). Because no understanding of any text is stable, as each new reading is subject to the deconstruction of any meaning it appears to have established, it follows that criticism can be a kind of game, either playful or serious, as each critic ingeniously deconstructs the meanings established by others.

Decorum. Propriety, fitness, the quality of being appropriate. George Puttenham, in his *Arte of English Poesie* (1589), chides a translator of Virgil for his indecorum of having Aeneas "trudge," like a beggar, from Troy.

Defamiliarization. Turning the familiar to the strange by disrupting habitual ways of perceiving things. Derived from the thought of Victor Shklovsky and other Russian formalists, the idea is that art forces us to see things differently as we view them through the artist's sensibility, not our own.

Deism. A rational philosophy of religion, beginning with the theories of Lord Herbert of Cherbury, the "Father of Deism," in his *De Veritate* (1624). Deists generally held that God, the supreme Artisan, created a perfect clock of a universe, withdrew, and left it running, not to return to intervene in its natural works or the life of humankind; that the Bible is a moral guide, but neither historically accurate nor divinely authentic; and that reason guides human beings to virtuous conduct.

Denotation. The thing that a word stands for, the dictionary definition, an objective concept without emotional coloring. It is contrasted with the *connotation*, ideas, attitudes, or emotions associated with the word in the mind of user or hearer.

Dénouement. French for "unknotting": the unraveling of plot threads toward the end of a play, novel, or other narrative.

Determinism. The philosophical belief that events are shaped by forces beyond the control of human beings.

Dialect. A variety of language belonging to a particular time, place, or social group, as, for example, an 18th-century cockney dialect, a New England dialect, or a coal miner's dialect. A language other than one's own is for the most part unintelligible without study or translation; a dialect other than one's own can generally be understood, although pronunciation, vocabulary, and syntax seem strange.

Dialogue. Conversation between two or more persons, as represented in prose fiction, drama, or essays, as opposed to *monologue*, the speech of one person. Good dialogue characterizes each speaker by idiom and attitude as it advances the dramatic conflict. The dialogue as a form of speculative exposition, or dialectical argument, is often less careful to distinguish the diction and character of the speakers.

Diatribe. Greek for "a wearing away": a bitter and abusive criticism or invective, often lengthy, directed against a person, institution, or work.

Diction. Word choice in speech or writing, an important element of style.

Didactic. Greek for "teaching": instructive, or having the qualities of a teacher. Since ancient times, literature has been assumed to have two functions, instruction and entertainment, with sometimes one and sometimes the other dominant. Literature intended primarily for instruction or containing an important moralistic element is didactic.

Dirge. A lamenting funeral song.

Discourse. (1) A formal discussion of a subject. (2) The conventions of communication associated with specific areas, in usages such as "poetic discourse," "the discourse of the novel," or "historical discourse."

Dissenter. A term arising in the 1640s for a member of the clergy or a follower who dissented from the forms of the established Anglican church, particularly Puritans. Dissenters generally came from the lower middle classes, merchants who disapproved of aristocratic frivolity and ecclesiastical pomp.

Dissonance. (1) Harsh and jarring sound; discord. It is frequently an intentional effect, as in the poems of Robert Browning. (2) Occasionally a term for half rhyme or slant rhyme.

Distich. A couplet, or pair of rhymed metrical lines.

Dithyramb. A frenzied choral song and dance to honor Dionysus, Greek god of wine and the power of fertility. Any irregular, impassioned poetry may be called *dithyrambic*. The irregular ode also evolved from the dithyramb.

Doggerel. (1) Trivial verse clumsily aiming at meter, usually tetrameter. (2) Any verse facetiously low and loose in meter and rhyme.

Domesday Book. The recorded census and survey of landholders that William the Conqueror ordered in 1085; from "Doomsday," the Last Judgment.

Dramatic Irony. A character in drama or fiction unknowingly says or does something in ironic contrast to what the audience or reader knows or will learn.

Dramatic Monologue. A monologue in verse. A speaker addresses a silent listener, revealing, in dramatic irony, things about himself or herself of which the speaker is unaware.

Eclogue. A short poem, usually a pastoral, and often in the form of a dialogue or soliloquy. During the Renaissance, in the works of Spenser and others, the eclogue became a major form of verse, with shepherds exchanging verses of love, lament, or eulogy.

Edition. The form in which a book is published, including its physical qualities and its content. A *first edition* is the first form of a book, printed and bound; a *second edition* is a later form, usually with substantial changes in content. Between the two, there may be more than one printing or impression of the first edition, sometimes with minor corrections. The term *edition* also refers to the format of a book. For example, an *illustrated edition* or a *two-volume edition* may be identical in verbal content to one without pictures or bound in a single volume.

Edwardian Period (1901–1914). From the death of Queen Victoria to the outbreak of World War I, named for the reign of Victoria's son, Edward VII (1901–1910), a period generally reacting against Victorian propriety and convention.

Elegiac Stanza. An iambic pentameter quatrain rhyming *abab*. Taking its name from Thomas Gray's *Elegy Written in a Country Churchyard* (1751), it is identical to the heroic quatrain.

Elegy. Greek for "lament": a poem on death or on a serious loss; characteristically a sustained meditation expressing sorrow and, frequently, an explicit or implied consolation.

Elision. Latin for "striking out": the omission or slurring of an unstressed vowel at the end of a word to bring a line of poetry closer to a prescribed metrical pattern, as in John Milton's *Lycidas:* "Tempered to th'oaten flute." *See also* Meter; Syncope.

Elizabethan Drama. English drama of the reign of Elizabeth I (1558–1603). Strictly speaking, drama from the reign of James I (1603–1625) belongs to the Jacobean period and that from the reign of Charles I (1625–1642) to the Caroline period, but the term *Elizabethan* is sometimes extended to include works of later reigns, before the closing of the theaters in 1642.

Elizabethan Period (1558–1603). The years marked by the reign of Elizabeth I; the "Golden Age of English Literature," especially as exemplified by the lyric poetry and dramas of Christopher Marlowe, Edmund Spenser, Sir Philip Sidney, and William Shakespeare, as well as the early Ben Jonson and John Donne.

Ellipsis. The omission of words for rhetorical effect: "*Drop dead*" for "You drop dead."

Emblem. (1) A didactic pictorial and literary form consisting of a word or phrase (*mot* or *motto*), a symbolic woodcut or engraving, and a brief moralistic poem (*explicatio*). Collections of emblems in book form were popular in the 16th and 17th centuries. (2) A type or symbol.

Emendation. A change made in a literary text to remove faults that have appeared through tampering or by errors in reading, transcription, or printing from the manuscript.

Empathy. Greek for "feeling with": identification with the feelings or passions of another person, natural creature, or even an inanimate object conceived of as possessing human attributes. Empathy suggests emotional identification, whereas sympathy may be largely an intellectual appreciation of another's situation.

Emphasis. Stress placed on words, phrases, or ideas to show their importance, by *italics*, **boldface**, and punctuation "!!!"; by figurative language, meter, and rhyme; or by strategies of rhetoric, like climactic order, contrast, repetition, and position.

Empiricism. Greek for "experience": the belief that all knowledge comes from experience, that human understanding of general truth can be founded only on observation of particulars. Empiricism is basic to the scientific method and to literary naturalism. It is opposed to rationalism, which discovers truth through reason alone, without regard to experience.

Enclosed Rhyme. A couplet, or pair of rhyming lines, enclosed in rhyming lines to give the pattern *abba*.

Encomium. Originally a Greek choral song in praise of a hero; later, any formal expression of praise, in verse or prose.

End Rhyme. Rhyme at the end of a line of verse (the usual placement), as distinguished from *initial rhyme*, at the beginning, or *internal rhyme*, within the line.

Enjambment. Run-on lines in which grammatical sense runs from one line of poetry to the next without pause or punctuation. The opposite of an end-stopped line.

Enlightenment. A philosophical movement in the 17th and 18th centuries, particularly in France, characterized by the conviction that reason could achieve all knowledge, supplant organized religion, and ensure progress toward happiness and perfection.

Envoy (or Envoi). A concluding stanza, generally shorter than the earlier stanzas of a poem, giving a brief summary of theme, address to a prince or patron, or return to a refrain.

Epic. A long narrative poem, typically a recounting of history or legend or of the deeds of a national hero. During the Renaissance, critical theory emphasized two assumptions: (1) the encyclopedic knowledge needed for major poetry, and (2) an aristocracy of genres, according to which epic and tragedy, because they deal with heroes and ruling-class figures, were reserved for major poets. Romanticism revived both the long mythological poem and the verse romance, but the prestige of the encyclopedic epic still lingered. In his autobiographical poem *The Prelude*, Wordsworth self-consciously internalized the heroic argument of the epic.

Epic Simile. Sometimes called a *Homeric simile:* an extended simile, comparing one thing with another by lengthy description of the second, often beginning with "as when" and concluding with "so" or "such."

Epicurean. Often meaning hedonistic (*see also* Hedonism), devoted to sensual pleasure and ease. Actually, Epicurus (c. 341–270 B.C.) was a kind of puritanical Stoic, recommending detachment from pleasure and pain to avoid life's inevitable suffering, hence advocating serenity as the highest happiness, intellect over the senses.

Epigram. (1) A brief poetic and witty couching of a home truth. (2) An equivalent statement in prose.

Epigraph. (1) An inscription on a monument or building. (2) A quotation or motto heading a book or chapter.

Epilogue. (1) A poetic address to the audience at the end of a play. (2) The actor performing the address. (3) Any similar appendage to a literary work, usually describing what happens to the characters in the future.

Epiphany. In religious tradition, the revelation of a divinity. James Joyce adapted the term to signify a moment of profound or spiritual revelation, when even the stroke of a clock or a noise in the street brings sudden illumination, and "its soul, its whatness leaps to us from the vestment of its appearance." For Joyce, art was an epiphany.

Episode. An incident in a play or novel; a continuous event in action and dialogue. Originally the term referred to a section in Greek tragedy between two choric songs.

Episodic Structure. In narration, the incidental stringing of one episode upon another, as in *Don Quixote* or *Moll Flanders*, in which one episode follows another with no necessary causal connection or plot.

Epistle. (1) A letter, usually a formal or artistic one, like Saint Paul's Epistles in the New Testament, or Horace's verse *Epistles*, widely imitated in the late 17th and 18th centuries, most notably by Alexander Pope. (2) A dedication in a prefatory epistle to a play or book.

Epitaph. (1) An inscription on a tombstone or monument memorializing the person, or persons, buried there. (2) A literary epigram or brief poem epitomizing the dead.

Epithalamium (or Epithalamion). A lyric ode honoring a bride and groom.

Epithet. A term characterizing a person or thing: e.g., *Richard the Lion-Hearted*.

Epitome. (1) A summary, an abridgment, an abstract. (2) One that supremely represents an entire class.

Essay. A literary composition on a single subject; usually short, in prose, and nonexhaustive. The word derives from French *essai* "an attempt," first used in the modern sense by Michel de Montaigne, whose *Essais* (1580–1588) are classics of the genre. Francis Bacon's *Essays* (1597) brought the term and form to English.

Estates. The "three estates of the realm," recognized from feudal times onward: the clergy (Lords Spiritual), the nobility (Lords Temporal), and the burghers (the Commons). In *Heroes and Hero-Worship*, Thomas Carlyle says that Edmund Burke (member of Parliament from 1766 to 1794) added to Parliament's three estates "the Reporters' Gallery" where "sat a fourth Estate more important than they all" (Lecture V). The Fourth Estate is now the press and other media.

Eulogy. A speech or composition of praise, especially of a deceased person.

Euphemism. Greek for "good speech": an attractive substitute for a harsh or unpleasant word or concept; figurative language or circumlocution substituting an indirect or oblique reference for a direct one.

Euphony. Melodious sound, the opposite of cacophony. A major feature of verse, but also a consideration in prose, euphony results from smooth-flowing meter or sentence rhythm as well as attractive sounds.

Euphuism. An artificial, highly elaborate affected style that takes its name from John Lyly's *Euphues: The Anatomy of Wit* (1578). Euphuism is characterized by the heavy use of rhetorical devices such as balance and antithesis, by much attention to alliteration and other sound patterns, and by learned allusion.

Excursus. (1) A lengthy discussion of a point, appended to a literary work. (2) A long digression.

Exegesis. (1) A detailed analysis, explanation, and interpretation of a difficult text, especially the Bible. (2) A rhetorical figure, also called *explicatio,* which clarifies a thought.

Exemplum. Latin for "example": a story used to illustrate a moral point. *Exempla* were a characteristic feature of medieval sermons. Chaucer's *Pardoner's Tale* and *Nun's Priest's Tale* are famous secular examples.

Existentialism. A philosophy centered on individual existence as unique and unrepeatable, hence rejecting the past for present existence and its unique dilemmas. Existentialism rose to prominence in the 1930s and 1940s, particularly in France after World War II in the work of Jean-Paul Sartre.

Expressionism. An early 20th-century movement in art and literature, best understood as a reaction against conventional realism and naturalism, and especially as a revolt against conventional society. The expressionist looked inward for images, expressing in paint, on stage, or in prose or verse a distorted, nightmarish version of reality, things dreamed about rather than actually existing.

Eye Rhyme. A rhyme of words that look but do not sound the same: *one, stone; word, lord; teak, break.*

Fable. (1) A short, allegorical story in verse or prose, frequently of animals, told to illustrate a moral. (2) The story line or plot of a narrative or drama. (3) Loosely, any legendary or fabulous account.

Falling Meter. A meter beginning with a stress, running from heavy to light.

Farce. A wildly comic play, mocking dramatic and social conventions, frequently with satiric intent.

Feminine Ending. An extra unstressed syllable at the end of a metrical line, usually iambic.

Feminine Rhyme. A rhyme of both the stressed and the unstressed syllables of one feminine ending with another.

Feudalism. The political and social system prevailing in Europe from the ninth century until the 1400s. It was a system of independent holdings (*feud* is Germanic for "estate") in which autonomous lords pledged fealty and service to those more powerful in exchange for protection, as did villagers to the neighboring lord of the manor.

Fiction. An imagined creation in verse, drama, or prose. Fiction is a thing made, an invention. It is distinguished from nonfiction by its essentially imaginative nature, but elements of fiction appear in fundamentally nonfictional constructions such as essays, biographies, autobiographies, and histories. Fictional anecdotes and illustrations abound in the works of politicians, business leaders, the clergy, philosophers, and scientists. Although any invented person, place, event, or condition is a fiction, the term is now most frequently used to mean "prose fiction," as distinct from verse or drama.

Figurative Language. Language that is not literal, being either metaphorical or rhetorically patterned.

Figure of Speech. An expression extending language beyond its literal meaning, either pictorially through metaphor, simile, allusion, and the like, or rhetorically through repetition, balance, antithesis, and the like. A figure of speech is also called a *trope.*

Fin de Siècle. "The end of the century," especially the last decade of the 19th. The term, acquired with the French influence of the symbolists Stéphane Mallarmé and Charles Baudelaire, connotes preciosity and decadence.

First-Person Narration. Narration by a character involved in a story.

Flyting. Scottish for "scolding": a form of invective, or violent verbal assault, in verse; traditional in Scottish literature, possibly Celtic in origin. Typically, two poets exchange scurrilous and often exhaustive abuse.

Folio. From Latin for "leaf." (1) A sheet of paper, folded once. (2) The largest of the book sizes, made from standard printing sheets, folded once before trimming and binding.

Folk Song. A song forming part of the folklore of a community. Like the folktale and the legend, a folk song is a traditional creative expression, characteristically shaped by oral tradition into the form in which it is later recorded in manuscript or print.

Folktale. A story forming part of the folklore of a community, generally less serious than the stories called *myths*. In preliterate societies, virtually all narratives were either myths or folktales: oral histories of real wars, kings, heroes, great families, and the like accumulating large amounts of legendary material.

Foot. The metrical unit; in English, an accented syllable with accompanying light syllable or syllables.

Foreshadowing. The technique of suggesting or prefiguring a development in a literary work before it occurs.

Formula. A plot outline or set of characteristic ingredients used in the construction of a literary work or applied to a portion of one. Formula fiction is written to the requirements of a particular market, usually undistinguished by much imagination or originality in applying the formula.

Foul Copy. A manuscript that has been used for printing, bearing the marks of the proofreader, editor, and printer, as well as, frequently, the author's queries and comments.

Four Elements. In ancient and medieval cosmology, earth, air, fire, and water—the four ultimate, exclusive, and eternal constituents that, according to Empedocles (c. 493–c. 433 B.C.) made up the world.

Four Senses of Interpretation. A mode of medieval criticism in which a work is examined for four kinds of meaning. The *literal meaning* is related to fact or history. The *moral* or *tropological meaning* is the lesson of the work as applied to individual behavior. The *allegorical meaning* is the particular story in its application to people generally, with emphasis on their beliefs. The *anagogical meaning* is its spiritual or mystical truth, its universal significance. After the literal, each of the others represents a broader form of what is usually called allegory, moving from individual morality to social organization to God.

Fourteeners. Lines of 14 syllables—7 iambic feet, popular with the Elizabethans.

Frame Narrative. A narrative enclosing one or more separate stories. Characteristically, the frame narrative is created as a vehicle for the stories it contains.

Free Verse. French *vers libre*; poetry free of traditional metrical and stanzaic patterns.

Genre. A term often applied loosely to the larger forms of literary convention, roughly analogous to "species" in biology. The Greeks spoke of three main genres of poetry—lyric, epic, and drama. Within each major genre, there are subgenres. In written forms dominated by prose, for example, there is a broad distinction between works of fiction (e.g., the novel) and thematic works (e.g., the essay). Within the fictional category, we note a distinction between novel and romance, and other forms such as satire and confession. The object of making these distinctions in literary tradition is not simply to classify but to judge authors in terms of the conventions they themselves chose.

Georgian. (1) Pertaining to the reigns of the four Georges—1714–1830, particularly the reigns of the first three, up to the close of the 18th century. (2) The literature written during the early years (1910–1914) of the reign of George V.

Georgic. A poem about farming and annual rural labors, after Virgil's *Georgics*.

Gloss. An explanation (from Greek *glossa* "tongue, language"); originally, Latin synonyms in the margins of Greek manuscripts and vernacular synonyms in later manuscripts as scribes gave the reader some help.

Glossary. A list of words, with explanations or definitions. A glossary is ordinarily a partial dictionary, appended to the end of a book to explain technical or unfamiliar terms.

Gothic. Originally, pertaining to the Goths, then to any Germanic people. Because the Goths began warring with the Roman empire in the 3rd century A.D., eventually sacking Rome itself, the term later became a synonym for "barbaric," which the 18th century next applied to anything medieval, of the Dark Ages.

Gothic Novel. A type of fiction introduced and named by Horace Walpole's *Castle of Otranto, A Gothic Story* (1764). Walpole introduced supernatural terror, with a huge mysterious helmet, portraits that walk abroad, and statues with nosebleeds. Matthew Gregory Lewis, "Monk Lewis," added sexual depravity to the murderous supernatural mix (*The Monk*, 1796). Mary Shelley's *Frankenstein* (1818) transformed the Gothic into moral science fiction.

Grotesque. Anything unnaturally distorted, ugly, ludicrous, fanciful, or bizarre; especially, in the 19th century, literature exploiting the abnormal.

Hedonism. A philosophy that sees pleasure as the highest good.

Hegelianism. The philosophy of G. W. F. Hegel (1770–1831), who developed the system of thought known as Hegelian dialectic, in which a given concept, or *thesis*, generates its opposite, or *antithesis*, and from the interaction of the two arises a *synthesis*. The synthesis then forms a thesis for a new cycle. Hegelian dialectic suggests that history is not static but contains a rational progression, an idea influential on many later thinkers.

Heroic Couplet. The closed and balanced iambic pentameter couplet typical of the heroic plays of John Dryden; hence, any closed couplet.

Heroic Quatrain. A stanza in four lines of iambic pentameter, rhyming *abab* (*see also* Meter). Also known as the *heroic stanza* and the *elegiac stanza*.

Hexameter. Six-foot lines.

Historicism. (1) Historical relativism. (2) An approach to literature that emphasizes its historical environment, the climate of ideas, belief, and literary conventions surrounding and influencing the writer.

Homily. A religious discourse or sermon, especially one emphasizing practical spiritual or moral advice.

Hubris. From Greek *hybris*, "pride": prideful arrogance or insolence of the kind that causes the tragic hero to ignore the warnings that might turn aside the action that leads to disaster.

Humors. The *cardinal humors* of ancient medical theory: blood, phlegm, yellow bile (choler), black bile (melancholy). From ancient times until the 19th century, the humors were believed largely responsible for health and disposition. Hippocrates (c. 460–c. 370 B.C.) thought an imbalance produced illness. Galen (c. A.D. 130–300) suggested that character types are produced by dominance of fluids: *sanguine*, or kindly, cheerful, amorous; *phlegmatic*, or sluggish, unresponsive; *choleric*, or quick-tempered; and *melancholic*, or brooding, dejected. In literature, especially during the early modern period, characters were portrayed according to the humors that dominated them, as in the comedy of humors.

Hyperbole. Overstatement to make a point, as when a parent tells a child "I've told you a thousand times."

Iambus (or Iamb). A metrical foot: ⌣ – .

Idealism. (1) In philosophy and ethics, an emphasis on ideas and ideals, as opposed to the sensory emphasis of materialism. (2) Literary idealism follows from philosophical precepts, emphasizing a world in which the most important reality is a spiritual or transcendent truth not always reflected in the world of sense perception.

Idyll. A short poem of rustic pastoral serenity.

Image. A concrete picture, either literally descriptive, as in "Red roses covered the white wall," or figurative, as in "She is a rose," each carrying a sensual and emotive connotation. A figurative image may be an analogy, metaphor, simile, personification, or the like.

Impressionism. A literary style conveying subjective impressions rather than objective reality, taking its name from the movement in French painting in the mid–19th century, notably in the works of Manet, Monet, and Renoir. The Imagists represented impressionism in poetry; in fiction, writers like Virginia Woolf and James Joyce.

Industrial Revolution. The accelerated change, beginning in the 1760s, from an agricultural-shopkeeping society, using hand tools, to an industrial-mechanized one.

Influence. The apparent effect of literary works on subsequent writers and their work, as in Robert Browning's influence on T. S. Eliot.

Innuendo. An indirect remark or gesture, especially one implying something derogatory; an insinuation.

Interlocking Rhyme. Rhyme between stanzas; a word unrhymed in one stanza is used as a rhyme for the next, as in terza rima: *aba bcb cdc* and so on.

Internal Rhyme. Rhyme within a line, rather than at the beginning (*initial rhyme*) or end (*end rhyme*); also, rhyme matching sounds in the middle of a line with sounds at the end.

Intertextuality. (1) The relations between one literary text and others it evokes through such means as quotation, paraphrase, allusion, parody, and revision. (2) More broadly, the relations between a given text and all other texts, the potentially infinite sum of knowledge within which any text has its meaning.

Inversion. A reversal of sequence or position, as when the normal order of elements within a sentence is inverted for poetic or rhetorical effect.

Irony. In general, irony is the perception of a clash between appearance and reality, between *seems* and *is*, or between *ought* and *is*. The myriad shadings of irony seem to fall into three categories: (1) *Verbal irony*—saying something contrary to what it means; the appearance is what the words say, the reality is their contrary meaning. (2) *Dramatic irony*—saying or doing something while unaware of its ironic contrast with the whole truth; named for its frequency in drama, dramatic irony is a verbal irony with the speaker's awareness erased. (3) *Situational irony*—events turning to the opposite of what is expected or what should be. The ironic situation turns the speaker's unknowing words ironic. Situational irony is the essence of both comedy and tragedy: the young lovers run into the worst possible luck, until everything clears up happily; the most noble spirits go to their death, while the featherheads survive.

Italian Sonnet (or Petrarchan Sonnet). A sonnet composed of an octave and sestet, rhyming *abbaabba cdecde* (or *cdcdcd* or some variant, without a closing couplet).

Italic (or Italics). Type slanting upward to the right. *This sentence is italic.*

Jacobean Period (1603–1625). The reign of James I, *Jacobus* being the Latin for "James." A certain skepticism and even cynicism seeped into Elizabethan joy. The Puritans and the court party, the Cavaliers, grew more antagonistic. But it was in the Jacobean period that Shakespeare wrote his greatest tragedies and tragi-comedies, and Ben Jonson did his major work.

Jargon. (1) Language peculiar to a trade or calling, as, for example, the jargon of astronauts, lawyers, or literary critics. (2) Confused or confusing language. This kind of jargon does not communicate to anybody.

Jeremiad. A lament or complaint, especially one enumerating transgressions and predicting destruction of a people, of the kind found in the Book of Jeremiah.

Juvenilia. Youthful literary products.

Kenning. A compound figurative metaphor, a circumlocution, in Old English and Old Norse poetry: "whale-road," for the sea.

Lament. A grieving poem, an elegy, in Anglo-Saxon or Renaissance times. *Deor's Lament* (c. 980) records the actual grief of a scop, or court poet, at being displaced in his lord's hall.

Lampoon. A satirical, personal ridicule in verse or prose. The term probably derives from the French *lampons*, "Let's guzzle," a refrain in 17th-century drinking songs.

Lay (or Lai). (1) A ballad or related metrical romance originating with the Breton lay of French Brittany and retaining some of its Celtic magic and folklore.

Lexicon. A word list, a vocabulary, a dictionary.

Libretto. "The little book" (Italian): the text of an opera, cantata, or other musical drama.

Litany. A prayer with phrases spoken or sung by a leader alternated with responses from congregation or choir. *The Litany* is a group of such prayers in the Book of Common Prayer.

Literal. According to the letter (of the alphabet): the precise, plain meaning of a word or phrase in its simplest, original sense, considered apart from its sense as a metaphor or other figure of speech. Literal language is the opposite of figurative language.

Literature. Strictly defined, anything written. Therefore the oral culture of a people—its folklore, folk songs, folktales, and so on—is not literature until it is written down. The movies are not literature except in their printed scripts. By the same strict meaning, historical records, telephone books, and the like are all literature because they are written in letters of the alphabet, although they are not taught as literature in schools. In contrast to this strict, literal meaning, literature has come to be equated with *creative writing* or works of the imagination: chiefly poetry, prose fiction, and drama.

Lollards. From Middle Dutch, literally, "mumblers": a derisive term applied to the followers of John Wyclif (c. 1328–1384), the reformer behind the Wyclif Bible (1385), the first in English. Lollards preached against the abuses of the medieval church, setting up a standard of poverty and individual service as against wealth and hierarchical privilege.

Lyric. A poem, brief and discontinuous, emphasizing sound and pictorial imagery rather than narrative or dramatic movement.

Macaronic Verse. (1) Strictly, verse mixing words in a writer's native language with endings, phrases, and syntax of another language, usually Latin or Greek, creating a comic or burlesque effect. (2) Loosely, any verse mingling two or more languages.

Mannerism, Mannerist. (1) In architecture and painting, a style elongating and distorting human figures and spaces, deliberately confusing scale and perspective. (2) Literary or artistic affectation; a stylistic quality produced by excessively peculiar, ornamental, or ingenious devices.

Manners. Social behavior. In usages like comedy of manners and novel of manners, the term suggests an examination of the behavior, morals, and values of a particular time, place, or social class.

Manuscript. Literally, "written by hand": any handwritten document, as, for example, a letter or diary; also, a work submitted for publication.

Marginalia. Commentary, references, or other material written by a reader in the margins of a manuscript or book.

Masculine Ending. The usual iambic ending, on the accented foot: $\smile$ –.

Masculine Rhyme. The most common rhyme in English, on the last syllable of a line.

Masque. An allegorical, poetic, and musical dramatic spectacle popular in the English courts and mansions of the 16th and early 17th centuries. Figures from mythology, history, and romance mingled in a pastoral fantasy with fairies, fauns, satyrs, and witches, as masked amateurs from the court (including kings and queens) participated in dances and scenes.

Materialism. In philosophy, an emphasis upon the material world as the ultimate reality. Its opposite is *idealism*. Thomas Hobbes was an early materialist in 17th-century England. In the 19th century, materialism had evolved into naturalism, which emerged as an especially materialistic form of realism.

Melodrama. A play with dire ingredients—the mortgage foreclosed, the daughter tied to the railroad tracks—but with a happy ending. The typical emotions produced here result in romantic tremors, pity, and terror.

Menippean Satire. Satire on pedants, bigots, rapacious professional people, and other persons or institutions perceiving the world from a single framework. The focus is on intellectual limitations and mental attitudes. Typical ingredients include a rambling narrative; unusual settings; displays of erudition; and long digressions.

Metaphor. Greek for "transfer" (*meta* and *trans* meaning "across"; *phor* and *fer* meaning "carry"): to carry something across. Hence a metaphor treats something as if it were something else. Money becomes a *nest egg*; a sandwich, a *submarine*.

Metaphysical Poetry. Seventeenth-century poetry of wit and startling extended metaphor.

Meter. The measured pulse of poetry. English meters derive from four Greek and Roman quantitative meters (*see* also Quantitative Verse), which English stresses more sharply, although the patterns are the same. The unit of each pattern is the *foot*, containing one stressed syllable and one or two light ones. *Rising meter* goes from light to heavy; *falling meter*, from heavy to light. One meter—iambic—has dominated English poetry, with the three others lending an occasional foot, for variety, and producing a few poems.

Rising Meters

Iambic: ⌣ – (the iambus)
Anapestic: ⌣ ⌣ – (the anapest)

Falling Meters

Trochaic: – ⌣ (the trochee)
Dactylic: – ⌣ ⌣ (the dactyl)

The number of feet in a line also gives the verse a name:

1 foot: monometer
2 feet: dimeter
3 feet: trimeter
4 feet: tetrameter
5 feet: pentameter
6 feet: hexameter
7 feet: heptameter

All meters show some variations, and substitutions of other kinds of feet, but three variations in iambic writing are virtually standard:

Inverted foot: – ⌣ (a trochee)
Spondee: – –
Ionic double foot: ⌣ ⌣ – –

The *pyrrhic foot* of classical meters, two light syllables (⌣ ⌣), lives in the English line only in the Ionic double foot, although some prosodists scan a relatively light iambus as pyrrhic.

Examples of meters and scansion:

Iambic Tetrameter

An-ni- | hil-a- | ting all | that's made |
To a | green thought | in a | green shade. |

Andrew Marvell, "The Garden"

Iambic Tetrameter

(*with two inverted feet*)

Close to | the sun | in lone- | ly lands, |
Ringed with | the az- | ure world, | he stands. |

Alfred, Lord Tennyson, "The Eagle"

Iambic Pentameter

Love's not | Time's fool, | though ros- | y lips | and cheeks |
Within | his bend- | ing sick- | le's com- | pass come |

William Shakespeare, Sonnet 116

When to | the ses- | sions of | sweet si- | lent thought |

William Shakespeare, Sonnet 30

Anapestic Tetrameter
(trochees substituted)

The pop- | lars are felled; | farewell | to the shade |
And the whis- | pering sound | of the cool | colonnade |

William Cowper, "The Popular Field"

Trochaic Tetrameter

Tell me | not in | mournful | numbers |

Henry Wadsworth Longfellow, "A Psalm of Life"

Dactylic Hexameter

This is the | forest prim- | eval. The | murmuring | pines and the | hemlocks |
Bearded with | moss . . . .

Henry Wadsworth Longfellow, "Evangeline"

Metonymy. "Substitute naming." A figure of speech in which an associated idea stands in for the actual item: "The *pen* is mightier than the *sword*" for "Literature and propaganda accomplish more and survive longer than warfare," or "The *White House* announced" for "The President announced." *See also* synecdoche.

Metrics. The analysis and description of meter; also called *prosody*.

Middle English. The language of England from the middle of the 12th century to approximately 1500. English began to lose its inflectional endings and accepted many French words into its vocabulary, especially terms associated with the new social, legal, and governmental structures (*baron, judge, jury, marshal, parliament, prince*), and those in common use by the French upper classes (*mansion, chamber, veal, beef*).

Mimesis. A term meaning "imitation." It has been central to literary criticism since Aristotle's *Poetics*. The ordinary meaning of *imitation* as creating a resemblance to something else is clearly involved in Aristotle's definition of dramatic plot as *mimesis praxeos*, the imitation of an action. But there are many things that a work of literature may imitate, and hence many contexts of imitation. Works of literature may imitate other works of literature: this is the aspect of literature that comes into such conceptions as convention and genre. In a larger sense, every work of literature imitates, or finds its identity in, the entire "world of words," in Wallace Stevens's phrase, the sense of the whole of reality as potentially literary, as finding its end in a book, as Stéphane Mallarmé says.

Miracle Play. A medieval play based on a saint's life or story from the Bible.

Miscellany. A collection of various things. A literary miscellany is therefore a book collecting varied works, usually poems by different authors, a kind of anthology. The term is applied especially to the many books of this kind that appeared in the Elizabethan period.

Mock Epic. A poem in epic form and manner ludicrously elevating some trivial subject to epic grandeur.

Modernism. A collective term, generally associated with the first half of the 20th century, for various aesthetic and cultural attempts to place a "modern" face on experience. Modernism arose from a sense that the old ways were worn out. The new century opened with broad social, philosophical, religious, and cultural discussion and reform. For creative artists, the challenges of the new present meant that art became subject to change in every way, that the content, forms, and techniques inherited from the 19th century existed to be challenged, broken apart, and re-formed.

Monodrama. (1) A play with one character. (2) A closet drama or dramatic monologue.

Monody. (1) A Greek ode for one voice. (2) An elegiac lament, a dirge, in poetic soliloquy.

Monologue. (1) A poem or story in the form of a soliloquy. (2) Any extended speech.

Motif (or Motive). (1) A recurrent thematic element—word, image, symbol, object, phrase, action. (2) A conventional incident, situation, or device like the unknown knight of mysterious origin and low degree in the romance, or the baffling riddle in fairy tales.

Muse. The inspirer of poetry, on whom the poet calls for assistance. In Greek mythology the Muses were the nine daughters of Zeus and Mnemosyne ("Memory") presiding over the arts and sciences.

Mystery Play. Medieval religious drama; eventually performed in elaborate cycles of plays acted on pageant wagons or stages throughout city streets, with different guilds of artisans and merchants responsible for each.

Mysticism. A spiritual discipline in which sensory experience is expunged and the mind is devoted to deep contemplation and the reaching of a transcendental union with God.

Myth. From Greek *mythos*, "plot" or "narrative." The verbal culture of most if not all human societies began with stories, and certain stories have achieved a distinctive importance as being connected with what the society feels it most needs to know: stories illustrating the society's religion, history, class structure, or the origin of peculiar features of the natural environment.

Narrative Poem. One that tells a story, particularly the epic, metrical romance, and shorter narratives, like the ballad.

Naturalism. (1) Broadly, according to nature. In this sense, naturalism is opposed to idealism, emphasizing things accessible to the senses in this world in contrast to permanent or spiritual truths presumed to lie outside it. (2) More specifically, a literary movement of the late 19th century; an extension of realism, naturalism was a reaction against the restrictions inherent in the realistic emphasis on the ordinary, as naturalists insisted that the extraordinary is real, too.

Neoclassical Period. Generally, the span of time from the restoration of Charles II to his father's throne in 1660 until the publication of William Wordsworth and Samuel Taylor Coleridge's *Lyrical Ballads* (1798). Writers hoped to revive something like the classical Pax Romana, an era of peace and literary excellence.

Neologism. A word newly coined or introduced into a language, or a new meaning given to an old word.

New Criticism. An approach to criticism prominent in the United States after the publication of John Crowe Ransom's *New Criticism* (1941). Generally, the New Critics were agreed that a poem or story should be considered an organic unit, with each part working to support the whole. They worked by close analysis, considering the text as the final authority, and were distrustful, though not wholly neglectful, of considerations brought from outside the text, as, for example, from biography or history.

New Historicism. A cross-disciplinary approach fostered by the rise of feminist and multicultural studies as well as a renewed emphasis on historical perspective. Associated in particular with work on the early modern and the romantic periods in the United States and England, the approach emphasizes analysis of the relationship between history and literature, viewing writings in both fields as "texts" for study. New Historicism has tended to note political influences on literary and historical texts, to illuminate the role of the writer against the backdrop of social customs and assumptions, and to view history as changeable and interconnected instead of as a linear progressive evolution.

Nocturne. A night piece; writing evocative of evening or night.

Nominalism. In the Middle Ages, the belief that universals have no real being, but are only names, their existence limited to their presence in the minds and language of humans. This belief was opposed to the beliefs of medieval realists, who held that universals have an independent existence, at least in the mind of God.

Norman Conquest. The period of English history in which the Normans consolidated their hold on England after the defeat of the Saxon King Harold by William, Duke of Normandy, in 1066. French became the court language and Norman lords gained control of English lands, but Anglo-Saxon administrative and judicial systems remained largely in place.

Novel. The extended prose fiction that arose in the 18th century to become a major literary expression of the modern world. The term comes from the Italian *novella*, the short "new" tale of intrigue and moral comeuppance most eminently disseminated by Boccaccio's *Decameron* (1348–1353). The terms *novel* and *romance*, from the French *roman*, competed interchangeably for most of the 18th century.

Novella. (1) Originally, a short tale. (2) In modern usage, a term sometimes used interchangeably with short novel or for a fiction of middle length, between a short story and a novel. See Novel, above.

Octave. (1) The first unit in an Italian sonnet: eight lines of iambic pentameter, rhyming *abbaabba*. *See also* Meter. (2) A stanza in eight lines.

Octavo (Abbreviated 8vo). A book made from sheets folded to give signatures of eight leaves (16 pages), a book of average size.

Octet. An octastich or octave.

Octosyllabic. Eight-syllable.

Ode. A long, stately lyric poem in stanzas of varied metrical pattern.

Old English. The language brought to England, beginning in 449, by the Jute, Angle, and Saxon invaders from Denmark; the language base from which modern English evolved.

Old English Literature. The literature of England from the Anglo-Saxon invasion of the mid-5th century until the beginning of the Middle English period in the mid-12th century.

Omniscient Narrative. A narrative account untrammeled by constraints of time or space. An omniscient narrator perspective knows about the external and internal realities of characters as well as incidents unknown to them, and can interpret motivation and meaning.

Onomatopoeia. The use of words formed or sounding like what they signify—*buzz, crack, smack, whinny*—especially in an extensive capturing of sense by sound.

Orientalism. A term denoting Western portrayals of Oriental culture. In literature it refers to a varied body of work beginning in the 18th century that described for Western readers the history, language, politics, and culture of the area east of the Mediterranean.

Oxford Movement. A 19th-century movement to reform the Anglican church according to the high-church and more nearly Catholic ideals and rituals of the later 17th-century church.

Oxymoron. A pointed stupidity: *oxy,* "sharp," plus *moron.* One of the great ironic figures of speech—for example, "a fearful joy," or Milton's "darkness visible."

Paleography. The study and interpretation of ancient handwriting and manuscript styles.

Palimpsest. A piece of writing on secondhand vellum, parchment, or other surface carrying traces of erased previous writings.

Panegyric. A piece of writing in praise of a person, thing, or achievement.

Pantheism. A belief that God and the universe are identical, from the Greek words *pan* ("all") and *theos* ("god"). God is all; all is God.

Pantomime. A form of drama presented without words, in a dumb show.

Parable. (1) A short tale, such as those of Jesus in the gospels, encapsulating a moral or religious lesson. (2) Any saying, figure of speech, or narrative in which one thing is expressed in terms of another.

Paradox. An apparently untrue or self-contradictory statement or circumstance that proves true upon reflection or when examined in another light.

Paraphrase. A rendering in other words of the sense of a text or passage, as of a poem, essay, short story, or other writing.

Parody. Originally, "a song sung beside" another. From this idea of juxtaposition arose the two basic elements of parody, comedy and criticism. As comedy, parody exaggerates or distorts the prominent features of style or content in a work. As criticism, it mimics the work, borrowing words or phrases or characteristic turns of thought in order to highlight weaknesses of conception or expression.

Passion Play. Originally a play based on Christ's Passion; later, one including both Passion and Resurrection. Such plays began in the Middle Ages, performed from the 13th century onward, often as part of the pageants presented for the feast of Corpus Christi.

Pastiche. A literary or other artistic work created by assembling bits and pieces from other works.

Pastoral. From Latin *pastor*, a shepherd. The first pastoral poet was Theocritus, a Greek of the 3rd century B.C. The pastoral was especially popular in Europe from the 14th through the 18th centuries, with some fine examples still written in England in the 19th century. The pastoral mode is self-reflexive. Typically the poet echoes the conventions of earlier pastorals in order to put "the complex into the simple," as William Empson observed in *Some Versions of Pastoral* (1935). The poem is not really about shepherds, but about the complex society the poet and readers inhabit.

Pathetic Fallacy. The attribution of animate or human characteristics to nature, as, for example, when rocks, trees, or weather are portrayed as reacting in sympathy to human feelings or events.

Pathos. The feeling of pity, sympathy, tenderness, compassion, or sorrow evoked by someone or something that is helpless.

Pedantry. Ostentatious book learning: an accusation frequently hurled in scholarly disagreements.

Pentameter. A line of five metrical feet. (*See* Meter.)

Peripeteia (or Peripetia, Peripety). A sudden change in situation in a drama or fiction, a reversal of luck for good or ill.

Periphrasis. The practice of talking around the point; a wordy restatement; a circumlocution.

Peroration. (1) The summative conclusion of a formal oration. (2) Loosely, a grandiloquent speech.

Persona. A mask (in Latin); in poetry and fiction, the projected speaker or narrator of the work—that is, a mask for the actual author.

Personification. The technique of treating abstractions, things, or animals as persons. A kind of metaphor, personification turns abstract ideas, like love, into a physical beauty named Venus, or conversely, makes dumb animals speak and act like humans.

Petrarchan Sonnet. Another name for an Italian sonnet.

Philology. The study of ancient languages and literatures; also more broadly interpreted from its basic meaning, "love of the word," to include all literary studies. In the 19th century, the field of historical linguistics.

Phoneme. In linguistics, the smallest distinguishable unit of sound. Different for each language, phonemes are defined by determining which differences in sound function to signal a difference in meaning.

Phonetics. (1) The study of speech sounds and their production, transmission, and reception. (2) The phonetic system of a particular language. (3) Symbols used to represent speech sounds.

Picaresque Novel. A novel chronicling the adventures of a rogue (Spanish: *picaro*), typically presented as an autobiography, episodic in structure and panoramic in its coverage of time and place.

Picturesque, The. A quality in landscape, and in idealized landscape painting, admired in the second half of the 18th century and featuring crags, flaring and blasted trees, a torrent or winding stream, ruins, and perhaps a quiet cottage and cart, with contrasting light and shadow. It was considered an aesthetic mean between the poles of Edmund Burke's *A Philosophical Inquiry into the Sublime and the Beautiful* (1756).

Plagiarism. Literary kidnapping (Latin *plagiarius*, "kidnapper")—the seizing and presenting as one's own the ideas or writings of another.

Plain Style. The straightforward, unembellished style of preaching favored by 17th-century Puritans as well as by reformers within the Anglican church, as speaking God's word directly from the inspired heart as opposed to the high style of aristocratic oratory and courtliness, the vehicle of subterfuge. Plain style was simultaneously advocated for scientific accuracy by the Royal Society.

Platonism. Any reflection of Plato's philosophy, particularly the belief in the eternal reality of ideal forms, of which the diversities of the physical world are but transitory shadows.

Poetics. The theory, art, or science of poetry. Poetics is concerned with the nature and function of poetry and with identifying and explaining its types, forms, and techniques.

Poet Laureate. Since the 17th century, a title conferred by the monarch on English poets. At first, the laureate was required to write poems to commemorate special occasions, such as royal birthdays, national celebrations, and the like, but since the early 19th century the appointment has been for the most part honorary.

Poetry. Imaginatively intense language, usually in verse. Poetry is a form of fiction—"the supreme fiction," said Wallace Stevens. It is distinguished from other fictions by the compression resulting from its heavier use of figures of speech and allusion and, usually, by the music of its patterns of sounds.

Postmodernism. A term first used in relation to literature in the late 1940s by Randall Jarrell and John Berryman to proclaim a new sensibility arising to challenge the reigning assumptions and practices of modernism. The attitudes and literary devices of the modernists—stream of consciousness, for example—had taken on the patina of tradition. For many of the postmodernists, disillusionment seemed to have reached its fullest measure. Life had little meaning, art less, and a neat closure to expectations raised by the artist seemed impossible. Intruding into one's own fiction to ponder its powers became a hallmark of the 1960s and 1970s.

Poststructuralism. A mode of literary criticism and thought centered on Jacques Derrida's concept of deconstruction. Structuralists see language as the paradigm for all structures. Poststructuralists see language as based on differences—hence the analytical deconstruction of what seemed an immutable system. What language expresses is already absent. Poststructuralism challenges the New Criticism, which seeks a truth fixed within the "verbal icon," the text, in W. K. Wimsatt's term. Poststructuralism invites interpretations through the spaces left by the way words operate.

Pragmatism. In philosophy, the idea that the value of a belief is best judged by the acts that follow from it—its practical results.

Preciosity. Since the 19th century, a term for an affected or overingenious refinement of language.

Predestination. The belief that an omniscient God, at the Creation, destined all subsequent events, particularly, in Calvinist belief, the election for salvation and the damnation of individual souls.

Pre-Raphaelite. Characteristic of a small but influential group of mid-19th-century painters who hoped to recapture the spiritual vividness they saw in medieval painting before Raphael (1483–1520).

Presbyterianism. John Calvin's organization of ecclesiastical governance not by bishops representing the pope but by elders representing the congregation.

Proscenium. Originally, in Greece, the whole acting area ("in front of the scenery"); now, that part of the stage projecting in front of the curtain.

Prose. Ordinary writing patterned on speech, as distinct from verse.

Prose Poetry. Prose rich in cadenced and poetic effects like alliteration, assonance, consonance, and the like, and in imagery.

Prosody. The analysis and description of meters; metrics (*see also* Meter). Linguists apply the term to the study of patterns of accent in a language.

Protagonist. The leading character in a play or story; originally the leader of the chorus in the agon ("contest") of Greek drama, faced with the antagonist, the opposition.

Pseudonym. A fictitious name adopted by an author for public use, like George Eliot (Mary Ann/Marian Evans), and George Orwell (Eric Arthur Blair).

Psychoanalytic Criticism. A form of criticism that uses the insights of Freudian psychology to illuminate a work.

Ptolemaic Universe. The universe as perceived by Ptolemy, a Greco-Egyptian astronomer of the 2nd century A.D., whose theories were dominant until the Renaissance produced the Copernican universe. In Ptolemy's system, the universe was world-centered, with the sun, moon, planets, and stars understood as rotating around the earth in a series of concentric spheres, producing as they revolved the harmonious "music of the spheres."

Puritanism. A Protestant movement arising in the mid-16th century with the Reformation in England. Theocracy—the individual and the congregation governed directly under God through Christ—became primary, reflected in the centrality of the Scriptures and their exposition, direct confession through prayer and public confession to the congregation rather than through priests, and the direct individual experience of God's grace.

Quadrivium. The more advanced four of the seven liberal arts as studied in medieval universities: arithmetic, geometry, astronomy, and music.

Quantitative Verse. Verse that takes account of the quantity of the syllables (whether they take a long or short time to pronounce) rather than their stress patterns.

Quarto (Abbreviated 4to, 4o). A book made from sheets folded twice, giving signatures of four leaves (eight pages). Many of Shakespeare's plays were first printed individually in quarto editions, designated First Quarto, Second Quarto, etc.

Quatrain. A stanza of four lines, rhymed or unrhymed. With its many variations, it is the most common stanzaic form in English.

Rationalism. The theory that reason, rather than revelation or authority, provides knowledge, truth, the choice of good over evil, and an adequate understanding of God and the universe.

Reader-Response Theory. A form of criticism that arose during the 1970s; it postulates the essential active involvement of the reader with the text and focuses on the effect of the process of reading on the mind.

Realism (in literature). The faithful representation of life. Realism carries the conviction of true reports of phenomena observable by others.

Realism (in philosophy). (1) In the Middle Ages, the belief that universal concepts possess real existence apart from particular things and the human mind. They exist either as entities like Platonic forms or as concepts in the mind of God. Medieval realism was opposed to nominalism. (2) In later epistemology, the belief that things exist apart from our perception of them. In this sense, realism is opposed to idealism, which locates all reality in our minds.

Recension. (1) A process of editorial revision based on an examination of the various versions and sources of a literary text. (2) The text produced as a result of reconciling variant readings.

Recto. The right-hand page of an open book; the front of a leaf as opposed to the *verso* or back of a leaf.

Redaction. (1) A revised version. (2) A rewriting or condensing of an older work.

Refrain. A set phrase, or chorus, recurring throughout a song or poem, usually at the end of a stanza or other regular interval.

Relativism. The philosophical belief that nothing is absolute, that values are relative to circumstances. In criticism, relativism is either personal or historical.

Revenge Tragedy. The popular Elizabethan mode, initiated by Thomas Kyd's *Spanish Tragedy* (c. 1586), wherein the hero must revenge a ruler's murder of father, son, or lover.

Reversal. The thrilling change of luck for the protagonist at the last moment in comedy or tragedy—the *peripeteia*, which Aristotle first described in his *Poetics,* along with the discovery that usually sparks it.

Rhetoric. From Greek *rhetor,* "orator": the art of persuasion in speaking or writing. Since ancient times, rhetoric has been understood by some as a system of persuasive devices divorced from considerations of the merits of the case argued.

Rhetorical Figure. A figure of speech employing stylized patterns of word order or meaning for purposes of ornamentation or persuasion.

Rhetorical Question. A question posed for rhetorical effect, usually with a self-evident answer.

Rhyme (sometimes Rime, an older spelling). The effect created by matching sounds at the ends of words. The functions of rhyme are essentially four: pleasurable, mnemonic, structural, and rhetorical. Like meter and figurative language, rhyme provides a pleasure derived from fulfillment of a basic human desire to see similarity in dissimilarity, likeness with a difference.

Rhyme Royal. A stanza of seven lines of iambic pentameter, rhyming *ababbcc* (*see also* Meter).

Rhythm. The measured flow of repeated sound patterns, as, for example, the heavy stresses of accentual verse, the long and short syllables of quantitative verse, the balanced syntactical arrangements of parallelism in either verse or prose.

Romance. A continuous narrative in which the emphasis is on what happens in the plot, rather than on what is reflected from ordinary life or experience. Thus a central element in romance is adventure; at its most primitive, romance is an endless sequence of adventures.

Romanticism. A term describing qualities that colored most elements of European and American intellectual life in the late 18th and early 19th centuries, from literature, art, and music, through architecture, landscape gardening, philosophy, and politics. Within the social, political, and intellectual structures of society, the Romantics stressed the separateness of the person, celebrated individual perception and imagination, and embraced nature as a model for harmony in society and art. Their view was an egalitarian one, stressing the value of expressive abilities common to all, inborn rather than developed through training.

Roundheads. Adherents of the Parliamentary, or Puritan, party in the English Civil War, so called from their short haircuts, as opposed to the fashionable long wigs of the Cavaliers, supporters of King Charles I.

Rubric. From Latin *rubrica,* "red earth" (for coloring): in a book or manuscript, a heading, marginal notation, or other section distinguished for special attention by being printed in red ink or in distinctive type.

Run-on Line. A line of poetry whose sense does not stop at the end, with punctuation, but runs on to the next line.

Satire. Poking corrective ridicule at persons, types, actions, follies, mores, and beliefs.

Scop. An Anglo-Saxon bard, or court poet, a kind of poet laureate.

Semiotics. In anthropology, sociology, and linguistics, the study of signs, including words, other sounds, gestures, facial expressions, music, pictures, and other signals used in communication.

Senecan Tragedy. The bloody and bombastic tragedies of revenge inspired by Seneca's nine closet dramas, which had been discovered in Italy in the mid-16th century and soon thereafter translated into English.

Sensibility. Sensitive feeling, emotion. The term arose early in the 18th century to denote the tender undercurrent of feeling in the neoclassical period, continuing through Jane Austen's *Sense and Sensibility* (1811) and afterward.

Sequel. A literary work that explores later events in the lives of characters introduced elsewhere.

Serial. A narration presented in segments separated by time. Novels by Charles Dickens and other 19th-century writers were first serialized in magazines.

Seven Liberal Arts. The subjects studied in medieval universities, consisting of the *trivium* (grammar, logic, and rhetoric), for the B.A., and the *quadrivium* (arithmetic, geometry, astronomy, and music), for the M.A.

Shakespearean Sonnet (or English Sonnet). A sonnet in three quatrains and a couplet, rhyming *abab cdcd efef gg*.

Signified, Signifier. In structural linguistics, the *signified* is the idea in mind when a word is used, an entity separate from the *signifier*, the word itself.

Simile. A metaphor stating the comparison by use of *like*, *as*, or *as if*.

Slang. The special vocabulary of a class or group of people (as, for example, truck drivers, jazz musicians, salespeople, drug dealers), generally considered substandard, low, or offensive when measured against formal, educated usage.

Sonnet. A verse form of 14 lines, in English characteristically in iambic pentameter and most often in one of two rhyme schemes: the *Italian* (or *Petrarchan*) or *Shakespearean* (or *English*). An Italian sonnet is composed of an octave, rhyming *abbaabba*, and a sestet, rhyming *cdecde* or *cdcdcd*, or in some variant pattern, but with no closing couplet. A Shakespearean sonnet has three quatrains and a couplet, and rhymes *abab cdcd efef gg*. In both types, the content tends to follow the formal outline suggested by rhyme linkage, giving two divisions to the thought of an Italian sonnet and four to a Shakespearean one.

Sonnet Sequence. A group of sonnets thematically unified to create a longer work, although generally, unlike the stanza, each sonnet so connected can also be read as a meaningful separate unit.

Spondee. A metrical foot of two long, or stressed, syllables: – –.

Sprung Rhythm. Gerard Manley Hopkins's term to describe his variations of iambic meter to avoid the "same and tame." His feet, he said, vary from one to four syllables, with one stress per foot, on the first syllable.

Stanza. A term derived from an Italian word for "room" or "stopping place" and used, loosely, to designate any grouping of lines in a separate unit in a poem: a verse paragraph. More strictly, a stanza is a grouping of a prescribed number of lines in a given meter, usually with a particular rhyme scheme, repeated as a unit of structure. Poems in stanzas provide an instance of the aesthetic pleasure in repetition with a difference that also underlies the metrical and rhyming elements of poetry.

Stereotype. A character representing generalized racial or social traits repeated as typical from work to work, with no individualizing traits.

Stichomythia. Dialogue in alternate lines, favored in Greek tragedy and by Seneca and his imitators among the Elizabethans—including William Shakespeare.

Stock Characters. Familiar types repeated in literature to become symbolic of a particular genre, like the strong, silent hero of the western or the hard-boiled hero of the detective story.

Stoicism. (1) Generally, fortitude, repression of feeling, indifference to pleasure or pain. (2) Specifically, the philosophy of the Stoics, who, cultivating endurance and self-control, restrain passions such as joy and grief that place them in conflict with nature's dictates.

Stress. In poetry, the accent or emphasis given to certain syllables, indicated in scansion by a macron (–). In a trochee, for example, the stress falls on the first syllable: *sŭmmĕr*. *See also* Meter.

Structuralism. The study of social organizations and myths, of language, and of literature as structures. Each part is significant only as it relates to others in the total structure, with nothing meaningful by itself.

Structural Linguistics. Analysis and description of the grammatical structures of a spoken language.

Sublime. In literature, a quality attributed to lofty or noble ideas, grand or elevated expression, or (the ideal of sublimity) an inspiring combination of thought and language. In nature or art, it is a quality, as in a landscape or painting, that inspires awe or reverence.

Subplot. A sequence of events subordinate to the main story in a narrative or dramatic work.

Syllabic Verse. Poetry in which meter has been set aside and the line is controlled by a set number of syllables, regardless of stress.

Symbol. Something standing for its natural qualities in another context, with human meaning added: an eagle, standing for the soaring imperious dominance of Rome.

Symbolism. Any use of symbols, especially with a theoretical commitment, as when the French Symbolists of the 1880s and 1890s stressed, in Stéphane Mallarmé's words, not the thing but the effect, the subjective emotion implied by the surface rendering.

Syncopation. The effect produced in verse or music when two stress patterns play off against one another.

Synecdoche. The understanding of one thing by another—a kind of metaphor in which a part stands for the whole, or the whole for a part: *a hired hand* meaning "a laborer."

Synesthesia. Greek for "perceiving together": close association or confusion of sense impressions. The result is essentially a metaphor, transferring qualities of one sense to another, as in common phrases like "blue note" and "cold eye."

Synonyms. Words in the same language denoting the same thing, usually with different connotations: *female, woman, lady, dame; male, masculine, macho.*

Synopsis. A summary of a play, a narrative, or an argument.

Tenor and Vehicle. I. A. Richards's terms for the two aspects of metaphor, *tenor* being the actual thing projected figuratively in the *vehicle.* "She [tenor] is a rose [vehicle]."

Tercet (or Triplet). A verse unit of three lines, sometimes rhymed, sometimes not.

Terza Rima. A verse form composed of tercets with interlocking rhyme (*aba bcb cdc*, and so on), usually in iambic pentameter. Invented by Dante for his *Divine Comedy.*

Third-Person Narration. A method of storytelling in which someone who is not involved in the story, but stands somewhere outside it in space and time, tells of the events.

Topos. A commonplace, from Greek *topos* (plural *topoi*), "place." (1) A topic for argument, remembered by the classical system of placing it, in the mind's eye, in a place within a building and then proceeding mentally from one place to the next. (2) A rhetorical device, similarly remembered as a commonplace.

Tragedy. Fundamentally, a serious fiction involving the downfall of a hero or heroine. As a literary form, a basic mode of drama. Tragedy often involves the theme of isolation, in which a hero, a character of greater than ordinary human importance, becomes isolated from the community. Then there is the theme of the violation and reestablishment of order, in which the neutralizing of the violent act may take the form of revenge. Finally, a character may embody a passion too great for the cosmic order to tolerate, such as the passion of sexual love. Renaissance tragedy seems to be essentially a mixture of the heroic and the ironic. It tends to center on heroes who, though they cannot be of divine parentage in Christianized Western Europe, are still of titanic importance, with an articulateness and social authority beyond anything in our normal experience.

Tragic Irony. The essence of tragedy, in which the most noble and most deserving person, because of the very grounds of his or her excellence, dies in defeat. *See also* Irony.

Tragicomedy. (1) A tragedy with happy ending, frequently with penitent villain and romantic setting, disguises, and discoveries.

Travesty. Literally a "cross-dressing": a literary work so clothed, or presented, as to appear ludicrous; a grotesque image or likeness.

Trivium. The first three of the seven liberal arts as studied in medieval universities: grammar, logic, and rhetoric (including oratory).

Trochee. A metrical foot going $-\smile$.

Trope. Greek *tropos* for "a turn": a word or phrase turned from its usual meaning to an unusual one; hence, a figure of speech, or an expression turned beyond its literal meaning.

Type. (1) A literary genre. (2) One of the type characters. (3) A symbol or emblem. (4) In theology and literary criticism, an event in early Scriptures or literatures that is seen as prefiguring an event in later Scriptures or in history or literature generally.

Type Characters. Individuals endowed with traits that mark them more distinctly as representatives of a type or class than as standing apart from a type: the typical doctor or rakish aristocrat, for example. Type characters are the opposite of individualized characters.

Typology. The study of types. Typology springs from a theory of literature or history that recognizes events as duplicated in time.

Utopia. A word from two Greek roots (*outopia*, meaning "no place," and *eutopia*, meaning "good place"), pointing to the idea that a utopia is a nonexistent land of social perfection.

Verisimilitude (*vraisemblance* in French). The appearance of actuality.

Verso. The left-hand page of an open book; the back of a leaf of paper.

Vice. A stock character from the medieval morality play, a mischief-making tempter.

Vignette. (1) A brief, subtle, and intimate literary portrait, named for *vignette* portraiture, which is unbordered, shading off into the surrounding color at the edges, with features delicately rendered. (2) A short essay, sketch, or story, usually fewer than five hundred words.

Villanelle. One of the French verse forms, in five tercets, all rhyming *aba*, and a quatrain, rhyming *abaa*. The entire first and third lines are repeated alternately as the final lines of tercets 2, 3, 4, and 5, and together to conclude the quatrain.

Virgule. A "little rod"—the diagonal mark or slash used to indicate line ends in poetry printed continuously in running prose.

Vulgate. (1) A people's common vernacular language (Latin *vulgus*, "common people"). (2) The Vulgate Bible, translated by St. Jerome c. 383–405; the official Roman Catholic Bible.

Wit and Humor. *Wit* is intellectual acuity; *humor*, an amused indulgence of human deficiencies. Wit now denotes the acuity that produces laughter. It originally meant mere understanding, then quickness of understanding, then, beginning in the 17th century, quick perception coupled with creative fancy. Humor (British *humour*, from the four bodily humors) was simply a disposition, usually eccentric. In the 18th century, *humour* came to mean a laughable eccentricity and then a kindly amusement at such eccentricity.

Zeugma. The technique of using one word to yoke two or more others for ironic or amusing effect, achieved when at least one of the yoked is a misfit, as in Alexander Pope's "lose her Heart, or Necklace, at a Ball."

BIBLIOGRAPHY
The Restoration and the Eighteenth Century

Bibliographies and Guides to Research • Robin Alston et al., *The Eighteenth-Century Short-Title Catalogue (ESTC)*, online and on CD-ROM. • Margaret M. Duggan, *English Literature and Backgrounds, 1660–1700: A Selective Critical Guide*, 2 vols., 1990. • *The Eighteenth Century: A Current Bibliography for [1925–]*, annual. The bibliographies for 1925–1970 have been reprinted as *English Literature, 1660–1800: A Bibliography of Modern Studies*, 1950–1972. • Waldo Sumner Glock, *Eighteenth-Century English Literary Studies: A Bibliography*, 1984. • Roger D. Lund, *Restoration and Early Eighteenth-Century English Literature, 1660–1740: A Selected Bibliography of Resource Materials*, 1980. • Joanne Shattock, ed., *The Cambridge Bibliography of English Literature*, vol. 2, 1660–1800, 2003. • R. D. Spector, *Backgrounds to Restoration and Eighteenth-Century English Literature: An Annotated Bibliographical Guide to Modern Scholarship*, 1989. • *Studies in English Literature*, Annual review of "Recent Studies in the Restoration and Eighteenth Century" (Summer issue), 1961–.

Online Resources • Alan Liu et al., eds., *Voice of the Shuttle: Restoration and Eighteenth Century:* http://vos.ucsb.edu • Jack Lynch, ed., *Eighteenth-Century Resources:* http://andromeda.rutgers.edu/~jlynch/18th/ • James E. May, *The C-18L Bibliographies: Resources for Eighteenth-Century Studies across the Disciplines:* http://www.personal.psu.edu/special/C18/maytools.htm

Cultural and Intellectual Background • John Brewer, *The Pleasures of the Imagination: English Culture in the Eighteenth Century*, 1997. • James Engell, *The Creative Imagination: Enlightenment to Romanticism*, 1981. • James Engell, *Forming the Critical Mind: Dryden to Coleridge*, 1989. • Northrop Frye, "Towards Defining an Age of Sensibility," *English Literary History*, vol. 23, 1956; repr. in *Backgrounds to Eighteenth-Century Literature*, ed. Kathleen Williams, 1971. • Donald Greene, *The Age of Exuberance: Backgrounds to Eighteenth-Century English Literature*, 1970. • Jürgen Habermas, *The Structural Transformation of the Public Sphere*, 1962; trans., Thomas Burger, 1989. •

Jean H. Hagstrum, *Sex and Sensibility: Ideal and Erotic Love from Milton to Mozart*, 1980. • Tim Harris, *Popular Culture in Restoration England*, c. 1500–1800, 1995. • Lawrence Lipking, *The Ordering of the Arts in Eighteenth-Century England*, 1970. • Gerald MacLean, ed., *Culture and Society in the Stuart Restoration: Literature, Drama, History*, 1995. • C. A. Moore, *Backgrounds of English Literature, 1700–1760*, 1953. • John Mullan and Christopher Reid, eds., *Eighteenth-Century Popular Culture: A Selection*, 2000. • Ronald Paulson, *Breaking and Remaking: Aesthetic Practice in England, 1700–1820*, 1989. • Roy Porter, *The Creation of the Modern World: The British Enlightenment*, 2000. • Pat Rogers, ed., *The Context of English Literature: The Eighteenth Century*, 1978. • Pat Rogers, *Grub Street: Studies in a Subculture*, 1972. • James Sambrook, *The Eighteenth Century: The Intellectual and Cultural Context of English Literature, 1700–1789*, 2nd ed., 1993. • J. W. Yolton et al., eds., *The Blackwell Companion to the Enlightenment*, 1991. • Steven N. Zwicker, *The Cambridge Companion to English Literature, 1650–1740*, 1998.

History, Religion, and Political Thought • Jeremy Black, *An Illustrated History of Eighteenth-Century Britain*, 1996. • John Brewer, *The Sinews of Power: War, Money, and the English State, 1688–1783*, 1989. • J. C. D. Clark, *English Society, 1688–1832*, 1985. • Linda Colley, *Britons: Forging the Nation, 1707–1837*, 1992. • Peter Earle, *The Making of the English Middle Class*, 1989. • Jeremy Gregory and John Stevenson, *Britain in the Eighteenth Century, 1688–1820*, 2000. • Tim Harris, *Politics Under the Later Stuarts*, 1993. • Tim Harris, *The Politics of Religion in Restoration England*, 1990. • T. W. Heyck, *The Peoples of the British Isles*, vol. 2, 1688–1870, 1992. • Ronald Hutton, *Charles II*, 1989. • Ronald Hutton, *The Restoration*, 1985. • J. P. Kenyon, *The Stuart Constitution*, 2nd ed., 1986. • Mark Kishlansky, *A Monarchy Transformed: Britain 1603–1714*, 1996. • Paul Langford, *A Polite and Commercial People: England 1727–1783*, 1989. • Dorothy Marshall, *Eighteenth Century England*, 2nd. ed., 1962. • Neil McKendrick,

John Brewer, and J. H. Plumb, *The Birth of a Consumer Society: The Commercialization of Eighteenth-Century Britain*, 1982. • J. H. Plumb, *England in the Eighteenth Century*, 1972. • J. G. A. Pocock, *Politics, Language, and Time: Essays on Political Thought and History*, 1989. • J. G. A. Pocock, *Virtue, Commerce, and History*, 1985. • Roy Porter, *English Society in the Eighteenth Century*, rev. ed., 1990. • Isabel Rivers, *Reason, Grace, and Sentiment: A Study of the Language of Religion and Ethics in England, 1660–1780*, vol. 1, *Whichcote to Wesley*, 1991. • Richard B. Schwartz, *Daily Life in Johnson's London*, 1983. • W. A. Speck, *Stability and Strife: England, 1714–1760*, 1977. • John Spurr, *The Restoration Church of England*, 1991. • E. P. Thompson, *Albion's Fatal Tree: Crime and Society in Eighteenth-Century England*, 1976. • E. P. Thompson, *Customs in Common*, 1991. • John Wroughton, *The Longman Companion to the Stuart Age 1603–1714*, 1997.

Women, Writing, Politics, and Culture • George Ballard, *Memoirs of Several Ladies of Great Britain Who Have Been Celebrated for Their Writings or Skill in the Learned Languages, Arts, and Sciences*, 1752; ed. Ruth Perry, 1985. • Margaret J. M. Ezell, *Writing Women's Literary History*, 1993. • Catherine Gallagher, *Nobody's Story: The Vanishing Acts of Women Writers in the Marketplace, 1670–1820*, 1994. • Susan Greenfield and Carol Barash, eds., *Inventing Maternity*, 1999. • Isobel Grundy and Susan Wiseman, eds., *Women, Writing, and History: 1640–1799*, 1992. • Bridget Hill, *Eighteenth-Century Women: An Anthology*, 1984. • Bridget Hill, *Women, Work, and Sexual Politics in Eighteenth-Century England*, 1989. • Sylvia Meyers, *The Bluestocking Circle*, 1990. • Anita Pacheco, ed., *Early Women Writers: 1660–1720*, 1998. • Myra Reynolds, *The Learned Lady in England, 1650–1760*, 1920. • Mona Scheuermann, *Her Bread to Earn: Women, Money, and Society from Defoe to Austen*, 1993. • Hilda Smith, *Reason's Disciples: Seventeenth-Century English Feminists*, 1982. • Susan Staves, *Married Women's Separate Property in England, 1660–1833*, 1990. • Beth Fawkes Tobin, *History, Gender, and Eighteenth-Century Literature*, 1994. • Janet Todd, ed., *A Dictionary of British and American Women Writers, 1660–1800*, 1985. • Janet Todd, *The Sign of Angellica: Women, Writing, and Fiction, 1660–1800*, 1989. • Katherine Wilson and Frank J. Warnke, eds., *Women Writers of the Seventeenth Century*, 1989.

General Literature • Martin C. Battestin, *The Providence of Wit: Aspects of Form in Augustan Literature and the Arts*, 1974. • Richard Braverman, *Plots and Counterplots: Sexual Politics and the Body Politic in English Literature, 1660–1730*. • John Butt and Geoffrey Carnall, *English Literature in the Mid-Eighteenth Century*, 1979. • James L. Clifford, ed., *Eighteenth-Century English Literature: Modern Essays in Criticism*, 1959. • Leopold Damrosch, Jr., ed., *Modern Essays on Eighteenth-Century Literature*, 1988. • Robert DeMaria, Jr., ed., *British Literature, 11640–1789: A Critical Reader*, 1999. • Bonamy Dobrée, *English Literature in the Early Eighteenth Century, 1700–1740*, 1959. • Paul Fussell, *The Rhetorical World of Augustan Humanism*, 1965. • Roger Lonsdale, ed., *The Sphere History of Literature*, vol. 4, *Dryden to Johnson*, rev. ed., 1987. • Felicity Nussbaum and Laura Brown, eds., *The New Eighteenth Century: Theory, Politics, English Literature*, 1987. • Ronald Paulson, *Popular and Polite Art in the Age of Hogarth and Fielding*, 1979. • Martin Price, *To the Palace of Wisdom: Studies in Order and Energy from Dryden to Blake*, 1964. • Isabel Rivers, ed., *Books and Their Readers in Eighteenth-Century England*, 1982. • Isabel Rivers, ed., *Books and Their Readers in Eighteenth-Century England: New Essays*, 2002. • John Sitter, *Literary Loneliness in Mid-Eighteenth-Century England*, 1982. • James Sutherland, *English Literature of the Late Seventeenth Century*, 1969. • Howard Weinbrot, *Britannia's Issue: The Rise of British Literature from Dryden to Ossian*, 1993. • David Womersley, ed., *A Companion to Literature from Milton to Blake*, 2000. • Steven N. Zwicker, *Lines of Authority: Politics and English Literary Culture, 1649–1689*, 1993.

Drama • R. W. Bevis, *English Drama: Restoration and Eighteenth Century, 1660–1789*, 1988. Laura Brown, *English Dramatic Form, 1660–1760*, 1981. • J. Douglas Canfield and Deborah C. Payne, eds., *Cultural Readings of Restoration and Eighteenth-Century English Theater*, 1995. • T. W. Craik et al., eds., *The Revels History of Drama in English*, vol. 5, 1660–1750. • Deborah Payne Fiske, ed., *The Cambridge Companion to English Restoration Theatre*, Cambridge 2000. • Pat Gill, *Interpreting Ladies: Women, Wit, and Morality in the Restoration Comedy of Manners*, 1994. • John T. Harwood, *Critics, Values, and Restoration Comedy*, 1982. • Derek Hughes, *English Drama 1660–1700*, 1996. • Robert D. Hume, *The Development of English Drama in the Late Seventeenth Century*, 1976. • Robert D.

Hume, *The Rakish Stage: Studies in English Drama, 1660–1800*, 1983. • John Loftis, ed., *Restoration Drama*, 1966. • Robert Markley, *Two-Edg'd Weapons: Style and Ideology in the Comedies of Etherege, Wycherley, and Congreve*, 1988. • Earl Miner, ed., *Restoration Dramatists*, 1966. • Allardyce Nicoll, *A History of English Drama, 1660–1900*, vols. 1–3 (1660–1800) 1952. • Susan J. Owen, ed. *A Companion to Restoration Drama*, 2001. • David Roberts, *The Ladies: Female Patronage of Restoration Drama, 1660–1700*, 1989.

Fiction • Nancy Armstrong, *Desire and Domestic Fiction*, 1989. • Jerry C. Beasley, *English Fiction, 1660–1800: A Guide to Information Sources*, 1978. • John Bender, *Imaging the Penitentiary*, 1987. • Terry Castle, *Masquerade and Civilization*, 1986. • Leopold Damrosch, *God's Plot and Man's Stories*, 1985. • Lennard J. Davis, *Factual Fictions: The Origins of the English Novel*, 1983. • Margaret Anne Doody, *The True Story of the Novel*, 1996. • Christopher Flint, *Family Fictions: Narrative and Domestic Relations in Britain, 1688–1789*, 2000. • J. Paul Hunter, *Before Novels*, 1990. • Deidre Shauna Lynch, *The Economy of Character: Novels, Market Culture, and the Business of Inner Meaning*, 1998. • Michael McKeon, *The Origins of the English Novel, 1660–1740*, 1987. • John Richetti, ed., *The Cambridge Companion to the Eighteenth-Century Novel*, 1996. • John Richetti, *The English Novel in History 1700–1780*, 1999. • John Richetti, *Popular Fiction Before Richardson*, 1969. • Paul Salzman, *English Prose Fiction, 1558–1700: A Critical History*, 1985. • Mary Ann Schofield and Cecelia Macheski, *Fetter'd or Free? British Women Novelists, 1670–1815*, 1986. • Jane Spencer, *The Rise of the Woman Novelist*, 1986. • Ian Watt, *The Rise of the Novel: Studies in Defoe, Richardson, and Fielding*, 1957.

Poetry • Carol Barash, *English Women's Poetry, 1649–1714: Politics, Community, and Linguistic Authority*, 1997. • Margaret Doody, *The Daring Muse: Augustan Poetry Reconsidered*, 1985. • Germaine Greer et al., eds., *Kissing the Rod: An Anthology of Seventeenth-Century Women's Verse*, 1988. • Jean Hagstrum, *The Sister Arts: The Tradition of Literary Pictorialism and English Poetry from Dryden to Gray*, 1958. • Ian Jack, *Augustan Satire: Intention and Idiom in English Poetry, 1660–1750*, 1952. • Donna Landry, *The Muses of Resistance: Laboring-Class Women's Poetry in Britain, 1739–1796*, 1990. • Roger Lonsdale, ed., *The New Oxford Book of Eighteenth-*

Century Verse, 1984. • Roger Lonsdale, ed., *Eighteenth-Century Women Poets*, 1990. • Eric Rothstein, *Restoration and Eighteenth-Century Poetry, 1660–1800*, 1981. • Patricia Spacks, *The Poetry of Vision*, 1967. • James Sutherland, *A Preface to Eighteenth-Century Poetry*, 1948. • Howard Weinbrot, *The Formal Strain: Studies in Augustan Imitation and Satire*, 1969.

Satire • Ronald Paulson, *The Fictions of Satire*, 1967. • Claude Rawson, ed., *English Satire and the Satiric Tradition*, 1984. • Claude Rawson, *Order from Confusion Sprung*, 1985. • Michael Seidel, *Satiric Inheritance: Rabelais to Sterne*, 1979.

Letters, Diaries, Autobiography, Biography • Howard Anderson, Philip B. Daghlian, and Irvin Ehrenpreis, eds., *The Familiar Letter in the Eighteenth Century*, 1966. • William Epstein, *Recognizing Biography*, 1987. • Michael Mascuch, *Origins of the Individualist Self: Autobiography and Self-Identity in England, 1591–1791*, 1996. • Felicity Nussbaum, *The Autobiographical Subject: Gender and Ideology in Eighteenth-Century England*, 1989. • Bruce Redford, *The Converse of the Pen: Acts of Intimacy in the Eighteenth-Century Familiar Letter*, 1987. • Stuart Sherman, *Telling Time: Clocks, Diaries, and English Diurnal Form, 1660–1785*, 1996. • Patricia Meyer Spacks, *Imagining a Self: Autobiography and Novel in Eighteenth-Century England*, 1976. • Richard Wendorf, *The Elements of Life: Biography and Portrait Painting in Stuart and Georgian England*, 1990.

Perspectives: Mind and God (See also "Cultural and Intellectual Backgrounds") • Jonathan Bennett, *Locke, Berkeley, Hume: Central Themes*, 1971. • James Collins, *The British Empiricists*, 1967. • Peter Gay, ed., *The Enlightenment: A Comprehensive Anthology*, 1973. • John J. Richetti, *Philosophical Writing: Locke, Berkeley, Hume*, 1983. • Keith Thomas, ed., *The British Empiricists*, 1992. • Richard S. Westfall, *Science and Religion in Seventeenth-Century England*, 1958. • R. S. Woolhouse, *The Empiricists*, 1988. • John W. Yolton, *Perception and Reality: A History from Descartes to Kant*, 1996. • John W. Yolton, ed., *Philosophy, Religion, and Science in the Seventeenth and Eighteenth Centuries*, 1990.

Perspectives: Reading Papers • Jeremy Black, *The English Press in the Eighteenth Century*, 1986. • Donovan H. Bond and W. Reynolds McLeod, eds., *Newsletters to Newspapers: Eighteenth-*

Century Journalism, 1977. • Richmond P. Bond, ed., Studies in the Early English Periodical, 1957. • C. L. Carlson, The First Magazine: A History of The Gentleman's Magazine, 1938. • J. A. Downie and Thomas N. Corns, eds., Telling People What to Think: Early Eighteenth-Century Periodicals from The Review to The Rambler, 1993. • Walter Graham, English Literary Periodicals, 1930. • Joad Raymond, The Invention of the Newspaper, 1996. • Kathryn Shevelow, Women and Print Culture: The Construction of Femininity in the Early Periodical, 1989. • C. John Sommerville, The News Revolution in England, 1996. • James Sutherland, The Restoration Newspaper and its Development, 1986. • Katherine K. Weed and Richmond P. Bond, Studies of British Newspapers and Periodicals from Their Beginning to 1800: A Bibliography, 1946.

Perspectives: The Royal Society and the New Science • I. Bernard Cohen with K. E. Duffin and Stuart Strickland, eds., Puritanism and the Rise of Modern Science: The Merton Thesis, 1990. • Michael Hunter, Science and Society in Restoration England, 1981. • Michael Hunter, Science and the Shape of Orthodoxy: Intellectual Change in Late Seventeenth-Century Britain, 1995. • Michael Hunter, The Royal Society and Its Fellows, 1660–1700: The Morphology of an Early Scientific Institution, 2nd ed., 1994. • Lisa Jardine, Ingenious Pursuits: Building the Scientific Revolution, 2000. • Londa Schiebinger, The Mind Has No Sex: Women in the Origins of Modern Science, 1989. • Londa Schiebinger, Nature's Body: Gender in the Making of Modern Science, 1993. • Steven Shapin and Simon Schaffer, Leviathan and the Air-Pump: Hobbes, Boyle, and the Experimental Life, 1985. • Steven Shapin, The Scientific Revolution, 1996. • Steven Shapin, A Social History of Truth: Civility and Science in Seventeenth-Century England, 1994. • Larry R. Stewart, The Rise of Public Science: Rhetoric, Technology and Natural Philosophy in Newtonian Britain, 1660–1750, 1992. • Geoffrey V. Sutton, Science for a Polite Society: Gender, Culture, and the Demonstration of Enlightenment, 1995. • Catherine Wilson, The Invisible World: Early Modern Philosophy and the Invention of the Microscope, 1995. • John W. Yolton, ed., Philosophy, Religion, and Science in the Seventeenth and Eighteenth Centuries, 1990.

Joseph Addison and Richard Steele • Editions. • Donald F. Bond, ed., The Spectator, 5 vols., 1965. • Donald F. Bond, ed., The Tatler, 3 vols.,

1987. • Erin Mackie, ed., The Commerce of Everyday Life: Selections from The Tatler and The Spectator, 1998. • Angus Ross, ed., Selections from The Tatler and The Spectator, 1988.

Biographies. • George A. Aitken, The Life of Richard Steele, 2 vols., 1889. • Peter Smithers, The Life of Joseph Addison, 1954. • Calhoun Winton, Captain Steele: The Early Career of Richard Steele, 1964. • Calhoun Winton, Sir Richard Steele M.P.: The Later Career, 1970.

Criticism. • Scott Black, "Social and Literary Form in the Spectator," Eighteenth-Century Studies, vol. 33, 1999. • Edward A. Bloom and Lillian D. Bloom, eds., Addison and Steele, the Critical Heritage, 1980. • Edward A. Bloom, Joseph Addison's Sociable Animal, 1971. • Michael G. Ketcham, Transparent Designs: Reading, Performance and Form in the Spectator Papers, 1985. • Erin Mackie, Market à la Mode: Fashion, Commodity, and Gender in The Tatler and The Spectator, 1997.

Mary Astell • Editions. • Bridget Hill, ed., The First English Feminist: Reflections upon Marriage and Other Writings by Mary Astell, 1986. • Patricia Springborg, ed., Political Writings, 1996. • Patricia Springborg, ed., A Serious Proposal to the Ladies, parts I and II, 1997.

Biography. • Ruth Perry, The Celebrated Mary Astell: An Early English Feminist, 1986.

Criticism. • Catherine Gallagher, "Embracing the Absolute: The Politics of the Female Subject in Seventeenth-Century England," Gender, vol. 1, 1988.

John Aubrey • Editions. • Andrew Clark, ed., "Brief Lives," Chiefly of Contemporaries, Set Down by John Aubrey, Between the Years 1669 & 1696, 2 vols., 1898. • Oliver Lawson Dick, ed., Aubrey's Brief Lives, 1949.

Biographies. • Anthony Powell, John Aubrey and His Friends, 1988. • David Tylden-Wright, John Aubrey: A Life, 1991.

Criticism. • Michael Hunter, John Aubrey and the Realm of Learning, 1975.

Aphra Behn • Editions. • Catherine Gallagher, ed., Oroonoko, 2000. • Joanna Lipking, ed., Oroonoko: An Authoritative Text, Historical Backgrounds, Criticism, 1997. • Janet Todd, ed., Oroonoko, The Rover, and other Works, 1992. • Janet Todd, ed., The Works of Aphra Behn, 7 vols., 1992–1996.

Biography. • Janet Todd, *The Secret Life of Aphra Behn*, 1997.

Criticism. • Laura Brown, "The Romance of Empire: Oroonoko and the Trade in Slaves," *The New Eighteenth Century*, eds. Felicity Nussbaum and Laura Brown, 1987. • Margaret W. Ferguson, "Juggling the Categories of Race, Class and Gender: Aphra Behn's Oroonoko," *Women's Studies*, vol. 19, 1991. • Oddvar Holmesland, "Aphra Behn's Oroonoko: Cultural Dialectics and the Novel," *ELH*, vol. 68, 2001. • Catherine Gallagher, "The Author-Monarch and the Royal Slave: Oroonoko and the Blackness of Representation," *Nobody's Story: The Vanishing Acts of Women Writers in the Marketplace, 1670–1820*, 1994. • Heidi Hutner, ed., *Rereading Aphra Behn*, 1993. • Sara Heller Mendelson, *The Mental World of Stuart Women: Three Studies*, 1987. • Mary Ann O'Donnell, *Aphra Behn: An Annotated Bibliography*, 1986. • M. I. Stapleton, "Aphra Behn, Libertine," *Restoration*, vol. 24, 2000. • Janet Todd, ed., *Aphra Behn Studies*, 1996.

George Berkeley • Editions. • M. R. Ayers, ed., *Philosophical Works, Including the Works on Vision*, rev. ed., 1980. • A. A. Luce and T. E. Jessop, eds., *The Works of George Berkeley, Bishop of Cloyne*, 9 vols., 1948–1952.

Biography. • A. A. Luce, *The Life of George Berkeley, Bishop of Cloyne*, 1949.

Criticism. • David Berman, ed., *George Berkeley: Eighteenth-Century Responses*, 2 vols., 1989. • Jonathan Dancy, *Berkeley, an Introduction*, 1987. • A. C. Grayling, *Berkeley: The Central Arguments*, 1986. • K. P. Winkler, *Berkeley: An Interpretation*, 1989.

James Boswell • Editions. • R. W. Chapman, ed., *Life of Johnson*, rev. J. D. Fleeman. 1970. • G. B. Hill and L. F. Powell, eds., *Boswell's Life of Johnson*, 6 vols., 1934–1964. • Frederick A. Pottle, et al., eds., *The Yale Editions of the Private Papers of James Boswell*, 1950–. • Frederick A. Pottle, ed., *Boswell's London Journal, 1762–1763*, 1950. • Frederick A. Pottle and Charles H. Bennett, eds., *Boswell's Journal of a Tour to the Hebrides with Samuel Johnson, 1773*, 1963. • John Wain, ed., *The Journals of James Boswell, 1762–1795*, 1991.

Biographies. • Frank Brady, *James Boswell, the Later Years, 1769–1795*, 1984. • Mary Hyde, *The Impossible Friendship: Boswell and Mrs. Thrale*, 1972. • Peter Martin, *A Life of James Boswell*, 2000. • Frederick A. Pottle, *James Boswell, the Earlier Years, 1740–1769*, 1985. • Frederick A. Pottle, *The Literary Career of James Boswell*, 1929.

Criticism. • (See Also the Listings of Criticism on Samuel Johnson). • Hamilton Cochrane, *Boswell's Literary Art: An Annotated Bibliography of Critical Studies*, 1992. • James L. Clifford, ed., *Twentieth Century Interpretations of Boswell's* Life of Johnson, 1970. • Greg Clingham, ed., *New Light on Boswell: Critical and Historical Essays on the Occasion of the Bicentenary of* The Life of Johnson, 1991. • Irma S. Lustig, ed., *Boswell: Citizen of the World, Man of Letters*, 1995 • Adam Sisman, *Boswell's Presumptuous Task*, 2001. • John A. Vance, ed., *Boswell's Life of Johnson: New Questions, New Answers*, 1995.

Mary Carleton • Edition. • Janet Todd and Elizabeth Spearing, eds., "The Case of Madam Mary Carleton," *Counterfeit Ladies: The Life and Death of Moll Cutpurse, The Case of Mary Carleton*, 1994.

Criticism. • Hero Chalmers, "The Person I Am, or What They Made Me To Be: The Construction of the Feminine Subject in the Autobiographies of Mary Carleton," *Women, Texts and Histories 1575–1760*, eds. Clare Brant and Diane Purkiss, 1992. • Mihoko Suzuki, "The Case of Mary Carleton: Representing the Female Subject, 1663–1673," *Tulsa Studies in Women's Literature*, vol. 12, no. 1, 1993. • Janet Todd, "The German Princess: Criminalities of Gender and Class," in Rosamaria Loretellie and Roberto De Romanis, eds. *Narrating Transgression*, 1999.

Margaret Lucas Cavendish, Duchess of Newcastle • Editions. • Kate Lilley, ed., The Blazing World *and Other Writings*, 1994. • Paul Salzman, ed. The Blazing World, *An Anthology of Seventeenth-Century Fiction*, 1991.

Biography. • Kathleen Jones, *A Glorious Fame: The Life of Margaret Cavendish, Duchess of Newcastle*, 1988.

Criticism • Anna Battigelli, *Margaret Cavendish and the Exiles of the Mind*, 1998. • Catherine Gallagher, "Embracing the Absolute: The Politics of the Female Subject in Seventeenth-Century England," *Genders*, vol. 1, 1988. • Rosemary Kegl, "The World I Have Made: Margaret Cavendish, Feminism, and the Blazing World," *Feminist Readings of Early Modern Culture*, eds. Valerie Traub, M. Lindsay Kaplan, and Dympna Callaghan, 1996. • Eve Keller, "Producing Petty Gods: Margaret Cavendish's Critique of Experimental Science," *English Literary History*, vol. 64, no. 2, 1997. • Sara Heller Mendelson, *The Mental World of Stuart Women: Three Studies*, 1987. • John Rogers, *The Matter of Revolution: Science, Poetry, and Politics in the Age of Milton*, 1996.

Mary, Lady Chudleigh • Edition. • Margaret J. M. Ezell, ed., *The Poems and Prose of Mary, Lady Chudleigh*, 1993.

Criticism. • Carol Barash, *"The Native Liberty."*

William Collins • Editions. • Roger Lonsdale, ed., *The Poems of Gray, Collins and Goldsmith*, 1969. • Richard Wendorf and Charles Ryskamp, eds., *The Works of William Collins*, 1979.

Biography. • Edward Gay Ainsworth, *Poor Collins: His Life, His Art, and His Influence*, 1937. • P. L. Carver, *The Life of a Poet: A Biographical Sketch of William Collins*, 1967.

Criticism. • Richard Wendorf, *William Collins and Eighteenth-Century English Poetry*, 1981.

William Cowper • Editions. • John D. Baird and Charles Ryskamp, eds., *The Poems of William Cowper*, 3 vols., 1980–1995. • James King and Charles Ryskamp, eds., *The Letters and Prose Writings of William Cowper*, 5 vols., 1979–1986. • James Sambrook, ed., *"The Task" and Selected Other Poems*, 1994.

Biography. • James King, *William Cowper: A Biography*, 1986. • Charles Ryskamp, *William Cowper of the Inner Temple, Esq.*, 1959.

Criticism. • Morris Golden, *In Search of Stability: The Poetry of William Cowper*, 1960. • Vincent Newey, *Cowper's Poetry: A Critical Study and Reassessment*, 1982.

George Crabbe • Edition. • Norma Dalrymple-Champneys and Arthur Pollard, *George Crabbe: The Complete Poetical Works*, 3 vols., 1988.

Biography. • George Crabbe, *The Life of George Crabbe by His Son*, introd. Edmund Blunden, 1947.

Criticism. • Jerome McGann, "The Anachronism of George Crabbe," *English Literary History*, vol. 48, no. 3, 1981. • Peter New, *George Crabbe's Poetry*, 1976. • Mark Storey, "George Crabbe (1754–1832)," in *A Handbook to English Romanticism*, eds. Jean Raimond and J. R. Watson, 1992. • Frank Whitehead, "Crabbe,

'Realism', and Poetic Truth," *Essays in Criticism*, vol. 39, no. 1, 1989.

Daniel Defoe • Editions. • Paula Backscheider, ed., *A Journal of the Plague Year*, 1992. • P. N. Furbank and W. R. Owens, eds., The True-Born Englishman *and Other Writings*, 1997. • Louis Landa and David Roberts, eds., A Journal of the Plague Year: *Text, Backgrounds, Criticism*, 1990. • William L. Payne, ed., *The Best of Defoe's* Review: *An Anthology*, 1951. • Manuel Schonhorn, *Accounts of the Apparition of Mrs. Veal*, 1965.

Biography. • Paula R. Backscheider, *Daniel Defoe: His Life*, 1989. • Maximillian E. Novak, *Daniel Defoe, Master of Fictions*, 2001.

Criticism. • Paula R. Backscheider, *Daniel Defoe: Ambition and Innovation*, 1986. • Rodney Baine, *Daniel Defoe and the Supernatural*, 1979. • David Blewett, *Defoe's Art of Fiction*, 1979. • Lincoln B. Faller, *Crime and Defoe: A New Kind of Writing*, 1993. • P. N. Furbank and W. R. Owens, *The Canonisation of Daniel Defoe*, 1988. • J. Paul Hunter, *The Reluctant Pilgrim: Defoe's Emblematic Method and Quest for Form in Robinson Crusoe*, 1966. • Roger D. Lund, ed., *Critical Essays on Daniel Defoe*, 1997. • Watson Nicholson, *The Historical Sources of Defoe's* Journal of the Plague Year, 1919. • Watson Nicholson, *Realism, Myth and History in Defoe's Fiction*, 1983. • Maximillian E. Novak, *Economics and the Fiction of Daniel Defoe*, 1962. • Maximillian E. Novak, *Realism, Myth, and History in Defoe's Fiction*, 1983. • William Payne, *Mr. Review: Daniel Defoe as the Author of the* Review, 1961. • John J. Richetti, *Daniel Defoe*, 1987. • John J. Richetti, *Defoe's Narratives*, 1975. • Pat Rogers, ed., *Defoe, the Critical Heritage*, 1972.

John Dryden • Editions. • Paul Hammond, *The Poems of John Dryden*, 1995–. • James Kinsley, ed., *The Poems and Fables of John Dryden*, 1962. • H. T. Swedenberg, Jr. and Edward Niles Hooker, eds., *Works*, 20 vols., 1961–. • Keith Walker, ed., *John Dryden*, 1987. • George Watson, ed., *"Of Dramatick Poesy" and Other Critical Essays*, 2 vols., 1962. • Steven N. Zwicker, ed., *Selected Poems*, 2002.

Biographies. • Paul Hammond, *John Dryden: A Literary Life*, 1991. • James Anderson Winn, *John Dryden and His World*, 1987.

Criticism. • Reuben Brower, "An Allusion to Europe: Dryden and Poetic Tradition," *English Literary History*, vol. 19, 1952. • David A. Bywaters, *Dryden in Revolutionary England*, 1991. • Michael Werth Gelber, *The Just and the Lively: The Literary Criticism of John Dryden*, 1999. • Phillip Harth, *Contexts of Dryden's Thought*, 1968. • Geoffrey Hill, *The Enemy's Country*, 1991. • David Hopkins, *John Dryden*, 1986. • Robert Hume, *Dryden's Criticism*, 1970. • James and Helen Kinsley, *Dryden: The Critical Heritage*, 1971. • Earl Miner, *Dryden's Poetry*, 1967. • Earl Miner, ed., *John Dryden*, 1972. • H. T. Swedenborg, ed., *Essential Articles for the Study of John Dryden*, 1966. • James A. Winn, ed., *Critical Essays on John Dryden*, 1997. • David Wykes, *A Preface to Dryden*, 1977. • Steven N. Zwicker, *Dryden's Political Poetry: The Typology of King and Nation*, 1972. • Steven N. Zwicker, *Politics and Language in Dryden's Poetry: The Arts of Disguise*, 1984.

John Evelyn • Editions. • John Bowie, *The Diary of John Evelyn*, 1983. • E. S. de Beer, *The Diary of John Evelyn*, 6 vols., 1955.

Biography. • John Bowie, *John Evelyn and His World*, 1981.

Anne Finch, Countess of Winchilsea • Editions. • Myra Reynolds, ed., *The Poems of Anne, Countess of Winchilsea*, 1903. • Katherine M. Rogers, ed., *Selected Poems of Anne Finch, Countess of Winchilsea*, 1979.

Biography. • Barbara McGovern, *Anne Finch and Her Poetry: A Critical Biography*, 1992.

Criticism. • Charles H. Hinnant, *The Poetry of Anne Finch*, 1994.

John Gay • Editions. • Vinton A. Dearing and Charles Beckwith, eds., *John Gay: Poetry and Prose*, 2 vols., 1974. • John Fuller, *John Gay: Dramatic Works*, 2 vols., 1983. • Bryan Loughery and T. O. Treadwell, eds., *The Beggar's Opera*, 1987. • Edgar V. Roberts, ed., *The Beggar's Opera*, 1969.

Biography. • David Nokes, *John Gay: A Profession of Friendship*, 1995.

Criticism. • Sven Armens, *John Gay, Social Critic*, 1954. Dianne Dugaw, *"Deep Play": John Gay and the Invention of Modernity*, 2001. • William Empson, "The Beggar's Opera: Mock-Pastoral as the Cult of Independence," *Some Versions of Pastoral*, 1935. • Michael Friedman, "He Was Just a Macheath: Boswell and The Beggar's Opera," *Age of Johnson*, vol. 4, 1991. • Peter Elfed Lewis, *John Gay: The Beggar's Opera*, 1976. • Peter Lewis and Nigel

Wood, eds., *John Gay and the Scriblerians*, 1988. • Yvonne Noble, ed., *Twentieth-Century Interpretations of* The Beggar's Opera: *A Collection of Critical Essays*, 1975. • Calhoun Winton, *John Gay and the London Theatre*, 1993.

Oliver Goldsmith • Editions. • Arthur Friedman, ed., *Collected Works of Oliver Goldsmith*, 5 vols., 1966. • Roger Lonsdale, ed., *The Poems of Gray, Collins and Goldsmith*, 1969.

Biography. • Ralph M. Wardle, *Oliver Goldsmith*, 1957.

Criticism. • John Barrell, *The Dark Side of the Landscape: The Rural Poor in English Painting, 1730–1840*, 1980. • Howard J. Bell, Jr., "The Deserted Village and Goldsmith's Social Doctrines," *PMLA*, vol. 59, 1944. • Peter Dixon, *Oliver Goldsmith Revisited*, 1991. • Alfred Lutz, "The Deserted Village, and the Politics of Genre," *Modern Language Quarterly*, vol. 55, no. 2, 1994. • G. S. Rousseau, ed., *Goldsmith, the Critical Heritage*, 1974. • Andrew Swarbrick, ed., *The Art of Oliver Goldsmith*, 1984.

Thomas Gray • Editions. • Roger Lonsdale, ed., *The Poems of Gray, Collins and Goldsmith*, 1969. • Alastair Macdonald, ed., *An Elegy Wrote in a Country Church Yard*, 1976. • H. W. Starr and J. R. Hendrickson, eds., *The Complete Poems of Thomas Gray: English, Latin and Greek*, 1966. • Paget Toynbee and Leonard Whibley, eds., *The Correspondence of Thomas Gray*, rev. ed., 1971.

Biography. • Robert L. Mack, *Thomas Gray: A Life*, 2000. • R. W. Ketton-Cremer, *Thomas Gray*, 1955.

Criticism. • F. W. Hilles and Harold Bloom, eds., *From Sensibility to Romanticism*, 1965. • James Downey and Ben Jones, eds., *Fearful Joy: Papers from the Thomas Gray Bicentenary Conference*, 1974. • Robert F. Gleckner, *Gray Agonistes: Thomas Gray and Masculine Friendship*, 1997. • Morris Golden, *Thomas Gray*, 1988. • W. B. Hutchings and William Ruddick, eds., *Thomas Gray: Contemporary Essays*, 1993. • Suvir Kaul, *Thomas Gray and Literary Authority: A Study in Ideology and Poetics*, 1992. • Vincent Newey, "The Selving of Thomas Gray," *Centring the Self: Subjectivity, Society, and Reading from Thomas Gray to Thomas Hardy*, 1995. • Herbert W. Starr, *Twentieth-Century Interpretations of Gray's Elegy*, 1968. • Frank A. Vaughan, *Again to the Life of Eternity: William Blake's Illustrations of the Poems of Thomas Gray*, 1995. • Henry

Winefield, *The Poet Without a Name: Gray's Elegy and the Problem of History*, 1991.

Eliza Haywood • Editions. • *The Female Spectator*, 1745–1746. • Gabrielle M. Firmager, ed., The Female Spectator: *Being Selections from Mrs. Eliza Haywood's Periodical, First Published in Monthly Parts (1744–6)*, 1993. • Mary Priestley, The Female Spectator: *Being Selections from Mrs. Eliza Haywood's Periodical*, 1929.

Biography. • Mary Anne Schofield, *Eliza Haywood*, 1985.

Criticism. • James Hodges, "The Female Spectator: A Courtesy Periodical," *Studies in the Early English Periodical*, ed. Richmond Bond, 1957. • Helene Koon, "Eliza Haywood and *The Female Spectator*," *Huntington Library Quarterly*, vol. 42, 1978–1979. • Kathryn Shevelow, "Re-Writing the Moral Essay: Eliza Haywood's *Female Spectator*," *Reader*, vol. 13, 1985.

William Hogarth • Editions. • Ronald Paulson, ed., *The Analysis of Beauty*, 1998. • Ronald Paulson, ed., *Hogarth's Graphic Works*, 3rd ed., 1989. • Sean Shesgreen, ed., *Engravings by Hogarth*, 1973.

Biographies. • Ronald Paulson, *Hogarth*, 3 vols., 1991–1993. • Jenny Uglow, *Hogarth: A Life and a World*, 1997.

Criticism. • David Bindman, *Hogarth*, 1981. • David Dabydeen, *Hogarth, Walpole, and Commercial Britain*, 1987. • Bernadette Fort and Angela Rosenthal, eds., *The Other Hogarth: Aesthetics of Difference*, 2001. • Ronald Paulson, *The Art of Hogarth*, 1975.

Robert Hooke • Criticism. • Ellen Tan Drake, *Restless Genius: Robert Hooke and his Earthly Thoughts*, 1996. • Michael Hunter and Simon Schaffer, eds., *Robert Hooke: New Studies*, 1989.

David Hume • Editions. • Antony Flew, ed., *An Enquiry Concerning Human Understanding*, 1988. • Selby-Bigge and P. H. Nidditch, eds., *Enquiries Concerning Human Understanding and Concerning the Principles of Morals*, 3rd ed., 1975. • Selby-Bigge and P. H. Nidditch, eds., *A Treatise of Human Nature*, 2nd ed., 1978.

Biography. • E. E. Mossner, *The Life of David Hume*, 1954.

Criticism. • A. J. Ayer, *Hume*, 1980. • John Bricke, *Hume's Philosophy of Mind*, 1980. •

V. C. Chappell, ed., *Hume*, 1966. • Jerome Christensen, *Practicing Enlightenment: Hume and the Formation of a Literary Career*, 1987. • Antony Flew, *David Hume, Philosopher of Moral Science*, 1986. • J. C. A. Gaskin, *Hume's Philosophy of Religion*, rev. ed. 1988. • Norman Kemp Smith, *The Philosophy of David Hume*, 1941. • David Fate Norton, ed., *The Cambridge Companion to Hume*, 1993.

Samuel Johnson • Editions. • Frank Brady and W. K. Wimsatt, eds., *Selected Poetry and Prose*, 1977. • J. D. Fleeman, *A Journey to the Western Islands of Scotland*, 1985. • Donald Greene, ed., *Samuel Johnson*, 1984. • G. B. Hill, ed., *Johnson's Lives of the English Poets*, 3 vols., 1905. • Peter Levi, A Journey to the Western Islands of Scotland *and* The Journal of a Tour to the Hebrides, 1984. • E. L. McAdam, Jr. and George Milne, *Johnson's Dictionary: A Modern Selection*, 1963. • E. L. McAdam, Jr. et al., eds., *The Yale Edition of the Works of Samuel Johnson*, 14 vols., 1958–. • Anne McDermott, ed., *A Dictionary of the English Language* on CD-ROM [computer file], 1996. • Bruce Redford, ed., *The Letters of Samuel Johnson*, 5 vols., 1992–1994. • Pat Rogers, *Johnson and Boswell in Scotland: A Journey to the Hebrides*, 1993.

Biographies. • Walter Jackson Bate, *Samuel Johnson*, 1977. • James Boswell, *Boswell's Life of Johnson*, eds. G. B. Hill and L. F. Powell, 6 vols., 1934–1964. • O. M. Brack, Jr. and Robert E. Kelley, *The Early Biographies of Samuel Johnson*, 1974. • James L. Clifford, *Dictionary Johnson: The Middle Years of Samuel Johnson*, 1979. • James L. Clifford, *Young Sam Johnson*, 1955. • Robert DeMaria, Jr., *The Life of Samuel Johnson: A Critical Biography*, 1993. • John Hawkins, *The Life of Samuel Johnson, LL.D.*, ed. Bertram Davis, 1961. • G. B. Hill, ed., *Johnsonian Miscellanies*, 2 vols., 1897. • Thomas Kaminski, *The Early Career of Samuel Johnson*, 1987. • Lawrence I. Lipking, *Samuel Johnson: The Life of an Author*, 2000. • John Wain, *Samuel Johnson*, 1974.

Criticism. • Walter Jackson Bate, *The Achievement of Samuel Johnson*, 1955. • Harold Bloom, ed., *Modern Critical Views: Dr. Samuel Johnson and James Boswell*, 1986. • James T. Boulton, ed., *Johnson, the Critical Heritage*, 1971. • Jonathan Clark and Howard Erskine-Hill, eds., *Samuel Johnson in Historical Context*, 2002. • James L. Clifford and Donald Greene, *Johnsonian Studies, 1887–1950: A Survey and Bibliography*, 1951. • Greg Clingham, *The*

Cambridge Companion to Samuel Johnson, 1997. • Leopold Damrosch, *The Uses of Johnson's Criticism*, 1976. • Philip Davis, *In Mind of Johnson: A Study of Johnson the Rambler*, 1989. • Robert DeMaria, Jr., *Johnson's, Dictionary, and the Language of Learning*, 1986. • Robert DeMaria, Jr., *Samuel Johnson and the Life of Reading*, 1997. • Robert Folkenflik, *Samuel Johnson, Biographer*, 1978. • Paul Fussell, *Samuel Johnson and the Life of Writing*, 1971. • Donald Greene, *The Politics of Samuel Johnson*, 2nd ed., 1990. • Donald Greene and John A. Vance, *A Bibliography of Johnsonian Studies, 1970–1985*, 1987. • Isobel Grundy, ed., *Samuel Johnson: New Critical Essays*, 1984. • Jean H. Hagstrum, *Samuel Johnson's Literary Criticism*, 1967. • Kevin Hart, *Samuel Johnson and the Culture of Property*, 1999. • Nicholas Hudson, *Samuel Johnson and Eighteenth-Century Thought*, 1988. • Paul J. Korshin, ed., *Johnson after Two Hundred Years*, 1986. • Jack Lynch, *A Bibliography of Johnson Studies, 1986–1998*, 2000. • G. F. Parker, *Johnson's Shakespeare*, 1989. • Allen Reddick, *The Making of Johnson's Dictionary, 1746–1773*, 1996. • Pat Rogers, *Johnson and Boswell: The Transit of Caledonia*, 1995. • Pat Rogers, *The Samuel Johnson Encyclopedia*, 1996. • Arthur Sherbo, *Samuel Johnson's Critical Opinions: A Reexamination*, 1995. • James H. Sledd and Gwin J. Kolb, *Dr. Johnson's Dictionary: Essays in the Biography of a Book*, 1955. • Robert D. Spector, *Samuel Johnson and the Essay*, 1997. • David F. Venturo, *Johnson the Poet*, 1999. David Wheeler, ed., *Domestick Privacies*, 1987. • William K. Wimsatt, *Philosophic Words: A Study of Style and Meaning in the Rambler and Dictionary of Samuel Johnson*, 1948. • William K. Wimsatt, *The Prose Style of Samuel Johnson*, 1941. • Thomas M. Woodman, *A Preface to Samuel Johnson*, 1993.

Mary Leapor • Biography and Criticism. • Richard Greene, *Mary Leapor: A Study in Eighteenth-Century Women's Poetry*, 1993.

John Locke • Editions. • Peter H. Nidditch, ed., *An Essay Concerning Human Understanding*, 1975. • J. W. Yolton, *The Locke Reader*, 1977.

Criticism. • R. I. Aaron, *John Locke*, rev. ed., 1955. • Vere Chappell, ed., *The Cambridge Companion to Locke*, 1994. • John Dunn, *Locke*, 1984. • Christopher Fox, *Locke and the Scriblerians: Identity and Consciousness in Early Eighteenth-Century Britain*, 1988. • W. M. Spellman, *John Locke*, 1997. • John W. Yolton, *Locke: An Introduction*, 1985.

Lady Mary Wortley Montagu • Editions. • Robert Halsband, ed., *The Complete Letters of Lady Mary Wortley Montagu, 1965–1967*. • Robert Halsband and Isobel Grundy, eds., *Essays and Poems and Simplicity, a Comedy*, 1977. • Malcolm Jack, ed., *Turkish Embassy Letters*, 1993.

Biography. • Robert Halsband, *The Life of Lady Mary Wortley Montagu*, 1956.

Criticism. • Jill Campbell, "Lady Mary Wortley Montagu and the Historical Machinery of Female Identity," *History, Gender, and Eighteenth-Century Literature*, ed. Beth Fawkes Tobin, 1994. • Cynthia Lowenthal, *Lady Mary Wortley Montagu and the Eighteenth-Century Familiar Letter*, 1994. • Ruth Bernard Yeazell, "Public Baths and Private Harems: Lady Mary Wortley Montagu and the Origins of Ingres's *Bain Ture*," *Yale Journal of Criticism*, vol. 7, no. 1, 1994.

Sir Isaac Newton • Editions. • I. Bernard Cohen and Richard S. Westfall, eds., *Newton: Texts, Backgrounds, Commentaries*, 1995. • H. W. Turnbull, *The Correspondence of Isaac Newton*, 7 vols., 1959–1977.

Biography. • Richard S. Westfall, *Never at Rest*, 1980.

Criticism. • D. Gjertsen, *The Newton Handbook*, 1986. • F. E. Manuel, *The Religion of Isaac Newton*, 1974. • Marjorie Hope Nicolson, *Newton Demands the Muse: Newton's Opticks and the Eighteenth-Century Poets*, 1946.

Samuel Pepys • Editions. • Robert Latham, ed., *The Illustrated Pepys*, 1983. • Robert Latham, ed., *The Shorter Pepys*, 1985. • Robert Latham and William Matthews, eds., *The Diary of Samuel Pepys*, 11 vols., 1970–1983.

Biographies. • Arthur Bryant, *Samuel Pepys*, 3 vols., 3rd ed., 1967. • Richard Ollard, *Pepys: A Biography*, 1975. • J. R. Tanner, *Samuel Pepys and the Royal Navy*, 1920.

Criticism. • Francis Barker, *The Tremulous Private Body: Essays on Subjection*, rev. ed., 1995. • Harry Berger, Jr., "The Pepys Show: Ghost-Writing and Documentary Desire in the Diary," *ELH*, vol. 65, 1998. • Marjorie Hope Nicolson, *Pepys' Diary and the New Science*, 1965. • Robert Louis Stevenson, "Samuel Pepys," *Familiar Studies of Men and Books*, 1895. • Stuart Sherman, " 'In the Fullness of Time': Pepys and His Predecessors" and

"'With My Minute Wach in My Hand': The Diary as Timekeeper," *Telling Time: Clocks, Diaries, and English Diurnal Form, 1660–1785*, 1996. • James Grantham Turner, "Pepys and the Private Parts of Monarchy," in *Culture and Society in the Restoration*, ed. Gerald MacLean, 1995.

Hester Lynch Thrale Piozzi • Editions. • Katherine C. Balderston, ed., Thraliana; *the Diary of Mrs. Hester Lynch Thrale (later Mrs. Piozzi) 1776–1809*, 2nd ed., 1951. • Edward A. Bloom and Lillian D. Bloom, eds., *The Piozzi Letters*, 1989–. • A. Hayward, ed., *Autobiography, Letters and Literary Remains of Mrs. Piozzi (Thrale)*, 2 vols., 1975. • Mary Hyde, ed., *The Thrales of Streatham Park*, 1977.

Biographies. • James L. Clifford, *Hester Lynch Piozzi (Mrs. Thrale)*, rev. ed., 1968. • William McCarthy, *Hester Thrale Piozzi, Portrait of a Literary Woman*, 1985.

Criticism. • Martine Watson Brownely, "Eighteenth-Century Women's Images and Roles: The Case of Hester Thrale Piozzi," *Biography*, vol. 3, 1980. • Felicity A. Nussbaum, "Managing Women: Thrale's *Family Book* and *Thraliana*," *The Autobiographical Subject: Gender and Ideology in Eighteenth-Century England*, 1989. • John Riely, "Johnson and Mrs. Thrale: The Beginning and the End," *Johnson and His Age*, ed. James Engell, 1984. • Judy Simons, "The Unfixed Text: Narrative and Identity in Women's Private Writings," *The Representation of the Self in Women's Autobiography*, eds. Vita Fortunati and Gabriella Morisco, 1993.

Alexander Pope • Editions. • John Butt et al., eds., *The Twickenham Edition of the Poems of Alexander Pope*, 11 vols., 1940–1969. • John Butt, ed., *The Poems of Alexander Pope*, 1963. • George Sherburn, ed., *The Correspondence of Alexander Pope*, 5 vols., 1956. • Cynthia Wall, ed., *The Rape of the Lock*, 1998. • Aubrey Williams, ed., *Poetry and Prose of Alexander Pope*, 1969.

Biographies. • Maynard Mack, *Alexander Pope: A Life*, 1985. • George Sherburn, *The Early Career of Alexander Pope*, 1934. • Joseph Spence, *Observations, Anecdotes, and Characters of Books and Men*, ed. James M. Osborn, 2 vols., 1966.

Criticism. • Paul Baines, *The Complete Critical Guide to Alexander Pope*, 2001. • Reuben Brower, *Alexander Pope: The Poetry of Allusion*, 1959. • Laura Brown, *Alexander Pope*, 1985. • Morris Brownell, *Alexander Pope and the Arts of Georgian England*, 1978. • Helen Deutsch, *Resemblance and Disgrace: Alexander Pope and the Deformation of Culture*, 1996. • Howard Erskine-Hill, ed., *Alexander Pope: World and Word*, 1998. • Howard Erskine-Hill, *The Social Milieu of Alexander Pope*, 1978. • David Fairer, ed., *Pope: New Contexts*, 1990. • David Fairer, *Pope's Imagination*, 1984. • David F. Foxon, *Pope and the Eighteenth-Century Book Trade*, 1991. • Bertrand A. Goldgar, *Literary Criticism of Alexander Pope*, 1965. • Dustin Griffin, *Alexander Pope: The Poet in the Poems*, 1978. • Brean Hammond, ed., *Longman Critical Readers: Pope*, 1966. • J. Paul Hunter, "Pope and the Ideology of the Couplet," *Ideas*, vol. 4, no. 1, 1996. • Maynard Mack, *The Garden and the City: Retirement and Politics in the Later Poetry of Pope*, 1969. • Maynard Mack, ed., *Essential Articles for the Study of Alexander Pope*, 1968. • Maynard Mack and James Winn, eds., *Pope: Recent Essays by Several Hands*, 1980. • David B. Morris, *Alexander Pope: The Genius of Sense*, 1984. • Marjorie Hope Nicolson and G. S. Rousseau, "*This Long Disease, My Life*": *Alexander Pope and the Sciences*, 1968. • Valerie Rumbold, *Women's Place in Pope's World*, 1989. • Geoffrey Tillotson, *On the Poetry of Pope*, 2nd. ed., 1950. • Howard Weinbrot, *Alexander Pope and the Tradition of Formal Verse Satire*, 1982. • Aubrey L. Williams, *Pope's Dunciad: A Study of Its Meaning*, 1955.

Richard Brinsley Sheridan • Editions • F. W. Bateson, ed., *The School for Scandal*, 2nd. ed., 1995. • Cecil Price, ed., *The Dramatic Works of Richard Brinsley Sheridan*, 1973. • Bruce Redford, ed., *The Origins of The School for Scandal*, 1986.

Biographies • James Morwood, *The Life and Works of Richard Brinsley Sheridan*, 1985. • Fintan O'Toole, *A Traitor's Kiss*, 1998.

Criticism • Mark. S. Auburn, *Sheridan's Comedies*, 1977. • Peter Davidson, ed., *Sheridan's Comedies: A Casebook*, 1986. • Jack D. Durant, *Richard Brinsley Sheridan: A Reference Guide*, 1981. • John Loftis, *Sheridan and the Drama of Georgian England*, 1976. • James

Morwood and David Crane, *Sheridan Studies*, 1995.

Christopher Smart • Editions. • Karina Williamson, ed., *The Poetical Works of Christopher Smart*, 5 vols., 1980–1996. • Karina Williamson and Marcus Walsh, eds., *Selected Poems*, 1990.

Biographies. • Christopher Devlin, *Poor Kit Smart*, 1961. • Arthur Sherbo, *Christopher Smart, Scholar of the University*, 1967.

Criticism. • Moira Dearnely, *The Poetry of Christopher Smart*, 1967. • Harriet Guest, *A Form of Sound Words: The Religious Poetry of Christopher Smart*, 1989. • Geoffrey H. Hartmann, "Christopher Smart's, 'Magnificat',: Towards a Theory of Representation," *English Literary History*, vol. 41, 1974. • Clement Hawes, *Mania and Literary Style: The Rhetoric of Enthusiasm from the Ranters to Christopher Smart*, 1996.

Jonathan Swift • Editions. • Herbert Davis, ed., *The Prose Works of Jonathan Swift*, 14 vols., 1939–1968. • Christopher Fox, ed., *Gulliver's Travels: Complete, Authoritative Text with Biographical and Historical Contexts, Critical History, and Essays from Five Contemporary Critical Perspectives*, 1995. • A. C. Guthkelch and D. Nichol Smith, eds., *"A Tale of a Tub," to Which Is Added "The Battle of the Books," and the "Mechanical Operation of the Spirit,"* 2nd ed., 1958. • Pat Rogers, ed., *The Complete Poems*, 1983. • Harold Williams, ed., *The Correspondence of Jonathan Swift*, 5 vols., 1963–1965. • Harold Williams, ed., *Journal to Stella*, 2 vols., 1948. • Harold Williams, ed., *The Poems of Jonathan Swift*, 2nd ed., 3 vols., 1958.

Biographies. • Irvin Ehrenpreis, *Swift: The Man, His Works, and the Age*, 3 vols., 1962–1983. • Victoria Glendinning, *Jonathan Swift: A Portrait*, 1999. • David Nokes, *Jonathan Swift, A Hypocrite Reversed: A Critical Biography*, 1985.

Criticism. • Frank Boyle, *Swift as Nemesis: Modernity and Its Satirist*, 2000. • J. A. Downie, *Jonathan Swift: Political Writer*, 1985. • Robert C. Elliott, *The Power of Satire: Magic, Ritual, Art*, 1960. • Oliver W. Ferguson, *Jonathan Swift and Ireland*, 1962. • H. J. Real Fischer and J. Wooley, eds., *Swift and His Contexts*, 1989. • John Irwin Fischer and Donald C. Mell Jr., eds., *Contemporary Studies of Swift's Poetry*, 1980. • Carol Houlihan Flynn, *The Body in Swift and Defoe*, 1990. • Christopher Fox, ed., *Walking Naboth's Vineyard: New Studies of Swift*, 1995. • Nora Crow Jaffe, *The Poet Swift*, 1977. • Ellen Pollak, *The Poetics of Sexual Myth: Gender and Ideology in the Verse of Swift and Pope*, 1985. • Martin Price, *Swift's Rhetorical Art: A Study in Structure and Meaning*, 1953. • C. J. Rawson, ed., *The Character of Swift's Satire*, 1983. • Richard H. Rodino, *Swift Studies, 1965–1980: An Annotated Bibliography*, 1984. • Edward W. Rosenheim, *Swift and the Satirist's Art*, 1963. • Edward W. Said, "Swift as Intellectual" and "Swift's Tory Anarchy," *The World, the Text, and the Critic*, 1983. • Brian Vickers, ed., *The World of Jonathan Swift: Essays for the Tercentenary*, 1968. • David M. Vieth, *Swift's Poetry 1900–1980: An Annotated Bibliography of Studies*, 1982. • Kathleen Williams, ed., *Swift: The Critical Heritage*, 1970.

James Thomson • Editions. • James Sambrook, ed., *Liberty, The Castle of Indolence, and Other Poems*, 1986. • James Sambrook, ed., *The Seasons*, 1981. • James Sambrook, ed., *The Seasons and The Castle of Indolence*, 1972.

Biographies. • A. D. McKillop, *James Thomson: Letters and Documents*, 1958. • James Sambrook, *James Thomson, 1700–1748: A Life*, 1991. • Mary Jane W. Scott, *James Thomson, Anglo-Scot*, 1988.

Criticism. • John Barrell, *English Literature in History, 1730–1780*, 1983. • Ralph Cohen, *The Art of Discrimination: Thomson's The Seasons and the Language of Criticism*, 1964. • Ralph Cohen, *The Unfolding of The Seasons*, 1970. • Patricia Meyer Spacks, *The Varied God*, 1959.

Isaac Watts • Editions. • Bennett A. Brockman, ed., *Divine Songs Attempted in an Easy Language for the Use of Children*, 1978. • Bennett A. Brockman, *The Psalms and Hymns of Isaac Watts: With All the Additional Hymns and Complete Indexes*, 1997.

Biography. • Arthur Paul Davis, *Isaac Watts: His Life and Work*, 1943.

Criticism. • Donald Davie, *The Eighteenth-Century Hymn in England*, 1993. • Madeleine Forell Marshall and Janet Todd, *English Congregational Hymns in the Eighteenth Century*, 1982. • J. R. Watson, *The English Hymn: A Critical and Historical Study*, 1997.

John Wilmot, Earl of Rochester • Editions. • Frank H. Ellis, ed., *The Complete Works*, 1994. • Jeremy Treglown, *The Letters of John Wilmot, Earl of Rochester*, 1980. • David M. Vieth, ed., *The Complete Poems of John Wilmot, Earl of Rochester*, 1968. • Keith Walker, ed., *The Poems of John Wilmot, Earl of Rochester*, 1984.

Biographies. • John Adlard, *The Debt to Pleasure*, 1974. • Graham Greene, *Lord Rochester's Monkey; Being the Life of John Wilmot, Second Earl of Rochester*, 1974. • Jeremy Lamb, *So Idle a Rogue: The Life and Death of Lord Rochester*, 1993. • Vivian de Sola Pinto, *Enthusiast in Wit: A Portrait of John Wilmot, Earl of Rochester*, 1962.

Criticism. • David Farley-Hills, *Rochester's Poetry*, 1978. • David Farley-Hills, ed., *Rochester: The Critical Heritage*, 1972. • Nicholas Fisher, ed., *That Second Bottle: Essays on John Wilmot, Earl of Rochester*, 2000. • Dustin Griffin, *Satires Against Man: The Poems of Rochester*, 1973. • Marianne Thormählen, *Rochester: The Poems in Context*, 1993. • Jeremy Treglown, ed., *Spirit of Wit: Reconsiderations of Rochester*, 1982. • David M. Vieth, ed., *John Wilmot, Earl of Rochester: Critical Essays*, 1988.

William Wycherley • Editions. • Arthur Friedman, ed., *The Plays of William Wycherley*, 1979. • Peter Holland, ed., *The Plays of William Wycherley*, 1981. • James Ogdon, ed., *The Country Wife*, 2nd ed., 1991.

Biography. • Eugene B. McCarthy, *William Wycherley: A Biography*, 1979.

Criticism. • Douglas Ford, "The Country Wife: Rake Hero as Artist," *Restoration* vol. 17, 1993. • Peggy A. Knapp, "The 'Plyant' Discourse of Wycherley's *The Country Wife*," *Studies in English Literature*, vol. 40, 2000. • H. W. Matalene, "What Happens in *The Country Wife*," *Studies in English Literature*, vol. 22, 1982. • Judith Milhous and Robert D. Hume, "The Country Wife," in *Producible Interpretations*, 1985. • Michael Neill, "Horned Beasts and China Oranges: Reading the Signs in *The Country Wife*," *Eighteenth-Century Life*, vol. 12, 1988. • Deborah C. Payne, "Reading the Signs in *The Country Wife*," *Studies in English Literature*, vol. 26, 1986. • Jocelyn Powell, "The Country Wife," in *Restoration Theatre Production*, 1984. • Eve Kosofsky Sedgwick, "The Country Wife: Anatomies of Male Homosocial Desire," in *Between Men*, 1985. • James Thompson, *Language in Wycherley's Plays*, 1984. • Rose Zimbardo, *Wycherley's Drama: A Link in the Development of English Satire*, 1965.

Edward Young • Edition. • Stephen Cornford, *Edward Young: Night Thoughts*, 1989.

Biography. • Isabel St. John Bliss, *Edward Young*, 1969.

Criticism. • Vincent Newey, "Edward Young," in *A Handbook to English Romanticism*, eds. Jean Raimond and J. R. Watson, 1992.

CREDITS